Black Jack

Volume 2

Osamu Tezuka

VERTICAL.

Translation—Camellia Nieh
Production—Glen Isip
Akane Ishida
Lawrence Leung
Copyright © 2008 by Tezuka Productions
Translation Copyright © 2008 by Camellia Nieh and Vertical, Inc.

Published by Vertical, Inc., New York.

Originally published in Japanese as *Burakku Jakku 2*
by Akita Shoten, Tokyo, 1987.
Burakku Jakku first serialized in *Shukan Shonen Champion*,
Akita Shoten, 1973-83.

Hardcover ISBN: 978-1-934287-53-8
Paperback ISBN: 978-1-934287-28-6

Manufactured in the United States of America

First Edition

Vertical, Inc.
1185 Avenue of the Americas 32nd Floor
New York, NY 10036
www.vertical-inc.com

CONTENTS

NEEDLE

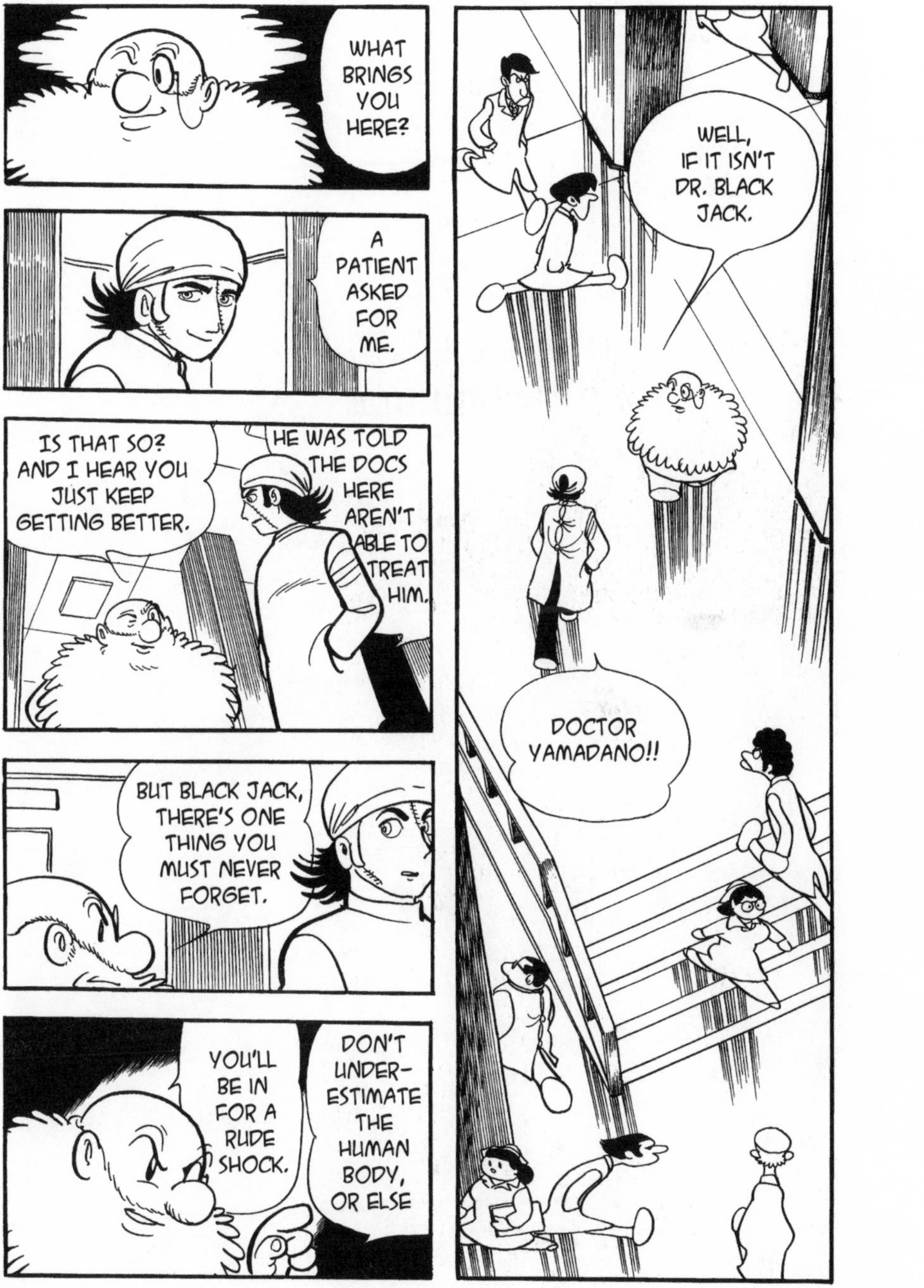
WELL, IF IT ISN'T DR. BLACK JACK.
DOCTOR YAMADANO!!
WHAT BRINGS YOU HERE?
A PATIENT ASKED FOR ME.
HE WAS TOLD THE DOCS HERE AREN'T ABLE TO TREAT HIM.
IS THAT SO? AND I HEAR YOU JUST KEEP GETTING BETTER.
BUT BLACK JACK, THERE'S ONE THING YOU MUST NEVER FORGET.
DON'T UNDER-ESTIMATE THE HUMAN BODY, OR ELSE
YOU'LL BE IN FOR A RUDE SHOCK.

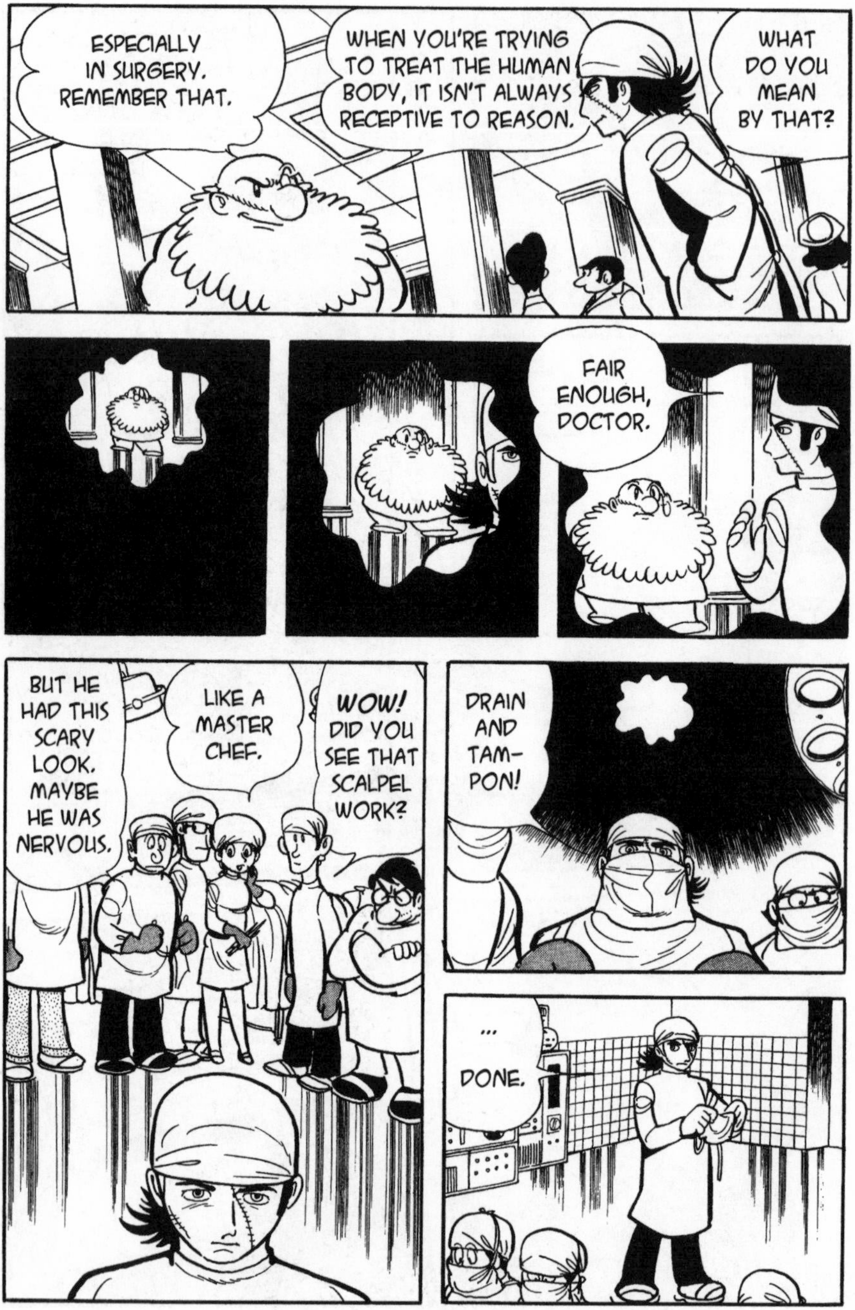
WHAT DO YOU MEAN BY THAT?
WHEN YOU'RE TRYING TO TREAT THE HUMAN BODY, IT ISN'T ALWAYS RECEPTIVE TO REASON.
ESPECIALLY IN SURGERY. REMEMBER THAT.
FAIR ENOUGH, DOCTOR.
DRAIN AND TAM-PON!
... DONE.
WOW! DID YOU SEE THAT SCALPEL WORK?
LIKE A MASTER CHEF.
BUT HE HAD THIS SCARY LOOK. MAYBE HE WAS NERVOUS.

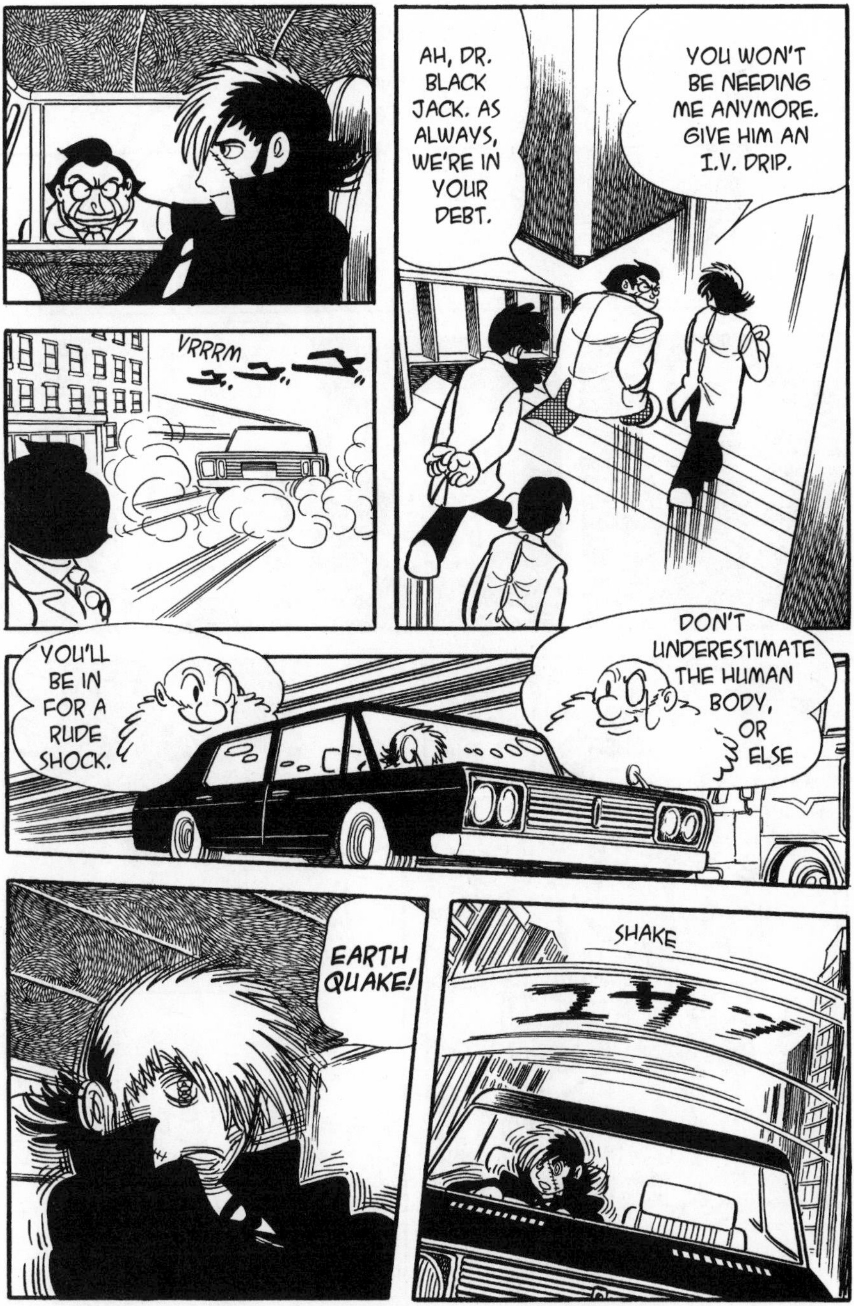
YOU WON'T BE NEEDING ME ANYMORE. GIVE HIM AN I.V. DRIP.
AH, DR. BLACK JACK. AS ALWAYS, WE'RE IN YOUR DEBT.
VRRRM
DON'T UNDERESTIMATE THE HUMAN BODY, OR ELSE
YOU'LL BE IN FOR A RUDE SHOCK.
SHAKE
EARTH QUAKE!

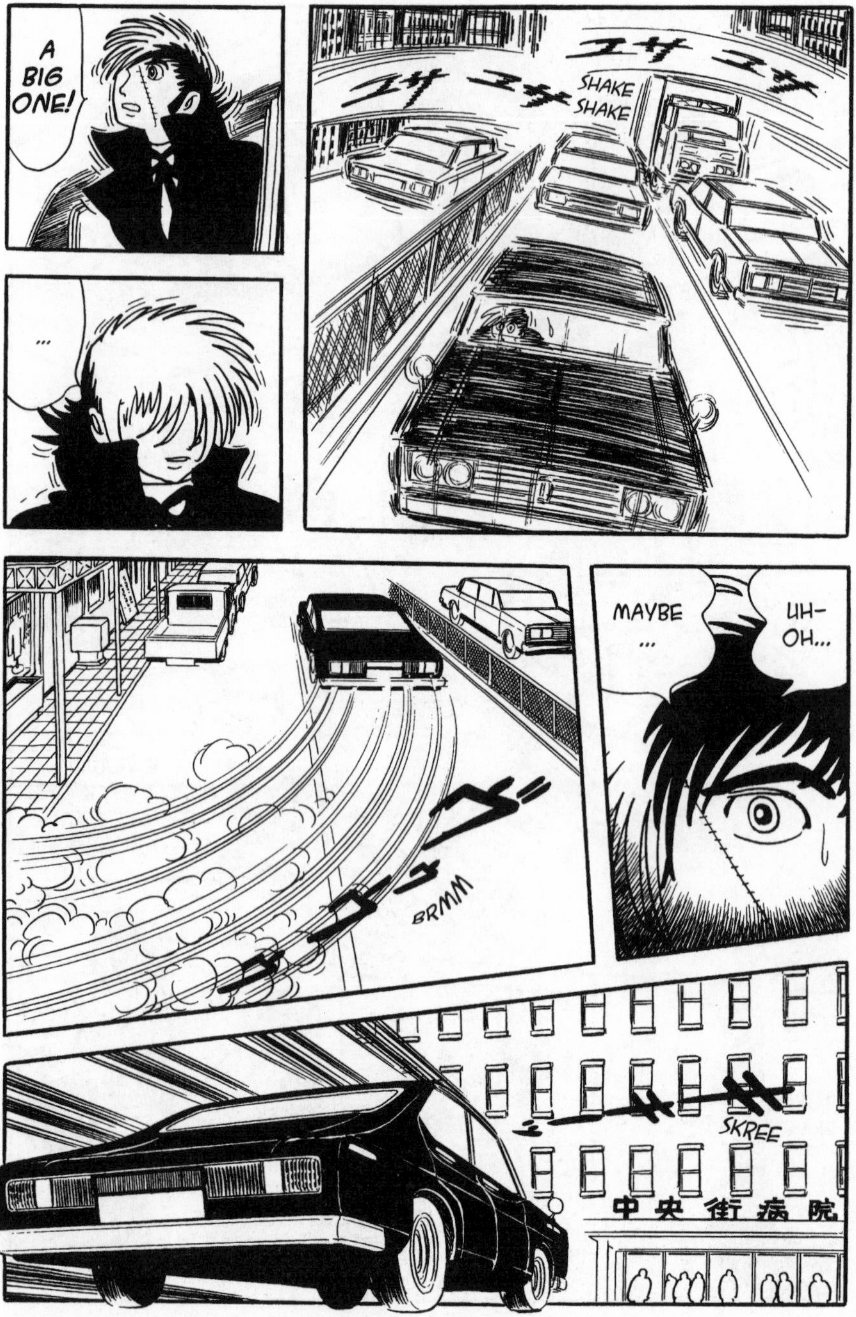

A BIG ONE!
...
ユサ ユサ ユサ ユサ
SHAKE SHAKE
MAYBE ...
UH-OH...
BRMM
SKREE
中央街病院

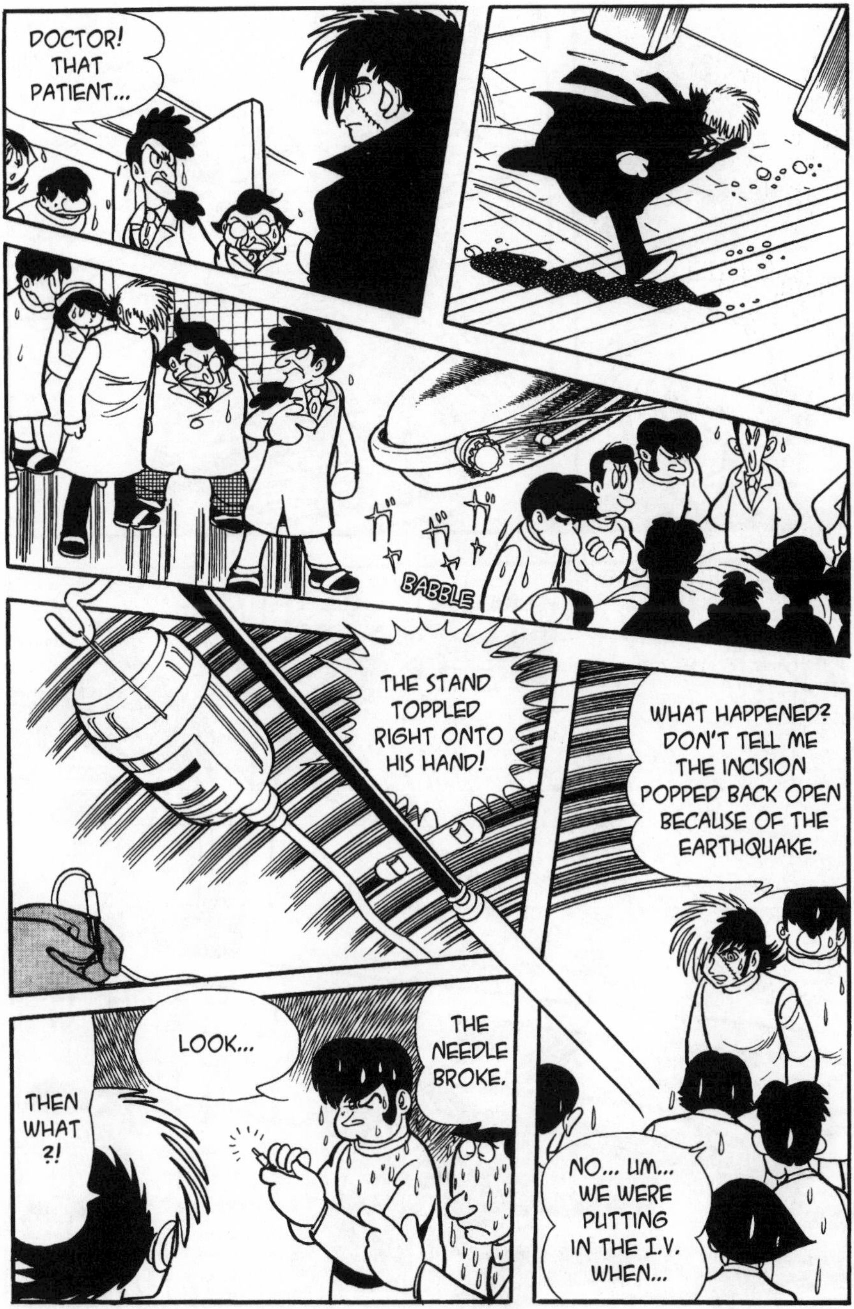
DOCTOR! THAT PATIENT...
ガヤ ガヤ ガヤ
BABBLE
WHAT HAPPENED? DON'T TELL ME THE INCISION POPPED BACK OPEN BECAUSE OF THE EARTHQUAKE.
NO... UM... WE WERE PUTTING IN THE I.V. WHEN...
THE STAND TOPPLED RIGHT ONTO HIS HAND!
THE NEEDLE BROKE.
LOOK...
THEN WHAT ?!

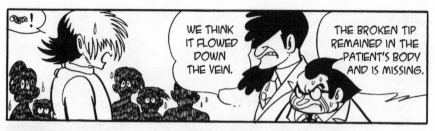

THE BROKEN TIP REMAINED IN THE PATIENT'S BODY AND IS MISSING.
WE THINK IT FLOWED DOWN THE VEIN.
HOGWASH!
NO REASON AN INJECTION NEEDLE SHOULD EVER SNAP!
HAVE A LOOK AT THIS X-RAY.
NOTHING LIKE THIS HAS EVER HAPPENED BEFORE.
THE NEEDLE TIP IS CLEARLY IN A VESSEL!
THIS ONE WAS TAKEN THIRTY SECONDS LATER.
THOUGH THE TIP SEEMS TO SNAG NOW AND THEN, SLOWLY BUT SURELY IT'S FLOWING TOWARDS THE PATIENT'S HEART.

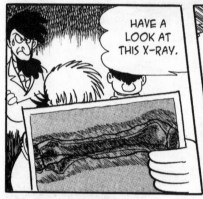

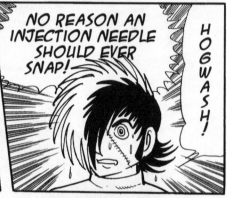

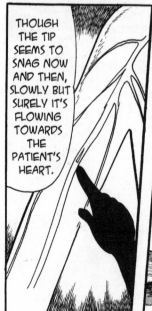

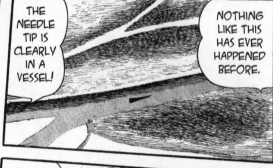

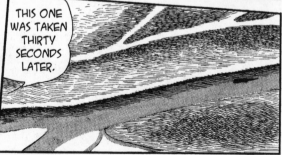

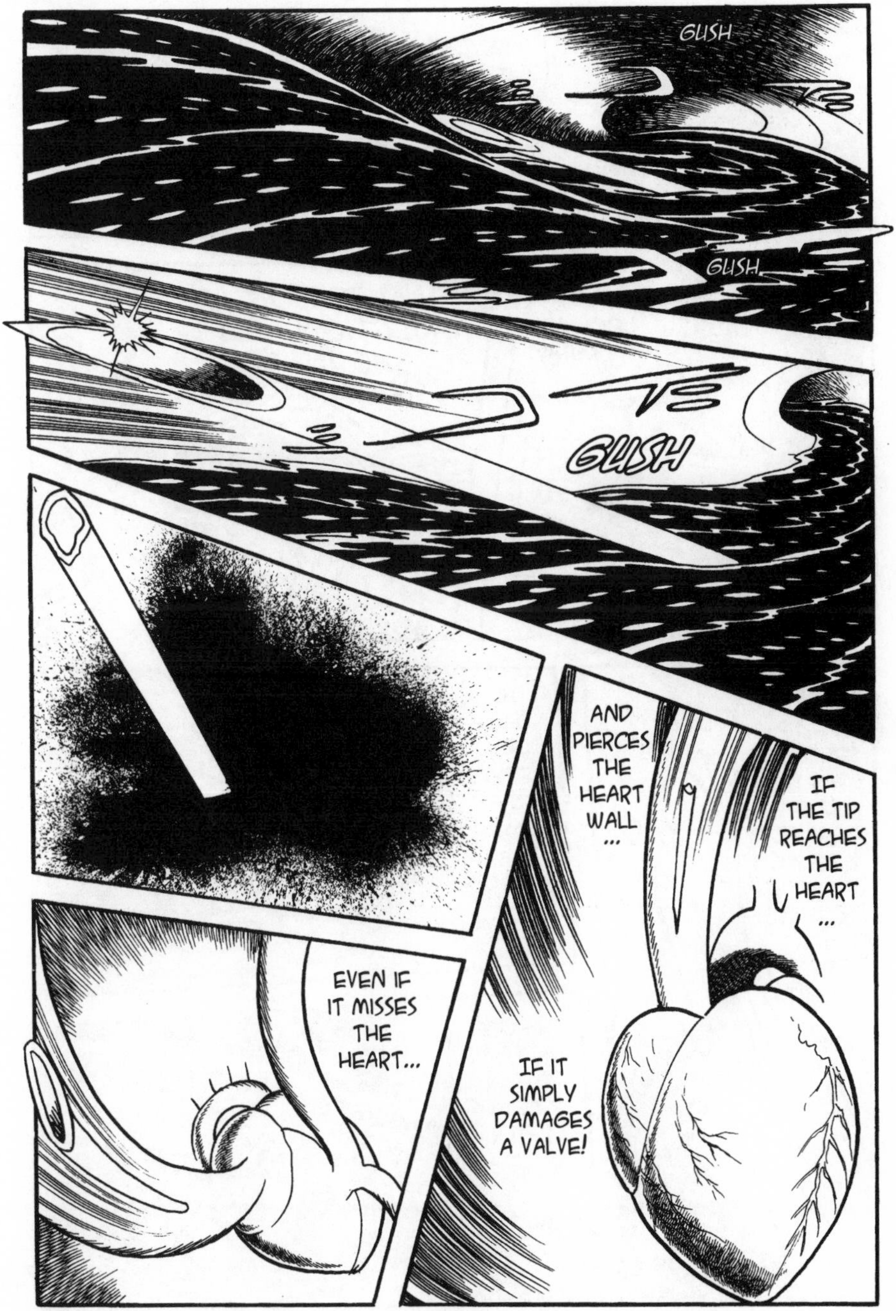
GUSH
GUSH
GUSH
IF THE TIP REACHES THE HEART ...
AND PIERCES THE HEART WALL ...
EVEN IF IT MISSES THE HEART...
IF IT SIMPLY DAMAGES A VALVE!

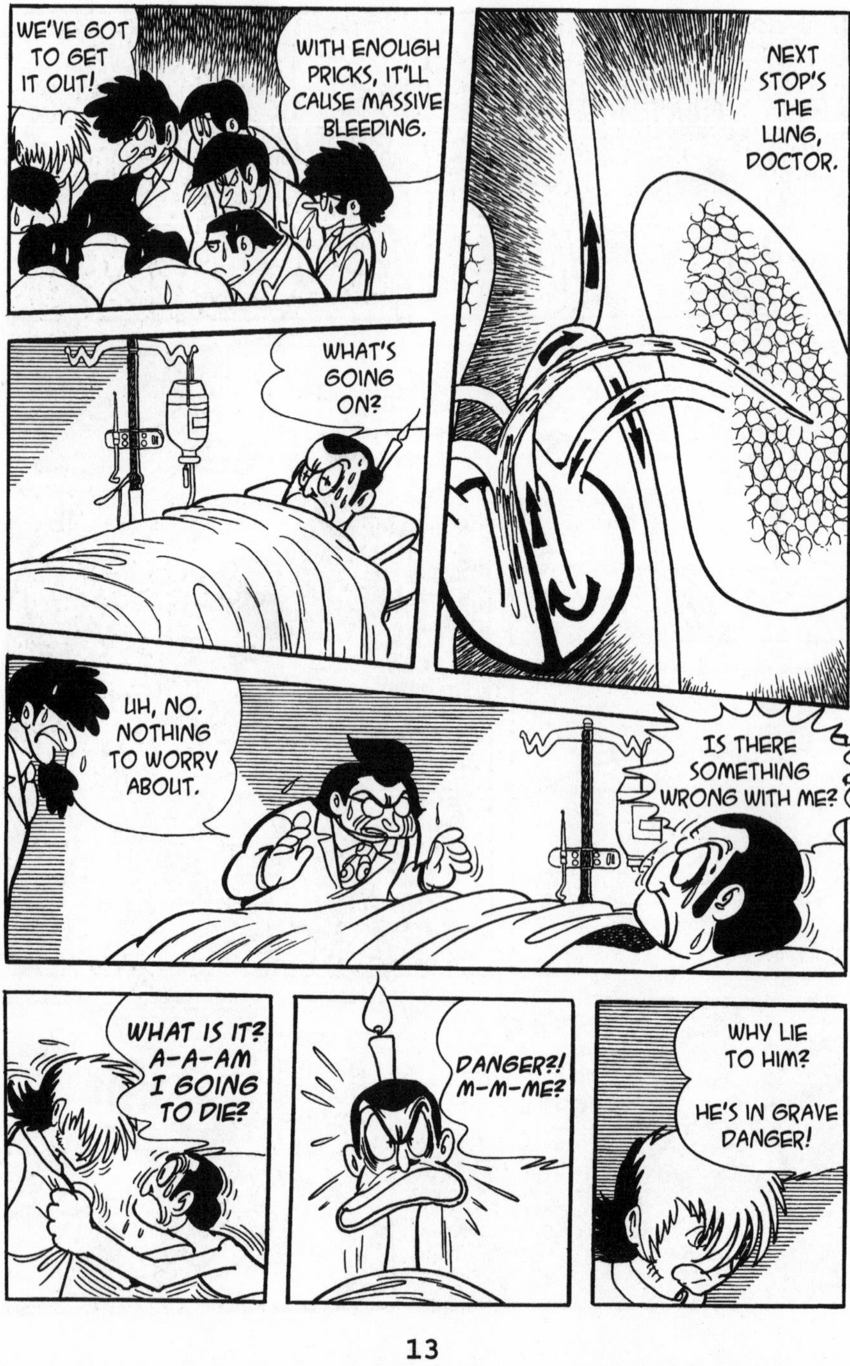
WE'VE GOT TO GET IT OUT!
WITH ENOUGH PRICKS, IT'LL CAUSE MASSIVE BLEEDING.
WHAT'S GOING ON?
NEXT STOP'S THE LUNG, DOCTOR.
UH, NO. NOTHING TO WORRY ABOUT.
IS THERE SOMETHING WRONG WITH ME?
WHAT IS IT? A-A-AM I GOING TO DIE?
DANGER?! M-M-ME?
WHY LIE TO HIM?
HE'S IN GRAVE DANGER!

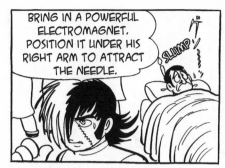

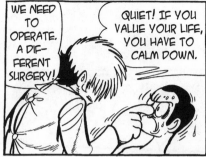

WE NEED TO OPERATE. A DIF-FERENT SURGERY!
QUIET! IF YOU VALUE YOUR LIFE, YOU HAVE TO CALM DOWN.
BRING IN A POWERFUL ELECTROMAGNET. POSITION IT UNDER HIS RIGHT ARM TO ATTRACT THE NEEDLE.
SLUMP
SET UP MINIATURE RADARS TO TRACK ITS LOCATION.
WE'LL OPEN THE VEIN AND EXTRACT THE NEEDLE BEFORE IT REACHES HIS HEART!
TOOT
TOOT
TOOT
THERE IT IS.
IT'S HEADED FOR THE VENA CAVA AND THE HEART.
ONCE IT ENTERS THE VC, IT'LL BE TOO LATE TO OPERATE!
TOOT

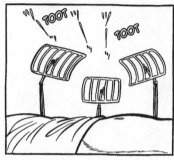

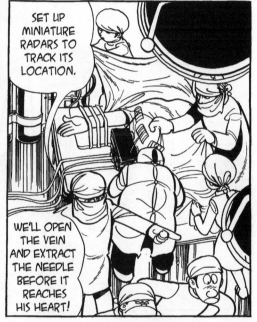

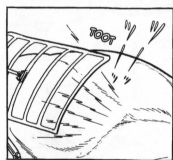

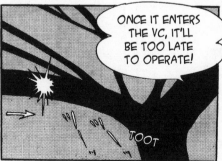

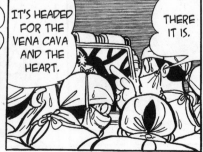

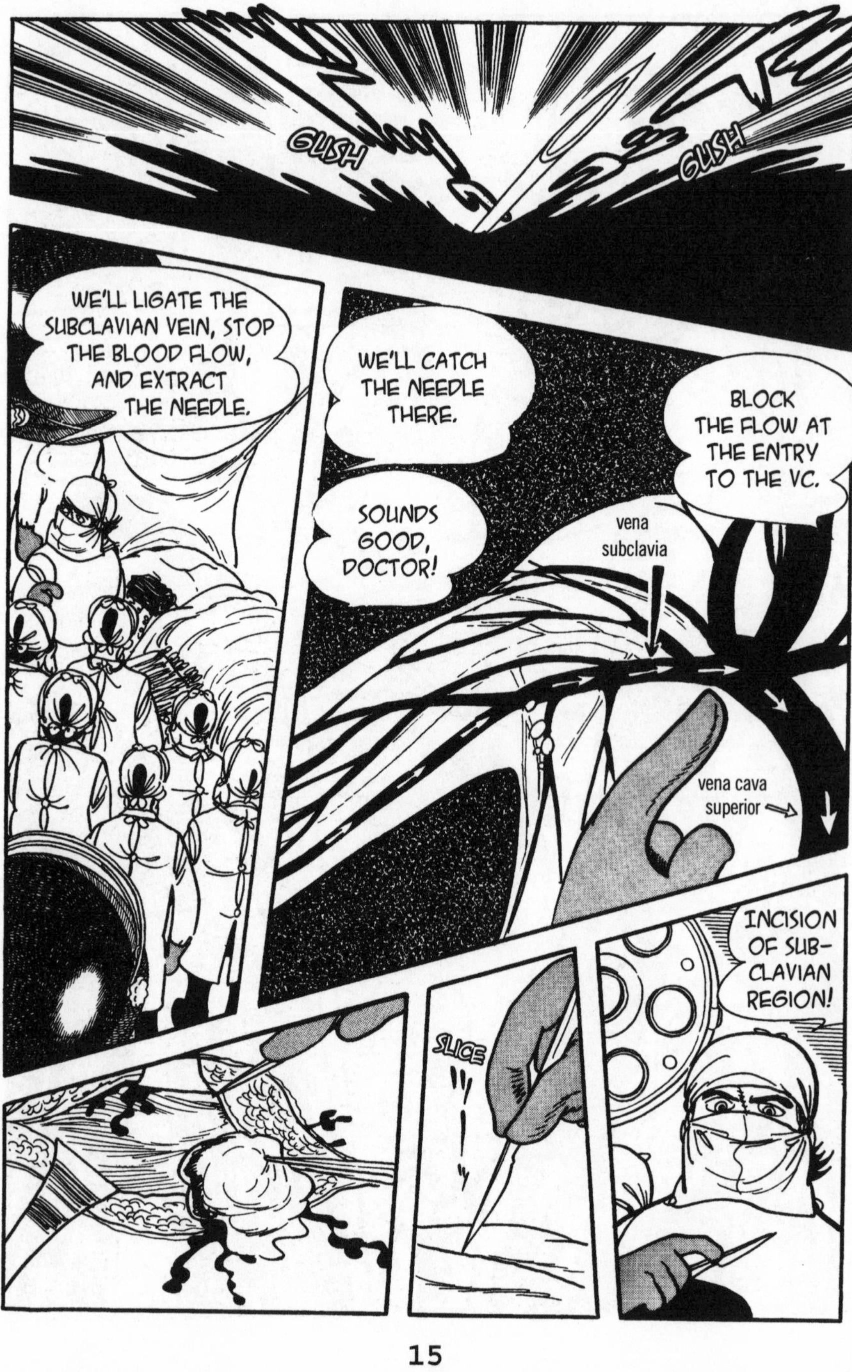
GUSH
GUSH
BLOCK THE FLOW AT THE ENTRY TO THE VC.
WE'LL CATCH THE NEEDLE THERE.
SOUNDS GOOD, DOCTOR!
vena subclavia
vena cava superior
WE'LL LIGATE THE SUBCLAVIAN VEIN, STOP THE BLOOD FLOW, AND EXTRACT THE NEEDLE.
INCISION OF SUB-CLAVIAN REGION!
SLICE

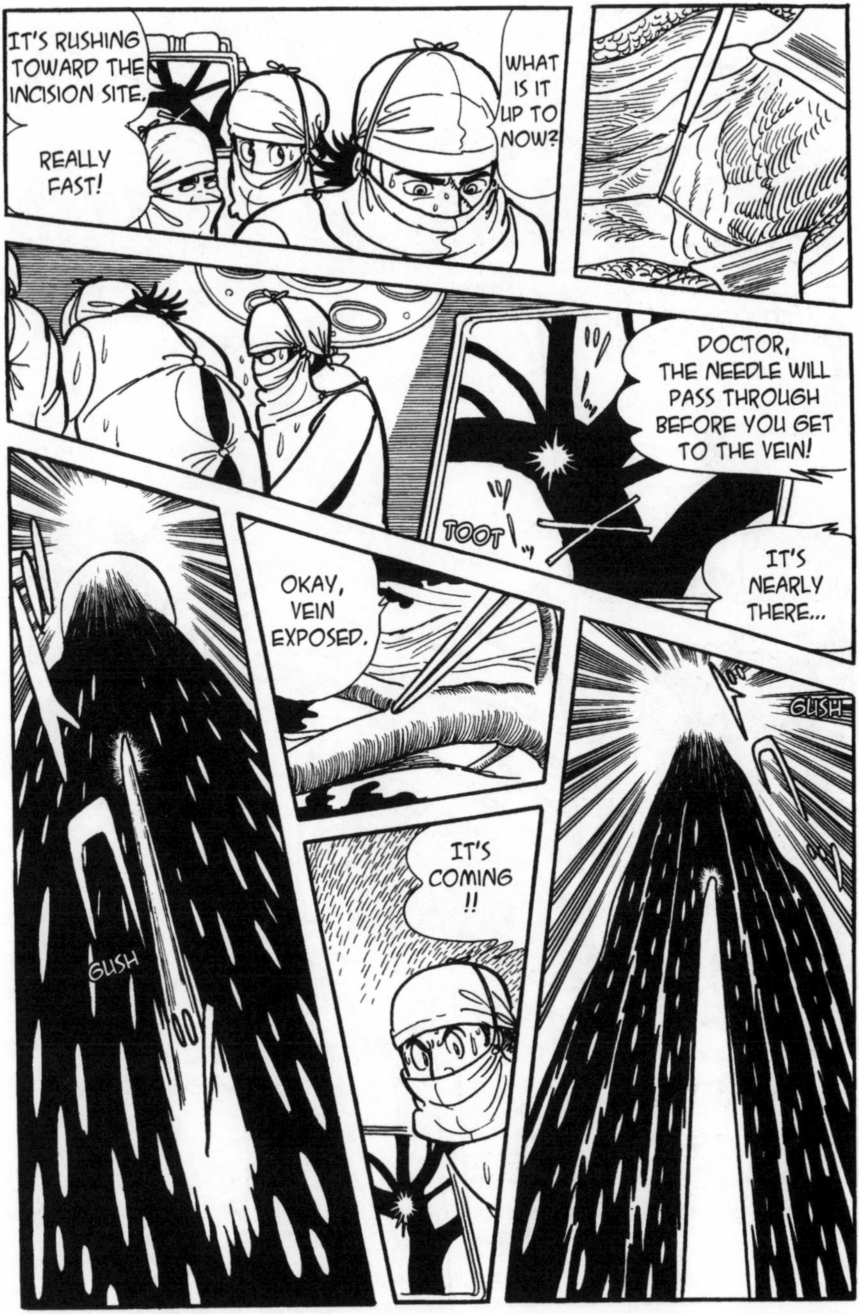
IT'S RUSHING TOWARD THE INCISION SITE.
REALLY FAST!
WHAT IS IT UP TO NOW?
DOCTOR, THE NEEDLE WILL PASS THROUGH BEFORE YOU GET TO THE VEIN!
TOOT
IT'S NEARLY THERE...
GUSH
OKAY, VEIN EXPOSED.
IT'S COMING !!
GUSH

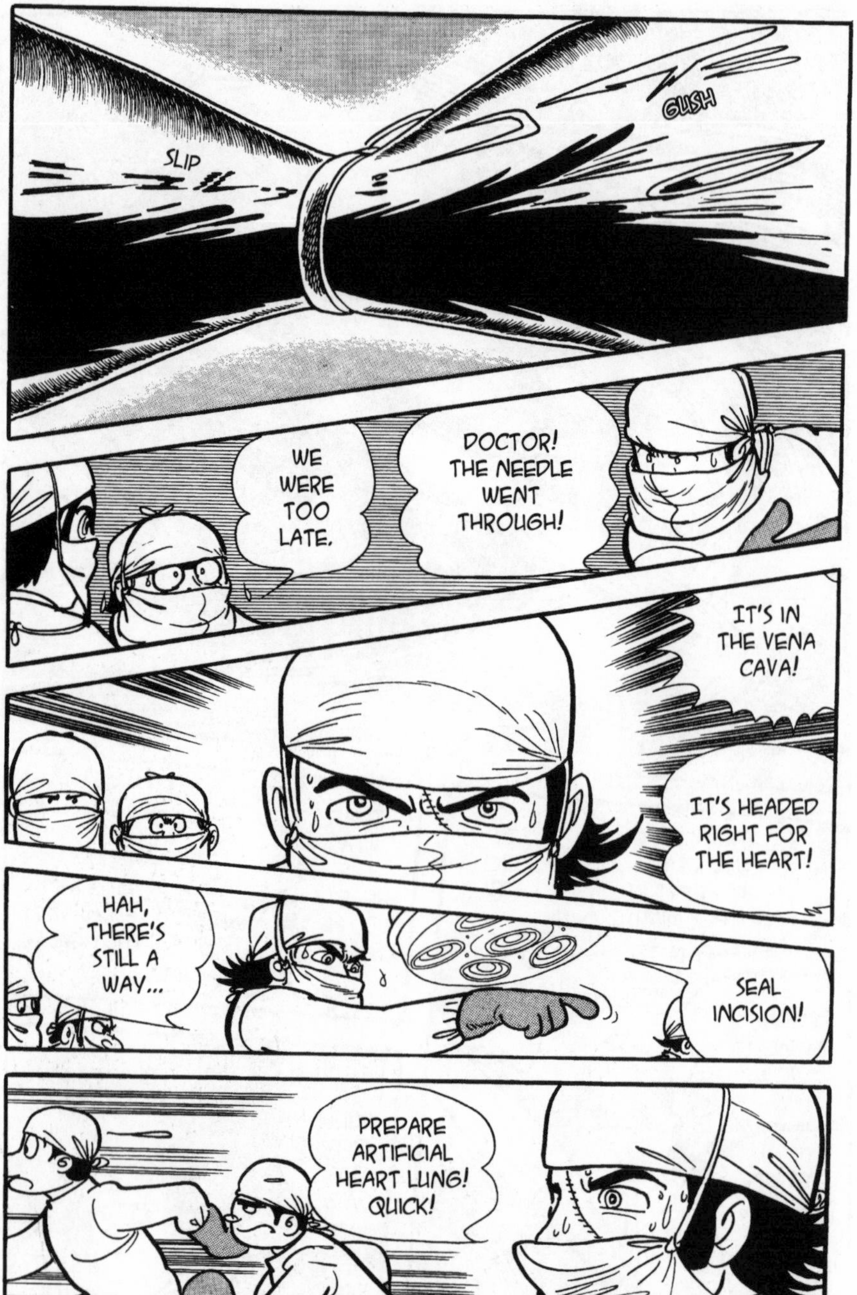
GUSH
SLIP
DOCTOR! THE NEEDLE WENT THROUGH!
WE WERE TOO LATE.
IT'S IN THE VENA CAVA!
IT'S HEADED RIGHT FOR THE HEART!
SEAL INCISION!
HAH, THERE'S STILL A WAY...
PREPARE ARTIFICIAL HEART LUNG! QUICK!

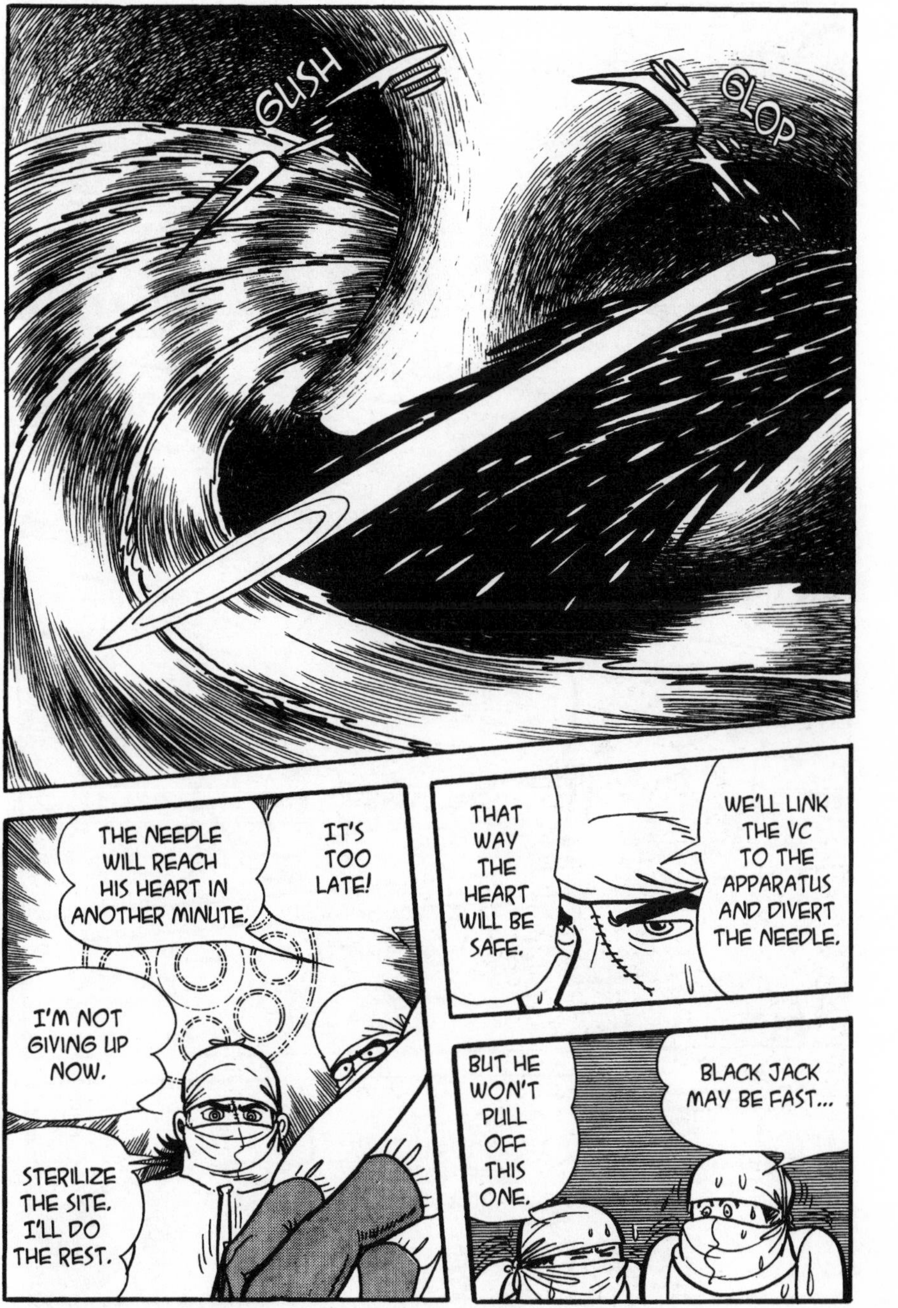
GLOP
GUSH
WE'LL LINK THE VC TO THE APPARATUS AND DIVERT THE NEEDLE.
THAT WAY THE HEART WILL BE SAFE.
BLACK JACK MAY BE FAST...
BUT HE WON'T PULL OFF THIS ONE.
IT'S TOO LATE!
THE NEEDLE WILL REACH HIS HEART IN ANOTHER MINUTE.
I'M NOT GIVING UP NOW.
STERILIZE THE SITE. I'LL DO THE REST.

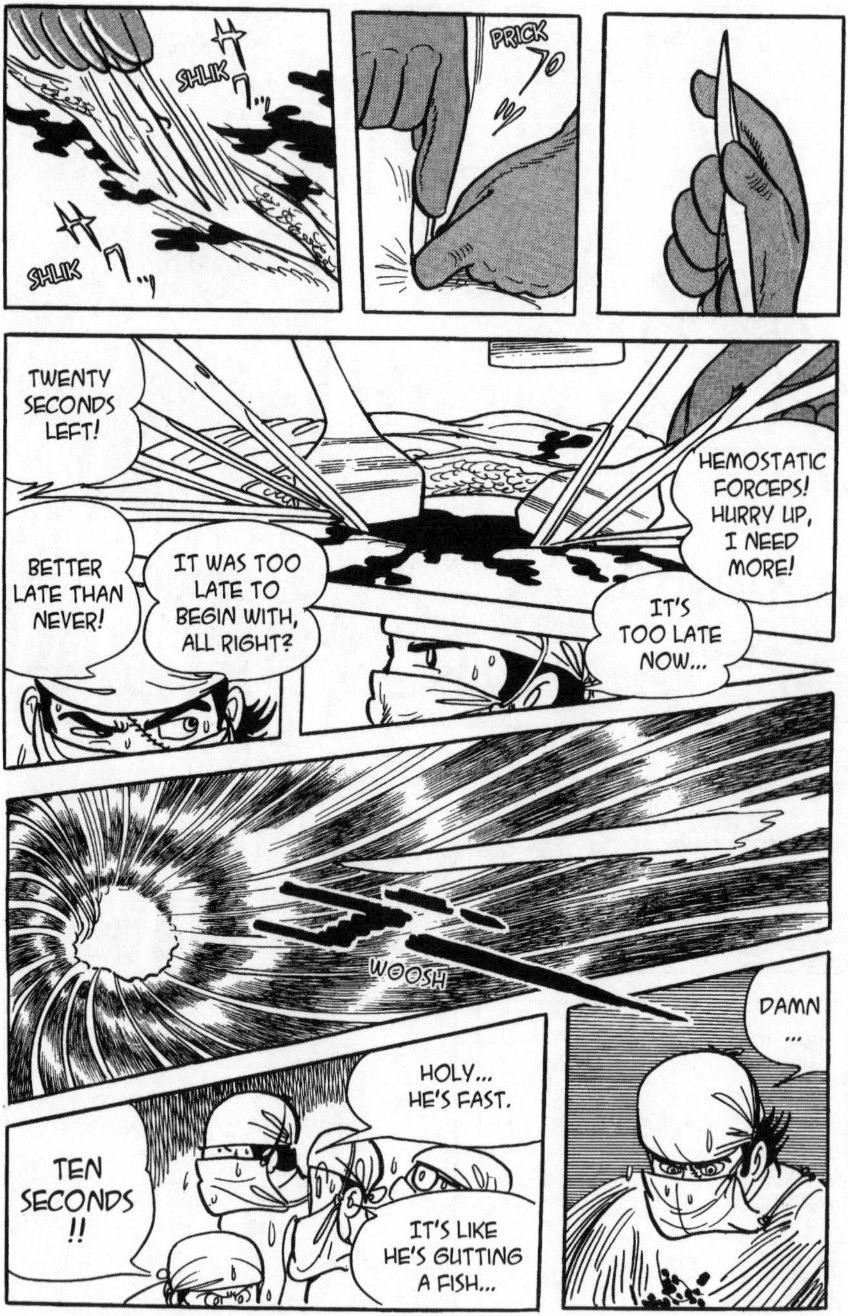
PRICK
SHLIK
SHLIK
HEMOSTATIC FORCEPS! HURRY UP, I NEED MORE!
TWENTY SECONDS LEFT!
IT'S TOO LATE NOW...
IT WAS TOO LATE TO BEGIN WITH, ALL RIGHT?
BETTER LATE THAN NEVER!
WOOSH
DAMN ...
HOLY... HE'S FAST.
IT'S LIKE HE'S GUTTING A FISH...
TEN SECONDS !!

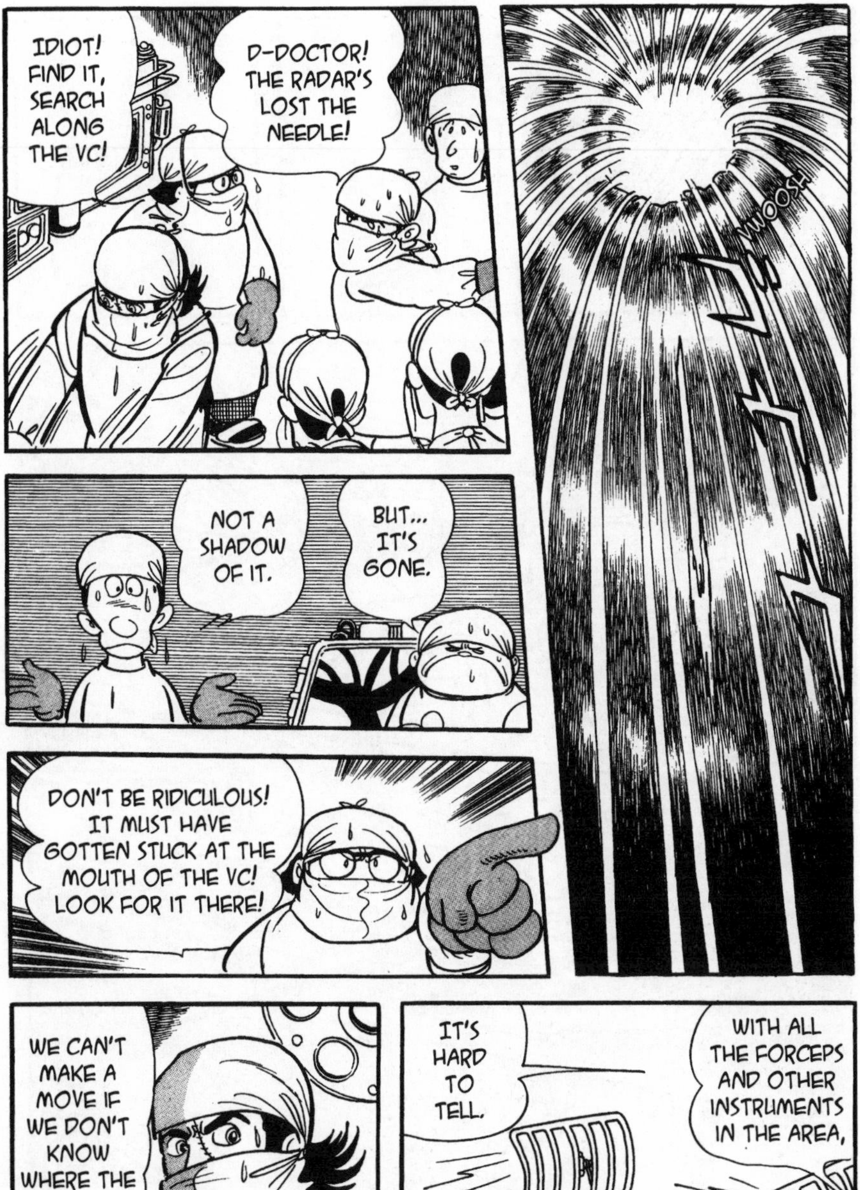
WOOSH
D-DOCTOR! THE RADAR'S LOST THE NEEDLE!
IDIOT! FIND IT, SEARCH ALONG THE VC!
BUT... IT'S GONE.
NOT A SHADOW OF IT.
DON'T BE RIDICULOUS! IT MUST HAVE GOTTEN STUCK AT THE MOUTH OF THE VC! LOOK FOR IT THERE!
WITH ALL THE FORCEPS AND OTHER INSTRUMENTS IN THE AREA,
IT'S HARD TO TELL.
WE CAN'T MAKE A MOVE IF WE DON'T KNOW WHERE THE NEEDLE IS!

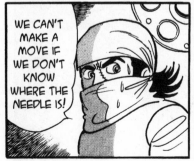

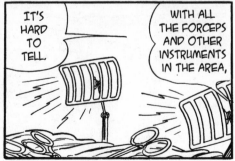

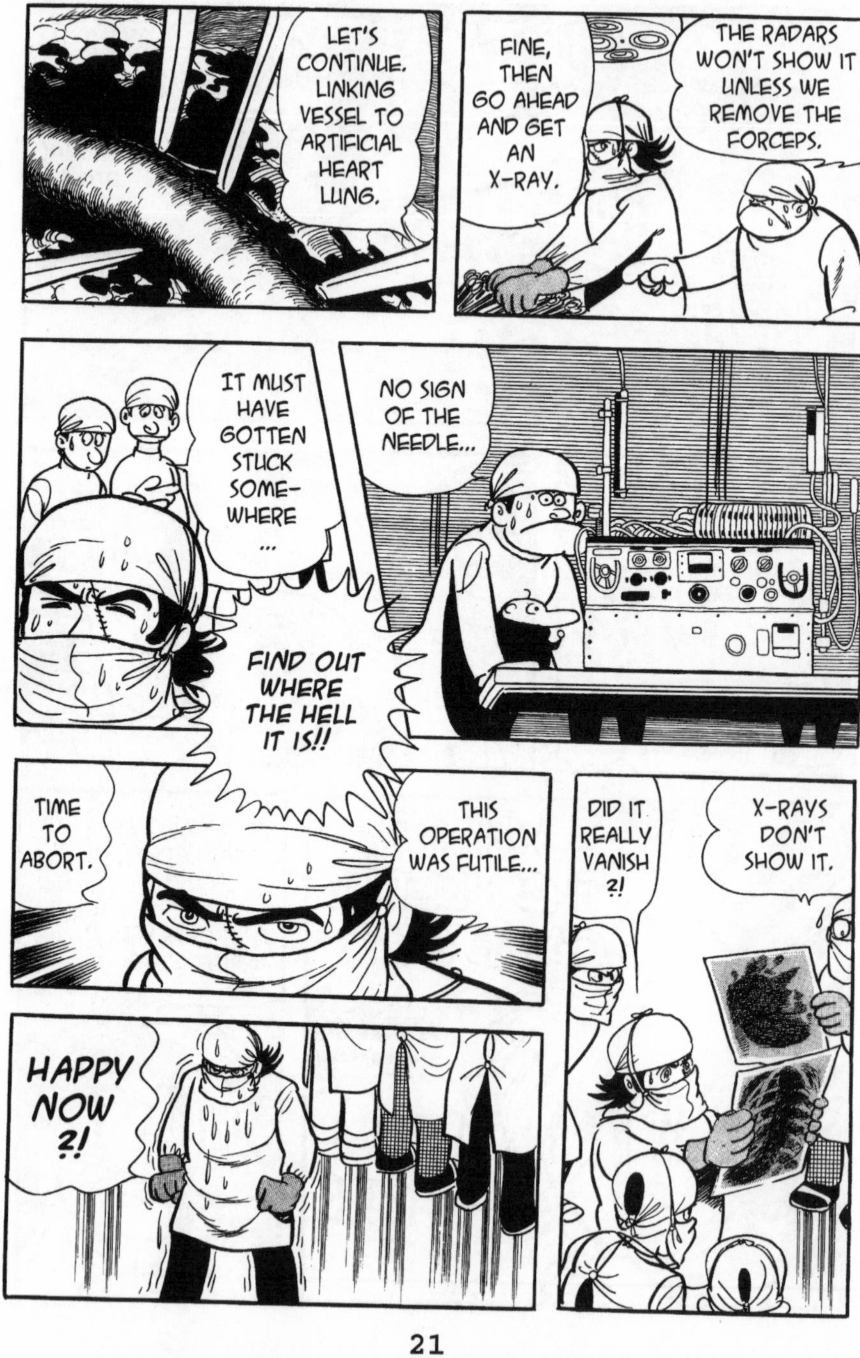
THE RADARS WON'T SHOW IT UNLESS WE REMOVE THE FORCEPS.
FINE, THEN GO AHEAD AND GET AN X-RAY.
LET'S CONTINUE. LINKING VESSEL TO ARTIFICIAL HEART LUNG.
NO SIGN OF THE NEEDLE...
IT MUST HAVE GOTTEN STUCK SOME-WHERE ...
FIND OUT WHERE THE HELL IT IS!!
X-RAYS DON'T SHOW IT.
DID IT REALLY VANISH ?!
THIS OPERATION WAS FUTILE...
TIME TO ABORT.
HAPPY NOW ?!

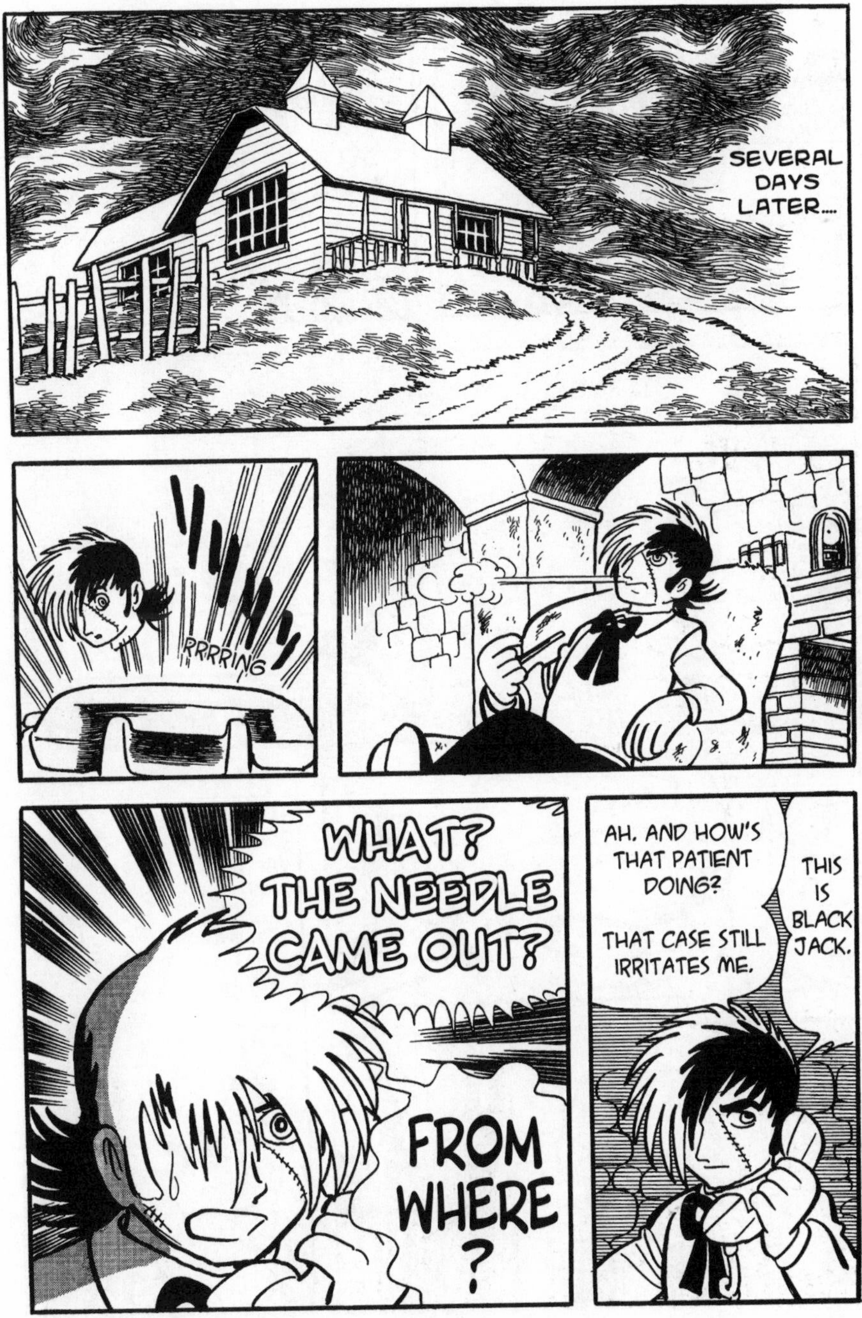
SEVERAL DAYS LATER....
RRRRING
THIS IS BLACK JACK.
AH. AND HOW'S THAT PATIENT DOING?
THAT CASE STILL IRRITATES ME.
WHAT? THE NEEDLE CAME OUT?
FROM WHERE?

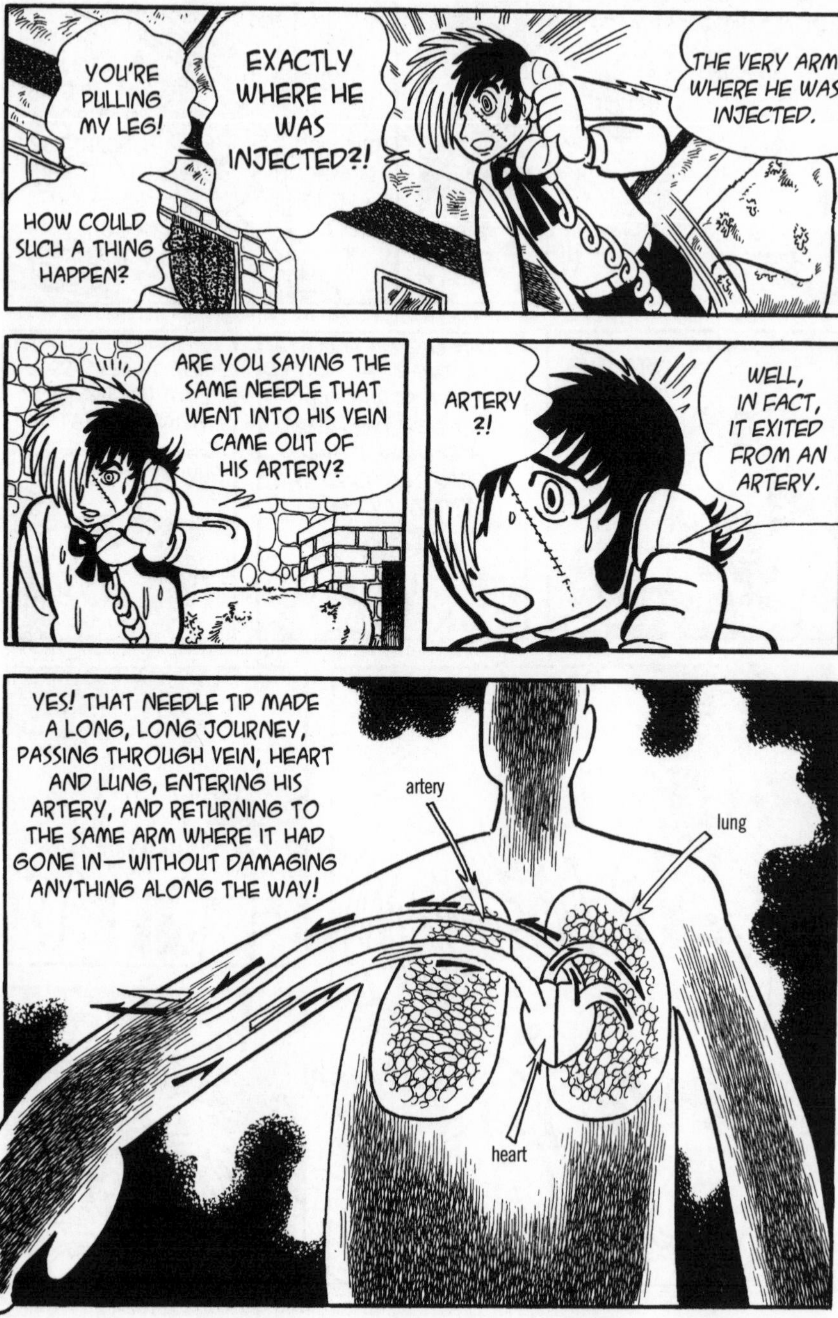
THE VERY ARM WHERE HE WAS INJECTED.
EXACTLY WHERE HE WAS INJECTED?!
YOU'RE PULLING MY LEG!
HOW COULD SUCH A THING HAPPEN?
WELL, IN FACT, IT EXITED FROM AN ARTERY.
ARTERY ?!
ARE YOU SAYING THE SAME NEEDLE THAT WENT INTO HIS VEIN CAME OUT OF HIS ARTERY?
YES! THAT NEEDLE TIP MADE A LONG, LONG JOURNEY, PASSING THROUGH VEIN, HEART AND LUNG, ENTERING HIS ARTERY, AND RETURNING TO THE SAME ARM WHERE IT HAD GONE IN—WITHOUT DAMAGING ANYTHING ALONG THE WAY!
artery
lung
heart

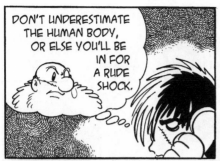

YOU'RE TELLING ME HIS BODY JUST SPIT IT BACK OUT
LIKE YOU OR I MIGHT SPIT OUT FOUL-TASTING FOOD?
DON'T UNDERESTIMATE THE HUMAN BODY, OR ELSE YOU'LL BE IN FOR A RUDE SHOCK.
ONE THING I STILL DON'T UNDERSTAND: HOW DID THAT NEEDLE DISAPPEAR DURING SURGERY?
I CAN ONLY SPECULATE, BUT I THINK THE NEEDLE TIP JUST WHIPPED THROUGH THE HEART AND LUNG; IT HAD ALREADY ENTERED THE ARTERY BY THEN.
GIVE THE PATIENT MY CONGRAT-ULATIONS!
...
ha ha ha
DAMN IT!

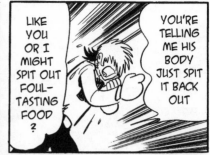

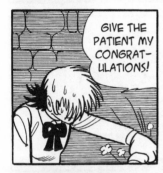

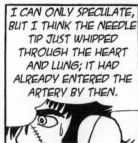

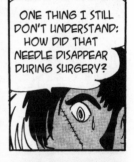

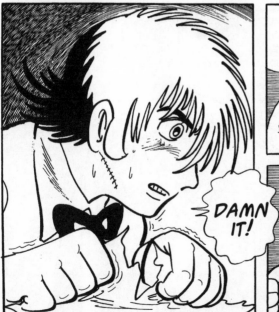

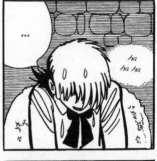

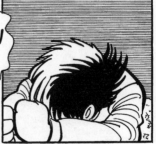

GRANNY

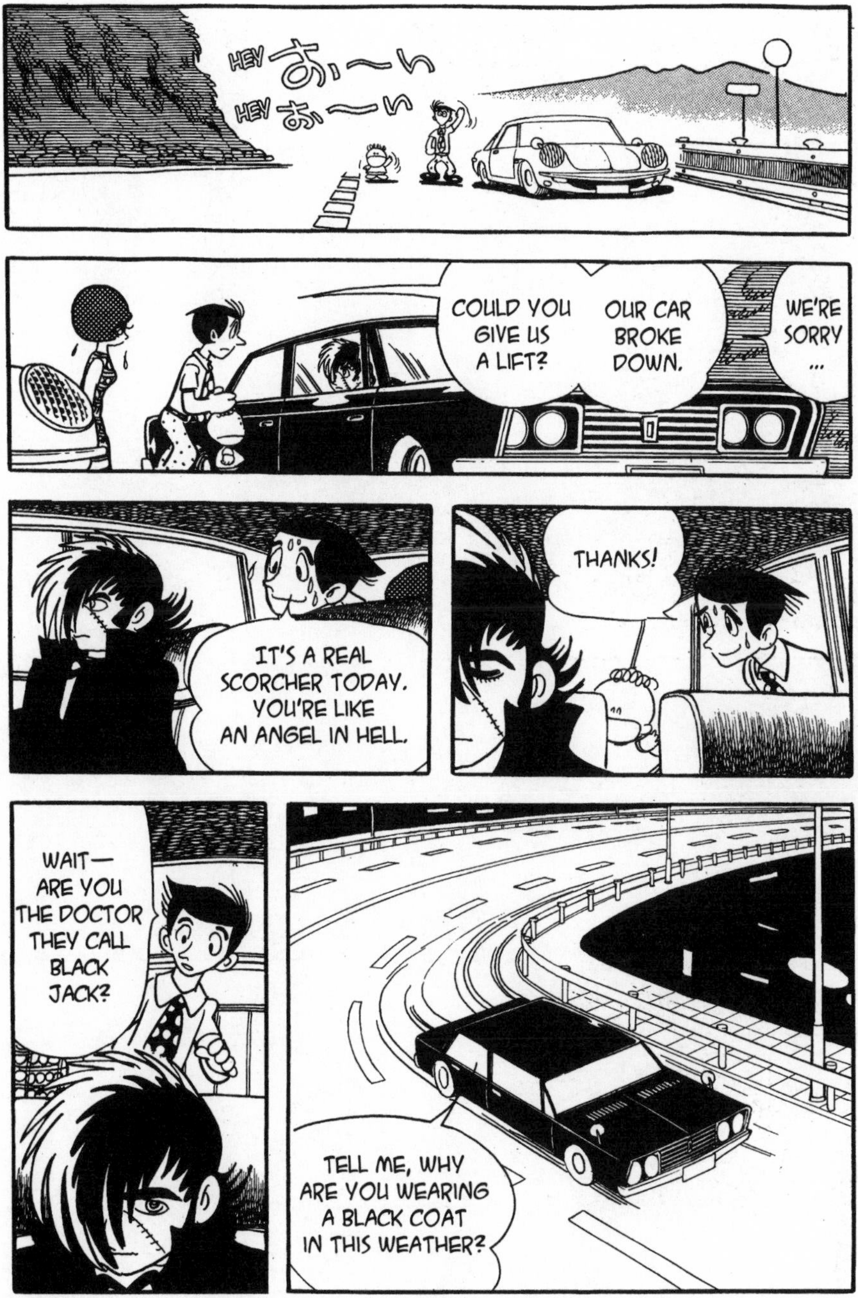
HEY おーい
HEY おーい
WE'RE SORRY ...
OUR CAR BROKE DOWN.
COULD YOU GIVE US A LIFT?
THANKS!
IT'S A REAL SCORCHER TODAY. YOU'RE LIKE AN ANGEL IN HELL.
TELL ME, WHY ARE YOU WEARING A BLACK COAT IN THIS WEATHER?
WAIT— ARE YOU THE DOCTOR THEY CALL BLACK JACK?

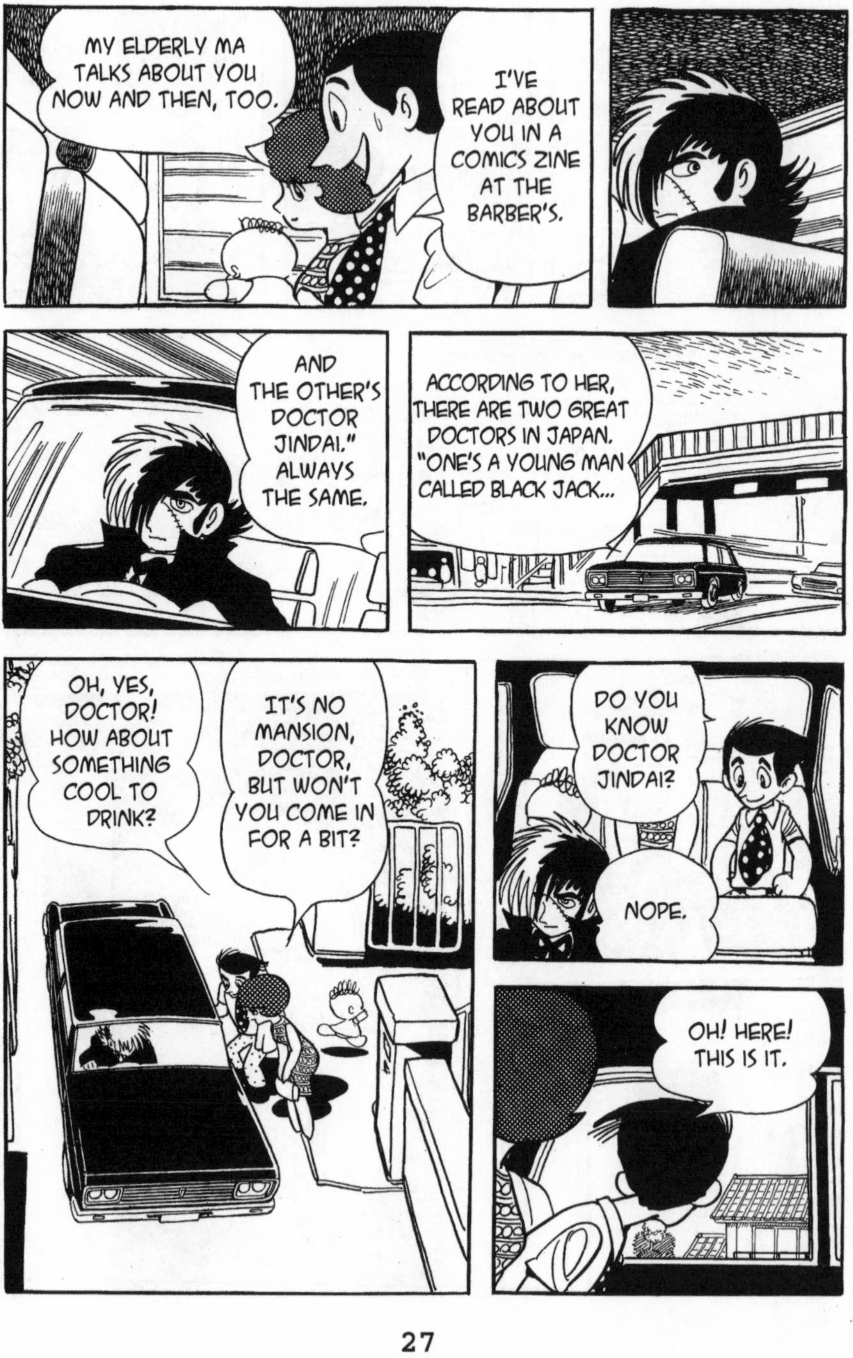
I'VE READ ABOUT YOU IN A COMICS ZINE AT THE BARBER'S.
MY ELDERLY MA TALKS ABOUT YOU NOW AND THEN, TOO.
ACCORDING TO HER, THERE ARE TWO GREAT DOCTORS IN JAPAN. "ONE'S A YOUNG MAN CALLED BLACK JACK...
AND THE OTHER'S DOCTOR JINDAI." ALWAYS THE SAME.
DO YOU KNOW DOCTOR JINDAI?
NOPE.
OH! HERE! THIS IS IT.
IT'S NO MANSION, DOCTOR, BUT WON'T YOU COME IN FOR A BIT?
OH, YES, DOCTOR! HOW ABOUT SOMETHING COOL TO DRINK?

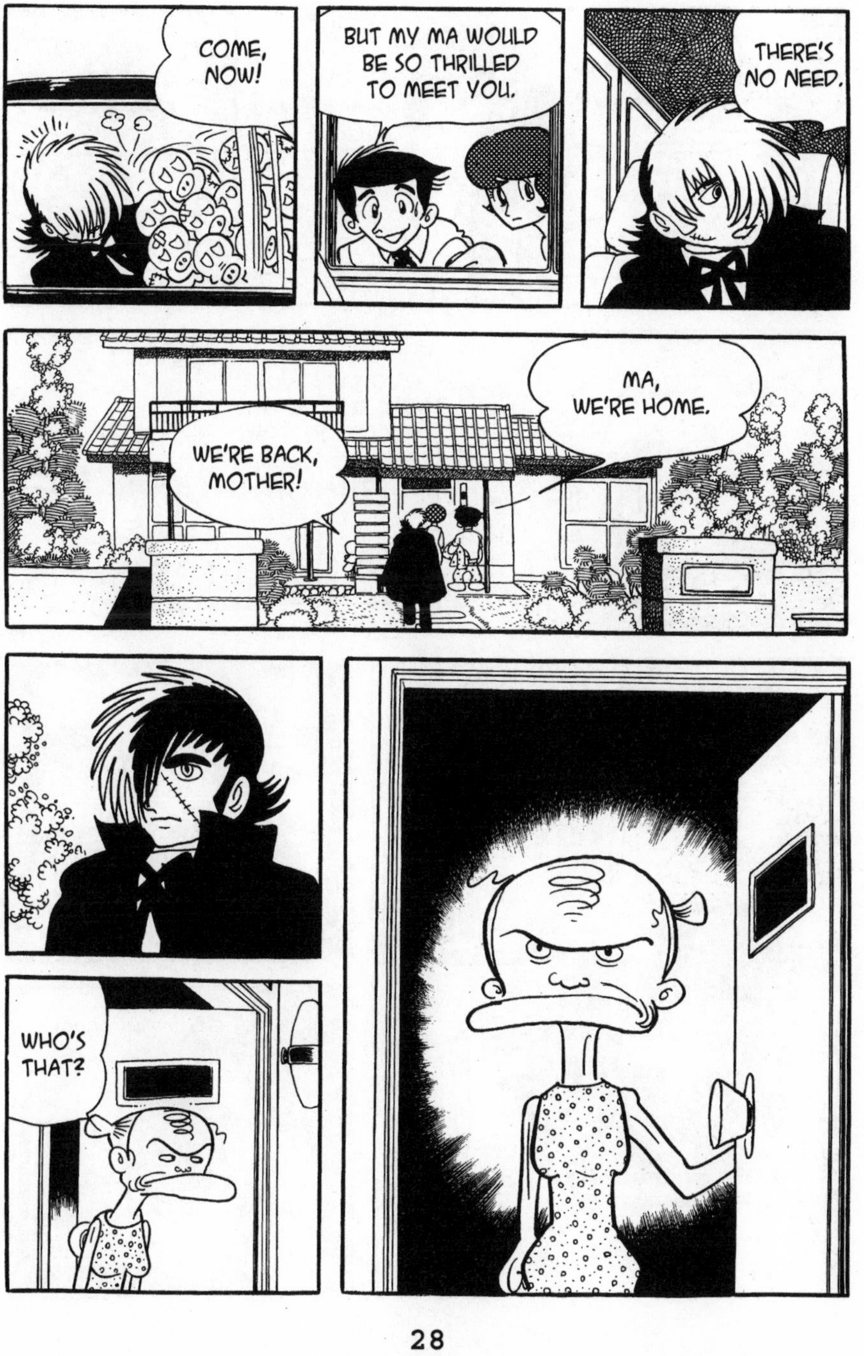
COME, NOW!
BUT MY MA WOULD BE SO THRILLED TO MEET YOU.
THERE'S NO NEED.
WE'RE BACK, MOTHER!
MA, WE'RE HOME.
WHO'S THAT?

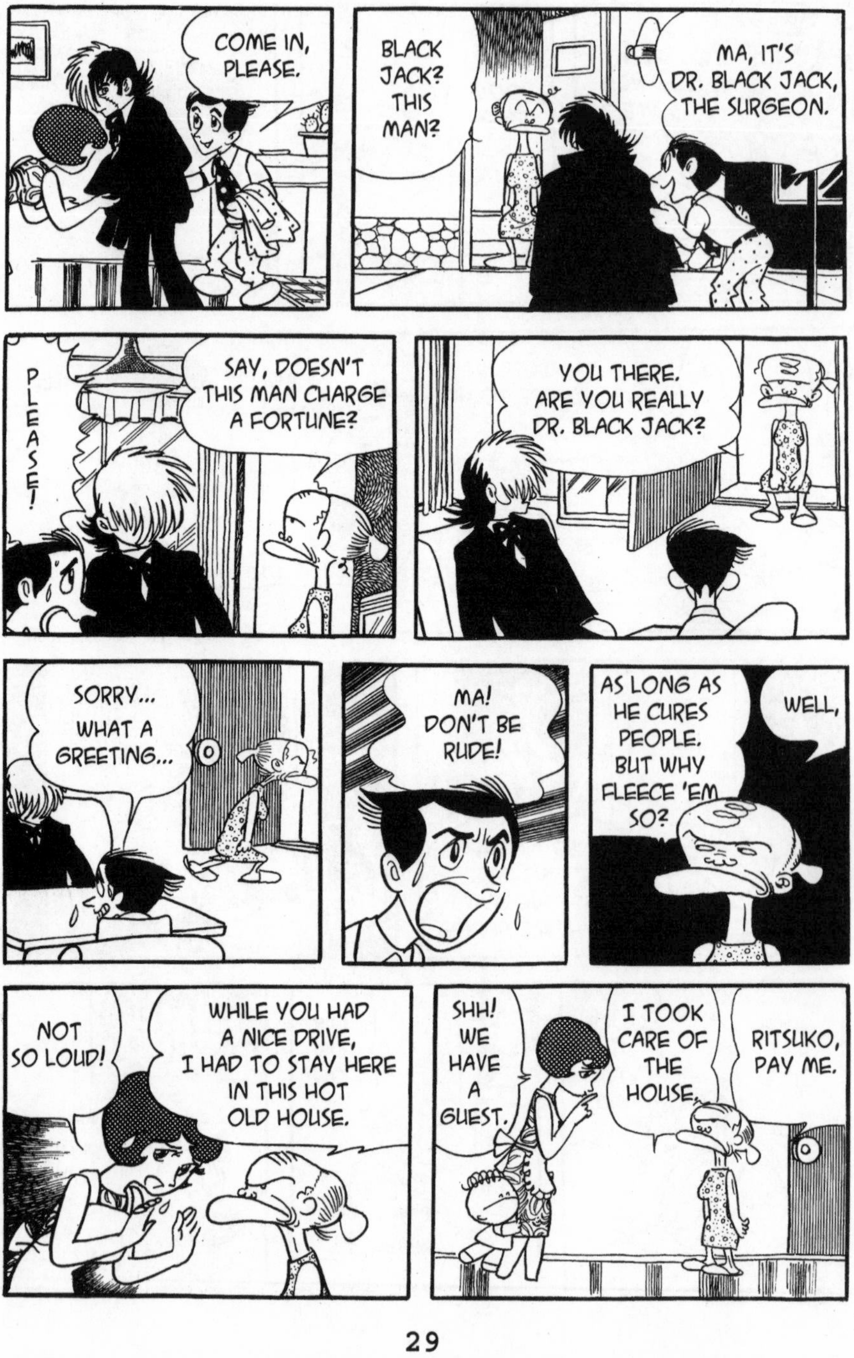
MA, IT'S DR. BLACK JACK, THE SURGEON.
BLACK JACK? THIS MAN?
COME IN, PLEASE.
YOU THERE. ARE YOU REALLY DR. BLACK JACK?
SAY, DOESN'T THIS MAN CHARGE A FORTUNE?
PLEASE!
WELL,
AS LONG AS HE CURES PEOPLE. BUT WHY FLEECE 'EM SO?
MA! DON'T BE RUDE!
SORRY... WHAT A GREETING...
RITSUKO, PAY ME.
I TOOK CARE OF THE HOUSE.
SHH! WE HAVE A GUEST.
WHILE YOU HAD A NICE DRIVE, I HAD TO STAY HERE IN THIS HOT OLD HOUSE.
NOT SO LOUD!

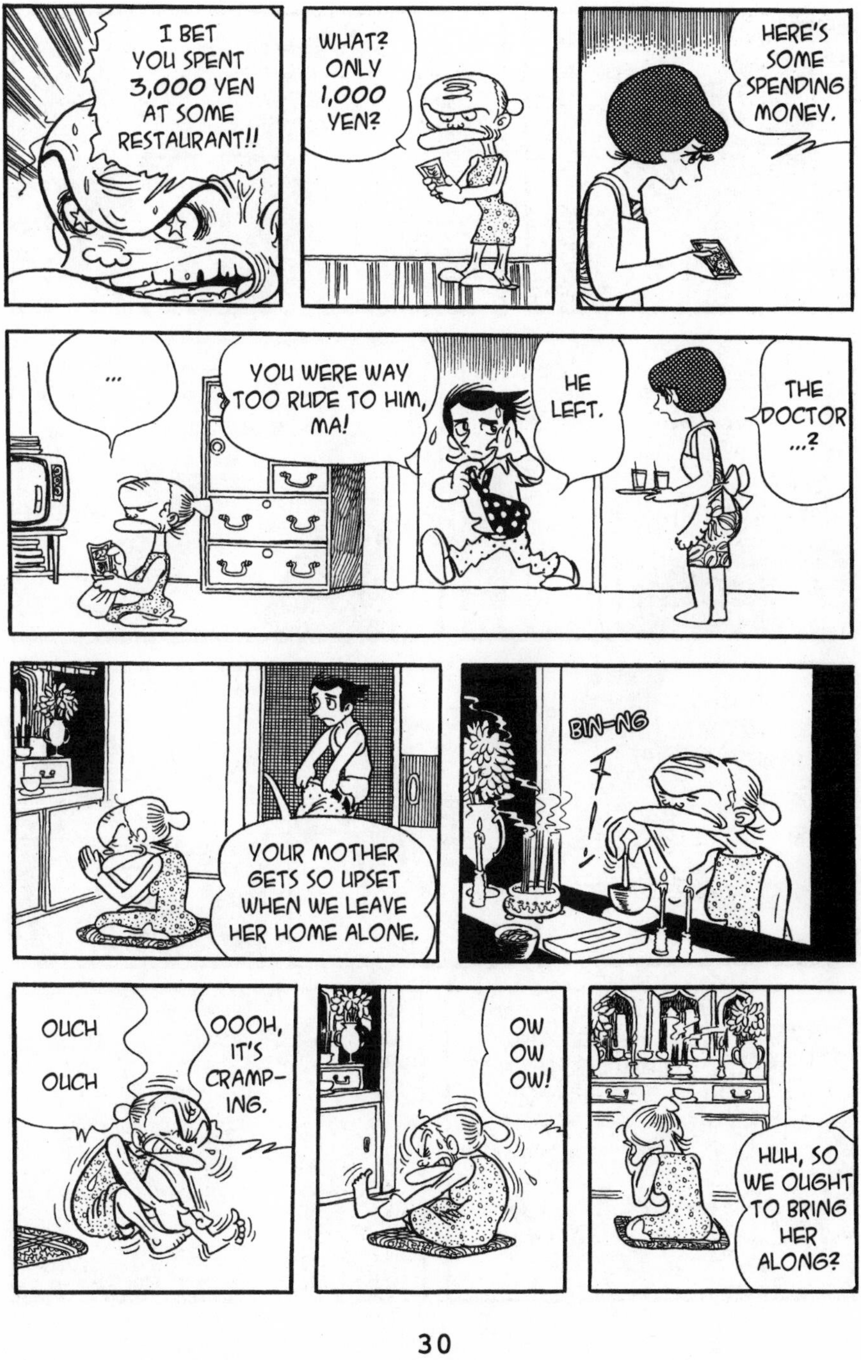
HERE'S SOME SPENDING MONEY.
WHAT? ONLY 1,000 YEN?
I BET YOU SPENT 3,000 YEN AT SOME RESTAURANT!!
THE DOCTOR ...?
HE LEFT.
YOU WERE WAY TOO RUDE TO HIM, MA!
...
BIN-NG
YOUR MOTHER GETS SO UPSET WHEN WE LEAVE HER HOME ALONE.
HUH, SO WE OUGHT TO BRING HER ALONG?
OW OW OW!
OOOH, IT'S CRAMP-ING.
OUCH OUCH

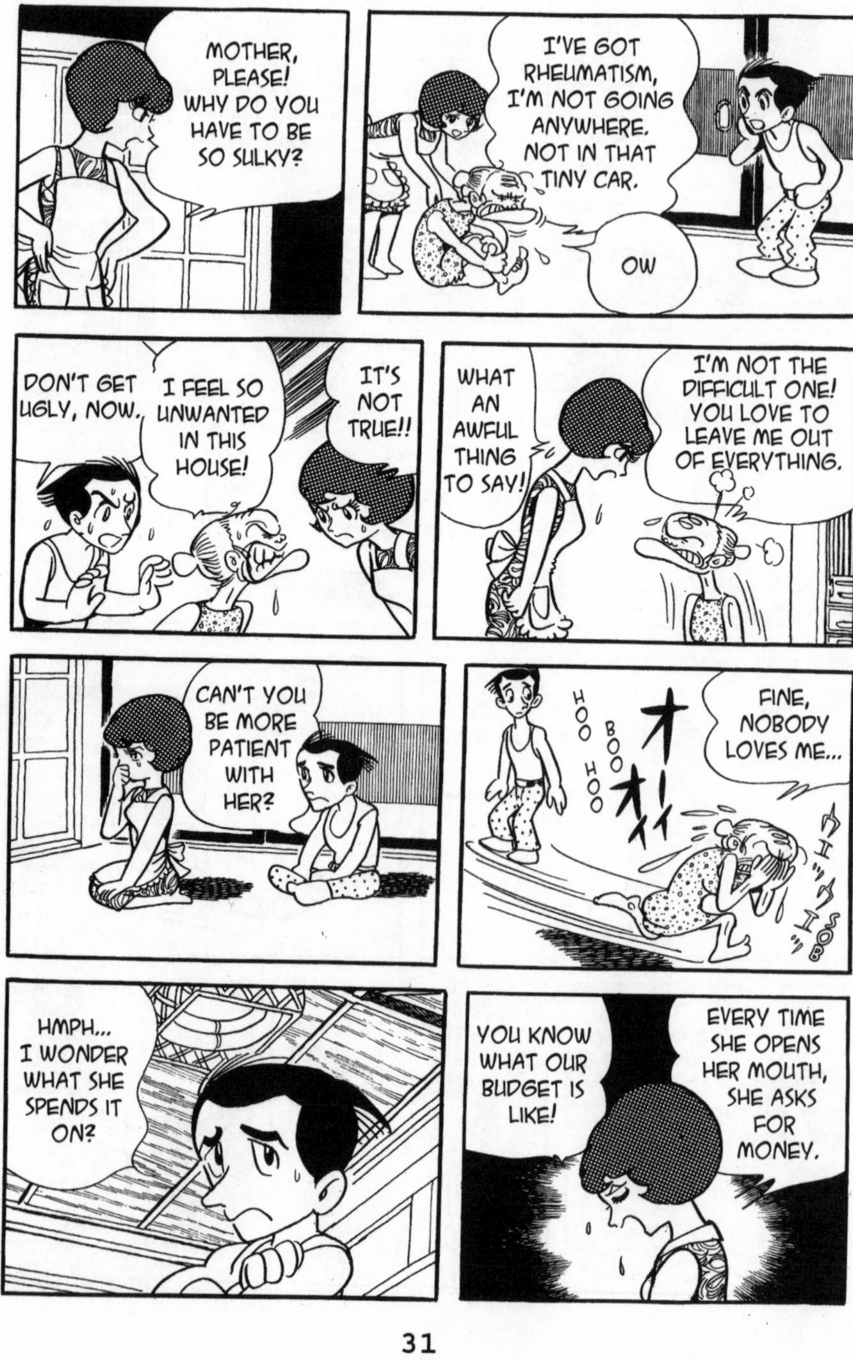
I'VE GOT RHEUMATISM, I'M NOT GOING ANYWHERE. NOT IN THAT TINY CAR.
OW
MOTHER, PLEASE! WHY DO YOU HAVE TO BE SO SULKY?
I'M NOT THE DIFFICULT ONE! YOU LOVE TO LEAVE ME OUT OF EVERYTHING.
WHAT AN AWFUL THING TO SAY!
IT'S NOT TRUE!!
I FEEL SO UNWANTED IN THIS HOUSE!
DON'T GET UGLY, NOW.
FINE, NOBODY LOVES ME...
SOB
BOO HOO
HOO HOO
CAN'T YOU BE MORE PATIENT WITH HER?
EVERY TIME SHE OPENS HER MOUTH, SHE ASKS FOR MONEY.
YOU KNOW WHAT OUR BUDGET IS LIKE!
HMPH... I WONDER WHAT SHE SPENDS IT ON?

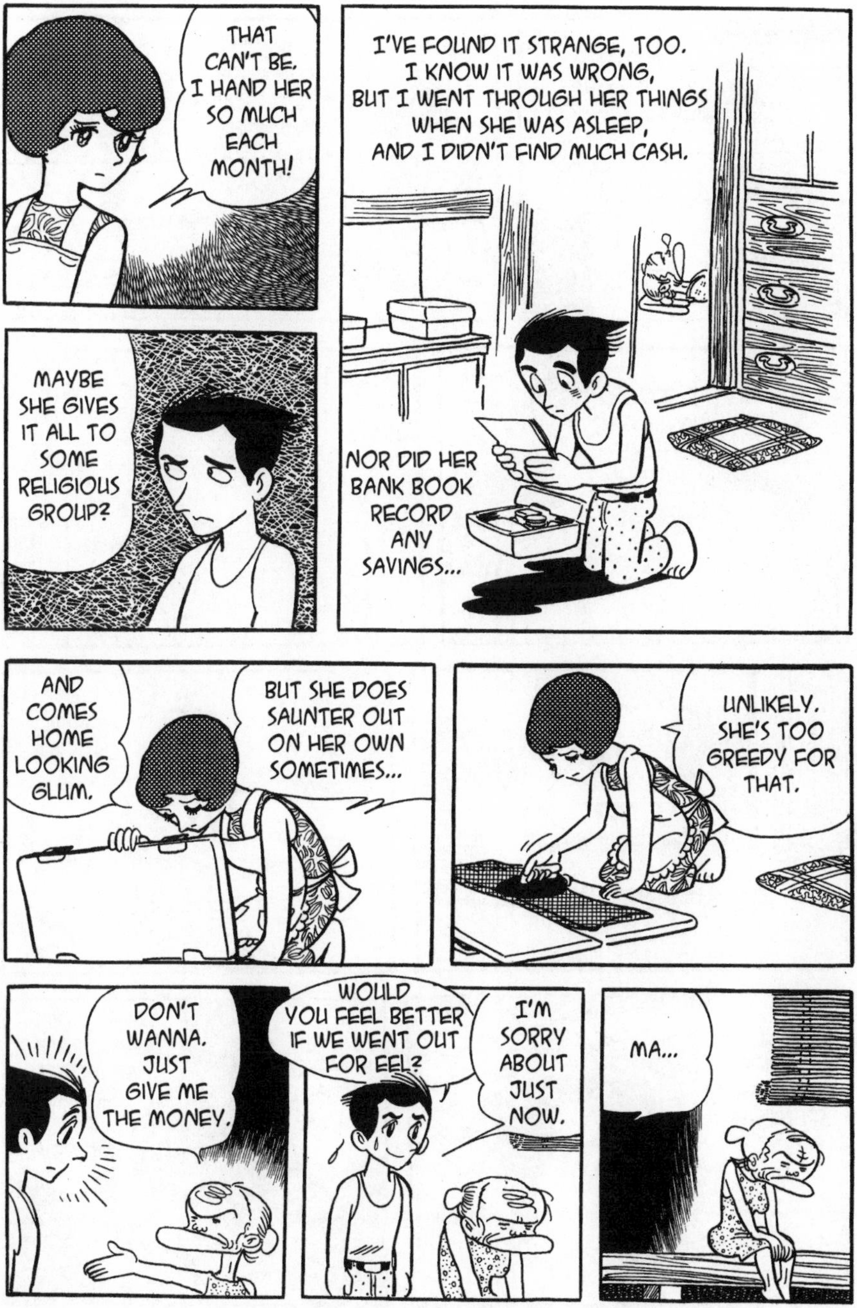
I'VE FOUND IT STRANGE, TOO. I KNOW IT WAS WRONG, BUT I WENT THROUGH HER THINGS WHEN SHE WAS ASLEEP, AND I DIDN'T FIND MUCH CASH.
NOR DID HER BANK BOOK RECORD ANY SAVINGS...
THAT CAN'T BE. I HAND HER SO MUCH EACH MONTH!
MAYBE SHE GIVES IT ALL TO SOME RELIGIOUS GROUP?
UNLIKELY. SHE'S TOO GREEDY FOR THAT.
BUT SHE DOES SAUNTER OUT ON HER OWN SOMETIMES...
AND COMES HOME LOOKING GLUM.
MA...
I'M SORRY ABOUT JUST NOW.
WOULD YOU FEEL BETTER IF WE WENT OUT FOR EEL?
DON'T WANNA. JUST GIVE ME THE MONEY.

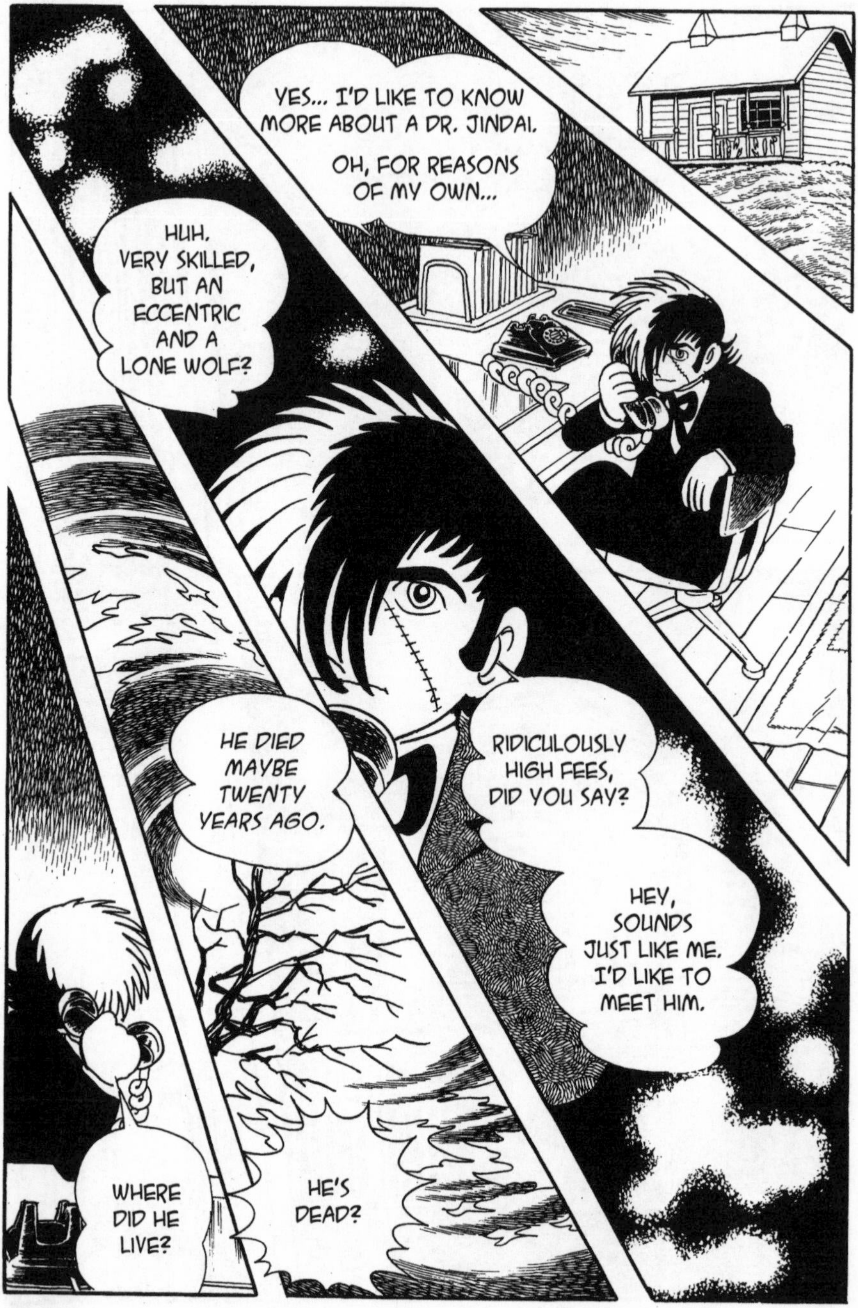
YES... I'D LIKE TO KNOW MORE ABOUT A DR. JINDAI.
OH, FOR REASONS OF MY OWN...
HUH. VERY SKILLED, BUT AN ECCENTRIC AND A LONE WOLF?
RIDICULOUSLY HIGH FEES, DID YOU SAY?
HEY, SOUNDS JUST LIKE ME. I'D LIKE TO MEET HIM.
HE DIED MAYBE TWENTY YEARS AGO.
HE'S DEAD?
WHERE DID HE LIVE?

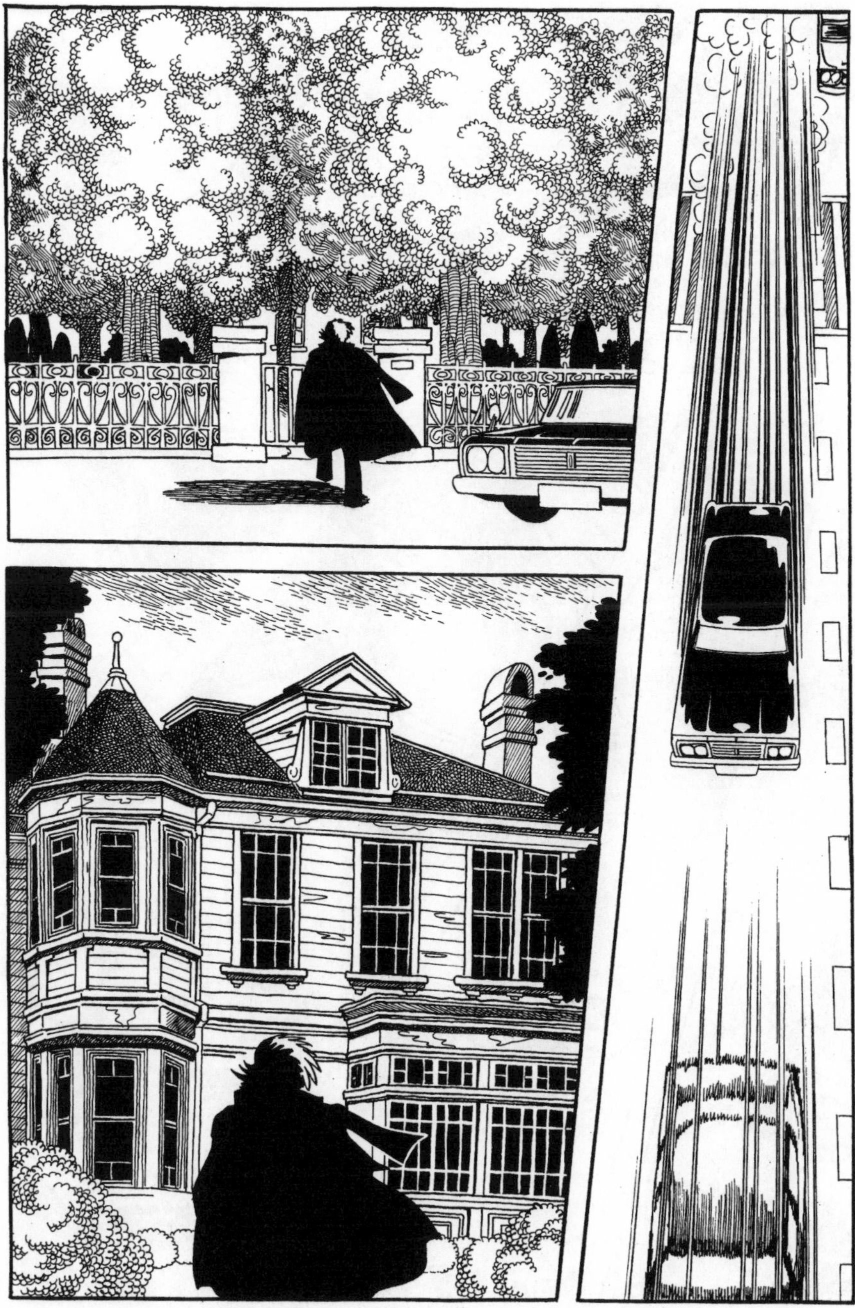

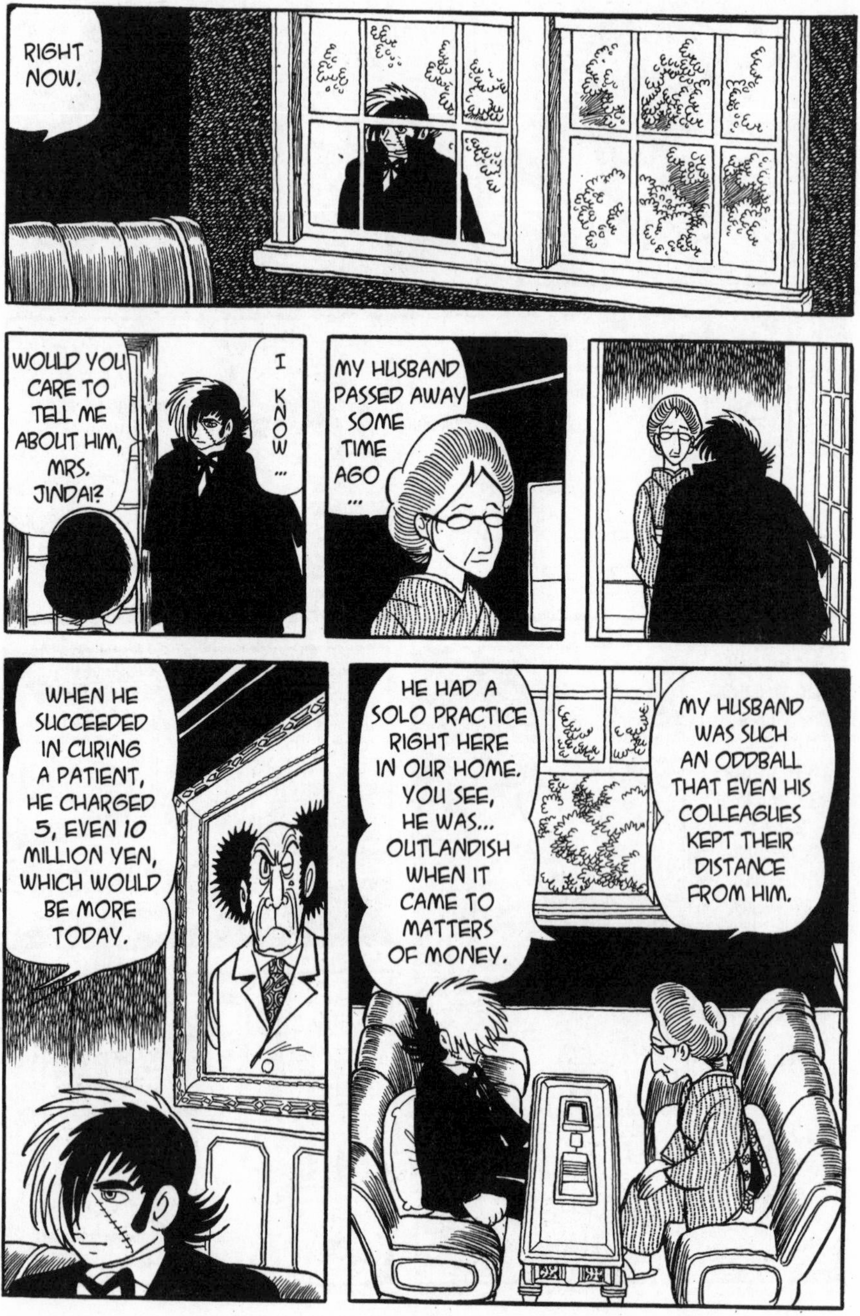
RIGHT NOW.
MY HUSBAND PASSED AWAY SOME TIME AGO ...
I KNOW ...
WOULD YOU CARE TO TELL ME ABOUT HIM, MRS. JINDAI?
MY HUSBAND WAS SUCH AN ODDBALL THAT EVEN HIS COLLEAGUES KEPT THEIR DISTANCE FROM HIM.
HE HAD A SOLO PRACTICE RIGHT HERE IN OUR HOME. YOU SEE, HE WAS... OUTLANDISH WHEN IT CAME TO MATTERS OF MONEY.
WHEN HE SUCCEEDED IN CURING A PATIENT, HE CHARGED 5, EVEN 10 MILLION YEN, WHICH WOULD BE MORE TODAY.

THAT *IS* STRANGE.

WELL ...

WHAT IS IT?

HA HA ...

IT SOUNDS LIKE I HAD A PEER IN DR. JINDAI!

I THOUGHT I WAS THE GREEDIEST MAN EVER.

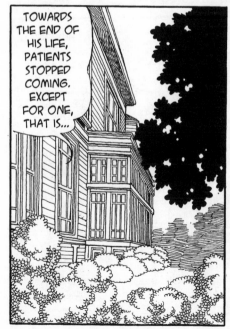

TOWARDS THE END OF HIS LIFE, PATIENTS STOPPED COMING. EXCEPT FOR ONE, THAT IS...

HE MUST HAVE BEEN ...

VERY, VERY SKILLED.

36

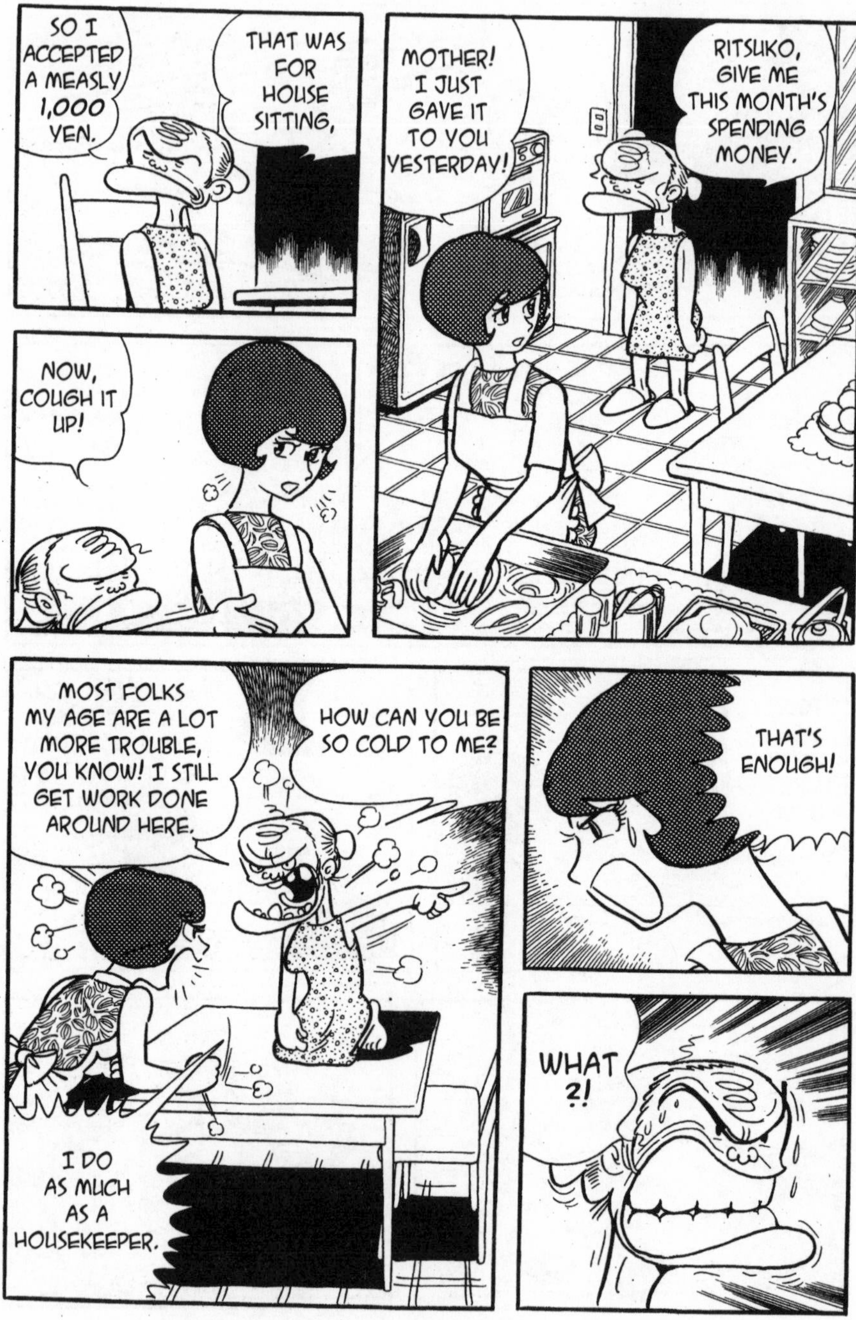
RITSUKO, GIVE ME THIS MONTH'S SPENDING MONEY.
MOTHER! I JUST GAVE IT TO YOU YESTERDAY!
THAT WAS FOR HOUSE SITTING,
SO I ACCEPTED A MEASLY 1,000 YEN.
NOW, COUGH IT UP!
THAT'S ENOUGH!
WHAT ?!
HOW CAN YOU BE SO COLD TO ME?
MOST FOLKS MY AGE ARE A LOT MORE TROUBLE, YOU KNOW! I STILL GET WORK DONE AROUND HERE.
I DO AS MUCH AS A HOUSEKEEPER.

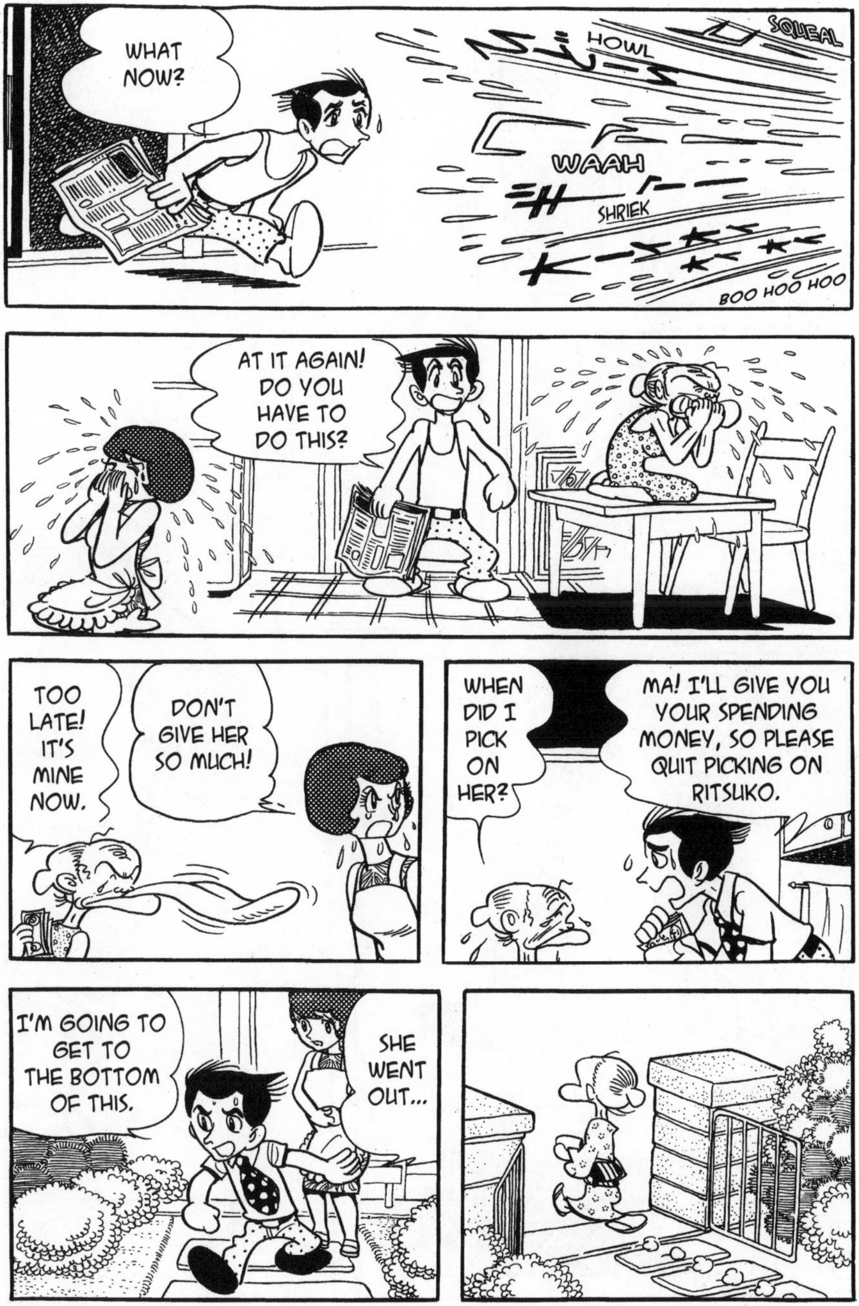
SQUEAL
HOWL
WAAH
SHRIEK
BOO HOO HOO
WHAT NOW?
AT IT AGAIN! DO YOU HAVE TO DO THIS?
MA! I'LL GIVE YOU YOUR SPENDING MONEY, SO PLEASE QUIT PICKING ON RITSUKO.
WHEN DID I PICK ON HER?
DON'T GIVE HER SO MUCH!
TOO LATE! IT'S MINE NOW.
SHE WENT OUT...
I'M GOING TO GET TO THE BOTTOM OF THIS.

INTERNAL AND
PEDIATRIC MEDICINE

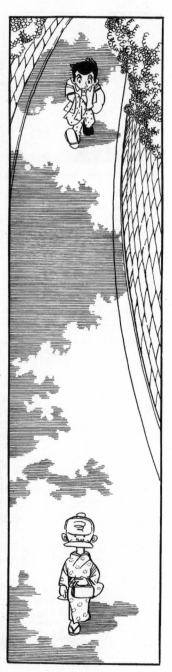

WHY, THIS IS...

39

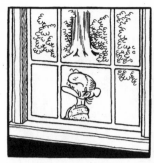

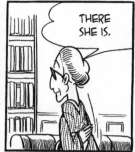

DING DONG
THERE SHE IS.
THANK YOU, AS ALWAYS.
I BELIEVE THIS IS MY LAST PAYMENT?
...SO IT IS! WE ARE DONE.
PHEW... THAT'S A LOAD OFF MY MIND.
IT'S BEEN EXACTLY THIRTY YEARS!
YOU CAME EVERY MONTH, WITHOUT FAIL...
I GAVE MY WORD TO DR. JINDAI
THAT I'D PAY HIS FEE IF IT TOOK MY WHOLE LIFE. NOW I'M FREE TO DIE.
DEAR ME...
DON'T SAY THAT.
PLEASE GIVE MY BEST REGARDS TO YOUR SON.
I'LL BE ON MY WAY NOW...

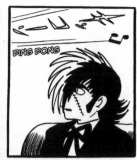

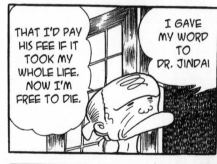

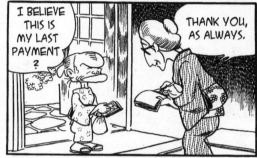

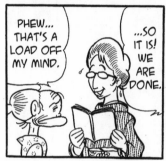

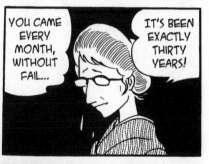

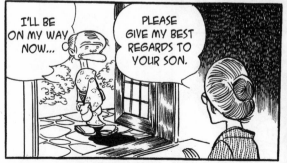

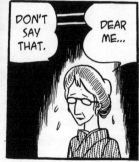

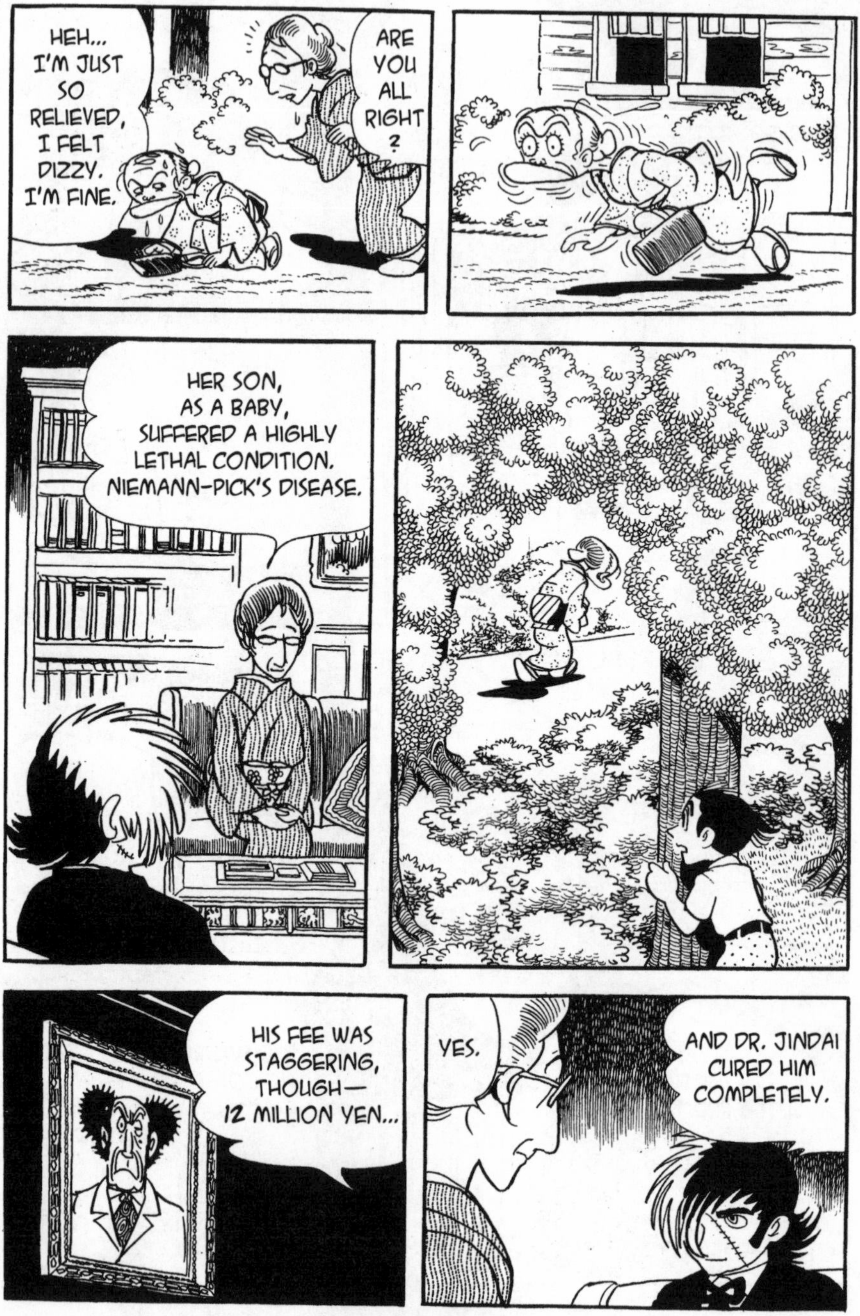
ARE YOU ALL RIGHT?
HEH... I'M JUST SO RELIEVED, I FELT DIZZY. I'M FINE.
HER SON, AS A BABY, SUFFERED A HIGHLY LETHAL CONDITION. NIEMANN-PICK'S DISEASE.
AND DR. JINDAI CURED HIM COMPLETELY.
YES.
HIS FEE WAS STAGGERING, THOUGH— 12 MILLION YEN...

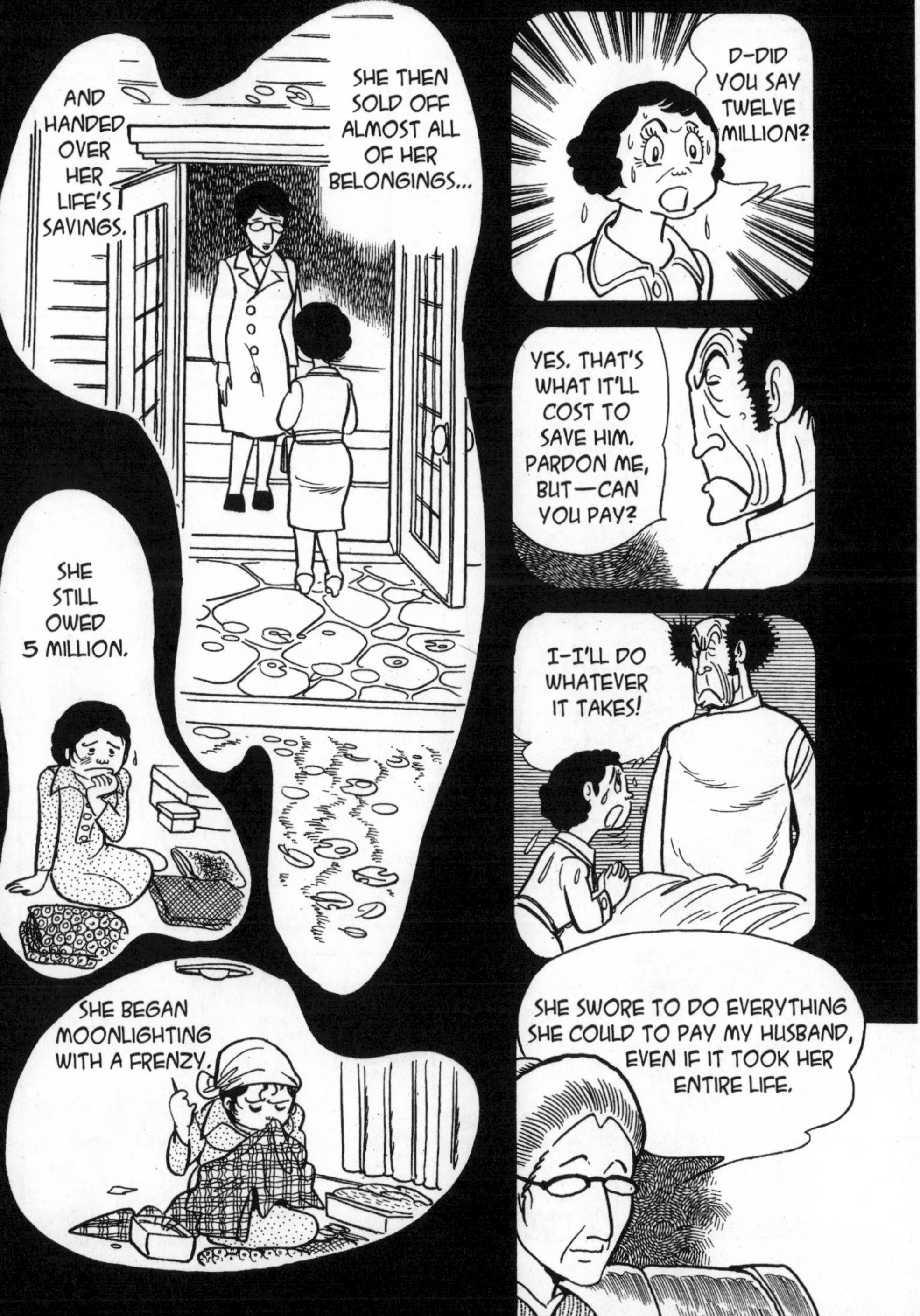
D-DID YOU SAY TWELVE MILLION?
YES. THAT'S WHAT IT'LL COST TO SAVE HIM. PARDON ME, BUT—CAN YOU PAY?
I-I'LL DO WHATEVER IT TAKES!
SHE SWORE TO DO EVERYTHING SHE COULD TO PAY MY HUSBAND, EVEN IF IT TOOK HER ENTIRE LIFE.
SHE THEN SOLD OFF ALMOST ALL OF HER BELONGINGS...
AND HANDED OVER HER LIFE'S SAVINGS.
SHE STILL OWED 5 MILLION.
SHE BEGAN MOONLIGHTING WITH A FRENZY.

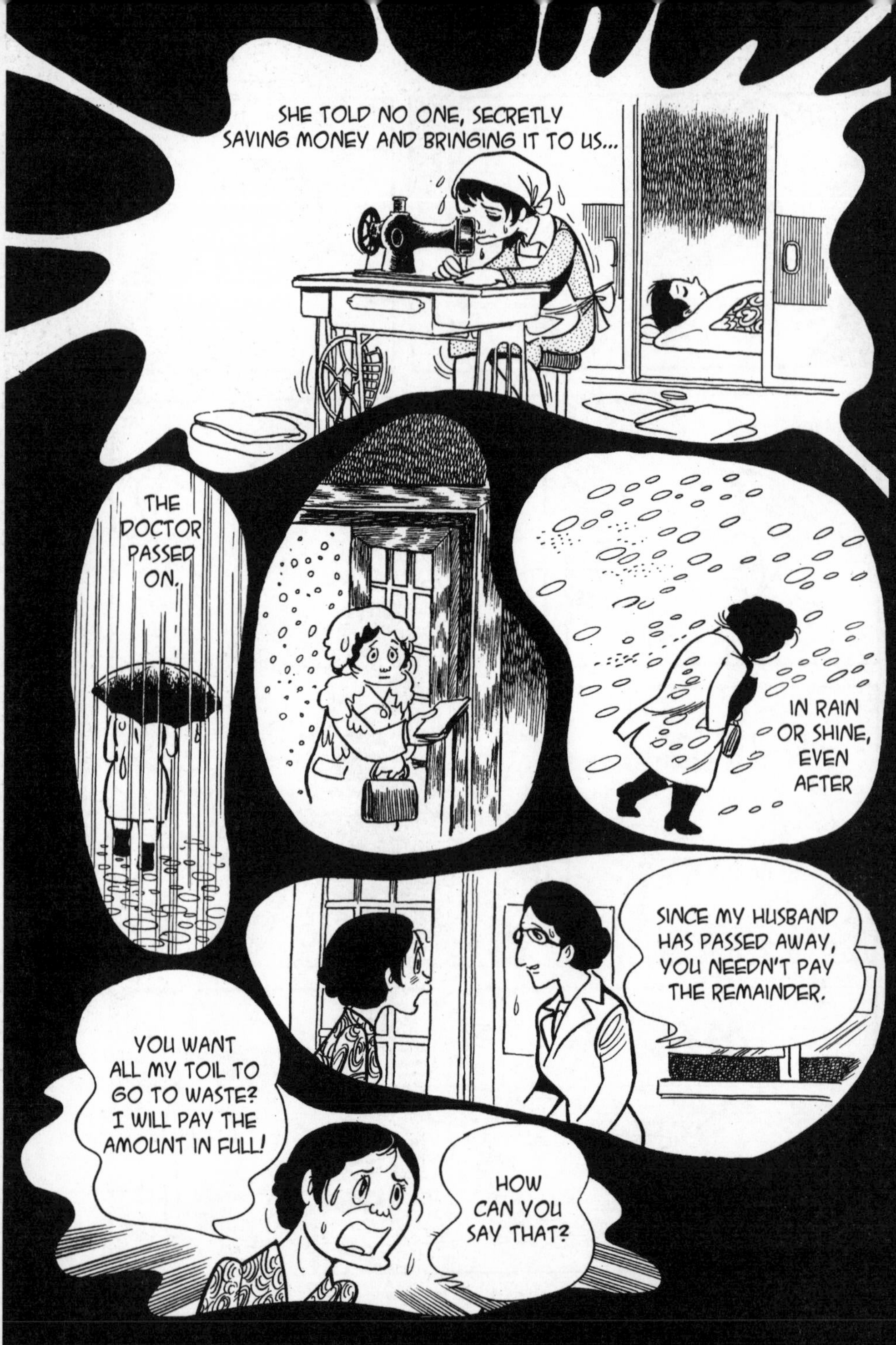
SHE TOLD NO ONE, SECRETLY SAVING MONEY AND BRINGING IT TO US...
IN RAIN OR SHINE, EVEN AFTER
THE DOCTOR PASSED ON.
SINCE MY HUSBAND HAS PASSED AWAY, YOU NEEDN'T PAY THE REMAINDER.
HOW CAN YOU SAY THAT?
YOU WANT ALL MY TOIL TO GO TO WASTE? I WILL PAY THE AMOUNT IN FULL!

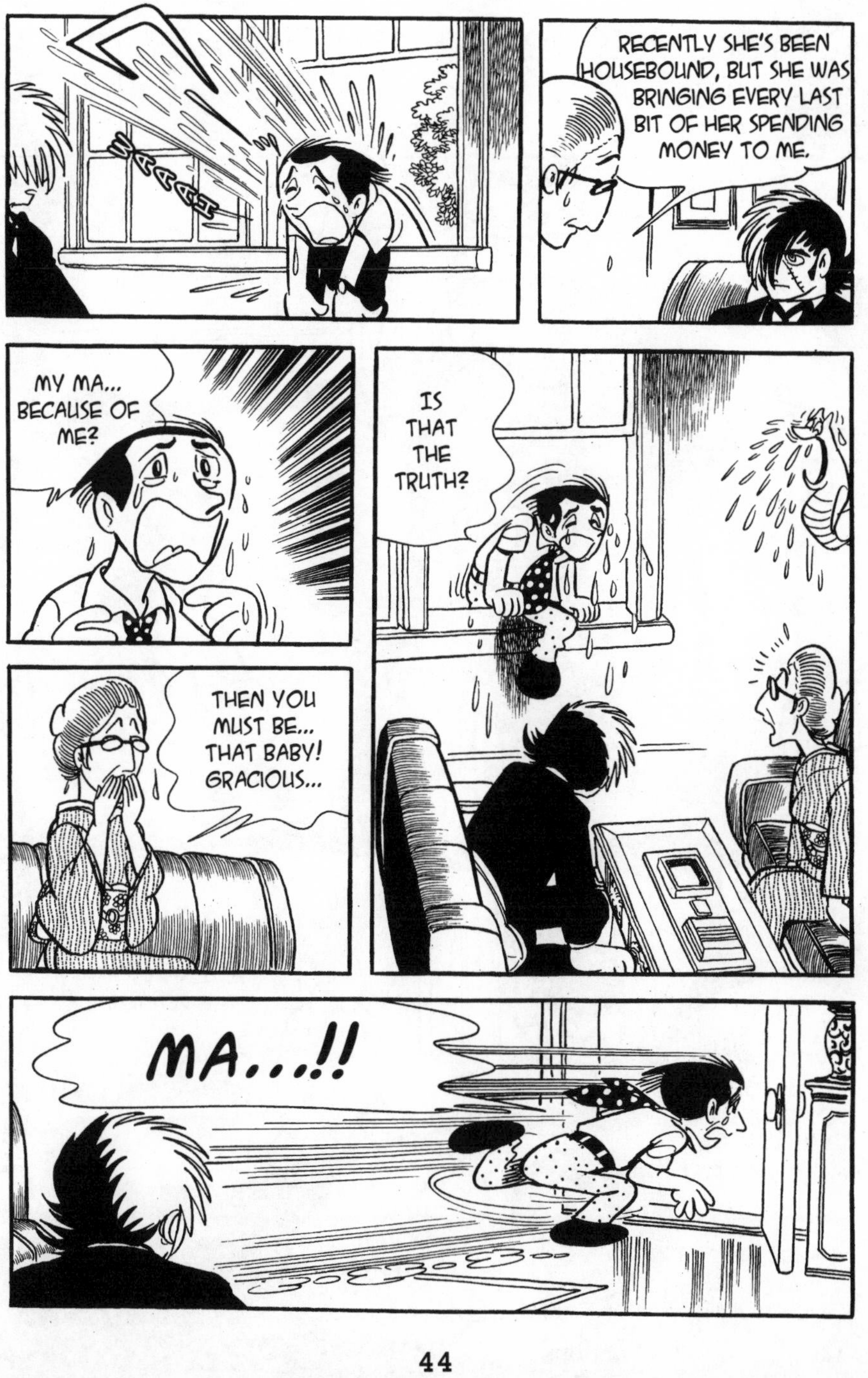
RECENTLY SHE'S BEEN HOUSEBOUND, BUT SHE WAS BRINGING EVERY LAST BIT OF HER SPENDING MONEY TO ME.
IS THAT THE TRUTH?
MY MA... BECAUSE OF ME?
THEN YOU MUST BE... THAT BABY! GRACIOUS...
MA...!!

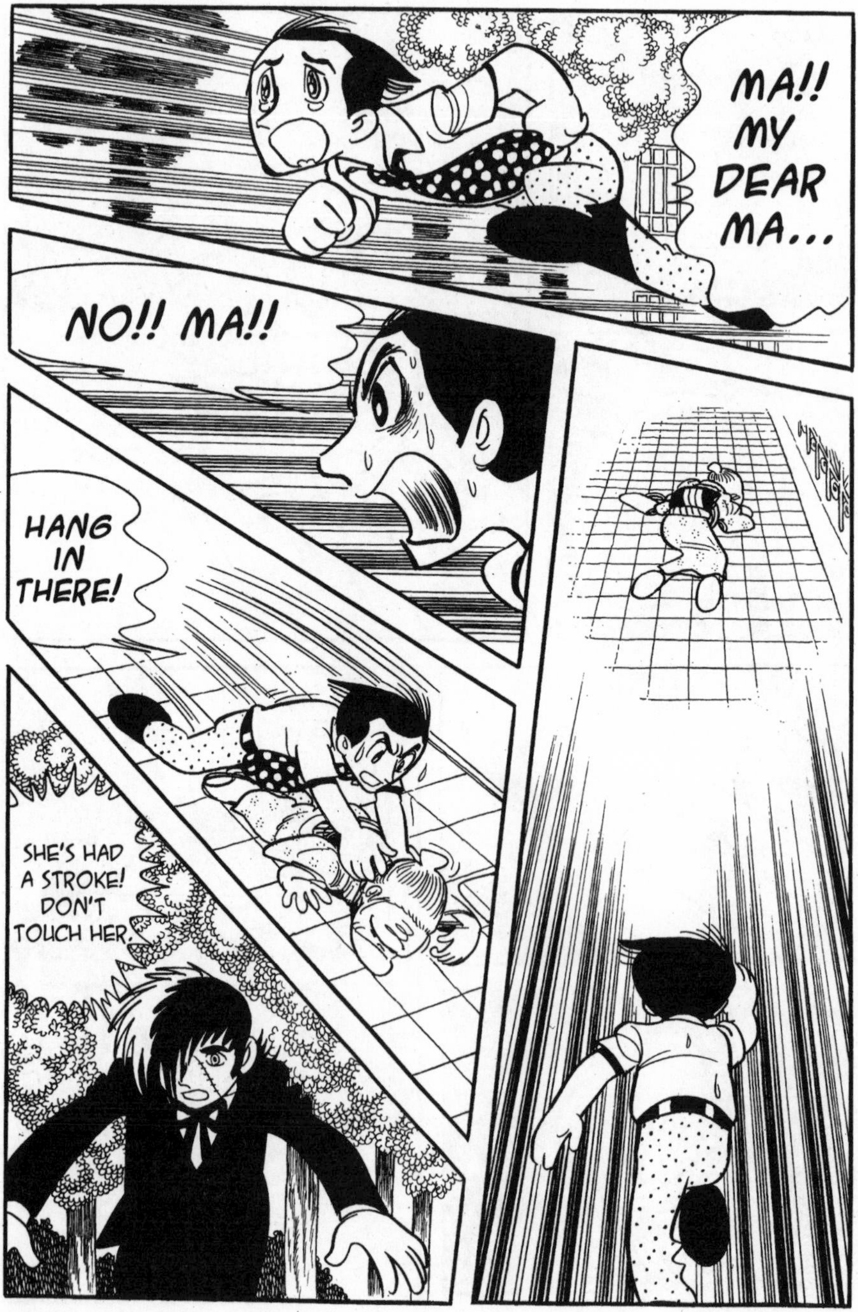

MA!! MY DEAR MA...
NO!! MA!!
HANG IN THERE!
SHE'S HAD A STROKE! DON'T TOUCH HER.

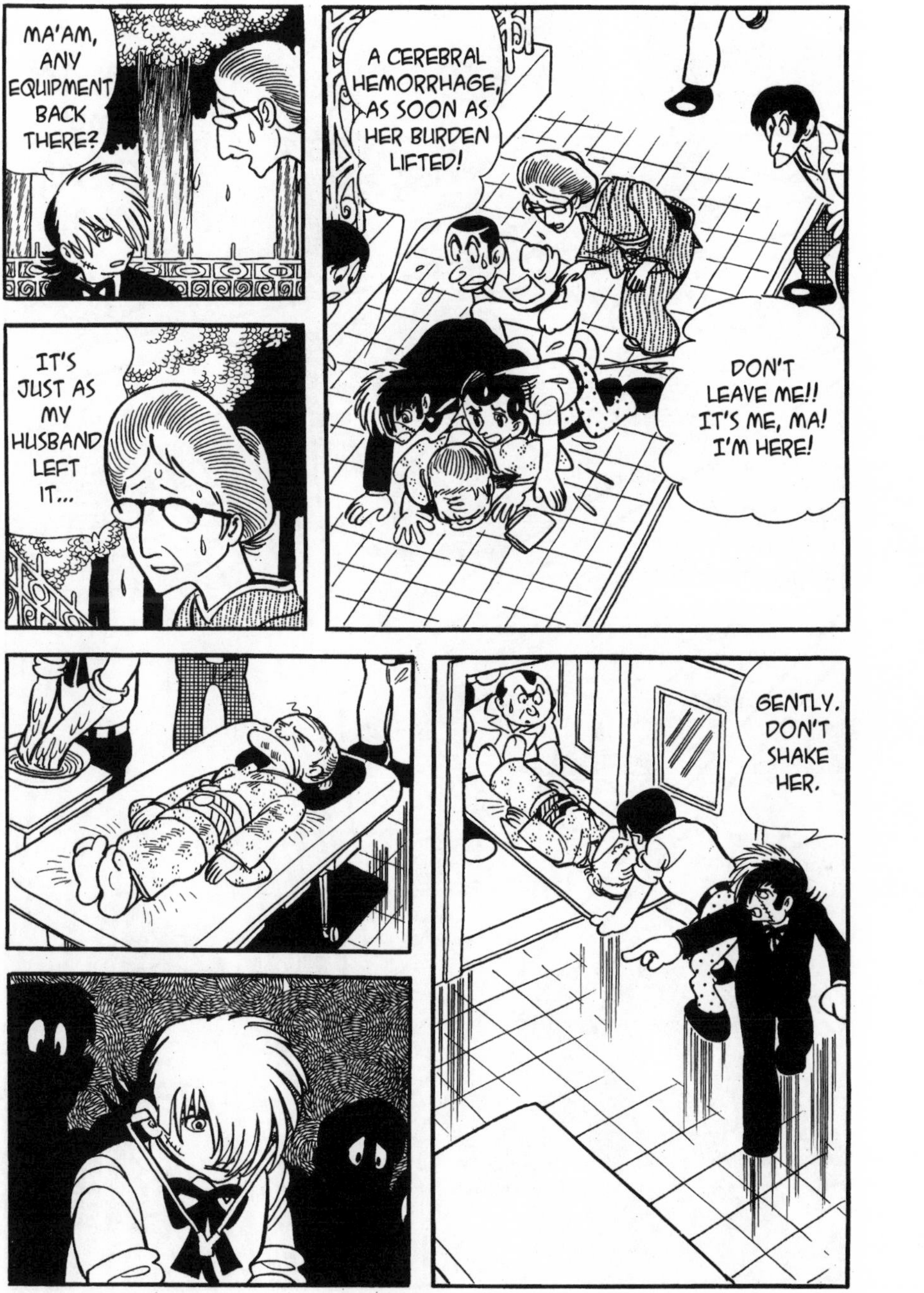
A CEREBRAL HEMORRHAGE, AS SOON AS HER BURDEN LIFTED!
DON'T LEAVE ME!! IT'S ME, MA! I'M HERE!
MA'AM, ANY EQUIPMENT BACK THERE?
IT'S JUST AS MY HUSBAND LEFT IT...
GENTLY. DON'T SHAKE HER.

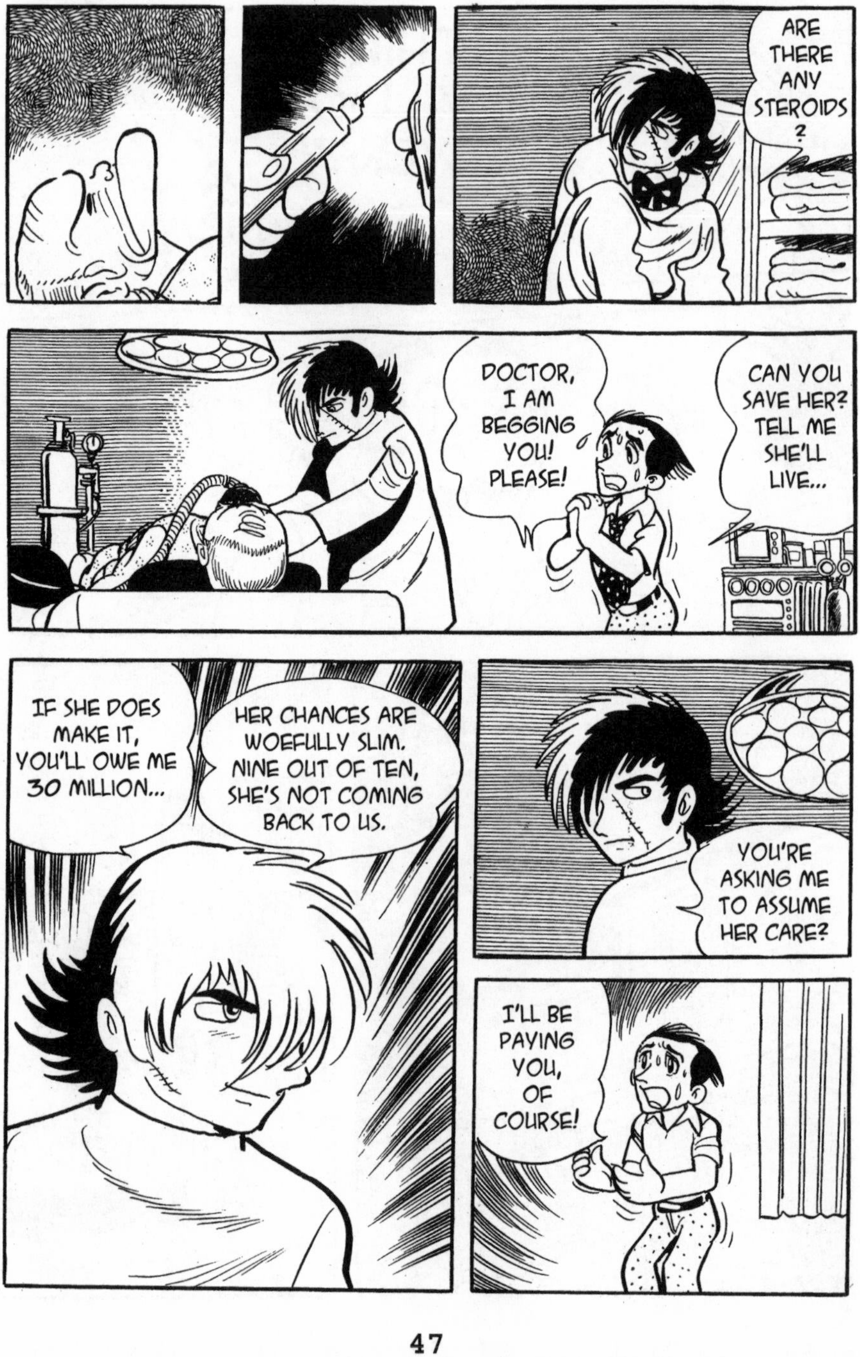
ARE THERE ANY STEROIDS?
CAN YOU SAVE HER? TELL ME SHE'LL LIVE...
DOCTOR, I AM BEGGING YOU! PLEASE!
YOU'RE ASKING ME TO ASSUME HER CARE?
I'LL BE PAYING YOU, OF COURSE!
HER CHANCES ARE WOEFULLY SLIM. NINE OUT OF TEN, SHE'S NOT COMING BACK TO US.
IF SHE DOES MAKE IT, YOU'LL OWE ME 30 MILLION...

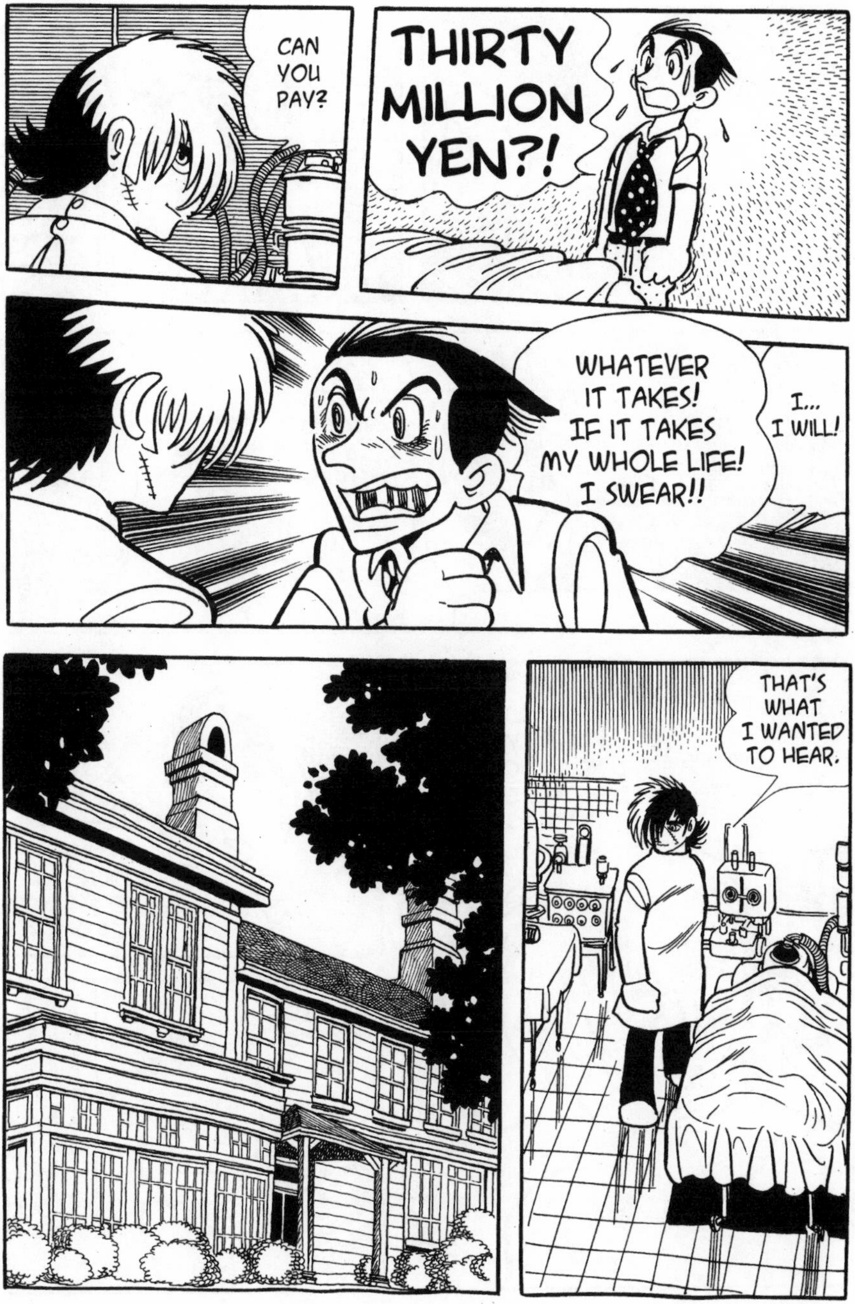
THIRTY MILLION YEN?!
CAN YOU PAY?
I... I WILL!
WHATEVER IT TAKES! IF IT TAKES MY WHOLE LIFE! I SWEAR!!
THAT'S WHAT I WANTED TO HEAR.

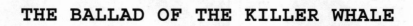

THE BALLAD OF THE KILLER WHALE

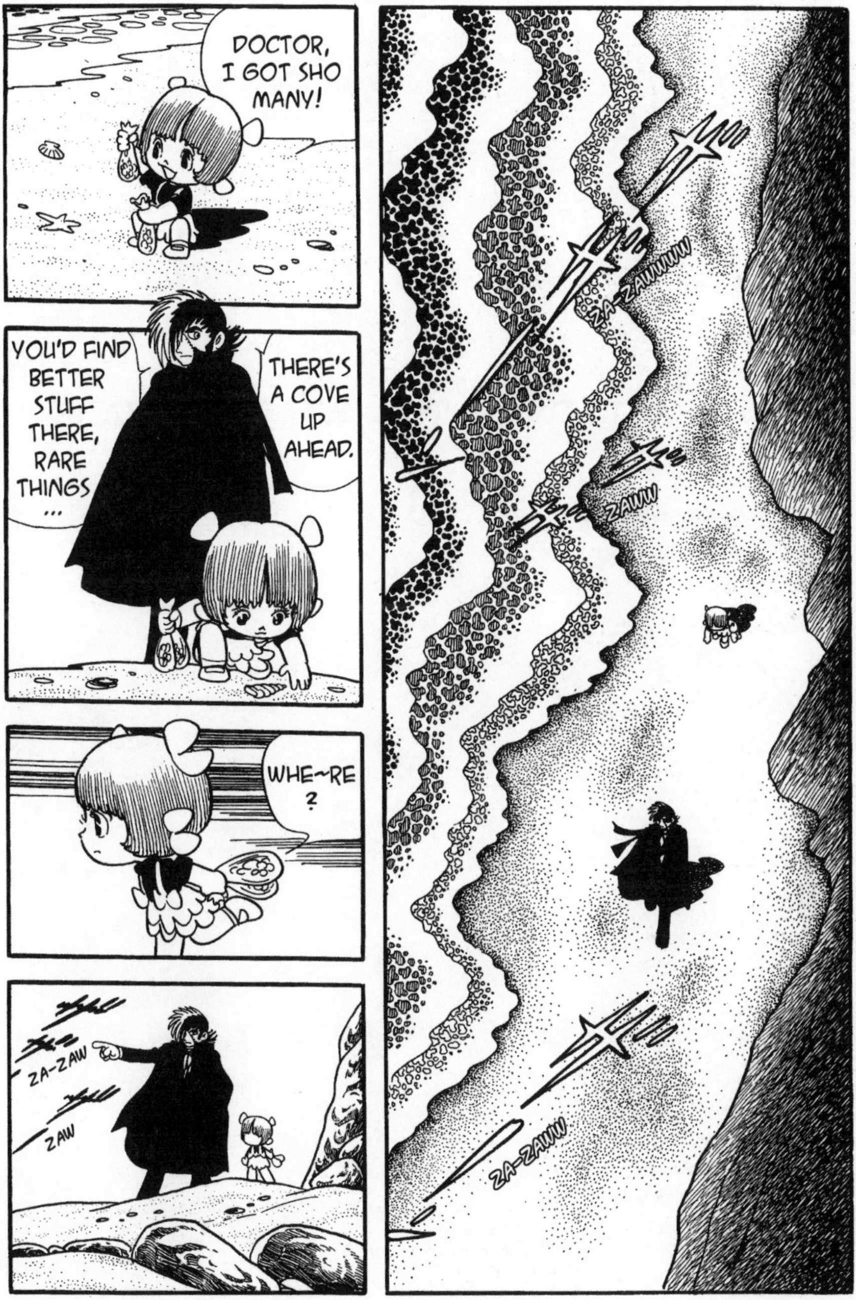
DOCTOR, I GOT SHO MANY!
THERE'S A COVE UP AHEAD.
YOU'D FIND BETTER STUFF THERE, RARE THINGS ...
WHE~RE ?
ZA-ZAW
ZAW
ZA-ZAWWW
ZAWW
ZA-ZAWW

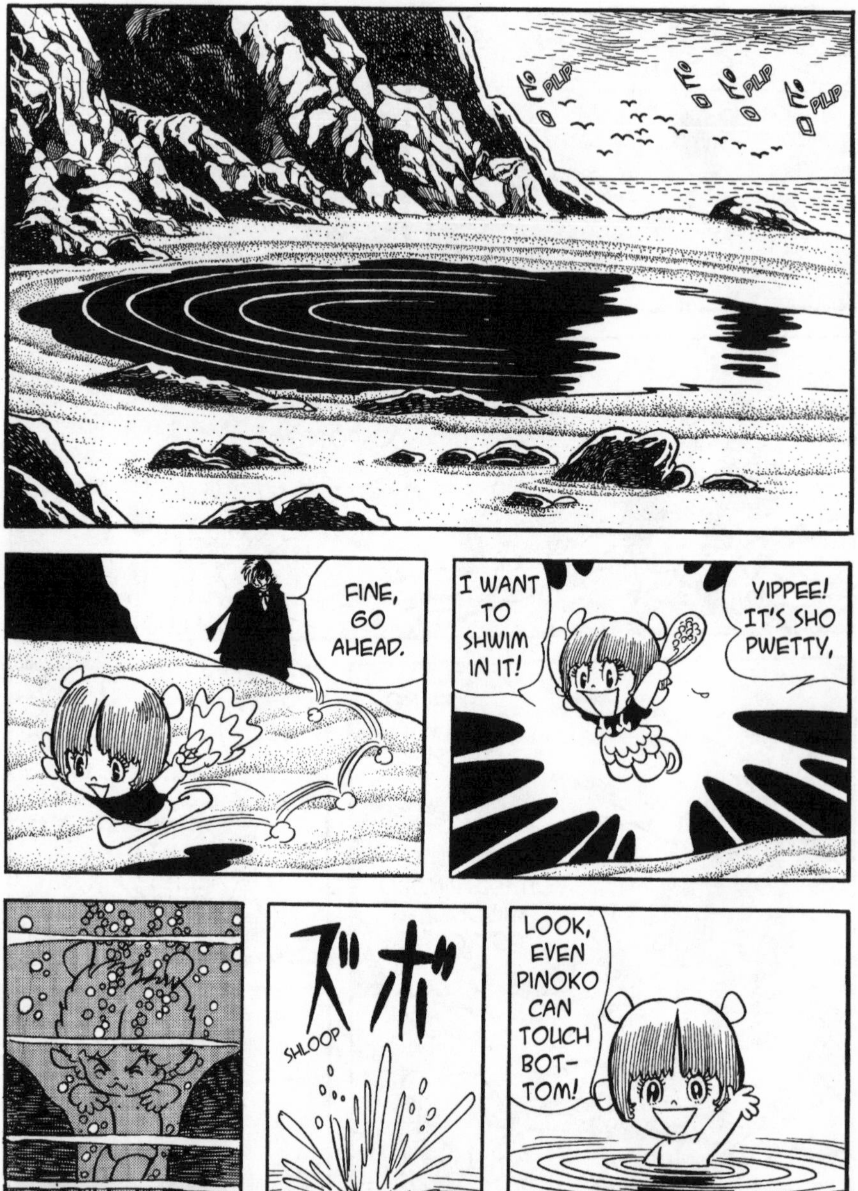
PLIP
PLIP
PLIP
YIPPEE! IT'S SHO PWETTY,
I WANT TO SHWIM IN IT!
FINE, GO AHEAD.
LOOK, EVEN PINOKO CAN TOUCH BOT-TOM!
ズボ
SHLOOP

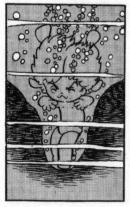

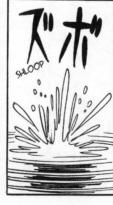

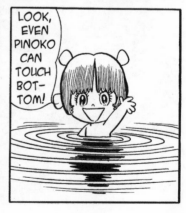

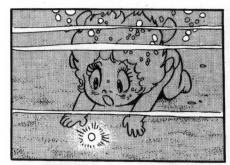

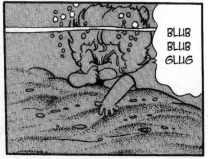

BLUB BLUB GLUG
LOOK, A PEAWL!
I FOUND IT ON THE BOTTOM!
DID YOU, NOW.
LOOK! IS THIS COWAL? IS IT WEAL?
I'D SAY SO.
CAN TAKE?
TAKE ALL YOU LIKE.
HOW DO YOU KNOW THIS PLACE?
ZAWWW
ZVVV
ZA-
WHY DIDN'T YOU TELL PINOKO SHOONER, DOCTOR?
I DIDN'T WANT TO TELL ANYONE.

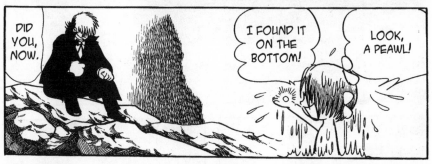

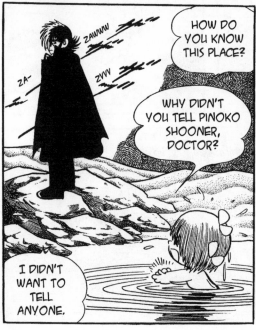

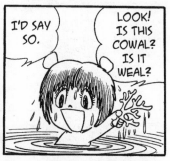

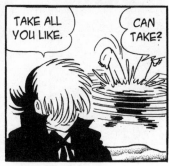

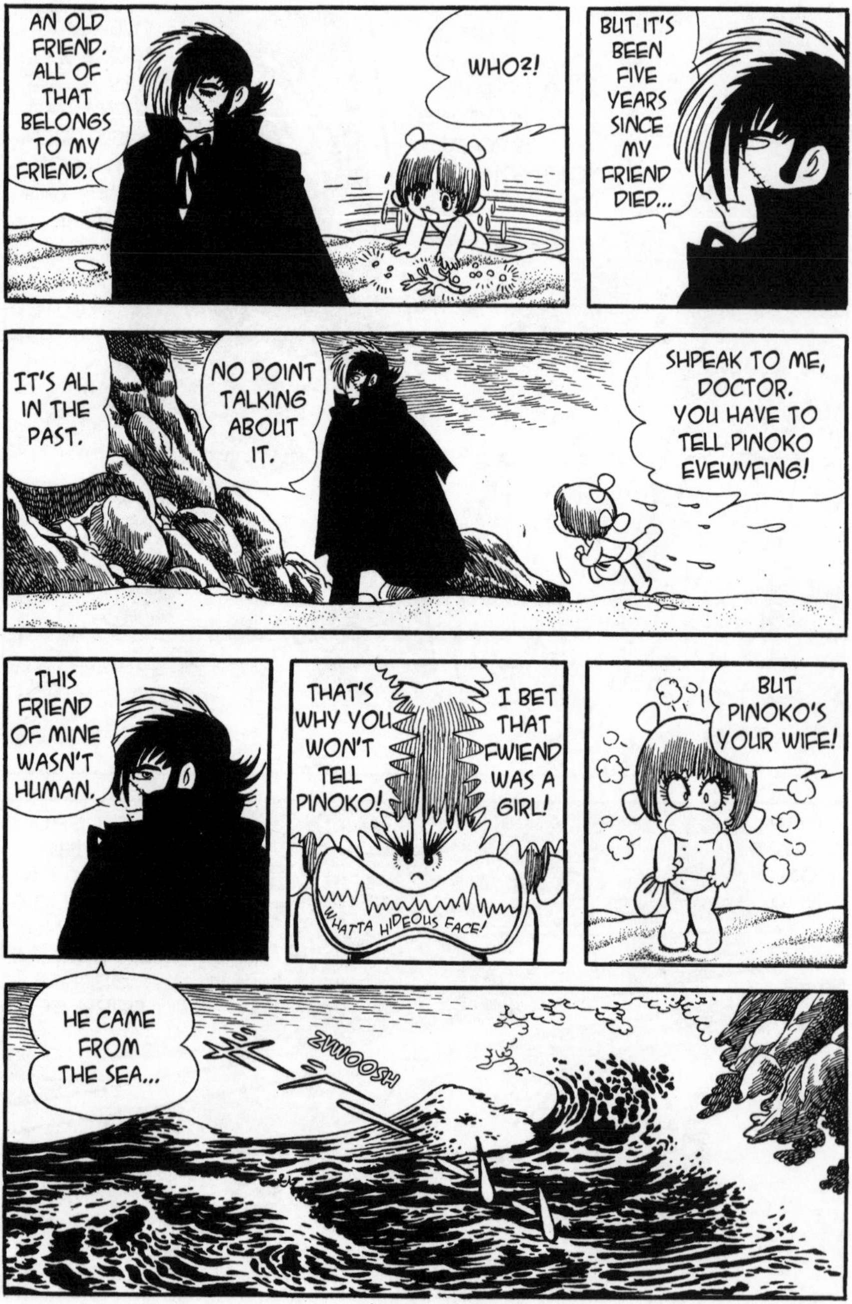
AN OLD FRIEND. ALL OF THAT BELONGS TO MY FRIEND.
WHO?!
BUT IT'S BEEN FIVE YEARS SINCE MY FRIEND DIED...
IT'S ALL IN THE PAST.
NO POINT TALKING ABOUT IT.
SHPEAK TO ME, DOCTOR. YOU HAVE TO TELL PINOKO EVEWYFING!
THIS FRIEND OF MINE WASN'T HUMAN.
THAT'S WHY YOU WON'T TELL PINOKO!
I BET THAT FWIEND WAS A GIRL!
WHATTA HIDEOUS FACE!
BUT PINOKO'S YOUR WIFE!
HE CAME FROM THE SEA...
ZWOOSH
HSOOWZ

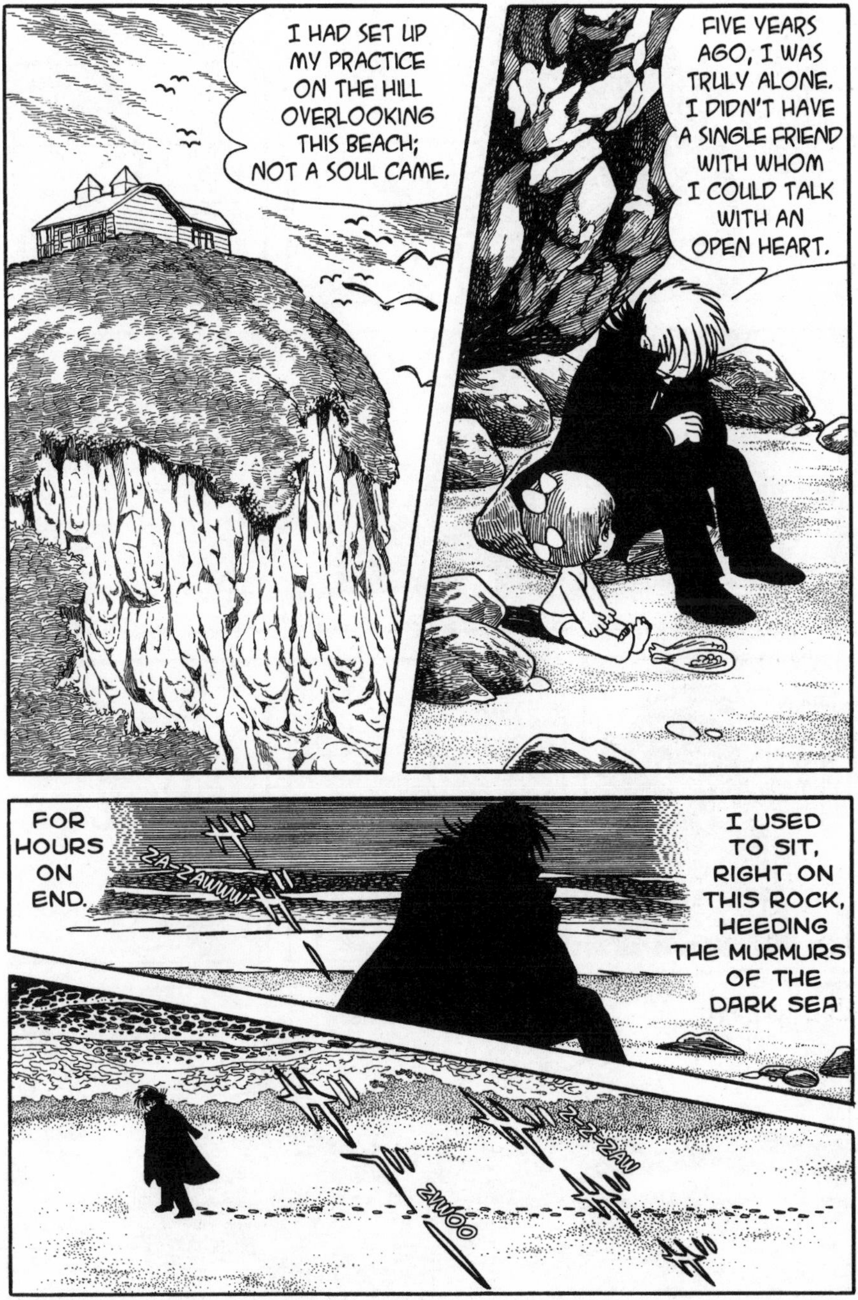
FIVE YEARS AGO, I WAS TRULY ALONE. I DIDN'T HAVE A SINGLE FRIEND WITH WHOM I COULD TALK WITH AN OPEN HEART.
I HAD SET UP MY PRACTICE ON THE HILL OVERLOOKING THIS BEACH; NOT A SOUL CAME.
I USED TO SIT, RIGHT ON THIS ROCK, HEEDING THE MURMURS OF THE DARK SEA
FOR HOURS ON END.
ZA-ZAWWW
ZA-ZA-ZAW

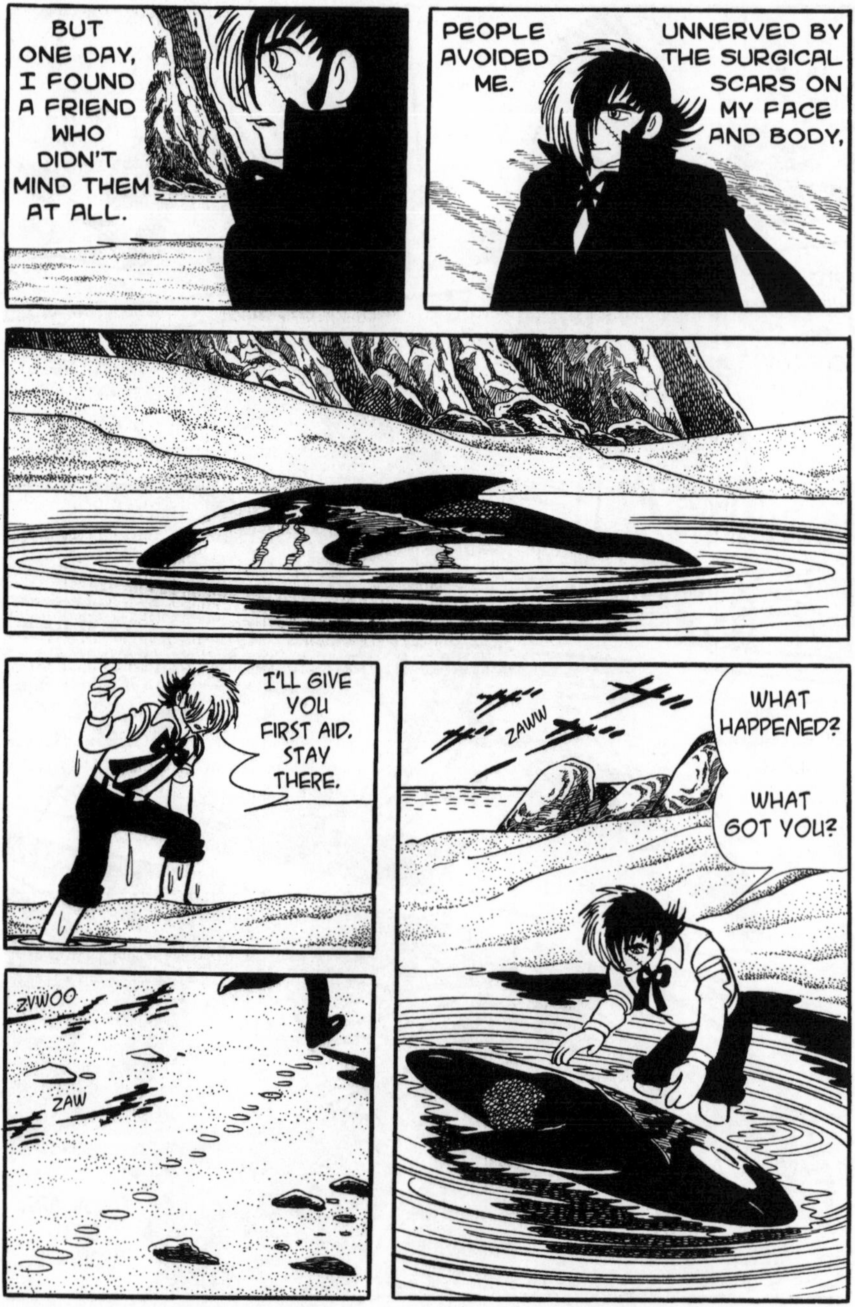
UNNERVED BY THE SURGICAL SCARS ON MY FACE AND BODY,
PEOPLE AVOIDED ME.
BUT ONE DAY, I FOUND A FRIEND WHO DIDN'T MIND THEM AT ALL.
ZAWW
WHAT HAPPENED?
WHAT GOT YOU?
I'LL GIVE YOU FIRST AID. STAY THERE.
ZVWOO
ZAW

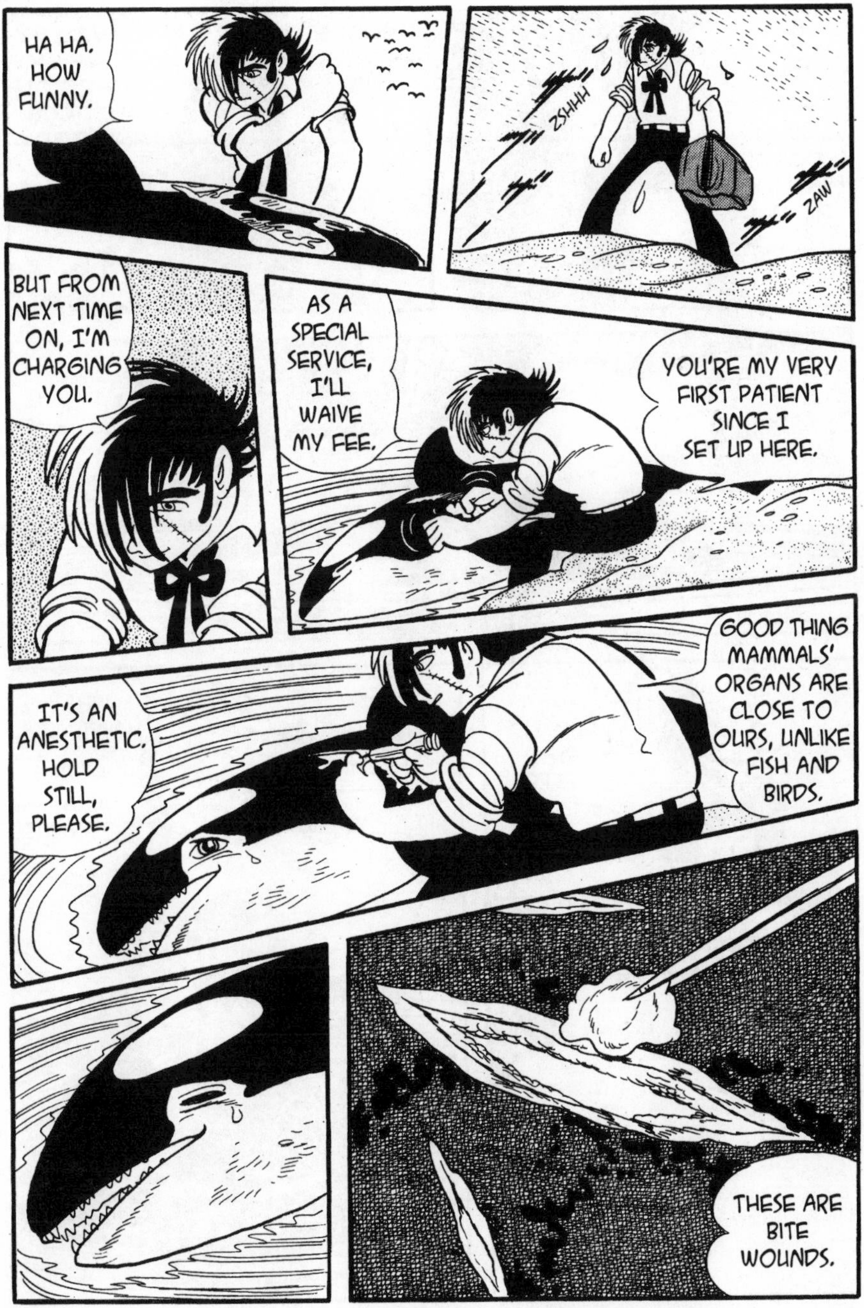
ZSHHH
ZAW
HA HA. HOW FUNNY.
YOU'RE MY VERY FIRST PATIENT SINCE I SET UP HERE.
AS A SPECIAL SERVICE, I'LL WAIVE MY FEE.
BUT FROM NEXT TIME ON, I'M CHARGING YOU.
GOOD THING MAMMALS' ORGANS ARE CLOSE TO OURS, UNLIKE FISH AND BIRDS.
IT'S AN ANESTHETIC. HOLD STILL, PLEASE.
THESE ARE BITE WOUNDS.

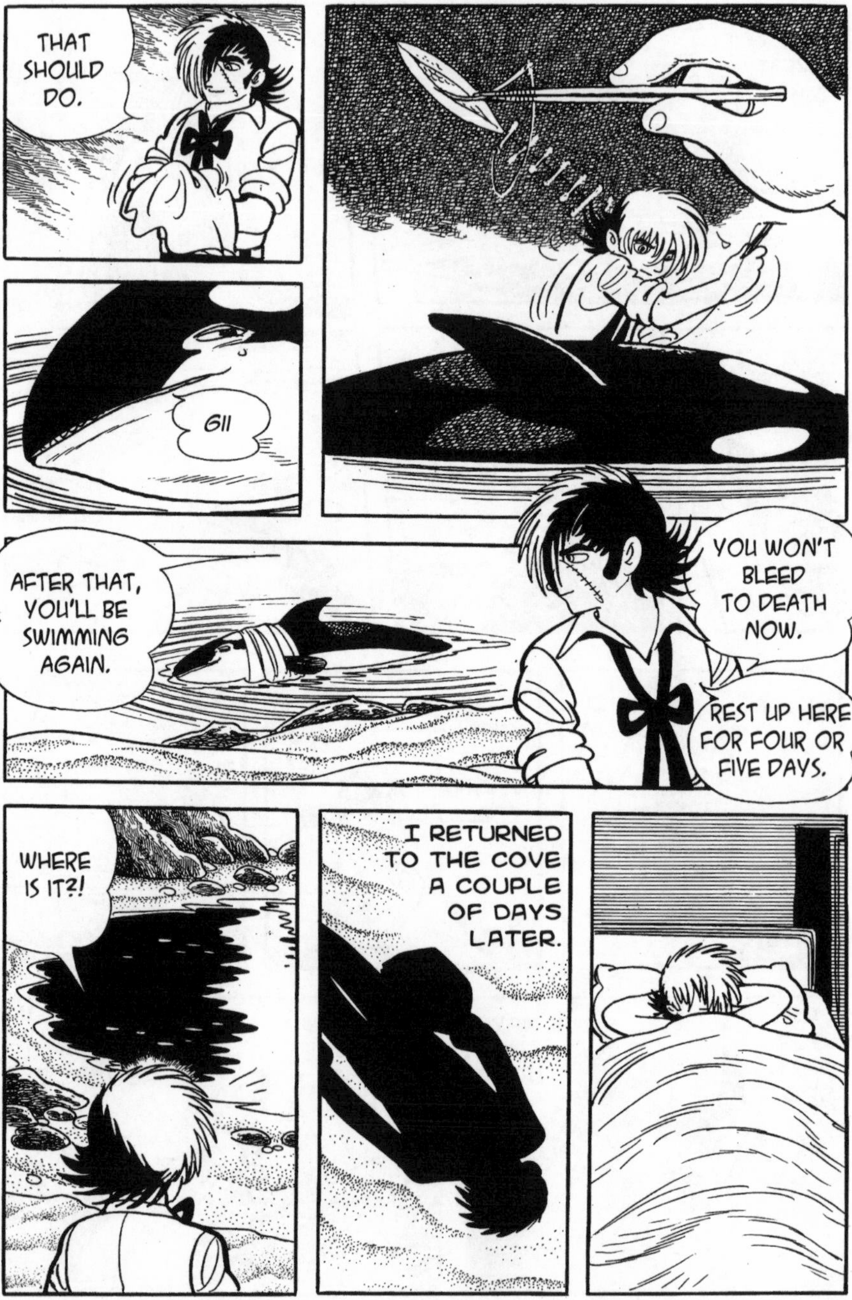
THAT SHOULD DO.
GII
YOU WON'T BLEED TO DEATH NOW.
REST UP HERE FOR FOUR OR FIVE DAYS.
AFTER THAT, YOU'LL BE SWIMMING AGAIN.
I RETURNED TO THE COVE A COUPLE OF DAYS LATER.
WHERE IS IT?!

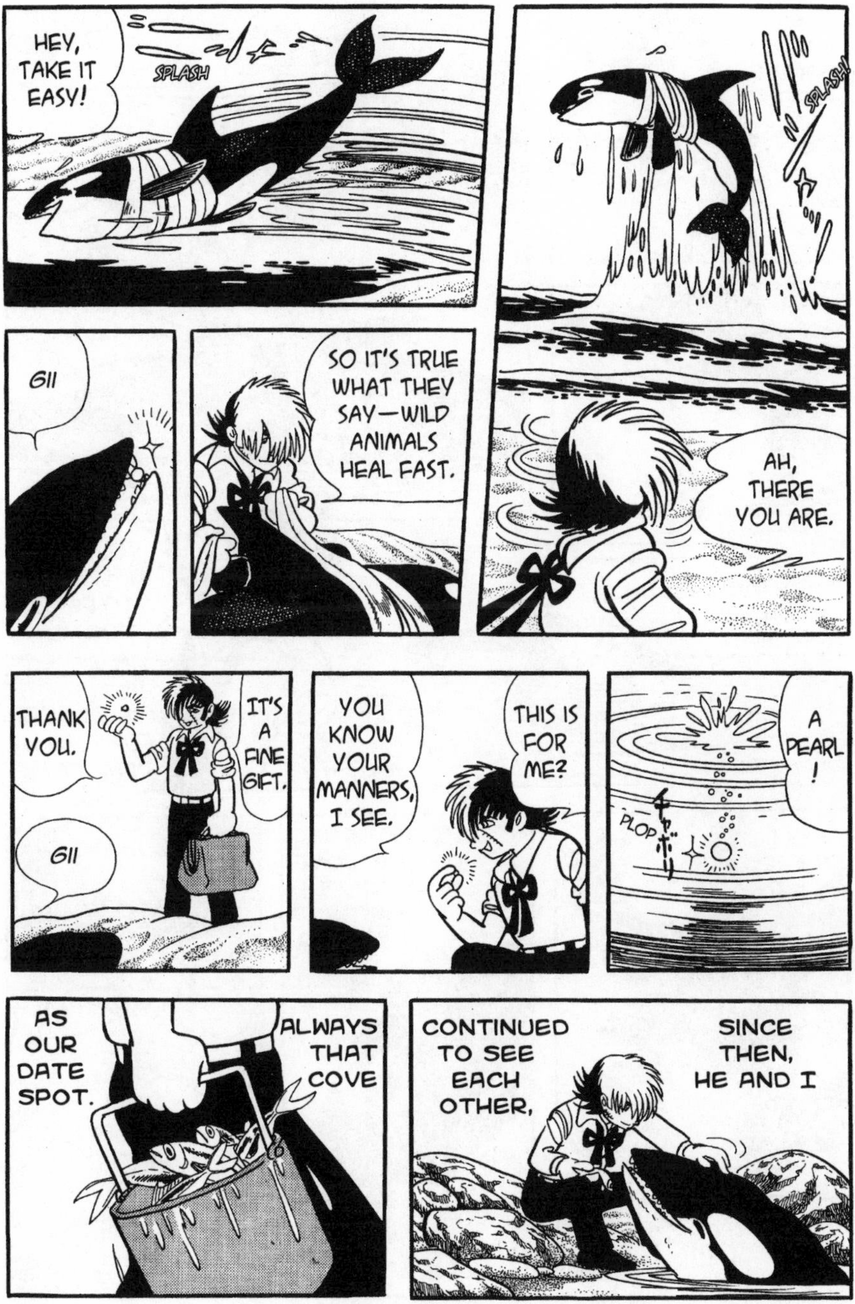
SPLASH!
AH, THERE YOU ARE.
HEY, TAKE IT EASY!
SPLASH
SO IT'S TRUE WHAT THEY SAY—WILD ANIMALS HEAL FAST.
GII
A PEARL!
PLOP
THIS IS FOR ME?
YOU KNOW YOUR MANNERS, I SEE.
IT'S A FINE GIFT.
THANK YOU.
GII
SINCE THEN, HE AND I
CONTINUED TO SEE EACH OTHER,
ALWAYS THAT COVE
AS OUR DATE SPOT.

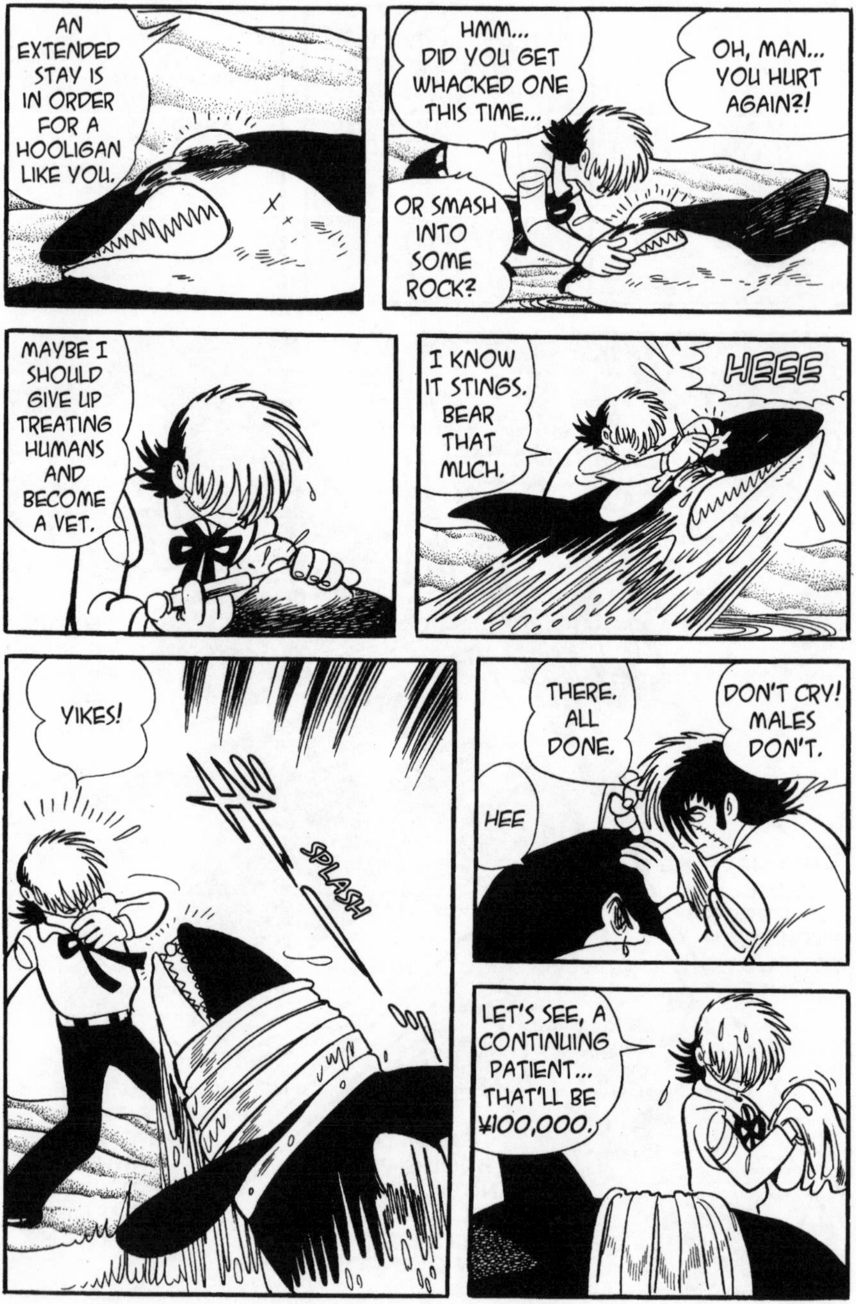
OH, MAN... YOU HURT AGAIN?!
HMM... DID YOU GET WHACKED ONE THIS TIME...
OR SMASH INTO SOME ROCK?
AN EXTENDED STAY IS IN ORDER FOR A HOOLIGAN LIKE YOU.
HEEE
I KNOW IT STINGS. BEAR THAT MUCH.
MAYBE I SHOULD GIVE UP TREATING HUMANS AND BECOME A VET.
DON'T CRY! MALES DON'T.
THERE. ALL DONE.
HEE
LET'S SEE, A CONTINUING PATIENT... THAT'LL BE ¥100,000.
YIKES!
SPLASH

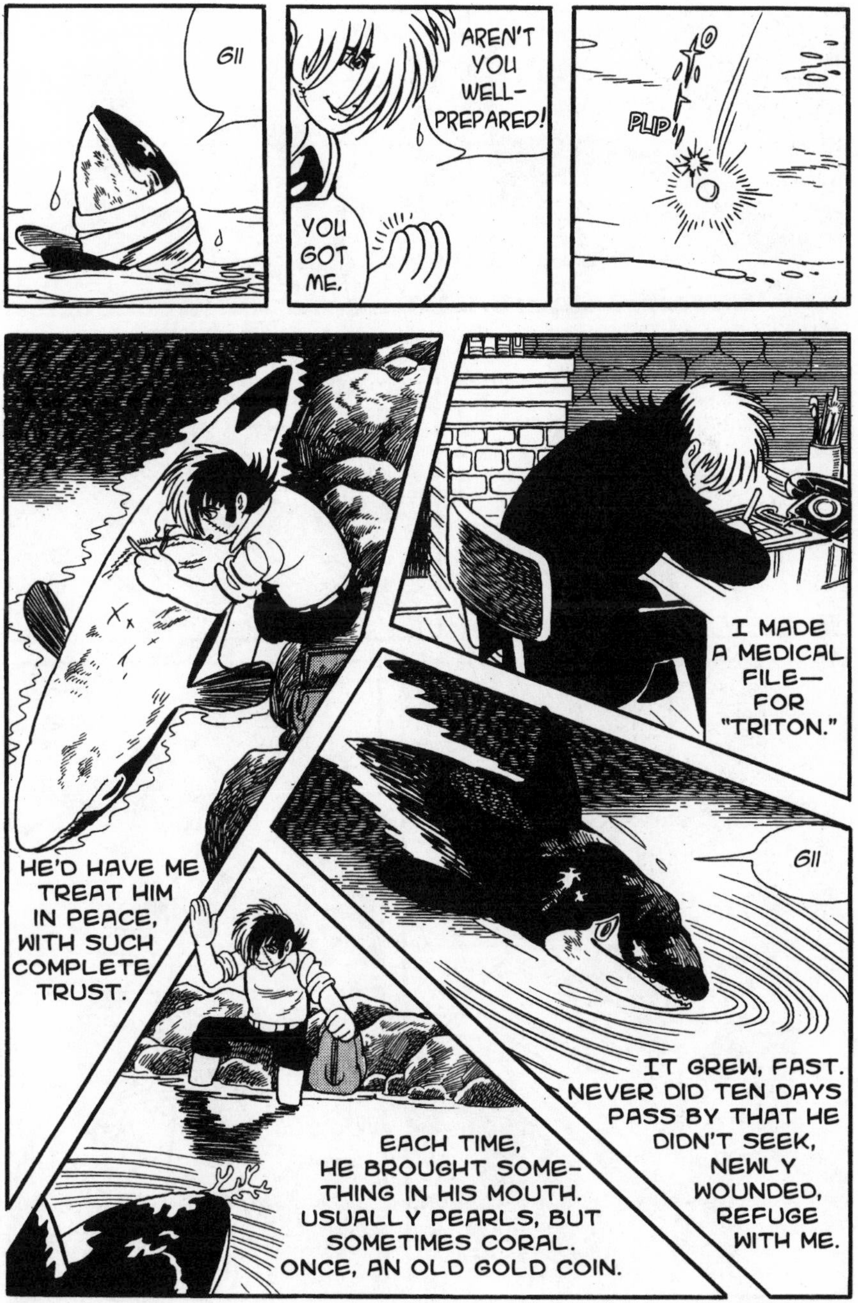
GII
AREN'T YOU WELL-PREPARED!
YOU GOT ME.
PLIP
HE'D HAVE ME TREAT HIM IN PEACE, WITH SUCH COMPLETE TRUST.
I MADE A MEDICAL FILE— FOR "TRITON."
GII
IT GREW, FAST. NEVER DID TEN DAYS PASS BY THAT HE DIDN'T SEEK, NEWLY WOUNDED, REFUGE WITH ME.
EACH TIME, HE BROUGHT SOME-THING IN HIS MOUTH. USUALLY PEARLS, BUT SOMETIMES CORAL. ONCE, AN OLD GOLD COIN.

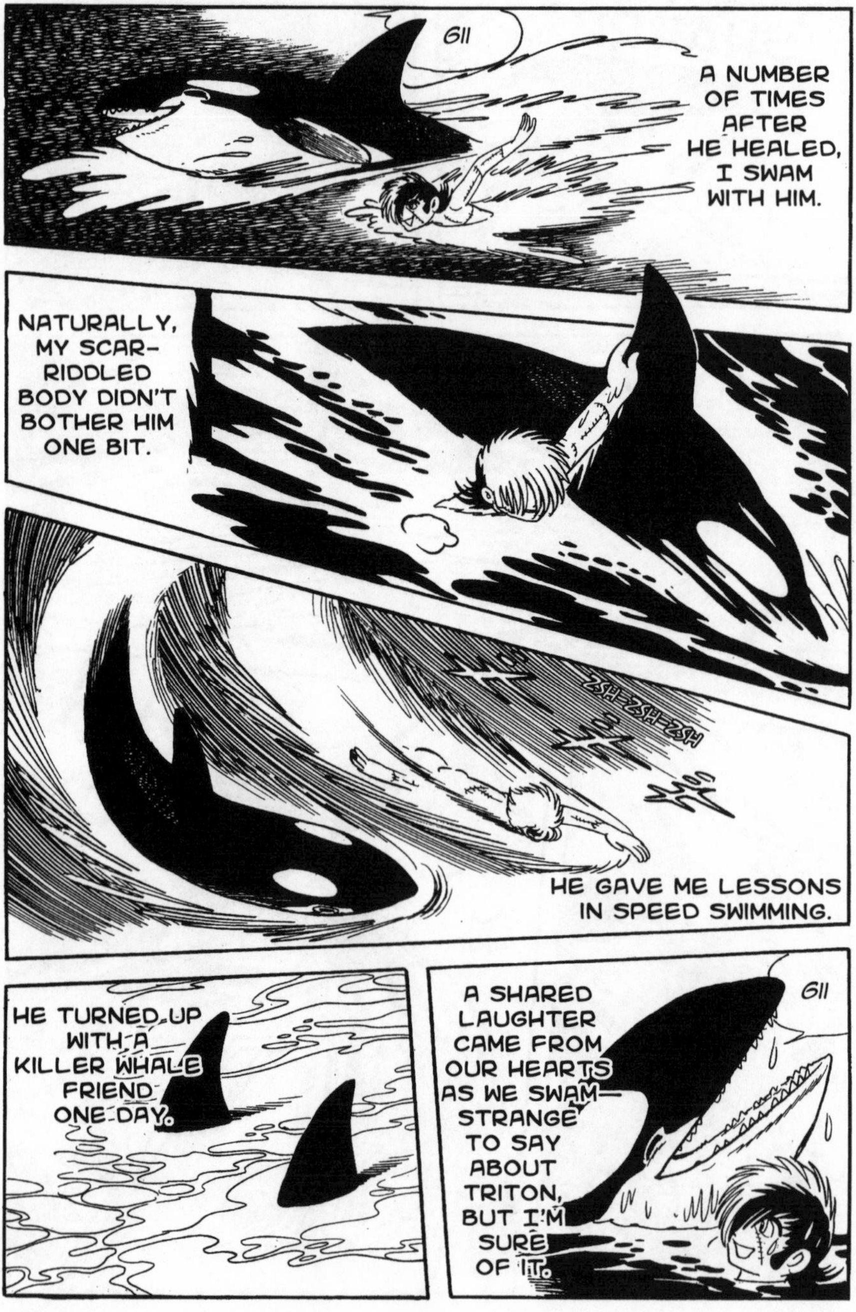
GII
A NUMBER OF TIMES AFTER HE HEALED, I SWAM WITH HIM.
NATURALLY, MY SCAR-RIDDLED BODY DIDN'T BOTHER HIM ONE BIT.
HSZ-HSZ-HSZ
HE GAVE ME LESSONS IN SPEED SWIMMING.
HE TURNED UP WITH A KILLER WHALE FRIEND ONE DAY.
GII
A SHARED LAUGHTER CAME FROM OUR HEARTS AS WE SWAM—STRANGE TO SAY ABOUT TRITON, BUT I'M SURE OF IT.

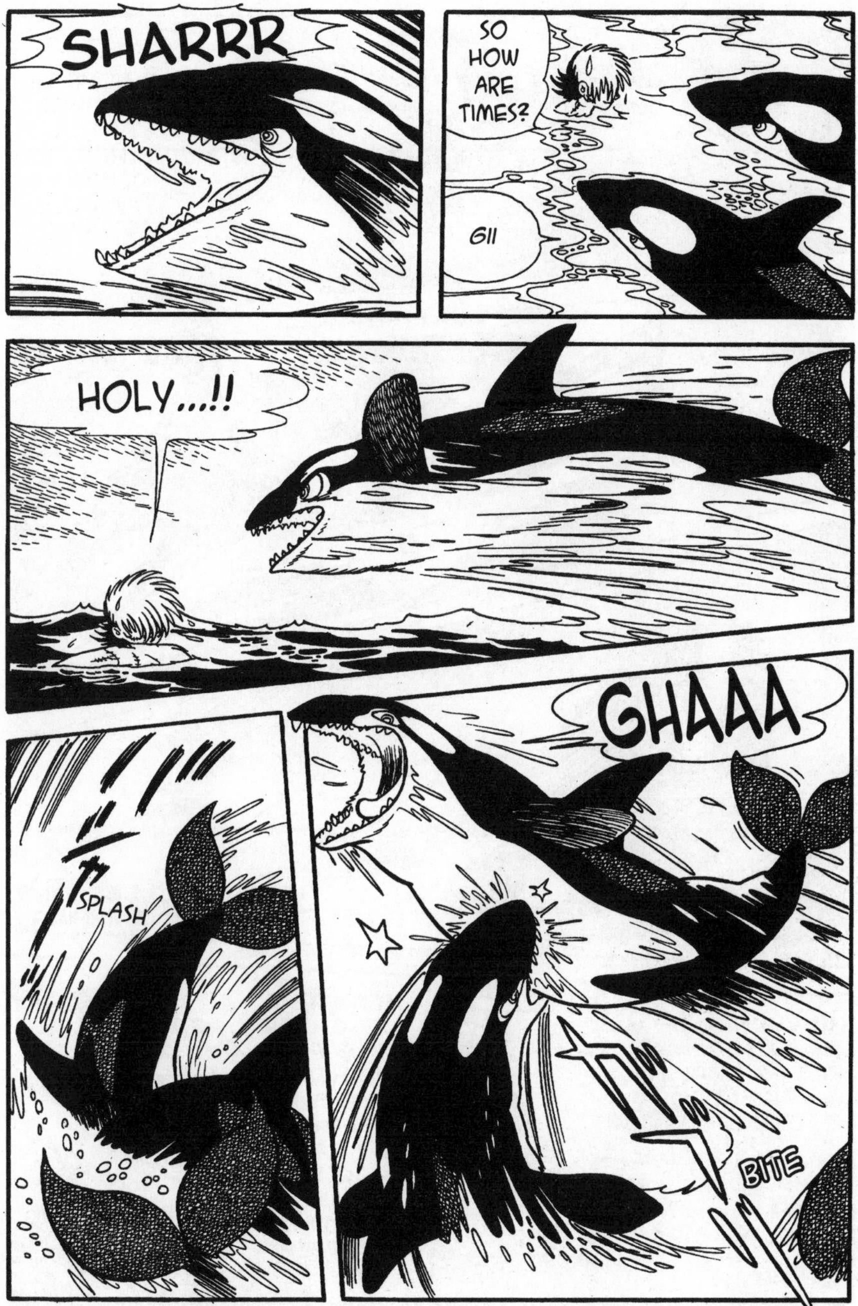
SO HOW ARE TIMES?
GII
SHARRR
HOLY...!!
GHAAA
BITE
SPLASH

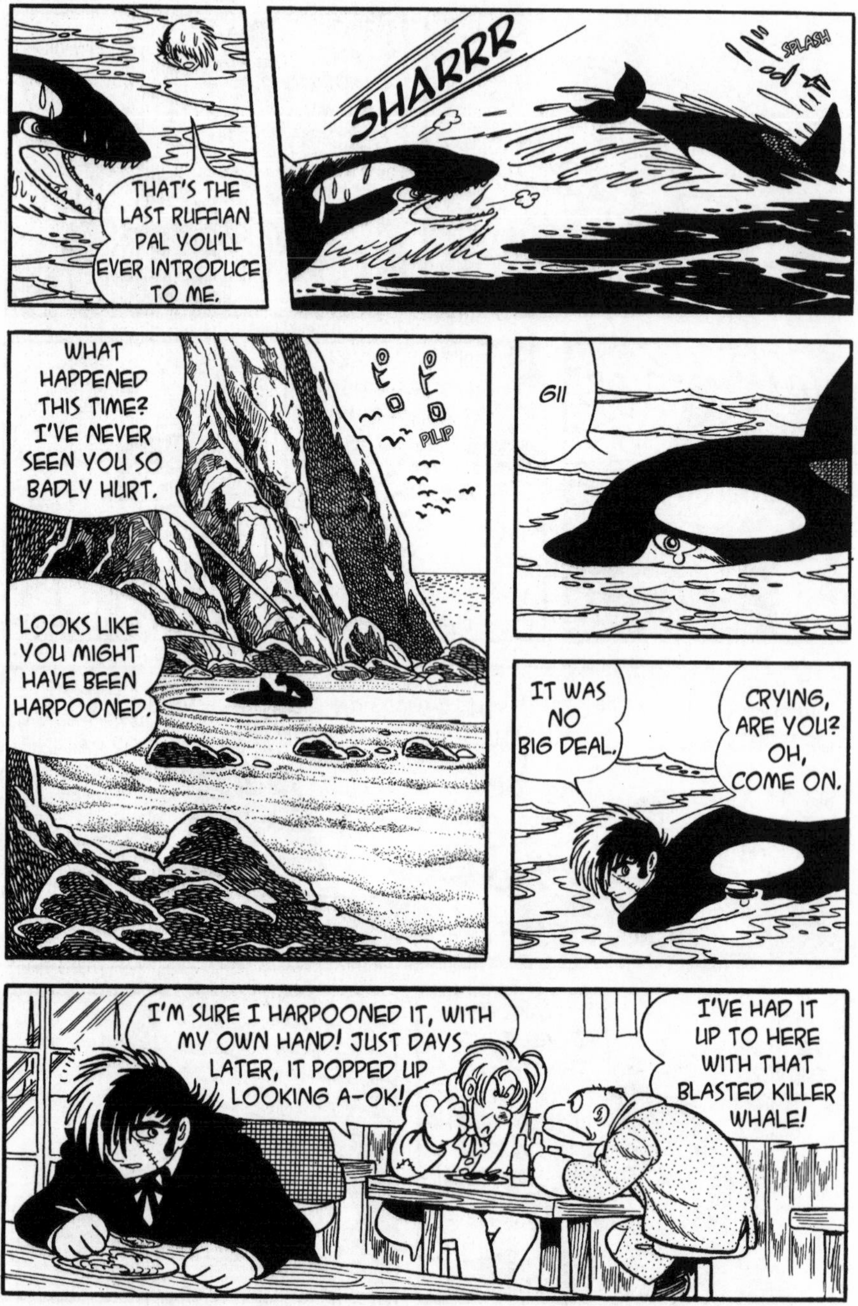
THAT'S THE LAST RUFFIAN PAL YOU'LL EVER INTRODUCE TO ME.
SHARRR
SPLASH
WHAT HAPPENED THIS TIME? I'VE NEVER SEEN YOU SO BADLY HURT.
PILP
LOOKS LIKE YOU MIGHT HAVE BEEN HARPOONED.
GII
IT WAS NO BIG DEAL.
CRYING, ARE YOU? OH, COME ON.
I'M SURE I HARPOONED IT, WITH MY OWN HAND! JUST DAYS LATER, IT POPPED UP LOOKING A-OK!
I'VE HAD IT UP TO HERE WITH THAT BLASTED KILLER WHALE!

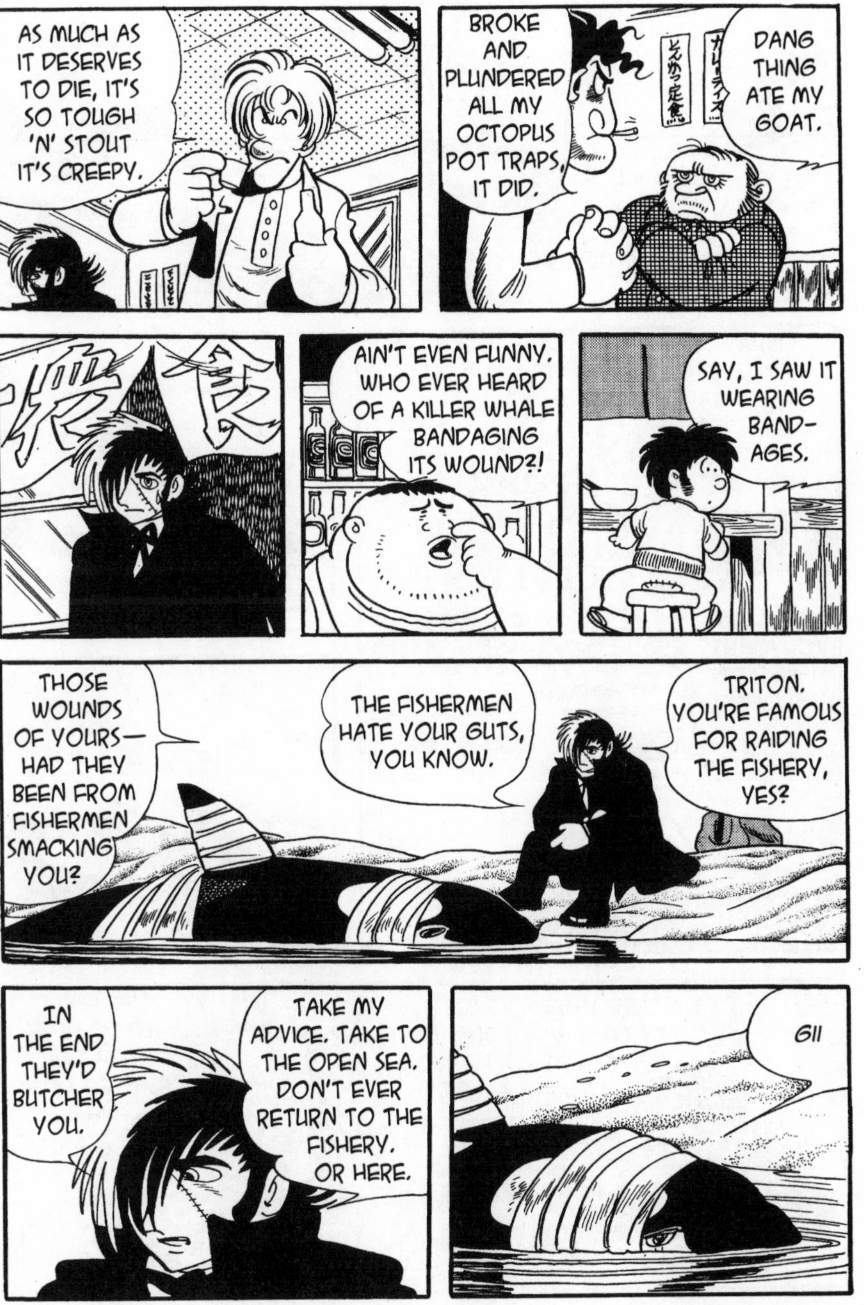
DANG THING ATE MY GOAT.
カレーライス
とんかつ定食
BROKE AND PLUNDERED ALL MY OCTOPUS POT TRAPS, IT DID.
AS MUCH AS IT DESERVES TO DIE, IT'S SO TOUGH 'N' STOUT IT'S CREEPY.
SAY, I SAW IT WEARING BAND-AGES.
AIN'T EVEN FUNNY. WHO EVER HEARD OF A KILLER WHALE BANDAGING ITS WOUND?!
TRITON. YOU'RE FAMOUS FOR RAIDING THE FISHERY, YES?
THE FISHERMEN HATE YOUR GUTS, YOU KNOW.
THOSE WOUNDS OF YOURS— HAD THEY BEEN FROM FISHERMEN SMACKING YOU?
GII
TAKE MY ADVICE. TAKE TO THE OPEN SEA. DON'T EVER RETURN TO THE FISHERY. OR HERE.
IN THE END THEY'D BUTCHER YOU.

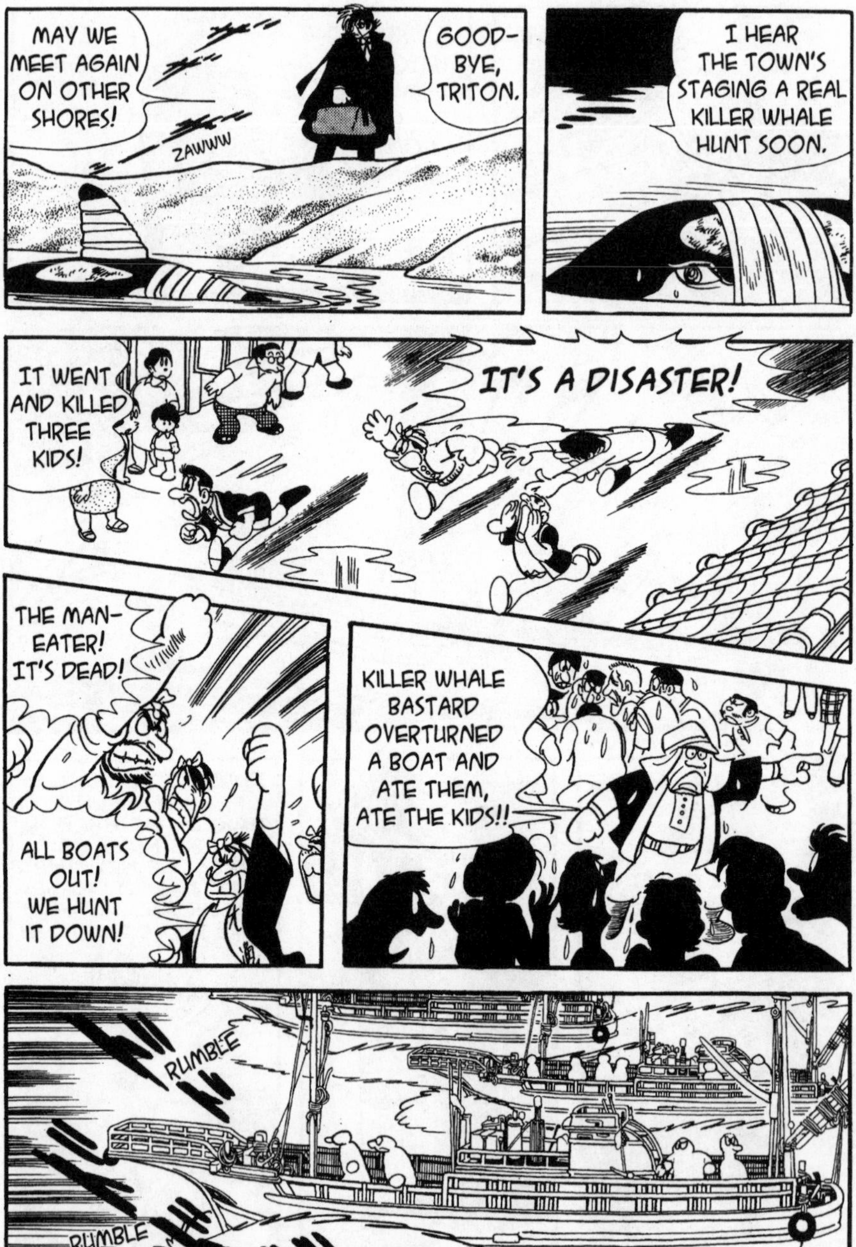
MAY WE MEET AGAIN ON OTHER SHORES!
ZAWWW
GOOD-BYE, TRITON.
I HEAR THE TOWN'S STAGING A REAL KILLER WHALE HUNT SOON.
IT'S A DISASTER!
IT WENT AND KILLED THREE KIDS!
THE MAN-EATER! IT'S DEAD!
ALL BOATS OUT! WE HUNT IT DOWN!
KILLER WHALE BASTARD OVERTURNED A BOAT AND ATE THEM, ATE THE KIDS!!
RUMBLE
RUMBLE

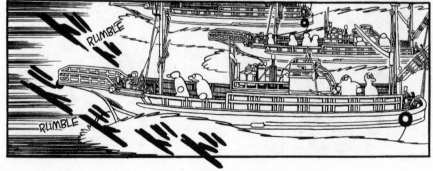

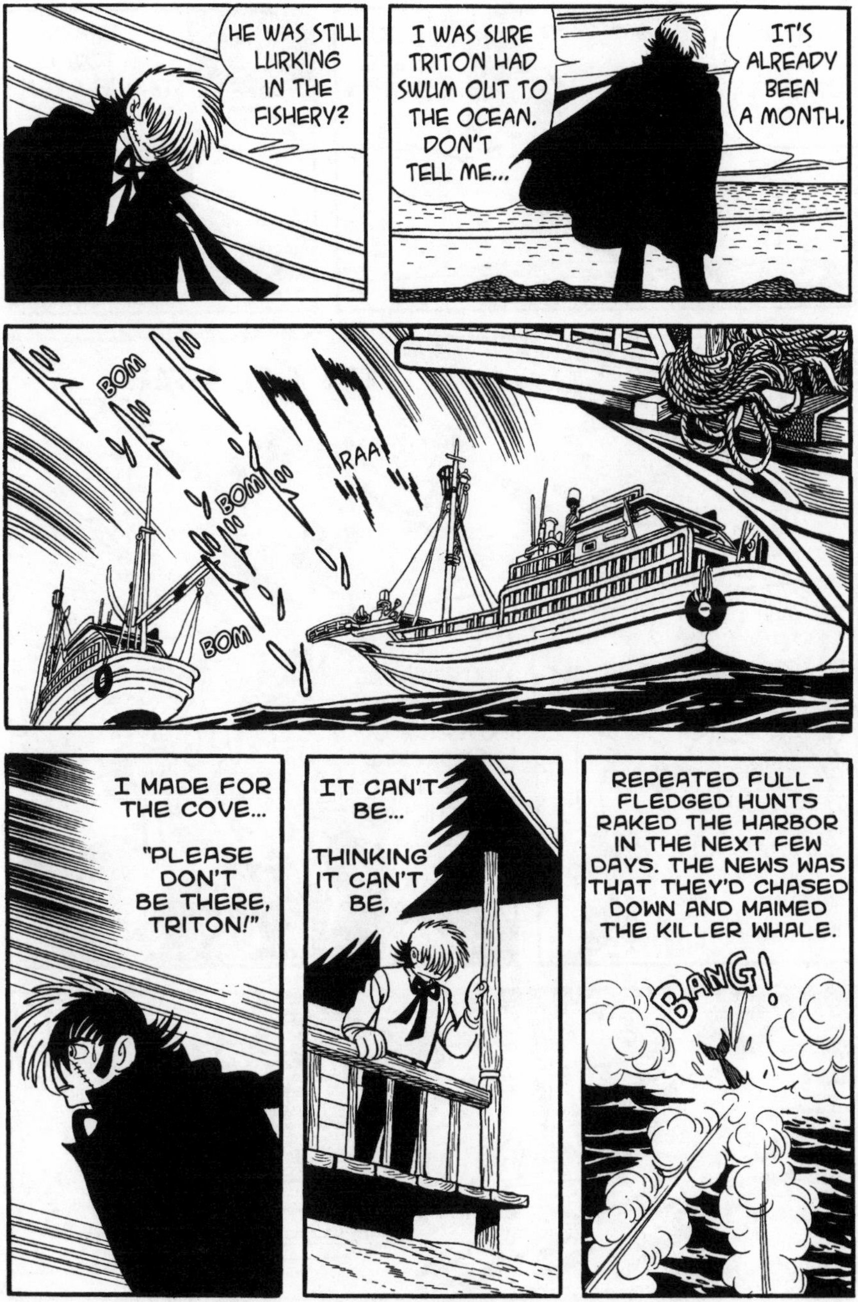
HE WAS STILL LURKING IN THE FISHERY?
I WAS SURE TRITON HAD SWUM OUT TO THE OCEAN. DON'T TELL ME...
IT'S ALREADY BEEN A MONTH.
BOM
RAA
BOM
BOM
I MADE FOR THE COVE...
"PLEASE DON'T BE THERE, TRITON!"
IT CAN'T BE...
THINKING IT CAN'T BE,
REPEATED FULL-FLEDGED HUNTS RAKED THE HARBOR IN THE NEXT FEW DAYS. THE NEWS WAS THAT THEY'D CHASED DOWN AND MAIMED THE KILLER WHALE.
BANG!

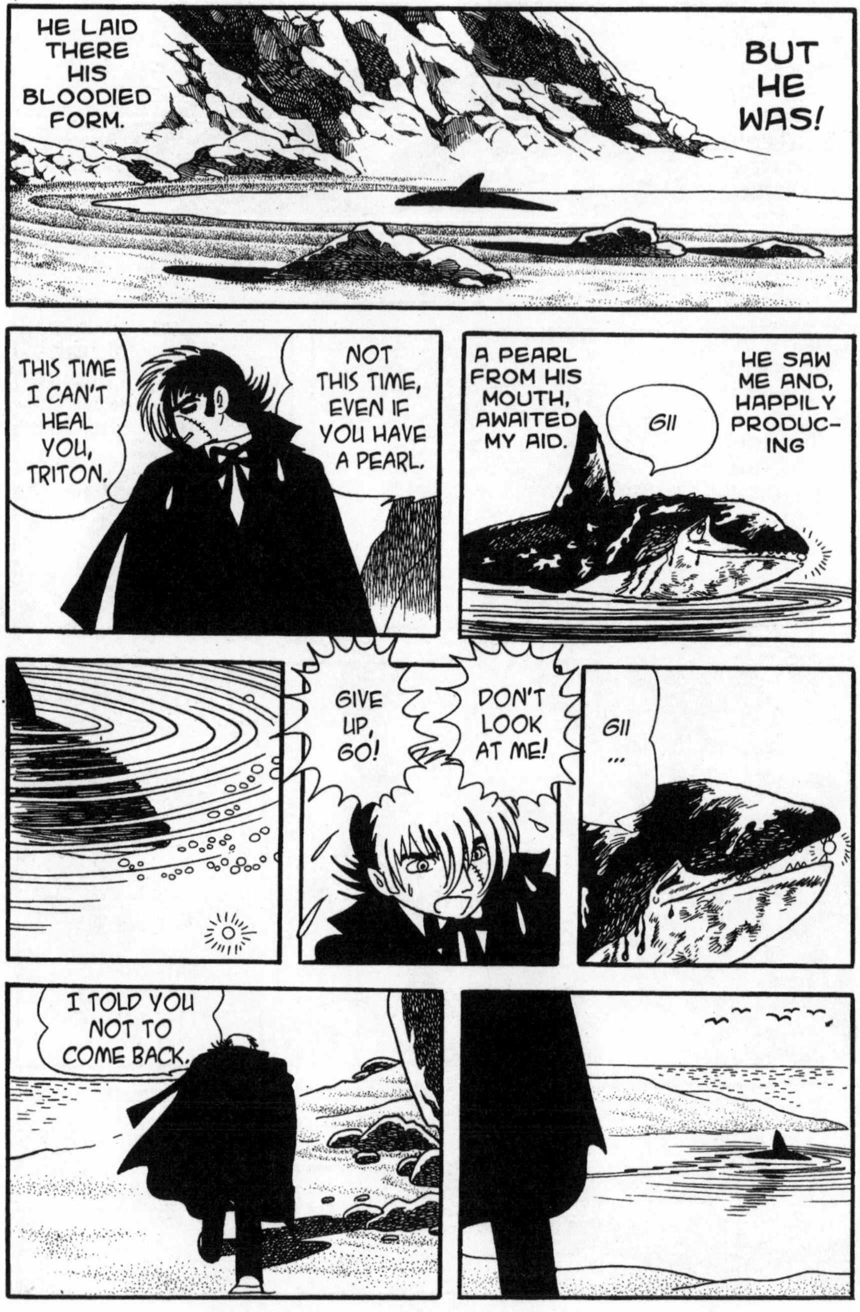
BUT HE WAS!
HE LAID THERE HIS BLOODIED FORM.
HE SAW ME AND, HAPPILY PRODUC-ING
GII
A PEARL FROM HIS MOUTH, AWAITED MY AID.
NOT THIS TIME, EVEN IF YOU HAVE A PEARL.
THIS TIME I CAN'T HEAL YOU, TRITON.
GII ...
DON'T LOOK AT ME!
GIVE UP, GO!
I TOLD YOU NOT TO COME BACK.

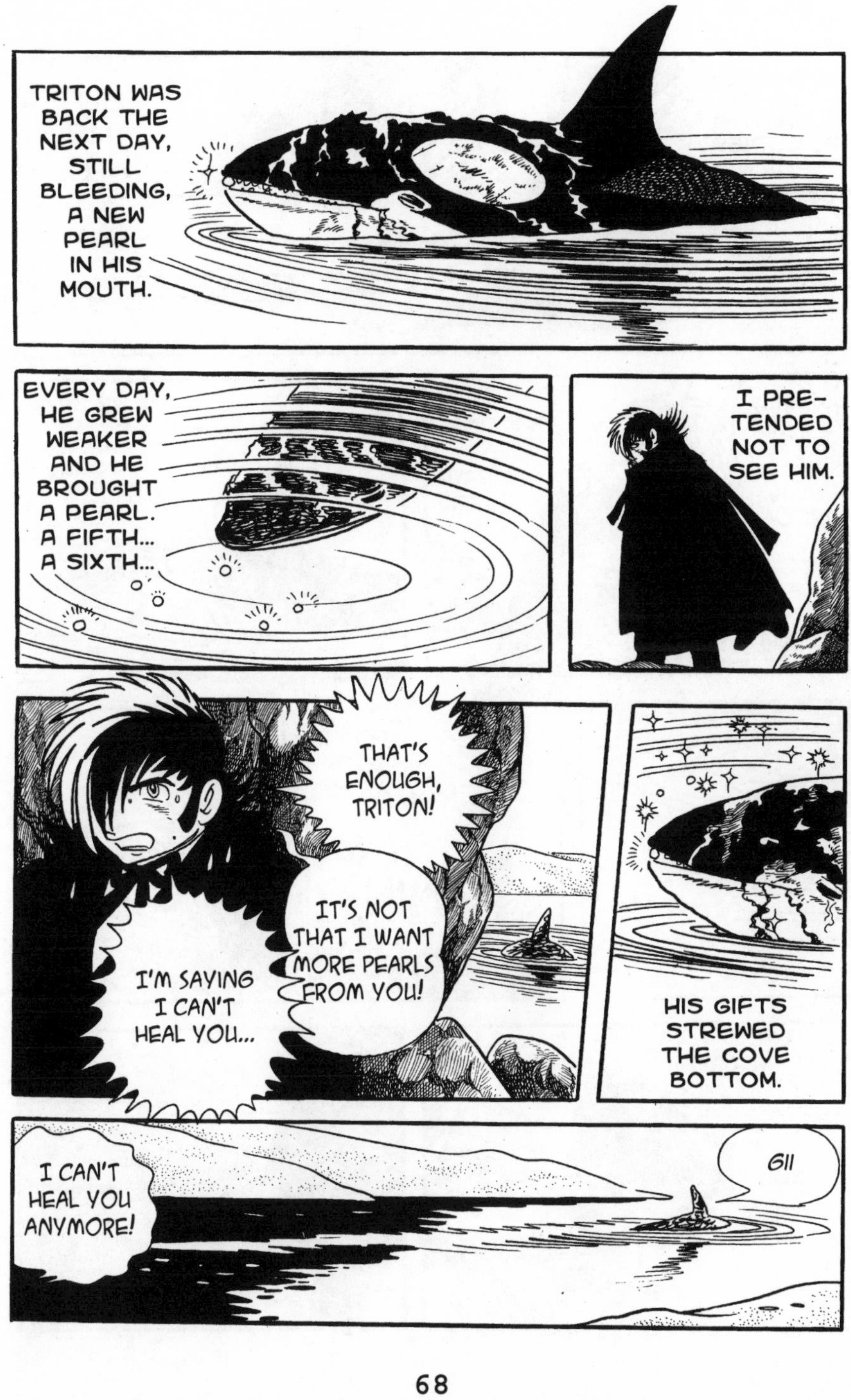
TRITON WAS BACK THE NEXT DAY, STILL BLEEDING, A NEW PEARL IN HIS MOUTH.
EVERY DAY, HE GREW WEAKER AND HE BROUGHT A PEARL. A FIFTH... A SIXTH...
I PRE-TENDED NOT TO SEE HIM.
THAT'S ENOUGH, TRITON!
IT'S NOT THAT I WANT MORE PEARLS FROM YOU!
I'M SAYING I CAN'T HEAL YOU...
HIS GIFTS STREWED THE COVE BOTTOM.
I CAN'T HEAL YOU ANYMORE!
GII

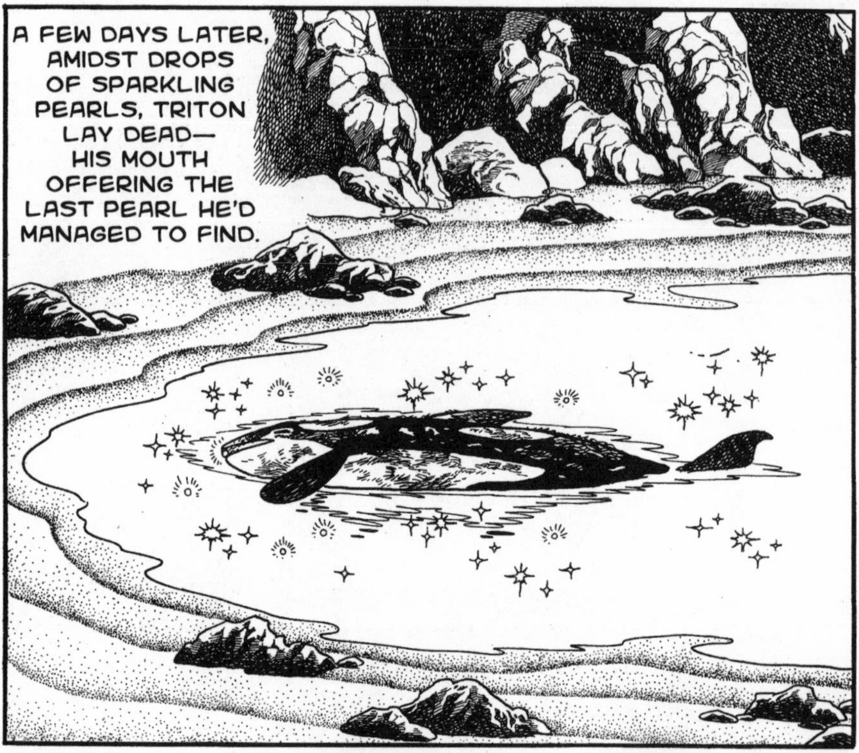
A FEW DAYS LATER, AMIDST DROPS OF SPARKLING PEARLS, TRITON LAY DEAD— HIS MOUTH OFFERING THE LAST PEARL HE'D MANAGED TO FIND.

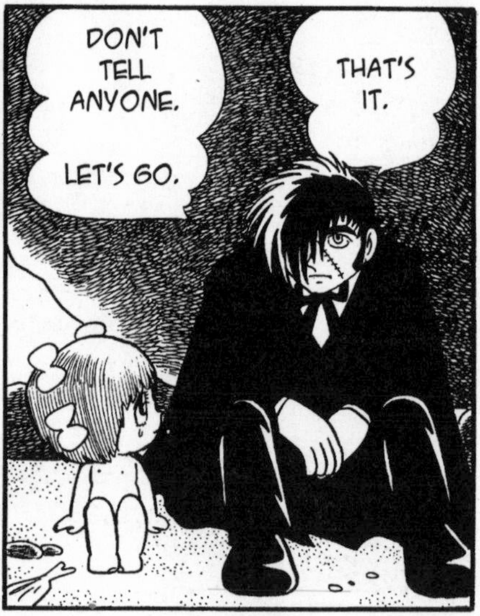
THAT'S IT.
DON'T TELL ANYONE.
LET'S GO.

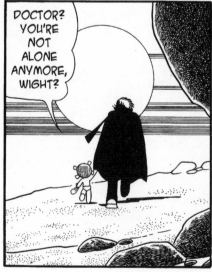

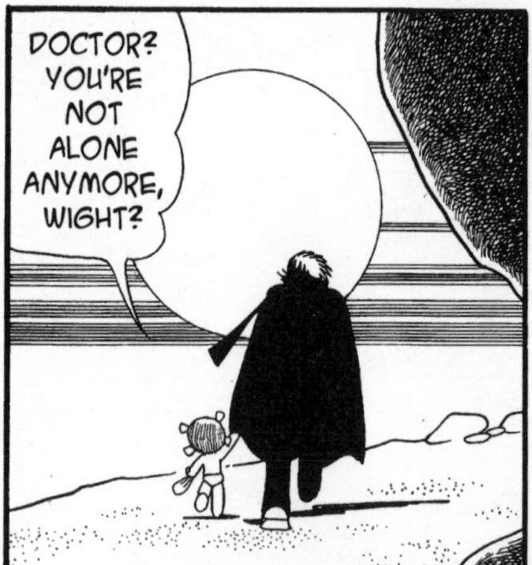
DOCTOR? YOU'RE NOT ALONE ANYMORE, WIGHT?

TO EACH HIS OWN

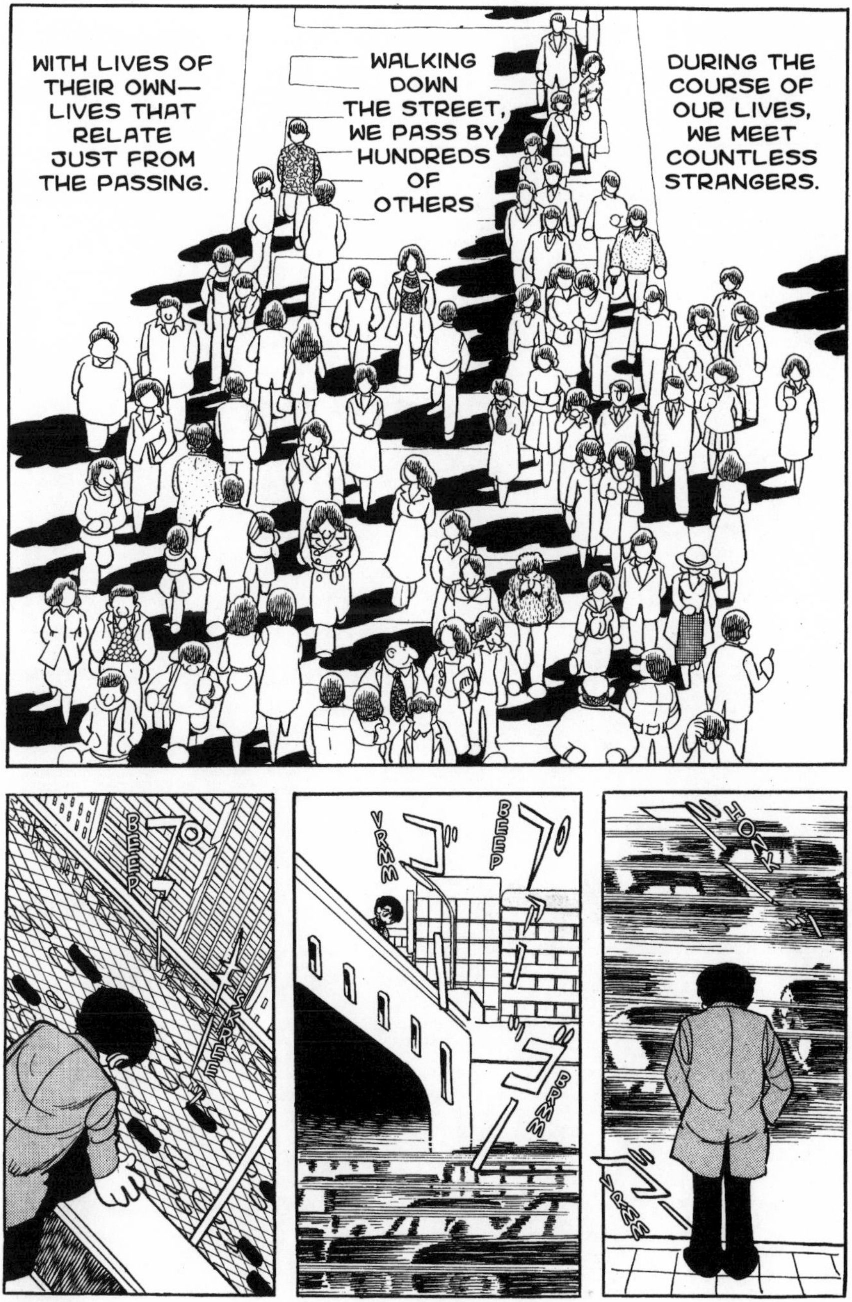
DURING THE COURSE OF OUR LIVES, WE MEET COUNTLESS STRANGERS.
WALKING DOWN THE STREET, WE PASS BY HUNDREDS OF OTHERS
WITH LIVES OF THEIR OWN— LIVES THAT RELATE JUST FROM THE PASSING.
HONK
VRMM
BEEP
VRMM
BRMM
BEEP
SKREE

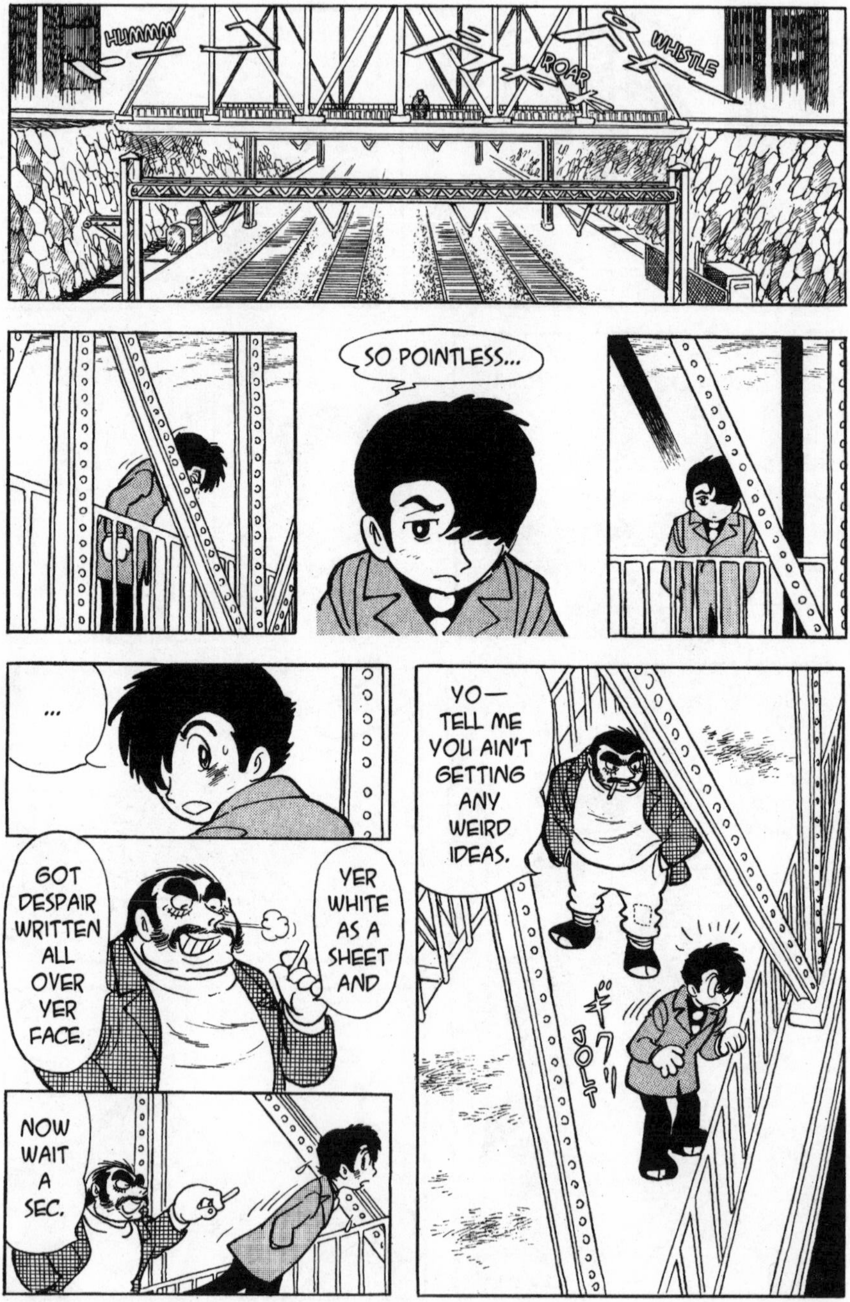
WHISTLE
ROAR
HUMMM
SO POINTLESS...
YO— TELL ME YOU AIN'T GETTING ANY WEIRD IDEAS.
JOLT
...
YER WHITE AS A SHEET AND
GOT DESPAIR WRITTEN ALL OVER YER FACE.
NOW WAIT A SEC.

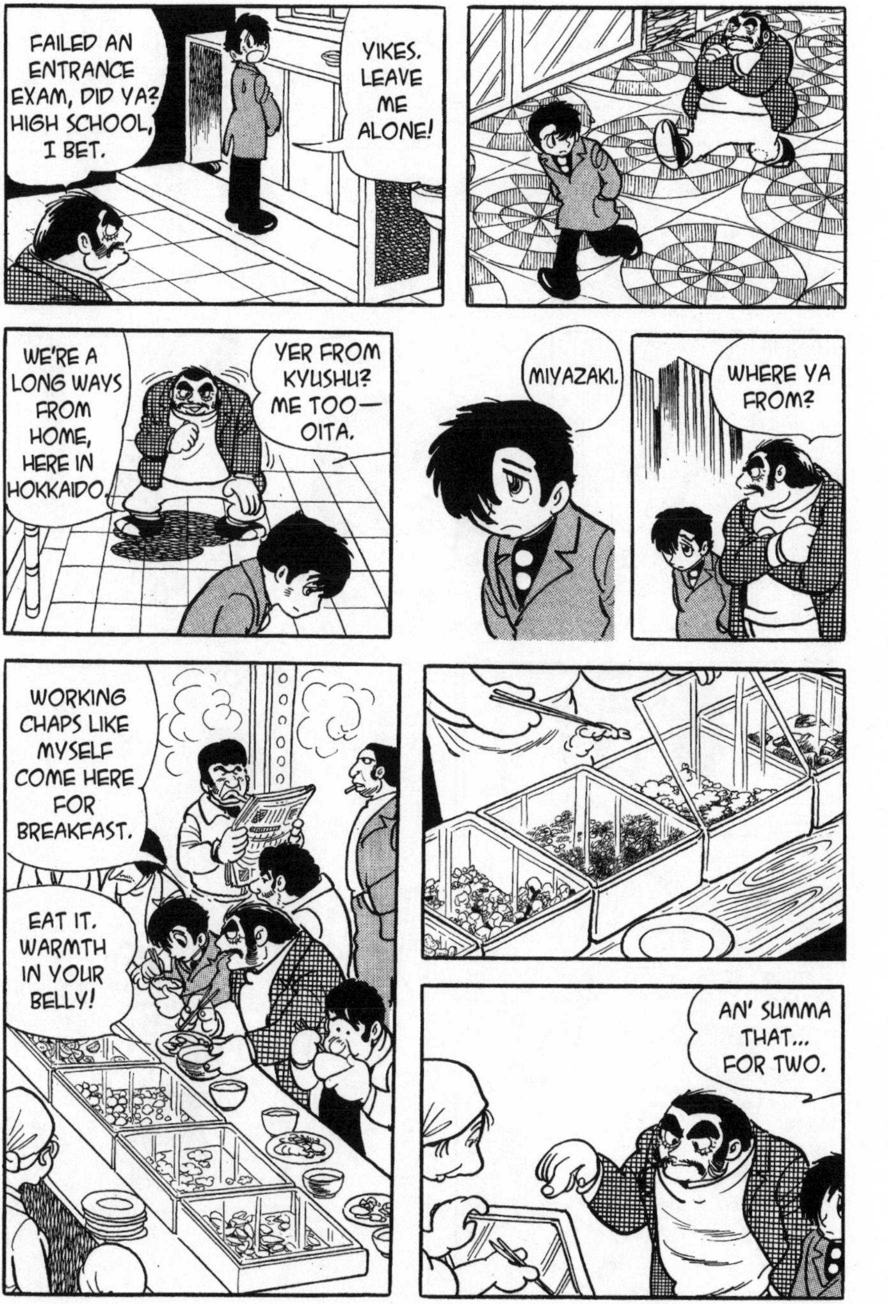
FAILED AN ENTRANCE EXAM, DID YA? HIGH SCHOOL, I BET.
YIKES. LEAVE ME ALONE!
WHERE YA FROM?
MIYAZAKI.
YER FROM KYUSHU? ME TOO— OITA.
WE'RE A LONG WAYS FROM HOME, HERE IN HOKKAIDO.
AN' SUMMA THAT... FOR TWO.
WORKING CHAPS LIKE MYSELF COME HERE FOR BREAKFAST.
EAT IT. WARMTH IN YOUR BELLY!

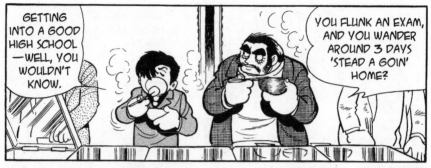

YOU FLUNK AN EXAM, AND YOU WANDER AROUND 3 DAYS 'STEAD A GOIN' HOME?
GETTING INTO A GOOD HIGH SCHOOL —WELL, YOU WOULDN'T KNOW.
IT'S A MATTER OF LIFE AND DEATH...
AND I'M AS GOOD AS DEAD NOW.
LIFE AND DEATH ?!
IDIOT! THOSE AIN'T WORDS TO PLAY WITH.
I KNOW YOU LIVE IN A DIFFERENT WORLD.
PEOPLE WOULD KILL TO GET INTO A TOP SCHOOL. IT'S LIKE WAR!
THE EXAM WARS, EH?
WHY'S IT GOT TO BE A TOP SCHOOL?
SO I CAN BECOME A DOCTOR. MY DAD'S SET ON IT.

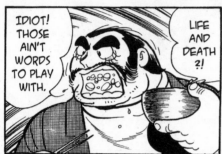

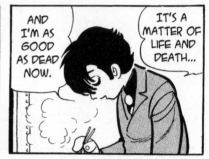

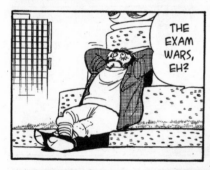

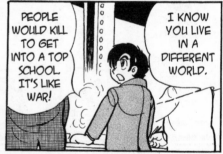

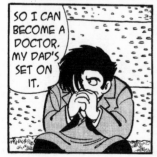

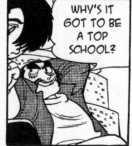

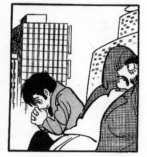

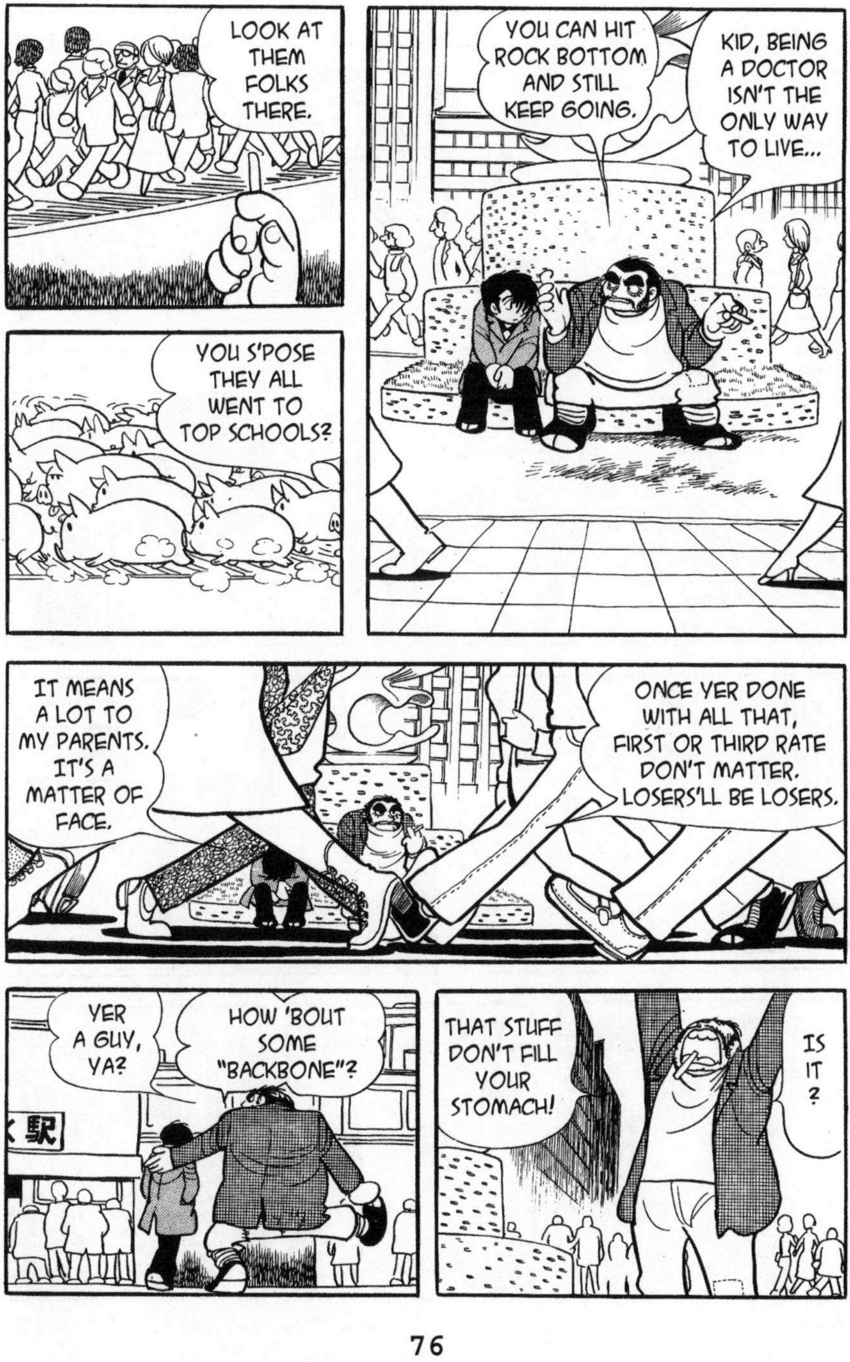
LOOK AT THEM FOLKS THERE.
YOU S'POSE THEY ALL WENT TO TOP SCHOOLS?
KID, BEING A DOCTOR ISN'T THE ONLY WAY TO LIVE...
YOU CAN HIT ROCK BOTTOM AND STILL KEEP GOING.
IT MEANS A LOT TO MY PARENTS. IT'S A MATTER OF FACE.
ONCE YER DONE WITH ALL THAT, FIRST OR THIRD RATE DON'T MATTER. LOSERS'LL BE LOSERS.
YER A GUY, YA?
HOW 'BOUT SOME "BACKBONE"?
THAT STUFF DON'T FILL YOUR STOMACH!
IS IT?

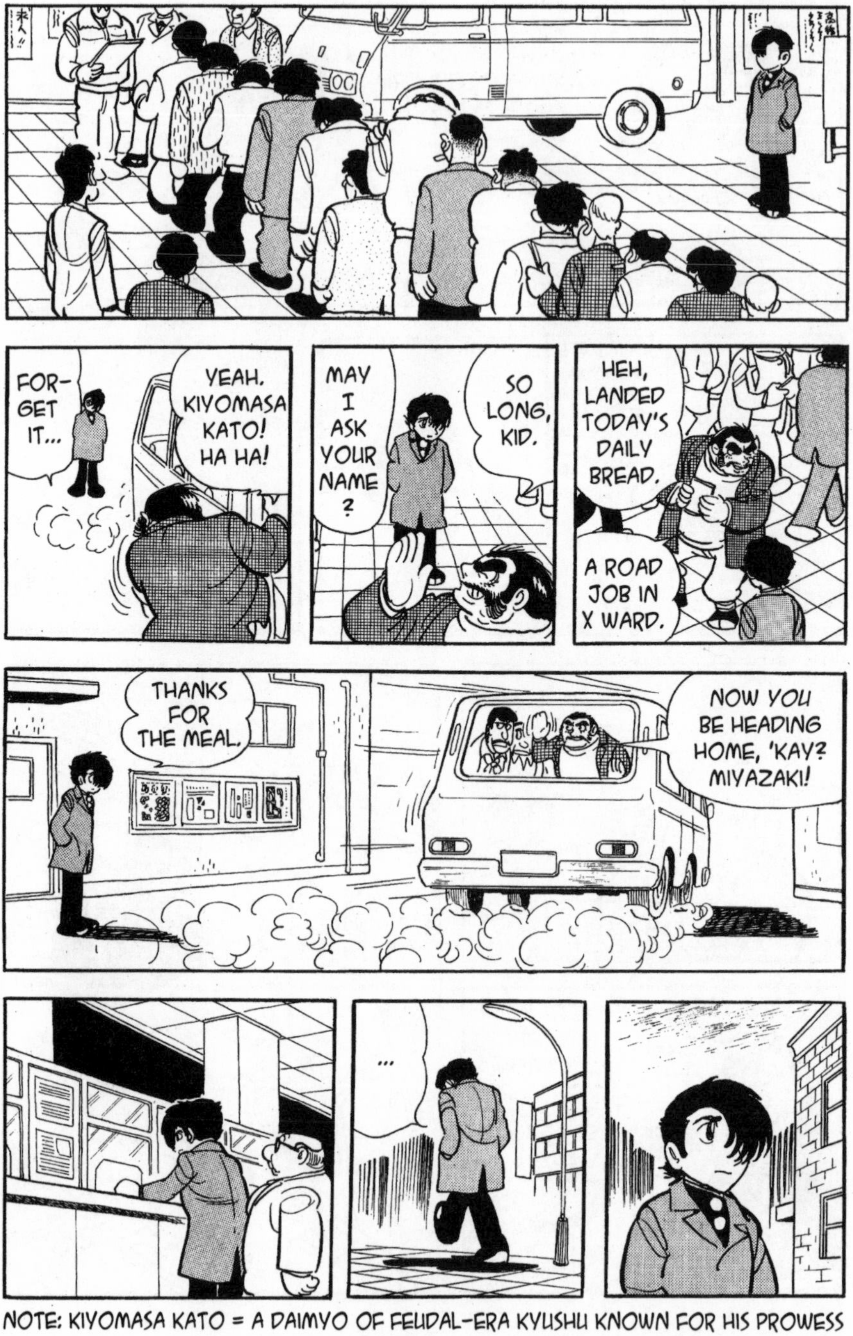
HEH, LANDED TODAY'S DAILY BREAD.
A ROAD JOB IN X WARD.
SO LONG, KID.
MAY I ASK YOUR NAME?
YEAH. KIYOMASA KATO! HA HA!
FOR-GET IT...
NOW YOU BE HEADING HOME, 'KAY? MIYAZAKI!
THANKS FOR THE MEAL.
...

NOTE: KIYOMASA KATO = A DAIMYO OF FEUDAL-ERA KYUSHU KNOWN FOR HIS PROWESS

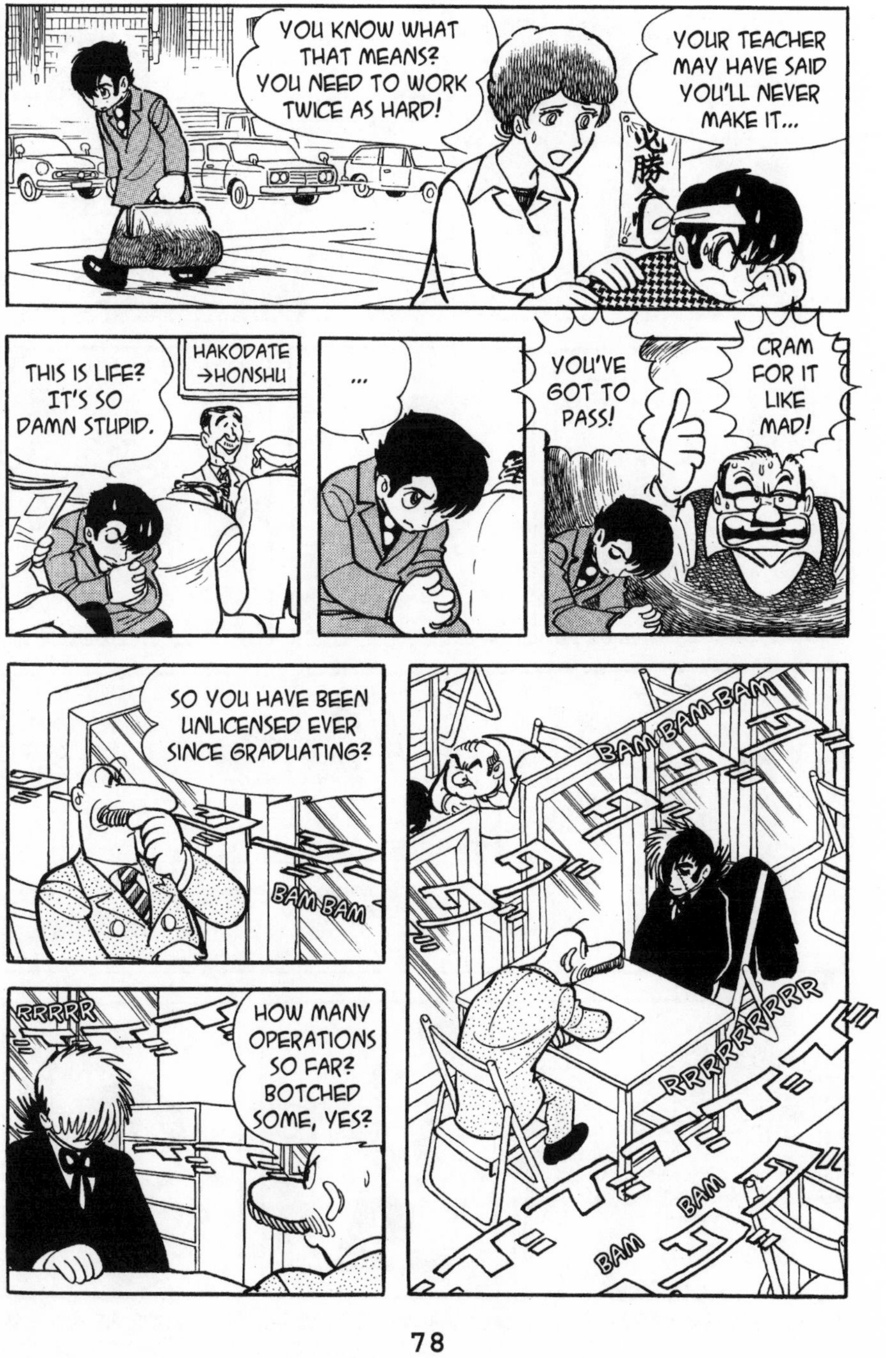
YOUR TEACHER MAY HAVE SAID YOU'LL NEVER MAKE IT...
必勝合
YOU KNOW WHAT THAT MEANS? YOU NEED TO WORK TWICE AS HARD!
CRAM FOR IT LIKE MAD!
YOU'VE GOT TO PASS!
...
HAKODATE →HONSHU
THIS IS LIFE? IT'S SO DAMN STUPID.
BAM BAM BAM
RRRRRRRRR
BAM
BAM
SO YOU HAVE BEEN UNLICENSED EVER SINCE GRADUATING?
BAM BAM
RRRRR
HOW MANY OPERATIONS SO FAR? BOTCHED SOME, YES?

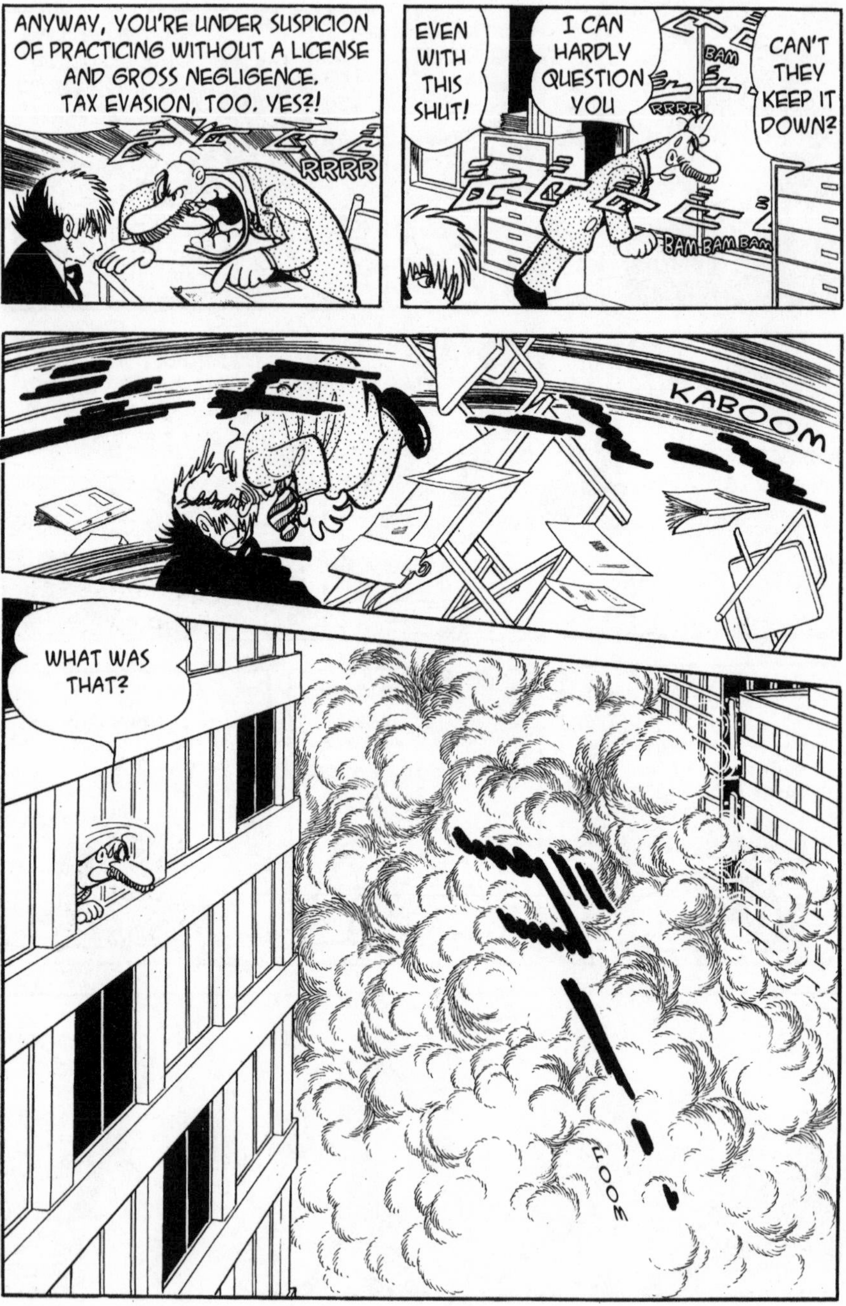
CAN'T THEY KEEP IT DOWN?
BAM
RRRR
I CAN HARDLY QUESTION YOU
EVEN WITH THIS SHUT!
BAM BAM BAM
ANYWAY, YOU'RE UNDER SUSPICION OF PRACTICING WITHOUT A LICENSE AND GROSS NEGLIGENCE. TAX EVASION, TOO. YES?!
RRRR
KABOOM
WHAT WAS THAT?
FOOM

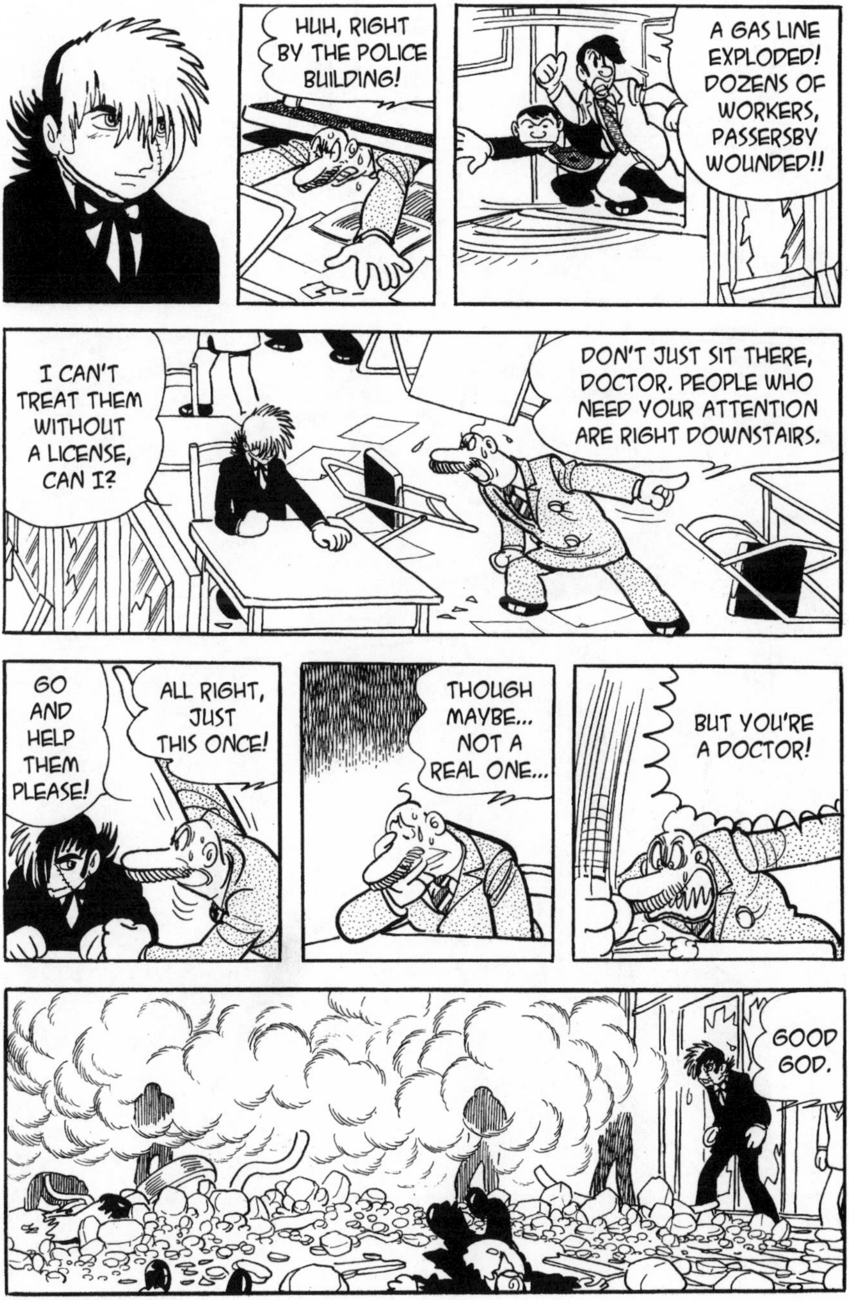
A GAS LINE EXPLODED! DOZENS OF WORKERS, PASSERSBY WOUNDED!!
HUH, RIGHT BY THE POLICE BUILDING!
DON'T JUST SIT THERE, DOCTOR. PEOPLE WHO NEED YOUR ATTENTION ARE RIGHT DOWNSTAIRS.
I CAN'T TREAT THEM WITHOUT A LICENSE, CAN I?
BUT YOU'RE A DOCTOR!
THOUGH MAYBE... NOT A REAL ONE...
GO AND HELP THEM PLEASE!
ALL RIGHT, JUST THIS ONCE!
GOOD GOD.

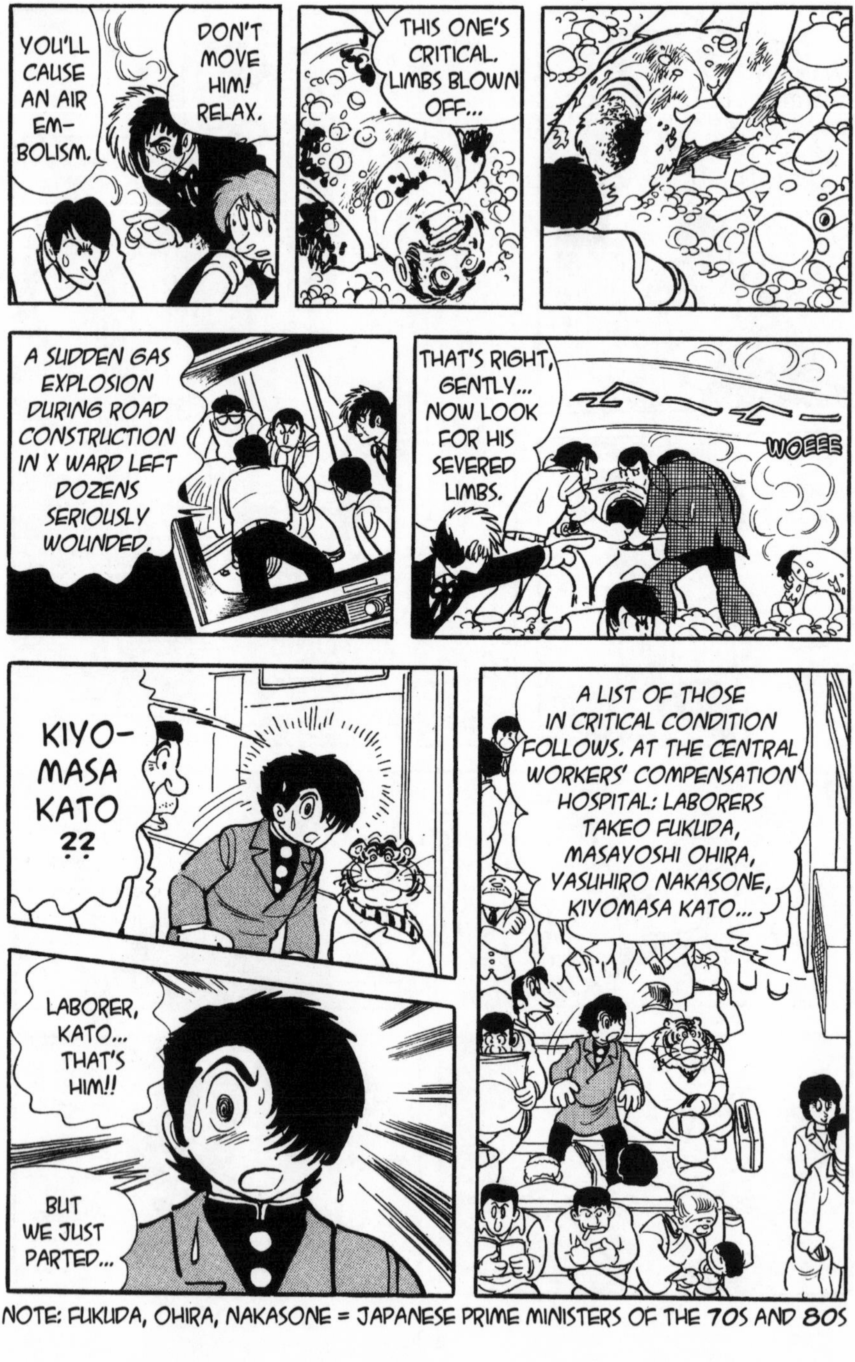
THIS ONE'S CRITICAL. LIMBS BLOWN OFF...
DON'T MOVE HIM! RELAX.
YOU'LL CAUSE AN AIR EM-BOLISM.
THAT'S RIGHT, GENTLY... NOW LOOK FOR HIS SEVERED LIMBS.
WOEEE
A SUDDEN GAS EXPLOSION DURING ROAD CONSTRUCTION IN X WARD LEFT DOZENS SERIOUSLY WOUNDED.
A LIST OF THOSE IN CRITICAL CONDITION FOLLOWS. AT THE CENTRAL WORKERS' COMPENSATION HOSPITAL: LABORERS TAKEO FUKUDA, MASAYOSHI OHIRA, YASUHIRO NAKASONE, KIYOMASA KATO...
KIYO-MASA KATO ??
LABORER, KATO... THAT'S HIM!!
BUT WE JUST PARTED...

NOTE: FUKUDA, OHIRA, NAKASONE = JAPANESE PRIME MINISTERS OF THE 70S AND 80S

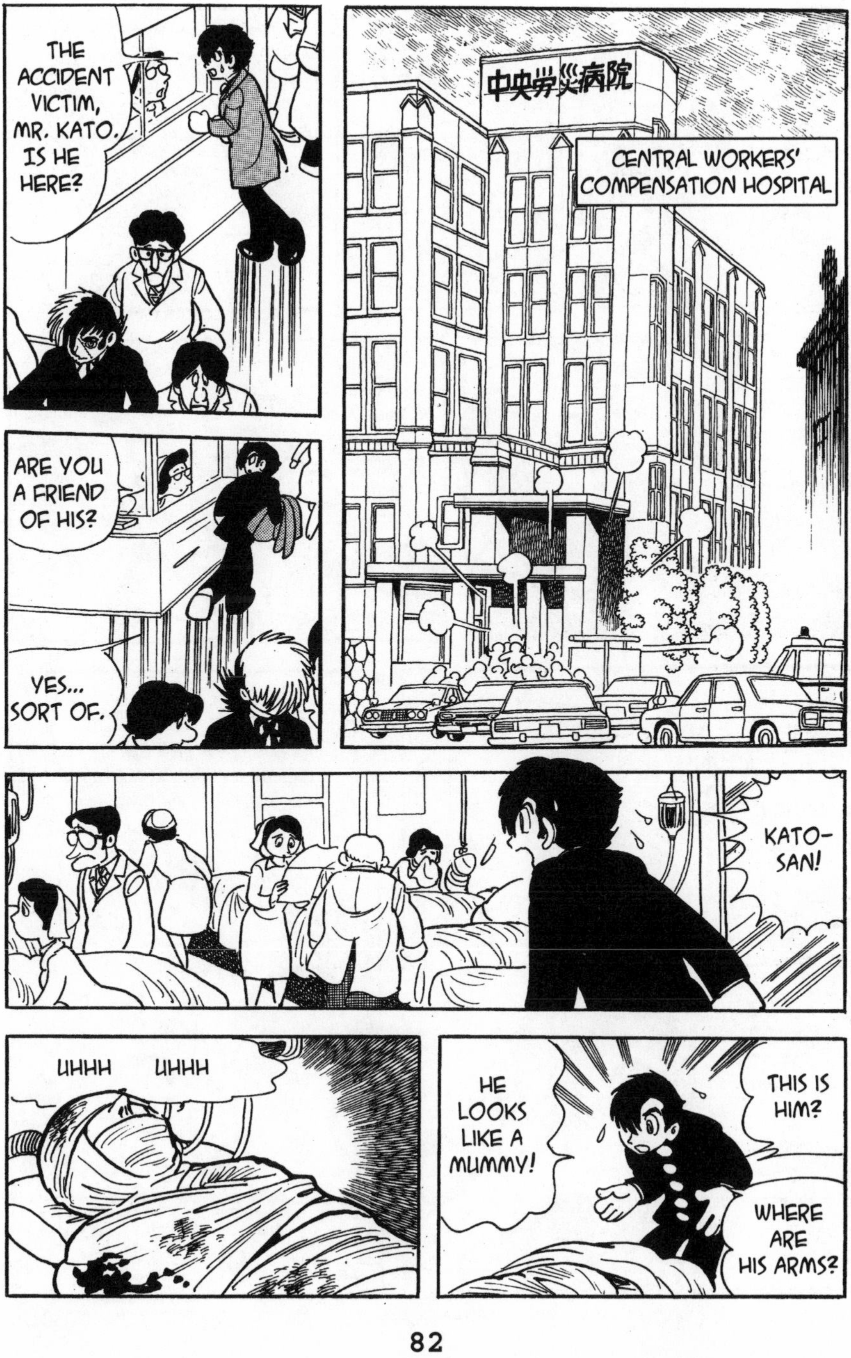
中央労災病院
CENTRAL WORKERS' COMPENSATION HOSPITAL
THE ACCIDENT VICTIM, MR. KATO. IS HE HERE?
ARE YOU A FRIEND OF HIS?
YES... SORT OF.
KATO-SAN!
THIS IS HIM?
HE LOOKS LIKE A MUMMY!
WHERE ARE HIS ARMS?
UHHH UHHH

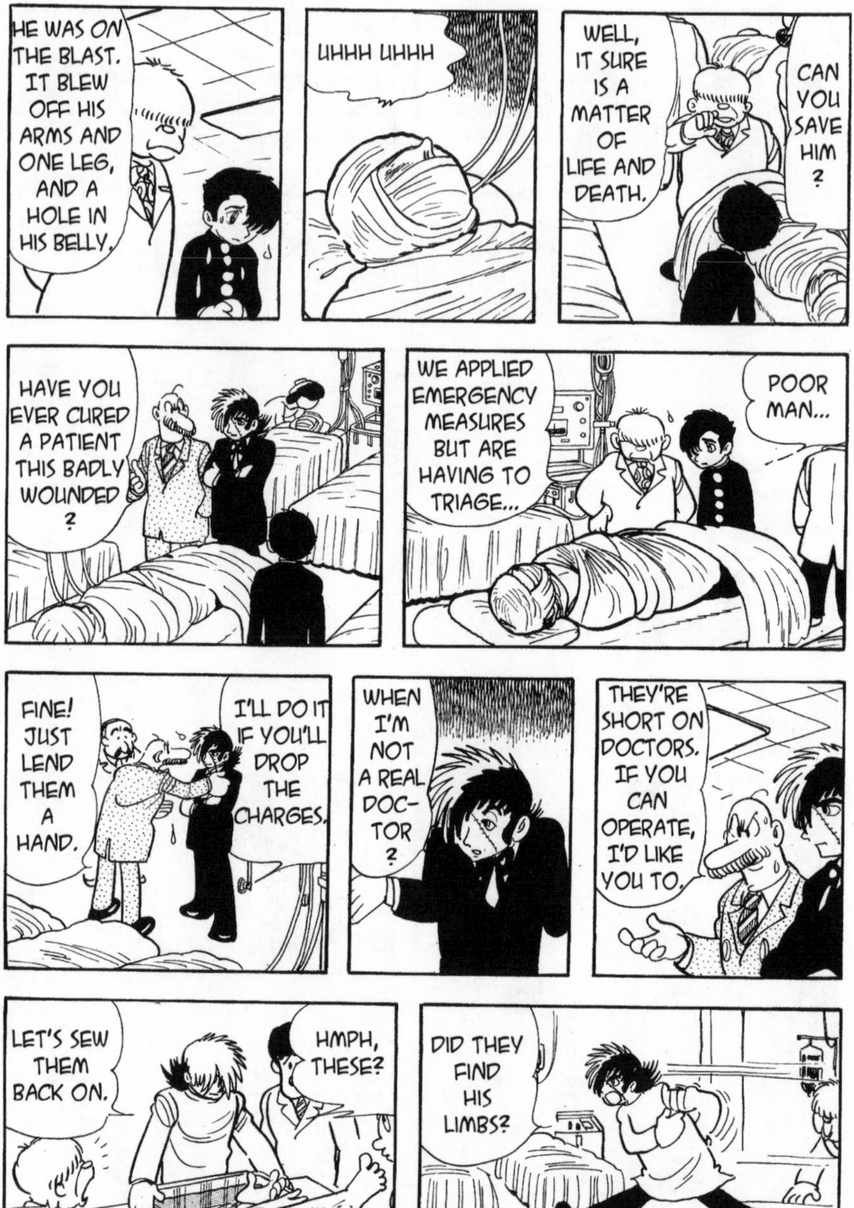
CAN YOU SAVE HIM ?
WELL, IT SURE IS A MATTER OF LIFE AND DEATH.
UHHH UHHH
HE WAS ON THE BLAST. IT BLEW OFF HIS ARMS AND ONE LEG, AND A HOLE IN HIS BELLY.
POOR MAN...
WE APPLIED EMERGENCY MEASURES BUT ARE HAVING TO TRIAGE...
HAVE YOU EVER CURED A PATIENT THIS BADLY WOUNDED ?
THEY'RE SHORT ON DOCTORS. IF YOU CAN OPERATE, I'D LIKE YOU TO.
WHEN I'M NOT A REAL DOC-TOR ?
I'LL DO IT IF YOU'LL DROP THE CHARGES.
FINE! JUST LEND THEM A HAND.
DID THEY FIND HIS LIMBS?
HMPH, THESE?
LET'S SEW THEM BACK ON.
WHAT?!

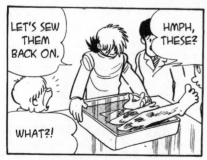

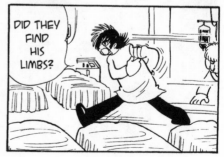

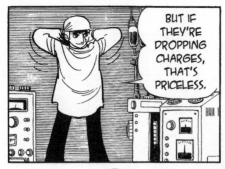

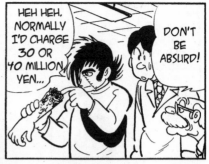

HEH HEH. NORMALLY I'D CHARGE 30 OR 40 MILLION YEN...
DON'T BE ABSURD!
BUT IF THEY'RE DROPPING CHARGES, THAT'S PRICELESS.
IS HE INSANE? WE'RE NOT TALKING ABOUT A DOLL...
WHAT IS IT, SON?
I'D... LIKE TO WATCH...
THIS ONE ISN'T PUBLIC!
I MEAN TO PRACTICE ONE DAY...
FINE BY ME. THE SEVERITY OF A LIFE IN THE BALANCE OUGHT TO TEACH HIM A LESSON.
LISTEN, KID... WHEN I WAS EVEN YOUNGER THAN YOU ARE, AN ACCIDENT LEFT ME IN PIECES, TOO.

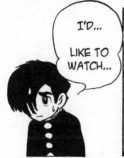

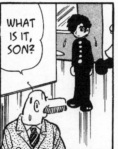

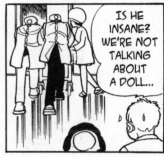

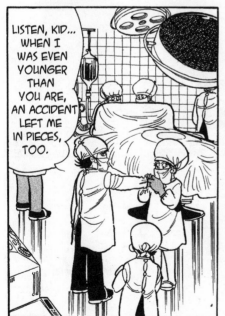

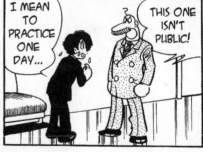

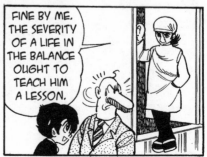

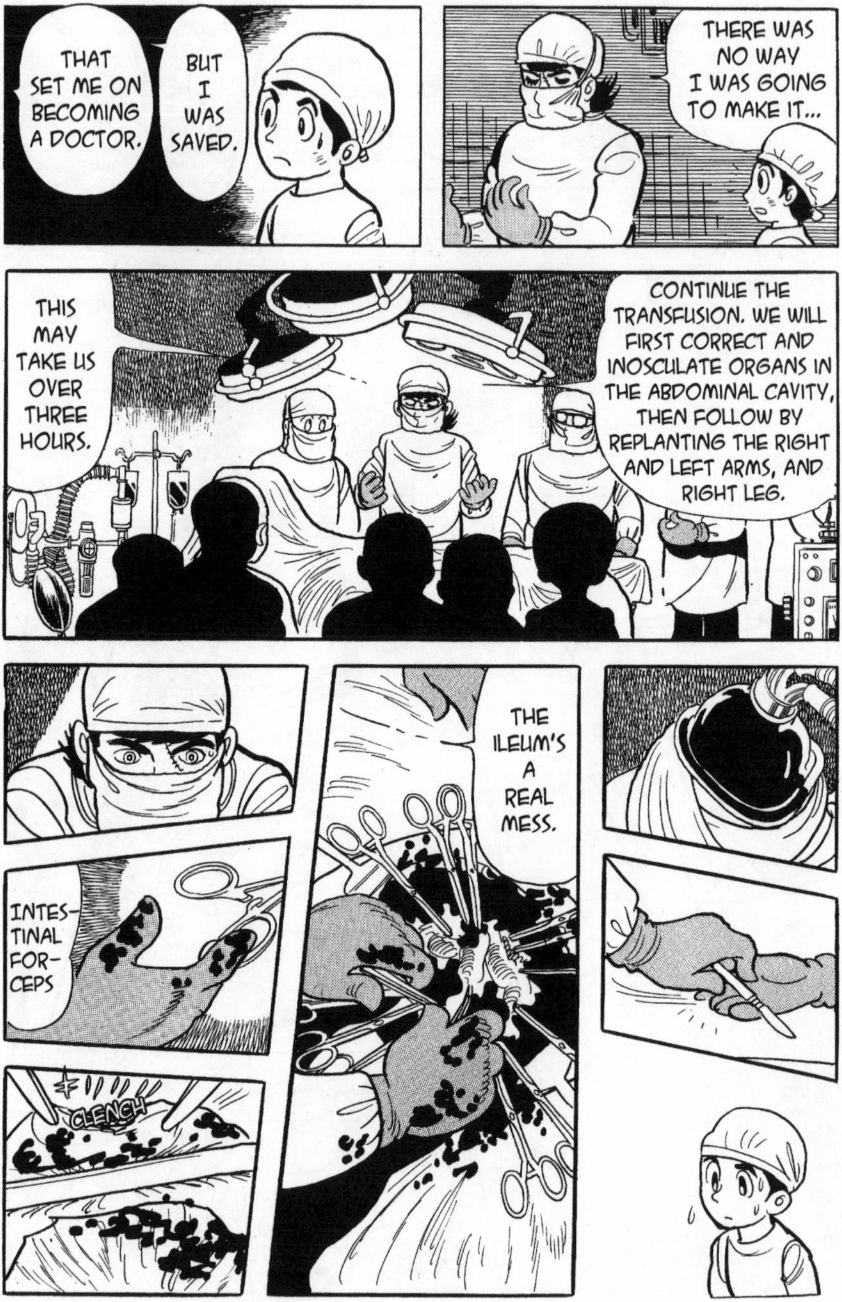
THERE WAS NO WAY I WAS GOING TO MAKE IT...
BUT I WAS SAVED.
THAT SET ME ON BECOMING A DOCTOR.
CONTINUE THE TRANSFUSION. WE WILL FIRST CORRECT AND INOSCULATE ORGANS IN THE ABDOMINAL CAVITY, THEN FOLLOW BY REPLANTING THE RIGHT AND LEFT ARMS, AND RIGHT LEG.
THIS MAY TAKE US OVER THREE HOURS.
THE ILEUM'S A REAL MESS.
INTES-TINAL FOR-CEPS
CLENCH

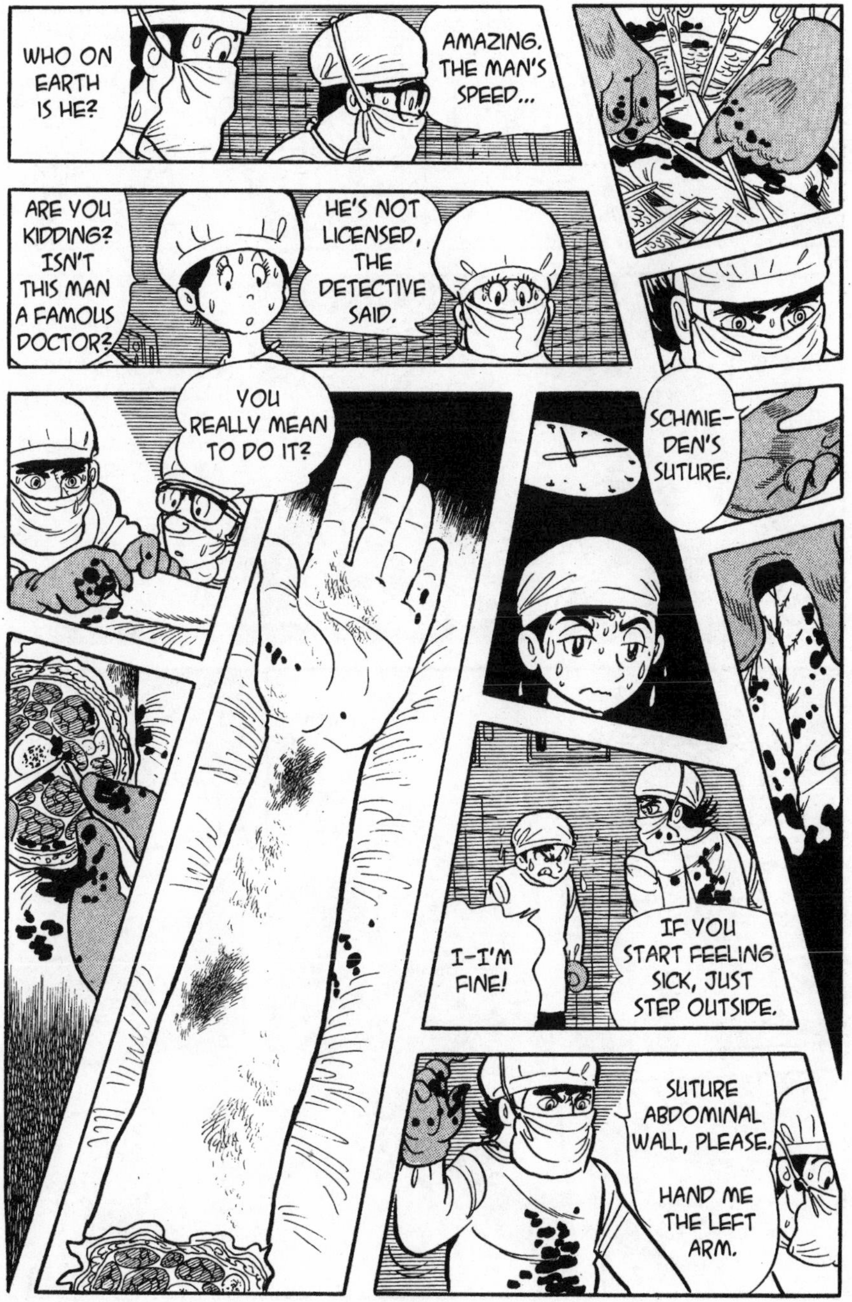
WHO ON EARTH IS HE?
AMAZING. THE MAN'S SPEED...
ARE YOU KIDDING? ISN'T THIS MAN A FAMOUS DOCTOR?
HE'S NOT LICENSED, THE DETECTIVE SAID.
SCHMIEDEN'S SUTURE.
YOU REALLY MEAN TO DO IT?
IF YOU START FEELING SICK, JUST STEP OUTSIDE.
I-I'M FINE!
SUTURE ABDOMINAL WALL, PLEASE.
HAND ME THE LEFT ARM.

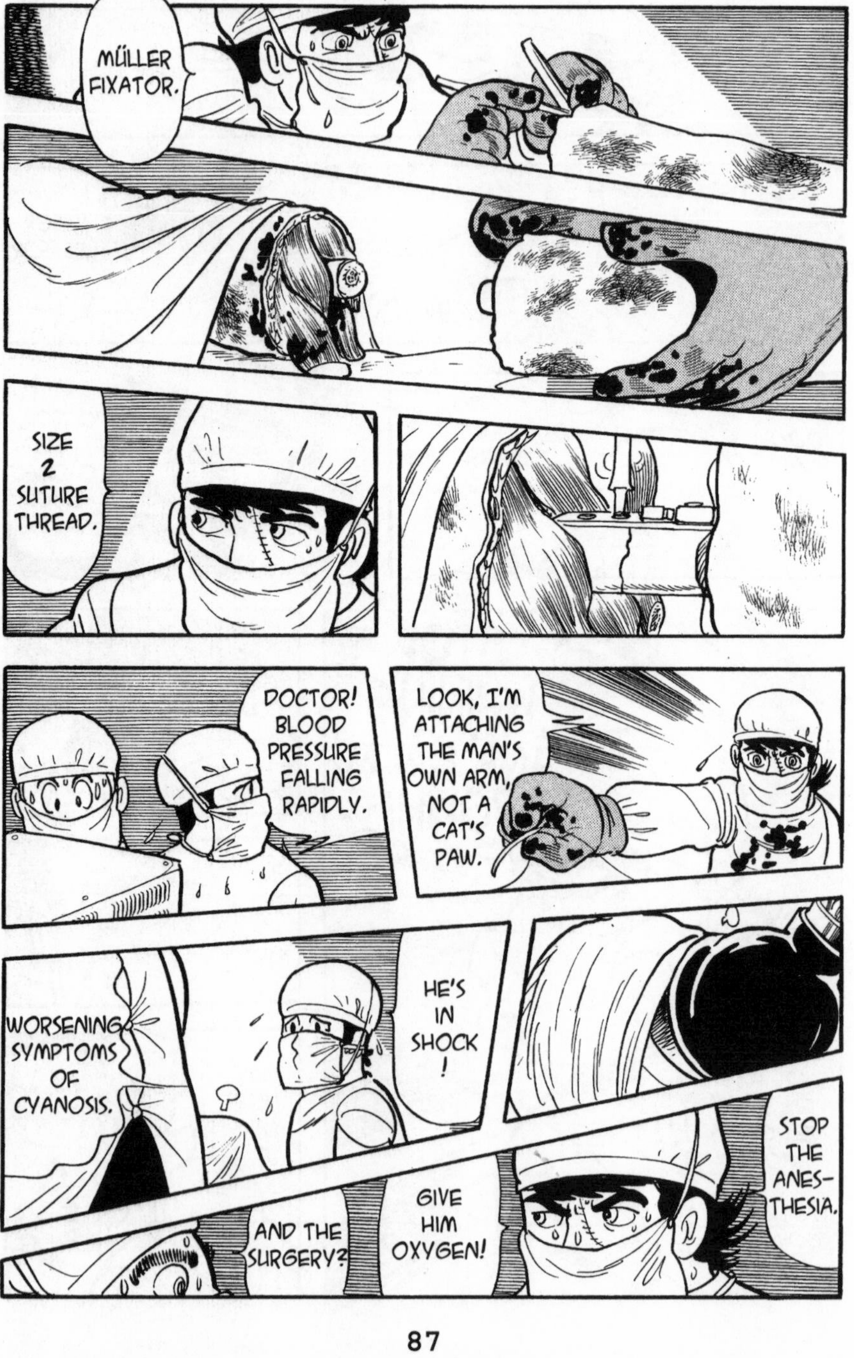
MÜLLER FIXATOR.
SIZE 2 SUTURE THREAD.
DOCTOR! BLOOD PRESSURE FALLING RAPIDLY.
LOOK, I'M ATTACHING THE MAN'S OWN ARM, NOT A CAT'S PAW.
WORSENING SYMPTOMS OF CYANOSIS.
HE'S IN SHOCK!
AND THE SURGERY?
GIVE HIM OXYGEN!
STOP THE ANES-THESIA.

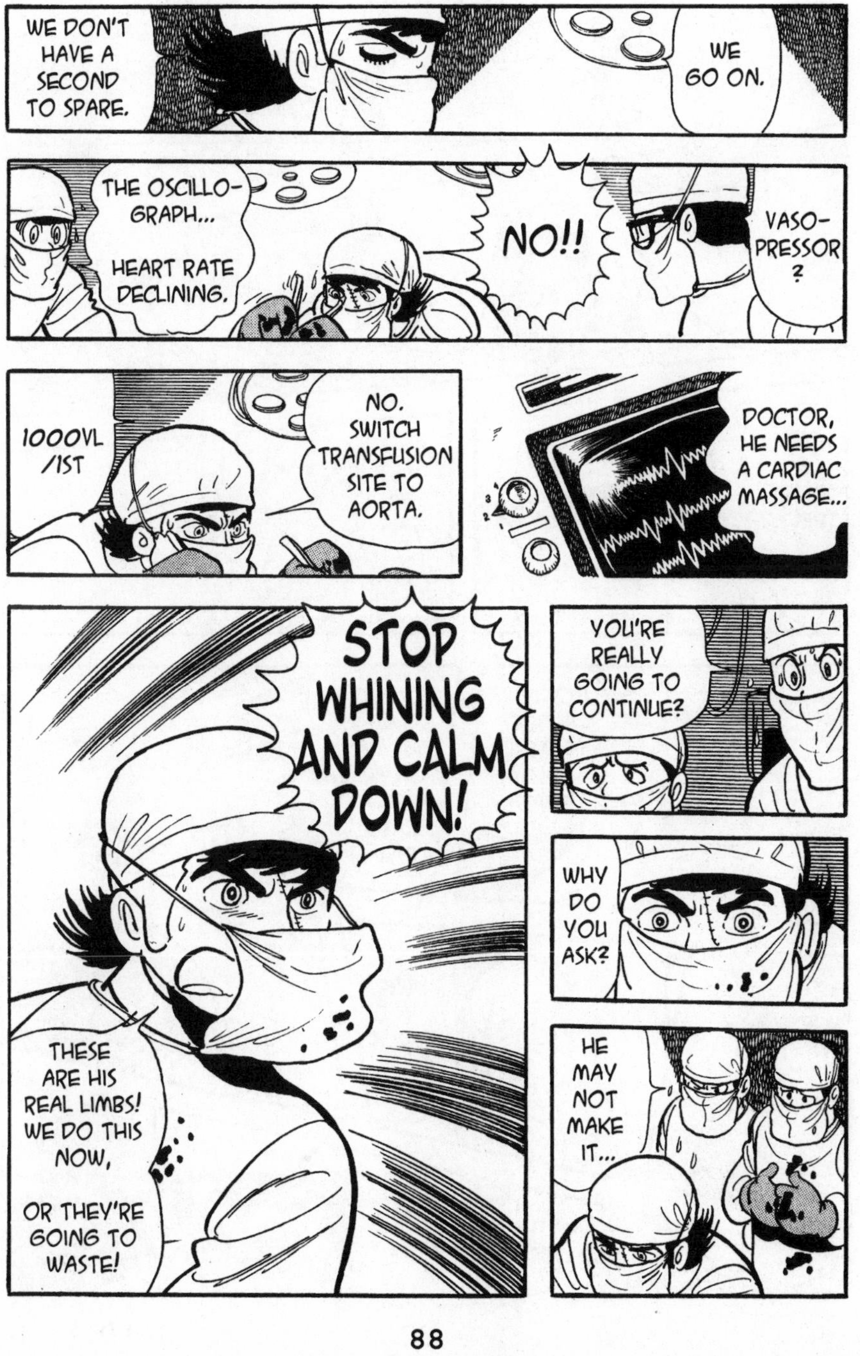
WE GO ON.
WE DON'T HAVE A SECOND TO SPARE.
VASO-PRESSOR?
NO!!
THE OSCILLO-GRAPH... HEART RATE DECLINING.
DOCTOR, HE NEEDS A CARDIAC MASSAGE...
NO. SWITCH TRANSFUSION SITE TO AORTA.
1000VL /1ST
YOU'RE REALLY GOING TO CONTINUE?
WHY DO YOU ASK?
HE MAY NOT MAKE IT...
STOP WHINING AND CALM DOWN!
THESE ARE HIS REAL LIMBS! WE DO THIS NOW,
OR THEY'RE GOING TO WASTE!

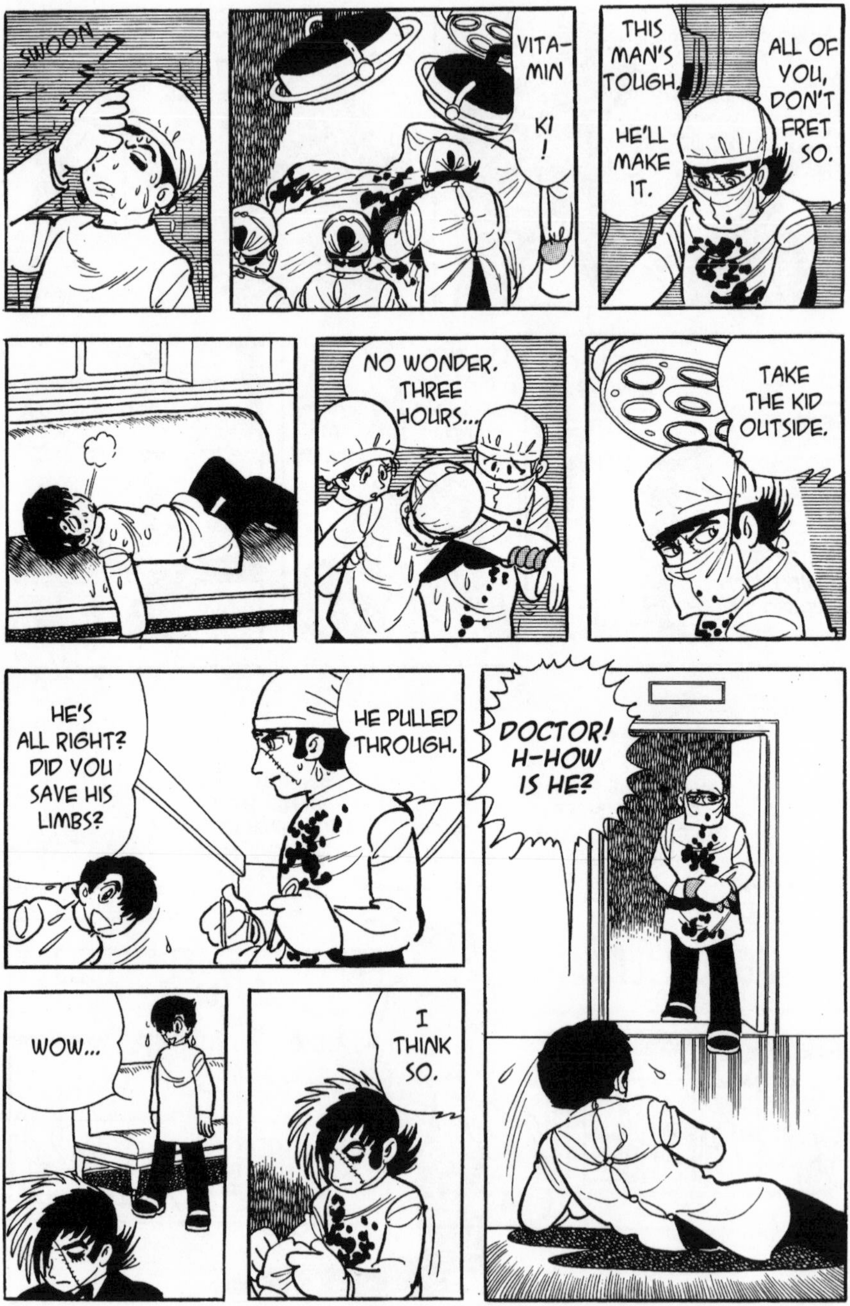
ALL OF YOU, DON'T FRET SO.
THIS MAN'S TOUGH.
HE'LL MAKE IT.
VITA-MIN KI!
SWOON
TAKE THE KID OUTSIDE.
NO WONDER. THREE HOURS...
DOCTOR! H-HOW IS HE?
HE PULLED THROUGH.
HE'S ALL RIGHT? DID YOU SAVE HIS LIMBS?
I THINK SO.
WOW...

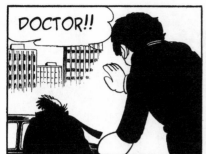

DETECTIVE, I GET OFF SCOT-FREE, YES?
SO LONG ...
DOCTOR!!
DOCTOR! JUST THIS MORNING, I WAS READY TO DIE.
WHY?
I FAILED MY EXAM. BUT...
IT'S NOT A MATTER OF LIFE AND DEATH.
WHAT'S SO FUNNY?
JUST MY OWN DAMN STUPIDITY.
THE YOUTH, BLACK JACK, AND KATO WILL PROBABLY NEVER MEET AGAIN.
YET, FOR THE YOUTH, THAT BRIEF TIME COULD NOT BUT HAVE BEEN FRUITFUL.

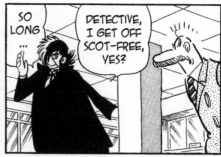

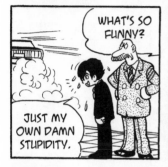

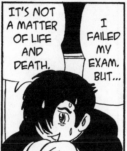

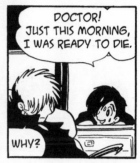

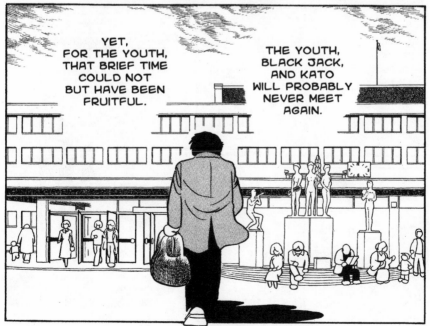

EMERGENCY SHELTER

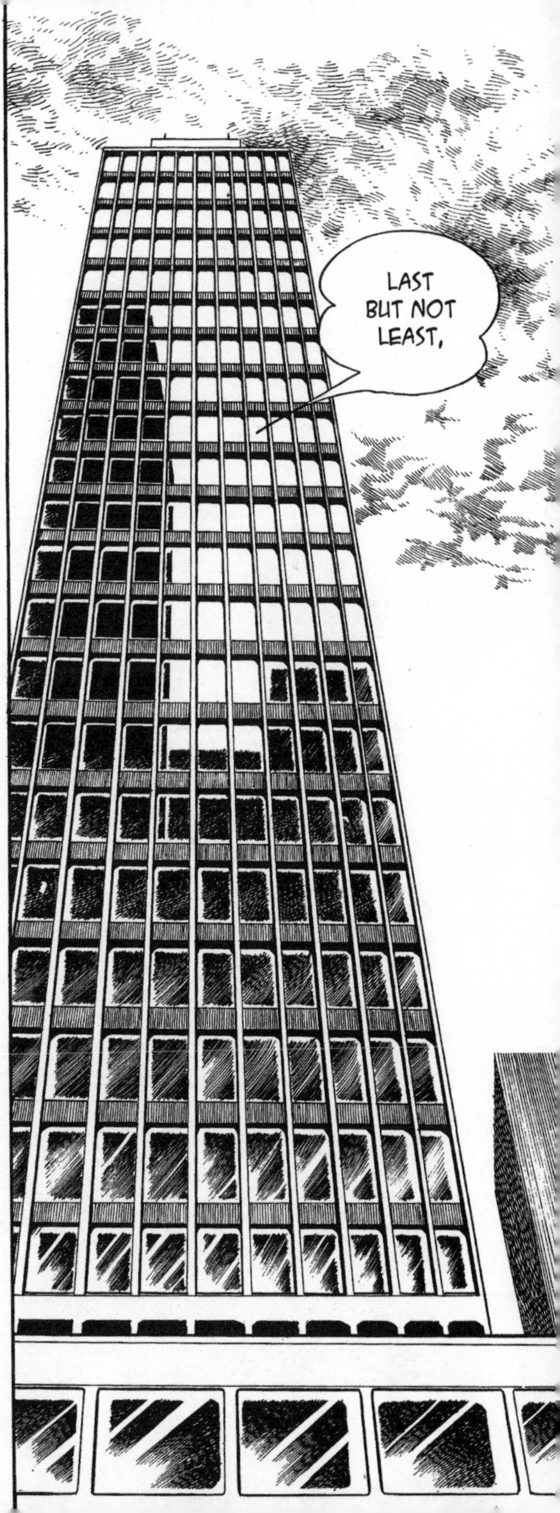
LAST BUT NOT LEAST,
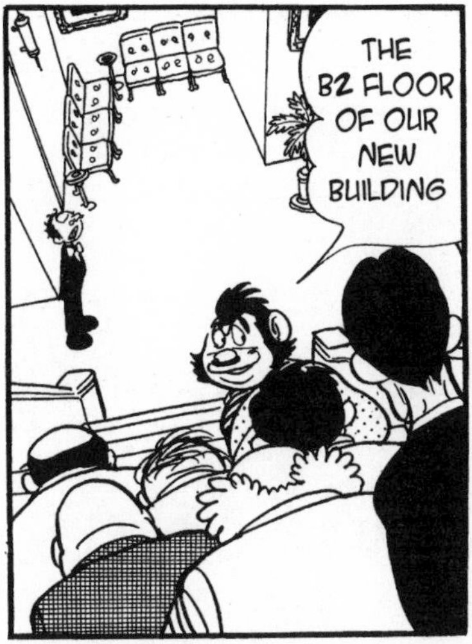
THE B2 FLOOR OF OUR NEW BUILDING
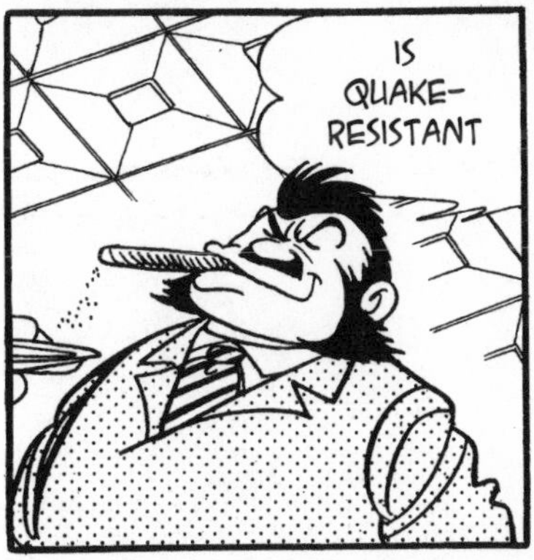
IS QUAKE-RESISTANT
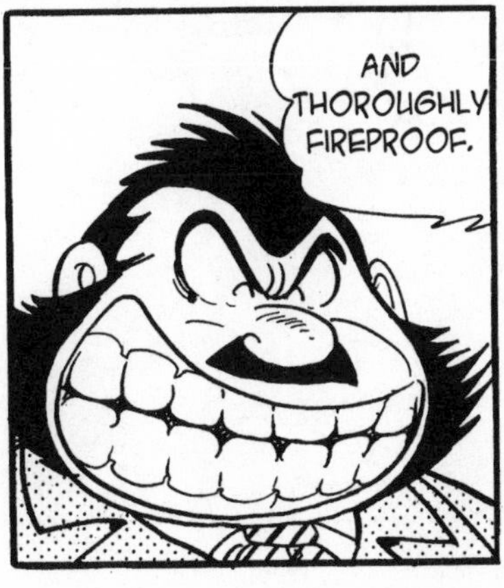
AND THOROUGHLY FIREPROOF.

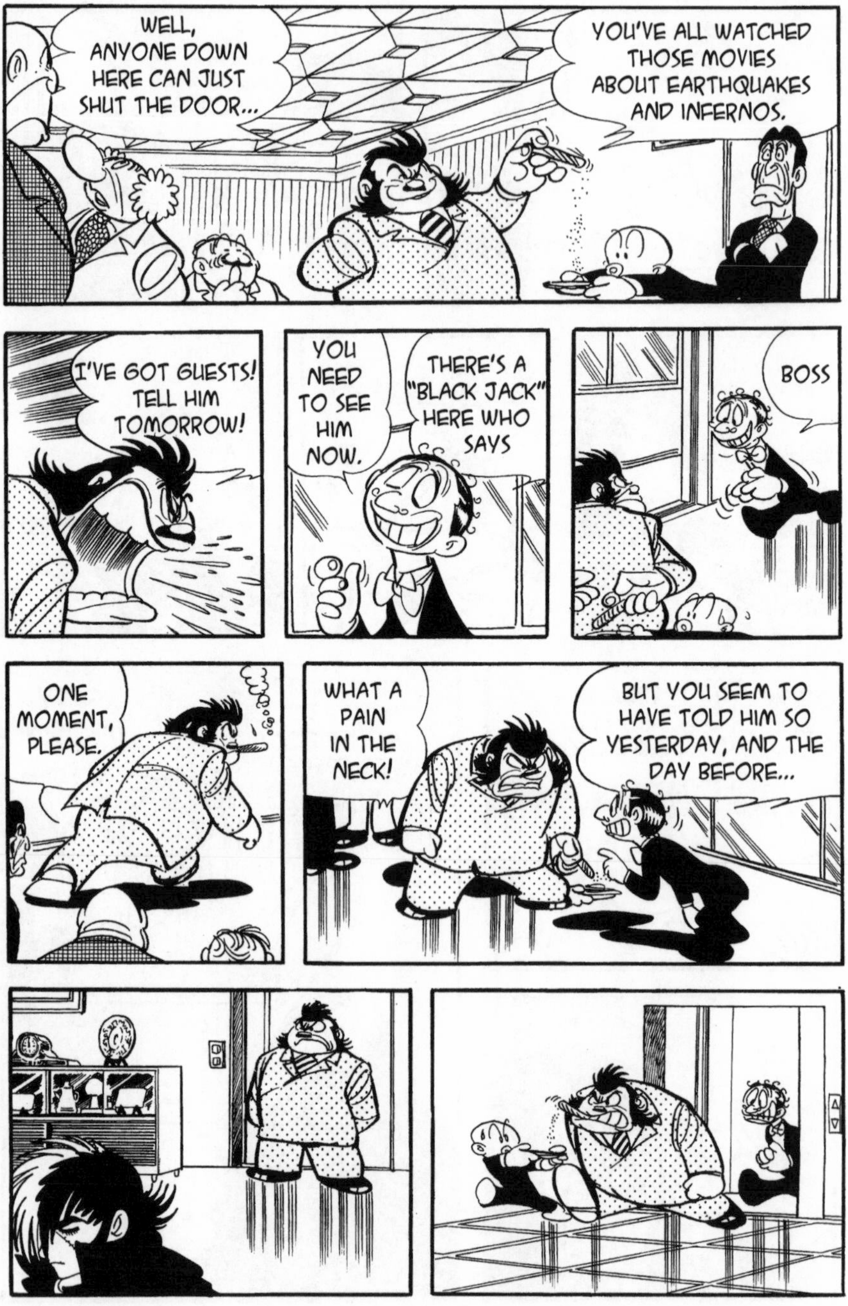
YOU'VE ALL WATCHED THOSE MOVIES ABOUT EARTHQUAKES AND INFERNOS.
WELL, ANYONE DOWN HERE CAN JUST SHUT THE DOOR...
BOSS
THERE'S A "BLACK JACK" HERE WHO SAYS
YOU NEED TO SEE HIM NOW.
I'VE GOT GUESTS! TELL HIM TOMORROW!
BUT YOU SEEM TO HAVE TOLD HIM SO YESTERDAY, AND THE DAY BEFORE...
WHAT A PAIN IN THE NECK!
ONE MOMENT, PLEASE.

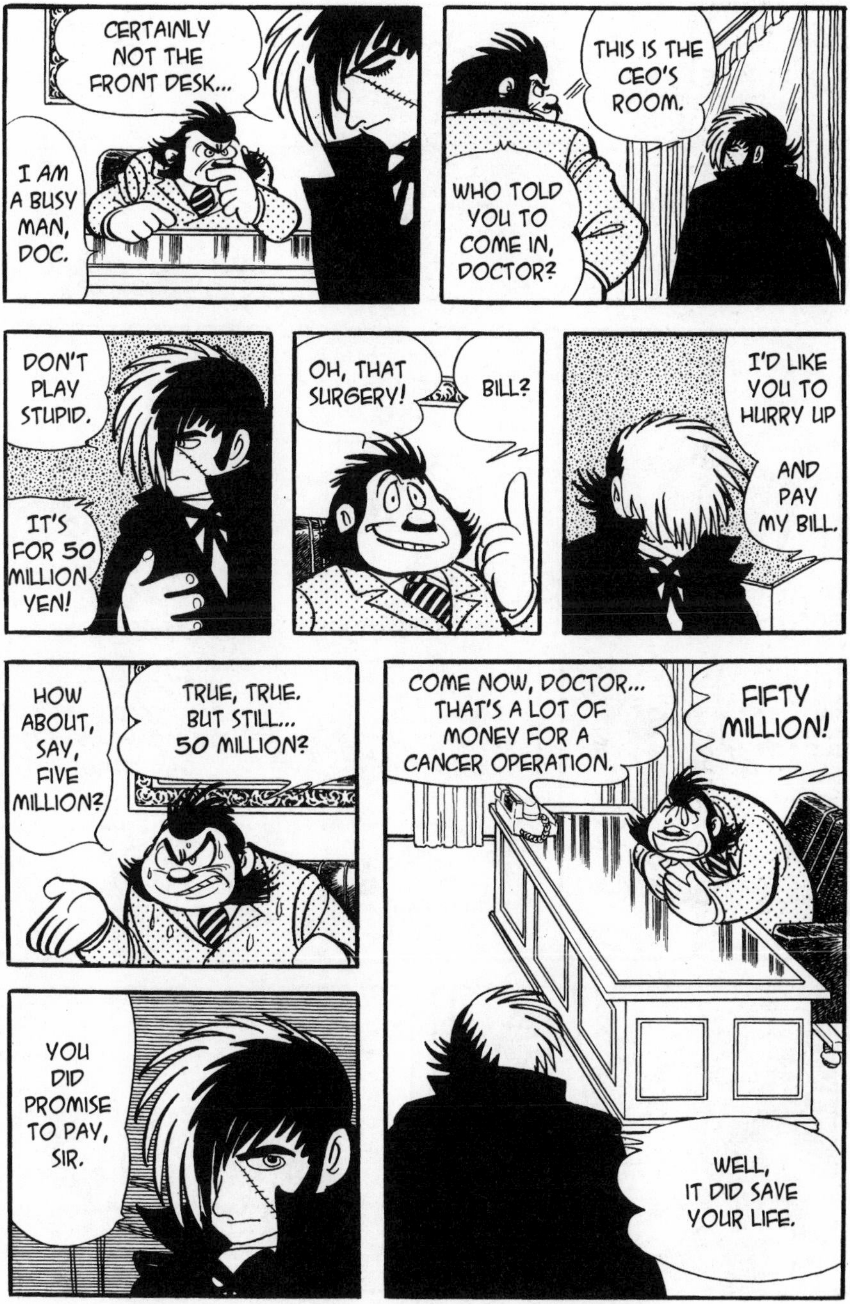
THIS IS THE CEO'S ROOM.
WHO TOLD YOU TO COME IN, DOCTOR?
CERTAINLY NOT THE FRONT DESK...
I AM A BUSY MAN, DOC.
I'D LIKE YOU TO HURRY UP
AND PAY MY BILL.
BILL?
OH, THAT SURGERY!
DON'T PLAY STUPID.
IT'S FOR 50 MILLION YEN!
FIFTY MILLION!
COME NOW, DOCTOR... THAT'S A LOT OF MONEY FOR A CANCER OPERATION.
WELL, IT DID SAVE YOUR LIFE.
TRUE, TRUE. BUT STILL... 50 MILLION?
HOW ABOUT, SAY, FIVE MILLION?
YOU DID PROMISE TO PAY, SIR.

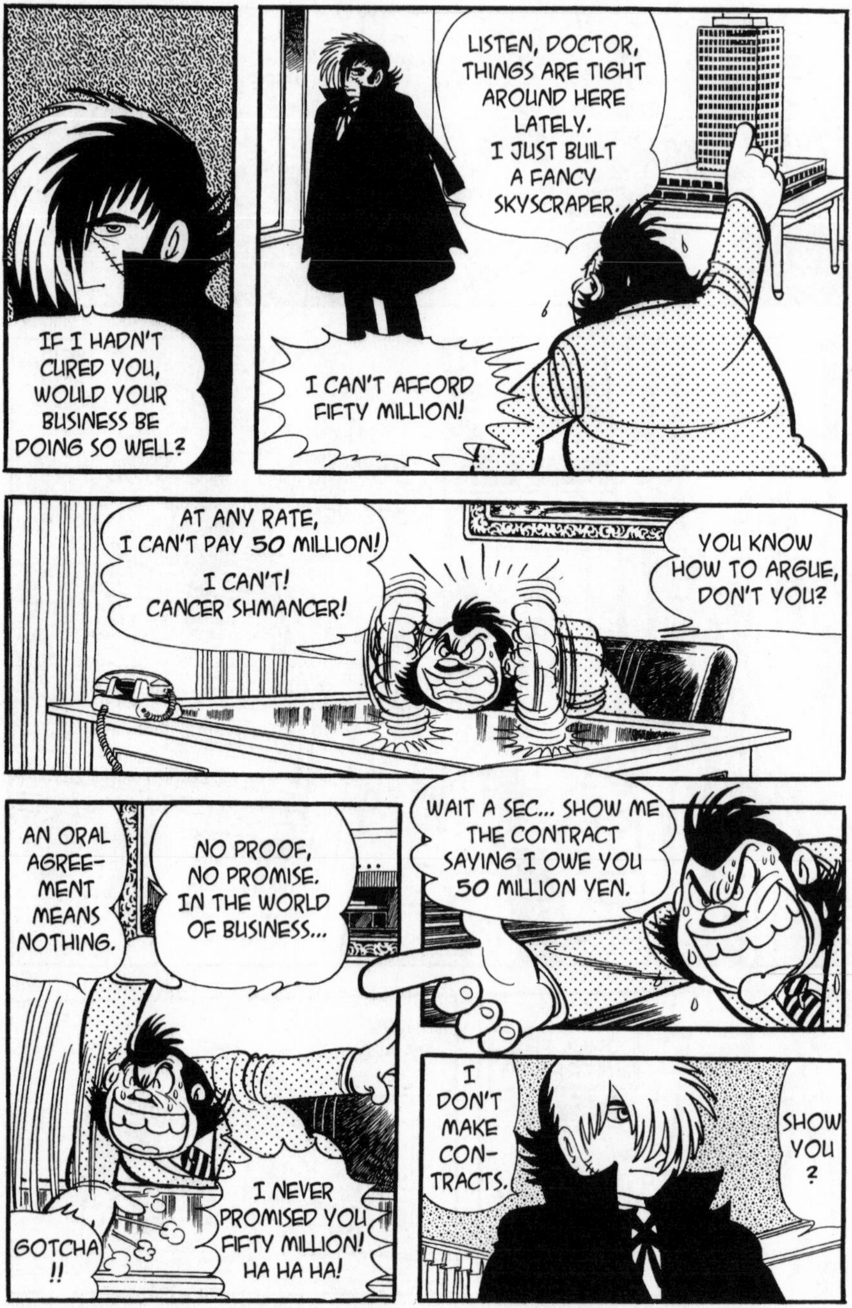
LISTEN, DOCTOR, THINGS ARE TIGHT AROUND HERE LATELY. I JUST BUILT A FANCY SKYSCRAPER.
I CAN'T AFFORD FIFTY MILLION!
IF I HADN'T CURED YOU, WOULD YOUR BUSINESS BE DOING SO WELL?
AT ANY RATE, I CAN'T PAY 50 MILLION!
I CAN'T! CANCER SHMANCER!
YOU KNOW HOW TO ARGUE, DON'T YOU?
WAIT A SEC... SHOW ME THE CONTRACT SAYING I OWE YOU 50 MILLION YEN.
SHOW YOU?
I DON'T MAKE CON-TRACTS.
GOTCHA!!
I NEVER PROMISED YOU FIFTY MILLION! HA HA HA!
NO PROOF, NO PROMISE. IN THE WORLD OF BUSINESS...
AN ORAL AGREE-MENT MEANS NOTHING.

I WON'T NOT PAY.

I THINK THAT'S A VERY CRUDE WAY TO PUT IT...

JUST NOT TODAY!

SO YOU WERE LYING?

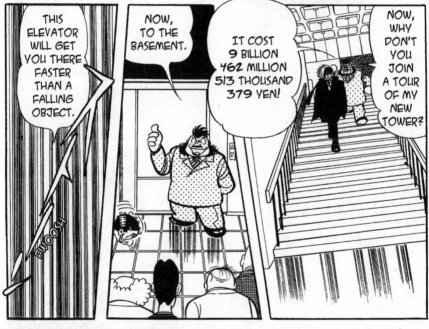

THIS ELEVATOR WILL GET YOU THERE FASTER THAN A FALLING OBJECT.

FWOOSH

NOW, TO THE BASEMENT.

IT COST 9 BILLION 462 MILLION 513 THOUSAND 379 YEN!

NOW, WHY DON'T YOU JOIN A TOUR OF MY NEW TOWER?

VREEE

BEEP

SHELTER ENTRANCE

HERE WE ARE.

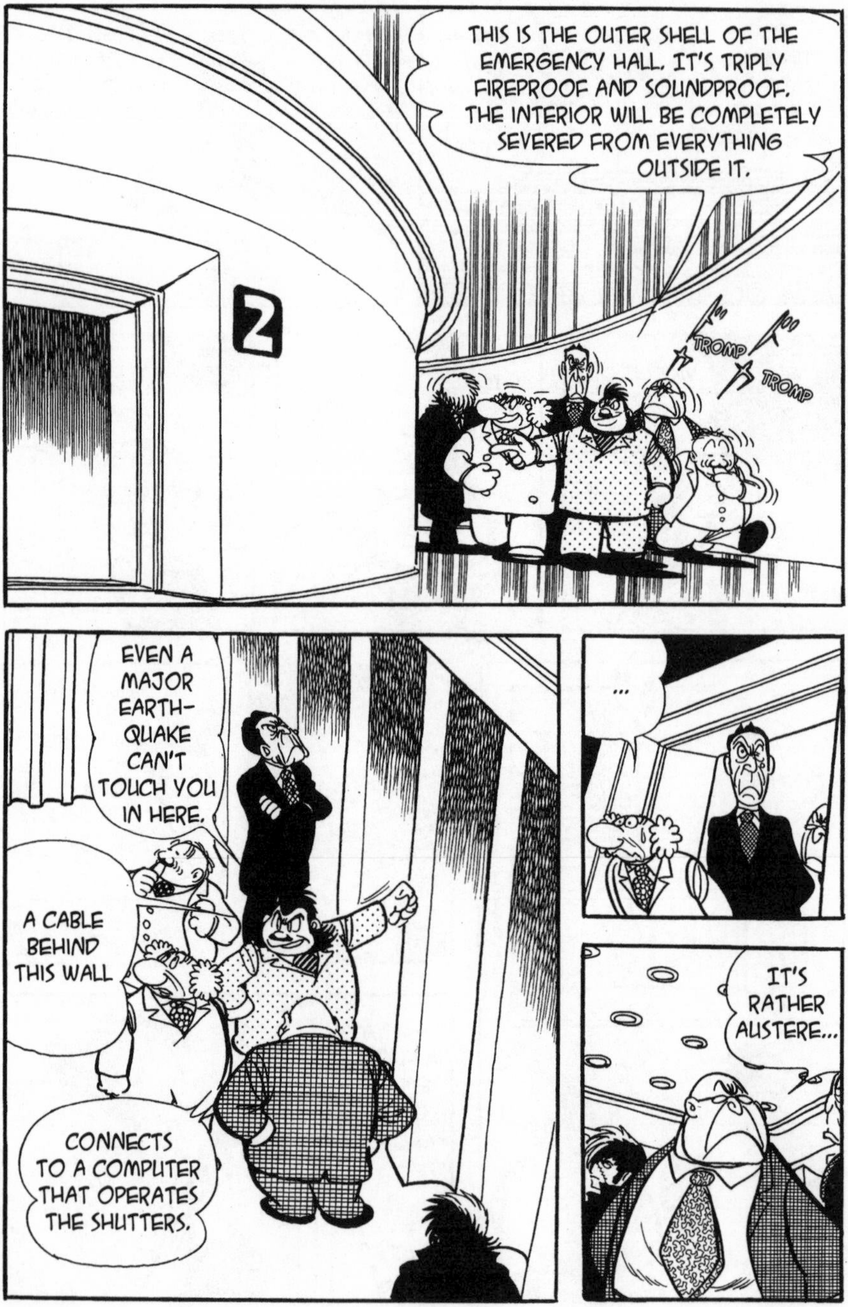
THIS IS THE OUTER SHELL OF THE EMERGENCY HALL. IT'S TRIPLY FIREPROOF AND SOUNDPROOF. THE INTERIOR WILL BE COMPLETELY SEVERED FROM EVERYTHING OUTSIDE IT.
TROMP
TROMP
EVEN A MAJOR EARTH-QUAKE CAN'T TOUCH YOU IN HERE.
A CABLE BEHIND THIS WALL
CONNECTS TO A COMPUTER THAT OPERATES THE SHUTTERS.
...
IT'S RATHER AUSTERE...

TELL THE COMPUTER TO CLOSE THE SHUTTERS!
IT'LL DO THAT ONLY IN A CRISIS.
THAT'S WHY I WANT TO RUN A TEST.
JUST PUNCH IN DATA TO SIMULATE A DISASTER.
YOU WANT TO TRICK THE COMPUTER?
NO! I WANT TO RUN A TEST!
WATCH YOUR TONGUE!
WOULD OUR COMPUTER BELIEVE A LIE?
AN EARTH-QUAKE OF MAGNITUDE 7, INTENSITY 5, AT A DEPTH OF 30 KM!
RATTLE
RATTLE
RATTLE
BING!
SIR, LOOK! IT'S COMING DOWN.
SHHP
I SIMULATED A MAJOR EARTH-QUAKE.

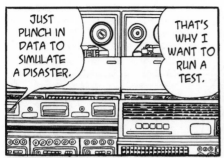

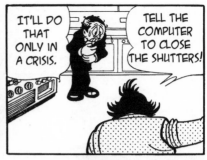

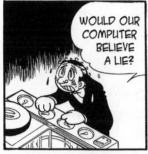

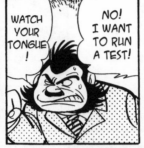

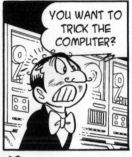

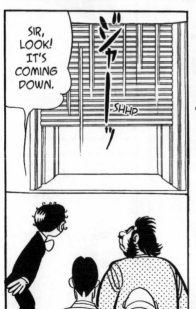

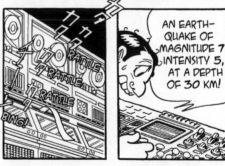

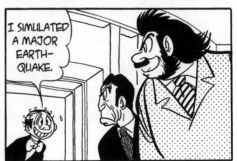

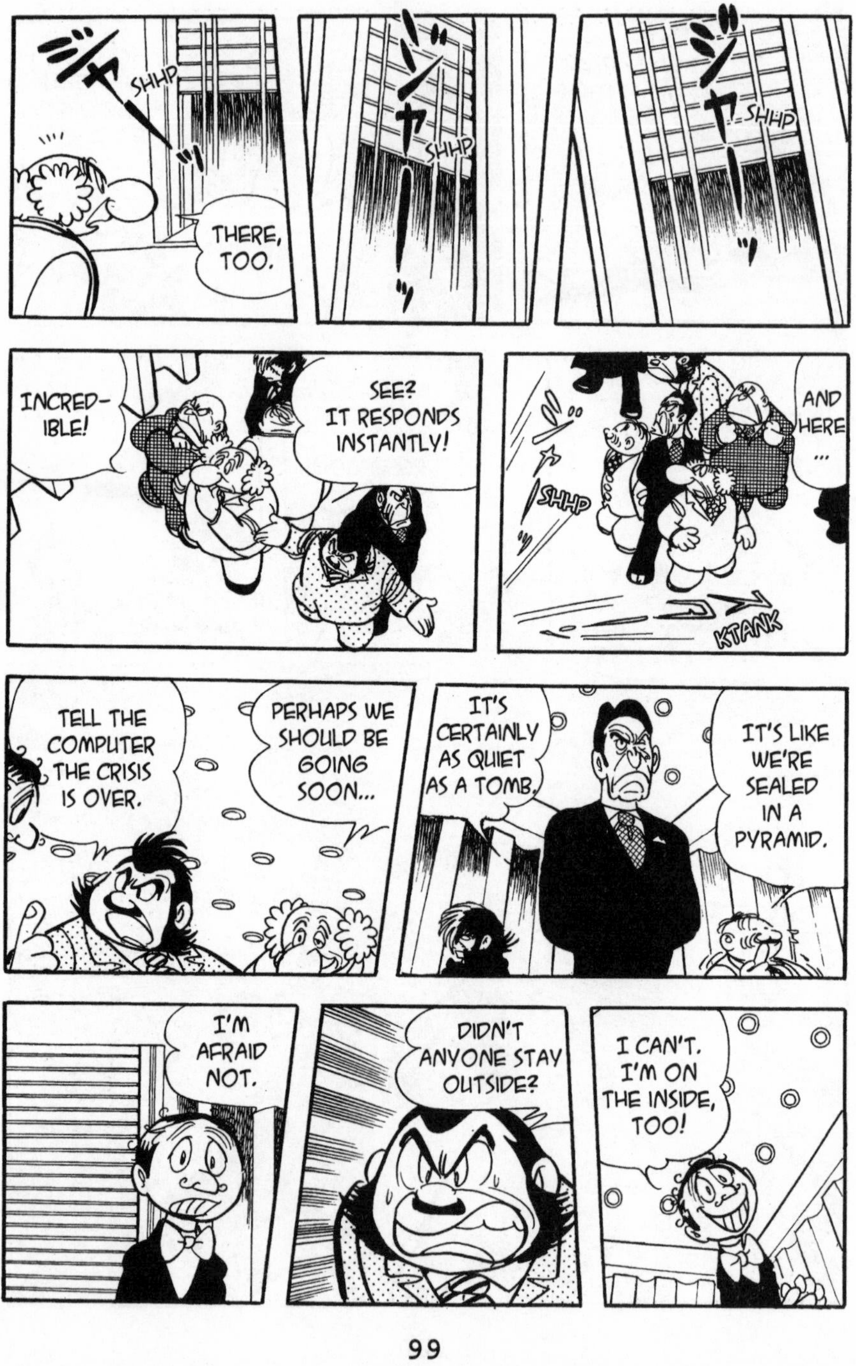
ジャッ
SHHP
THERE, TOO.
ジャーッ
SHHP
ジャーッ
SHHP
INCRED-IBLE!
SEE? IT RESPONDS INSTANTLY!
AND HERE...
SHHP
KTANK
TELL THE COMPUTER THE CRISIS IS OVER.
PERHAPS WE SHOULD BE GOING SOON...
IT'S CERTAINLY AS QUIET AS A TOMB.
IT'S LIKE WE'RE SEALED IN A PYRAMID.
I'M AFRAID NOT.
DIDN'T ANYONE STAY OUTSIDE?
I CAN'T. I'M ON THE INSIDE, TOO!

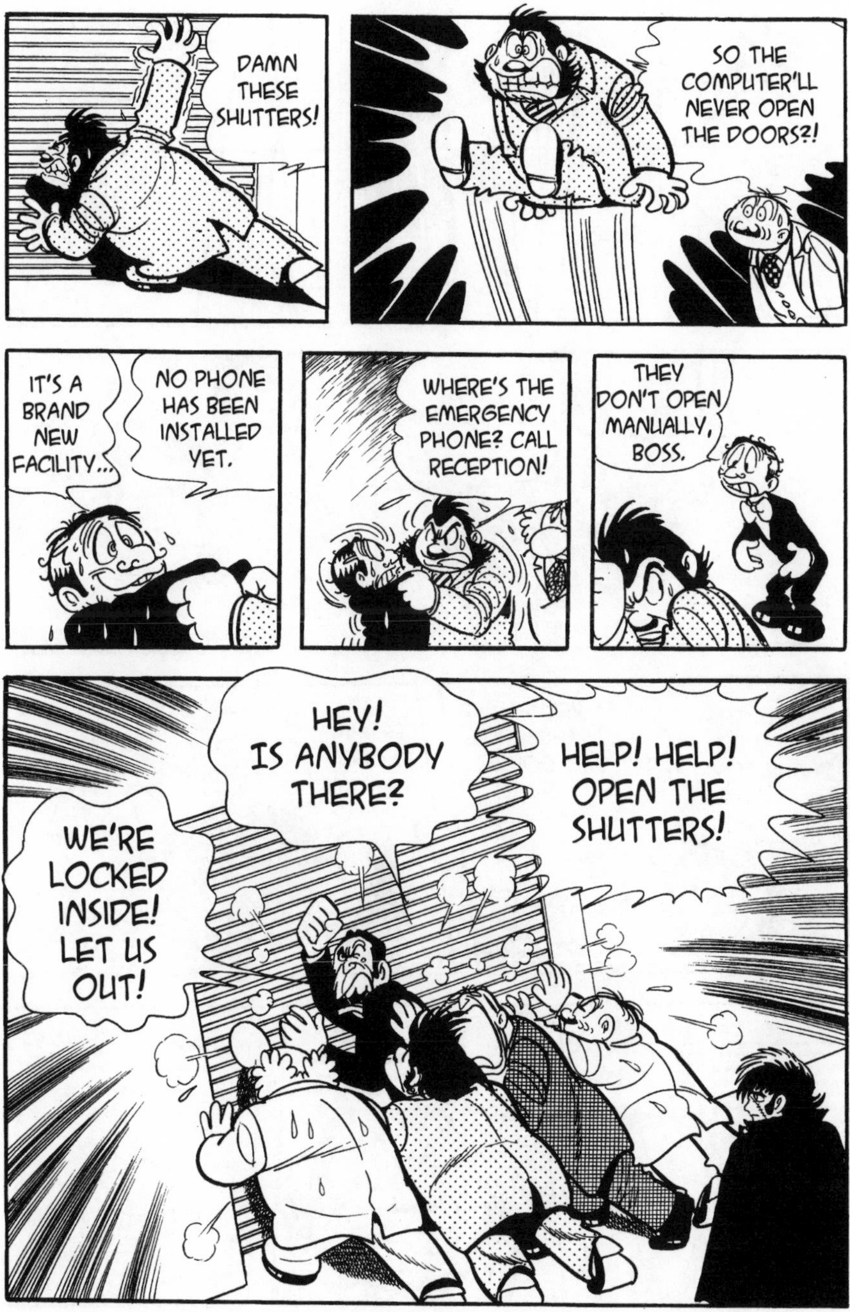
SO THE COMPUTER'LL NEVER OPEN THE DOORS?!
DAMN THESE SHUTTERS!
THEY DON'T OPEN MANUALLY, BOSS.
WHERE'S THE EMERGENCY PHONE? CALL RECEPTION!
IT'S A BRAND NEW FACILITY...
NO PHONE HAS BEEN INSTALLED YET.
HELP! HELP! OPEN THE SHUTTERS!
HEY! IS ANYBODY THERE?
WE'RE LOCKED INSIDE! LET US OUT!

LET'S ALL YELL AT ONCE!
ONE, TWO, THREE!
LET US OUT!
IT'S NO USE. A THOUSAND TRUMPETING ELEPHANTS WOULDN'T BE HEARD ACROSS THESE SOUNDPROOF WALLS.
EXECUTIVE DIRECTOR! IT'S YOUR FAULT!
FIGURE OUT HOW TO OPEN THEM.
DON'T KEEP BLAMING THIS ON ME!
THIS IS *YOUR* FAULT, BOSS!
NO, IT'S BECAUSE YOU'RE A BLITHERING NINCOMPOOP!
THIS IS NO TIME FOR BICKERING.
WHAT'S TO BECOME OF US IF THE DOORS NEVER OPEN?!
THERE ISN'T A DROP OF FOOD OR WATER DOWN HERE!

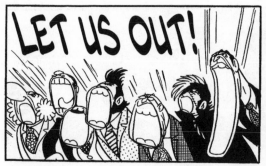

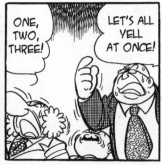

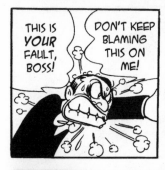

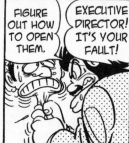

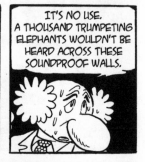

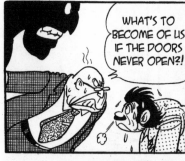

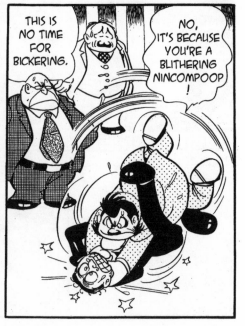

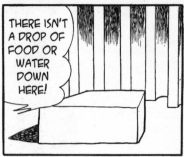

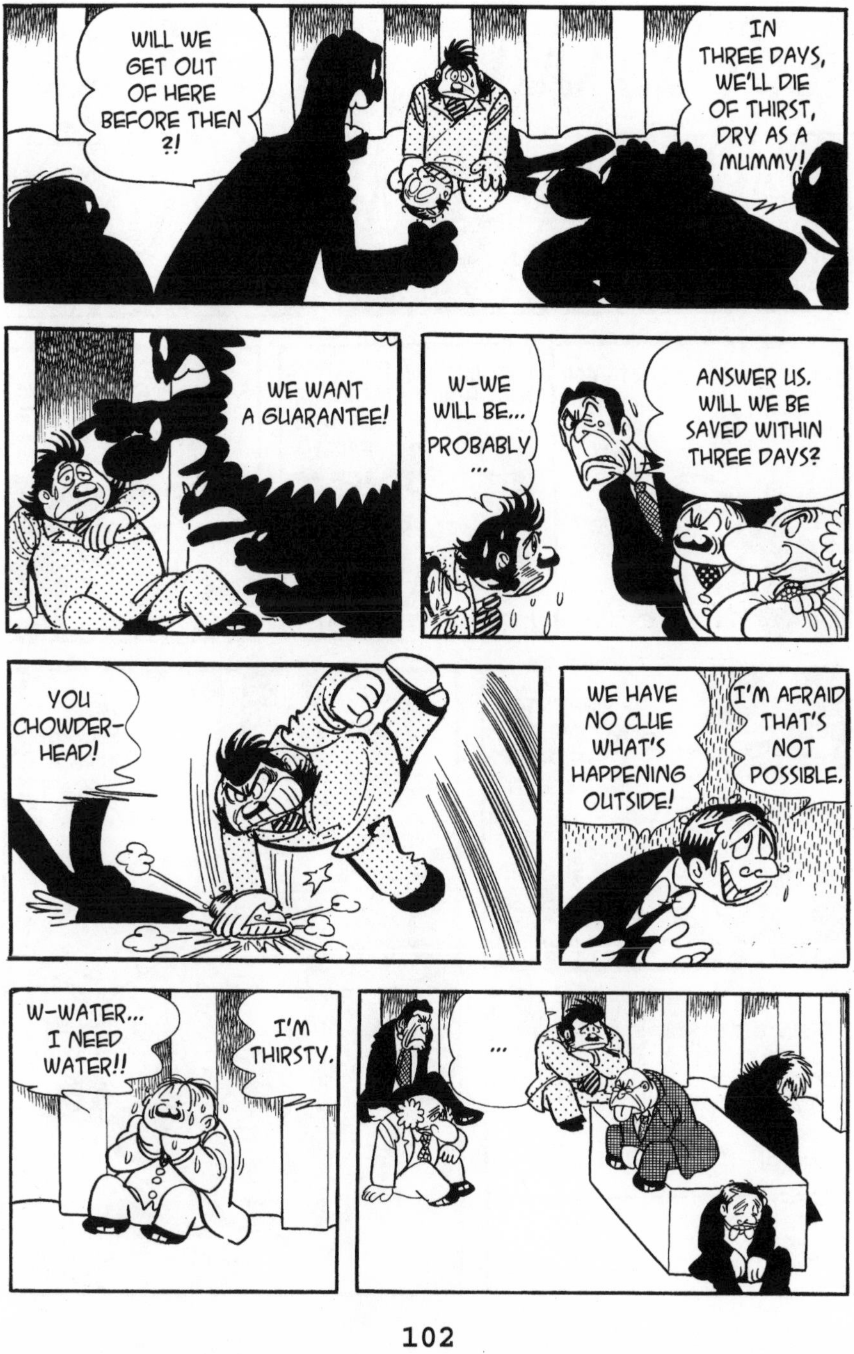
IN THREE DAYS, WE'LL DIE OF THIRST, DRY AS A MUMMY!
WILL WE GET OUT OF HERE BEFORE THEN ?!
ANSWER US. WILL WE BE SAVED WITHIN THREE DAYS?
W-WE WILL BE... PROBABLY ...
WE WANT A GUARANTEE!
I'M AFRAID THAT'S NOT POSSIBLE.
WE HAVE NO CLUE WHAT'S HAPPENING OUTSIDE!
YOU CHOWDER-HEAD!
...
I'M THIRSTY.
W-WATER... I NEED WATER!!

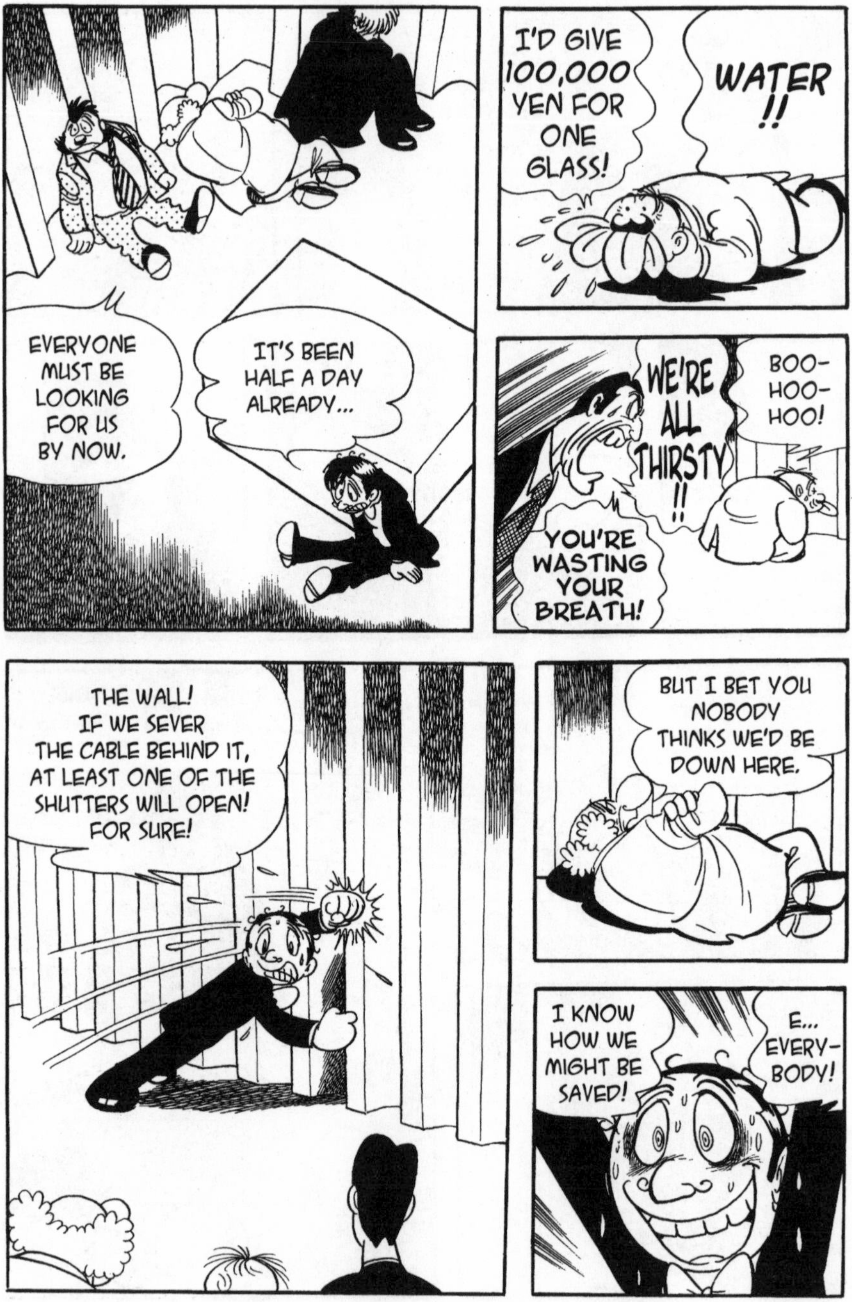
WATER !!
I'D GIVE 100,000 YEN FOR ONE GLASS!
BOO-HOO-HOO!
WE'RE ALL THIRSTY !!
YOU'RE WASTING YOUR BREATH!
IT'S BEEN HALF A DAY ALREADY...
EVERYONE MUST BE LOOKING FOR US BY NOW.
BUT I BET YOU NOBODY THINKS WE'D BE DOWN HERE.
E... EVERY-BODY!
I KNOW HOW WE MIGHT BE SAVED!
THE WALL! IF WE SEVER THE CABLE BEHIND IT, AT LEAST ONE OF THE SHUTTERS WILL OPEN! FOR SURE!

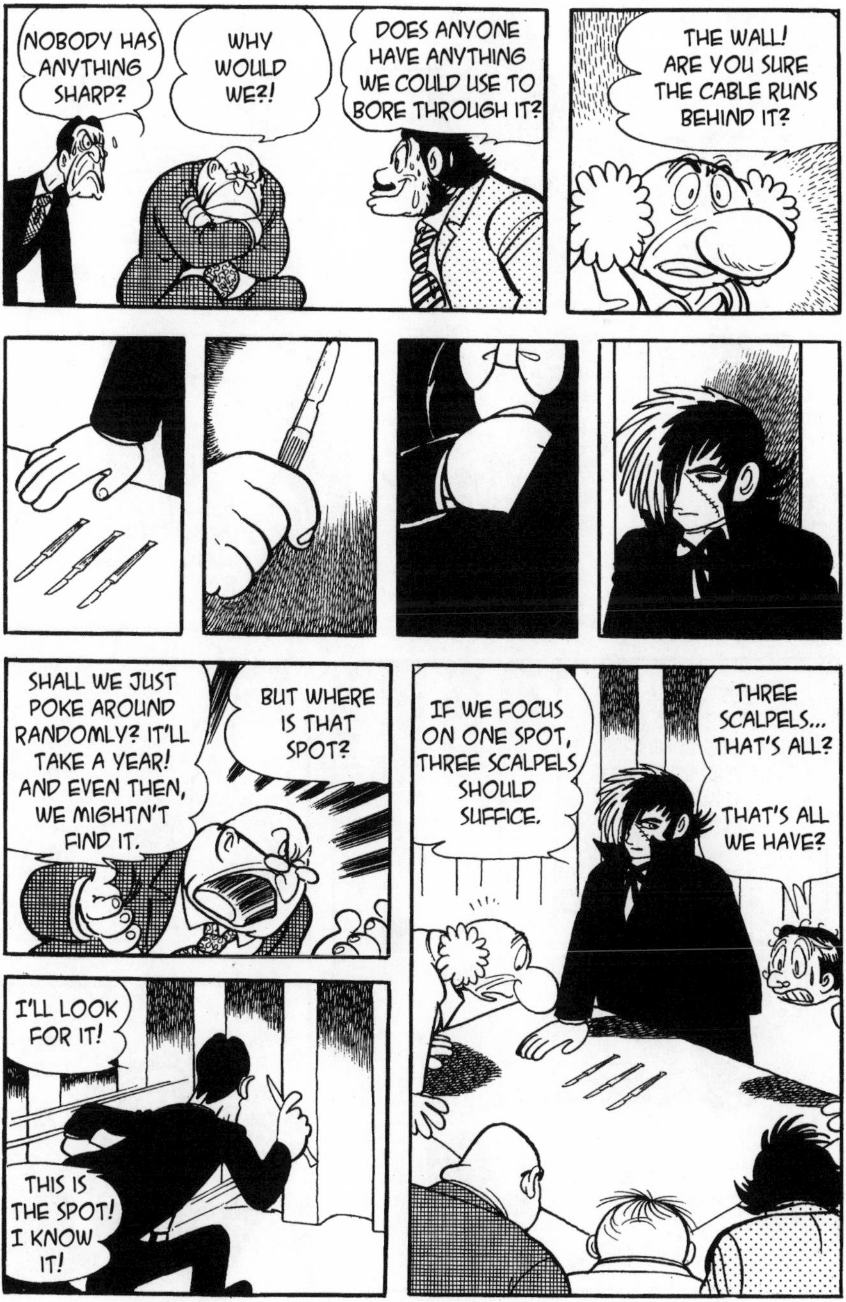
THE WALL! ARE YOU SURE THE CABLE RUNS BEHIND IT?
DOES ANYONE HAVE ANYTHING WE COULD USE TO BORE THROUGH IT?
WHY WOULD WE?!
NOBODY HAS ANYTHING SHARP?
THREE SCALPELS... THAT'S ALL?
THAT'S ALL WE HAVE?
IF WE FOCUS ON ONE SPOT, THREE SCALPELS SHOULD SUFFICE.
BUT WHERE IS THAT SPOT?
SHALL WE JUST POKE AROUND RANDOMLY? IT'LL TAKE A YEAR! AND EVEN THEN, WE MIGHTN'T FIND IT.
I'LL LOOK FOR IT!
THIS IS THE SPOT! I KNOW IT!

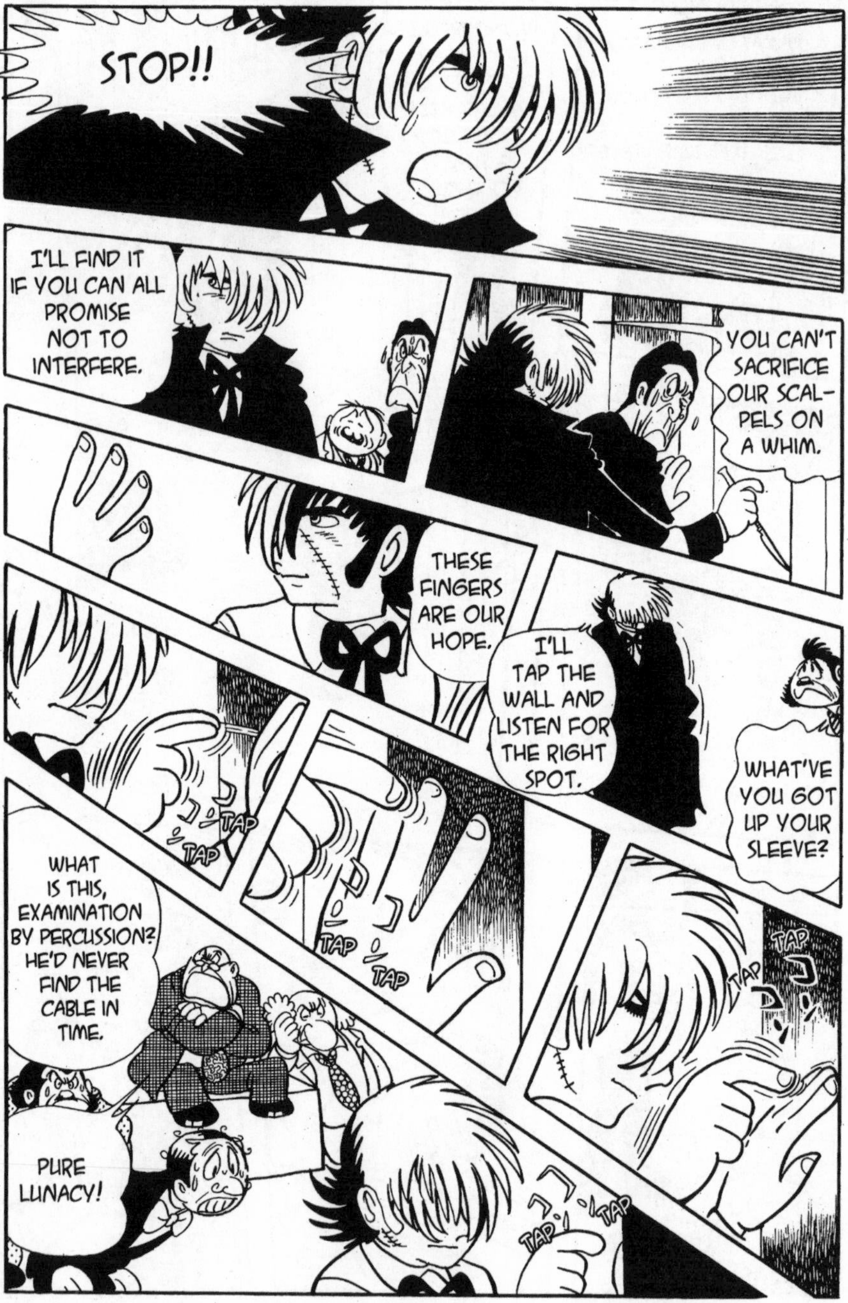
STOP!!
YOU CAN'T SACRIFICE OUR SCAL-PELS ON A WHIM.
I'LL FIND IT IF YOU CAN ALL PROMISE NOT TO INTERFERE.
WHAT'VE YOU GOT UP YOUR SLEEVE?
THESE FINGERS ARE OUR HOPE.
I'LL TAP THE WALL AND LISTEN FOR THE RIGHT SPOT.
TAP
TAP
TAP
TAP
TAP
TAP
TAP
TAP
WHAT IS THIS, EXAMINATION BY PERCUSSION? HE'D NEVER FIND THE CABLE IN TIME.
PURE LUNACY!

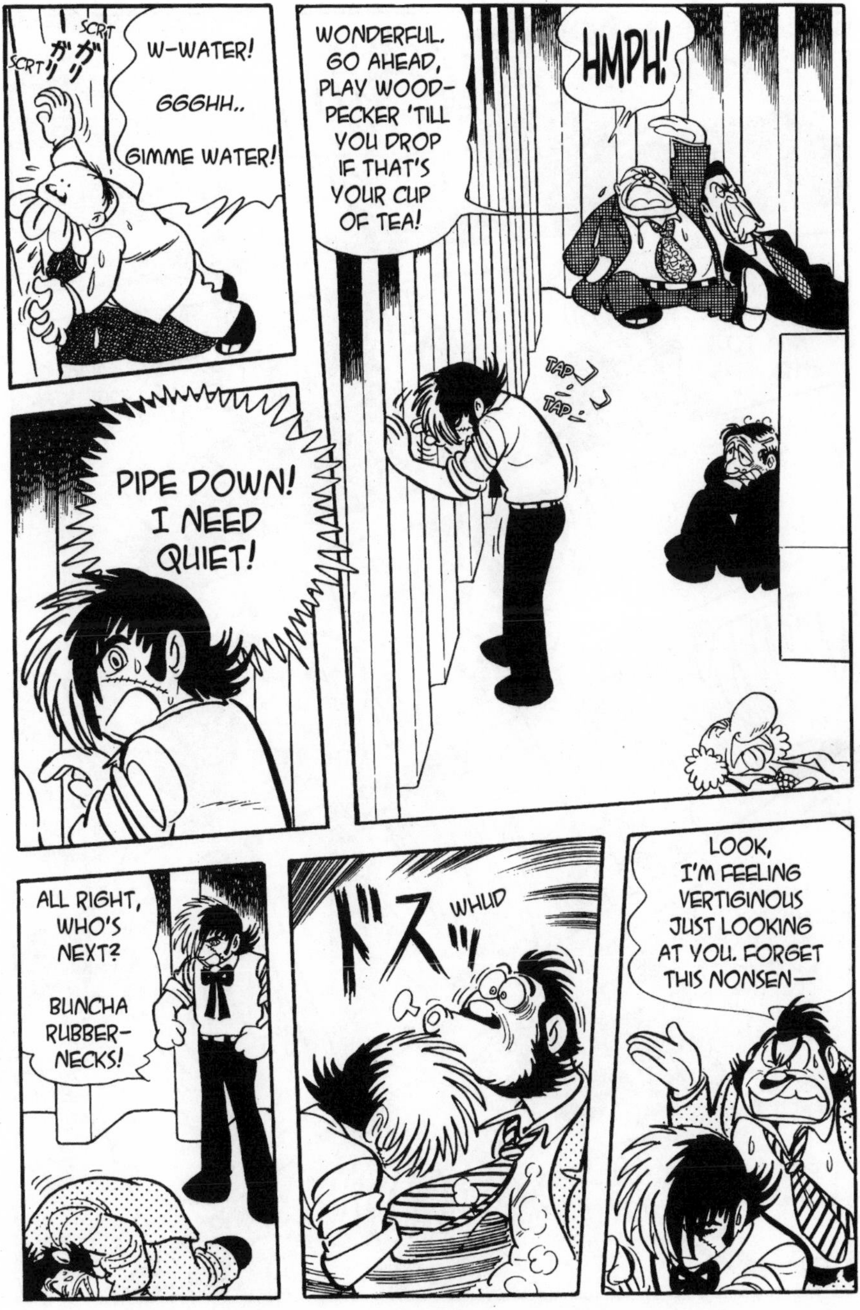
HMPH!
WONDERFUL. GO AHEAD, PLAY WOOD-PECKER 'TILL YOU DROP IF THAT'S YOUR CUP OF TEA!
TAP
TAP
W-WATER! GGGHH.. GIMME WATER!
SCRT
ガリ
SCRT
ガリ
PIPE DOWN! I NEED QUIET!
LOOK, I'M FEELING VERTIGINOUS JUST LOOKING AT YOU. FORGET THIS NONSEN—
WHUD
ドスッ
ALL RIGHT, WHO'S NEXT?
BUNCHA RUBBER-NECKS!

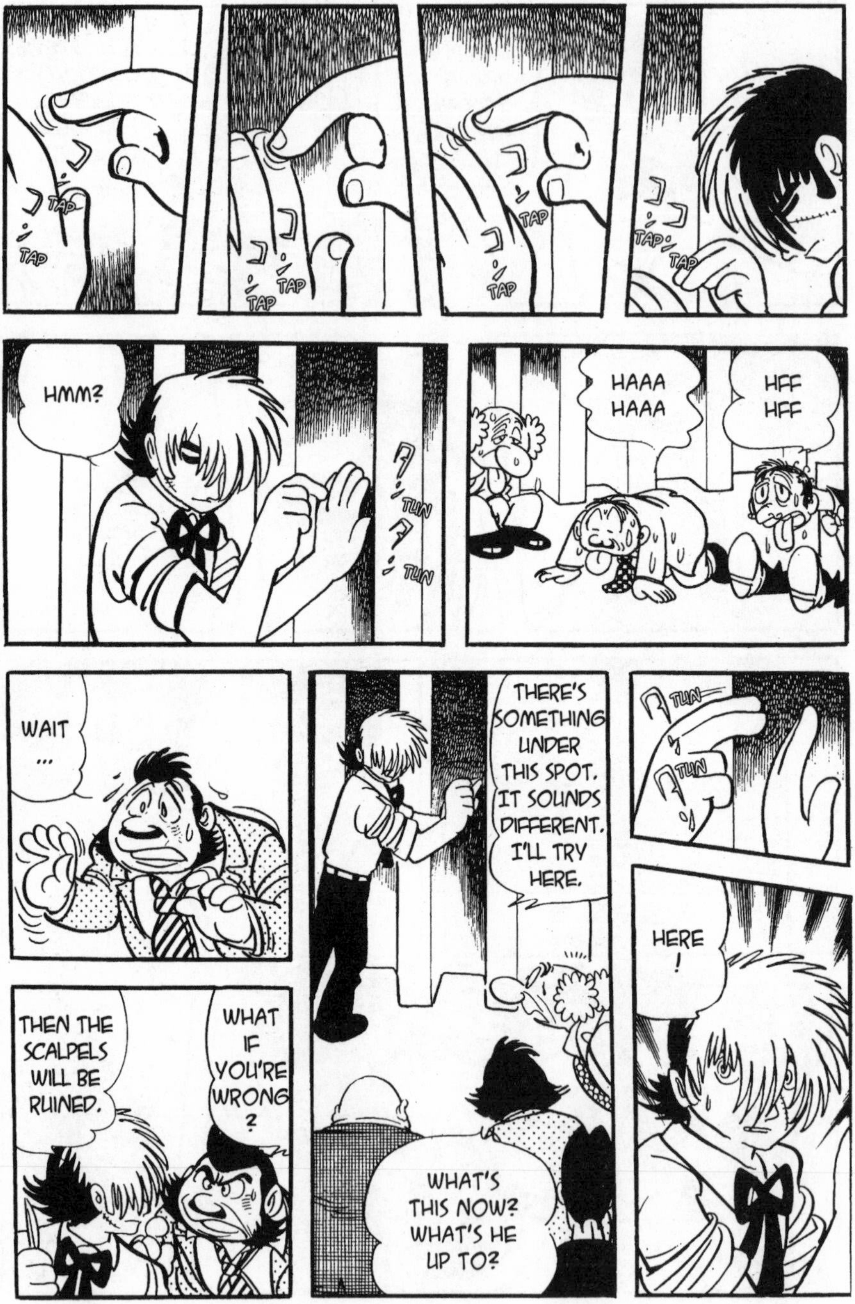
TAP
TAP
TAP
TAP
TAP
TAP
TAP
TAP
HFF HFF
HAAA HAAA
HMM?
TUN
TUN
TUN
TUN
HERE!
THERE'S SOMETHING UNDER THIS SPOT. IT SOUNDS DIFFERENT. I'LL TRY HERE.
WHAT'S THIS NOW? WHAT'S HE UP TO?
WAIT ...
WHAT IF YOU'RE WRONG?
THEN THE SCALPELS WILL BE RUINED.

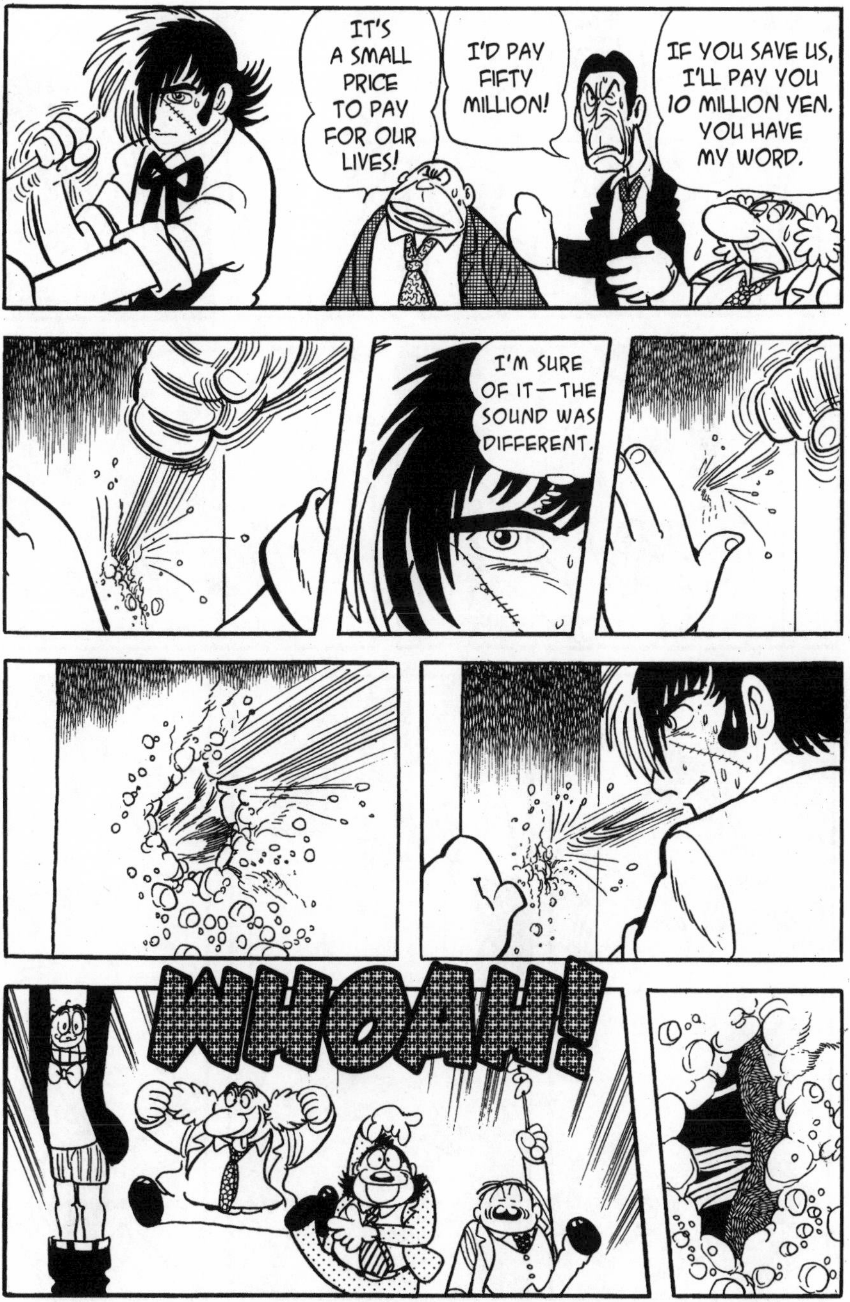
IF YOU SAVE US, I'LL PAY YOU 10 MILLION YEN. YOU HAVE MY WORD.
I'D PAY FIFTY MILLION!
IT'S A SMALL PRICE TO PAY FOR OUR LIVES!
I'M SURE OF IT—THE SOUND WAS DIFFERENT.
WHOAH!

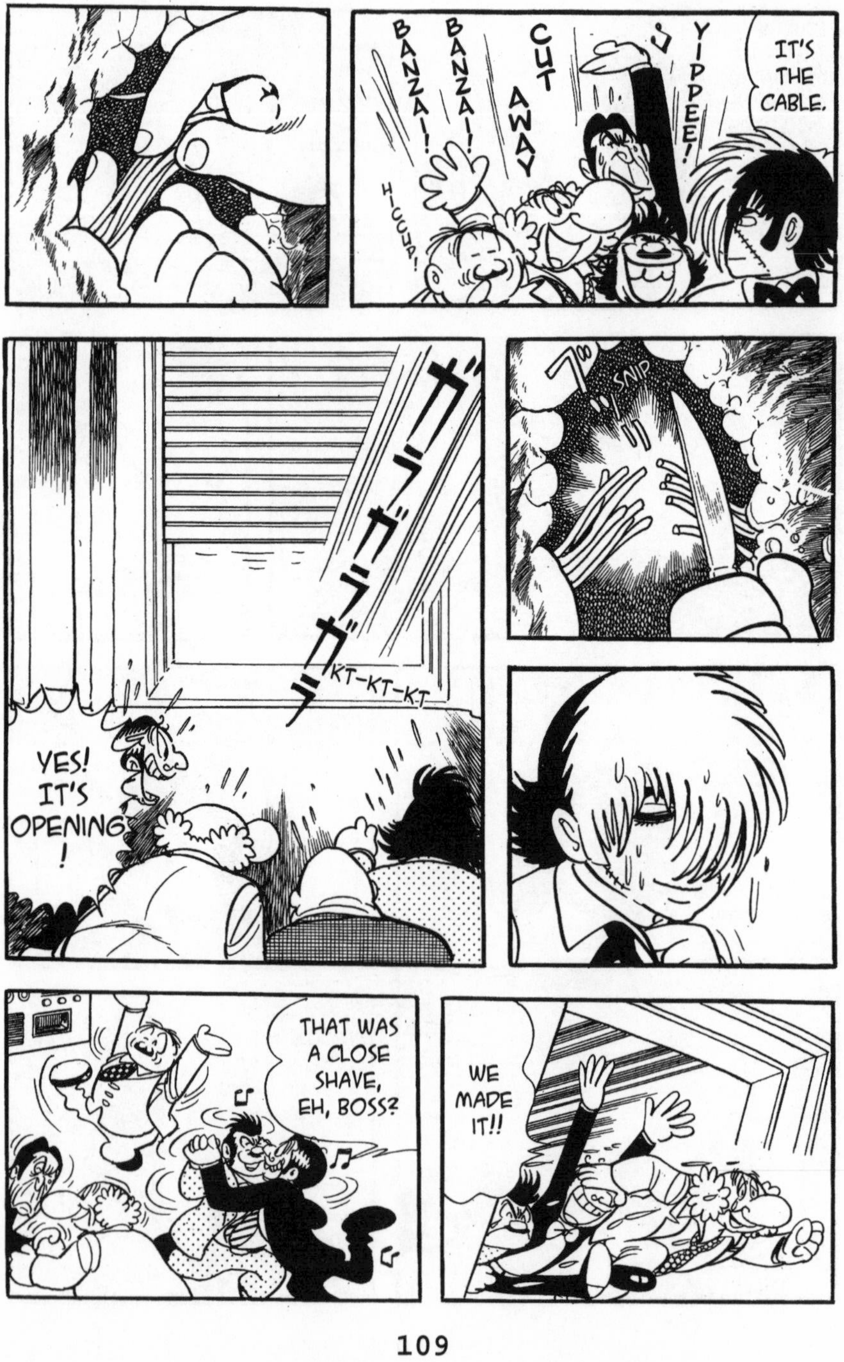
IT'S THE CABLE.
YIPPEE!
CUT AWAY
BANZAI!
BANZAI!
HICCUP!
SNIP
YES! IT'S OPENING!
ガラガラガラ
KT-KT-KT
WE MADE IT!!
THAT WAS A CLOSE SHAVE, EH, BOSS?

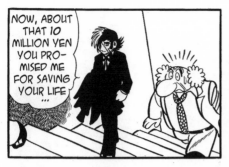

PLEASE GET SOME REST UPSTAIRS.
I'LL HAVE MY FILL OF WATER!
NOW, ABOUT THAT 10 MILLION YEN YOU PRO-MISED ME FOR SAVING YOUR LIFE ...
I-I GOT A BIT CARRIED AWAY, SEE... HEH-HEH...
WE CERTAINLY DO OWE YOU... BUT ALLOW US TO TALK IT OVER A BIT FIRST.
MAYBE A MILLION YEN ?
I KNEW IT. DON'T THINK...
I COUNTED ON IT.
APPARENTLY YOU'RE A BUNCH OF MEN WHO VALUE PAPER CONTRACTS OVER YOUR OWN LIVES.

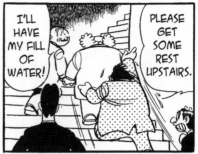

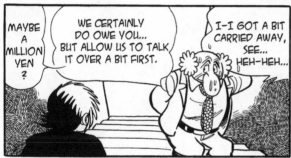

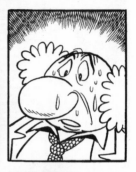

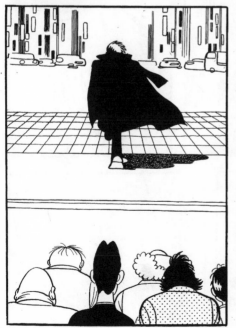

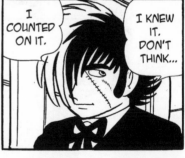

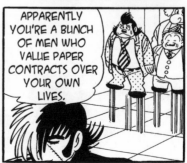

DIRTJACKED

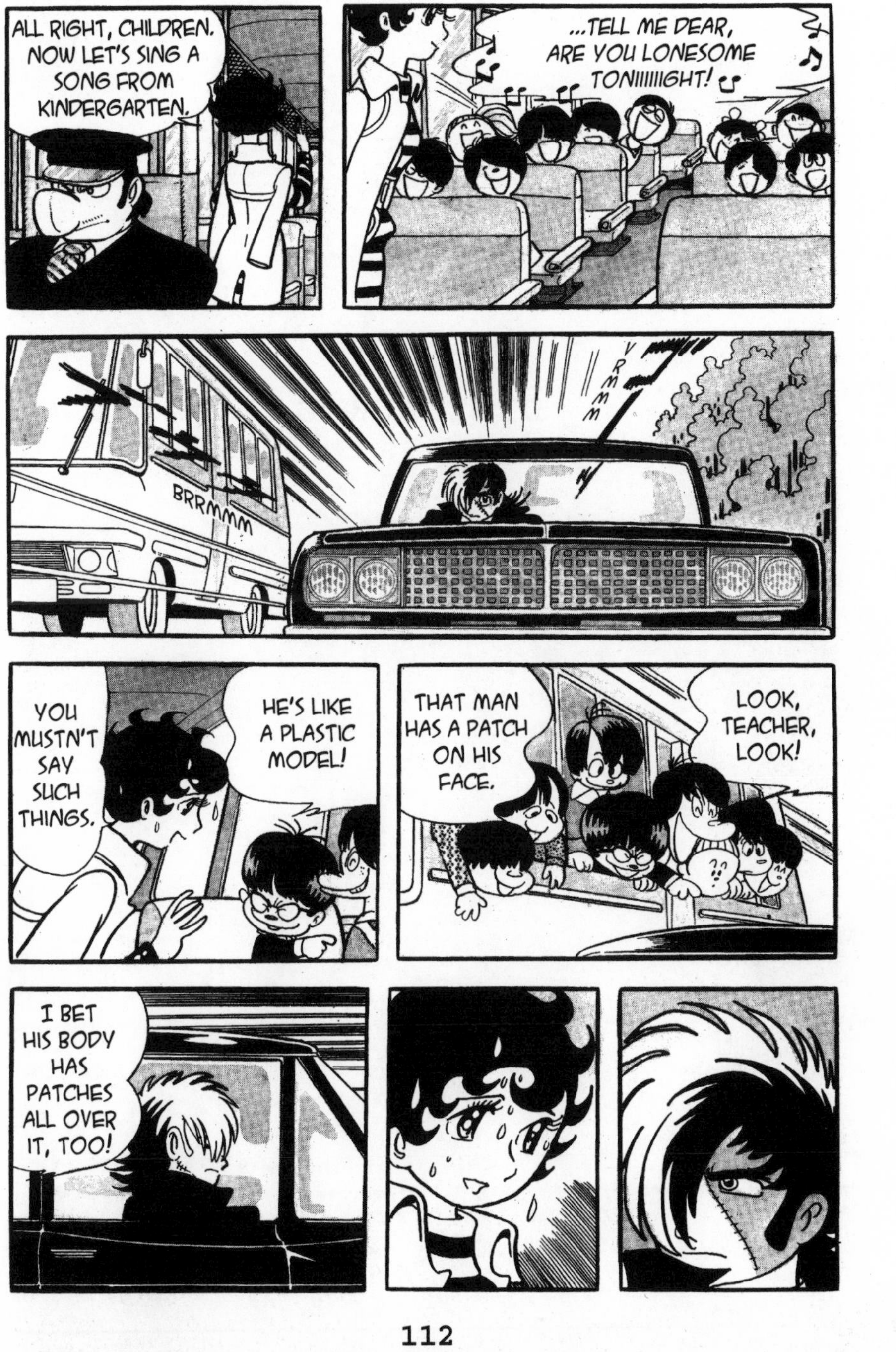
...TELL ME DEAR, ARE YOU LONESOME TONIIIIIIGHT!
ALL RIGHT, CHILDREN. NOW LET'S SING A SONG FROM KINDERGARTEN.
VRMMM
BRRMMM
LOOK, TEACHER, LOOK!
THAT MAN HAS A PATCH ON HIS FACE.
HE'S LIKE A PLASTIC MODEL!
YOU MUSTN'T SAY SUCH THINGS.
I BET HIS BODY HAS PATCHES ALL OVER IT, TOO!

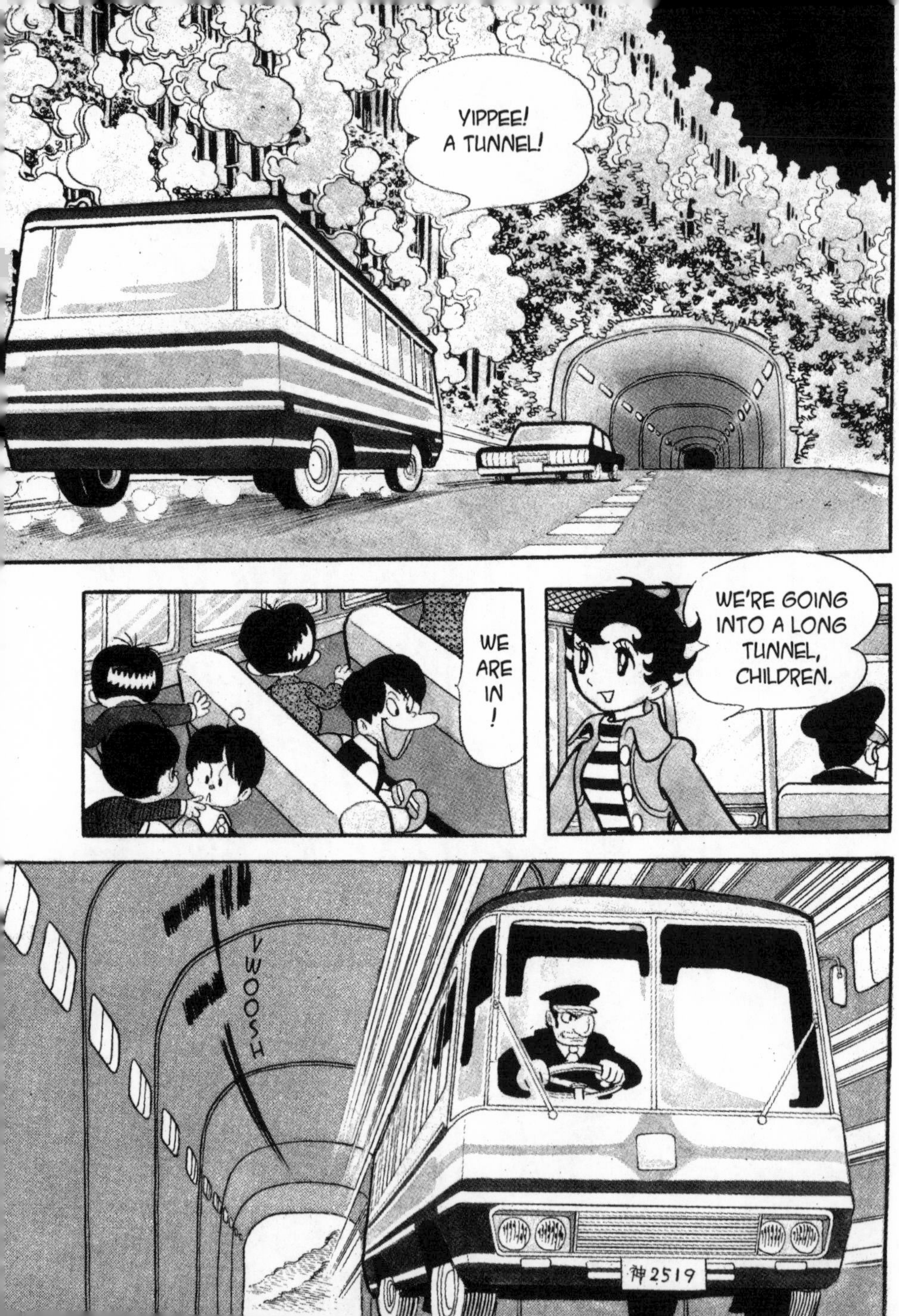
YIPPEE! A TUNNEL!
WE'RE GOING INTO A LONG TUNNEL, CHILDREN.
WE ARE IN!
VWOOSH
神2519

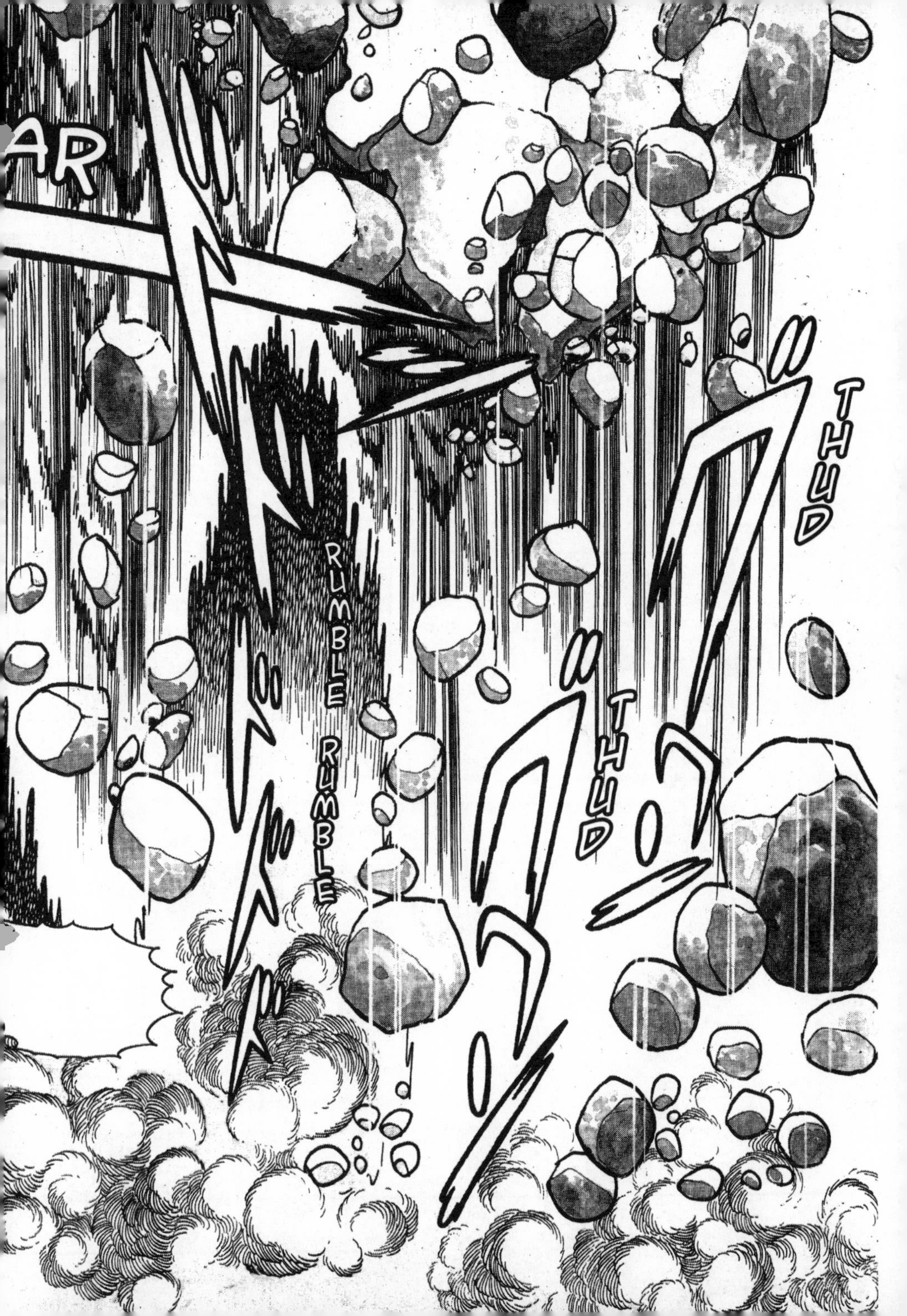
AR
RUMBLE RUMBLE
THUD
THUD

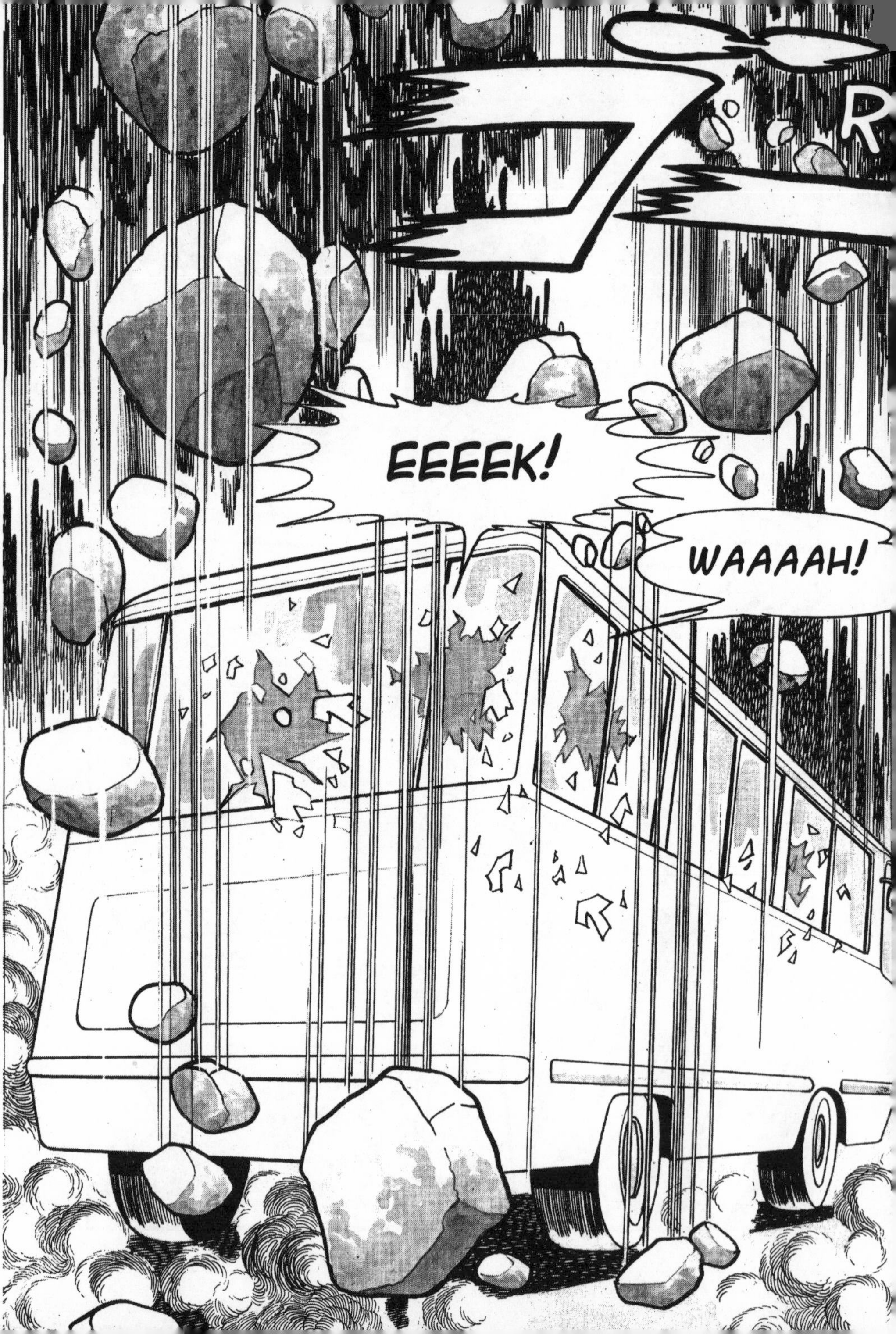

R
EEEEK!
WAAAAH!

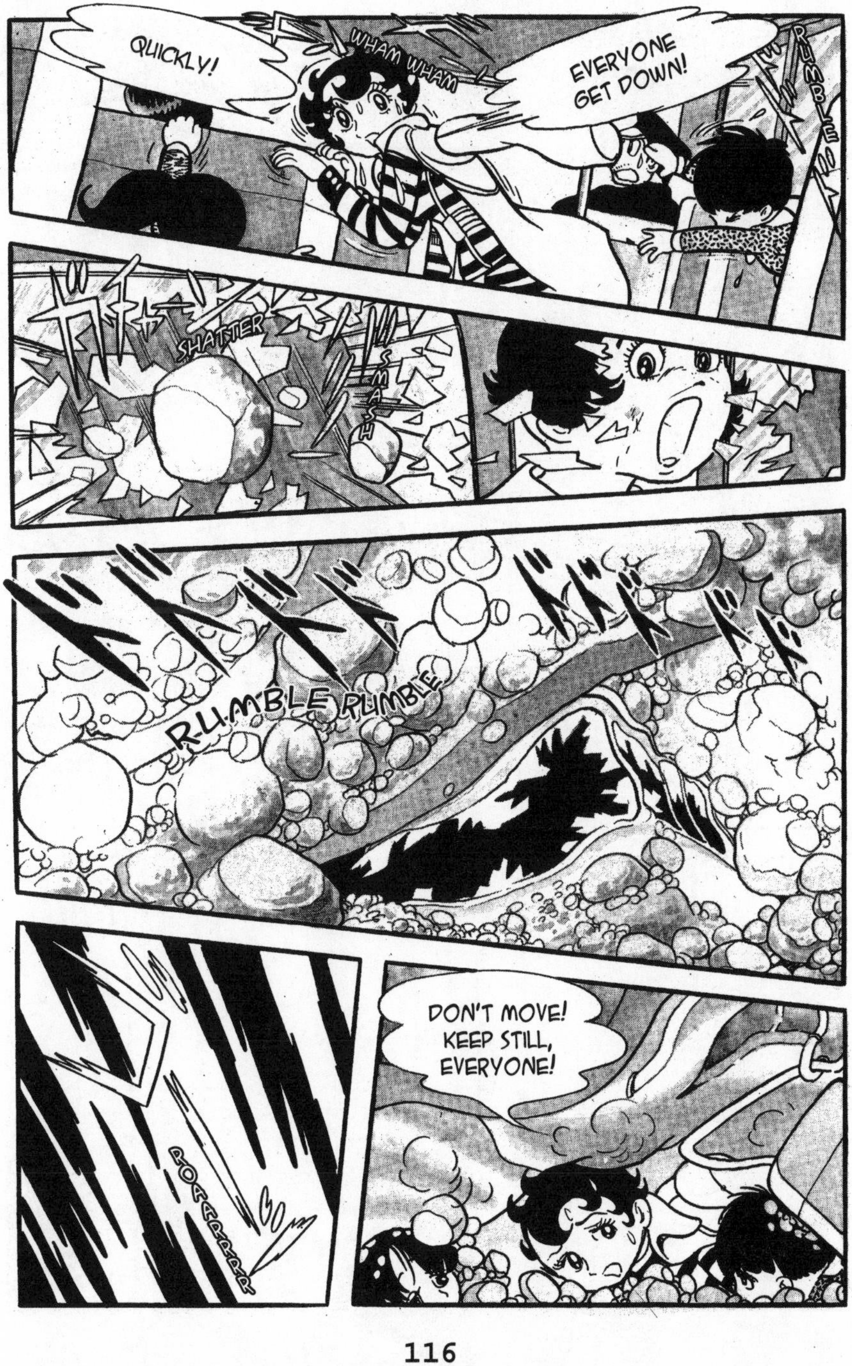
RUMBLE
EVERYONE GET DOWN!
WHAM WHAM
QUICKLY!
SMASH
SHATTER
RUMBLE RUMBLE
DON'T MOVE! KEEP STILL, EVERYONE!
ROAARRRR

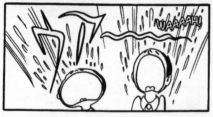

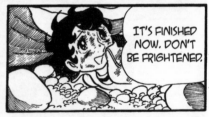

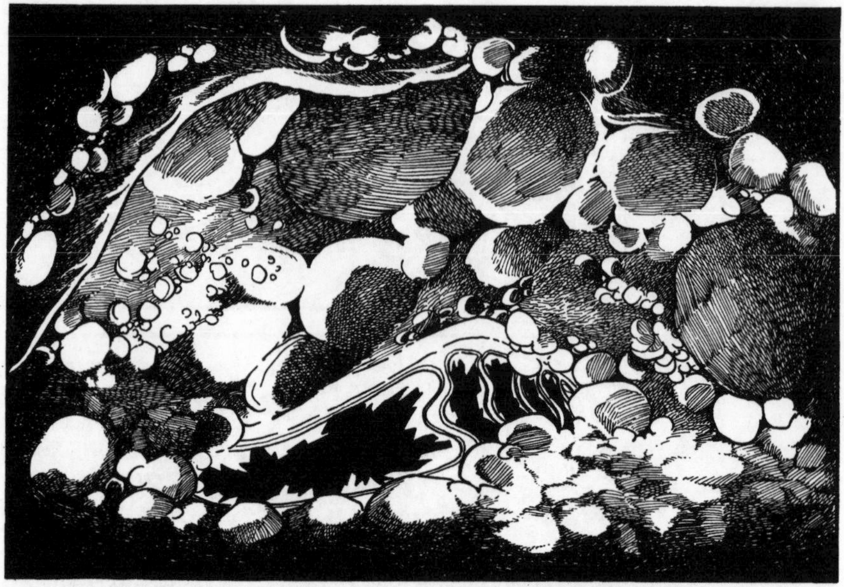
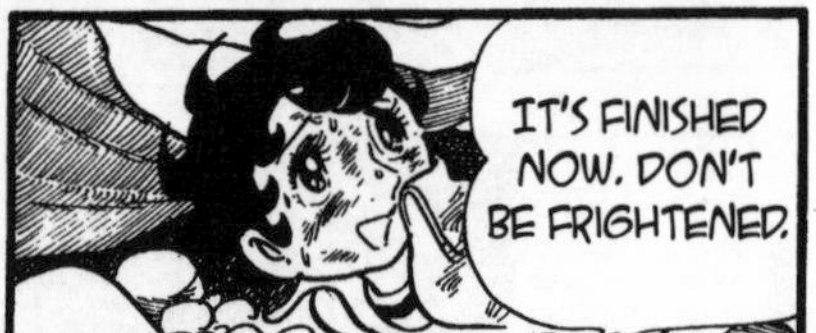
IT'S FINISHED NOW. DON'T BE FRIGHTENED.
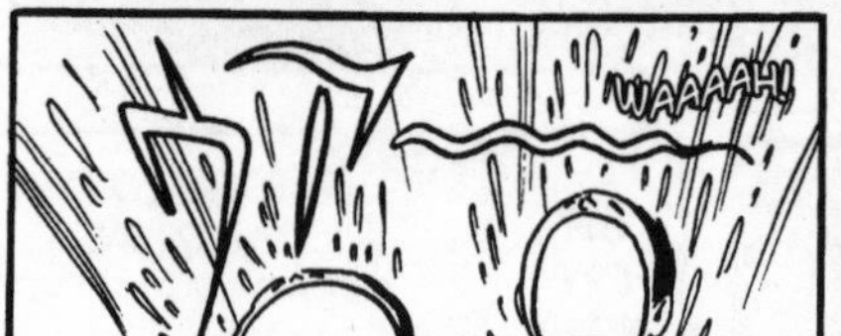
WAAAAH!
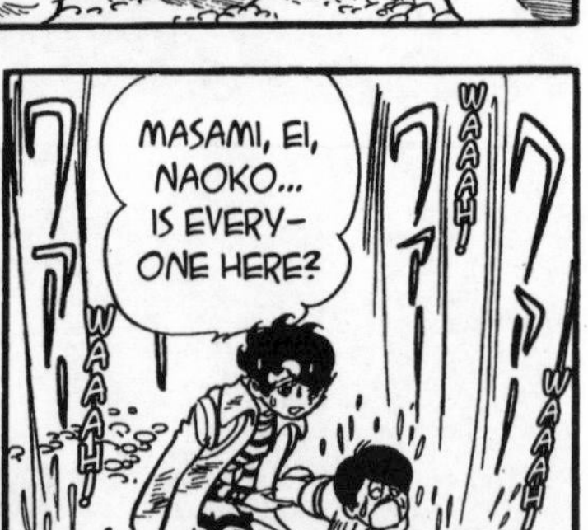
MASAMI, EI, NAOKO... IS EVERY-ONE HERE?
WAAAAH!
WAAAAH!
WAAAAH!
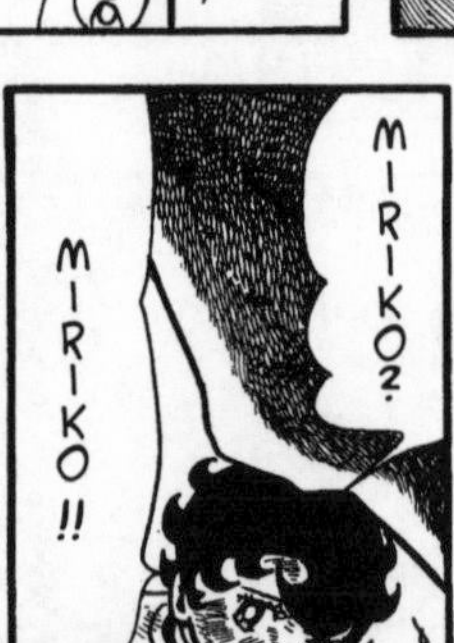
MIRIKO?
MIRIKO!!
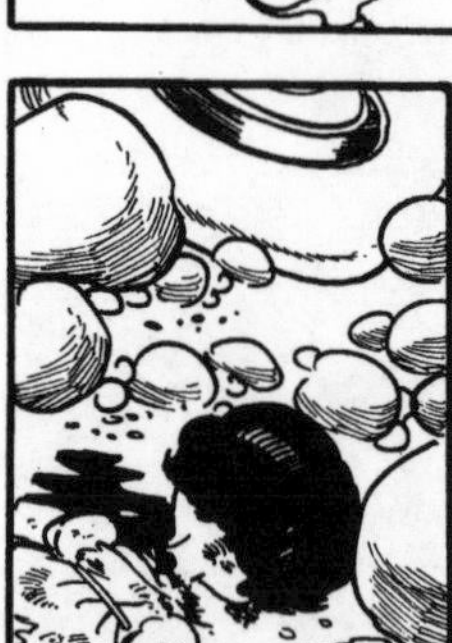

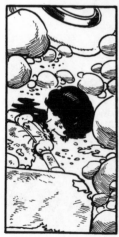

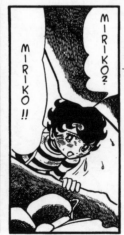

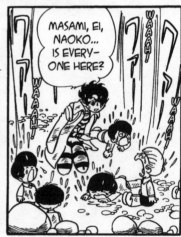

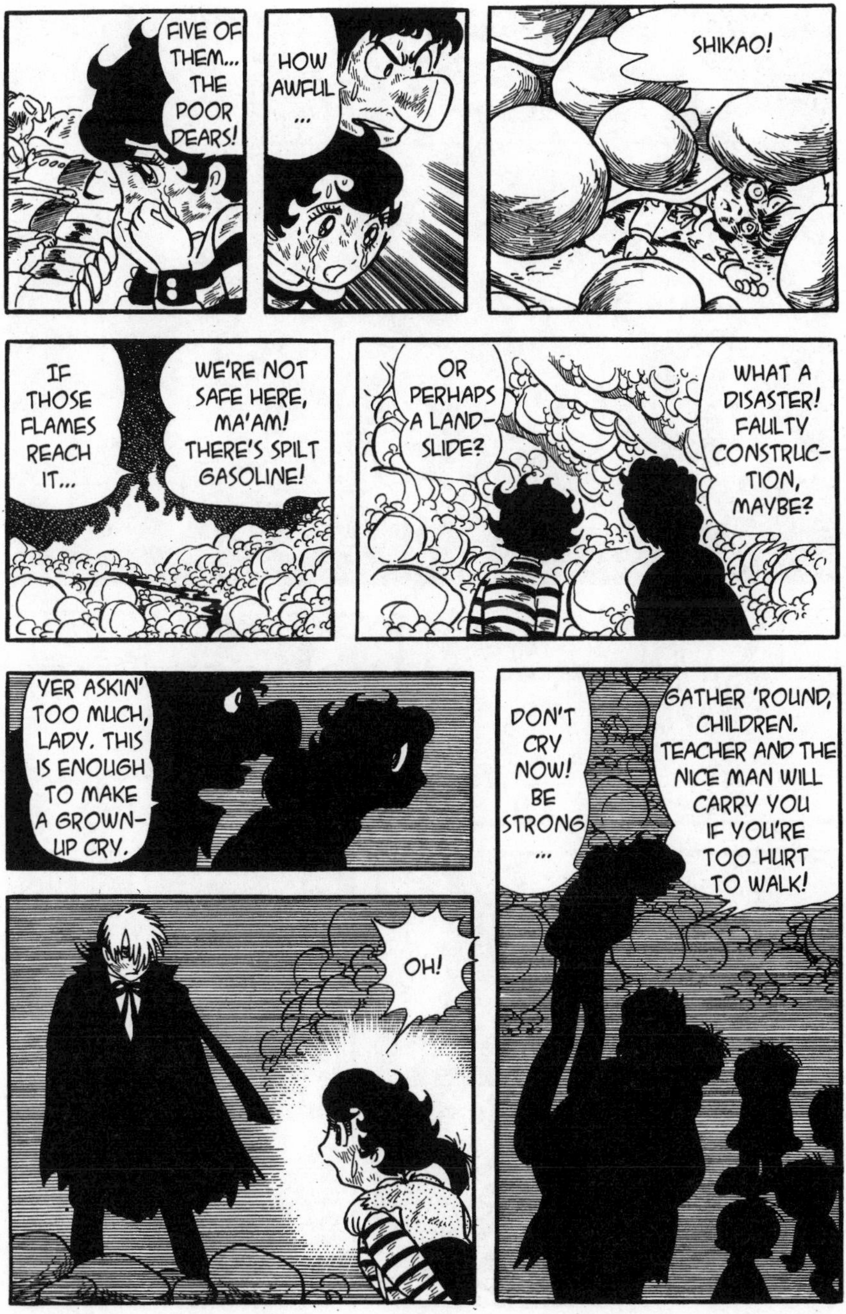
SHIKAO!
HOW AWFUL ...
FIVE OF THEM... THE POOR DEARS!
WHAT A DISASTER! FAULTY CONSTRUCTION, MAYBE?
OR PERHAPS A LANDSLIDE?
WE'RE NOT SAFE HERE, MA'AM! THERE'S SPILT GASOLINE!
IF THOSE FLAMES REACH IT...
GATHER 'ROUND, CHILDREN. TEACHER AND THE NICE MAN WILL CARRY YOU IF YOU'RE TOO HURT TO WALK!
DON'T CRY NOW! BE STRONG ...
YER ASKIN' TOO MUCH, LADY. THIS IS ENOUGH TO MAKE A GROWN-UP CRY.
OH!

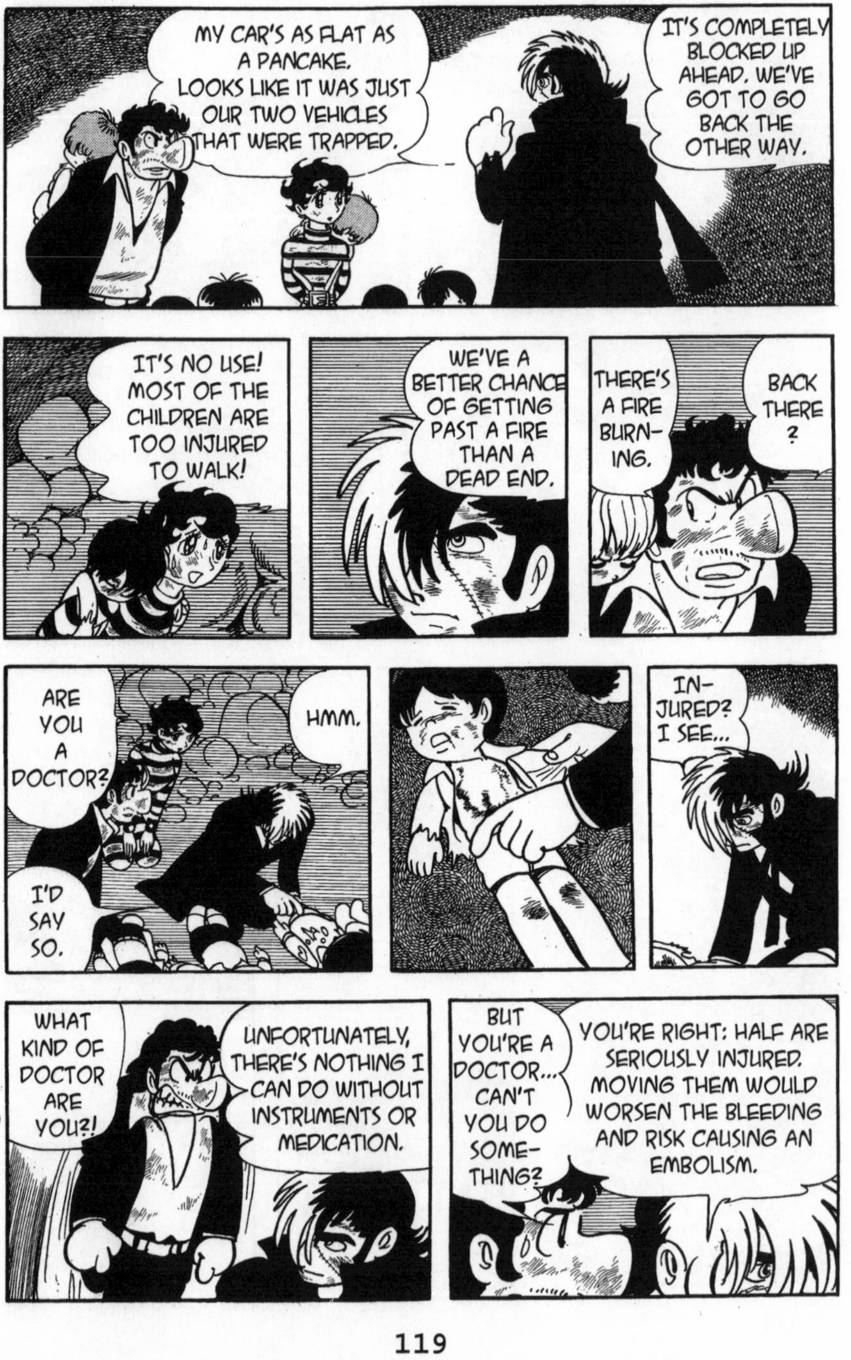
IT'S COMPLETELY BLOCKED UP AHEAD. WE'VE GOT TO GO BACK THE OTHER WAY.
MY CAR'S AS FLAT AS A PANCAKE. LOOKS LIKE IT WAS JUST OUR TWO VEHICLES THAT WERE TRAPPED.
BACK THERE?
THERE'S A FIRE BURN-ING.
WE'VE A BETTER CHANCE OF GETTING PAST A FIRE THAN A DEAD END.
IT'S NO USE! MOST OF THE CHILDREN ARE TOO INJURED TO WALK!
IN-JURED? I SEE...
HMM.
ARE YOU A DOCTOR?
I'D SAY SO.
YOU'RE RIGHT: HALF ARE SERIOUSLY INJURED. MOVING THEM WOULD WORSEN THE BLEEDING AND RISK CAUSING AN EMBOLISM.
BUT YOU'RE A DOCTOR... CAN'T YOU DO SOME-THING?
UNFORTUNATELY, THERE'S NOTHING I CAN DO WITHOUT INSTRUMENTS OR MEDICATION.
WHAT KIND OF DOCTOR ARE YOU?!

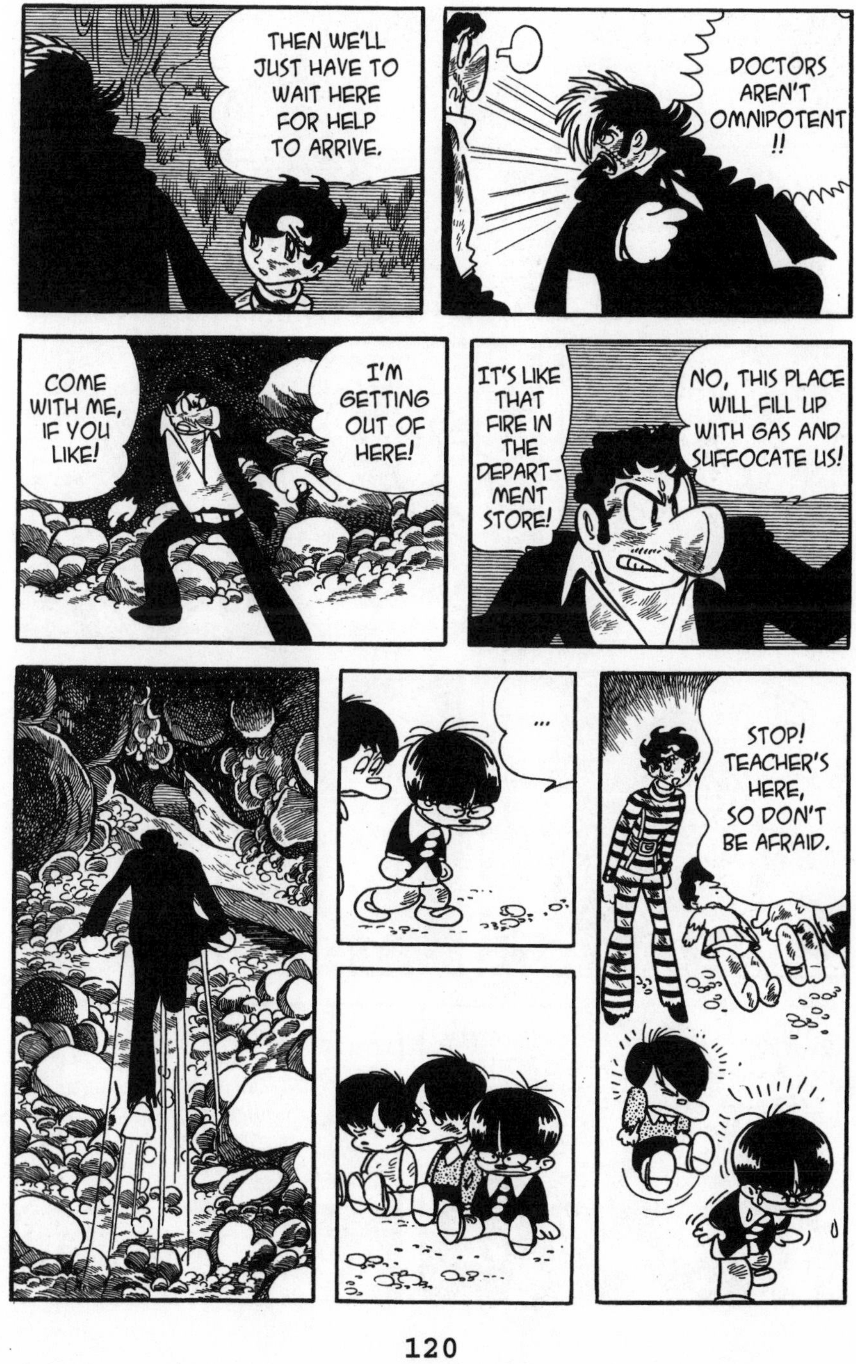
DOCTORS AREN'T OMNIPOTENT !!
THEN WE'LL JUST HAVE TO WAIT HERE FOR HELP TO ARRIVE.
NO, THIS PLACE WILL FILL UP WITH GAS AND SUFFOCATE US!
IT'S LIKE THAT FIRE IN THE DEPART-MENT STORE!
I'M GETTING OUT OF HERE!
COME WITH ME, IF YOU LIKE!
STOP! TEACHER'S HERE, SO DON'T BE AFRAID.
...

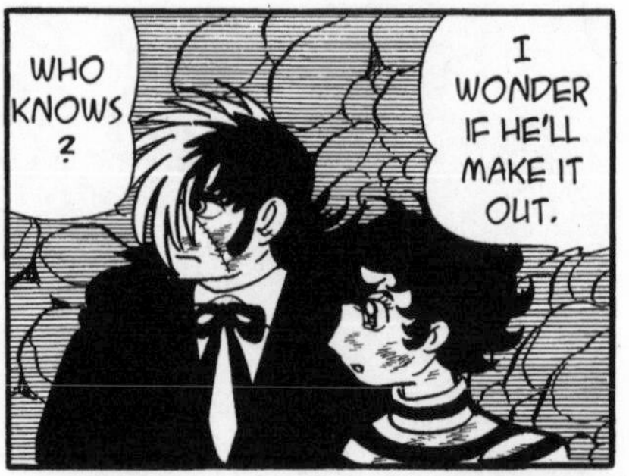
I WONDER IF HE'LL MAKE IT OUT.
WHO KNOWS?
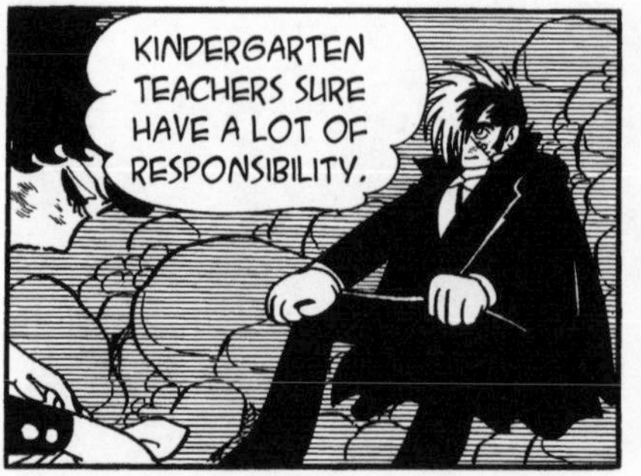
KINDERGARTEN TEACHERS SURE HAVE A LOT OF RESPONSIBILITY.
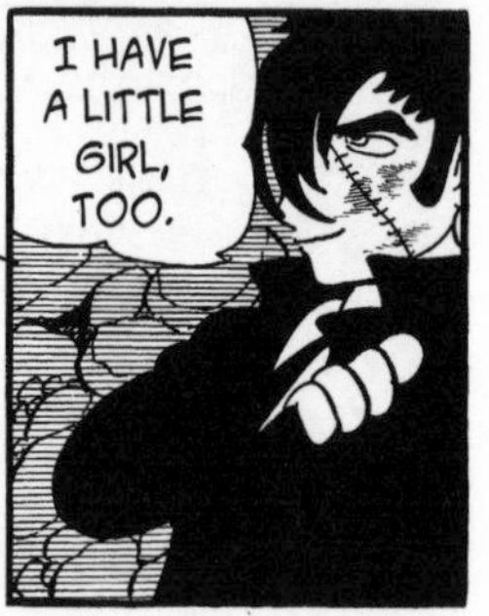
I HAVE A LITTLE GIRL, TOO.
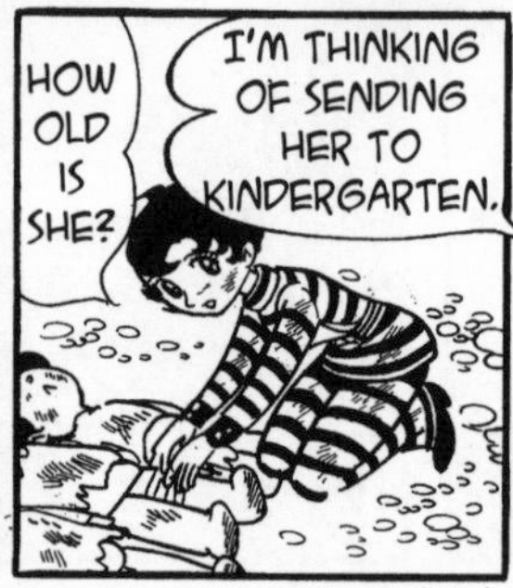
I'M THINKING OF SENDING HER TO KINDERGARTEN.
HOW OLD IS SHE?
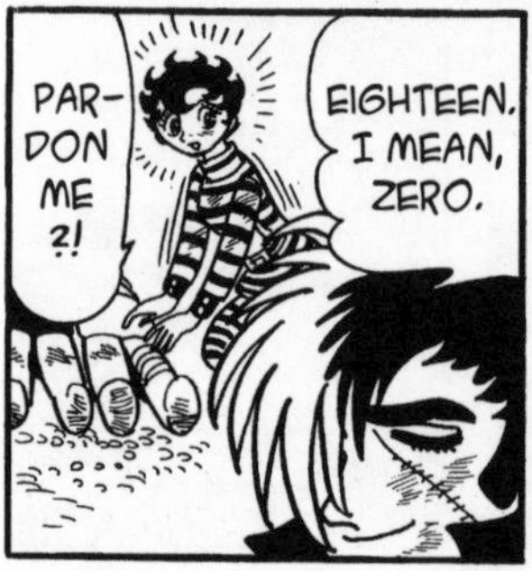
EIGHTEEN. I MEAN, ZERO.
PAR-DON ME ?!
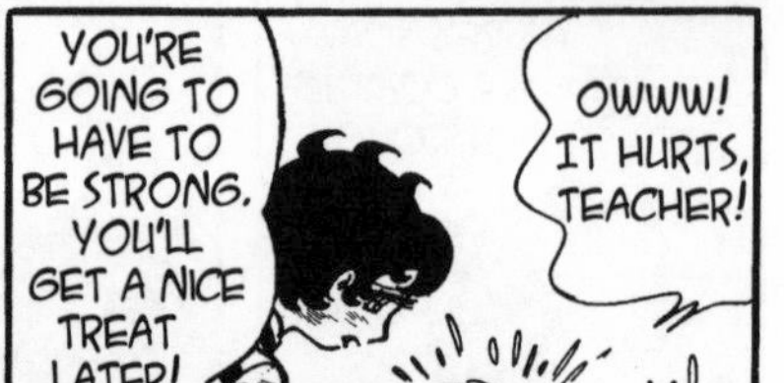
OWWW! IT HURTS, TEACHER!
YOU'RE GOING TO HAVE TO BE STRONG. YOU'LL GET A NICE TREAT LATER!
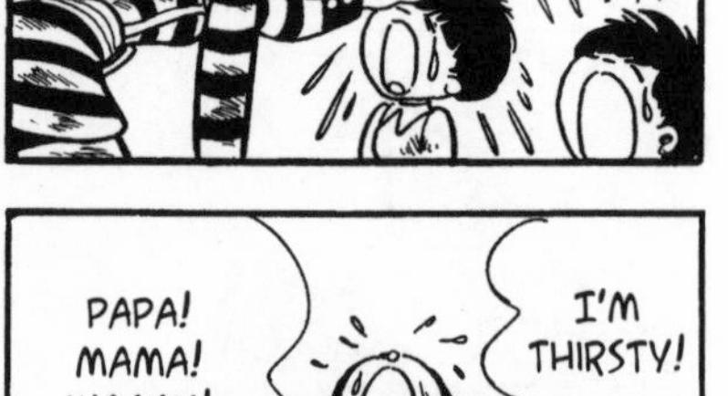
I'M THIRSTY!
PAPA! MAMA! WAAAH!
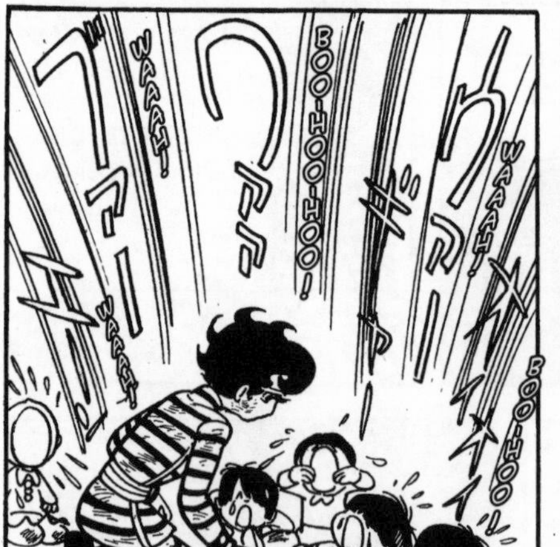
BOO-HOO!
WAAAAH!
BOO-HOO-HOO-HOO!
WAAAH!
WAAAH!

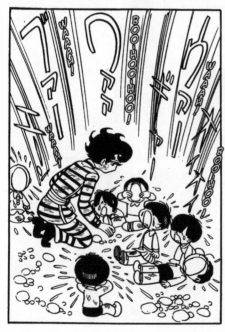

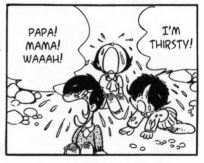

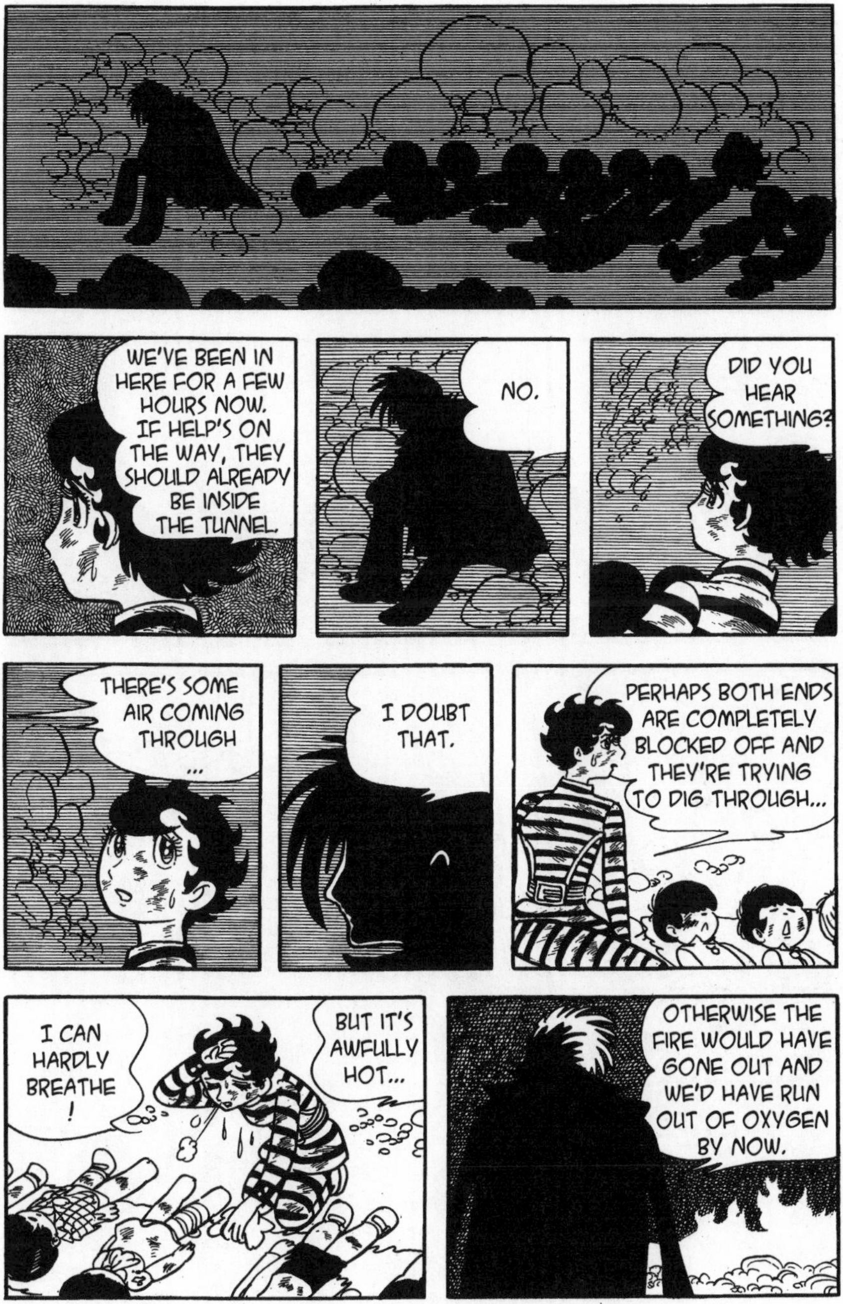
DID YOU HEAR SOMETHING?
NO.
WE'VE BEEN IN HERE FOR A FEW HOURS NOW. IF HELP'S ON THE WAY, THEY SHOULD ALREADY BE INSIDE THE TUNNEL.
PERHAPS BOTH ENDS ARE COMPLETELY BLOCKED OFF AND THEY'RE TRYING TO DIG THROUGH...
I DOUBT THAT.
THERE'S SOME AIR COMING THROUGH ...
OTHERWISE THE FIRE WOULD HAVE GONE OUT AND WE'D HAVE RUN OUT OF OXYGEN BY NOW.
BUT IT'S AWFULLY HOT...
I CAN HARDLY BREATHE !

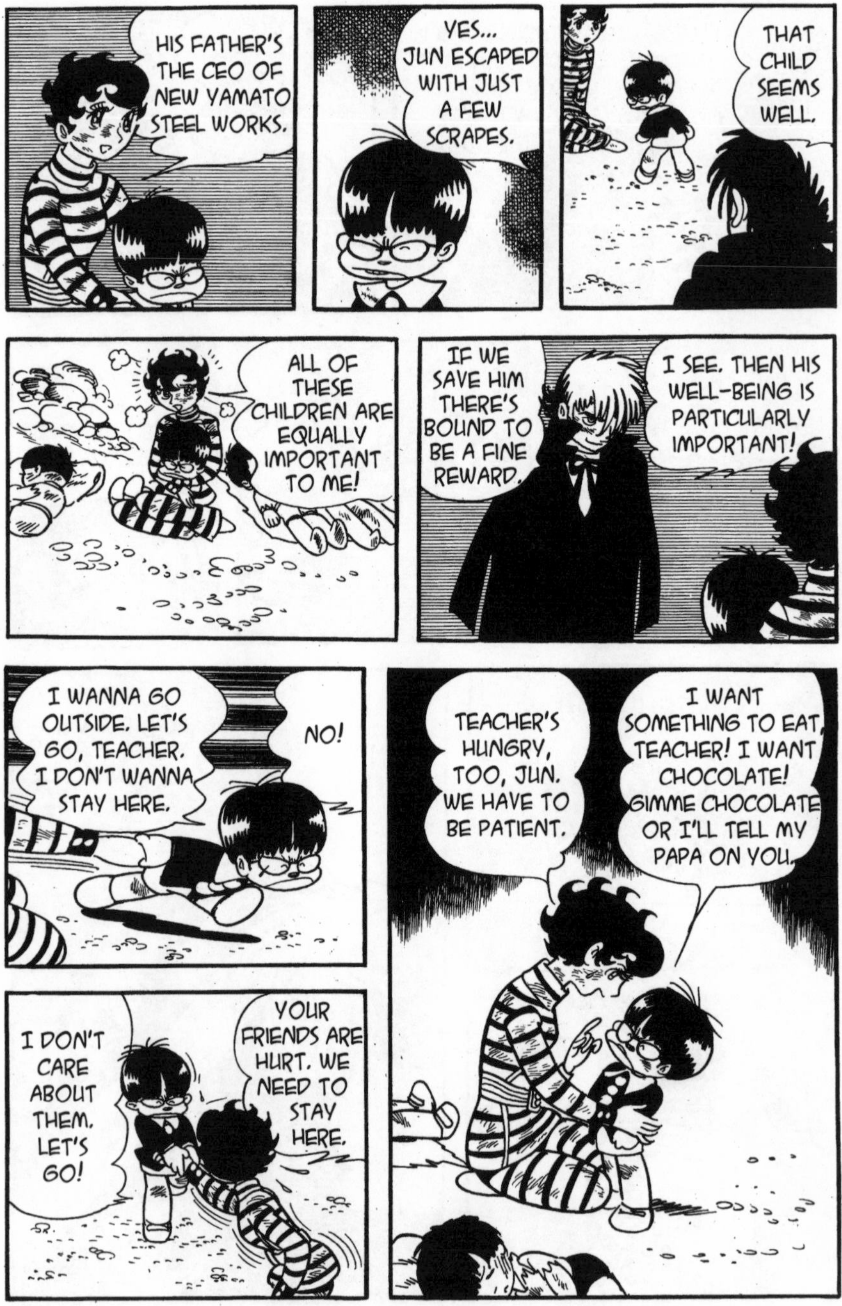
THAT CHILD SEEMS WELL.
YES... JUN ESCAPED WITH JUST A FEW SCRAPES.
HIS FATHER'S THE CEO OF NEW YAMATO STEEL WORKS.
I SEE. THEN HIS WELL-BEING IS PARTICULARLY IMPORTANT!
IF WE SAVE HIM THERE'S BOUND TO BE A FINE REWARD.
ALL OF THESE CHILDREN ARE EQUALLY IMPORTANT TO ME!
I WANT SOMETHING TO EAT, TEACHER! I WANT CHOCOLATE! GIMME CHOCOLATE OR I'LL TELL MY PAPA ON YOU.
TEACHER'S HUNGRY, TOO, JUN. WE HAVE TO BE PATIENT.
I WANNA GO OUTSIDE. LET'S GO, TEACHER. I DON'T WANNA STAY HERE.
NO!
YOUR FRIENDS ARE HURT. WE NEED TO STAY HERE.
I DON'T CARE ABOUT THEM. LET'S GO!

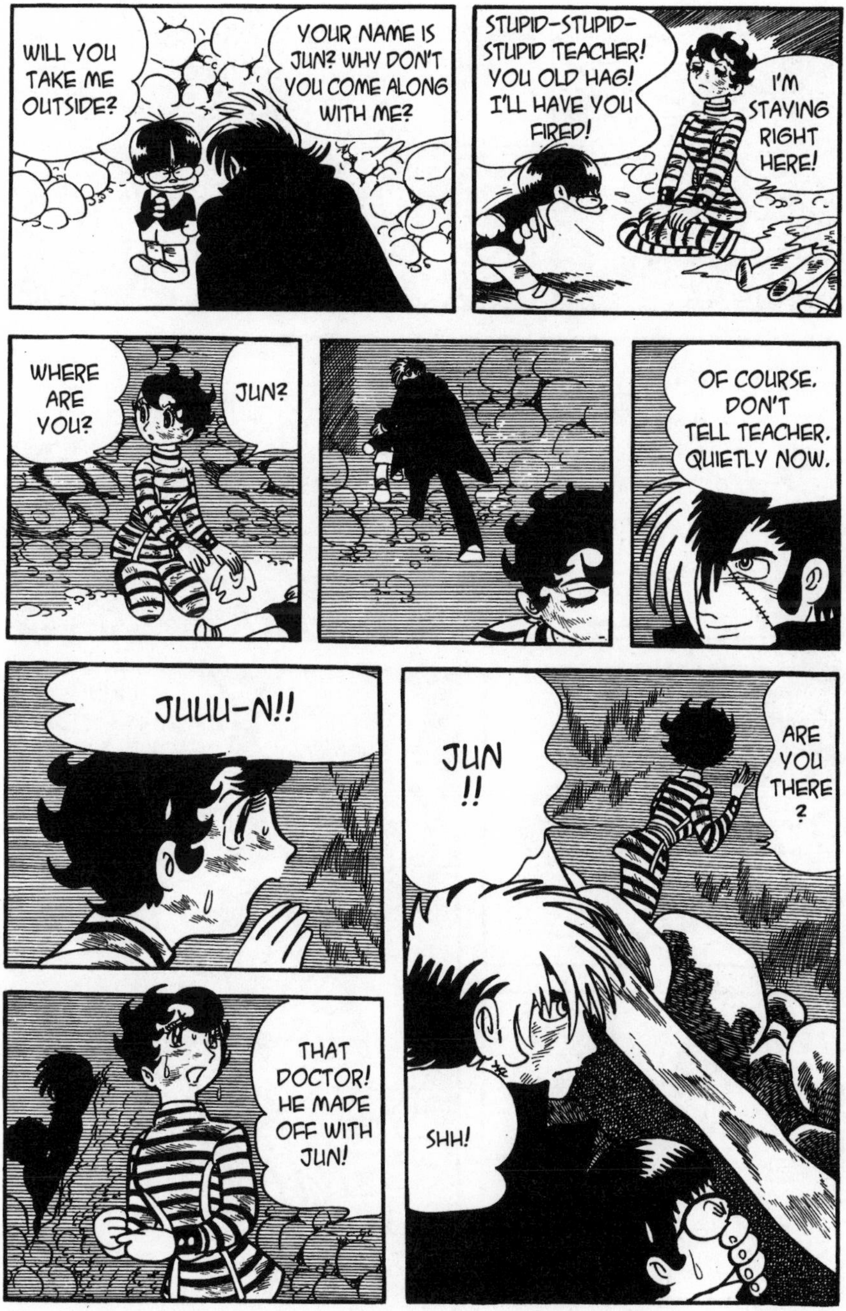
WILL YOU TAKE ME OUTSIDE?
YOUR NAME IS JUN? WHY DON'T YOU COME ALONG WITH ME?
STUPID-STUPID-STUPID TEACHER! YOU OLD HAG! I'LL HAVE YOU FIRED!
I'M STAYING RIGHT HERE!
WHERE ARE YOU?
JUN?
OF COURSE. DON'T TELL TEACHER. QUIETLY NOW.
JUUU-N!!
THAT DOCTOR! HE MADE OFF WITH JUN!
JUN !!
ARE YOU THERE ?
SHH!

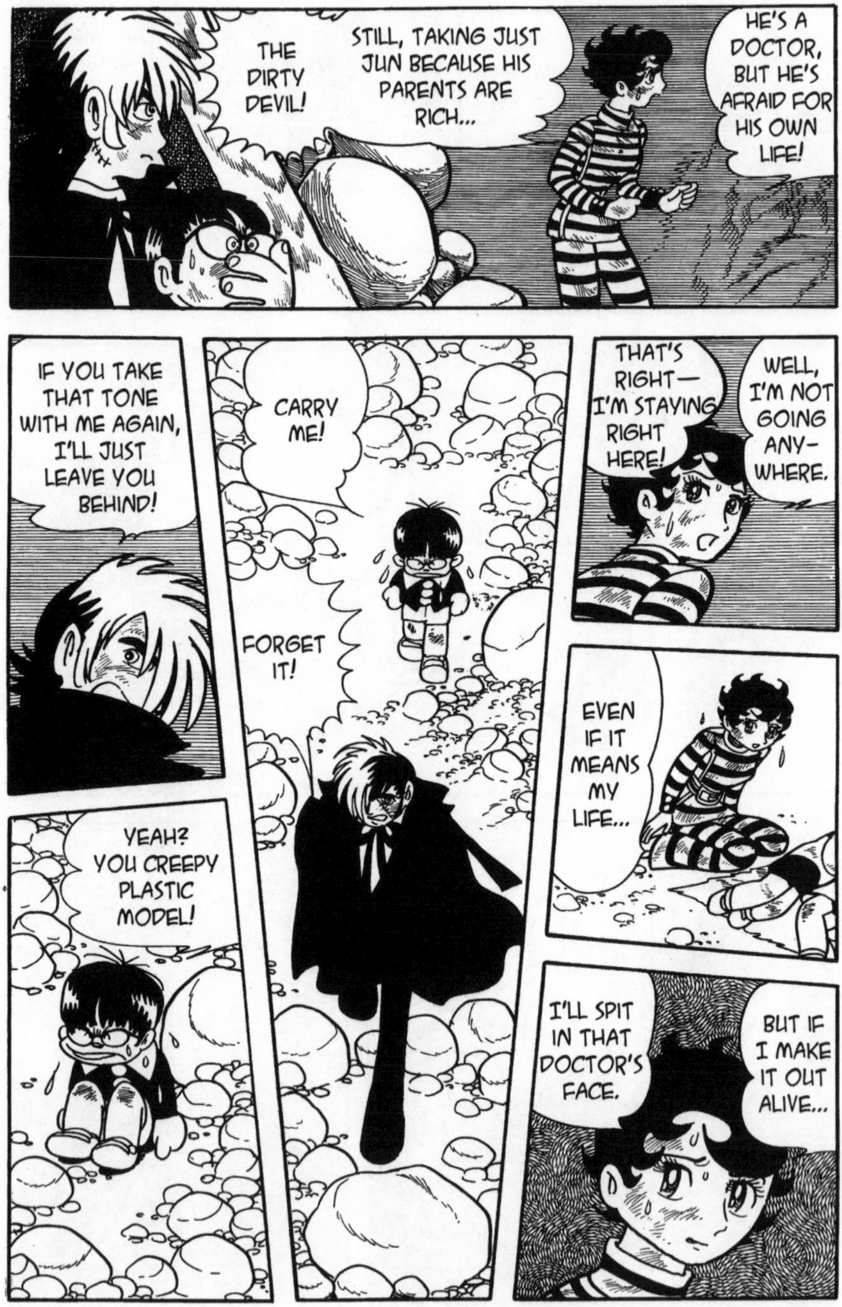
HE'S A DOCTOR, BUT HE'S AFRAID FOR HIS OWN LIFE!
STILL, TAKING JUST JUN BECAUSE HIS PARENTS ARE RICH...
THE DIRTY DEVIL!
WELL, I'M NOT GOING ANY-WHERE.
THAT'S RIGHT— I'M STAYING RIGHT HERE!
EVEN IF IT MEANS MY LIFE...
BUT IF I MAKE IT OUT ALIVE...
I'LL SPIT IN THAT DOCTOR'S FACE.
CARRY ME!
FORGET IT!
IF YOU TAKE THAT TONE WITH ME AGAIN, I'LL JUST LEAVE YOU BEHIND!
YEAH? YOU CREEPY PLASTIC MODEL!

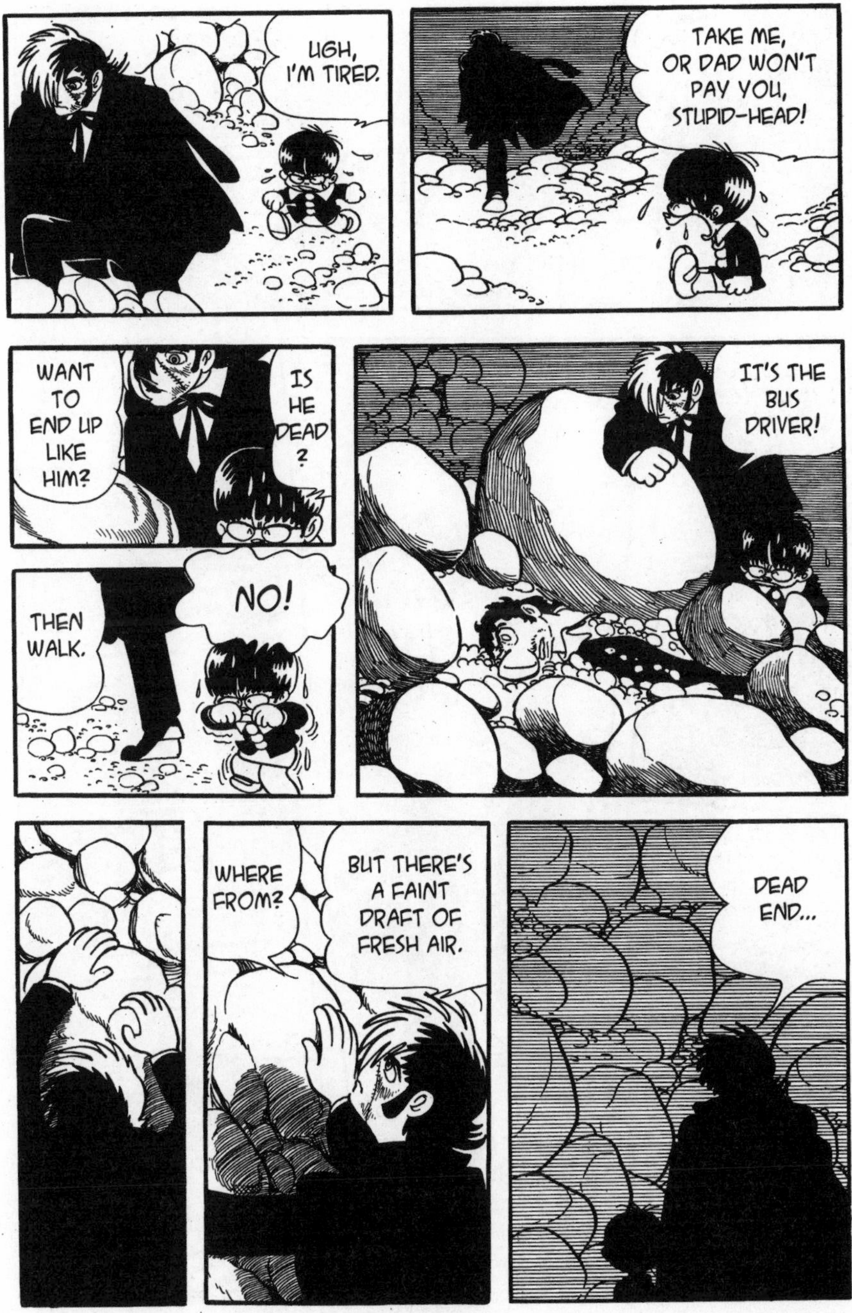
TAKE ME, OR DAD WON'T PAY YOU, STUPID-HEAD!
UGH, I'M TIRED.
IT'S THE BUS DRIVER!
IS HE DEAD?
WANT TO END UP LIKE HIM?
NO!
THEN WALK.
DEAD END...
BUT THERE'S A FAINT DRAFT OF FRESH AIR.
WHERE FROM?

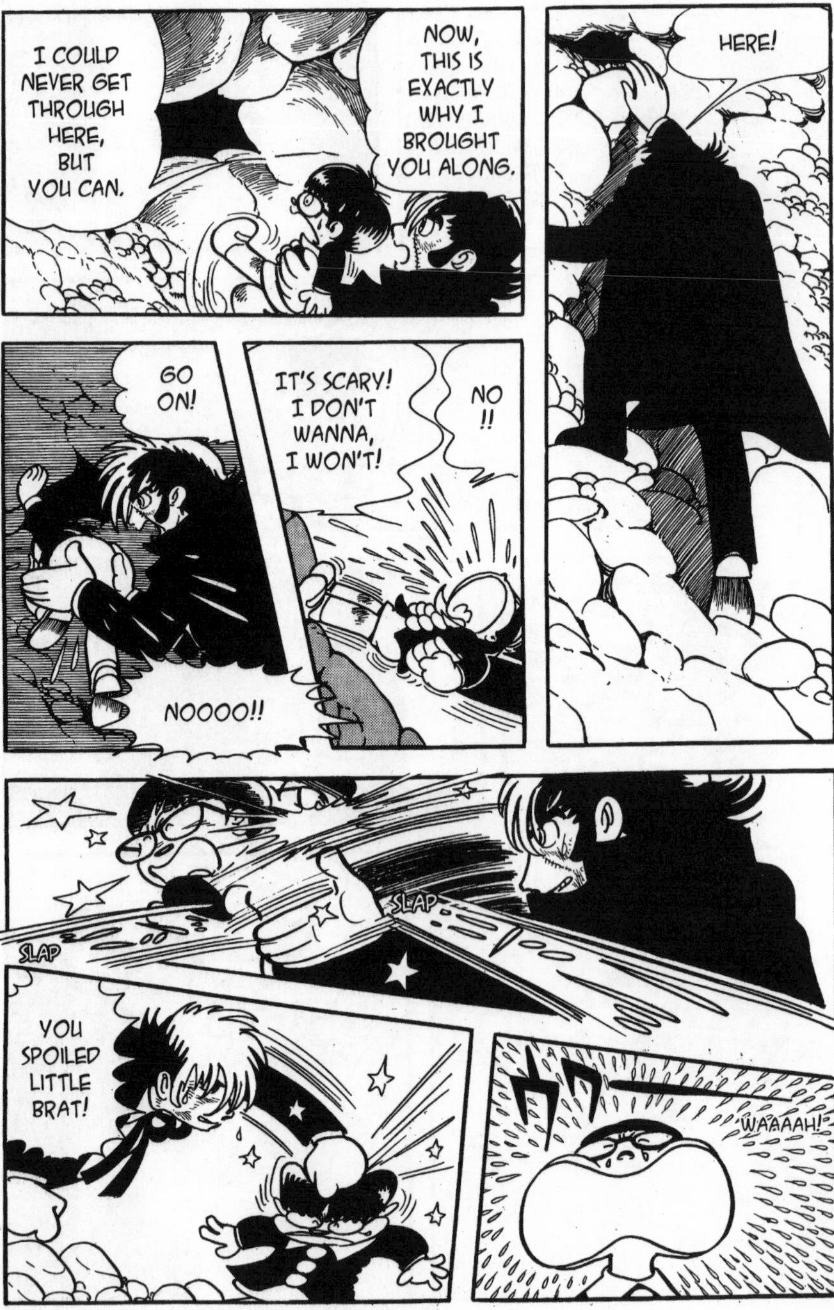
HERE!
NOW, THIS IS EXACTLY WHY I BROUGHT YOU ALONG.
I COULD NEVER GET THROUGH HERE, BUT YOU CAN.
NO !!
IT'S SCARY! I DON'T WANNA, I WON'T!
GO ON!
NOOOO!!
SLAP
SLAP
WAAAAH!
YOU SPOILED LITTLE BRAT!

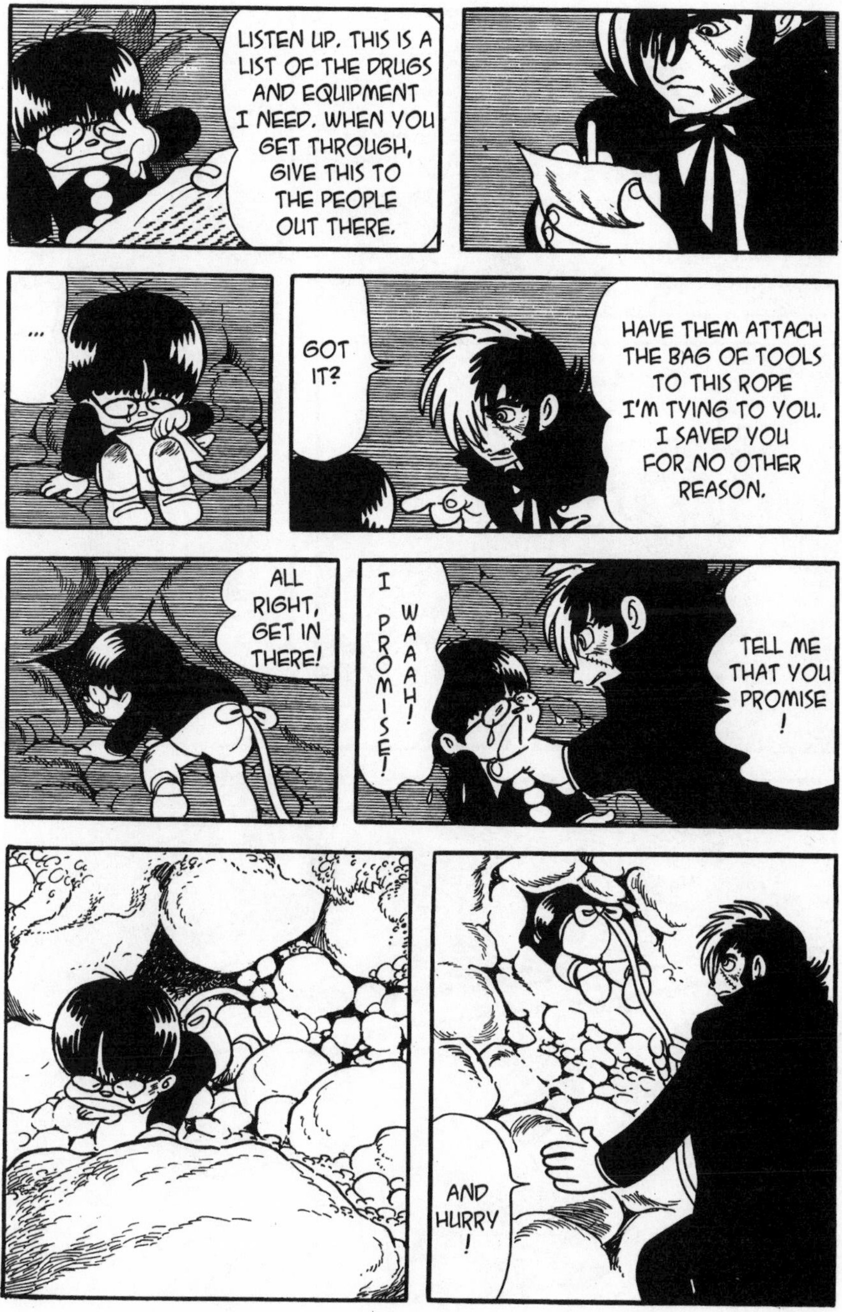
LISTEN UP. THIS IS A LIST OF THE DRUGS AND EQUIPMENT I NEED. WHEN YOU GET THROUGH, GIVE THIS TO THE PEOPLE OUT THERE.
HAVE THEM ATTACH THE BAG OF TOOLS TO THIS ROPE I'M TYING TO YOU. I SAVED YOU FOR NO OTHER REASON.
GOT IT?
...
TELL ME THAT YOU PROMISE!
WAAAH!
I PROMISE!
ALL RIGHT, GET IN THERE!
AND HURRY!

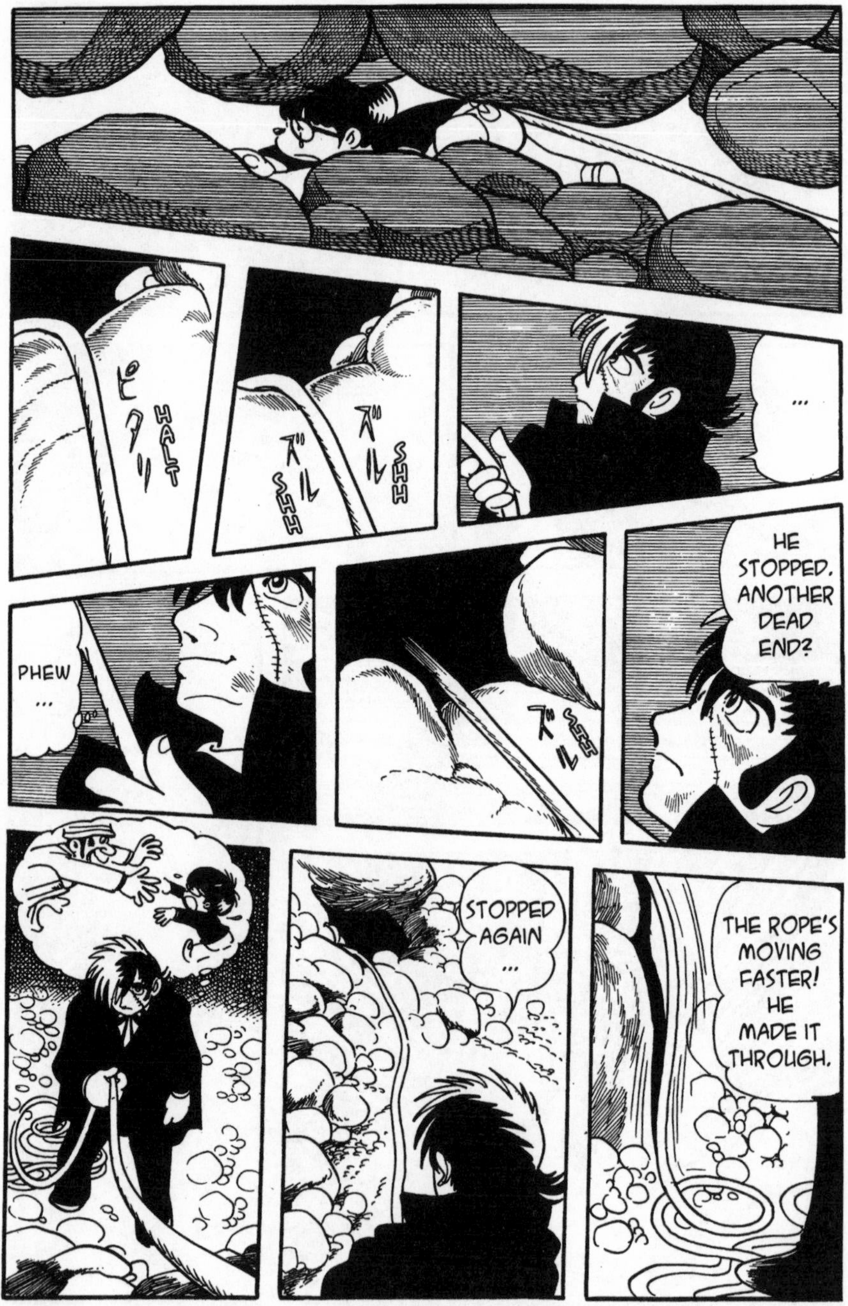
...
ズルズル
SHH SHH
ピタッ
HALT
HE STOPPED. ANOTHER DEAD END?
ズル
SHH
PHEW ...
THE ROPE'S MOVING FASTER! HE MADE IT THROUGH.
STOPPED AGAIN ...

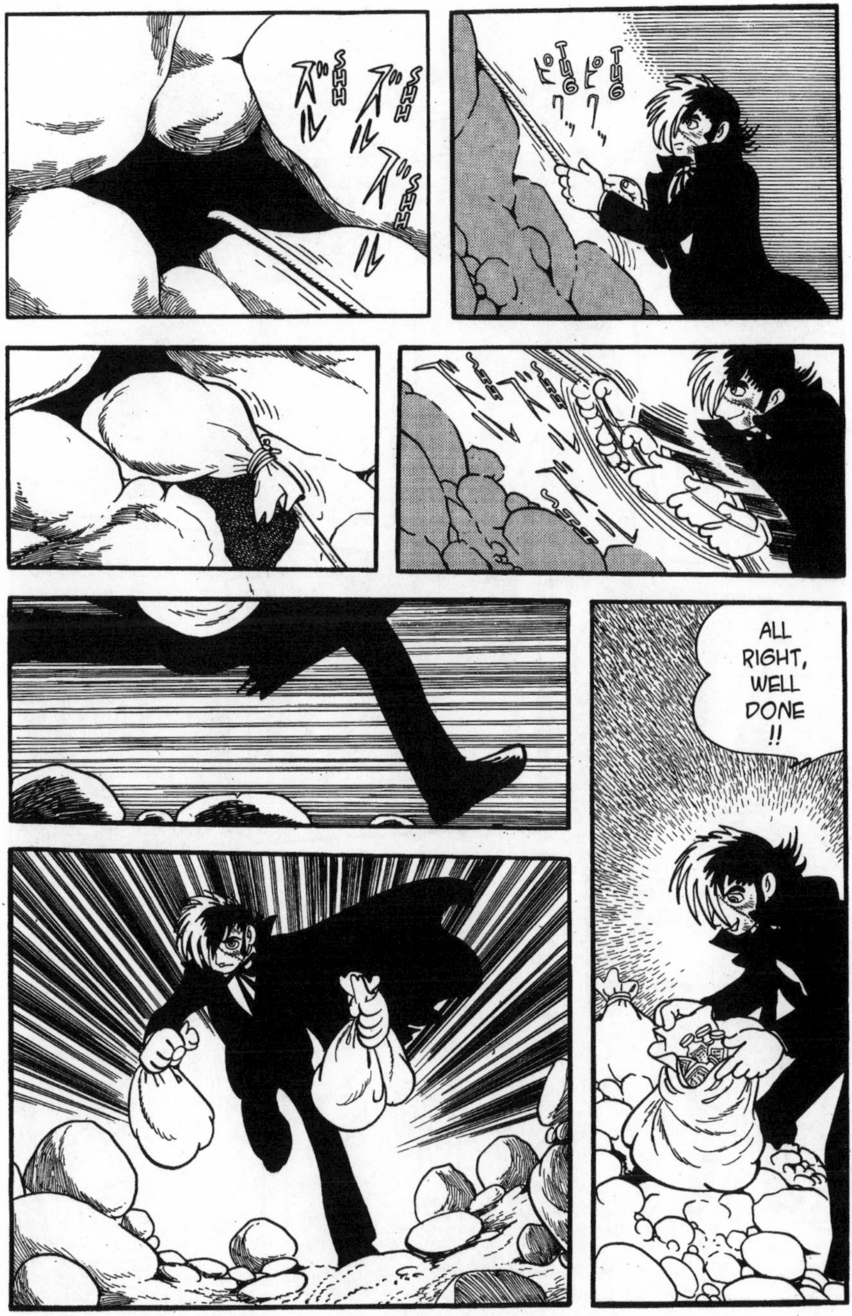
TUG
TUG
SHH
SHH
SHH
ALL RIGHT, WELL DONE !!

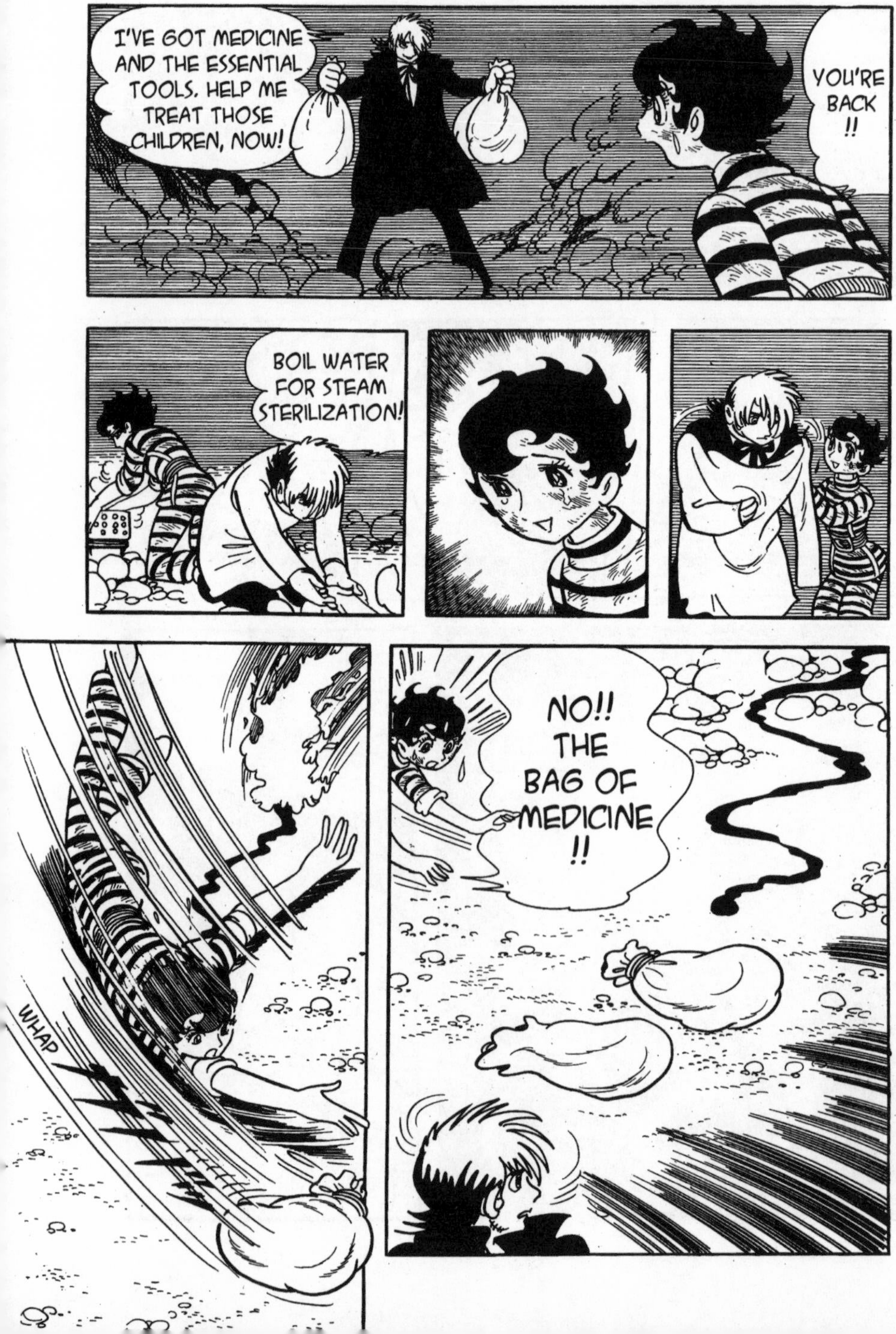
YOU'RE BACK !!
I'VE GOT MEDICINE AND THE ESSENTIAL TOOLS. HELP ME TREAT THOSE CHILDREN, NOW!
BOIL WATER FOR STEAM STERILIZATION!
NO!! THE BAG OF MEDICINE !!
WHAP

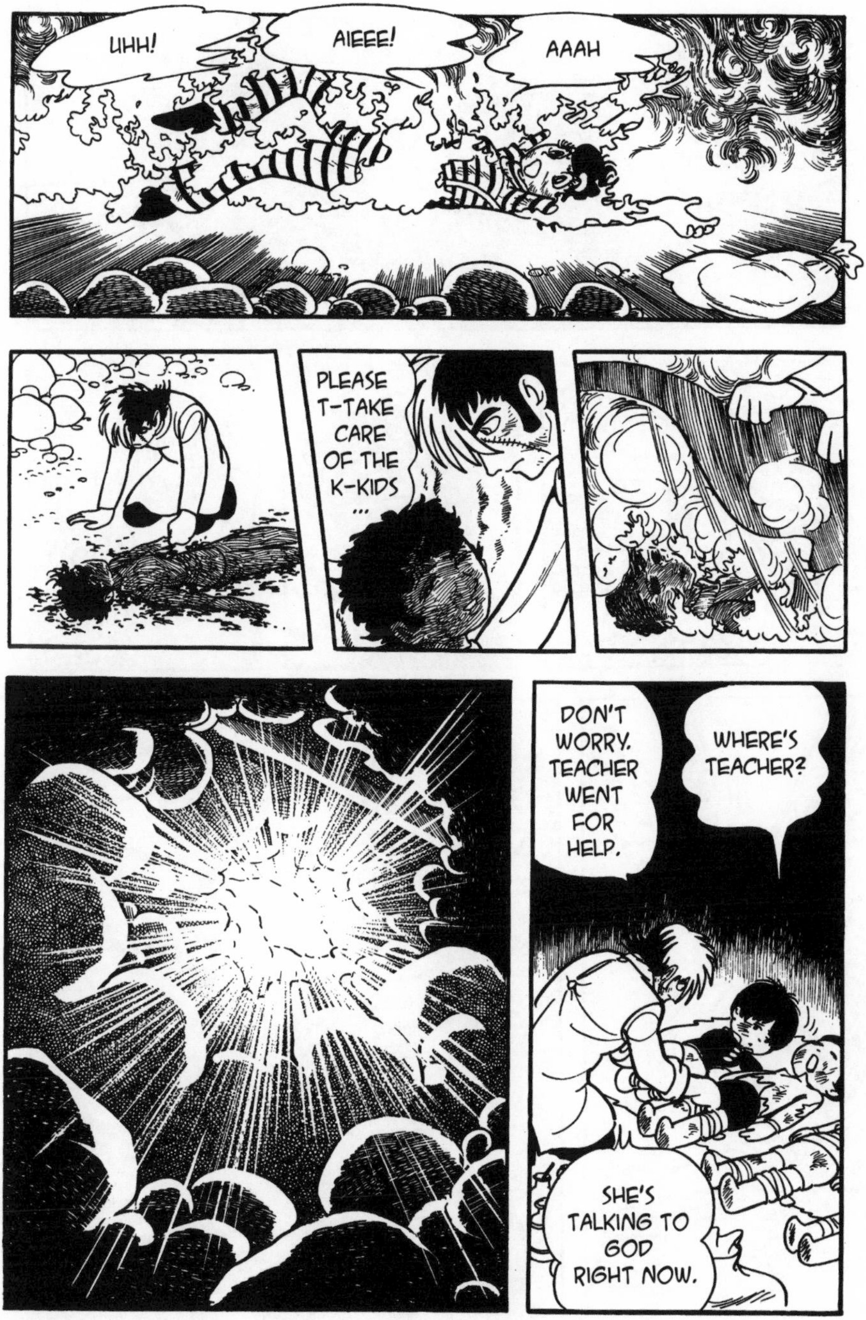
AAAH
AIEEE!
UHH!
PLEASE T-TAKE CARE OF THE K-KIDS ...
WHERE'S TEACHER?
DON'T WORRY. TEACHER WENT FOR HELP.
SHE'S TALKING TO GOD RIGHT NOW.

WHERE ART THOU, FRIEND?

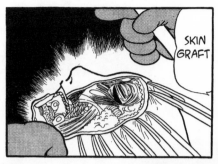

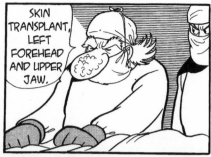

SKIN TRANSPLANT, LEFT FOREHEAD AND UPPER JAW.
SKIN GRAFT
I CAN'T USE THIS.
LOOK...
IT'LL JUST NECROSE AND ROT RIGHT OFF!
WE HAVE AN EMERGENCY. WE NEED A FRESH GRAFT IMMEDIATELY!
I'LL TRY TO ROUND UP A DONOR.
I'LL HELP.

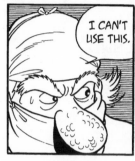

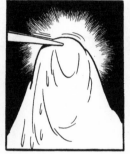

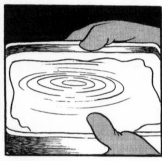

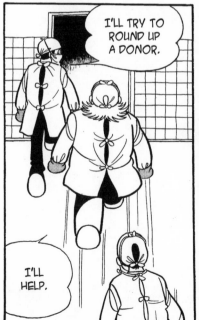

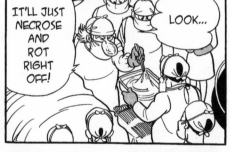

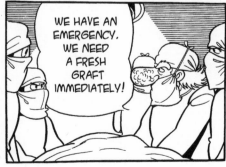

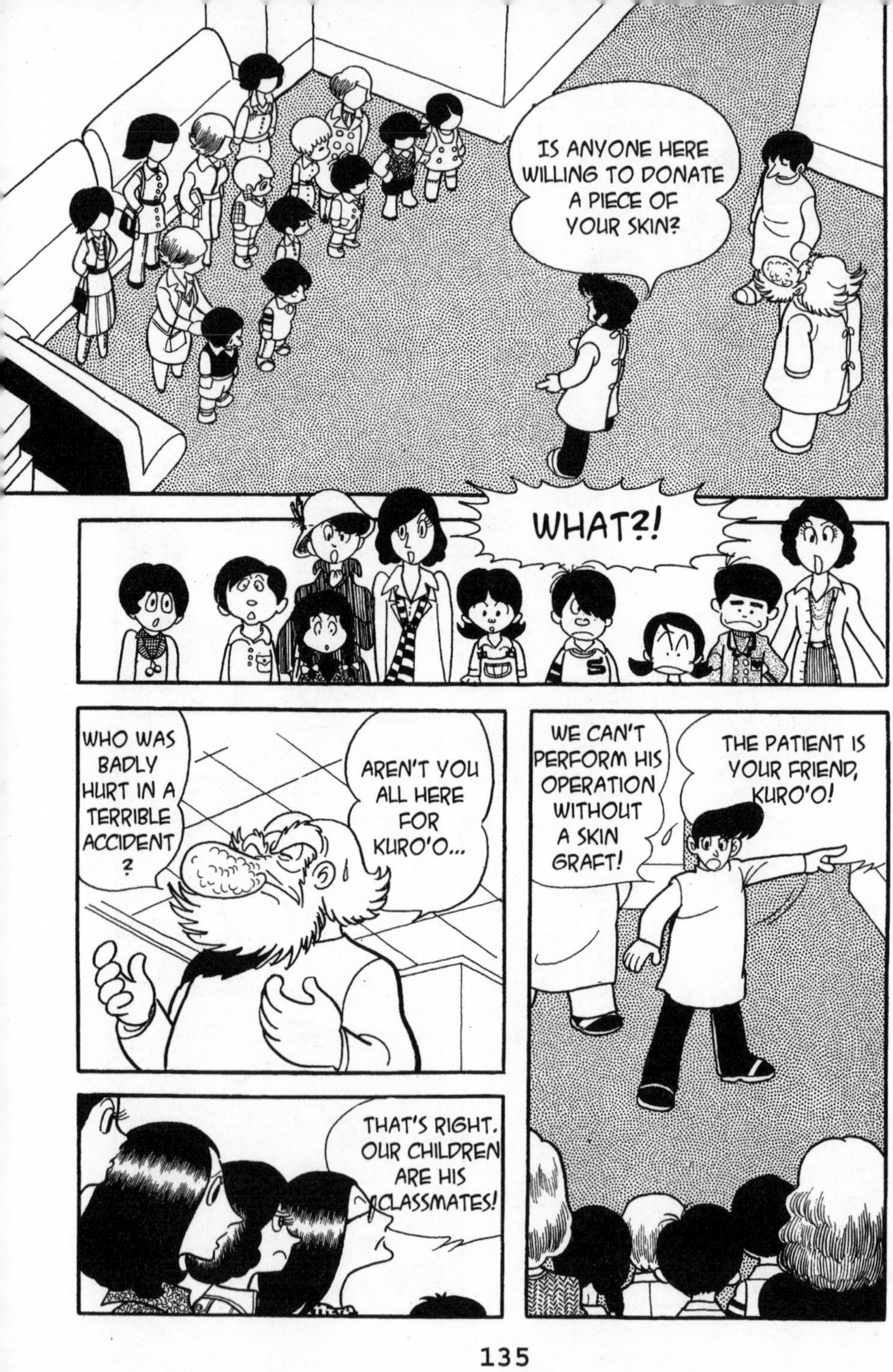
IS ANYONE HERE WILLING TO DONATE A PIECE OF YOUR SKIN?
WHAT?!
THE PATIENT IS YOUR FRIEND, KURO'O!
WE CAN'T PERFORM HIS OPERATION WITHOUT A SKIN GRAFT!
AREN'T YOU ALL HERE FOR KURO'O...
WHO WAS BADLY HURT IN A TERRIBLE ACCIDENT?
THAT'S RIGHT. OUR CHILDREN ARE HIS CLASSMATES!

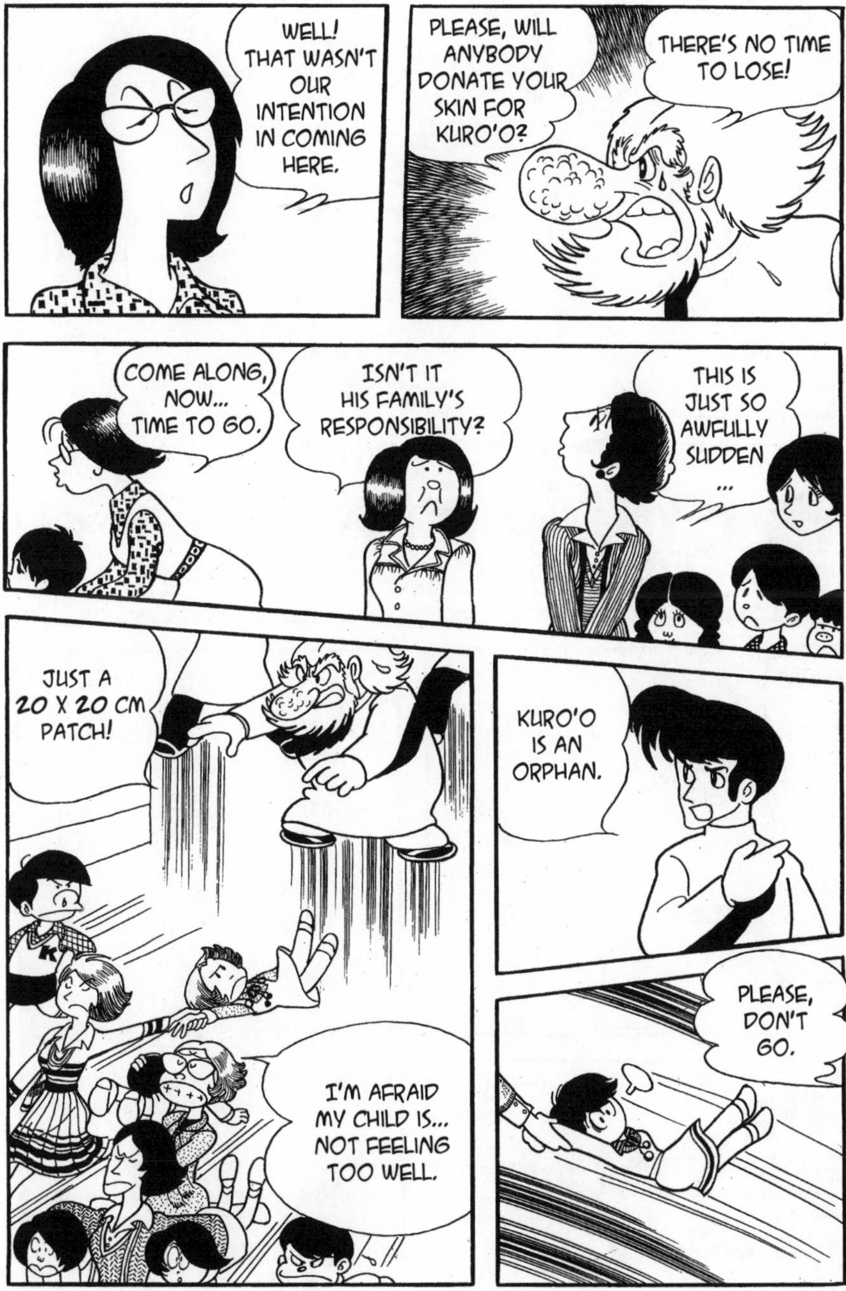
THERE'S NO TIME TO LOSE!
PLEASE, WILL ANYBODY DONATE YOUR SKIN FOR KURO'O?
WELL! THAT WASN'T OUR INTENTION IN COMING HERE.
THIS IS JUST SO AWFULLY SUDDEN ...
ISN'T IT HIS FAMILY'S RESPONSIBILITY?
COME ALONG, NOW... TIME TO GO.
KURO'O IS AN ORPHAN.
PLEASE, DON'T GO.
JUST A 20 X 20 CM PATCH!
I'M AFRAID MY CHILD IS... NOT FEELING TOO WELL.

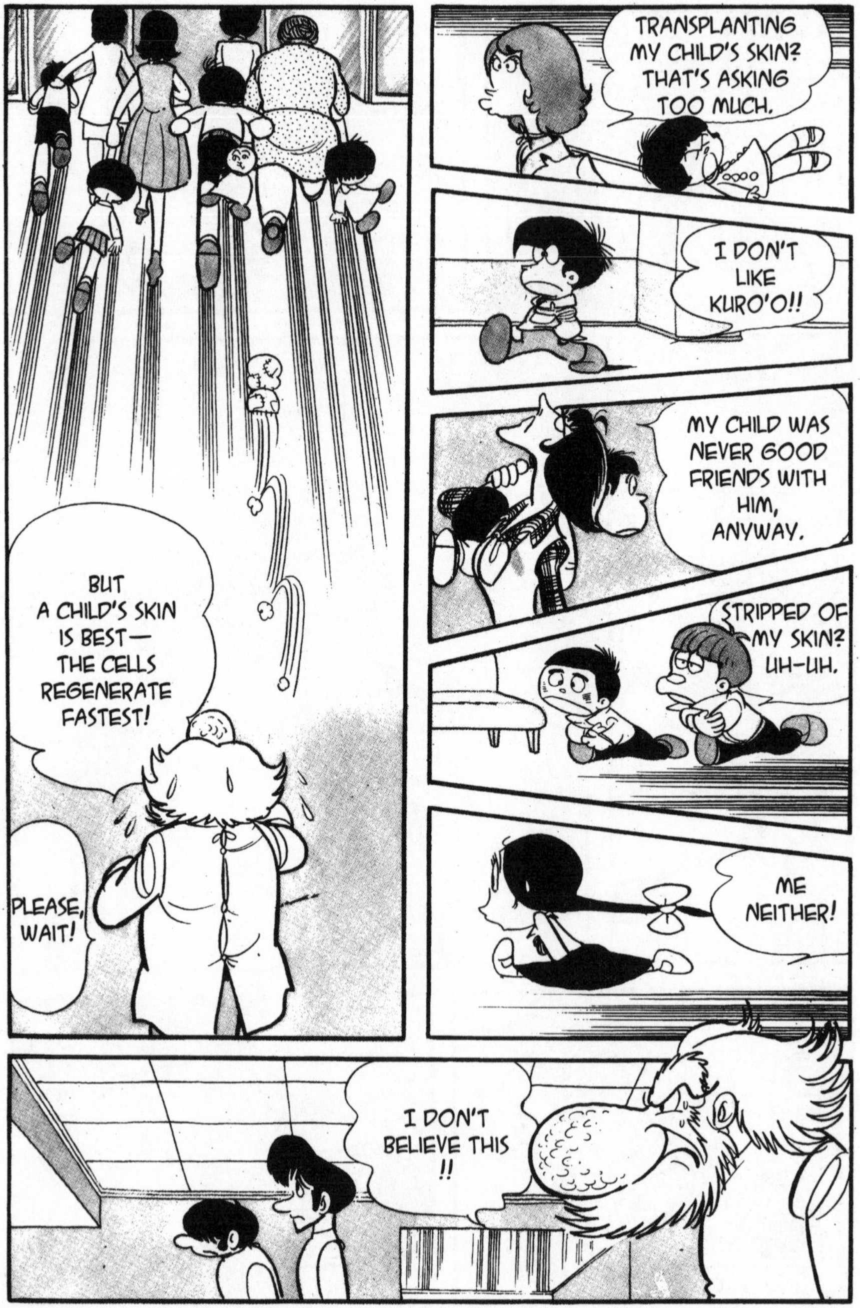
TRANSPLANTING MY CHILD'S SKIN? THAT'S ASKING TOO MUCH.
I DON'T LIKE KURO'O!!
MY CHILD WAS NEVER GOOD FRIENDS WITH HIM, ANYWAY.
STRIPPED OF MY SKIN? UH-UH.
ME NEITHER!
BUT A CHILD'S SKIN IS BEST— THE CELLS REGENERATE FASTEST!
PLEASE, WAIT!
I DON'T BELIEVE THIS !!

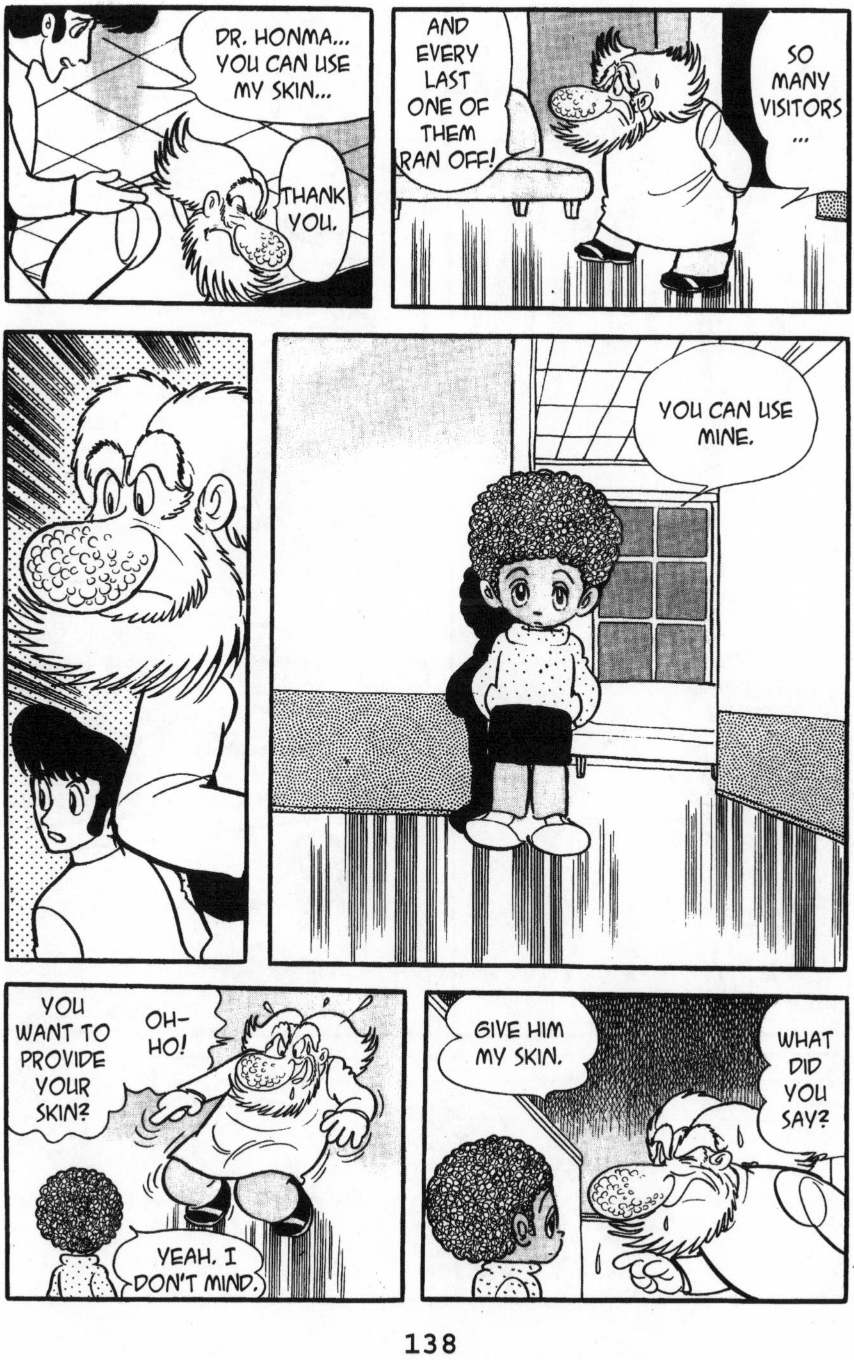
SO MANY VISITORS ...
AND EVERY LAST ONE OF THEM RAN OFF!
DR. HONMA... YOU CAN USE MY SKIN...
THANK YOU.
YOU CAN USE MINE.
WHAT DID YOU SAY?
GIVE HIM MY SKIN.
OH-HO!
YOU WANT TO PROVIDE YOUR SKIN?
YEAH. I DON'T MIND.

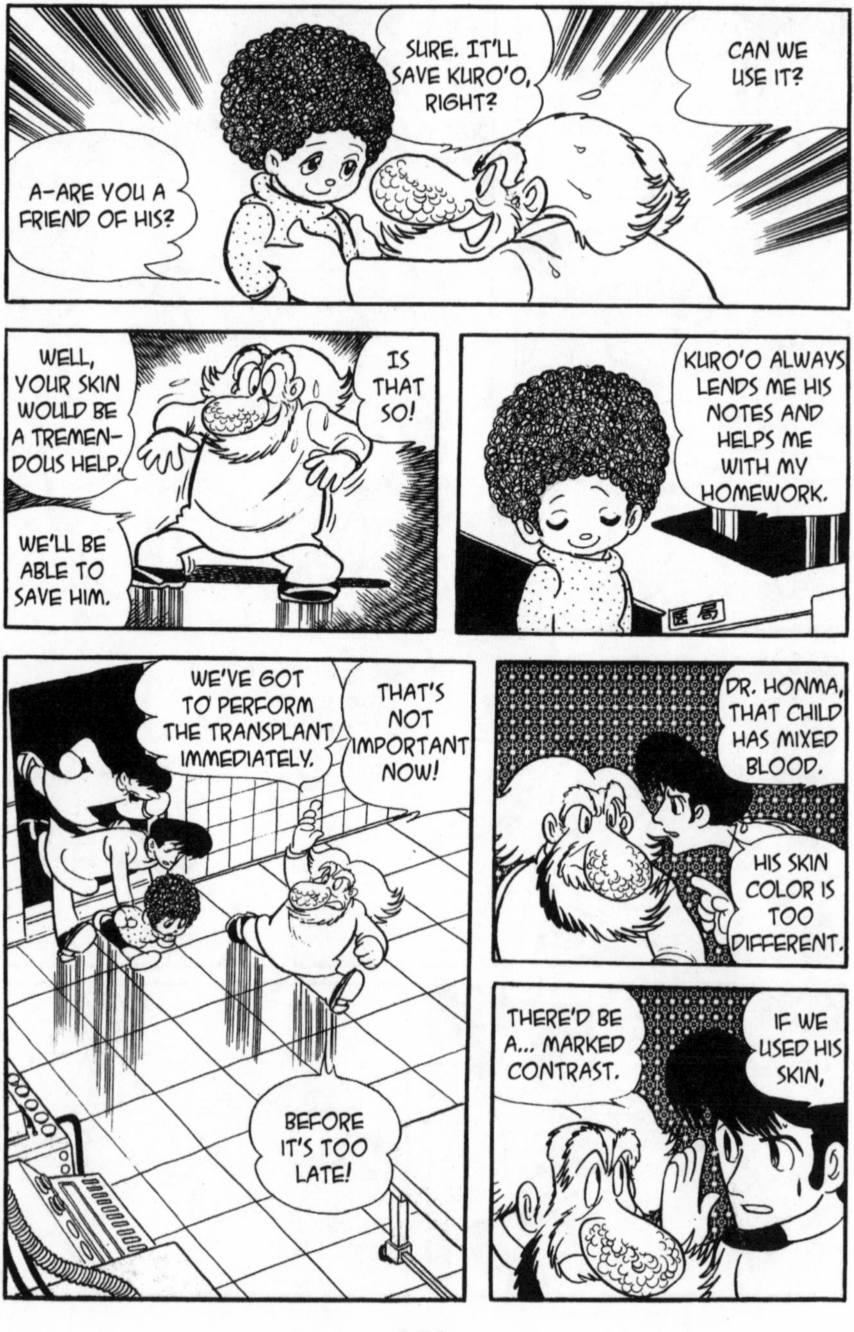
CAN WE USE IT?
SURE. IT'LL SAVE KURO'O, RIGHT?
A-ARE YOU A FRIEND OF HIS?
KURO'O ALWAYS LENDS ME HIS NOTES AND HELPS ME WITH MY HOMEWORK.
医局
IS THAT SO!
WELL, YOUR SKIN WOULD BE A TREMENDOUS HELP.
WE'LL BE ABLE TO SAVE HIM.
DR. HONMA, THAT CHILD HAS MIXED BLOOD.
HIS SKIN COLOR IS TOO DIFFERENT.
IF WE USED HIS SKIN,
THERE'D BE A... MARKED CONTRAST.
THAT'S NOT IMPORTANT NOW!
WE'VE GOT TO PERFORM THE TRANSPLANT IMMEDIATELY.
BEFORE IT'S TOO LATE!

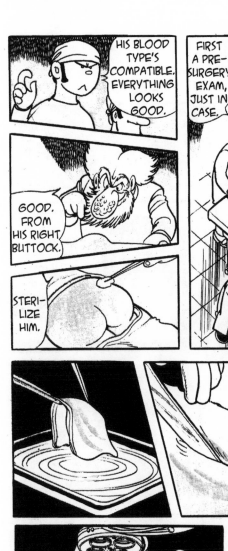

HIS BLOOD TYPE'S COMPATIBLE. EVERYTHING LOOKS GOOD.
FIRST A PRE-SURGERY EXAM, JUST IN CASE.
LIE DOWN HERE... THAT'S RIGHT, FACE DOWN.
GOOD. FROM HIS RIGHT BUTTOCK.
STERILIZE HIM.
REMOVE THE SUBCUTANEOUS TISSUE, TOO.
KRAUSE METHOD
WE'VE GOT IT!

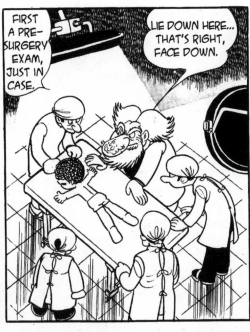

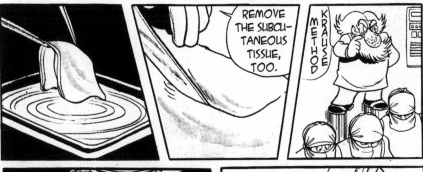

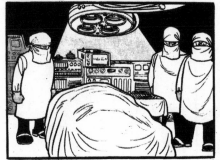

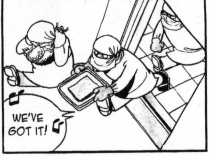

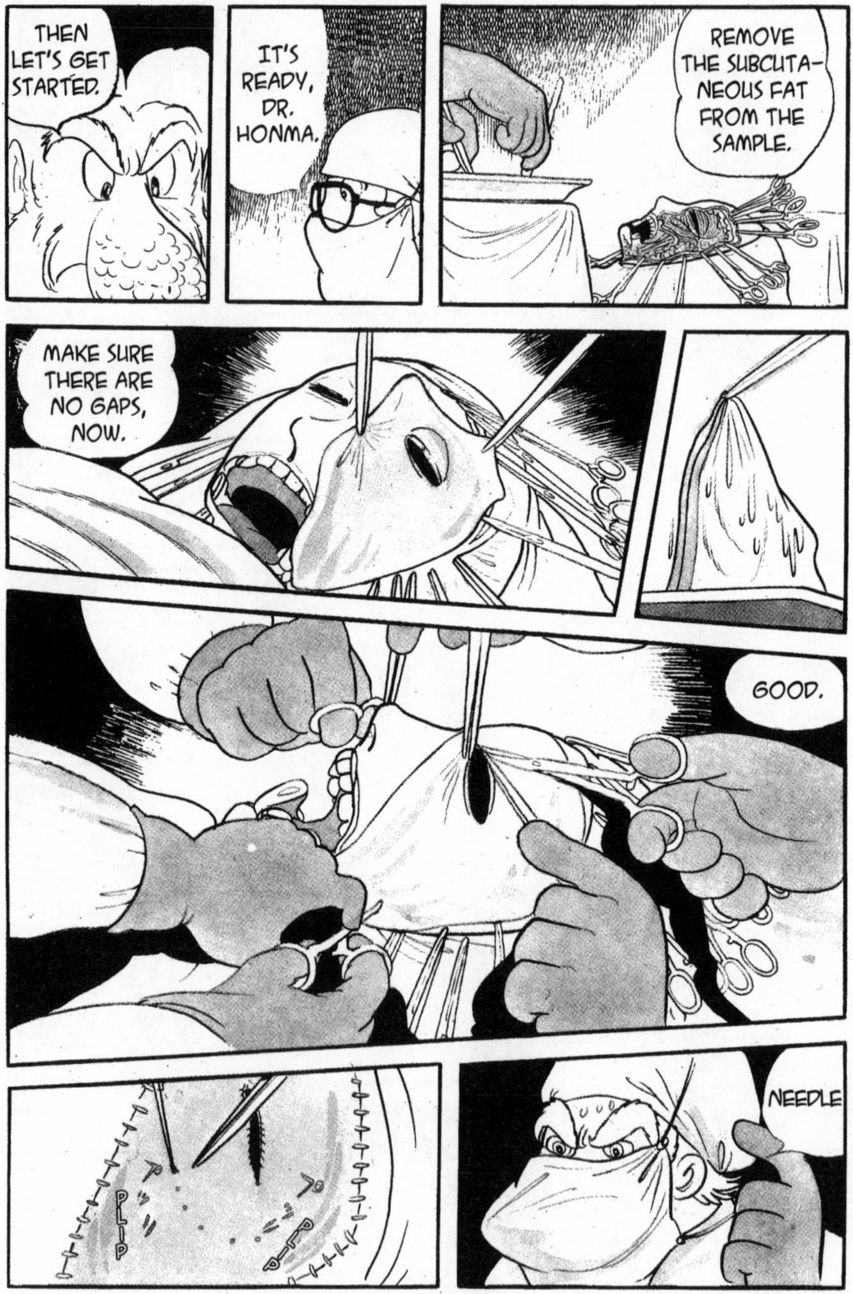
REMOVE THE SUBCUTA-NEOUS FAT FROM THE SAMPLE.
IT'S READY, DR. HONMA.
THEN LET'S GET STARTED.
MAKE SURE THERE ARE NO GAPS, NOW.
GOOD.
NEEDLE
PLIP
PLIP

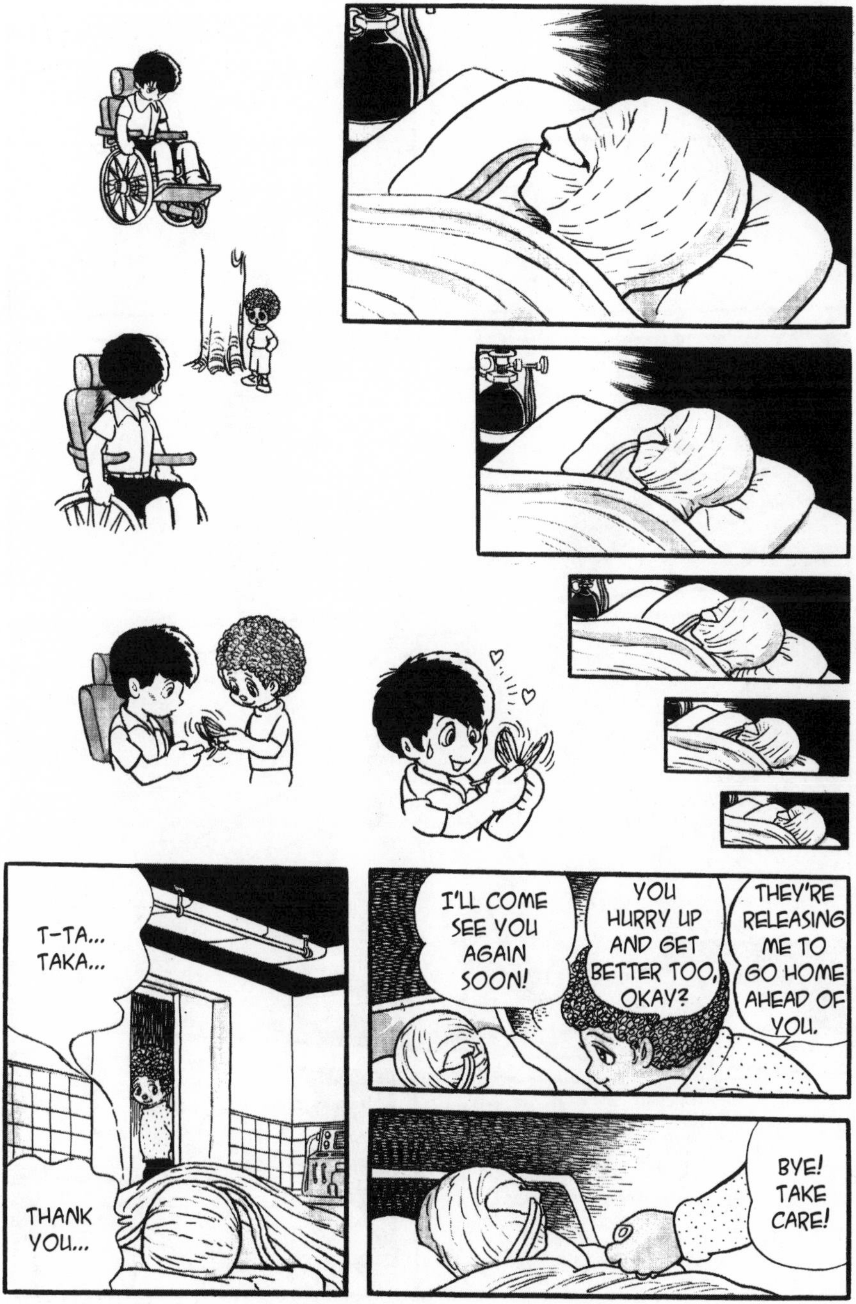
THEY'RE RELEASING ME TO GO HOME AHEAD OF YOU.
YOU HURRY UP AND GET BETTER TOO, OKAY?
I'LL COME SEE YOU AGAIN SOON!
BYE! TAKE CARE!
T-TA... TAKA...
THANK YOU...

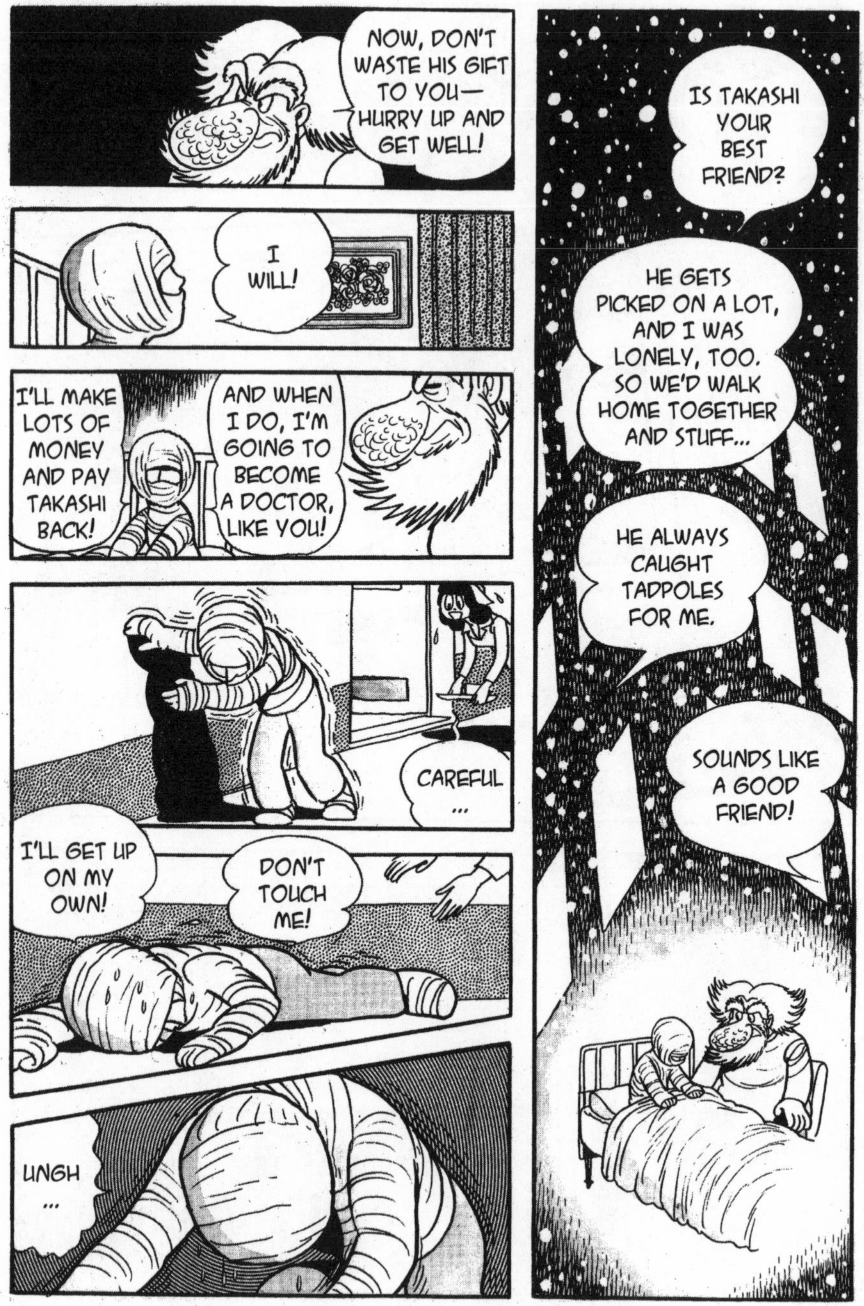
NOW, DON'T WASTE HIS GIFT TO YOU— HURRY UP AND GET WELL!
I WILL!
I'LL MAKE LOTS OF MONEY AND PAY TAKASHI BACK!
AND WHEN I DO, I'M GOING TO BECOME A DOCTOR, LIKE YOU!
CAREFUL ...
I'LL GET UP ON MY OWN!
DON'T TOUCH ME!
UNGH ...
IS TAKASHI YOUR BEST FRIEND?
HE GETS PICKED ON A LOT, AND I WAS LONELY, TOO. SO WE'D WALK HOME TOGETHER AND STUFF...
HE ALWAYS CAUGHT TADPOLES FOR ME.
SOUNDS LIKE A GOOD FRIEND!

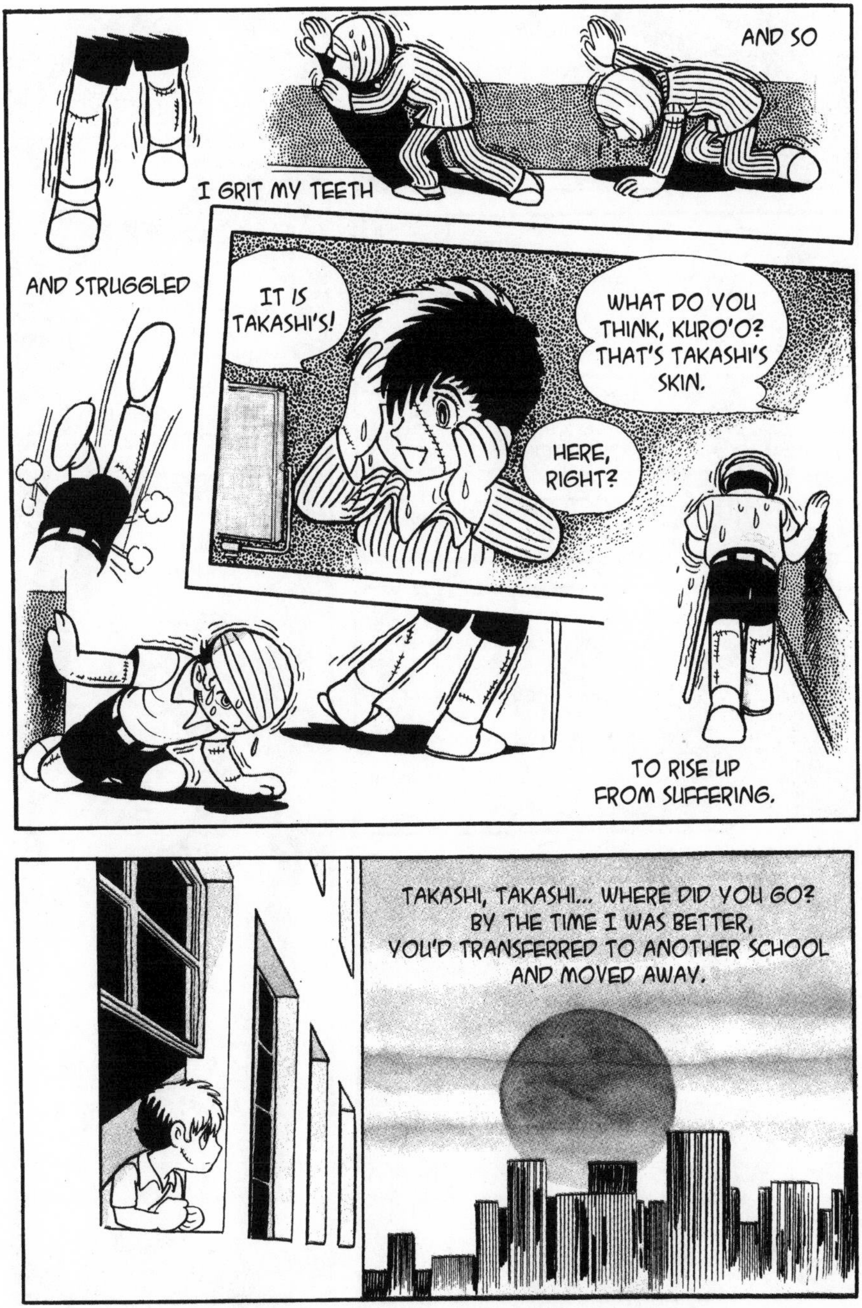
AND SO
I GRIT MY TEETH
AND STRUGGLED
WHAT DO YOU THINK, KURO'O? THAT'S TAKASHI'S SKIN.
IT IS TAKASHI'S!
HERE, RIGHT?
TO RISE UP FROM SUFFERING.
TAKASHI, TAKASHI... WHERE DID YOU GO? BY THE TIME I WAS BETTER, YOU'D TRANSFERRED TO ANOTHER SCHOOL AND MOVED AWAY.

NOTE: "KURO" MEANS *BLACK* AND "O" IS A COMMON ENDING FOR MALE NAMES; IN OTHER WORDS, *BLACK JACK*.

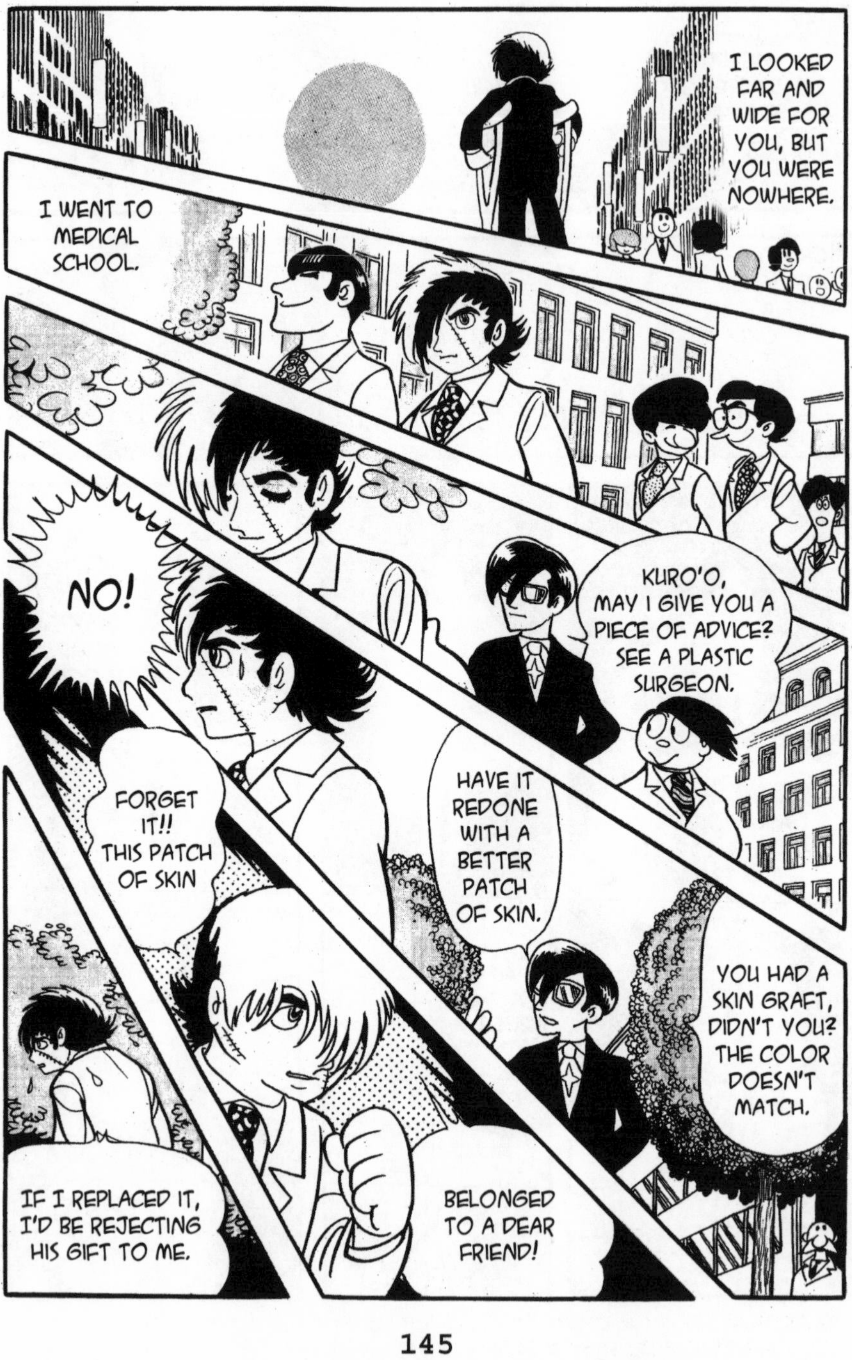
I LOOKED FAR AND WIDE FOR YOU, BUT YOU WERE NOWHERE.
I WENT TO MEDICAL SCHOOL.
KURO'O, MAY I GIVE YOU A PIECE OF ADVICE? SEE A PLASTIC SURGEON.
NO!
YOU HAD A SKIN GRAFT, DIDN'T YOU? THE COLOR DOESN'T MATCH.
HAVE IT REDONE WITH A BETTER PATCH OF SKIN.
FORGET IT!! THIS PATCH OF SKIN
BELONGED TO A DEAR FRIEND!
IF I REPLACED IT, I'D BE REJECTING HIS GIFT TO ME.

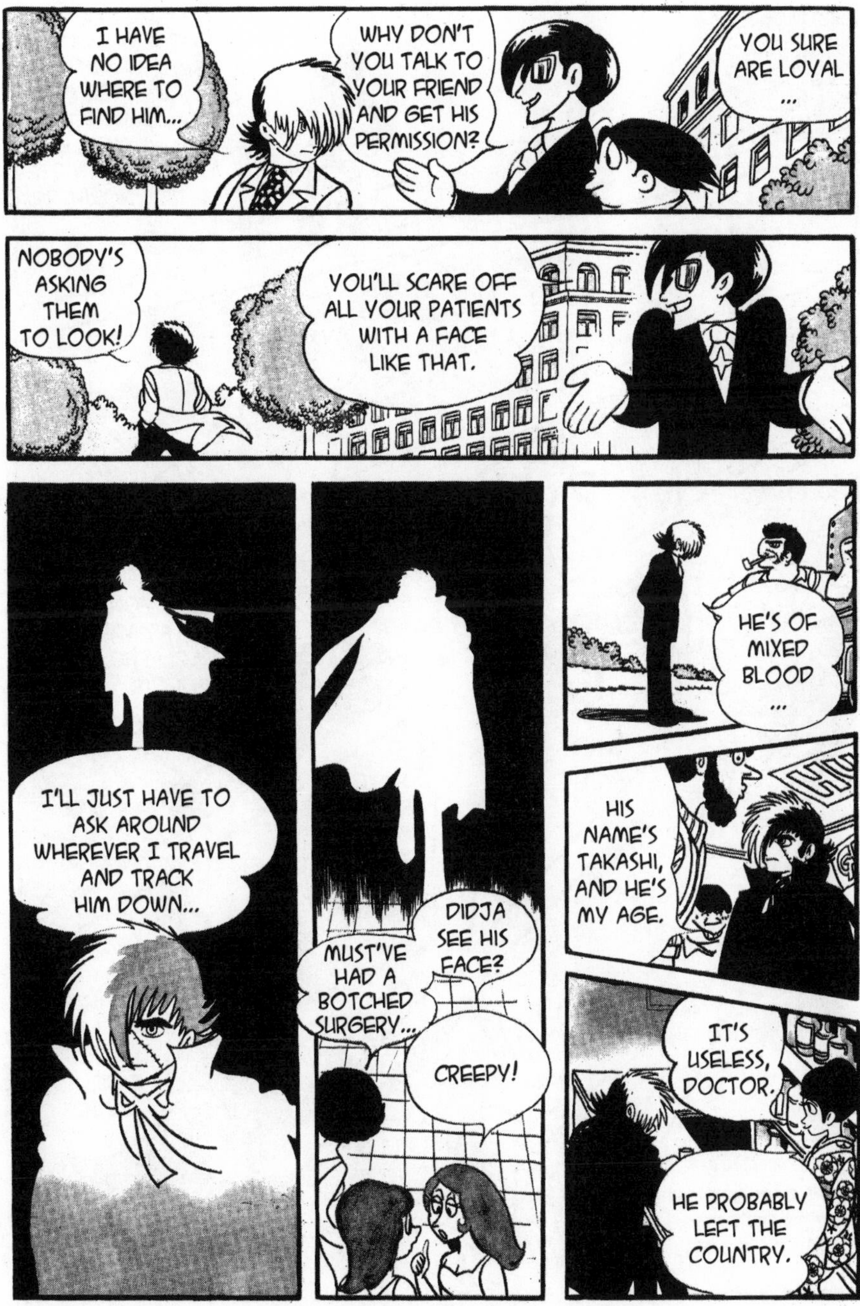
YOU SURE ARE LOYAL ...
WHY DON'T YOU TALK TO YOUR FRIEND AND GET HIS PERMISSION?
I HAVE NO IDEA WHERE TO FIND HIM...
YOU'LL SCARE OFF ALL YOUR PATIENTS WITH A FACE LIKE THAT.
NOBODY'S ASKING THEM TO LOOK!
HE'S OF MIXED BLOOD ...
HIS NAME'S TAKASHI, AND HE'S MY AGE.
IT'S USELESS, DOCTOR.
HE PROBABLY LEFT THE COUNTRY.
DIDJA SEE HIS FACE?
MUST'VE HAD A BOTCHED SURGERY...
CREEPY!
I'LL JUST HAVE TO ASK AROUND WHEREVER I TRAVEL AND TRACK HIM DOWN...

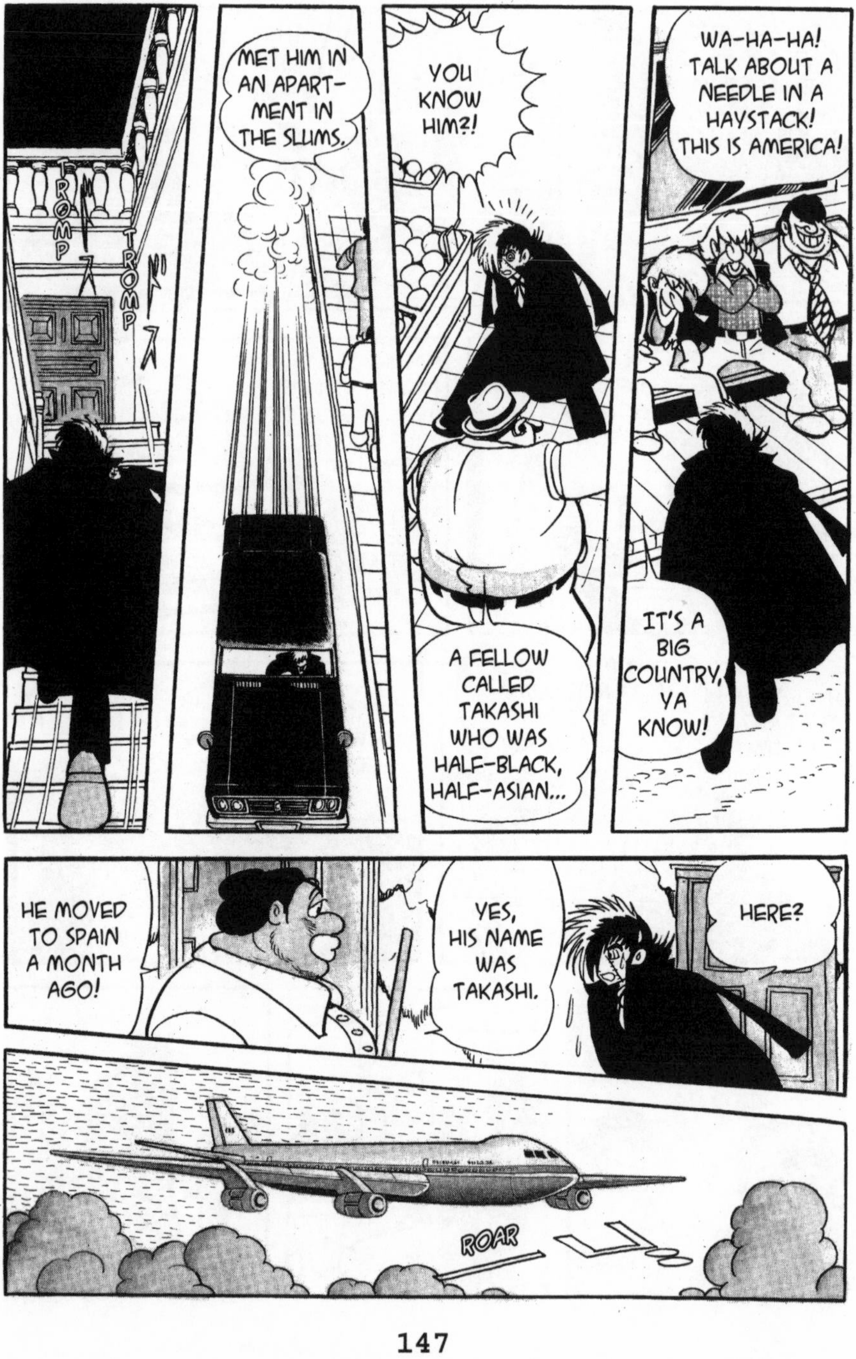
WA-HA-HA! TALK ABOUT A NEEDLE IN A HAYSTACK! THIS IS AMERICA!
IT'S A BIG COUNTRY, YA KNOW!
A FELLOW CALLED TAKASHI WHO WAS HALF-BLACK, HALF-ASIAN...
YOU KNOW HIM?!
MET HIM IN AN APART-MENT IN THE SLUMS.
TROMP
TROMP
HERE?
YES, HIS NAME WAS TAKASHI.
HE MOVED TO SPAIN A MONTH AGO!
ROAR

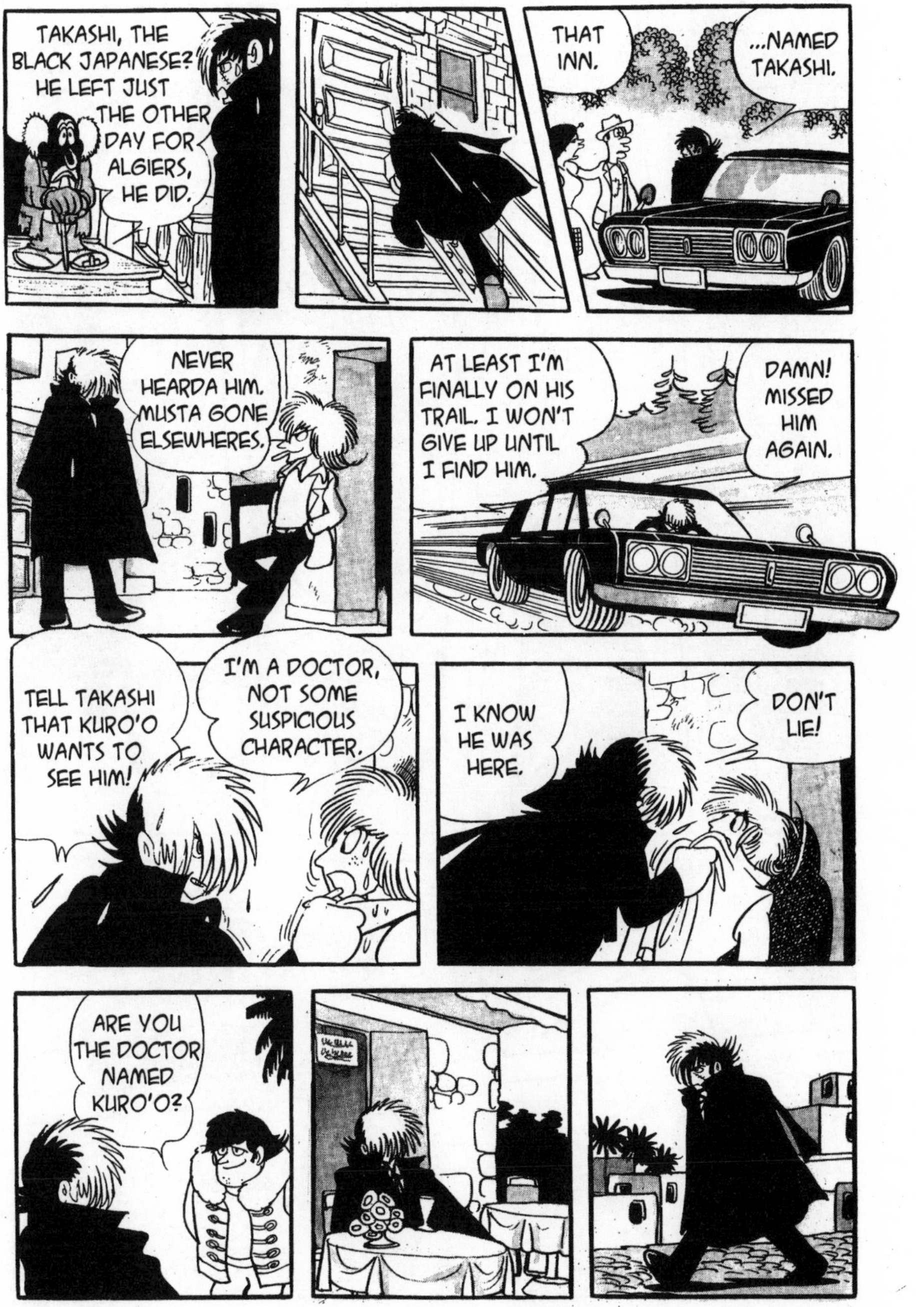
...NAMED TAKASHI.
THAT INN.
TAKASHI, THE BLACK JAPANESE? HE LEFT JUST THE OTHER DAY FOR ALGIERS, HE DID.
DAMN! MISSED HIM AGAIN.
AT LEAST I'M FINALLY ON HIS TRAIL. I WON'T GIVE UP UNTIL I FIND HIM.
NEVER HEARDA HIM. MUSTA GONE ELSEWHERES.
DON'T LIE!
I KNOW HE WAS HERE.
I'M A DOCTOR, NOT SOME SUSPICIOUS CHARACTER.
TELL TAKASHI THAT KURO'O WANTS TO SEE HIM!
ARE YOU THE DOCTOR NAMED KURO'O?

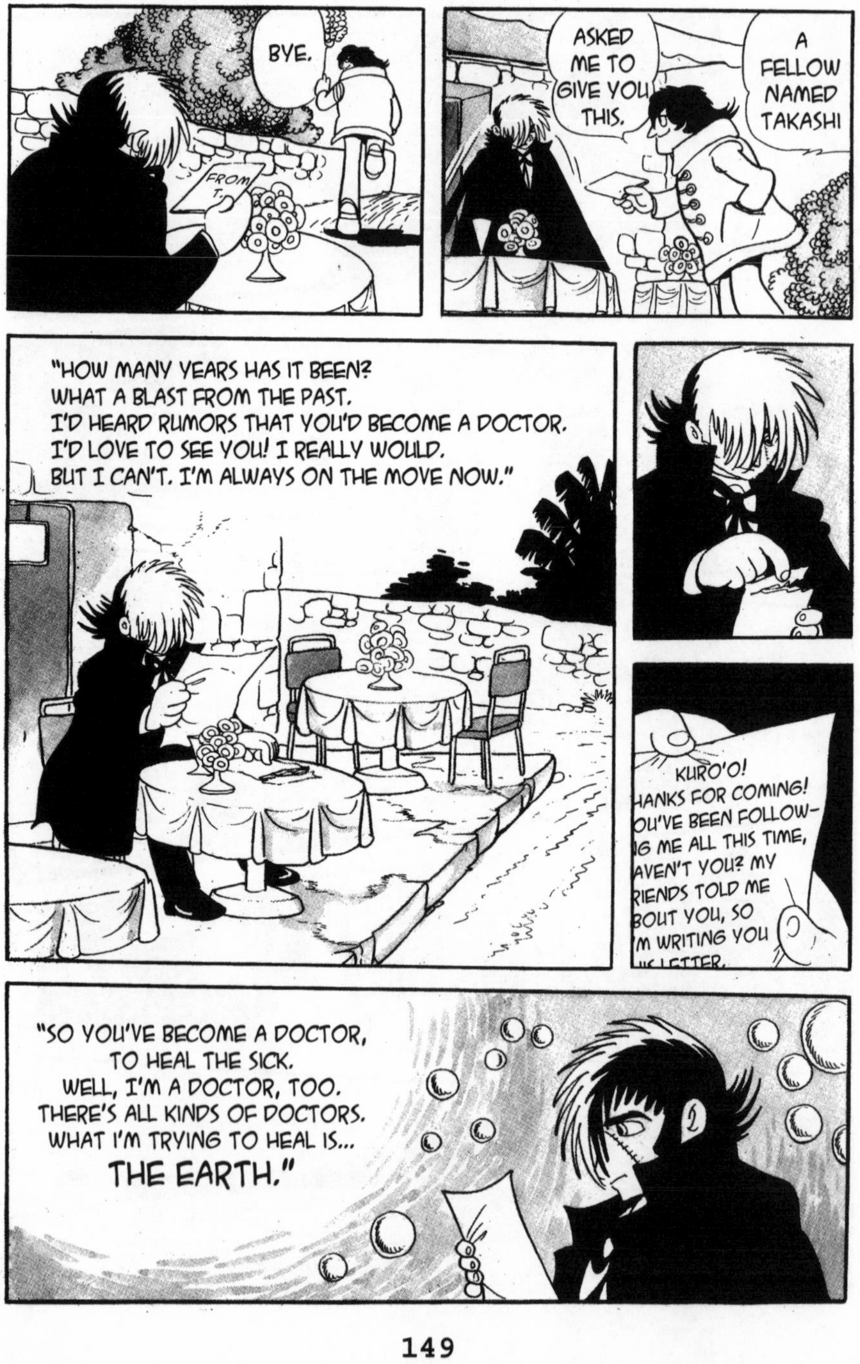
A FELLOW NAMED TAKASHI
ASKED ME TO GIVE YOU THIS.
BYE.
FROM T.
KURO'O!
HANKS FOR COMING!
OU'VE BEEN FOLLOW-
IG ME ALL THIS TIME,
AVEN'T YOU? MY
RIENDS TOLD ME
BOUT YOU, SO
'M WRITING YOU
"HOW MANY YEARS HAS IT BEEN? WHAT A BLAST FROM THE PAST. I'D HEARD RUMORS THAT YOU'D BECOME A DOCTOR. I'D LOVE TO SEE YOU! I REALLY WOULD. BUT I CAN'T. I'M ALWAYS ON THE MOVE NOW."
"SO YOU'VE BECOME A DOCTOR, TO HEAL THE SICK. WELL, I'M A DOCTOR, TOO. THERE'S ALL KINDS OF DOCTORS. WHAT I'M TRYING TO HEAL IS... THE EARTH."

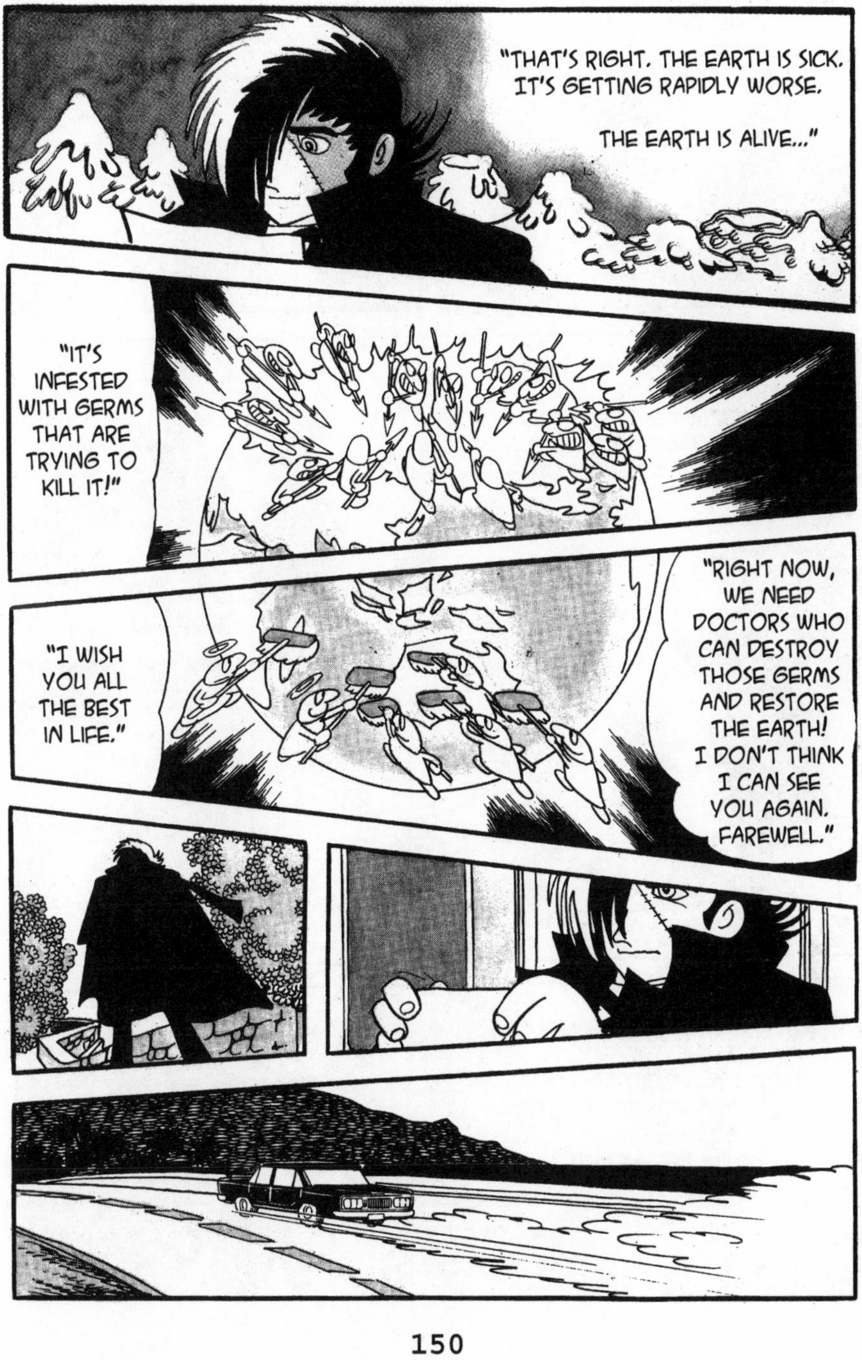
"THAT'S RIGHT. THE EARTH IS SICK. IT'S GETTING RAPIDLY WORSE.
THE EARTH IS ALIVE..."
"IT'S INFESTED WITH GERMS THAT ARE TRYING TO KILL IT!"
"RIGHT NOW, WE NEED DOCTORS WHO CAN DESTROY THOSE GERMS AND RESTORE THE EARTH! I DON'T THINK I CAN SEE YOU AGAIN. FAREWELL."
"I WISH YOU ALL THE BEST IN LIFE."

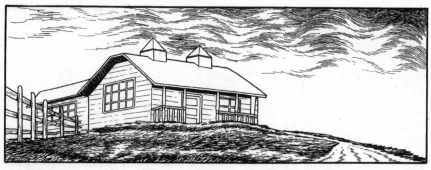

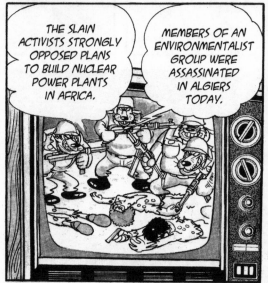

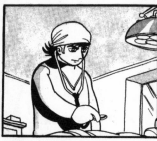

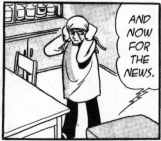

AND NOW FOR THE NEWS.
MEMBERS OF AN ENVIRONMENTALIST GROUP WERE ASSASSINATED IN ALGIERS TODAY.
THE SLAIN ACTIVISTS STRONGLY OPPOSED PLANS TO BUILD NUCLEAR POWER PLANTS IN AFRICA.
ONE OF THE VICTIMS, A HALF-JAPANESE MALE,
HAS AN OLD SURGICAL SCAR ON ONE BUTTOCK. THE EMBASSY IS TRYING TO ASCERTAIN...
THAT'S TAKASHI !!

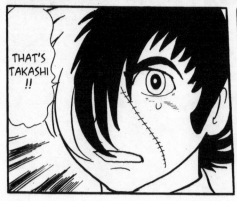

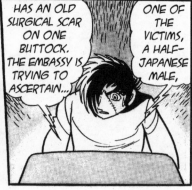

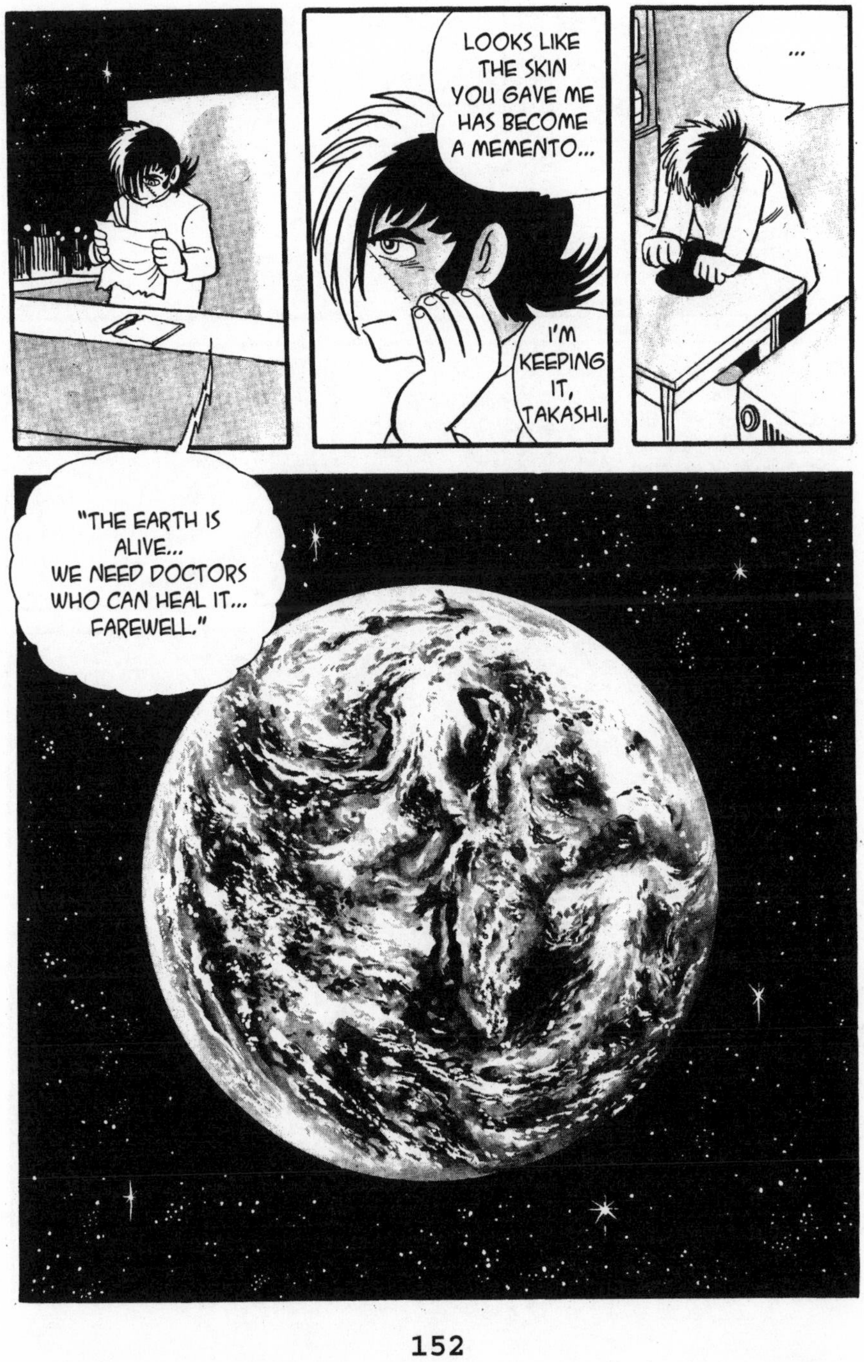
...
LOOKS LIKE THE SKIN YOU GAVE ME HAS BECOME A MEMENTO...
I'M KEEPING IT, TAKASHI.
"THE EARTH IS ALIVE... WE NEED DOCTORS WHO CAN HEAL IT... FAREWELL."

KIDNAPPING

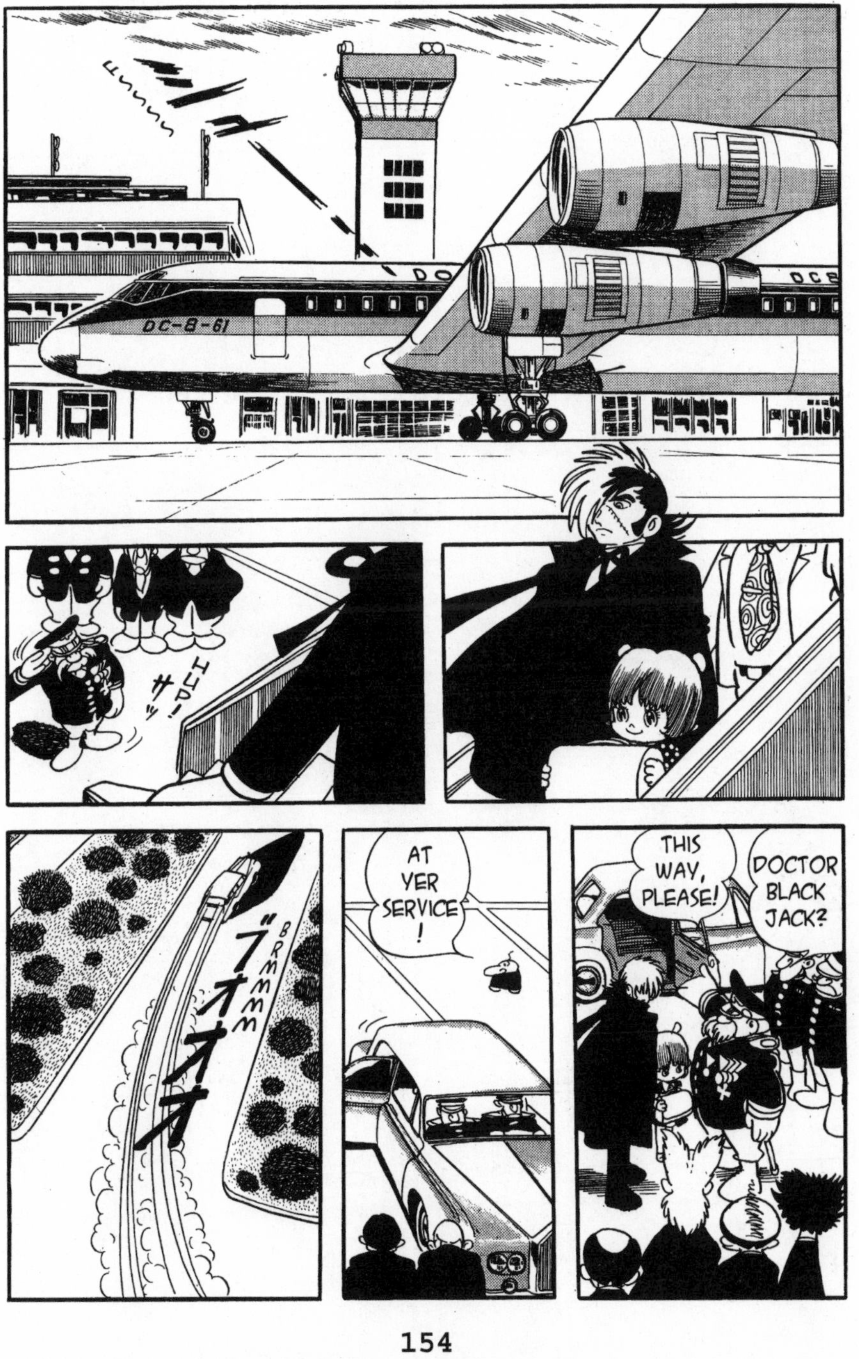
HUP!
サッ
DOCTOR BLACK JACK?
THIS WAY, PLEASE!
AT YER SERVICE!
BRMMMM
ブオオオ

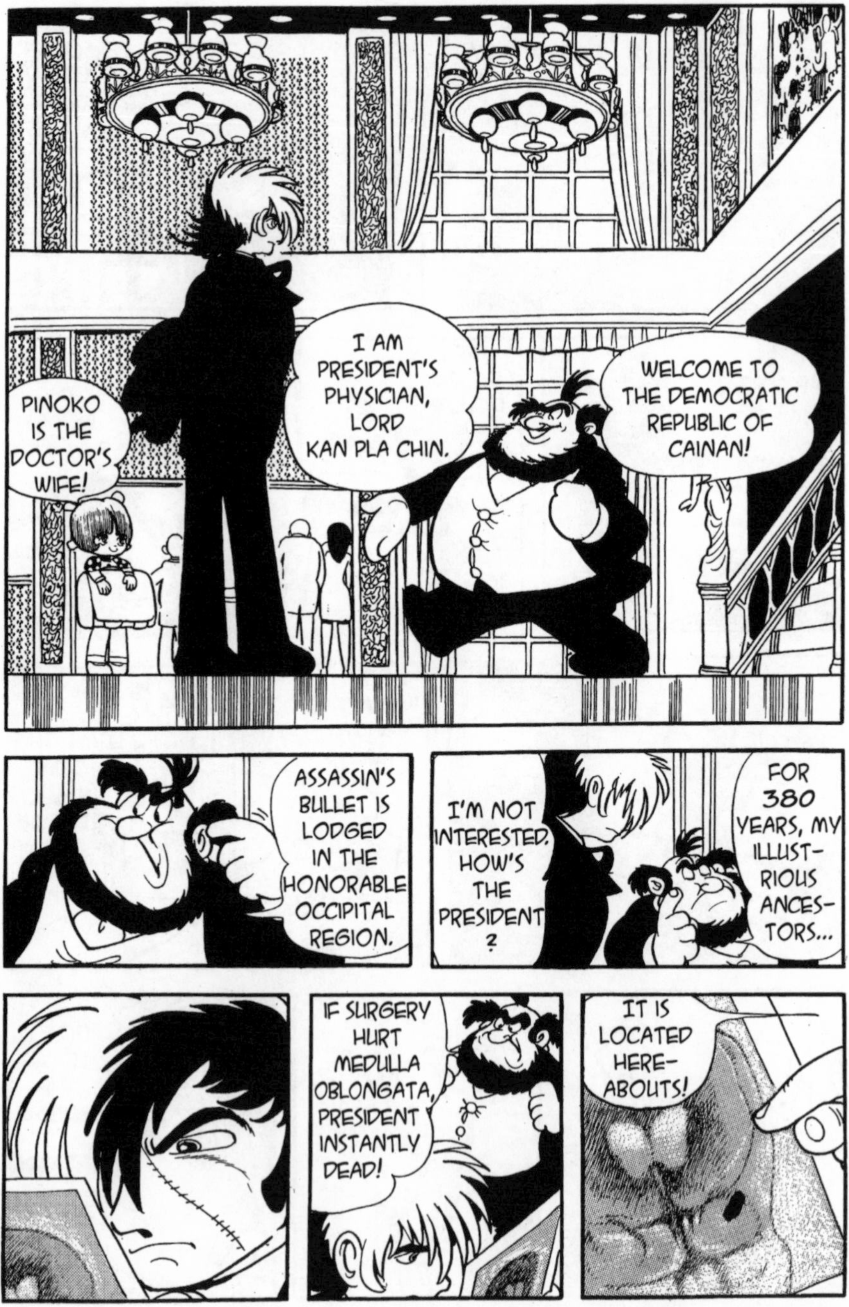
WELCOME TO THE DEMOCRATIC REPUBLIC OF CAINAN!
I AM PRESIDENT'S PHYSICIAN, LORD KAN PLA CHIN.
PINOKO IS THE DOCTOR'S WIFE!
FOR 380 YEARS, MY ILLUSTRIOUS ANCESTORS...
I'M NOT INTERESTED. HOW'S THE PRESIDENT?
ASSASSIN'S BULLET IS LODGED IN THE HONORABLE OCCIPITAL REGION.
IT IS LOCATED HEREABOUTS!
IF SURGERY HURT MEDULLA OBLONGATA, PRESIDENT INSTANTLY DEAD!

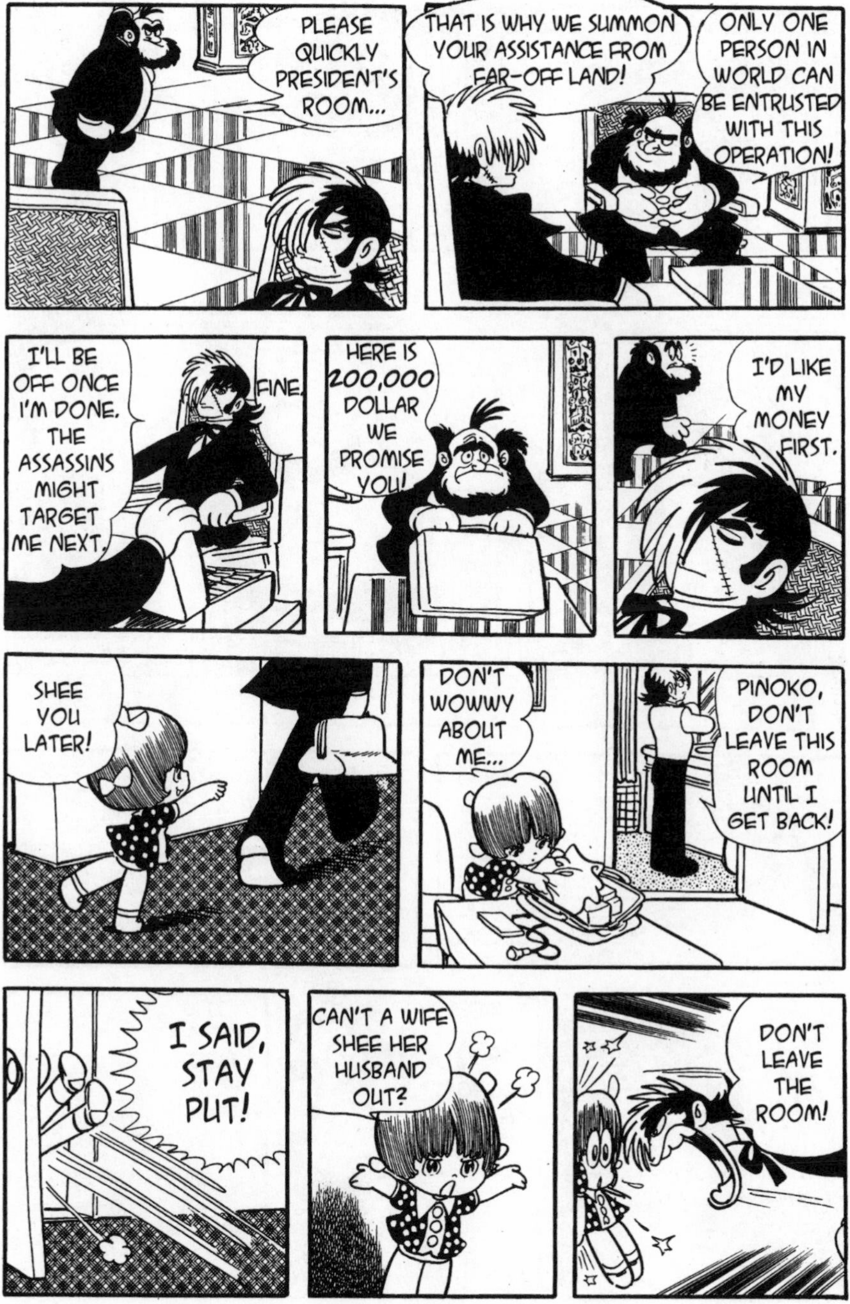
PLEASE QUICKLY PRESIDENT'S ROOM...
THAT IS WHY WE SUMMON YOUR ASSISTANCE FROM FAR-OFF LAND!
ONLY ONE PERSON IN WORLD CAN BE ENTRUSTED WITH THIS OPERATION!
I'LL BE OFF ONCE I'M DONE. THE ASSASSINS MIGHT TARGET ME NEXT.
FINE.
HERE IS 200,000 DOLLAR WE PROMISE YOU!
I'D LIKE MY MONEY FIRST.
SHEE YOU LATER!
DON'T WOWWY ABOUT ME...
PINOKO, DON'T LEAVE THIS ROOM UNTIL I GET BACK!
I SAID, STAY PUT!
CAN'T A WIFE SHEE HER HUSBAND OUT?
DON'T LEAVE THE ROOM!

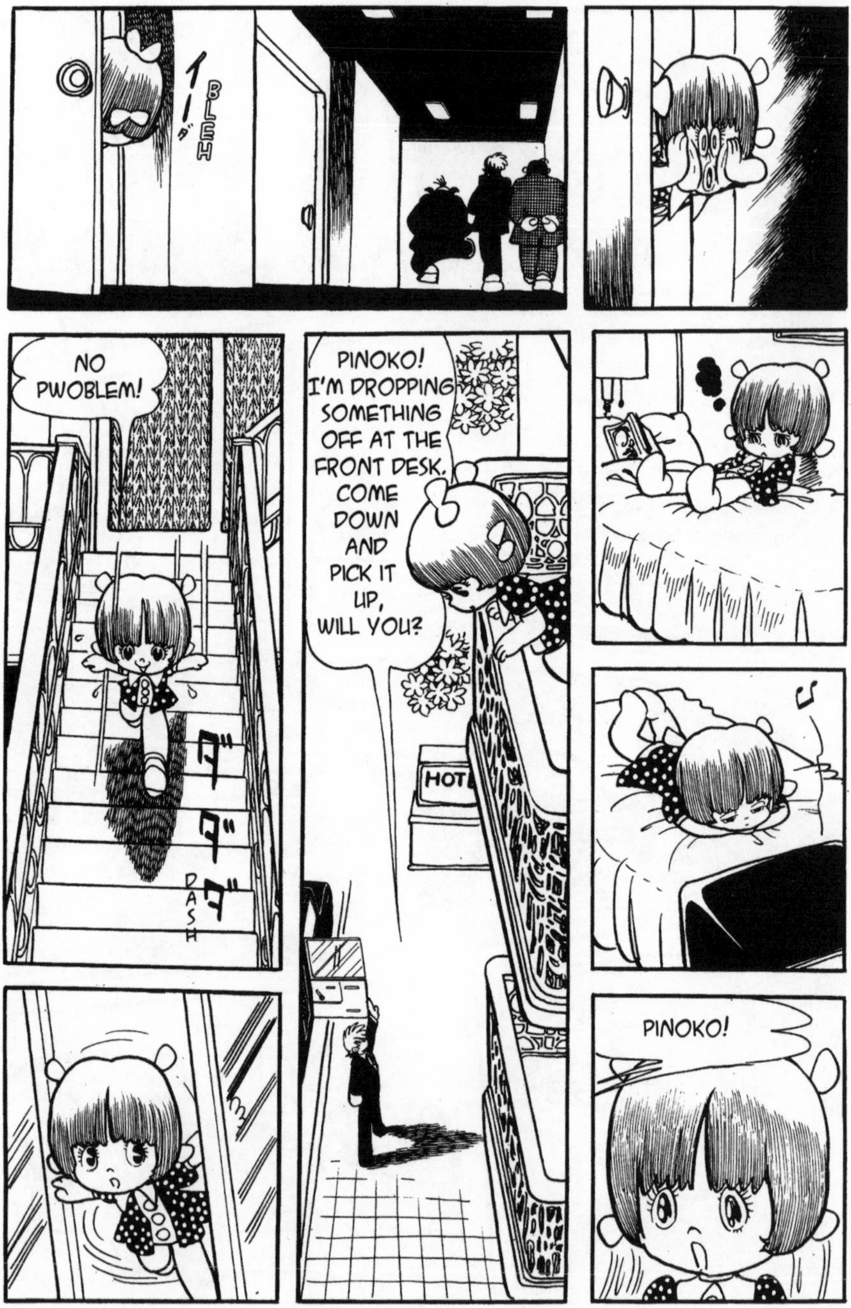
BLEH
PINOKO!
PINOKO! I'M DROPPING SOMETHING OFF AT THE FRONT DESK. COME DOWN AND PICK IT UP, WILL YOU?
NO PWOBLEM!
DASH

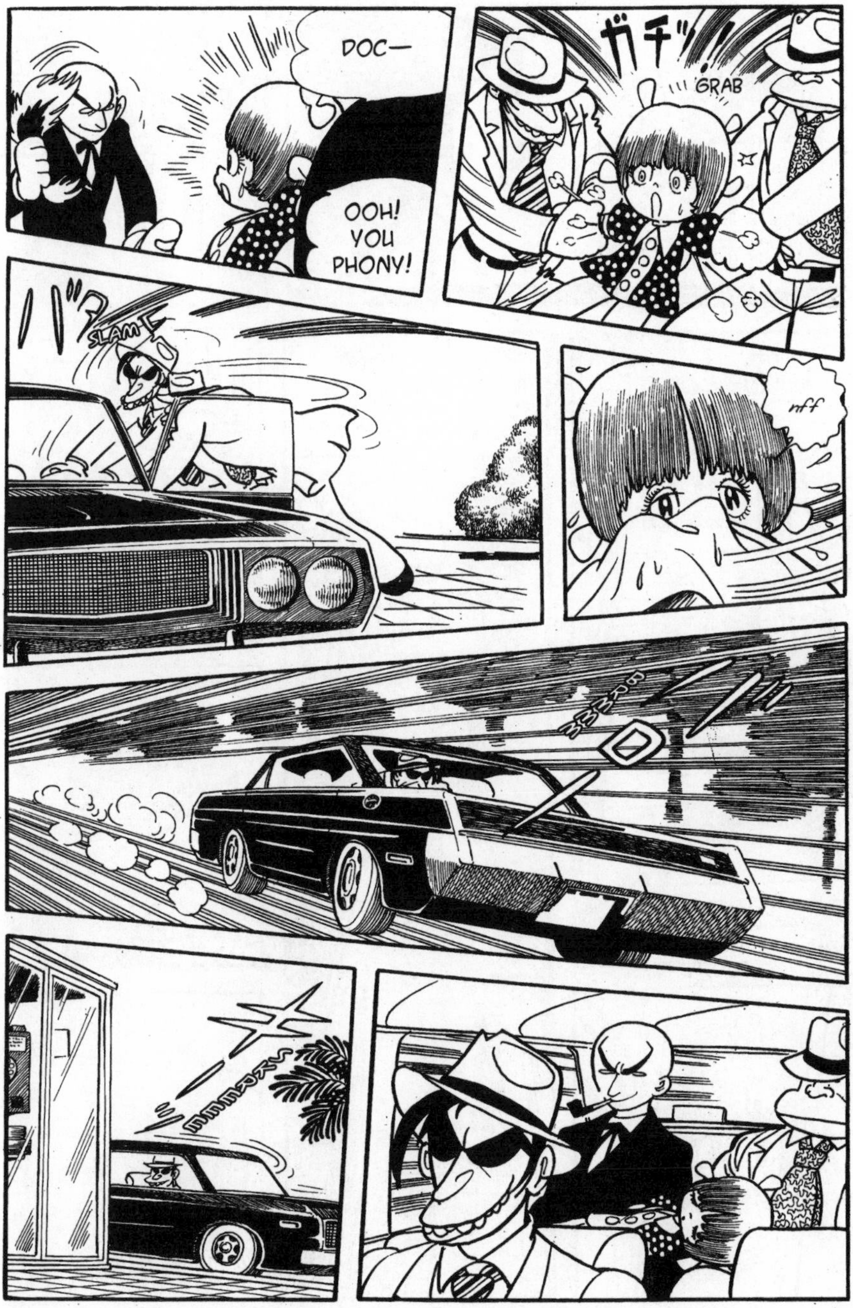
DOC—
OOH! YOU PHONY!
ガチッ
GRAB
SLAM
nff

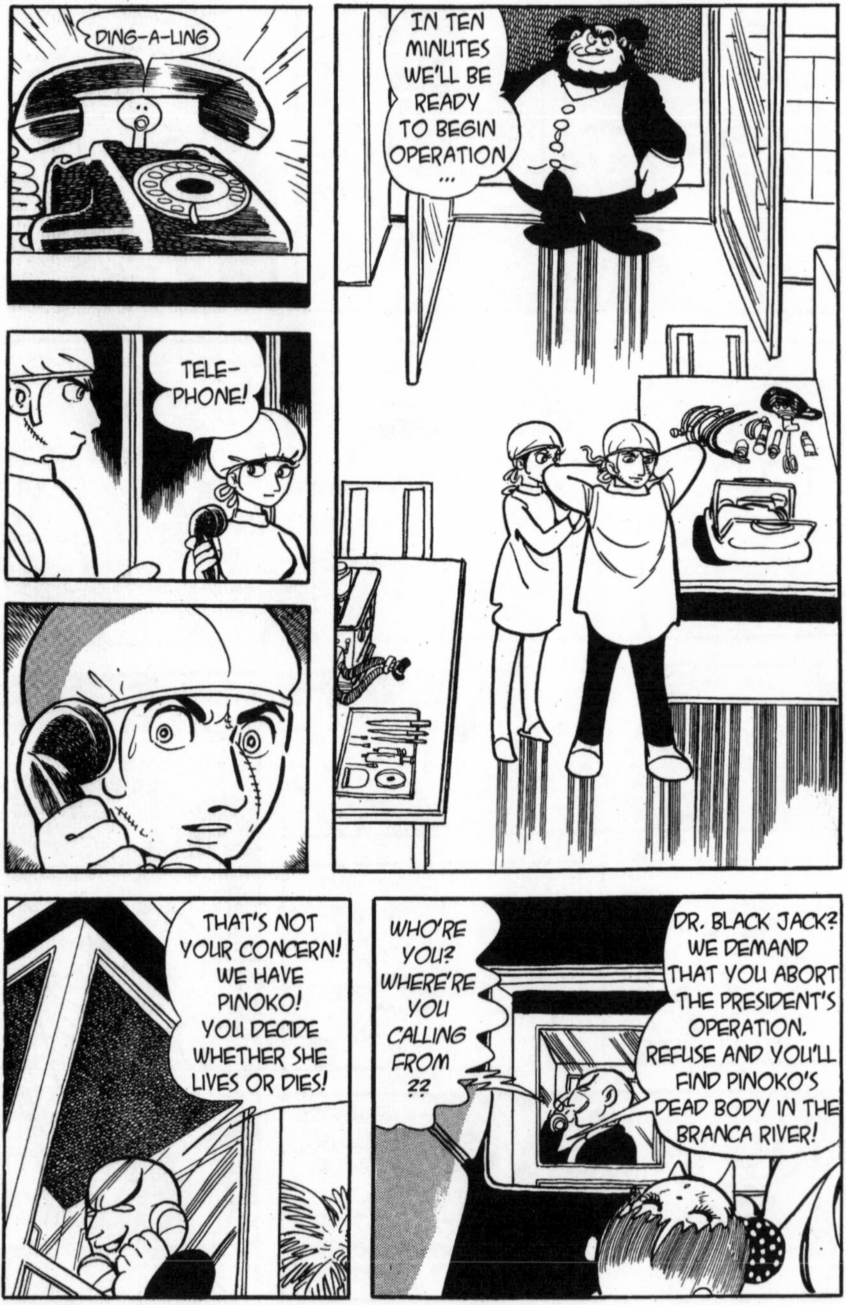
IN TEN MINUTES WE'LL BE READY TO BEGIN OPERATION ...
DING-A-LING
TELE-PHONE!
DR. BLACK JACK? WE DEMAND THAT YOU ABORT THE PRESIDENT'S OPERATION. REFUSE AND YOU'LL FIND PINOKO'S DEAD BODY IN THE BRANCA RIVER!
WHO'RE YOU? WHERE'RE YOU CALLING FROM ??
THAT'S NOT YOUR CONCERN! WE HAVE PINOKO! YOU DECIDE WHETHER SHE LIVES OR DIES!

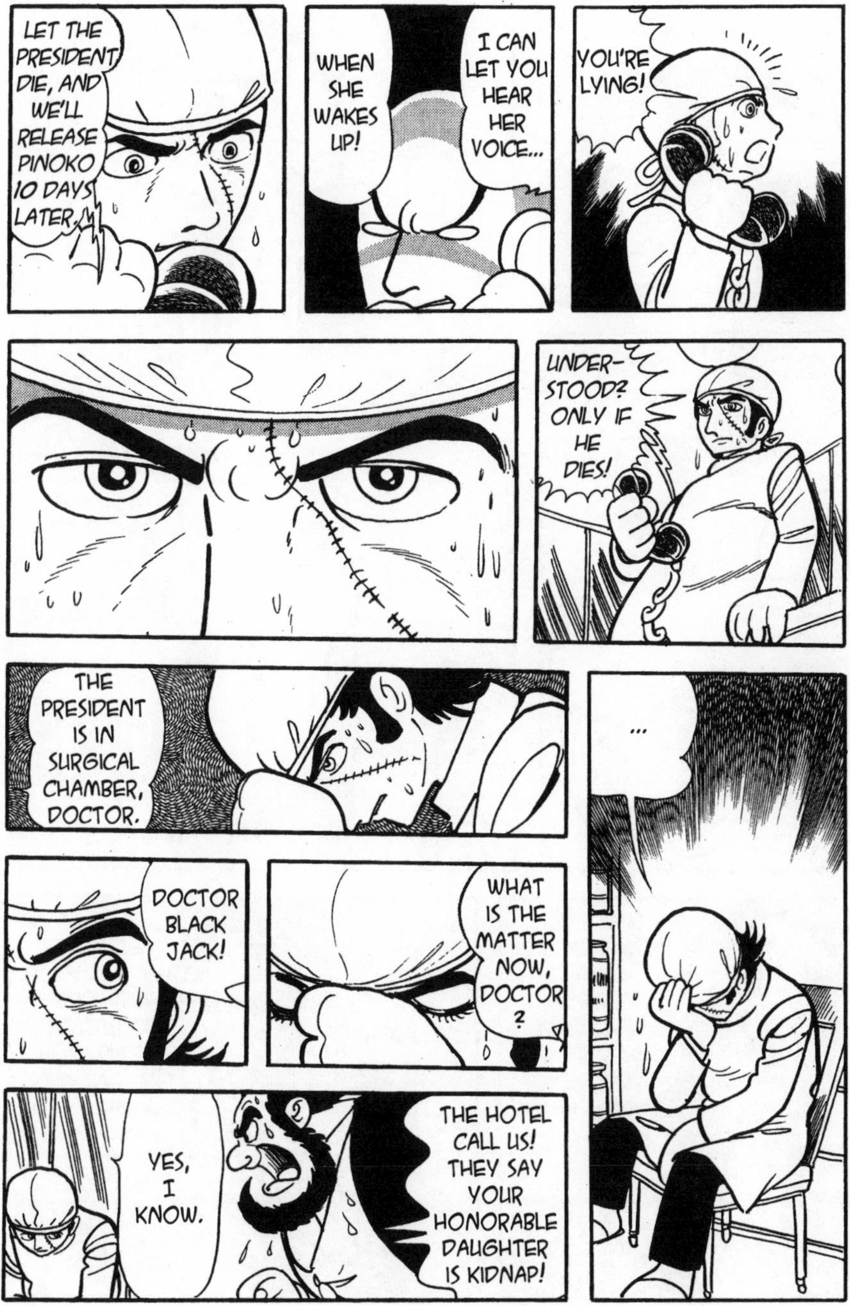
LET THE PRESIDENT DIE, AND WE'LL RELEASE PINOKO 10 DAYS LATER.
I CAN LET YOU HEAR HER VOICE...
WHEN SHE WAKES UP!
YOU'RE LYING!
UNDER-STOOD? ONLY IF HE DIES!
THE PRESIDENT IS IN SURGICAL CHAMBER, DOCTOR.
DOCTOR BLACK JACK!
WHAT IS THE MATTER NOW, DOCTOR?
THE HOTEL CALL US! THEY SAY YOUR HONORABLE DAUGHTER IS KIDNAP!
YES, I KNOW.
...

TERRIBLE! KIDNAPPER MUST BE ONE OF THE ASSASSINS!
THEY TOLD ME TO ABORT THE OPERATION IF I WANT HER BACK ALIVE.
THIS IS DISASTER!
IF OUR ILLUSTRIOUS PRESIDENT DIES, OUR GOVERNMENT WILL COLLAPSE!
DO I LET PINOKO DIE, OR THE PRESIDENT ?
PINOKO'S ONLY MY DAUGHTER
WHILE THE PRESIDENT'S LIFE IS WORTH 200,000 DOLLARS!
I'VE MADE UP MY MIND.
I'LL PERFORM THE OPERATION!
B-BUT... THEY WILL KILL PINOKO...!
THERE'S NO WAY I'M GIVING UP ON $200,000, HEH-HEH-HEH!

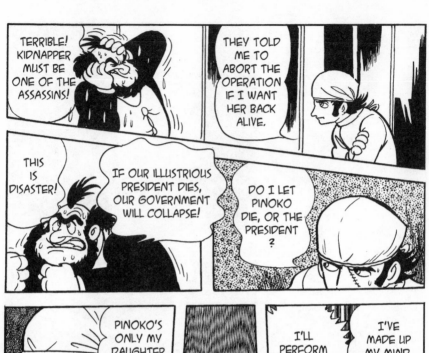

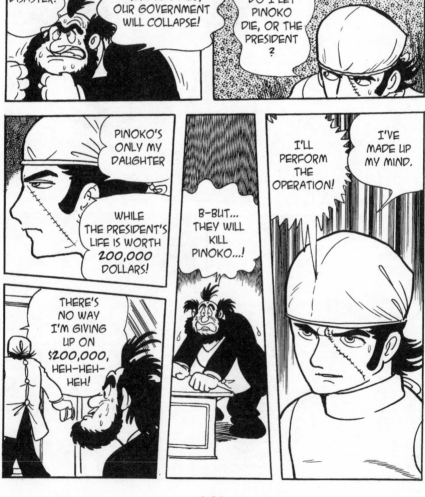

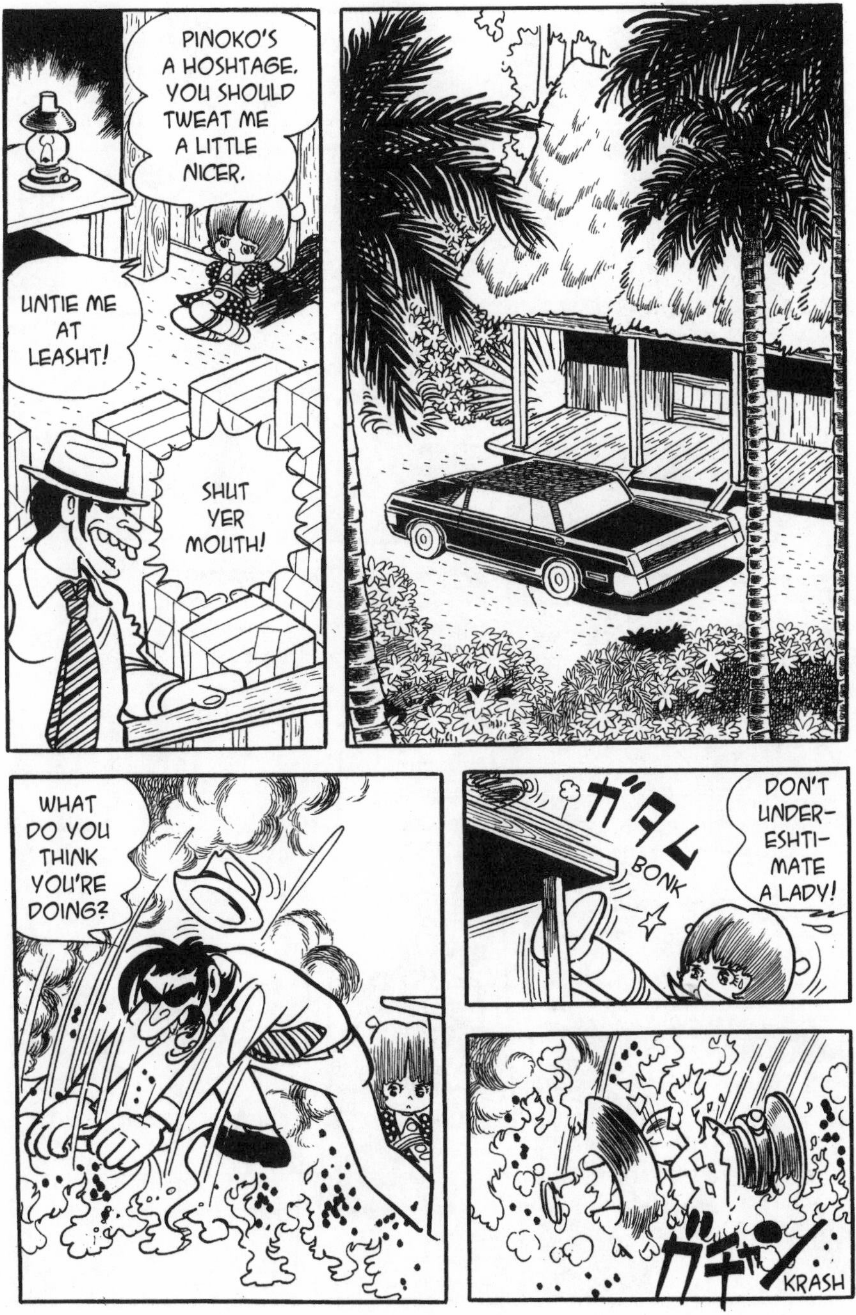
PINOKO'S A HOSHTAGE. YOU SHOULD TWEAT ME A LITTLE NICER.
UNTIE ME AT LEASHT!
SHUT YER MOUTH!
ガタム
BONK
DON'T UNDER-ESHTI-MATE A LADY!
ガチャン
KRASH
WHAT DO YOU THINK YOU'RE DOING?

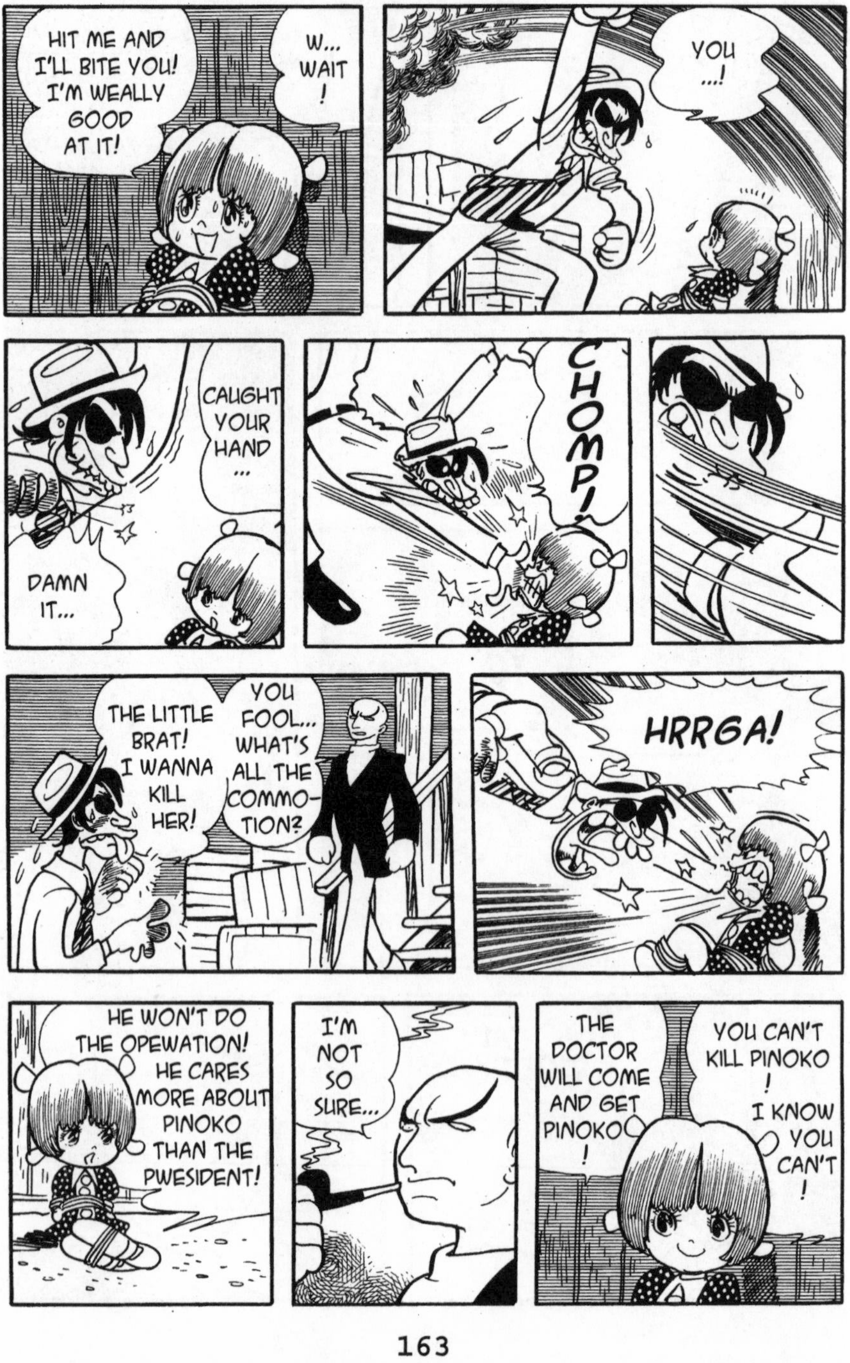
HIT ME AND I'LL BITE YOU! I'M WEALLY GOOD AT IT!
W... WAIT !
YOU ...!
CAUGHT YOUR HAND ...
DAMN IT...
CHOMP!
THE LITTLE BRAT! I WANNA KILL HER!
YOU FOOL... WHAT'S ALL THE COMMOTION?
HRRGA!
HE WON'T DO THE OPEWATION! HE CARES MORE ABOUT PINOKO THAN THE PWESIDENT!
I'M NOT SO SURE...
THE DOCTOR WILL COME AND GET PINOKO !
YOU CAN'T KILL PINOKO ! I KNOW YOU CAN'T !

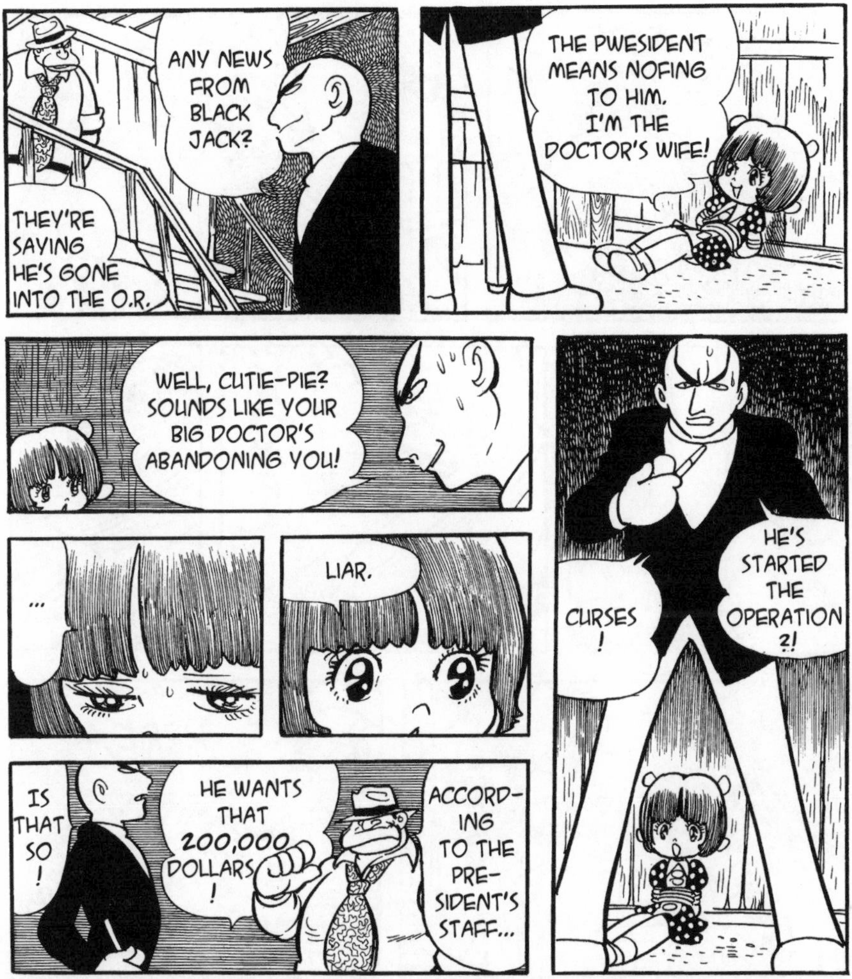
THE PWESIDENT MEANS NOFING TO HIM. I'M THE DOCTOR'S WIFE!
ANY NEWS FROM BLACK JACK?
THEY'RE SAYING HE'S GONE INTO THE O.R.
HE'S STARTED THE OPERATION ?!
CURSES !
WELL, CUTIE-PIE? SOUNDS LIKE YOUR BIG DOCTOR'S ABANDONING YOU!
LIAR.
...
ACCORD-ING TO THE PRE-SIDENT'S STAFF...
HE WANTS THAT 200,000 DOLLARS !
IS THAT SO !
GUESS HE CARES MORE ABOUT MONEY
THAN ABOUT YOUR LIFE.
THAT'S NOT TWUE!!
THE PWESIDENT'S MORE IMPORTANT THAN PINOKO!
FINK ABOUT IT A LITTLE !

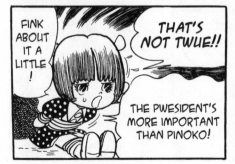

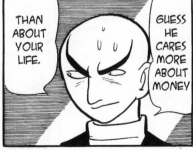

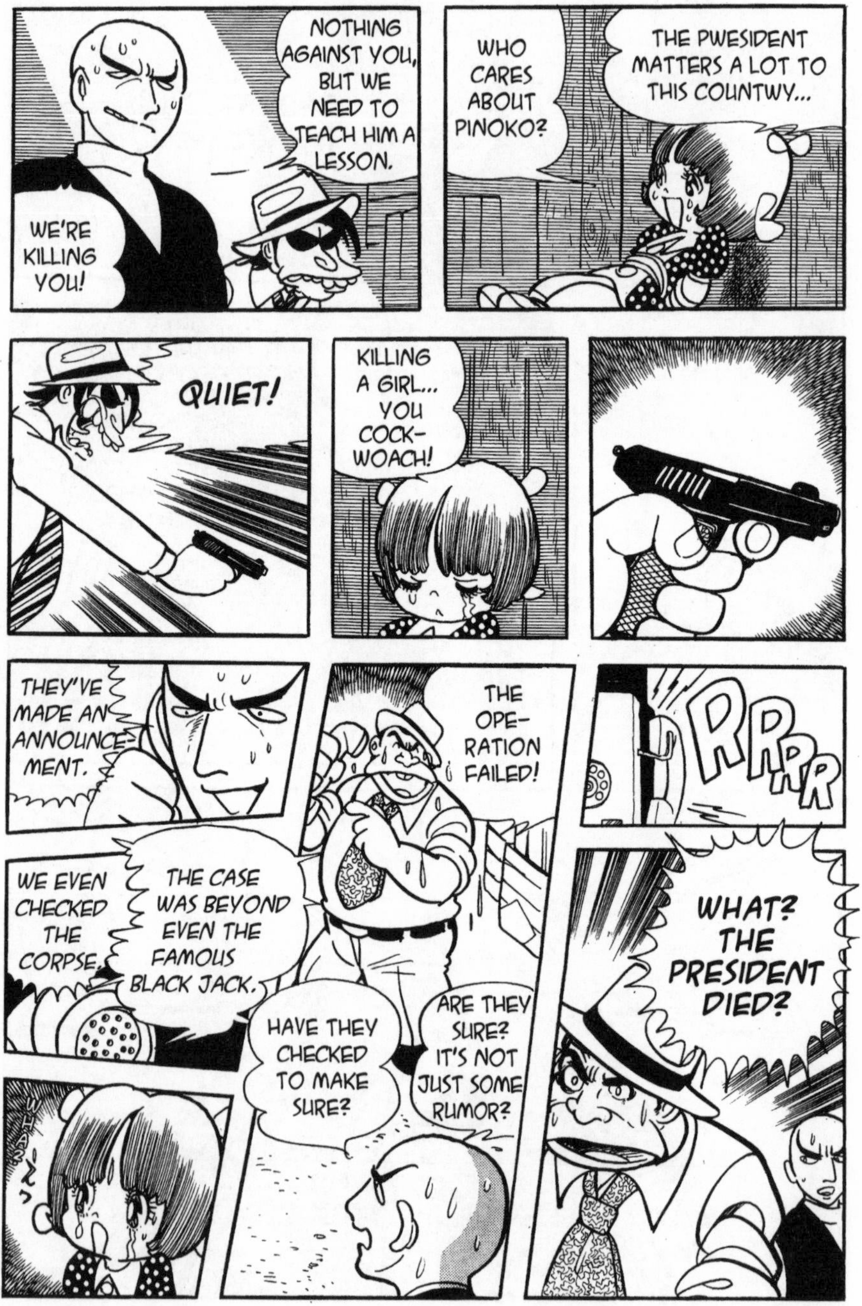
THE PWESIDENT MATTERS A LOT TO THIS COUNTWY...
WHO CARES ABOUT PINOKO?
NOTHING AGAINST YOU, BUT WE NEED TO TEACH HIM A LESSON.
WE'RE KILLING YOU!
KILLING A GIRL... YOU COCK-WOACH!
QUIET!
RRRRR
THE OPE-RATION FAILED!
THEY'VE MADE AN ANNOUNCE-MENT.
WHAT? THE PRESIDENT DIED?
ARE THEY SURE? IT'S NOT JUST SOME RUMOR?
HAVE THEY CHECKED TO MAKE SURE?
THE CASE WAS BEYOND EVEN THE FAMOUS BLACK JACK.
WE EVEN CHECKED THE CORPSE.

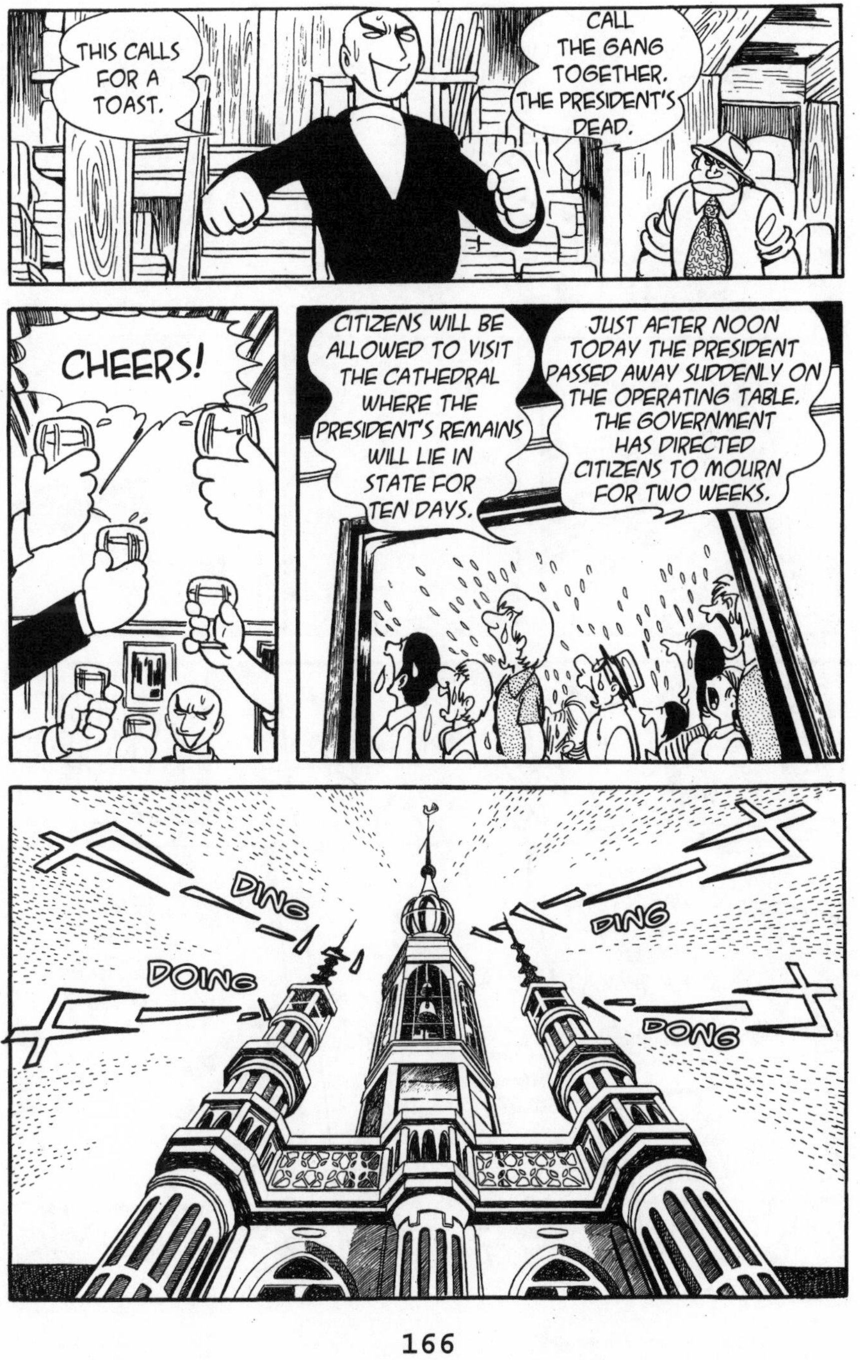
CALL THE GANG TOGETHER. THE PRESIDENT'S DEAD.
THIS CALLS FOR A TOAST.
JUST AFTER NOON TODAY THE PRESIDENT PASSED AWAY SUDDENLY ON THE OPERATING TABLE. THE GOVERNMENT HAS DIRECTED CITIZENS TO MOURN FOR TWO WEEKS.
CITIZENS WILL BE ALLOWED TO VISIT THE CATHEDRAL WHERE THE PRESIDENT'S REMAINS WILL LIE IN STATE FOR TEN DAYS.
CHEERS!
DING
DING
DOING
DONG

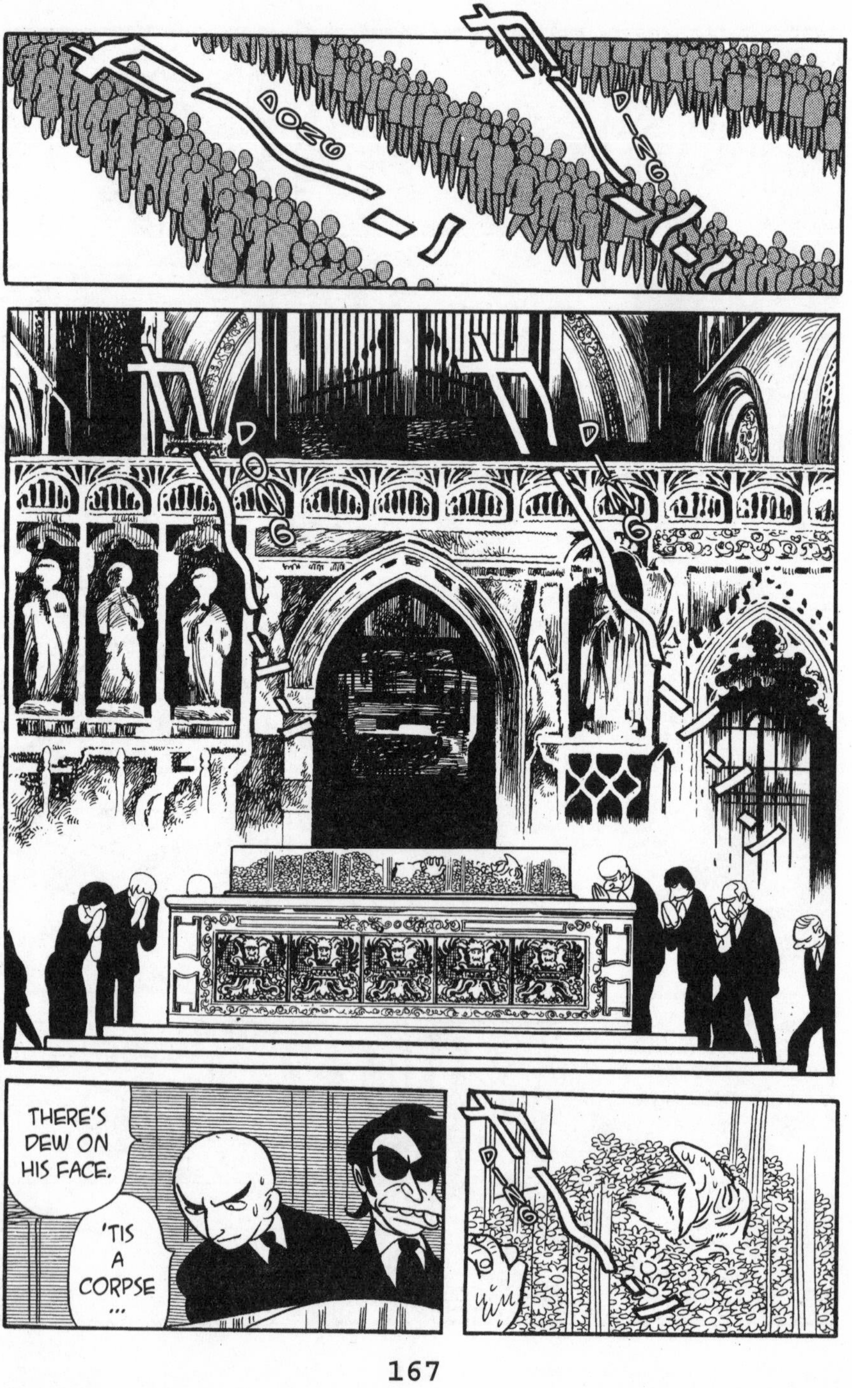
DING
DONG
DING
DONG
DING
THERE'S DEW ON HIS FACE.
'TIS A CORPSE ...

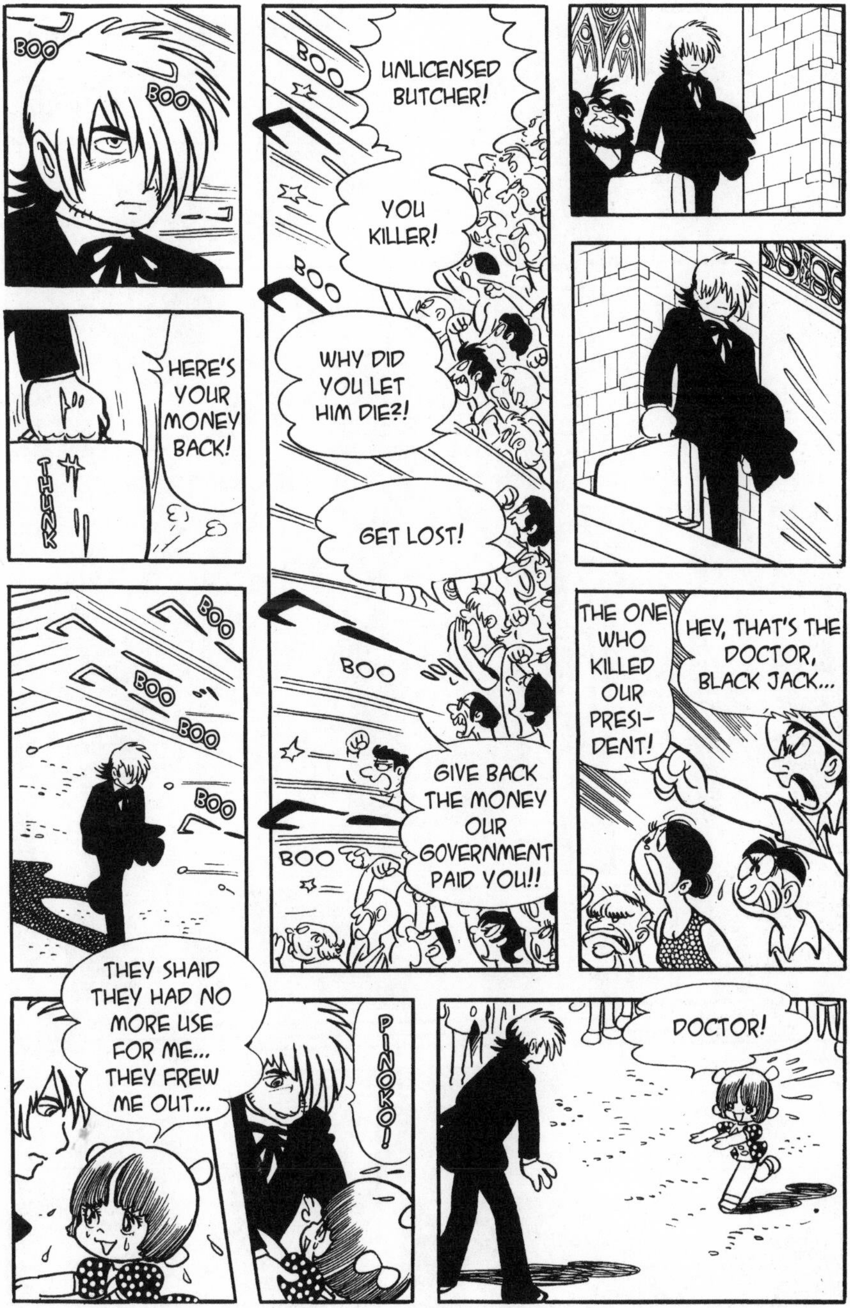
HEY, THAT'S THE DOCTOR, BLACK JACK...
THE ONE WHO KILLED OUR PRESI-DENT!
BOO
UNLICENSED BUTCHER!
YOU KILLER!
BOO
WHY DID YOU LET HIM DIE?!
GET LOST!
BOO
GIVE BACK THE MONEY OUR GOVERNMENT PAID YOU!!
BOO
BOO
BOO
HERE'S YOUR MONEY BACK!
THUNK
BOO
BOO
BOO
BOO
DOCTOR!
PINOKO!
THEY SHAID THEY HAD NO MORE USE FOR ME... THEY FREW ME OUT...

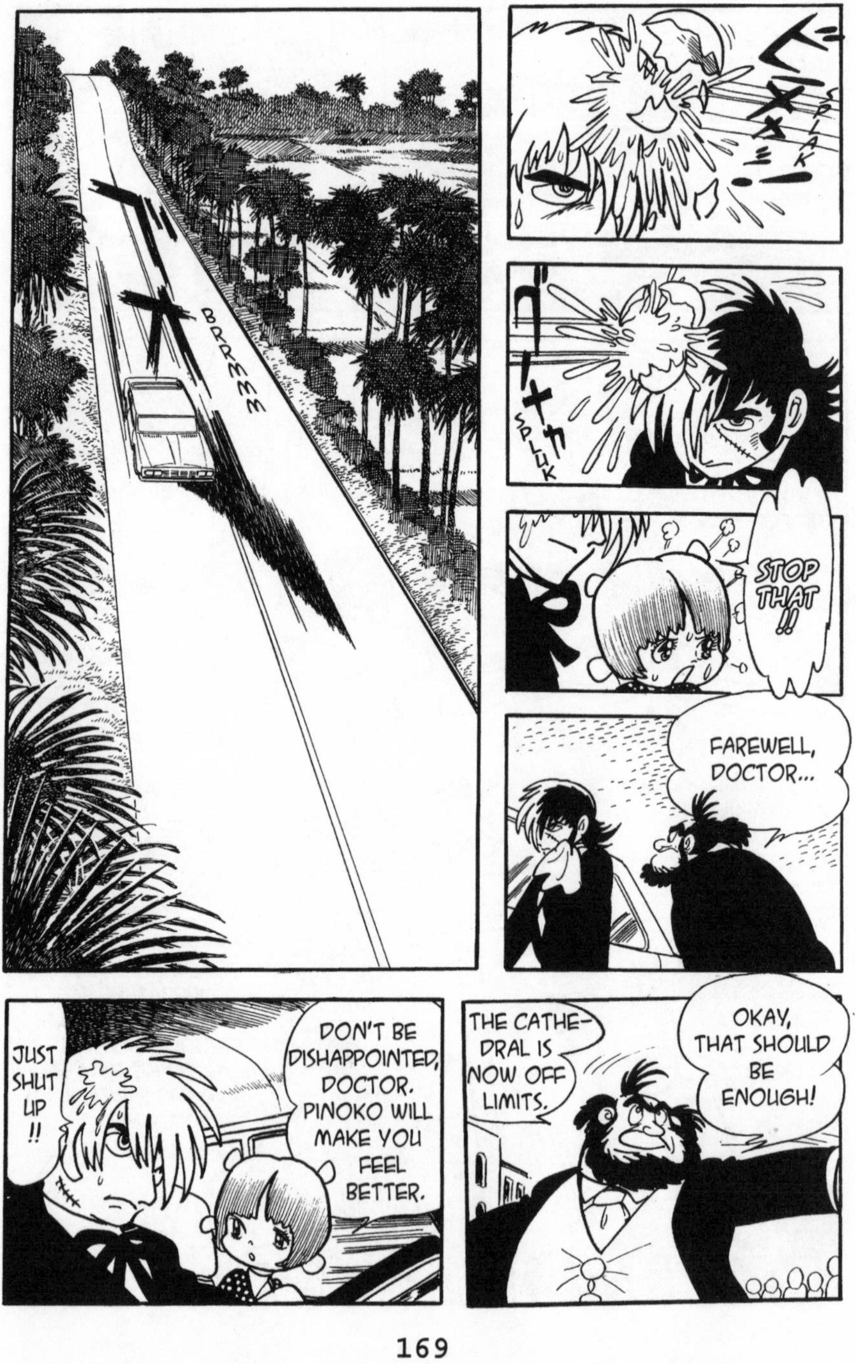
SPLAK
SPLUK
STOP THAT !!
FAREWELL, DOCTOR...
BRRMMM
OKAY, THAT SHOULD BE ENOUGH!
THE CATHE-DRAL IS NOW OFF LIMITS.
DON'T BE DISHAPPOINTED, DOCTOR. PINOKO WILL MAKE YOU FEEL BETTER.
JUST SHUT UP !!

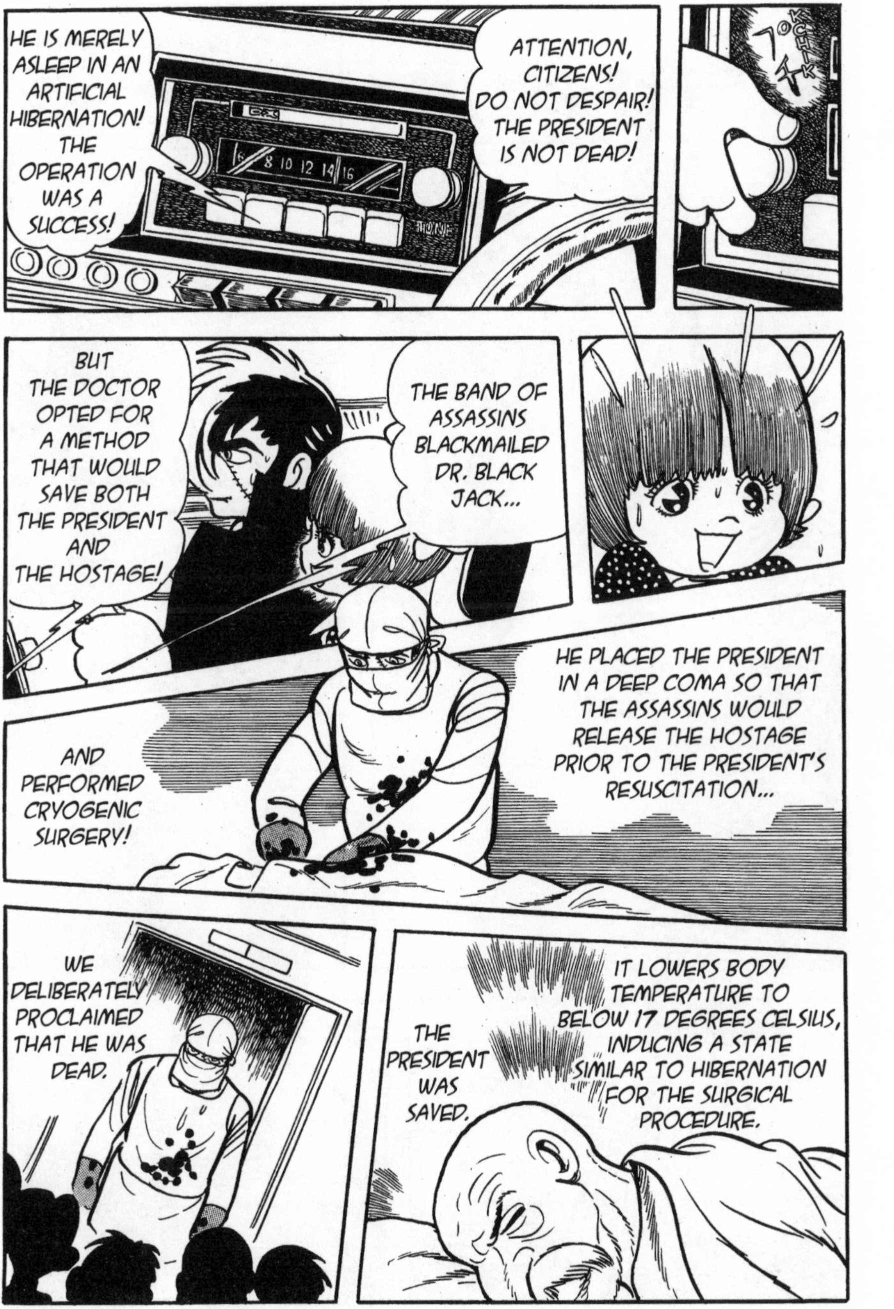
KCHIK
ATTENTION, CITIZENS! DO NOT DESPAIR! THE PRESIDENT IS NOT DEAD!
HE IS MERELY ASLEEP IN AN ARTIFICIAL HIBERNATION! THE OPERATION WAS A SUCCESS!
THE BAND OF ASSASSINS BLACKMAILED DR. BLACK JACK...
BUT THE DOCTOR OPTED FOR A METHOD THAT WOULD SAVE BOTH THE PRESIDENT AND THE HOSTAGE!
HE PLACED THE PRESIDENT IN A DEEP COMA SO THAT THE ASSASSINS WOULD RELEASE THE HOSTAGE PRIOR TO THE PRESIDENT'S RESUSCITATION...
AND PERFORMED CRYOGENIC SURGERY!
IT LOWERS BODY TEMPERATURE TO BELOW 17 DEGREES CELSIUS, INDUCING A STATE SIMILAR TO HIBERNATION FOR THE SURGICAL PROCEDURE.
THE PRESIDENT WAS SAVED.
WE DELIBERATELY PROCLAIMED THAT HE WAS DEAD.

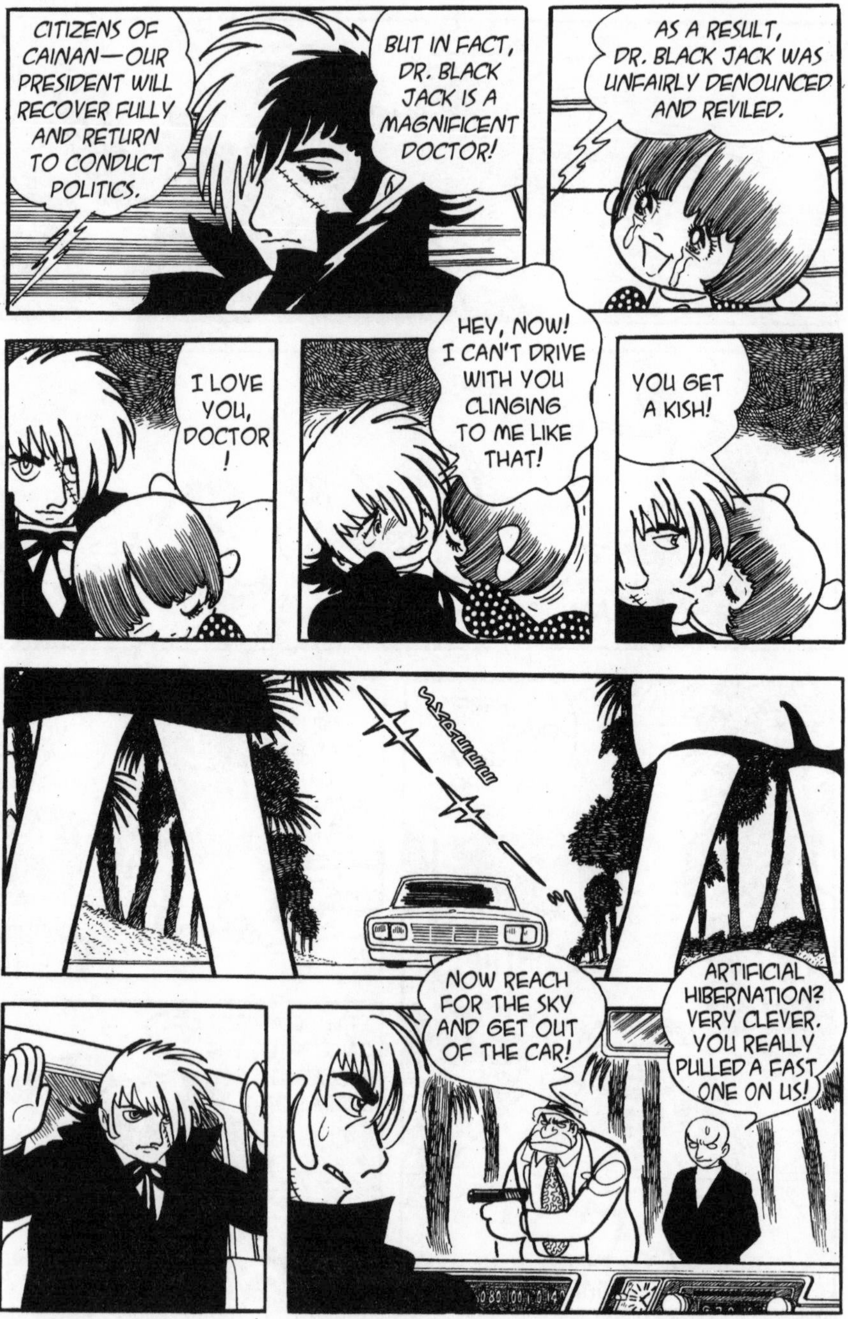
CITIZENS OF CAINAN—OUR PRESIDENT WILL RECOVER FULLY AND RETURN TO CONDUCT POLITICS.
BUT IN FACT, DR. BLACK JACK IS A MAGNIFICENT DOCTOR!
AS A RESULT, DR. BLACK JACK WAS UNFAIRLY DENOUNCED AND REVILED.
I LOVE YOU, DOCTOR!
HEY, NOW! I CAN'T DRIVE WITH YOU CLINGING TO ME LIKE THAT!
YOU GET A KISH!
NOW REACH FOR THE SKY AND GET OUT OF THE CAR!
ARTIFICIAL HIBERNATION? VERY CLEVER. YOU REALLY PULLED A FAST ONE ON US!

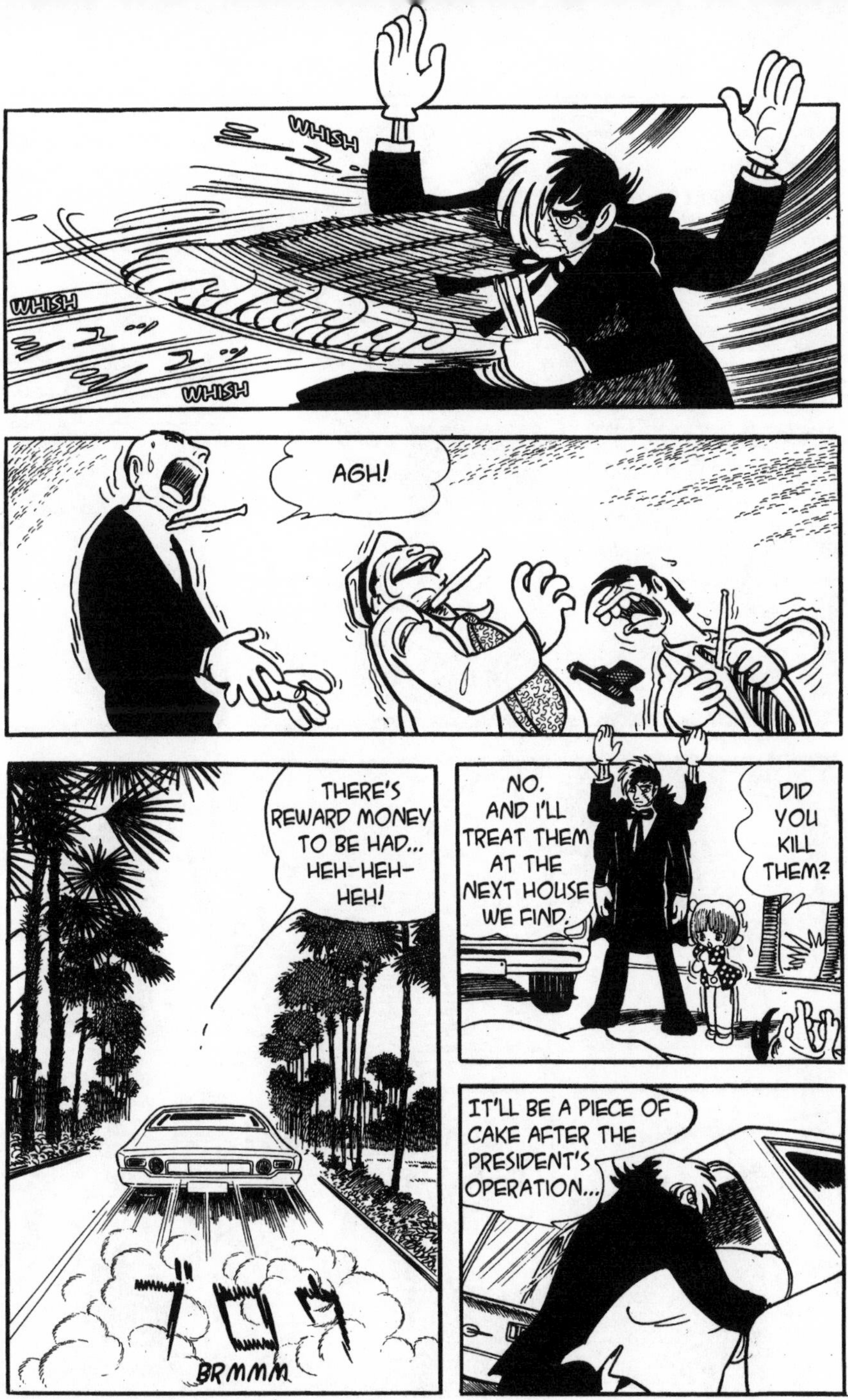
WHISH
WHISH
WHISH
AGH!
DID YOU KILL THEM?
NO. AND I'LL TREAT THEM AT THE NEXT HOUSE WE FIND.
IT'LL BE A PIECE OF CAKE AFTER THE PRESIDENT'S OPERATION...
THERE'S REWARD MONEY TO BE HAD... HEH-HEH-HEH!
BRMMM

ASSEMBLY LINE CARE

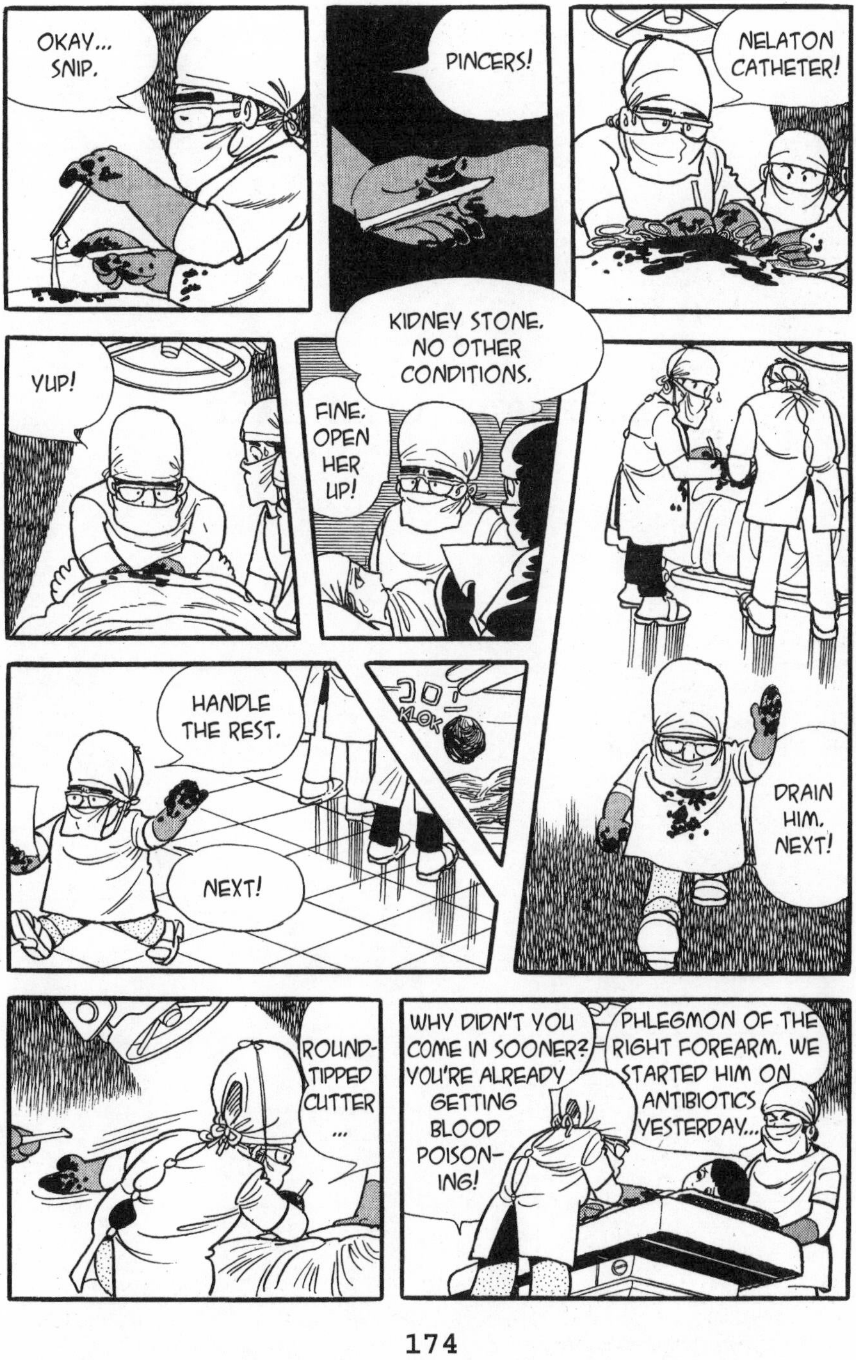
NELATON CATHETER!
PINCERS!
OKAY... SNIP.
DRAIN HIM. NEXT!
KIDNEY STONE. NO OTHER CONDITIONS.
FINE. OPEN HER UP!
YUP!
KLOK
HANDLE THE REST.
NEXT!
PHLEGMON OF THE RIGHT FOREARM. WE STARTED HIM ON ANTIBIOTICS YESTERDAY...
WHY DIDN'T YOU COME IN SOONER? YOU'RE ALREADY GETTING BLOOD POISONING!
ROUND-TIPPED CUTTER ...

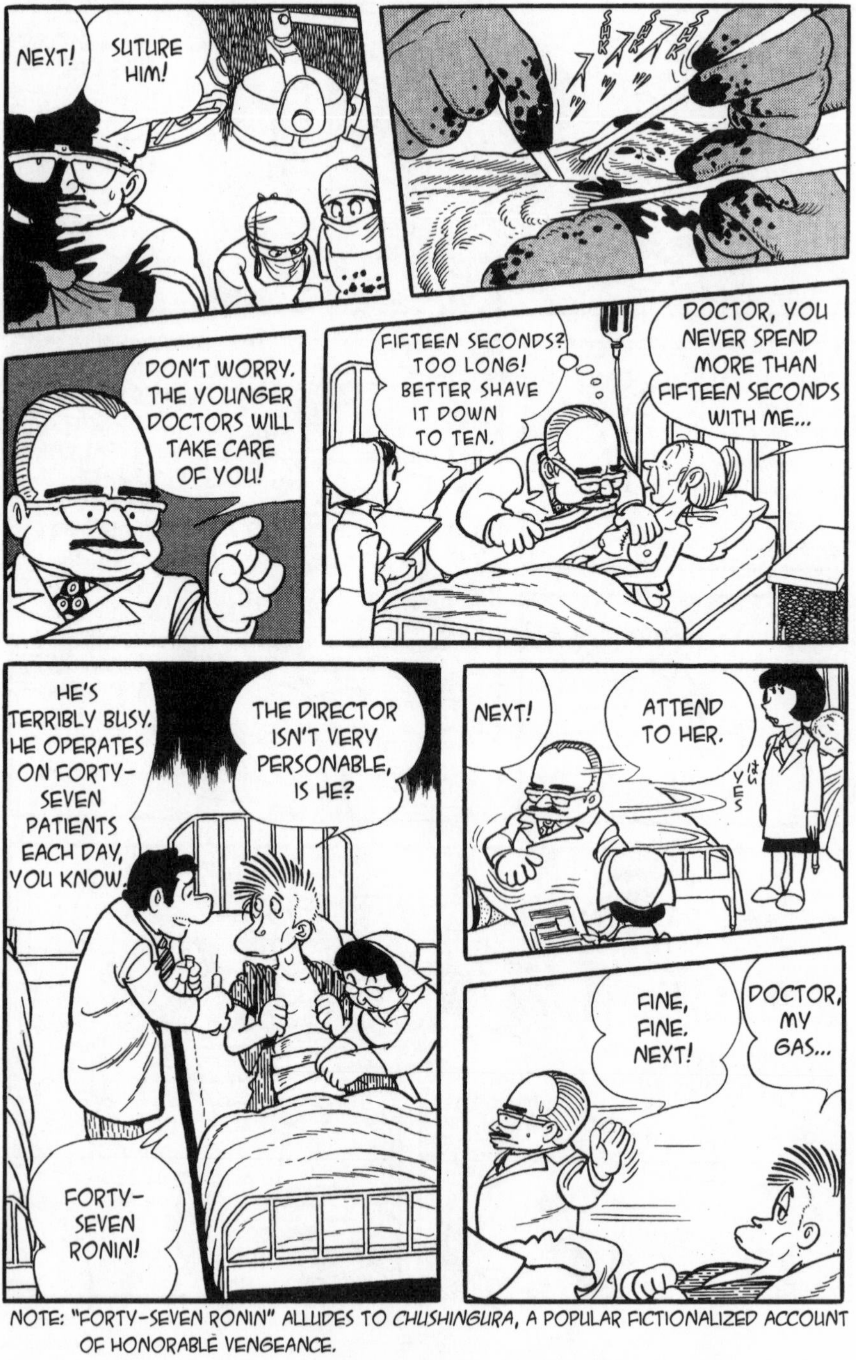
SHK SHK SHK
SUTURE HIM!
NEXT!
DOCTOR, YOU NEVER SPEND MORE THAN FIFTEEN SECONDS WITH ME...
FIFTEEN SECONDS? TOO LONG! BETTER SHAVE IT DOWN TO TEN.
DON'T WORRY. THE YOUNGER DOCTORS WILL TAKE CARE OF YOU!
ATTEND TO HER.
NEXT!
YES
DOCTOR, MY GAS...
FINE, FINE. NEXT!
THE DIRECTOR ISN'T VERY PERSONABLE, IS HE?
HE'S TERRIBLY BUSY. HE OPERATES ON FORTY-SEVEN PATIENTS EACH DAY, YOU KNOW.
FORTY-SEVEN RONIN!

NOTE: "FORTY-SEVEN RONIN" ALLUDES TO *CHUSHINGURA*, A POPULAR FICTIONALIZED ACCOUNT OF HONORABLE VENGEANCE.

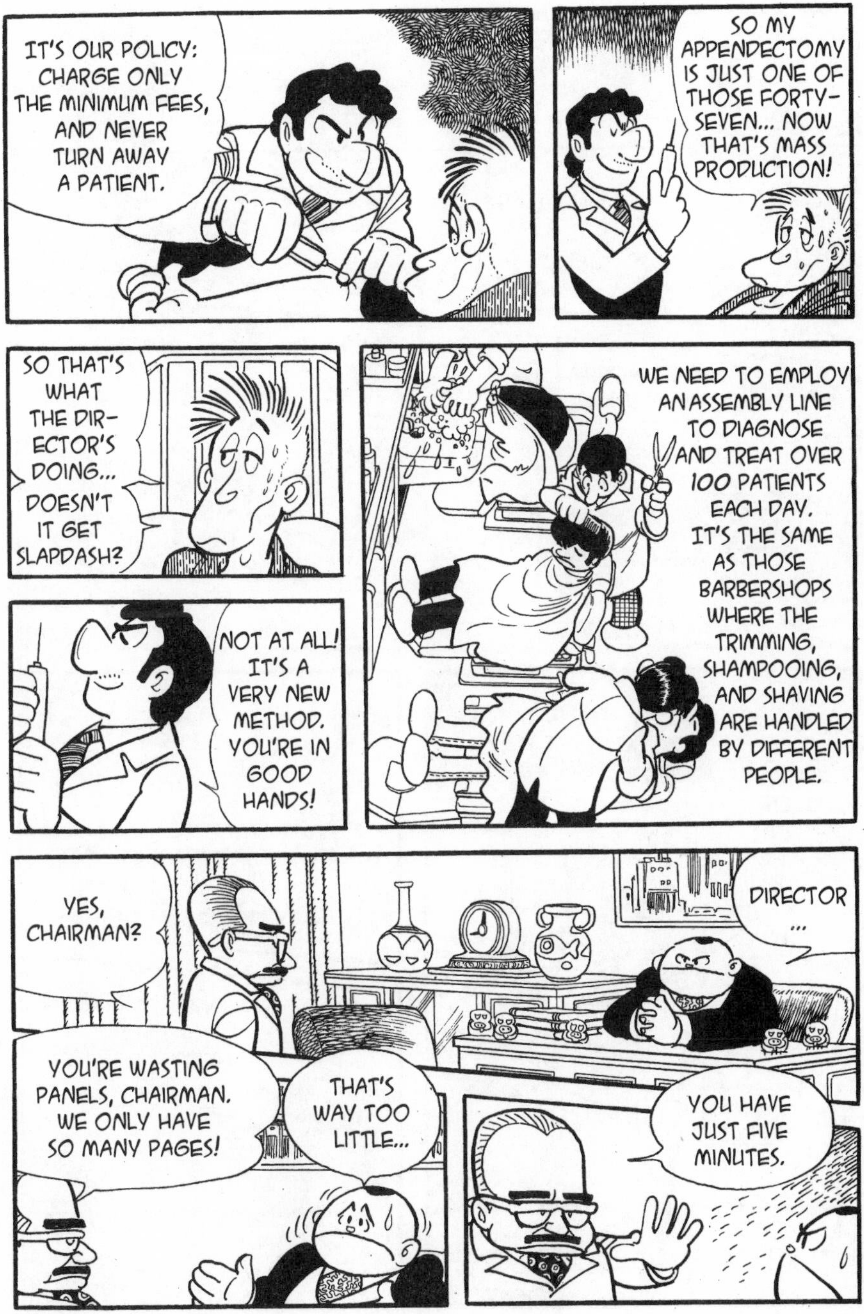
SO MY APPENDECTOMY IS JUST ONE OF THOSE FORTY-SEVEN... NOW THAT'S MASS PRODUCTION!
IT'S OUR POLICY: CHARGE ONLY THE MINIMUM FEES, AND NEVER TURN AWAY A PATIENT.
WE NEED TO EMPLOY AN ASSEMBLY LINE TO DIAGNOSE AND TREAT OVER 100 PATIENTS EACH DAY. IT'S THE SAME AS THOSE BARBERSHOPS WHERE THE TRIMMING, SHAMPOOING, AND SHAVING ARE HANDLED BY DIFFERENT PEOPLE.
SO THAT'S WHAT THE DIRECTOR'S DOING... DOESN'T IT GET SLAPDASH?
NOT AT ALL! IT'S A VERY NEW METHOD. YOU'RE IN GOOD HANDS!
DIRECTOR ...
YES, CHAIRMAN?
YOU HAVE JUST FIVE MINUTES.
THAT'S WAY TOO LITTLE...
YOU'RE WASTING PANELS, CHAIRMAN. WE ONLY HAVE SO MANY PAGES!

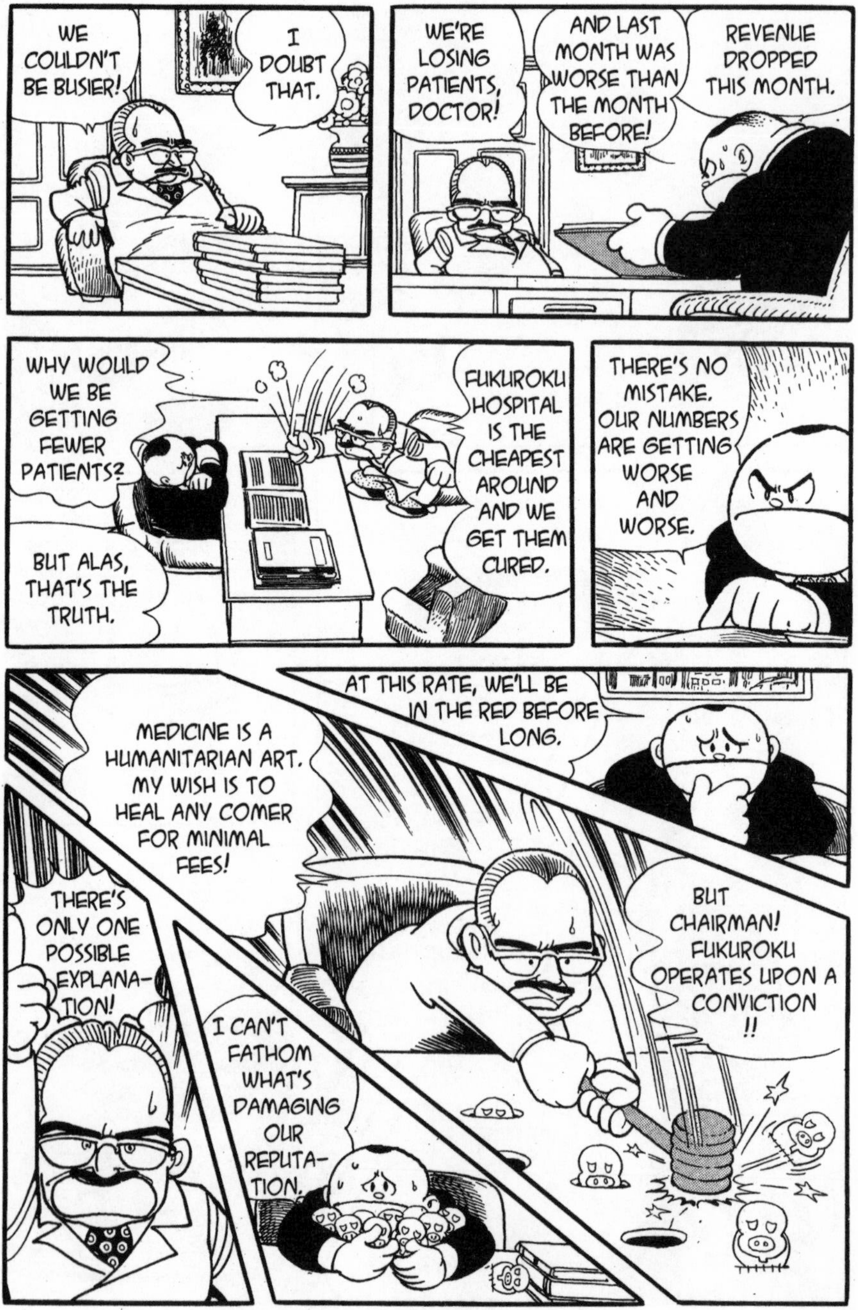
REVENUE DROPPED THIS MONTH.
AND LAST MONTH WAS WORSE THAN THE MONTH BEFORE!
WE'RE LOSING PATIENTS, DOCTOR!
I DOUBT THAT.
WE COULDN'T BE BUSIER!
THERE'S NO MISTAKE. OUR NUMBERS ARE GETTING WORSE AND WORSE.
FUKUROKU HOSPITAL IS THE CHEAPEST AROUND AND WE GET THEM CURED.
WHY WOULD WE BE GETTING FEWER PATIENTS?
BUT ALAS, THAT'S THE TRUTH.
AT THIS RATE, WE'LL BE IN THE RED BEFORE LONG.
MEDICINE IS A HUMANITARIAN ART. MY WISH IS TO HEAL ANY COMER FOR MINIMAL FEES!
BUT CHAIRMAN! FUKUROKU OPERATES UPON A CONVICTION !!
I CAN'T FATHOM WHAT'S DAMAGING OUR REPUTA-TION.
THERE'S ONLY ONE POSSIBLE EXPLANA-TION!

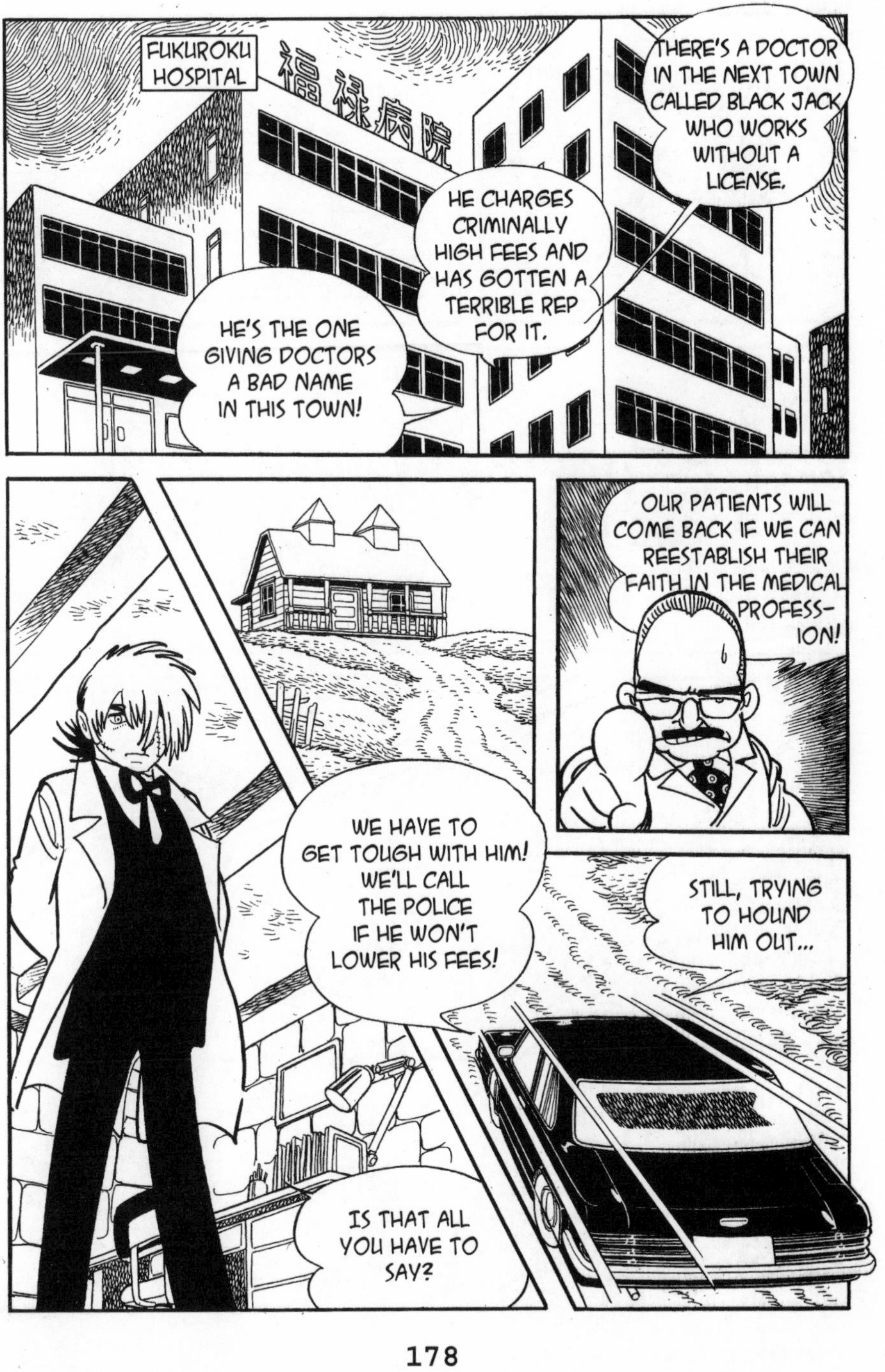
FUKUROKU HOSPITAL
福禄病院
THERE'S A DOCTOR IN THE NEXT TOWN CALLED BLACK JACK WHO WORKS WITHOUT A LICENSE.
HE CHARGES CRIMINALLY HIGH FEES AND HAS GOTTEN A TERRIBLE REP FOR IT.
HE'S THE ONE GIVING DOCTORS A BAD NAME IN THIS TOWN!
OUR PATIENTS WILL COME BACK IF WE CAN REESTABLISH THEIR FAITH IN THE MEDICAL PROFESS-ION!
WE HAVE TO GET TOUGH WITH HIM! WE'LL CALL THE POLICE IF HE WON'T LOWER HIS FEES!
STILL, TRYING TO HOUND HIM OUT...
IS THAT ALL YOU HAVE TO SAY?

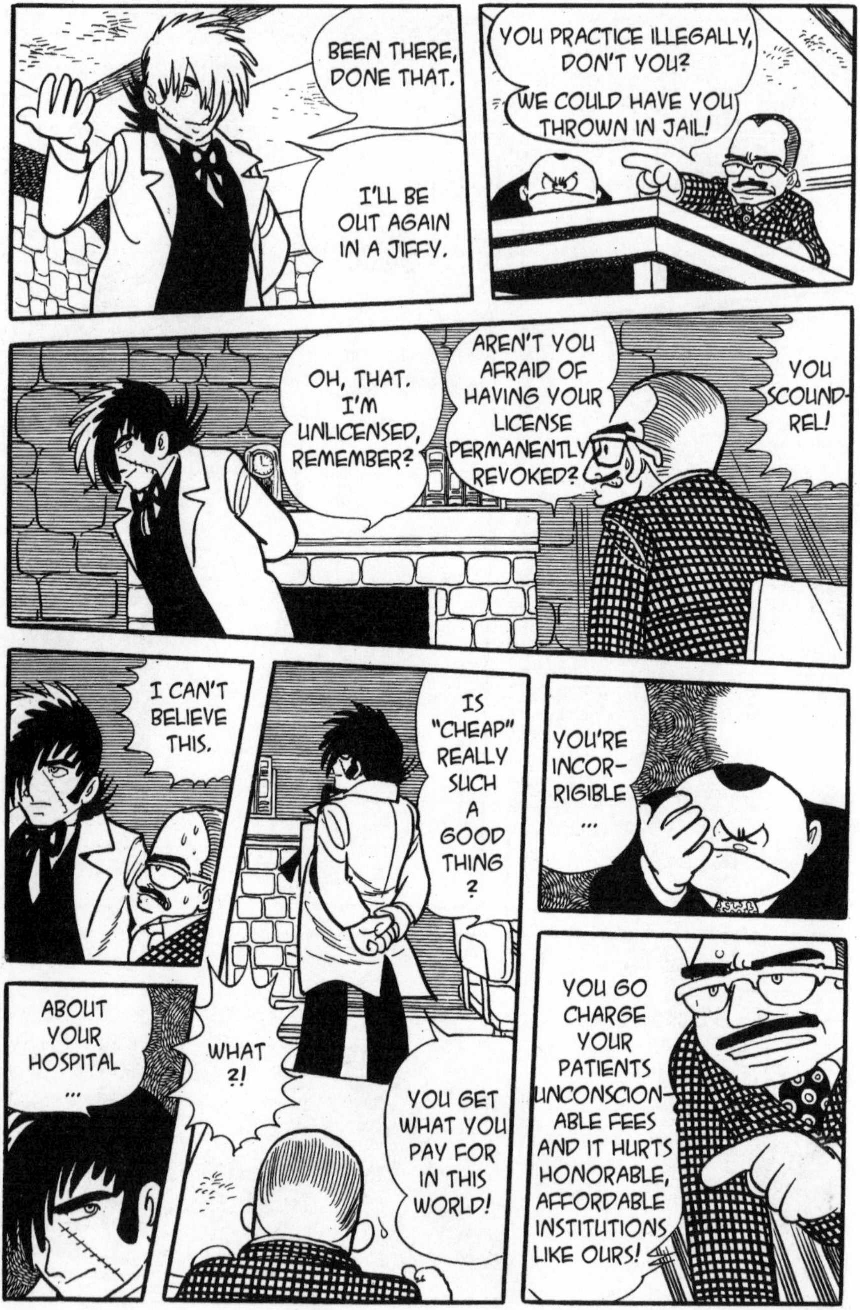
YOU PRACTICE ILLEGALLY, DON'T YOU?
WE COULD HAVE YOU THROWN IN JAIL!
BEEN THERE, DONE THAT.
I'LL BE OUT AGAIN IN A JIFFY.
YOU SCOUNDREL!
AREN'T YOU AFRAID OF HAVING YOUR LICENSE PERMANENTLY REVOKED?
OH, THAT. I'M UNLICENSED, REMEMBER?
YOU'RE INCORRIGIBLE ...
YOU GO CHARGE YOUR PATIENTS UNCONSCIONABLE FEES AND IT HURTS HONORABLE, AFFORDABLE INSTITUTIONS LIKE OURS!
IS "CHEAP" REALLY SUCH A GOOD THING?
YOU GET WHAT YOU PAY FOR IN THIS WORLD!
I CAN'T BELIEVE THIS.
ABOUT YOUR HOSPITAL ...
WHAT?!

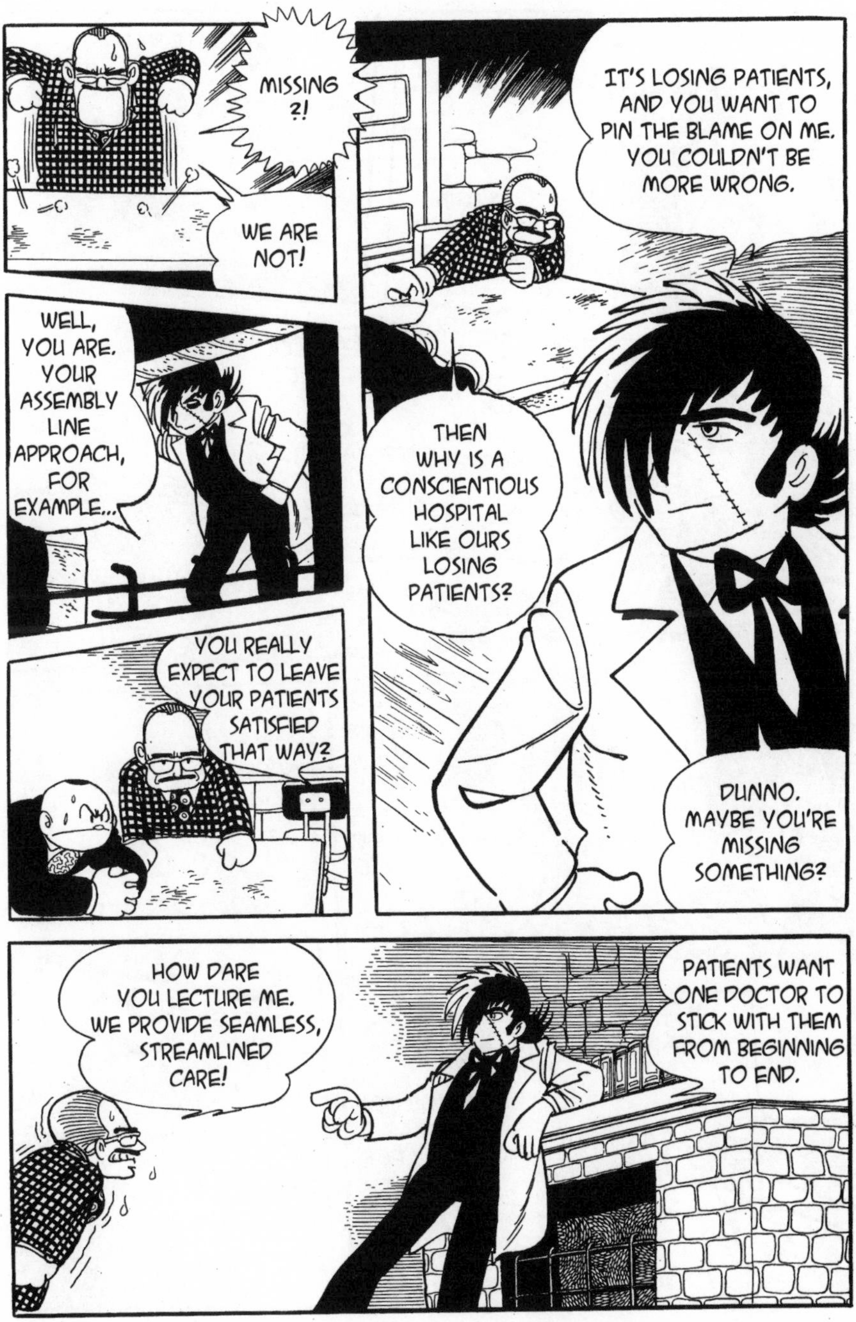
IT'S LOSING PATIENTS, AND YOU WANT TO PIN THE BLAME ON ME. YOU COULDN'T BE MORE WRONG.
THEN WHY IS A CONSCIENTIOUS HOSPITAL LIKE OURS LOSING PATIENTS?
DUNNO. MAYBE YOU'RE MISSING SOMETHING?
MISSING ?!
WE ARE NOT!
WELL, YOU ARE. YOUR ASSEMBLY LINE APPROACH, FOR EXAMPLE...
YOU REALLY EXPECT TO LEAVE YOUR PATIENTS SATISFIED THAT WAY?
PATIENTS WANT ONE DOCTOR TO STICK WITH THEM FROM BEGINNING TO END.
HOW DARE YOU LECTURE ME. WE PROVIDE SEAMLESS, STREAMLINED CARE!

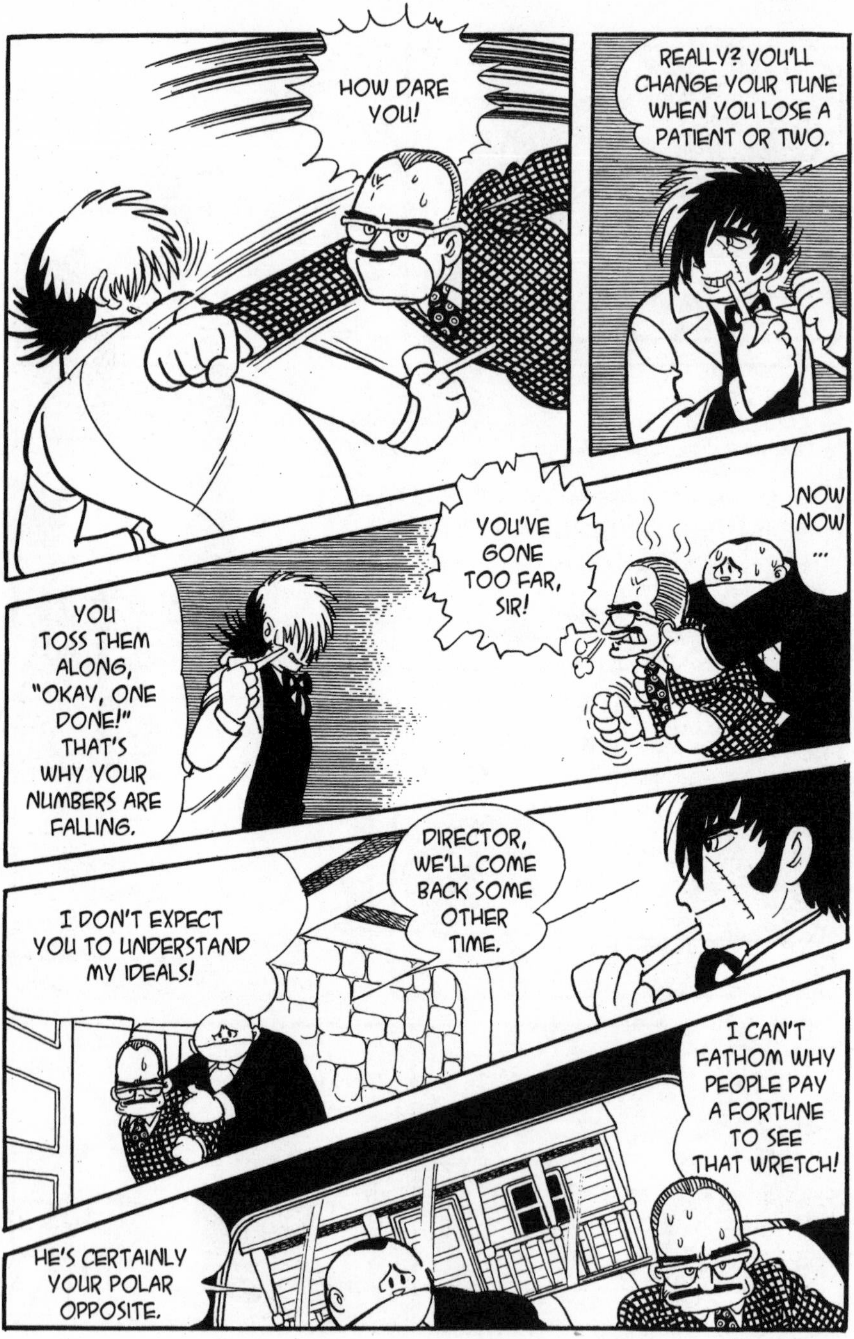
REALLY? YOU'LL CHANGE YOUR TUNE WHEN YOU LOSE A PATIENT OR TWO.
HOW DARE YOU!
NOW NOW ...
YOU'VE GONE TOO FAR, SIR!
YOU TOSS THEM ALONG, "OKAY, ONE DONE!" THAT'S WHY YOUR NUMBERS ARE FALLING.
DIRECTOR, WE'LL COME BACK SOME OTHER TIME.
I DON'T EXPECT YOU TO UNDERSTAND MY IDEALS!
I CAN'T FATHOM WHY PEOPLE PAY A FORTUNE TO SEE THAT WRETCH!
HE'S CERTAINLY YOUR POLAR OPPOSITE.

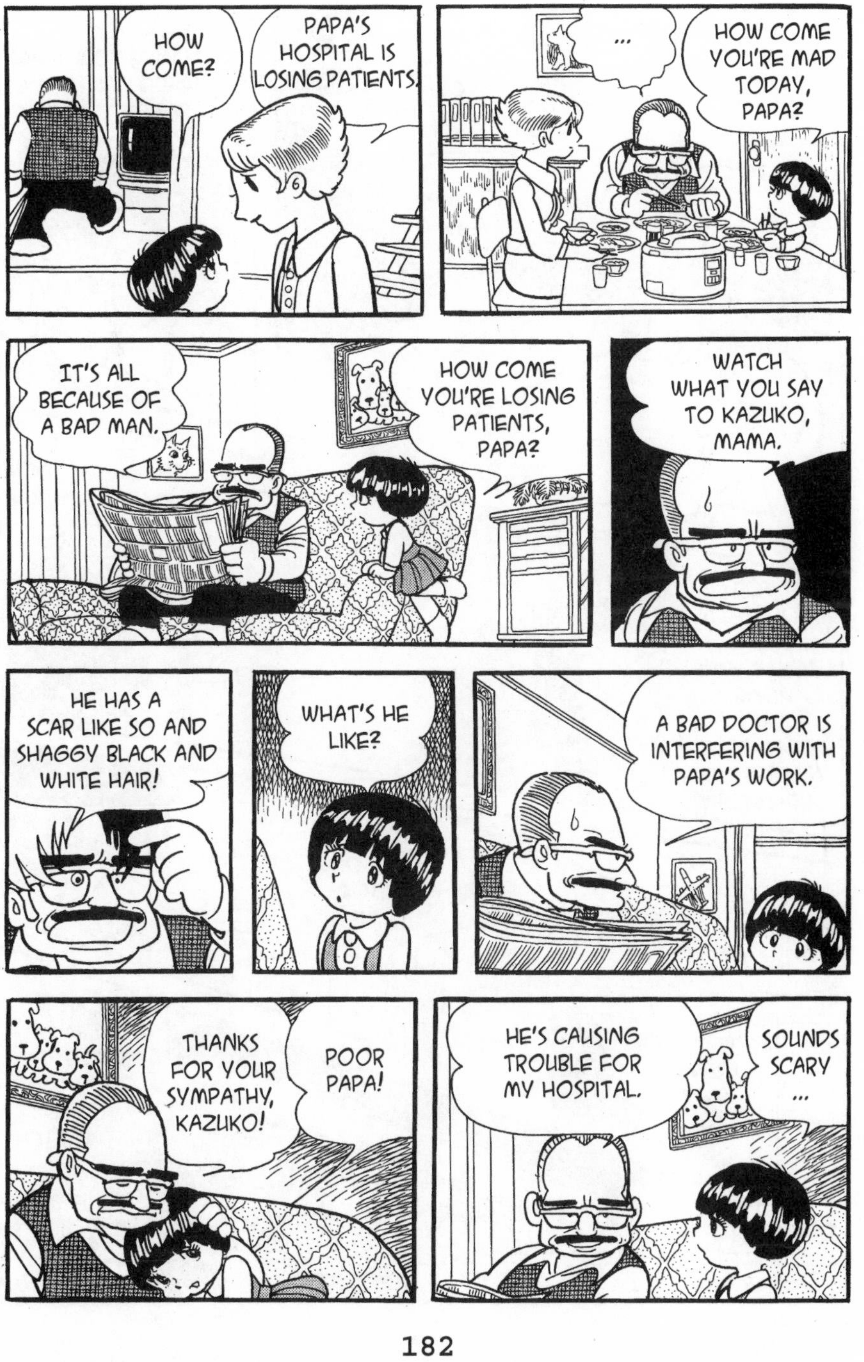
HOW COME YOU'RE MAD TODAY, PAPA?
...
PAPA'S HOSPITAL IS LOSING PATIENTS.
HOW COME?
WATCH WHAT YOU SAY TO KAZUKO, MAMA.
HOW COME YOU'RE LOSING PATIENTS, PAPA?
IT'S ALL BECAUSE OF A BAD MAN.
A BAD DOCTOR IS INTERFERING WITH PAPA'S WORK.
WHAT'S HE LIKE?
HE HAS A SCAR LIKE SO AND SHAGGY BLACK AND WHITE HAIR!
SOUNDS SCARY ...
HE'S CAUSING TROUBLE FOR MY HOSPITAL.
POOR PAPA!
THANKS FOR YOUR SYMPATHY, KAZUKO!

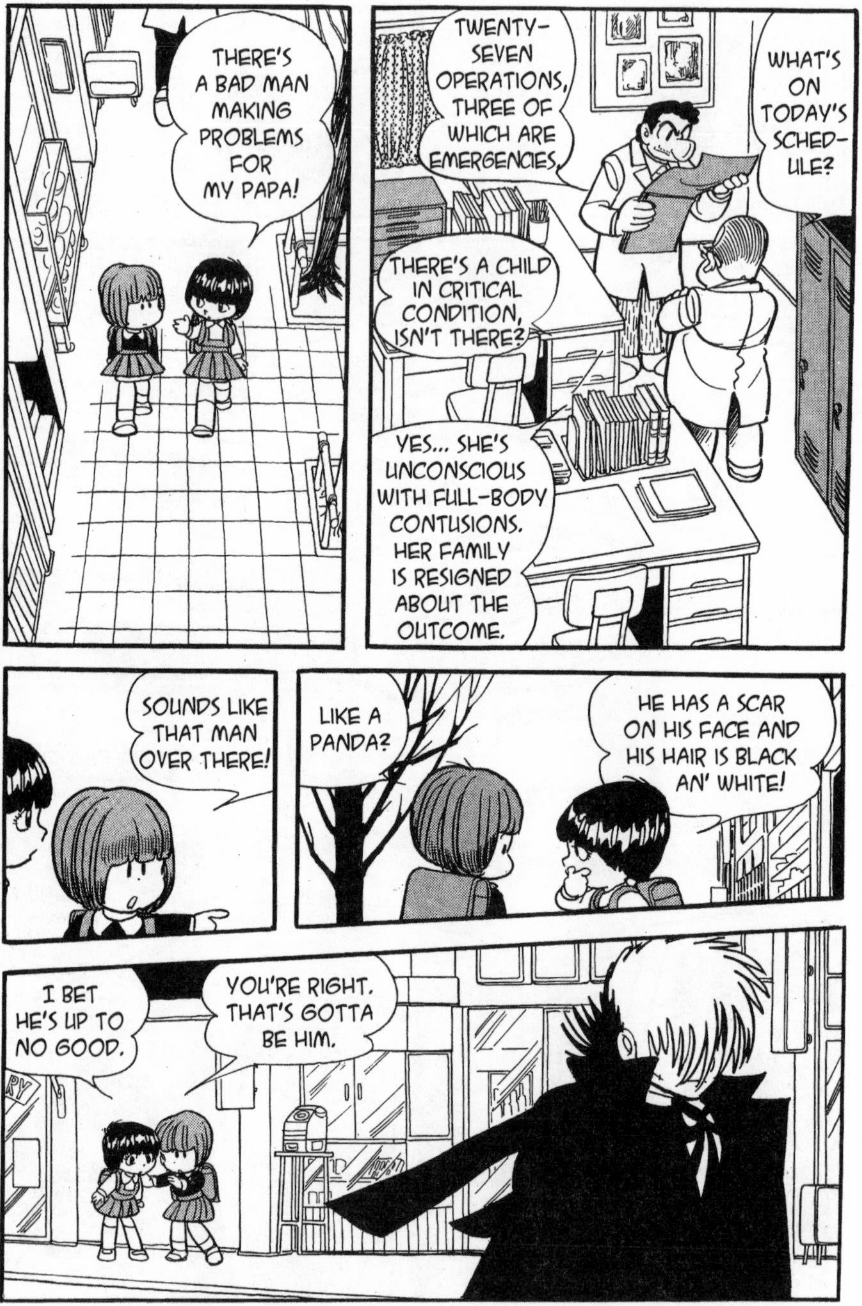
WHAT'S ON TODAY'S SCHED-ULE?
TWENTY-SEVEN OPERATIONS, THREE OF WHICH ARE EMERGENCIES.
THERE'S A CHILD IN CRITICAL CONDITION, ISN'T THERE?
YES... SHE'S UNCONSCIOUS WITH FULL-BODY CONTUSIONS. HER FAMILY IS RESIGNED ABOUT THE OUTCOME.
THERE'S A BAD MAN MAKING PROBLEMS FOR MY PAPA!
HE HAS A SCAR ON HIS FACE AND HIS HAIR IS BLACK AN' WHITE!
LIKE A PANDA?
SOUNDS LIKE THAT MAN OVER THERE!
YOU'RE RIGHT. THAT'S GOTTA BE HIM.
I BET HE'S UP TO NO GOOD.

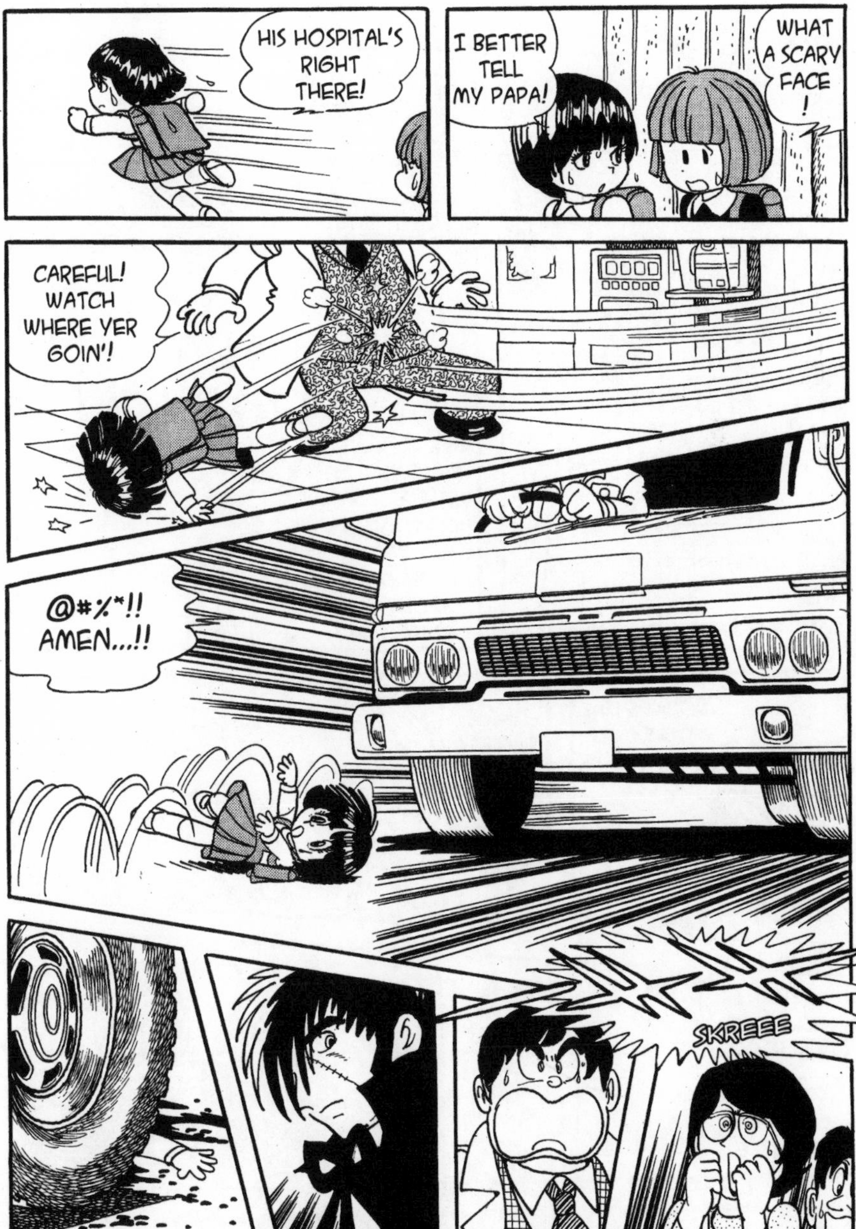
WHAT A SCARY FACE!
I BETTER TELL MY PAPA!
HIS HOSPITAL'S RIGHT THERE!
CAREFUL! WATCH WHERE YER GOIN'!
@#%*!! AMEN...!!
SKREEE

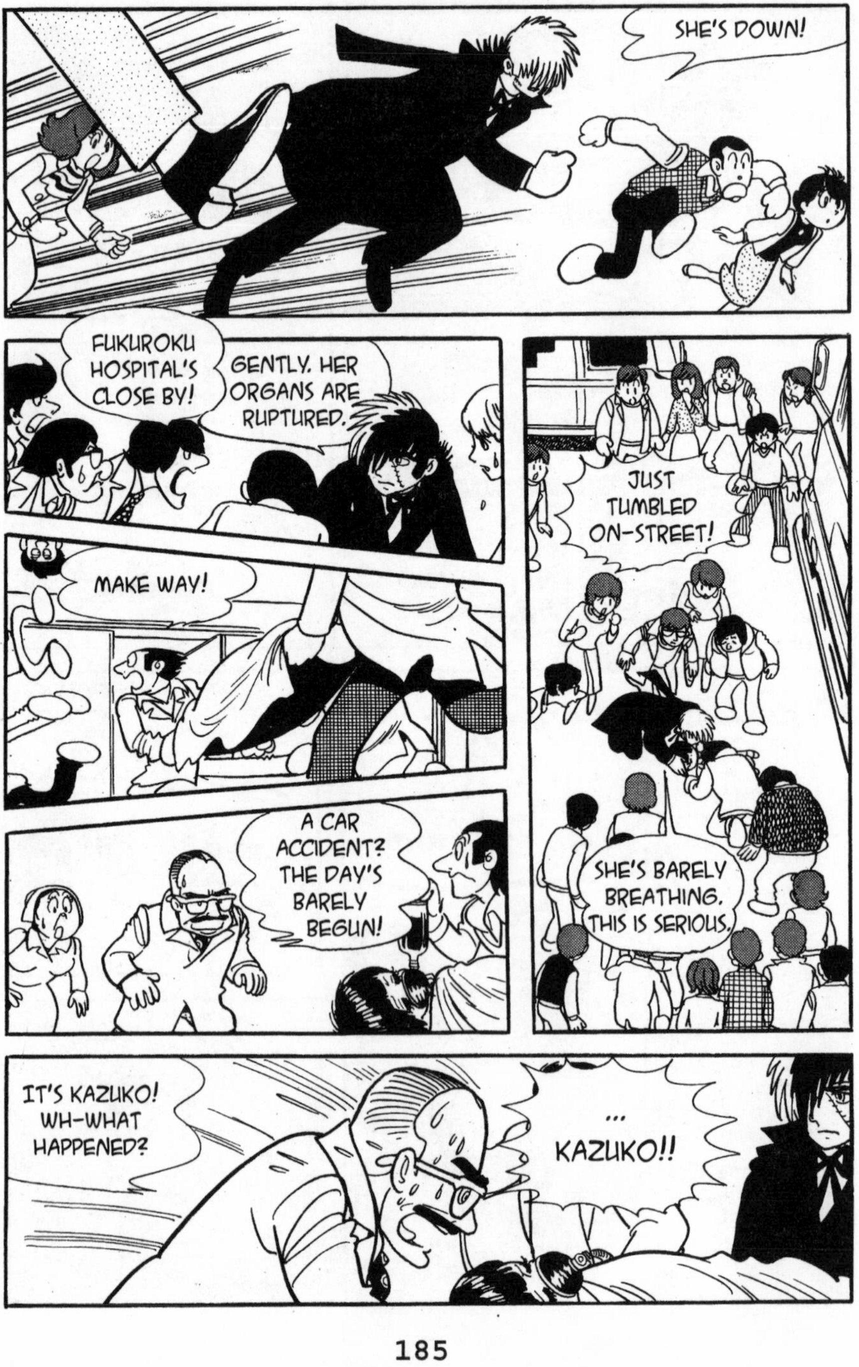
SHE'S DOWN!
JUST TUMBLED ON-STREET!
SHE'S BARELY BREATHING. THIS IS SERIOUS.
GENTLY. HER ORGANS ARE RUPTURED.
FUKUROKU HOSPITAL'S CLOSE BY!
MAKE WAY!
A CAR ACCIDENT? THE DAY'S BARELY BEGUN!
... KAZUKO!!
IT'S KAZUKO! WH-WHAT HAPPENED?

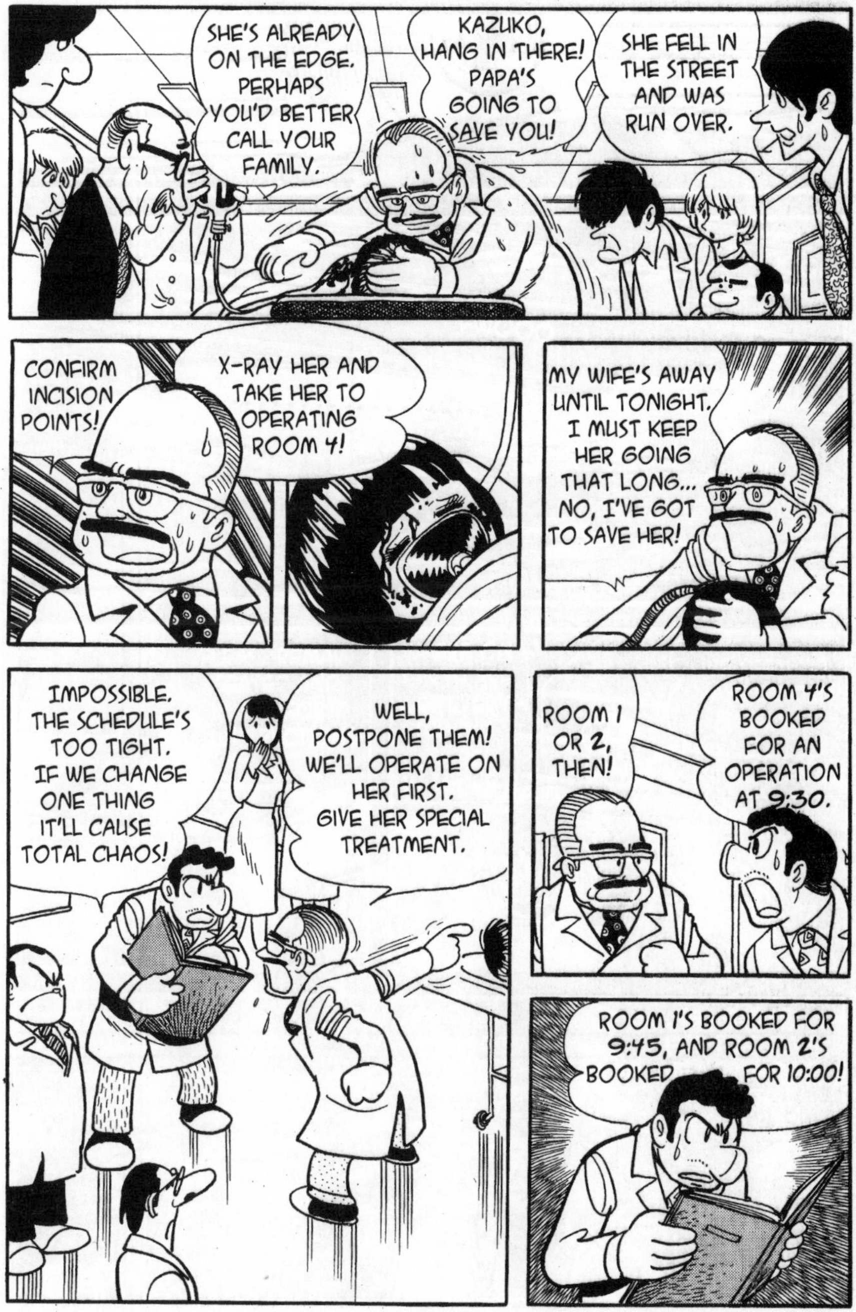
SHE FELL IN THE STREET AND WAS RUN OVER.
KAZUKO, HANG IN THERE! PAPA'S GOING TO SAVE YOU!
SHE'S ALREADY ON THE EDGE. PERHAPS YOU'D BETTER CALL YOUR FAMILY.
MY WIFE'S AWAY UNTIL TONIGHT. I MUST KEEP HER GOING THAT LONG... NO, I'VE GOT TO SAVE HER!
X-RAY HER AND TAKE HER TO OPERATING ROOM 4!
CONFIRM INCISION POINTS!
ROOM 4'S BOOKED FOR AN OPERATION AT 9:30.
ROOM 1 OR 2, THEN!
ROOM 1'S BOOKED FOR 9:45, AND ROOM 2'S BOOKED FOR 10:00!
WELL, POSTPONE THEM! WE'LL OPERATE ON HER FIRST. GIVE HER SPECIAL TREATMENT.
IMPOSSIBLE. THE SCHEDULE'S TOO TIGHT. IF WE CHANGE ONE THING IT'LL CAUSE TOTAL CHAOS!

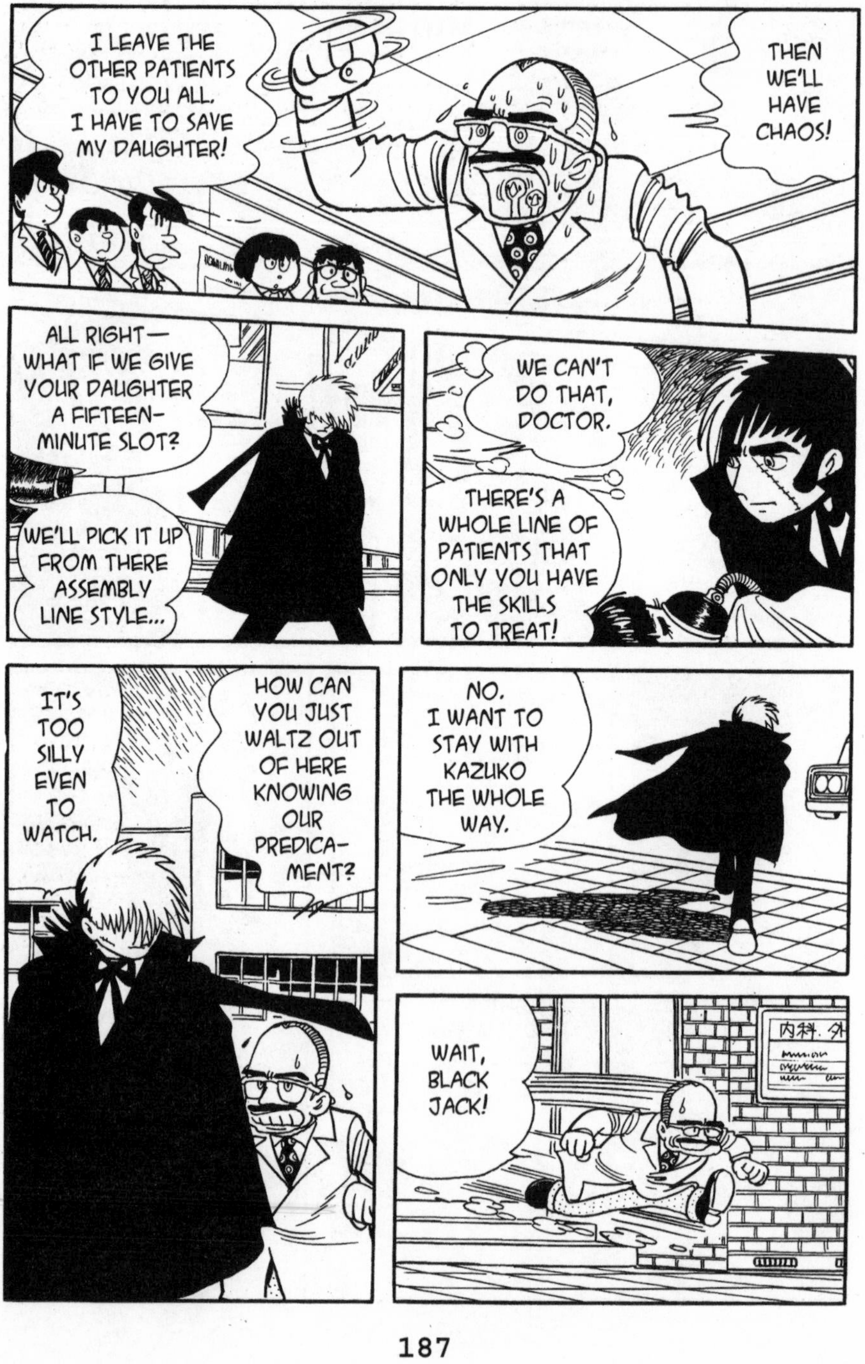
I LEAVE THE OTHER PATIENTS TO YOU ALL. I HAVE TO SAVE MY DAUGHTER!
THEN WE'LL HAVE CHAOS!
ALL RIGHT— WHAT IF WE GIVE YOUR DAUGHTER A FIFTEEN-MINUTE SLOT?
WE'LL PICK IT UP FROM THERE ASSEMBLY LINE STYLE...
WE CAN'T DO THAT, DOCTOR.
THERE'S A WHOLE LINE OF PATIENTS THAT ONLY YOU HAVE THE SKILLS TO TREAT!
IT'S TOO SILLY EVEN TO WATCH.
HOW CAN YOU JUST WALTZ OUT OF HERE KNOWING OUR PREDICA-MENT?
NO. I WANT TO STAY WITH KAZUKO THE WHOLE WAY.
内科. 外
WAIT, BLACK JACK!

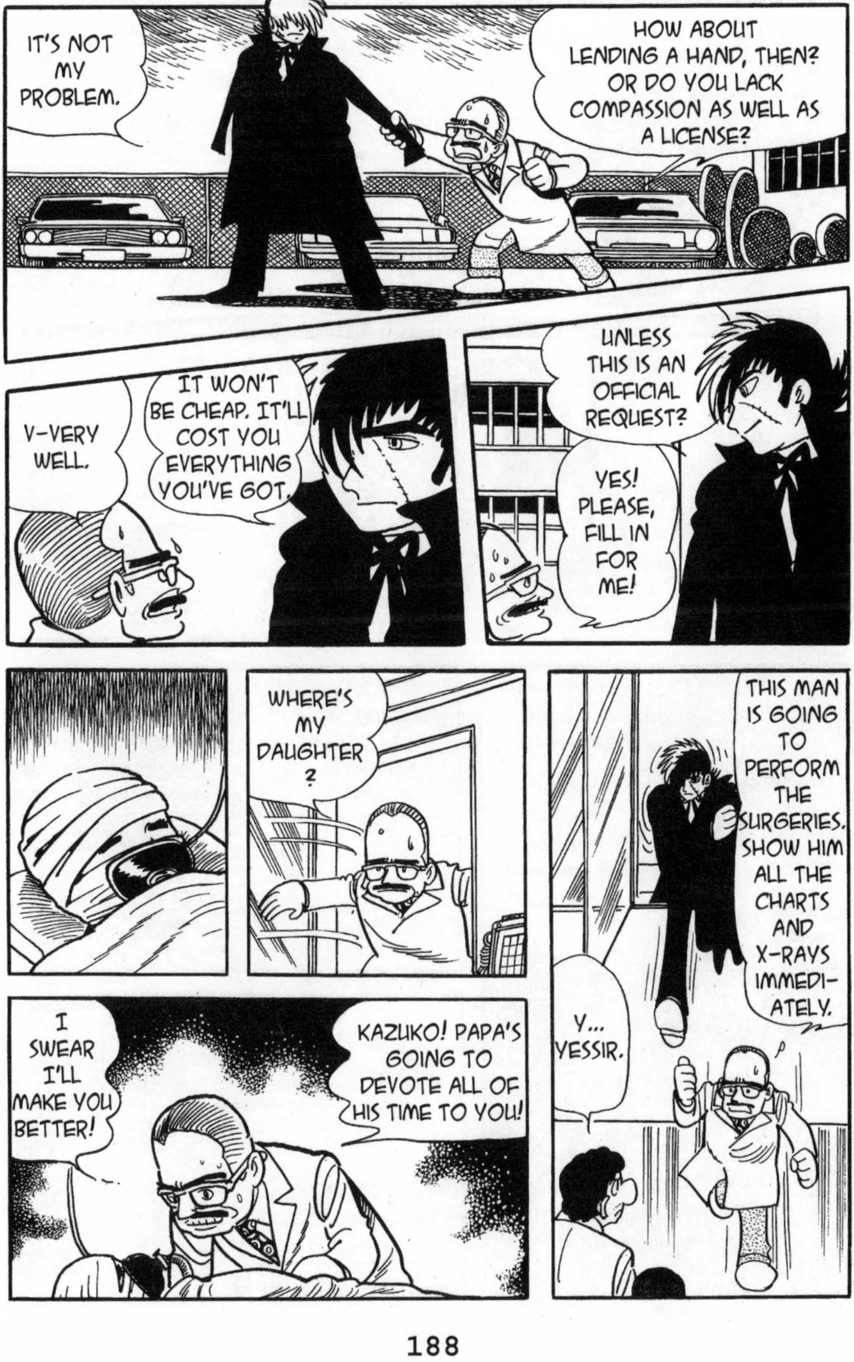
IT'S NOT MY PROBLEM.
HOW ABOUT LENDING A HAND, THEN? OR DO YOU LACK COMPASSION AS WELL AS A LICENSE?
UNLESS THIS IS AN OFFICIAL REQUEST?
YES! PLEASE, FILL IN FOR ME!
IT WON'T BE CHEAP. IT'LL COST YOU EVERYTHING YOU'VE GOT.
V-VERY WELL.
THIS MAN IS GOING TO PERFORM THE SURGERIES. SHOW HIM ALL THE CHARTS AND X-RAYS IMMEDI-ATELY.
Y... YESSIR.
WHERE'S MY DAUGHTER?
KAZUKO! PAPA'S GOING TO DEVOTE ALL OF HIS TIME TO YOU!
I SWEAR I'LL MAKE YOU BETTER!

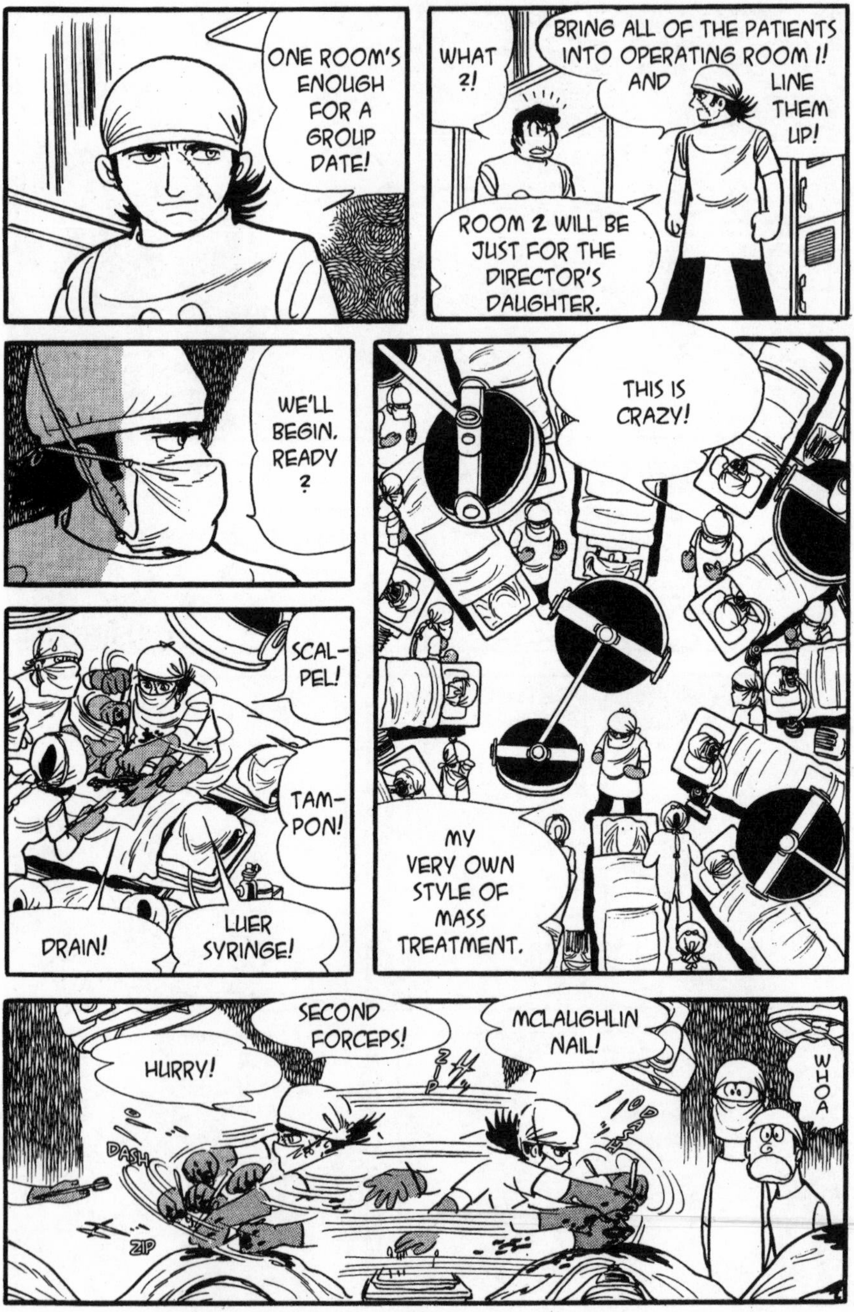
ONE ROOM'S ENOUGH FOR A GROUP DATE!
BRING ALL OF THE PATIENTS INTO OPERATING ROOM 1! AND LINE THEM UP!
WHAT ?!
ROOM 2 WILL BE JUST FOR THE DIRECTOR'S DAUGHTER.
WE'LL BEGIN. READY ?
SCAL-PEL!
TAM-PON!
DRAIN!
LUER SYRINGE!
THIS IS CRAZY!
MY VERY OWN STYLE OF MASS TREATMENT.
HURRY!
SECOND FORCEPS!
MCLAUGHLIN NAIL!
ZIP
DASH
DASH
ZIP
WHOA

TWO KOCHER CLAMPS!
WHERE'S THE REAMER?
THREE-FLANGED NAIL, ON THE DOUBLE!
WHP
WHP
SUTURES OVER HERE! SUCCINYLCHOLINE FOR HIM!
I CAN'T BELIEVE HE'S DOING THEM ALL AT ONCE...
HE'S SO FAST!
HER HEART'S WEAKEN-ING!
OH, GOD!
HER BLOOD PRESSURE'S FALLING, DOCTOR! SHE'S IN DANGER.
I WON'T LET YOU DIE, KAZUKO... PAPA'S HERE...
N-NO MATTER WHAT...
PLEASE... PLEASE... DON'T DIE... I'M BEGGING YOU...
PUMP
PUMP
PUMP
GIVE HER ARTIFICIAL RESPIRATION.
IS THIS THE END...?

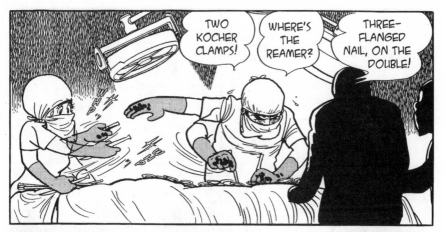

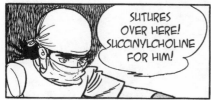

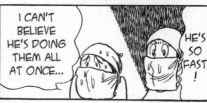

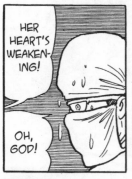

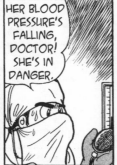

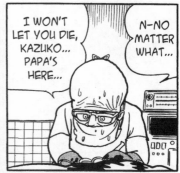

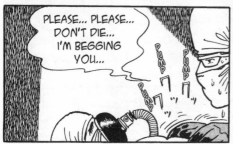

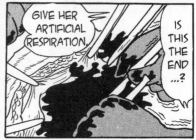

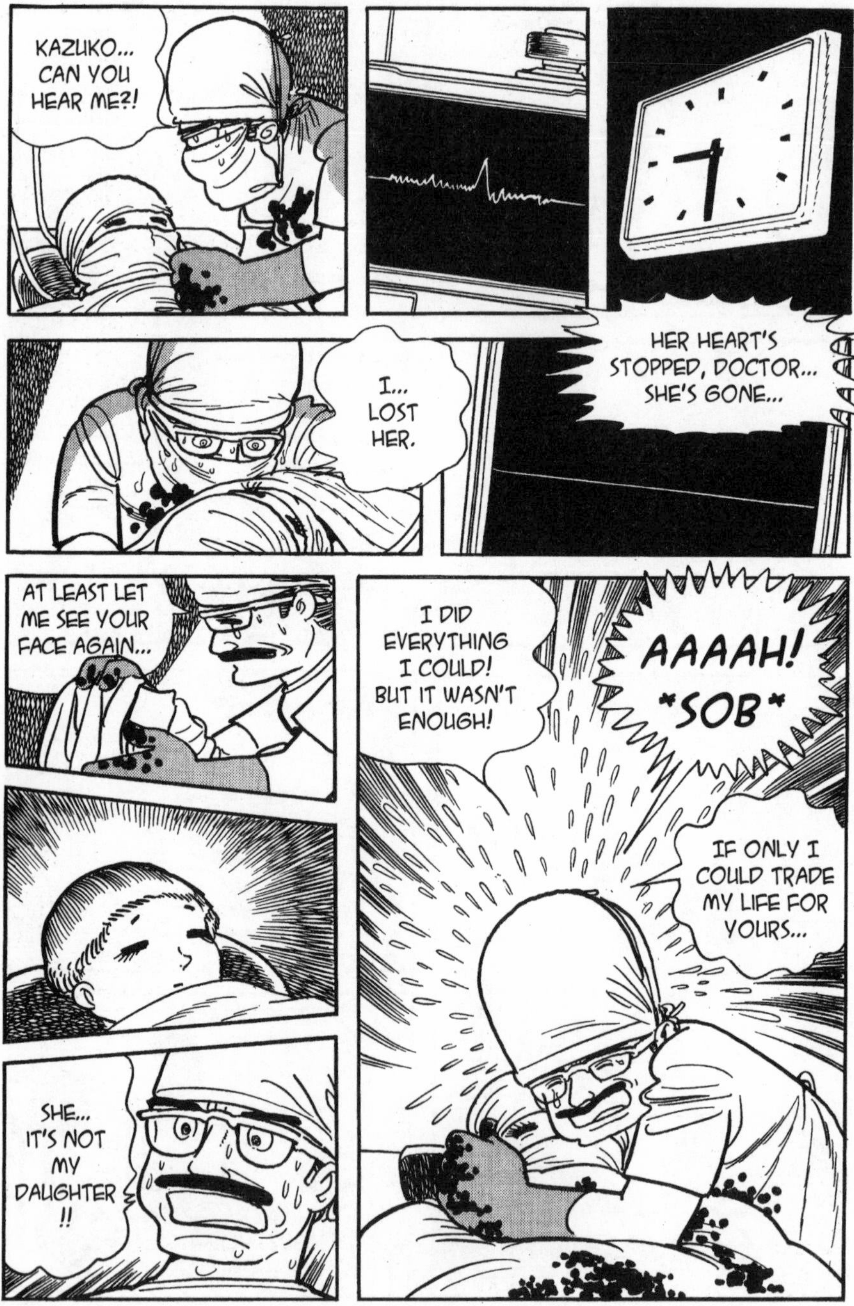
KAZUKO... CAN YOU HEAR ME?!
HER HEART'S STOPPED, DOCTOR... SHE'S GONE...
I... LOST HER.
I DID EVERYTHING I COULD! BUT IT WASN'T ENOUGH!
AAAAH! *SOB*
IF ONLY I COULD TRADE MY LIFE FOR YOURS...
AT LEAST LET ME SEE YOUR FACE AGAIN...
SHE... IT'S NOT MY DAUGHTER!!

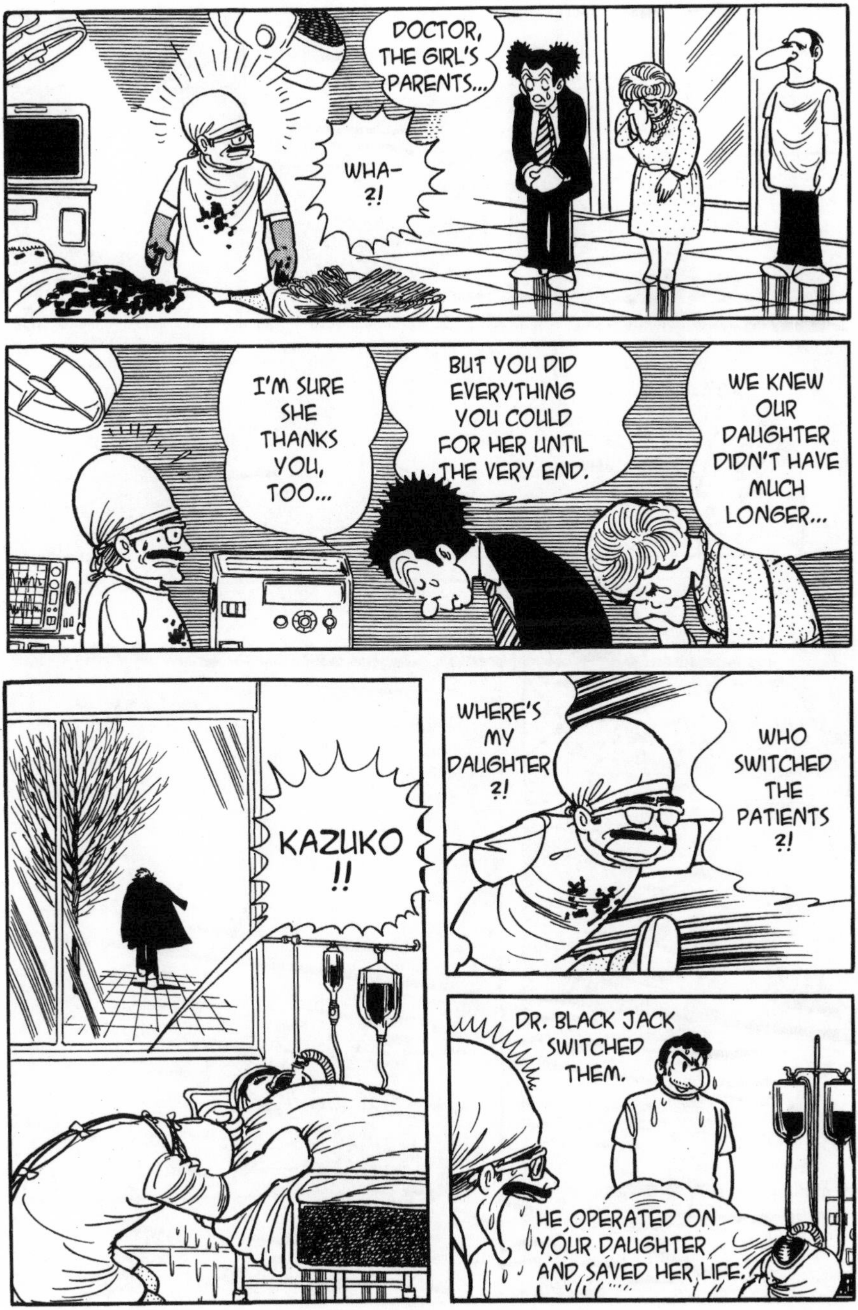
DOCTOR, THE GIRL'S PARENTS...
WHA-?!
WE KNEW OUR DAUGHTER DIDN'T HAVE MUCH LONGER...
BUT YOU DID EVERYTHING YOU COULD FOR HER UNTIL THE VERY END.
I'M SURE SHE THANKS YOU, TOO...
WHO SWITCHED THE PATIENTS?!
WHERE'S MY DAUGHTER?!
DR. BLACK JACK SWITCHED THEM.
HE OPERATED ON YOUR DAUGHTER AND SAVED HER LIFE.
KAZUKO!!

HELPING EACH OTHER

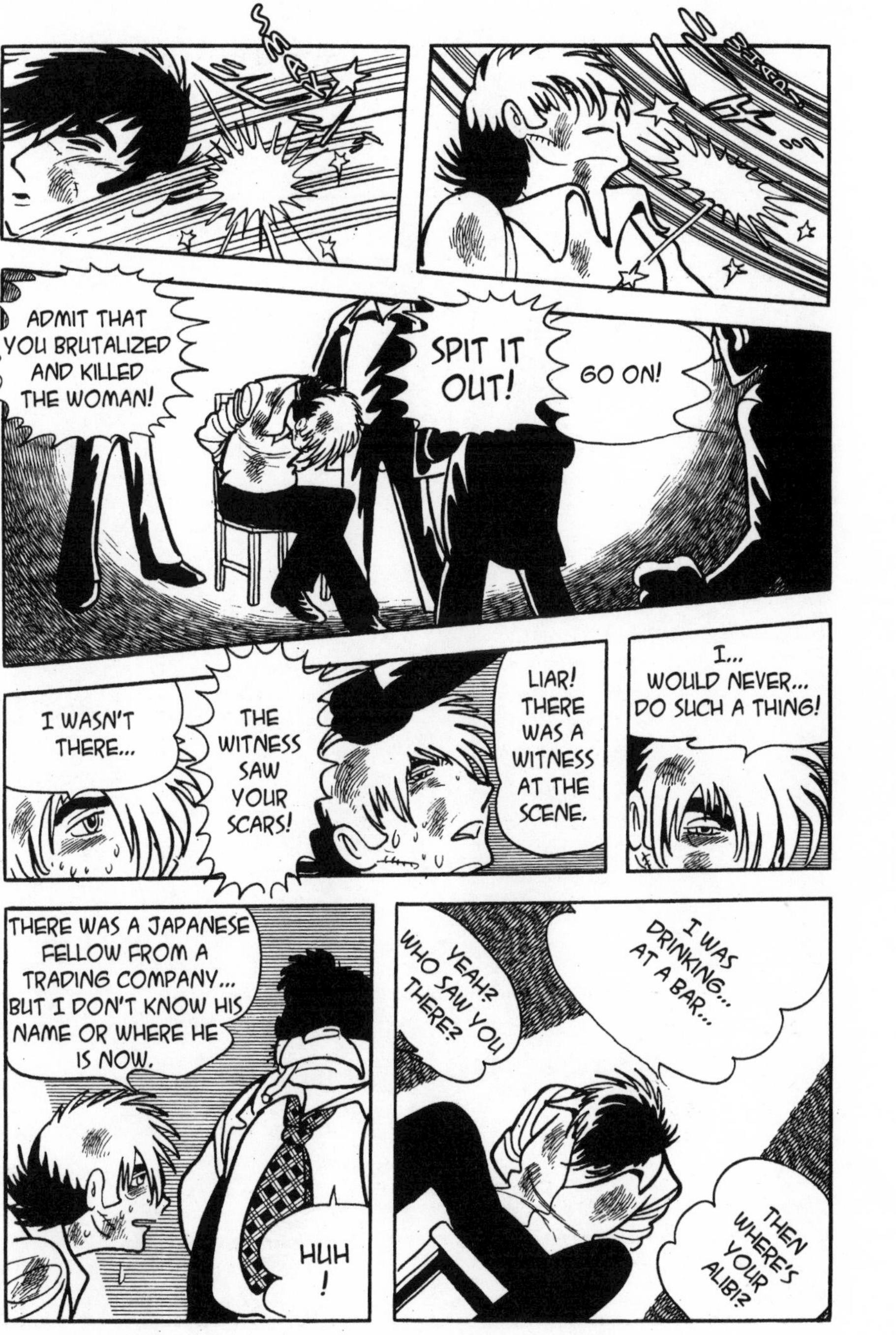
SMACK
GO ON!
SPIT IT OUT!
ADMIT THAT YOU BRUTALIZED AND KILLED THE WOMAN!
I... WOULD NEVER... DO SUCH A THING!
LIAR! THERE WAS A WITNESS AT THE SCENE.
THE WITNESS SAW YOUR SCARS!
I WASN'T THERE...
THEN WHERE'S YOUR ALIBI!?
I WAS DRINKING... AT A BAR...
YEAH? WHO SAW YOU THERE?
THERE WAS A JAPANESE FELLOW FROM A TRADING COMPANY... BUT I DON'T KNOW HIS NAME OR WHERE HE IS NOW.
HUH!

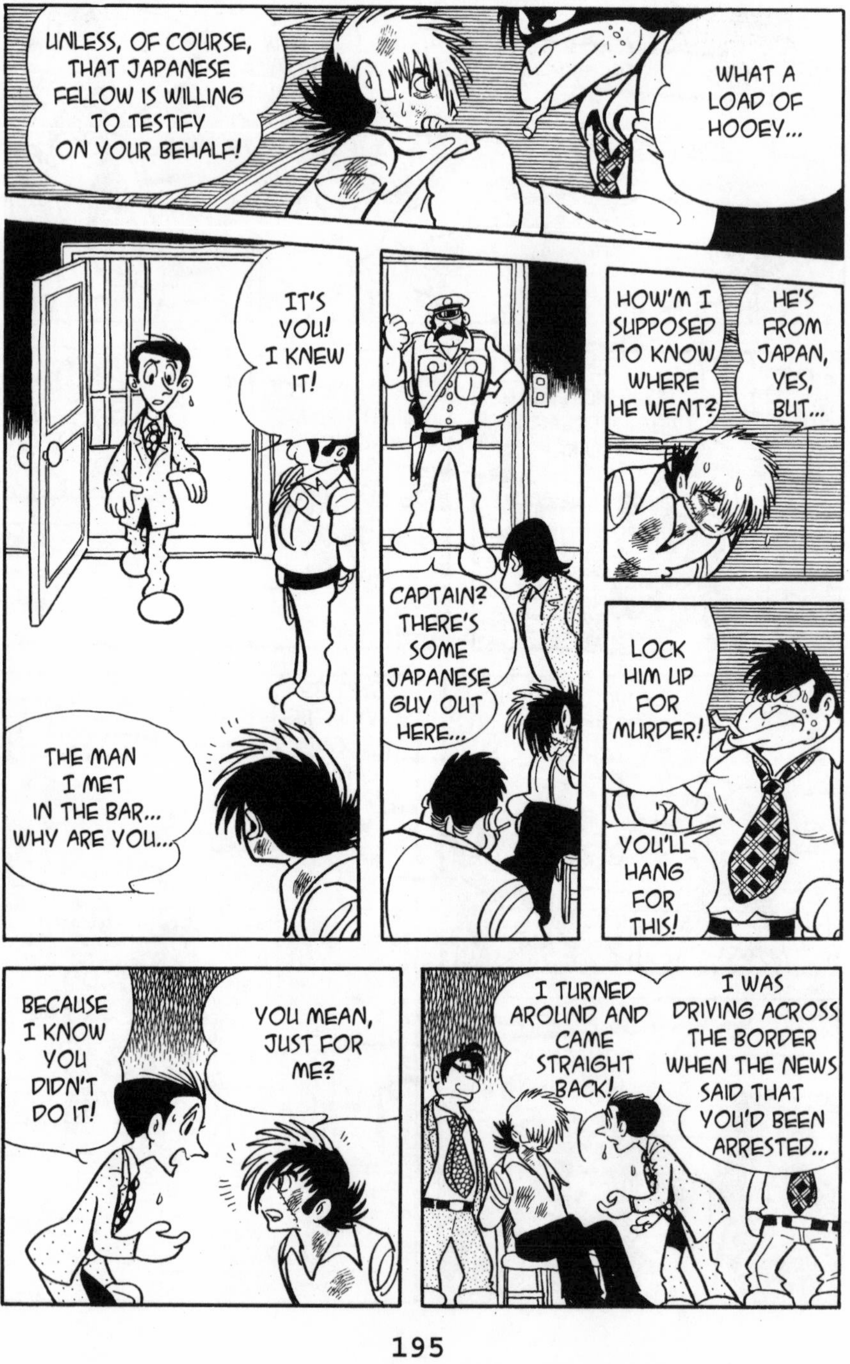
WHAT A LOAD OF HOOEY...
UNLESS, OF COURSE, THAT JAPANESE FELLOW IS WILLING TO TESTIFY ON YOUR BEHALF!
HE'S FROM JAPAN, YES, BUT...
HOW'M I SUPPOSED TO KNOW WHERE HE WENT?
LOCK HIM UP FOR MURDER!
YOU'LL HANG FOR THIS!
CAPTAIN? THERE'S SOME JAPANESE GUY OUT HERE...
IT'S YOU! I KNEW IT!
THE MAN I MET IN THE BAR... WHY ARE YOU...
I WAS DRIVING ACROSS THE BORDER WHEN THE NEWS SAID THAT YOU'D BEEN ARRESTED...
I TURNED AROUND AND CAME STRAIGHT BACK!
YOU MEAN, JUST FOR ME?
BECAUSE I KNOW YOU DIDN'T DO IT!

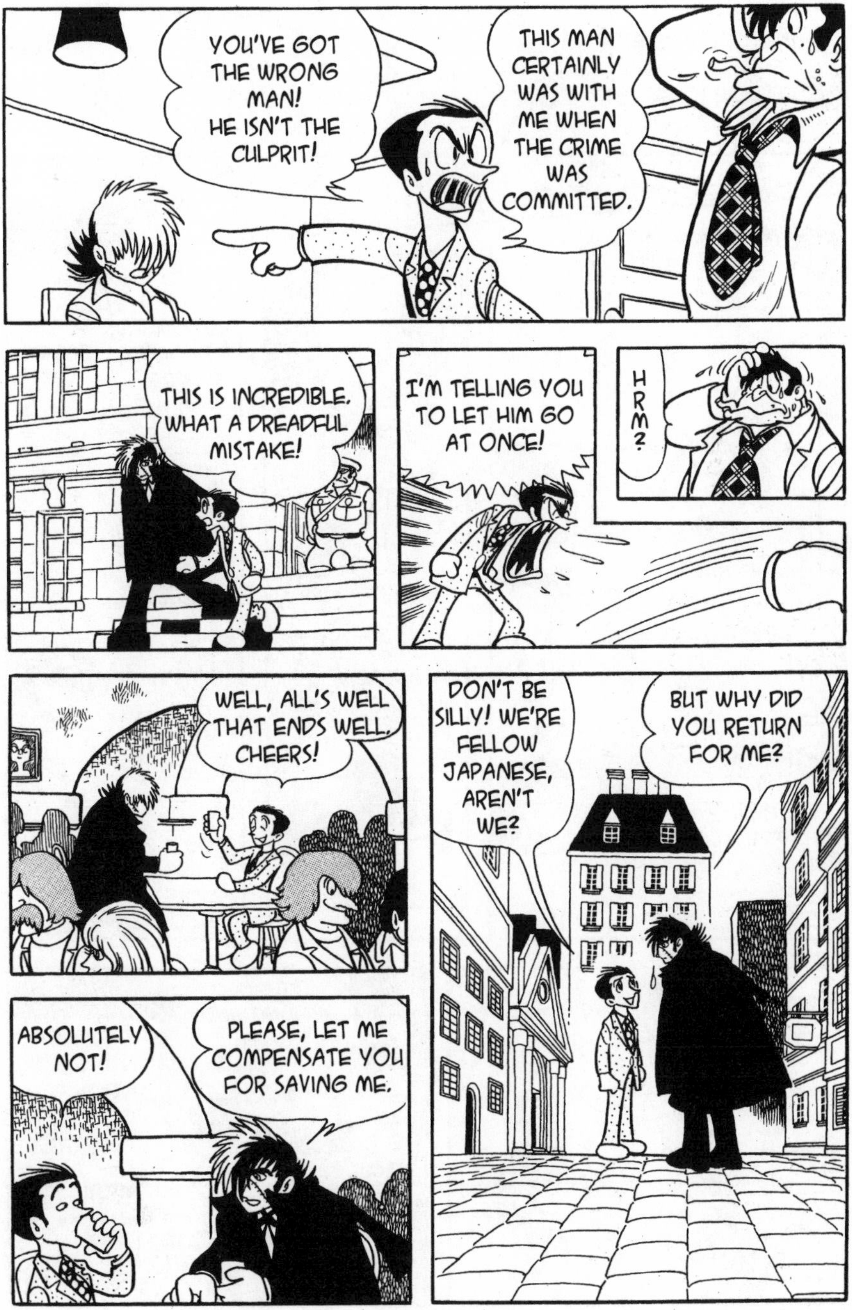
THIS MAN CERTAINLY WAS WITH ME WHEN THE CRIME WAS COMMITTED.
YOU'VE GOT THE WRONG MAN! HE ISN'T THE CULPRIT!
HRM?
I'M TELLING YOU TO LET HIM GO AT ONCE!
THIS IS INCREDIBLE. WHAT A DREADFUL MISTAKE!
BUT WHY DID YOU RETURN FOR ME?
DON'T BE SILLY! WE'RE FELLOW JAPANESE, AREN'T WE?
WELL, ALL'S WELL THAT ENDS WELL. CHEERS!
PLEASE, LET ME COMPENSATE YOU FOR SAVING ME.
ABSOLUTELY NOT!

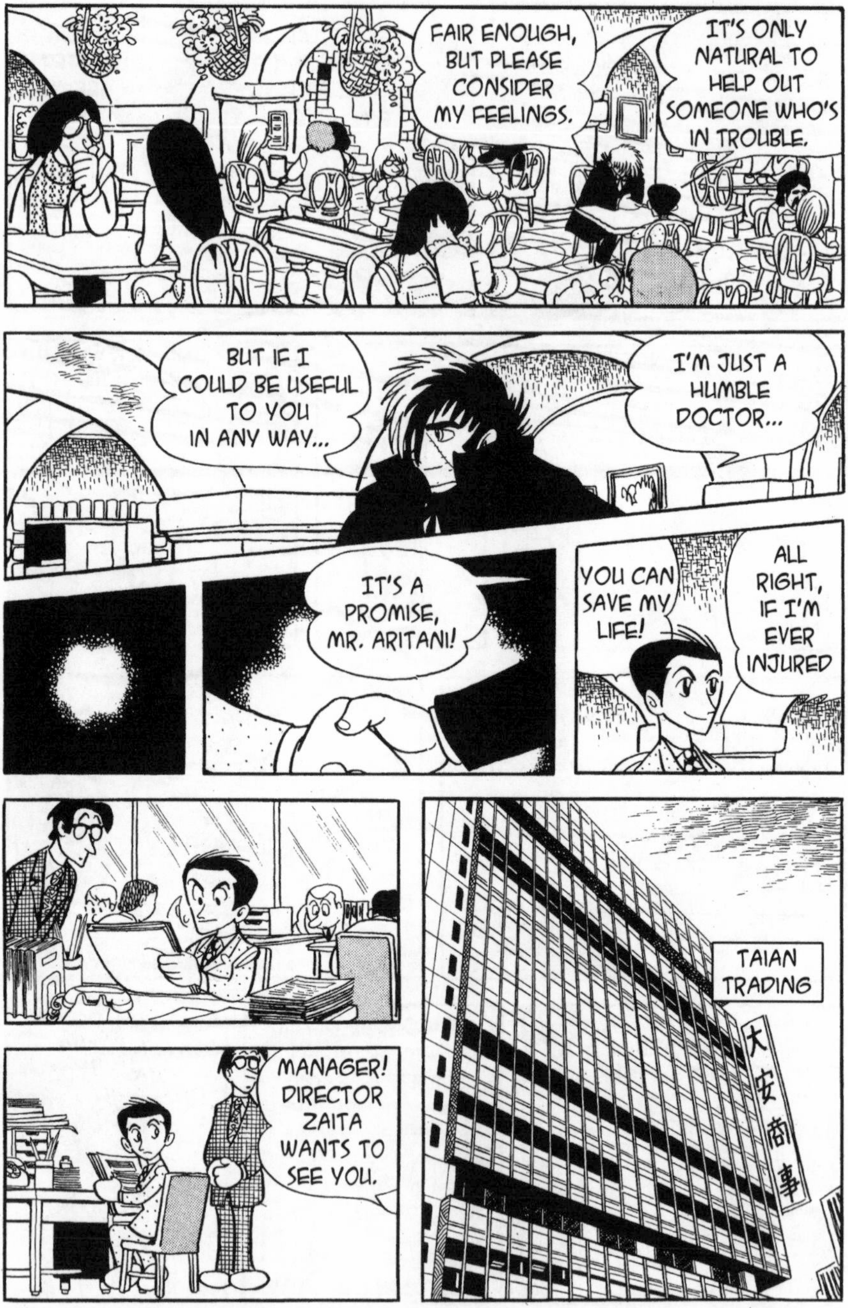
IT'S ONLY NATURAL TO HELP OUT SOMEONE WHO'S IN TROUBLE.
FAIR ENOUGH, BUT PLEASE CONSIDER MY FEELINGS.
I'M JUST A HUMBLE DOCTOR...
BUT IF I COULD BE USEFUL TO YOU IN ANY WAY...
ALL RIGHT, IF I'M EVER INJURED
YOU CAN SAVE MY LIFE!
IT'S A PROMISE, MR. ARITANI!
TAIAN TRADING
大安商事
MANAGER! DIRECTOR ZAITA WANTS TO SEE YOU.

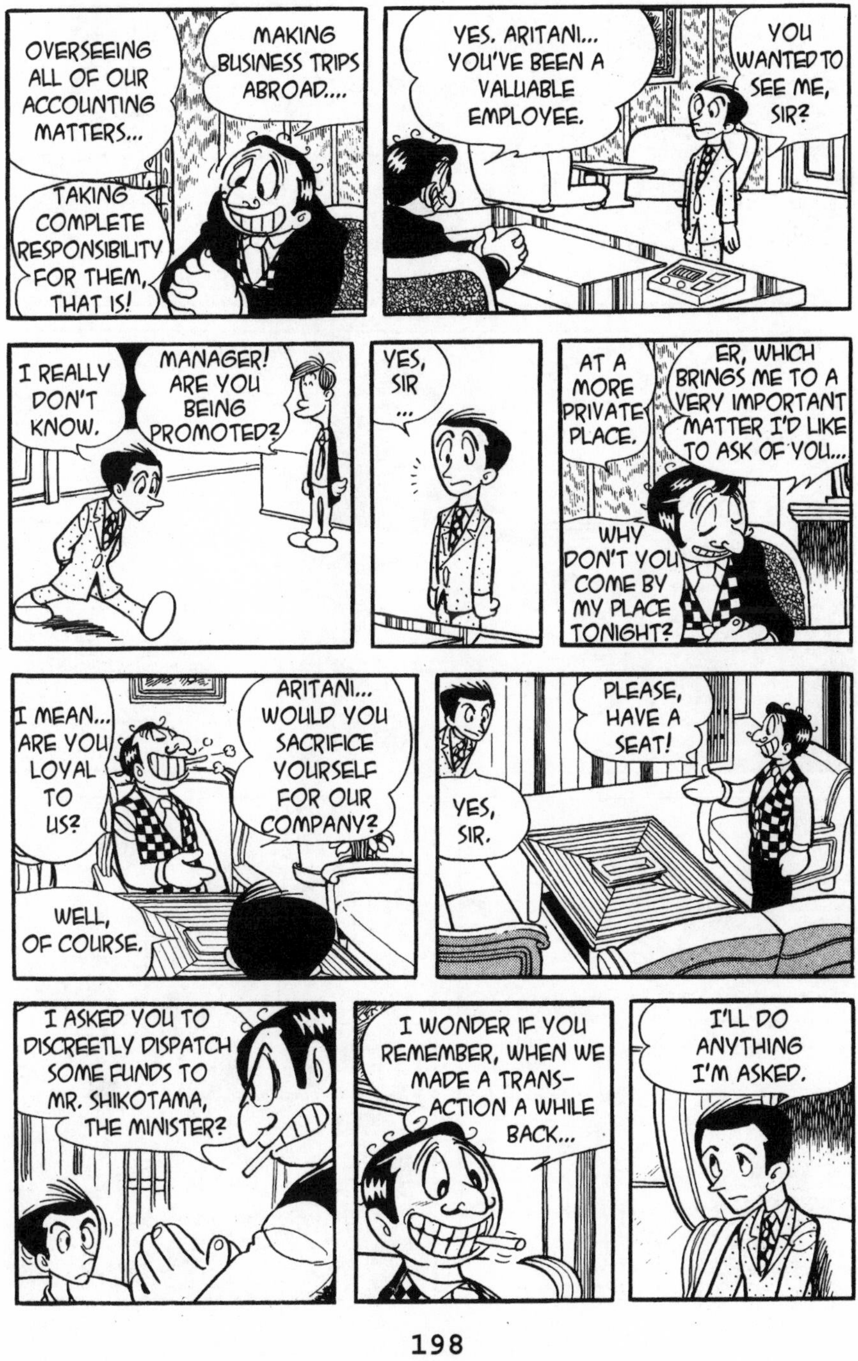
YOU WANTED TO SEE ME, SIR?
YES. ARITANI... YOU'VE BEEN A VALUABLE EMPLOYEE.
MAKING BUSINESS TRIPS ABROAD....
OVERSEEING ALL OF OUR ACCOUNTING MATTERS...
TAKING COMPLETE RESPONSIBILITY FOR THEM, THAT IS!
ER, WHICH BRINGS ME TO A VERY IMPORTANT MATTER I'D LIKE TO ASK OF YOU...
AT A MORE PRIVATE PLACE.
WHY DON'T YOU COME BY MY PLACE TONIGHT?
YES, SIR ...
MANAGER! ARE YOU BEING PROMOTED?
I REALLY DON'T KNOW.
PLEASE, HAVE A SEAT!
YES, SIR.
ARITANI... WOULD YOU SACRIFICE YOURSELF FOR OUR COMPANY?
I MEAN... ARE YOU LOYAL TO US?
WELL, OF COURSE.
I'LL DO ANYTHING I'M ASKED.
I WONDER IF YOU REMEMBER, WHEN WE MADE A TRANS-ACTION A WHILE BACK...
I ASKED YOU TO DISCREETLY DISPATCH SOME FUNDS TO MR. SHIKOTAMA, THE MINISTER?

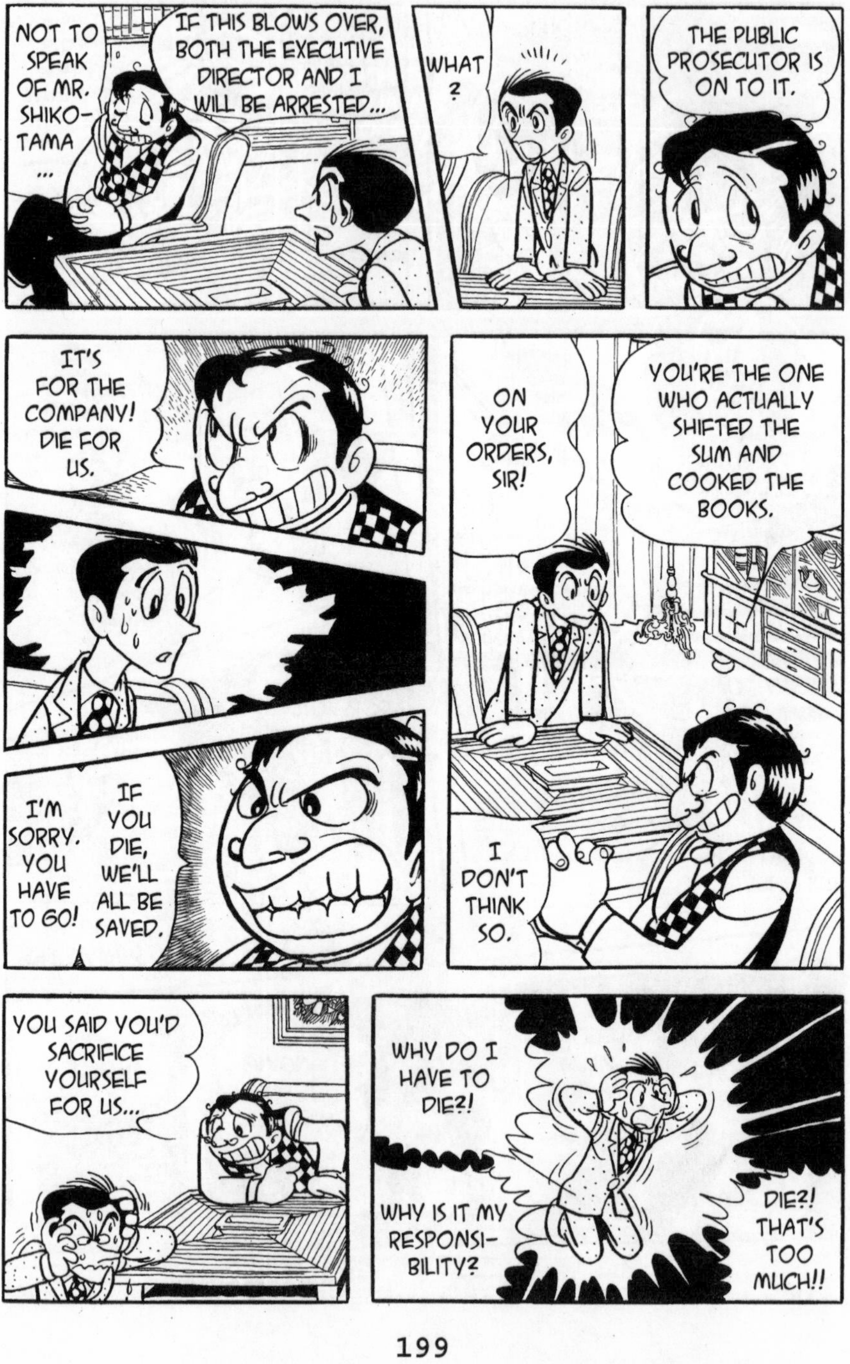
THE PUBLIC PROSECUTOR IS ON TO IT.
WHAT?
IF THIS BLOWS OVER, BOTH THE EXECUTIVE DIRECTOR AND I WILL BE ARRESTED...
NOT TO SPEAK OF MR. SHIKO-TAMA ...
YOU'RE THE ONE WHO ACTUALLY SHIFTED THE SUM AND COOKED THE BOOKS.
ON YOUR ORDERS, SIR!
I DON'T THINK SO.
IT'S FOR THE COMPANY! DIE FOR US.
IF YOU DIE, WE'LL ALL BE SAVED.
I'M SORRY. YOU HAVE TO GO!
WHY DO I HAVE TO DIE?!
DIE?! THAT'S TOO MUCH!!
WHY IS IT MY RESPONSI-BILITY?
YOU SAID YOU'D SACRIFICE YOURSELF FOR US...

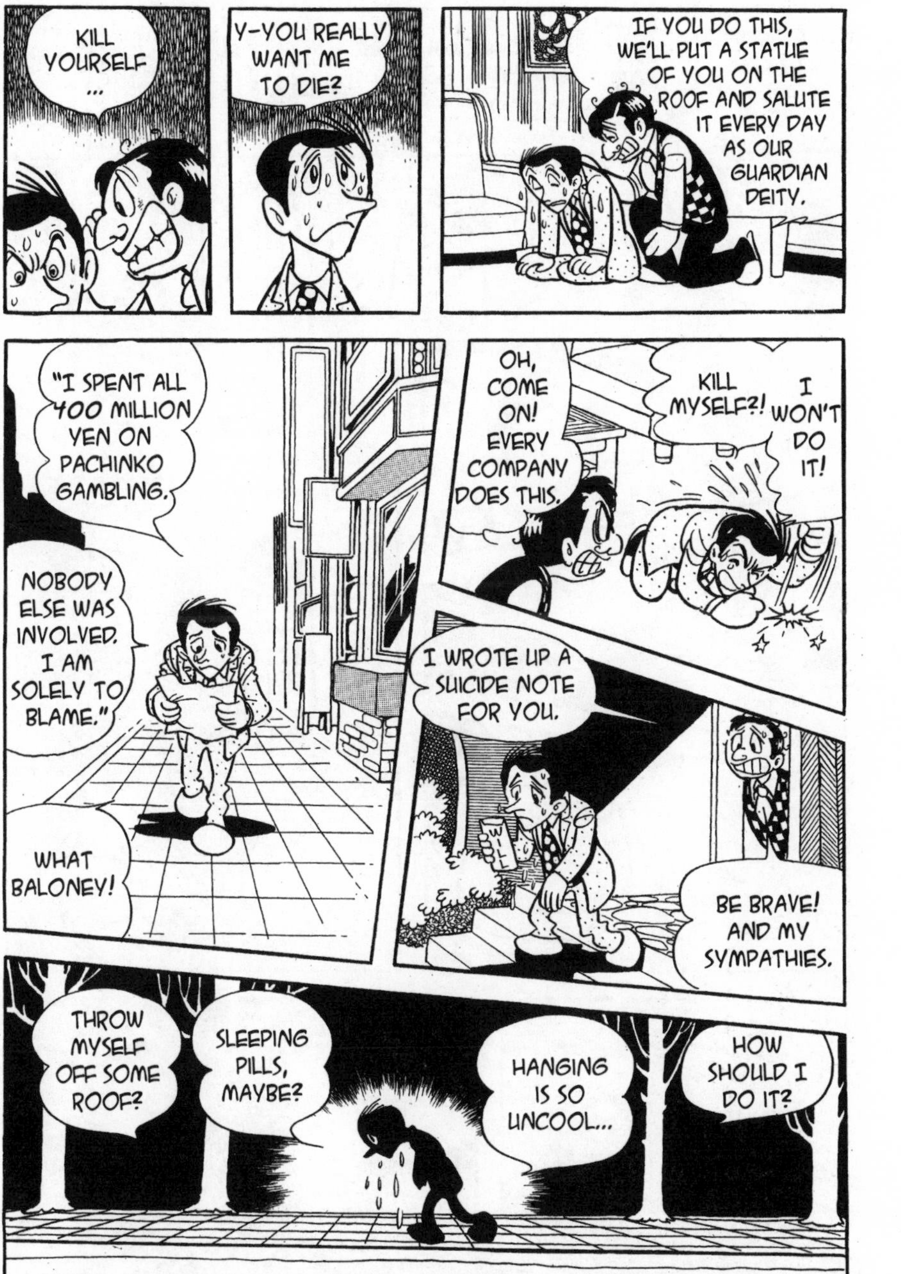
KILL YOURSELF ...
Y-YOU REALLY WANT ME TO DIE?
IF YOU DO THIS, WE'LL PUT A STATUE OF YOU ON THE ROOF AND SALUTE IT EVERY DAY AS OUR GUARDIAN DEITY.
"I SPENT ALL 400 MILLION YEN ON PACHINKO GAMBLING.
NOBODY ELSE WAS INVOLVED. I AM SOLELY TO BLAME."
WHAT BALONEY!
KILL MYSELF?!
I WON'T DO IT!
OH, COME ON! EVERY COMPANY DOES THIS.
I WROTE UP A SUICIDE NOTE FOR YOU.
WILL
BE BRAVE! AND MY SYMPATHIES.
THROW MYSELF OFF SOME ROOF?
SLEEPING PILLS, MAYBE?
HANGING IS SO UNCOOL...
HOW SHOULD I DO IT?

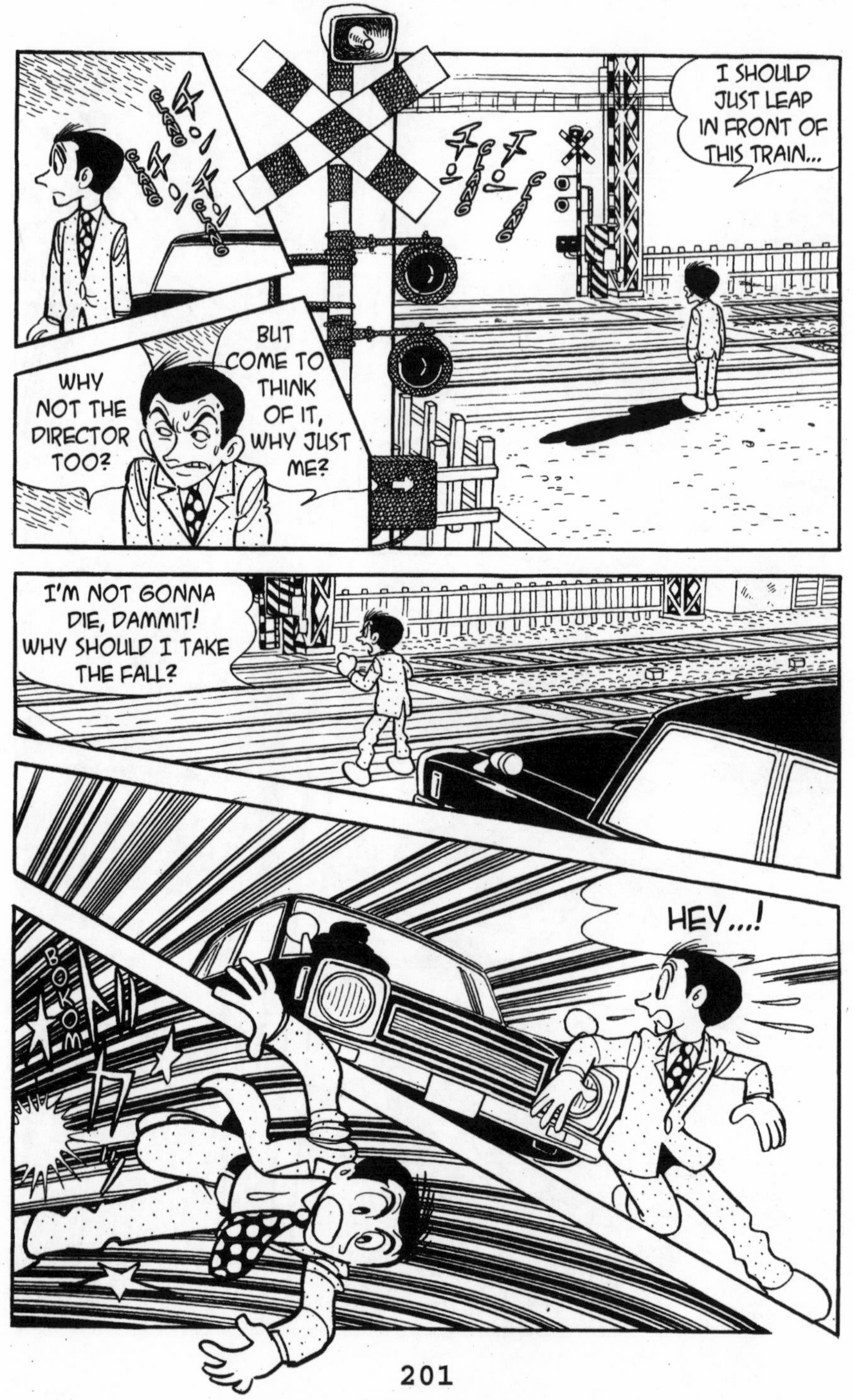
CLANG CLANG
I SHOULD JUST LEAP IN FRONT OF THIS TRAIN...
CLANG CLANG CLANG CLANG
BUT COME TO THINK OF IT, WHY JUST ME?
WHY NOT THE DIRECTOR TOO?
I'M NOT GONNA DIE, DAMMIT! WHY SHOULD I TAKE THE FALL?
HEY...!
BOKOM

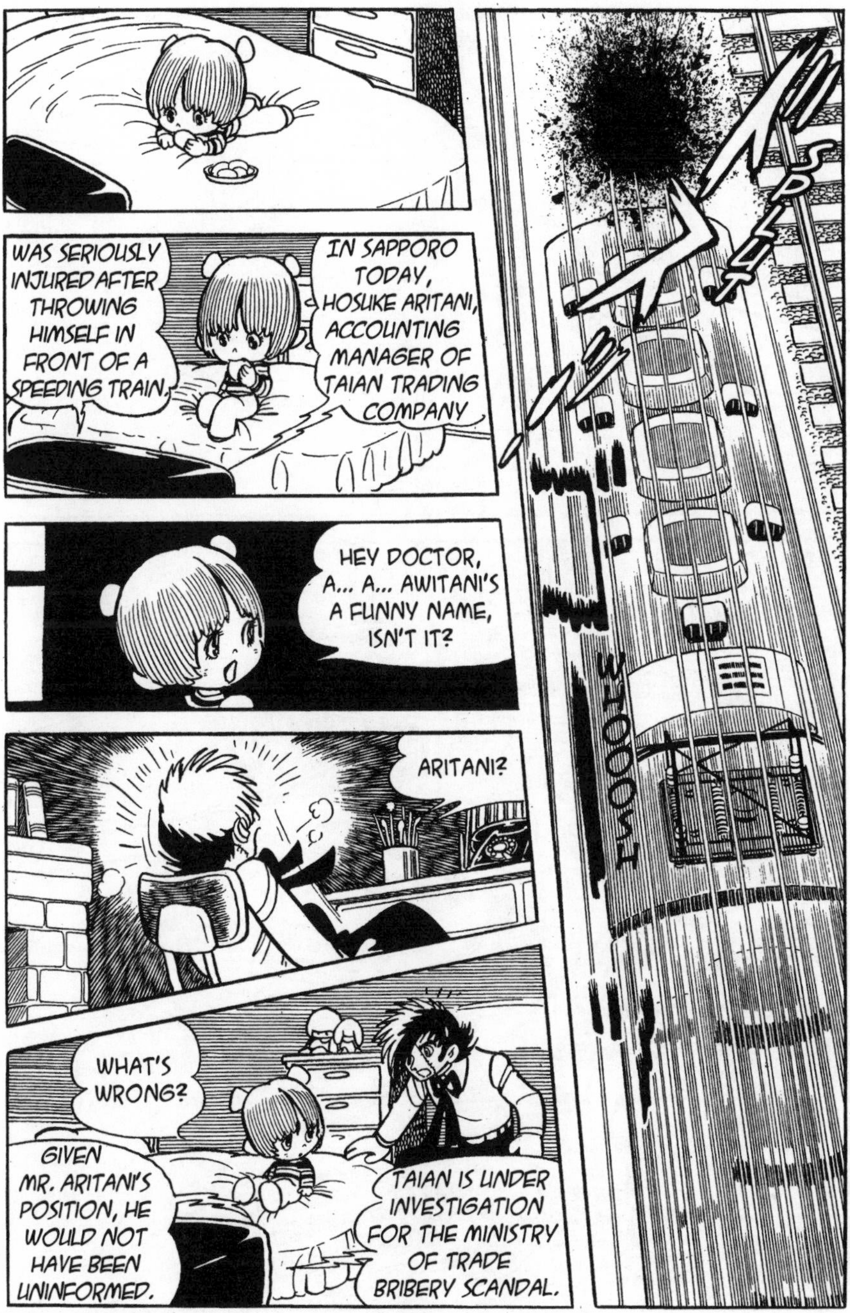
SPLUT
WHOOOSH
IN SAPPORO TODAY, HOSUKE ARITANI, ACCOUNTING MANAGER OF TAIAN TRADING COMPANY
WAS SERIOUSLY INJURED AFTER THROWING HIMSELF IN FRONT OF A SPEEDING TRAIN.
HEY DOCTOR, A... A... AWITANI'S A FUNNY NAME, ISN'T IT?
ARITANI?
WHAT'S WRONG?
TAIAN IS UNDER INVESTIGATION FOR THE MINISTRY OF TRADE BRIBERY SCANDAL.
GIVEN MR. ARITANI'S POSITION, HE WOULD NOT HAVE BEEN UNINFORMED.

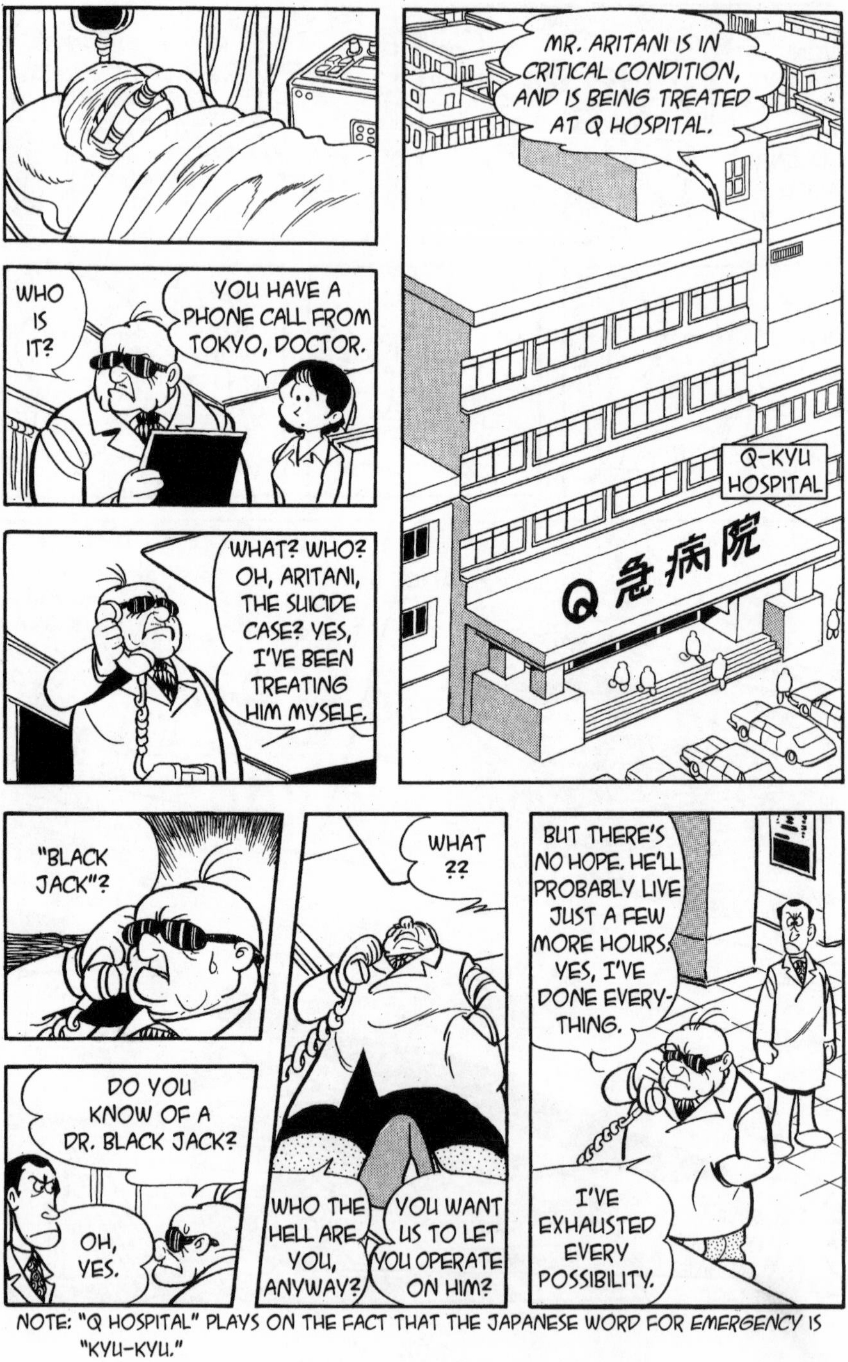
MR. ARITANI IS IN CRITICAL CONDITION, AND IS BEING TREATED AT Q HOSPITAL.
Q-KYU HOSPITAL
Q 急病院
YOU HAVE A PHONE CALL FROM TOKYO, DOCTOR.
WHO IS IT?
WHAT? WHO? OH, ARITANI, THE SUICIDE CASE? YES, I'VE BEEN TREATING HIM MYSELF.
BUT THERE'S NO HOPE. HE'LL PROBABLY LIVE JUST A FEW MORE HOURS. YES, I'VE DONE EVERY-THING.
I'VE EXHAUSTED EVERY POSSIBILITY.
WHAT ??
YOU WANT US TO LET YOU OPERATE ON HIM?
WHO THE HELL ARE YOU, ANYWAY?
"BLACK JACK"?
DO YOU KNOW OF A DR. BLACK JACK?
OH, YES.

NOTE: "Q HOSPITAL" PLAYS ON THE FACT THAT THE JAPANESE WORD FOR EMERGENCY IS "KYU-KYU."

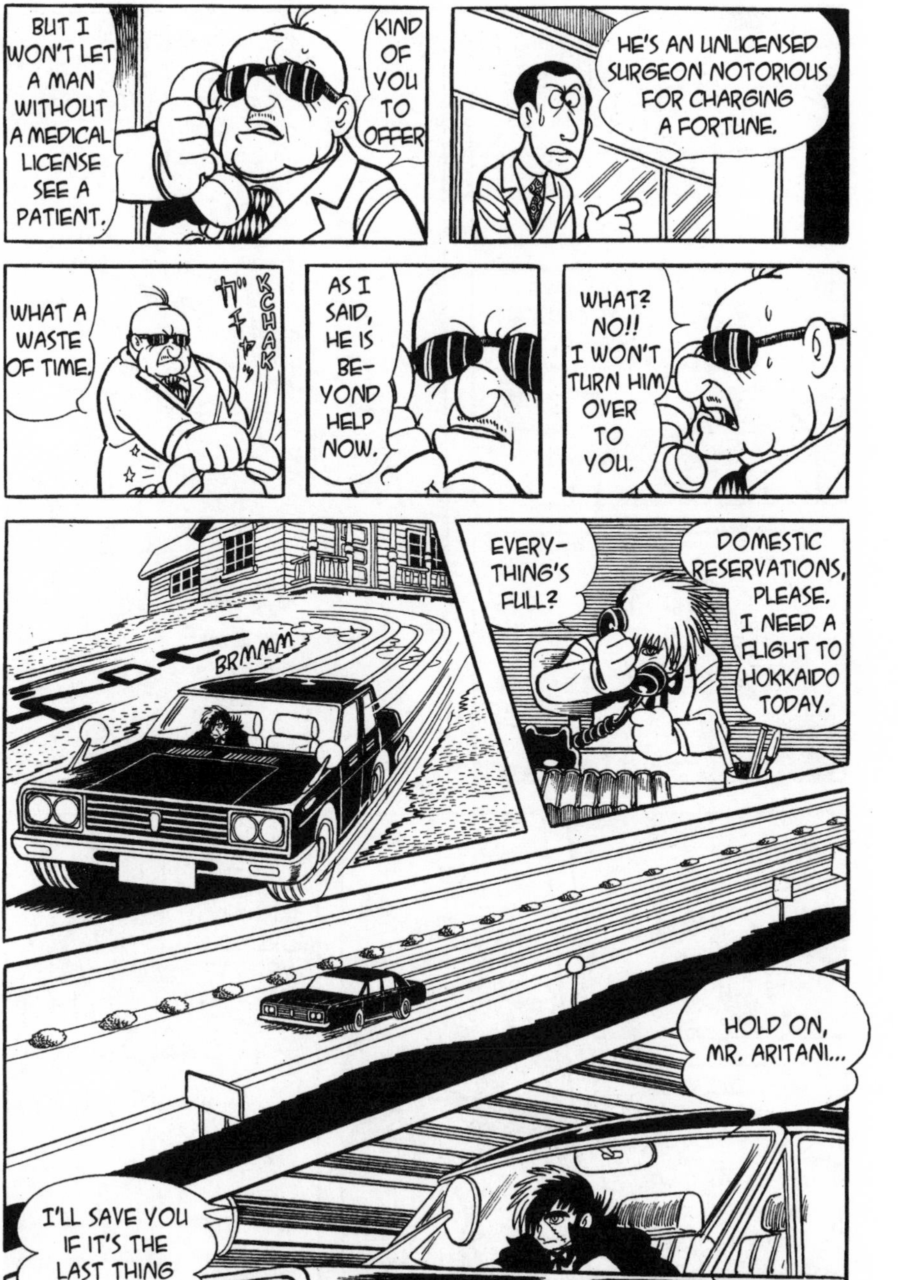
HE'S AN UNLICENSED SURGEON NOTORIOUS FOR CHARGING A FORTUNE.
KIND OF YOU TO OFFER
BUT I WON'T LET A MAN WITHOUT A MEDICAL LICENSE SEE A PATIENT.
WHAT? NO!! I WON'T TURN HIM OVER TO YOU.
AS I SAID, HE IS BE-YOND HELP NOW.
KCHAK
WHAT A WASTE OF TIME.
DOMESTIC RESERVATIONS, PLEASE. I NEED A FLIGHT TO HOKKAIDO TODAY.
EVERY-THING'S FULL?
BRMMM
HOLD ON, MR. ARITANI...
I'LL SAVE YOU IF IT'S THE LAST THING I DO!

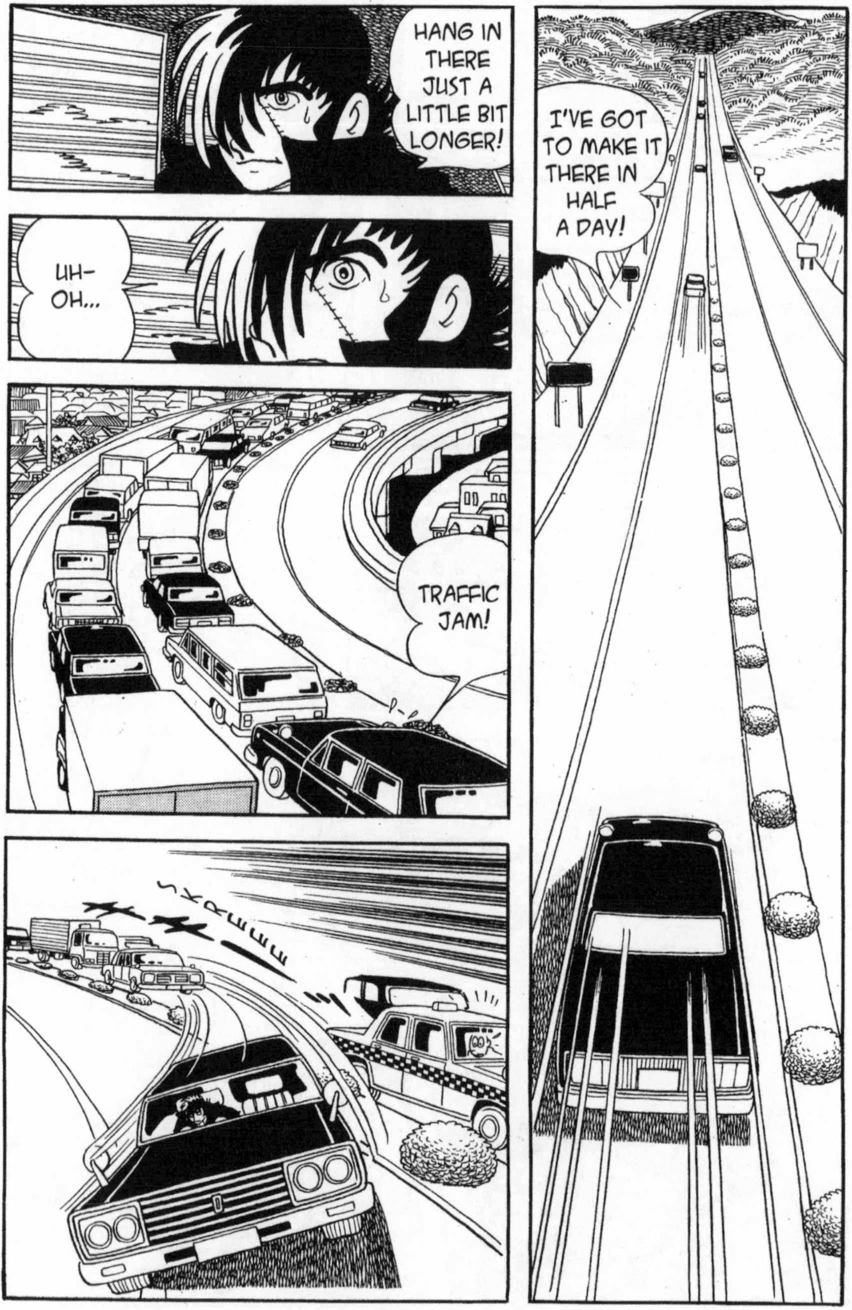
HANG IN THERE JUST A LITTLE BIT LONGER!
UH-OH...
TRAFFIC JAM!
SKREEEE
I'VE GOT TO MAKE IT THERE IN HALF A DAY!

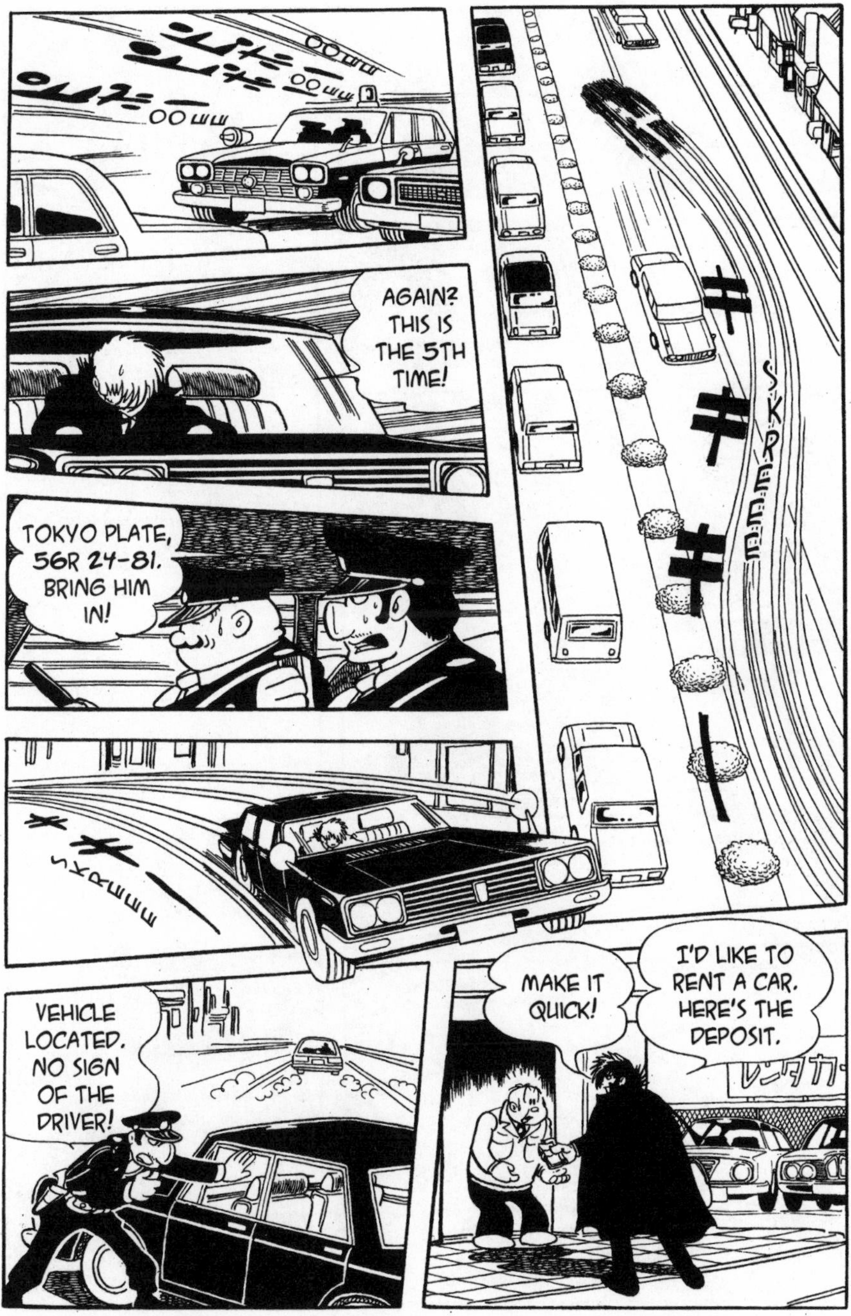
AGAIN? THIS IS THE 5TH TIME!
TOKYO PLATE, 56R 24-81. BRING HIM IN!
SKREEEE
SKREEEE
VEHICLE LOCATED. NO SIGN OF THE DRIVER!
I'D LIKE TO RENT A CAR. HERE'S THE DEPOSIT.
MAKE IT QUICK!

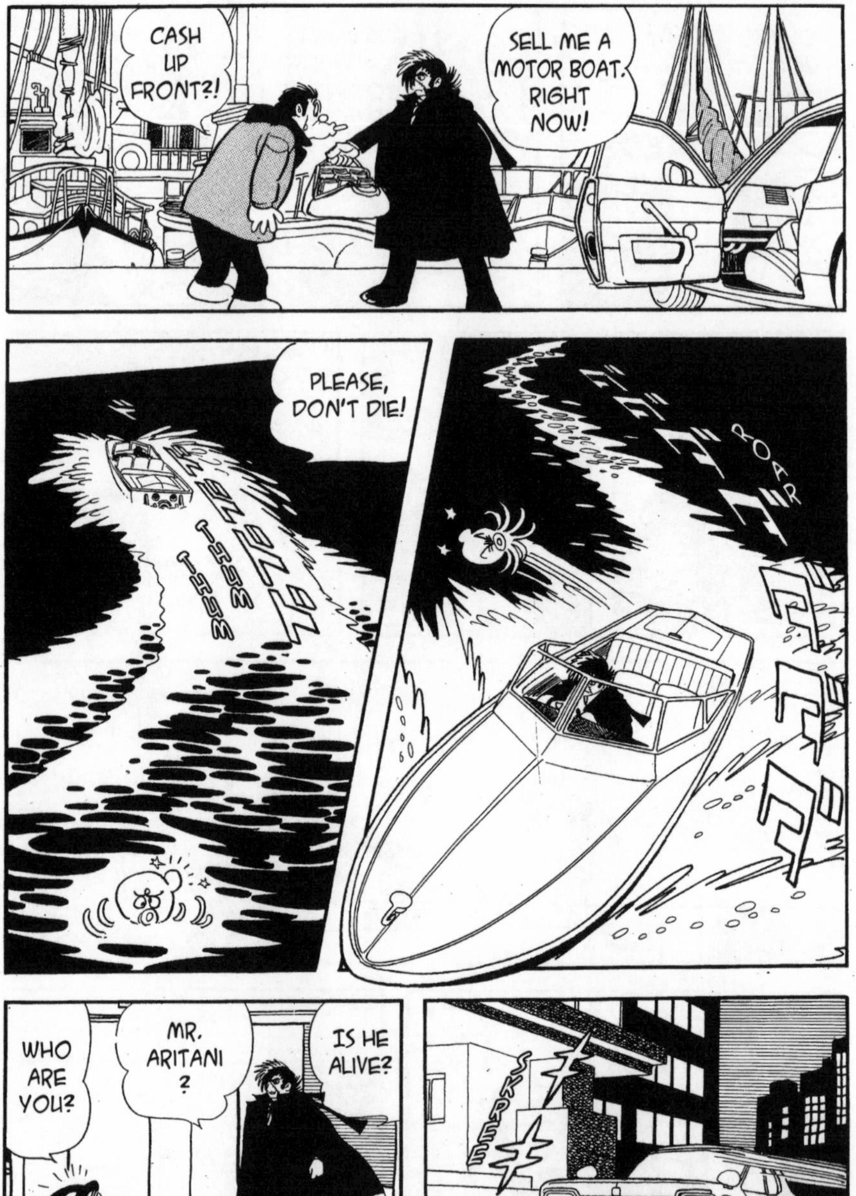
SELL ME A MOTOR BOAT. RIGHT NOW!
CASH UP FRONT?!
ROAR
PLEASE, DON'T DIE!
SKREE
IS HE ALIVE?
MR. ARITANI?
WHO ARE YOU?

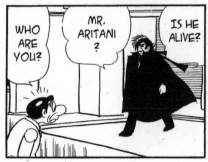

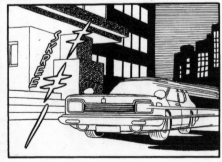

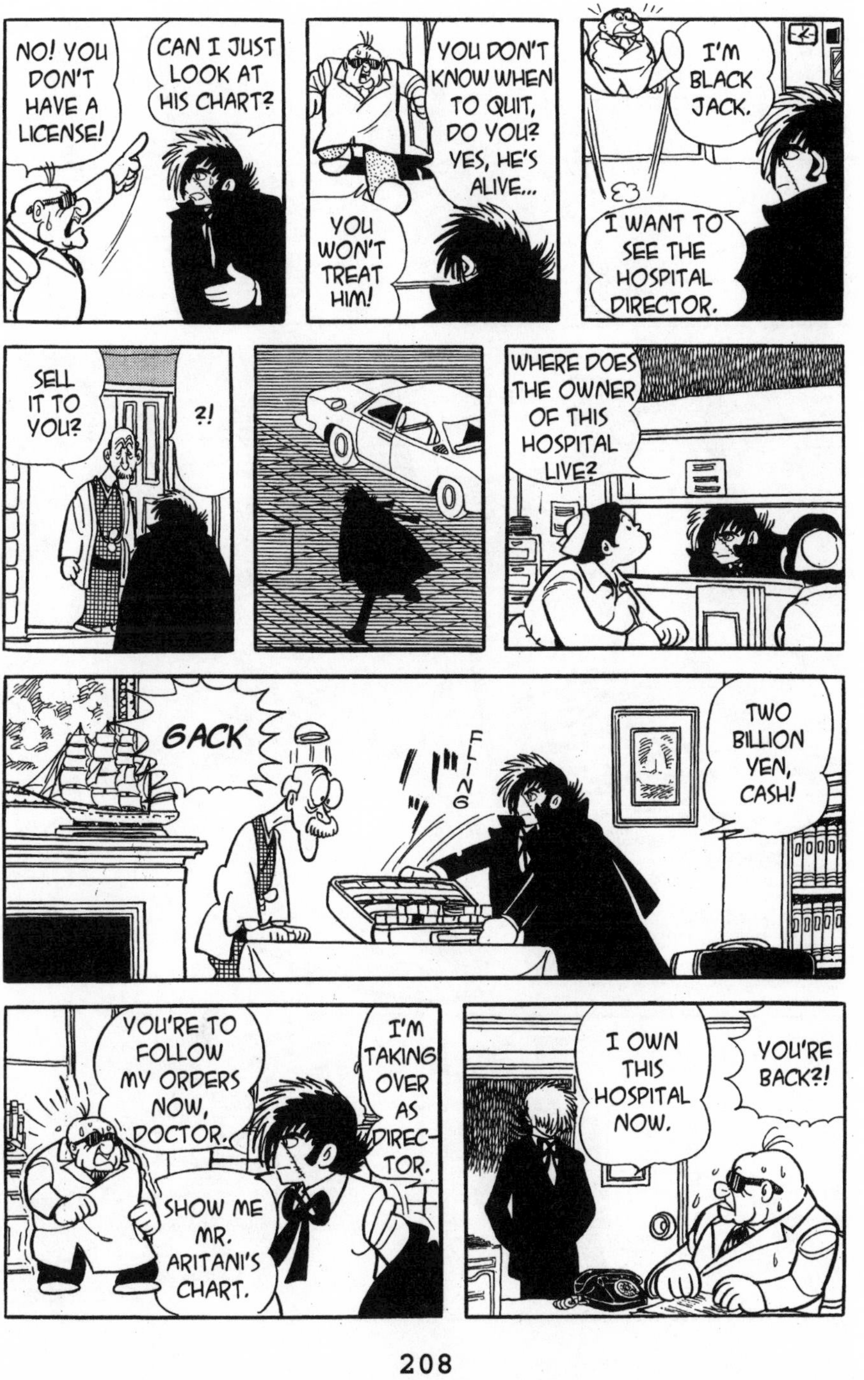
I'M BLACK JACK.
I WANT TO SEE THE HOSPITAL DIRECTOR.
YOU DON'T KNOW WHEN TO QUIT, DO YOU? YES, HE'S ALIVE...
YOU WON'T TREAT HIM!
CAN I JUST LOOK AT HIS CHART?
NO! YOU DON'T HAVE A LICENSE!
WHERE DOES THE OWNER OF THIS HOSPITAL LIVE?
?!
SELL IT TO YOU?
TWO BILLION YEN, CASH!
FLING
GACK
YOU'RE BACK?!
I OWN THIS HOSPITAL NOW.
I'M TAKING OVER AS DIRECTOR.
YOU'RE TO FOLLOW MY ORDERS NOW, DOCTOR.
SHOW ME MR. ARITANI'S CHART.

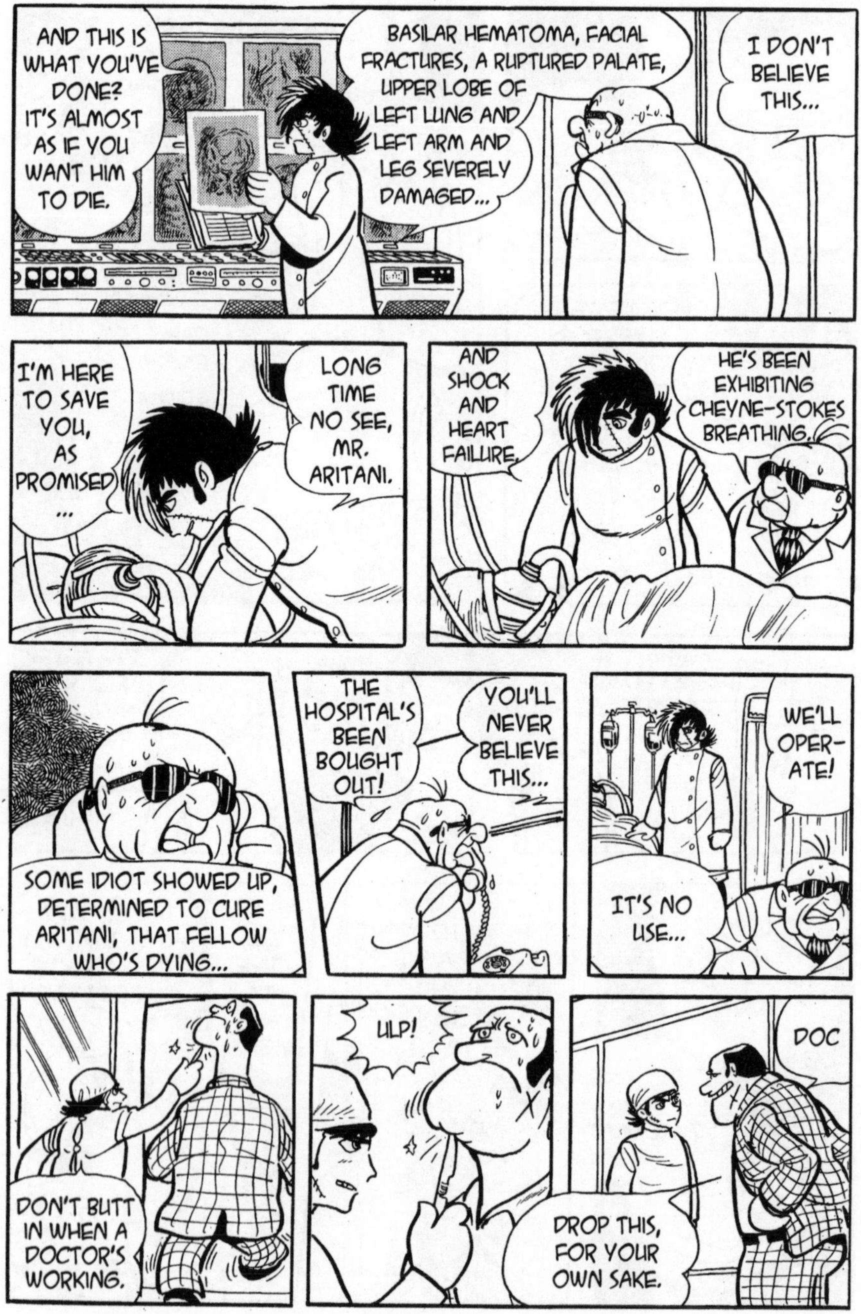
I DON'T BELIEVE THIS...
BASILAR HEMATOMA, FACIAL FRACTURES, A RUPTURED PALATE, UPPER LOBE OF LEFT LUNG AND LEFT ARM AND LEG SEVERELY DAMAGED...
AND THIS IS WHAT YOU'VE DONE? IT'S ALMOST AS IF YOU WANT HIM TO DIE.
HE'S BEEN EXHIBITING CHEYNE-STOKES BREATHING.
AND SHOCK AND HEART FAILURE.
LONG TIME NO SEE, MR. ARITANI.
I'M HERE TO SAVE YOU, AS PROMISED...
WE'LL OPER-ATE!
IT'S NO USE...
YOU'LL NEVER BELIEVE THIS...
THE HOSPITAL'S BEEN BOUGHT OUT!
SOME IDIOT SHOWED UP, DETERMINED TO CURE ARITANI, THAT FELLOW WHO'S DYING...
DOC
DROP THIS, FOR YOUR OWN SAKE.
ULP!
DON'T BUTT IN WHEN A DOCTOR'S WORKING.

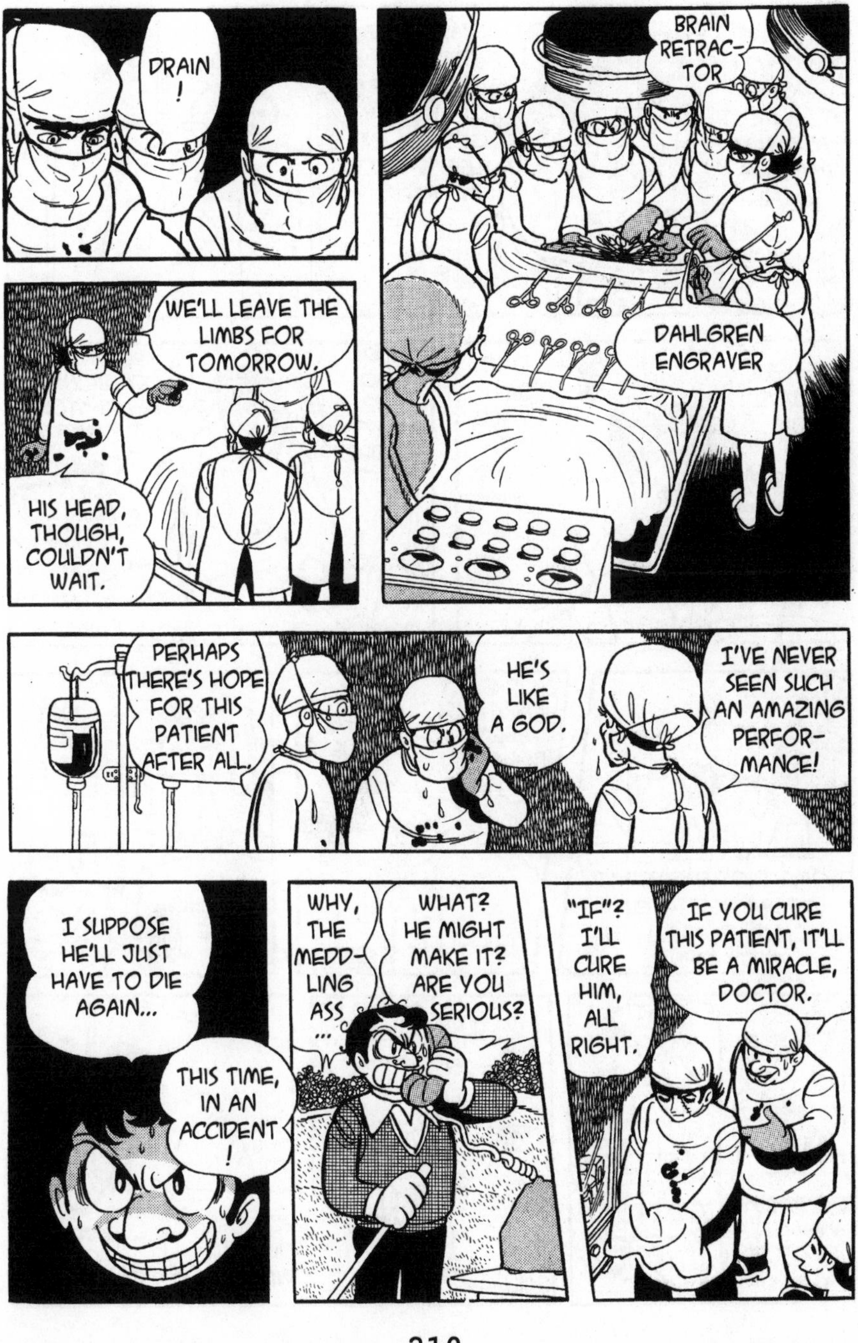
BRAIN RETRACTOR
DAHLGREN ENGRAVER
DRAIN!
WE'LL LEAVE THE LIMBS FOR TOMORROW.
HIS HEAD, THOUGH, COULDN'T WAIT.
I'VE NEVER SEEN SUCH AN AMAZING PERFORMANCE!
HE'S LIKE A GOD.
PERHAPS THERE'S HOPE FOR THIS PATIENT AFTER ALL.
IF YOU CURE THIS PATIENT, IT'LL BE A MIRACLE, DOCTOR.
"IF"? I'LL CURE HIM, ALL RIGHT.
WHAT? HE MIGHT MAKE IT? ARE YOU SERIOUS?
WHY, THE MEDDLING ASS...
I SUPPOSE HE'LL JUST HAVE TO DIE AGAIN...
THIS TIME, IN AN ACCIDENT!

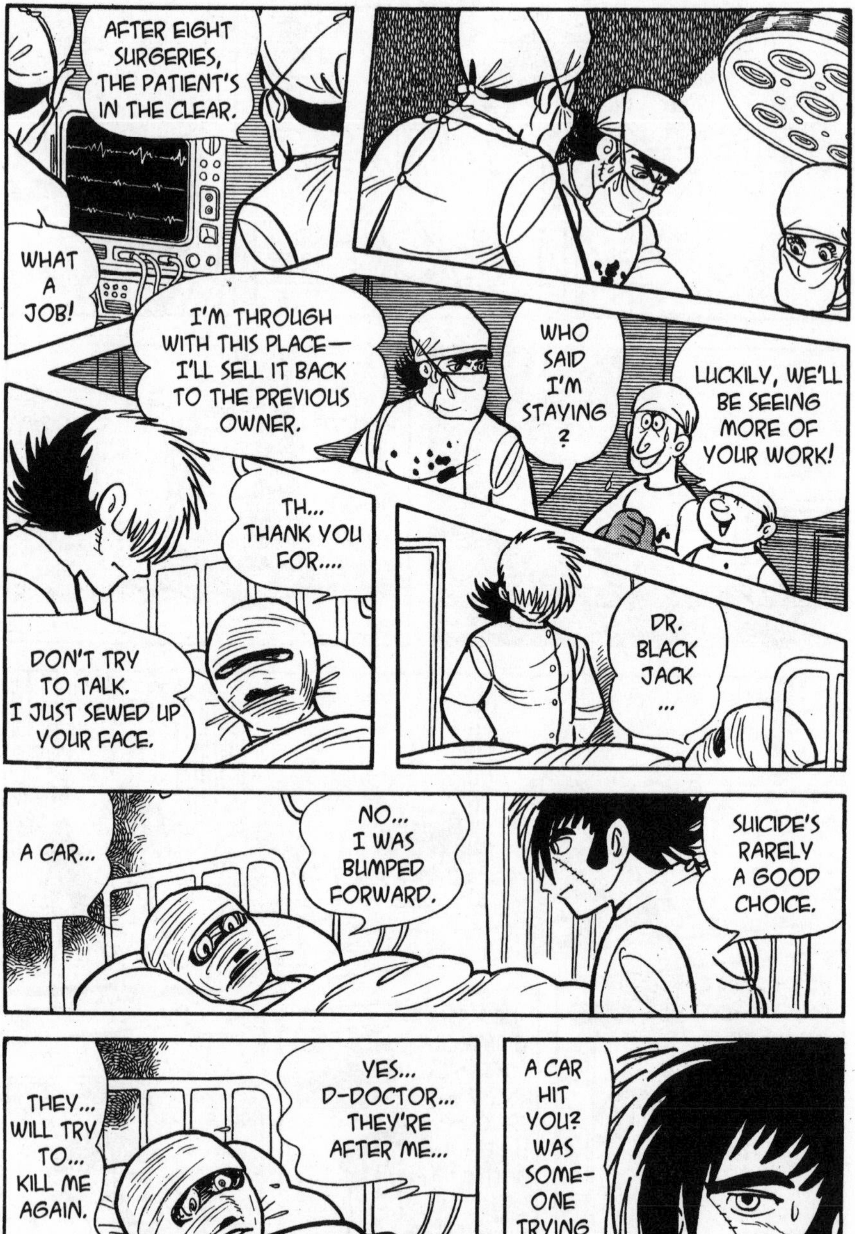
AFTER EIGHT SURGERIES, THE PATIENT'S IN THE CLEAR.
WHAT A JOB!
LUCKILY, WE'LL BE SEEING MORE OF YOUR WORK!
WHO SAID I'M STAYING?
I'M THROUGH WITH THIS PLACE— I'LL SELL IT BACK TO THE PREVIOUS OWNER.
DR. BLACK JACK ...
TH... THANK YOU FOR....
DON'T TRY TO TALK. I JUST SEWED UP YOUR FACE.
SUICIDE'S RARELY A GOOD CHOICE.
NO... I WAS BUMPED FORWARD.
A CAR...
A CAR HIT YOU? WAS SOME-ONE TRYING TO KILL YOU?
YES... D-DOCTOR... THEY'RE AFTER ME...
THEY... WILL TRY TO... KILL ME AGAIN.

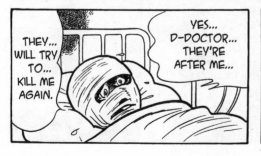

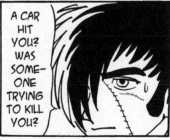

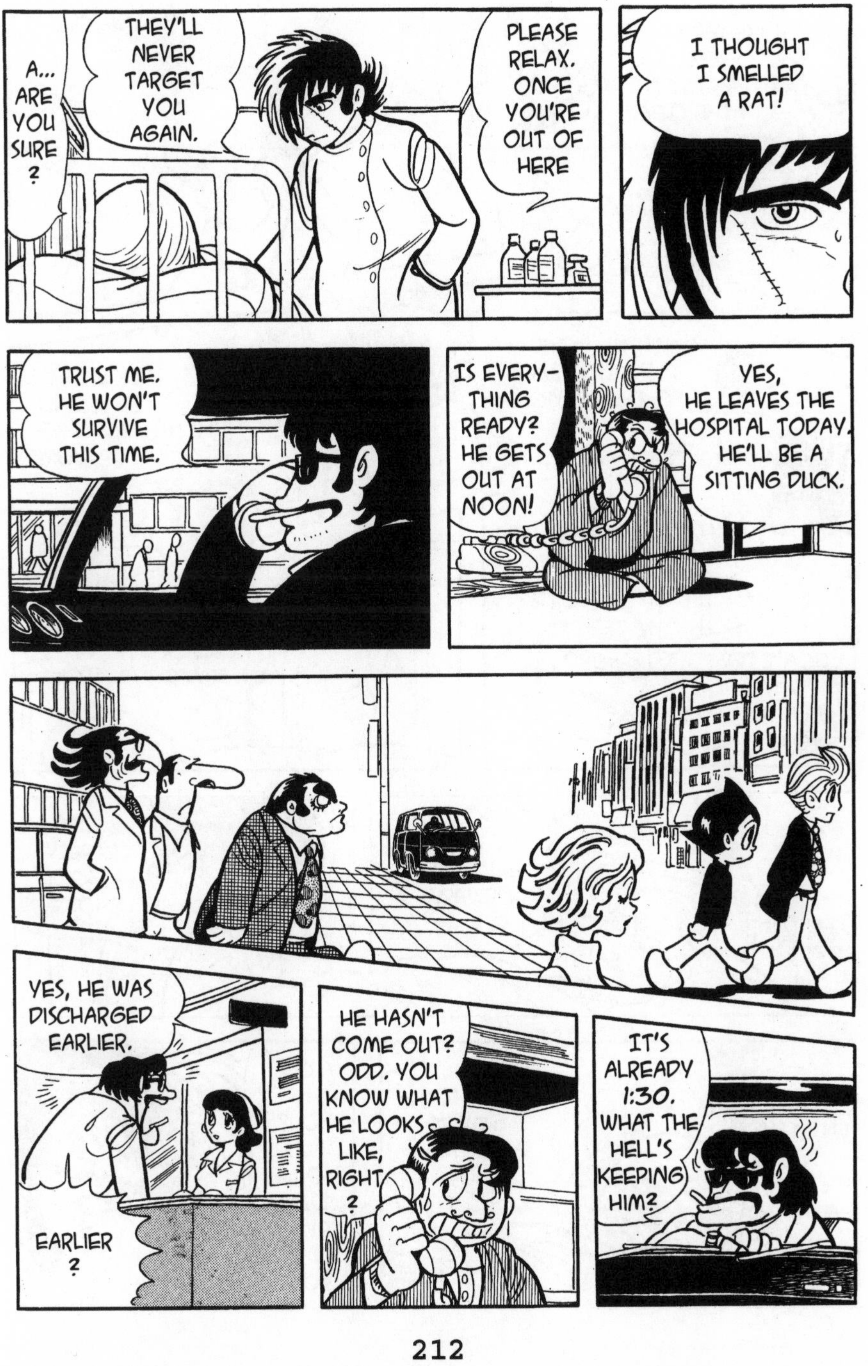
I THOUGHT I SMELLED A RAT!
PLEASE RELAX. ONCE YOU'RE OUT OF HERE
THEY'LL NEVER TARGET YOU AGAIN.
A... ARE YOU SURE?
YES, HE LEAVES THE HOSPITAL TODAY. HE'LL BE A SITTING DUCK.
IS EVERY-THING READY? HE GETS OUT AT NOON!
TRUST ME. HE WON'T SURVIVE THIS TIME.
IT'S ALREADY 1:30. WHAT THE HELL'S KEEPING HIM?
HE HASN'T COME OUT? ODD. YOU KNOW WHAT HE LOOKS LIKE, RIGHT?
YES, HE WAS DISCHARGED EARLIER.
EARLIER?

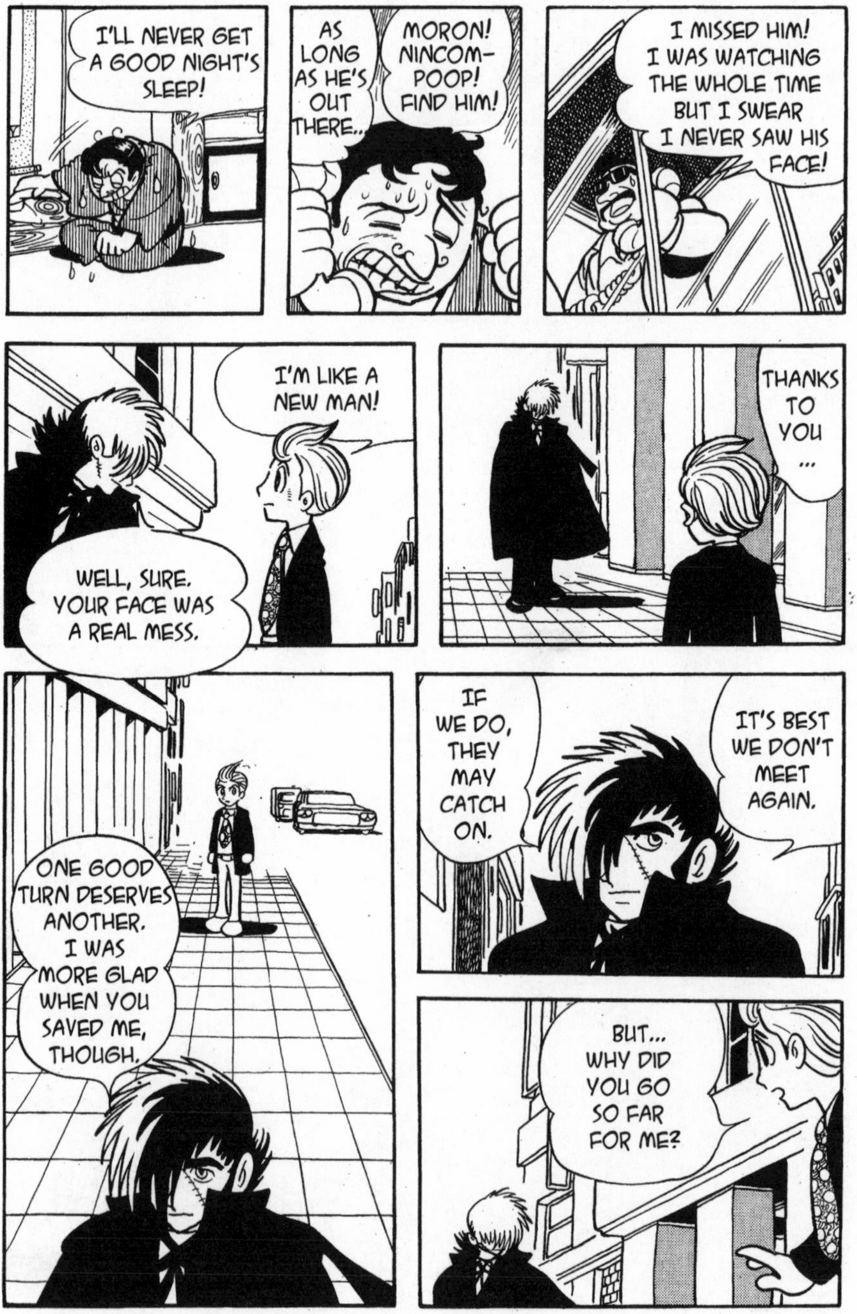
I MISSED HIM! I WAS WATCHING THE WHOLE TIME BUT I SWEAR I NEVER SAW HIS FACE!
MORON! NINCOM-POOP! FIND HIM!
AS LONG AS HE'S OUT THERE..
I'LL NEVER GET A GOOD NIGHT'S SLEEP!
THANKS TO YOU ...
I'M LIKE A NEW MAN!
WELL, SURE. YOUR FACE WAS A REAL MESS.
IT'S BEST WE DON'T MEET AGAIN.
IF WE DO, THEY MAY CATCH ON.
BUT... WHY DID YOU GO SO FAR FOR ME?
ONE GOOD TURN DESERVES ANOTHER. I WAS MORE GLAD WHEN YOU SAVED ME, THOUGH.

STRADIVARIUS

VWOOOSH
グオーーン
WHAT?!
BUT WHERE ARE WE?
IT BEATS CRASHING...
DUE TO INSTRUMENT FAILURE, WE'LL MAKE AN EMERGENCY LANDING!
BZZZ
BZZZ
BWOOOSH

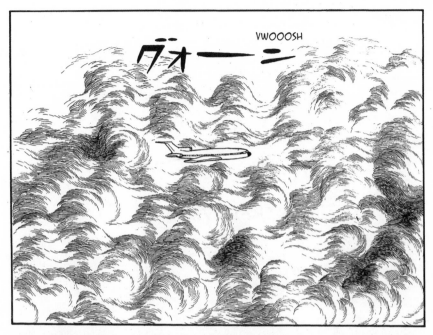

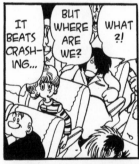

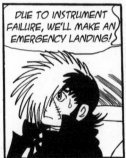

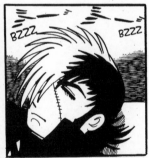

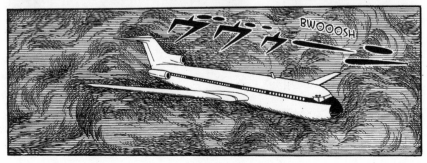

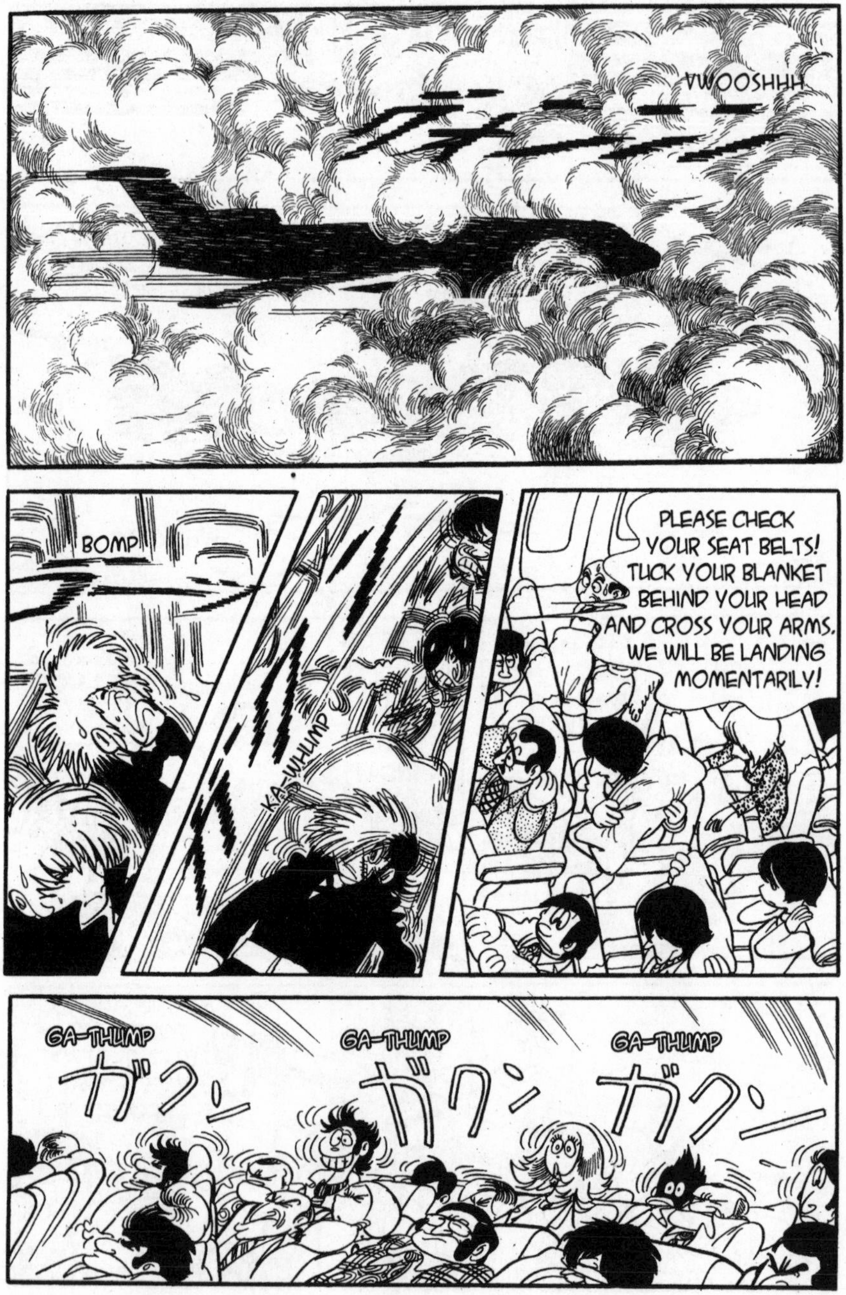
VWOOSHHH
PLEASE CHECK YOUR SEAT BELTS! TUCK YOUR BLANKET BEHIND YOUR HEAD AND CROSS YOUR ARMS. WE WILL BE LANDING MOMENTARILY!
KA-WHUMP
BOMP
GA-THUMP
GA-THUMP
GA-THUMP

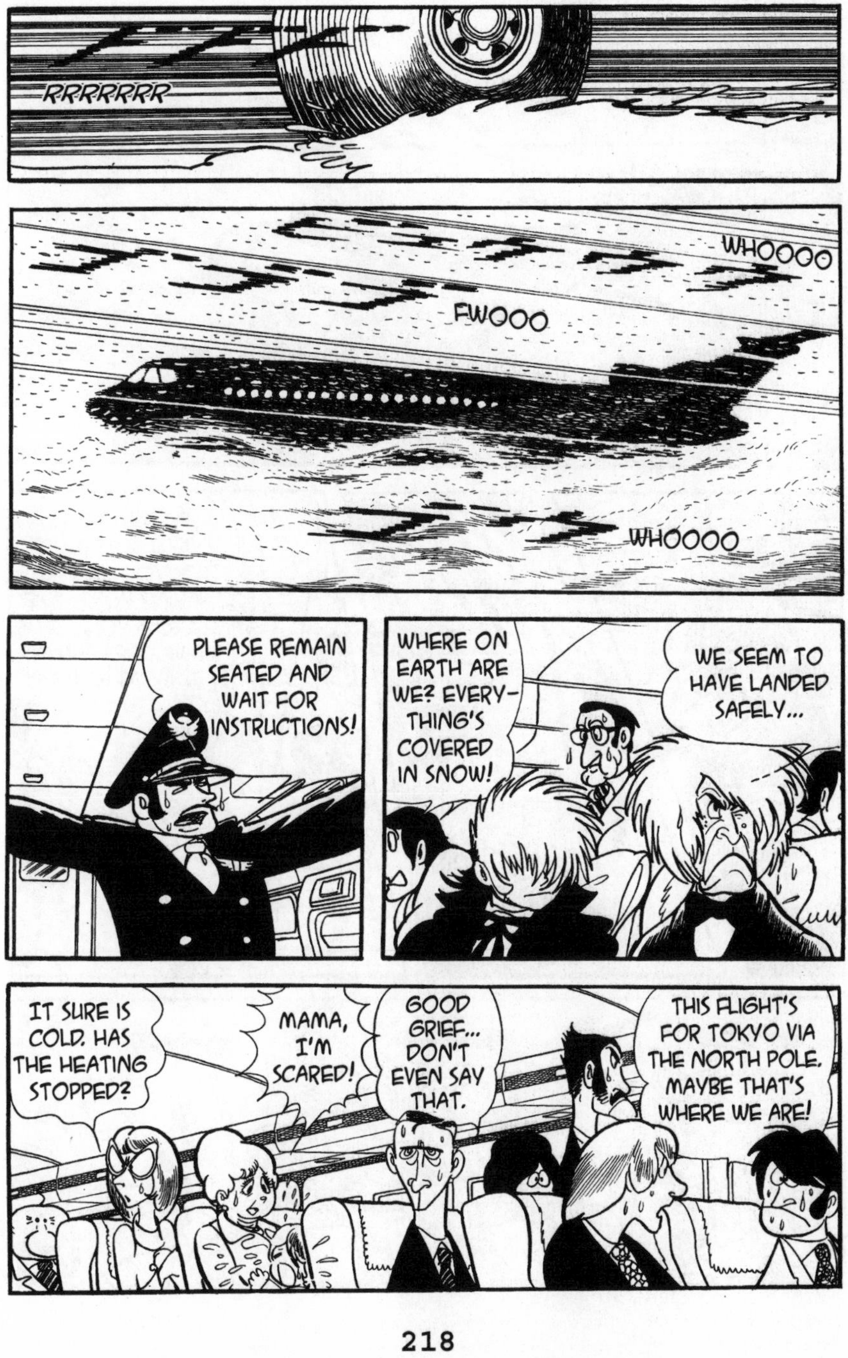
RRRRRRRR
WHOOOO
FWOOO
WHOOOO
WE SEEM TO HAVE LANDED SAFELY...
WHERE ON EARTH ARE WE? EVERYTHING'S COVERED IN SNOW!
PLEASE REMAIN SEATED AND WAIT FOR INSTRUCTIONS!
THIS FLIGHT'S FOR TOKYO VIA THE NORTH POLE. MAYBE THAT'S WHERE WE ARE!
GOOD GRIEF... DON'T EVEN SAY THAT.
MAMA, I'M SCARED!
IT SURE IS COLD. HAS THE HEATING STOPPED?

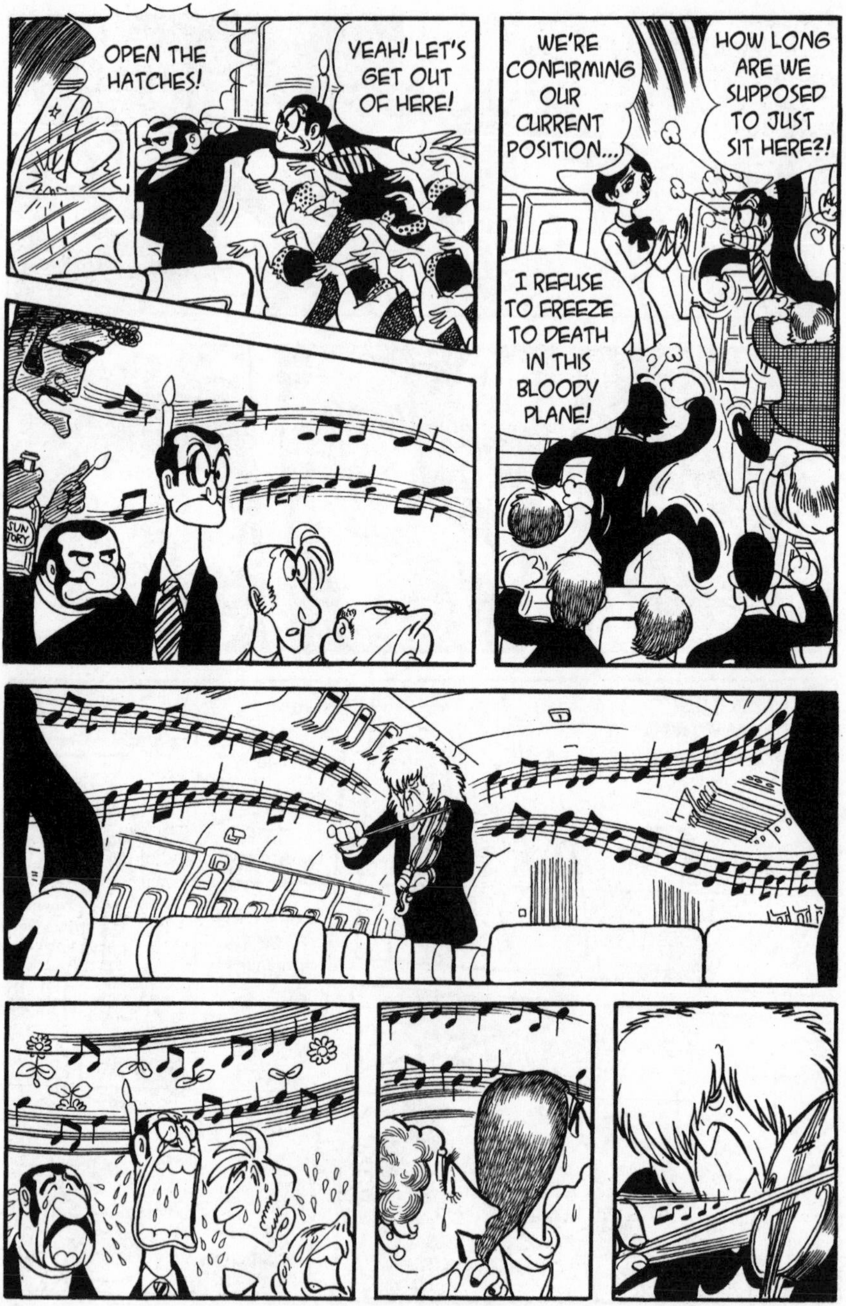
OPEN THE HATCHES!
YEAH! LET'S GET OUT OF HERE!
WE'RE CONFIRMING OUR CURRENT POSITION...
HOW LONG ARE WE SUPPOSED TO JUST SIT HERE?!
I REFUSE TO FREEZE TO DEATH IN THIS BLOODY PLANE!
SUNTORY

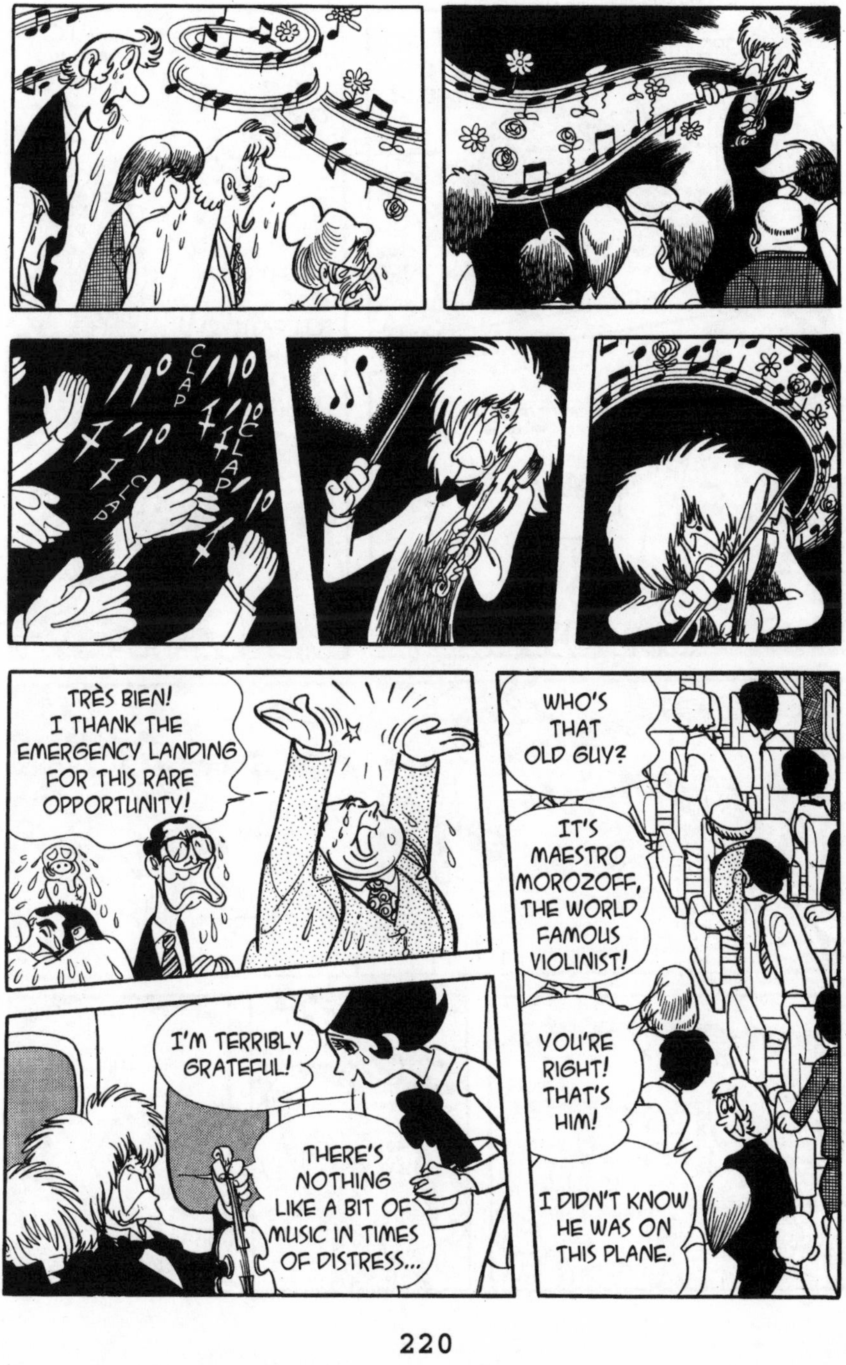
CLAP
CLAP
CLAP
CLAP
TRÈS BIEN! I THANK THE EMERGENCY LANDING FOR THIS RARE OPPORTUNITY!
I'M TERRIBLY GRATEFUL!
THERE'S NOTHING LIKE A BIT OF MUSIC IN TIMES OF DISTRESS...
WHO'S THAT OLD GUY?
IT'S MAESTRO MOROZOFF, THE WORLD FAMOUS VIOLINIST!
YOU'RE RIGHT! THAT'S HIM!
I DIDN'T KNOW HE WAS ON THIS PLANE.

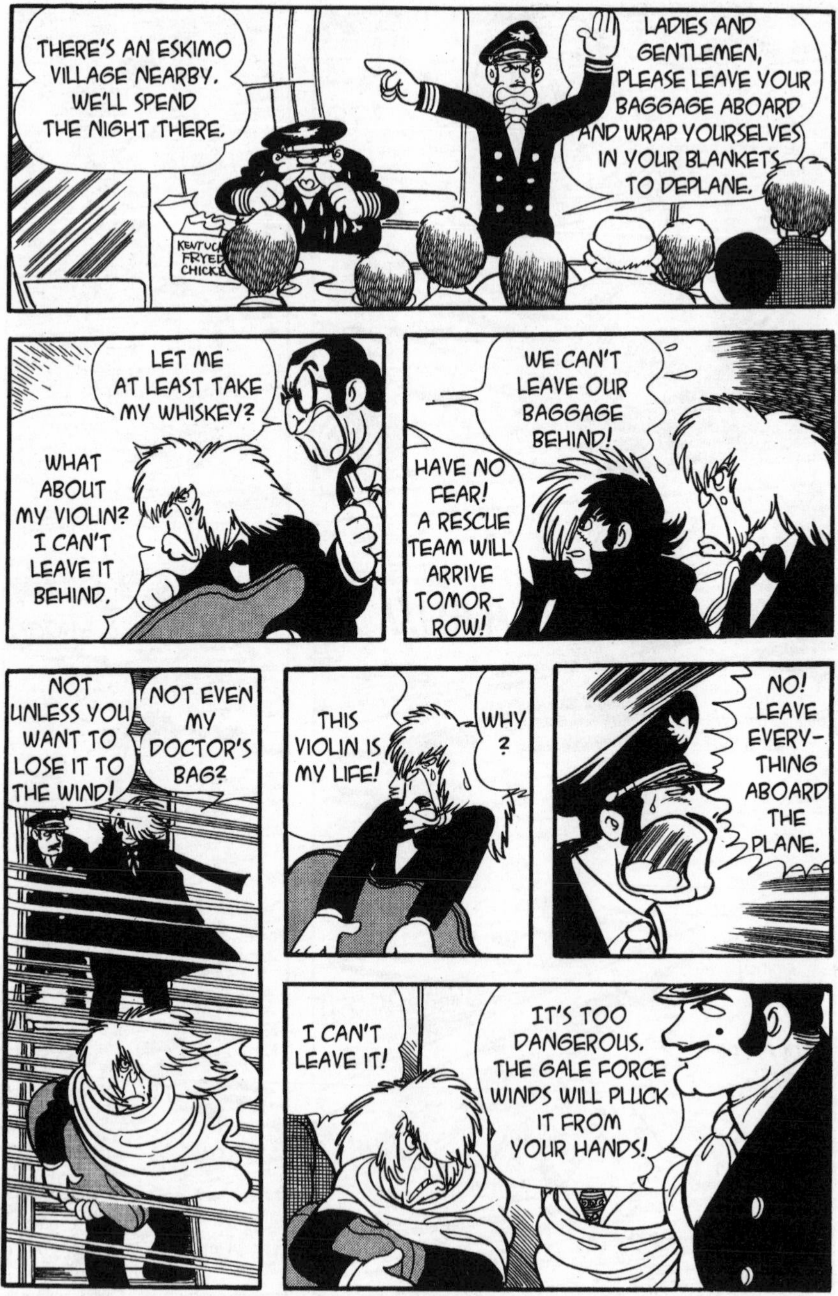
LADIES AND GENTLEMEN, PLEASE LEAVE YOUR BAGGAGE ABOARD AND WRAP YOURSELVES IN YOUR BLANKETS TO DEPLANE.
THERE'S AN ESKIMO VILLAGE NEARBY. WE'LL SPEND THE NIGHT THERE.
KENTUCK FRYED CHICKE
WE CAN'T LEAVE OUR BAGGAGE BEHIND!
HAVE NO FEAR! A RESCUE TEAM WILL ARRIVE TOMOR-ROW!
LET ME AT LEAST TAKE MY WHISKEY?
WHAT ABOUT MY VIOLIN? I CAN'T LEAVE IT BEHIND.
NO! LEAVE EVERY-THING ABOARD THE PLANE.
WHY ?
THIS VIOLIN IS MY LIFE!
IT'S TOO DANGEROUS. THE GALE FORCE WINDS WILL PLUCK IT FROM YOUR HANDS!
I CAN'T LEAVE IT!
NOT EVEN MY DOCTOR'S BAG?
NOT UNLESS YOU WANT TO LOSE IT TO THE WIND!

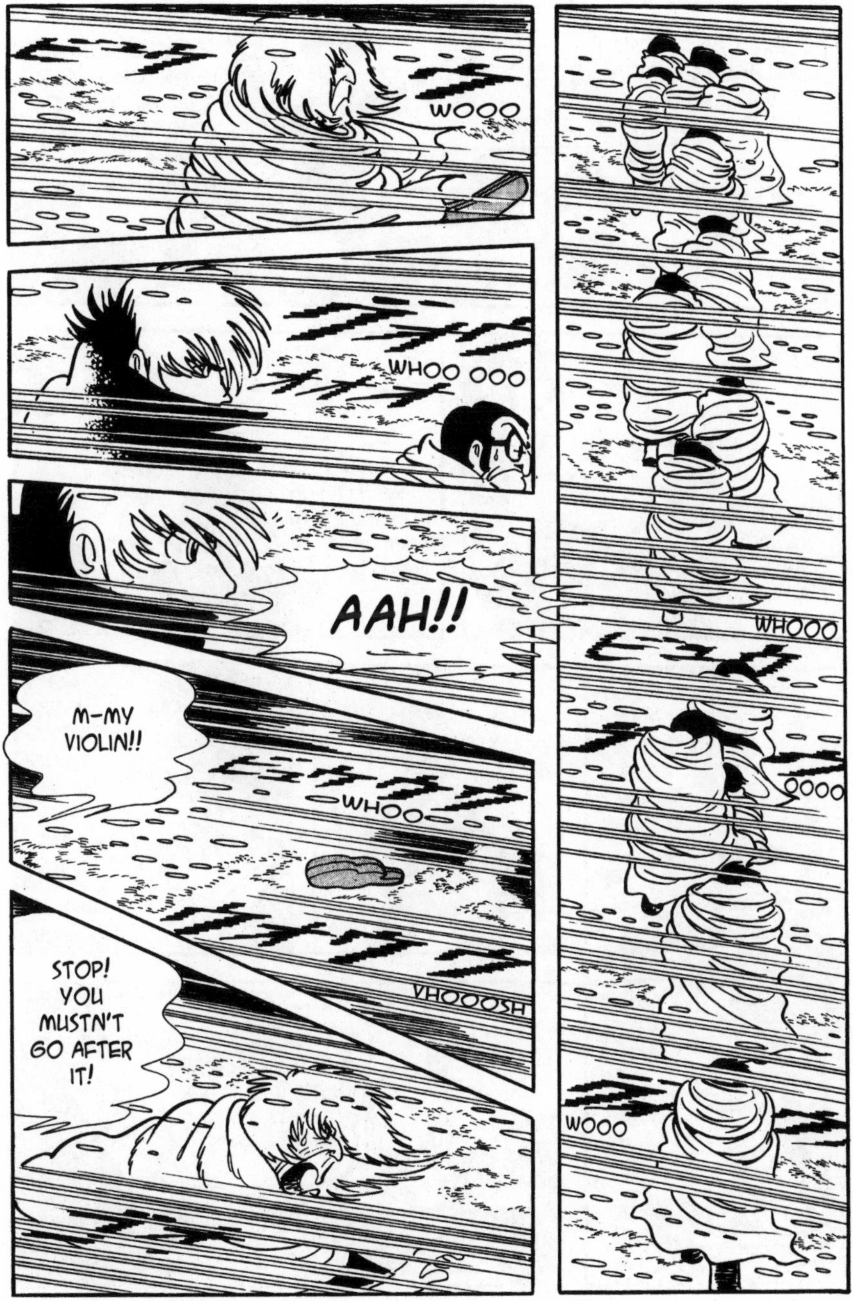
WHOOO
OOOO
WOOO
WOOO
WHOO OOO
AAH!!
M-MY VIOLIN!!
WHOO
VHOOOSH
STOP! YOU MUSTN'T GO AFTER IT!

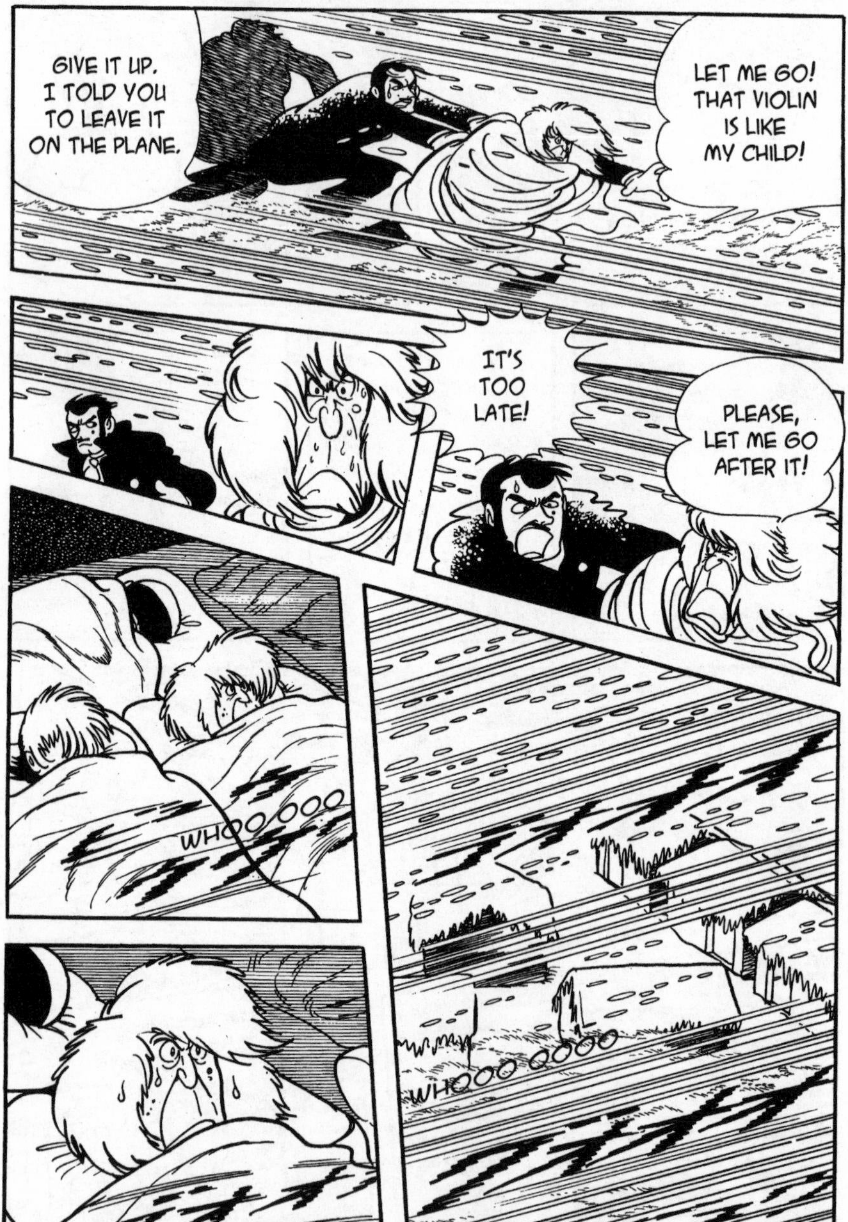
LET ME GO! THAT VIOLIN IS LIKE MY CHILD!
GIVE IT UP. I TOLD YOU TO LEAVE IT ON THE PLANE.
PLEASE, LET ME GO AFTER IT!
IT'S TOO LATE!
WHOOO OOOO
WHOOOOOO
WHOO

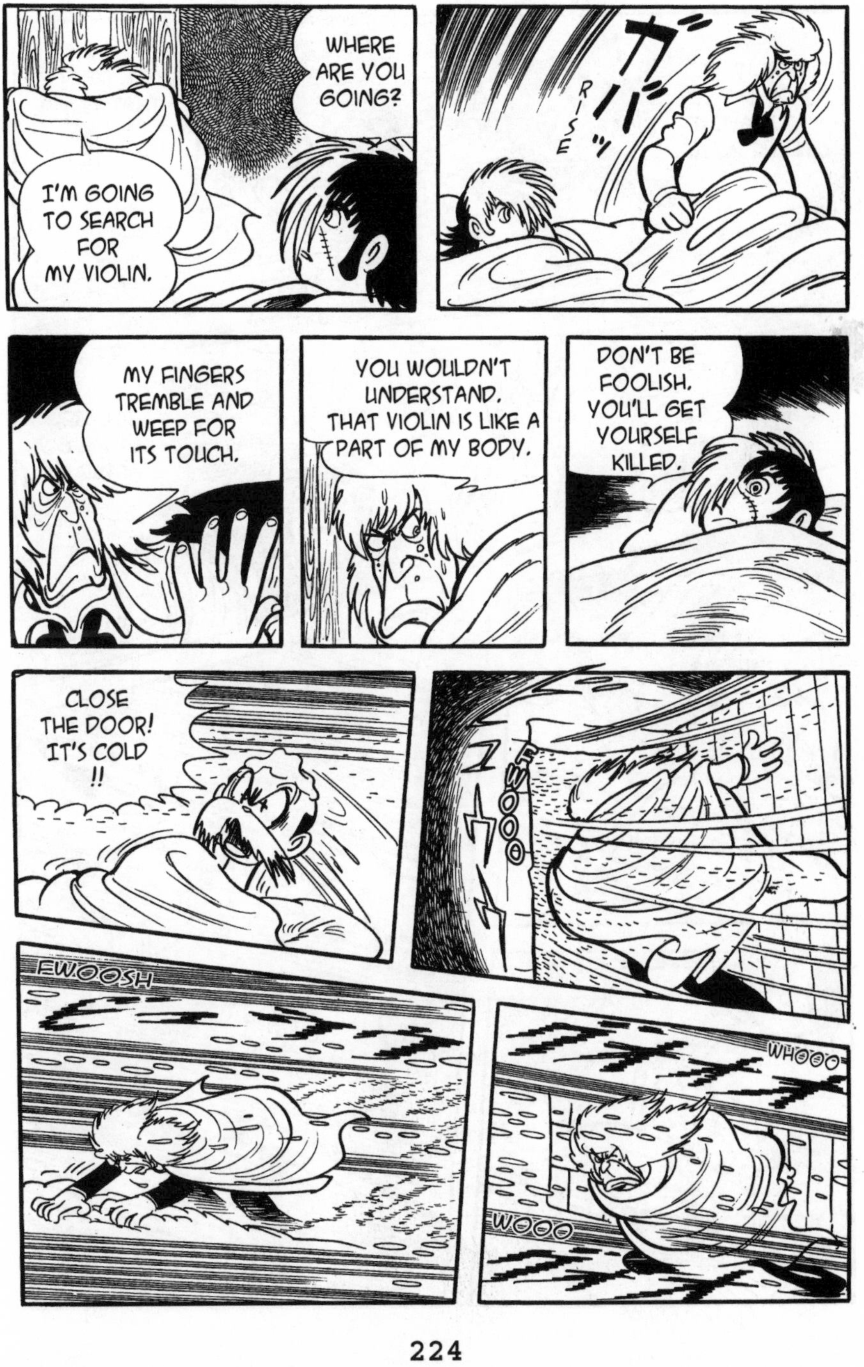
RISE
WHERE ARE YOU GOING?
I'M GOING TO SEARCH FOR MY VIOLIN.
DON'T BE FOOLISH. YOU'LL GET YOURSELF KILLED.
YOU WOULDN'T UNDERSTAND. THAT VIOLIN IS LIKE A PART OF MY BODY.
MY FINGERS TREMBLE AND WEEP FOR ITS TOUCH.
FWOOO
CLOSE THE DOOR! IT'S COLD !!
WHOOO
WOOO
FWOOSH

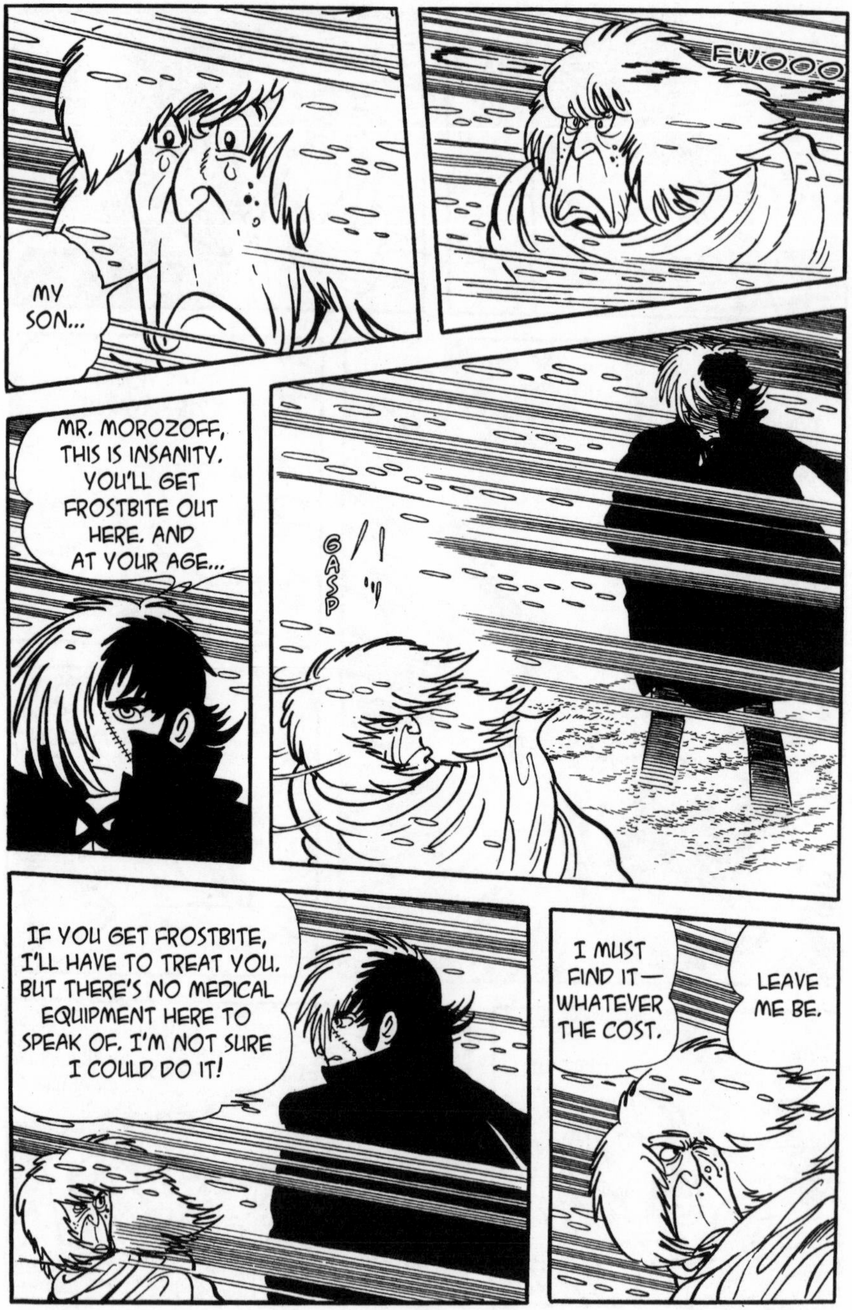
MY SON...
FWOOO
MR. MOROZOFF, THIS IS INSANITY. YOU'LL GET FROSTBITE OUT HERE. AND AT YOUR AGE...
GASP
IF YOU GET FROSTBITE, I'LL HAVE TO TREAT YOU. BUT THERE'S NO MEDICAL EQUIPMENT HERE TO SPEAK OF. I'M NOT SURE I COULD DO IT!
I MUST FIND IT— WHATEVER THE COST.
LEAVE ME BE.

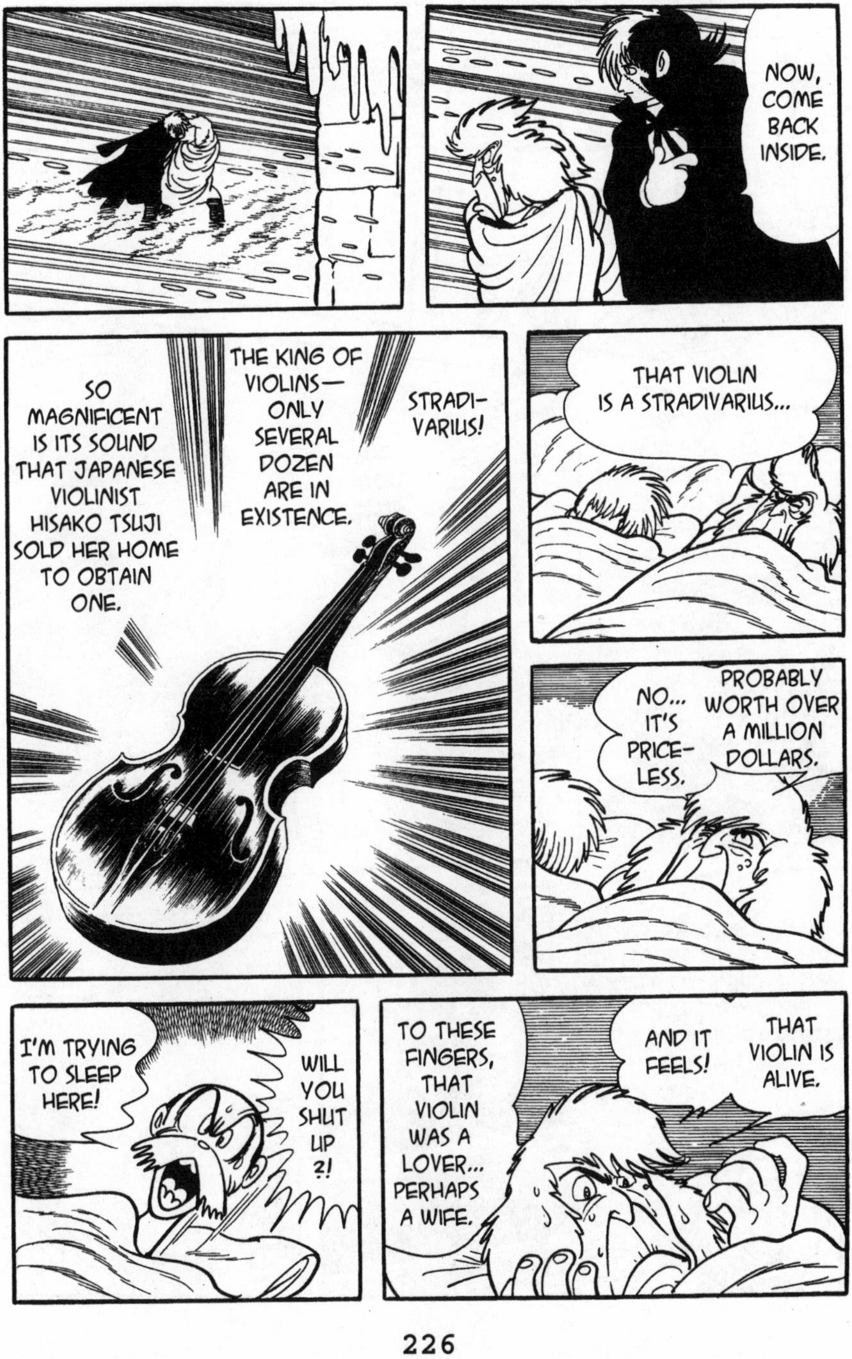

NOW, COME BACK INSIDE.
THAT VIOLIN IS A STRADIVARIUS...
PROBABLY WORTH OVER A MILLION DOLLARS.
NO... IT'S PRICE-LESS.
STRADI-VARIUS!
THE KING OF VIOLINS—ONLY SEVERAL DOZEN ARE IN EXISTENCE.
SO MAGNIFICENT IS ITS SOUND THAT JAPANESE VIOLINIST HISAKO TSUJI SOLD HER HOME TO OBTAIN ONE.
THAT VIOLIN IS ALIVE.
AND IT FEELS!
TO THESE FINGERS, THAT VIOLIN WAS A LOVER... PERHAPS A WIFE.
WILL YOU SHUT UP ?!
I'M TRYING TO SLEEP HERE!

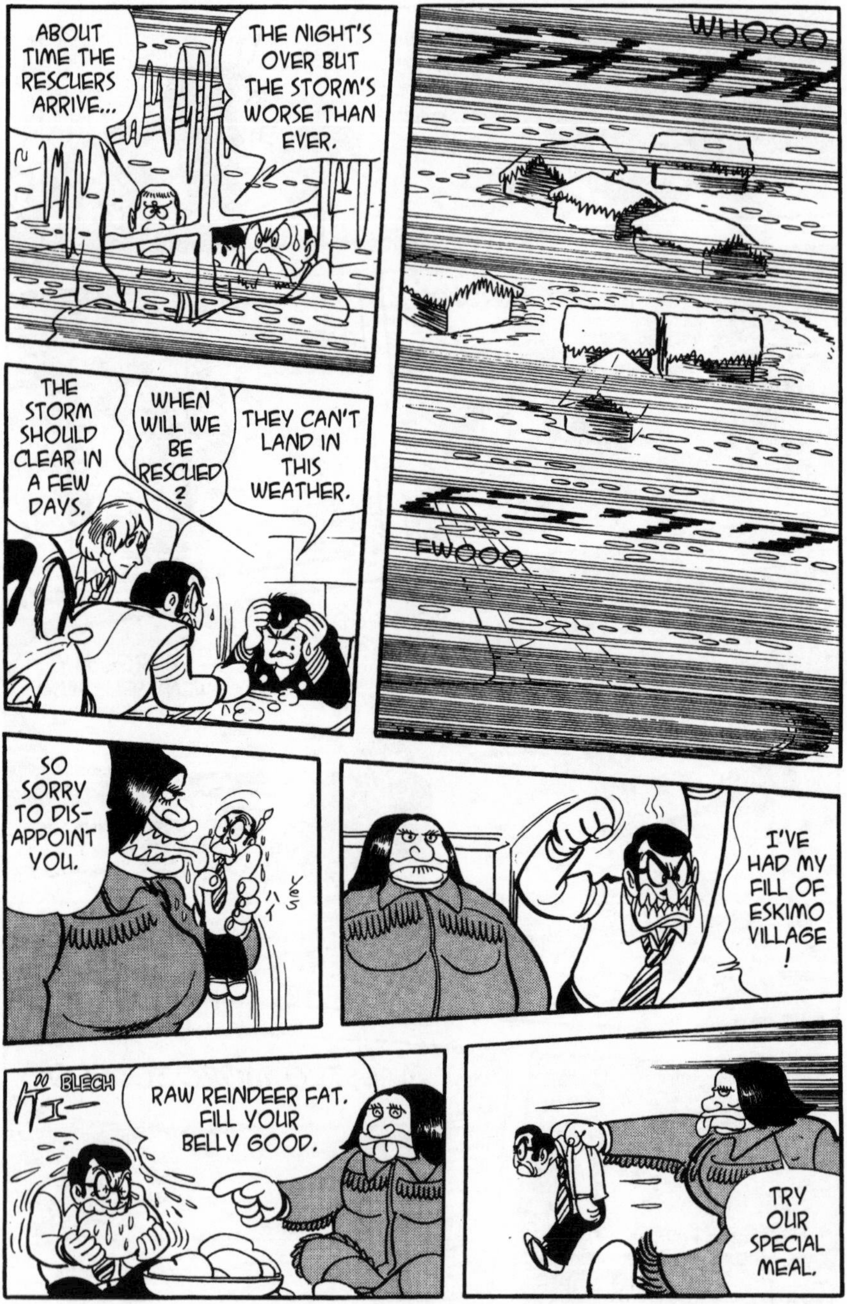
WHOOO
FWOOO
THE NIGHT'S OVER BUT THE STORM'S WORSE THAN EVER.
ABOUT TIME THE RESCUERS ARRIVE...
THEY CAN'T LAND IN THIS WEATHER.
WHEN WILL WE BE RESCUED?
THE STORM SHOULD CLEAR IN A FEW DAYS.
I'VE HAD MY FILL OF ESKIMO VILLAGE!
SO SORRY TO DIS-APPOINT YOU.
TRY OUR SPECIAL MEAL.
RAW REINDEER FAT. FILL YOUR BELLY GOOD.
BLECH

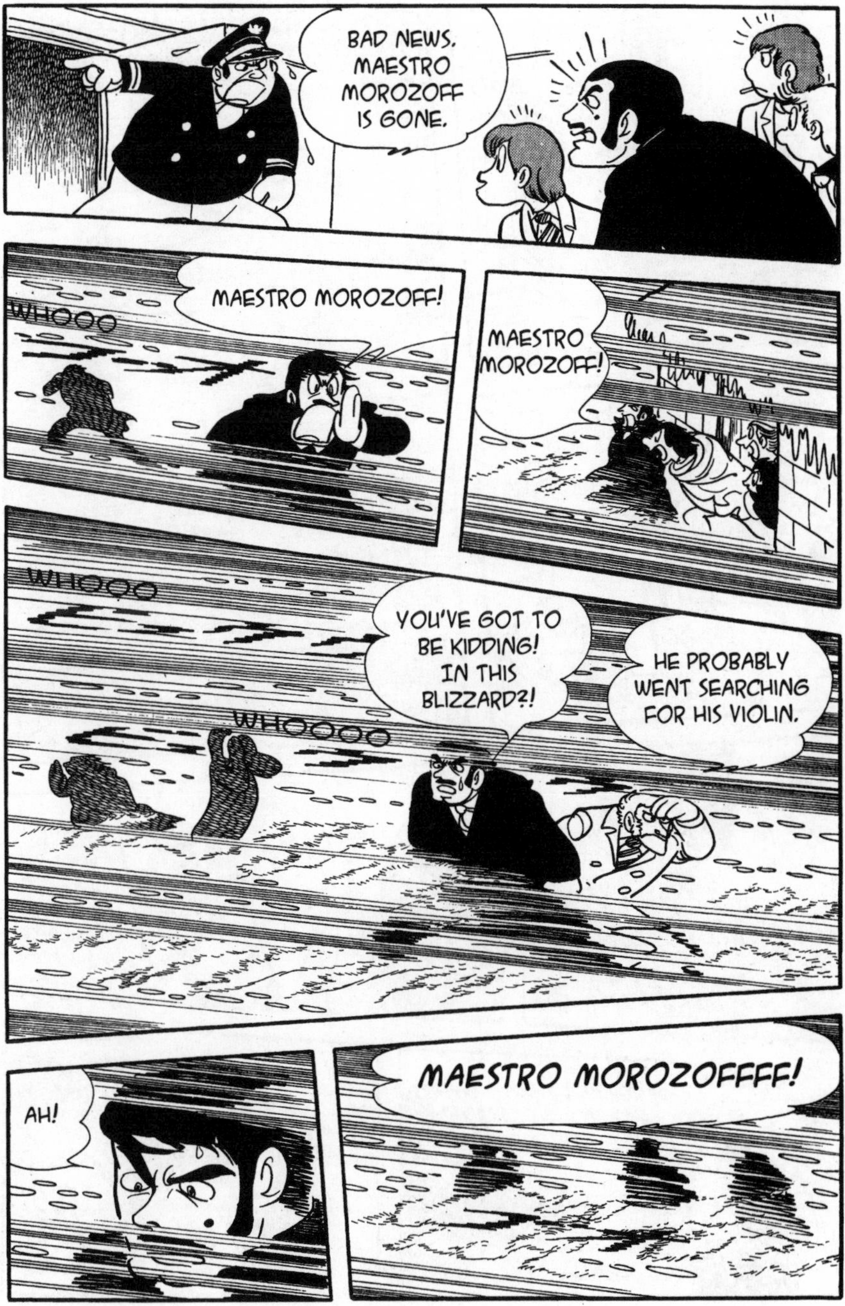
BAD NEWS. MAESTRO MOROZOFF IS GONE.
MAESTRO MOROZOFF!
MAESTRO MOROZOFF!
WHOOO
HE PROBABLY WENT SEARCHING FOR HIS VIOLIN.
YOU'VE GOT TO BE KIDDING! IN THIS BLIZZARD?!
WHOOO
WHOOOO
MAESTRO MOROZOFFFF!
AH!

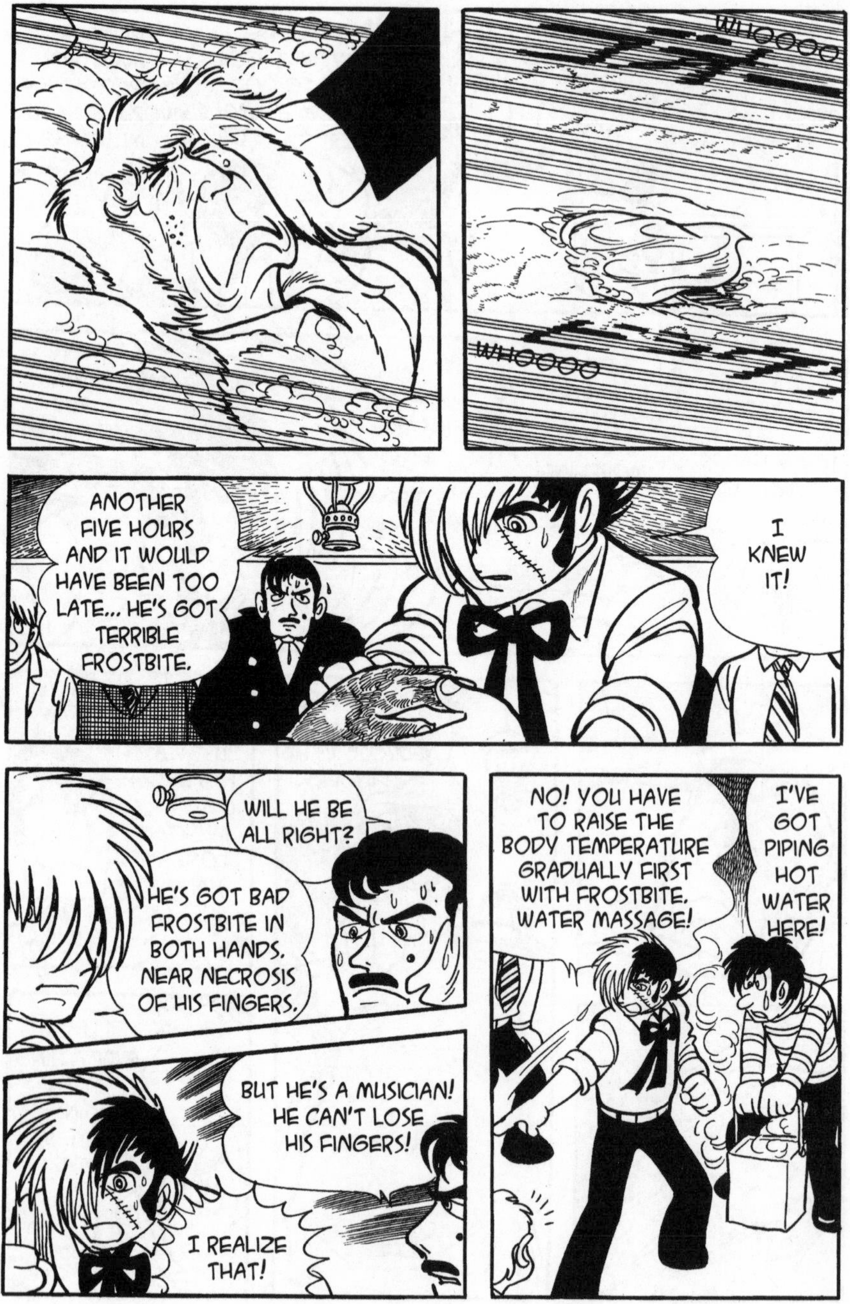
WHOOOO
WHOOOO
ANOTHER FIVE HOURS AND IT WOULD HAVE BEEN TOO LATE... HE'S GOT TERRIBLE FROSTBITE.
I KNEW IT!
WILL HE BE ALL RIGHT?
HE'S GOT BAD FROSTBITE IN BOTH HANDS. NEAR NECROSIS OF HIS FINGERS.
BUT HE'S A MUSICIAN! HE CAN'T LOSE HIS FINGERS!
I REALIZE THAT!
NO! YOU HAVE TO RAISE THE BODY TEMPERATURE GRADUALLY FIRST WITH FROSTBITE. WATER MASSAGE!
I'VE GOT PIPING HOT WATER HERE!

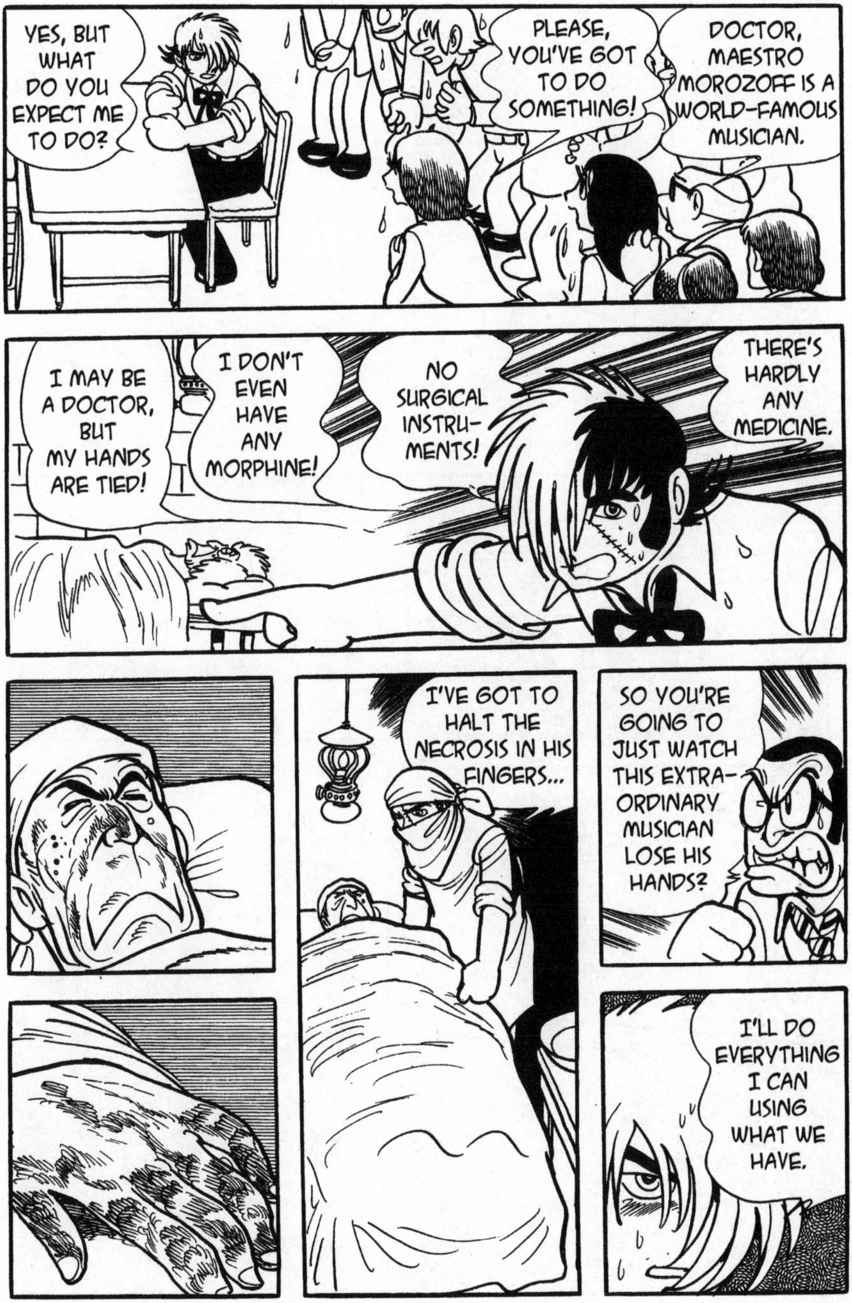
DOCTOR, MAESTRO MOROZOFF IS A WORLD-FAMOUS MUSICIAN.
PLEASE, YOU'VE GOT TO DO SOMETHING!
YES, BUT WHAT DO YOU EXPECT ME TO DO?
THERE'S HARDLY ANY MEDICINE.
NO SURGICAL INSTRU-MENTS!
I DON'T EVEN HAVE ANY MORPHINE!
I MAY BE A DOCTOR, BUT MY HANDS ARE TIED!
SO YOU'RE GOING TO JUST WATCH THIS EXTRA-ORDINARY MUSICIAN LOSE HIS HANDS?
I'LL DO EVERYTHING I CAN USING WHAT WE HAVE.
I'VE GOT TO HALT THE NECROSIS IN HIS FINGERS...

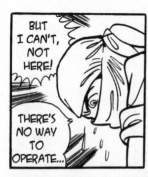

ON THE VERGE OF NECROSIS ...
IT'S USE-LESS!
SEVER THE SYMPATHETIC GANGLIA IN HIS LOWER BACK...
BUT I CAN'T, NOT HERE!
THERE'S NO WAY TO OPERATE...
I KNOW! THAT CHINESE DOCTOR, PROFESSOR YO, GAVE ME A BOOK ON ACUPUNCTURE ANESTHESIA...
THEIR ACUPUNCTURE TREATMENT IS ADVANCED.
MY MEMO ON WHERE TO INSERT THE NEEDLES!
FEELS LIKE GRASP-ING AT STRAWS ...
ONE...
TWO ...
LET THIS WORK,
ANES-THESIA ...

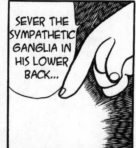

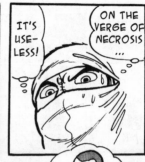

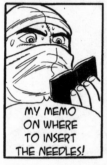

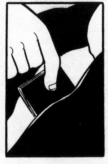

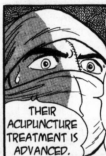

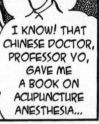

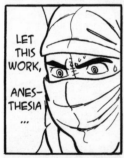

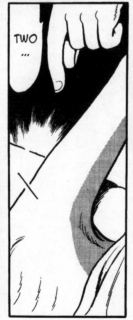

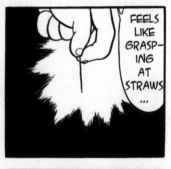

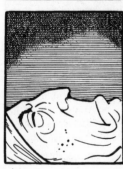

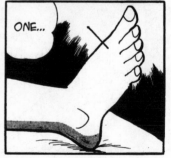

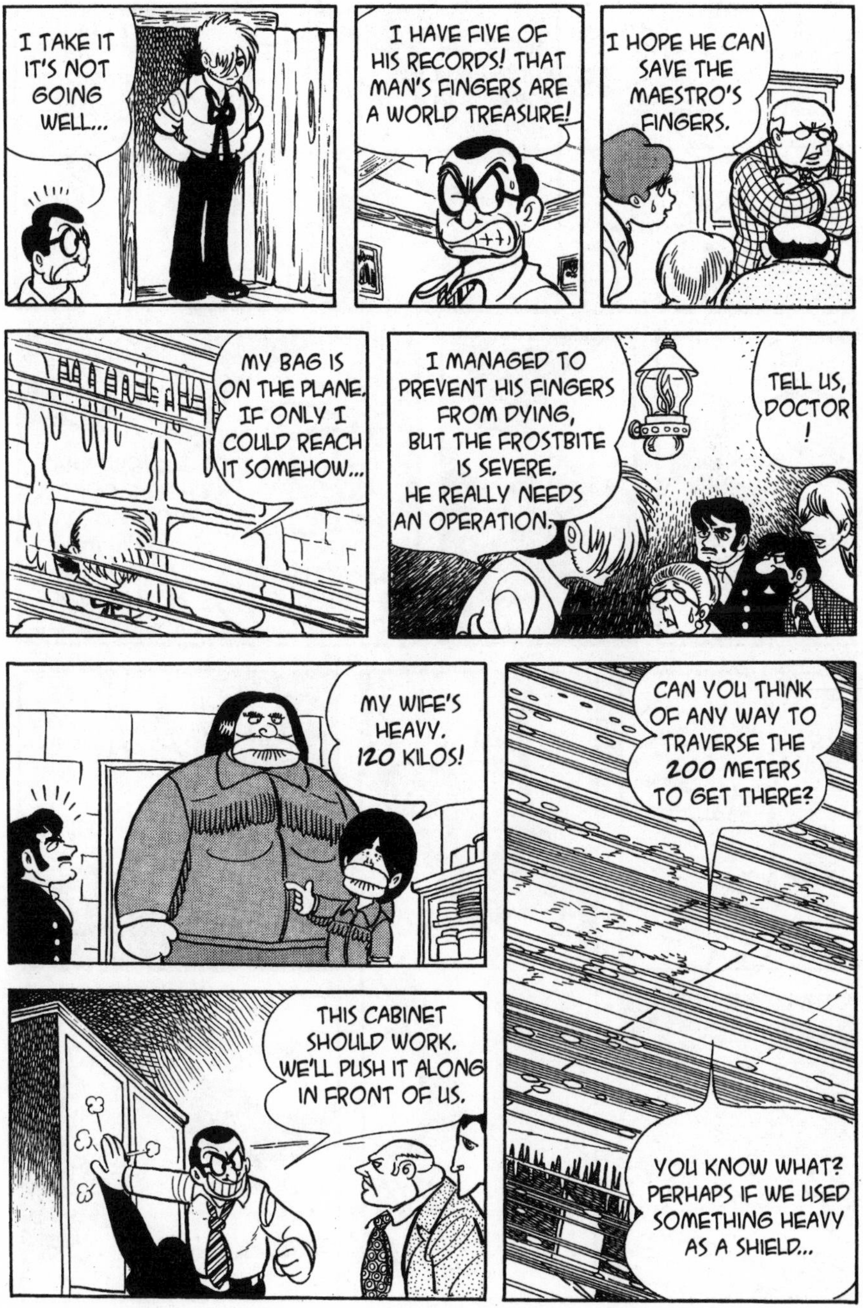
I HOPE HE CAN SAVE THE MAESTRO'S FINGERS.
I HAVE FIVE OF HIS RECORDS! THAT MAN'S FINGERS ARE A WORLD TREASURE!
I TAKE IT IT'S NOT GOING WELL...
TELL US, DOCTOR!
I MANAGED TO PREVENT HIS FINGERS FROM DYING, BUT THE FROSTBITE IS SEVERE. HE REALLY NEEDS AN OPERATION.
MY BAG IS ON THE PLANE. IF ONLY I COULD REACH IT SOMEHOW...
CAN YOU THINK OF ANY WAY TO TRAVERSE THE 200 METERS TO GET THERE?
YOU KNOW WHAT? PERHAPS IF WE USED SOMETHING HEAVY AS A SHIELD...
MY WIFE'S HEAVY. 120 KILOS!
THIS CABINET SHOULD WORK. WE'LL PUSH IT ALONG IN FRONT OF US.

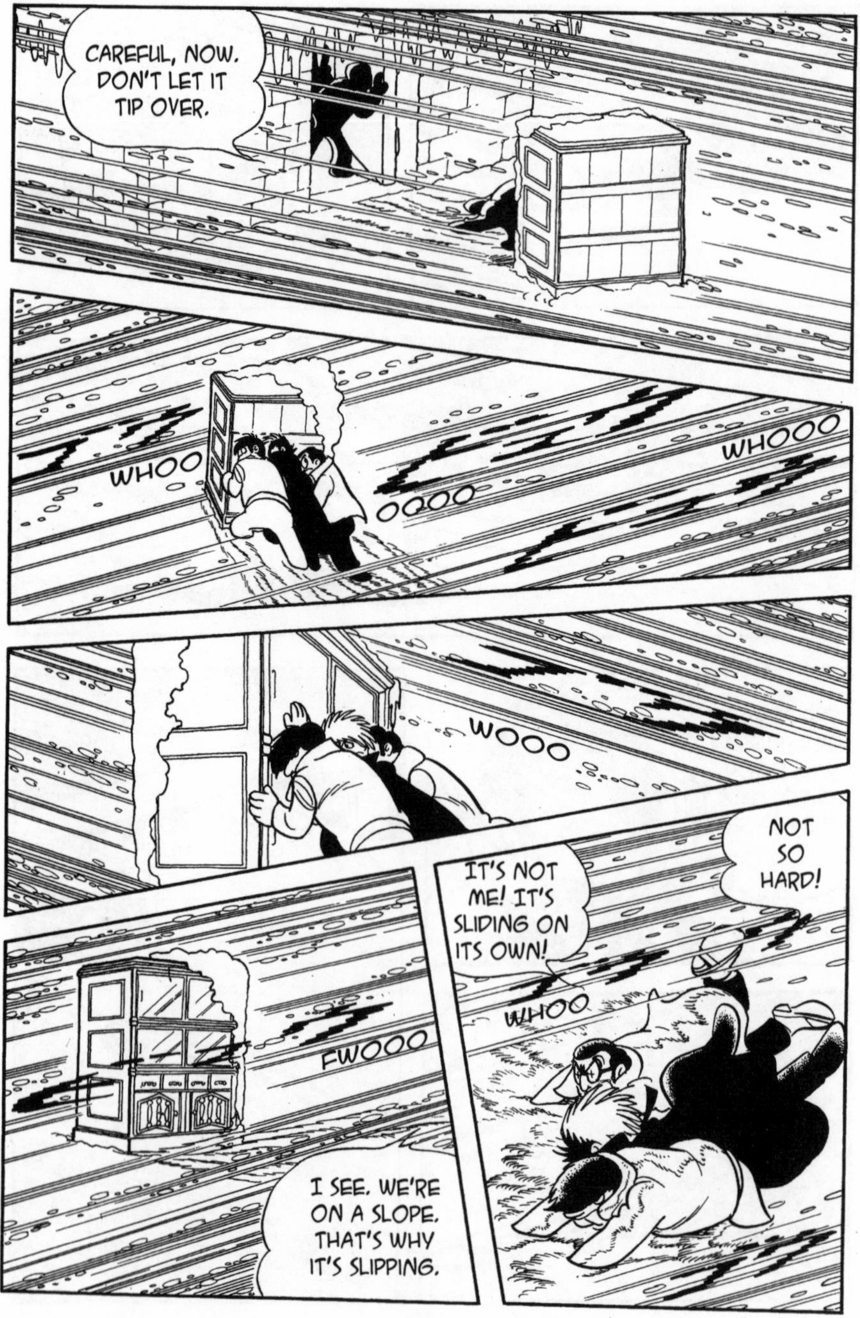
CAREFUL, NOW. DON'T LET IT TIP OVER.
WHOOO
OOOO
WHOO
WOOO
NOT SO HARD!
IT'S NOT ME! IT'S SLIDING ON ITS OWN!
WHOO
FWOOO
I SEE. WE'RE ON A SLOPE. THAT'S WHY IT'S SLIPPING.

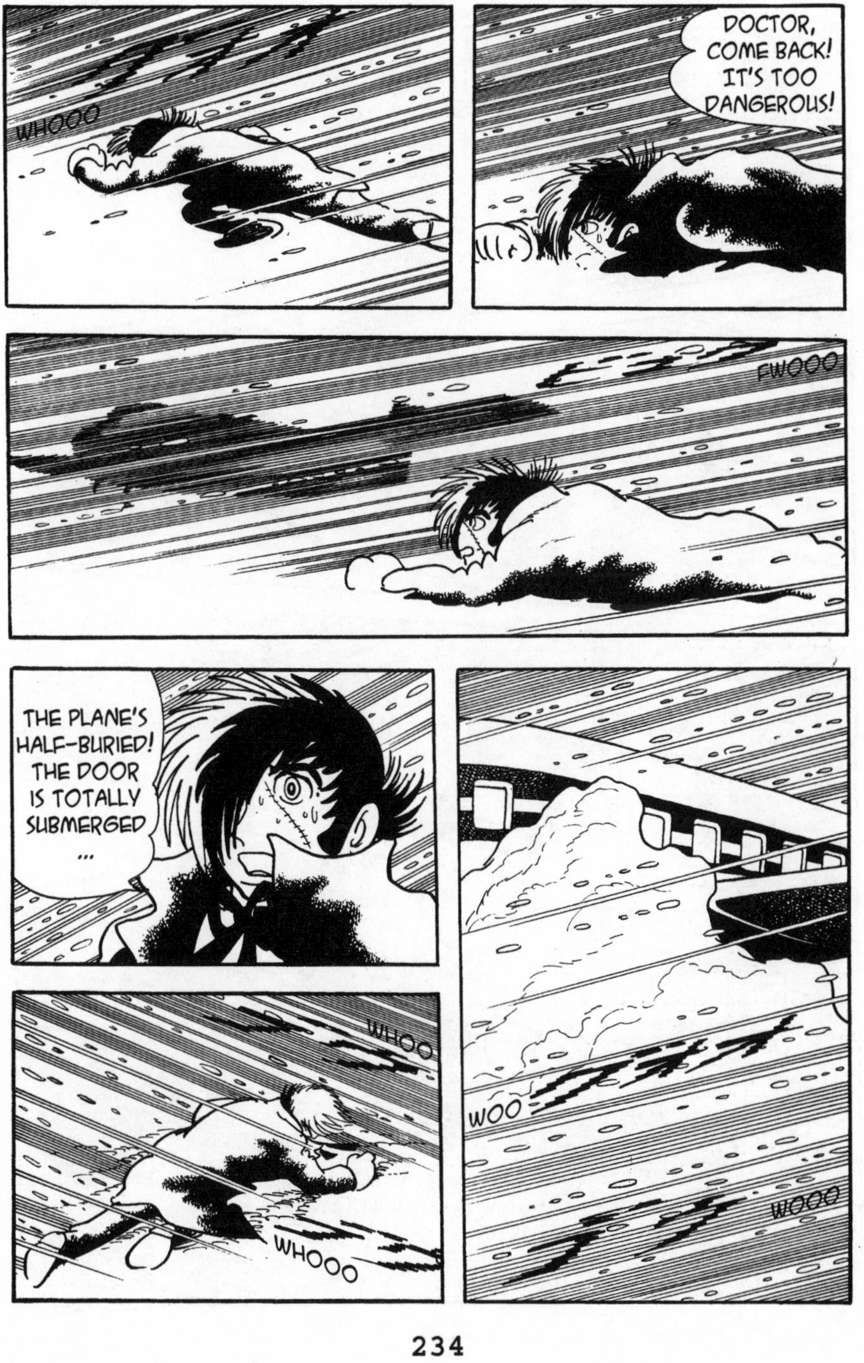
DOCTOR, COME BACK! IT'S TOO DANGEROUS!
WHOOO
FWOOO
WOOO
WOO
THE PLANE'S HALF-BURIED! THE DOOR IS TOTALLY SUBMERGED ...
WHOO
WHOOO

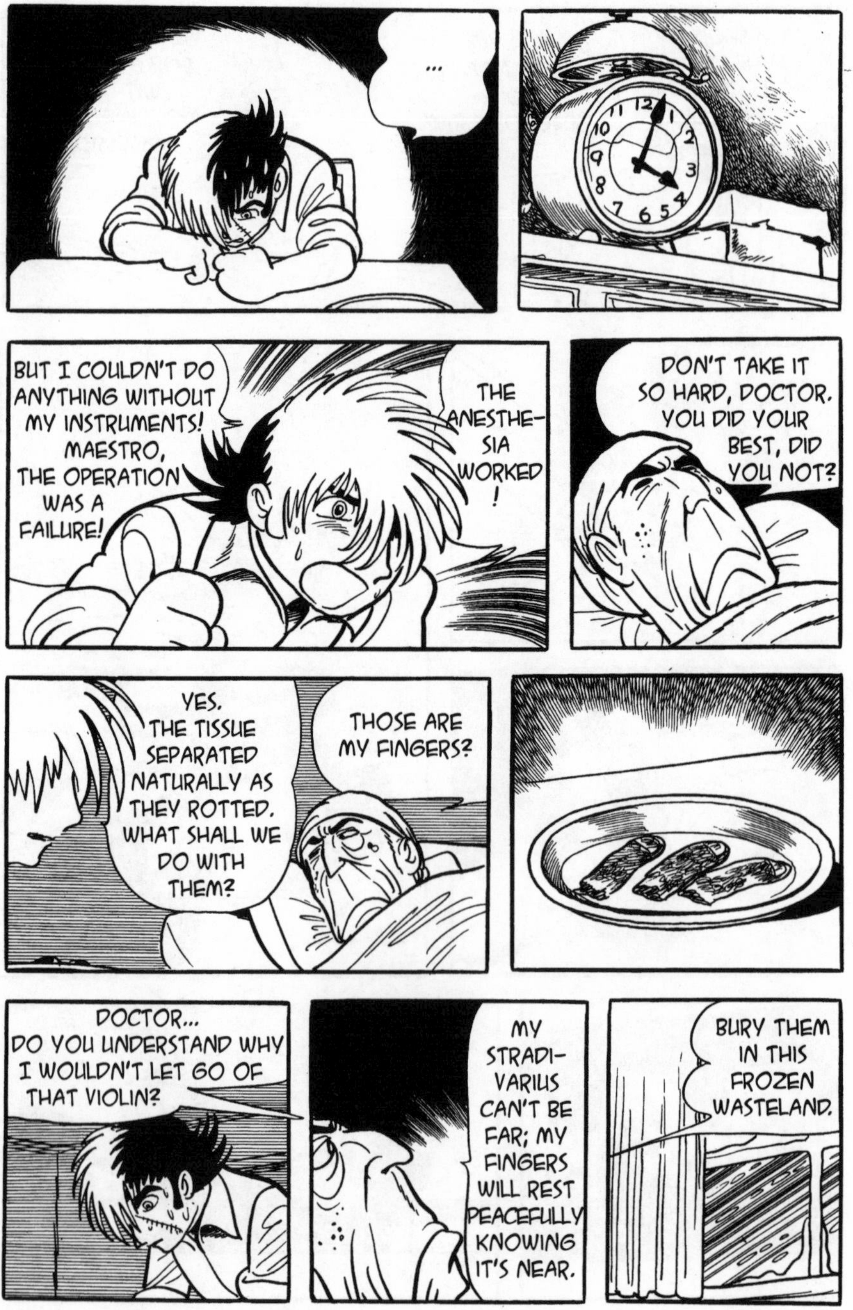
...
THE ANESTHESIA WORKED!
BUT I COULDN'T DO ANYTHING WITHOUT MY INSTRUMENTS! MAESTRO, THE OPERATION WAS A FAILURE!
DON'T TAKE IT SO HARD, DOCTOR. YOU DID YOUR BEST, DID YOU NOT?
THOSE ARE MY FINGERS?
YES. THE TISSUE SEPARATED NATURALLY AS THEY ROTTED. WHAT SHALL WE DO WITH THEM?
DOCTOR... DO YOU UNDERSTAND WHY I WOULDN'T LET GO OF THAT VIOLIN?
MY STRADIVARIUS CAN'T BE FAR; MY FINGERS WILL REST PEACEFULLY KNOWING IT'S NEAR.
BURY THEM IN THIS FROZEN WASTELAND.

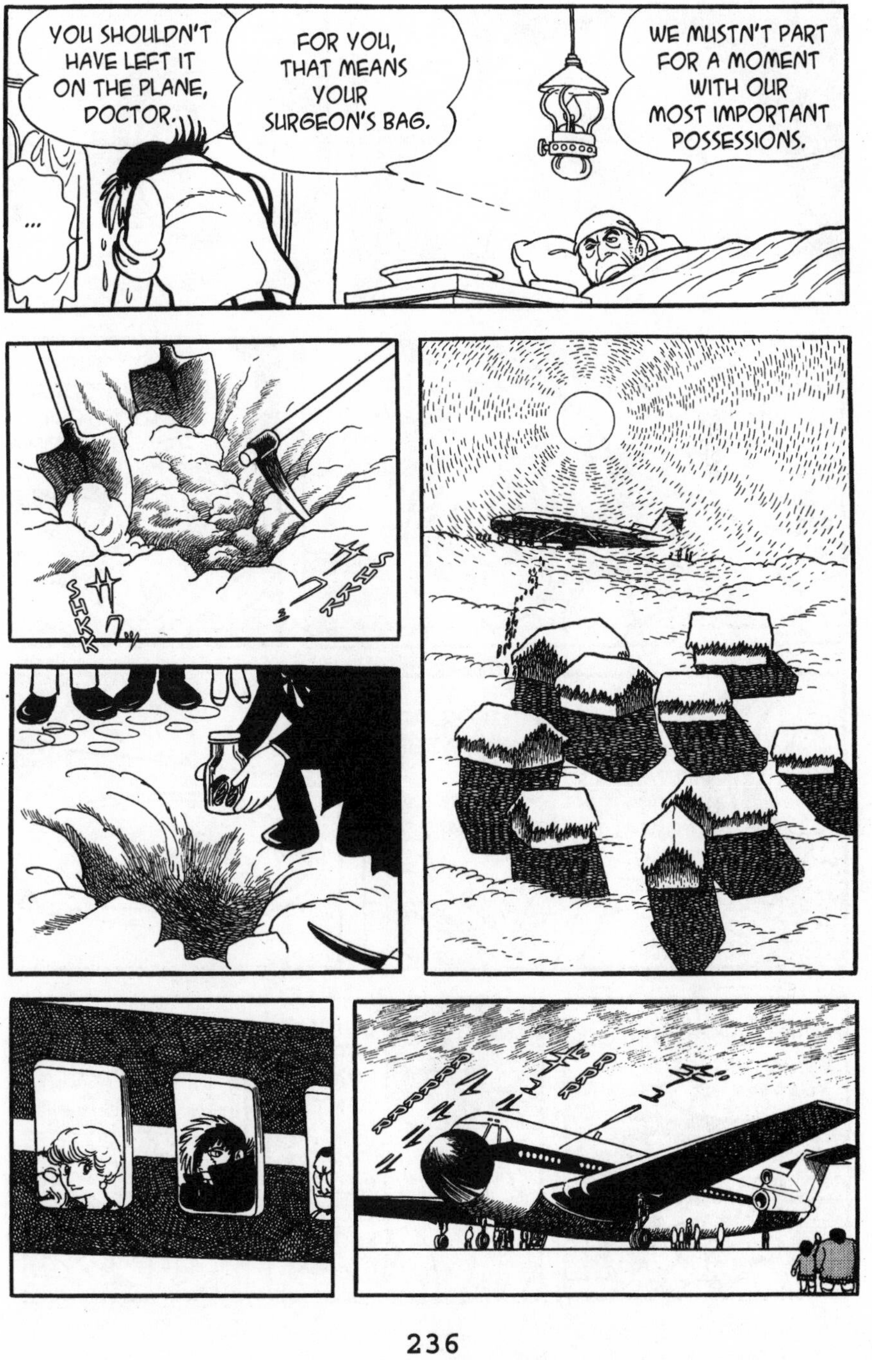
WE MUSTN'T PART FOR A MOMENT WITH OUR MOST IMPORTANT POSSESSIONS.
FOR YOU, THAT MEANS YOUR SURGEON'S BAG.
YOU SHOULDN'T HAVE LEFT IT ON THE PLANE, DOCTOR.
...
SHKK

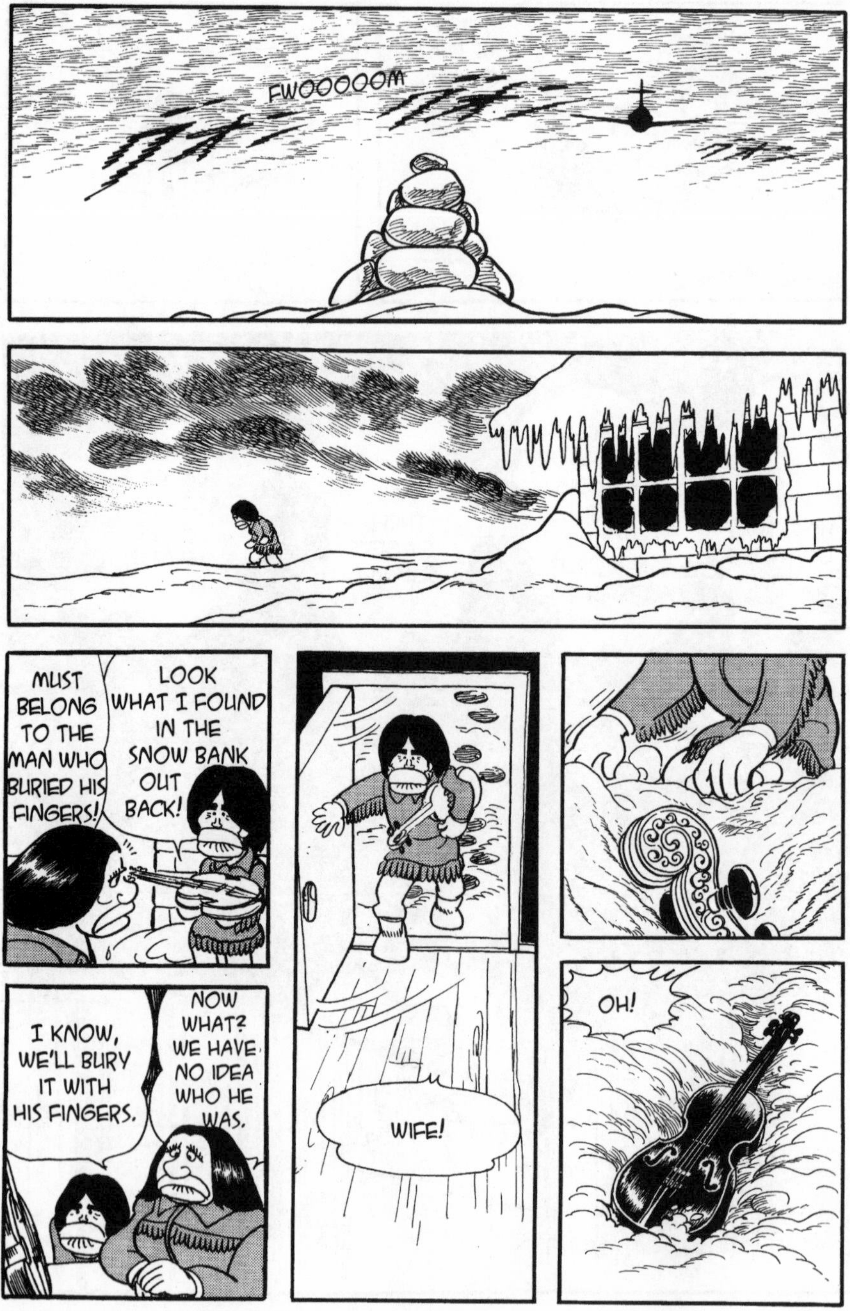
FWOOOOOM
OH!
WIFE!
LOOK WHAT I FOUND IN THE SNOW BANK OUT BACK!
MUST BELONG TO THE MAN WHO BURIED HIS FINGERS!
NOW WHAT? WE HAVE NO IDEA WHO HE WAS.
I KNOW, WE'LL BURY IT WITH HIS FINGERS.

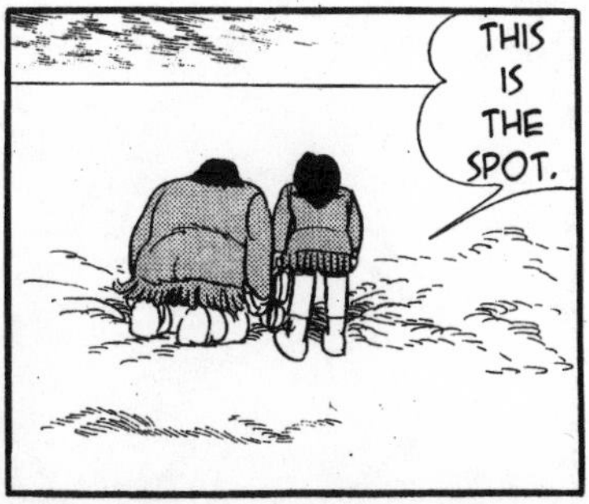
THIS IS THE SPOT.

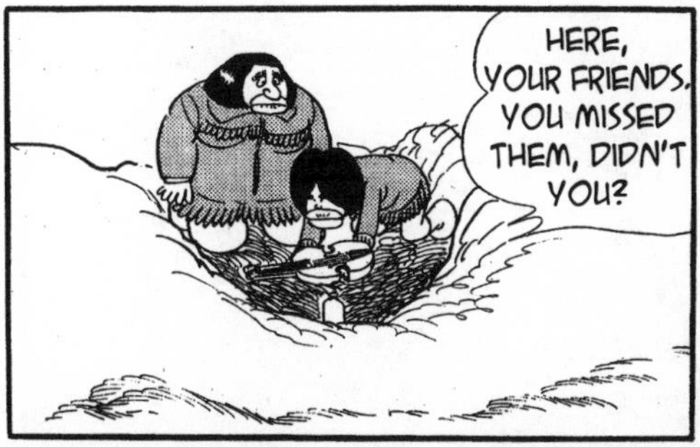
HERE, YOUR FRIENDS. YOU MISSED THEM, DIDN'T YOU?

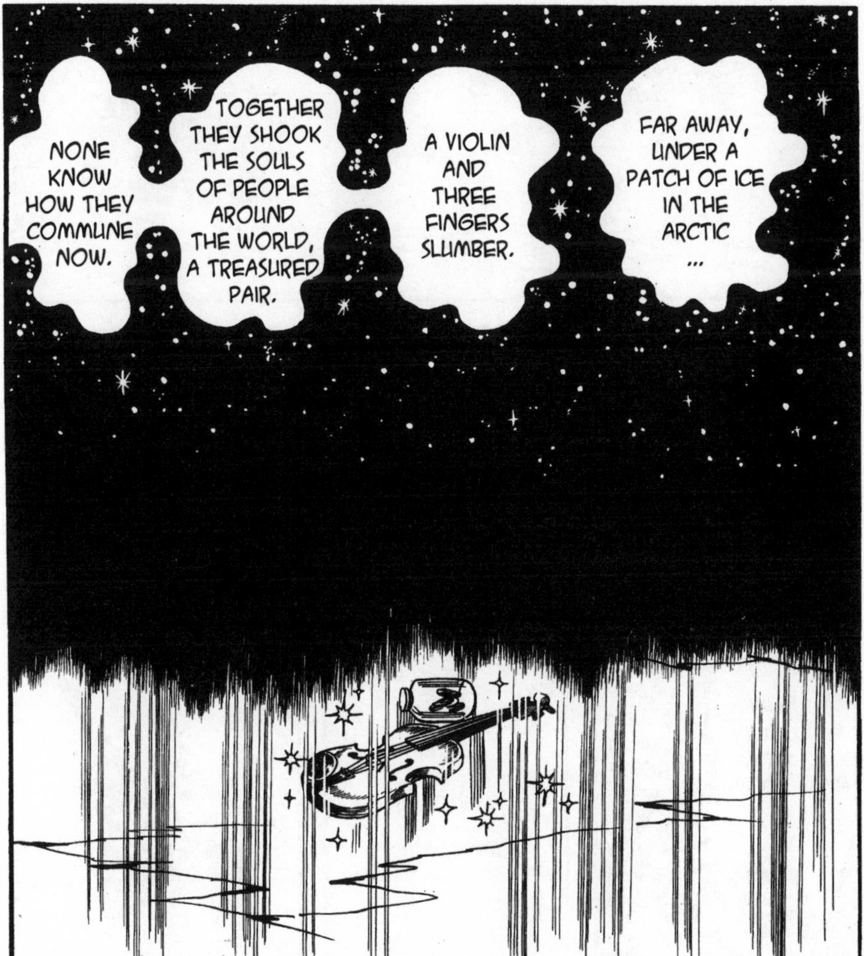
FAR AWAY, UNDER A PATCH OF ICE IN THE ARCTIC ...
A VIOLIN AND THREE FINGERS SLUMBER.
TOGETHER THEY SHOOK THE SOULS OF PEOPLE AROUND THE WORLD, A TREASURED PAIR.
NONE KNOW HOW THEY COMMUNE NOW.

PINOKO'S CHALLENGE

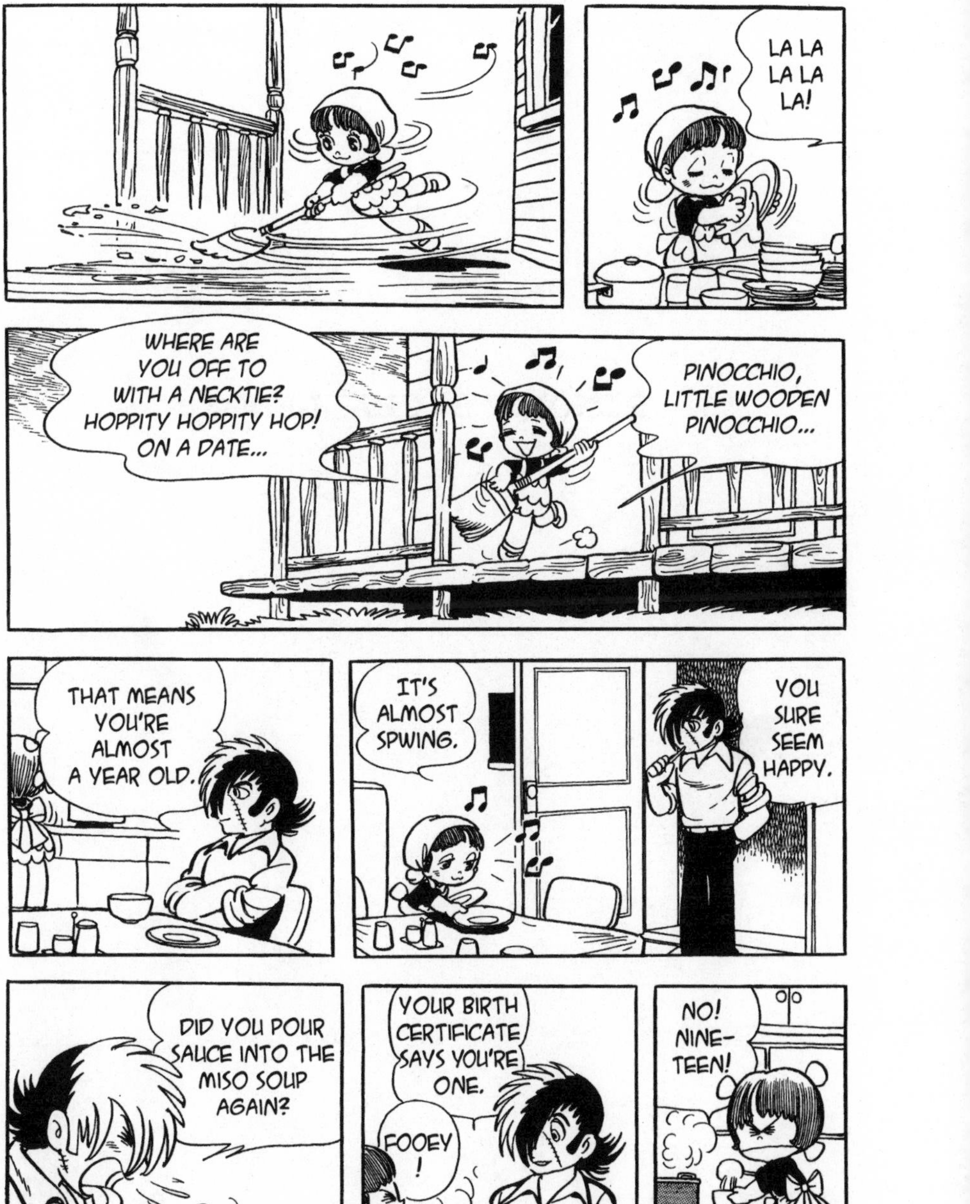
LA LA LA LA LA!
PINOCCHIO, LITTLE WOODEN PINOCCHIO...
WHERE ARE YOU OFF TO WITH A NECKTIE? HOPPITY HOPPITY HOP! ON A DATE...
YOU SURE SEEM HAPPY.
IT'S ALMOST SPWING.
THAT MEANS YOU'RE ALMOST A YEAR OLD.
NO! NINE-TEEN!
YOUR BIRTH CERTIFICATE SAYS YOU'RE ONE.
FOOEY!
DID YOU POUR SAUCE INTO THE MISO SOUP AGAIN?

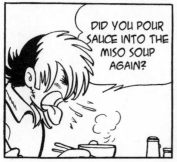

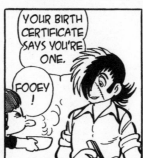

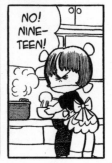

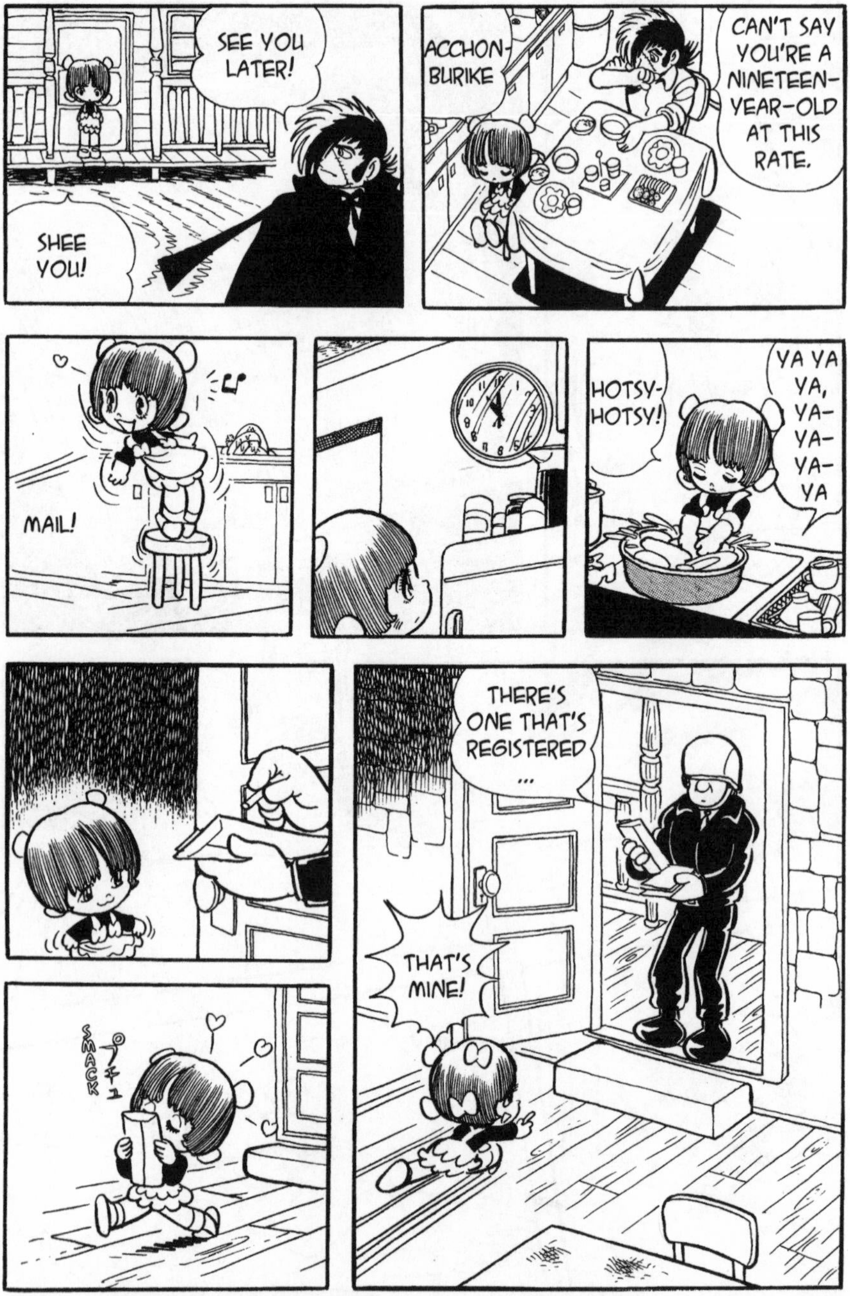
CAN'T SAY YOU'RE A NINETEEN-YEAR-OLD AT THIS RATE.
ACCHON-BURIKE
SEE YOU LATER!
SHEE YOU!
YA YA YA, YA-YA-YA-YA
HOTSY-HOTSY!
MAIL!
THERE'S ONE THAT'S REGISTERED ...
THAT'S MINE!
SMACK

NOTE: THE PINOKO-ISM "ACCHONBURIKE" IS, LIKE MANY WORDS COINED BY CHILDREN, DEVOID OF ANY KNOWN FIXED MEANING.

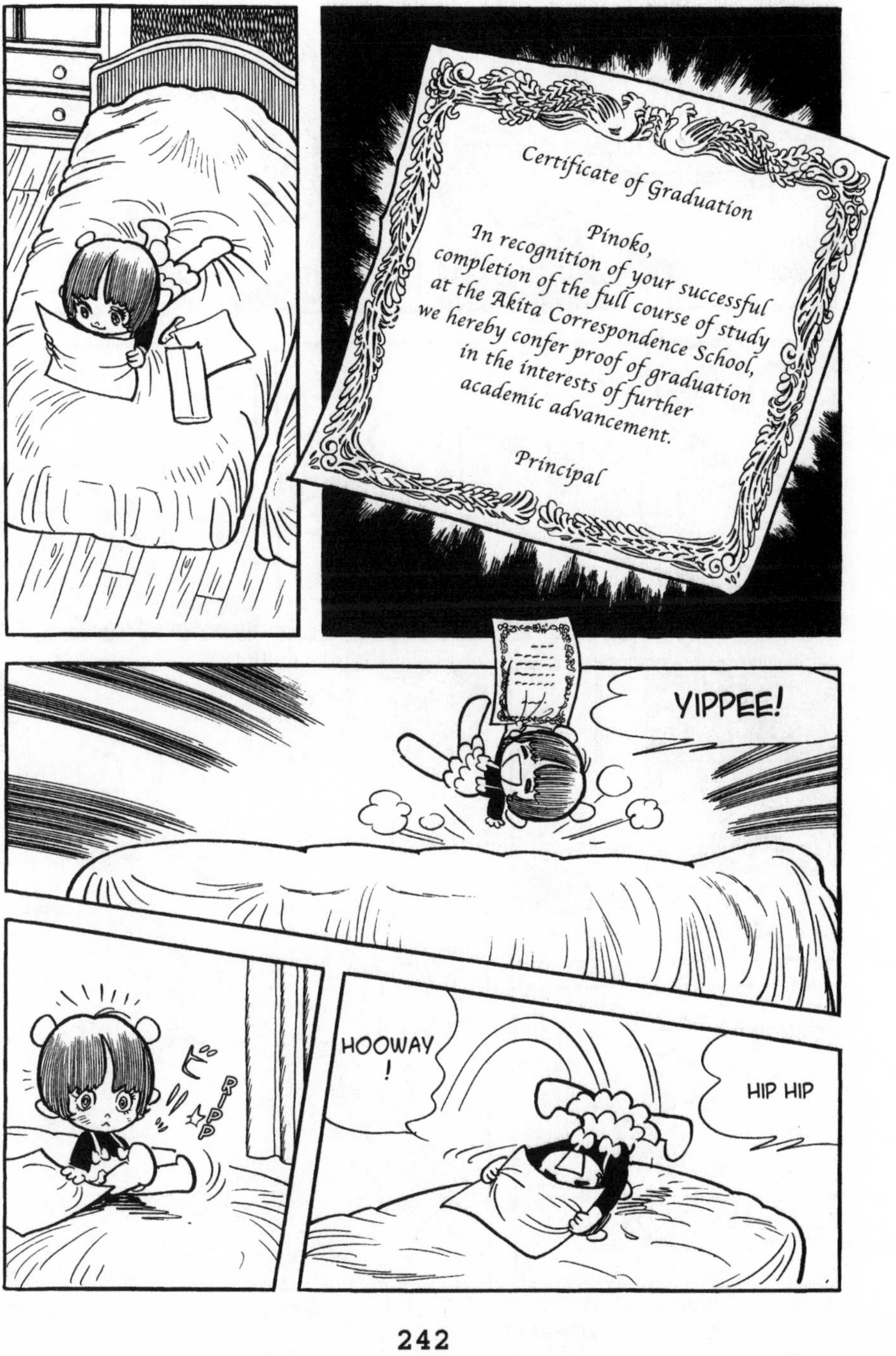
Certificate of Graduation
Pinoko,
In recognition of your successful completion of the full course of study at the Akita Correspondence School, we hereby confer proof of graduation in the interests of further academic advancement.
Principal
YIPPEE!
HIP HIP
HOOWAY!
RIPP

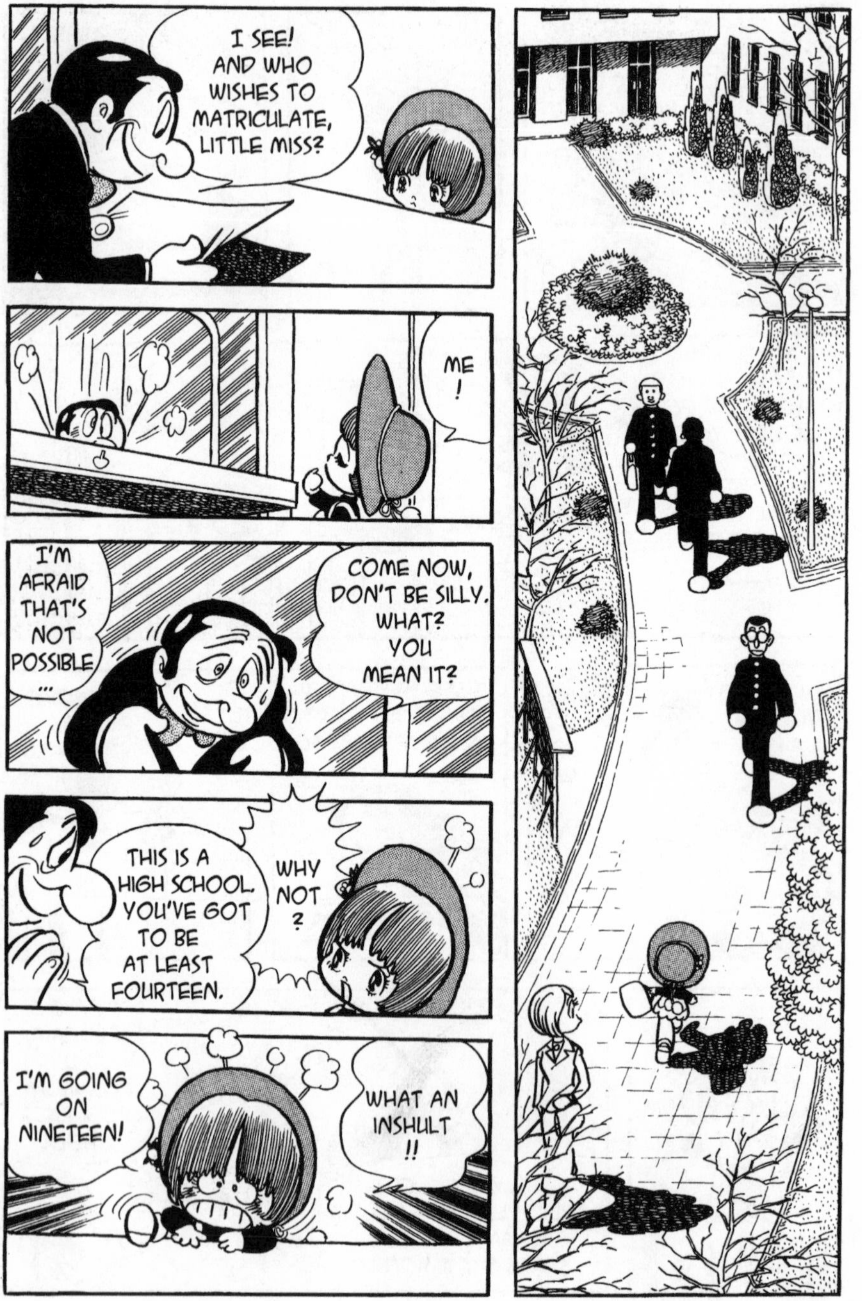
I SEE! AND WHO WISHES TO MATRICULATE, LITTLE MISS?
ME!
COME NOW, DON'T BE SILLY. WHAT? YOU MEAN IT?
I'M AFRAID THAT'S NOT POSSIBLE ...
WHY NOT?
THIS IS A HIGH SCHOOL. YOU'VE GOT TO BE AT LEAST FOURTEEN.
WHAT AN INSHULT !!
I'M GOING ON NINETEEN!

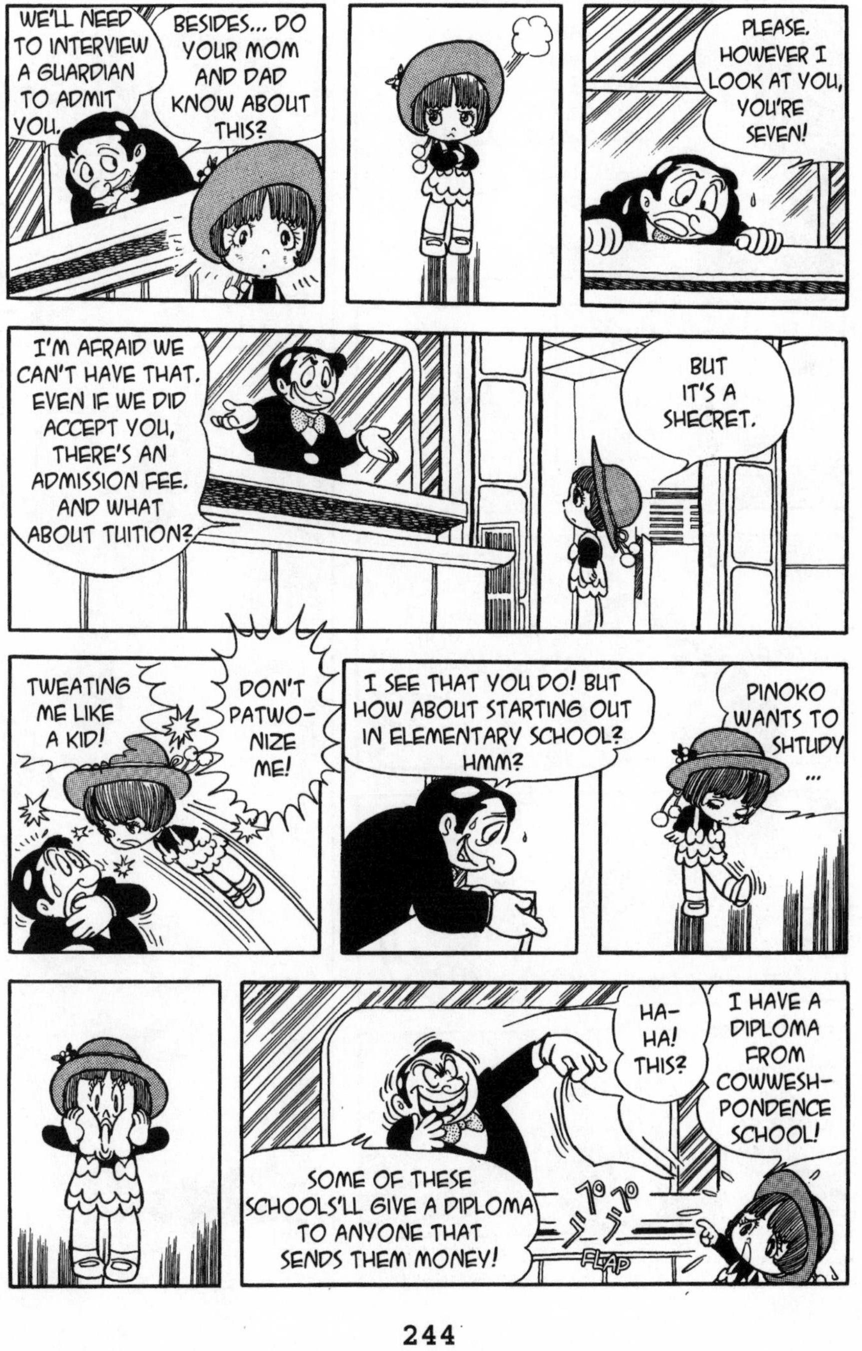
PLEASE. HOWEVER I LOOK AT YOU, YOU'RE SEVEN!
WE'LL NEED TO INTERVIEW A GUARDIAN TO ADMIT YOU.
BESIDES... DO YOUR MOM AND DAD KNOW ABOUT THIS?
BUT IT'S A SHECRET.
I'M AFRAID WE CAN'T HAVE THAT. EVEN IF WE DID ACCEPT YOU, THERE'S AN ADMISSION FEE. AND WHAT ABOUT TUITION?
PINOKO WANTS TO SHTUDY ...
I SEE THAT YOU DO! BUT HOW ABOUT STARTING OUT IN ELEMENTARY SCHOOL? HMM?
DON'T PATWONIZE ME!
TWEATING ME LIKE A KID!
I HAVE A DIPLOMA FROM COWWESH-PONDENCE SCHOOL!
HA-HA! THIS?
SOME OF THESE SCHOOLS'LL GIVE A DIPLOMA TO ANYONE THAT SENDS THEM MONEY!
FLAP

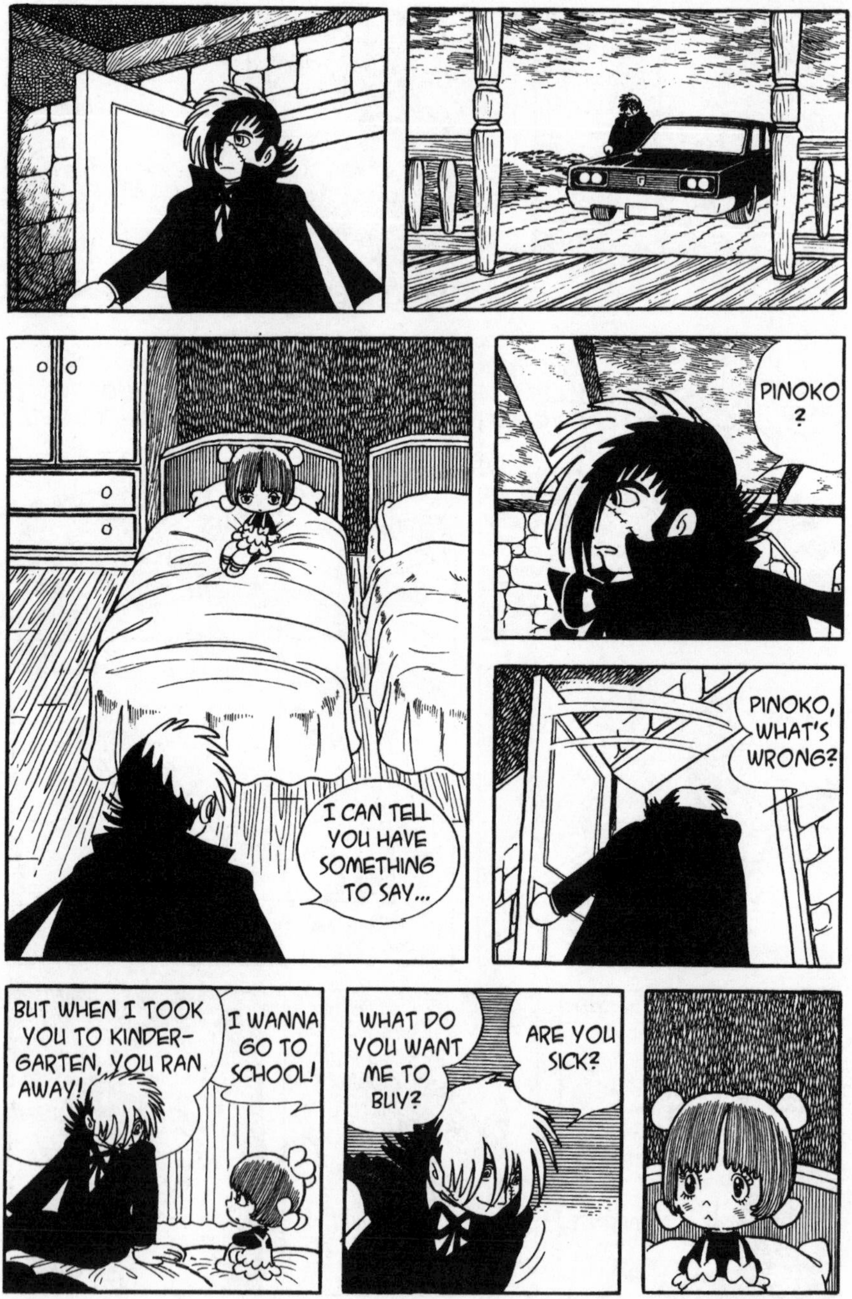
PINOKO?
PINOKO, WHAT'S WRONG?
I CAN TELL YOU HAVE SOMETHING TO SAY...
ARE YOU SICK?
WHAT DO YOU WANT ME TO BUY?
I WANNA GO TO SCHOOL!
BUT WHEN I TOOK YOU TO KINDER-GARTEN, YOU RAN AWAY!

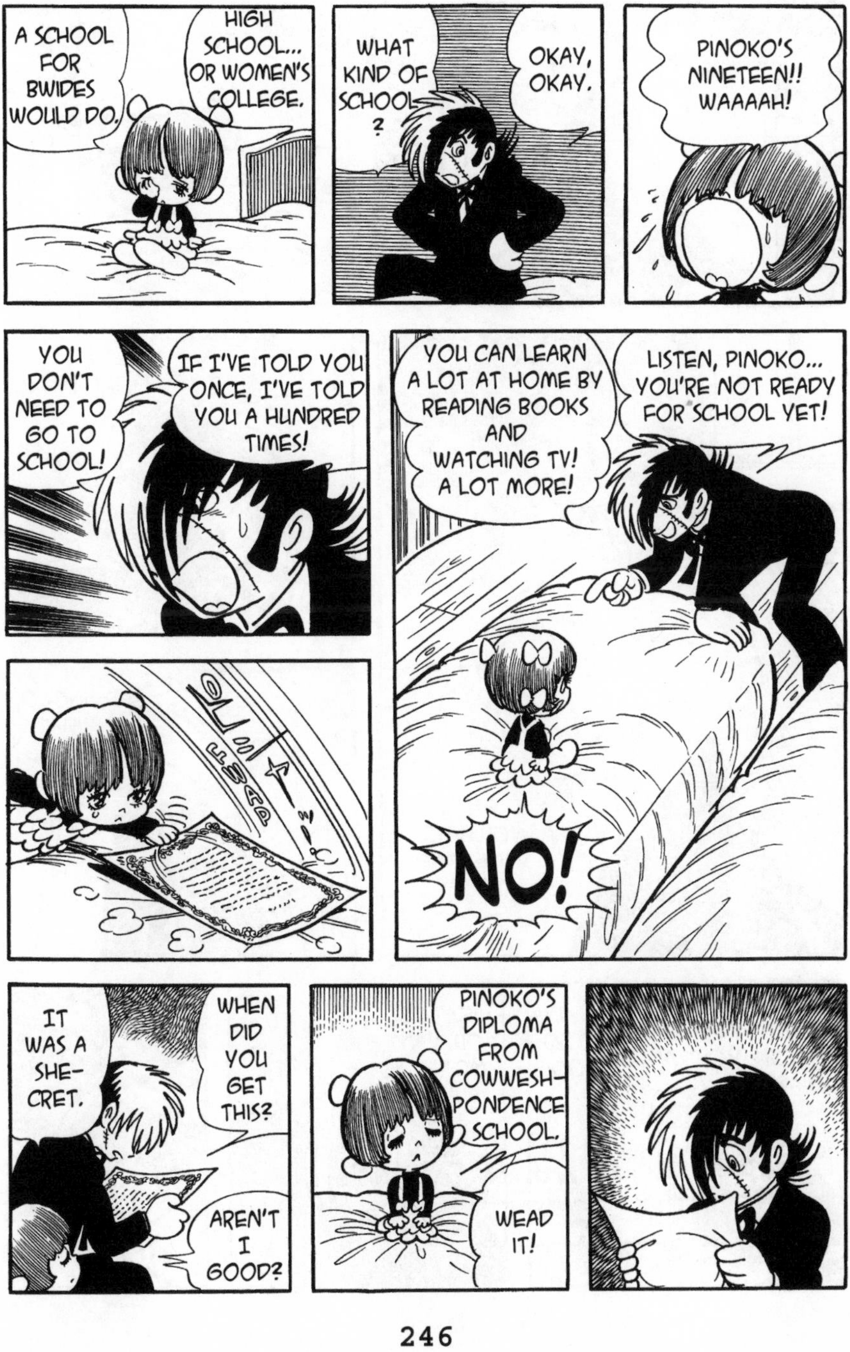
PINOKO'S NINETEEN!! WAAAAH!
OKAY, OKAY.
WHAT KIND OF SCHOOL?
HIGH SCHOOL... OR WOMEN'S COLLEGE.
A SCHOOL FOR BWIDES WOULD DO.
LISTEN, PINOKO... YOU'RE NOT READY FOR SCHOOL YET!
YOU CAN LEARN A LOT AT HOME BY READING BOOKS AND WATCHING TV! A LOT MORE!
NO!
IF I'VE TOLD YOU ONCE, I'VE TOLD YOU A HUNDRED TIMES!
YOU DON'T NEED TO GO TO SCHOOL!
SWAP
PINOKO'S DIPLOMA FROM COWWESH-PONDENCE SCHOOL.
WEAD IT!
WHEN DID YOU GET THIS?
IT WAS A SHE-CRET.
AREN'T I GOOD?

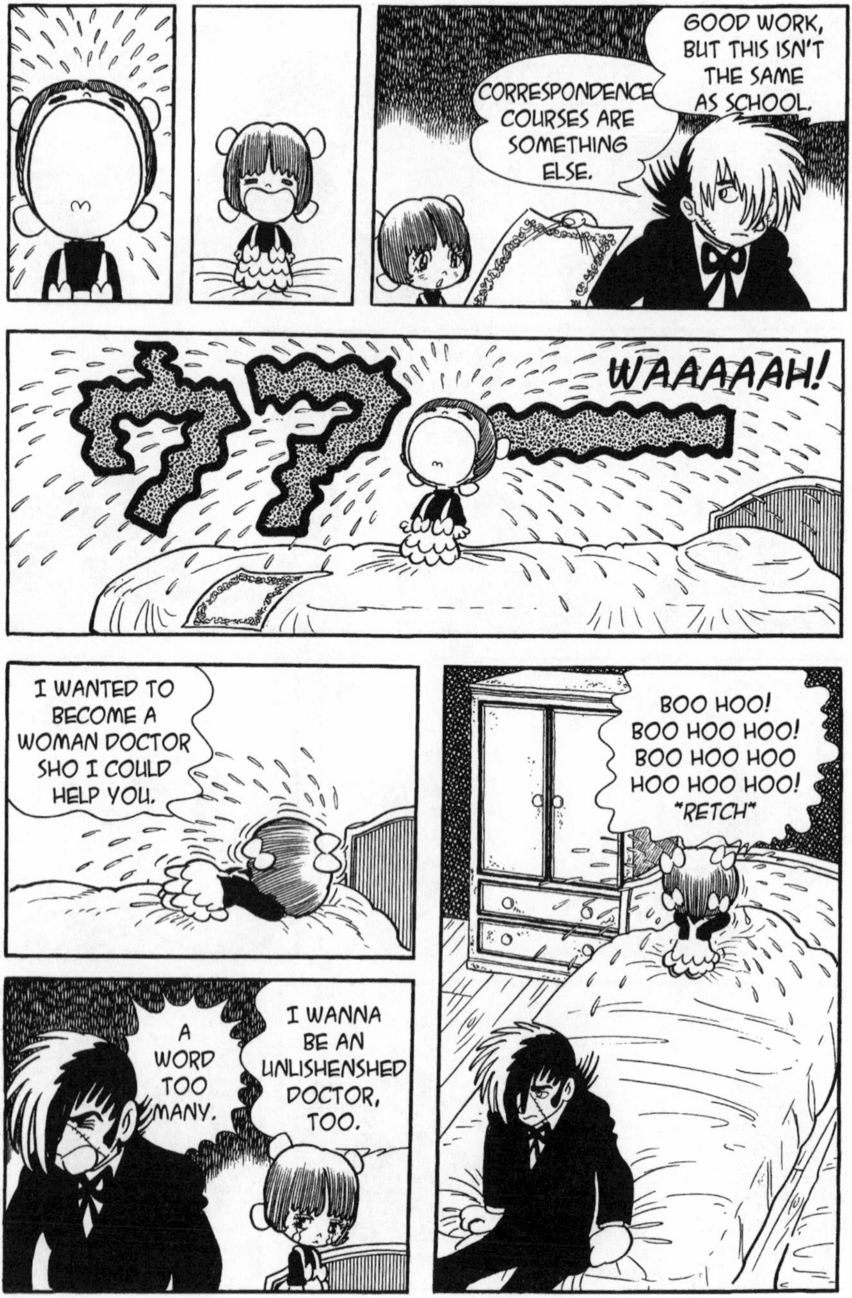
GOOD WORK, BUT THIS ISN'T THE SAME AS SCHOOL.
CORRESPONDENCE COURSES ARE SOMETHING ELSE.
WAAAAAH!
BOO HOO! BOO HOO HOO! BOO HOO HOO HOO HOO HOO! *RETCH*
I WANTED TO BECOME A WOMAN DOCTOR SHO I COULD HELP YOU.
I WANNA BE AN UNLISHENSHED DOCTOR, TOO.
A WORD TOO MANY.

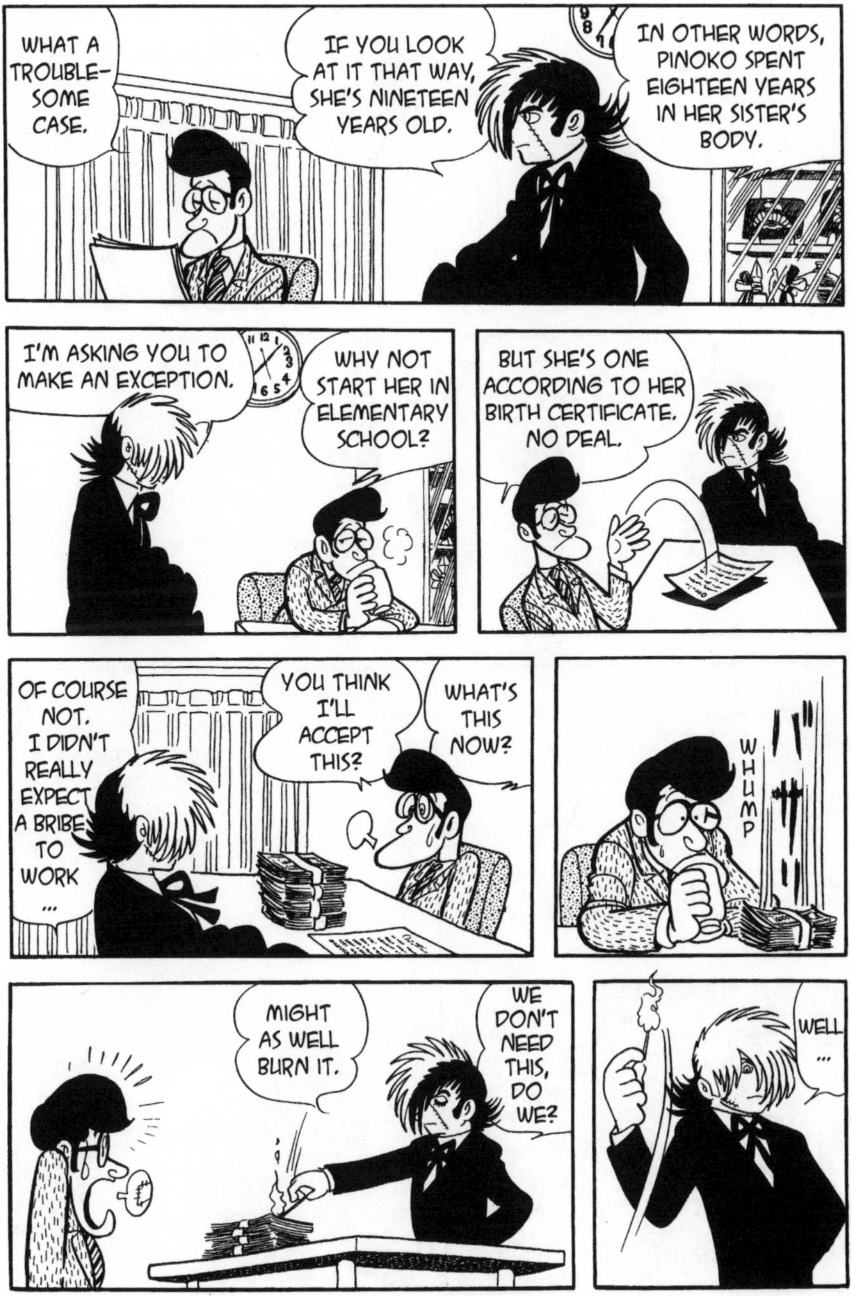
IN OTHER WORDS, PINOKO SPENT EIGHTEEN YEARS IN HER SISTER'S BODY.
IF YOU LOOK AT IT THAT WAY, SHE'S NINETEEN YEARS OLD.
WHAT A TROUBLE-SOME CASE.
BUT SHE'S ONE ACCORDING TO HER BIRTH CERTIFICATE. NO DEAL.
WHY NOT START HER IN ELEMENTARY SCHOOL?
I'M ASKING YOU TO MAKE AN EXCEPTION.
WHUMP
WHAT'S THIS NOW?
YOU THINK I'LL ACCEPT THIS?
OF COURSE NOT. I DIDN'T REALLY EXPECT A BRIBE TO WORK ...
WELL ...
WE DON'T NEED THIS, DO WE?
MIGHT AS WELL BURN IT.

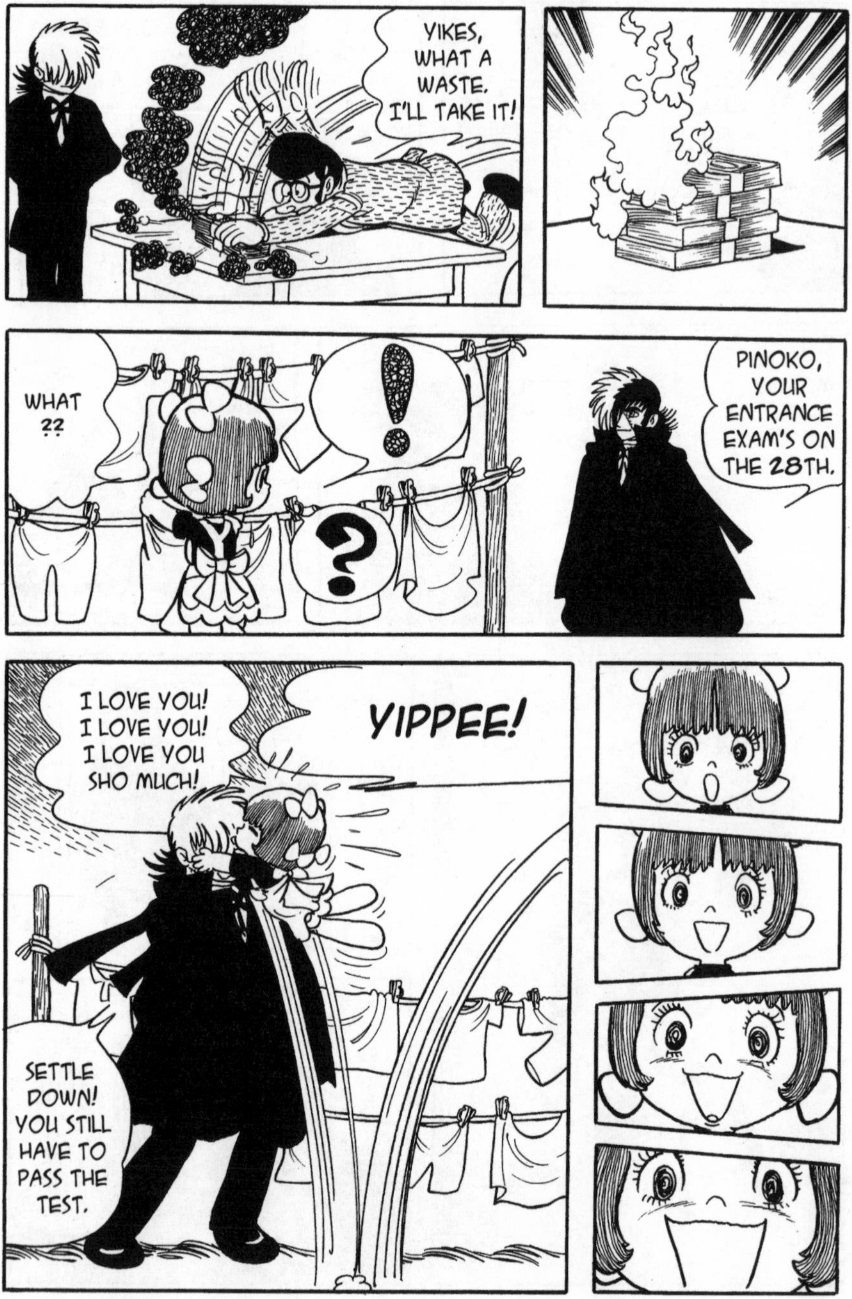
YIKES, WHAT A WASTE. I'LL TAKE IT!
PINOKO, YOUR ENTRANCE EXAM'S ON THE 28TH.
!
WHAT ??
?
YIPPEE!
I LOVE YOU! I LOVE YOU! I LOVE YOU SHO MUCH!
SETTLE DOWN! YOU STILL HAVE TO PASS THE TEST.

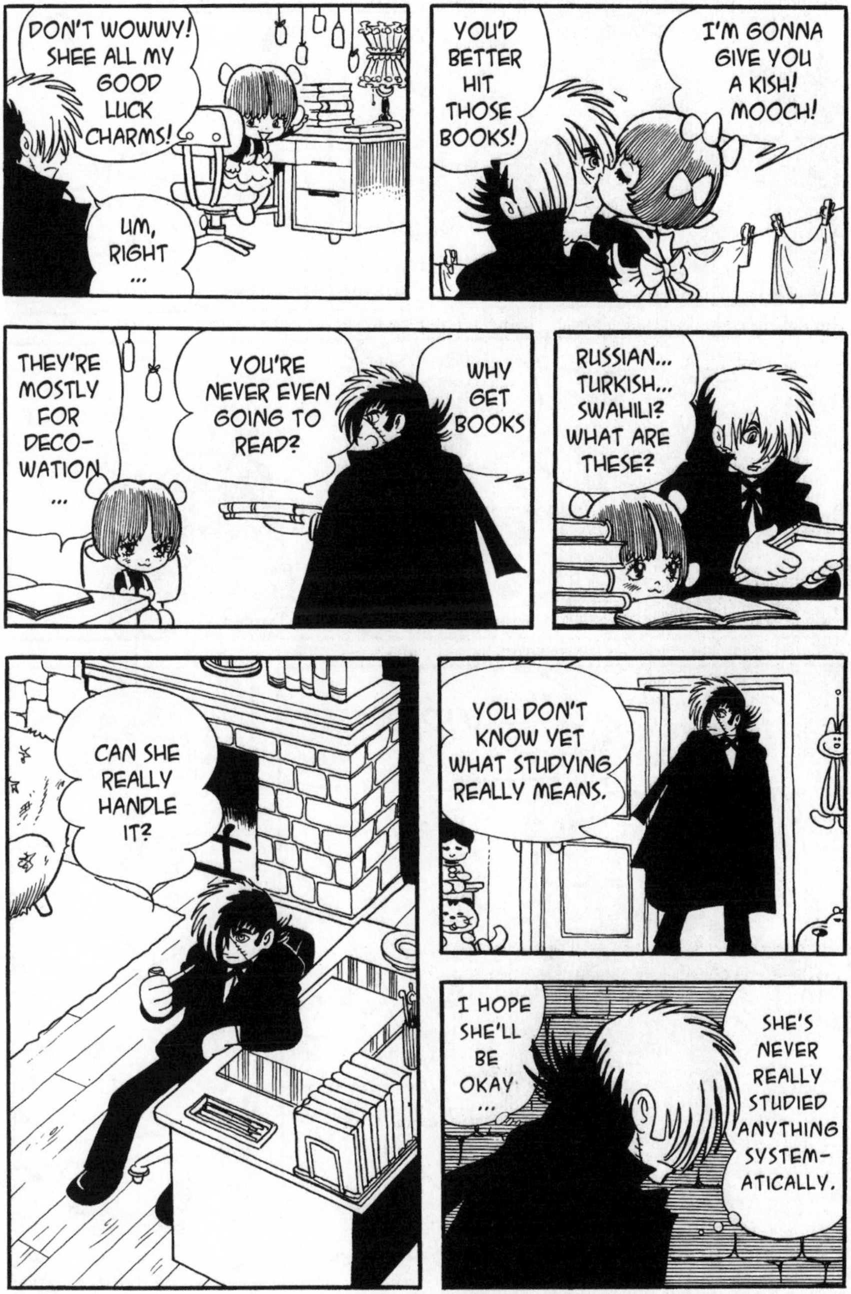
I'M GONNA GIVE YOU A KISH! MOOCH!
YOU'D BETTER HIT THOSE BOOKS!
DON'T WOWWY! SHEE ALL MY GOOD LUCK CHARMS!
UM, RIGHT ...
RUSSIAN... TURKISH... SWAHILI? WHAT ARE THESE?
WHY GET BOOKS
YOU'RE NEVER EVEN GOING TO READ?
THEY'RE MOSTLY FOR DECO-WATION ...
YOU DON'T KNOW YET WHAT STUDYING REALLY MEANS.
SHE'S NEVER REALLY STUDIED ANYTHING SYSTEM-ATICALLY.
I HOPE SHE'LL BE OKAY ...
CAN SHE REALLY HANDLE IT?

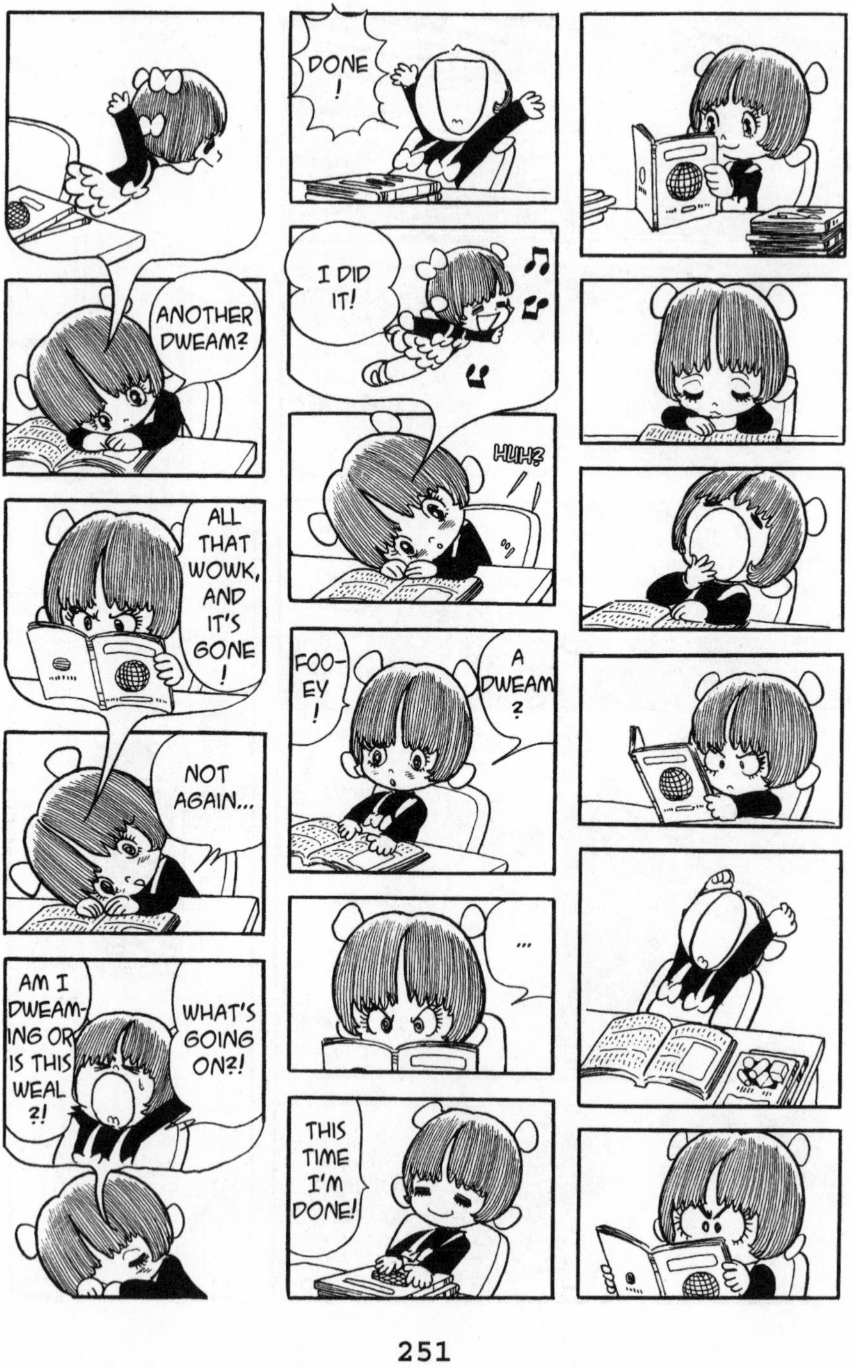
DONE!
I DID IT!
HUH?
A DWEAM?
FOO-EY!
...
THIS TIME I'M DONE!
ANOTHER DWEAM?
ALL THAT WOWK, AND IT'S GONE!
NOT AGAIN...
WHAT'S GOING ON?!
AM I DWEAM-ING OR IS THIS WEAL?!

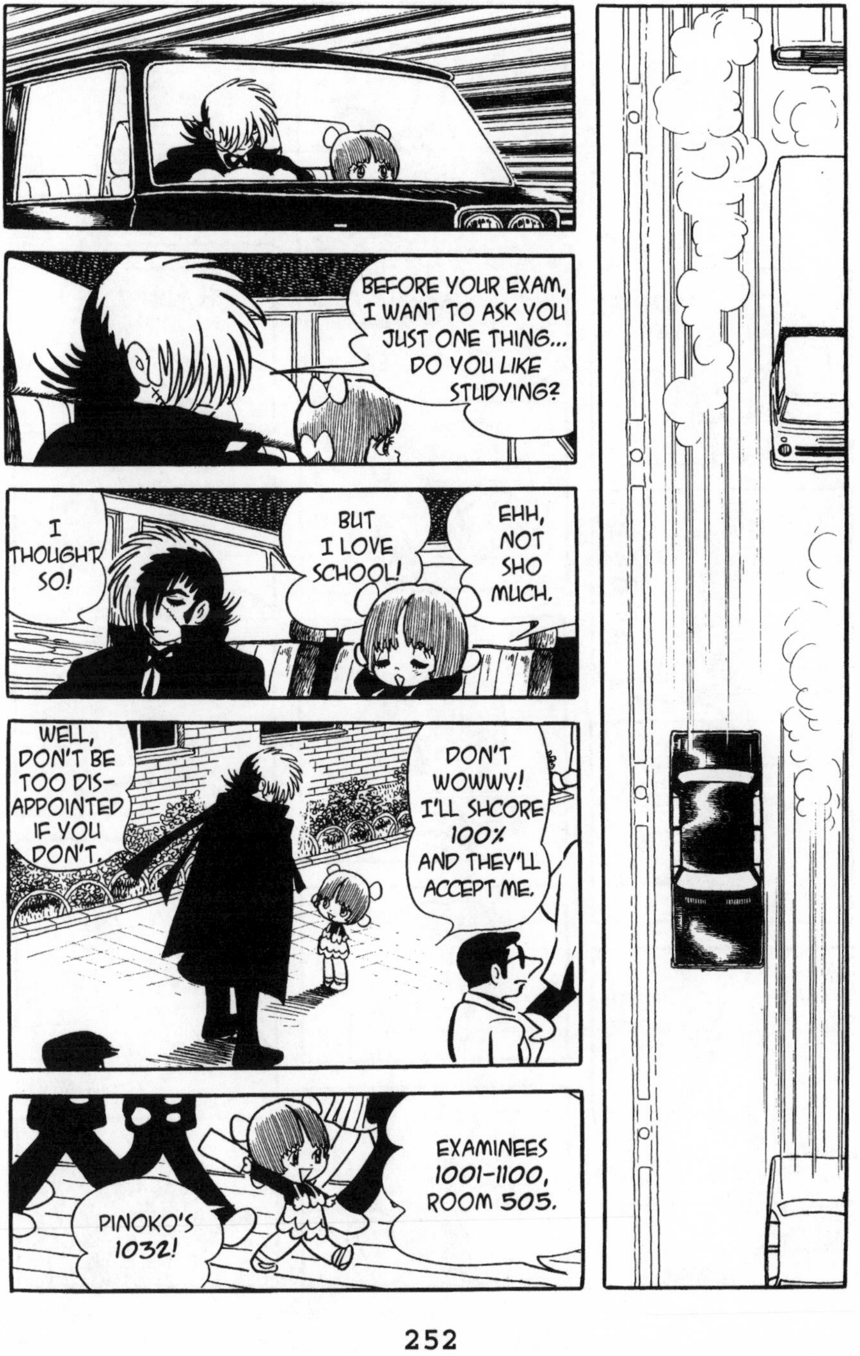
BEFORE YOUR EXAM, I WANT TO ASK YOU JUST ONE THING... DO YOU LIKE STUDYING?
EHH, NOT SHO MUCH.
BUT I LOVE SCHOOL!
I THOUGHT SO!
DON'T WOWWY! I'LL SHCORE 100% AND THEY'LL ACCEPT ME.
WELL, DON'T BE TOO DIS-APPOINTED IF YOU DON'T.
EXAMINEES 1001-1100, ROOM 505.
PINOKO'S 1032!

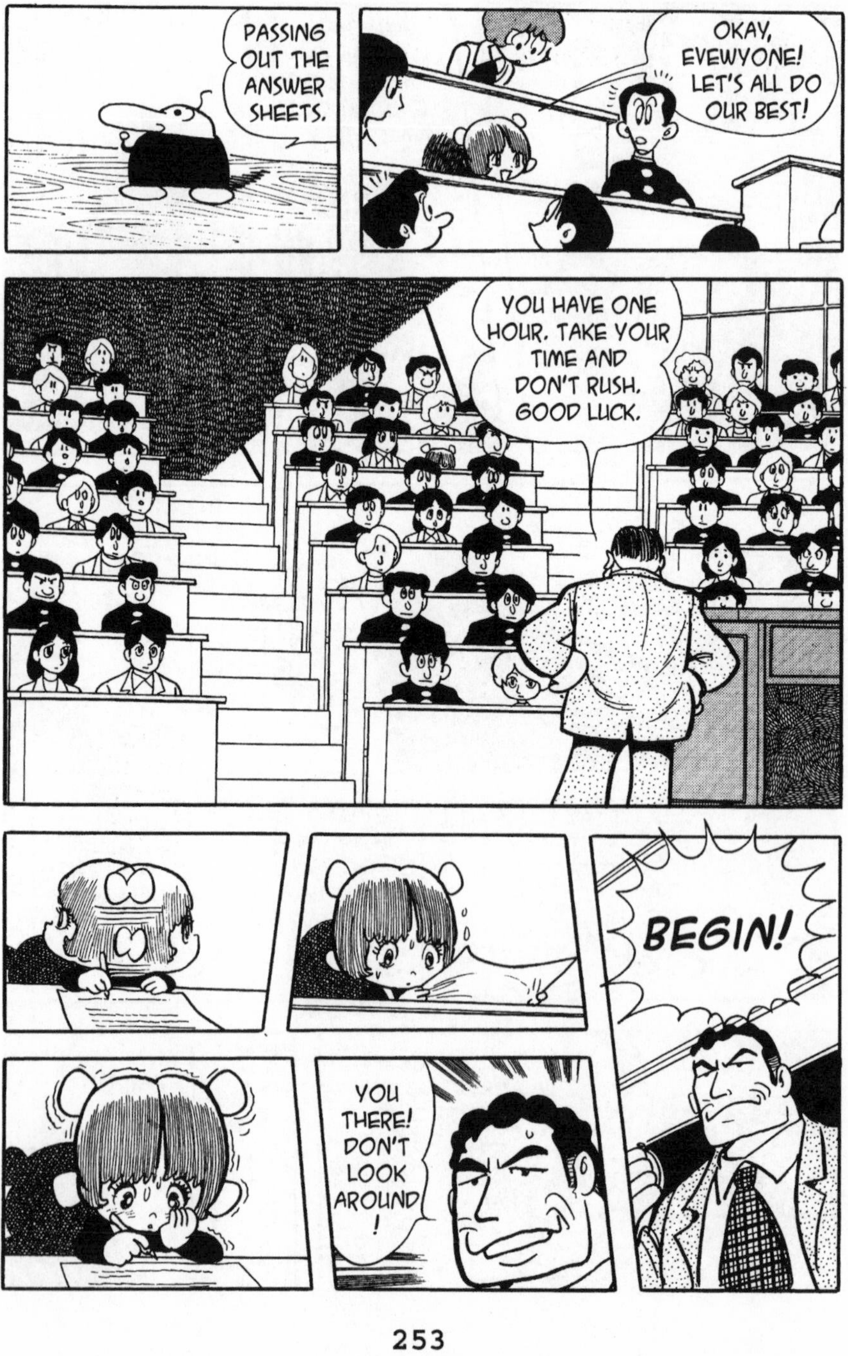
PASSING OUT THE ANSWER SHEETS.
OKAY, EVEWYONE! LET'S ALL DO OUR BEST!
YOU HAVE ONE HOUR. TAKE YOUR TIME AND DON'T RUSH. GOOD LUCK.
BEGIN!
YOU THERE! DON'T LOOK AROUND!

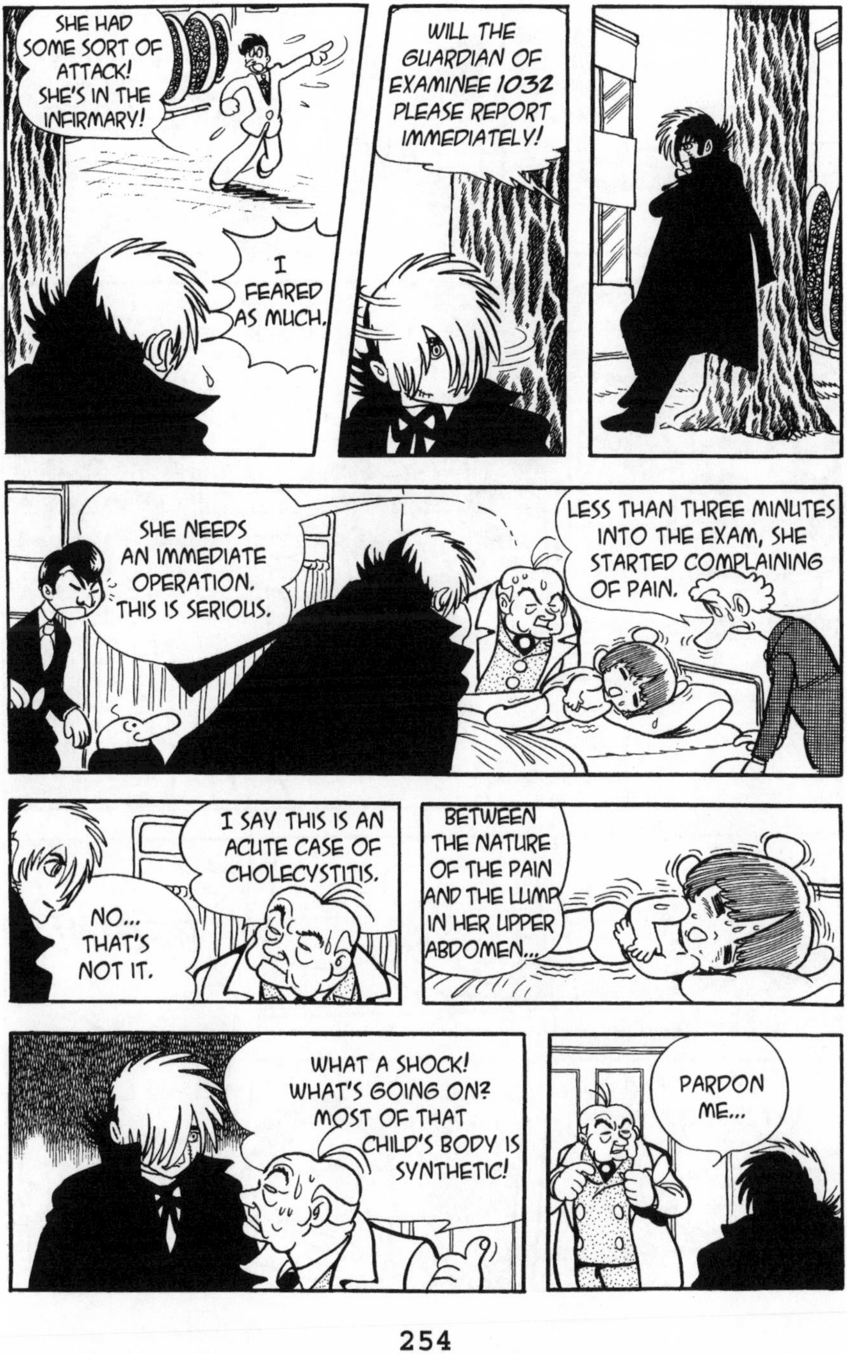
WILL THE GUARDIAN OF EXAMINEE 1032 PLEASE REPORT IMMEDIATELY!
SHE HAD SOME SORT OF ATTACK! SHE'S IN THE INFIRMARY!
I FEARED AS MUCH.
LESS THAN THREE MINUTES INTO THE EXAM, SHE STARTED COMPLAINING OF PAIN.
SHE NEEDS AN IMMEDIATE OPERATION. THIS IS SERIOUS.
BETWEEN THE NATURE OF THE PAIN AND THE LUMP IN HER UPPER ABDOMEN...
I SAY THIS IS AN ACUTE CASE OF CHOLECYSTITIS.
NO... THAT'S NOT IT.
PARDON ME...
WHAT A SHOCK! WHAT'S GOING ON? MOST OF THAT CHILD'S BODY IS SYNTHETIC!

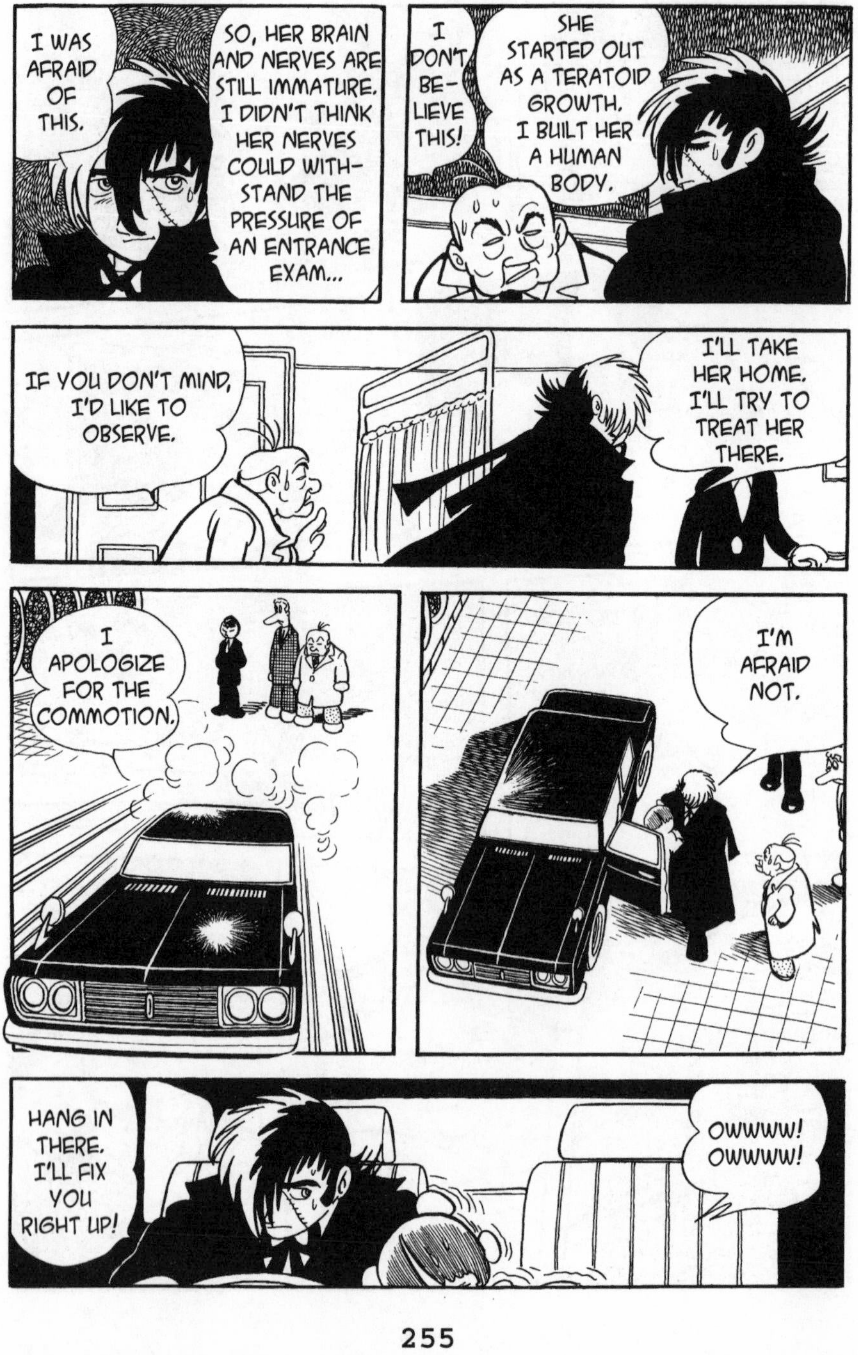
I WAS AFRAID OF THIS.
SO, HER BRAIN AND NERVES ARE STILL IMMATURE. I DIDN'T THINK HER NERVES COULD WITH-STAND THE PRESSURE OF AN ENTRANCE EXAM...
I DON'T BE-LIEVE THIS!
SHE STARTED OUT AS A TERATOID GROWTH. I BUILT HER A HUMAN BODY.
IF YOU DON'T MIND, I'D LIKE TO OBSERVE.
I'LL TAKE HER HOME. I'LL TRY TO TREAT HER THERE.
I APOLOGIZE FOR THE COMMOTION.
I'M AFRAID NOT.
HANG IN THERE. I'LL FIX YOU RIGHT UP!
OWWWW! OWWWW!

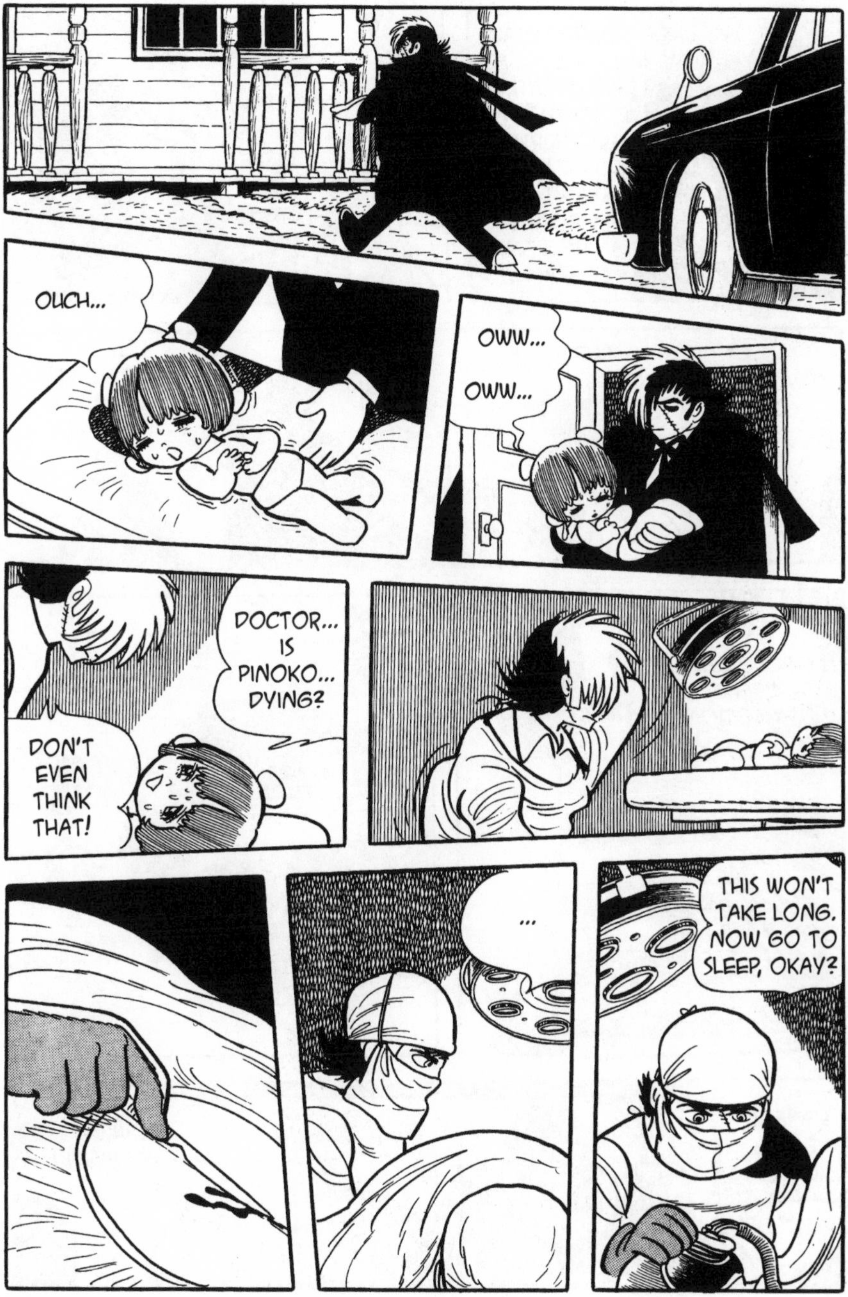
OUCH...
OWW...
OWW...
DOCTOR... IS PINOKO... DYING?
DON'T EVEN THINK THAT!
...
THIS WON'T TAKE LONG. NOW GO TO SLEEP, OKAY?

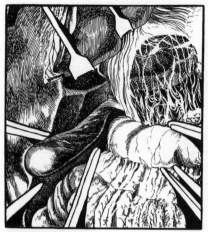

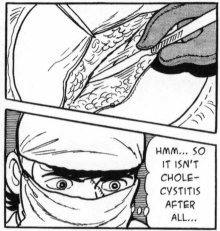

HMM... SO IT ISN'T CHOLE-CYSTITIS AFTER ALL...
HER GALL BLADDER'S FINE. NO STENOSIS OR STONE IN THE BILE DUCT, AND HER LIVER'S FINE, TOO.
THEN WHY ALL THE PAIN AND NAUSEA?
RIGHT— HER NERVES!!
THIS LOOKS LIKE BILIARY DYSKINESIA.
THE EXTREME TENSION IN HER GALL BLADDER CAUSED A BLOCKAGE.
THIS CAN ONLY BE TREATED PSYCHO-LOGICALLY!

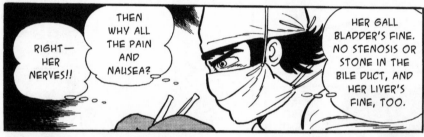

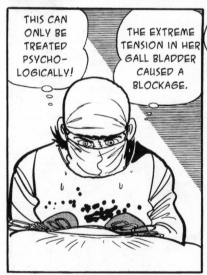

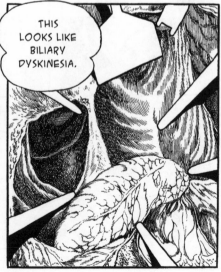

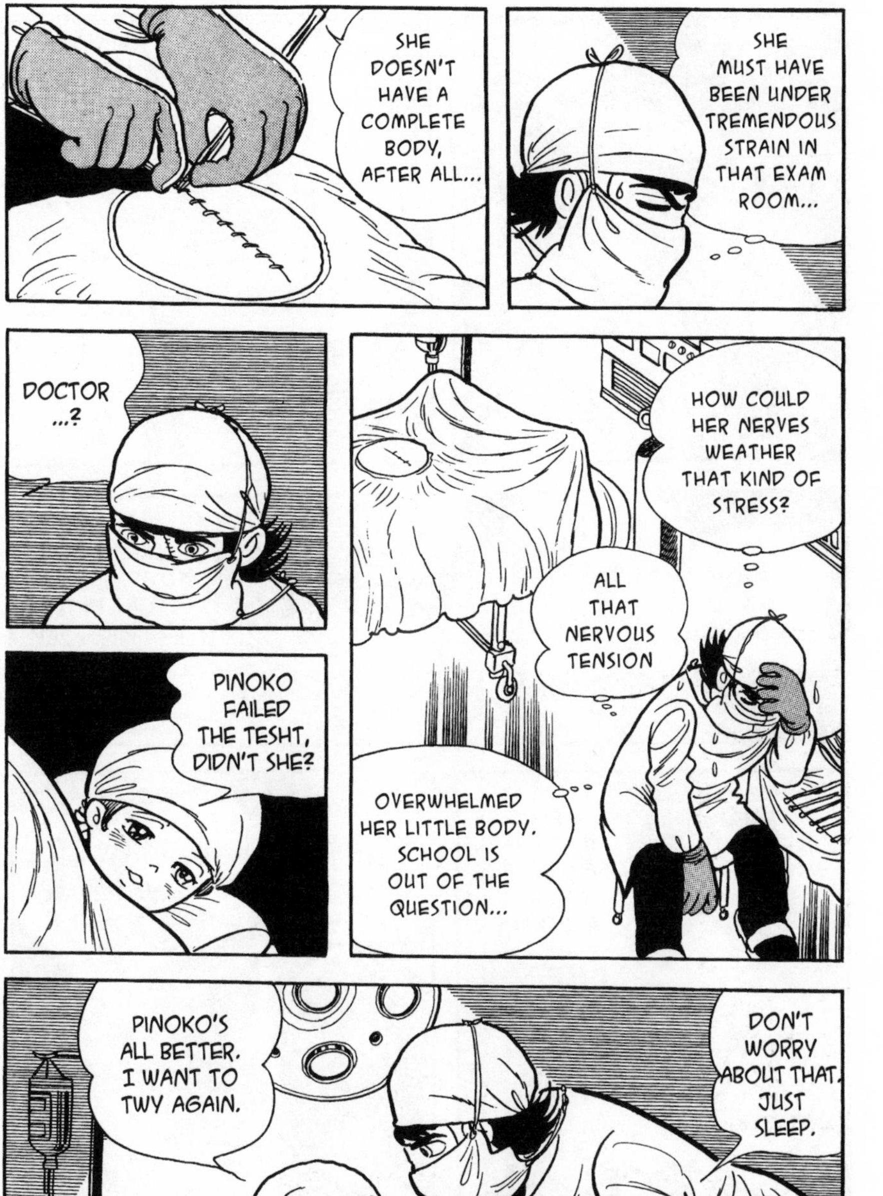
SHE DOESN'T HAVE A COMPLETE BODY, AFTER ALL...
SHE MUST HAVE BEEN UNDER TREMENDOUS STRAIN IN THAT EXAM ROOM...
DOCTOR ...?
PINOKO FAILED THE TESHT, DIDN'T SHE?
HOW COULD HER NERVES WEATHER THAT KIND OF STRESS?
ALL THAT NERVOUS TENSION
OVERWHELMED HER LITTLE BODY. SCHOOL IS OUT OF THE QUESTION...
PINOKO'S ALL BETTER. I WANT TO TWY AGAIN.
DON'T WORRY ABOUT THAT. JUST SLEEP.

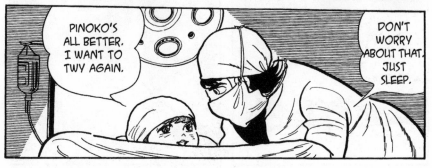

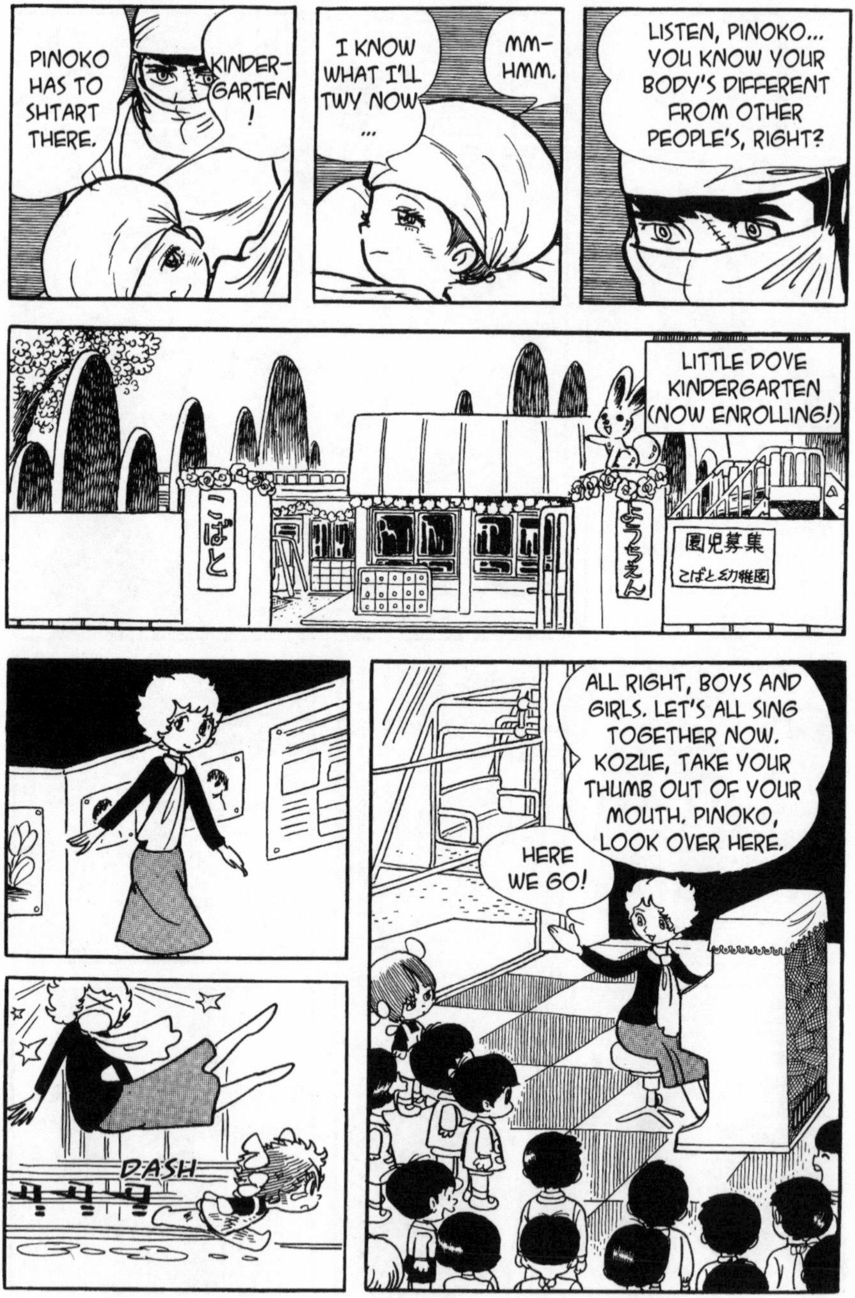
LISTEN, PINOKO... YOU KNOW YOUR BODY'S DIFFERENT FROM OTHER PEOPLE'S, RIGHT?
MM-HMM.
I KNOW WHAT I'LL TWY NOW ...
KINDER-GARTEN!
PINOKO HAS TO SHTART THERE.
LITTLE DOVE KINDERGARTEN (NOW ENROLLING!)
ようちえん
園児募集
こばと幼稚園
こばと
ALL RIGHT, BOYS AND GIRLS. LET'S ALL SING TOGETHER NOW. KOZUE, TAKE YOUR THUMB OUT OF YOUR MOUTH. PINOKO, LOOK OVER HERE.
HERE WE GO!
DASH

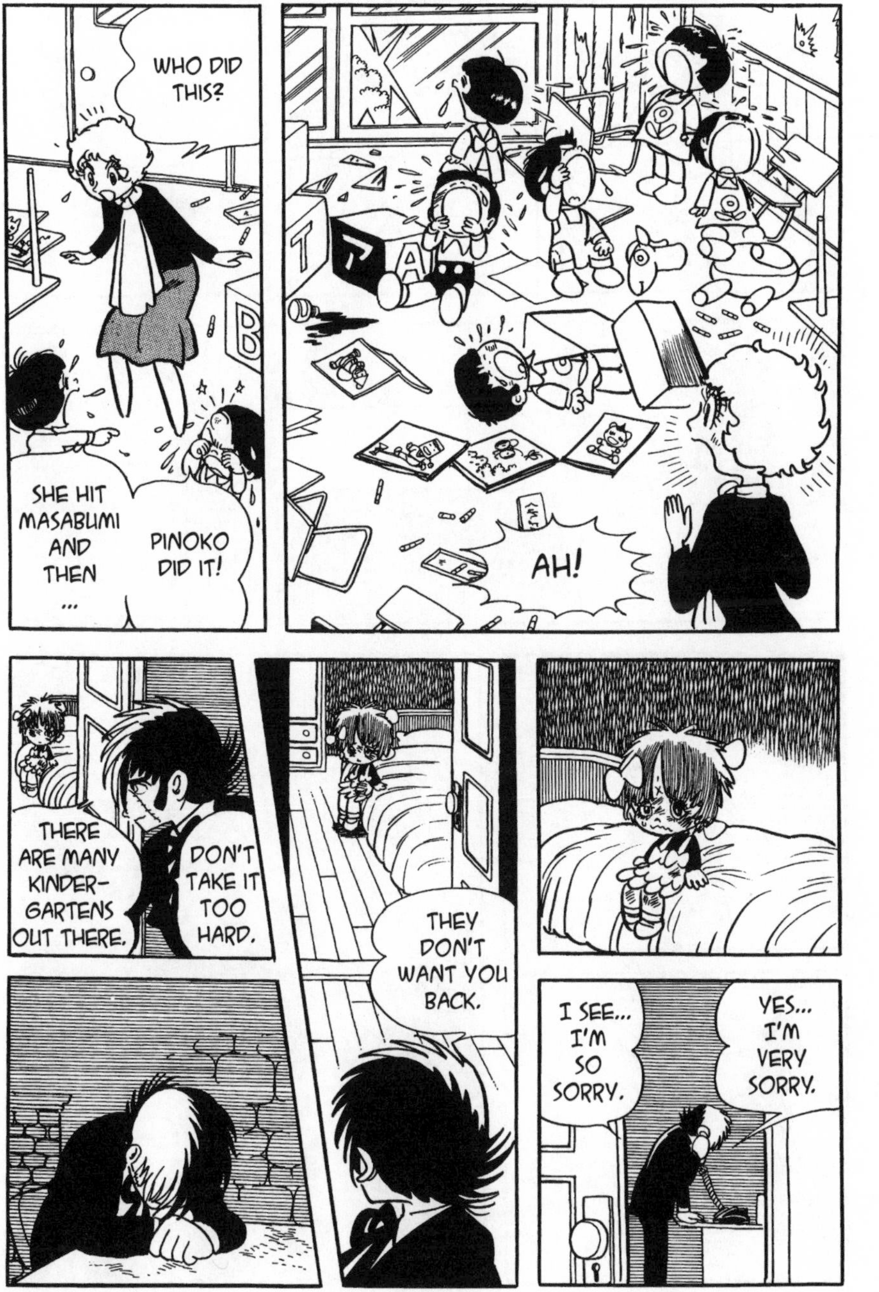
AH!
WHO DID THIS?
PINOKO DID IT!
SHE HIT MASABUMI AND THEN ...
YES... I'M VERY SORRY.
I SEE... I'M SO SORRY.
THEY DON'T WANT YOU BACK.
DON'T TAKE IT TOO HARD.
THERE ARE MANY KINDER-GARTENS OUT THERE.

HOSPITAL JACK

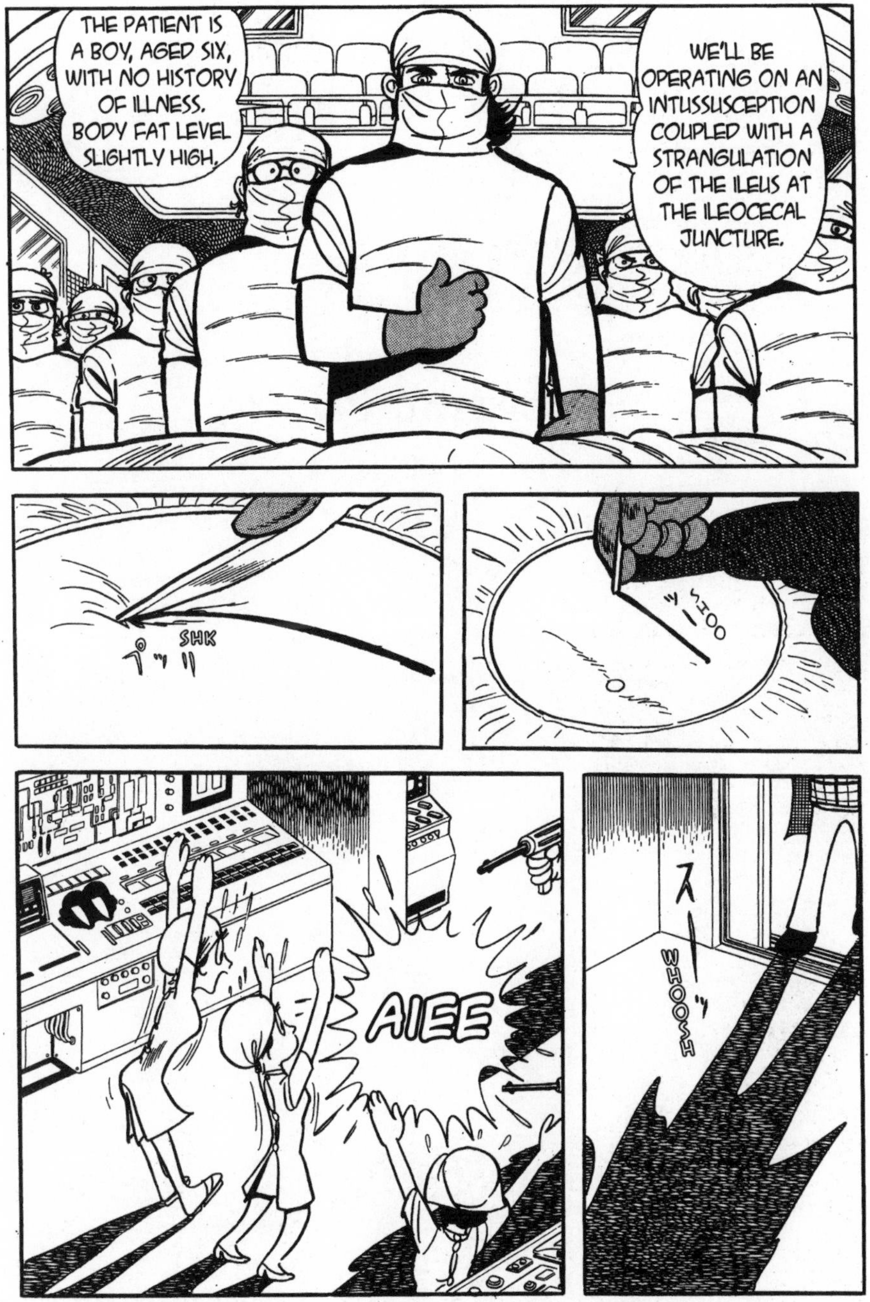
WE'LL BE OPERATING ON AN INTUSSUSCEPTION COUPLED WITH A STRANGULATION OF THE ILEUS AT THE ILEOCECAL JUNCTURE.
THE PATIENT IS A BOY, AGED SIX, WITH NO HISTORY OF ILLNESS. BODY FAT LEVEL SLIGHTLY HIGH.
SHK
WHOOSH
AIEE

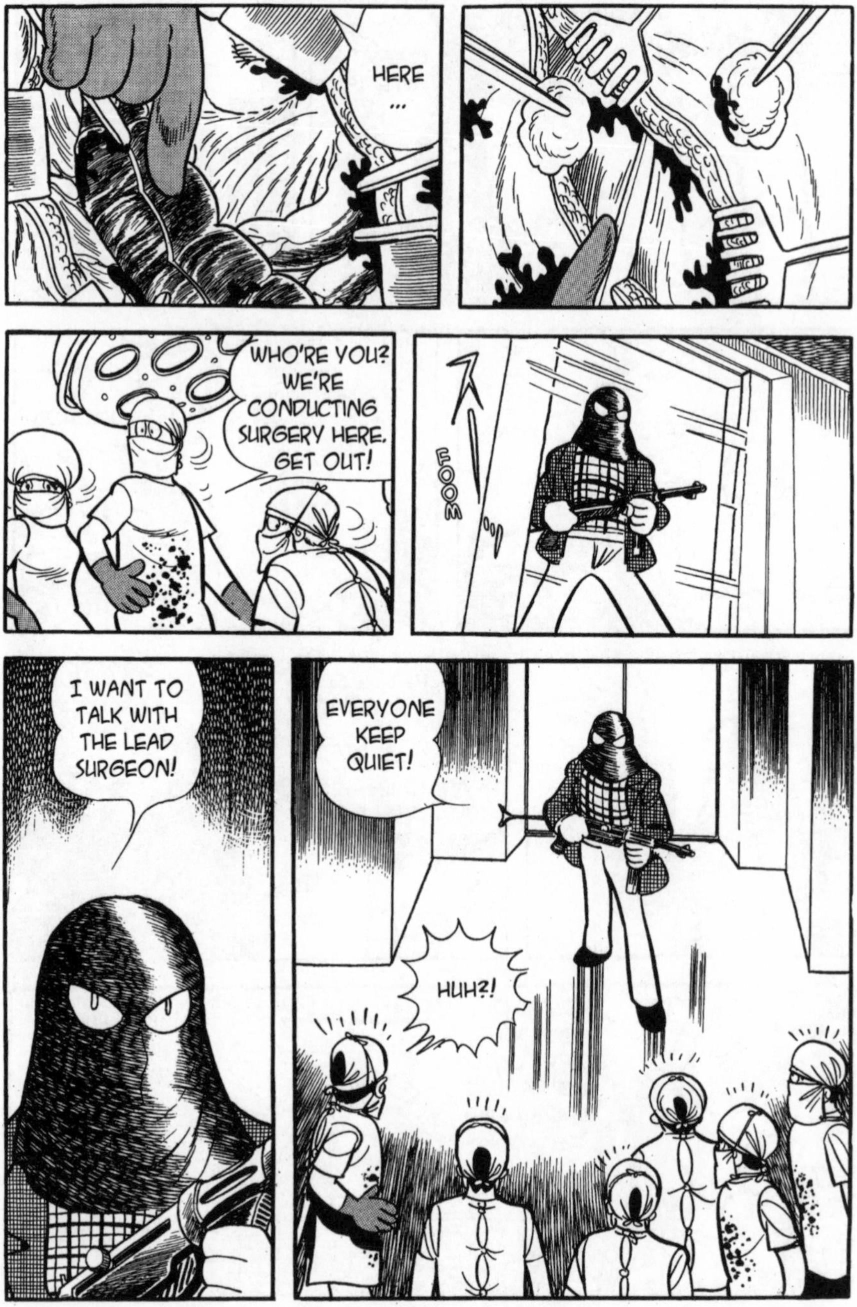
HERE ...
FOOM
WHO'RE YOU? WE'RE CONDUCTING SURGERY HERE. GET OUT!
EVERYONE KEEP QUIET!
HUH?!
I WANT TO TALK WITH THE LEAD SURGEON!

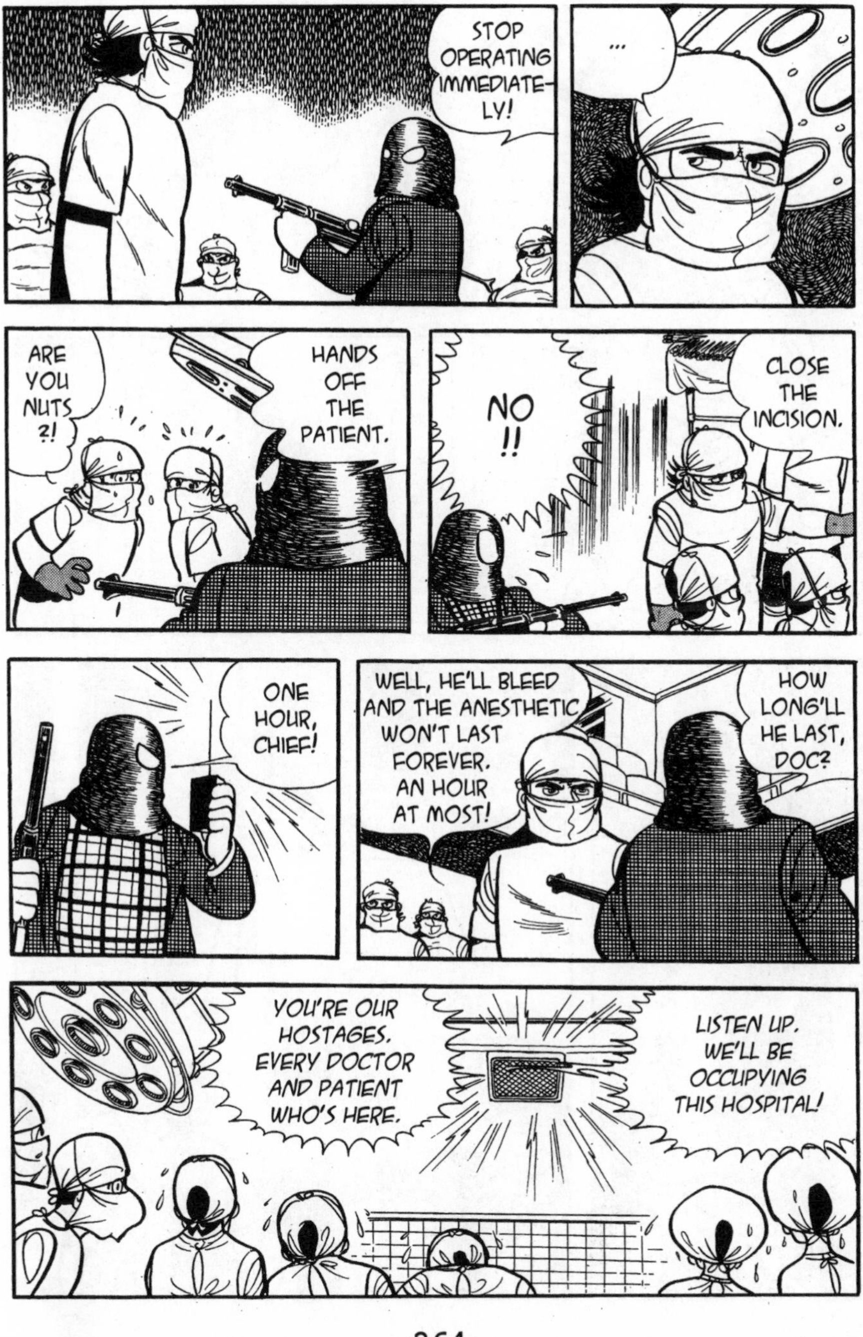
...
STOP OPERATING IMMEDIATE-LY!
CLOSE THE INCISION.
NO !!
HANDS OFF THE PATIENT.
ARE YOU NUTS ?!
HOW LONG'LL HE LAST, DOC?
WELL, HE'LL BLEED AND THE ANESTHETIC WON'T LAST FOREVER. AN HOUR AT MOST!
ONE HOUR, CHIEF!
LISTEN UP. WE'LL BE OCCUPYING THIS HOSPITAL!
YOU'RE OUR HOSTAGES. EVERY DOCTOR AND PATIENT WHO'S HERE.

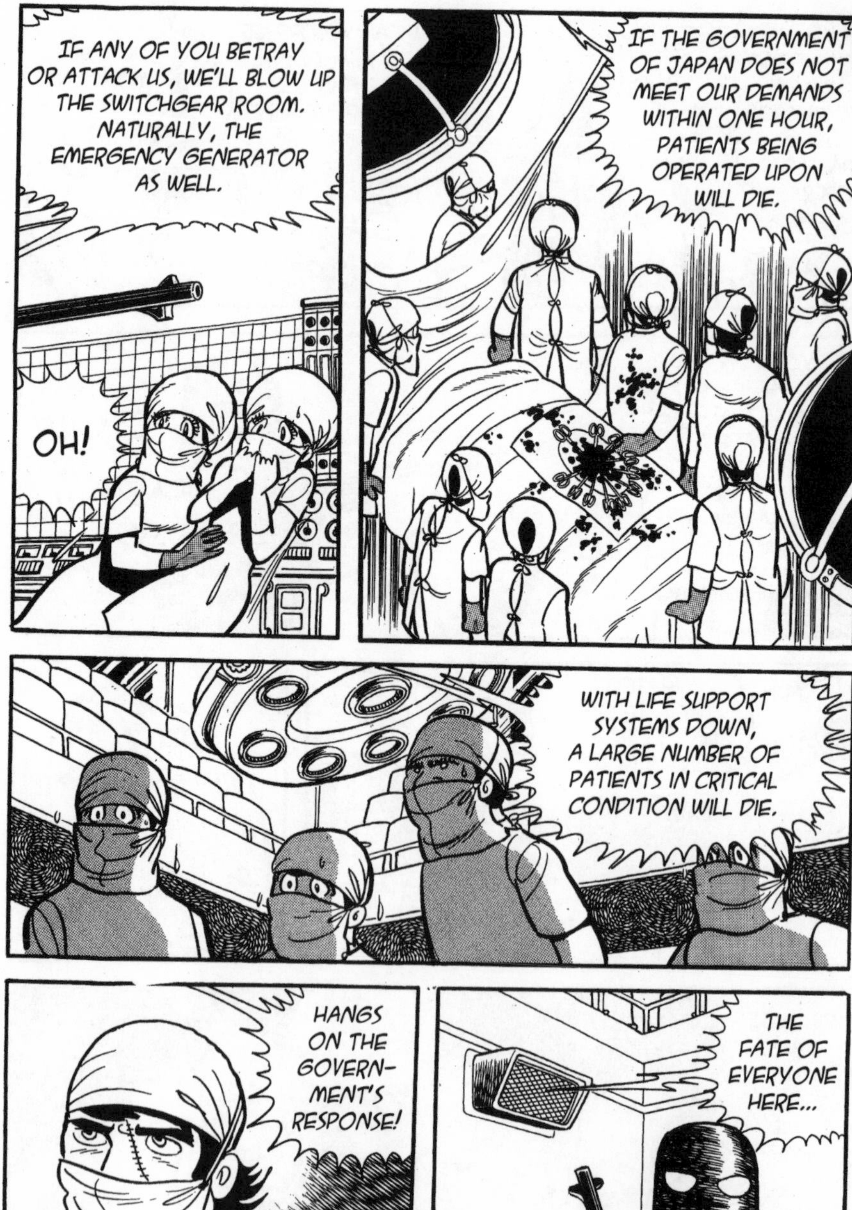
IF THE GOVERNMENT OF JAPAN DOES NOT MEET OUR DEMANDS WITHIN ONE HOUR, PATIENTS BEING OPERATED UPON WILL DIE.
IF ANY OF YOU BETRAY OR ATTACK US, WE'LL BLOW UP THE SWITCHGEAR ROOM. NATURALLY, THE EMERGENCY GENERATOR AS WELL.
OH!
WITH LIFE SUPPORT SYSTEMS DOWN, A LARGE NUMBER OF PATIENTS IN CRITICAL CONDITION WILL DIE.
THE FATE OF EVERYONE HERE...
HANGS ON THE GOVERNMENT'S RESPONSE!

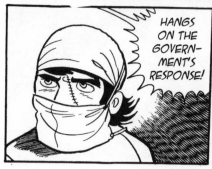

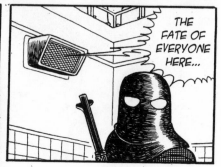

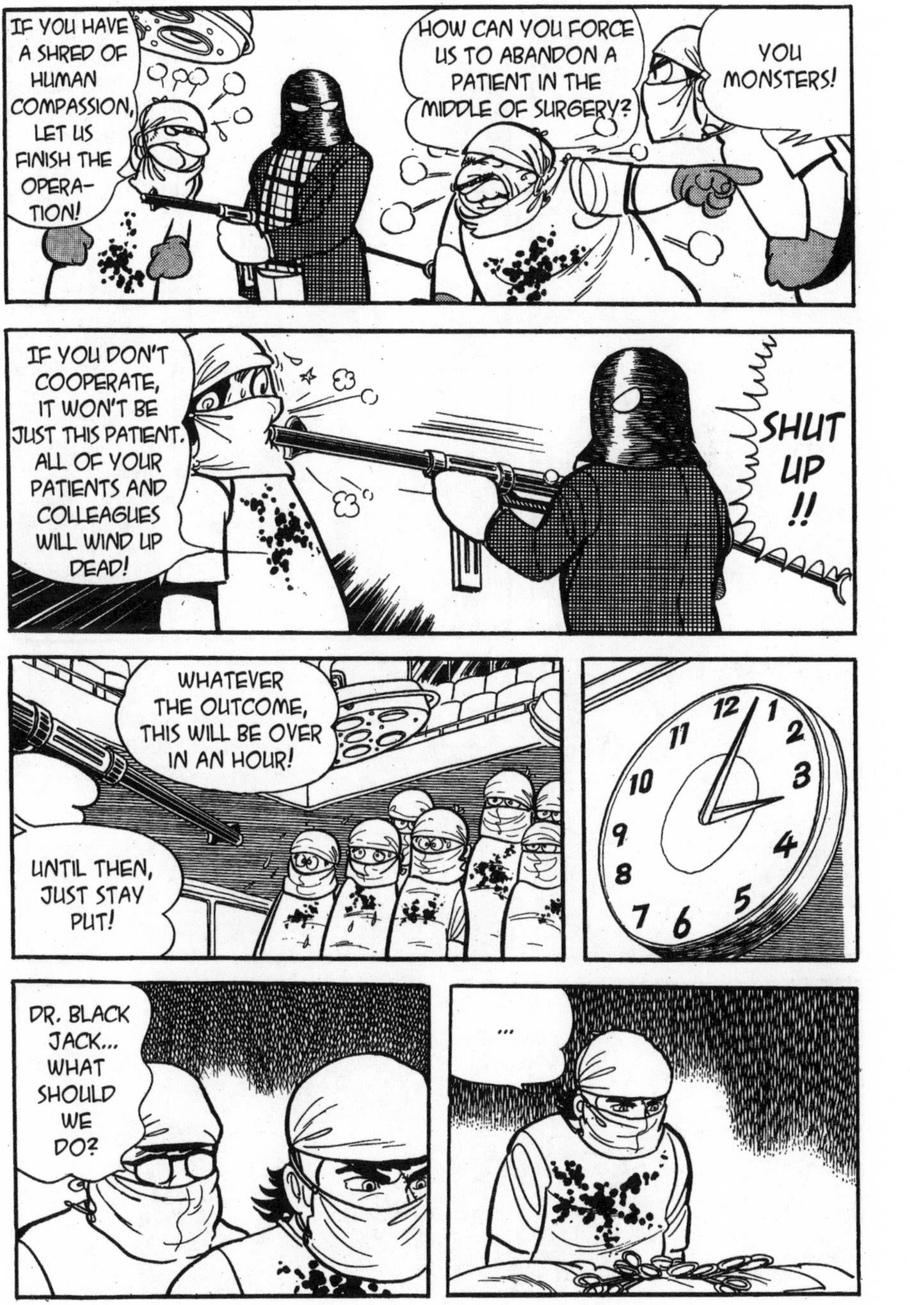
IF YOU HAVE A SHRED OF HUMAN COMPASSION, LET US FINISH THE OPERA-TION!
HOW CAN YOU FORCE US TO ABANDON A PATIENT IN THE MIDDLE OF SURGERY?
YOU MONSTERS!
IF YOU DON'T COOPERATE, IT WON'T BE JUST THIS PATIENT. ALL OF YOUR PATIENTS AND COLLEAGUES WILL WIND UP DEAD!
SHUT UP !!
WHATEVER THE OUTCOME, THIS WILL BE OVER IN AN HOUR!
UNTIL THEN, JUST STAY PUT!
12 1 2 3 4 5 6 7 8 9 10 11
DR. BLACK JACK... WHAT SHOULD WE DO?
...

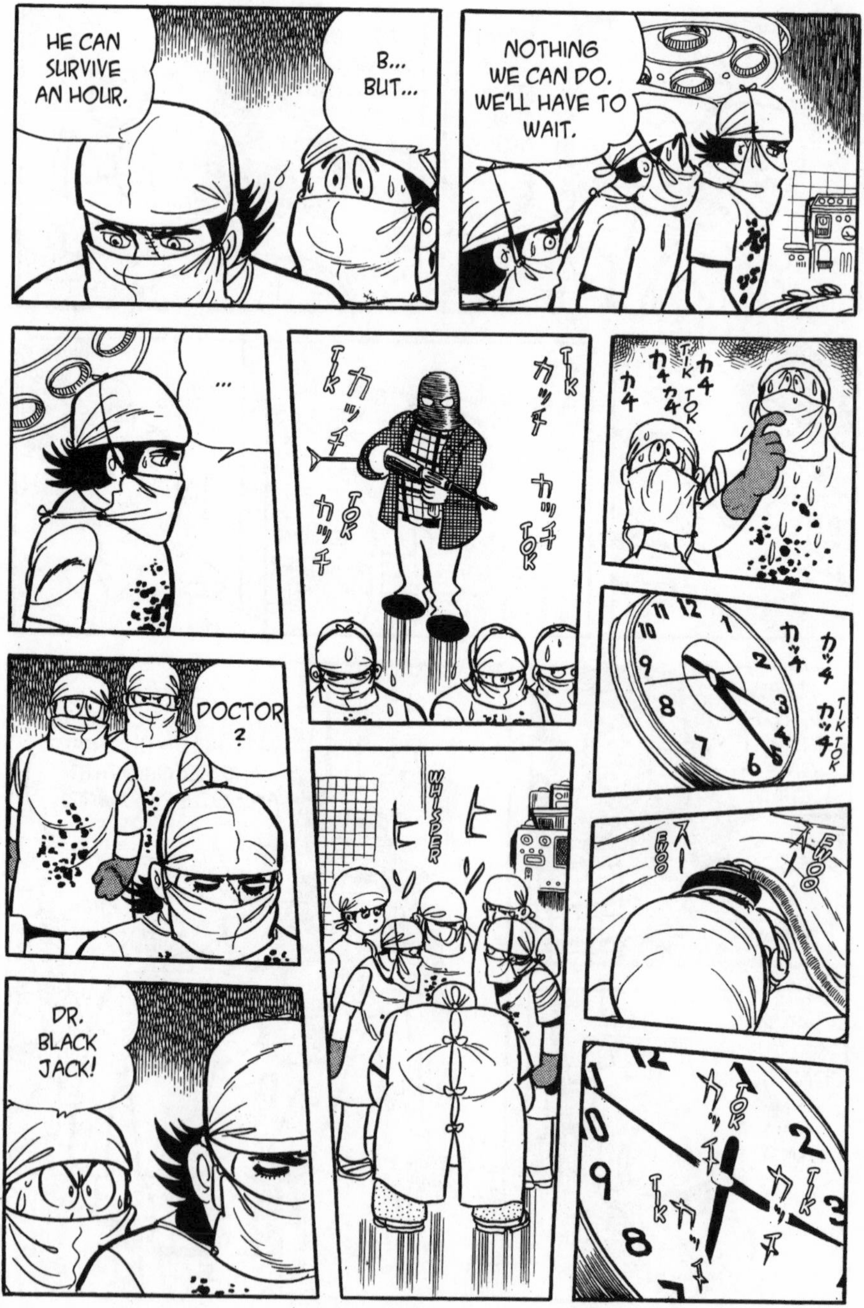
HE CAN SURVIVE AN HOUR.
B... BUT...
NOTHING WE CAN DO. WE'LL HAVE TO WAIT.
...
TIK TOK
カッチ
TIK TOK
カチ
TIK TOK
カッチ
DOCTOR?
WHISPER
SWOO
DR. BLACK JACK!
TIK TOK
カッチ

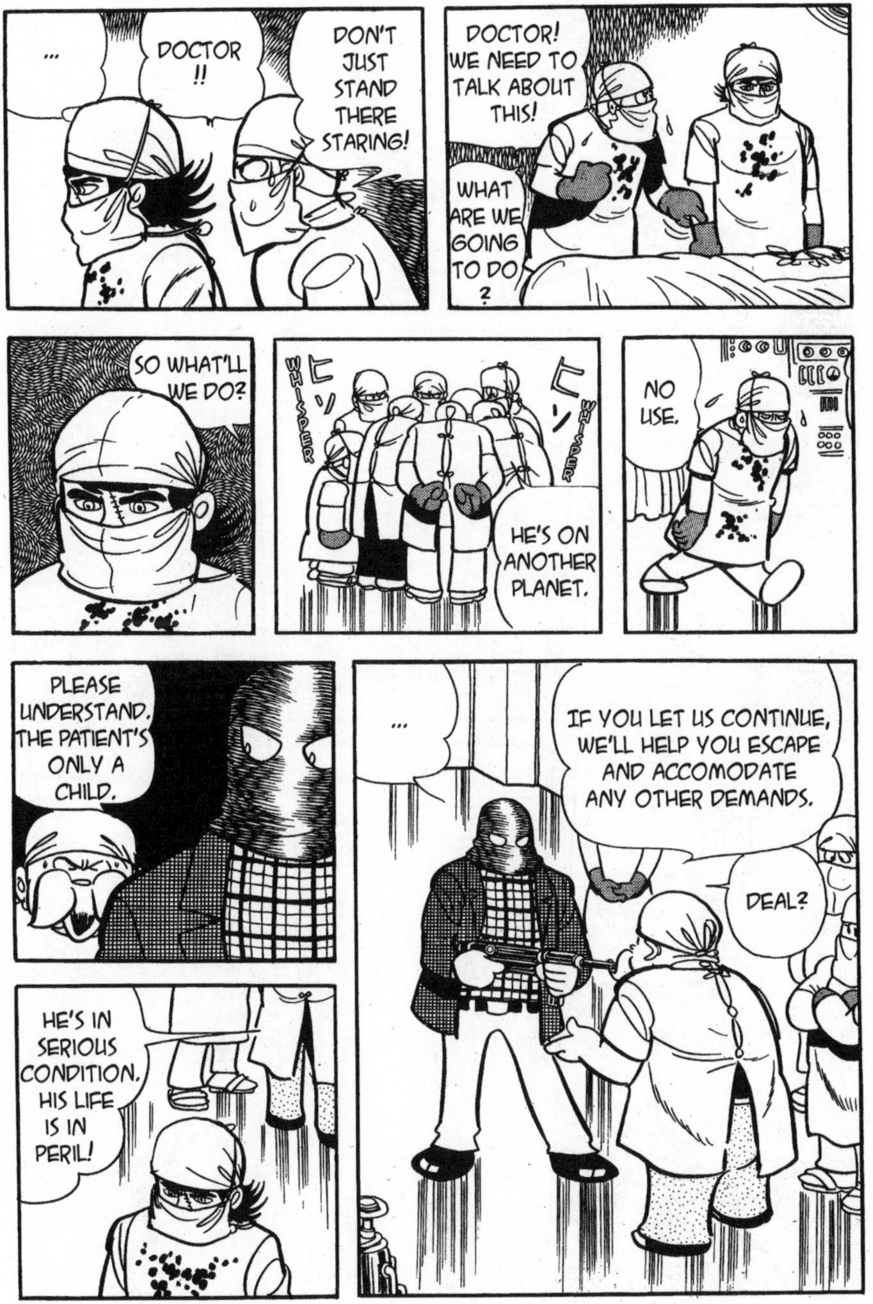
...
DOCTOR !!
DON'T JUST STAND THERE STARING!
DOCTOR! WE NEED TO TALK ABOUT THIS!
WHAT ARE WE GOING TO DO ?
SO WHAT'LL WE DO?
ヒソ WHISPER
ヒソ WHISPER
HE'S ON ANOTHER PLANET.
NO USE.
PLEASE UNDERSTAND. THE PATIENT'S ONLY A CHILD.
HE'S IN SERIOUS CONDITION. HIS LIFE IS IN PERIL!
...
IF YOU LET US CONTINUE, WE'LL HELP YOU ESCAPE AND ACCOMODATE ANY OTHER DEMANDS.
DEAL?

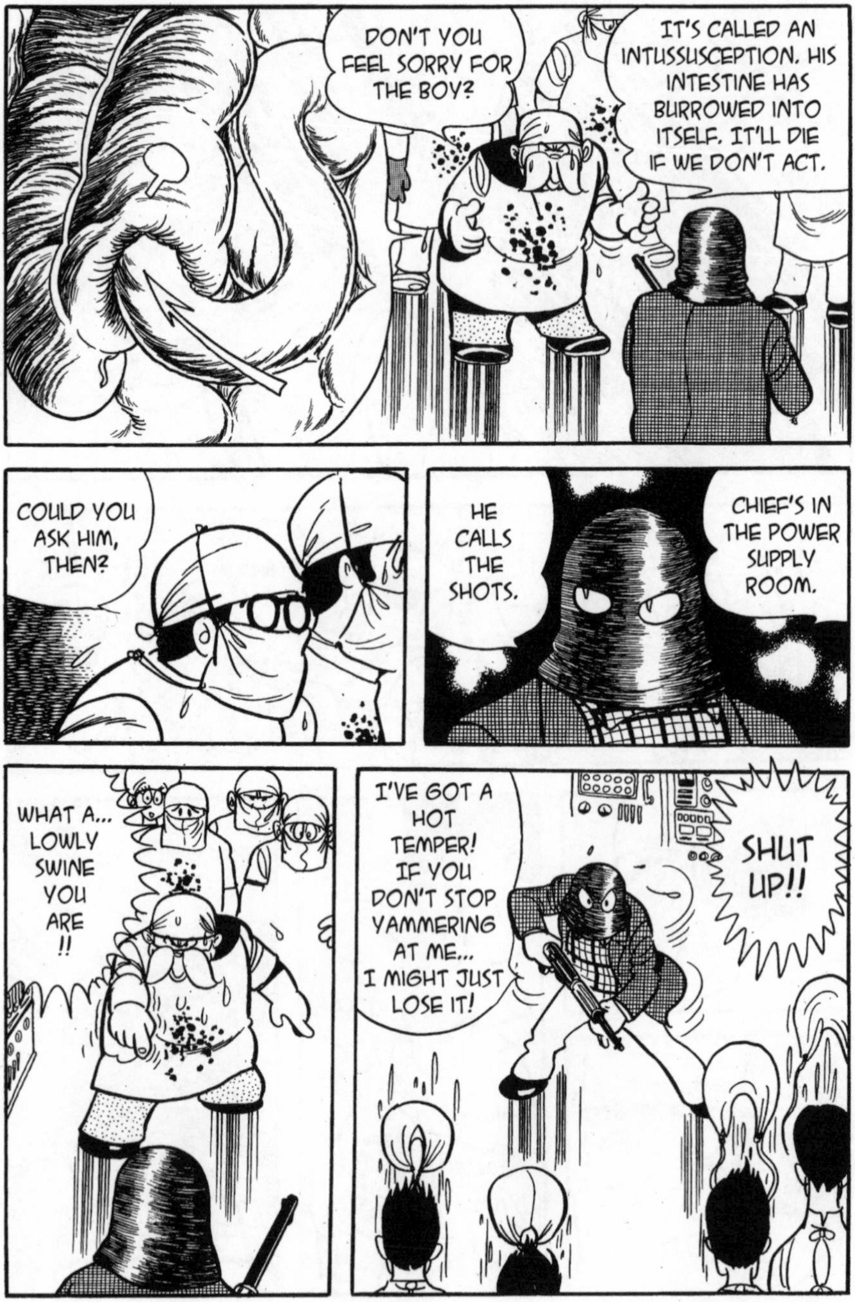
IT'S CALLED AN INTUSSUSCEPTION. HIS INTESTINE HAS BURROWED INTO ITSELF. IT'LL DIE IF WE DON'T ACT.
DON'T YOU FEEL SORRY FOR THE BOY?
CHIEF'S IN THE POWER SUPPLY ROOM.
HE CALLS THE SHOTS.
COULD YOU ASK HIM, THEN?
SHUT UP!!
I'VE GOT A HOT TEMPER! IF YOU DON'T STOP YAMMERING AT ME... I MIGHT JUST LOSE IT!
WHAT A... LOWLY SWINE YOU ARE !!

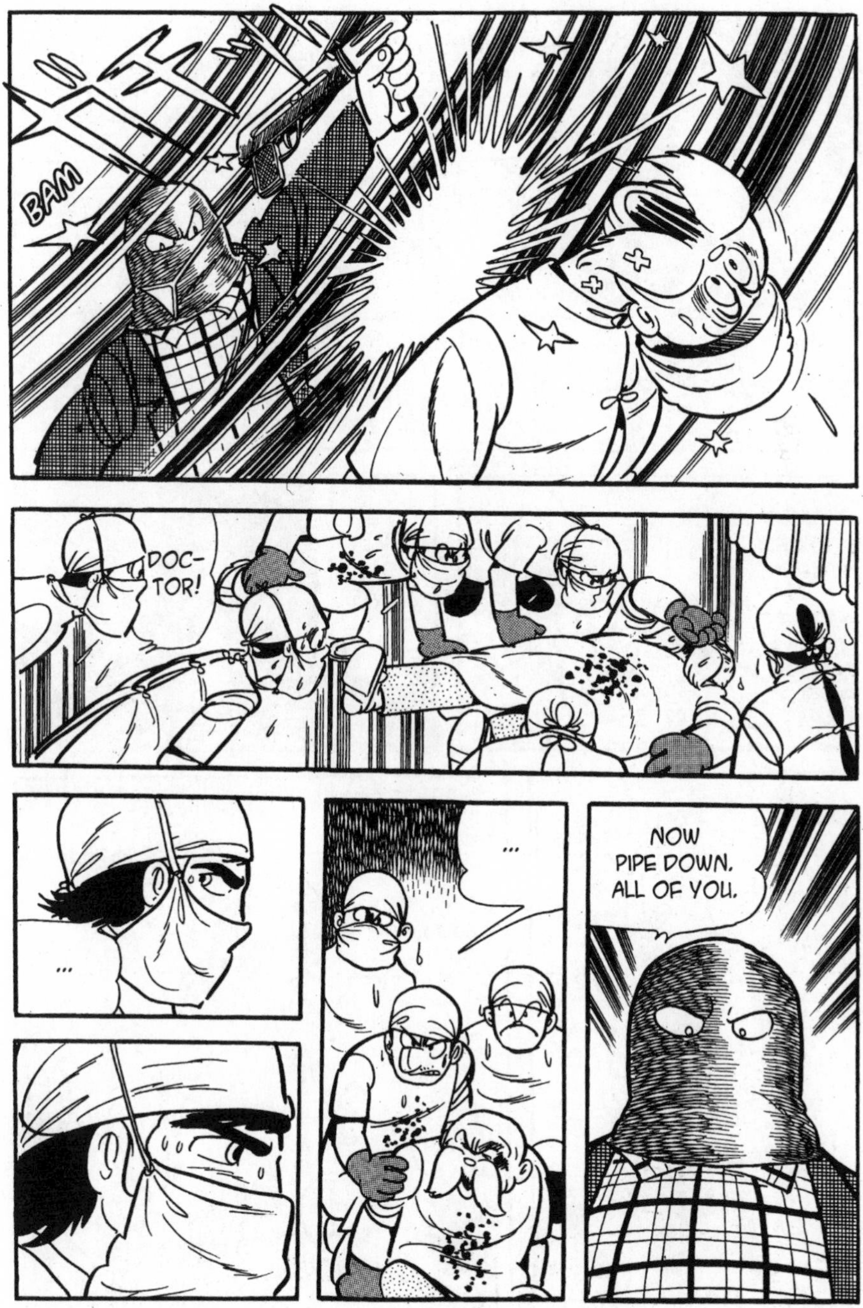
BAM
DOC-TOR!
NOW PIPE DOWN. ALL OF YOU.
...
...

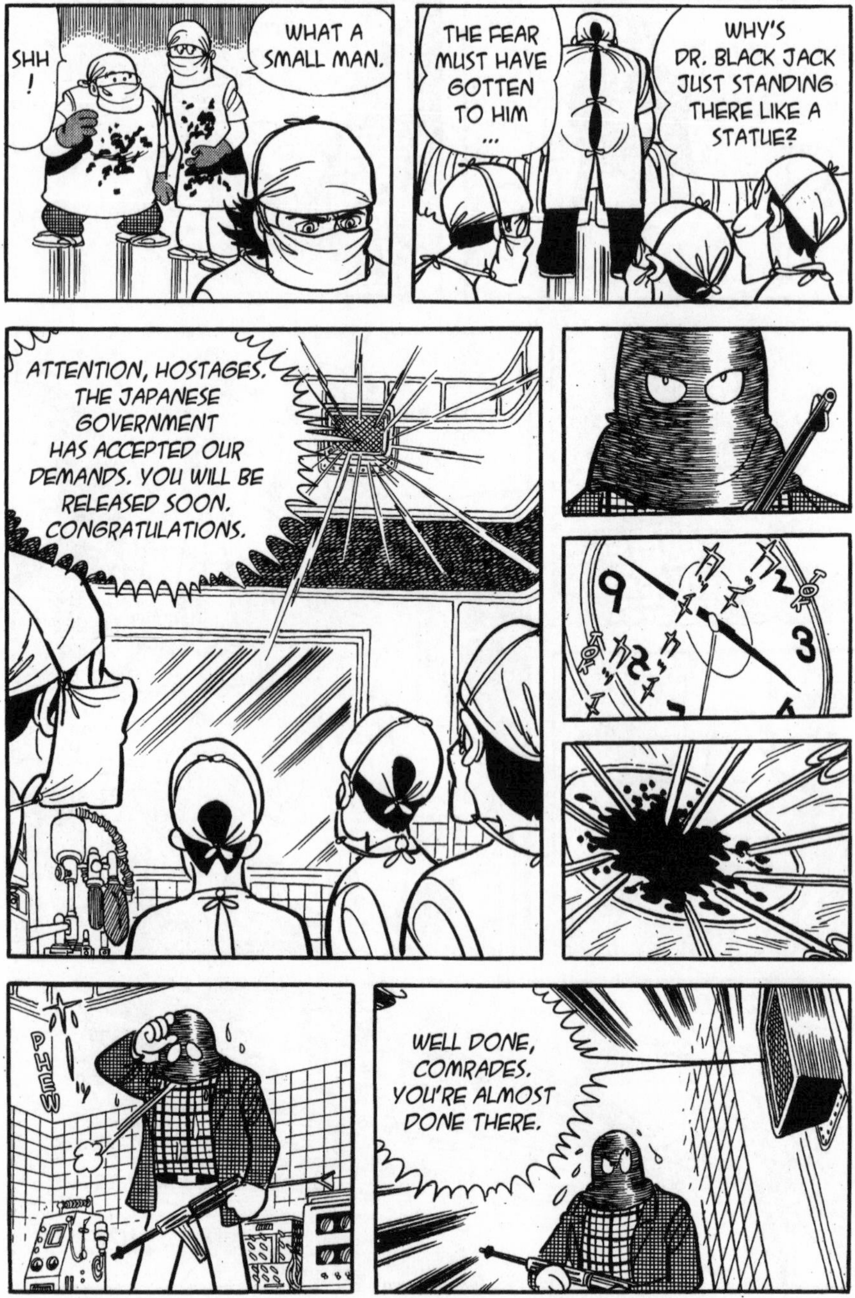
WHY'S DR. BLACK JACK JUST STANDING THERE LIKE A STATUE?
THE FEAR MUST HAVE GOTTEN TO HIM ...
WHAT A SMALL MAN.
SHH !
ATTENTION, HOSTAGES. THE JAPANESE GOVERNMENT HAS ACCEPTED OUR DEMANDS. YOU WILL BE RELEASED SOON. CONGRATULATIONS.
WELL DONE, COMRADES. YOU'RE ALMOST DONE THERE.
PHEW

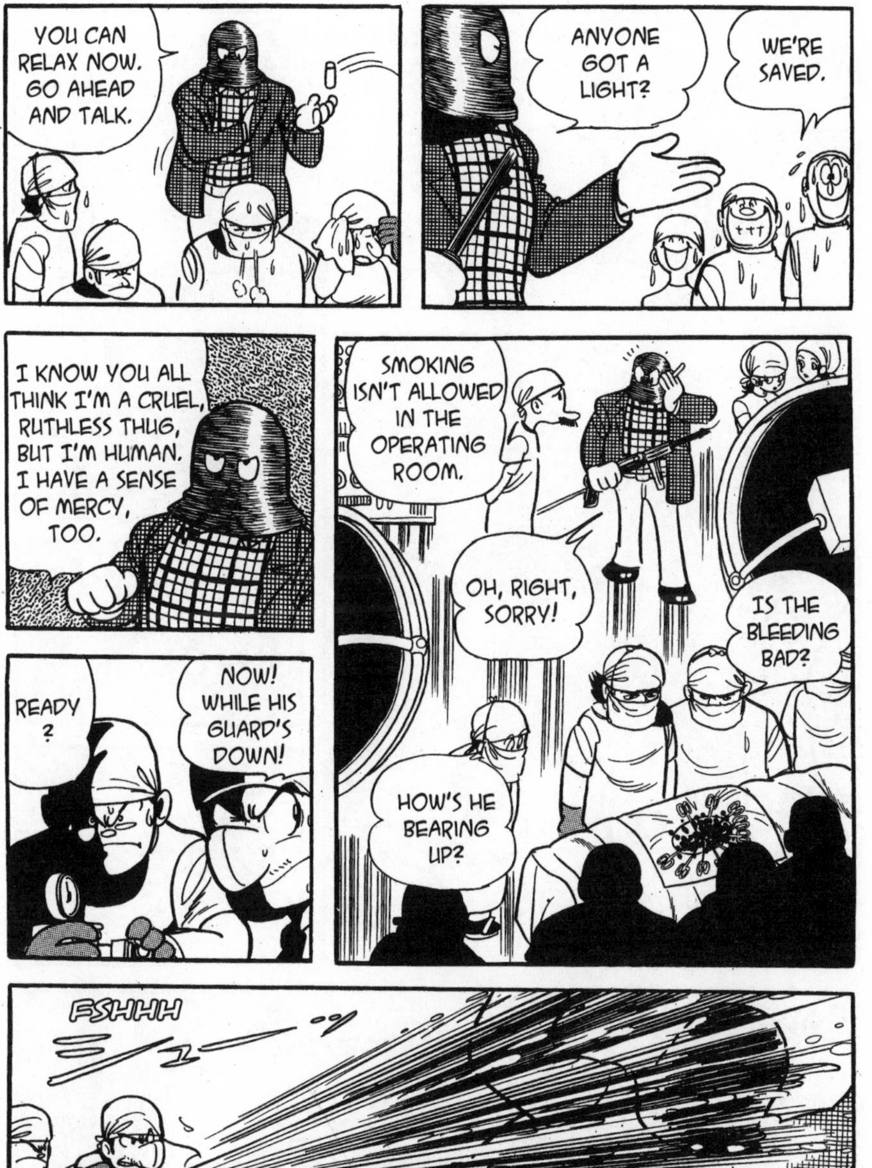
YOU CAN RELAX NOW. GO AHEAD AND TALK.
ANYONE GOT A LIGHT?
WE'RE SAVED.
I KNOW YOU ALL THINK I'M A CRUEL, RUTHLESS THUG, BUT I'M HUMAN. I HAVE A SENSE OF MERCY, TOO.
SMOKING ISN'T ALLOWED IN THE OPERATING ROOM.
OH, RIGHT, SORRY!
IS THE BLEEDING BAD?
HOW'S HE BEARING UP?
READY?
NOW! WHILE HIS GUARD'S DOWN!
FSHHH
URGH!

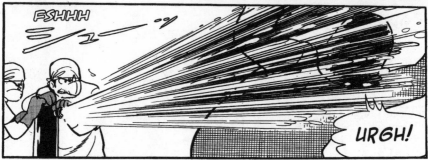

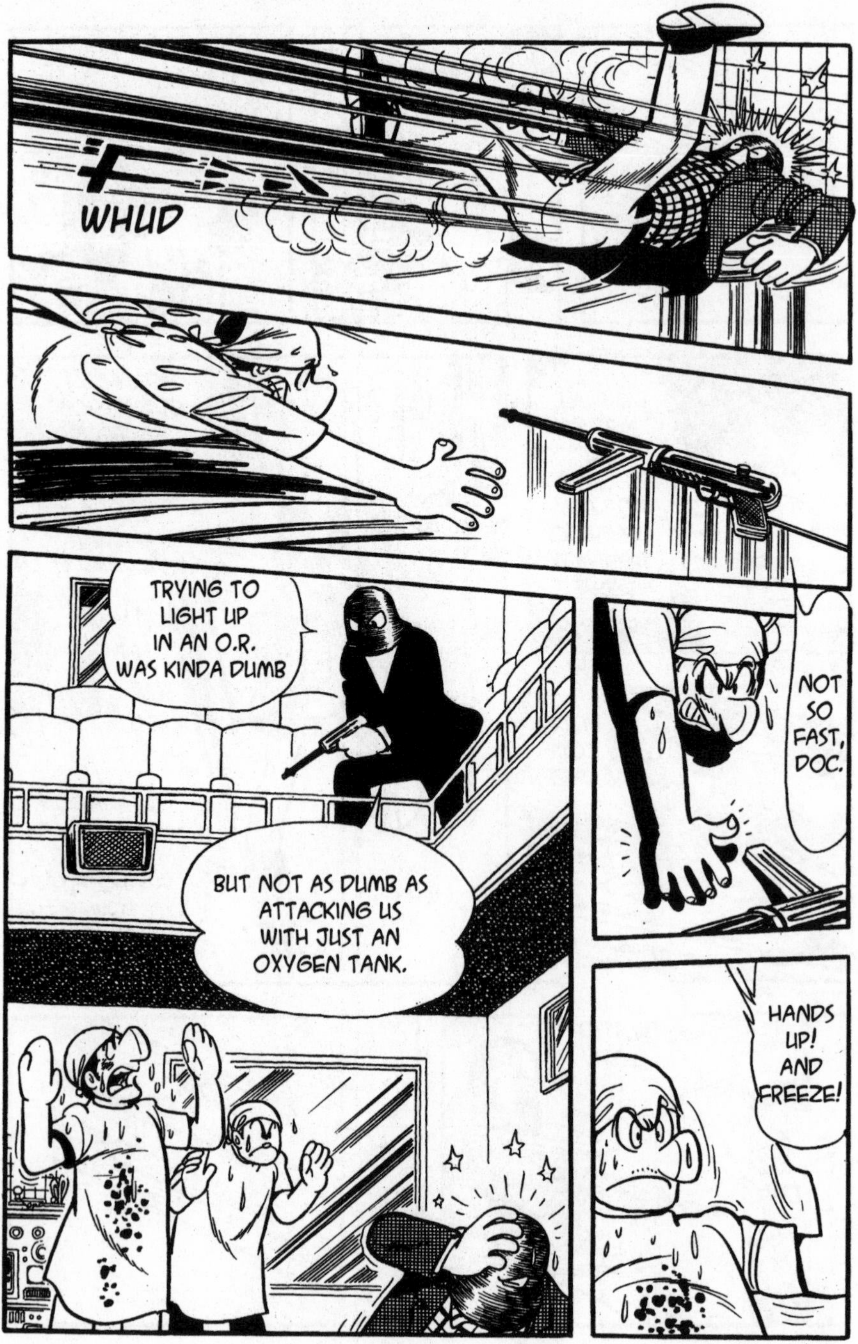
WHUD
NOT SO FAST, DOC.
HANDS UP! AND FREEZE!
TRYING TO LIGHT UP IN AN O.R. WAS KINDA DUMB
BUT NOT AS DUMB AS ATTACKING US WITH JUST AN OXYGEN TANK.

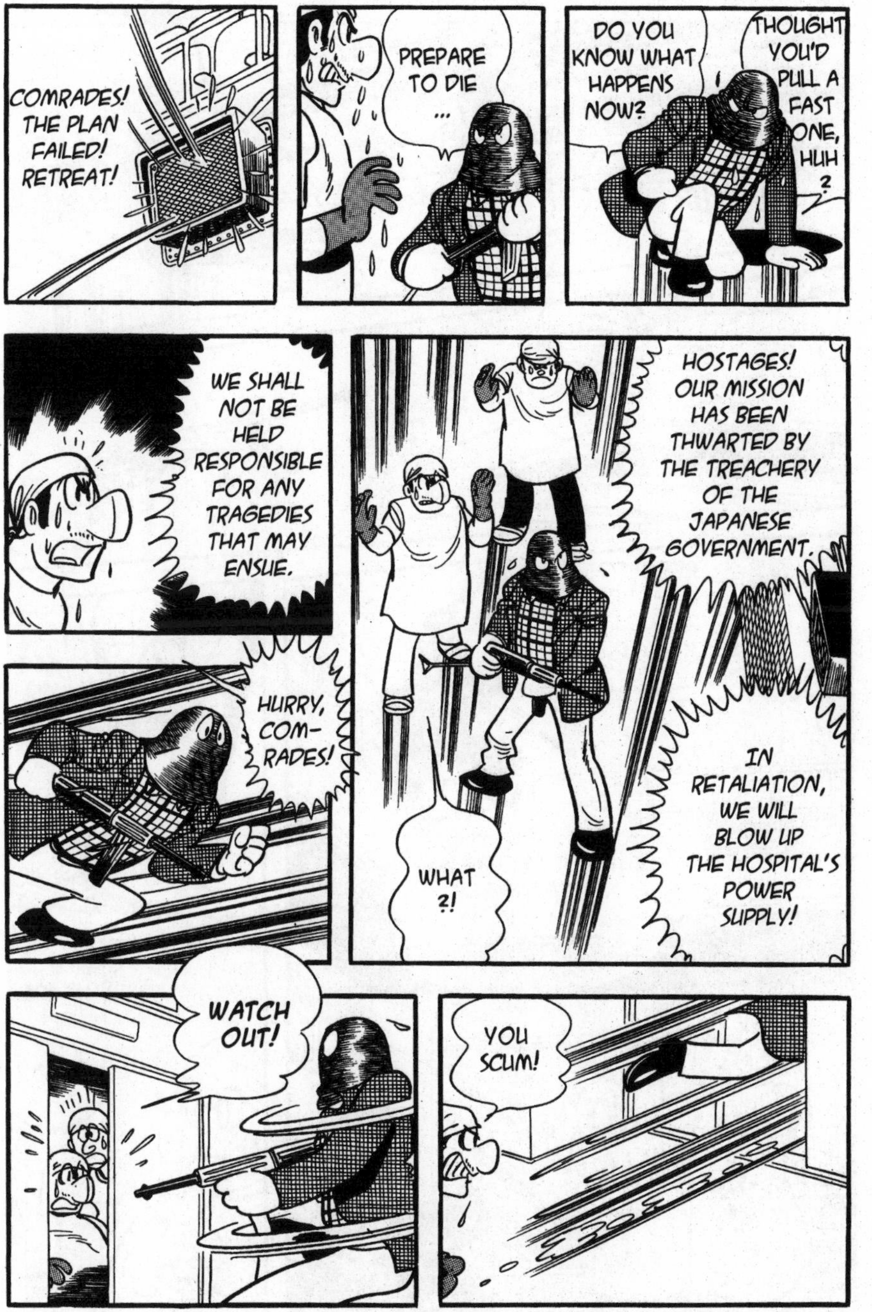
COMRADES! THE PLAN FAILED! RETREAT!
PREPARE TO DIE ...
THOUGHT YOU'D PULL A FAST ONE, HUH?
DO YOU KNOW WHAT HAPPENS NOW?
WE SHALL NOT BE HELD RESPONSIBLE FOR ANY TRAGEDIES THAT MAY ENSUE.
HURRY, COM-RADES!
HOSTAGES! OUR MISSION HAS BEEN THWARTED BY THE TREACHERY OF THE JAPANESE GOVERNMENT.
IN RETALIATION, WE WILL BLOW UP THE HOSPITAL'S POWER SUPPLY!
WHAT?!
WATCH OUT!
YOU SCUM!

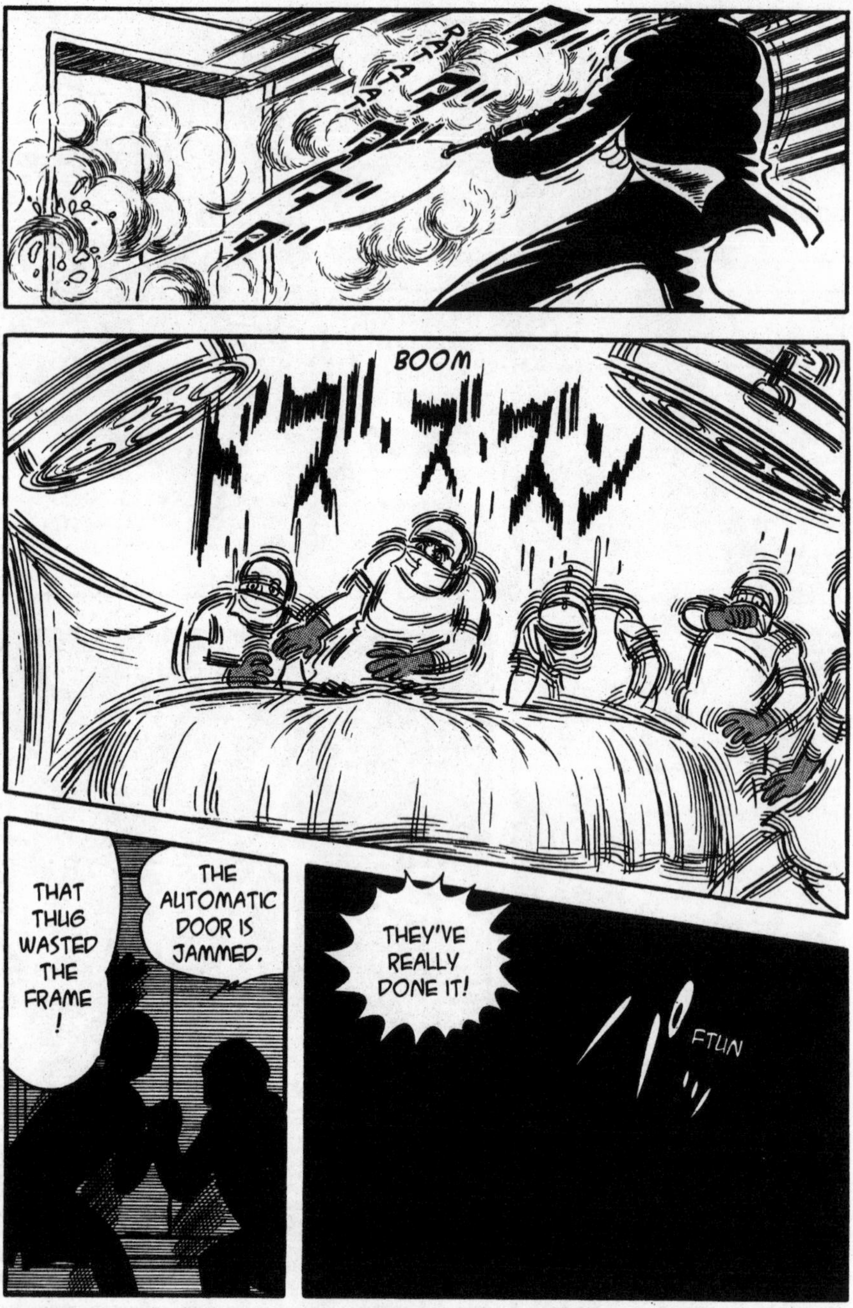
RATATATAT
BOOM
THEY'VE REALLY DONE IT!
FTUN
THE AUTOMATIC DOOR IS JAMMED.
THAT THUG WASTED THE FRAME!

DAMN! WE NEED LIGHT!
FAT CHANCE.
ANYONE GOT A MATCH?
I GAVE MINE TO THAT HOODED GUY!
THERE MUST BE A BOX SOME-WHERE!
HOW 'BOUT A LIGHTER?
READY, GO!
IT'S STUCK ...
HOW COULD THEY DO THIS? THIS CHILD'S LIFE WAS IN OUR HANDS!
LIGHT! ANY KIND!
HE'LL DIE IF WE DON'T RESUME SURGERY!
KRUNK
RATATAT
BLAM BLAM BLAM BLAM
VOOM
SOUNDS LIKE THE RIOT SQUAD'S HERE.

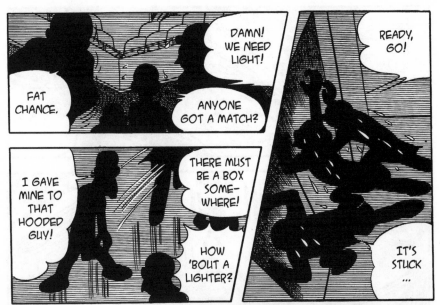

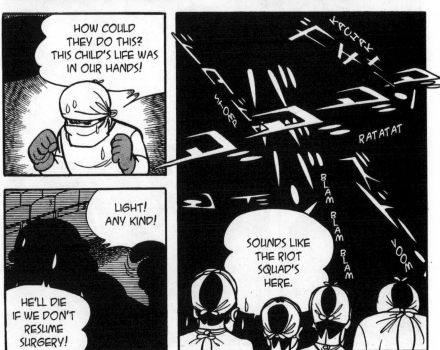

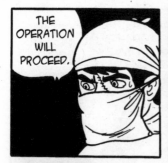

IT'S OVER, DR. BLACK JACK. WE CAN'T OPERATE LIKE THIS.
WHAT A SHAME! POOR KID ...
THE OPERATION WILL PROCEED.
WHAT, IN THIS PITCH DARK?
FEEL AROUND FOR THE INSTRU-MENTS AND HAND THEM TO ME.
WHAT ?!
YOU WANT TO OPERATE BLIND?!
IT CAN'T BE DONE!
HAND ME THE ILEUS TUBE.
ILEUS TUBE!!
YOU KNOW ITS SHAPE, DON'T YOU?

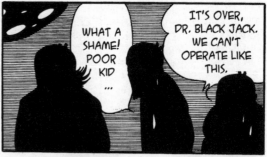

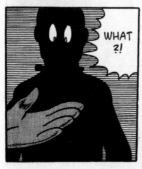

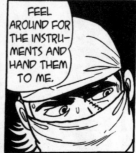

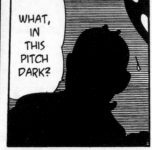

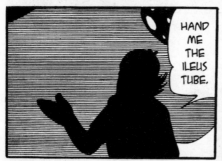

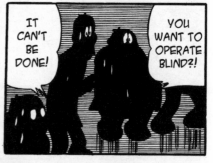

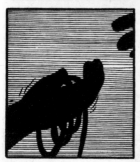

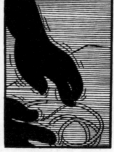

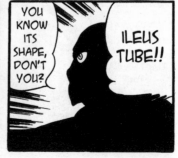

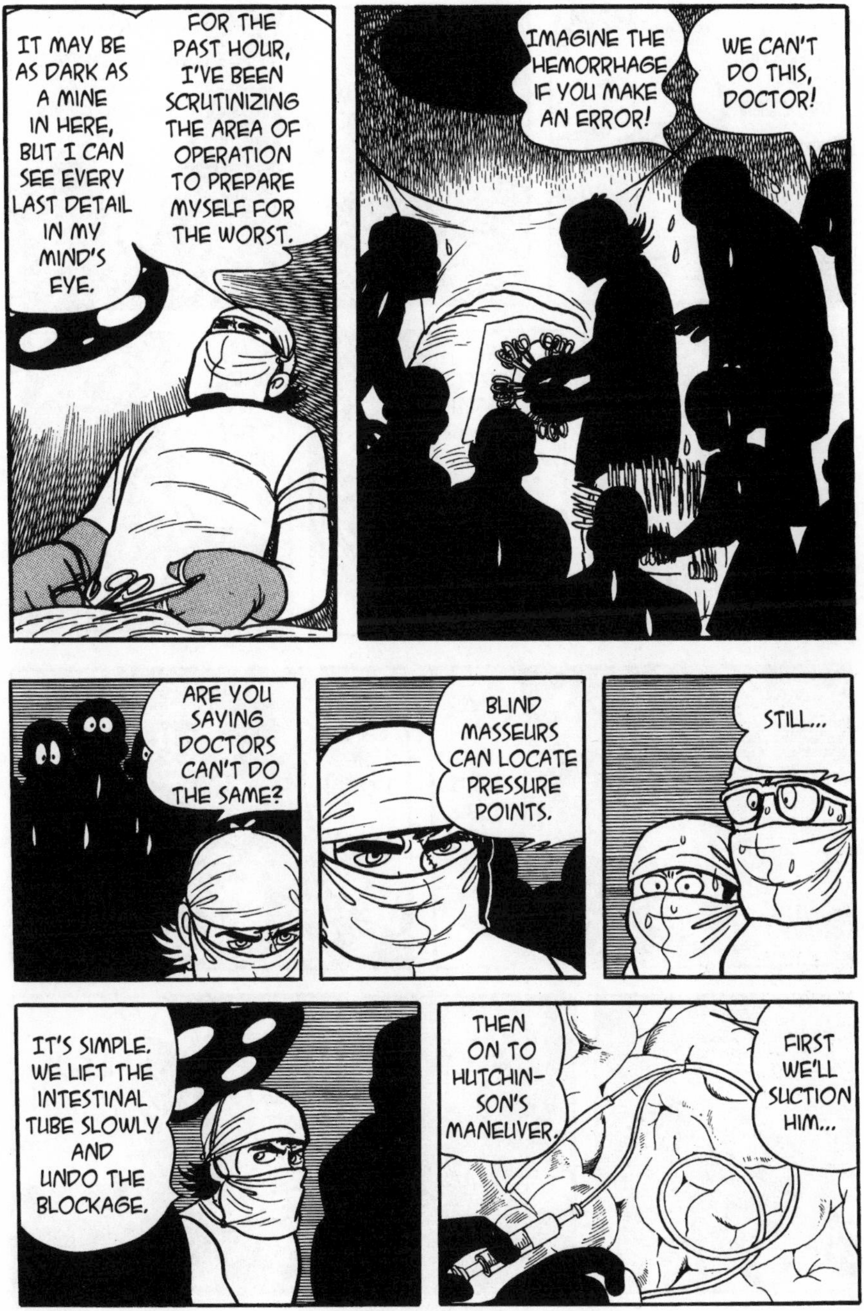
WE CAN'T DO THIS, DOCTOR!
IMAGINE THE HEMORRHAGE IF YOU MAKE AN ERROR!
FOR THE PAST HOUR, I'VE BEEN SCRUTINIZING THE AREA OF OPERATION TO PREPARE MYSELF FOR THE WORST.
IT MAY BE AS DARK AS A MINE IN HERE, BUT I CAN SEE EVERY LAST DETAIL IN MY MIND'S EYE.
STILL...
BLIND MASSEURS CAN LOCATE PRESSURE POINTS.
ARE YOU SAYING DOCTORS CAN'T DO THE SAME?
FIRST WE'LL SUCTION HIM...
THEN ON TO HUTCHIN-SON'S MANEUVER.
IT'S SIMPLE. WE LIFT THE INTESTINAL TUBE SLOWLY AND UNDO THE BLOCKAGE.

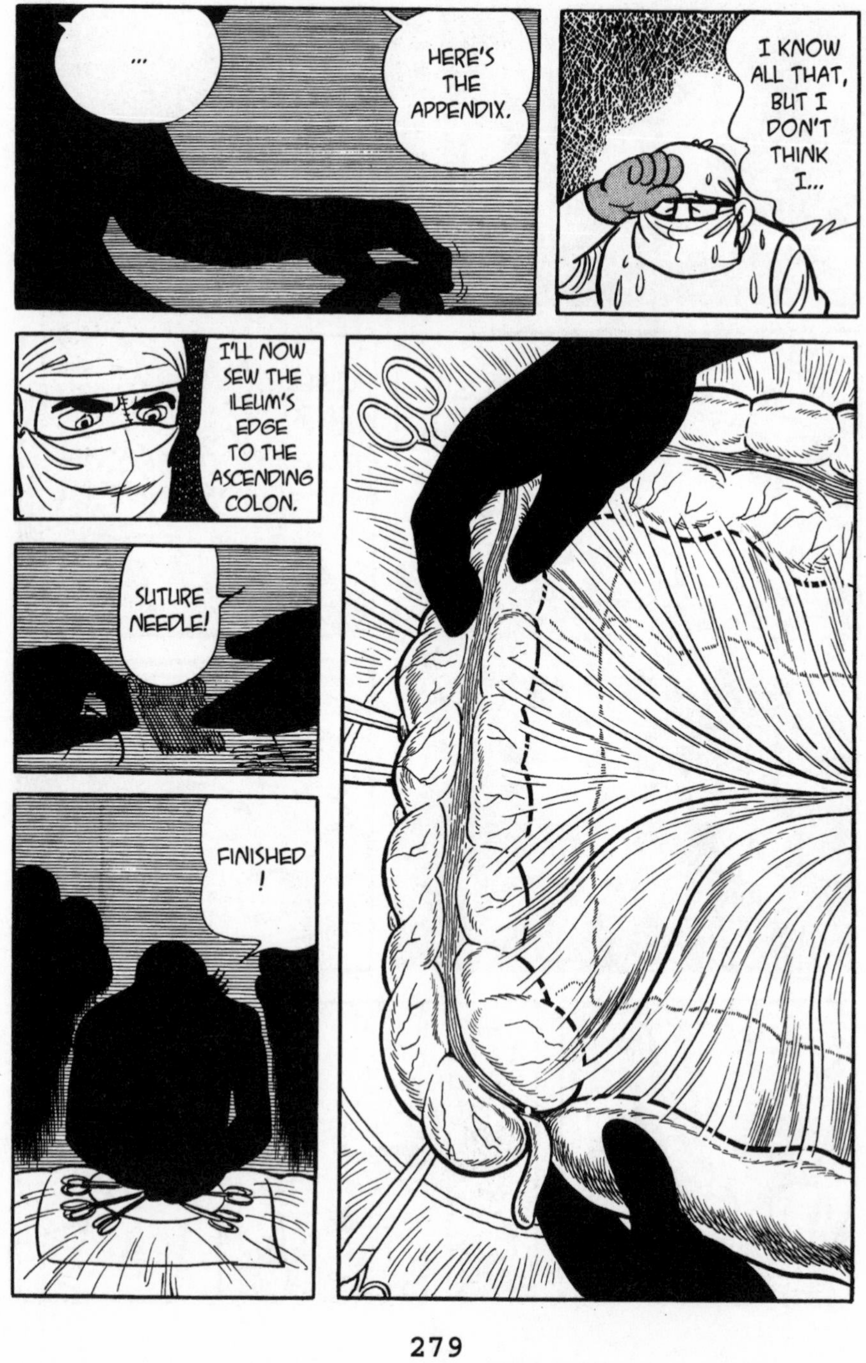
I KNOW ALL THAT, BUT I DON'T THINK I...
HERE'S THE APPENDIX.
...
I'LL NOW SEW THE ILEUM'S EDGE TO THE ASCENDING COLON.
SUTURE NEEDLE!
FINISHED!

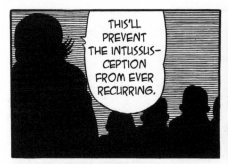

THIS'LL PREVENT THE INTUSSUS-CEPTION FROM EVER RECURRING.
LIGHT!
POWER'S BACK!
PTINK
THE PATIENT ?!
PERFECT WORK... D-DIVINE...
CHECK HIM AND MAKE SURE...
BUT I HAVE A HUNCH I DID JUST FINE.
CLAP
CLAP
CLAP

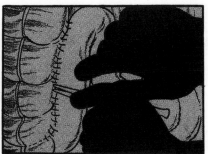

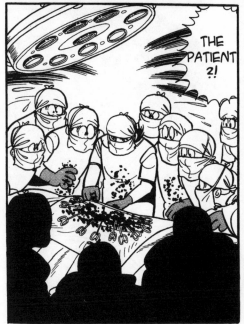

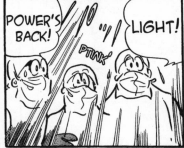

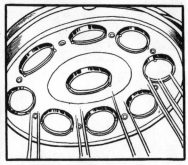

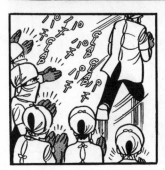

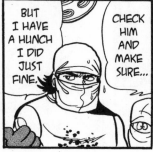

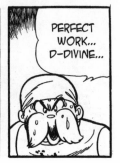

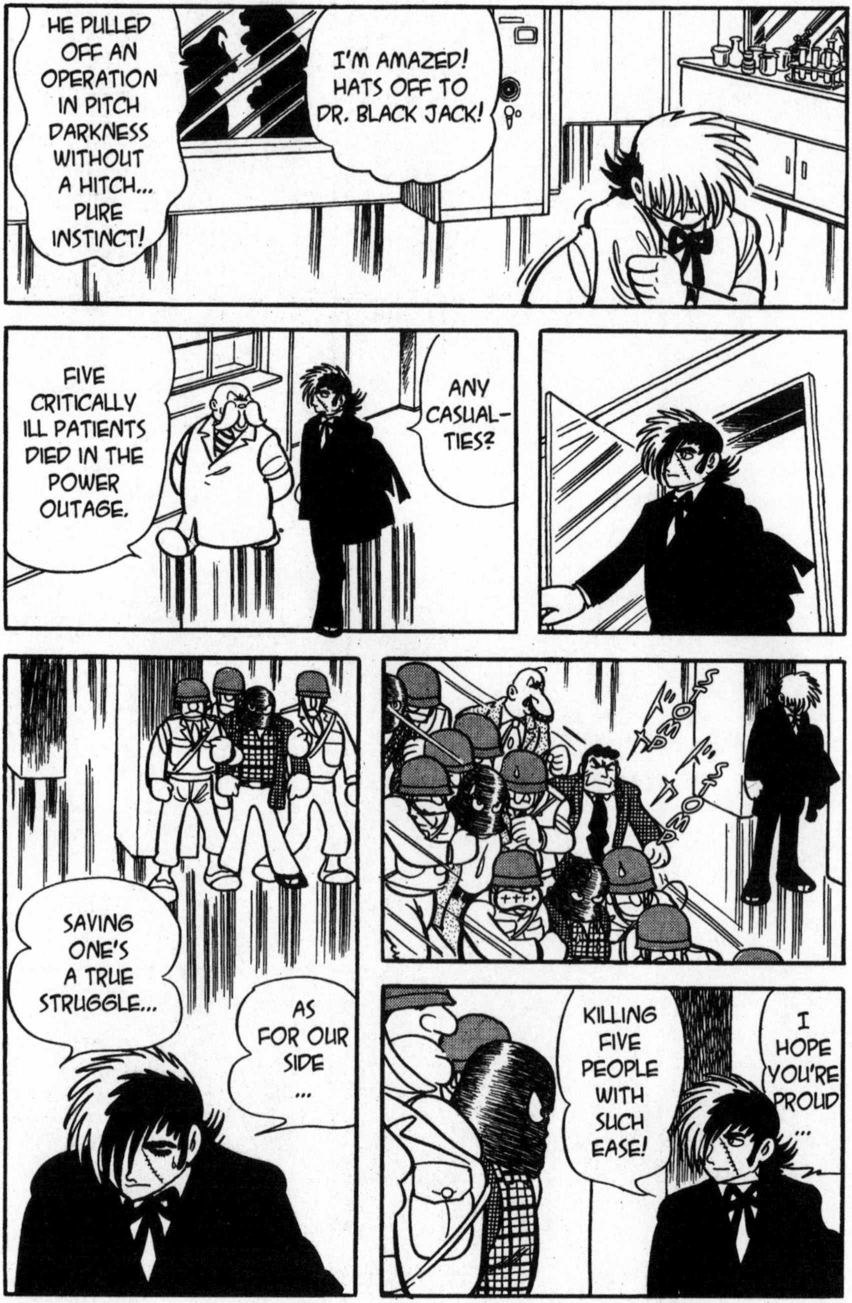
I'M AMAZED! HATS OFF TO DR. BLACK JACK!
HE PULLED OFF AN OPERATION IN PITCH DARKNESS WITHOUT A HITCH... PURE INSTINCT!
ANY CASUALTIES?
FIVE CRITICALLY ILL PATIENTS DIED IN THE POWER OUTAGE.
STOMP
STOMP
I HOPE YOU'RE PROUD...
KILLING FIVE PEOPLE WITH SUCH EASE!
AS FOR OUR SIDE...
SAVING ONE'S A TRUE STRUGGLE...

THE BLIND ACUPUNCTURIST

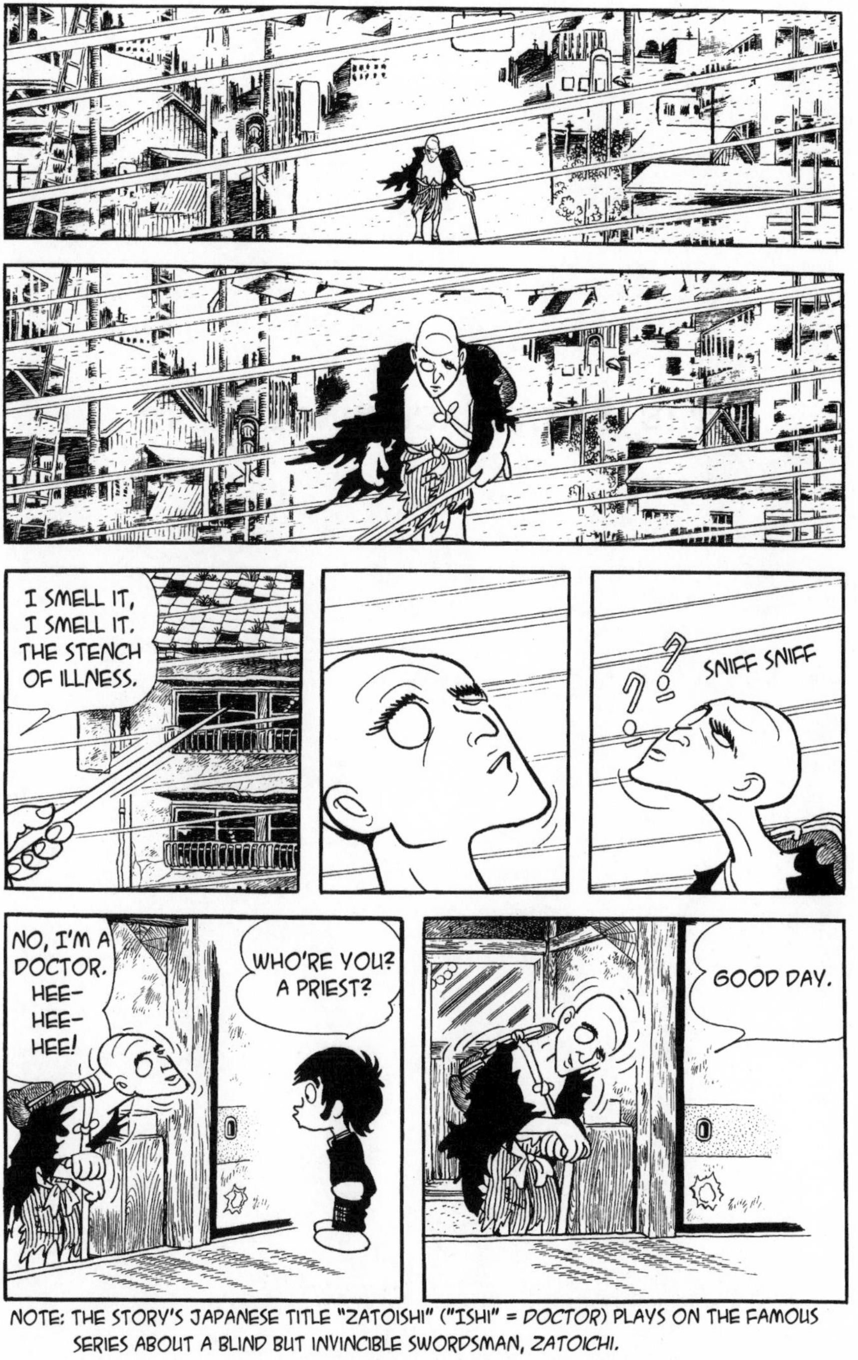
SNIFF SNIFF
I SMELL IT, I SMELL IT. THE STENCH OF ILLNESS.
GOOD DAY.
WHO'RE YOU? A PRIEST?
NO, I'M A DOCTOR. HEE-HEE-HEE!

NOTE: THE STORY'S JAPANESE TITLE "ZATOISHI" ("ISHI" = *DOCTOR*) PLAYS ON THE FAMOUS SERIES ABOUT A BLIND BUT INVINCIBLE SWORDSMAN, ZATOICHI.

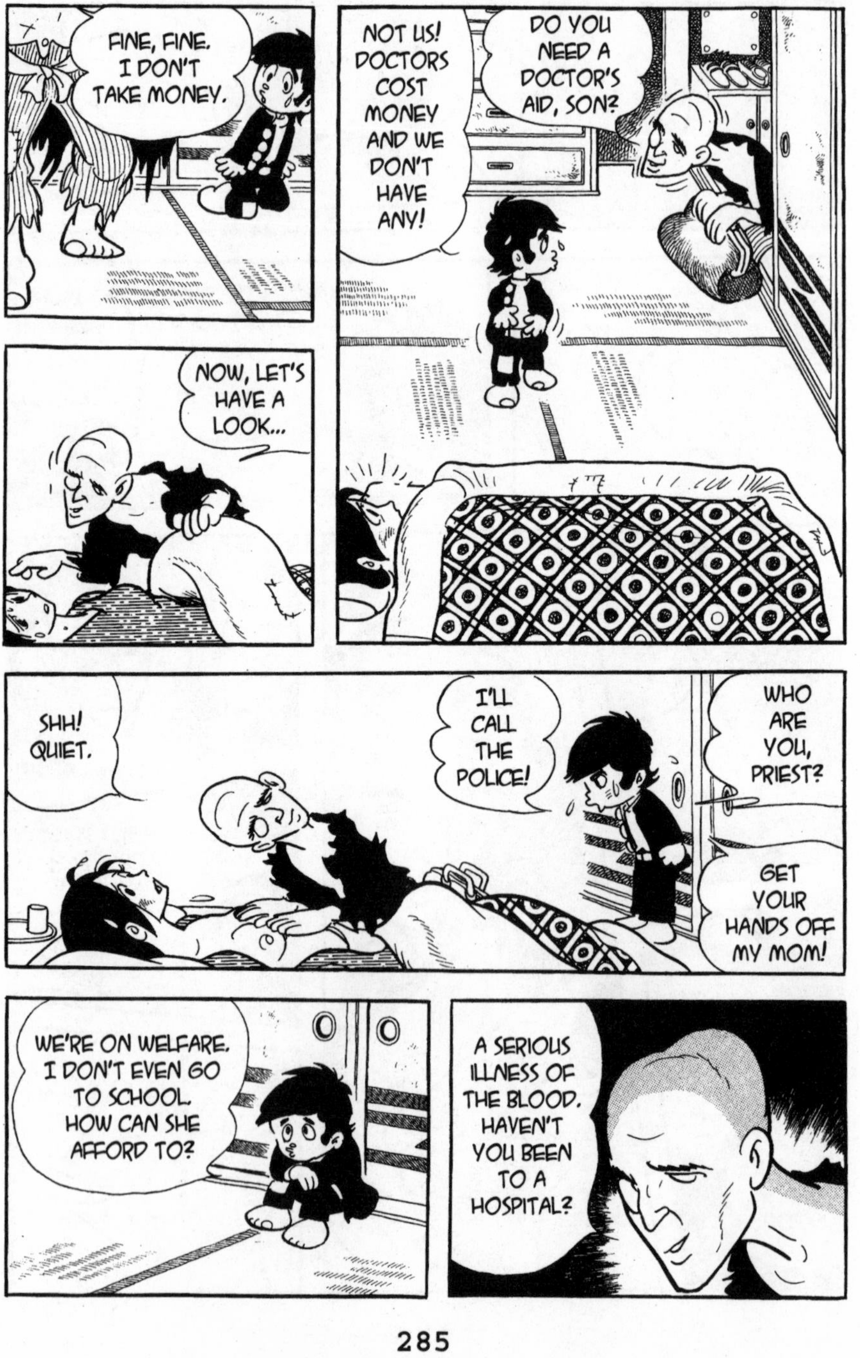
DO YOU NEED A DOCTOR'S AID, SON?
NOT US! DOCTORS COST MONEY AND WE DON'T HAVE ANY!
FINE, FINE. I DON'T TAKE MONEY.
NOW, LET'S HAVE A LOOK...
WHO ARE YOU, PRIEST?
GET YOUR HANDS OFF MY MOM!
I'LL CALL THE POLICE!
SHH! QUIET.
A SERIOUS ILLNESS OF THE BLOOD. HAVEN'T YOU BEEN TO A HOSPITAL?
WE'RE ON WELFARE. I DON'T EVEN GO TO SCHOOL. HOW CAN SHE AFFORD TO?

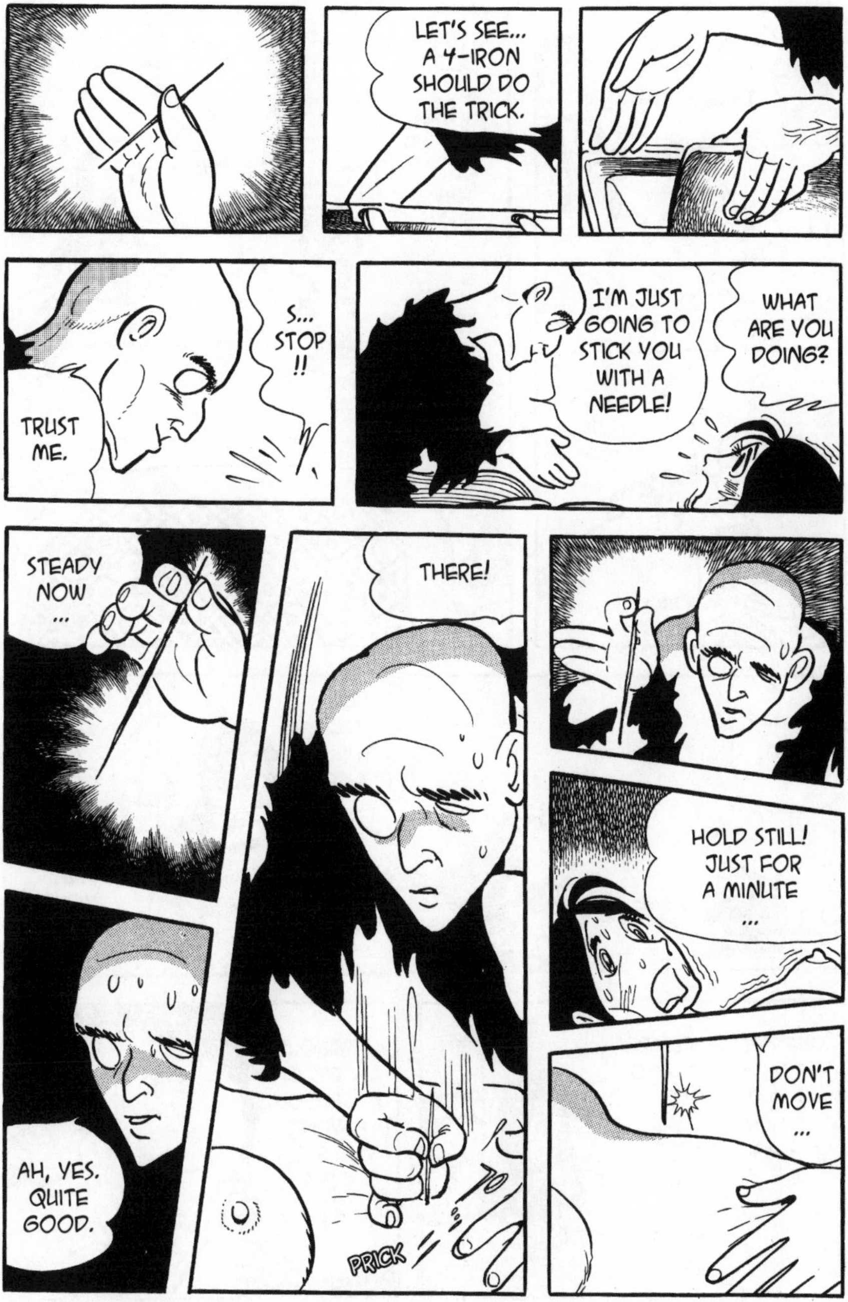
LET'S SEE... A 4-IRON SHOULD DO THE TRICK.
WHAT ARE YOU DOING?
I'M JUST GOING TO STICK YOU WITH A NEEDLE!
S... STOP !!
TRUST ME.
HOLD STILL! JUST FOR A MINUTE ...
DON'T MOVE ...
THERE!
PRICK
STEADY NOW ...
AH, YES. QUITE GOOD.

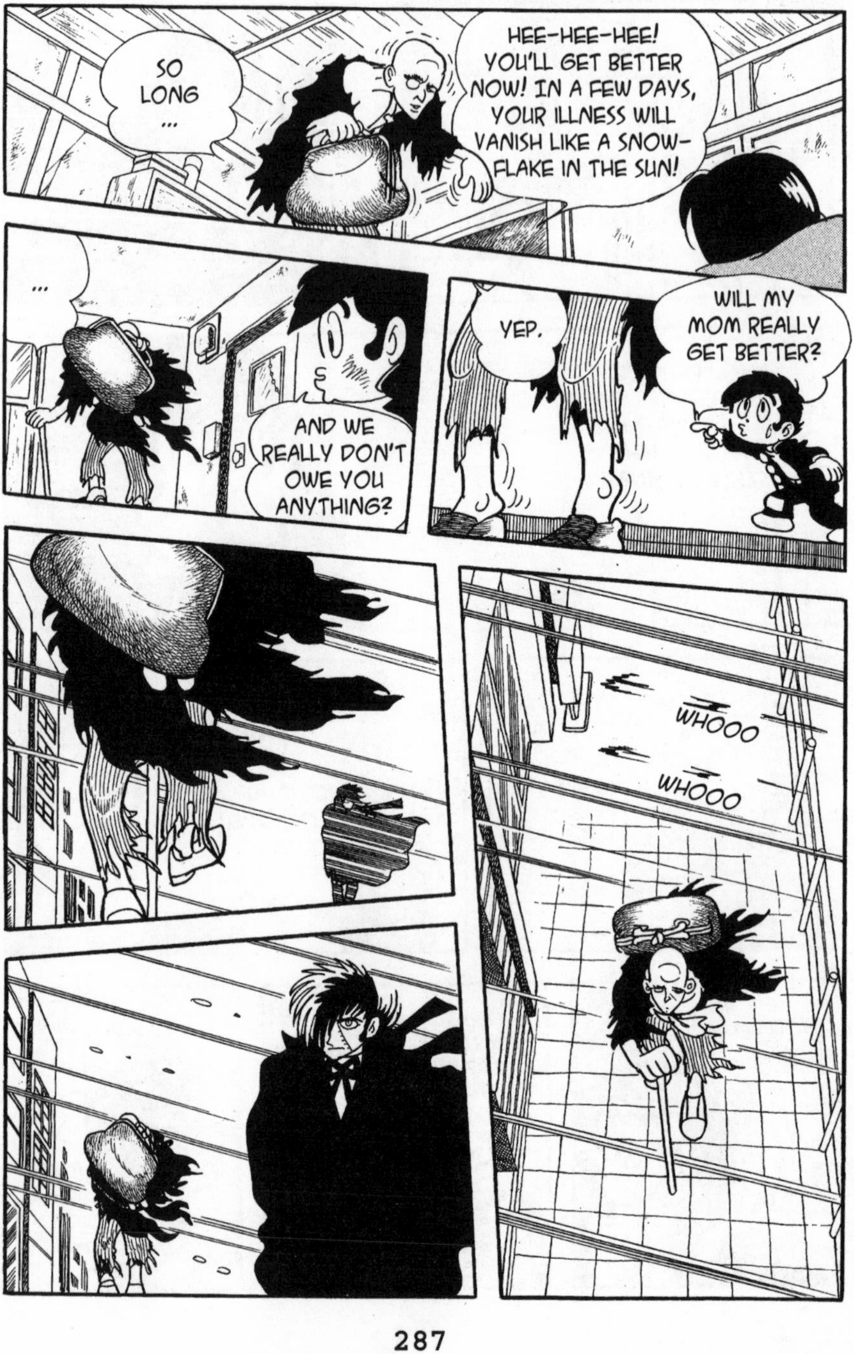
HEE-HEE-HEE! YOU'LL GET BETTER NOW! IN A FEW DAYS, YOUR ILLNESS WILL VANISH LIKE A SNOW-FLAKE IN THE SUN!
SO LONG ...
WILL MY MOM REALLY GET BETTER?
YEP.
AND WE REALLY DON'T OWE YOU ANYTHING?
...
WHOOO
WHOOO

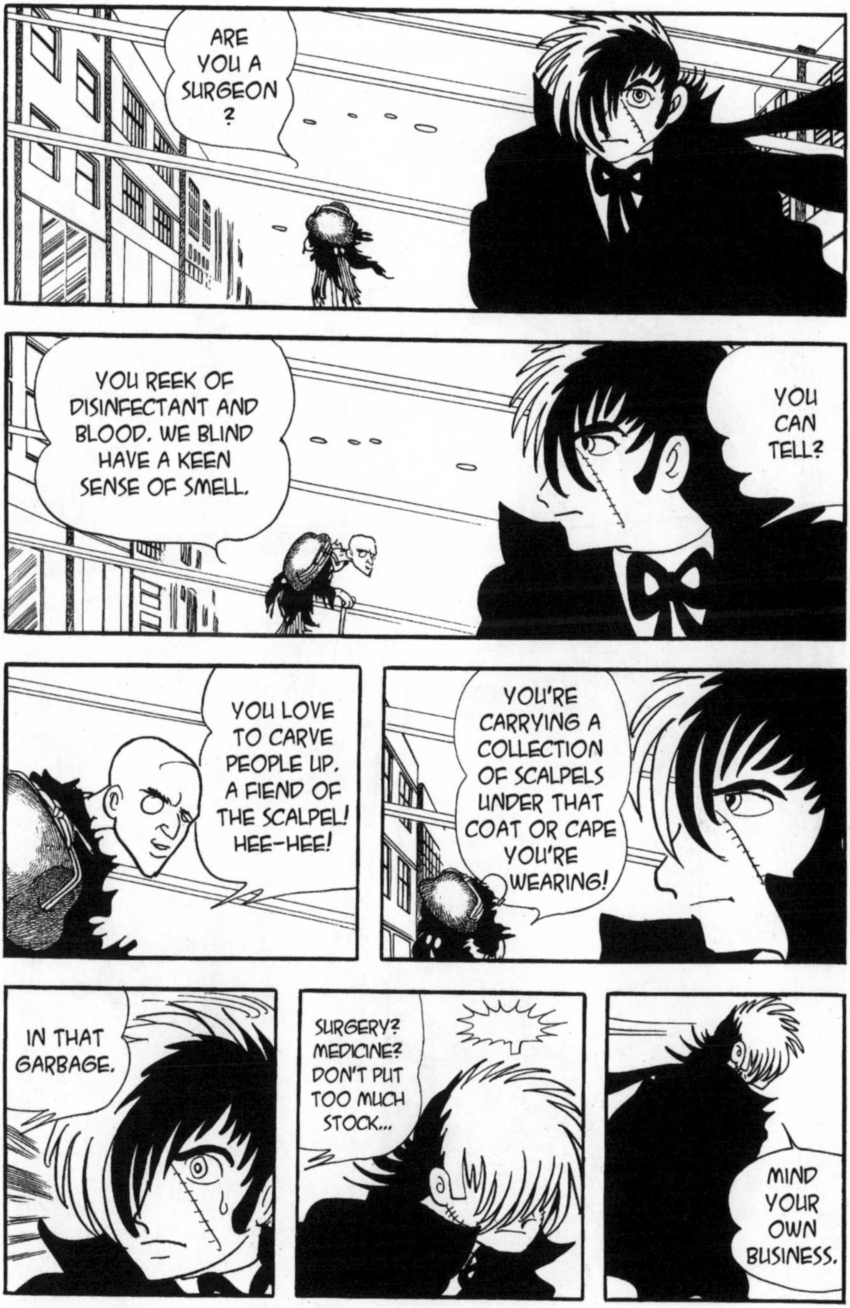
ARE YOU A SURGEON ?
YOU CAN TELL?
YOU REEK OF DISINFECTANT AND BLOOD. WE BLIND HAVE A KEEN SENSE OF SMELL.
YOU'RE CARRYING A COLLECTION OF SCALPELS UNDER THAT COAT OR CAPE YOU'RE WEARING!
YOU LOVE TO CARVE PEOPLE UP. A FIEND OF THE SCALPEL! HEE-HEE!
MIND YOUR OWN BUSINESS.
SURGERY? MEDICINE? DON'T PUT TOO MUCH STOCK...
IN THAT GARBAGE.

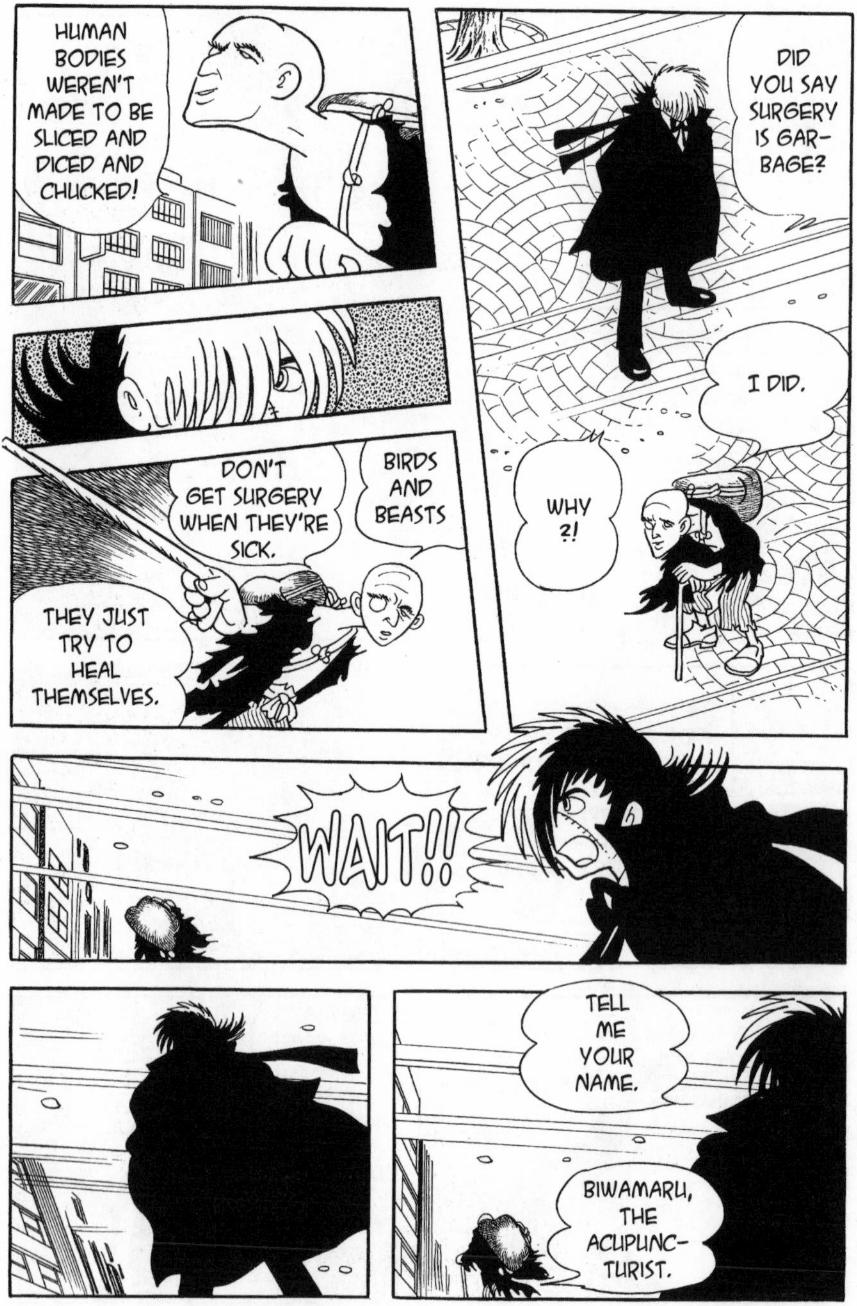
DID YOU SAY SURGERY IS GAR-BAGE?
I DID.
WHY ?!
HUMAN BODIES WEREN'T MADE TO BE SLICED AND DICED AND CHUCKED!
BIRDS AND BEASTS
DON'T GET SURGERY WHEN THEY'RE SICK.
THEY JUST TRY TO HEAL THEMSELVES.
WAIT!!
TELL ME YOUR NAME.
BIWAMARU, THE ACUPUNC-TURIST.

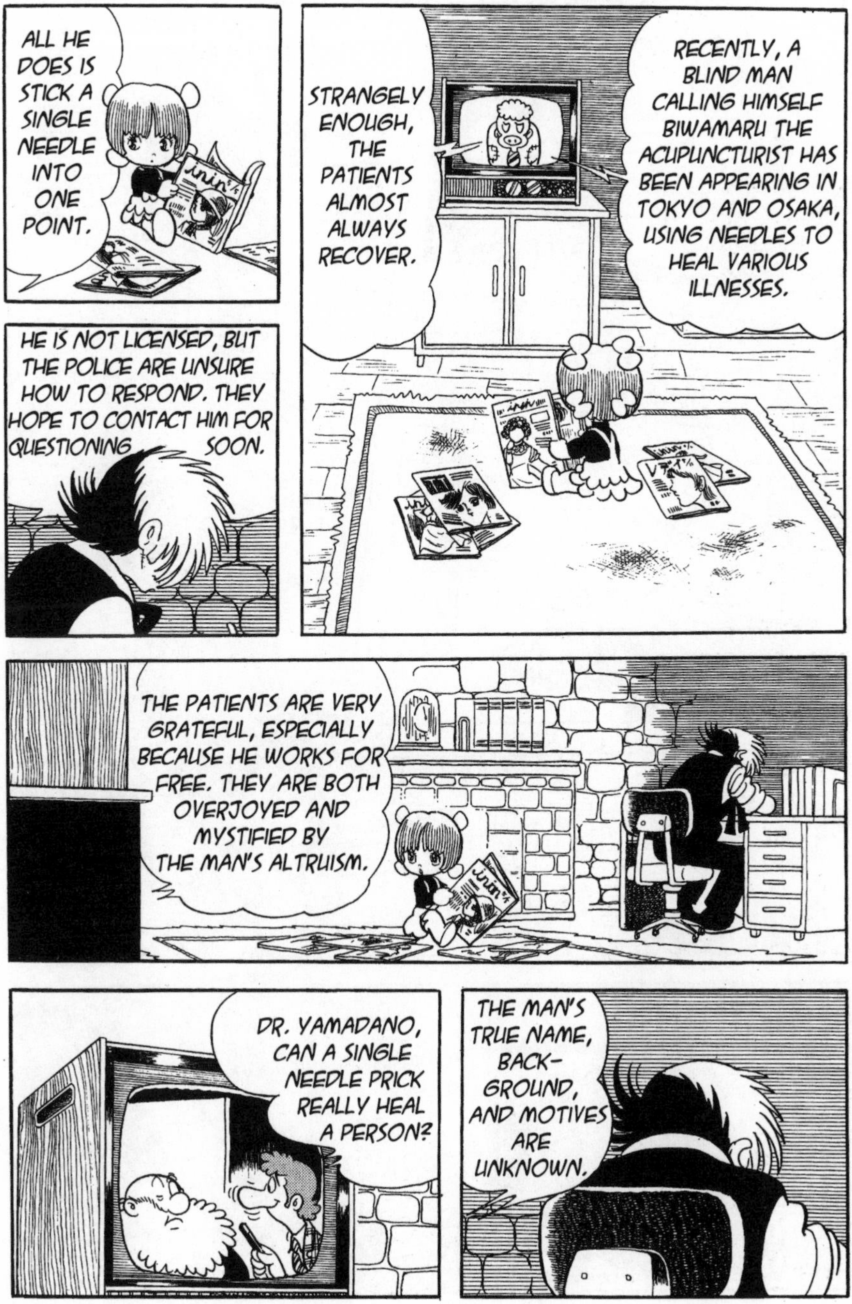
RECENTLY, A BLIND MAN CALLING HIMSELF BIWAMARU THE ACUPUNCTURIST HAS BEEN APPEARING IN TOKYO AND OSAKA, USING NEEDLES TO HEAL VARIOUS ILLNESSES.
STRANGELY ENOUGH, THE PATIENTS ALMOST ALWAYS RECOVER.
ALL HE DOES IS STICK A SINGLE NEEDLE INTO ONE POINT.
HE IS NOT LICENSED, BUT THE POLICE ARE UNSURE HOW TO RESPOND. THEY HOPE TO CONTACT HIM FOR QUESTIONING SOON.
THE PATIENTS ARE VERY GRATEFUL, ESPECIALLY BECAUSE HE WORKS FOR FREE. THEY ARE BOTH OVERJOYED AND MYSTIFIED BY THE MAN'S ALTRUISM.
THE MAN'S TRUE NAME, BACK-GROUND, AND MOTIVES ARE UNKNOWN.
DR. YAMADANO, CAN A SINGLE NEEDLE PRICK REALLY HEAL A PERSON?

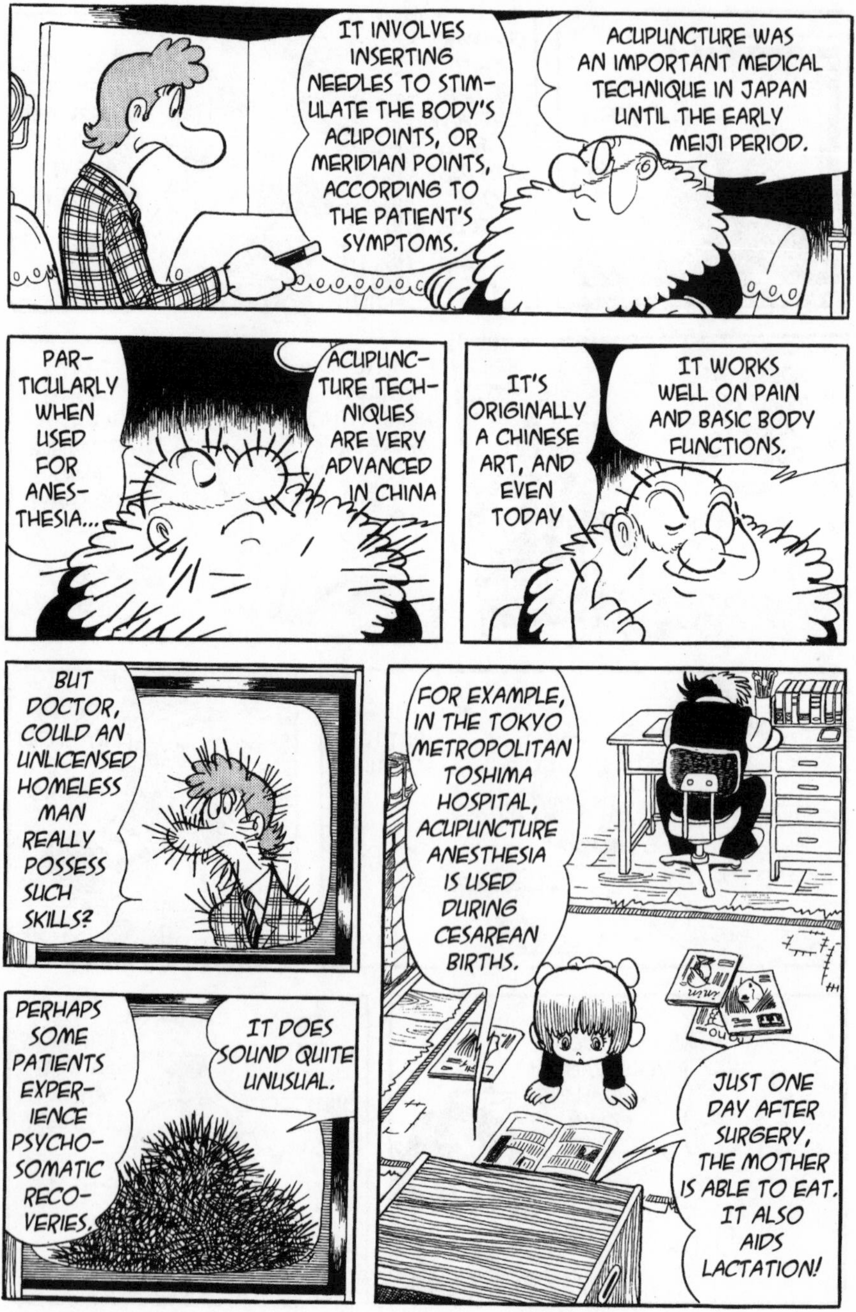
ACUPUNCTURE WAS AN IMPORTANT MEDICAL TECHNIQUE IN JAPAN UNTIL THE EARLY MEIJI PERIOD.
IT INVOLVES INSERTING NEEDLES TO STIM-ULATE THE BODY'S ACUPOINTS, OR MERIDIAN POINTS, ACCORDING TO THE PATIENT'S SYMPTOMS.
IT WORKS WELL ON PAIN AND BASIC BODY FUNCTIONS.
IT'S ORIGINALLY A CHINESE ART, AND EVEN TODAY
ACUPUNC-TURE TECH-NIQUES ARE VERY ADVANCED IN CHINA
PAR-TICULARLY WHEN USED FOR ANES-THESIA...
FOR EXAMPLE, IN THE TOKYO METROPOLITAN TOSHIMA HOSPITAL, ACUPUNCTURE ANESTHESIA IS USED DURING CESAREAN BIRTHS.
JUST ONE DAY AFTER SURGERY, THE MOTHER IS ABLE TO EAT. IT ALSO AIDS LACTATION!
BUT DOCTOR, COULD AN UNLICENSED HOMELESS MAN REALLY POSSESS SUCH SKILLS?
IT DOES SOUND QUITE UNUSUAL.
PERHAPS SOME PATIENTS EXPER-IENCE PSYCHO-SOMATIC RECO-VERIES.

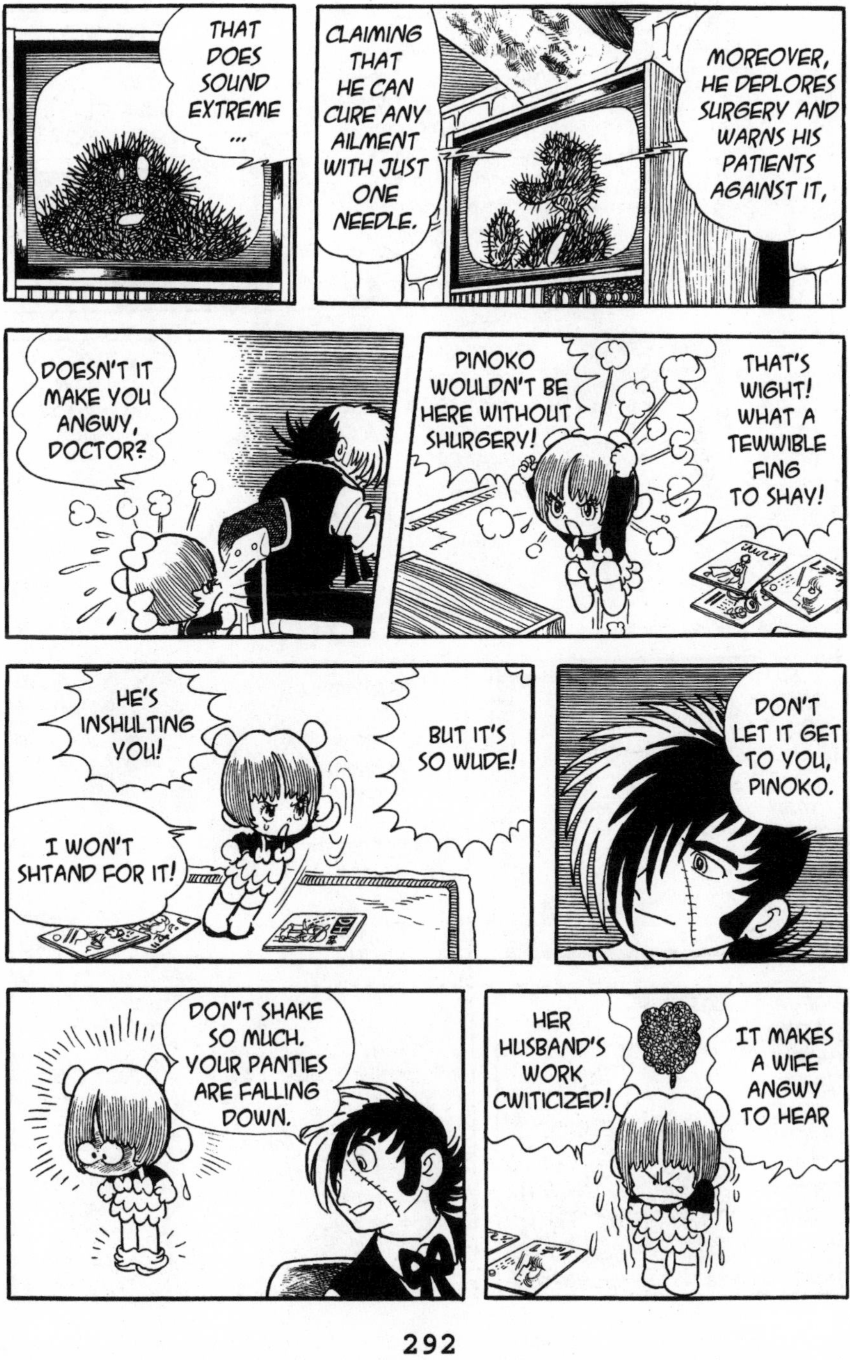
THAT DOES SOUND EXTREME ...
CLAIMING THAT HE CAN CURE ANY AILMENT WITH JUST ONE NEEDLE.
MOREOVER, HE DEPLORES SURGERY AND WARNS HIS PATIENTS AGAINST IT,
DOESN'T IT MAKE YOU ANGWY, DOCTOR?
PINOKO WOULDN'T BE HERE WITHOUT SHURGERY!
THAT'S WIGHT! WHAT A TEWWIBLE FING TO SHAY!
HE'S INSHULTING YOU!
BUT IT'S SO WUDE!
I WON'T SHTAND FOR IT!
DON'T LET IT GET TO YOU, PINOKO.
DON'T SHAKE SO MUCH. YOUR PANTIES ARE FALLING DOWN.
IT MAKES A WIFE ANGWY TO HEAR
HER HUSBAND'S WORK CWITICIZED!

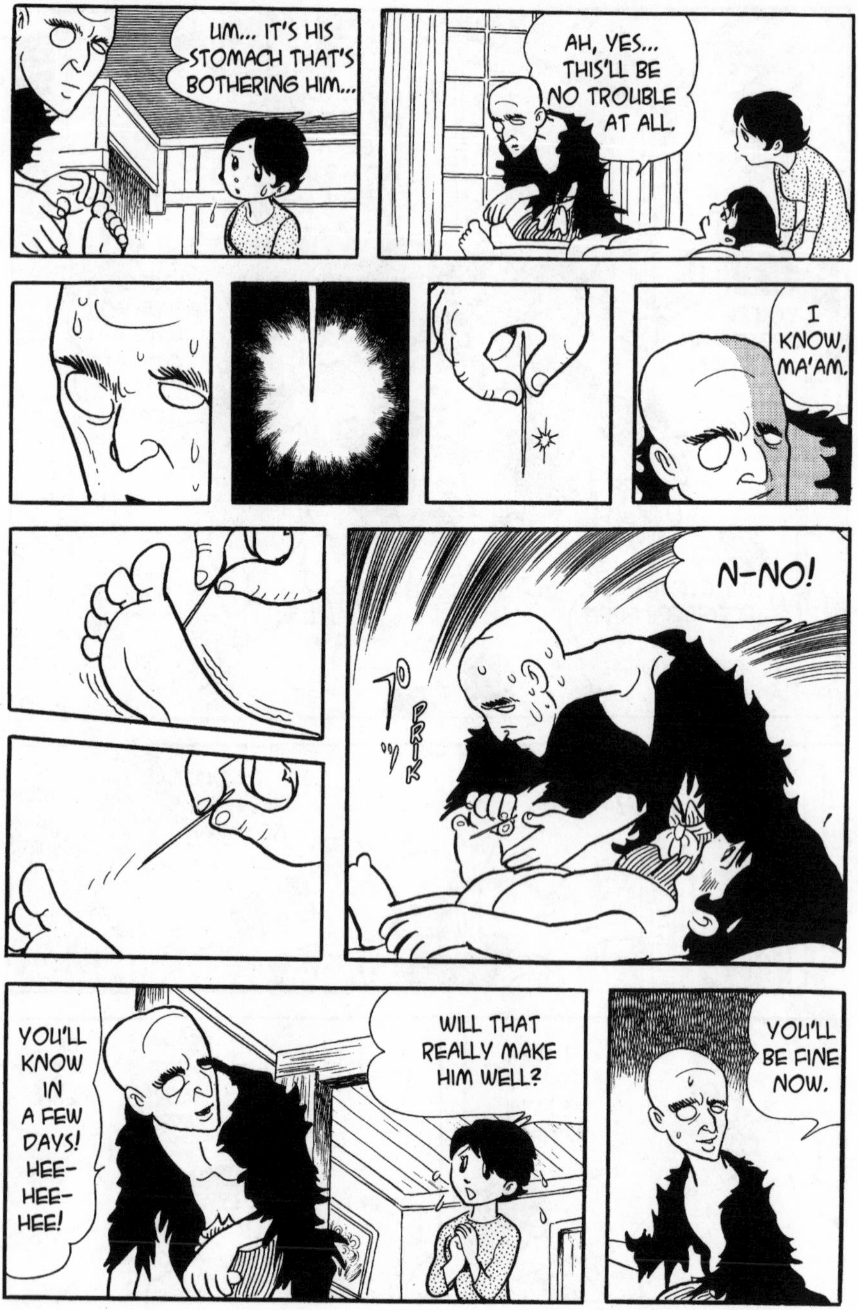
UM... IT'S HIS STOMACH THAT'S BOTHERING HIM...
AH, YES... THIS'LL BE NO TROUBLE AT ALL.
I KNOW, MA'AM.
N-NO!
PRIK
WILL THAT REALLY MAKE HIM WELL?
YOU'LL KNOW IN A FEW DAYS! HEE-HEE-HEE!
YOU'LL BE FINE NOW.

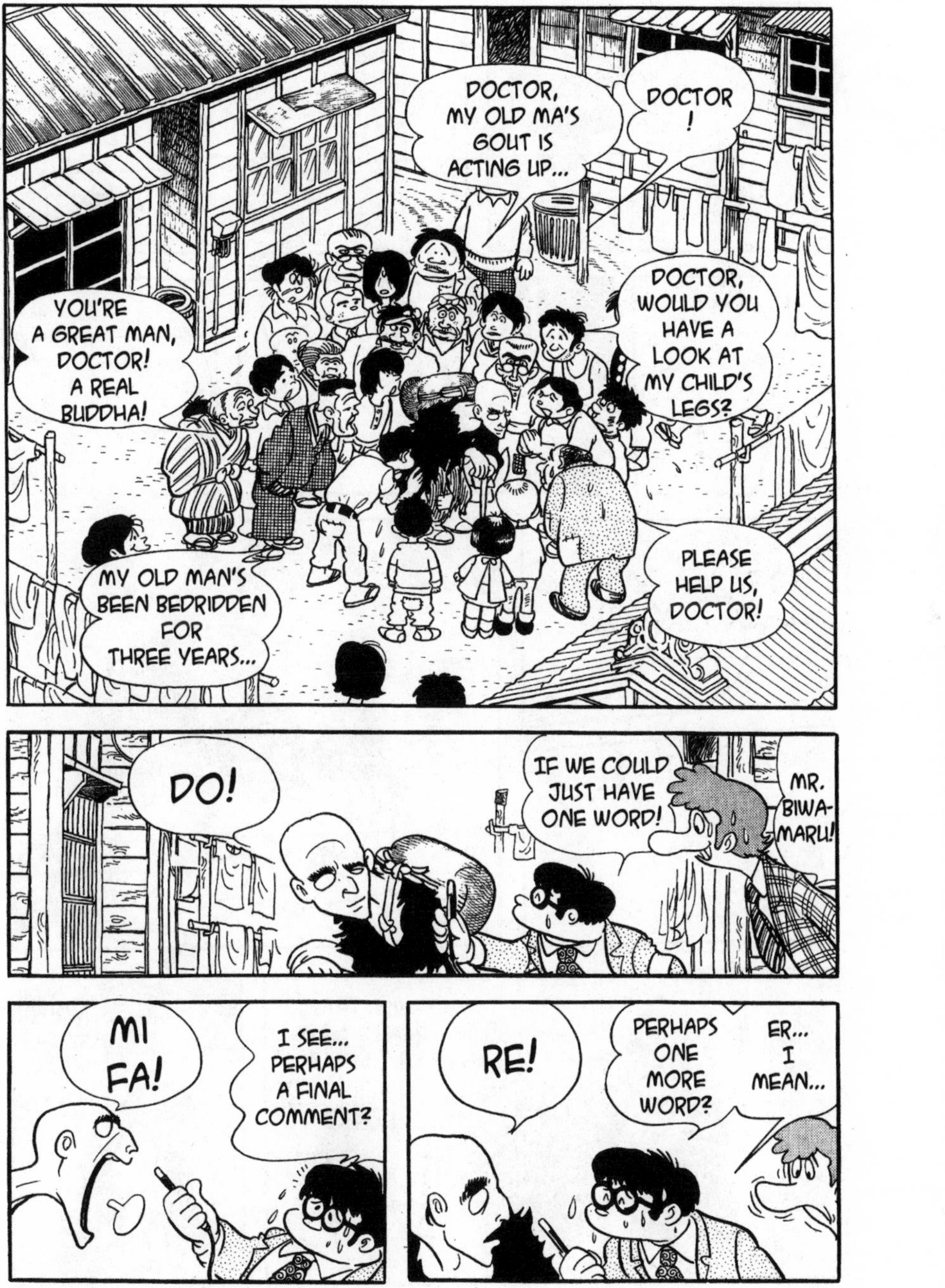
DOCTOR !
DOCTOR, MY OLD MA'S GOUT IS ACTING UP...
DOCTOR, WOULD YOU HAVE A LOOK AT MY CHILD'S LEGS?
YOU'RE A GREAT MAN, DOCTOR! A REAL BUDDHA!
PLEASE HELP US, DOCTOR!
MY OLD MAN'S BEEN BEDRIDDEN FOR THREE YEARS...
MR. BIWA-MARU!
IF WE COULD JUST HAVE ONE WORD!
DO!
ER... I MEAN...
PERHAPS ONE MORE WORD?
RE!
I SEE... PERHAPS A FINAL COMMENT?
MI FA!

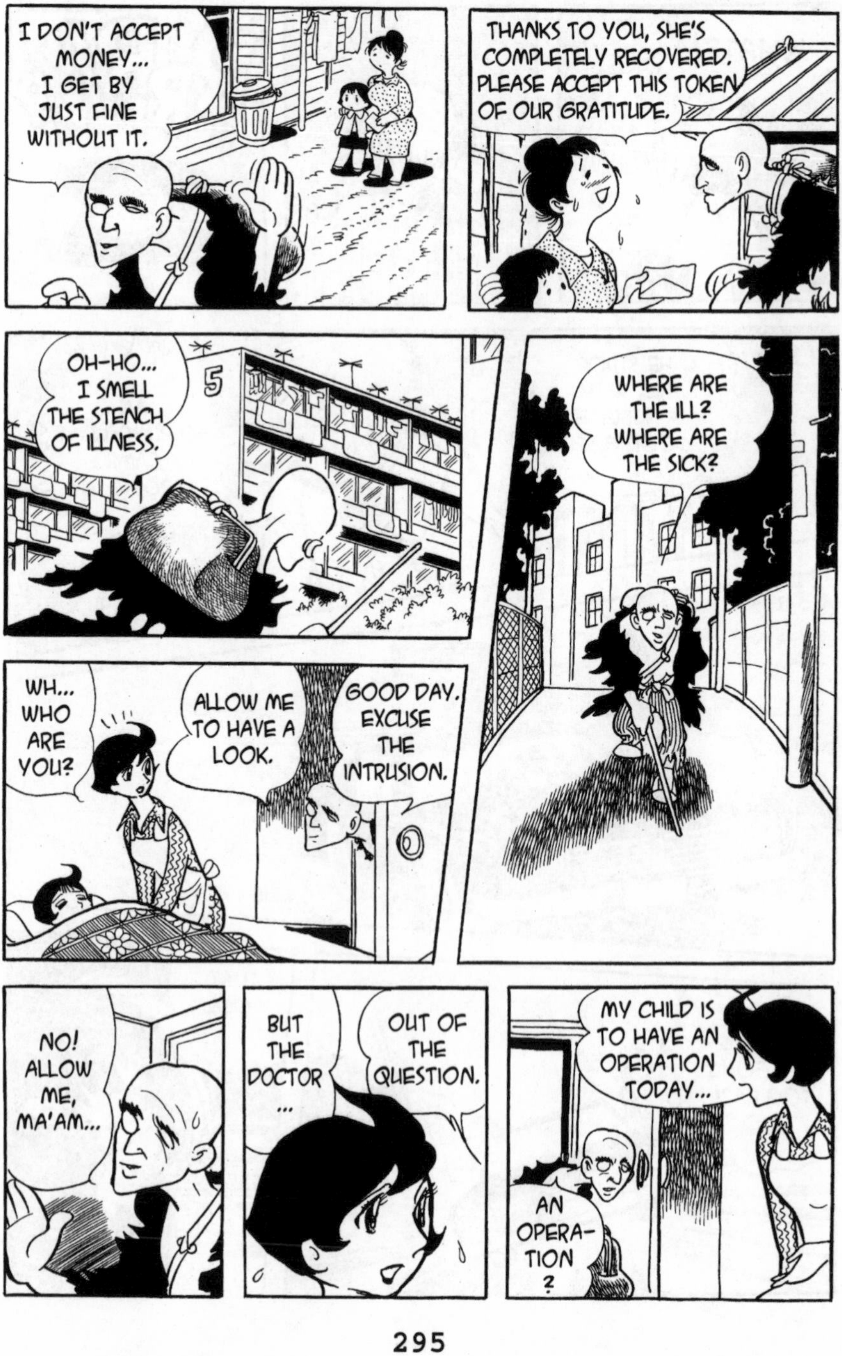
THANKS TO YOU, SHE'S COMPLETELY RECOVERED. PLEASE ACCEPT THIS TOKEN OF OUR GRATITUDE.
I DON'T ACCEPT MONEY... I GET BY JUST FINE WITHOUT IT.
WHERE ARE THE ILL? WHERE ARE THE SICK?
OH-HO... I SMELL THE STENCH OF ILLNESS.
5
GOOD DAY. EXCUSE THE INTRUSION.
ALLOW ME TO HAVE A LOOK.
WH... WHO ARE YOU?
MY CHILD IS TO HAVE AN OPERATION TODAY...
AN OPERA-TION ?
OUT OF THE QUESTION.
BUT THE DOCTOR ...
NO! ALLOW ME, MA'AM...

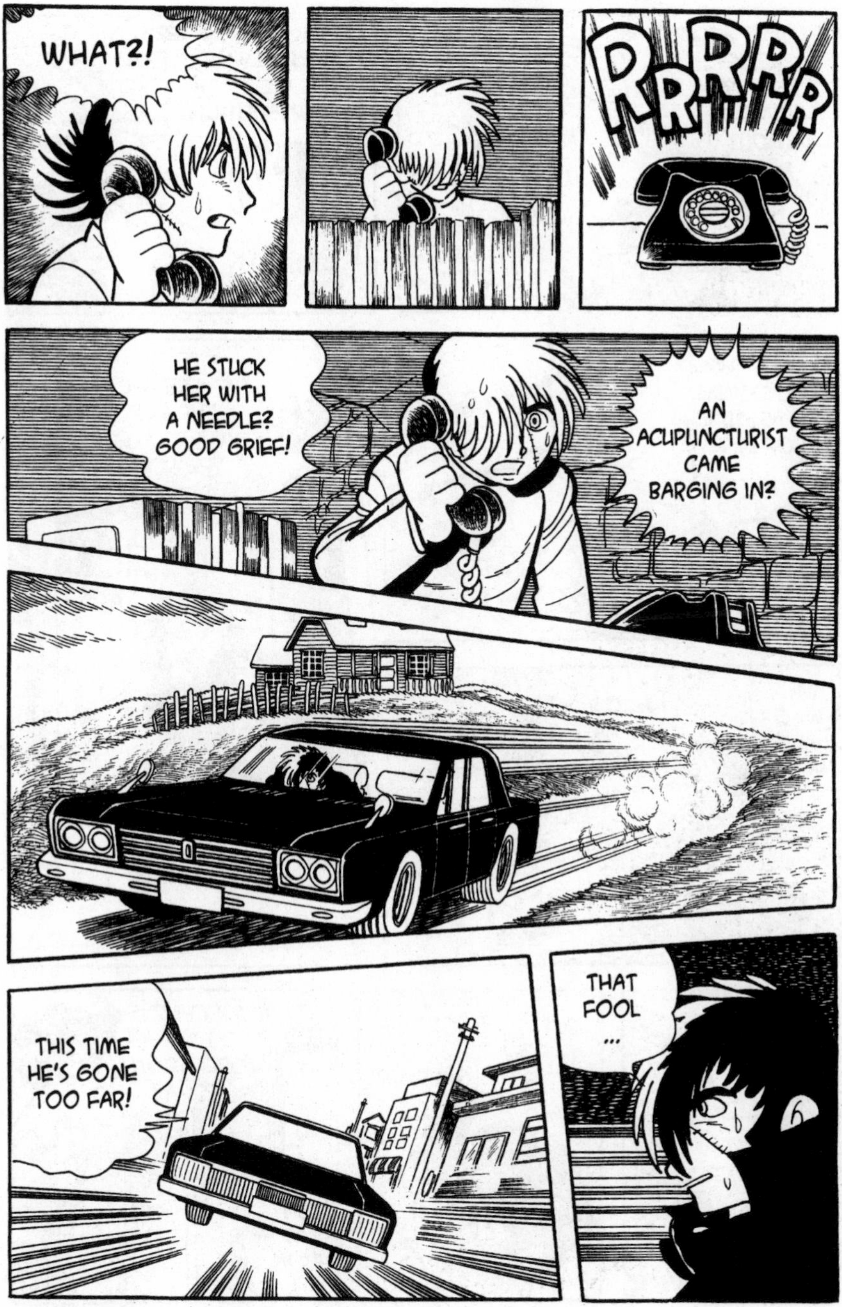
RRRRR
WHAT?!
AN ACUPUNCTURIST CAME BARGING IN?
HE STUCK HER WITH A NEEDLE? GOOD GRIEF!
THAT FOOL ...
THIS TIME HE'S GONE TOO FAR!

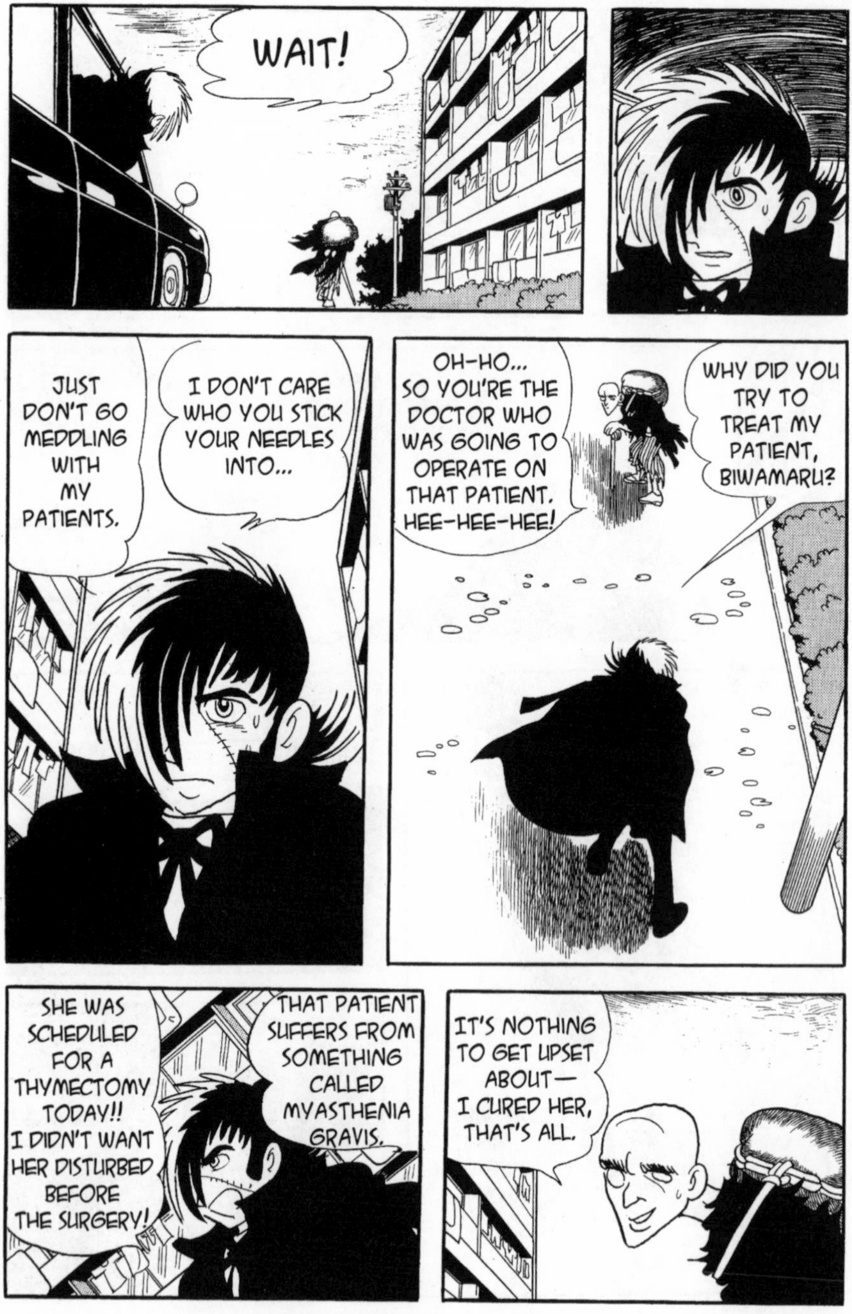
WAIT!
WHY DID YOU TRY TO TREAT MY PATIENT, BIWAMARU?
OH-HO... SO YOU'RE THE DOCTOR WHO WAS GOING TO OPERATE ON THAT PATIENT. HEE-HEE-HEE!
I DON'T CARE WHO YOU STICK YOUR NEEDLES INTO...
JUST DON'T GO MEDDLING WITH MY PATIENTS.
IT'S NOTHING TO GET UPSET ABOUT— I CURED HER, THAT'S ALL.
THAT PATIENT SUFFERS FROM SOMETHING CALLED MYASTHENIA GRAVIS.
SHE WAS SCHEDULED FOR A THYMECTOMY TODAY!! I DIDN'T WANT HER DISTURBED BEFORE THE SURGERY!

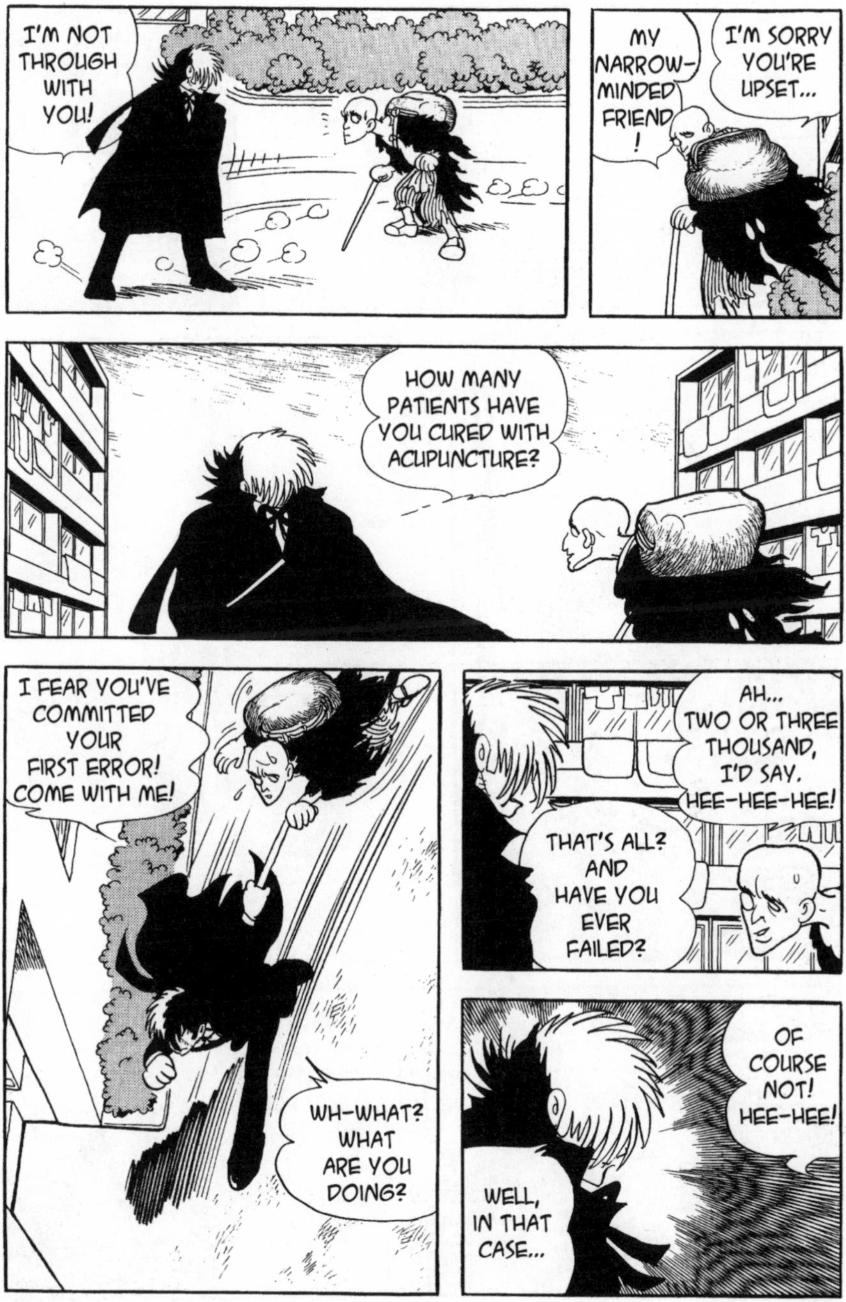
I'M NOT THROUGH WITH YOU!
I'M SORRY YOU'RE UPSET...
MY NARROW-MINDED FRIEND!
HOW MANY PATIENTS HAVE YOU CURED WITH ACUPUNCTURE?
AH... TWO OR THREE THOUSAND, I'D SAY. HEE-HEE-HEE!
THAT'S ALL? AND HAVE YOU EVER FAILED?
OF COURSE NOT! HEE-HEE!
WELL, IN THAT CASE...
I FEAR YOU'VE COMMITTED YOUR FIRST ERROR! COME WITH ME!
WH-WHAT? WHAT ARE YOU DOING?

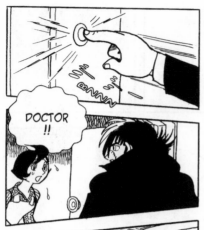

DOCTOR !!

QUICK!

TUMP
TUMP
TUMP
TUMP

GARA GARA GARA GARA GARA GARA

TREMBLE

HAND ME THAT FEEDING CUP!

JUST AS I THOUGHT!

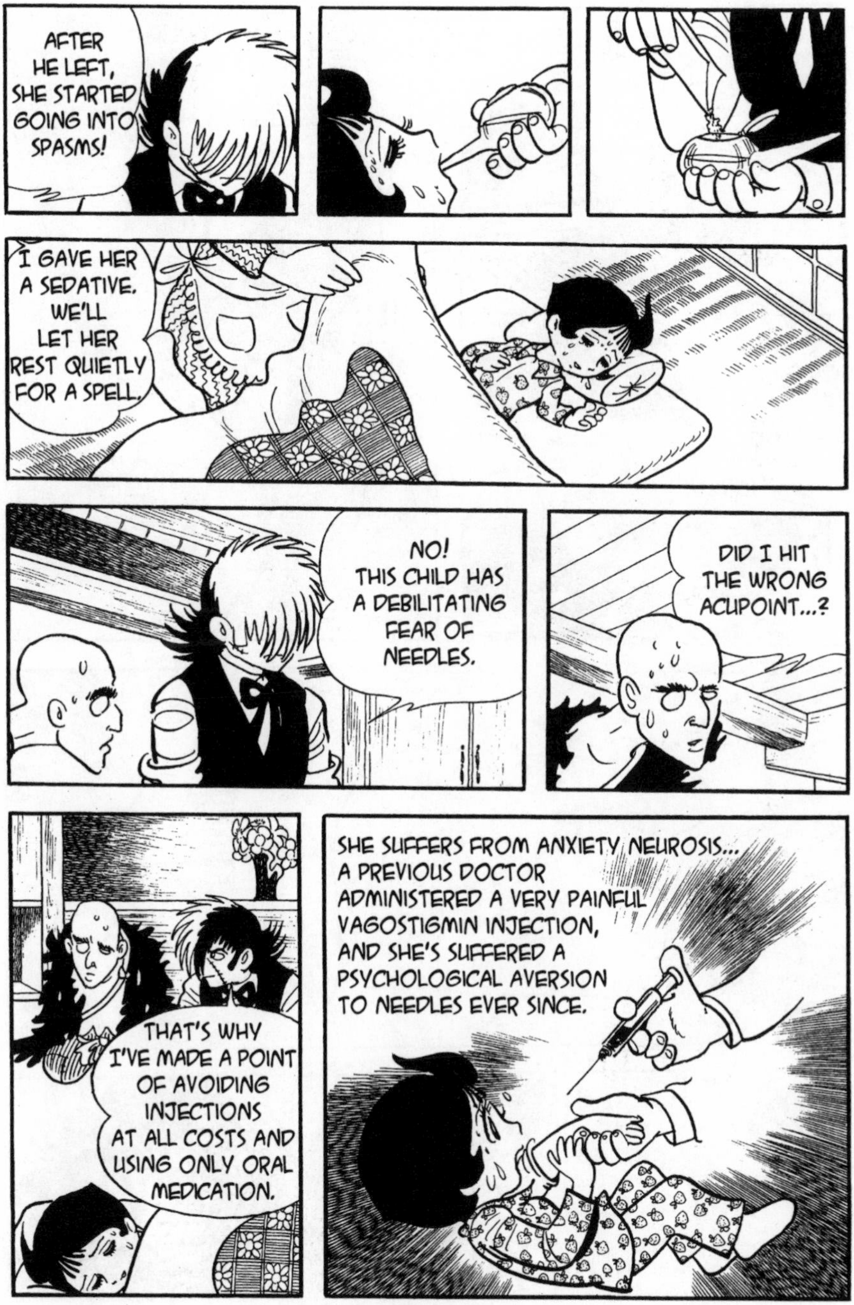
AFTER HE LEFT, SHE STARTED GOING INTO SPASMS!
I GAVE HER A SEDATIVE. WE'LL LET HER REST QUIETLY FOR A SPELL.
DID I HIT THE WRONG ACUPOINT...?
NO! THIS CHILD HAS A DEBILITATING FEAR OF NEEDLES.
SHE SUFFERS FROM ANXIETY NEUROSIS... A PREVIOUS DOCTOR ADMINISTERED A VERY PAINFUL VAGOSTIGMIN INJECTION, AND SHE'S SUFFERED A PSYCHOLOGICAL AVERSION TO NEEDLES EVER SINCE.
THAT'S WHY I'VE MADE A POINT OF AVOIDING INJECTIONS AT ALL COSTS AND USING ONLY ORAL MEDICATION.

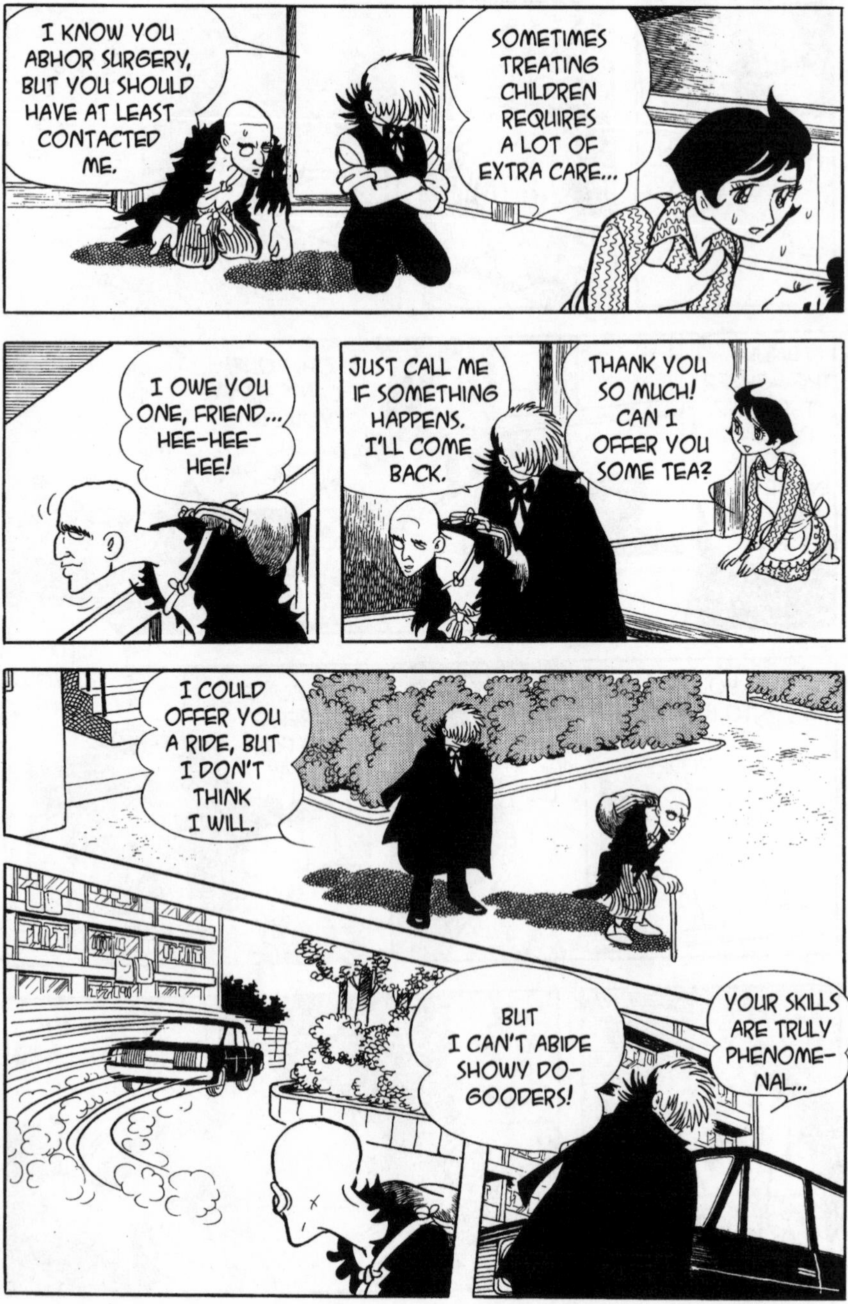
I KNOW YOU ABHOR SURGERY, BUT YOU SHOULD HAVE AT LEAST CONTACTED ME.
SOMETIMES TREATING CHILDREN REQUIRES A LOT OF EXTRA CARE...
I OWE YOU ONE, FRIEND... HEE-HEE-HEE!
JUST CALL ME IF SOMETHING HAPPENS. I'LL COME BACK.
THANK YOU SO MUCH! CAN I OFFER YOU SOME TEA?
I COULD OFFER YOU A RIDE, BUT I DON'T THINK I WILL.
YOUR SKILLS ARE TRULY PHENOME-NAL...
BUT I CAN'T ABIDE SHOWY DO-GOODERS!

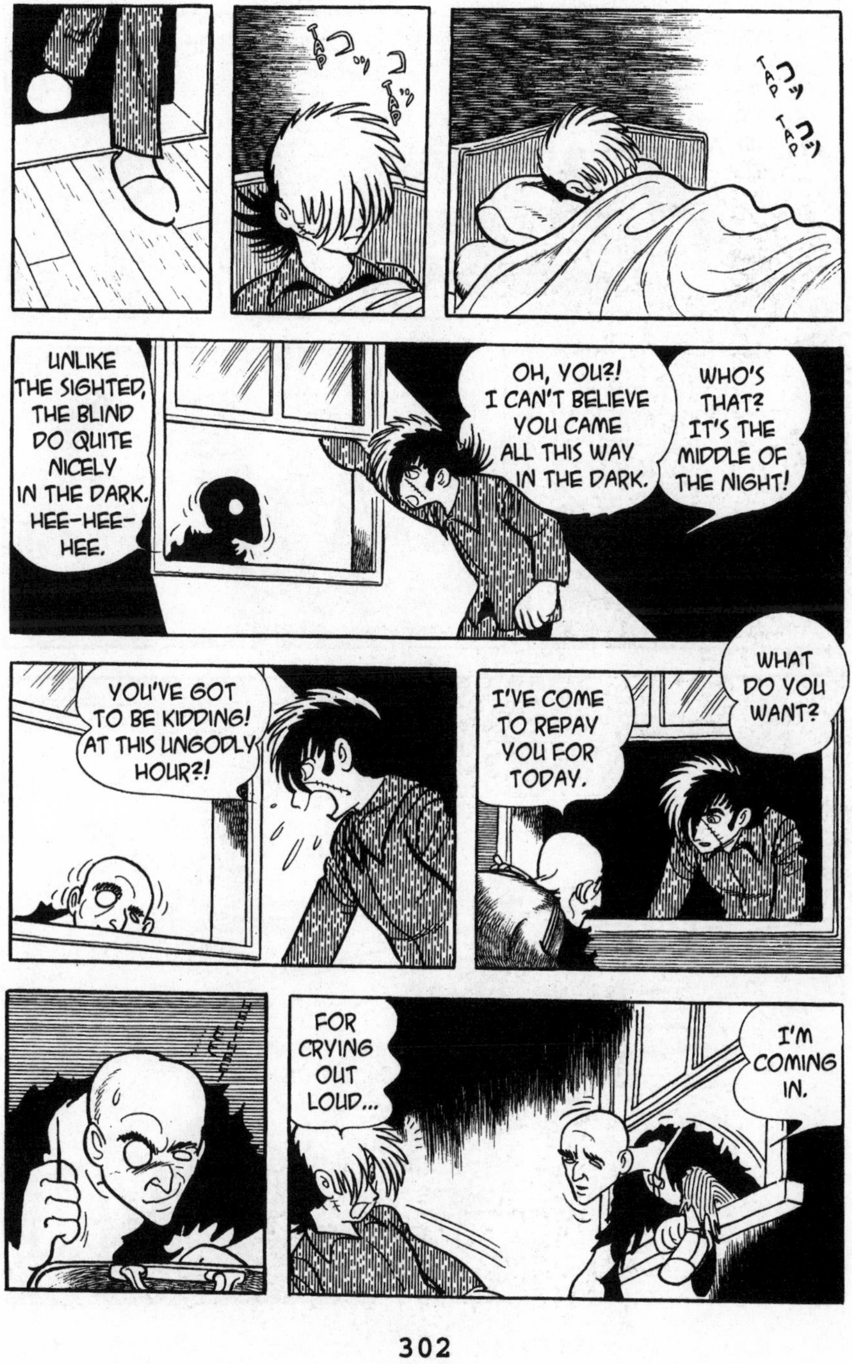
TAP コッ
TAP コッ
TAP コッ
TAP コッ
WHO'S THAT? IT'S THE MIDDLE OF THE NIGHT!
OH, YOU?! I CAN'T BELIEVE YOU CAME ALL THIS WAY IN THE DARK.
UNLIKE THE SIGHTED, THE BLIND DO QUITE NICELY IN THE DARK. HEE-HEE-HEE.
WHAT DO YOU WANT?
I'VE COME TO REPAY YOU FOR TODAY.
YOU'VE GOT TO BE KIDDING! AT THIS UNGODLY HOUR?!
I'M COMING IN.
FOR CRYING OUT LOUD...

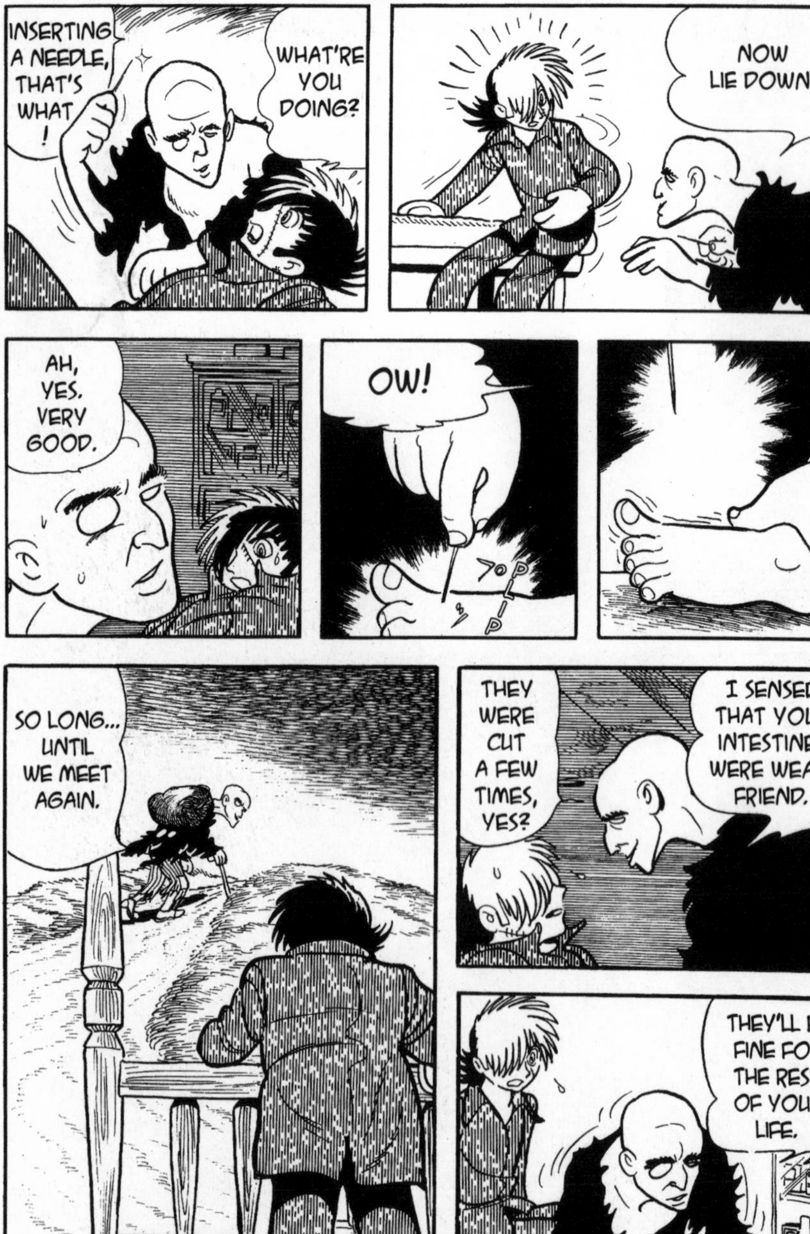
NOW LIE DOWN.
WHAT'RE YOU DOING?
INSERTING A NEEDLE, THAT'S WHAT!
OW!
PLIP
AH, YES. VERY GOOD.
I SENSED THAT YOUR INTESTINES WERE WEAK, FRIEND.
THEY WERE CUT A FEW TIMES, YES?
THEY'LL BE FINE FOR THE REST OF YOUR LIFE.
SO LONG... UNTIL WE MEET AGAIN.

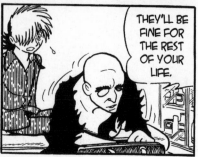

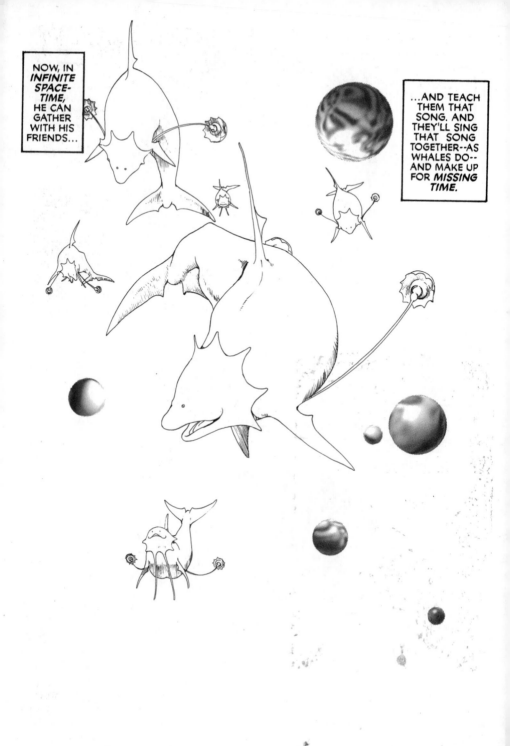

NOW, IN *INFINITE SPACE-TIME,* HE CAN GATHER WITH HIS FRIENDS...

...AND TEACH THEM THAT SONG. AND THEY'LL SING THAT SONG TOGETHER--AS WHALES DO-- AND MAKE UP FOR *MISSING TIME.*

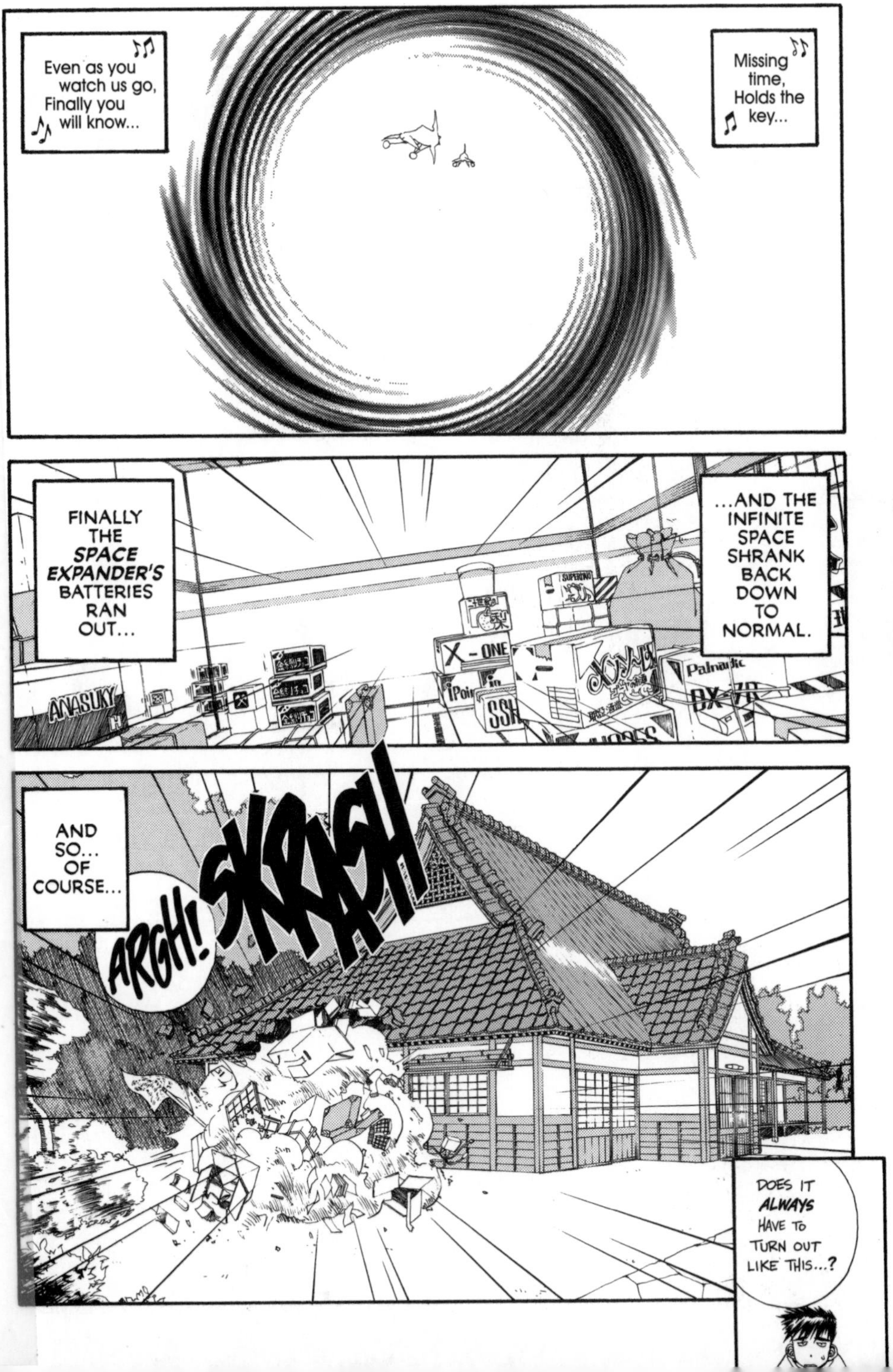
Even as you watch us go, Finally you will know...
Missing time, Holds the key...
FINALLY THE *SPACE EXPANDER'S* BATTERIES RAN OUT...
...AND THE INFINITE SPACE SHRANK BACK DOWN TO NORMAL.
X-ONE
ANASUKY
Palnadic
DX-7R
AND SO... OF COURSE...
ARGH!
SKRASH
DOES IT *ALWAYS* HAVE TO TURN OUT LIKE THIS...?

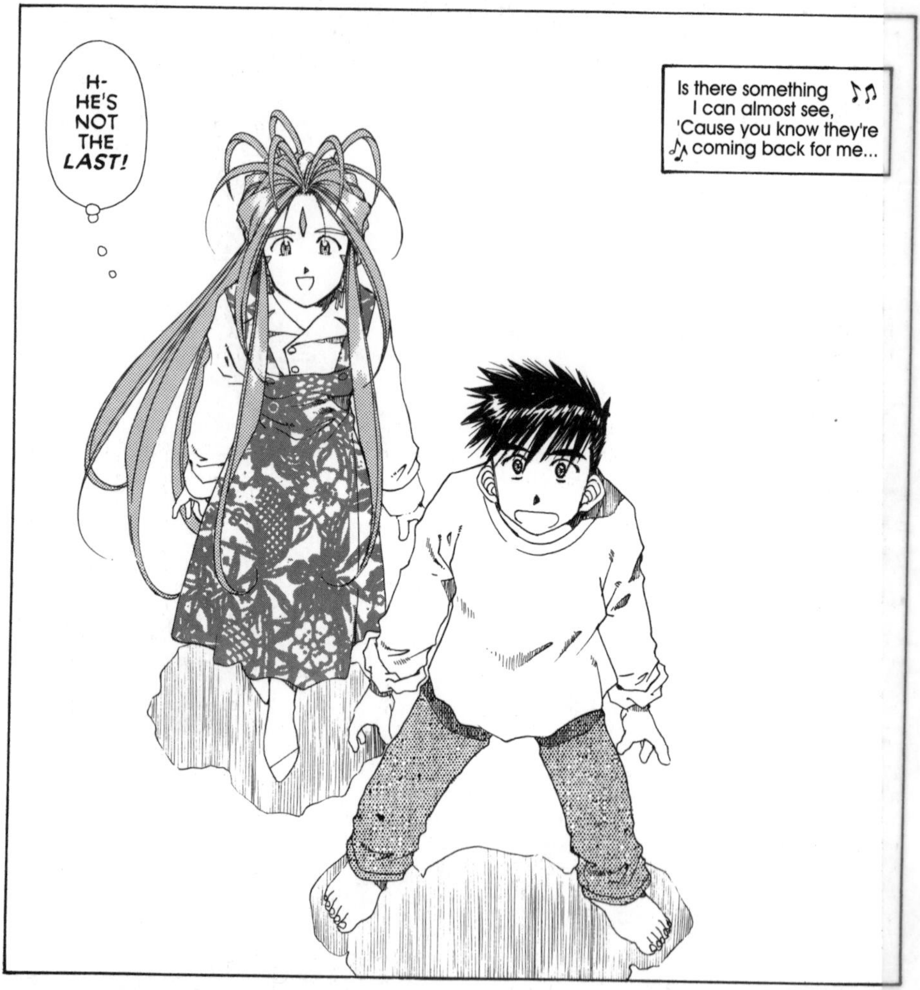
Is there something ♪♫ I can almost see, 'Cause you know they're ♪ coming back for me...
H-HE'S NOT THE *LAST!*

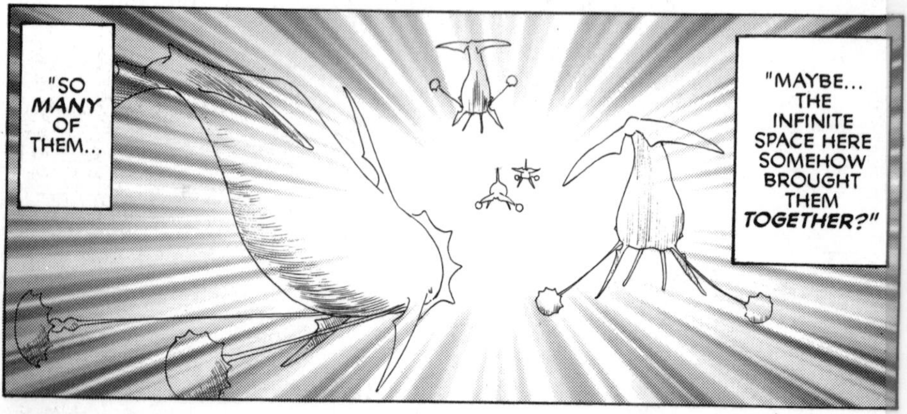
"MAYBE... THE INFINITE SPACE HERE SOMEHOW BROUGHT THEM *TOGETHER?"*
"SO *MANY* OF THEM...

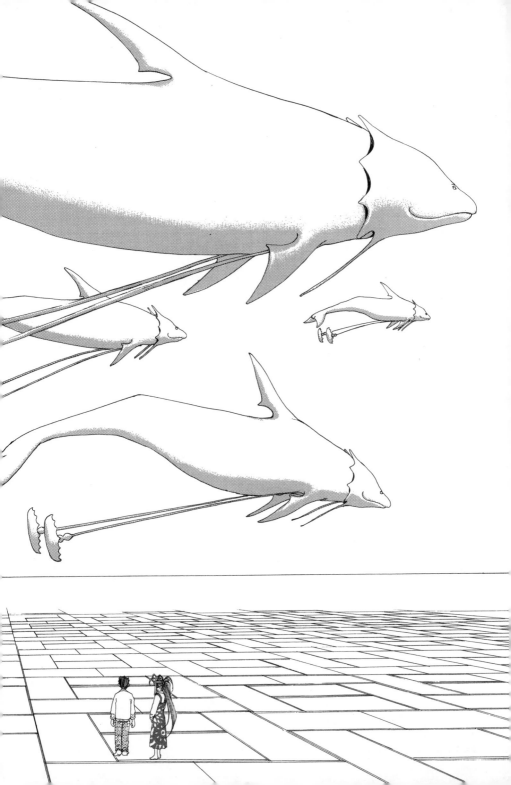

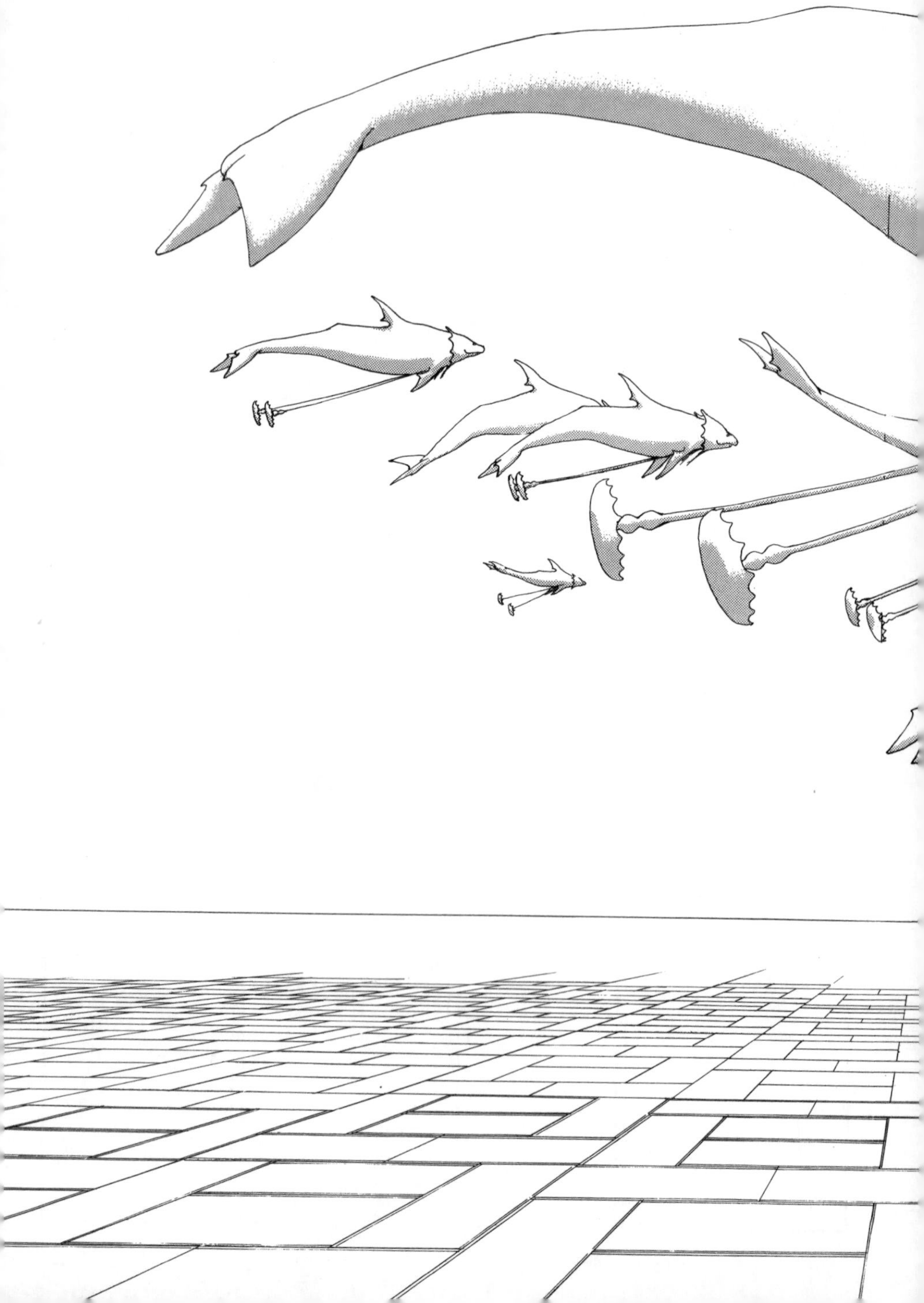

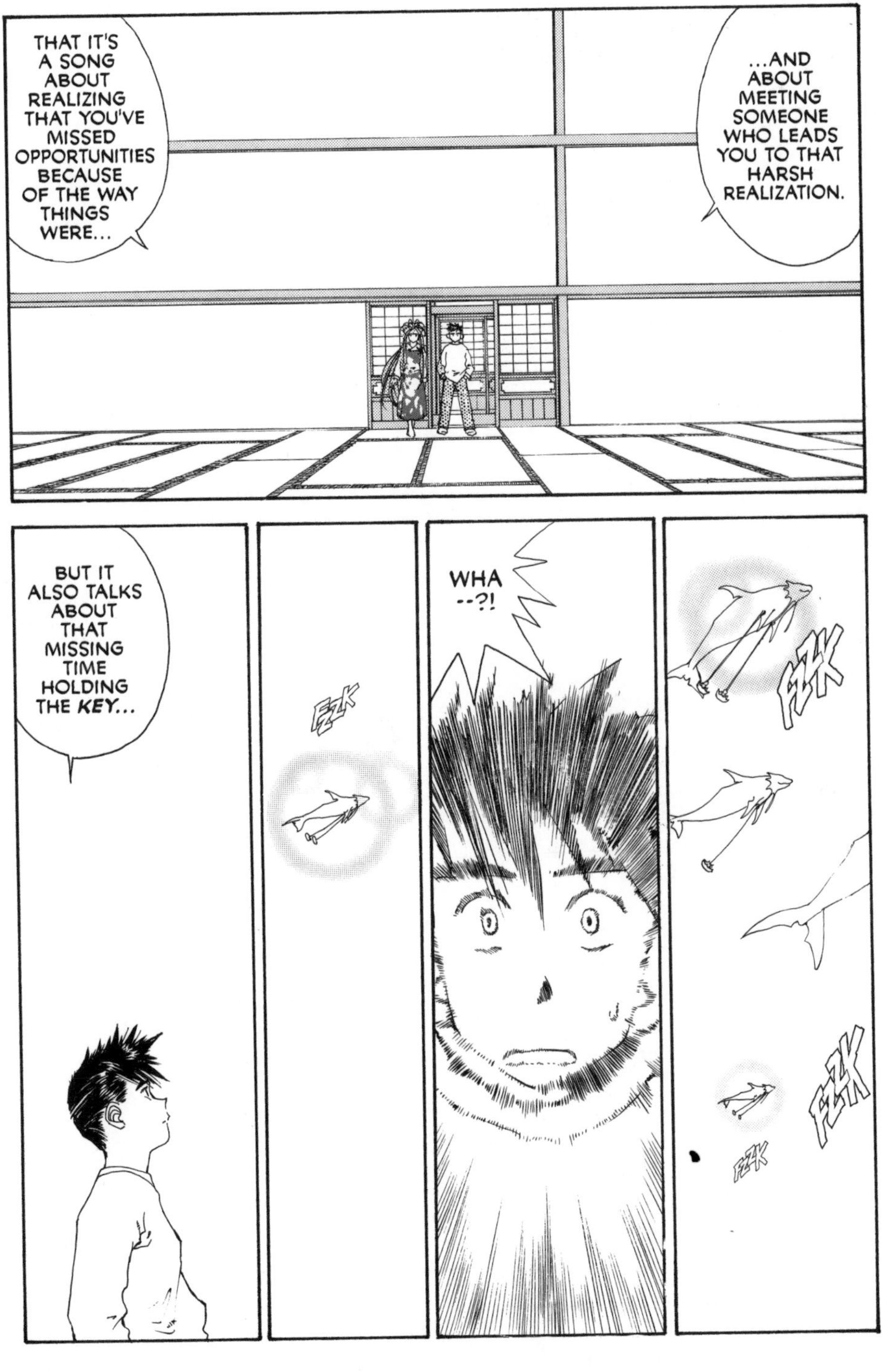
THAT IT'S A SONG ABOUT REALIZING THAT YOU'VE MISSED OPPORTUNITIES BECAUSE OF THE WAY THINGS WERE...
...AND ABOUT MEETING SOMEONE WHO LEADS YOU TO THAT HARSH REALIZATION.
BUT IT ALSO TALKS ABOUT THAT MISSING TIME HOLDING THE *KEY*...
FZK
WHA --?!
FZK
FZK
FZK

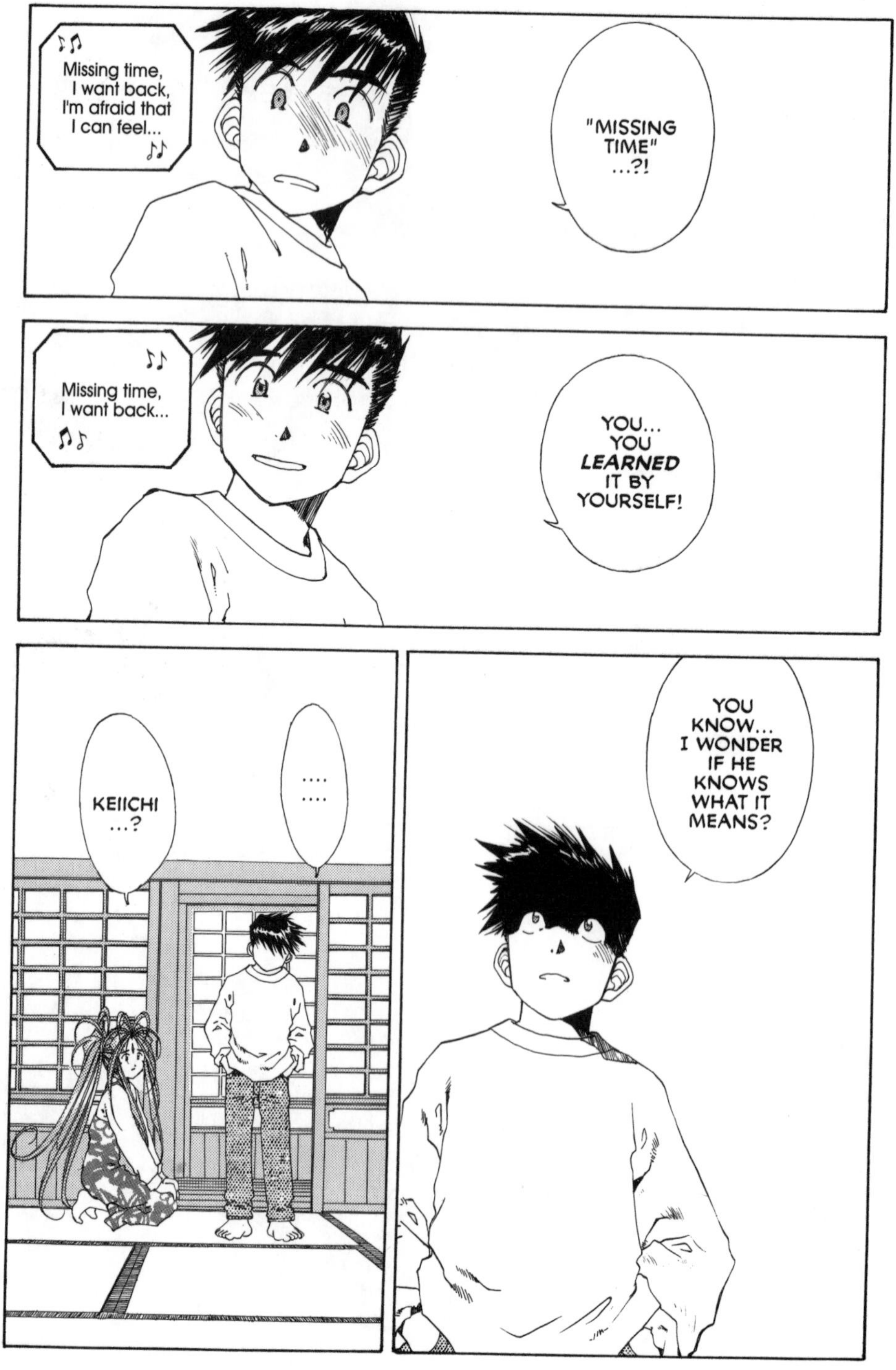
"MISSING TIME" ...?!
♪♫ Missing time, I want back, I'm afraid that I can feel... ♪♪
YOU... YOU *LEARNED* IT BY YOURSELF!
♪♪ Missing time, I want back... ♫♪
YOU KNOW... I WONDER IF HE KNOWS WHAT IT MEANS?
....
KEIICHI ...?

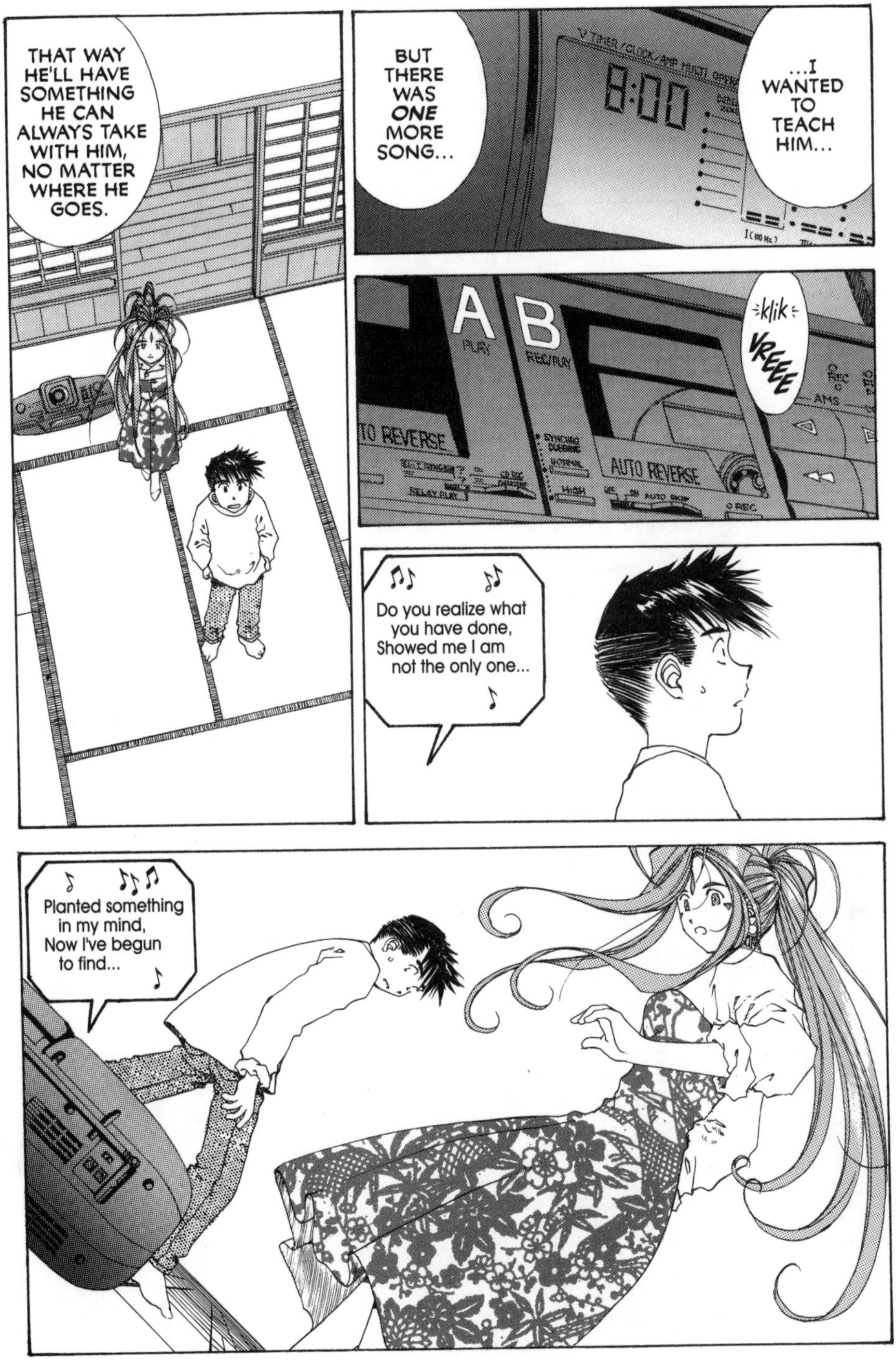

THAT WAY HE'LL HAVE SOMETHING HE CAN ALWAYS TAKE WITH HIM, NO MATTER WHERE HE GOES.
BUT THERE WAS ONE MORE SONG...
...I WANTED TO TEACH HIM...
8:00
A PLAY
B REC/PLAY
klik
VREEE
AUTO REVERSE
Do you realize what you have done, Showed me I am not the only one...
Planted something in my mind, Now I've begun to find...

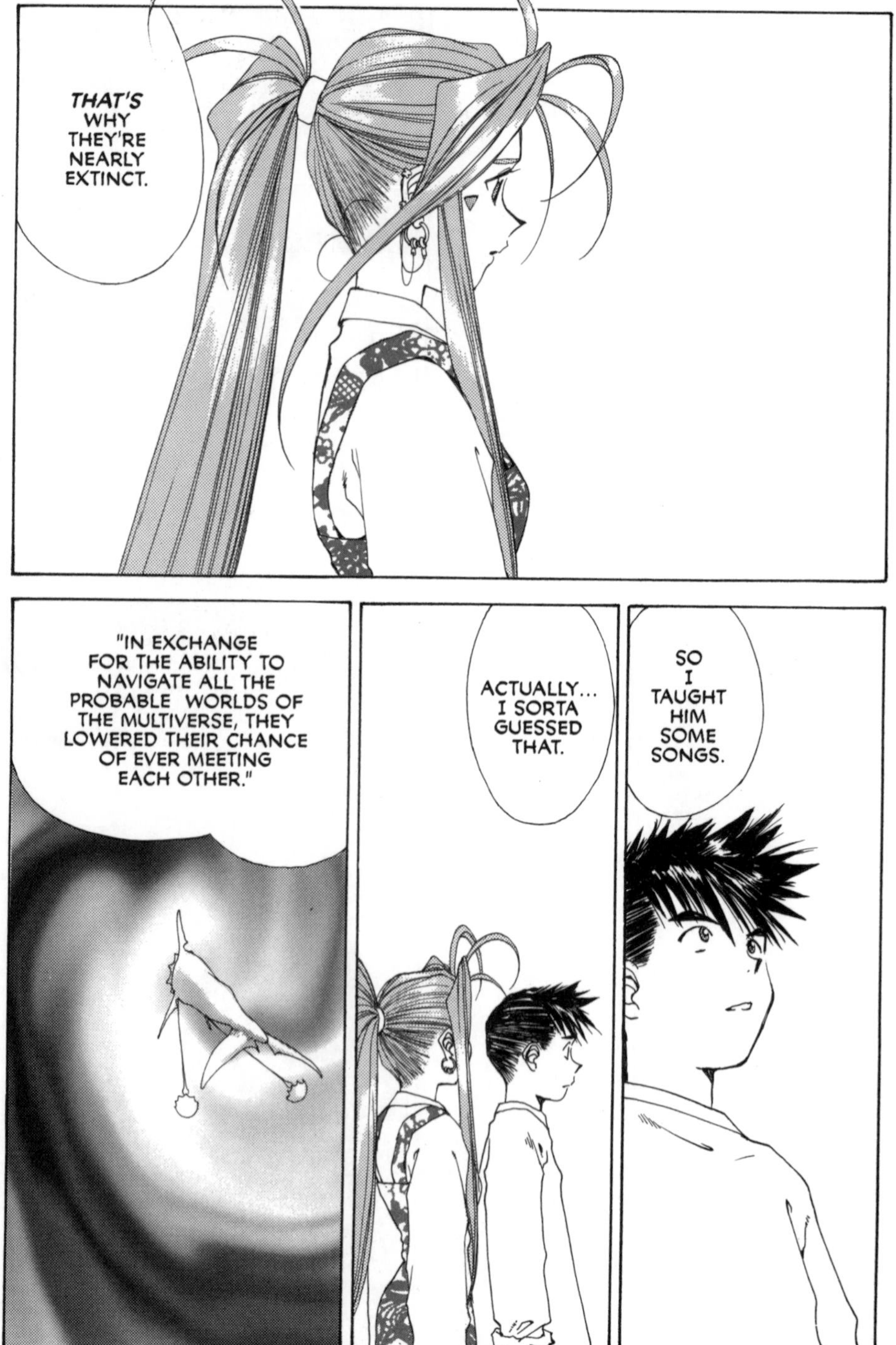
THAT'S WHY THEY'RE NEARLY EXTINCT.
"IN EXCHANGE FOR THE ABILITY TO NAVIGATE ALL THE PROBABLE WORLDS OF THE MULTIVERSE, THEY LOWERED THEIR CHANCE OF EVER MEETING EACH OTHER."
ACTUALLY... I SORTA GUESSED THAT.
SO I TAUGHT HIM SOME SONGS.

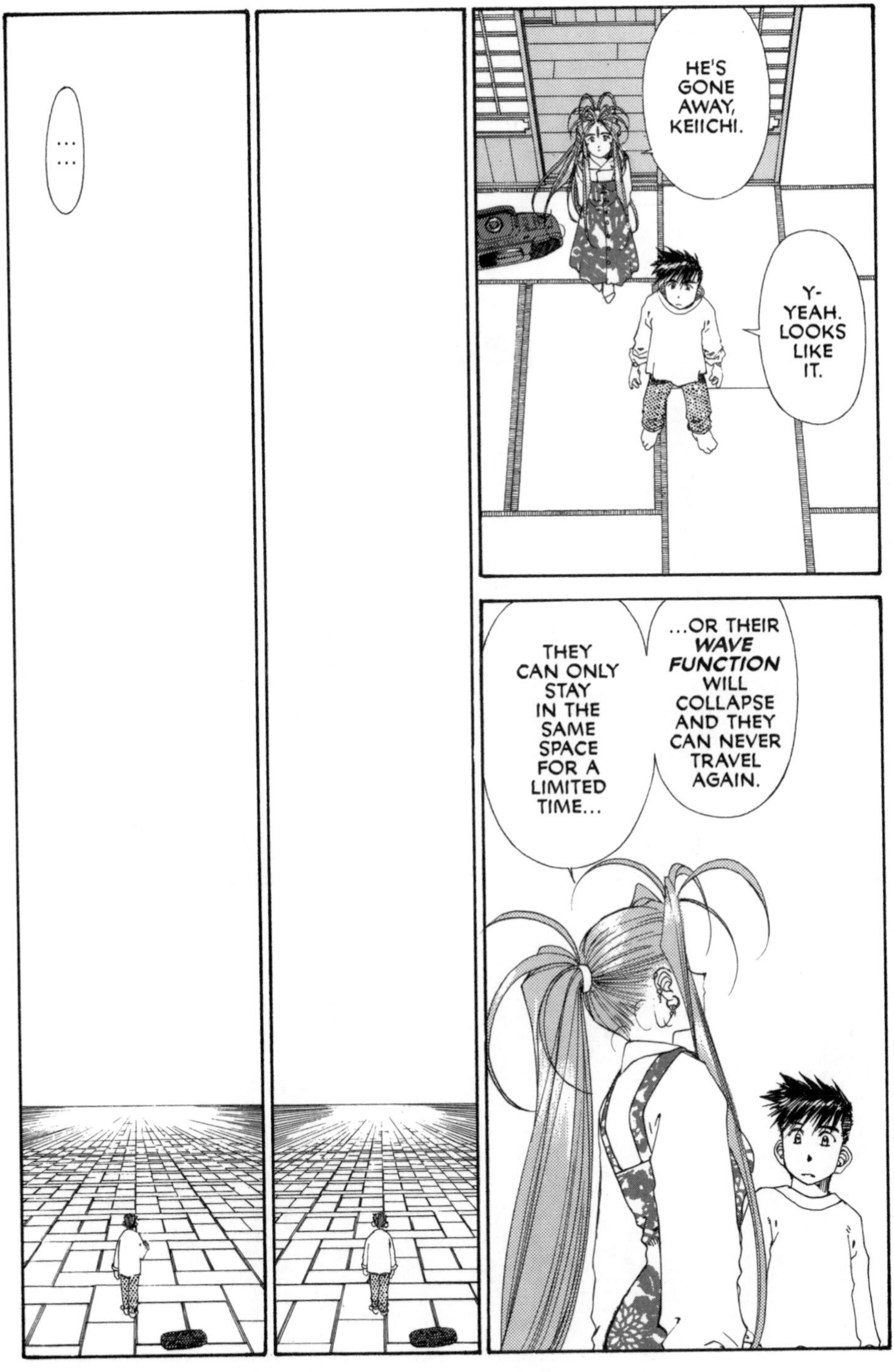
HE'S GONE AWAY, KEIICHI.
Y- YEAH. LOOKS LIKE IT.
THEY CAN ONLY STAY IN THE SAME SPACE FOR A LIMITED TIME...
...OR THEIR *WAVE FUNCTION* WILL COLLAPSE AND THEY CAN NEVER TRAVEL AGAIN.
......

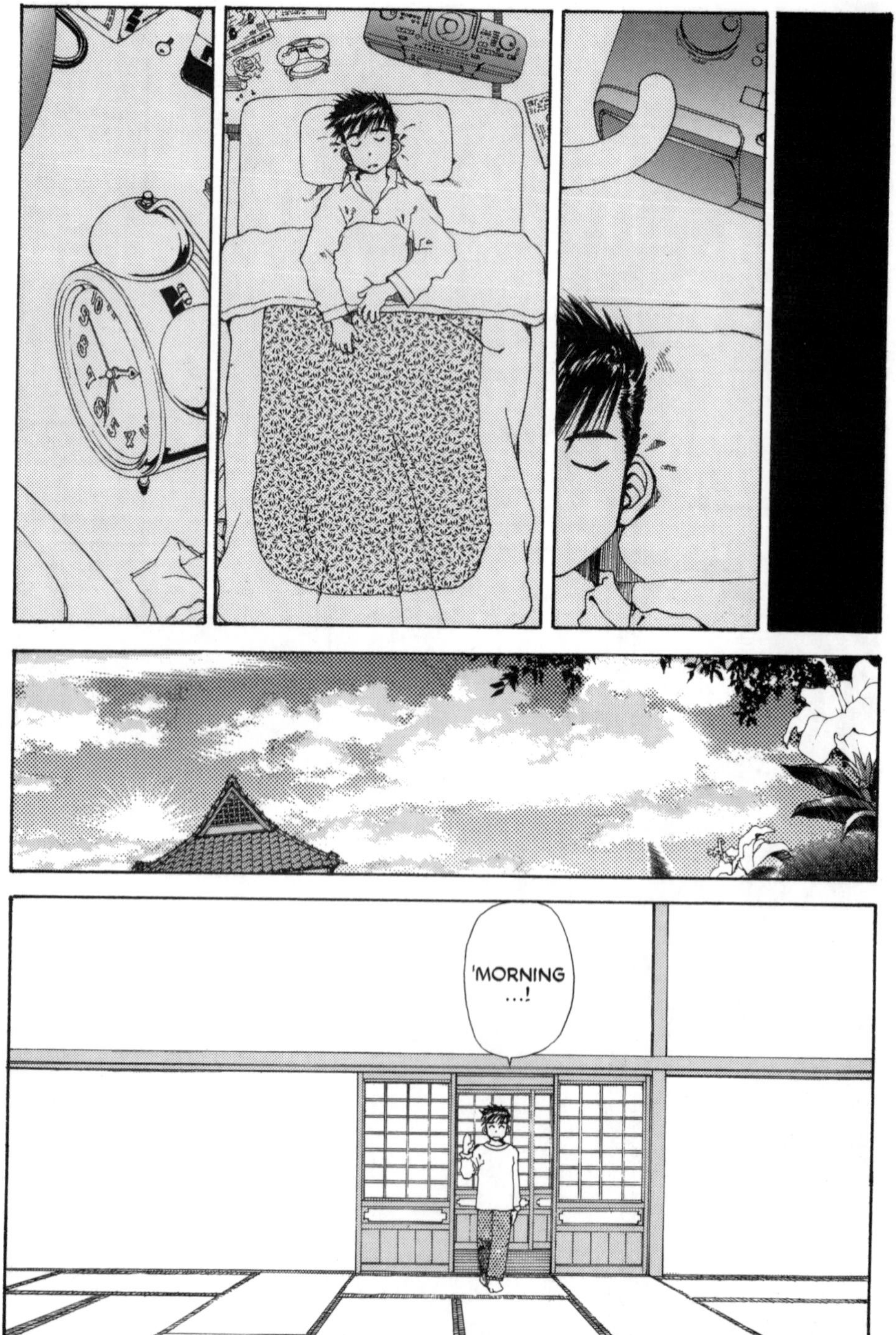
'MORNING ...!

"AND MAYBE THAT'S ***WHY...***"
....
TOMORROW WE'LL LEARN "MISSING TIME," OKAY?
AH, WELL! ***BED-TIME!***

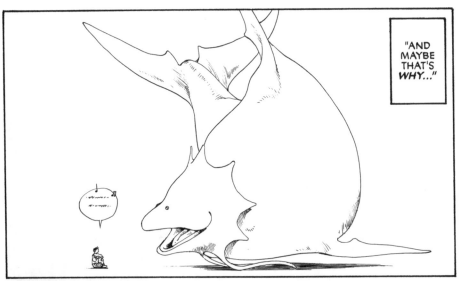

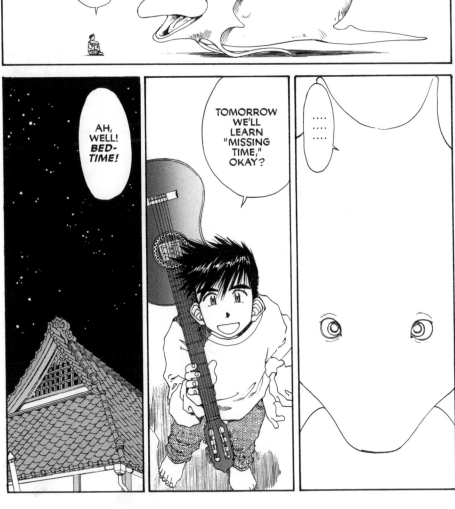

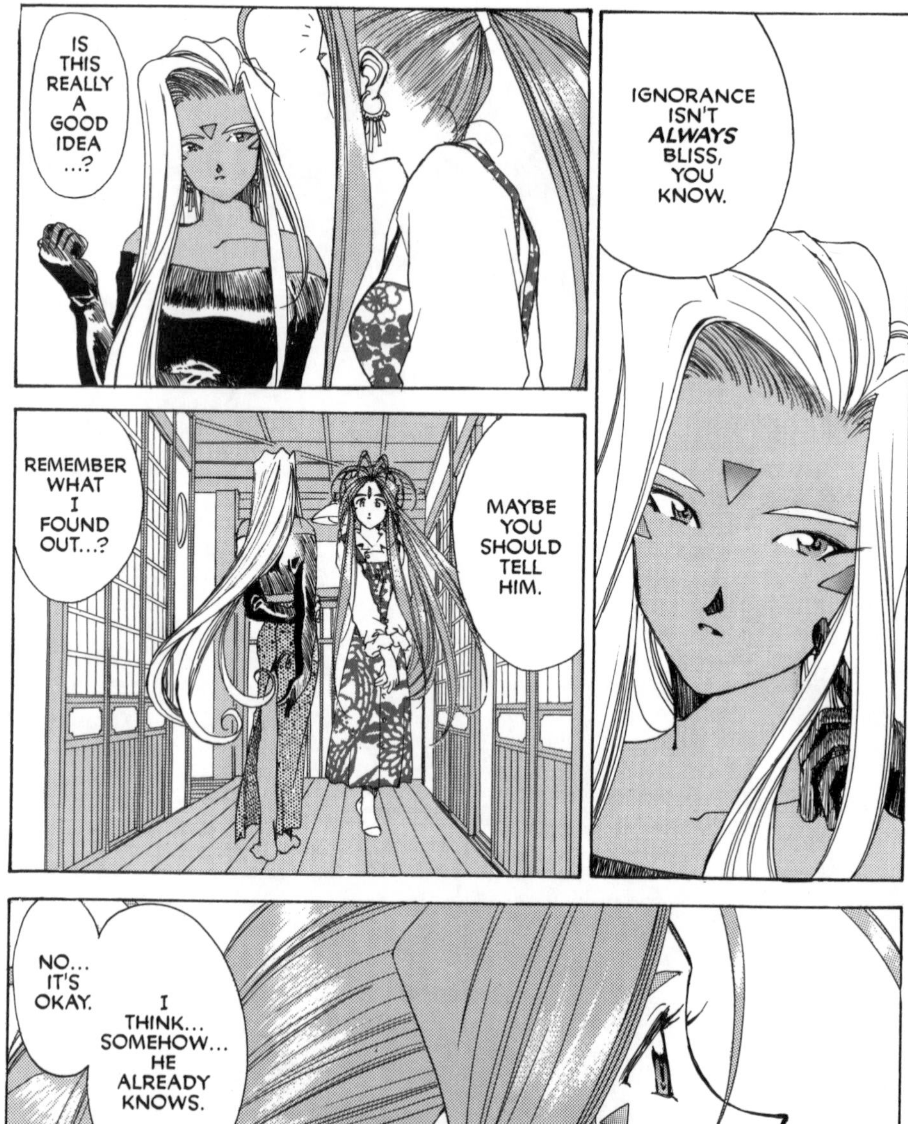
IS THIS REALLY A GOOD IDEA ...?
REMEMBER WHAT I FOUND OUT...?
MAYBE YOU SHOULD TELL HIM.
IGNORANCE ISN'T *ALWAYS* BLISS, YOU KNOW.
NO... IT'S OKAY.
I THINK... SOMEHOW... HE ALREADY KNOWS.

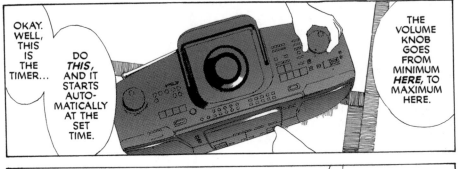

OKAY. WELL, THIS IS THE TIMER...

DO *THIS*, AND IT STARTS AUTOMATICALLY AT THE SET TIME.

THE VOLUME KNOB GOES FROM MINIMUM *HERE*, TO MAXIMUM HERE.

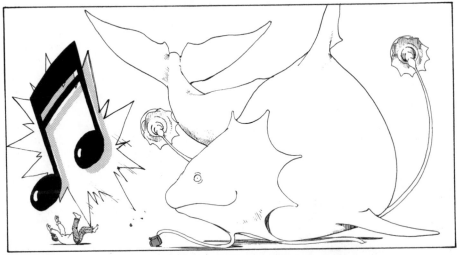

DON'T PUSH "PLAY" WHEN IT'S ON *MAX!*

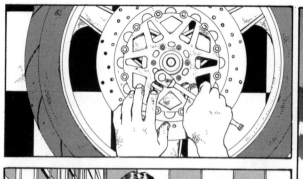

HUH
...?

YOU
WANT TO
KNOW
HOW IT
WORKS
...?

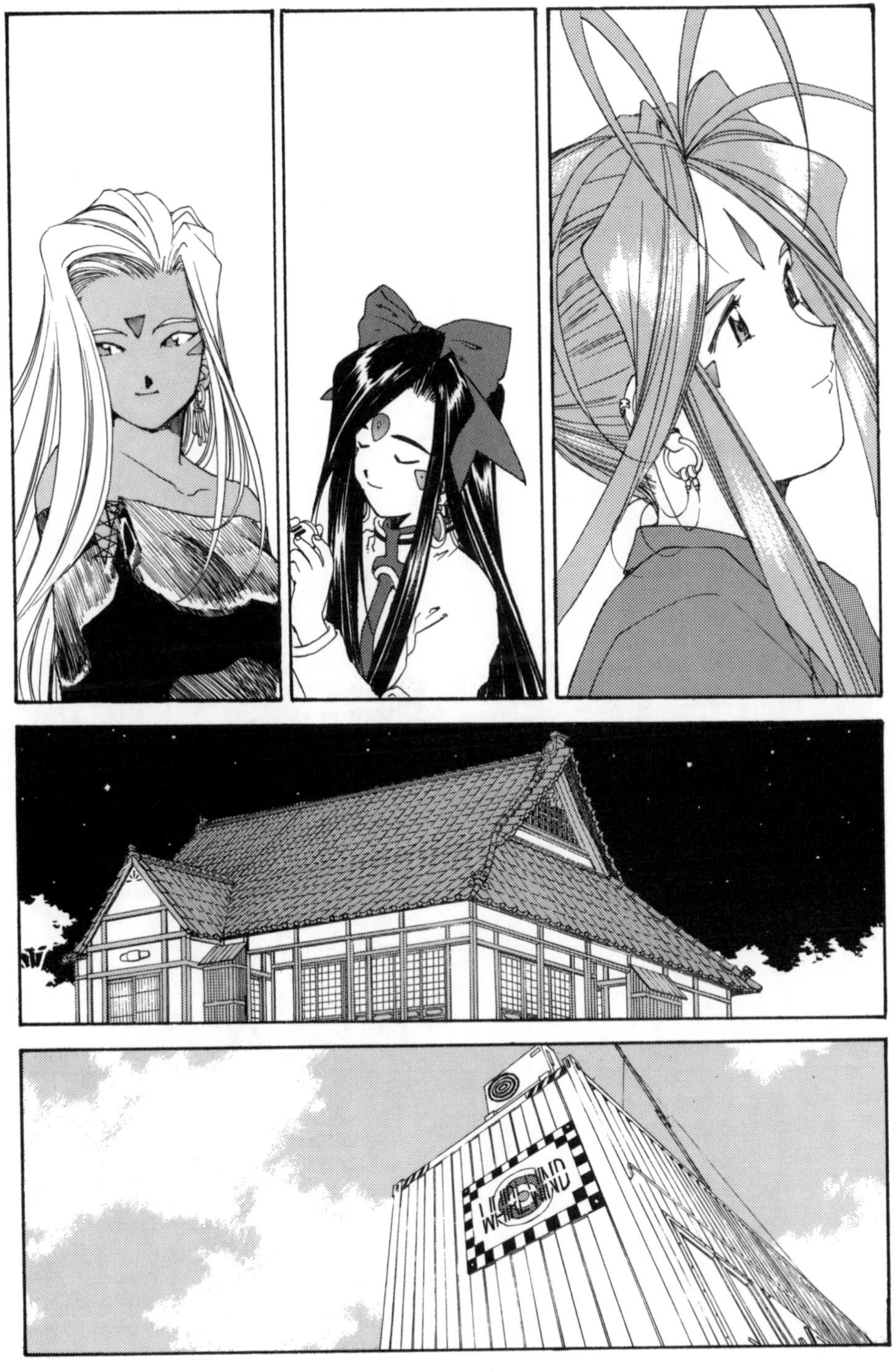

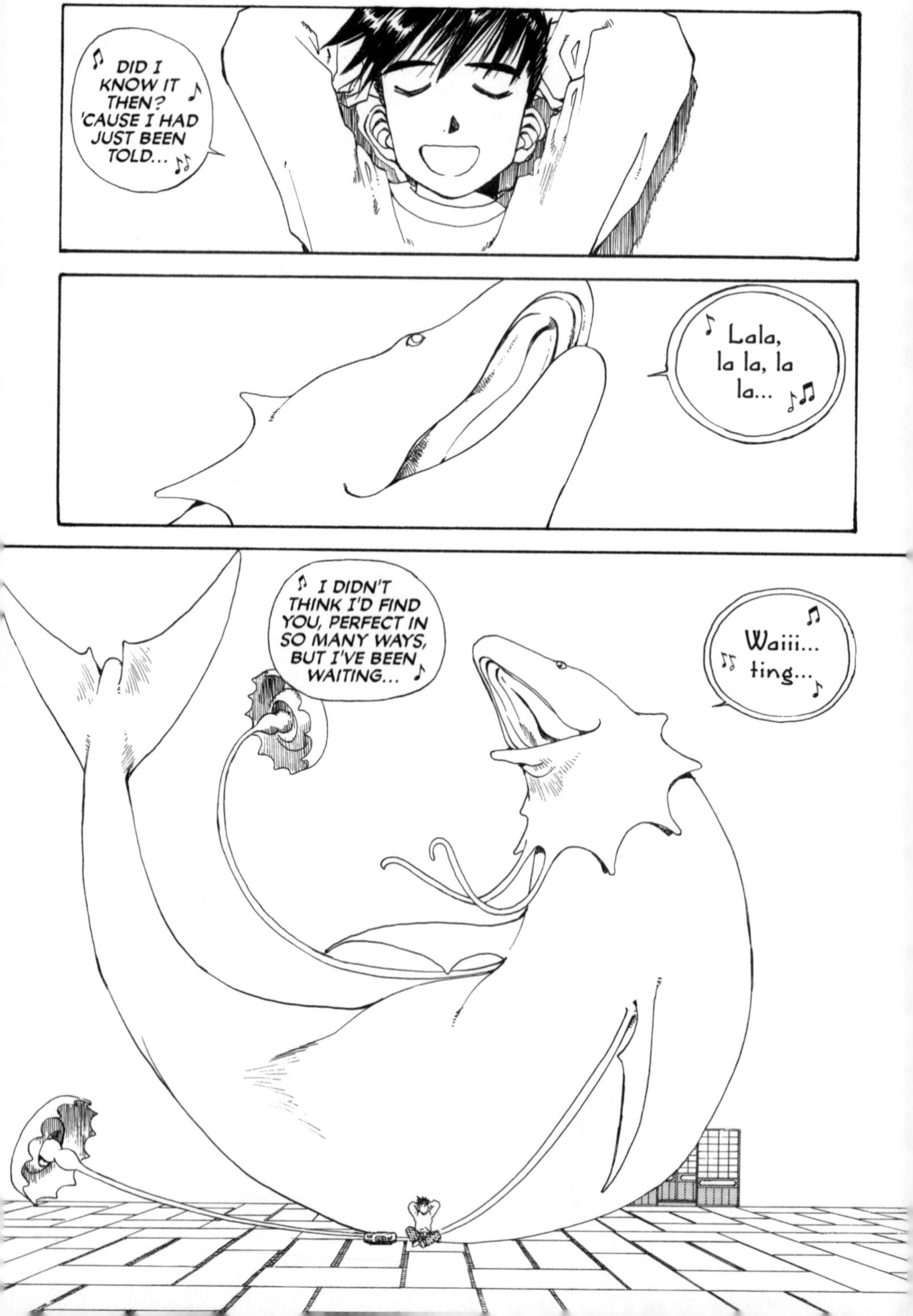
♪ DID I KNOW IT THEN? ♪ 'CAUSE I HAD JUST BEEN TOLD... ♫
♪ Lala, la la, la la... ♪♫
♪ I DIDN'T THINK I'D FIND YOU, PERFECT IN SO MANY WAYS, BUT I'VE BEEN WAITING... ♪
♫ Waiii... ♫ ting... ♪

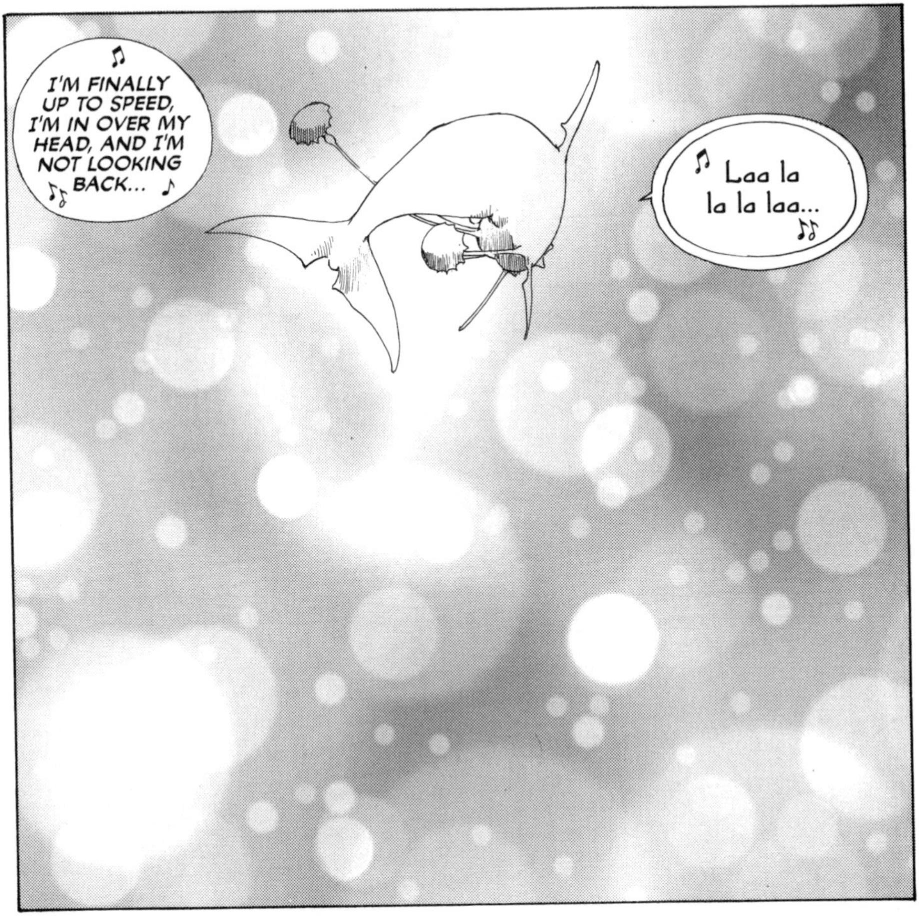
Laa la la la laa...
I'M FINALLY UP TO SPEED, I'M IN OVER MY HEAD, AND I'M NOT LOOKING BACK...

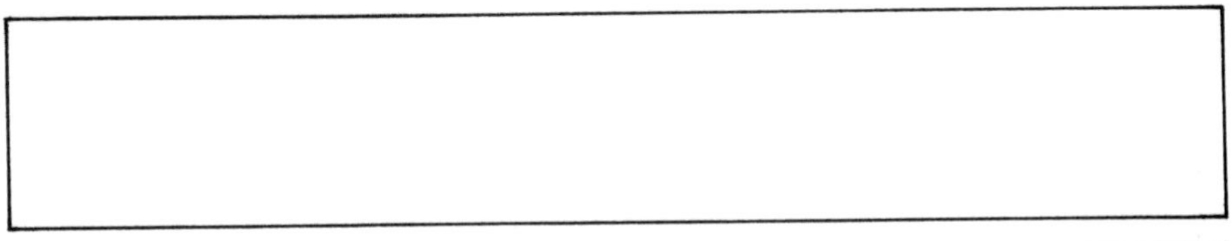

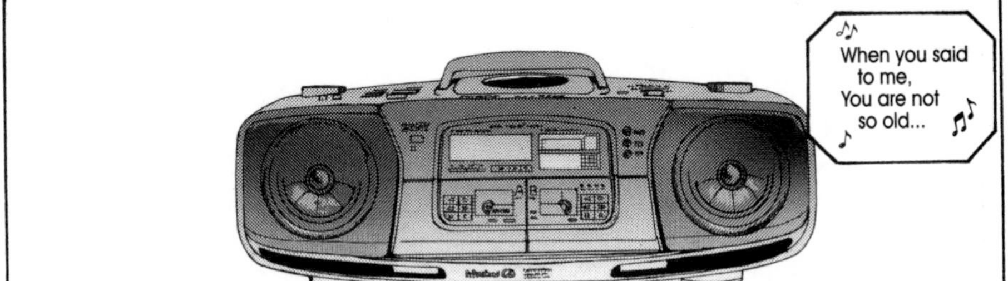
When you said to me, You are not so old...

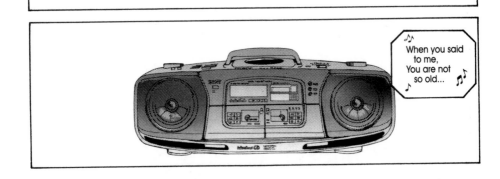

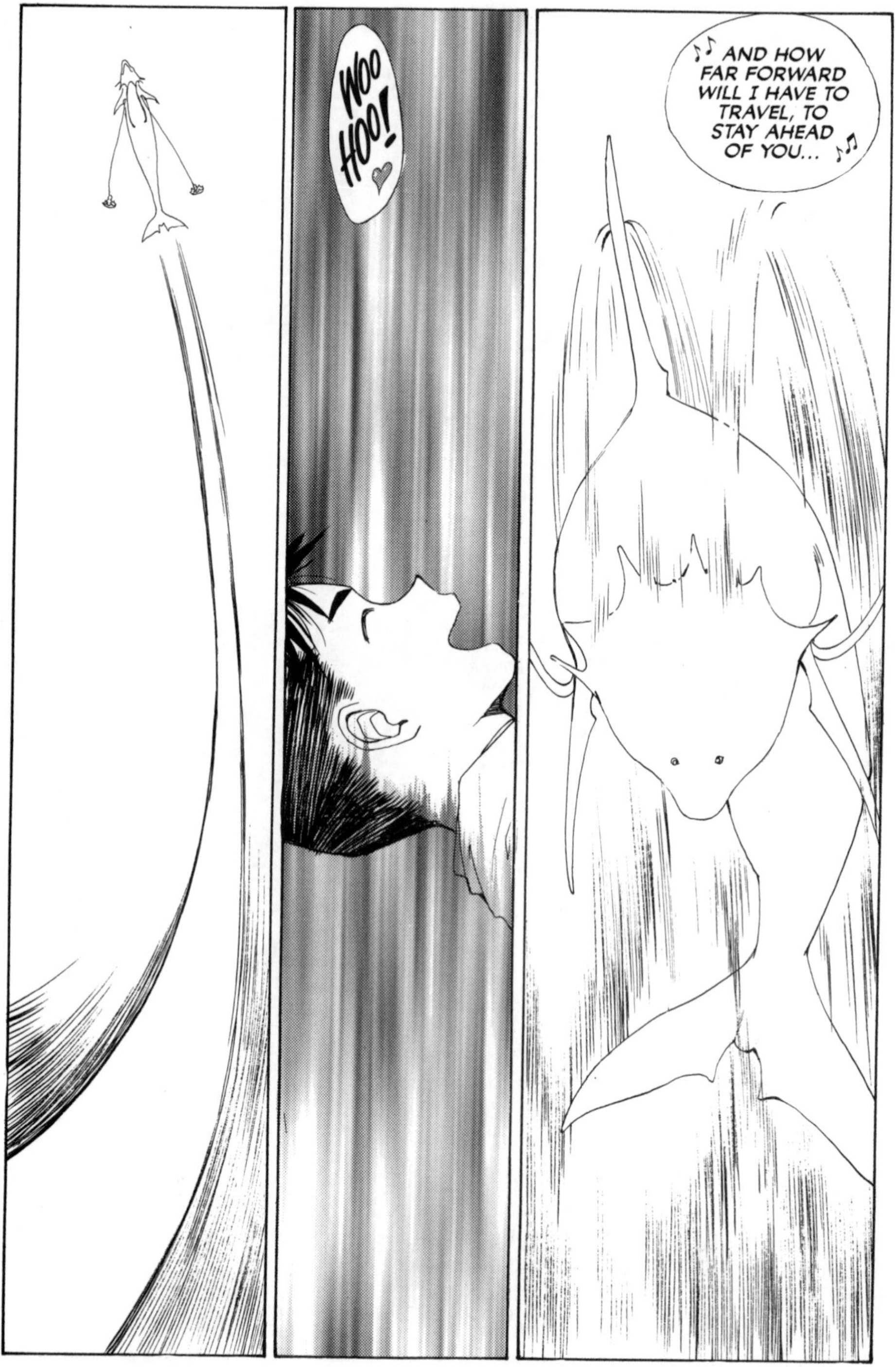
♪♪ AND HOW FAR FORWARD WILL I HAVE TO TRAVEL, TO STAY AHEAD OF YOU... ♪♫
WOO HOO! ♥

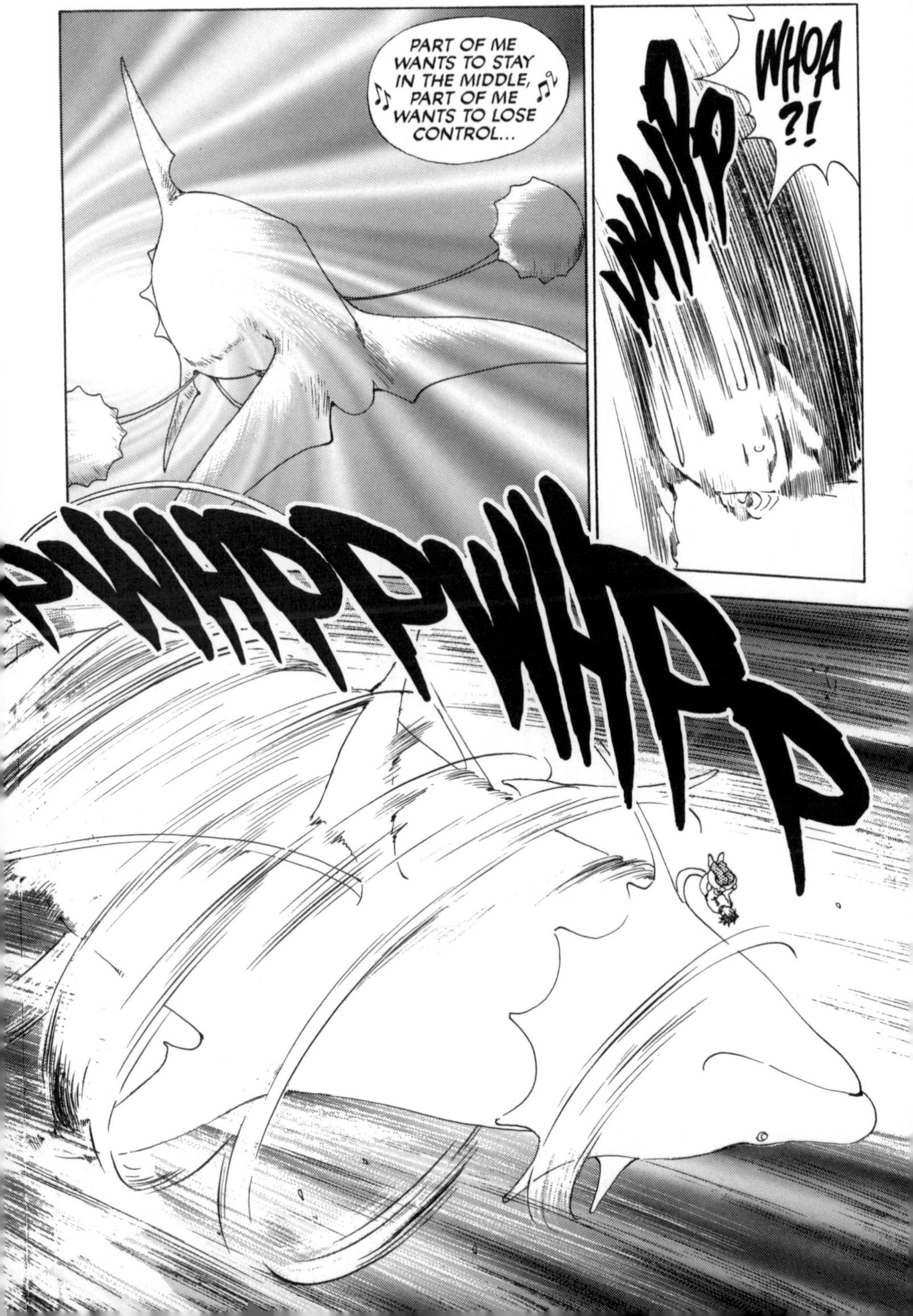
WHIPP
WHOA ?!
PART OF ME WANTS TO STAY IN THE MIDDLE, PART OF ME WANTS TO LOSE CONTROL...
PWHAPPWHAPP

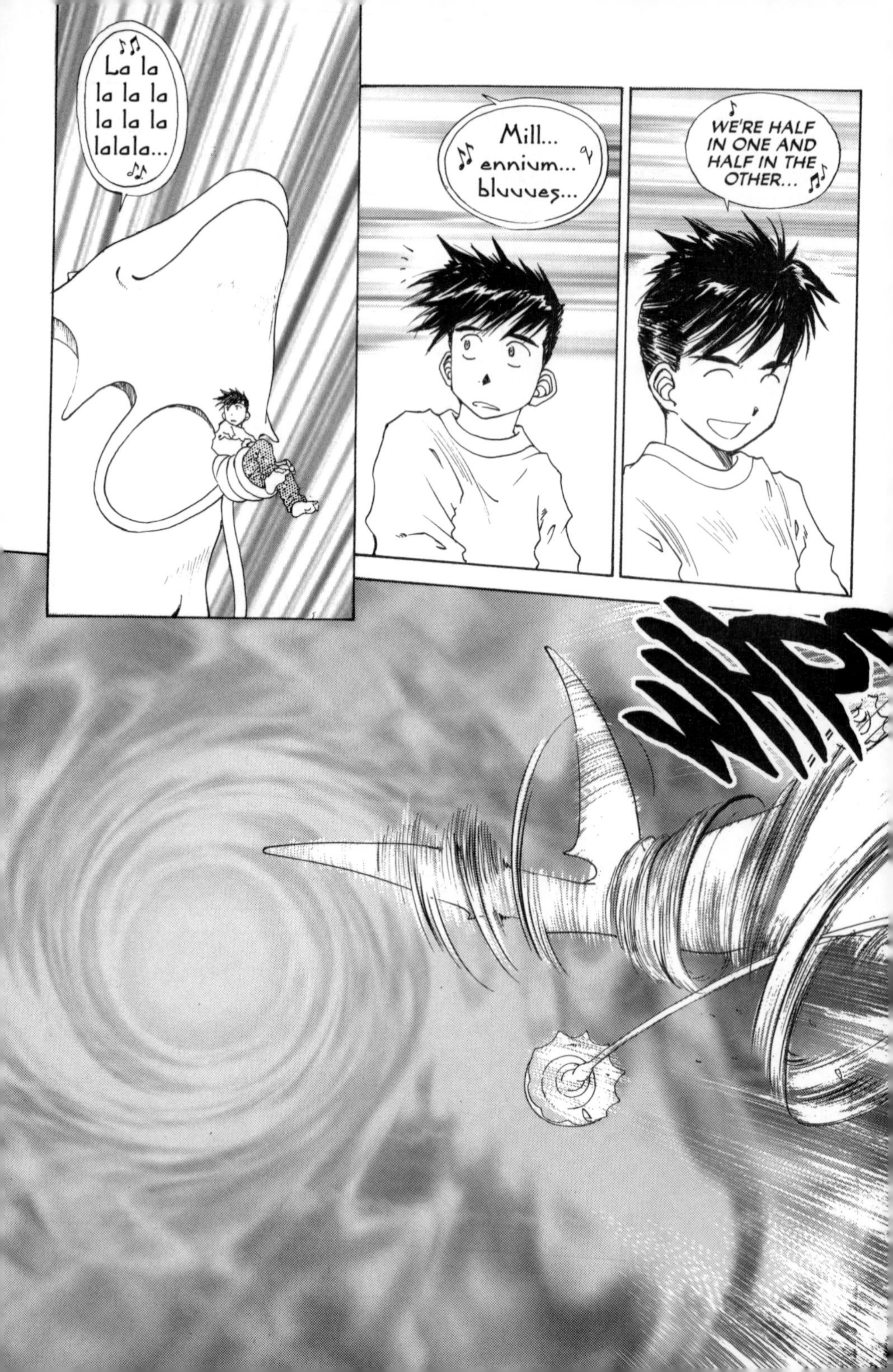

La la la la la la la la lalala...
Mill... ennium... bluuves...
WE'RE HALF IN ONE AND HALF IN THE OTHER...
WHP

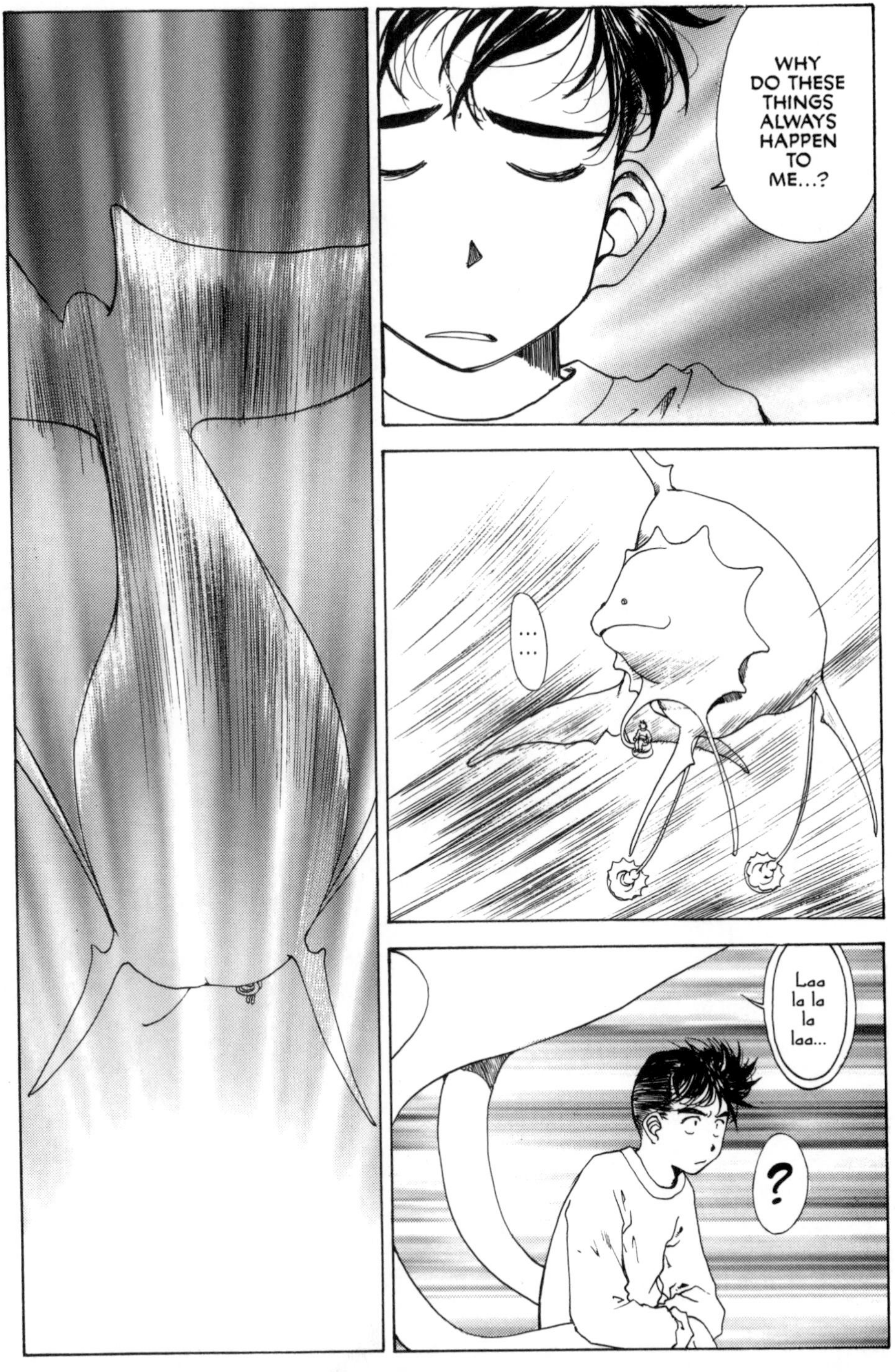
WHY DO THESE THINGS ALWAYS HAPPEN TO ME...?
......
Laa la la la la laa...
?

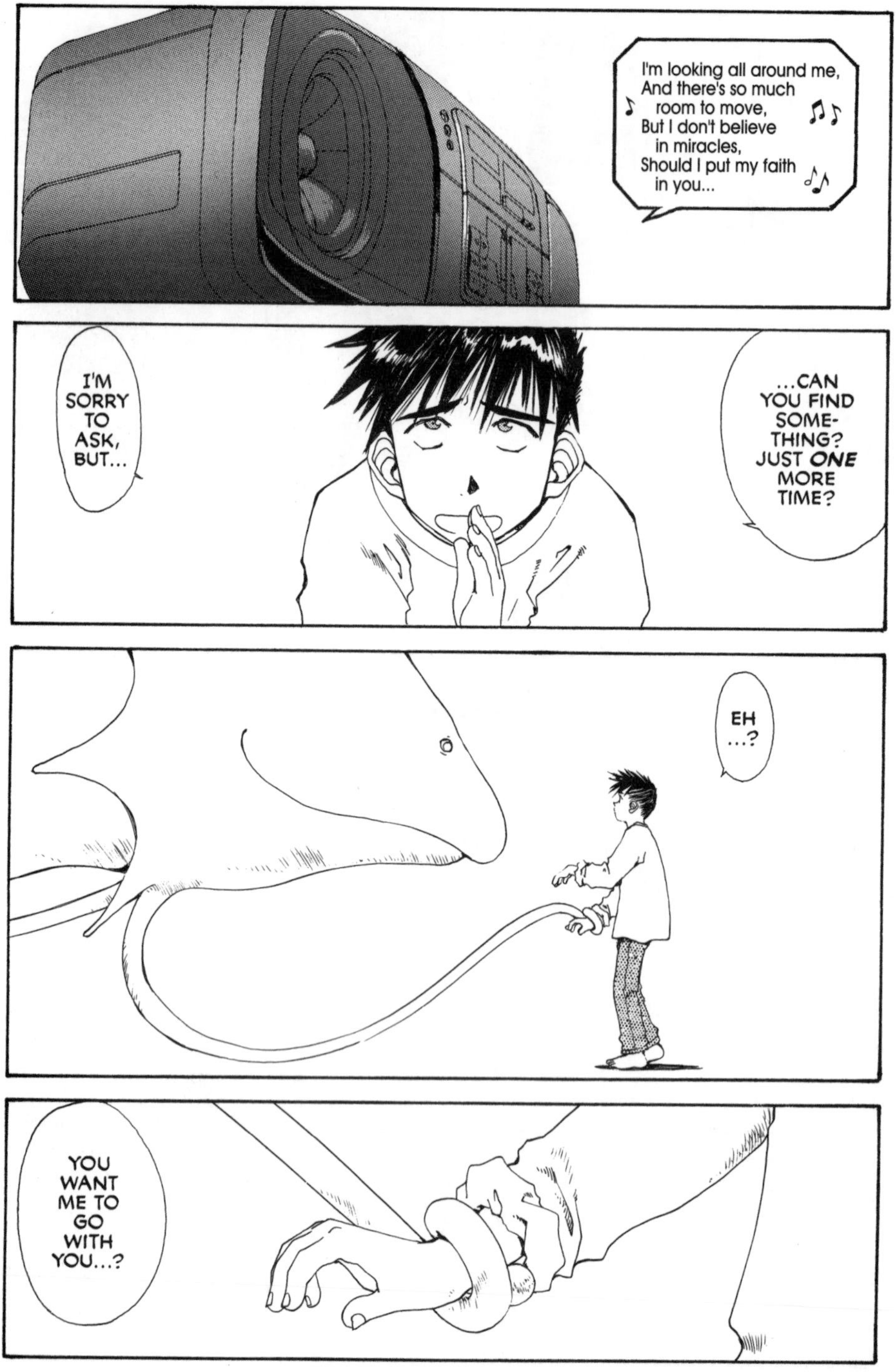
I'm looking all around me, And there's so much room to move, But I don't believe in miracles, Should I put my faith in you...
I'M SORRY TO ASK, BUT...
...CAN YOU FIND SOME-THING? JUST ONE MORE TIME?
EH ...?
YOU WANT ME TO GO WITH YOU...?

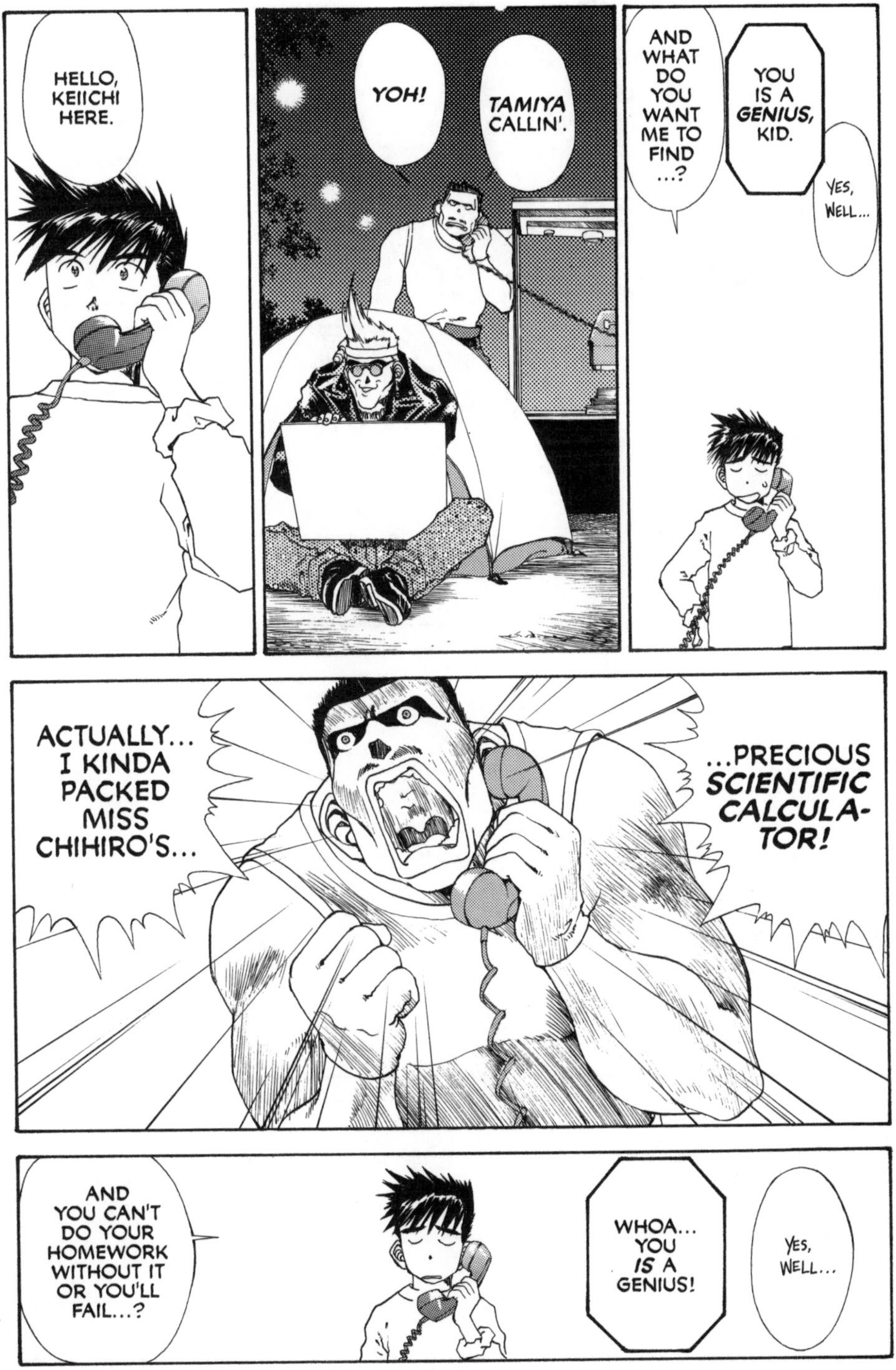
HELLO, KEIICHI HERE.
YOH!
TAMIYA CALLIN'.
AND WHAT DO YOU WANT ME TO FIND ...?
YOU IS A GENIUS, KID.
YES, WELL...
ACTUALLY... I KINDA PACKED MISS CHIHIRO'S...
...PRECIOUS SCIENTIFIC CALCULA-TOR!
AND YOU CAN'T DO YOUR HOMEWORK WITHOUT IT OR YOU'LL FAIL...?
WHOA... YOU IS A GENIUS!
YES, WELL...

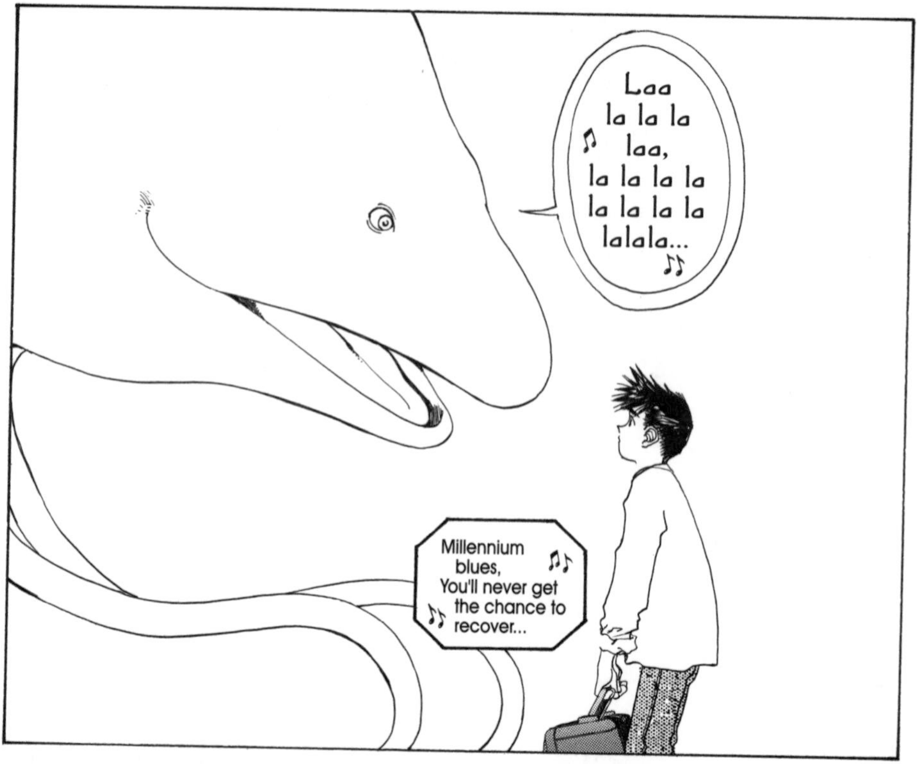
Laa la la la ♫ laa, la la la la la la la la lalala... ♫♫
Millennium blues, ♫♪ You'll never get the chance to ♫♪ recover...

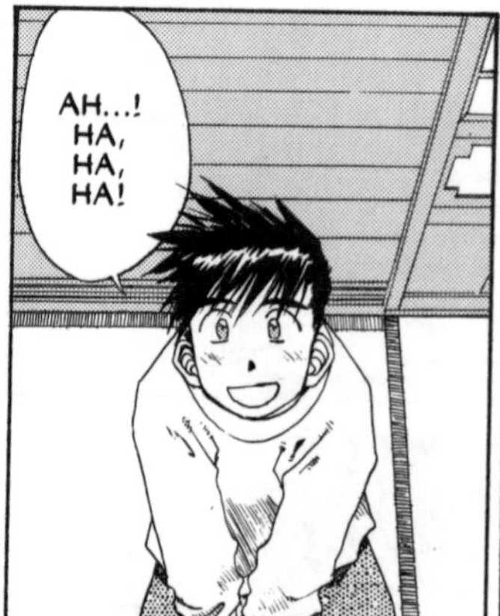
AH...! HA, HA, HA!

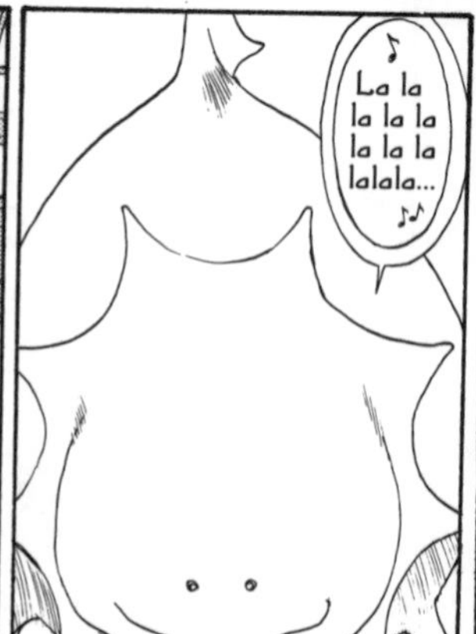
♪ La la la la la la la la lalala... ♫♪
They say ♫♫ it's not you ♪ anymore...

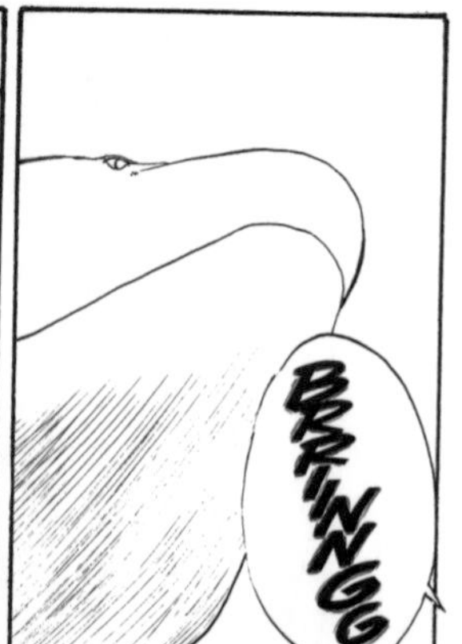
BRRINGG
WHOOPS ...!

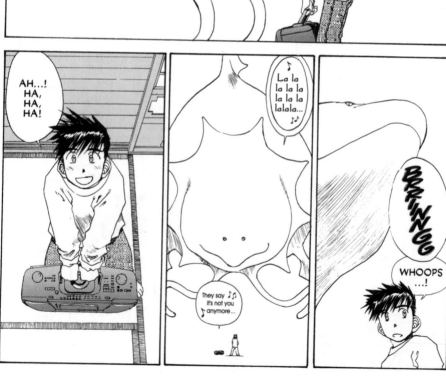

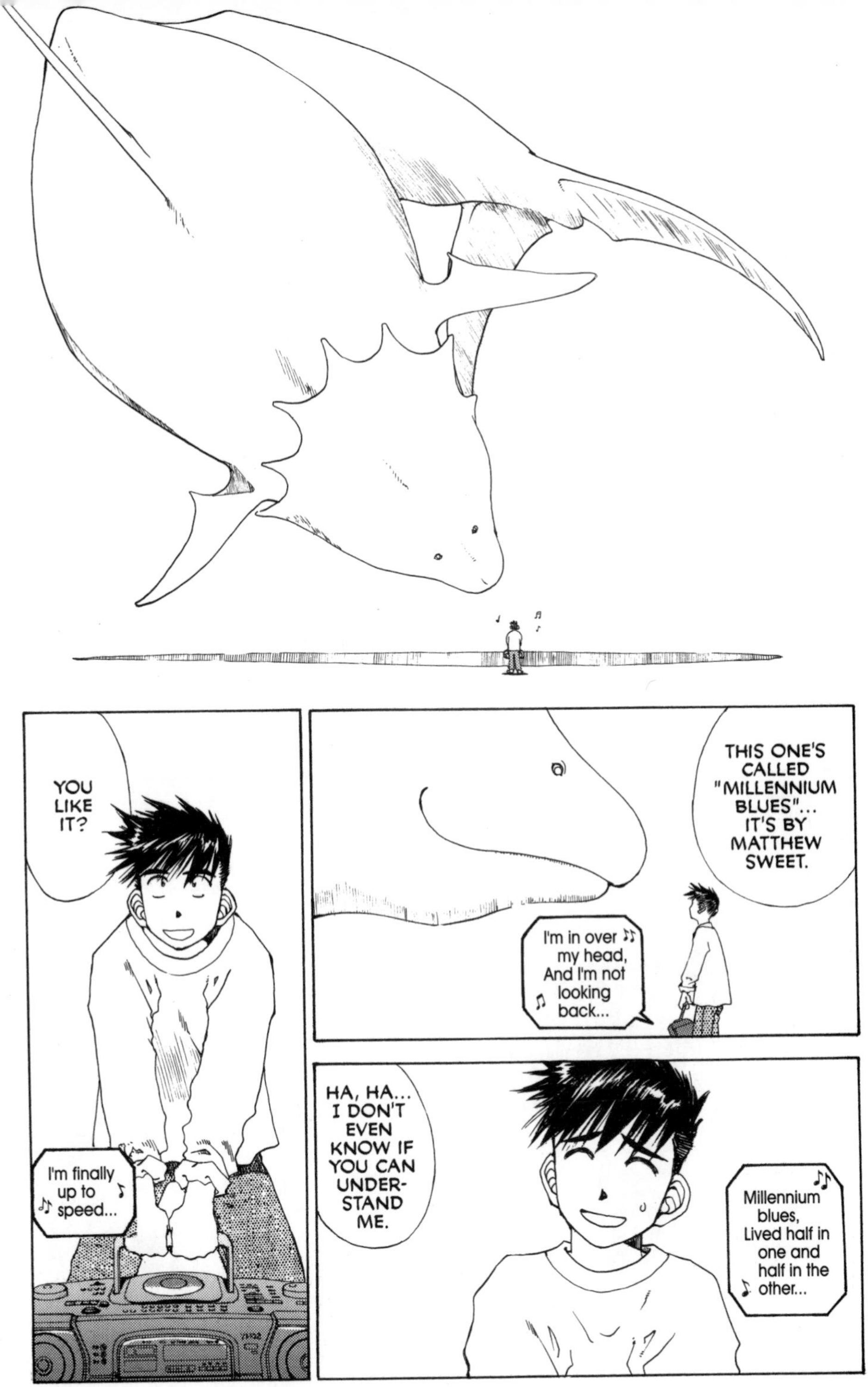
YOU LIKE IT?
I'm finally up to speed...
THIS ONE'S CALLED "MILLENNIUM BLUES"... IT'S BY MATTHEW SWEET.
I'm in over my head, And I'm not looking back...
HA, HA... I DON'T EVEN KNOW IF YOU CAN UNDER-STAND ME.
Millennium blues, Lived half in one and half in the other...

WAUGH!

♪ And how far forward will I have to travel, To stay ahead of you... ♪

?

THE *MUSIC?*

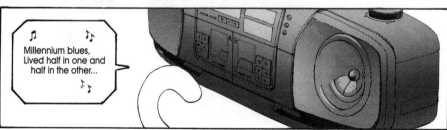

♪ Millennium blues, Lived half in one and half in the other... ♪

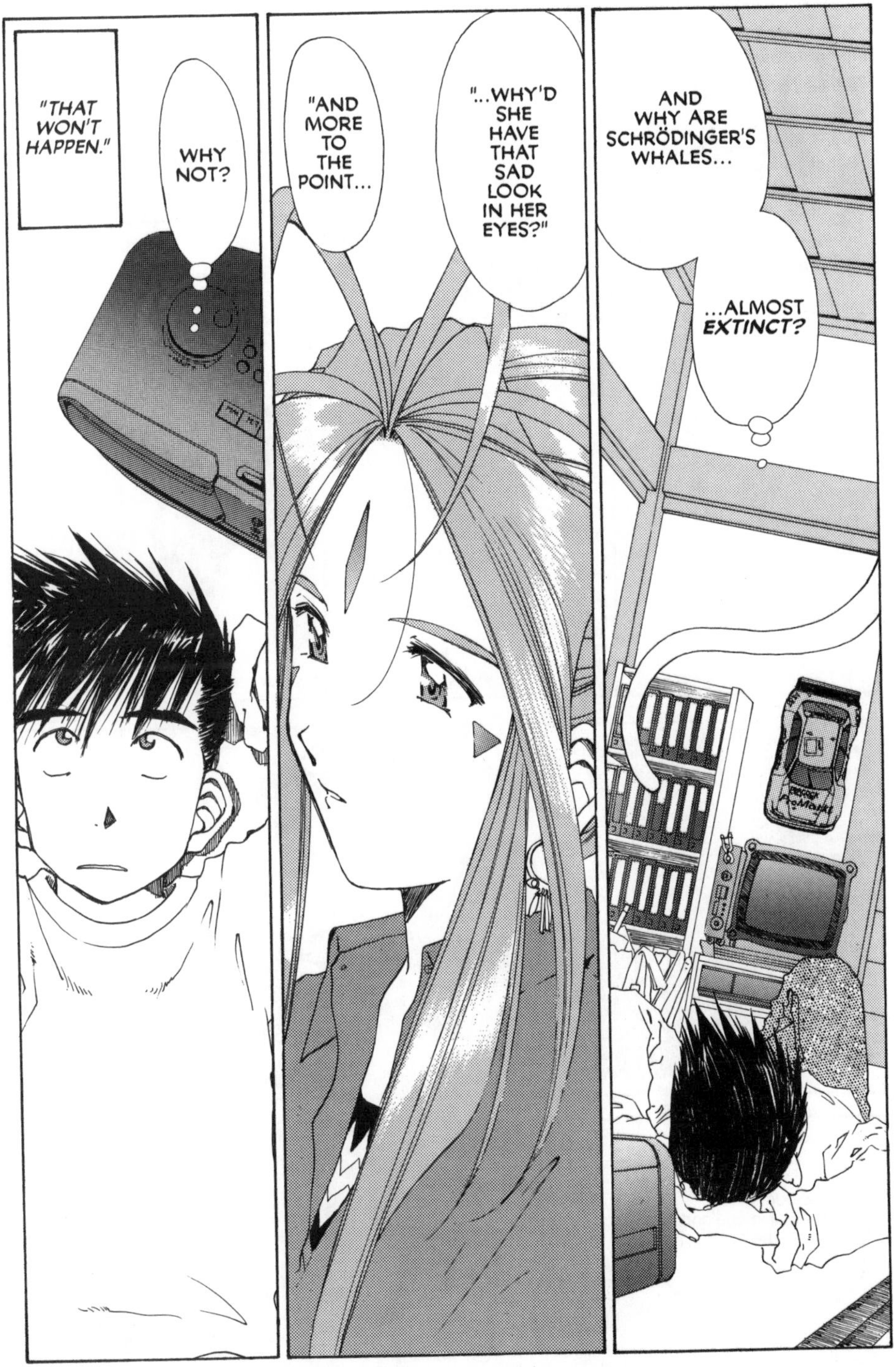
"THAT WON'T HAPPEN."
WHY NOT?
"AND MORE TO THE POINT...
"...WHY'D SHE HAVE THAT SAD LOOK IN HER EYES?"
AND WHY ARE SCHRÖDINGER'S WHALES...
...ALMOST *EXTINCT?*

KEIICHI'S SHOP
A VERY SPECIAL SELECTION
A B
Well you can make your way through living and loving, Looking good from where I sit...
06 01 00:
CD
TRACK OPERATON
INDEX DISPLAY
MINUTE
But with your great big eyes you see what is coming, And you're not a part of it...

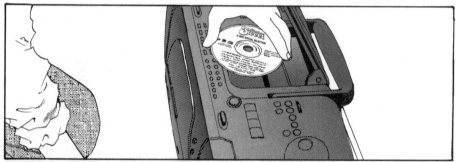

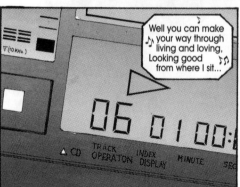

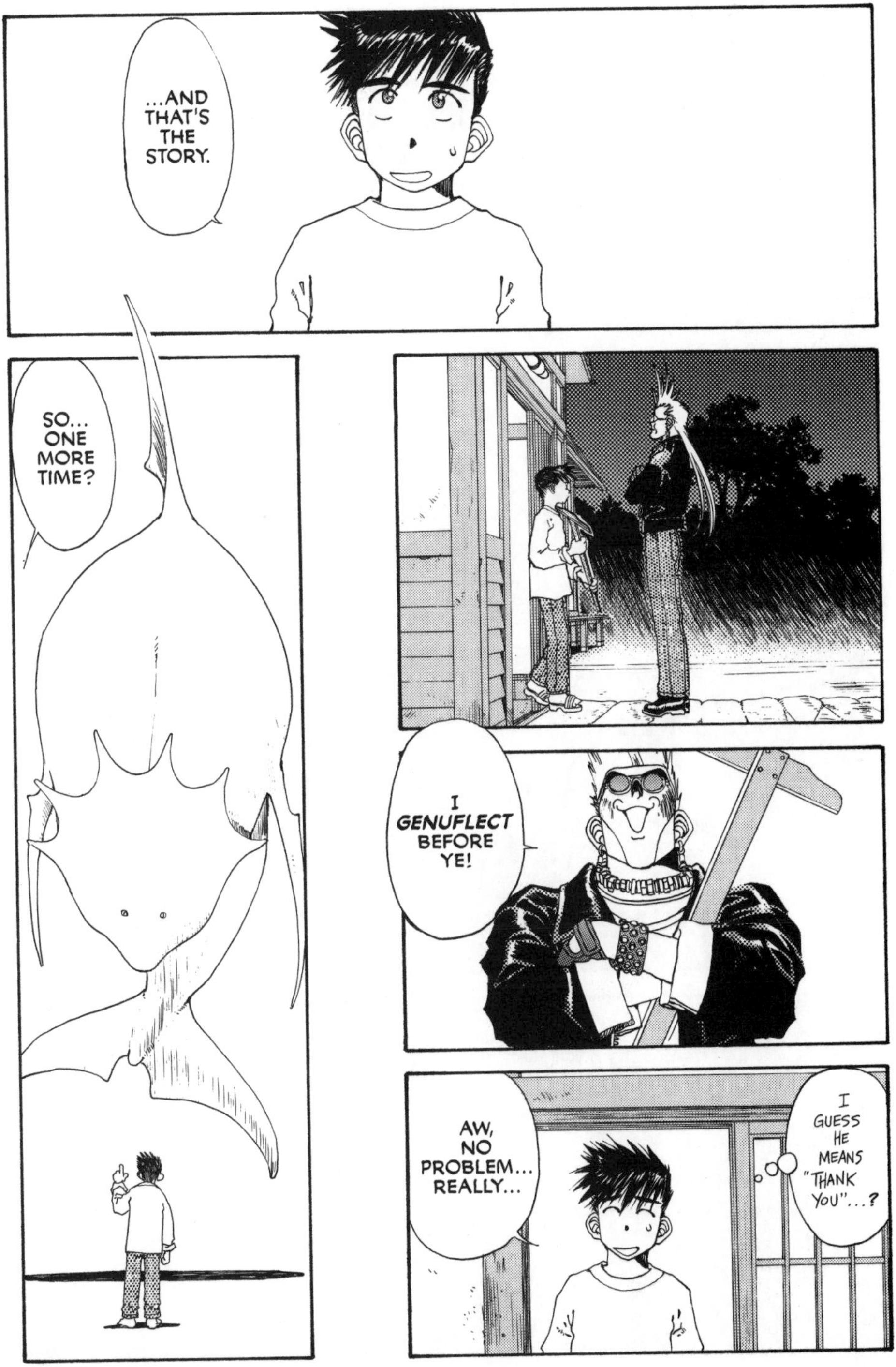
...AND THAT'S THE STORY.
I GENUFLECT BEFORE YE!
I GUESS HE MEANS "THANK YOU"...?
AW, NO PROBLEM... REALLY...
SO... ONE MORE TIME?

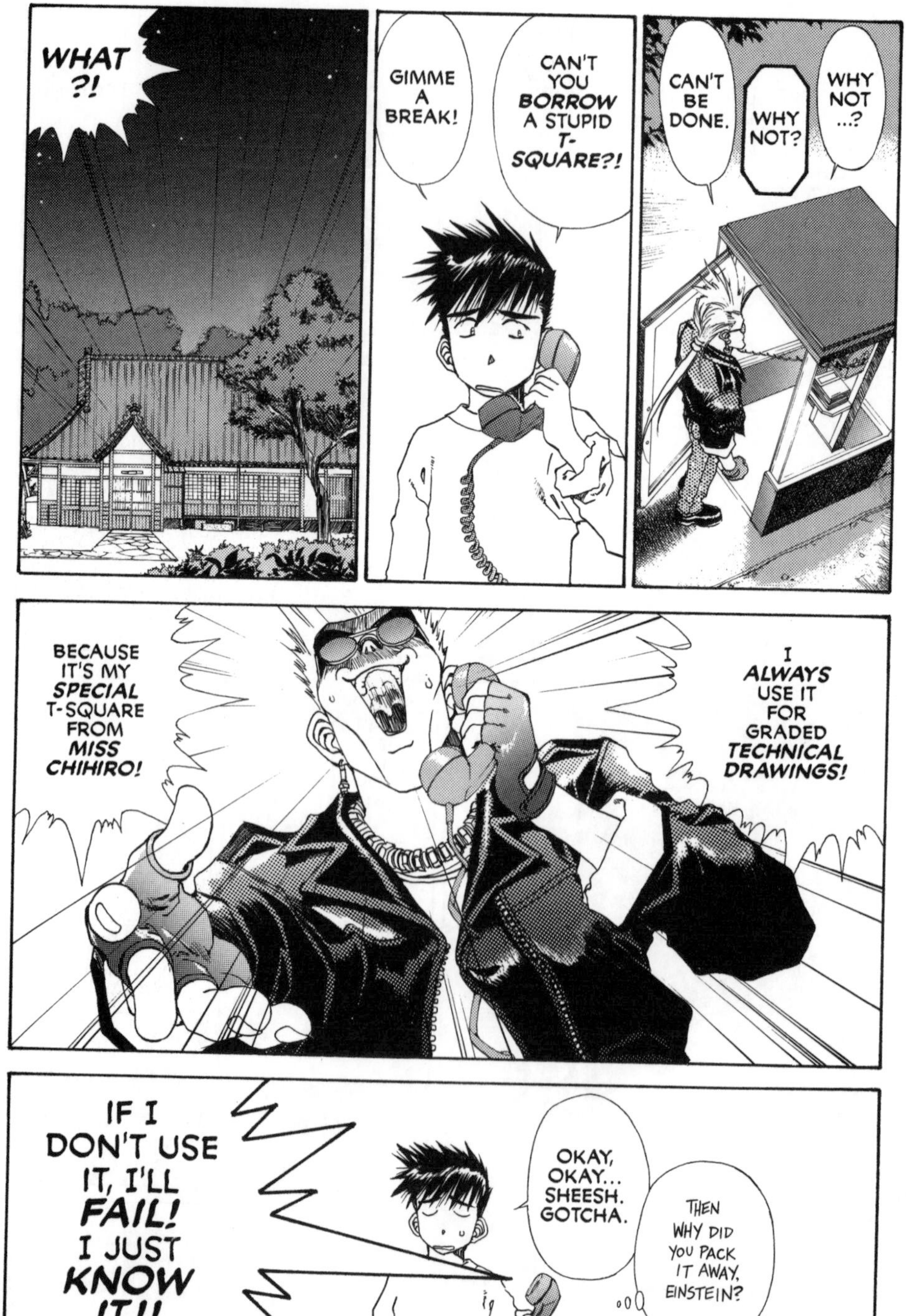
WHY NOT ...?
WHY NOT?
CAN'T BE DONE.
CAN'T YOU BORROW A STUPID T-SQUARE?!
GIMME A BREAK!
WHAT ?!
I ALWAYS USE IT FOR GRADED TECHNICAL DRAWINGS!
BECAUSE IT'S MY SPECIAL T-SQUARE FROM MISS CHIHIRO!
OKAY, OKAY... SHEESH. GOTCHA.
THEN WHY DID YOU PACK IT AWAY, EINSTEIN?
IF I DON'T USE IT, I'LL FAIL! I JUST KNOW IT!!

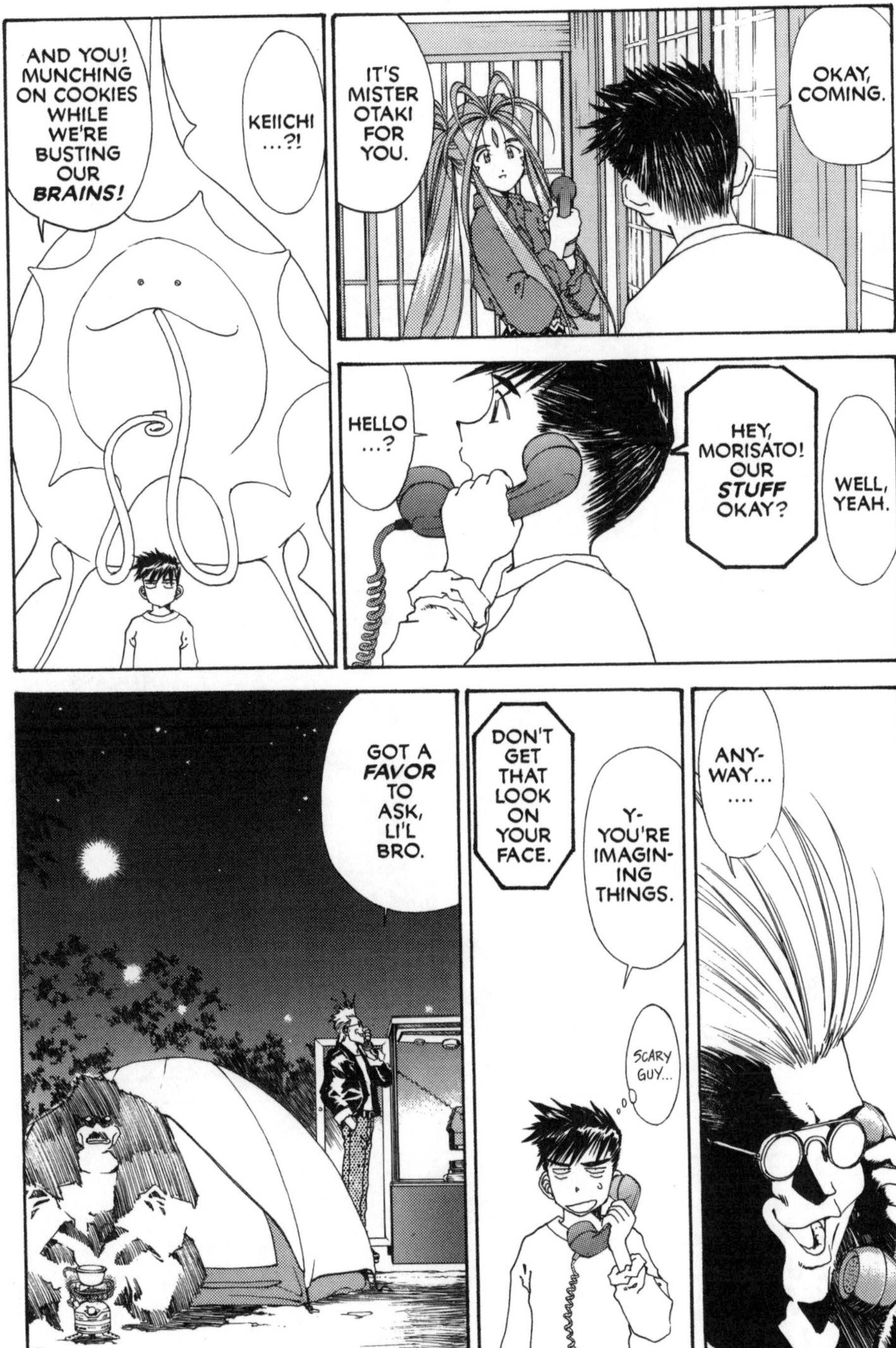
OKAY, COMING.
IT'S MISTER OTAKI FOR YOU.
HELLO ...?
HEY, MORISATO! OUR *STUFF* OKAY?
WELL, YEAH.
KEIICHI ...?!
AND YOU! MUNCHING ON COOKIES WHILE WE'RE BUSTING OUR ***BRAINS!***
ANY-WAY... ....
DON'T GET THAT LOOK ON YOUR FACE.
Y-YOU'RE IMAGIN-ING THINGS.
SCARY GUY...
GOT A ***FAVOR*** TO ASK, LI'L BRO.

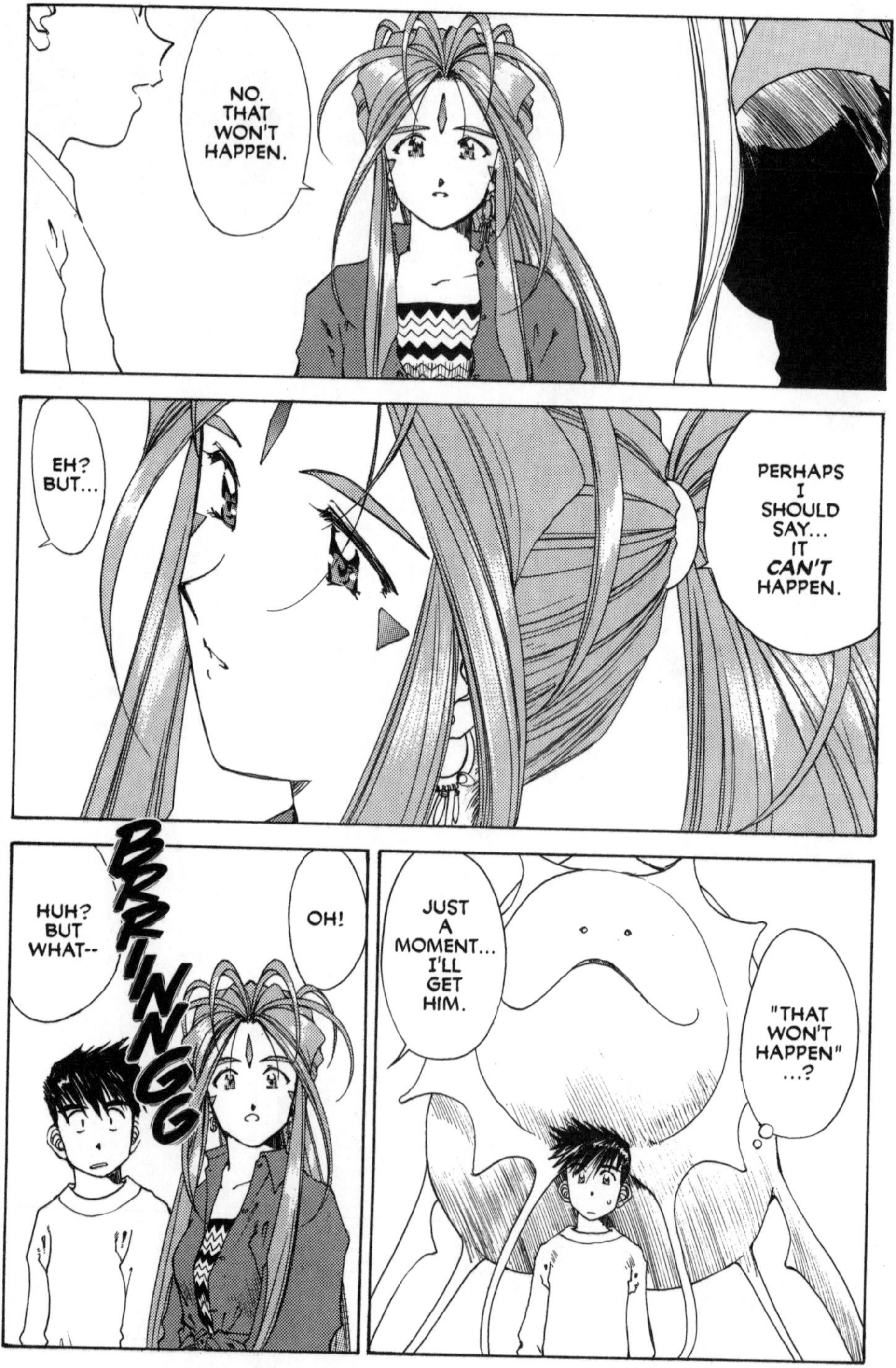
NO. THAT WON'T HAPPEN.
EH? BUT...
PERHAPS I SHOULD SAY... IT *CAN'T* HAPPEN.
HUH? BUT WHAT--
BRRIINGG
OH!
JUST A MOMENT... I'LL GET HIM.
"THAT WON'T HAPPEN" ...?

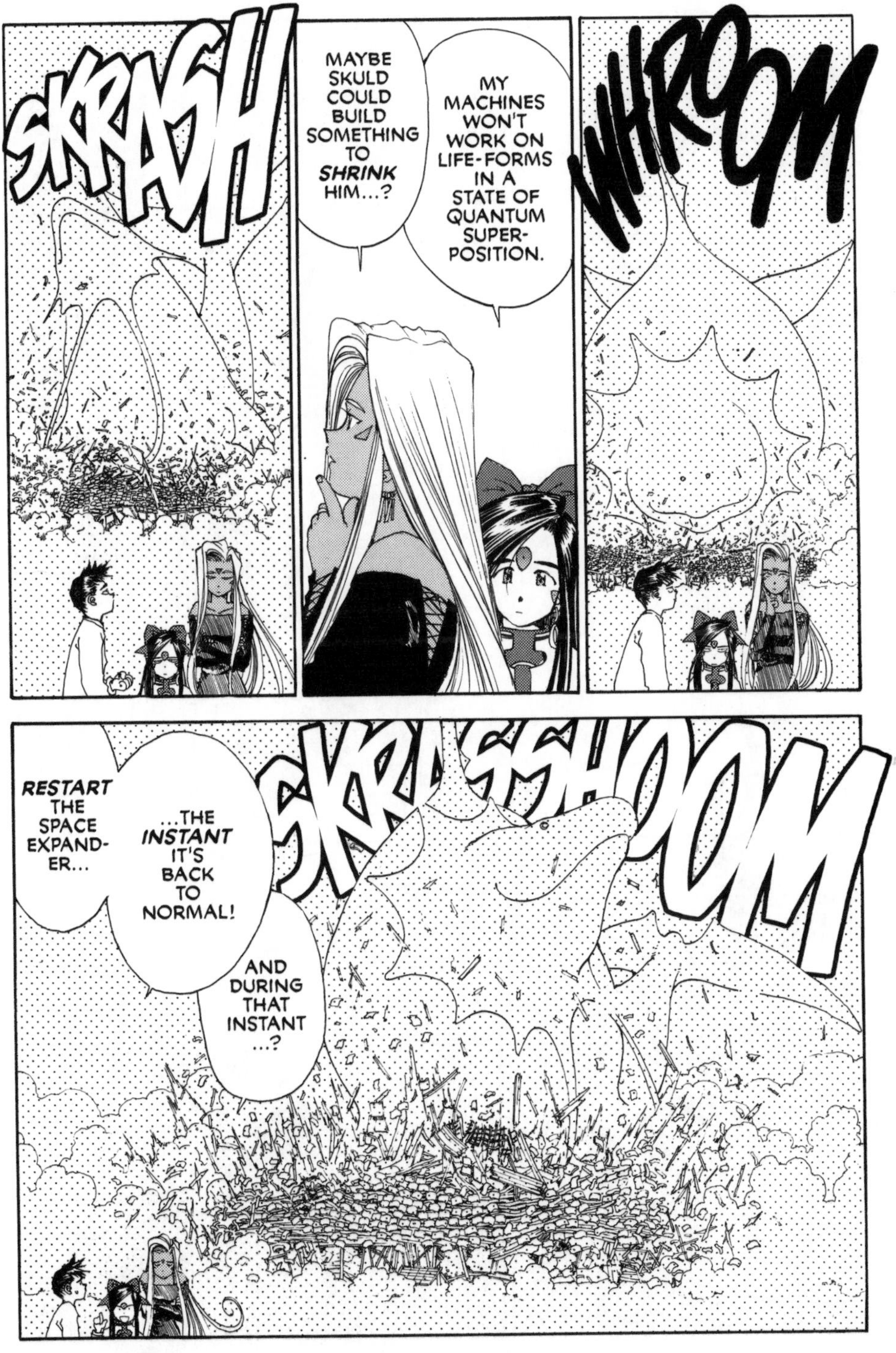
SKRASH
MAYBE SKULD COULD BUILD SOMETHING TO *SHRINK* HIM...?
MY MACHINES WON'T WORK ON LIFE-FORMS IN A STATE OF QUANTUM SUPER-POSITION.
WHROOM
RESTART THE SPACE EXPAND-ER...
...THE *INSTANT* IT'S BACK TO NORMAL!
AND DURING THAT INSTANT ...?
SKRASSHOOM

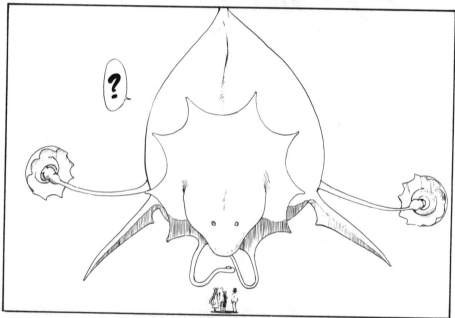

?

I KNOW!! WE JUST HAVE TO GET HIM OUT BEFORE IT HAPPENS!

THROUGH *THIS* DOOR? *HOW?*

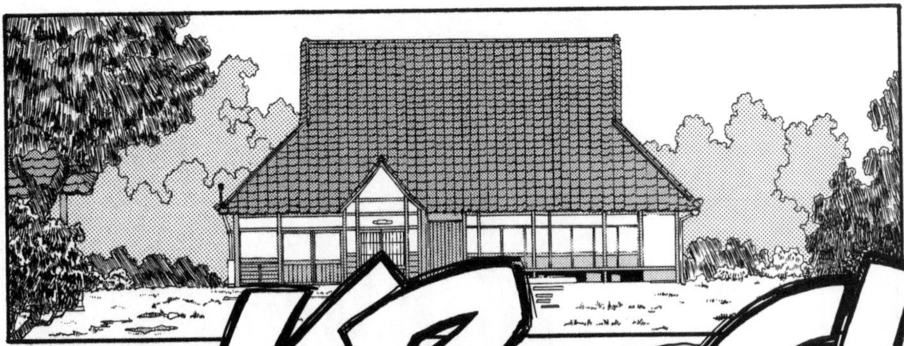

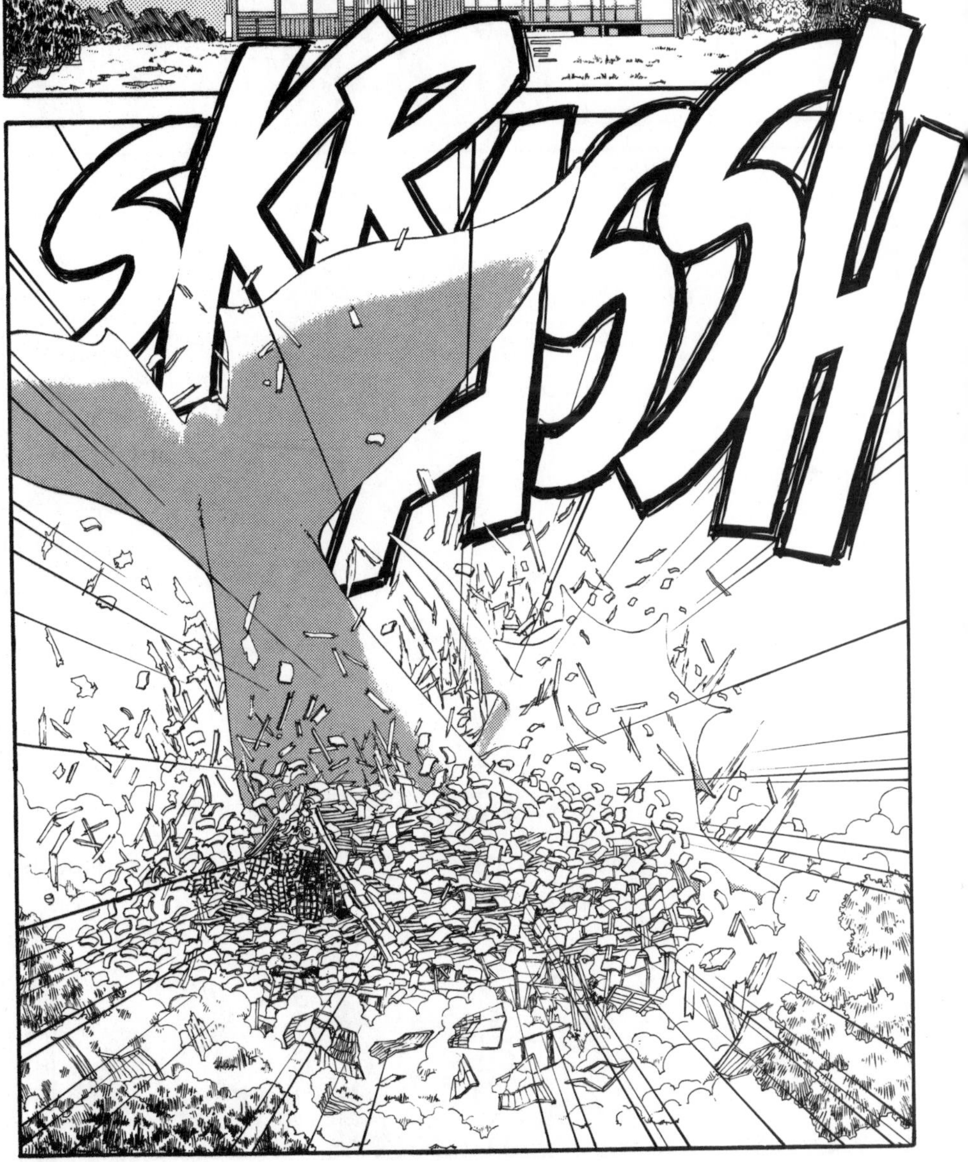
SKRASSH

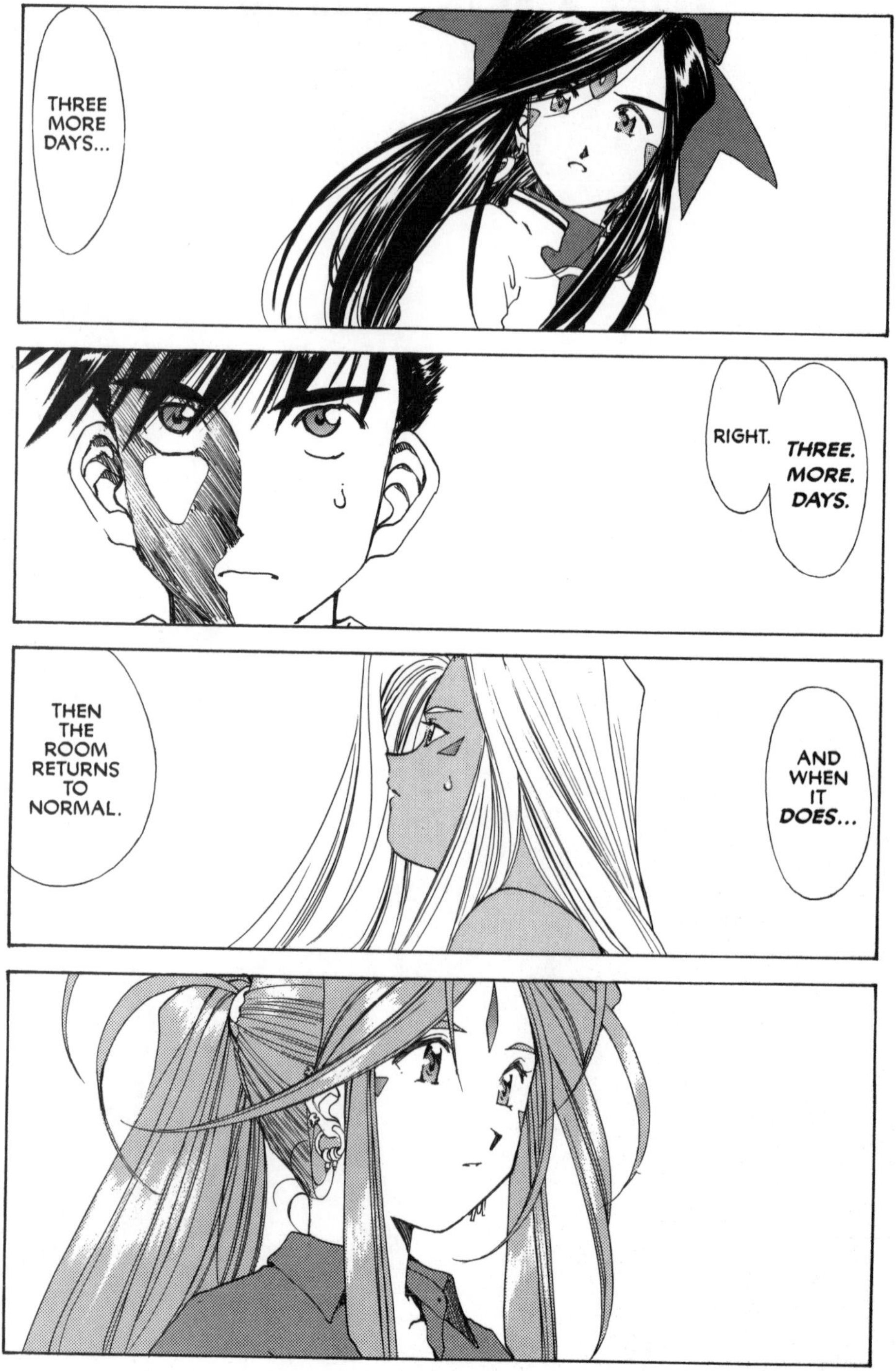
THREE MORE DAYS...
RIGHT. ***THREE. MORE. DAYS.***
THEN THE ROOM RETURNS TO NORMAL.
AND WHEN IT ***DOES...***

MISSING TIME

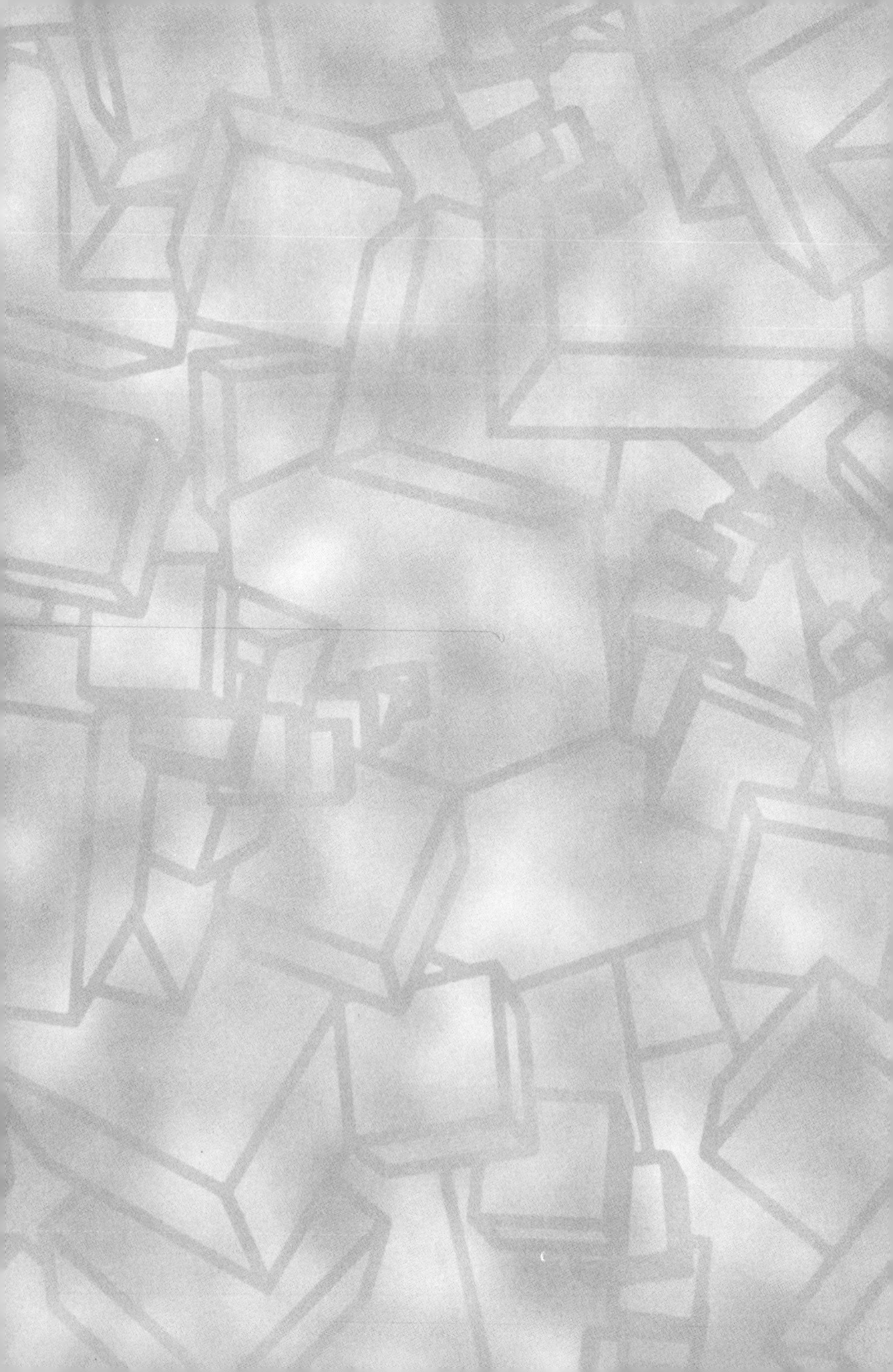

?
MNCH MNCH

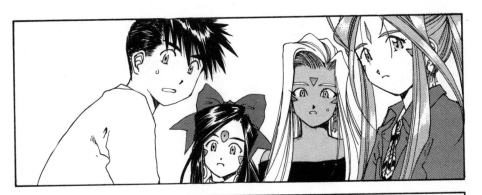

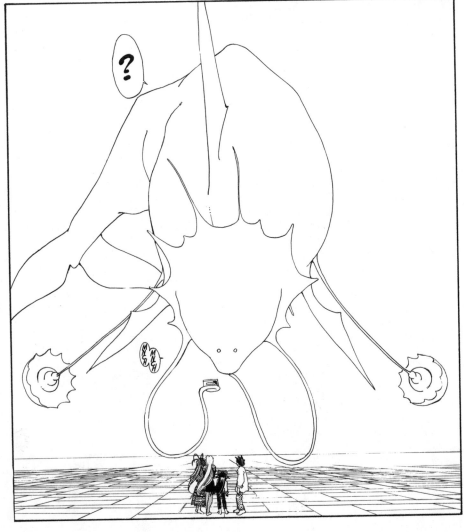

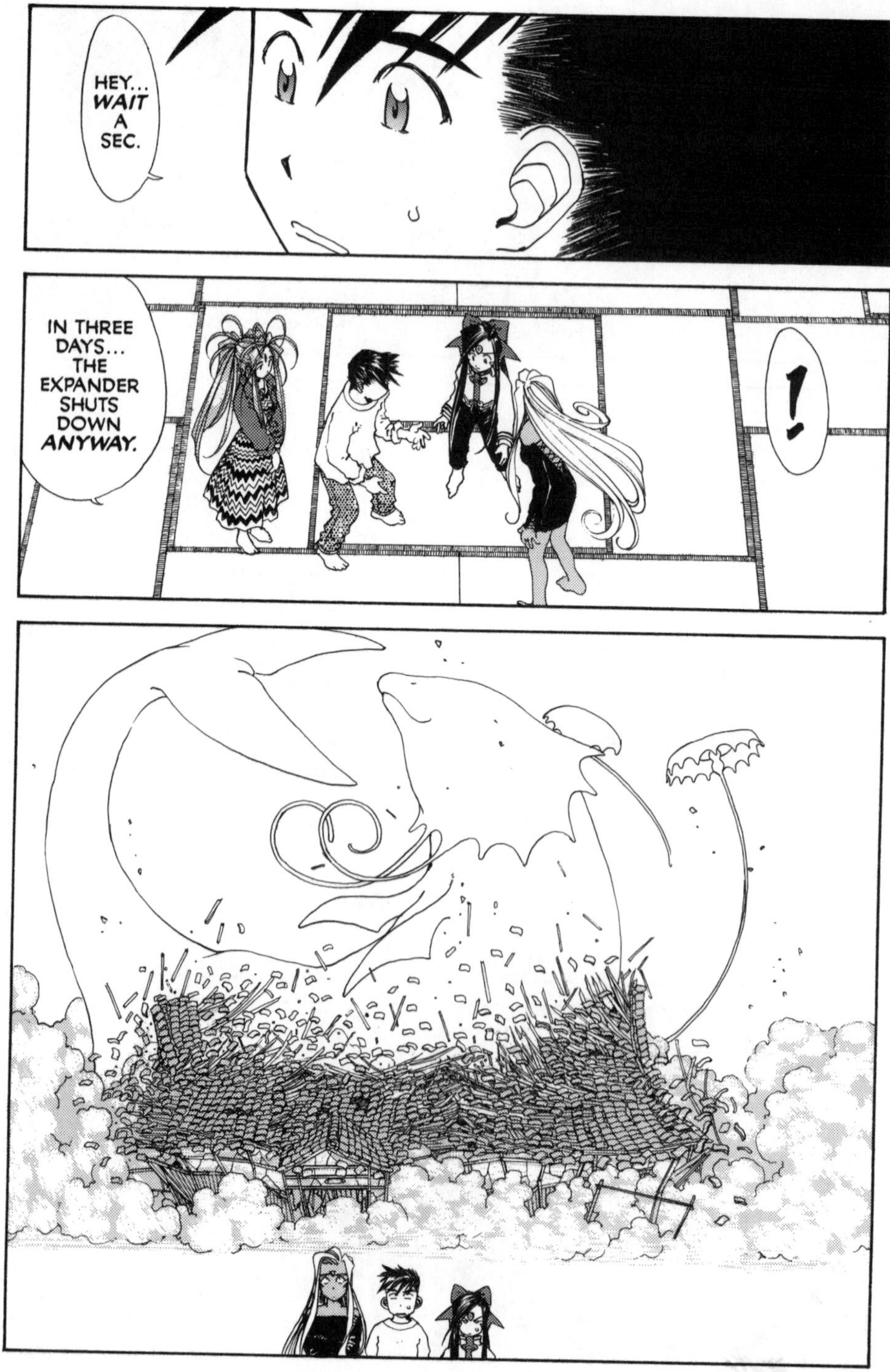
HEY... WAIT A SEC.
!
IN THREE DAYS... THE EXPANDER SHUTS DOWN ANYWAY.

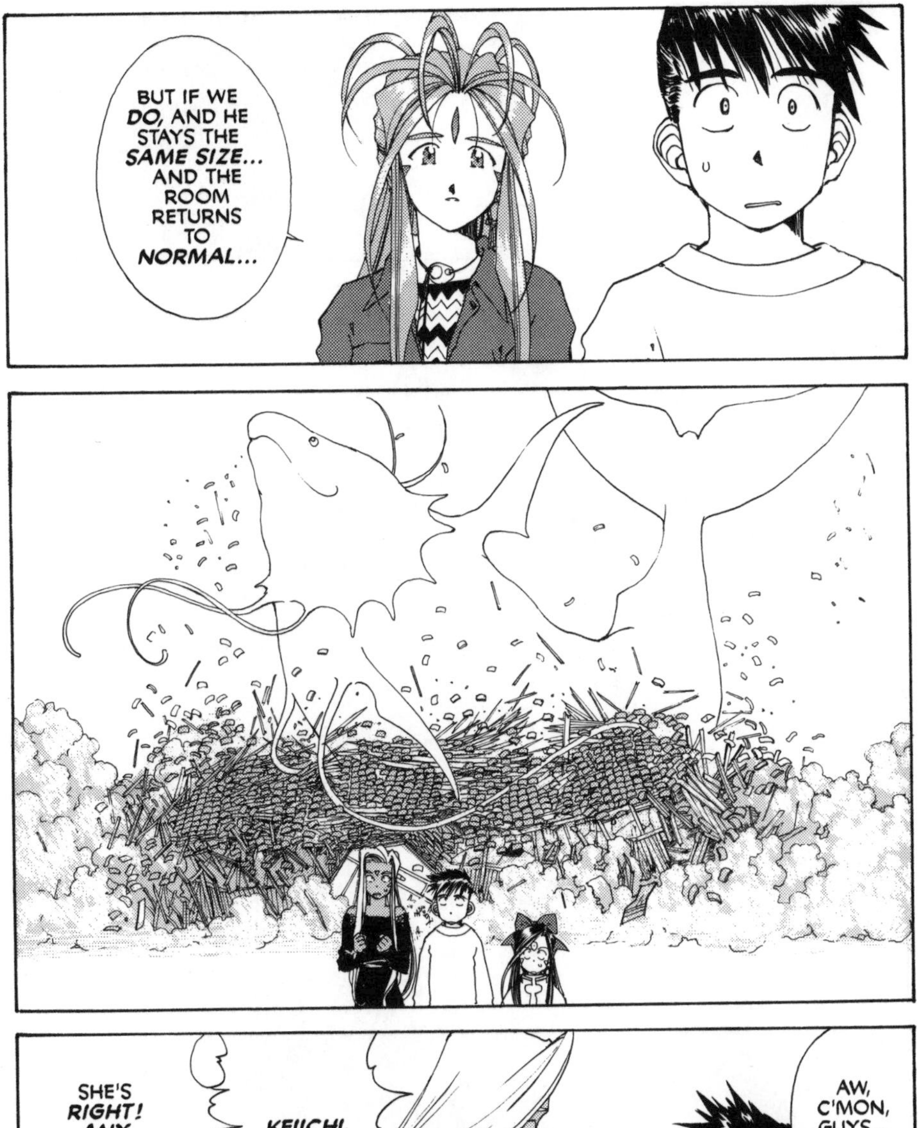
BUT IF WE *DO,* AND HE STAYS THE *SAME SIZE...* AND THE ROOM RETURNS TO *NORMAL...*
KEIICHI, YOU *IDIOT!*
SHE'S *RIGHT! ANY* DOOFUS COULD SEE *THAT!*
AW, C'MON, GUYS... GEEZ...

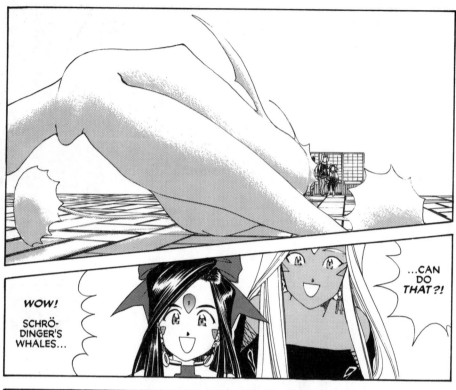

WOW!

SCHRÖ-DINGER'S WHALES...

...CAN DO THAT?!

I...I WANT THE TV!

I WANT MY BOTTLE OF SAKE!

MNCH MNCH

COULDN'T WE JUST HAVE HIM RESET THE SPACE EXPANDER...?

YES!! THAT WOULD SOLVE EVERYTHING!

KEIICHI! YOU GENIUS!

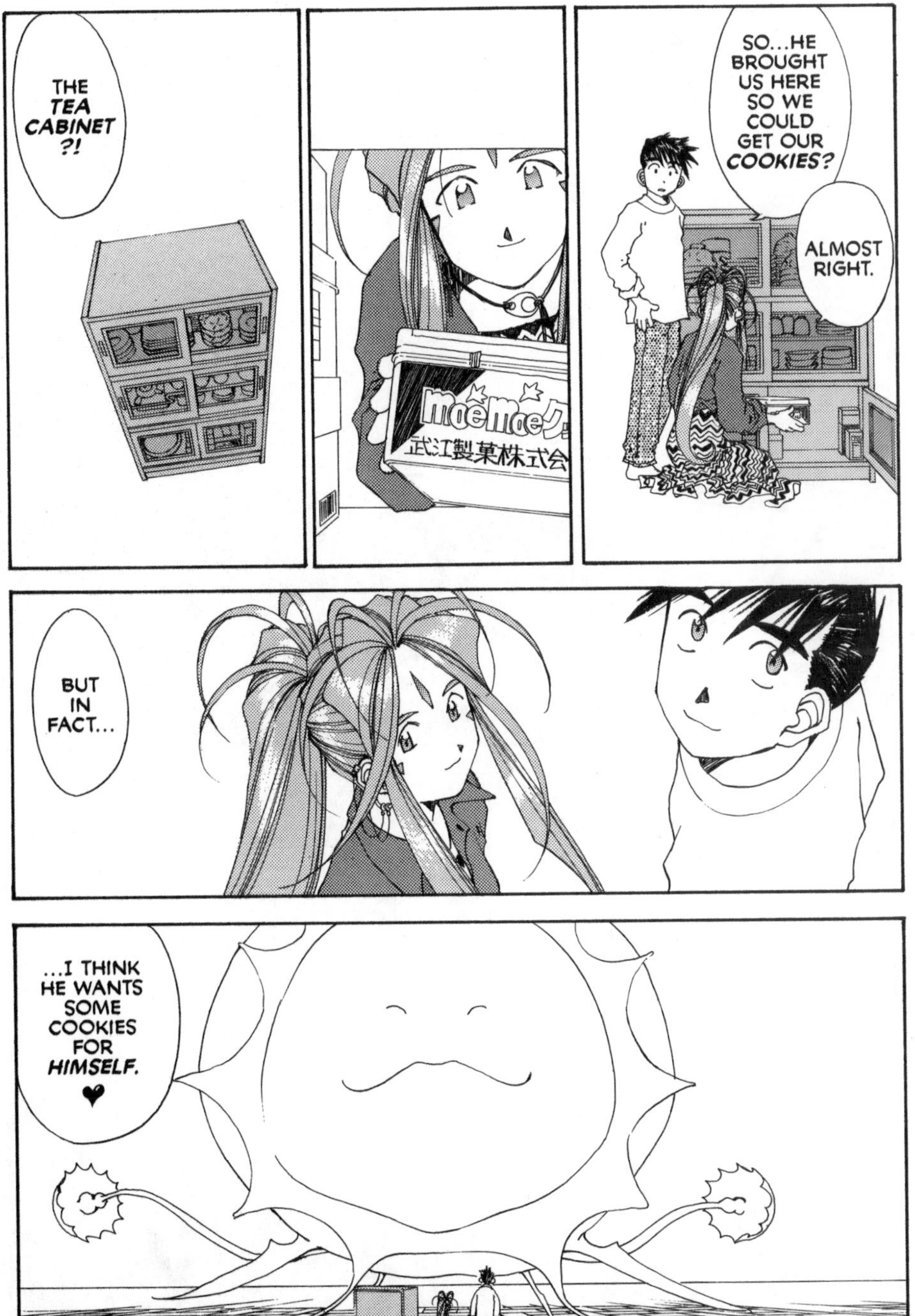
THE *TEA CABINET* ?!
SO...HE BROUGHT US HERE SO WE COULD GET OUR *COOKIES?*
ALMOST RIGHT.
BUT IN FACT...
...I THINK HE WANTS SOME COOKIES FOR *HIMSELF.* ❤

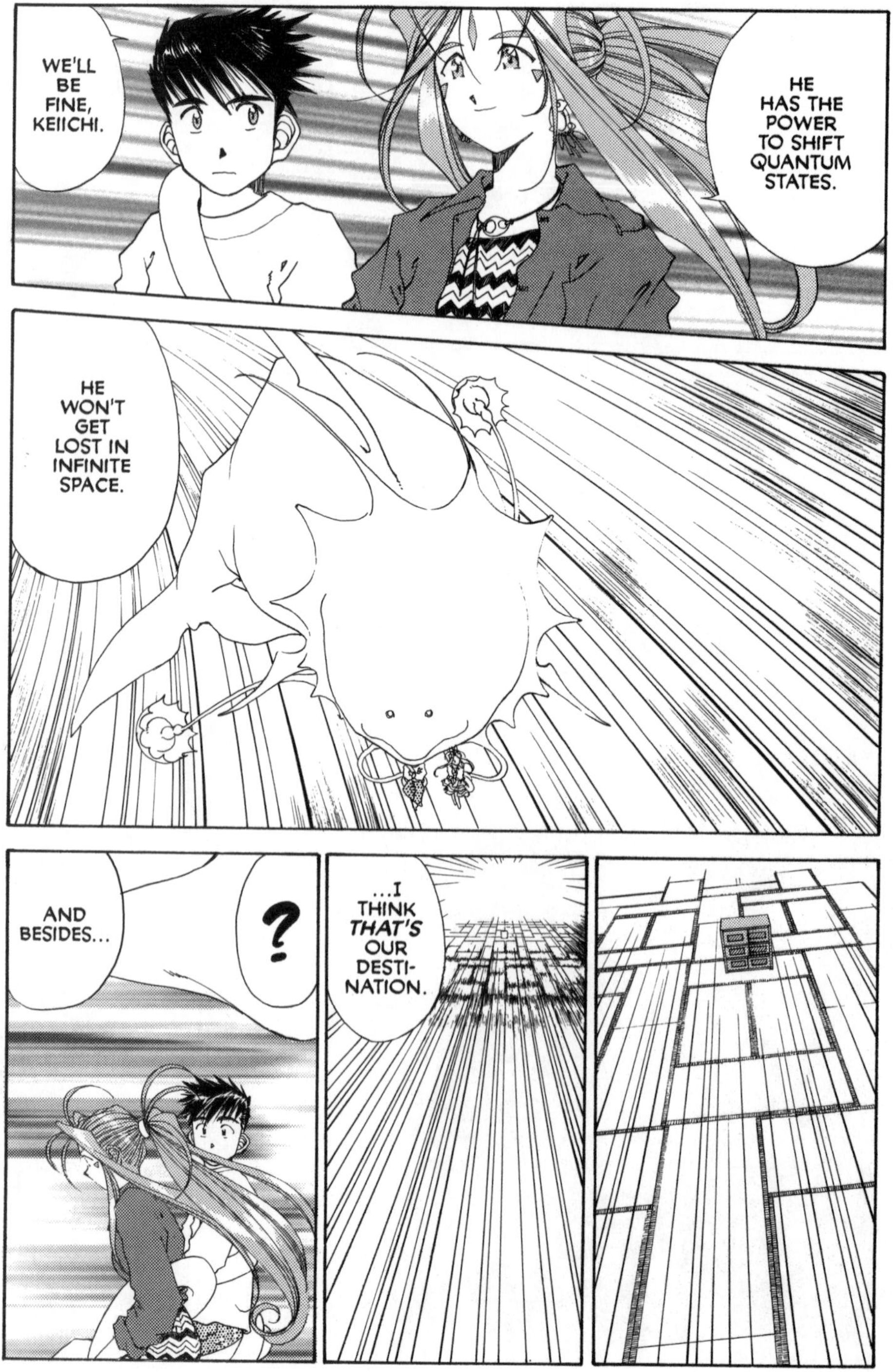
WE'LL BE FINE, KEIICHI.
HE HAS THE POWER TO SHIFT QUANTUM STATES.
HE WON'T GET LOST IN INFINITE SPACE.
AND BESIDES...
?
...I THINK *THAT'S* OUR DESTINATION.

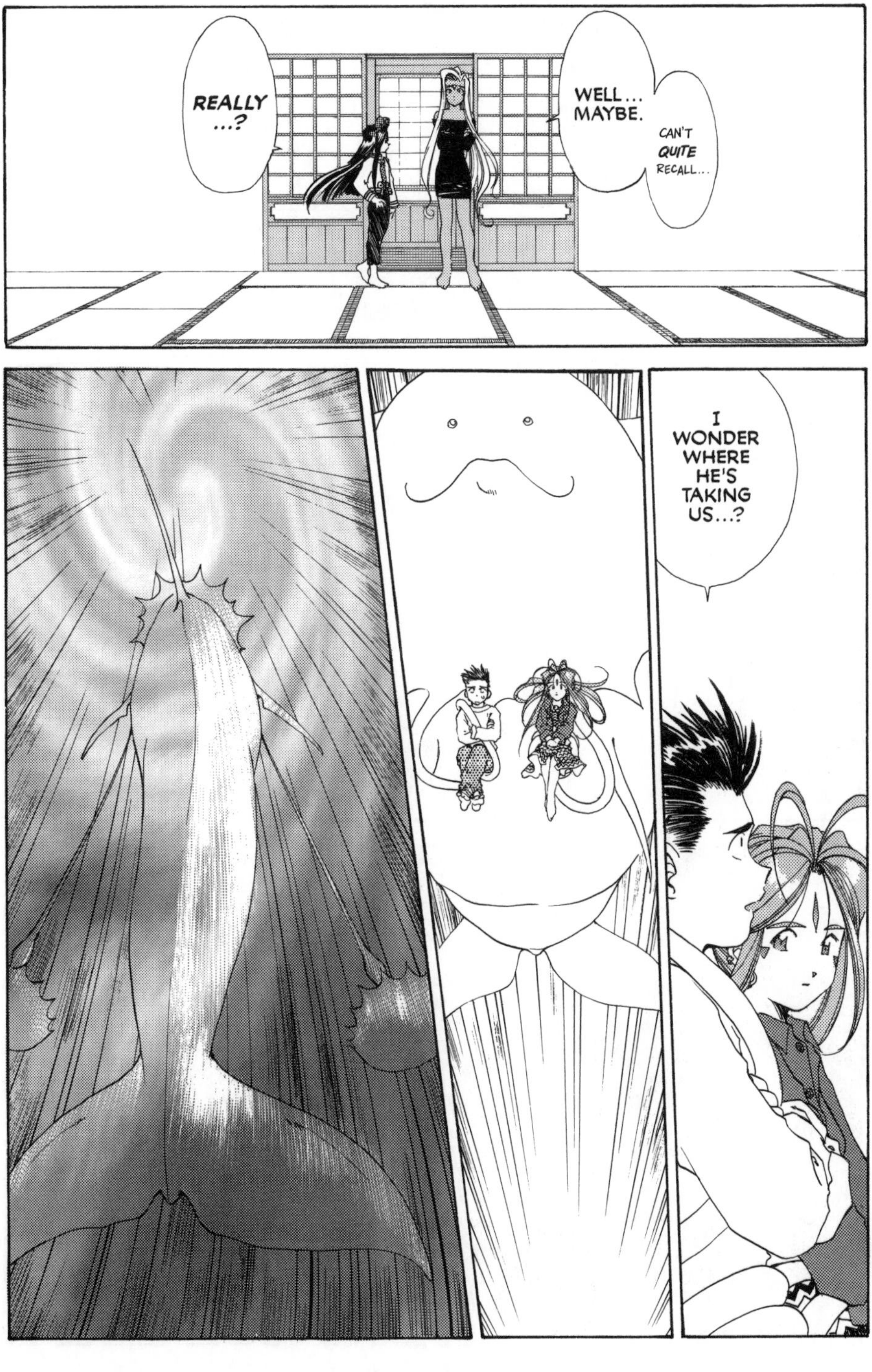
REALLY ...?
WELL... MAYBE.
CAN'T QUITE RECALL...
I WONDER WHERE HE'S TAKING US...?

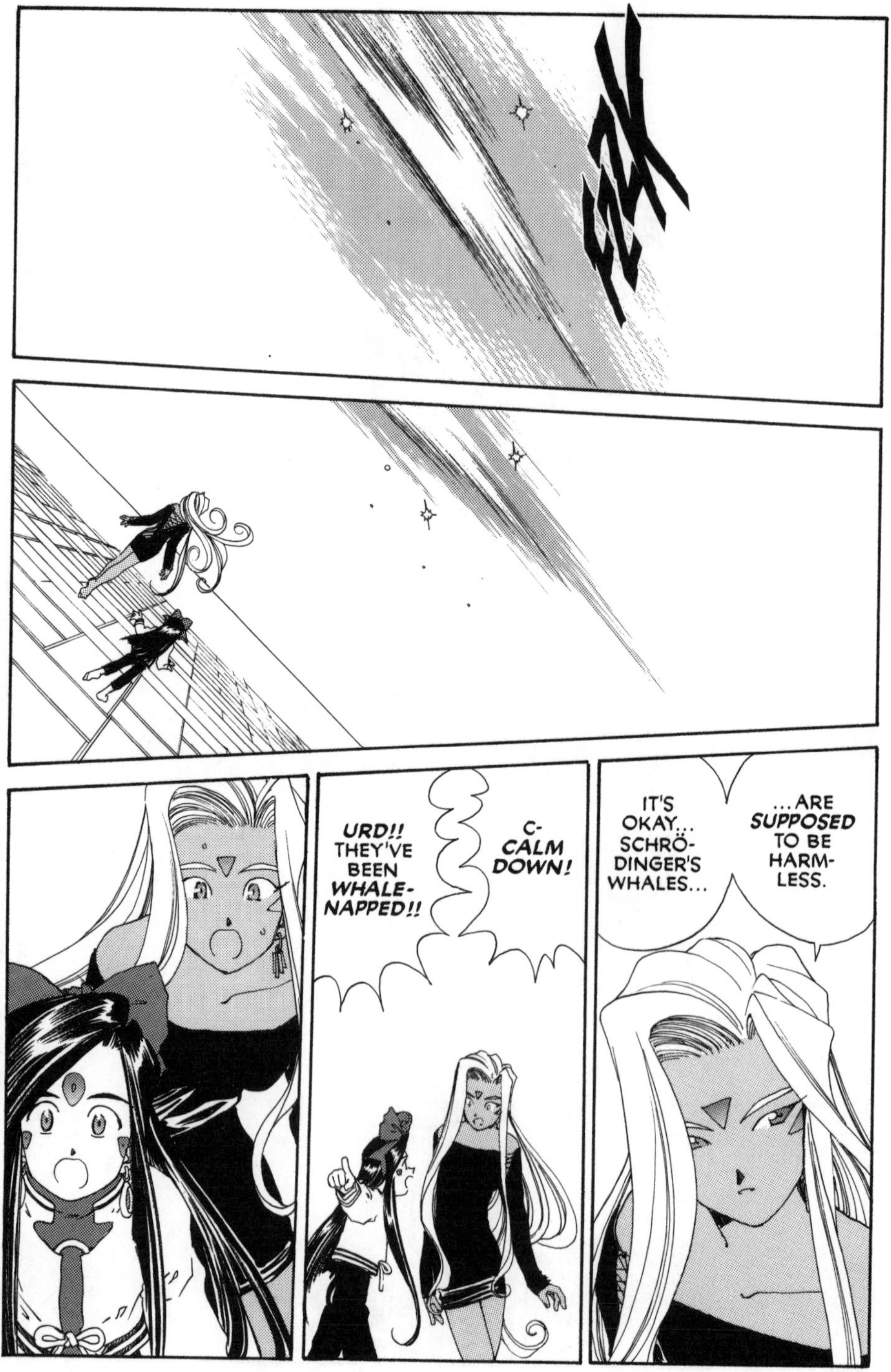
URD!! THEY'VE BEEN WHALE-NAPPED!!
C-CALM DOWN!
IT'S OKAY... SCHRÖDINGER'S WHALES...
...ARE SUPPOSED TO BE HARMLESS.

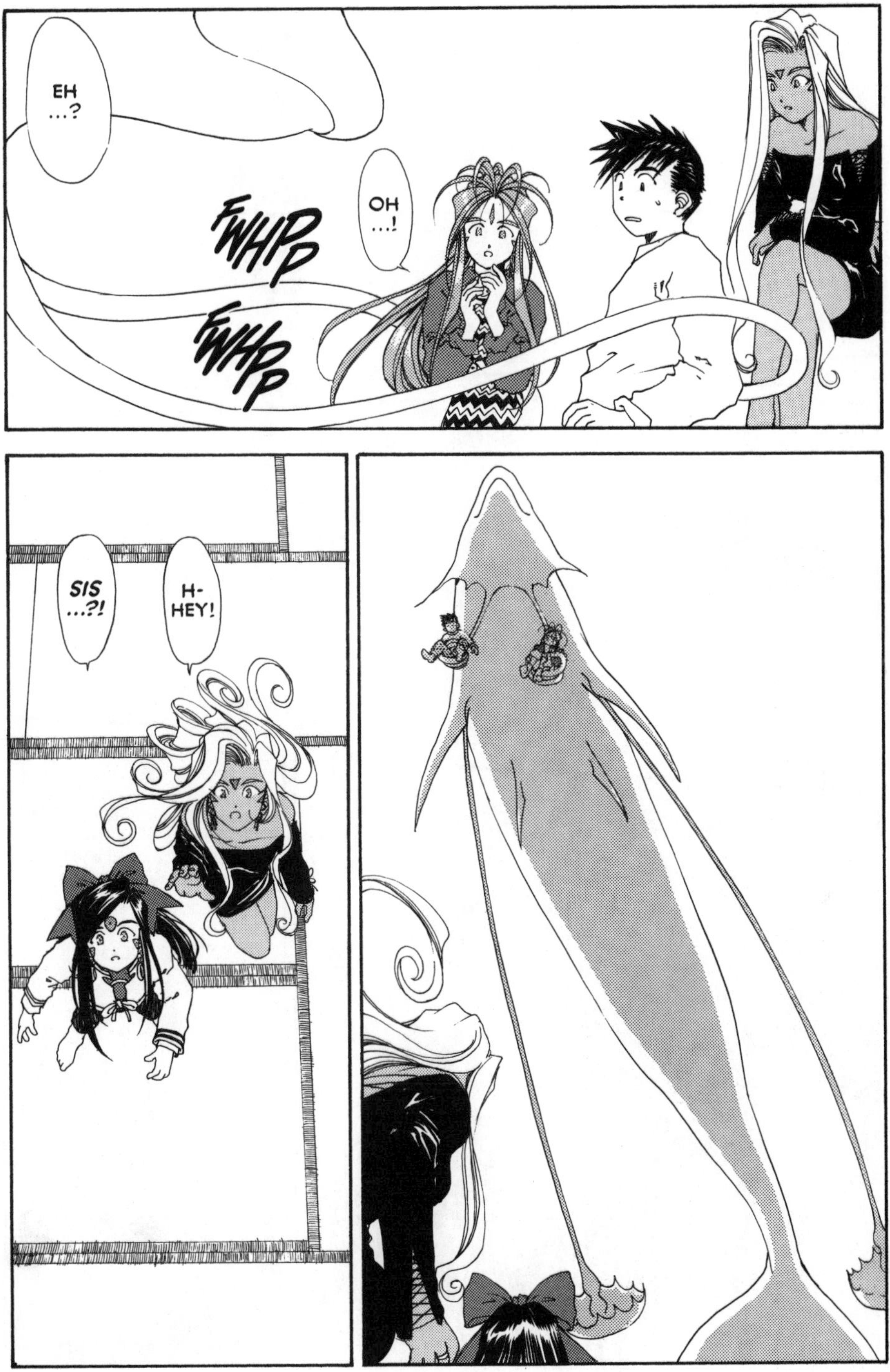
OH ...!
FWHPP
FWHPP
EH ...?
H-HEY!
SIS ...?!

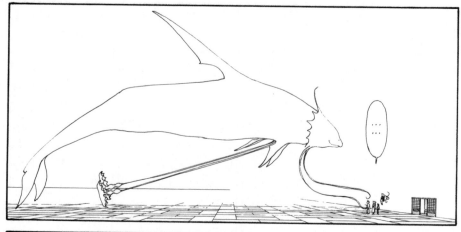

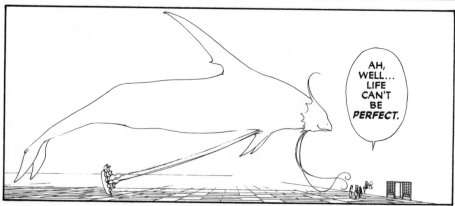

......
AH, WELL... LIFE CAN'T BE *PERFECT.*
...OUR COOKIES ARE OUT... *THERE,* SO WE WON'T HAVE SNACKS. IS THAT ALL RIGHT?
IF YOU'D LIKE, I'D *LOVE* TO OFFER YOU TEA. BUT I'M SORRY...

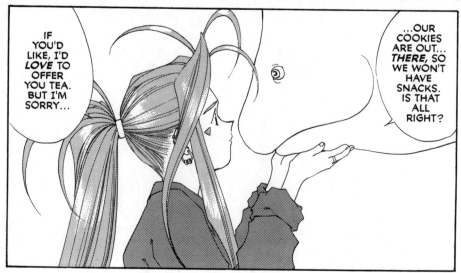

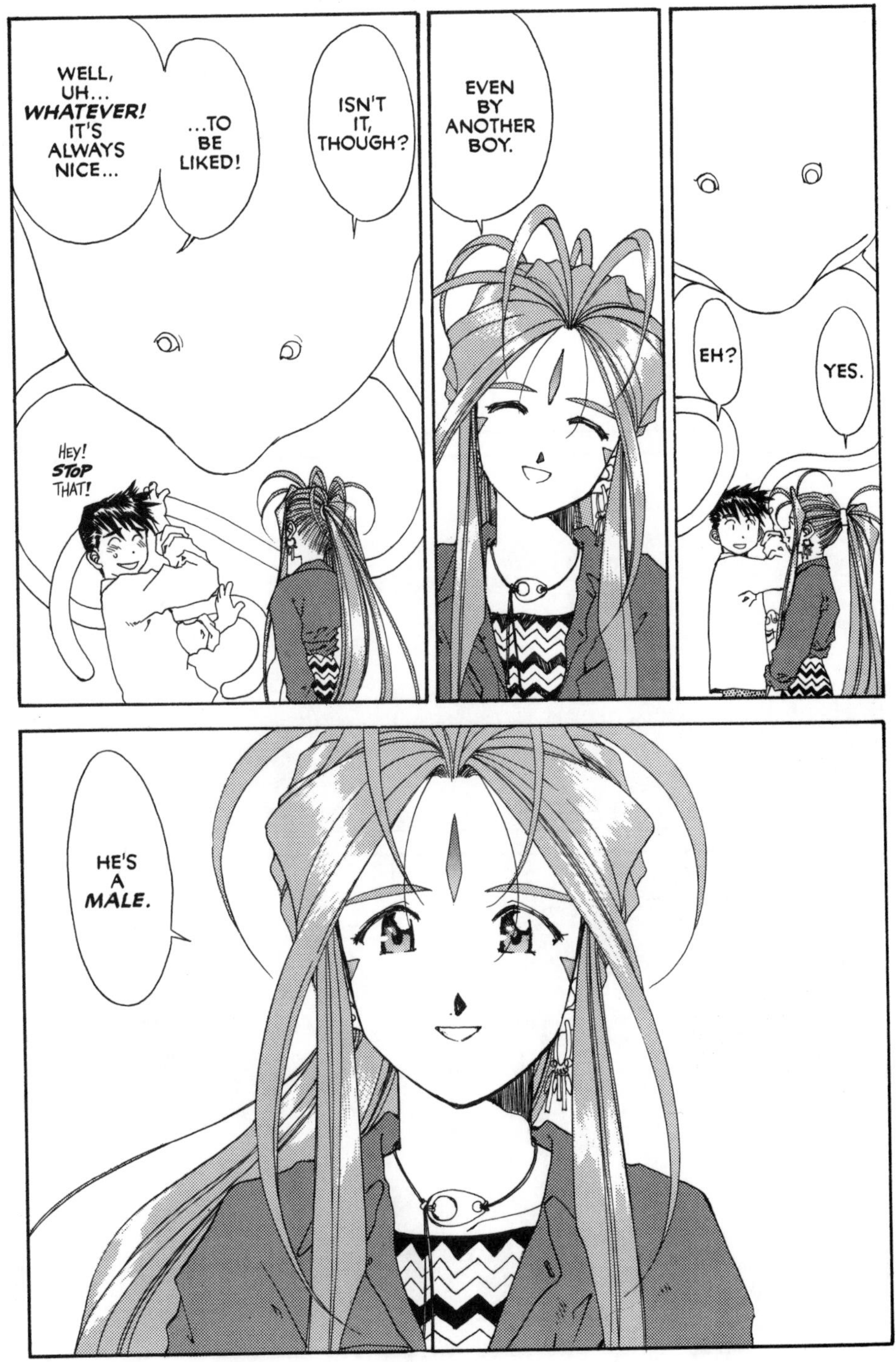
WELL, UH... WHATEVER! IT'S ALWAYS NICE...
...TO BE LIKED!
ISN'T IT, THOUGH?
HEY! STOP THAT!
EVEN BY ANOTHER BOY.
EH?
YES.
HE'S A MALE.

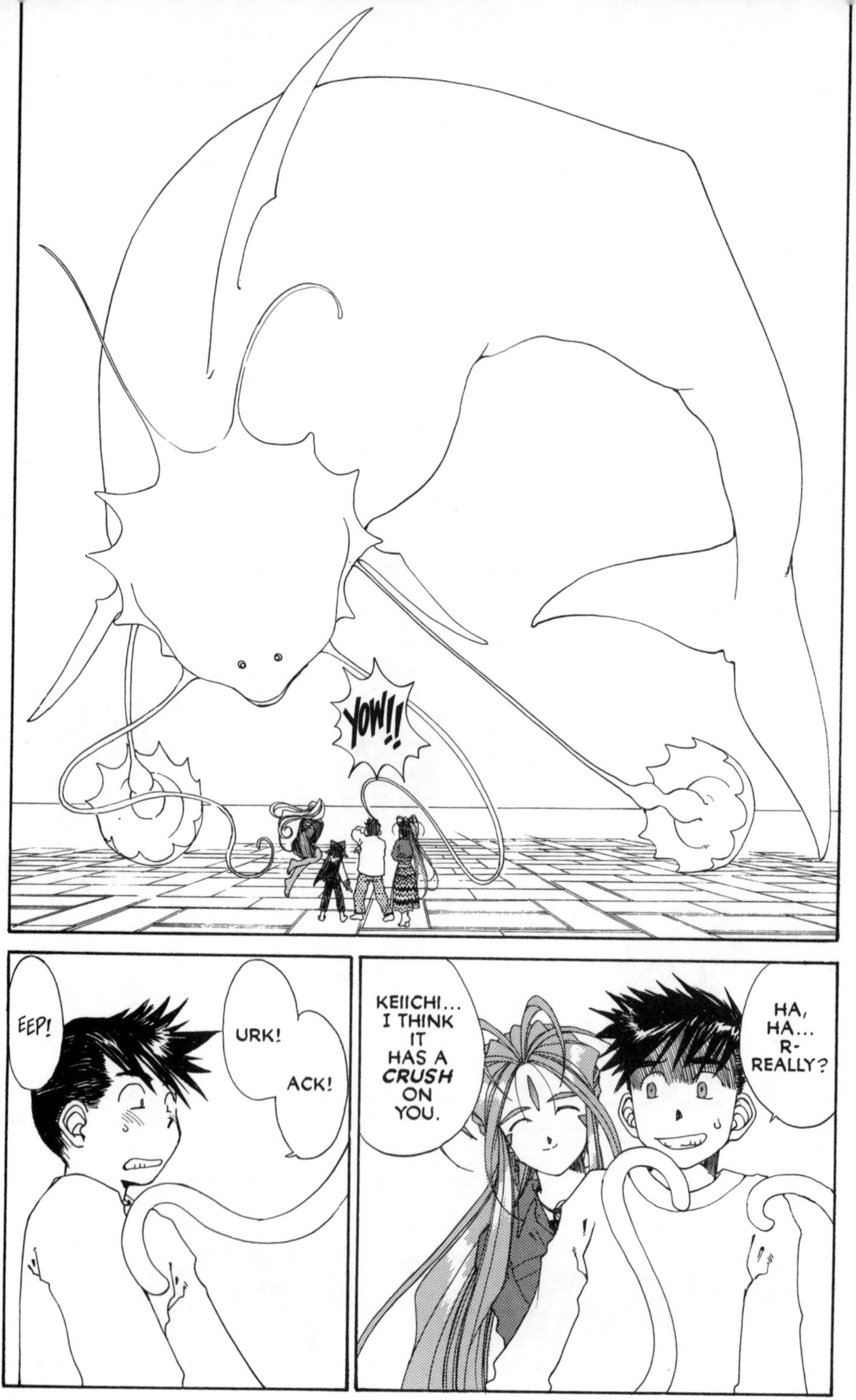
YOW!!
KEIICHI... I THINK IT HAS A CRUSH ON YOU.
HA, HA... R-REALLY?
URK!
ACK!
EEP!

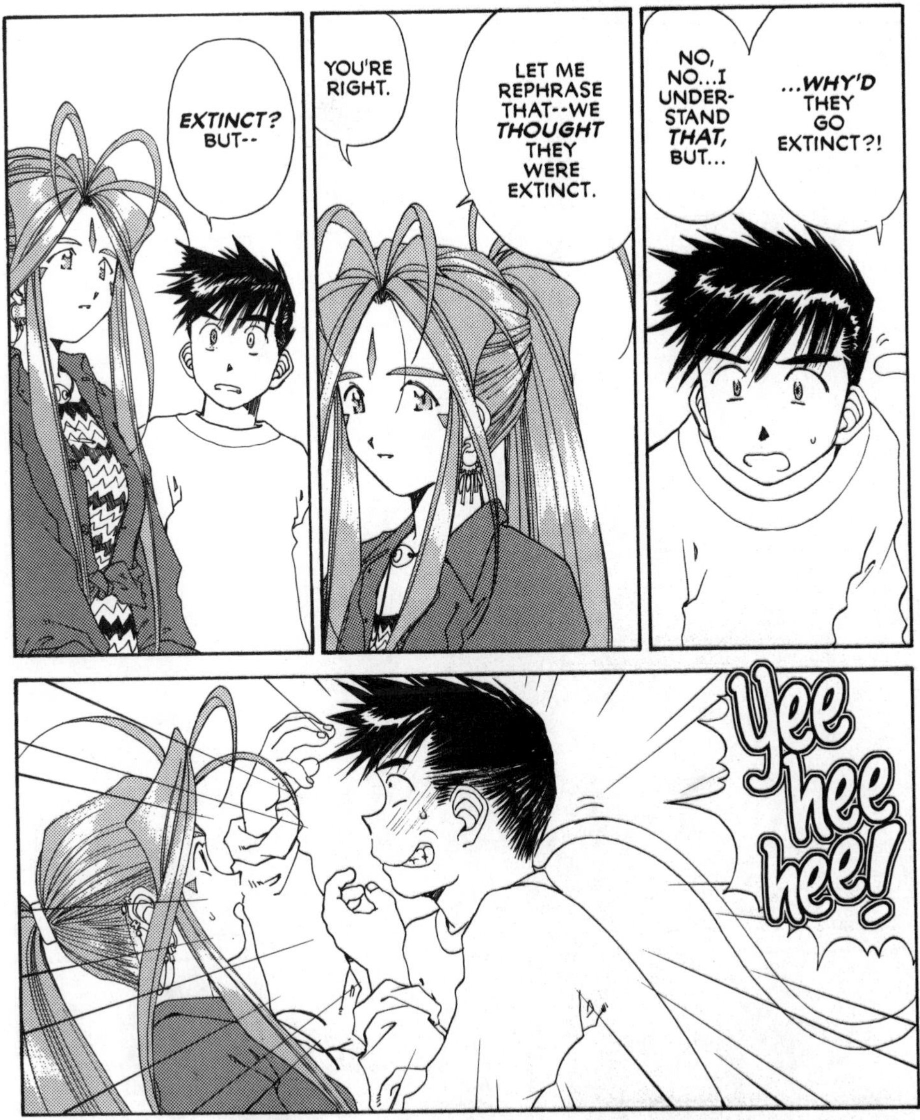
EXTINCT? BUT--
YOU'RE RIGHT.
LET ME REPHRASE THAT--WE *THOUGHT* THEY WERE EXTINCT.
NO, NO...I UNDERSTAND *THAT,* BUT...
...*WHY'D* THEY GO EXTINCT?!
Yee hee hee!
WHA... WHA...
WHO D-*DID* THAT?!

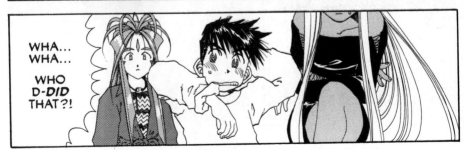

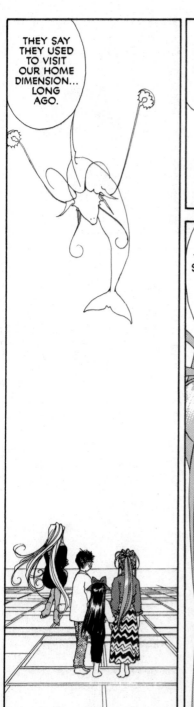

THEY SAY THEY USED TO VISIT OUR HOME DIMENSION... LONG AGO.

"LONG AGO" ...?

YES... BEFORE MY TIME.

YOU SEE... ....

THEY'RE EXTINCT.

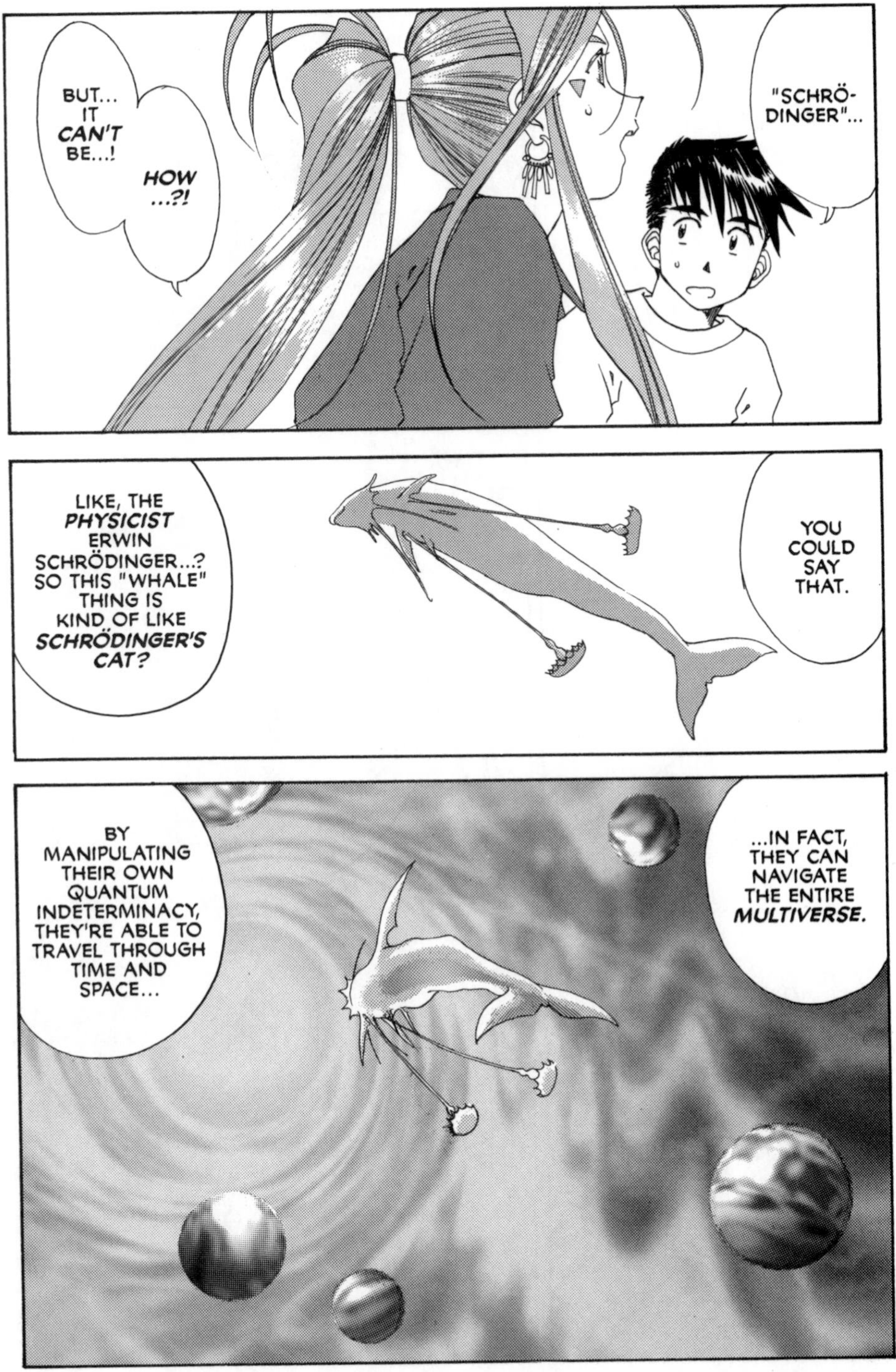
BUT... IT *CAN'T* BE...!
HOW ...?!
"SCHRÖ-DINGER"...
LIKE, THE *PHYSICIST* ERWIN SCHRÖDINGER...? SO THIS "WHALE" THING IS KIND OF LIKE *SCHRÖDINGER'S CAT?*
YOU COULD SAY THAT.
BY MANIPULATING THEIR OWN QUANTUM INDETERMINACY, THEY'RE ABLE TO TRAVEL THROUGH TIME AND SPACE...
...IN FACT, THEY CAN NAVIGATE THE ENTIRE *MULTIVERSE.*

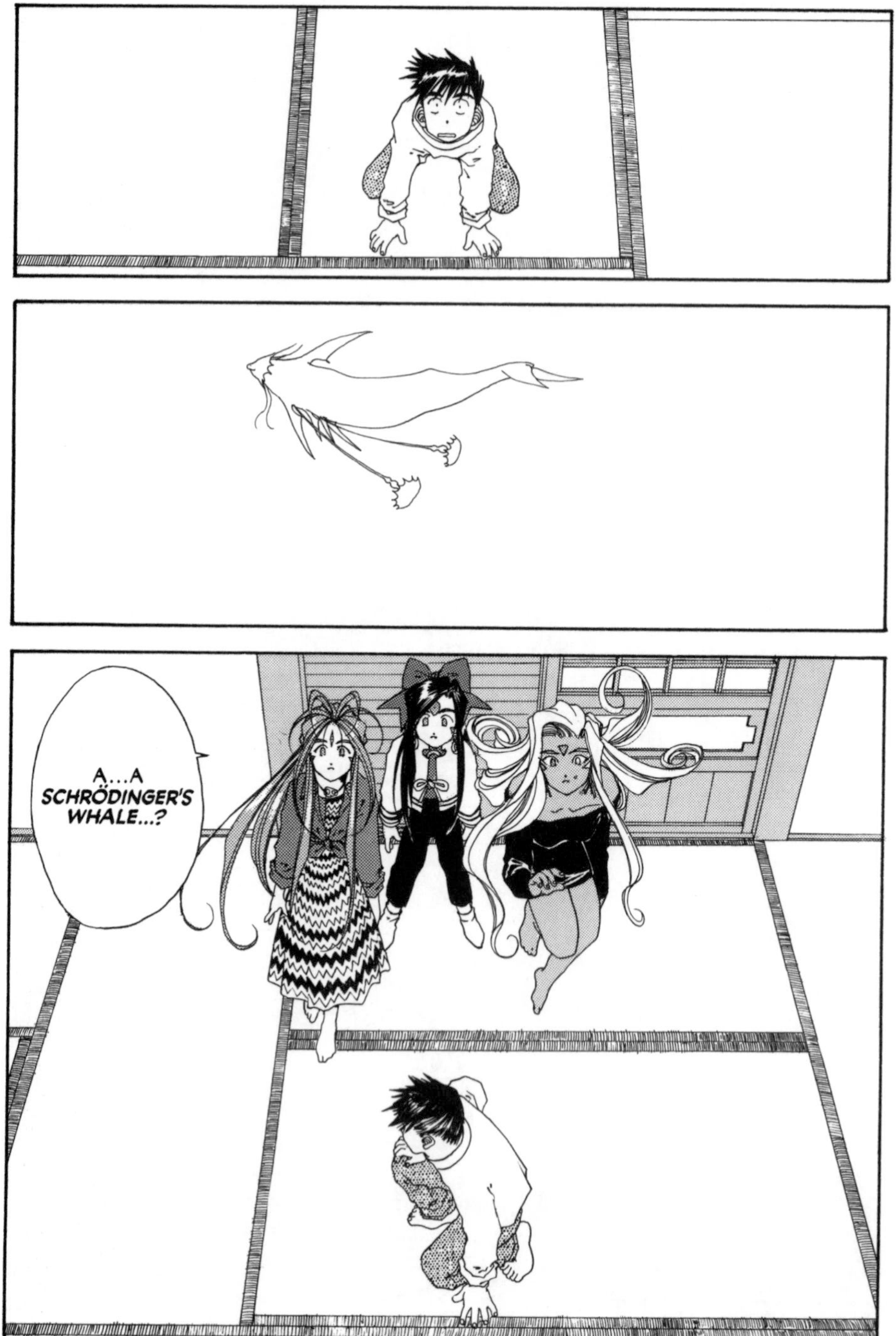
A...A SCHRÖDINGER'S WHALE...?

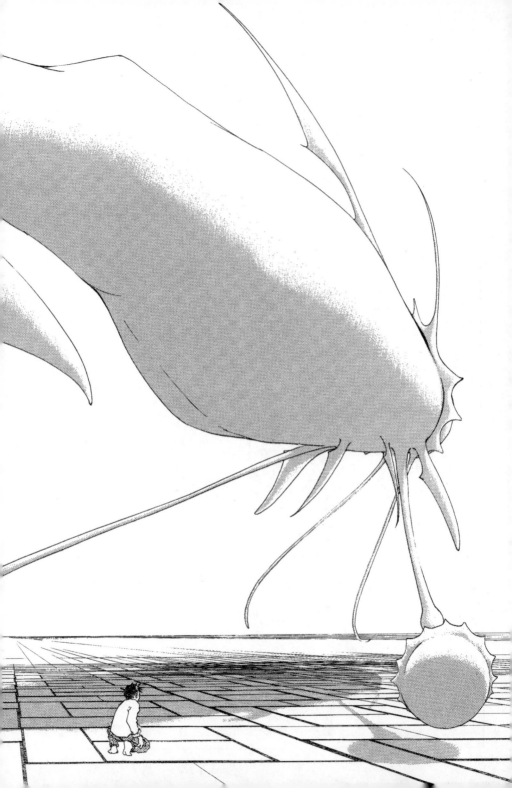

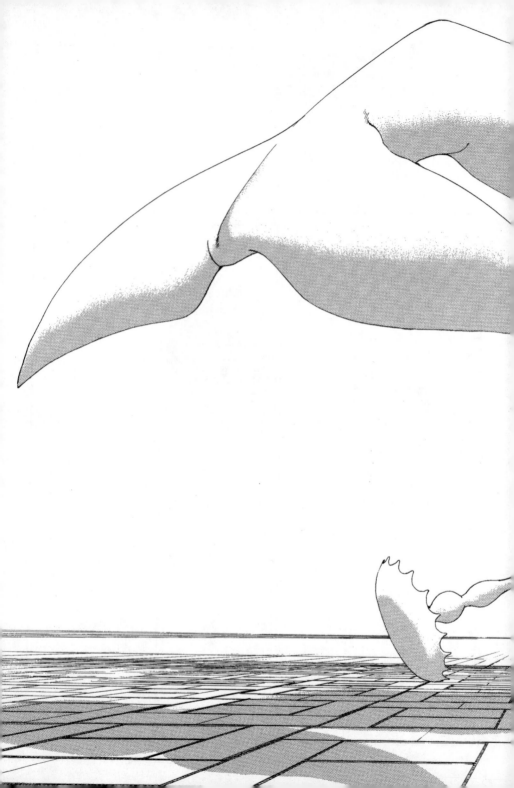

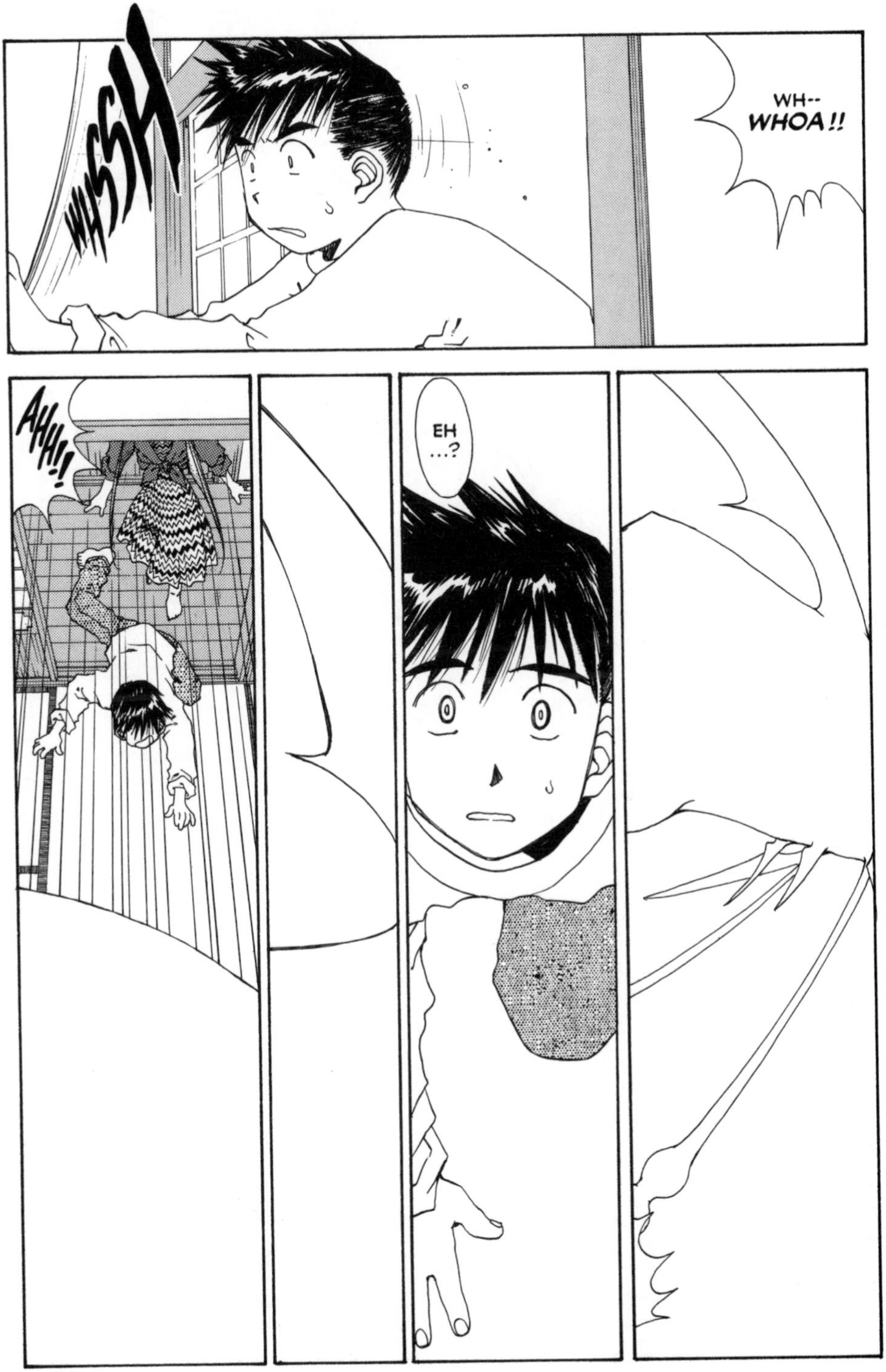
WH-- WHOA!!
WHSSH
EH ...?
AHH!!

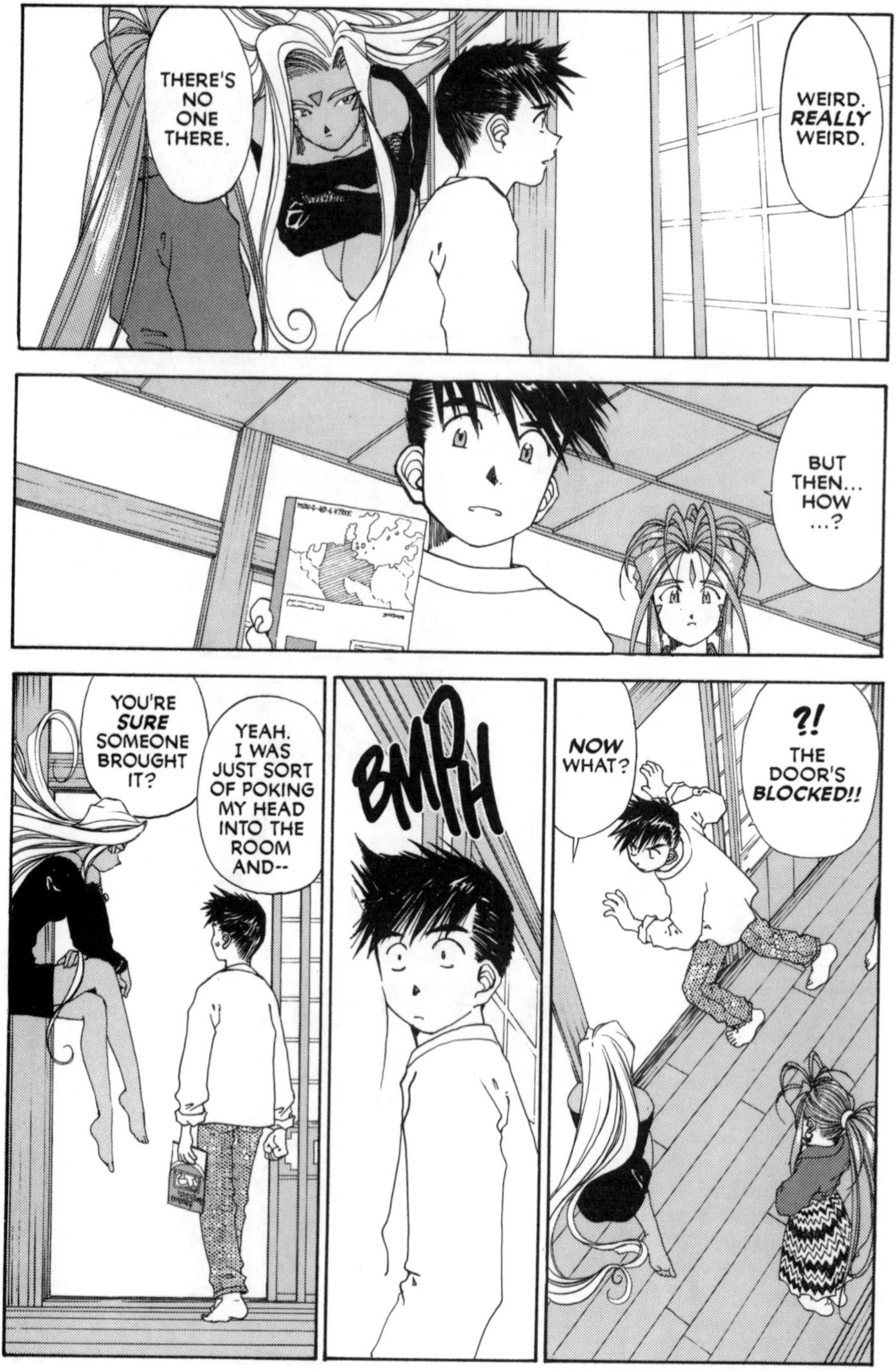
THERE'S NO ONE THERE.
WEIRD. REALLY WEIRD.
BUT THEN... HOW ...?
YOU'RE SURE SOMEONE BROUGHT IT?
YEAH. I WAS JUST SORT OF POKING MY HEAD INTO THE ROOM AND--
BMPH
NOW WHAT?
?! THE DOOR'S BLOCKED!!

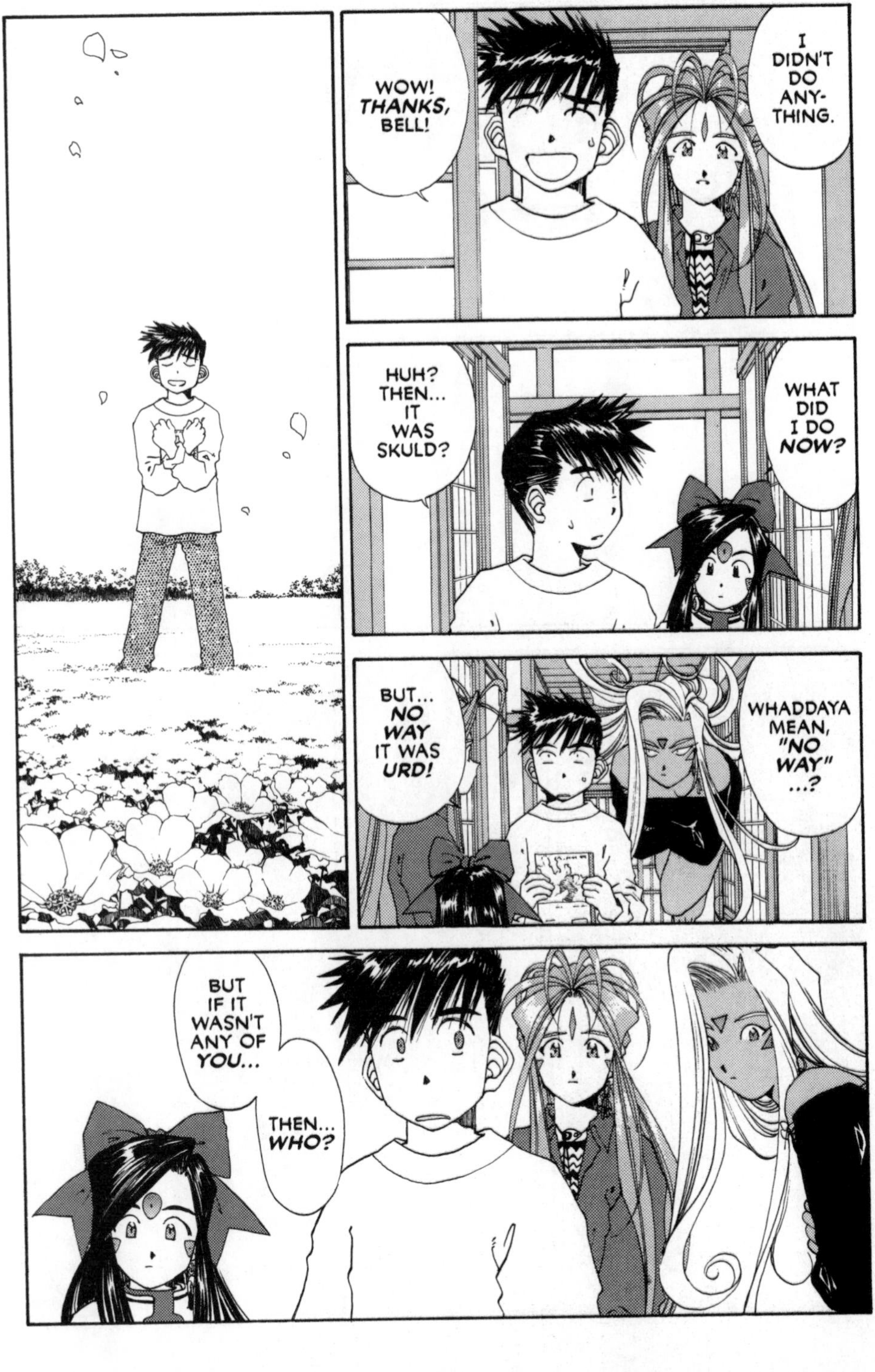
WOW! THANKS, BELL!
I DIDN'T DO ANY-THING.
HUH? THEN... IT WAS SKULD?
WHAT DID I DO NOW?
BUT... NO WAY IT WAS URD!
WHADDAYA MEAN, "NO WAY" ...?
BUT IF IT WASN'T ANY OF YOU...
THEN... WHO?

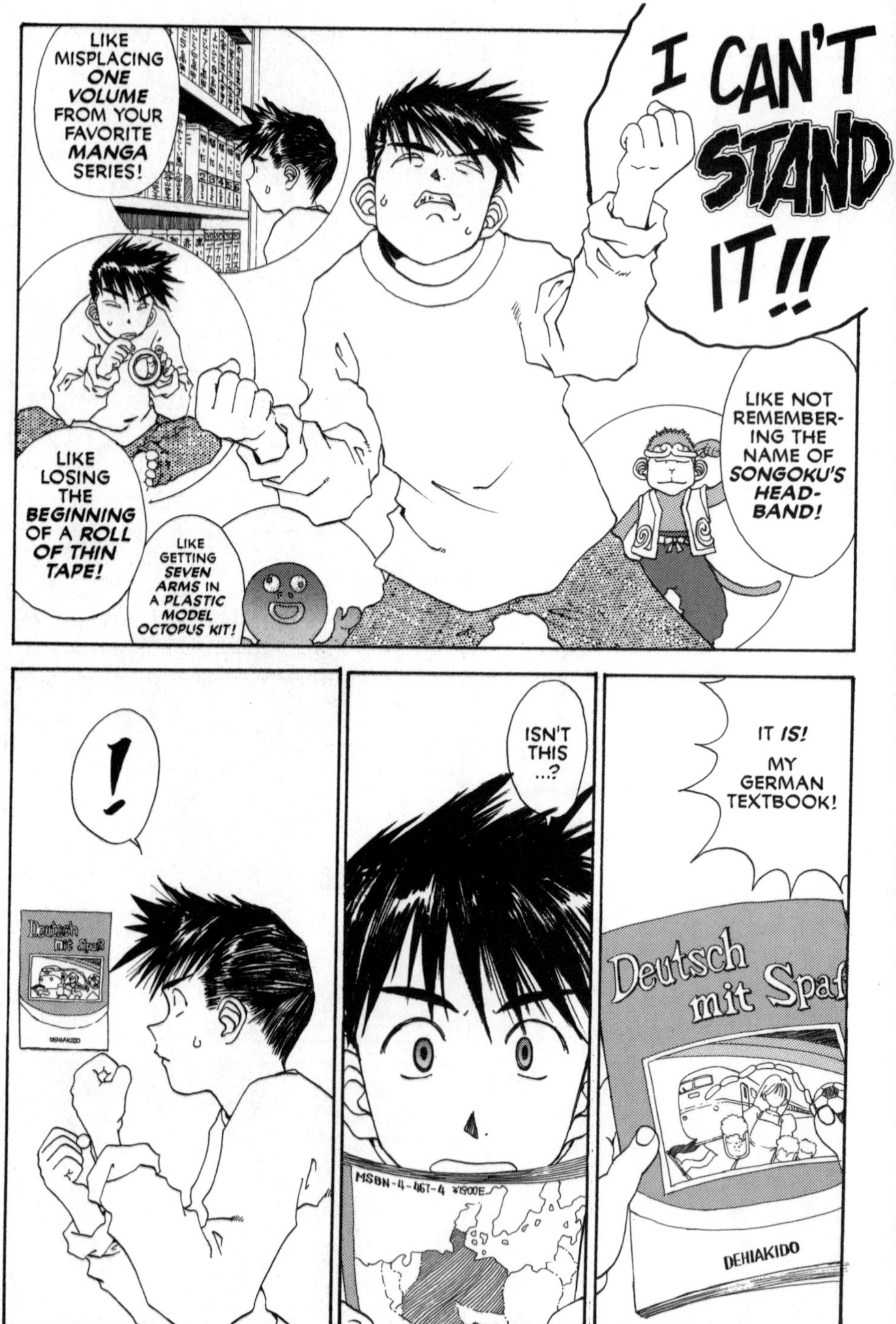
LIKE MISPLACING ONE VOLUME FROM YOUR FAVORITE MANGA SERIES!
LIKE LOSING THE BEGINNING OF A ROLL OF THIN TAPE!
LIKE GETTING SEVEN ARMS IN A PLASTIC MODEL OCTOPUS KIT!
I CAN'T STAND IT!!
LIKE NOT REMEMBERING THE NAME OF SONGOKU'S HEADBAND!
!
ISN'T THIS ...?
MSBN-4-467-4 ¥1900E
IT IS! MY GERMAN TEXTBOOK!
DEHIAKIDO

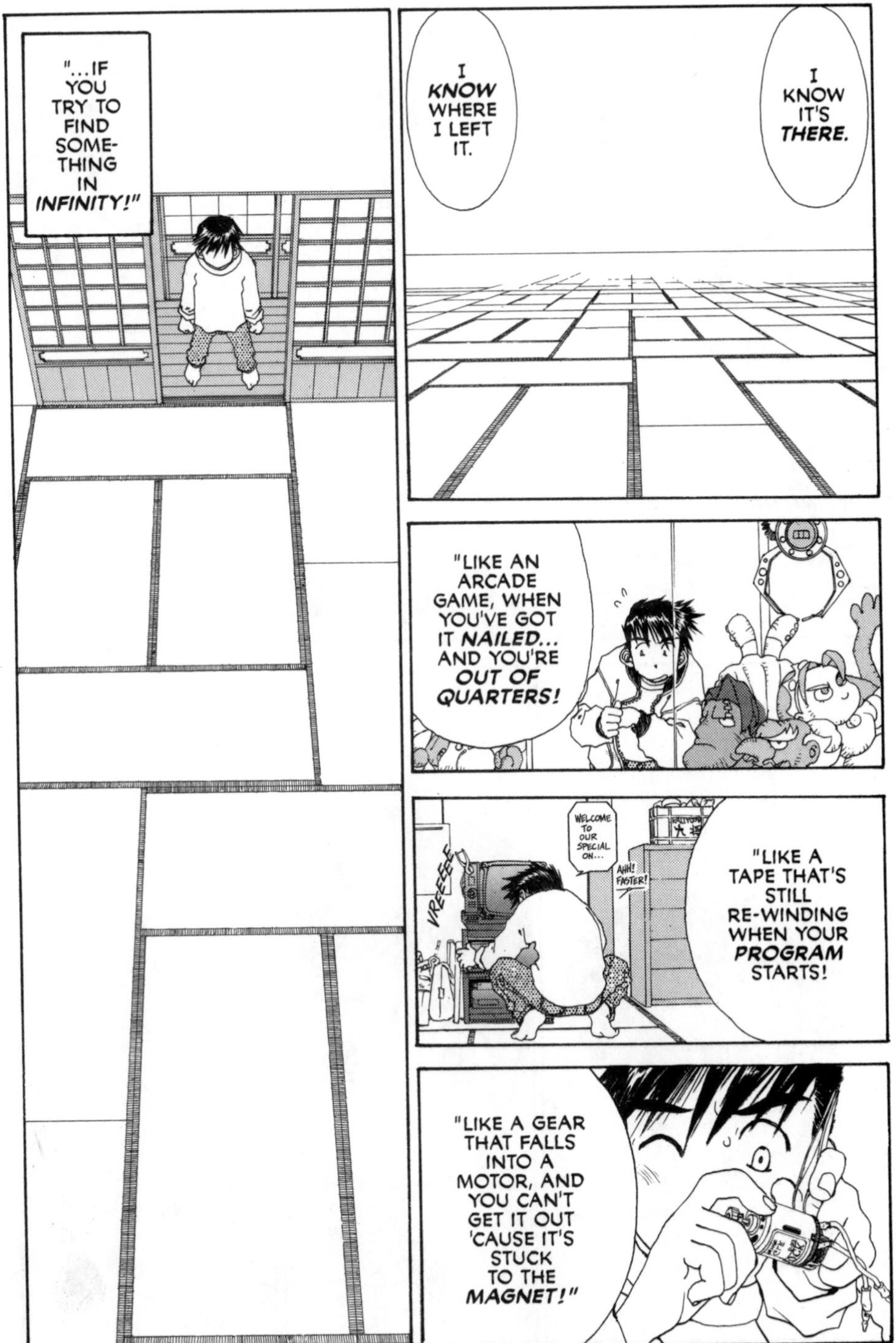
"...IF YOU TRY TO FIND SOME-THING IN INFINITY!"
I KNOW WHERE I LEFT IT.
I KNOW IT'S THERE.
"LIKE AN ARCADE GAME, WHEN YOU'VE GOT IT NAILED... AND YOU'RE OUT OF QUARTERS!
VREEEEE
WELCOME TO OUR SPECIAL ON...
AHH! FASTER!
"LIKE A TAPE THAT'S STILL RE-WINDING WHEN YOUR PROGRAM STARTS!
"LIKE A GEAR THAT FALLS INTO A MOTOR, AND YOU CAN'T GET IT OUT 'CAUSE IT'S STUCK TO THE MAGNET!"

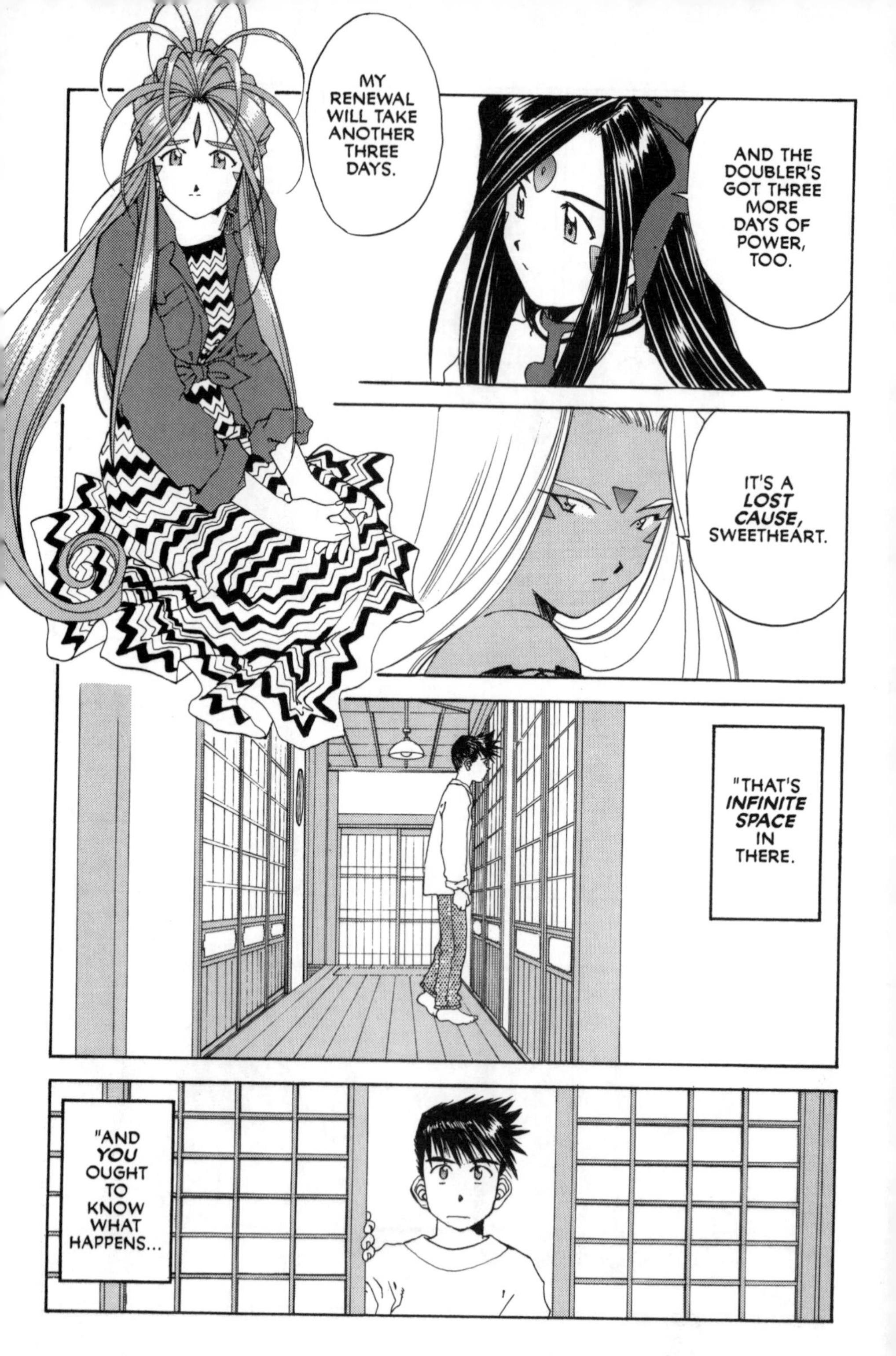
MY RENEWAL WILL TAKE ANOTHER THREE DAYS.
AND THE DOUBLER'S GOT THREE MORE DAYS OF POWER, TOO.
IT'S A *LOST CAUSE,* SWEETHEART.
"THAT'S *INFINITE SPACE* IN THERE.
"AND *YOU* OUGHT TO KNOW WHAT HAPPENS...

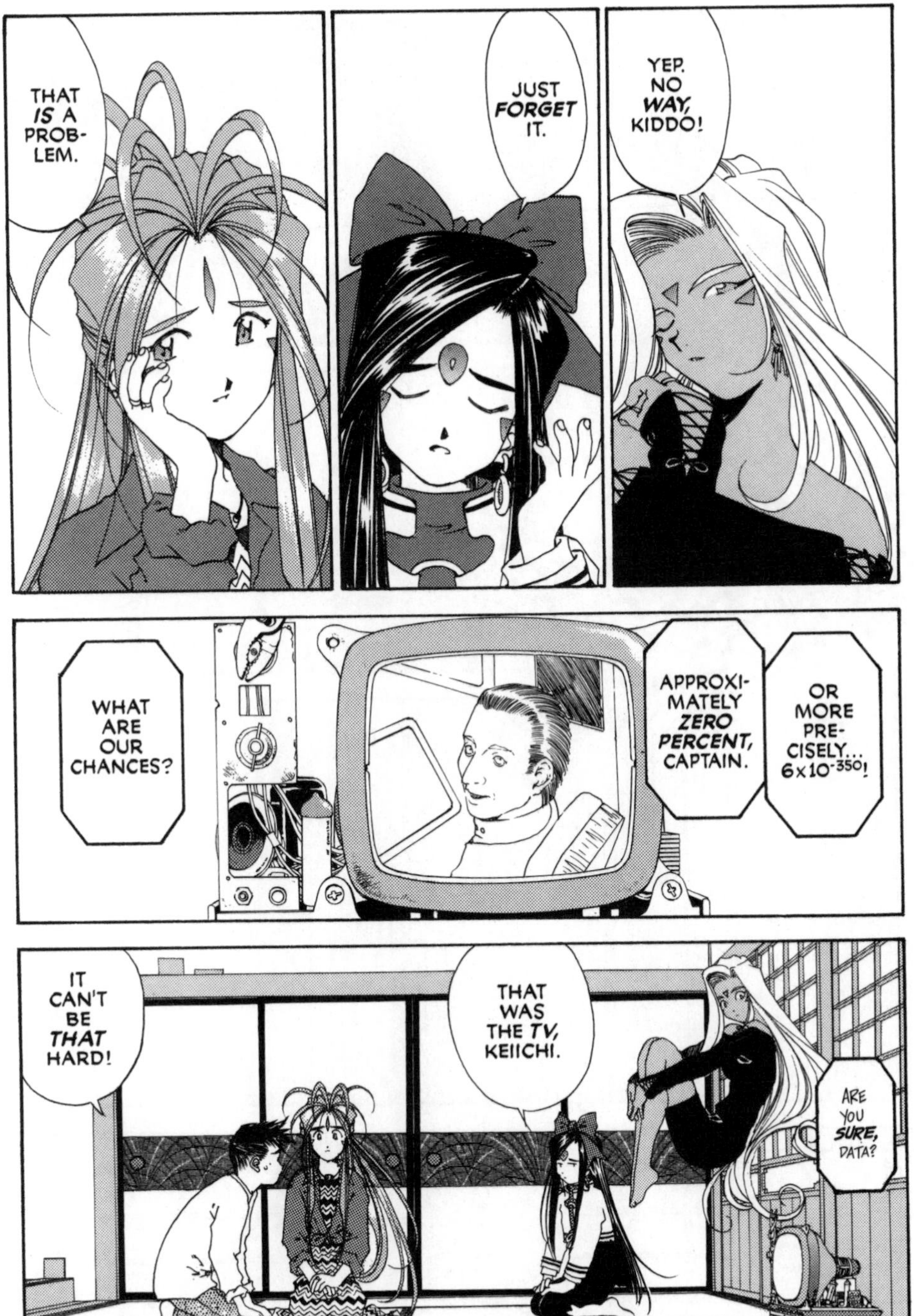
THAT *IS* A PROBLEM.
JUST *FORGET* IT.
YEP. NO *WAY,* KIDDO!
WHAT ARE OUR CHANCES?
APPROXIMATELY *ZERO PERCENT,* CAPTAIN.
OR MORE PRECISELY... 6×10^{-350}!
IT CAN'T BE *THAT* HARD!
THAT WAS THE *TV,* KEIICHI.
ARE YOU *SURE,* DATA?

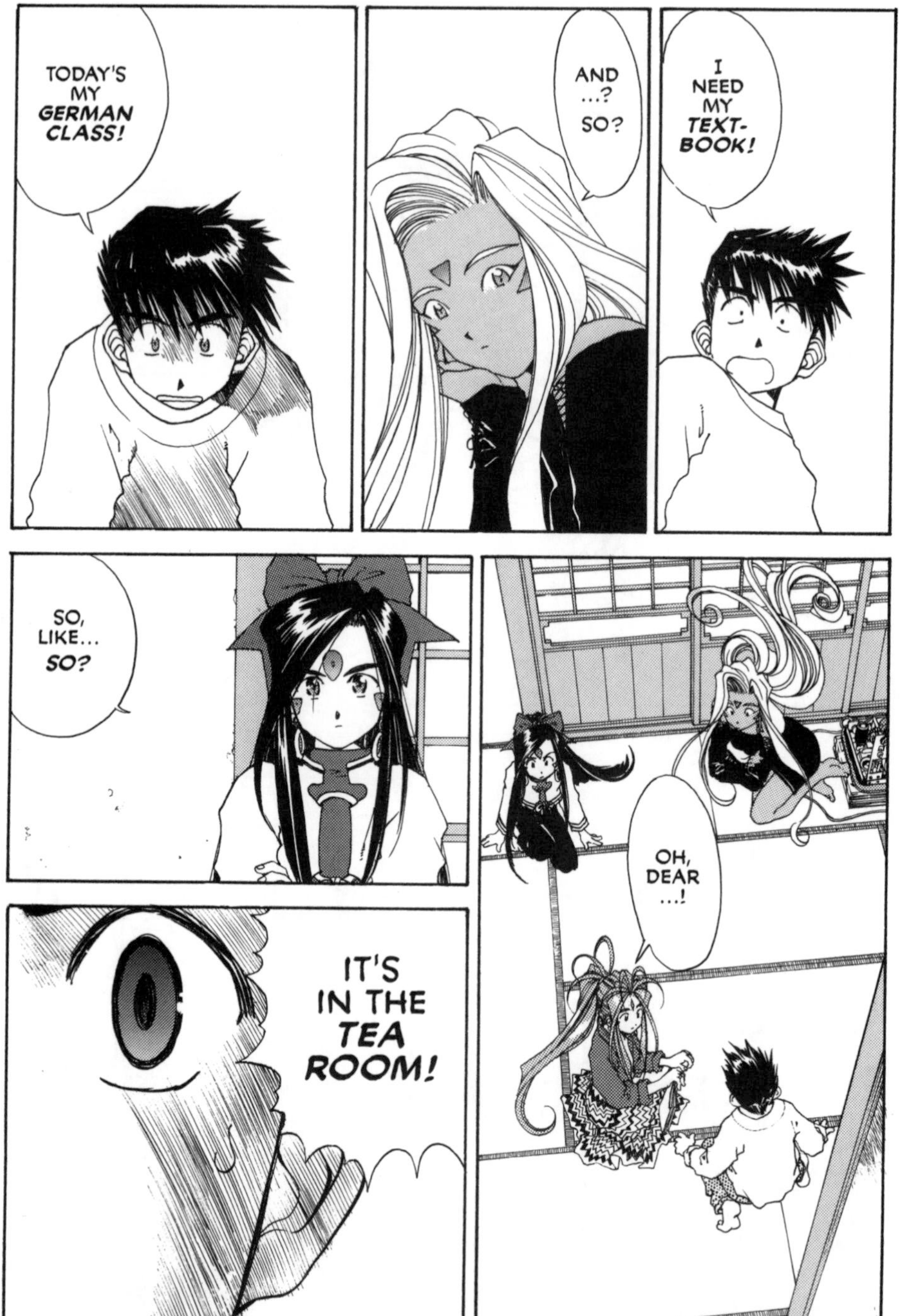
TODAY'S MY GERMAN CLASS!
AND ...? SO?
I NEED MY TEXT-BOOK!
SO, LIKE... SO?
IT'S IN THE TEA ROOM!
OH, DEAR ...!

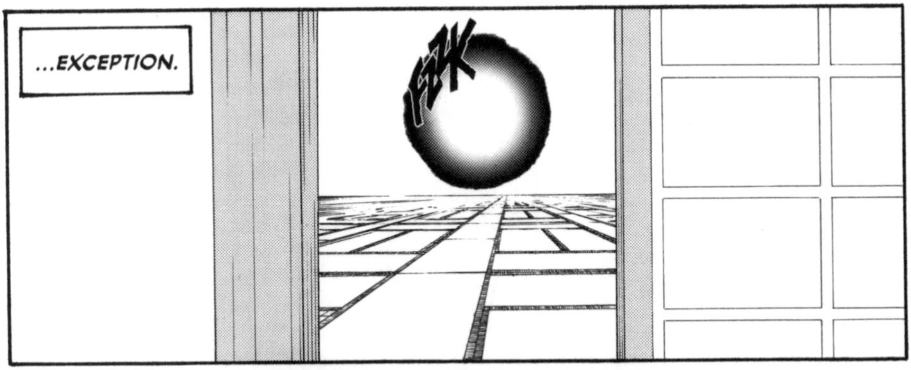
...EXCEPTION.
FZZK
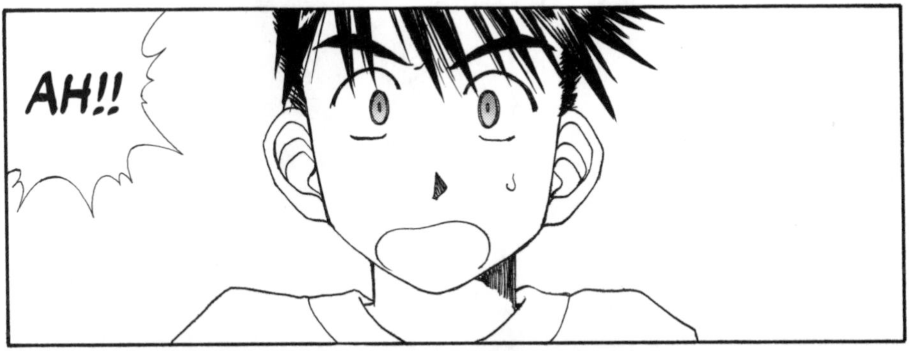
AH!!
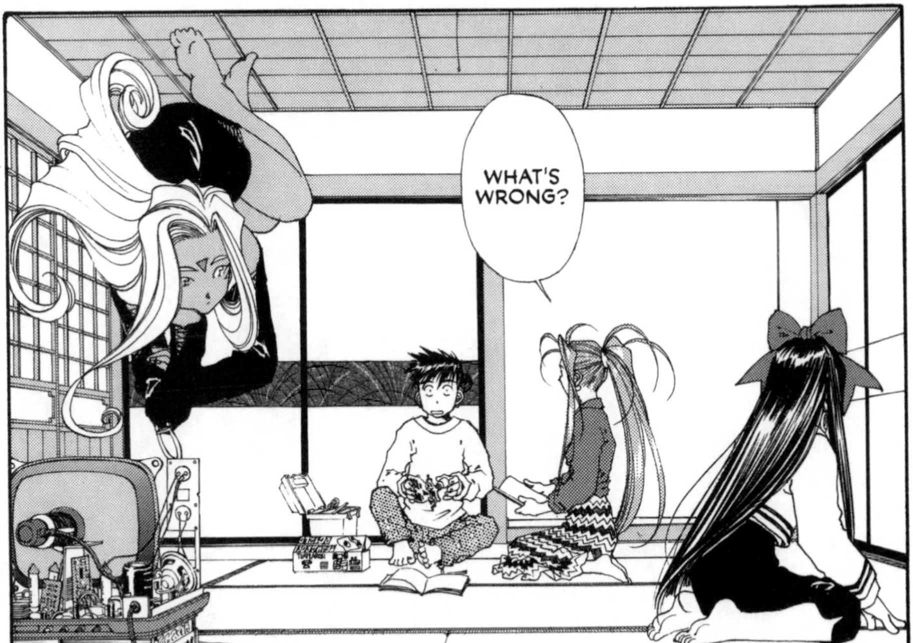
WHAT'S WRONG?

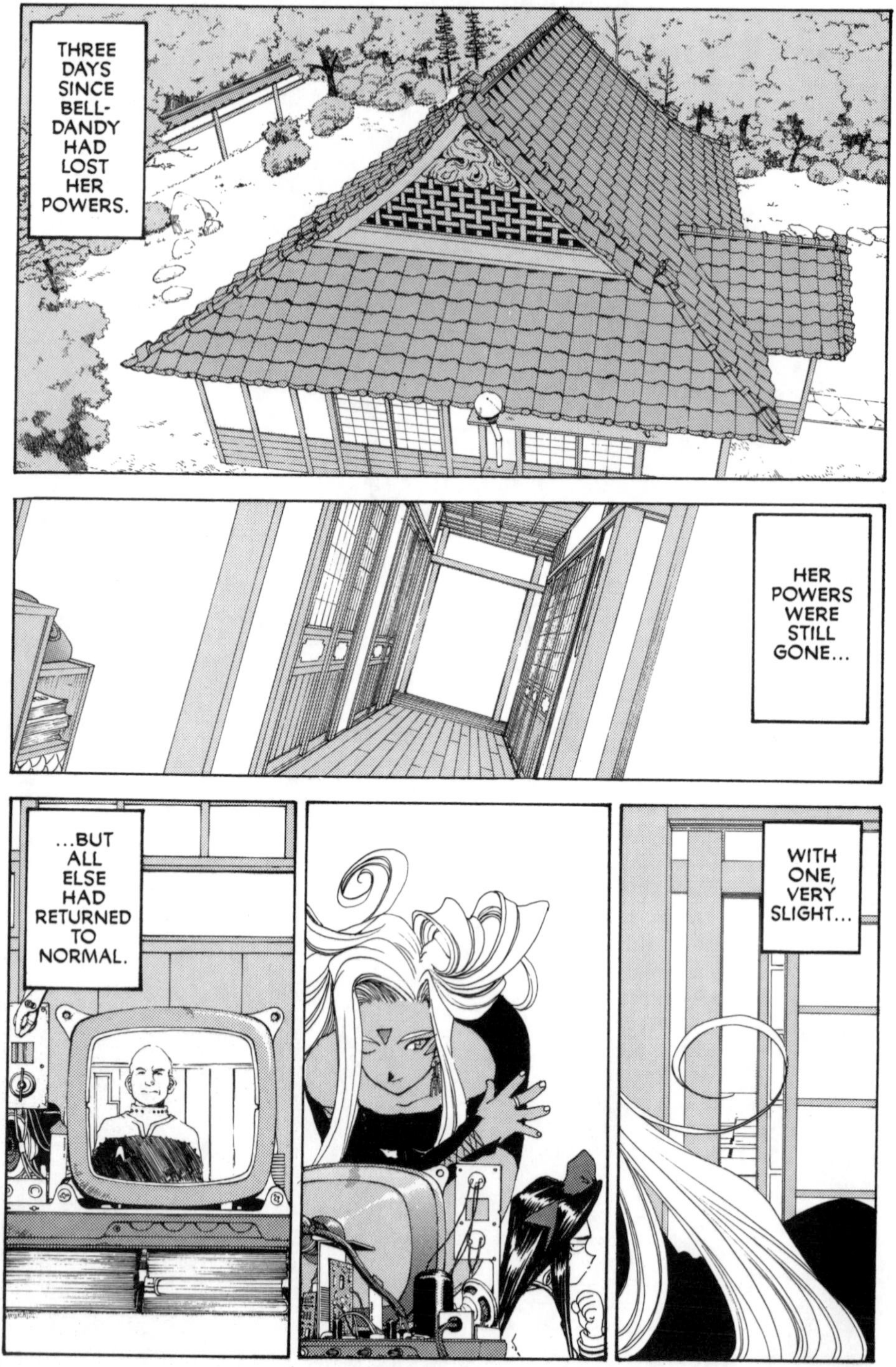
THREE DAYS SINCE BELL-DANDY HAD LOST HER POWERS.
HER POWERS WERE STILL GONE...
...BUT ALL ELSE HAD RETURNED TO NORMAL.
WITH ONE, VERY SLIGHT...

TRAVELER

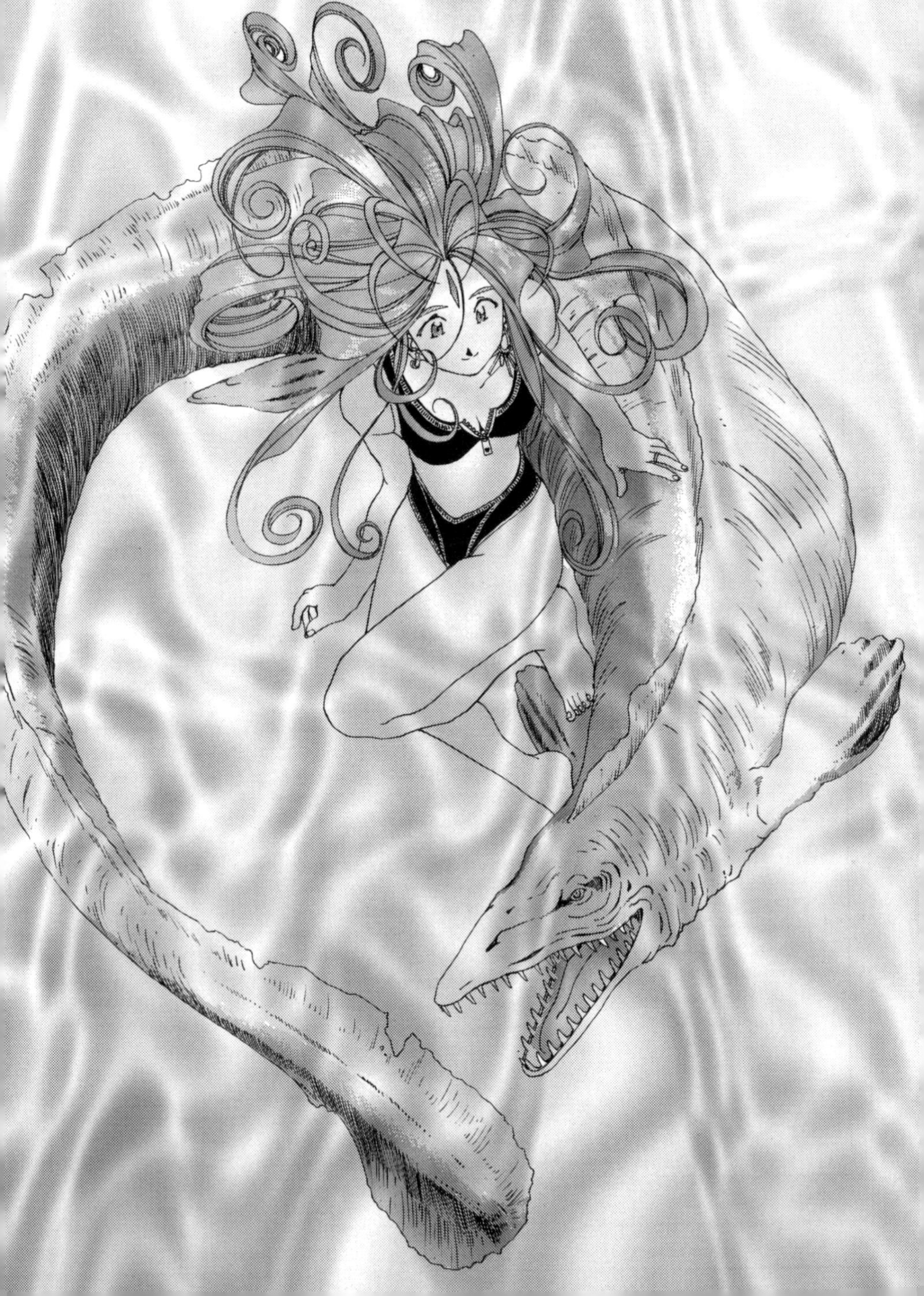

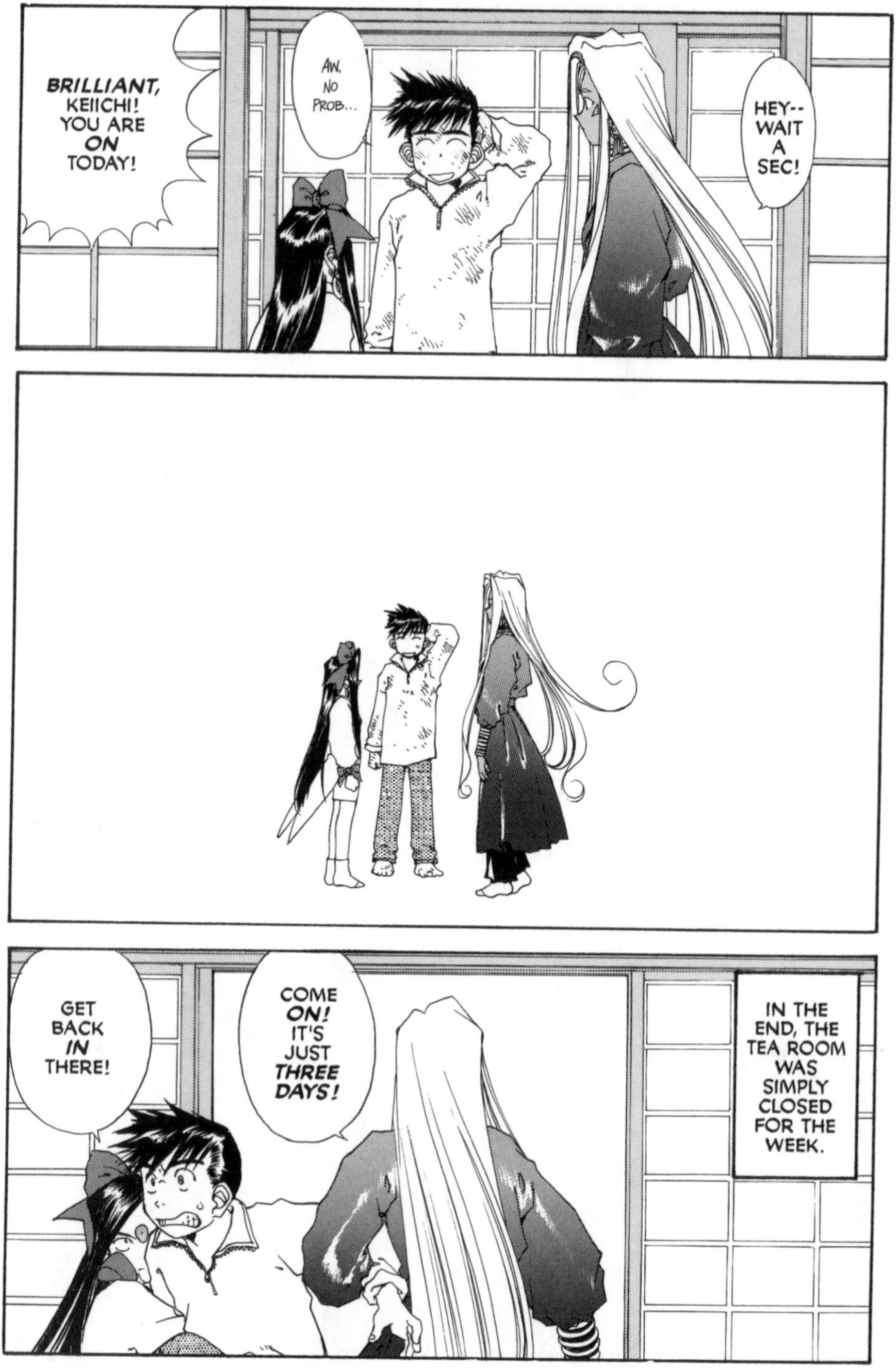
BRILLIANT, KEIICHI! YOU ARE ON TODAY!
AW, NO PROB...
HEY-- WAIT A SEC!
GET BACK IN THERE!
COME ON! IT'S JUST THREE DAYS!
IN THE END, THE TEA ROOM WAS SIMPLY CLOSED FOR THE WEEK.

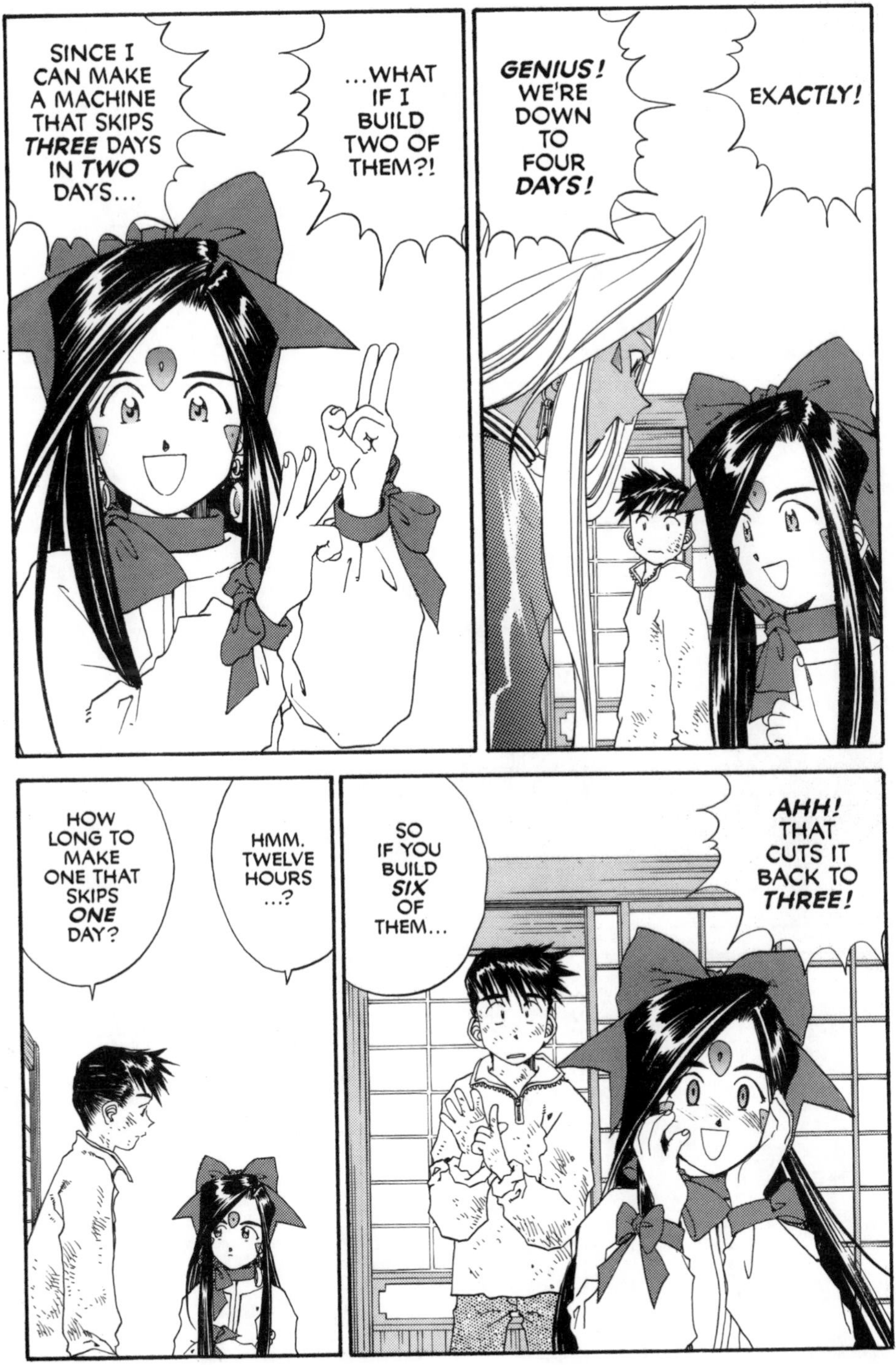
SINCE I CAN MAKE A MACHINE THAT SKIPS *THREE* DAYS IN *TWO* DAYS...
...WHAT IF I BUILD TWO OF THEM?!
GENIUS! WE'RE DOWN TO FOUR *DAYS!*
EX*ACTLY!*
HOW LONG TO MAKE ONE THAT SKIPS *ONE* DAY?
HMM. TWELVE HOURS ...?
SO IF YOU BUILD *SIX* OF THEM...
AHH! THAT CUTS IT BACK TO *THREE!*

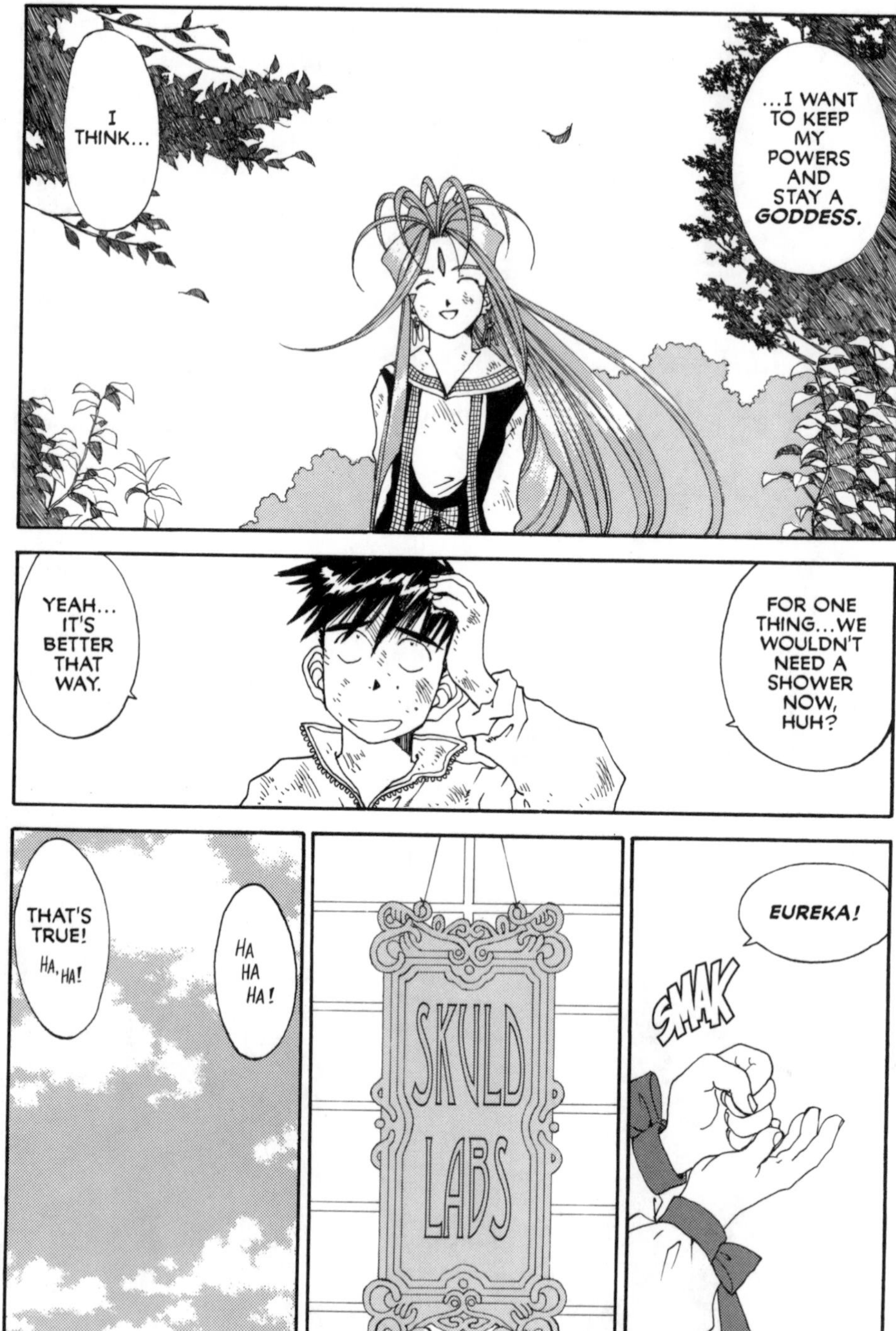
I THINK...
...I WANT TO KEEP MY POWERS AND STAY A *GODDESS.*
YEAH... IT'S BETTER THAT WAY.
FOR ONE THING...WE WOULDN'T NEED A SHOWER NOW, HUH?
THAT'S TRUE! HA, HA!
HA HA HA!
SKULD LABS
EUREKA!
SMAK

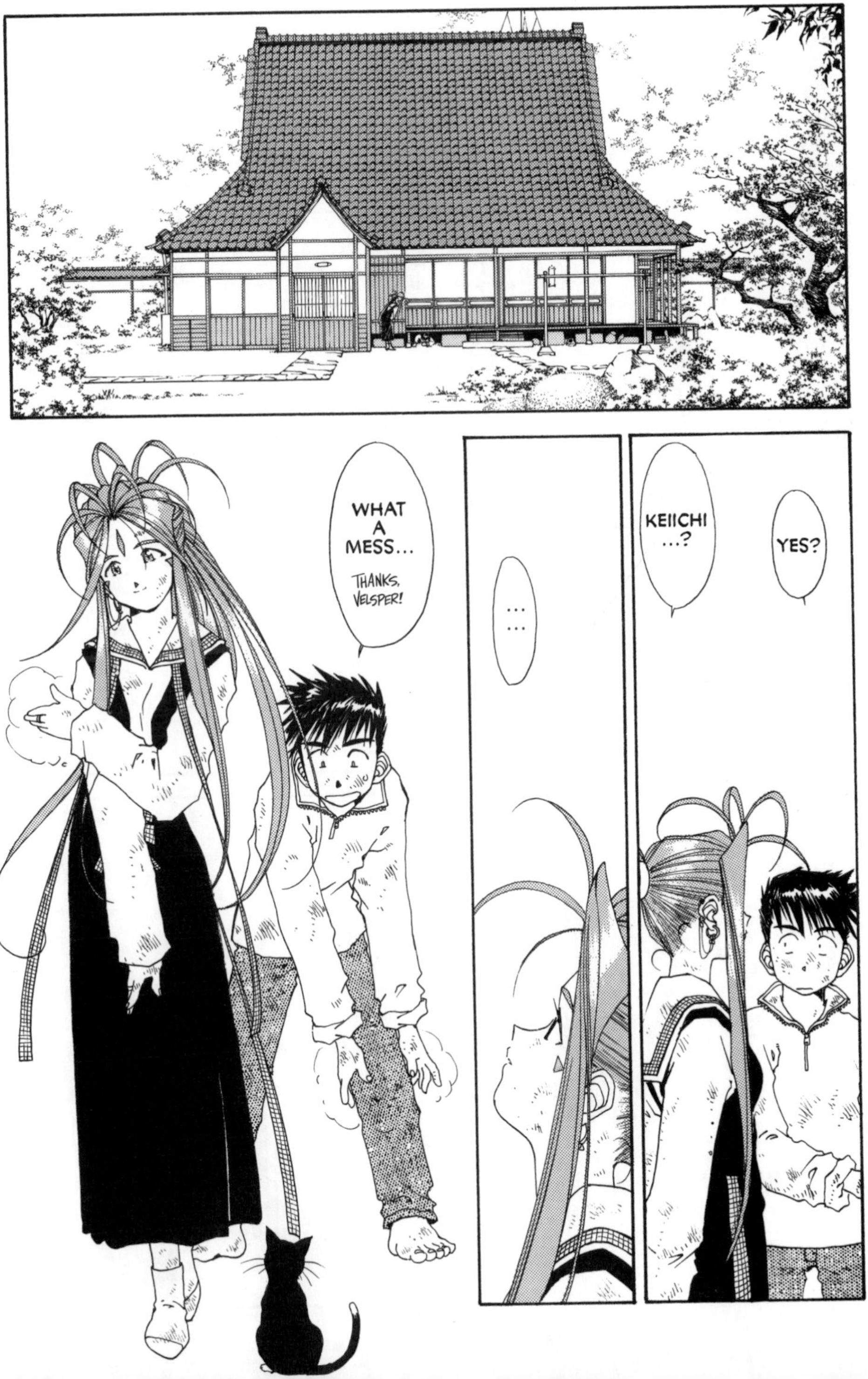
KEIICHI …?
YES?
… …
WHAT A MESS…
THANKS, VELSPER!

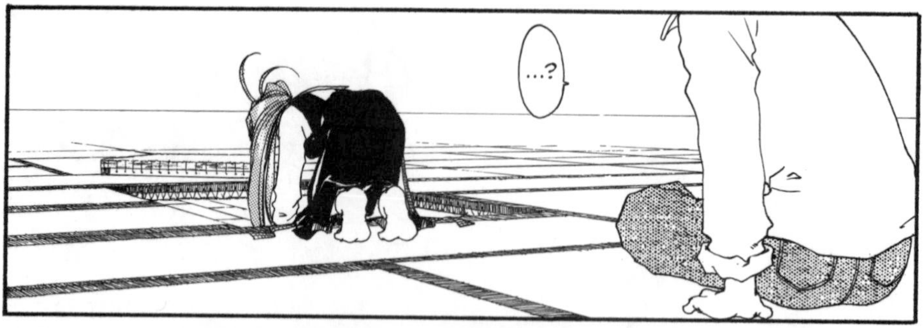
...?
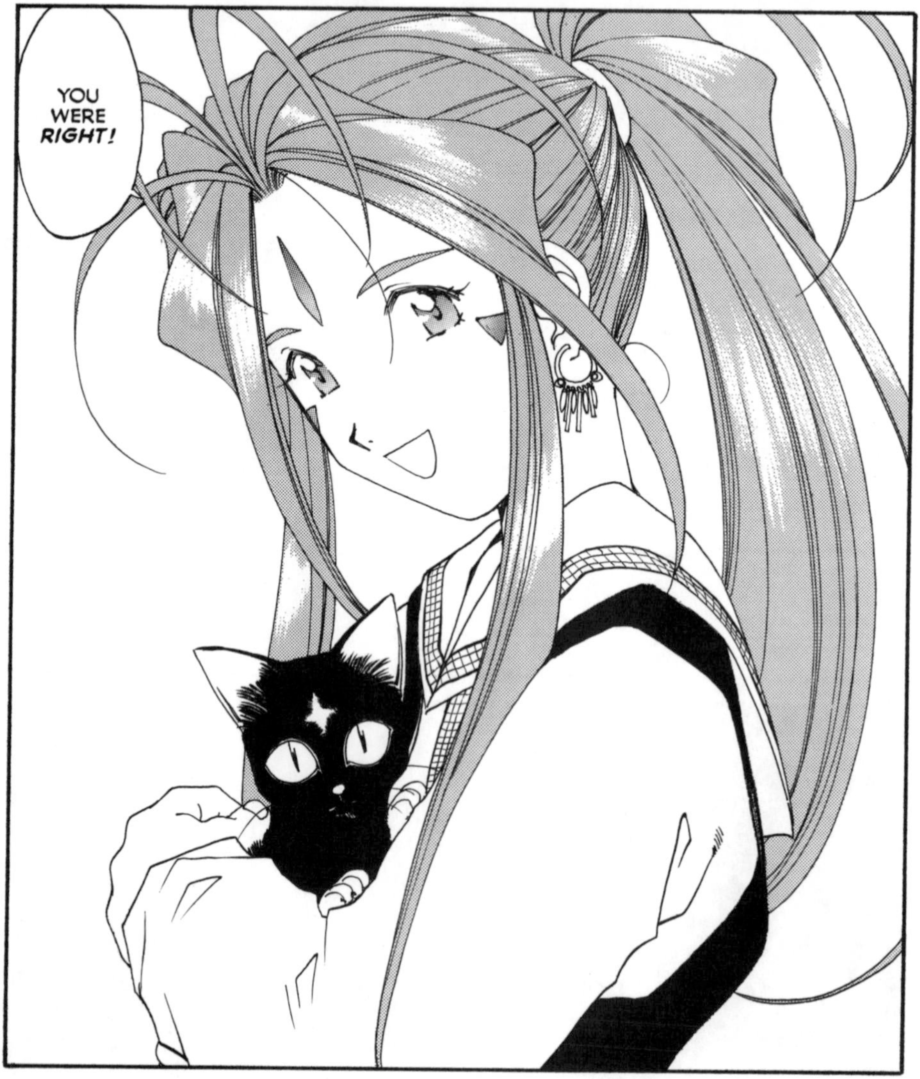
YOU WERE RIGHT!

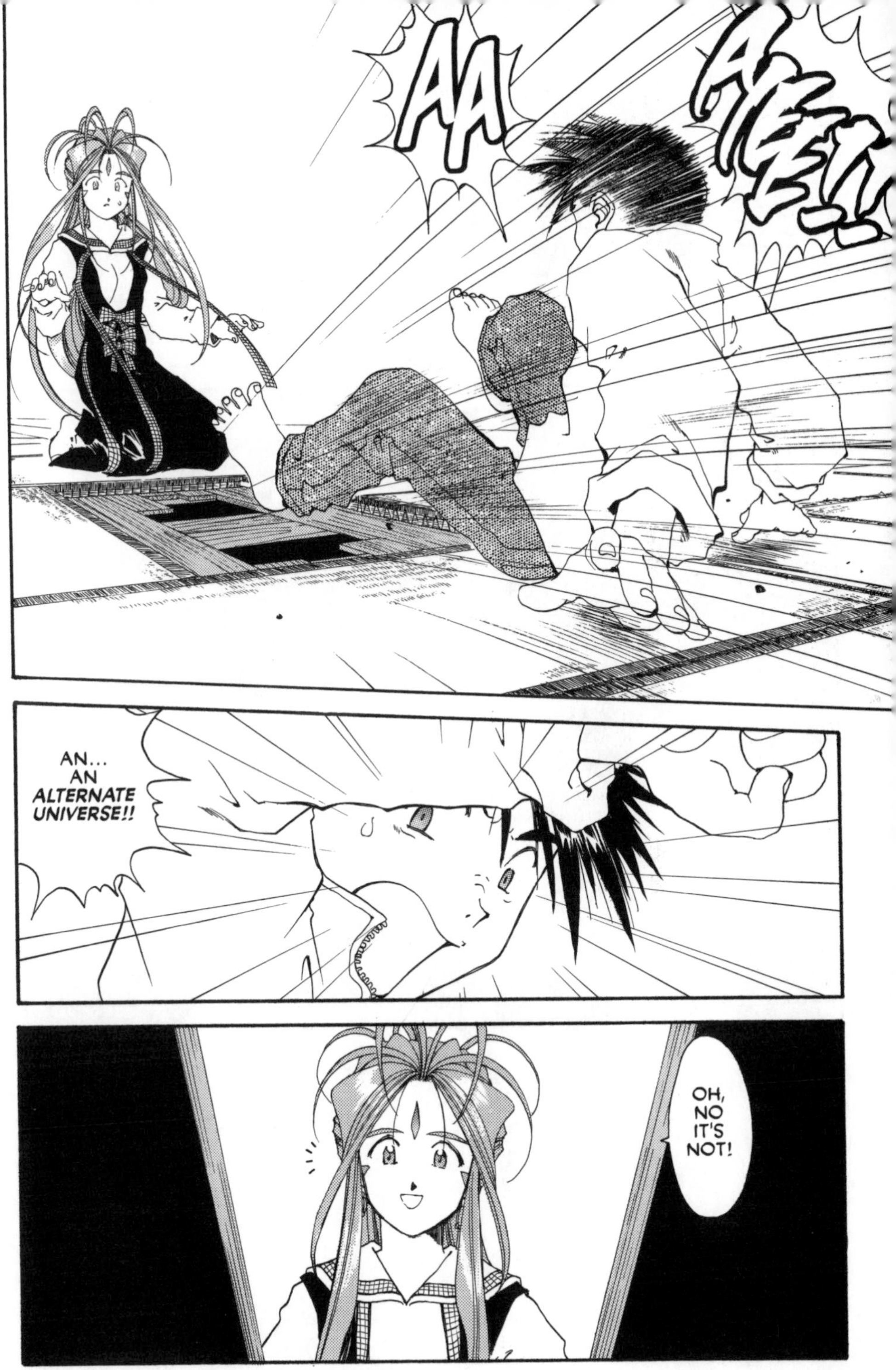
AAAIEE!!
AN... AN ALTERNATE UNIVERSE!!
OH, NO IT'S NOT!

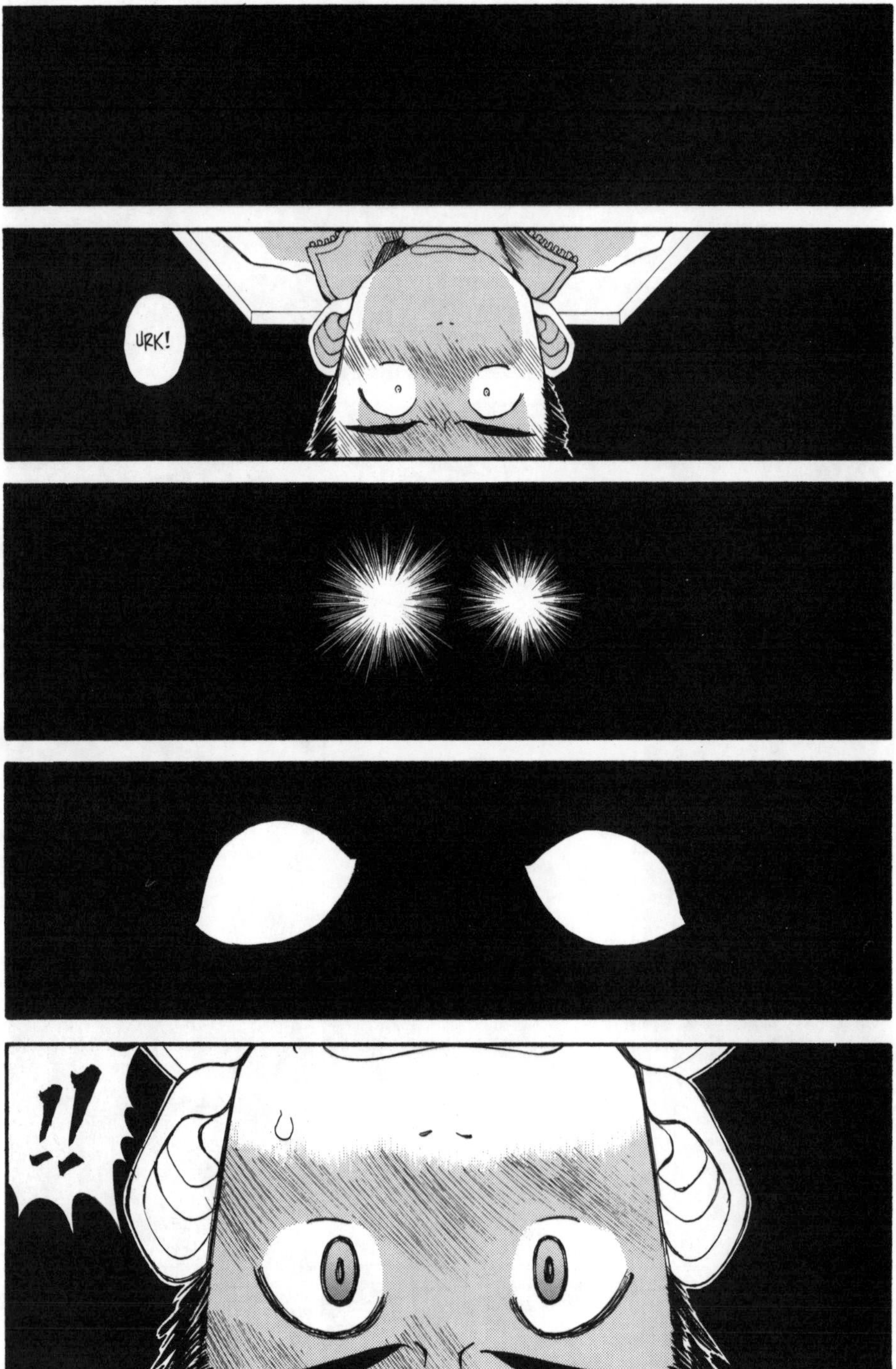
URK!
!!

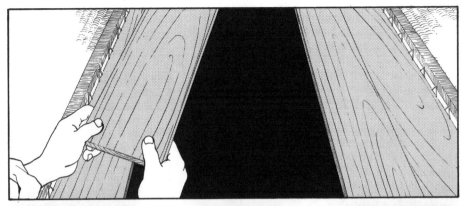

....?

OKAY... READY, SET--

GO!

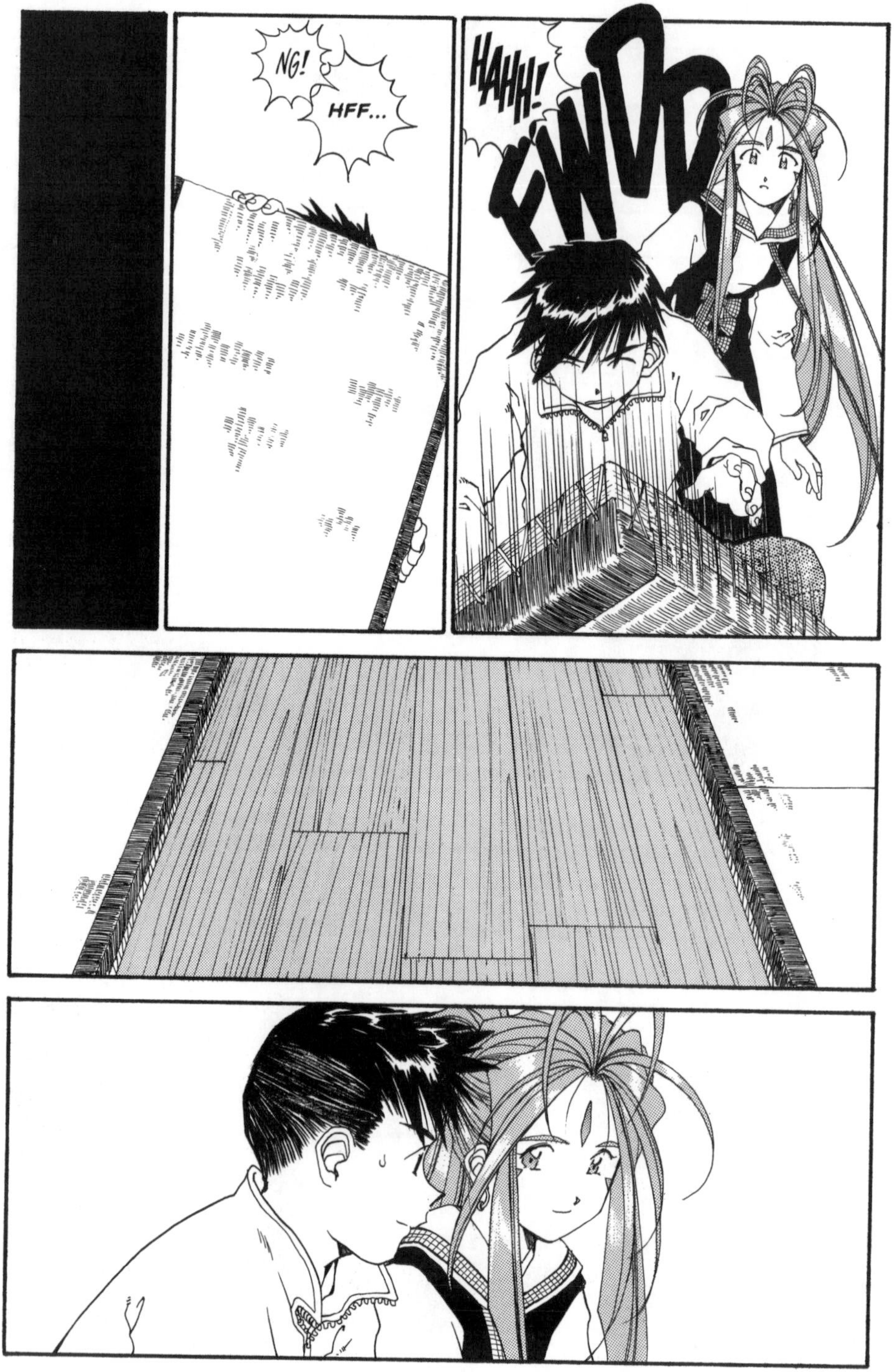
HAHH!
FWOP
NG!
HFF...

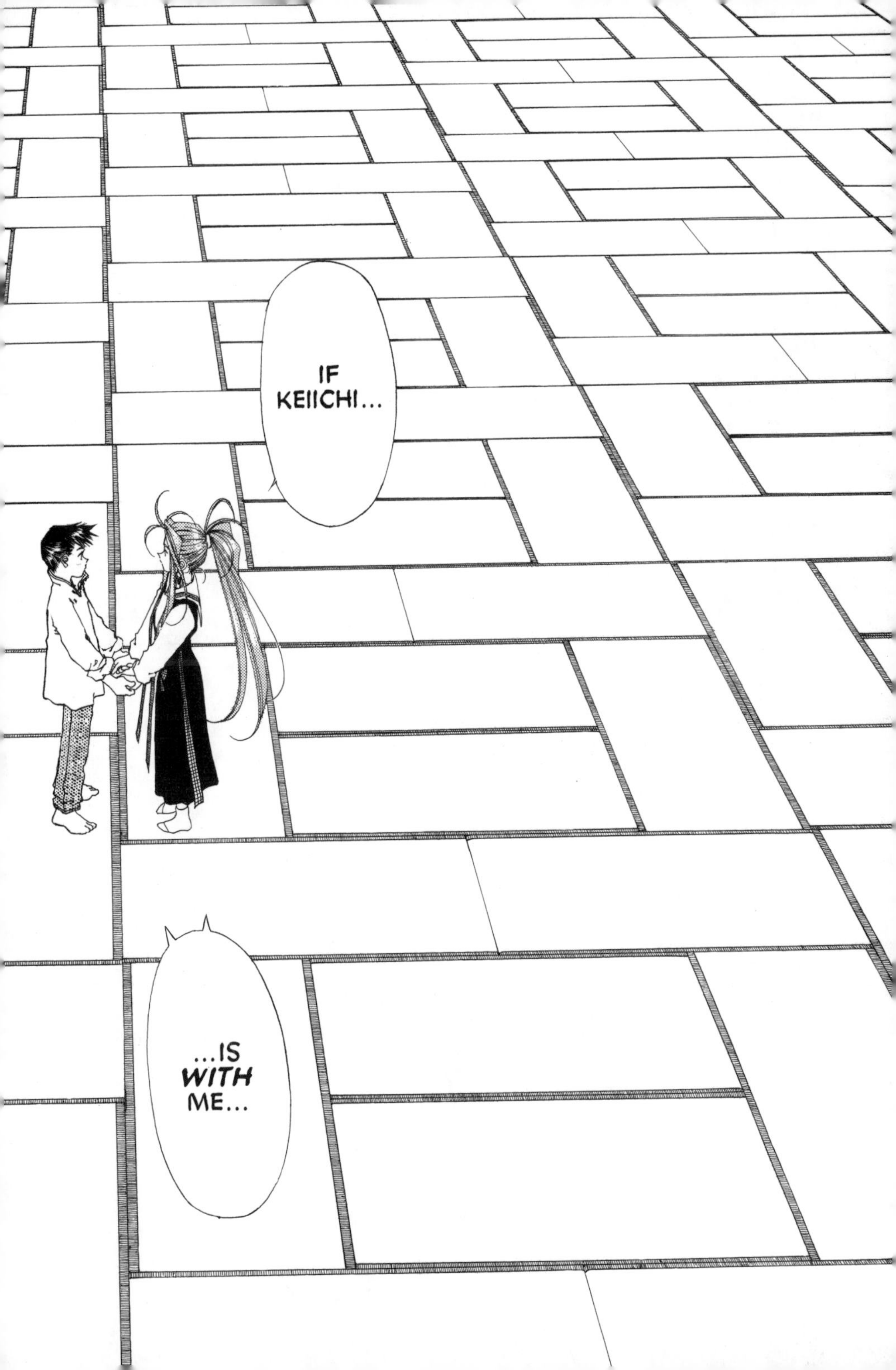
IF KEIICHI...
...IS WITH ME...

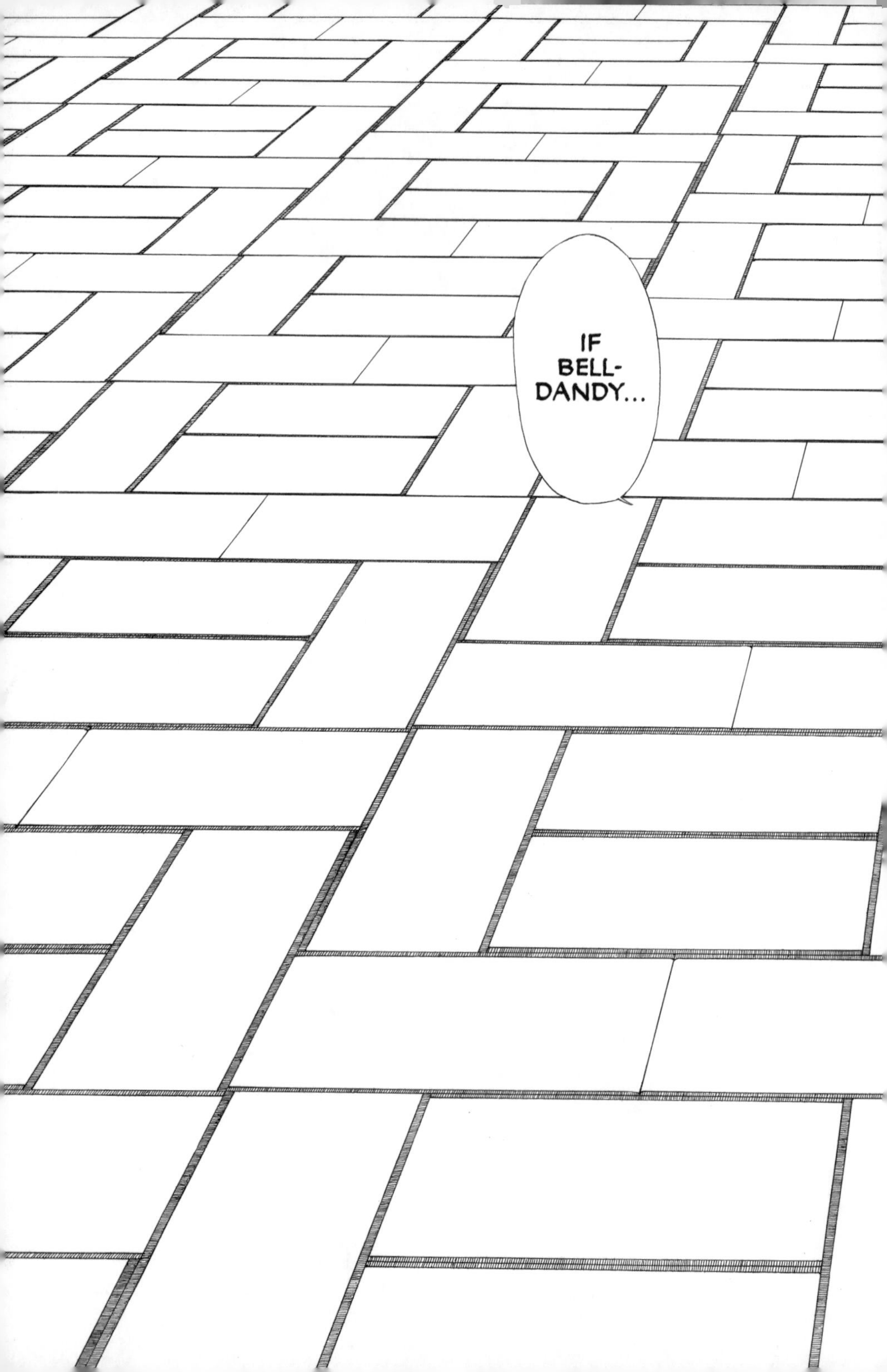
IF BELL-DANDY...

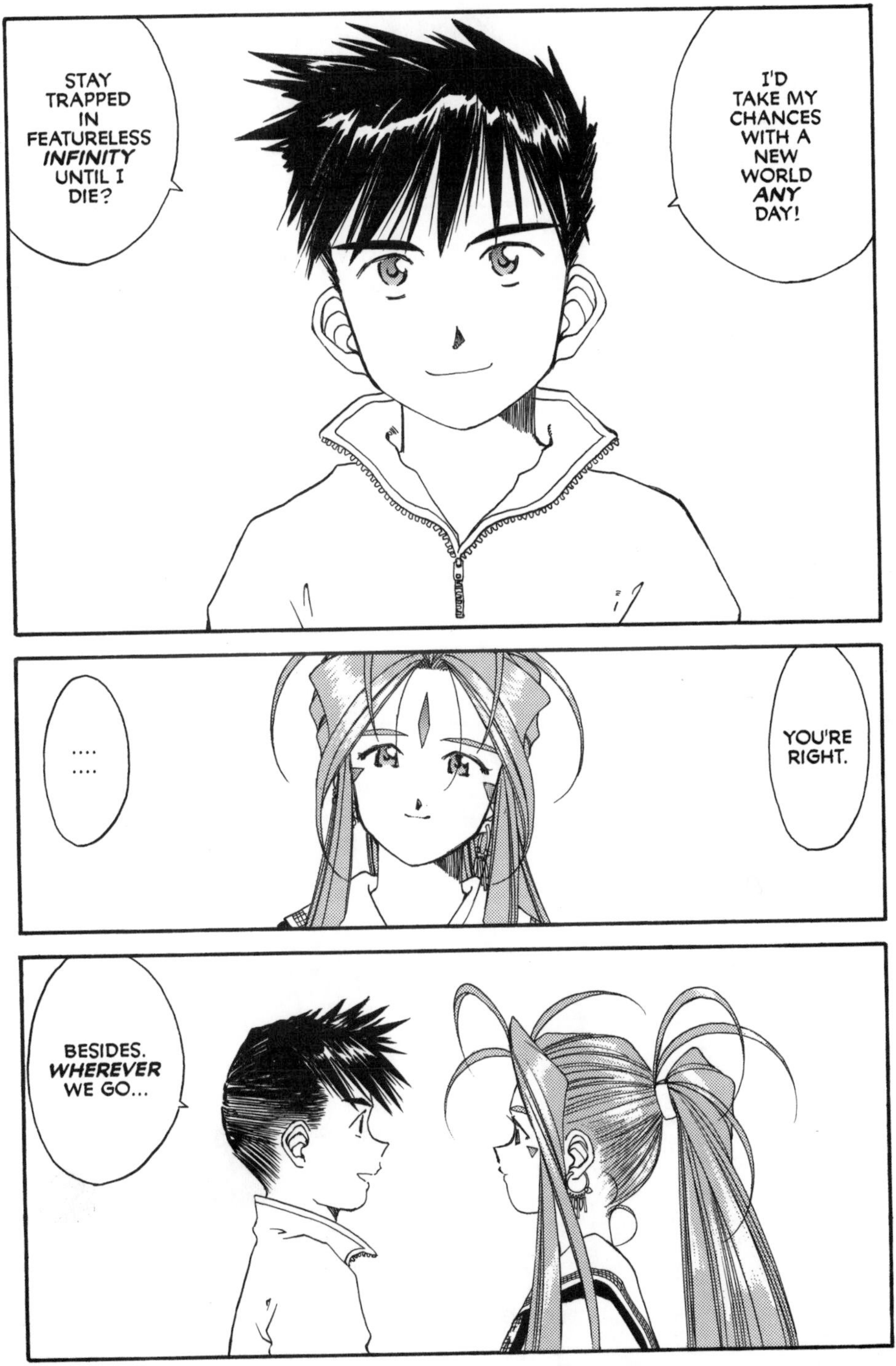

STAY TRAPPED IN FEATURELESS *INFINITY* UNTIL I DIE?
I'D TAKE MY CHANCES WITH A NEW WORLD *ANY* DAY!
....
....
YOU'RE RIGHT.
BESIDES. *WHEREVER* WE GO...

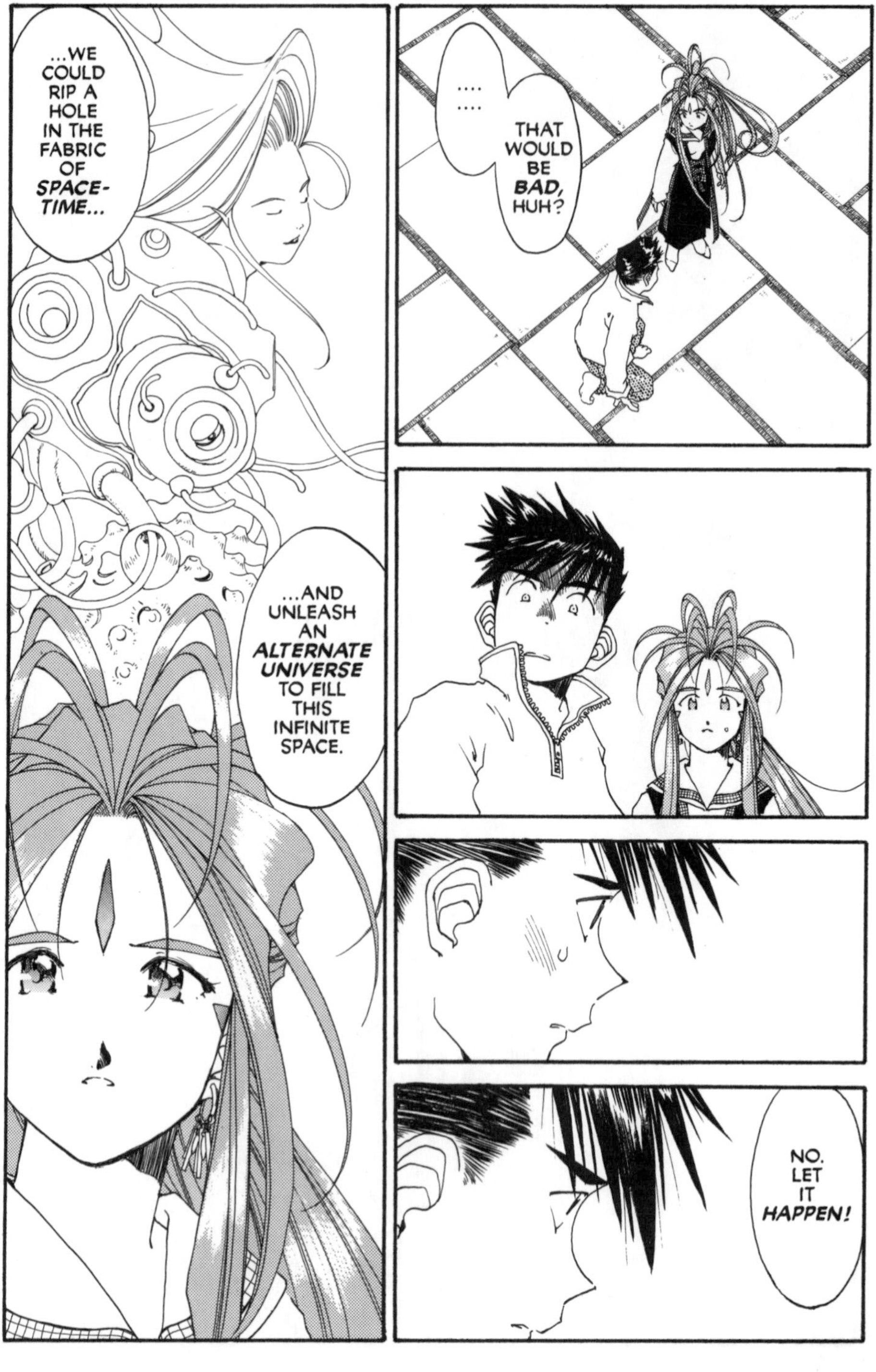
...WE COULD RIP A HOLE IN THE FABRIC OF *SPACE-TIME...*
...AND UNLEASH AN *ALTERNATE UNIVERSE* TO FILL THIS INFINITE SPACE.
....
THAT WOULD BE *BAD,* HUH?
NO. LET IT *HAPPEN!*

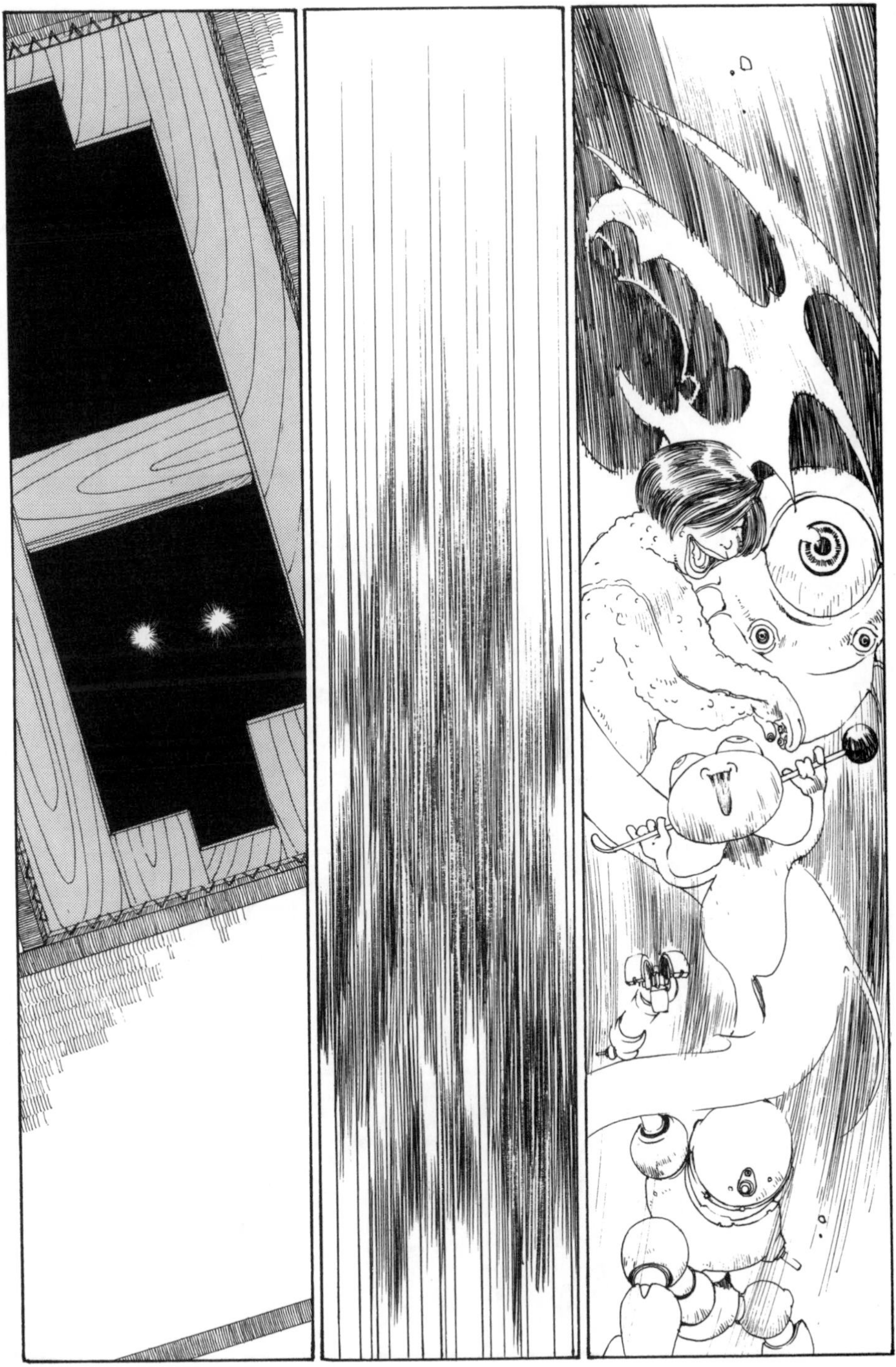

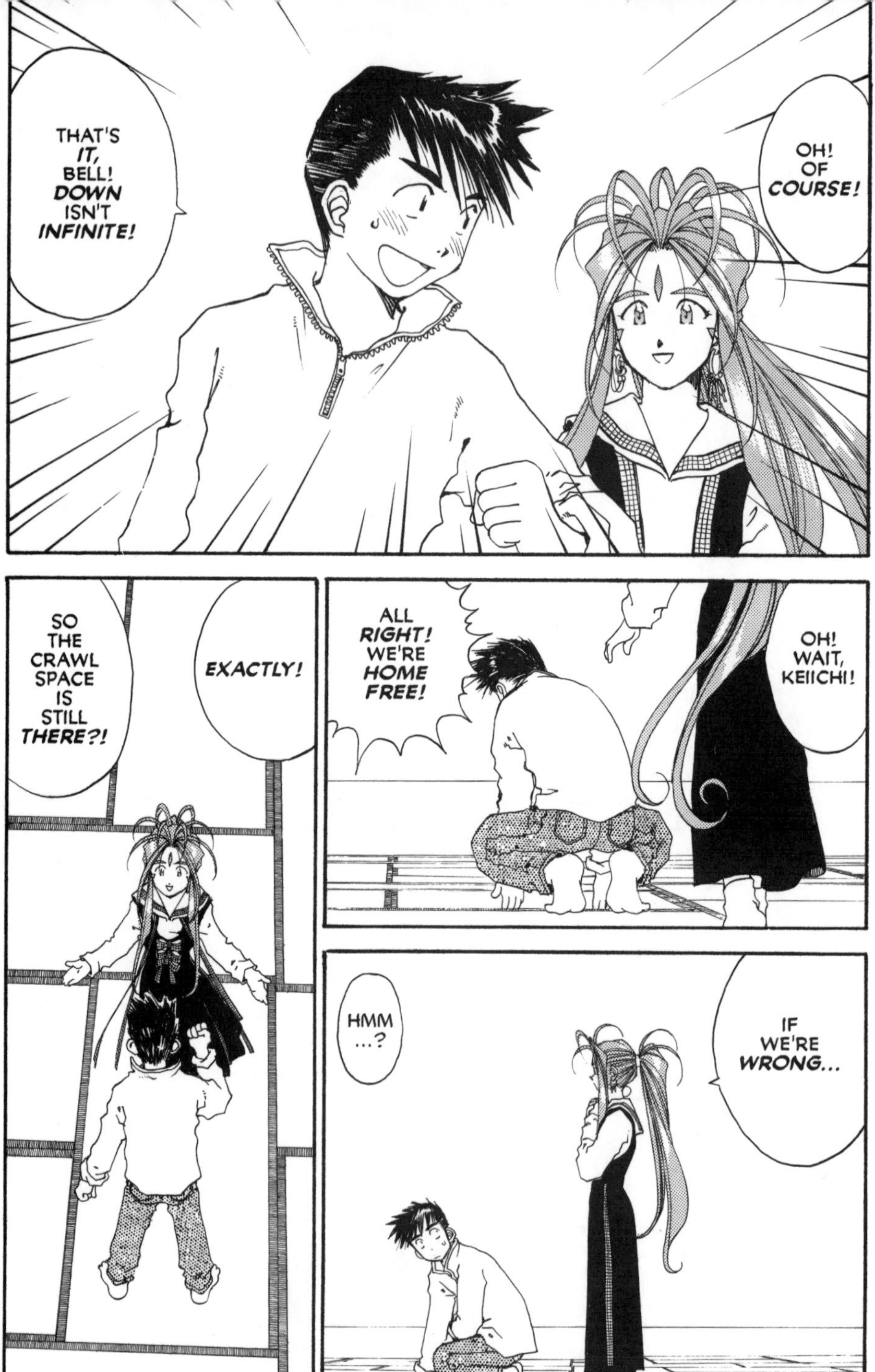
THAT'S *IT*, BELL! *DOWN* ISN'T *INFINITE!*
OH! OF *COURSE!*
SO THE CRAWL SPACE IS STILL *THERE?!*
EXACTLY!
ALL *RIGHT!* WE'RE *HOME FREE!*
OH! WAIT, KEIICHI!
HMM ...?
IF WE'RE *WRONG...*

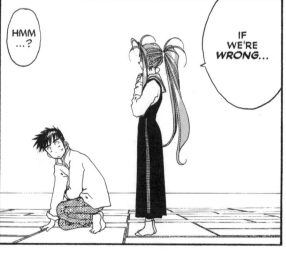

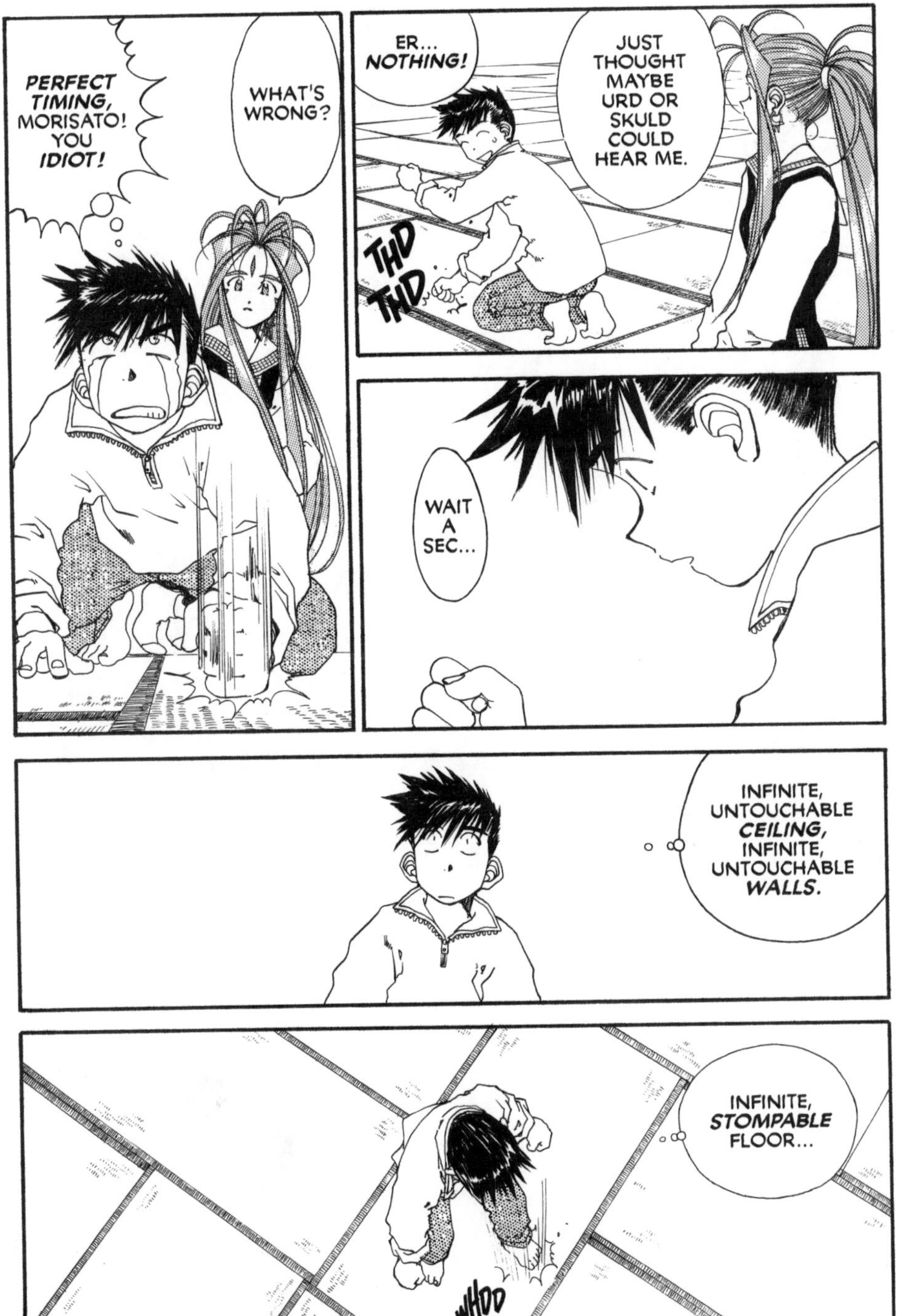

PERFECT TIMING, MORISATO! YOU IDIOT!
WHAT'S WRONG?
ER... NOTHING!
JUST THOUGHT MAYBE URD OR SKULD COULD HEAR ME.
THD THD
WAIT A SEC...
INFINITE, UNTOUCHABLE CEILING, INFINITE, UNTOUCHABLE WALLS.
INFINITE, STOMPABLE FLOOR...
WHOD

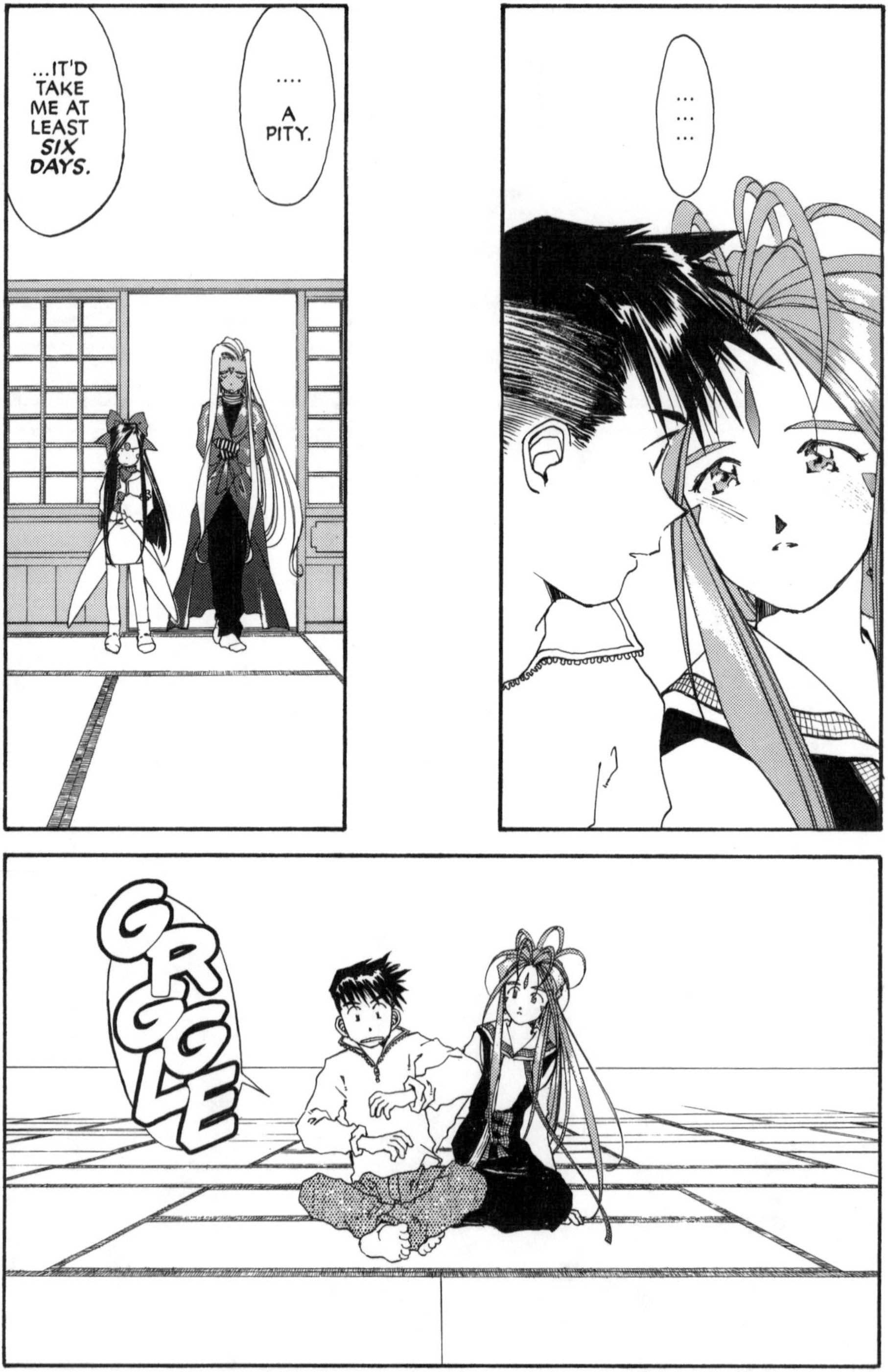
... ...
.... A PITY.
...IT'D TAKE ME AT LEAST *SIX DAYS.*
GRGGLE

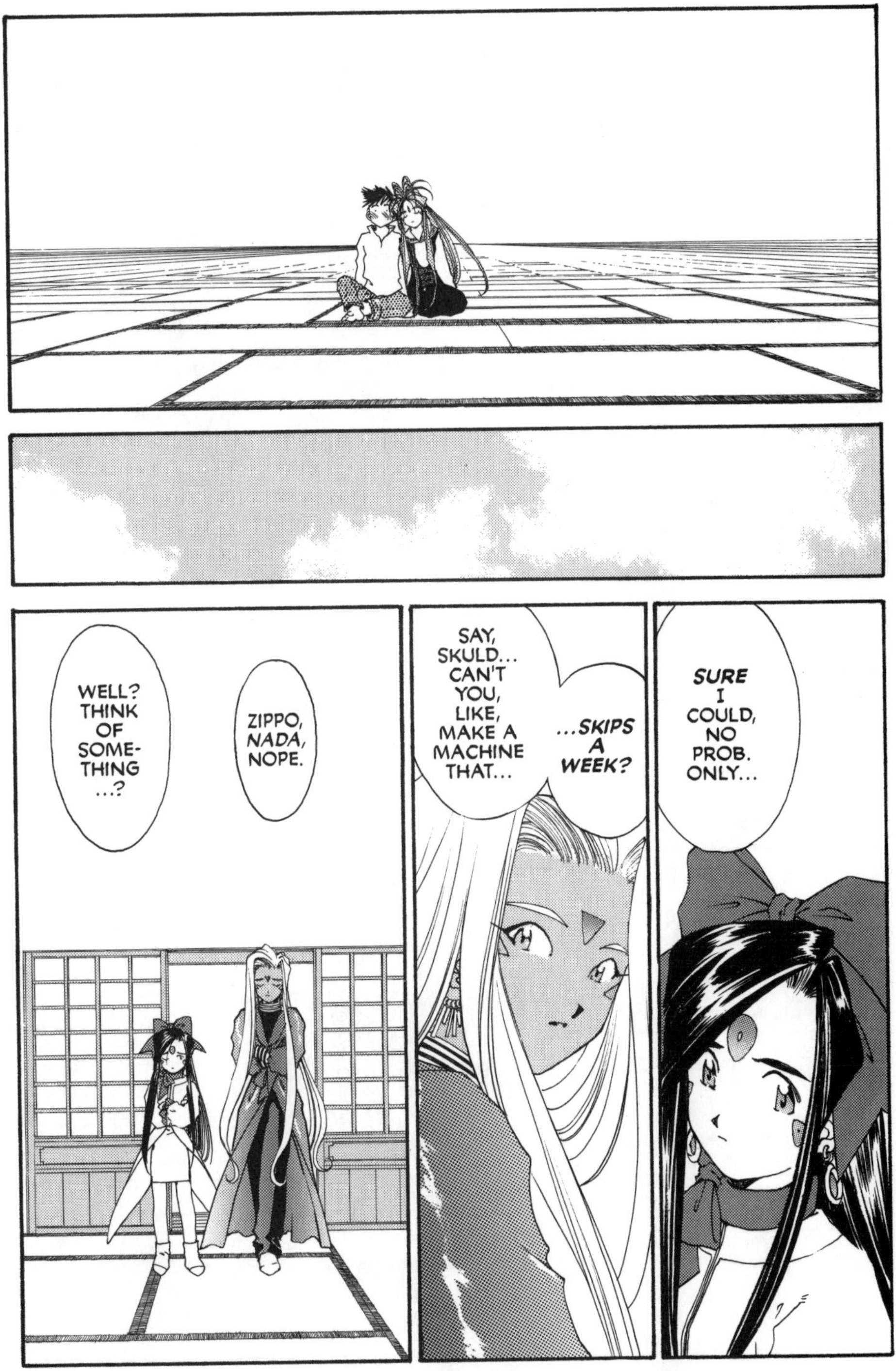
WELL? THINK OF SOME-THING ...?
ZIPPO, NADA, NOPE.
SAY, SKULD... CAN'T YOU, LIKE, MAKE A MACHINE THAT...
...SKIPS A WEEK?
SURE I COULD, NO PROB. ONLY...

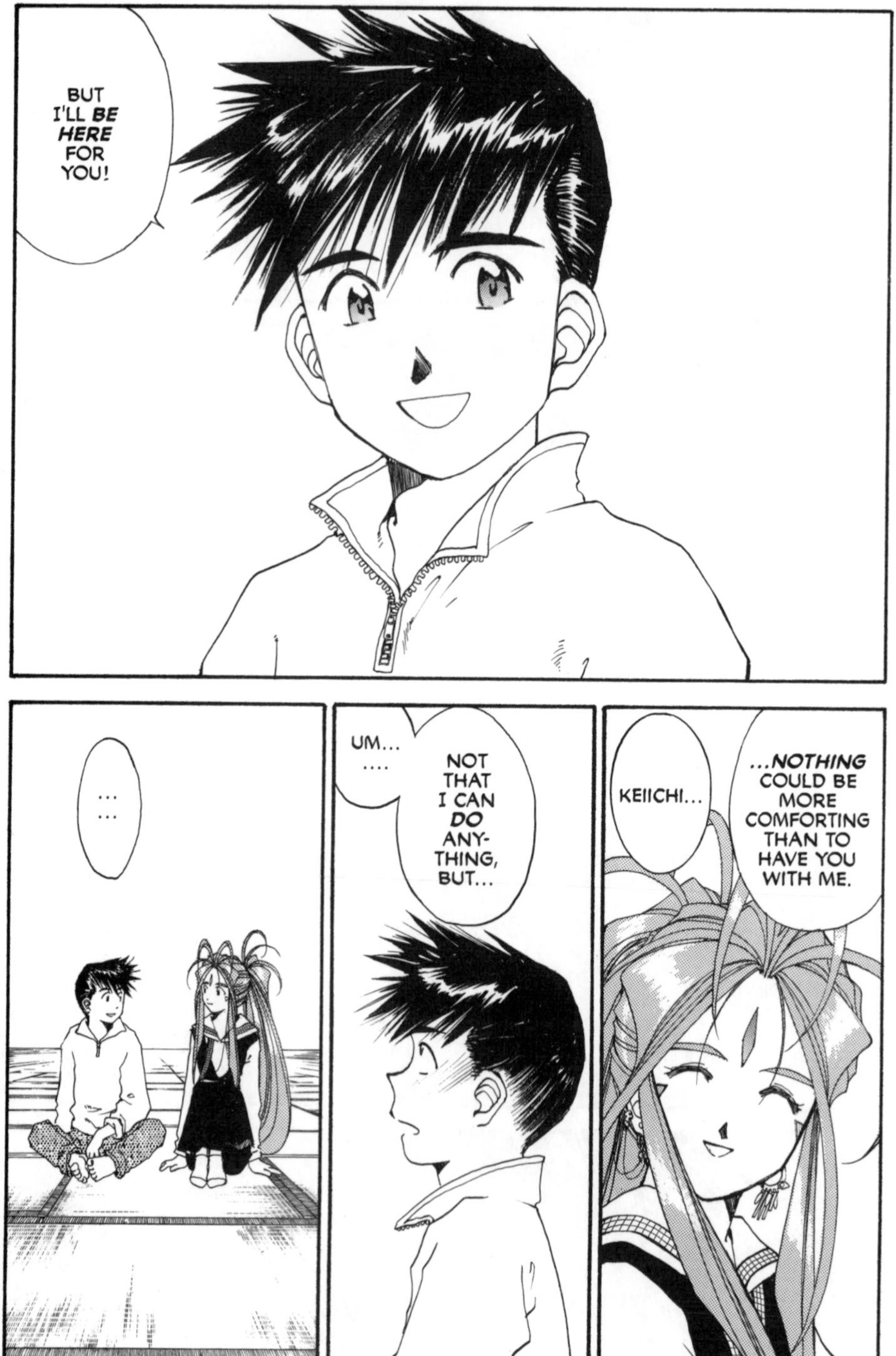
BUT I'LL BE HERE FOR YOU!
... ...
UM... ....
NOT THAT I CAN DO ANYTHING, BUT...
KEIICHI...
...NOTHING COULD BE MORE COMFORTING THAN TO HAVE YOU WITH ME.

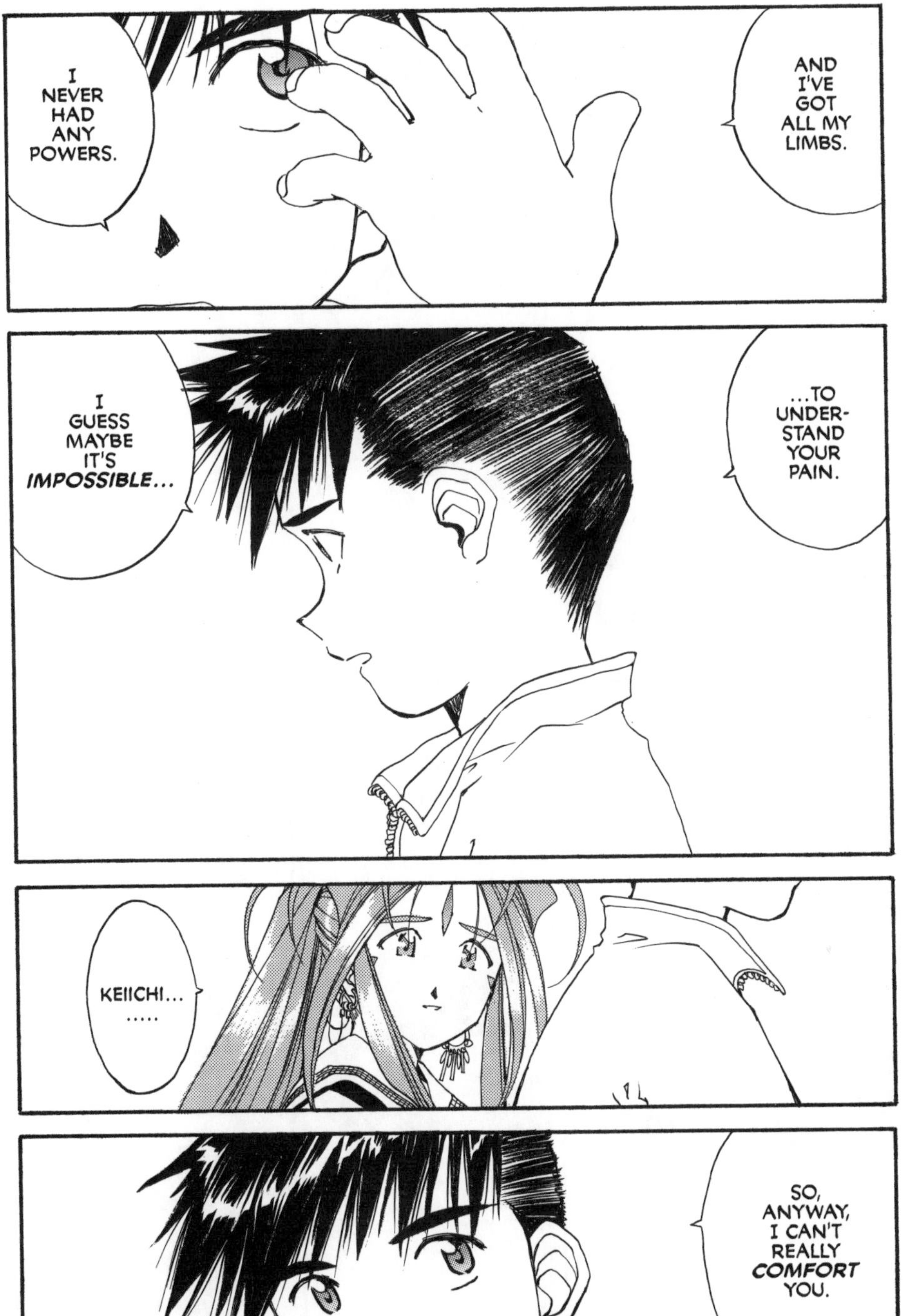
I NEVER HAD ANY POWERS.
AND I'VE GOT ALL MY LIMBS.
I GUESS MAYBE IT'S *IMPOSSIBLE...*
...TO UNDER-STAND YOUR PAIN.
KEIICHI... .....
SO, ANYWAY, I CAN'T REALLY *COMFORT* YOU.

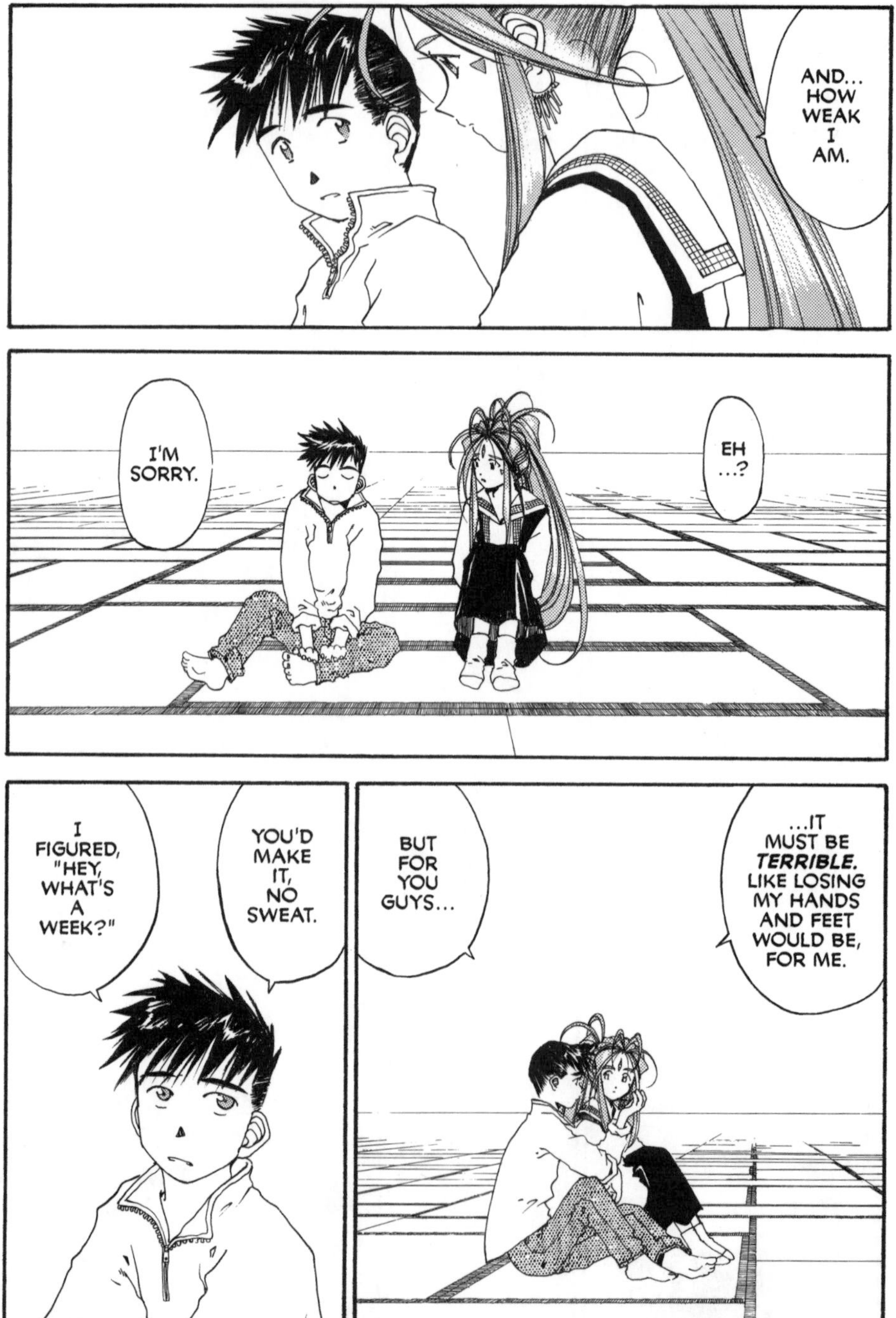

AND... HOW WEAK I AM.
I'M SORRY.
EH ...?
I FIGURED, "HEY, WHAT'S A WEEK?"
YOU'D MAKE IT, NO SWEAT.
BUT FOR YOU GUYS...
...IT MUST BE ***TERRIBLE.*** LIKE LOSING MY HANDS AND FEET WOULD BE, FOR ME.

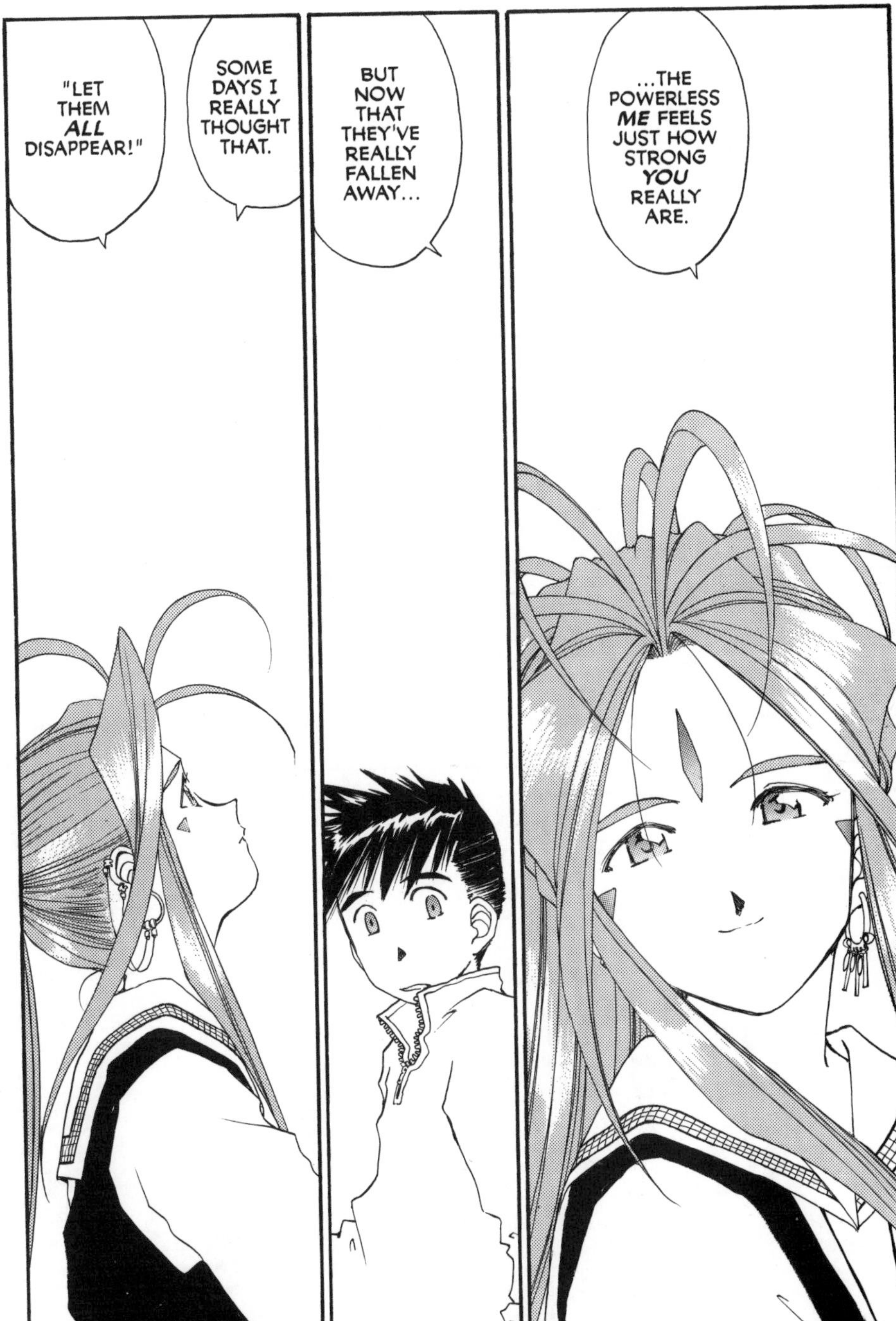
"LET THEM ALL DISAPPEAR!"
SOME DAYS I REALLY THOUGHT THAT.
BUT NOW THAT THEY'VE REALLY FALLEN AWAY...
...THE POWERLESS ME FEELS JUST HOW STRONG YOU REALLY ARE.

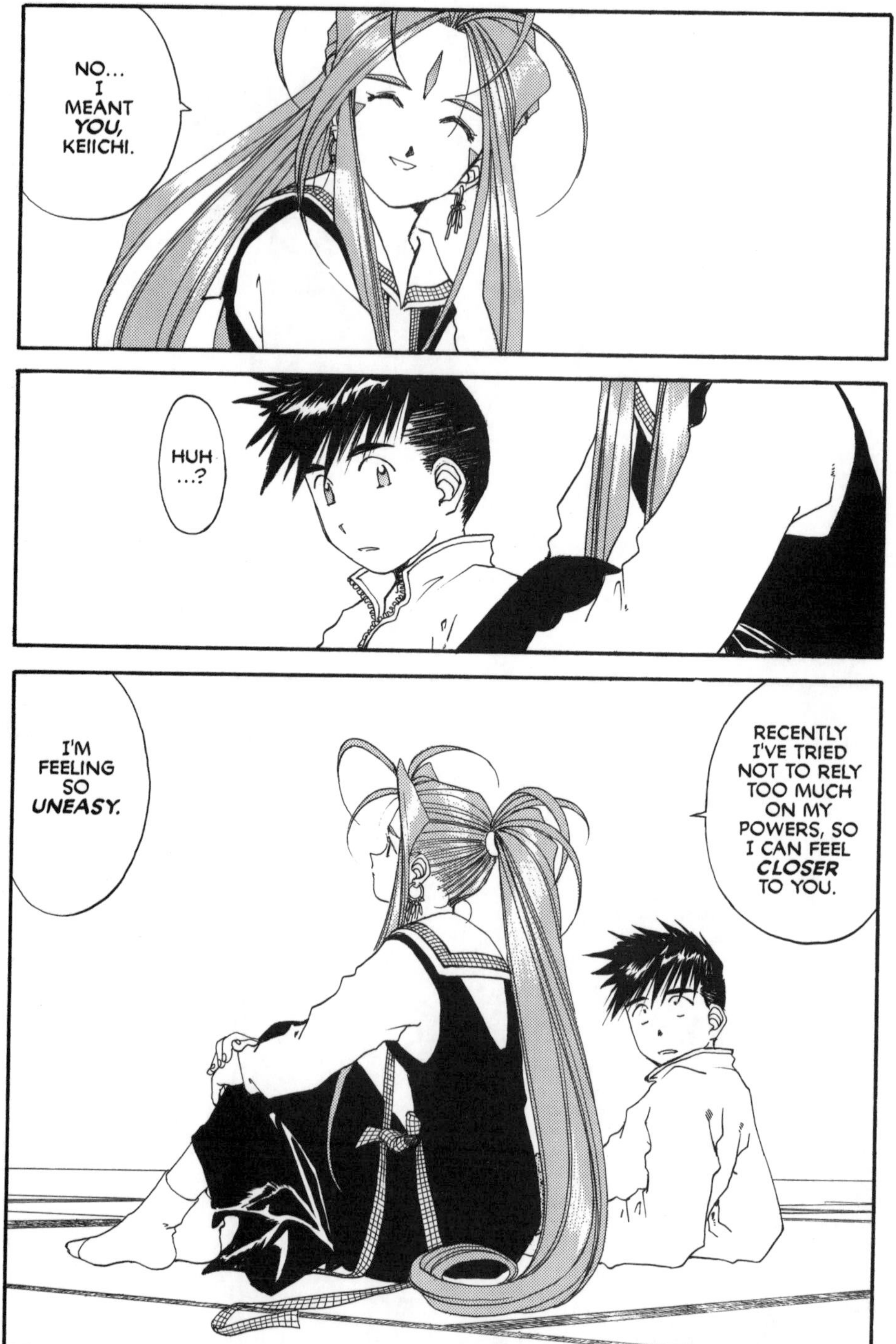
NO... I MEANT *YOU*, KEIICHI.
HUH ...?
RECENTLY I'VE TRIED NOT TO RELY TOO MUCH ON MY POWERS, SO I CAN FEEL *CLOSER* TO YOU.
I'M FEELING SO *UNEASY*.

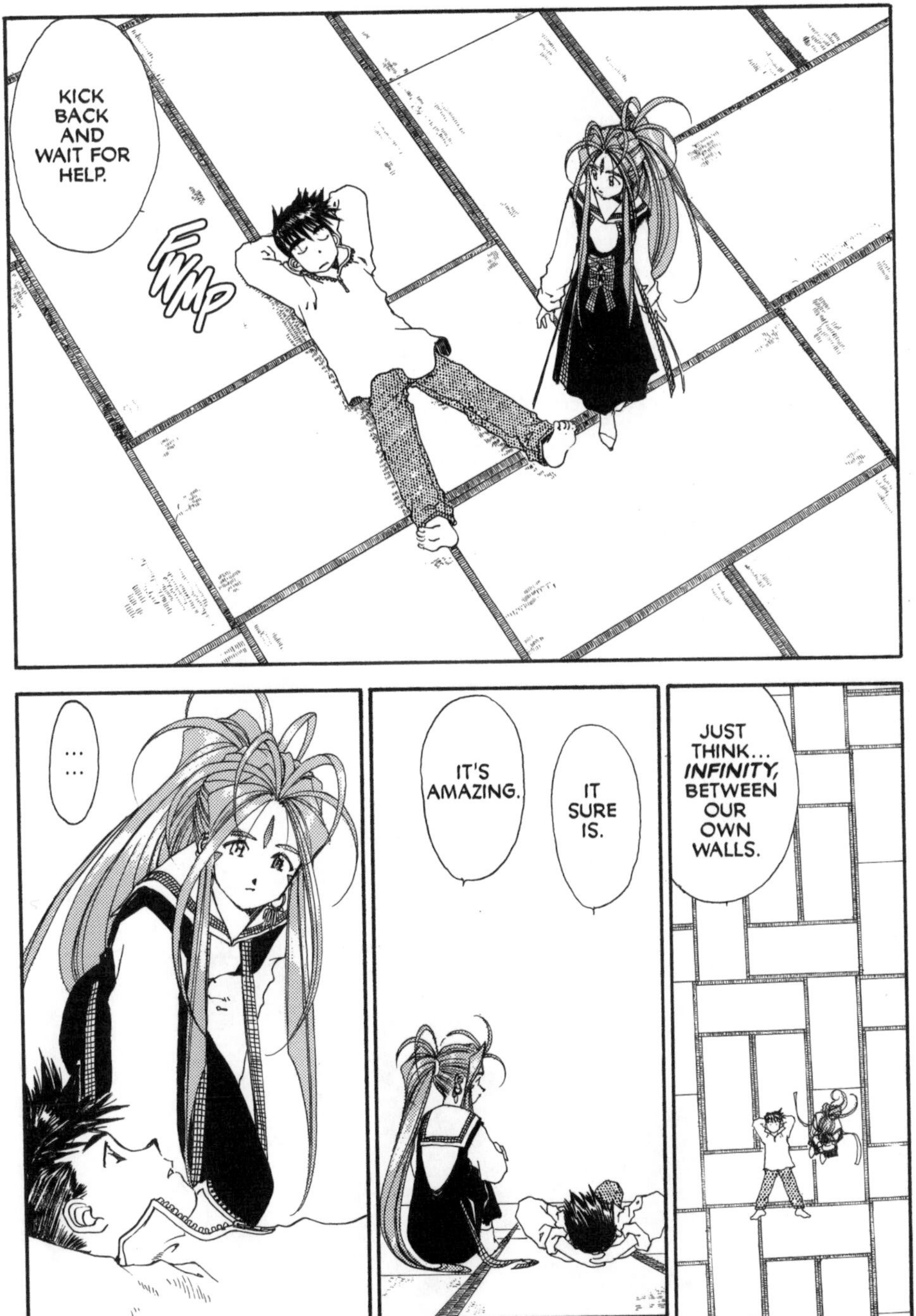
KICK BACK AND WAIT FOR HELP.
FWMP
JUST THINK... ***INFINITY,*** BETWEEN OUR OWN WALLS.
IT'S AMAZING.
IT SURE IS.
... ...

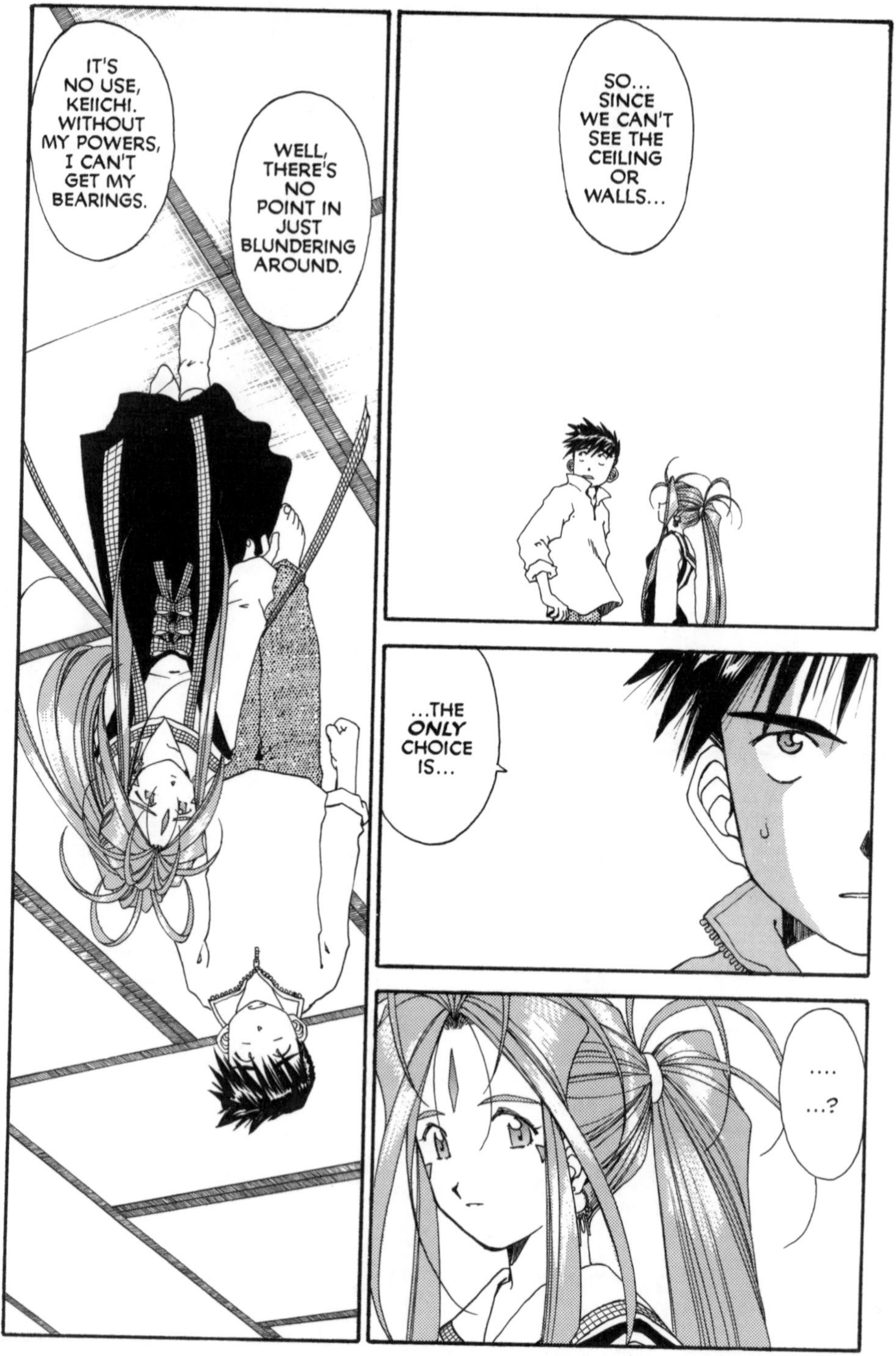
IT'S NO USE, KEIICHI. WITHOUT MY POWERS, I CAN'T GET MY BEARINGS.
WELL, THERE'S NO POINT IN JUST BLUNDERING AROUND.
SO... SINCE WE CAN'T SEE THE CEILING OR WALLS...
...THE *ONLY* CHOICE IS...
....
...?

AS LONG AS YOU'RE WITH ME...

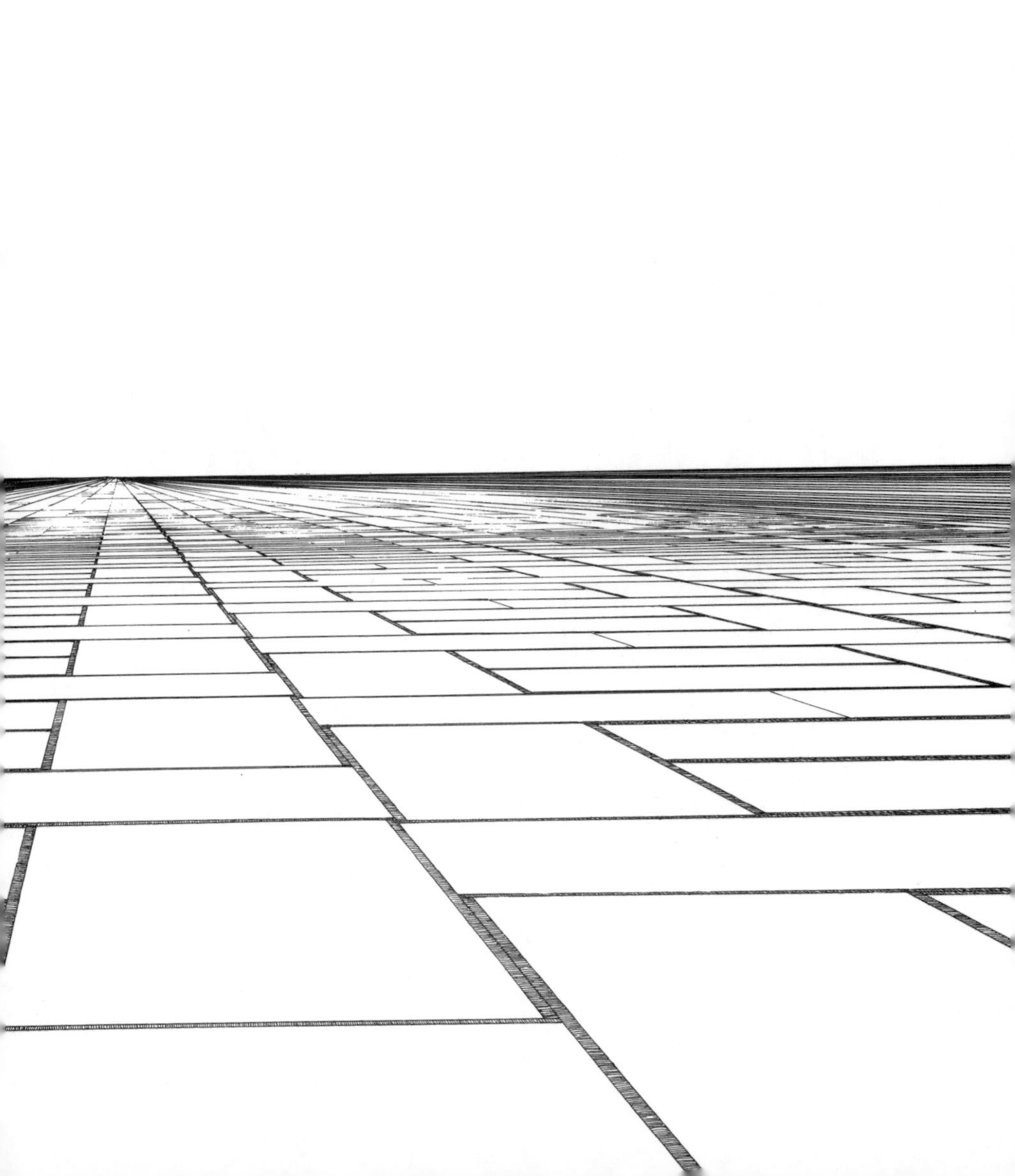

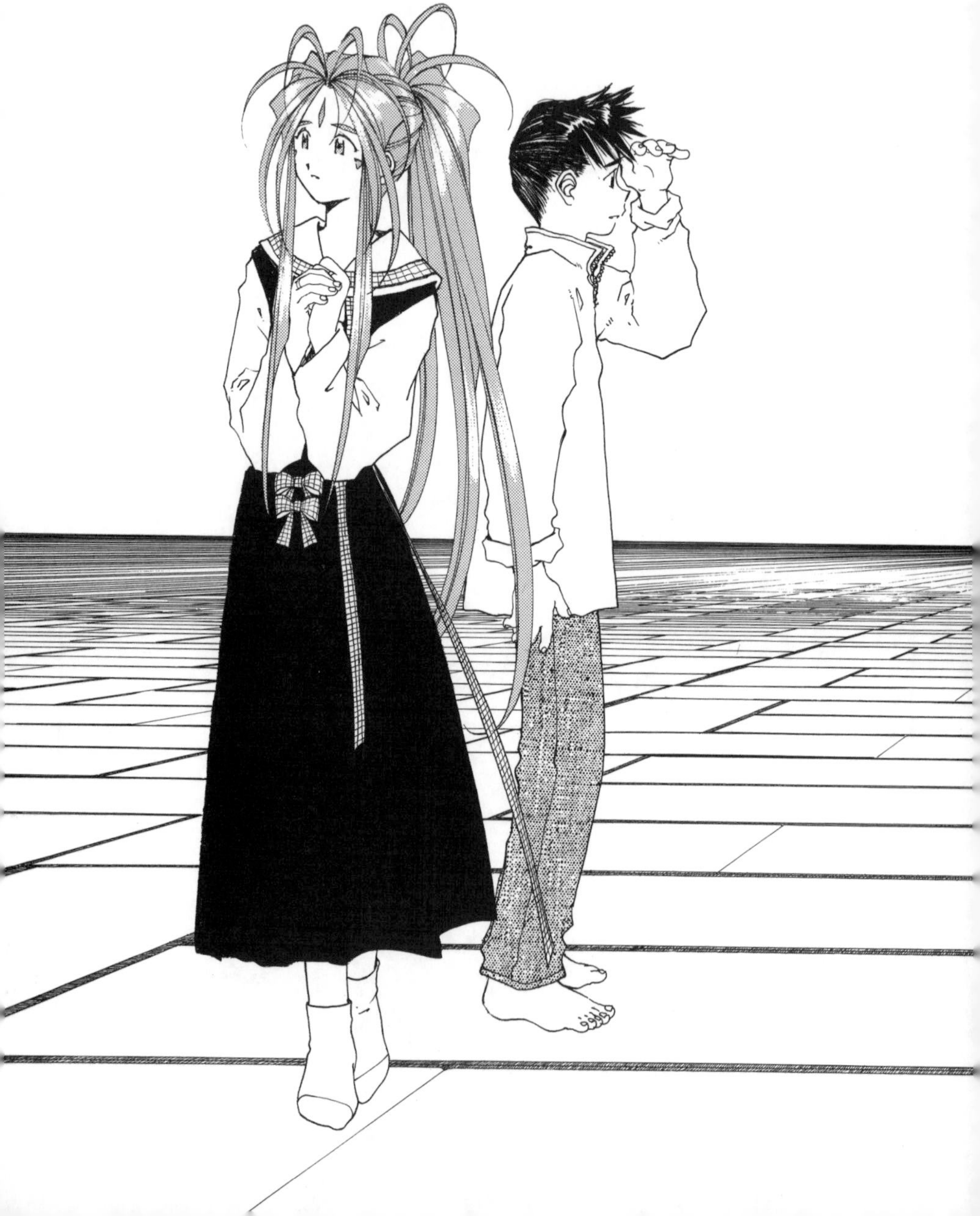

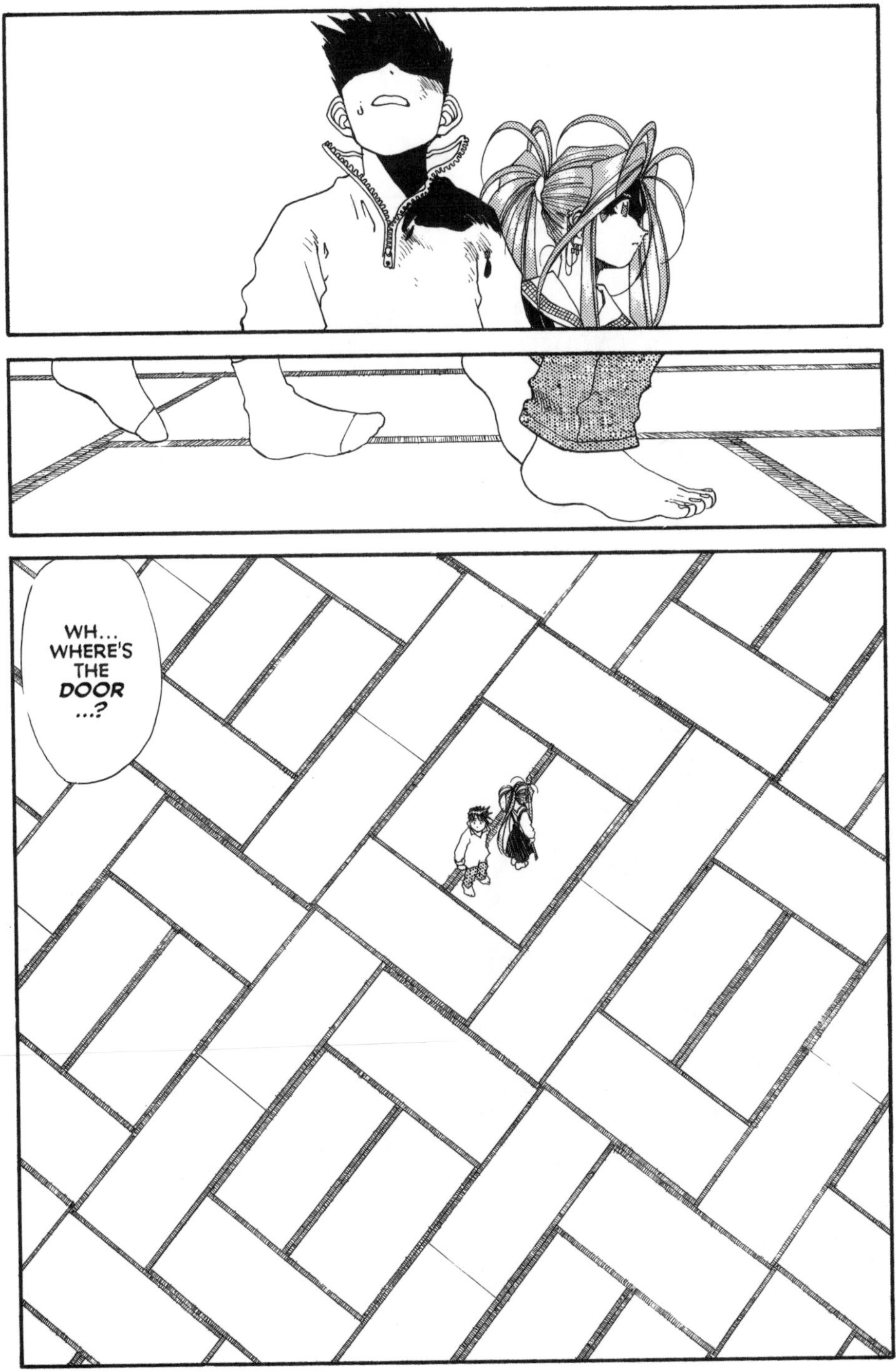
WH... WHERE'S THE *DOOR* ...?

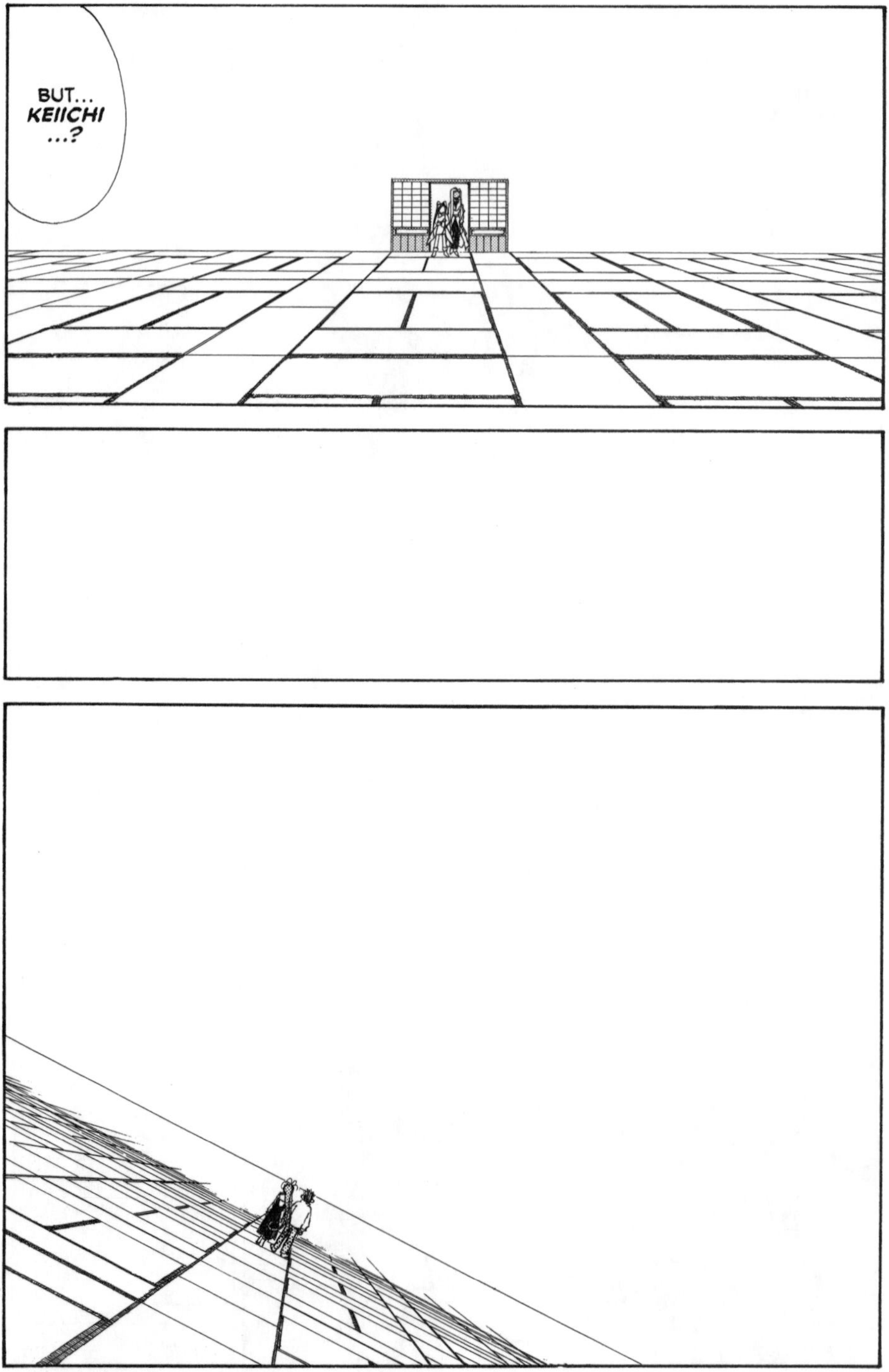
BUT... KEIICHI ...?

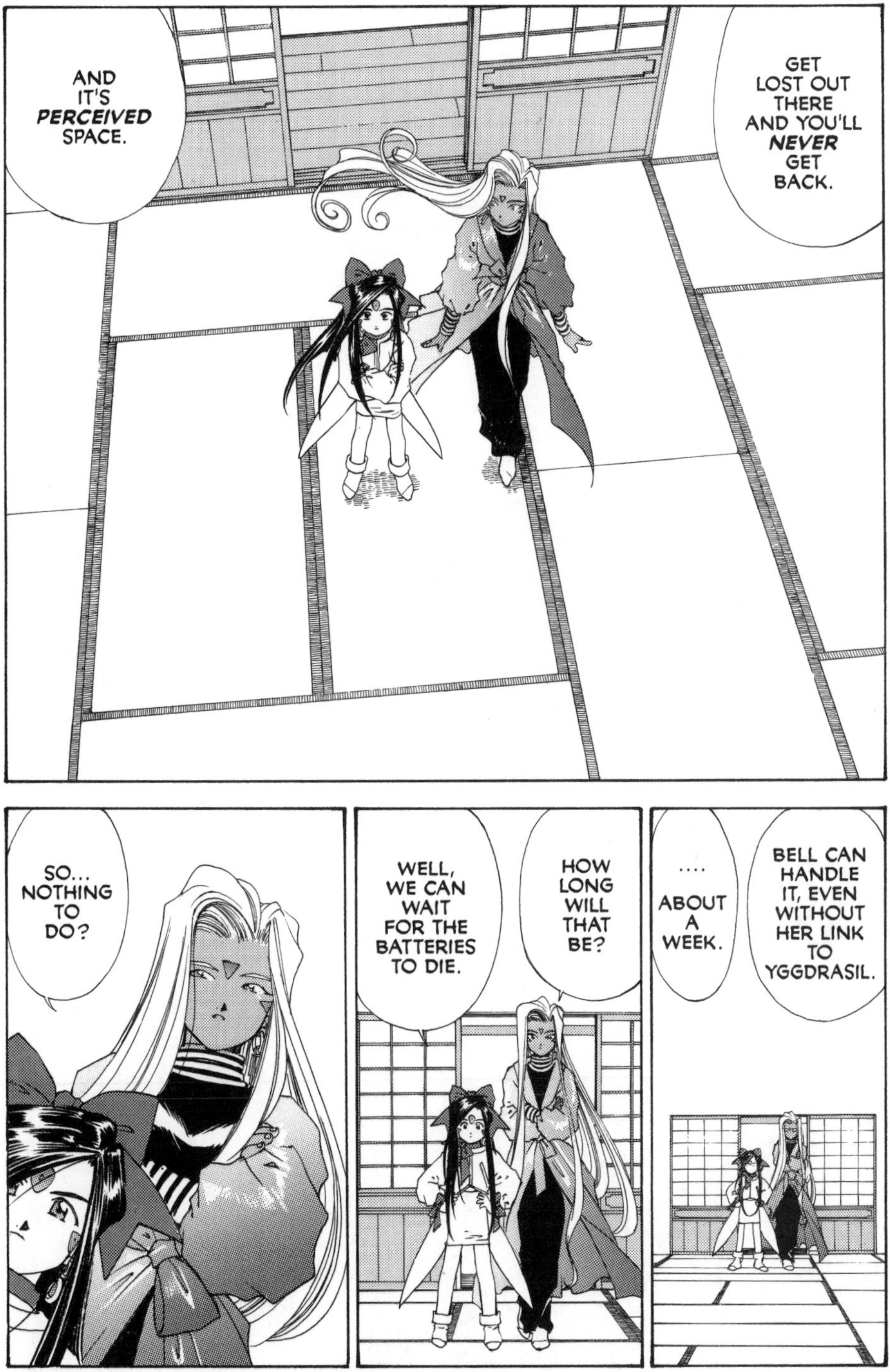
AND IT'S *PERCEIVED* SPACE.
GET LOST OUT THERE AND YOU'LL *NEVER* GET BACK.
SO... NOTHING TO DO?
WELL, WE CAN WAIT FOR THE BATTERIES TO DIE.
HOW LONG WILL THAT BE?
.... ABOUT A WEEK.
BELL CAN HANDLE IT, EVEN WITHOUT HER LINK TO YGGDRASIL.

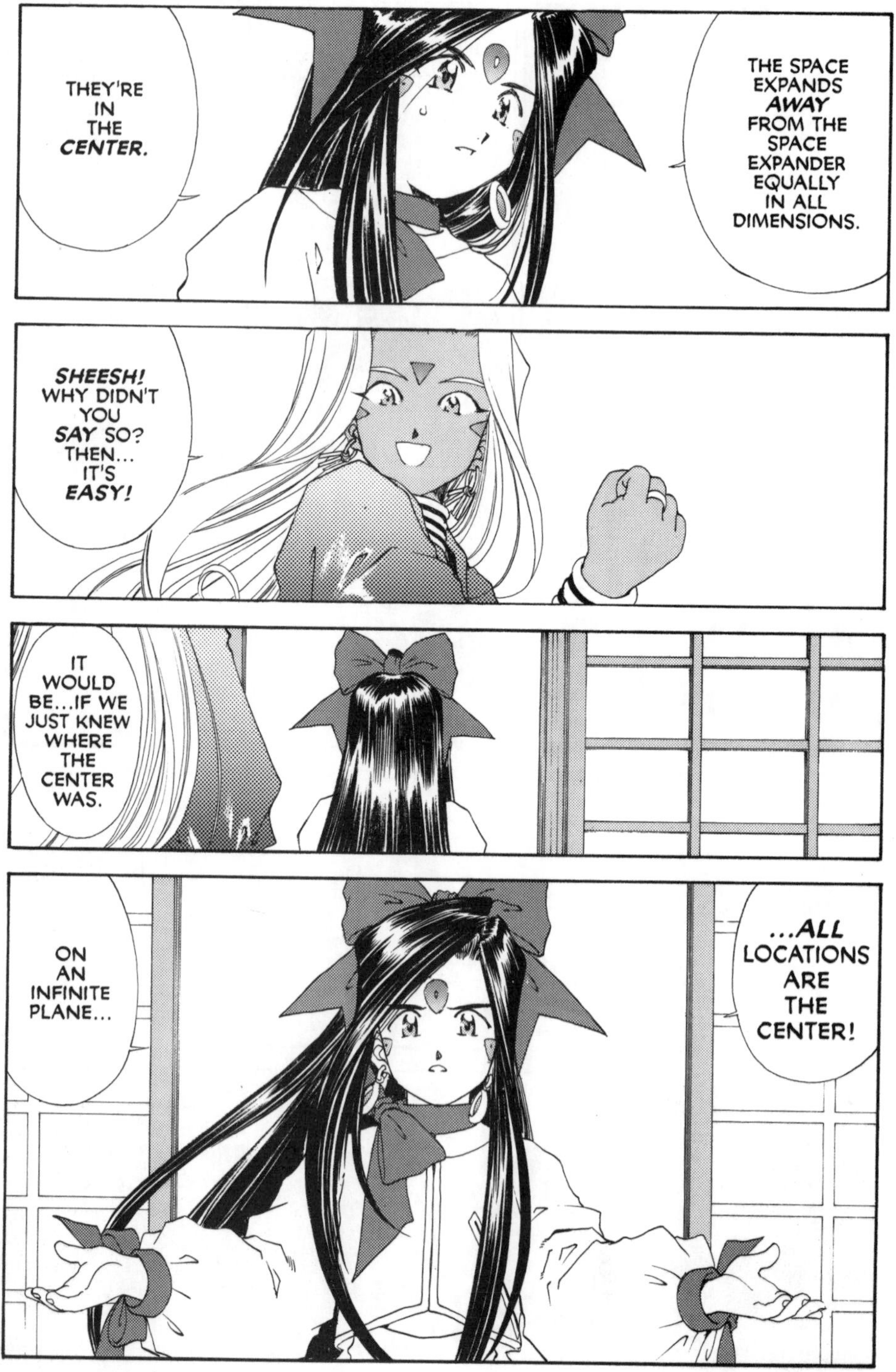
THEY'RE IN THE *CENTER.*
THE SPACE EXPANDS ***AWAY*** FROM THE SPACE EXPANDER EQUALLY IN ALL DIMENSIONS.
SHEESH! WHY DIDN'T YOU ***SAY*** SO? THEN... IT'S ***EASY!***
IT WOULD BE...IF WE JUST KNEW WHERE THE CENTER WAS.
ON AN INFINITE PLANE...
...ALL LOCATIONS ARE THE CENTER!

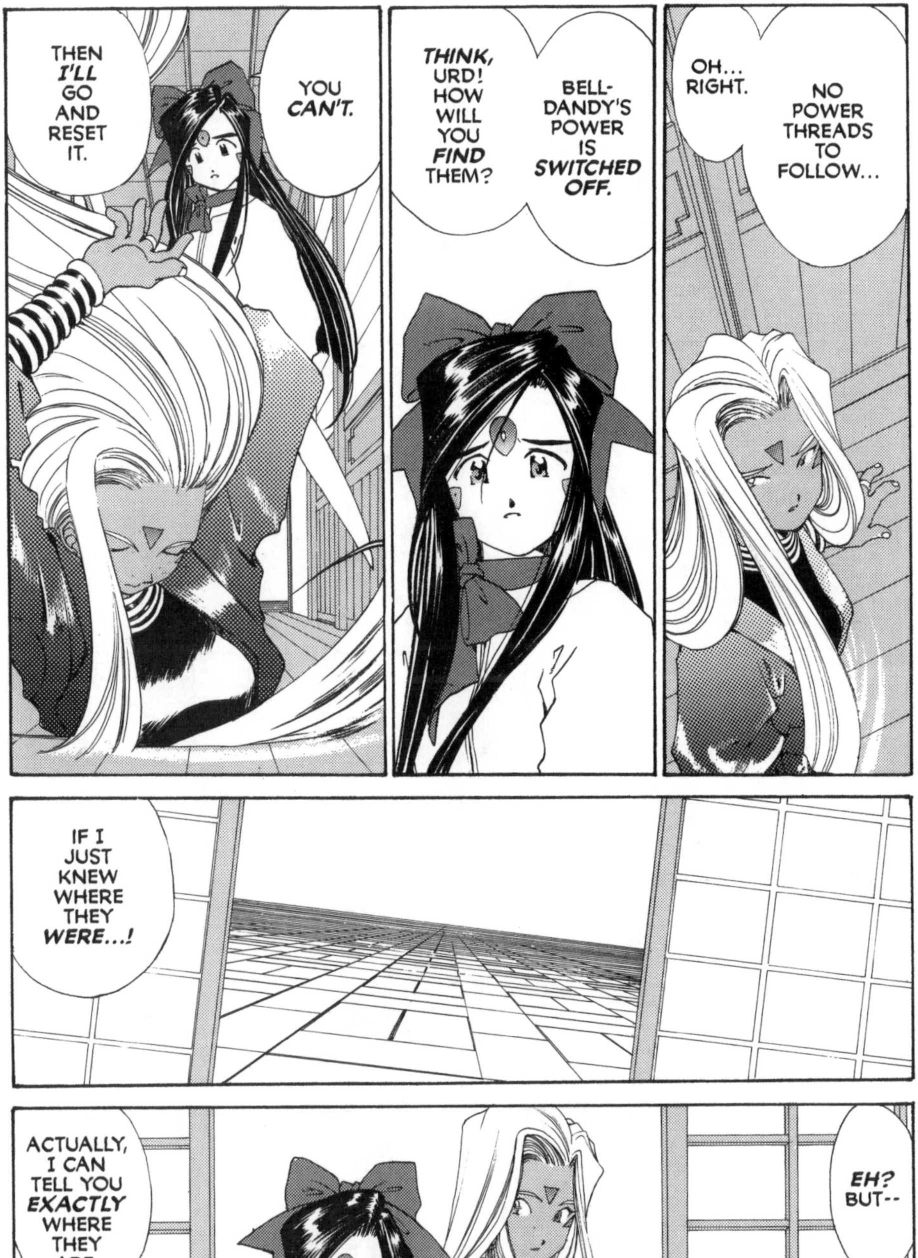
THEN I'LL GO AND RESET IT.
YOU CAN'T.
THINK, URD! HOW WILL YOU FIND THEM?
BELL-DANDY'S POWER IS SWITCHED OFF.
OH... RIGHT.
NO POWER THREADS TO FOLLOW...
IF I JUST KNEW WHERE THEY WERE...!
ACTUALLY, I CAN TELL YOU EXACTLY WHERE THEY ARE.
EH? BUT--

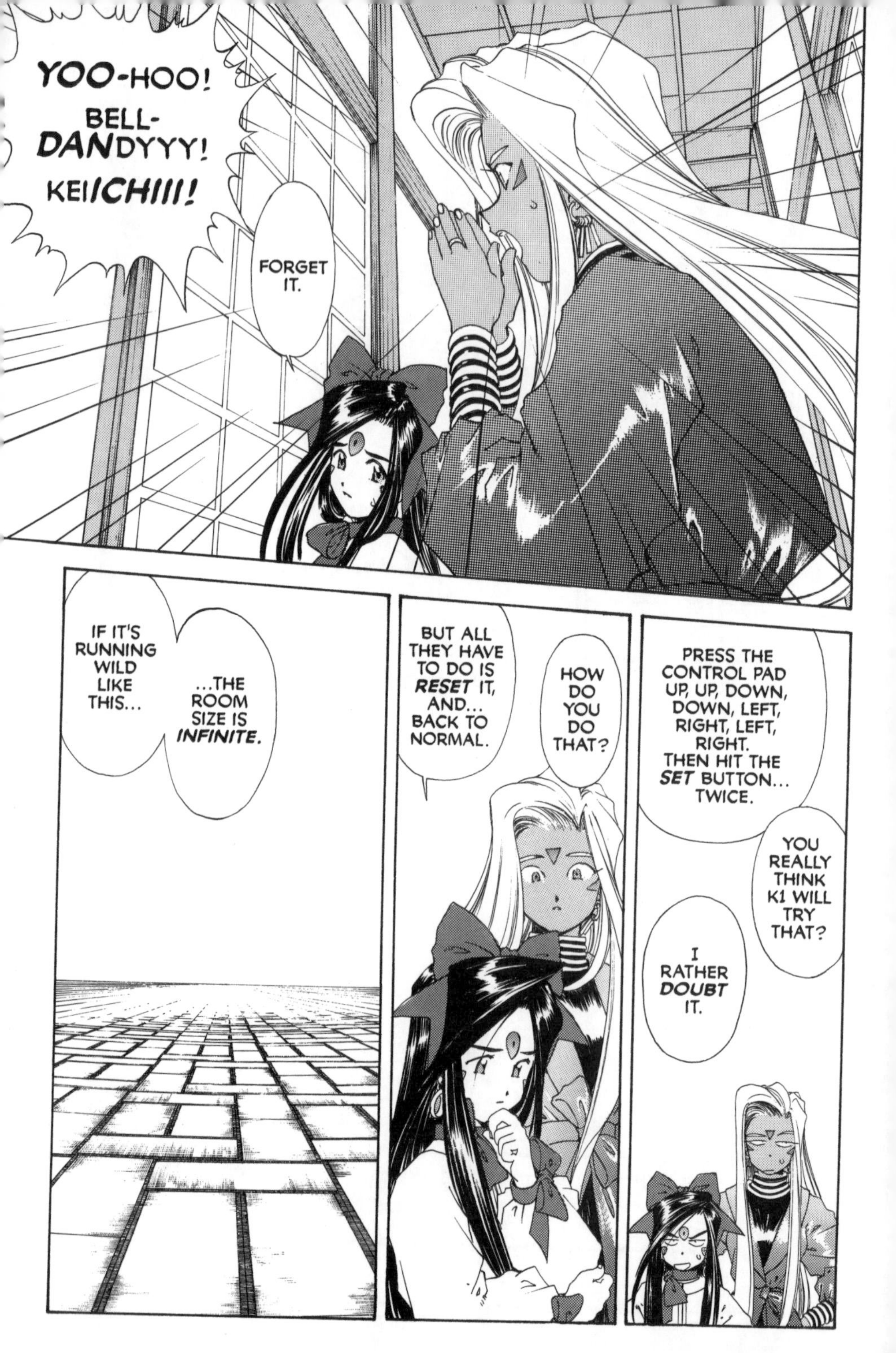
YOO-HOO! BELL-DANDYYY! KEIICHIII!
FORGET IT.
IF IT'S RUNNING WILD LIKE THIS...
...THE ROOM SIZE IS INFINITE.
BUT ALL THEY HAVE TO DO IS RESET IT, AND... BACK TO NORMAL.
HOW DO YOU DO THAT?
PRESS THE CONTROL PAD UP, UP, DOWN, DOWN, LEFT, RIGHT, LEFT, RIGHT. THEN HIT THE SET BUTTON... TWICE.
YOU REALLY THINK K1 WILL TRY THAT?
I RATHER DOUBT IT.

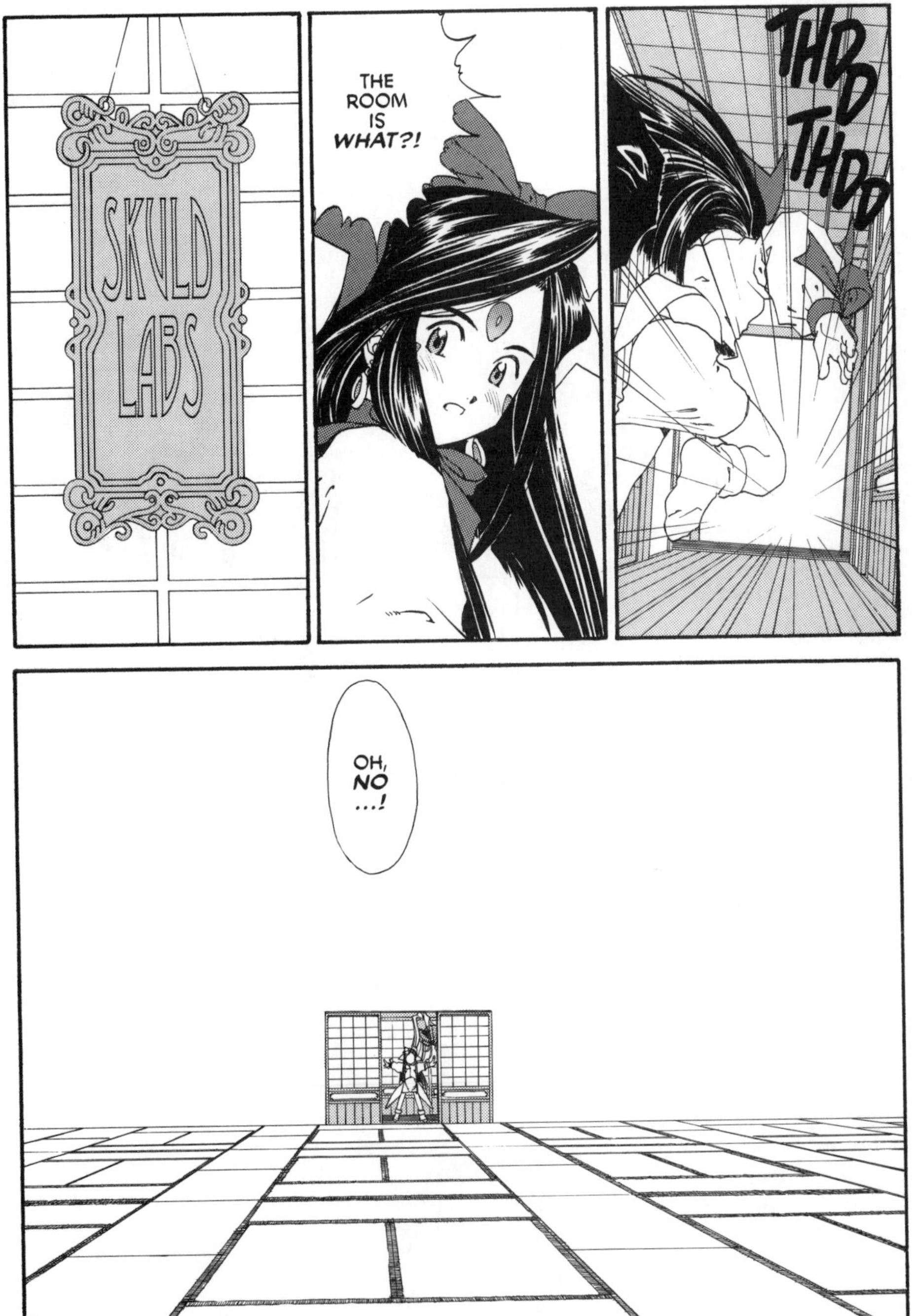
THDD THDD
THE ROOM IS WHAT?!
SKULD LABS
OH, NO ...!

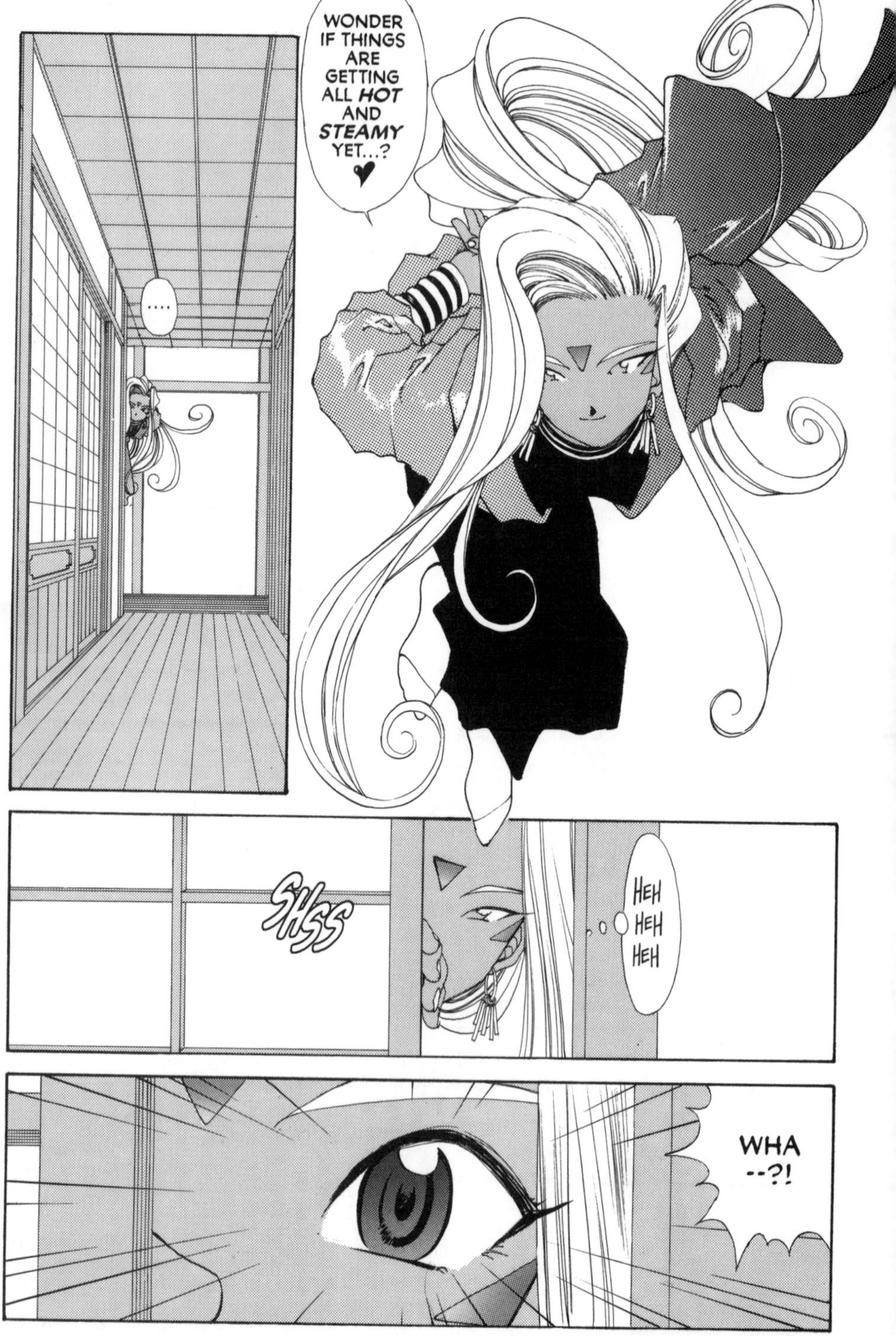
WONDER IF THINGS ARE GETTING ALL HOT AND STEAMY YET...? ♥
....
HEH HEH HEH
SHSS
WHA --?!

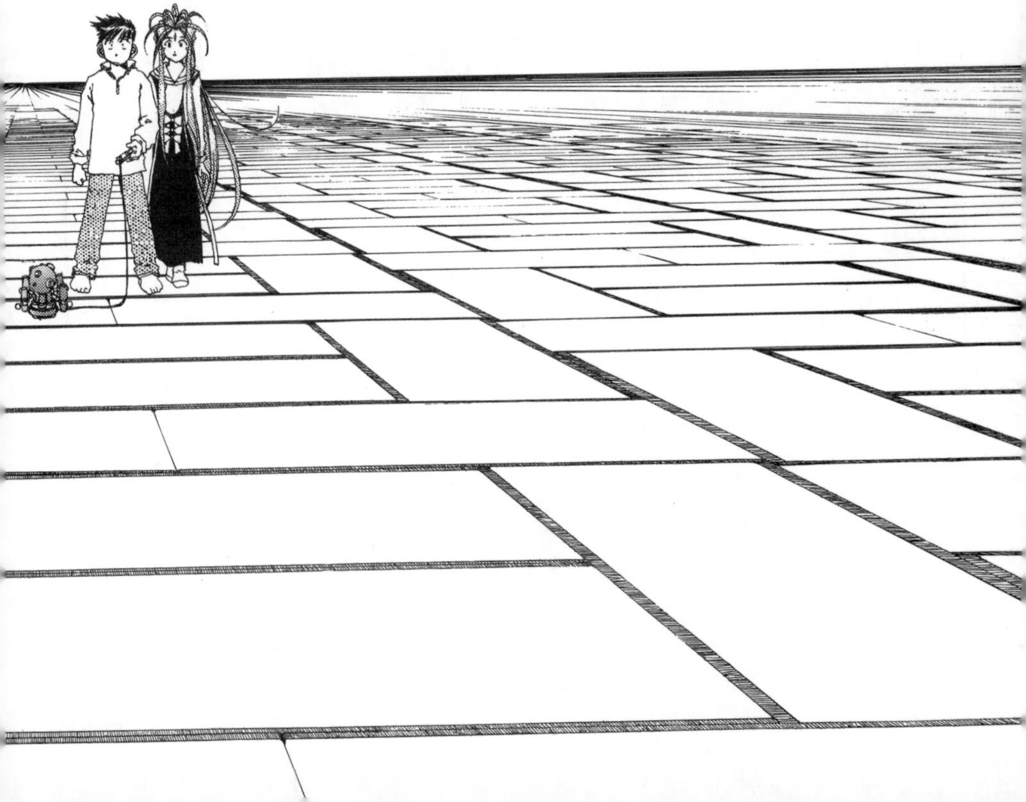

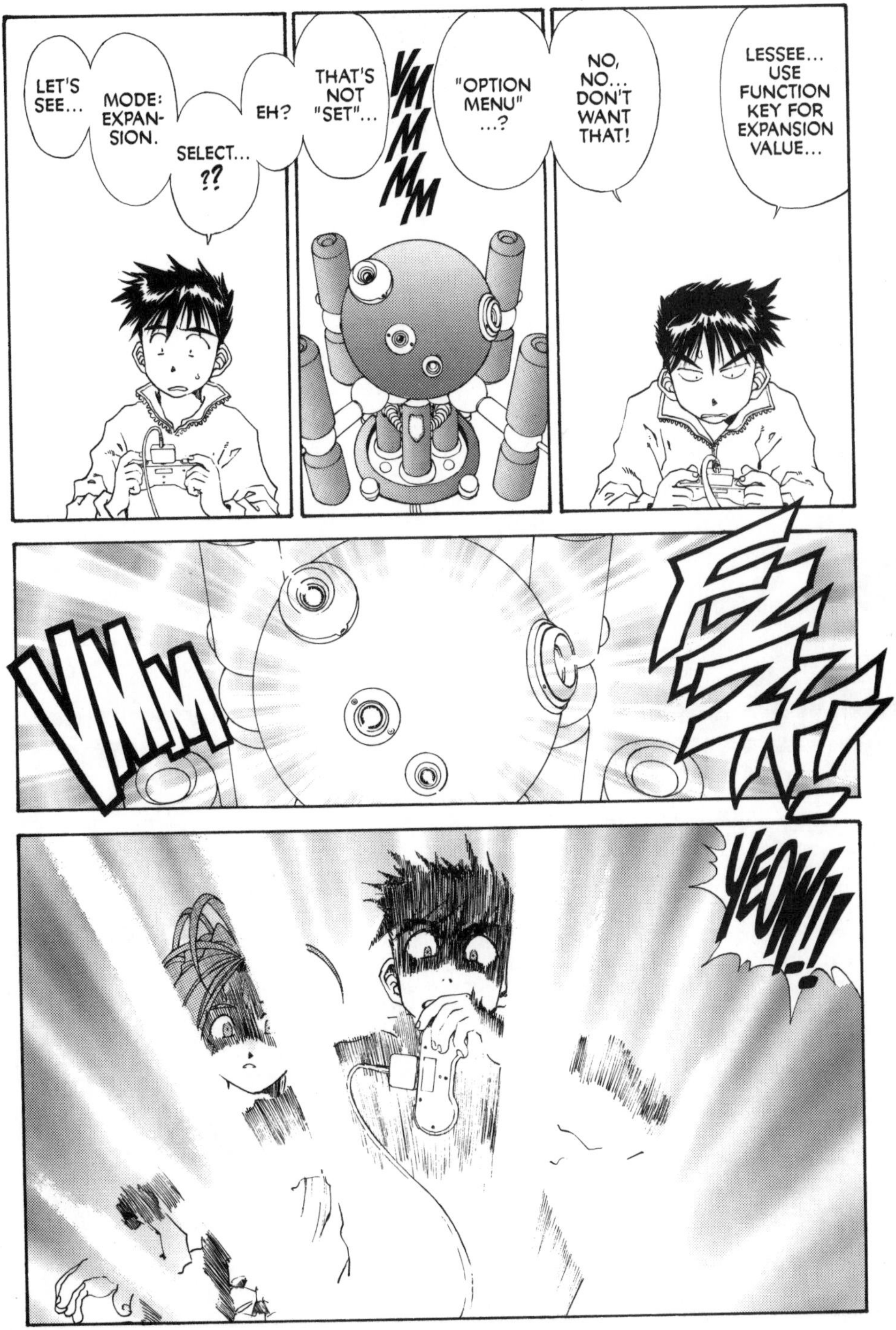
LET'S SEE...
MODE: EXPANSION.
SELECT... ??
EH?
THAT'S NOT "SET"...
VMMMMM
"OPTION MENU" ...?
NO, NO... DON'T WANT THAT!
LESSEE... USE FUNCTION KEY FOR EXPANSION VALUE...
VMM
FZZZT!
YEOW!!

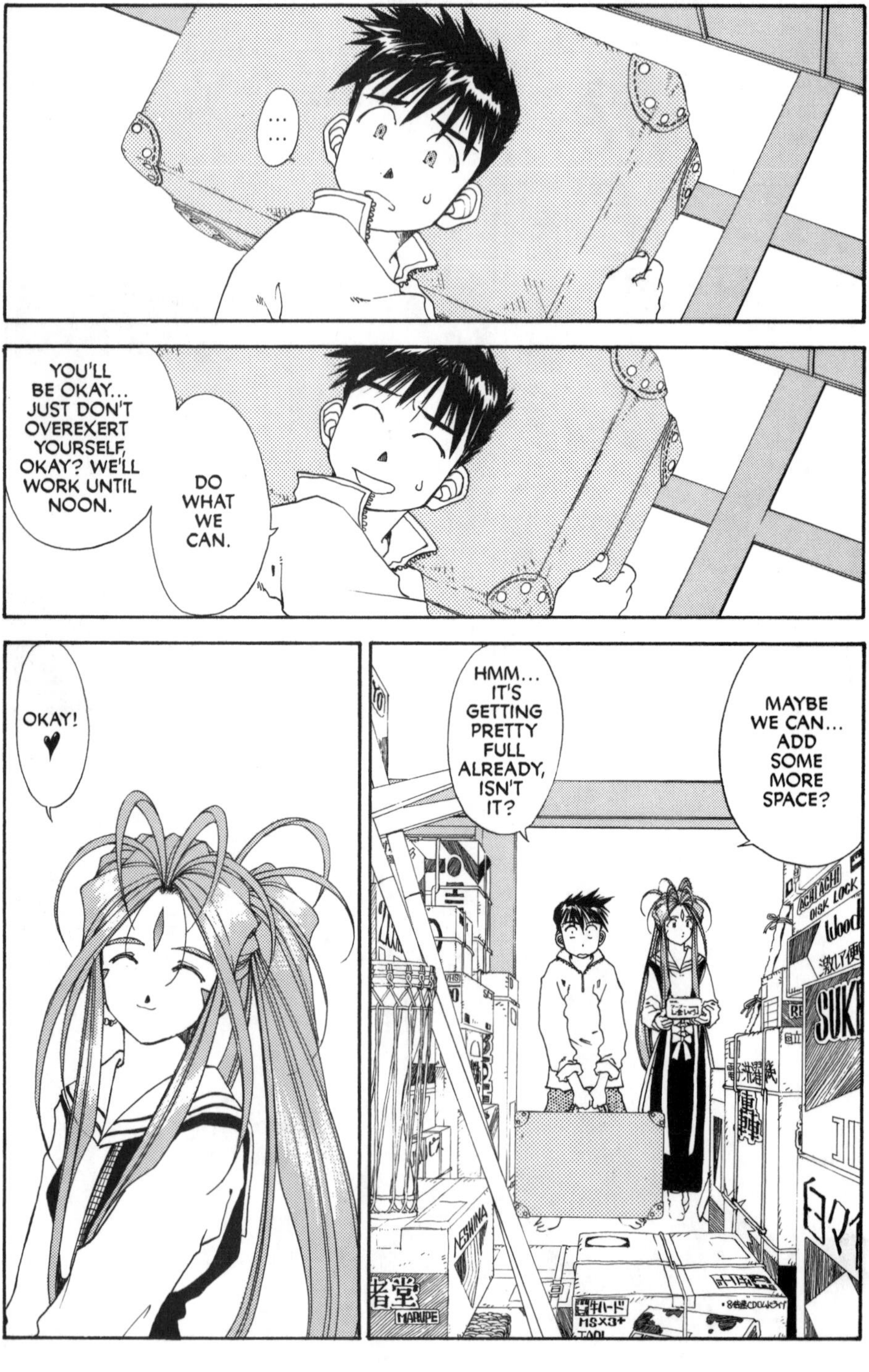
...
...
DO WHAT WE CAN.
YOU'LL BE OKAY... JUST DON'T OVEREXERT YOURSELF, OKAY? WE'LL WORK UNTIL NOON.
MAYBE WE CAN... ADD SOME MORE SPACE?
HMM... IT'S GETTING PRETTY FULL ALREADY, ISN'T IT?
ACHI ACHI
DISK LOCK
OKAY! ♥

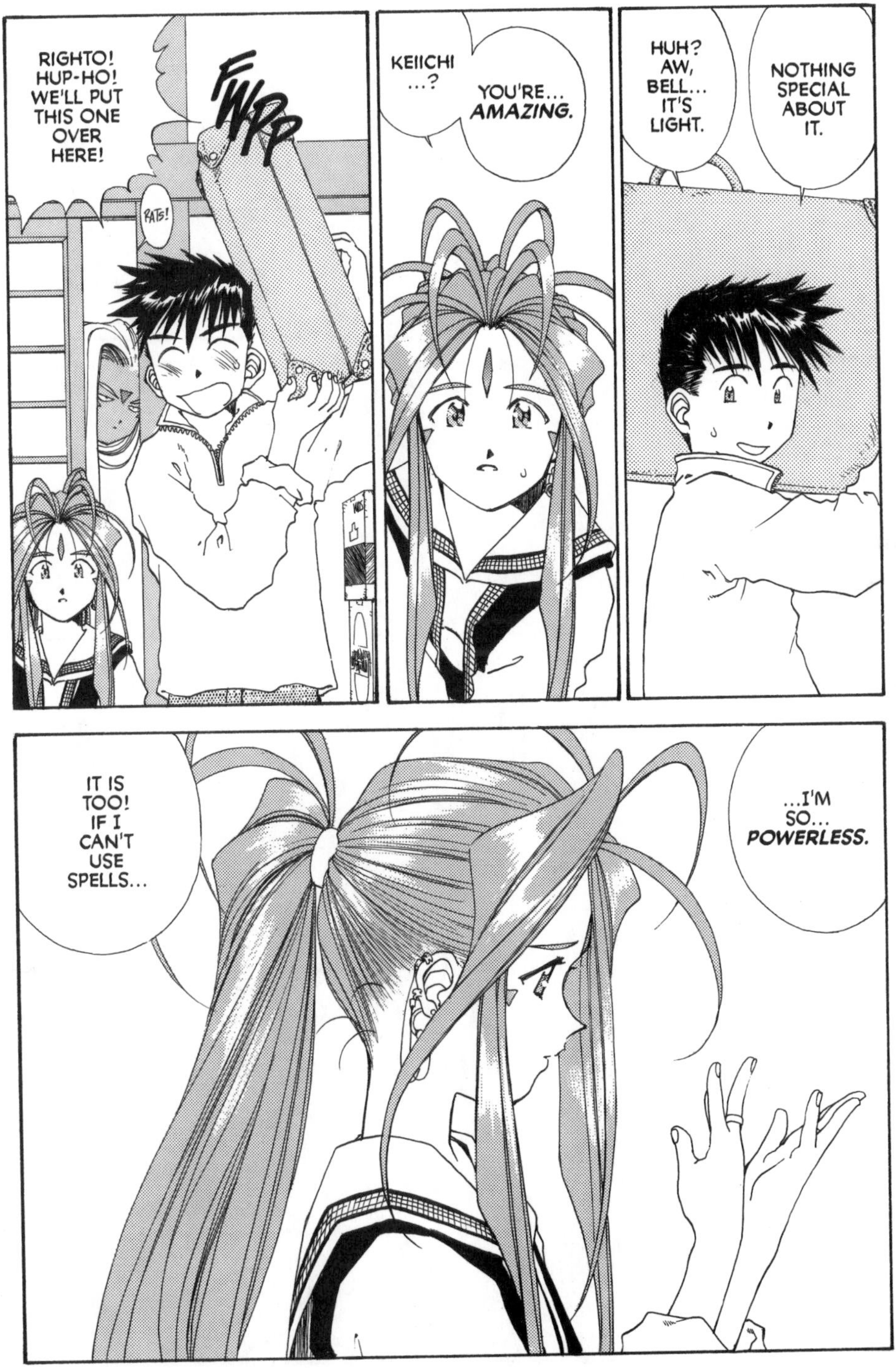
RIGHTO! HUP-HO! WE'LL PUT THIS ONE OVER HERE!
FWPP
RATS!
KEIICHI ...?
YOU'RE... AMAZING.
HUH? AW, BELL... IT'S LIGHT.
NOTHING SPECIAL ABOUT IT.
IT IS TOO! IF I CAN'T USE SPELLS...
...I'M SO... POWERLESS.

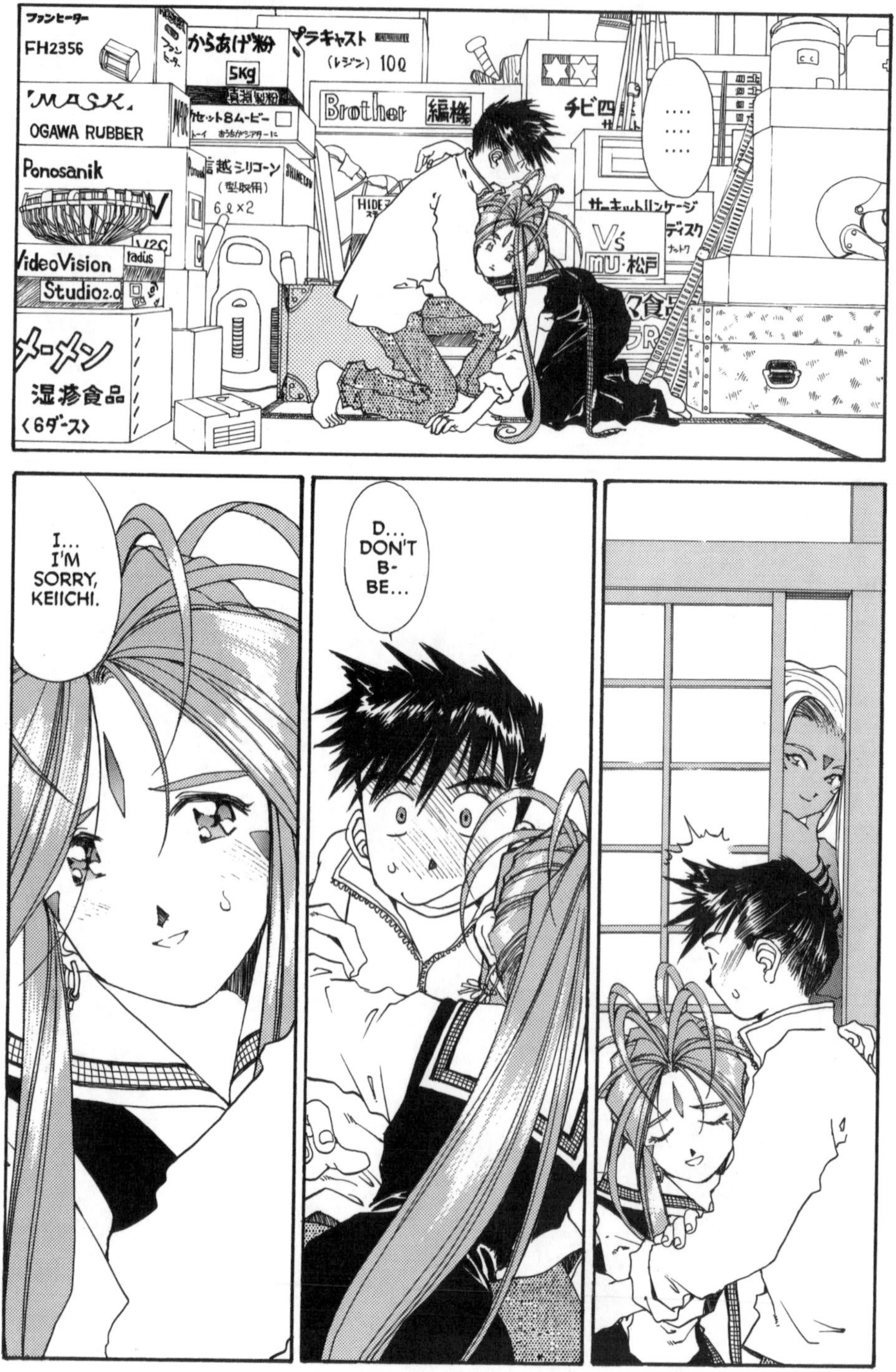
ファンヒーター
FH2356
からあげ粉
5kg
プラキャスト
(レジン) 10ℓ
Brother 編機
'MASK'
OGAWA RUBBER
Ponosanik
信越シリコーン
(型取用)
6ℓ×2
VideoVision
Studio2.0
メローメン
湿疹食品
〈6ダース〉
サーキットリンケージ
ディスク
V's
MU·松戸
....
....
....
D... DON'T B- BE...
I... I'M SORRY, KEIICHI.

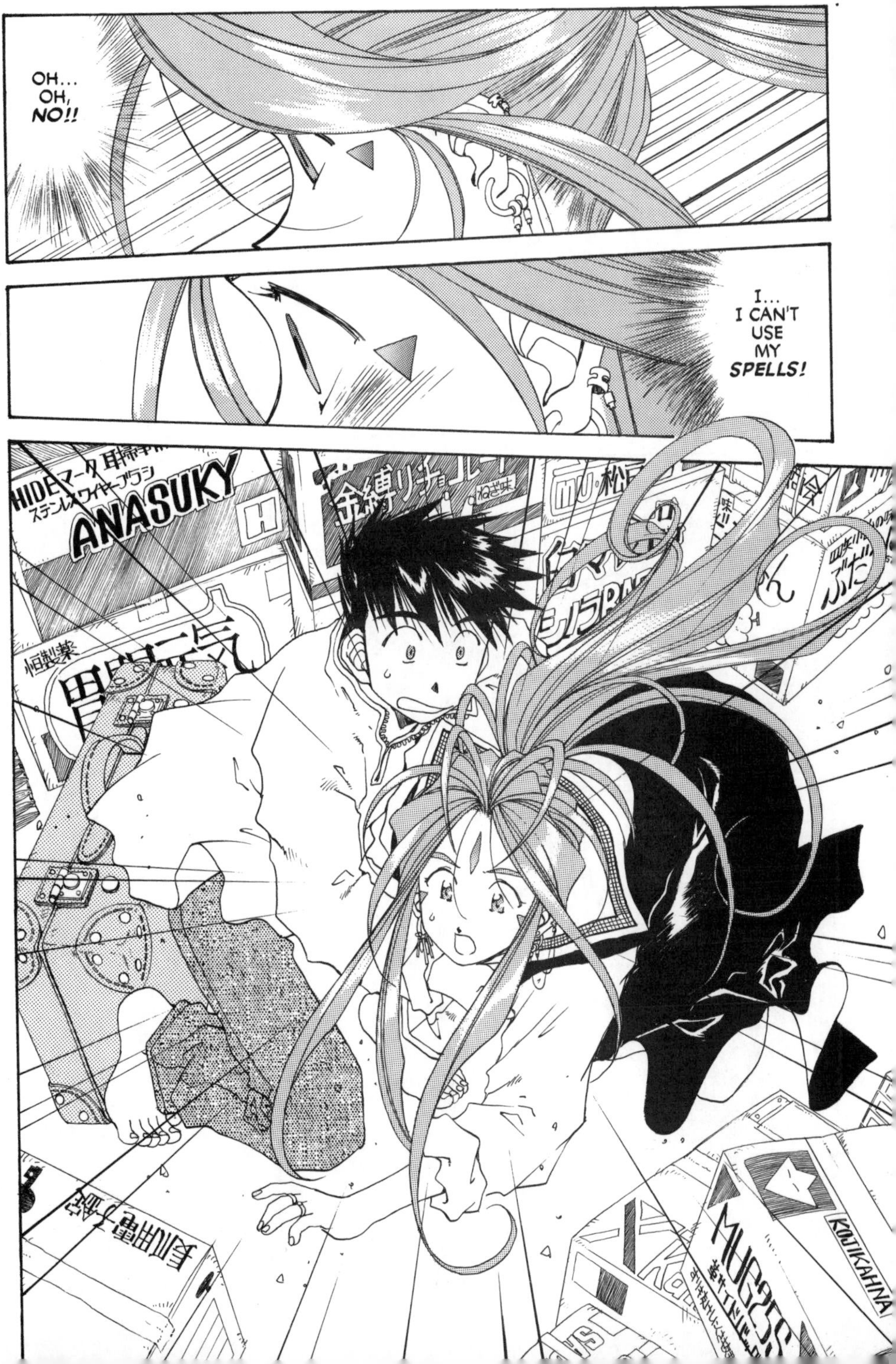
OH... OH, *NO!!*
I... I CAN'T USE MY *SPELLS!*
ANASUKY
KOJIKAHNA

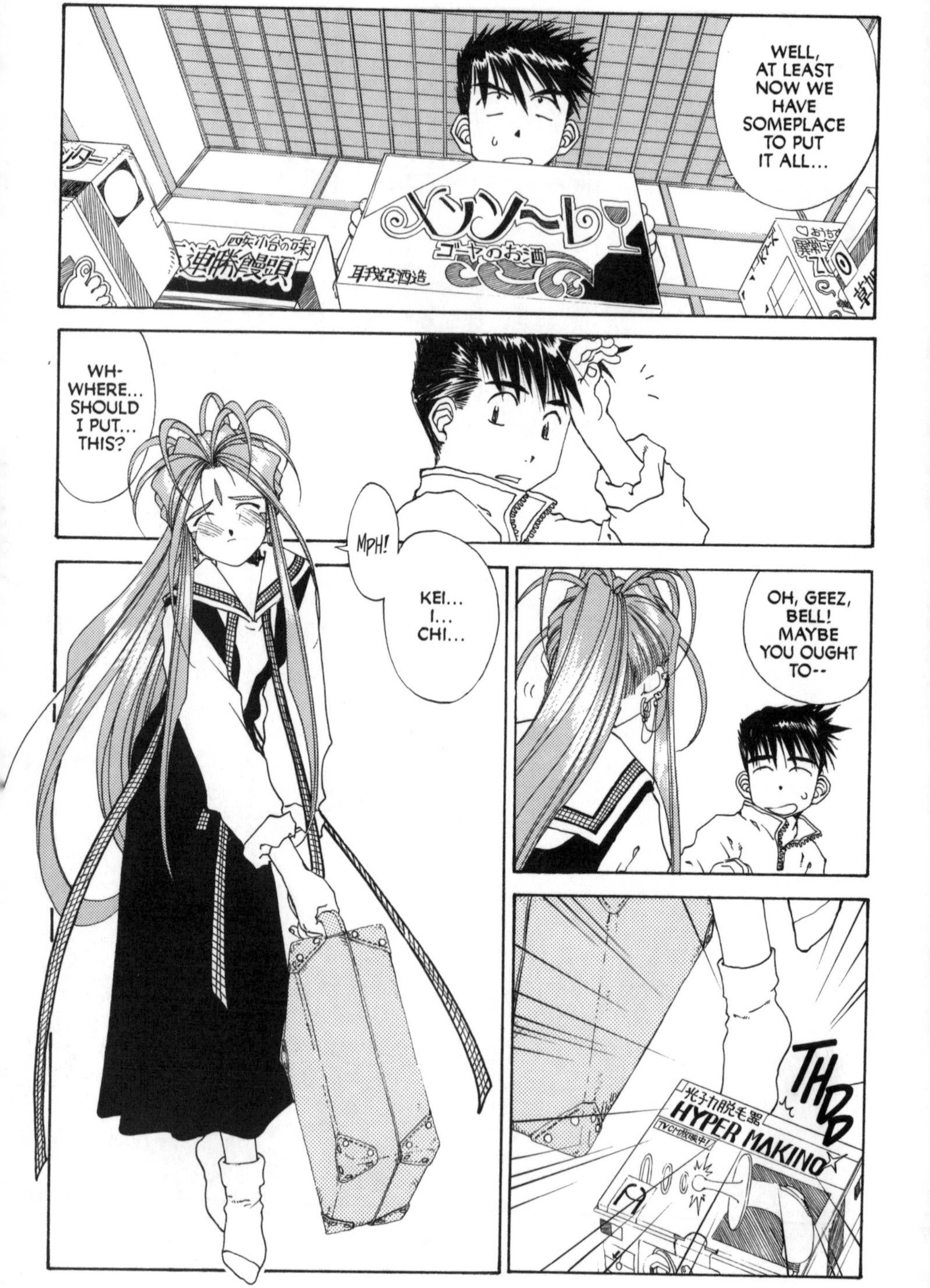
WELL, AT LEAST NOW WE HAVE SOMEPLACE TO PUT IT ALL...
ゴーヤのお酒
WH- WHERE... SHOULD I PUT... THIS?
MPH!
KEI... I... CHI...
OH, GEEZ, BELL! MAYBE YOU OUGHT TO--
THB
光子力脱毛器
HYPER MAKINO
TVCM放映中!

...BY *BORROW-ING* AGAINST *SPACE-TIME.*

I DON'T GET IT... BUT... *AMAZING!*

SO... HAVE FUN.

WHAT?! YOU'RE NOT *HELP-ING?*

OKAY, URD, YOU--

AH?!

DOOM

I'LL HELP, KEIICHI.

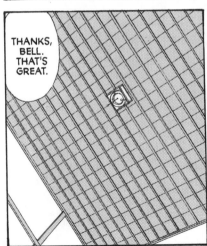

THANKS, BELL. THAT'S GREAT.

HEAVE

HO!!

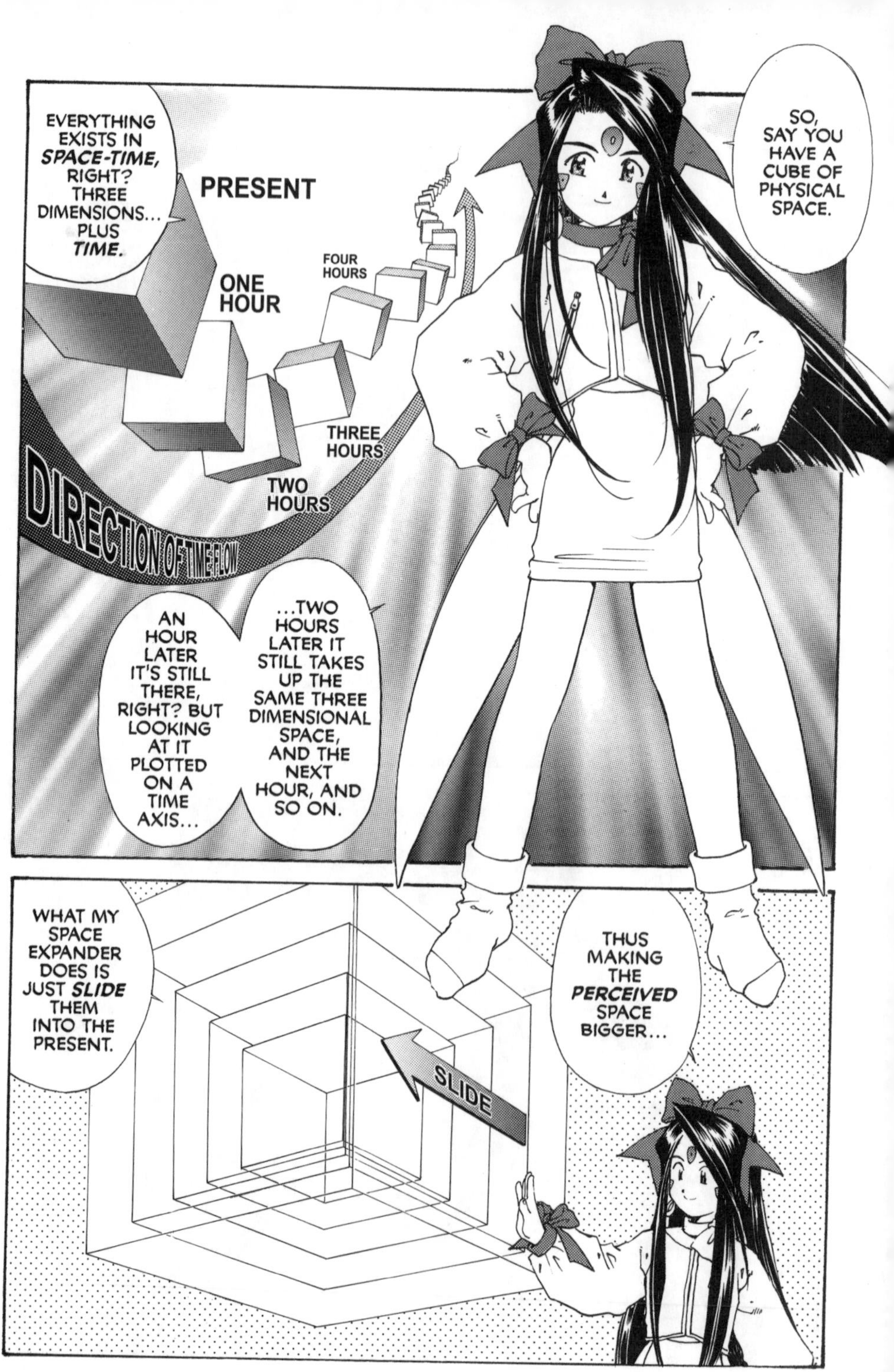
EVERYTHING EXISTS IN *SPACE-TIME,* RIGHT? THREE DIMENSIONS... PLUS *TIME.*
PRESENT
ONE HOUR
TWO HOURS
THREE HOURS
FOUR HOURS
DIRECTION OF TIME FLOW
SO, SAY YOU HAVE A CUBE OF PHYSICAL SPACE.
AN HOUR LATER IT'S STILL THERE, RIGHT? BUT LOOKING AT IT PLOTTED ON A TIME AXIS...
...TWO HOURS LATER IT STILL TAKES UP THE SAME THREE DIMENSIONAL SPACE, AND THE NEXT HOUR, AND SO ON.
WHAT MY SPACE EXPANDER DOES IS JUST *SLIDE* THEM INTO THE PRESENT.
SLIDE
THUS MAKING THE *PERCEIVED* SPACE BIGGER...

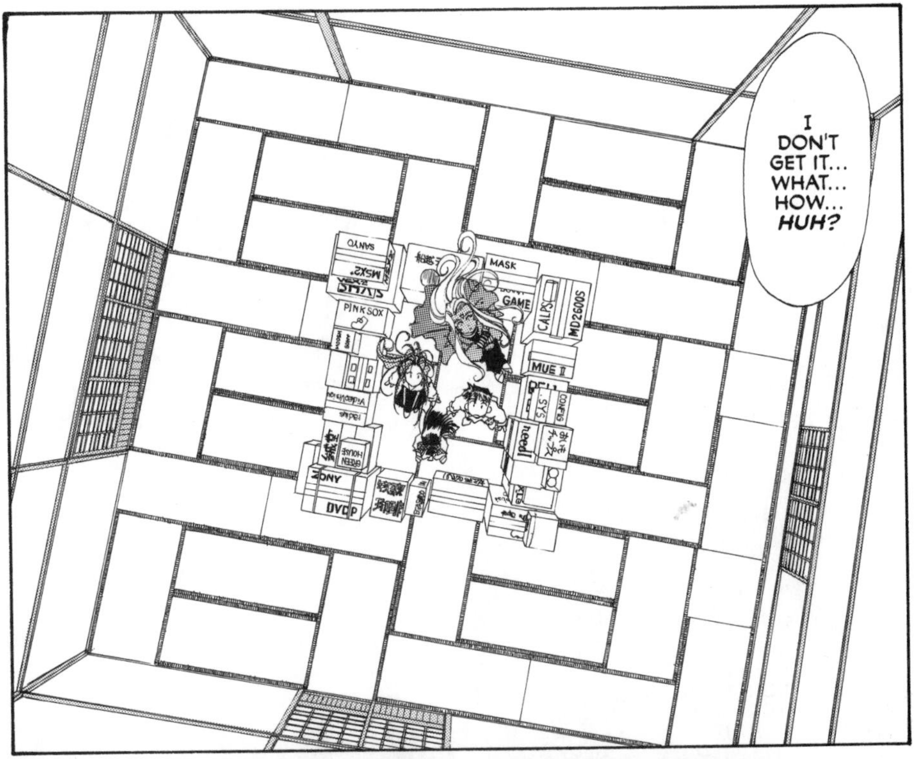
I DON'T GET IT... WHAT... HOW... ***HUH?***
MASK
GAME
PINKSOX
CALPS
MD2600S

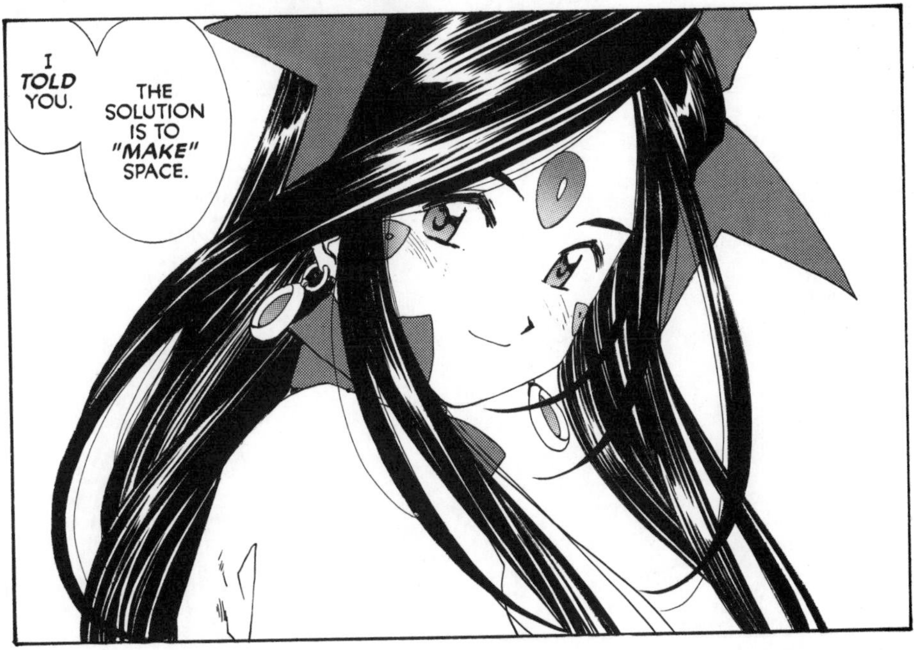
I ***TOLD*** YOU.
THE SOLUTION IS TO ***"MAKE"*** SPACE.

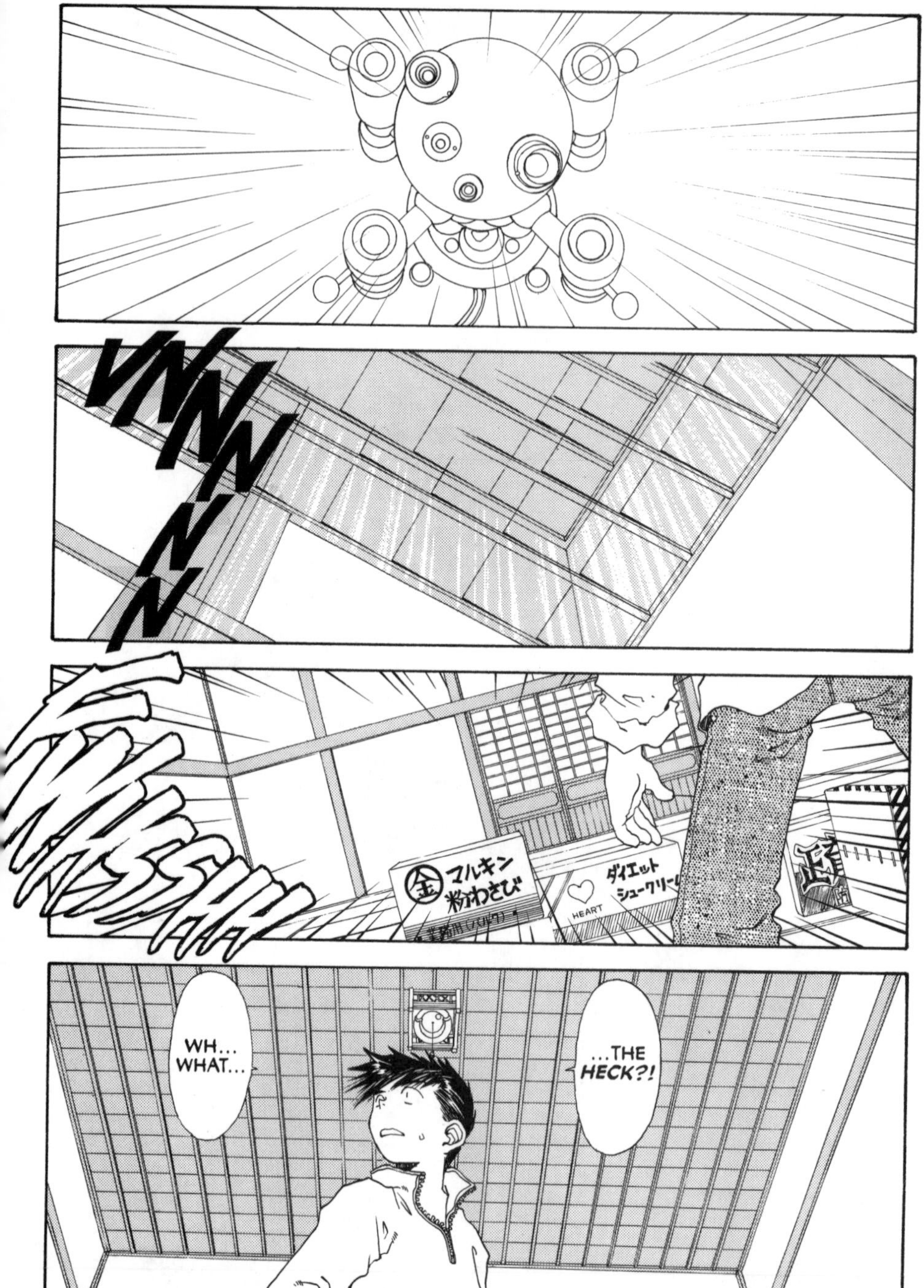
VNNNN
WHASSHH
マルキン
粉わさび
ダイエット
HEART
WH... WHAT...
...THE HECK?!

WIDE, WIDER, WIDEST

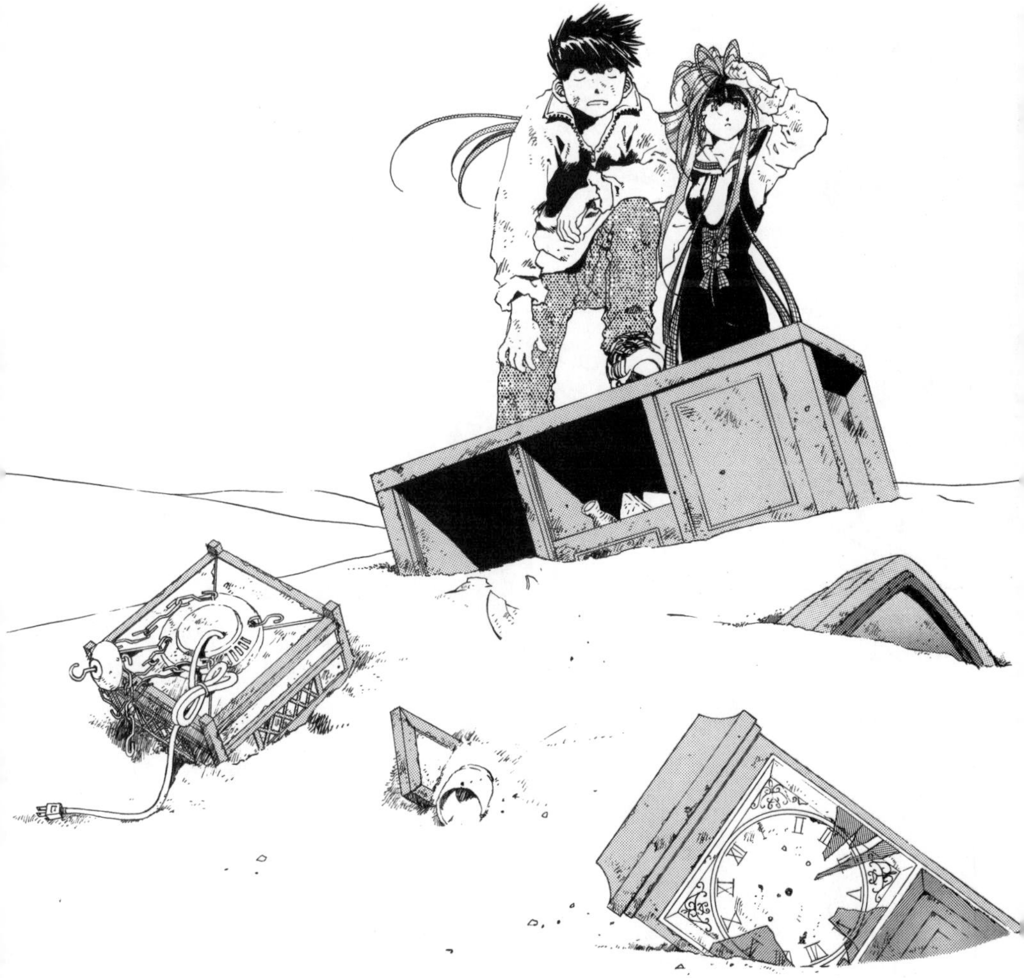

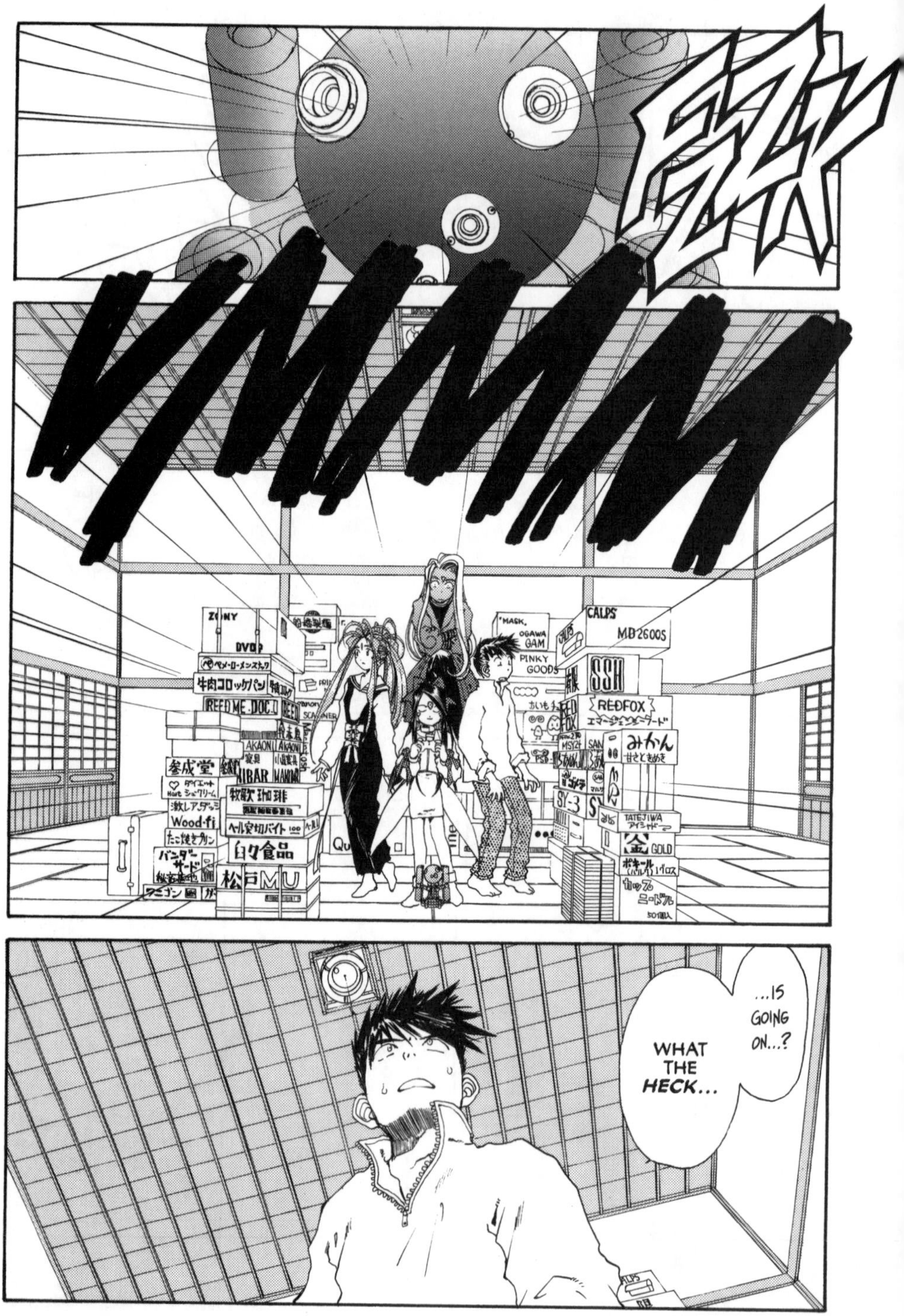
FZZK
WHAT THE HECK...
...IS GOING ON...?

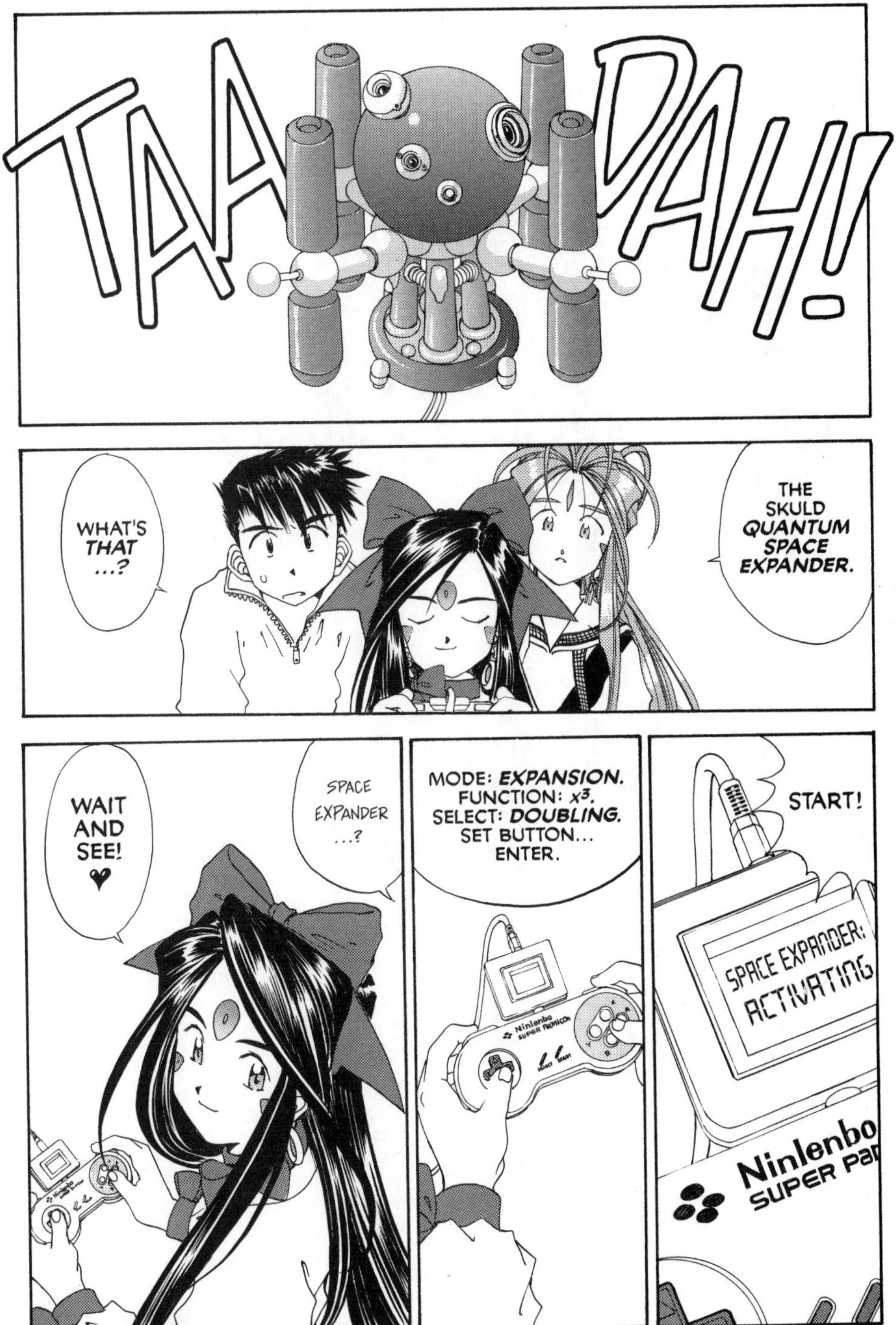
TAA DAH!!
WHAT'S *THAT* ...?
THE SKULD *QUANTUM SPACE EXPANDER.*
SPACE EXPANDER ...?
WAIT AND SEE! ♥
MODE: *EXPANSION.* FUNCTION: x^3. SELECT: *DOUBLING.* SET BUTTON... ENTER.
Ninlenbo SUPER FAMICOM
SELECT START
START!
SPACE EXPANDER: ACTIVATING
Ninlenbo SUPER PA

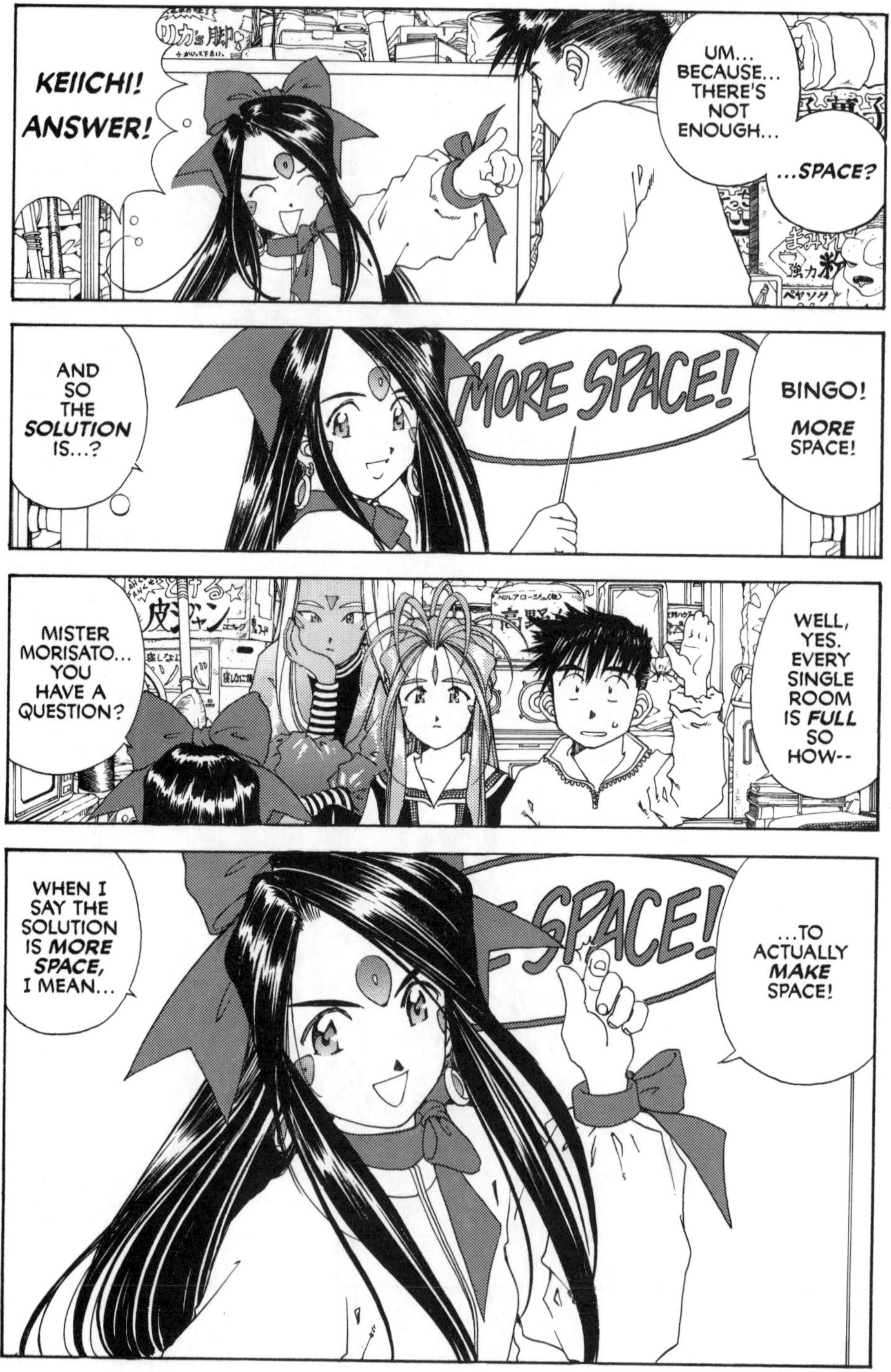
KEIICHI! ANSWER!
UM... BECAUSE... THERE'S NOT ENOUGH...
...SPACE?
AND SO THE SOLUTION IS...?
MORE SPACE!
BINGO! MORE SPACE!
MISTER MORISATO... YOU HAVE A QUESTION?
WELL, YES. EVERY SINGLE ROOM IS FULL SO HOW--
WHEN I SAY THE SOLUTION IS MORE SPACE, I MEAN...
...TO ACTUALLY MAKE SPACE!

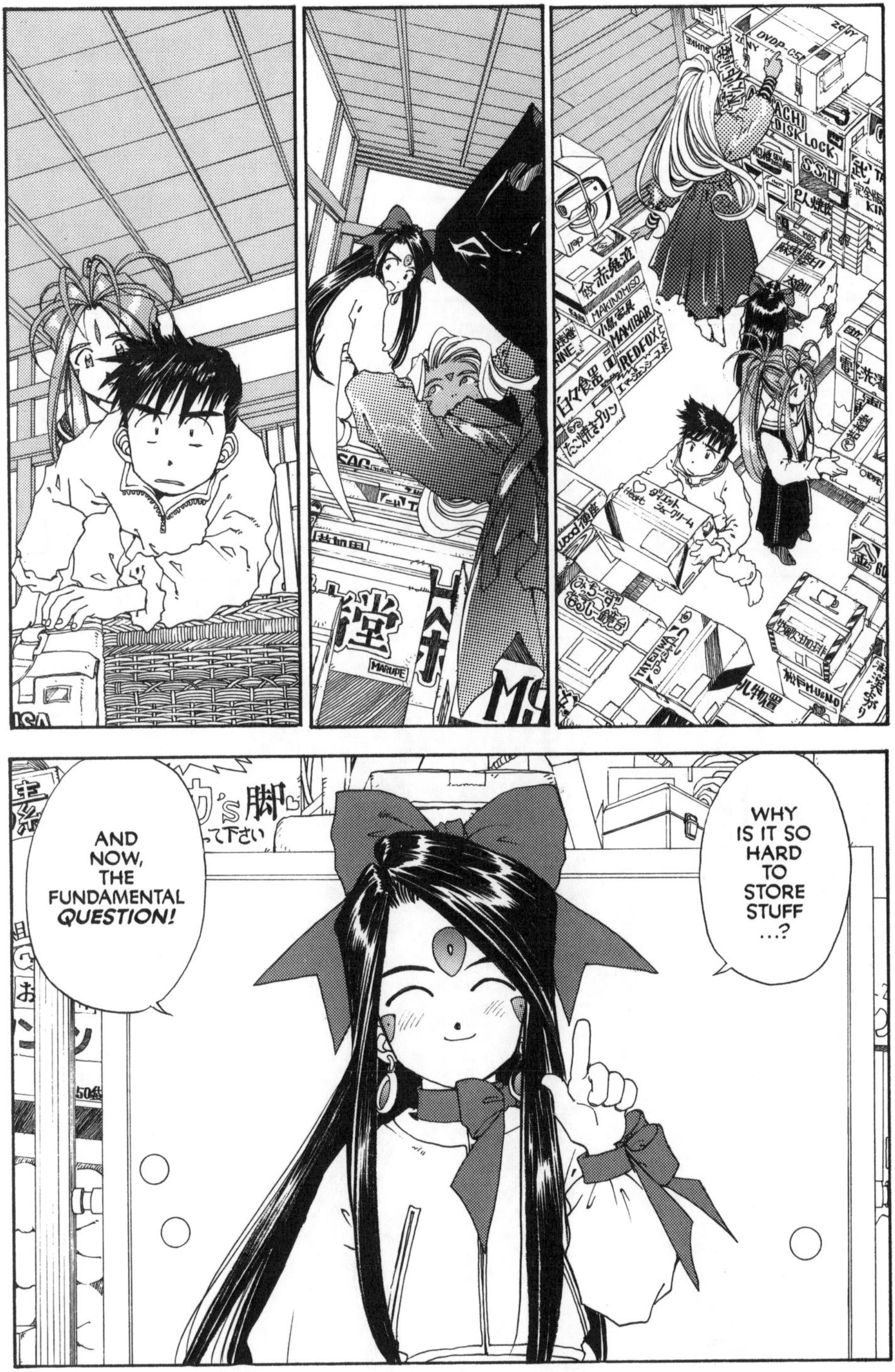
AND NOW, THE FUNDAMENTAL QUESTION!
WHY IS IT SO HARD TO STORE STUFF ...?

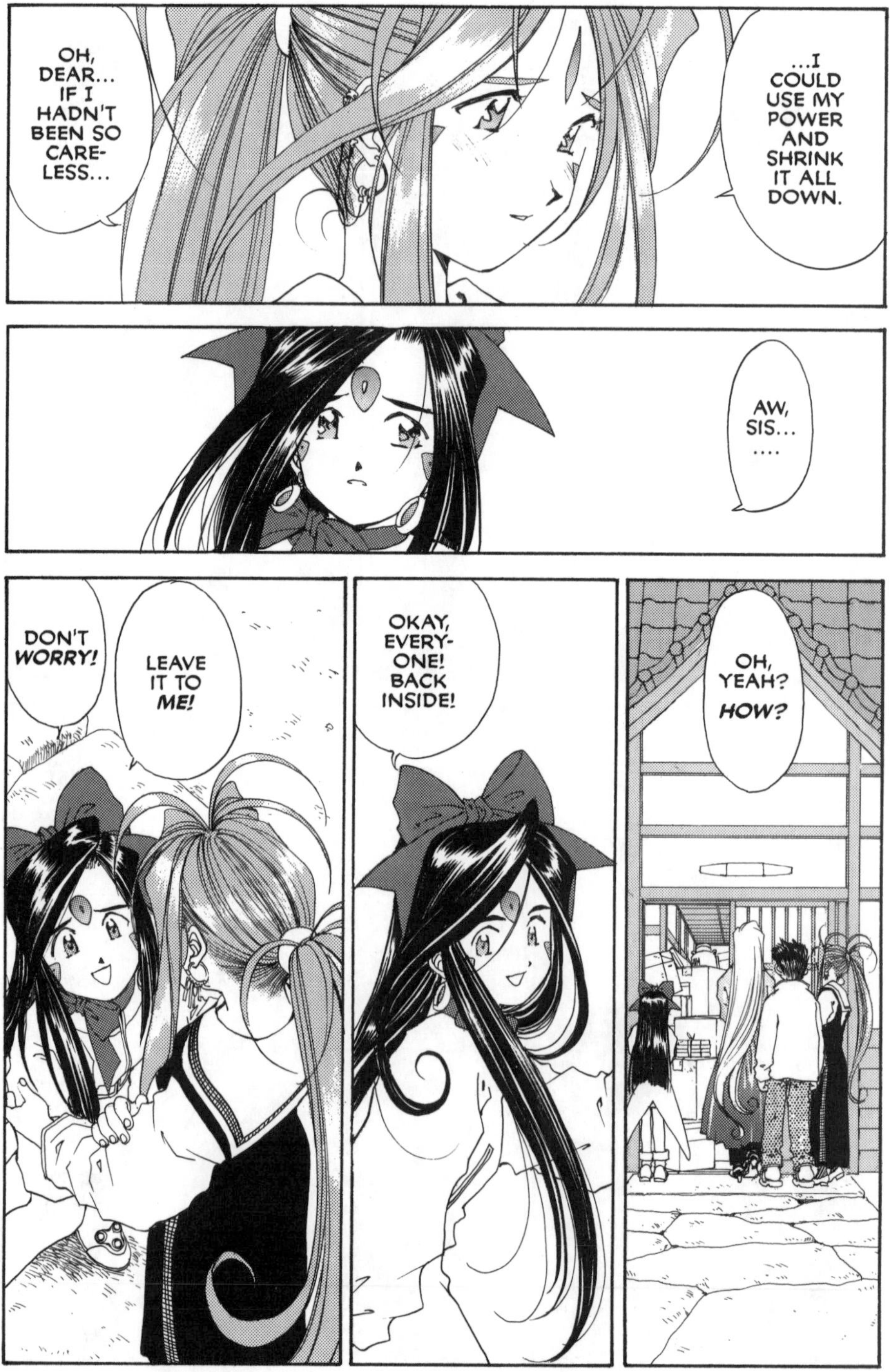
OH, DEAR... IF I HADN'T BEEN SO CARE-LESS...
...I COULD USE MY POWER AND SHRINK IT ALL DOWN.
AW, SIS... ....
DON'T *WORRY!*
LEAVE IT TO *ME!*
OKAY, EVERY-ONE! BACK INSIDE!
OH, YEAH? *HOW?*

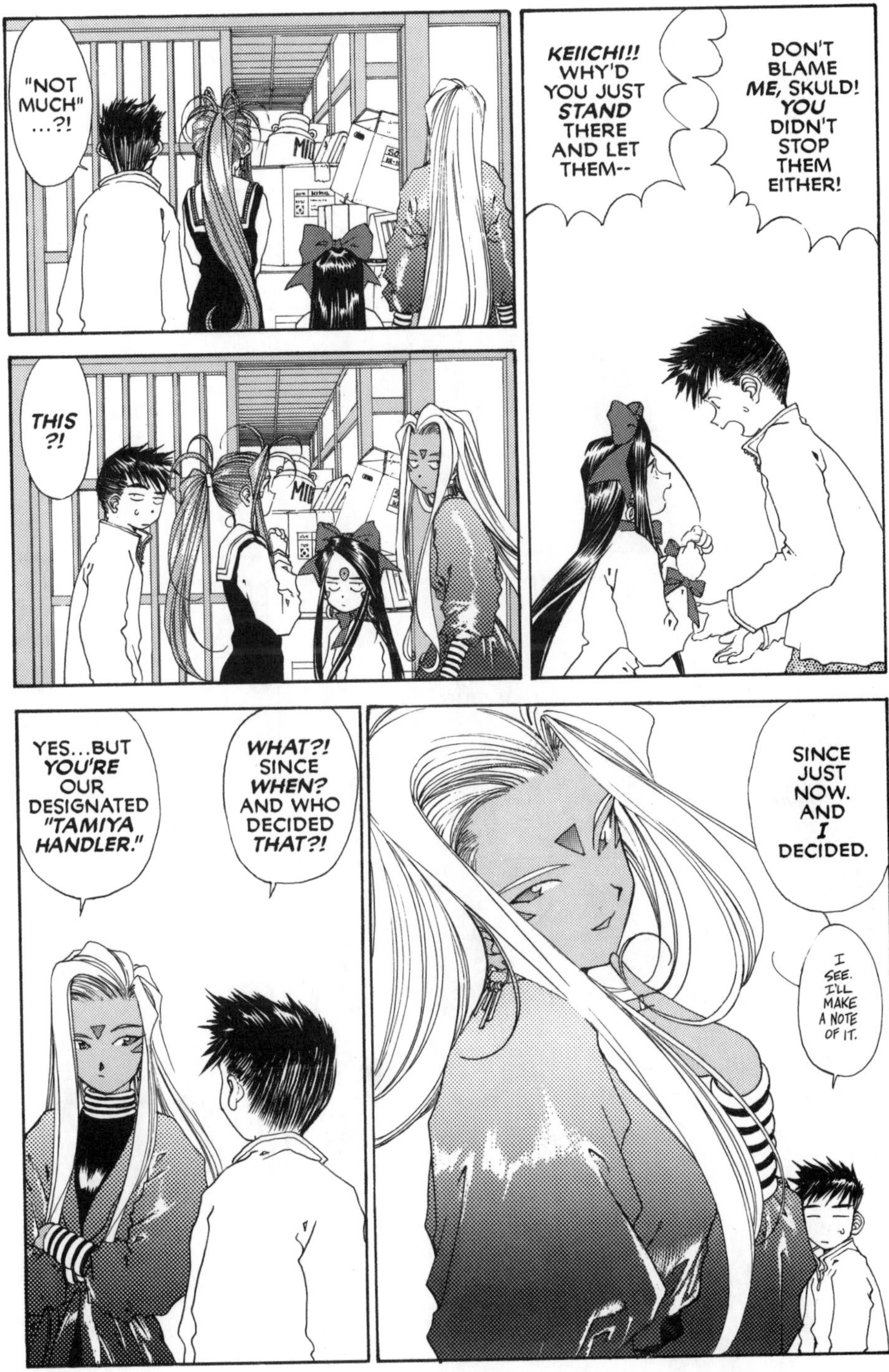
"NOT MUCH" ...?!
THIS ?!
KEIICHI!! WHY'D YOU JUST STAND THERE AND LET THEM--
DON'T BLAME ME, SKULD! YOU DIDN'T STOP THEM EITHER!
YES...BUT YOU'RE OUR DESIGNATED "TAMIYA HANDLER."
WHAT?! SINCE WHEN? AND WHO DECIDED THAT?!
SINCE JUST NOW. AND I DECIDED.
I SEE. I'LL MAKE A NOTE OF IT.

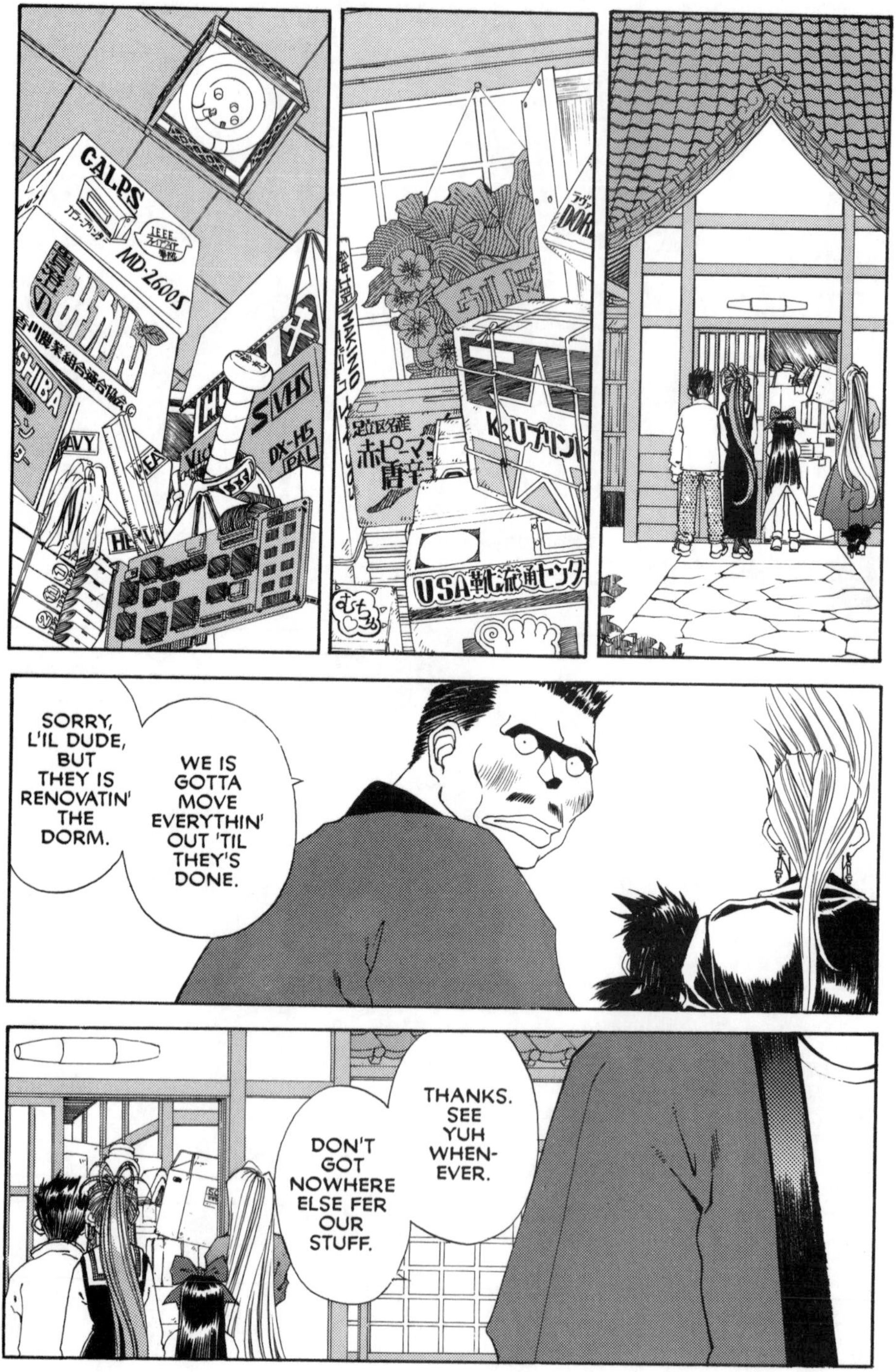
CALPS
MD-2600S
S-VHS
DX-H5 PAL
K&Uプリント
USA靴流通センター
SORRY, L'IL DUDE, BUT THEY IS RENOVATIN' THE DORM.
WE IS GOTTA MOVE EVERYTHIN' OUT 'TIL THEY'S DONE.
DON'T GOT NOWHERE ELSE FER OUR STUFF.
THANKS. SEE YUH WHEN-EVER.

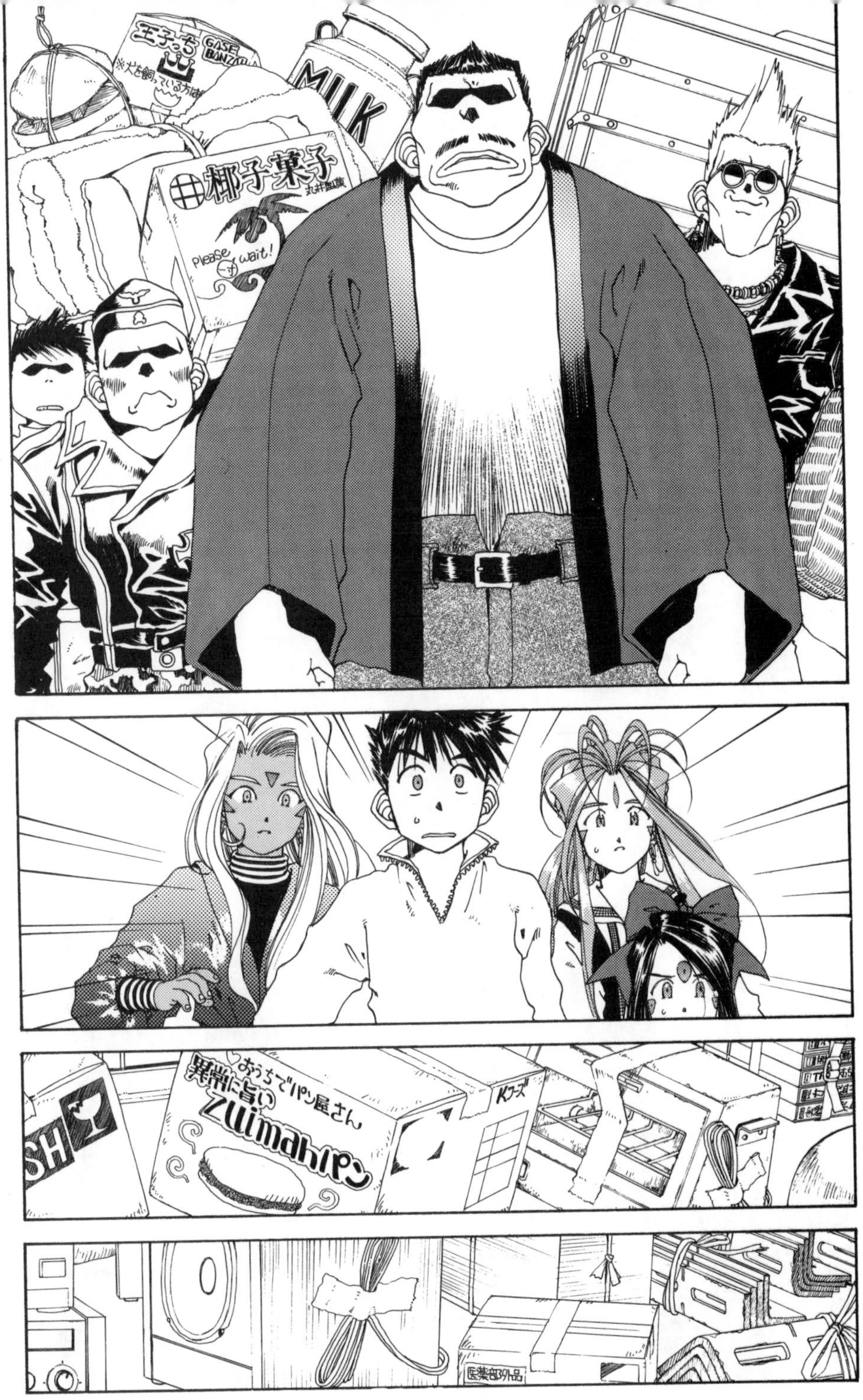
MILK
王子っち
GASE BANZAI
※犬を飼っている方は
椰子菓子
丸井製菓
please wait!
おうちでパン屋さん
異常に旨い
zuimahパン
Kフーズ
医薬部外品

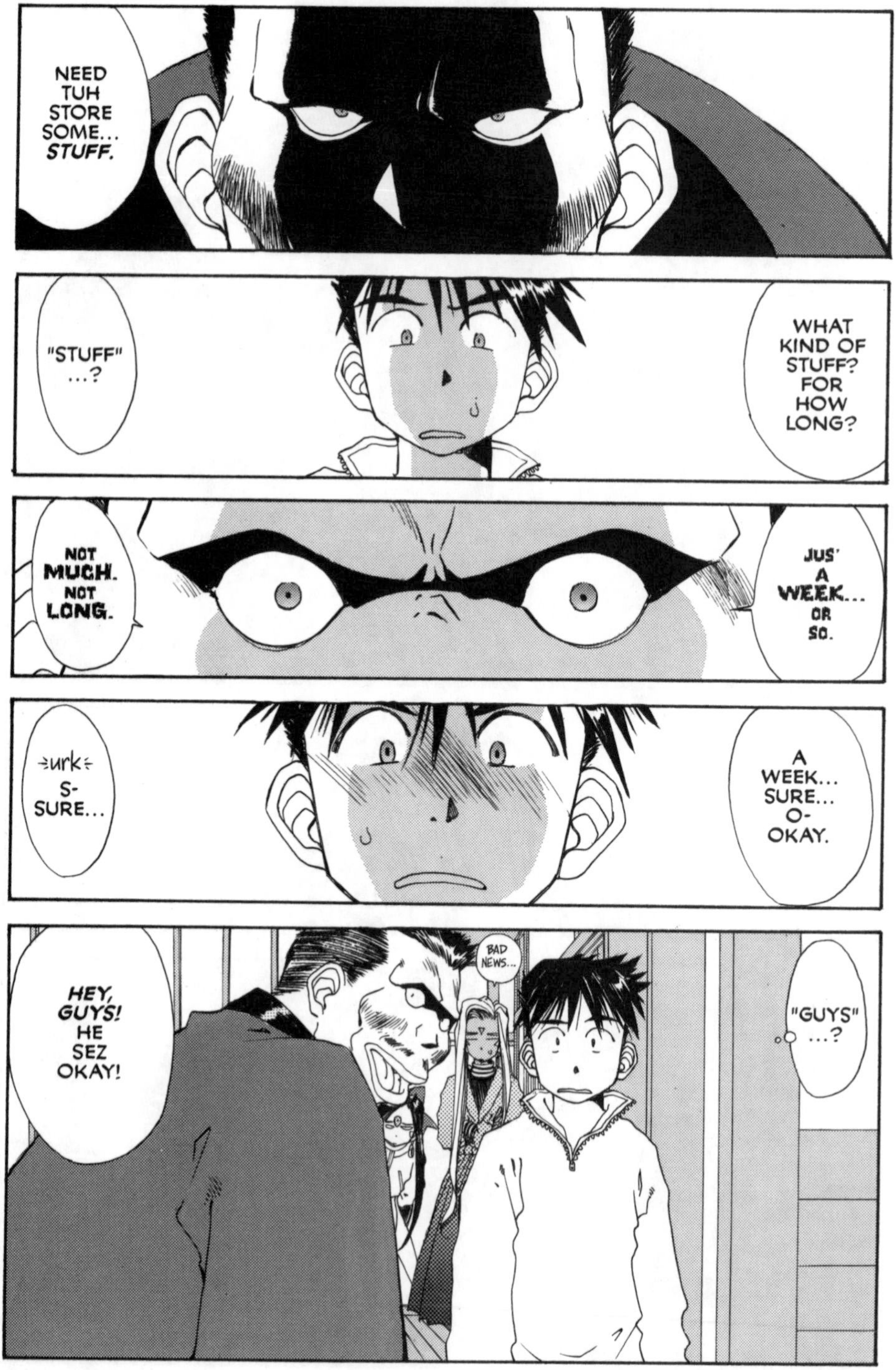
NEED TUH STORE SOME... *STUFF.*
"STUFF" ...?
WHAT KIND OF STUFF? FOR HOW LONG?
NOT MUCH. NOT LONG.
JUS' A WEEK... OR SO.
urk S-SURE...
A WEEK... SURE... O-OKAY.
HEY, GUYS! HE SEZ OKAY!
BAD NEWS...
"GUYS" ...?

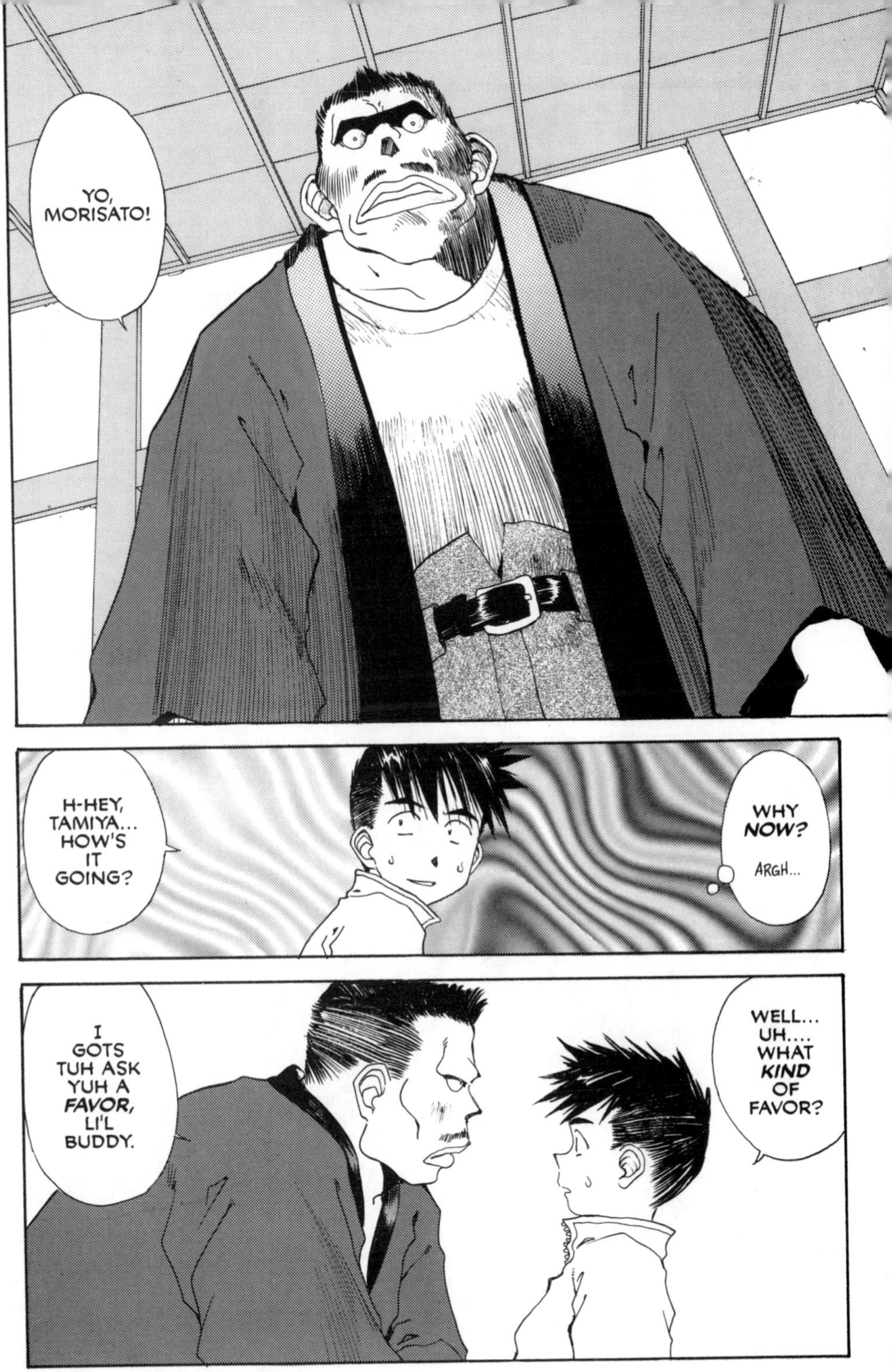
YO, MORISATO!
H-HEY, TAMIYA... HOW'S IT GOING?
WHY NOW? ARGH...
I GOTS TUH ASK YUH A FAVOR, LI'L BUDDY.
WELL... UH.... WHAT KIND OF FAVOR?

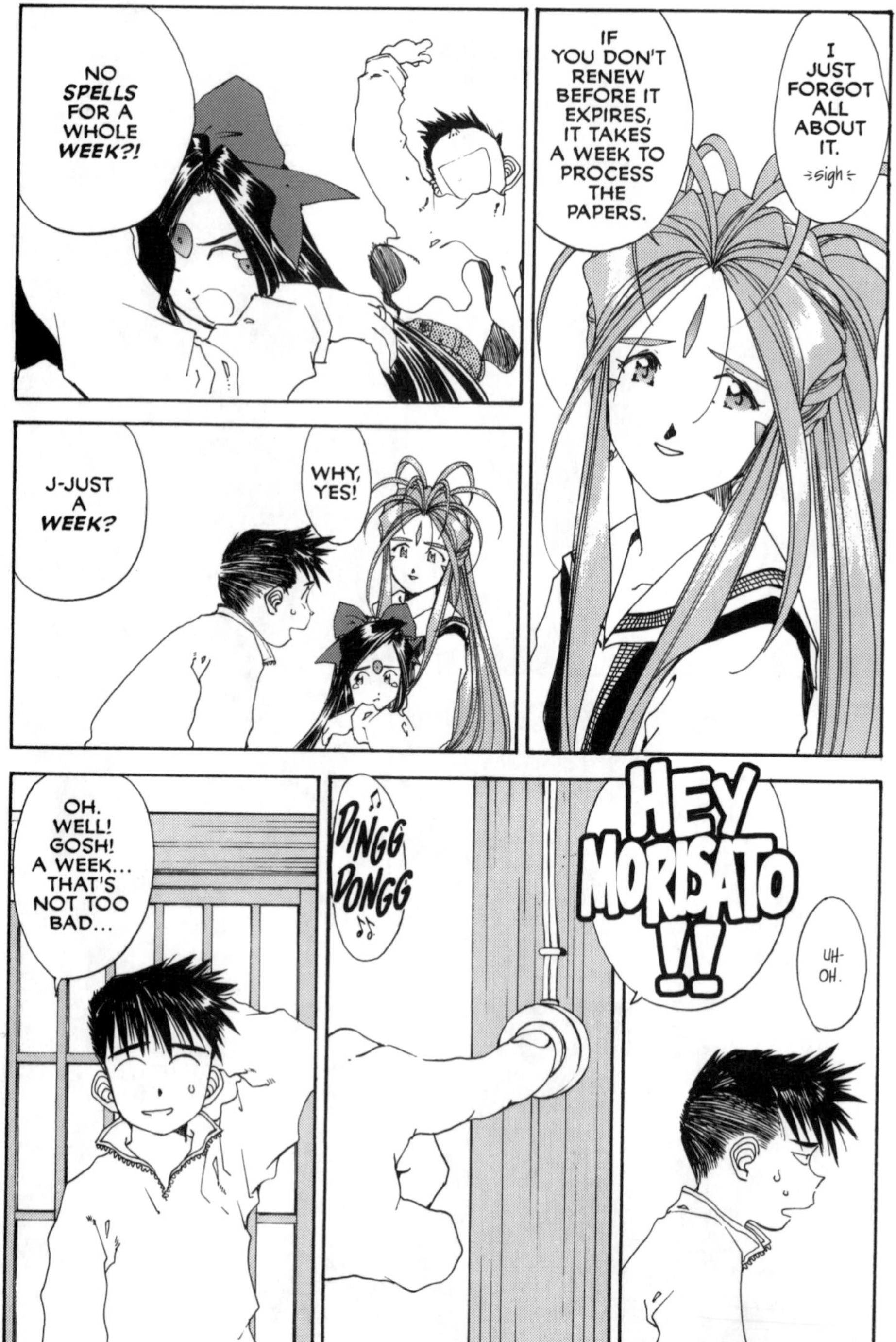
I JUST FORGOT ALL ABOUT IT.
sigh
IF YOU DON'T RENEW BEFORE IT EXPIRES, IT TAKES A WEEK TO PROCESS THE PAPERS.
NO SPELLS FOR A WHOLE WEEK?!
WHY, YES!
J-JUST A WEEK?
HEY MORISATO!!
UH-OH.
DINGG DONGG
OH. WELL! GOSH! A WEEK... THAT'S NOT TOO BAD...

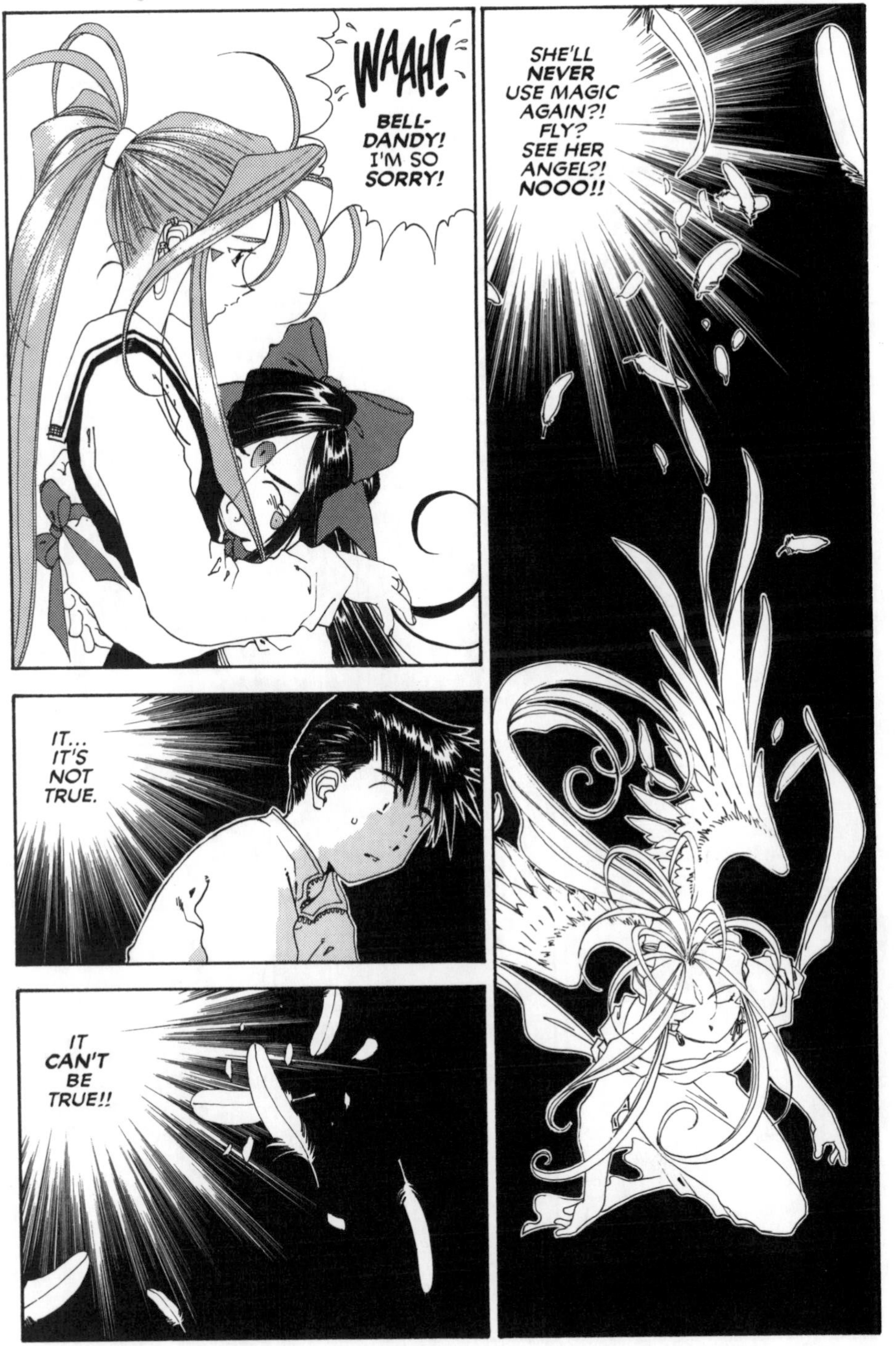
WAAH!
BELL-DANDY! I'M SO SORRY!
SHE'LL NEVER USE MAGIC AGAIN?! FLY? SEE HER ANGEL?! NOOO!!
IT... IT'S NOT TRUE.
IT CAN'T BE TRUE!!

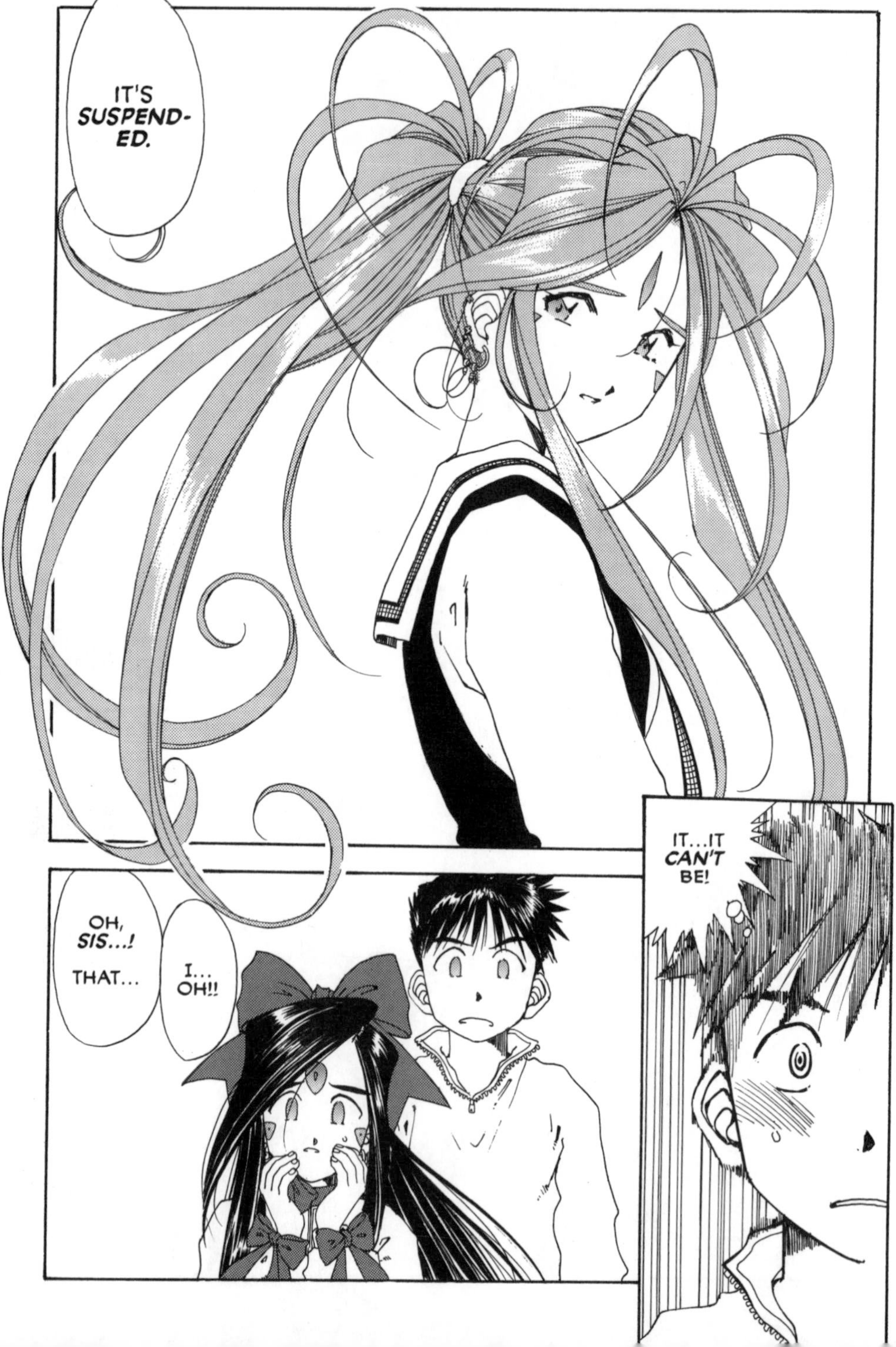
IT'S SUSPENDED.
OH, SIS...! THAT...
I... OH!!
IT...IT CAN'T BE!

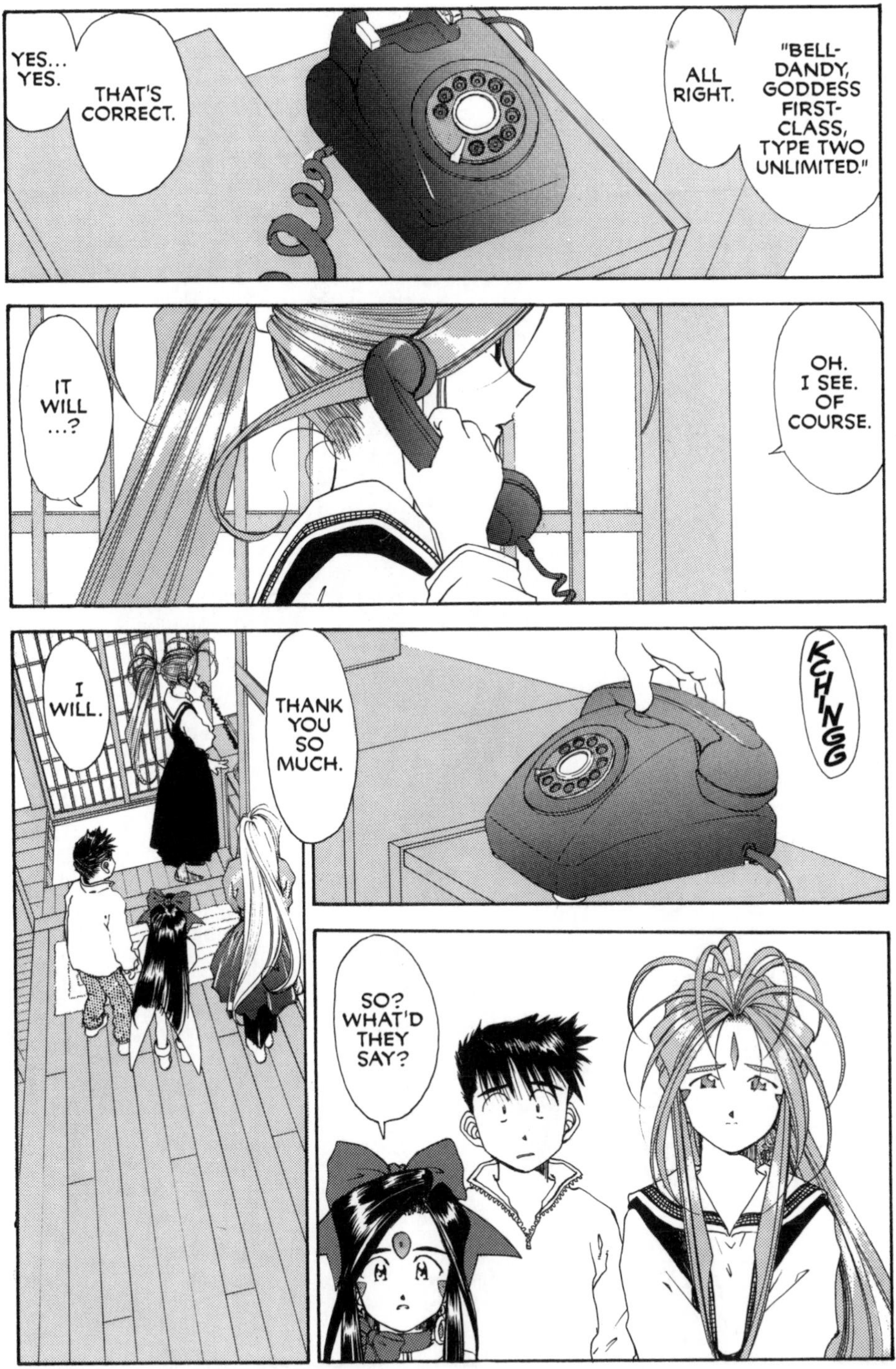
"BELL-DANDY, GODDESS FIRST-CLASS, TYPE TWO UNLIMITED."
ALL RIGHT.
THAT'S CORRECT.
YES... YES.
OH. I SEE. OF COURSE.
IT WILL ...?
I WILL.
THANK YOU SO MUCH.
KCHINGG
SO? WHAT'D THEY SAY?

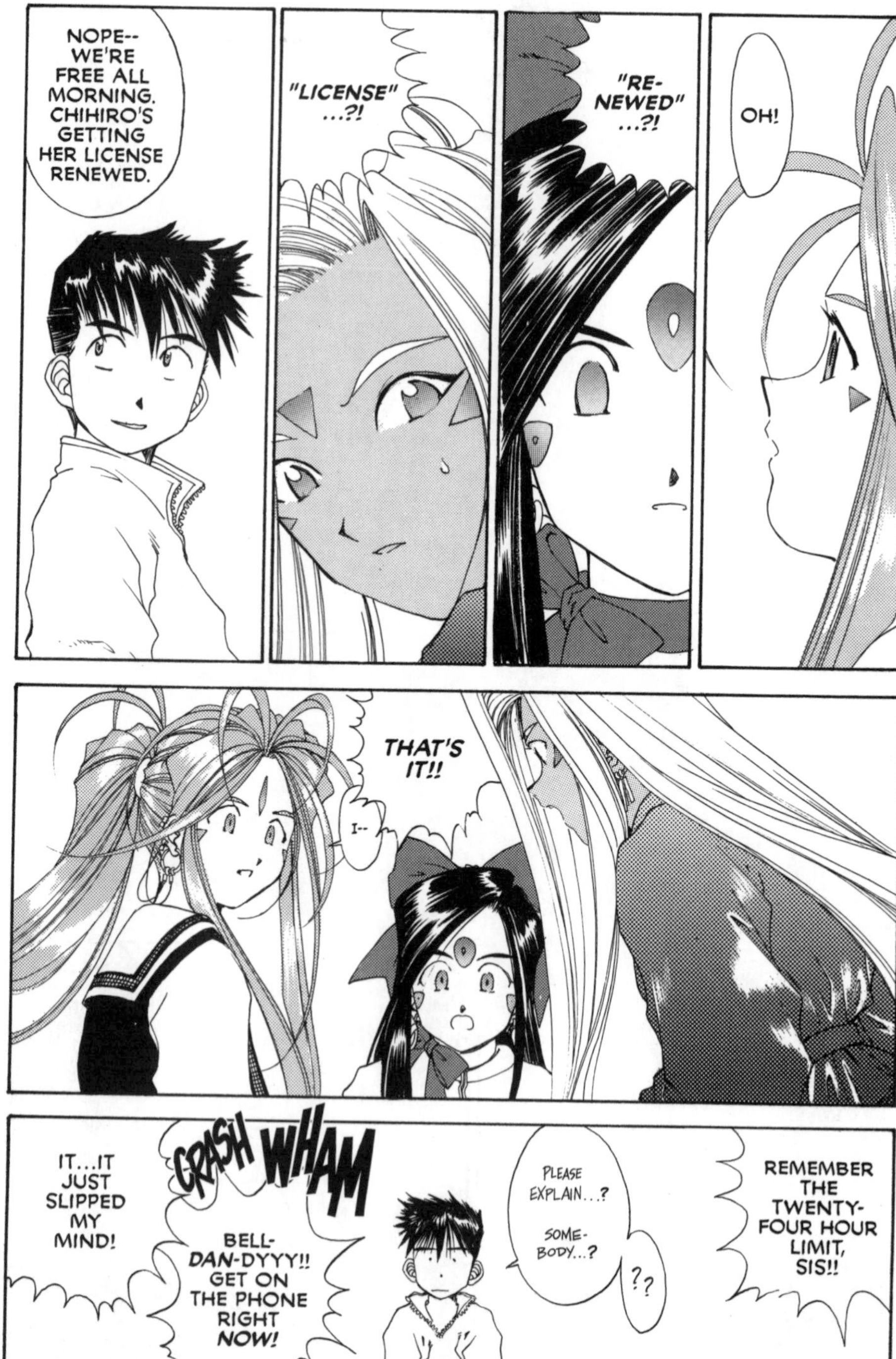
NOPE-- WE'RE FREE ALL MORNING. CHIHIRO'S GETTING HER LICENSE RENEWED.
"LICENSE" ...?!
"RE-NEWED" ...?!
OH!
I--
THAT'S IT!!
IT...IT JUST SLIPPED MY MIND!
CRASH
WHAM
BELL-DAN-DYYY!! GET ON THE PHONE RIGHT NOW!
PLEASE EXPLAIN...?
SOME-BODY...?
??
REMEMBER THE TWENTY-FOUR HOUR LIMIT, SIS!!

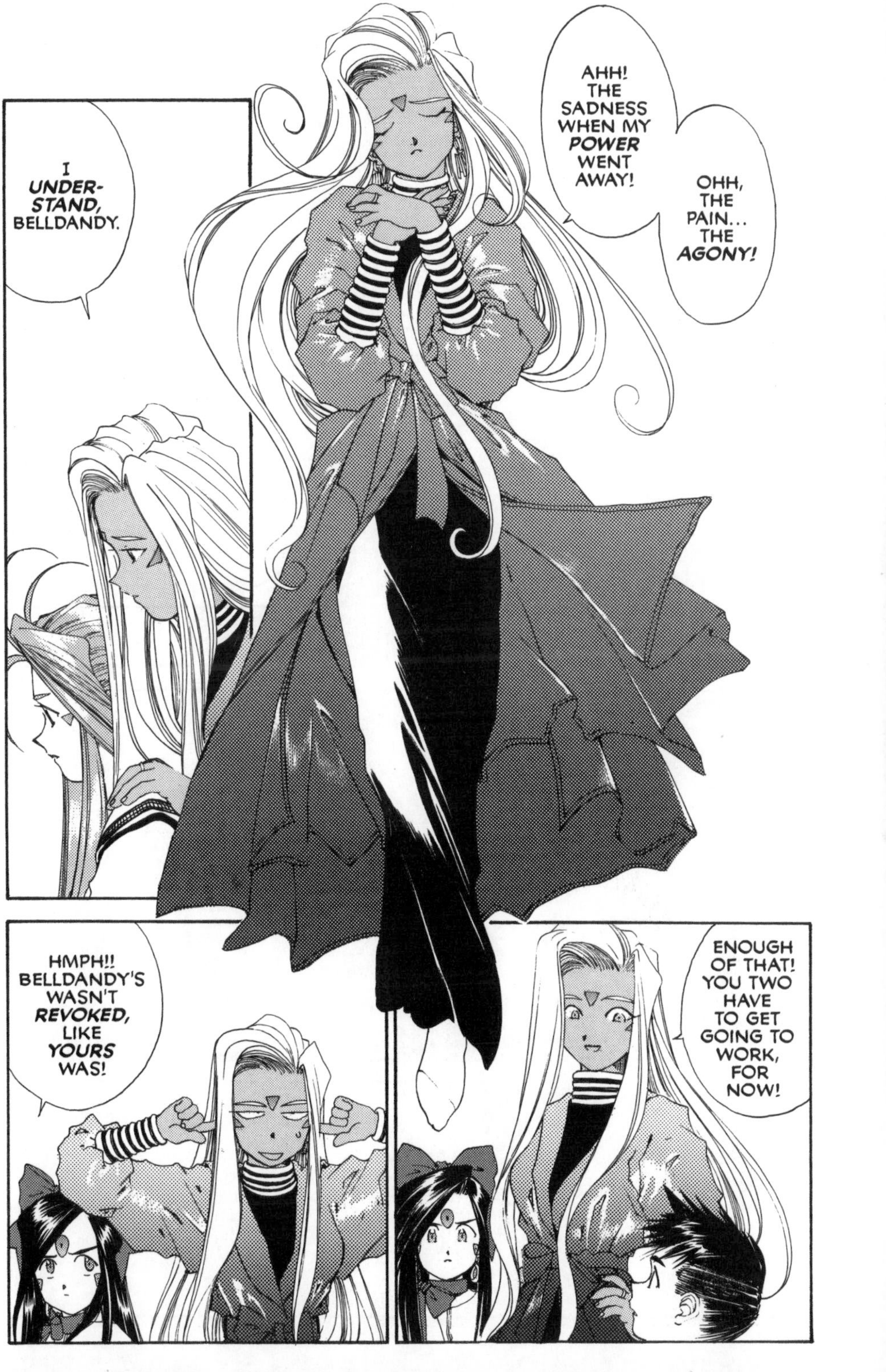
I *UNDER-STAND,* BELLDANDY.
AHH! THE SADNESS WHEN MY *POWER* WENT AWAY!
OHH, THE PAIN... THE *AGONY!*
HMPH!! BELLDANDY'S WASN'T *REVOKED,* LIKE *YOURS* WAS!
ENOUGH OF THAT! YOU TWO HAVE TO GET GOING TO WORK, FOR NOW!

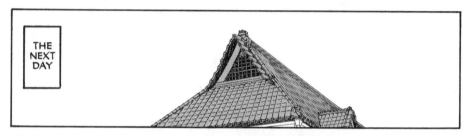

THE NEXT DAY

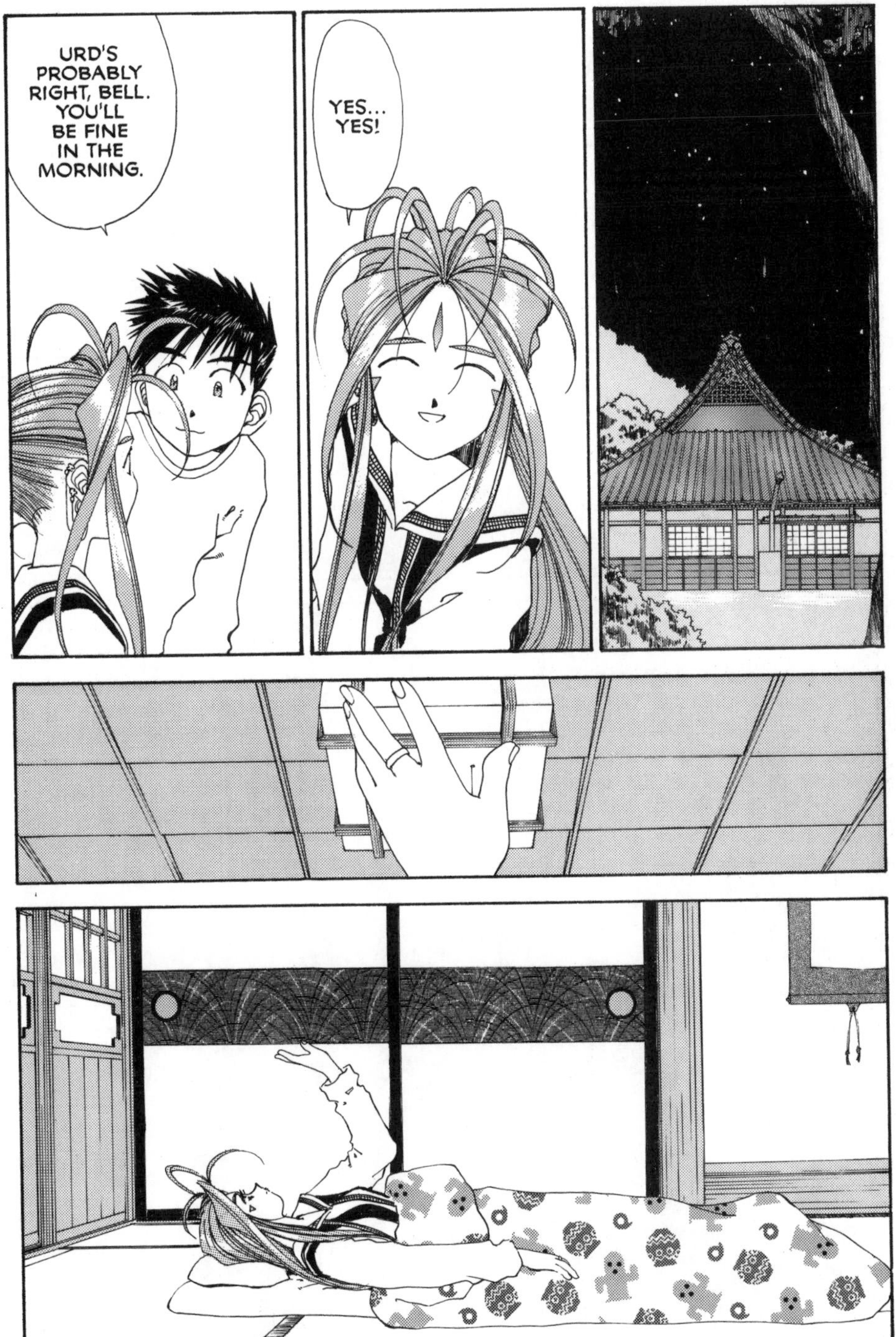
URD'S PROBABLY RIGHT, BELL. YOU'LL BE FINE IN THE MORNING.
YES... YES!

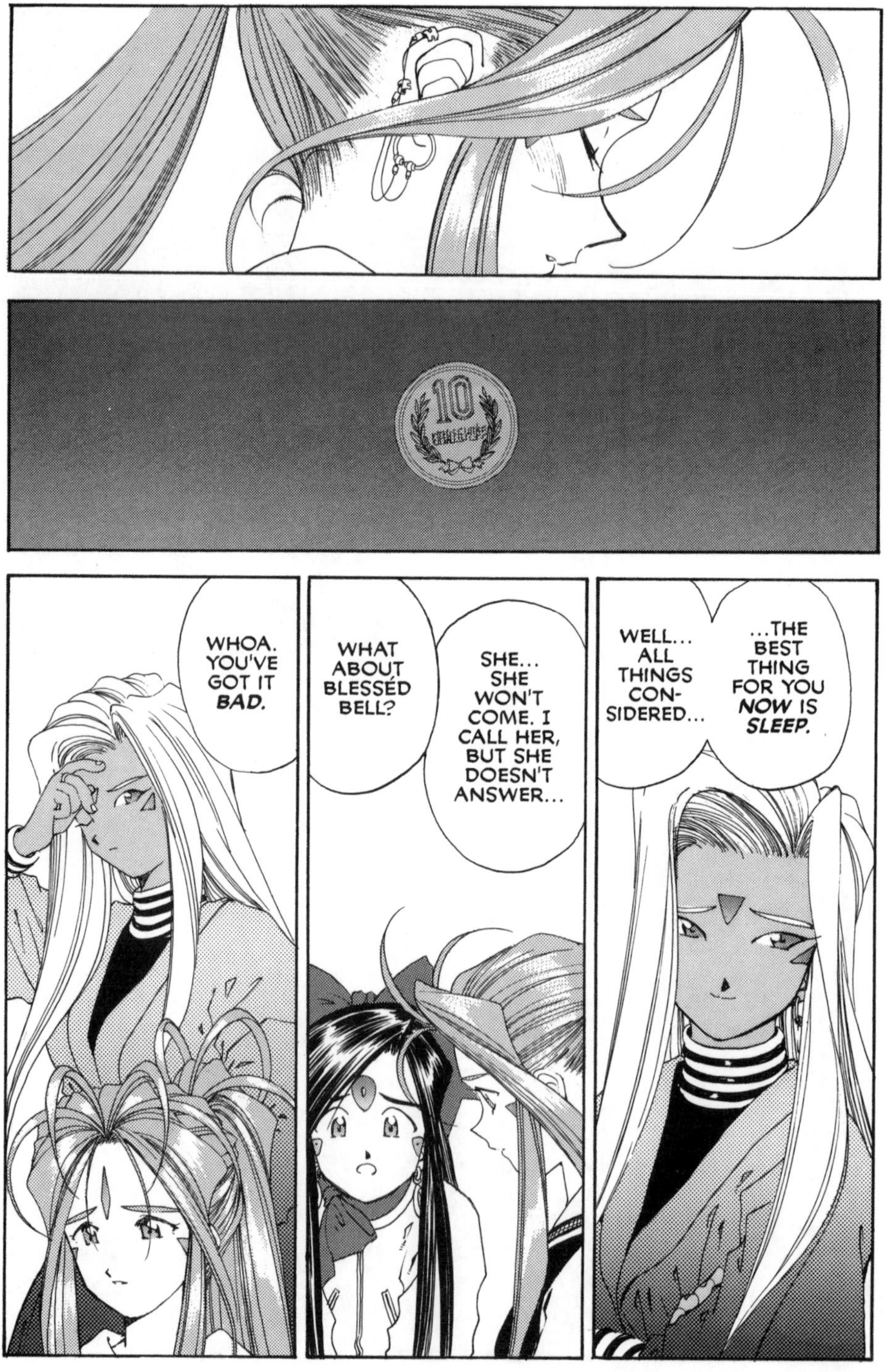
WHOA. YOU'VE GOT IT *BAD.*
WHAT ABOUT BLESSÉD BELL?
SHE... SHE WON'T COME. I CALL HER, BUT SHE DOESN'T ANSWER...
WELL... ALL THINGS CON-SIDERED...
...THE BEST THING FOR YOU *NOW* IS *SLEEP.*

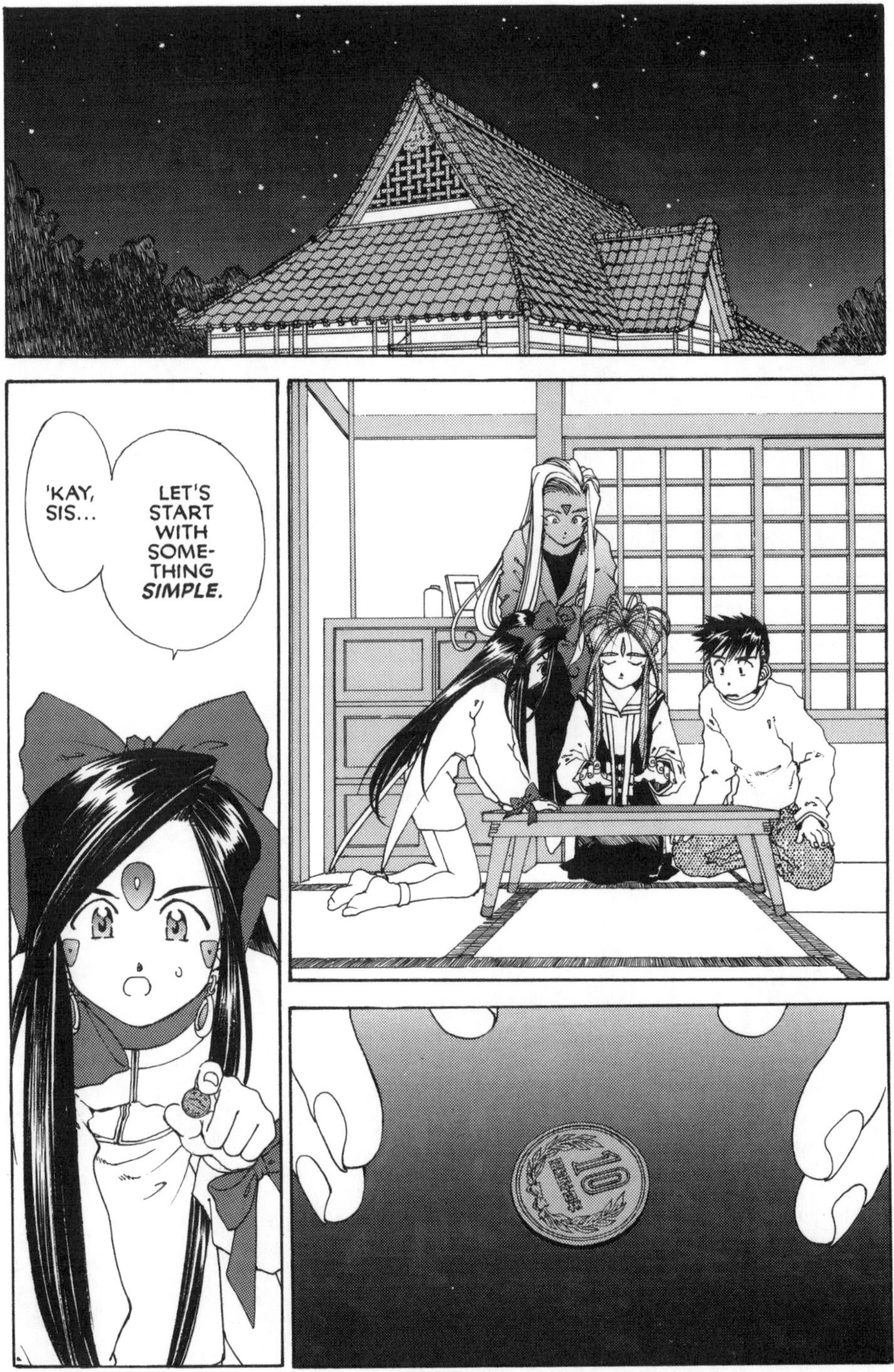
'KAY, SIS... LET'S START WITH SOME-THING SIMPLE.

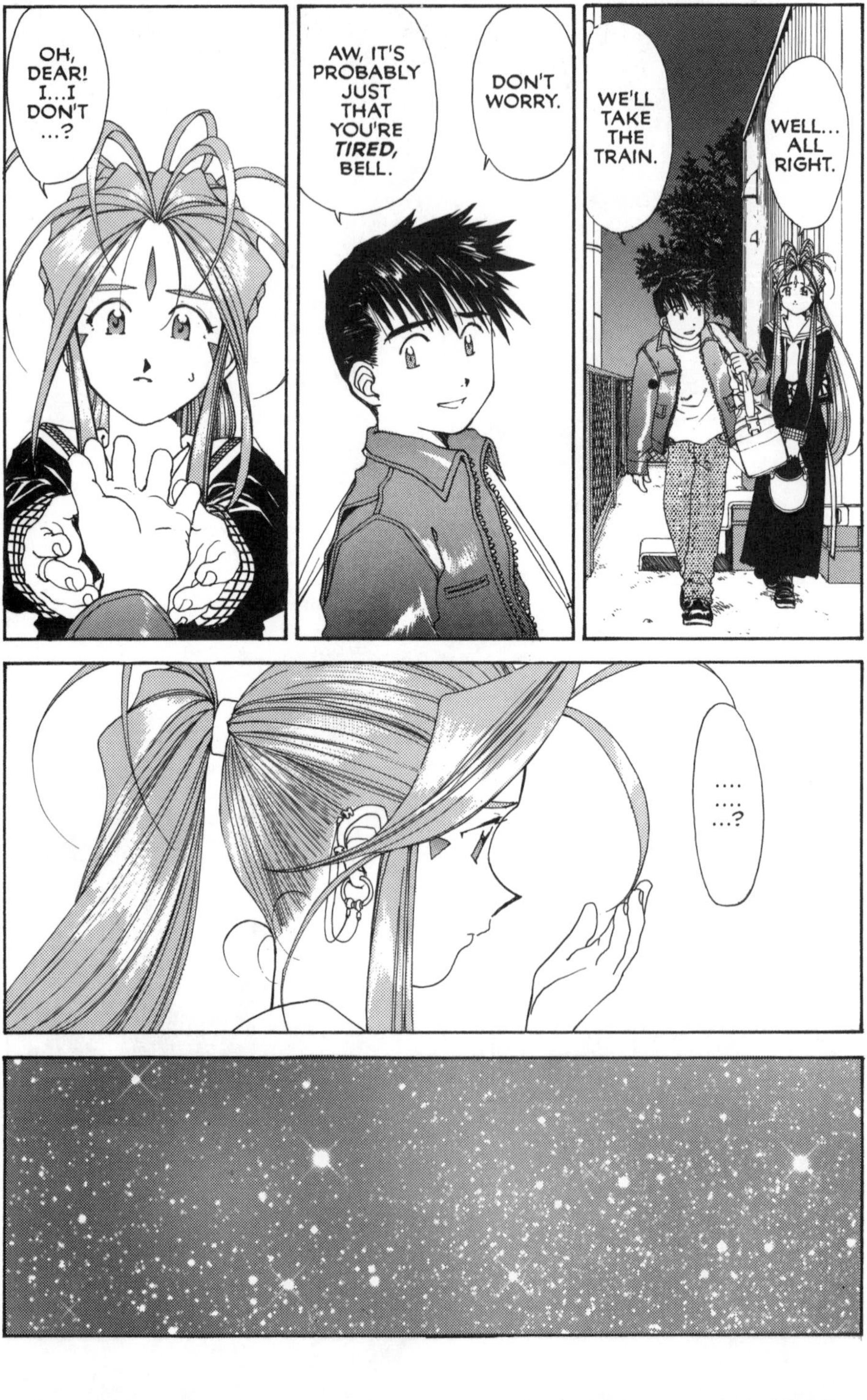
OH, DEAR! I...I DON'T ...?
AW, IT'S PROBABLY JUST THAT YOU'RE *TIRED,* BELL.
DON'T WORRY.
WE'LL TAKE THE TRAIN.
WELL... ALL RIGHT.
....?

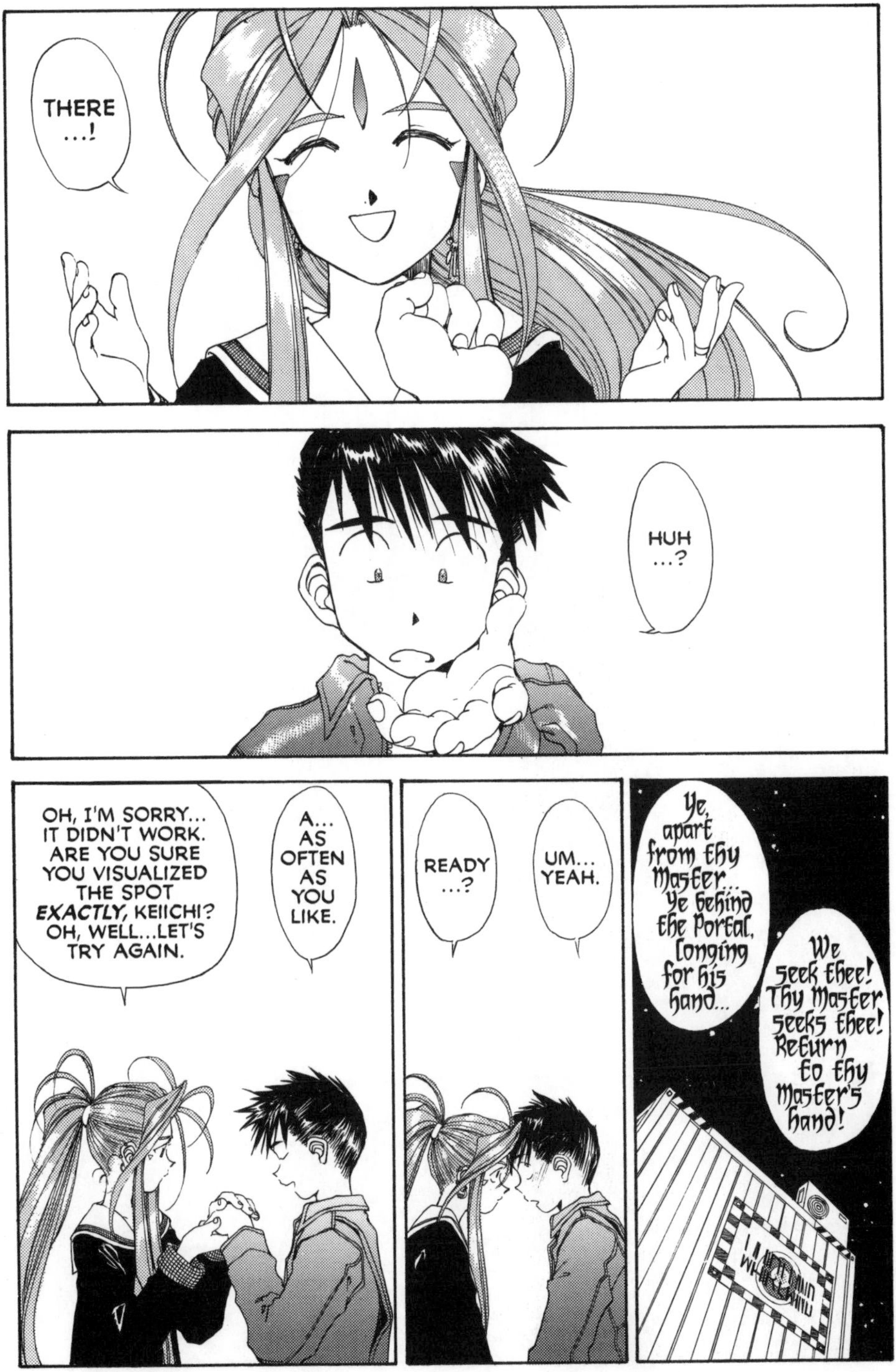
THERE ...!
HUH ...?
OH, I'M SORRY... IT DIDN'T WORK. ARE YOU SURE YOU VISUALIZED THE SPOT *EXACTLY,* KEIICHI? OH, WELL...LET'S TRY AGAIN.
A... AS OFTEN AS YOU LIKE.
READY ...?
UM... YEAH.
Ye, apart from thy Master... ye behind the Portal, longing for his hand...
We seek thee! Thy Master seeks thee! Return to thy Master's hand!

ARGH!

VRMMM

No!
W-
WAIT...!

KEIICHI
...?

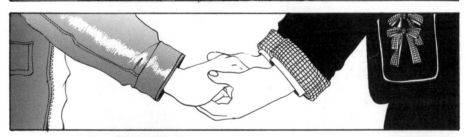

?!

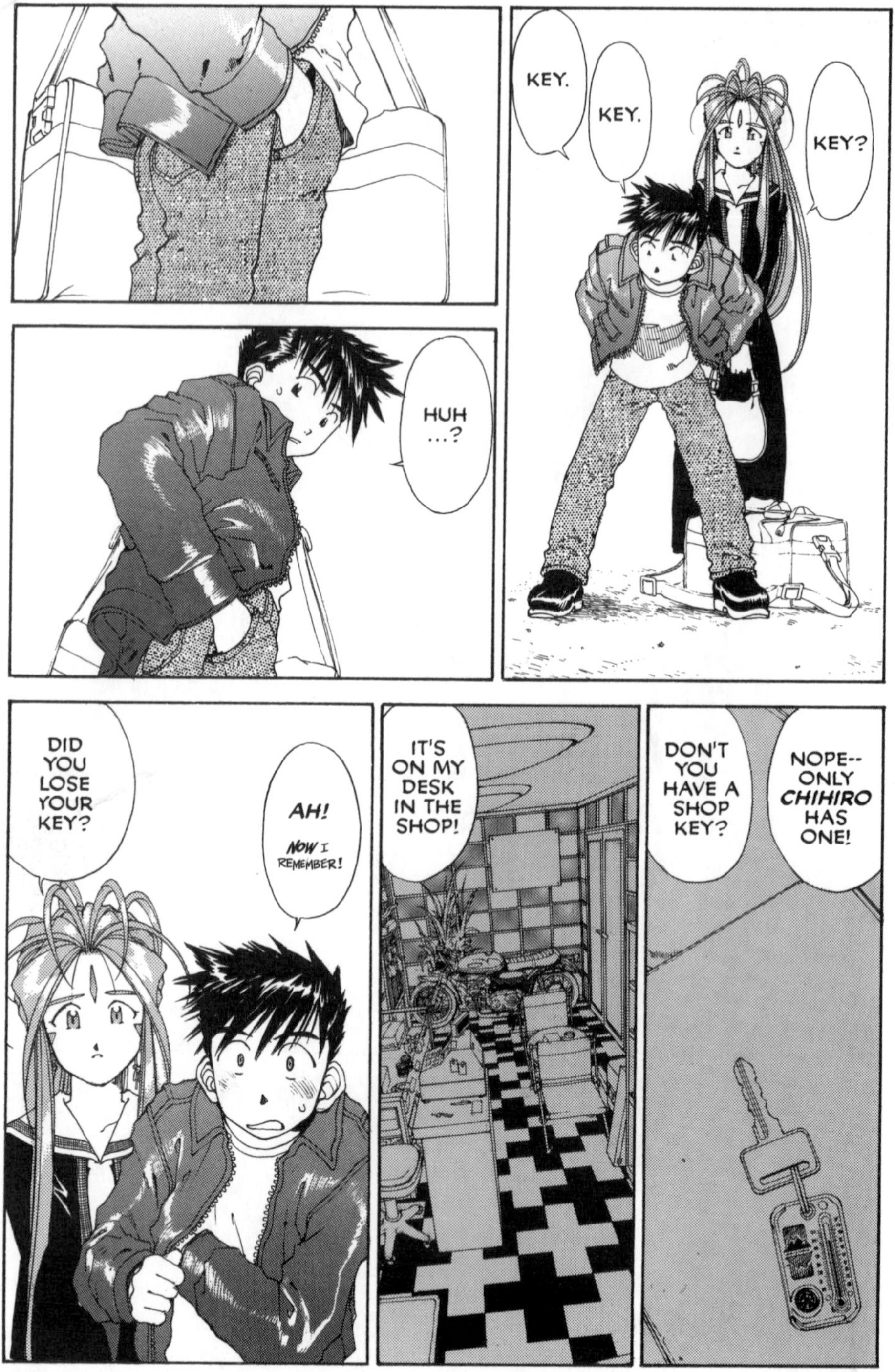
HUH ...?
KEY.
KEY.
KEY?
DID YOU LOSE YOUR KEY?
AH! NOW I REMEMBER!
IT'S ON MY DESK IN THE SHOP!
DON'T YOU HAVE A SHOP KEY?
NOPE-- ONLY CHIHIRO HAS ONE!

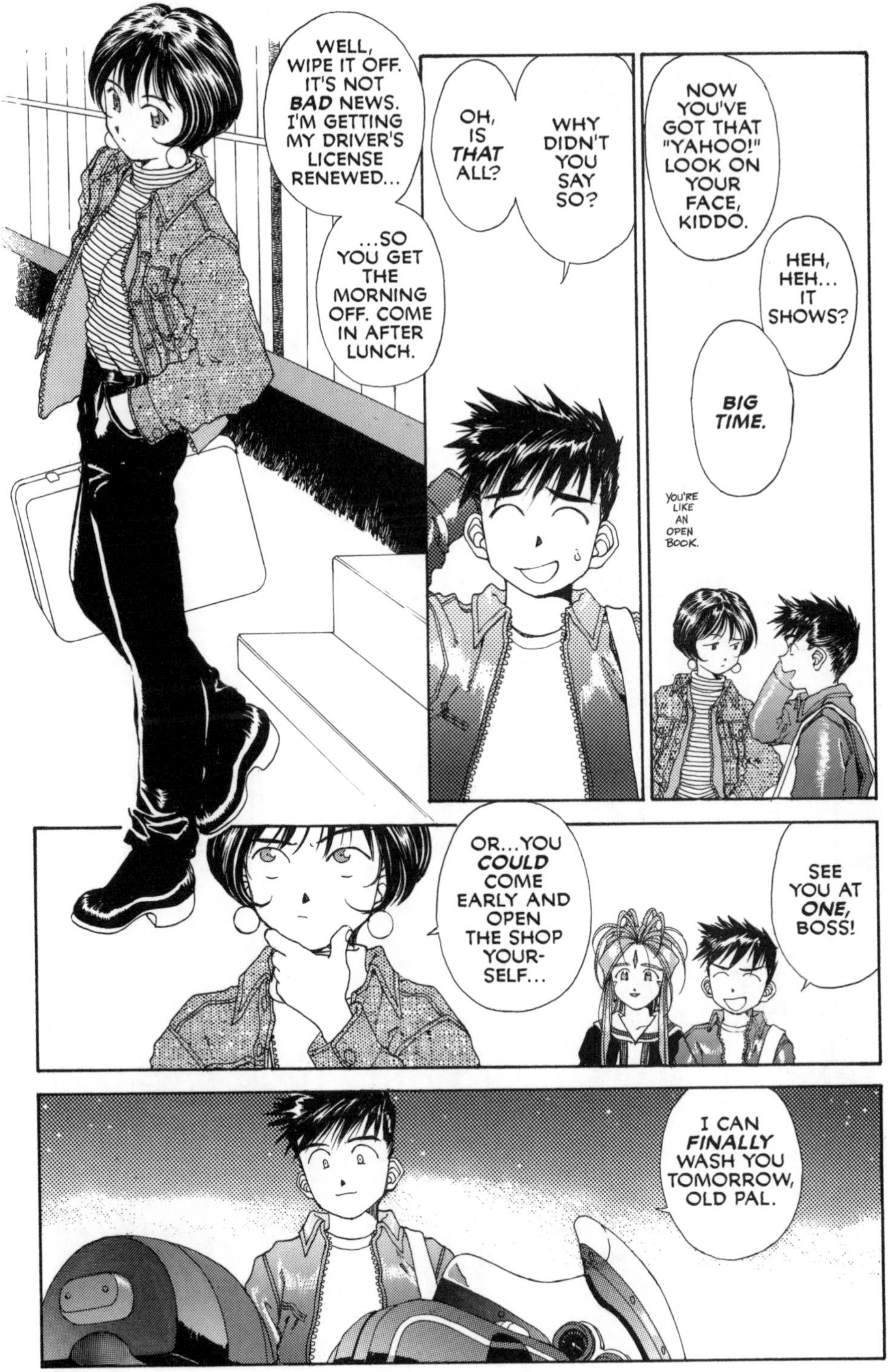
WELL, WIPE IT OFF. IT'S NOT *BAD* NEWS. I'M GETTING MY DRIVER'S LICENSE RENEWED...
...SO YOU GET THE MORNING OFF. COME IN AFTER LUNCH.
OH, IS *THAT* ALL?
WHY DIDN'T YOU SAY SO?
NOW YOU'VE GOT THAT "YAHOO!" LOOK ON YOUR FACE, KIDDO.
HEH, HEH... IT SHOWS?
BIG TIME.
YOU'RE LIKE AN OPEN BOOK.
OR...YOU *COULD* COME EARLY AND OPEN THE SHOP YOUR-SELF...
SEE YOU AT *ONE,* BOSS!
I CAN *FINALLY* WASH YOU TOMORROW, OLD PAL.

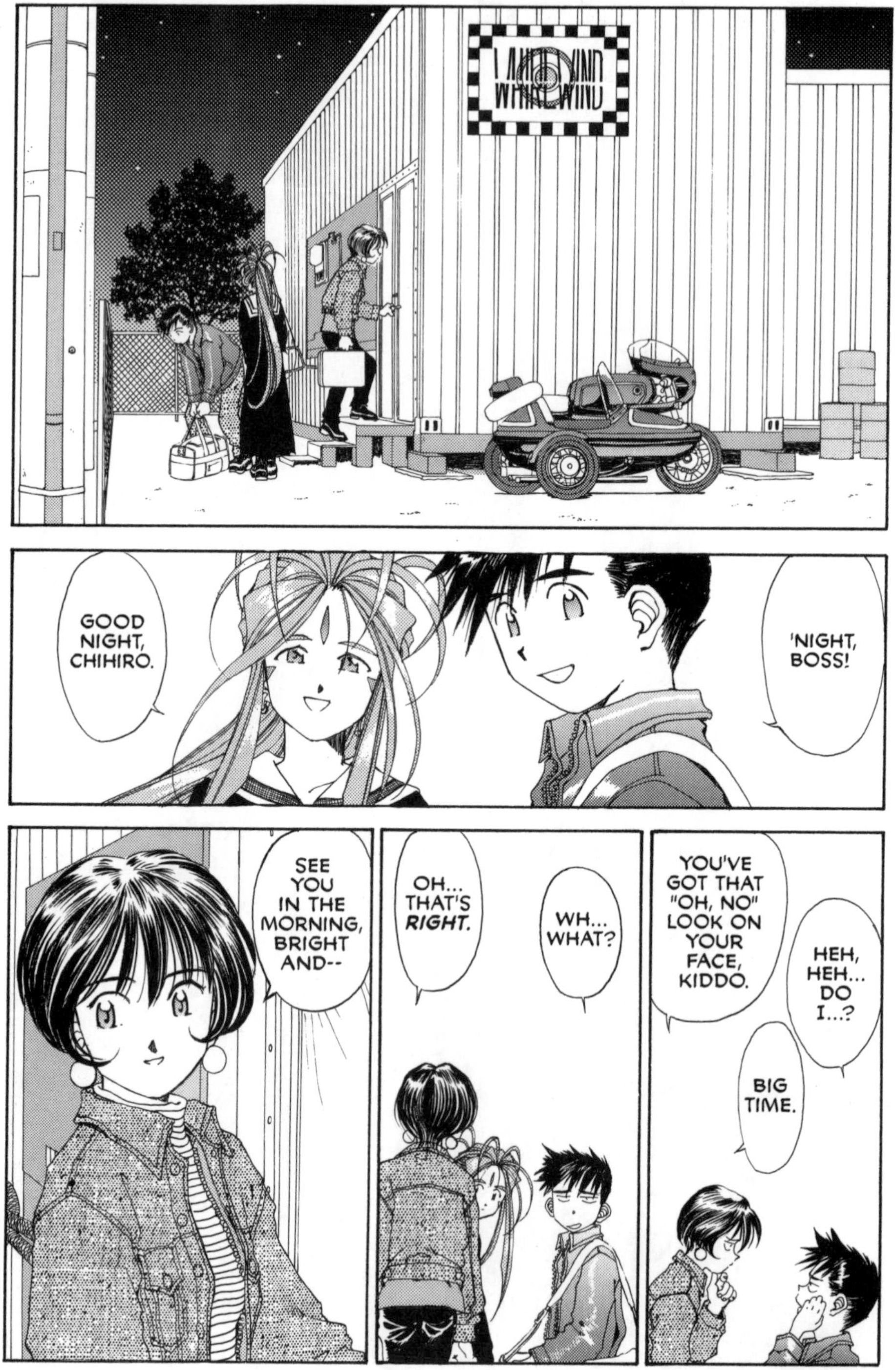
WHIRLWIND
GOOD NIGHT, CHIHIRO.
'NIGHT, BOSS!
SEE YOU IN THE MORNING, BRIGHT AND--
OH... THAT'S *RIGHT.*
WH... WHAT?
YOU'VE GOT THAT "OH, NO" LOOK ON YOUR FACE, KIDDO.
HEH, HEH... DO I...?
BIG TIME.

UNLICENSED GODDESS

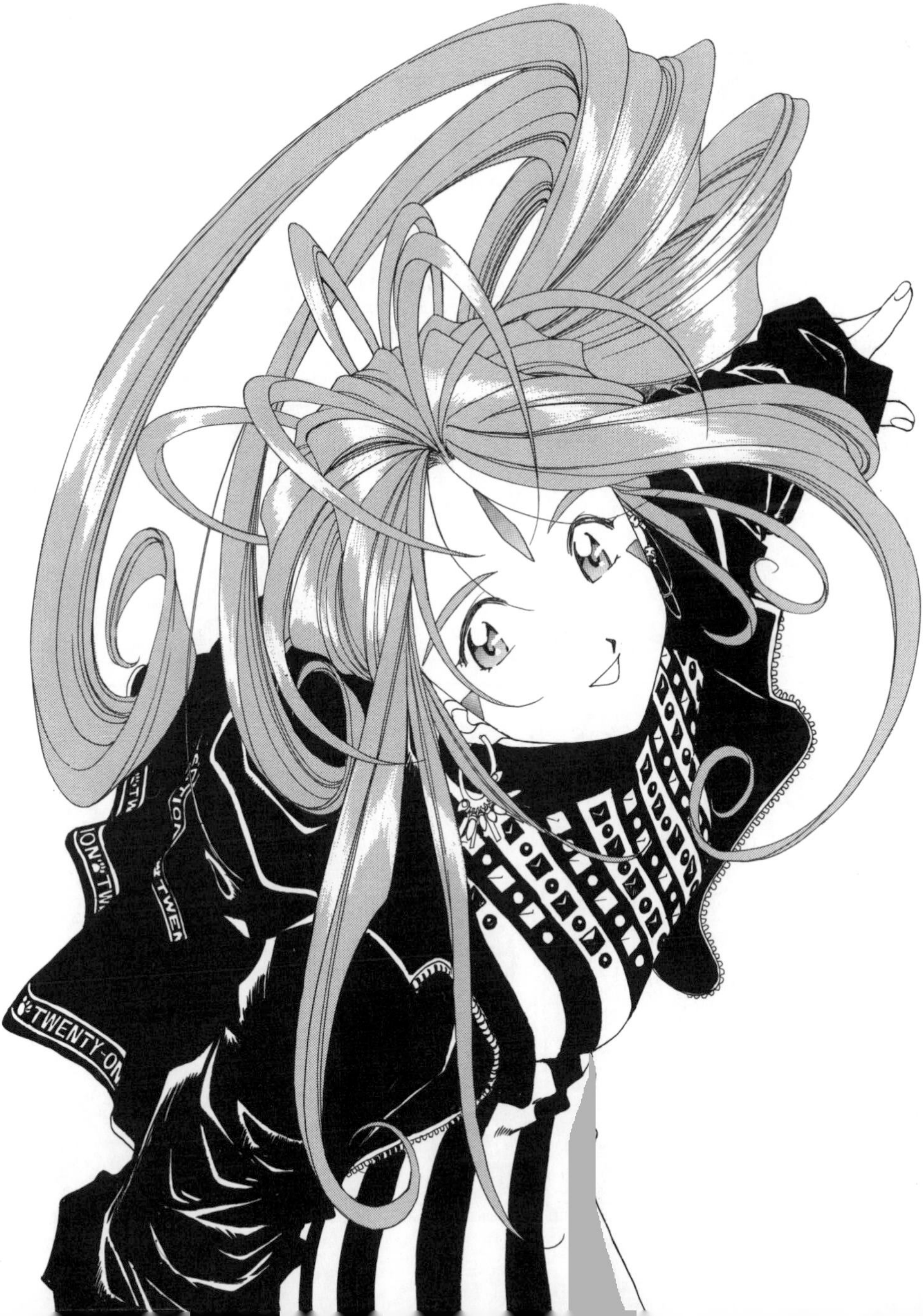

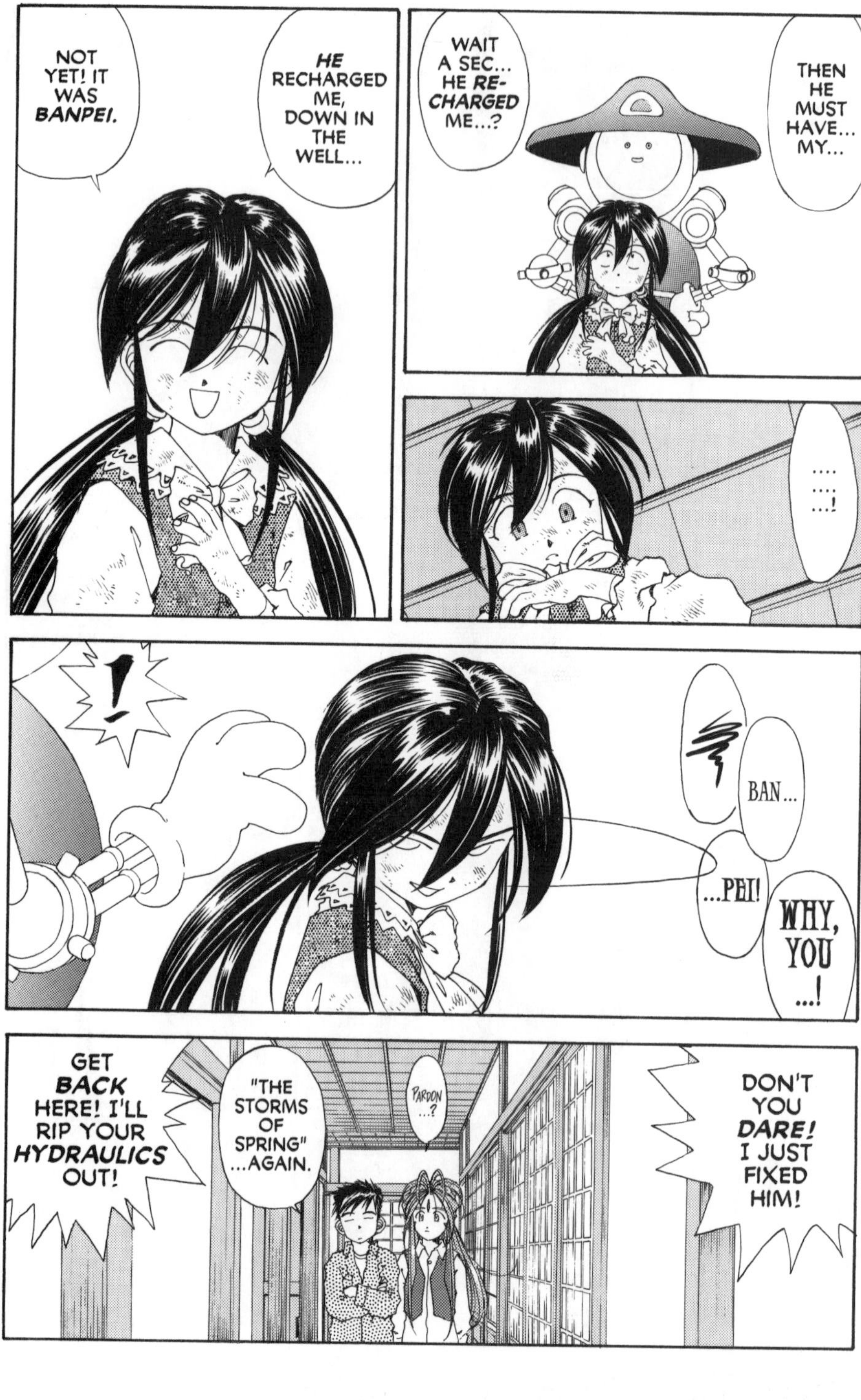
NOT YET! IT WAS BANPEI.
HE RECHARGED ME, DOWN IN THE WELL...
WAIT A SEC... HE RE-CHARGED ME...?
THEN HE MUST HAVE... MY...
....; ...!
!
BAN...
...PEI!
WHY, YOU ...!
GET BACK HERE! I'LL RIP YOUR HYDRAULICS OUT!
"THE STORMS OF SPRING" ...AGAIN.
PARDON ...?
DON'T YOU DARE! I JUST FIXED HIM!

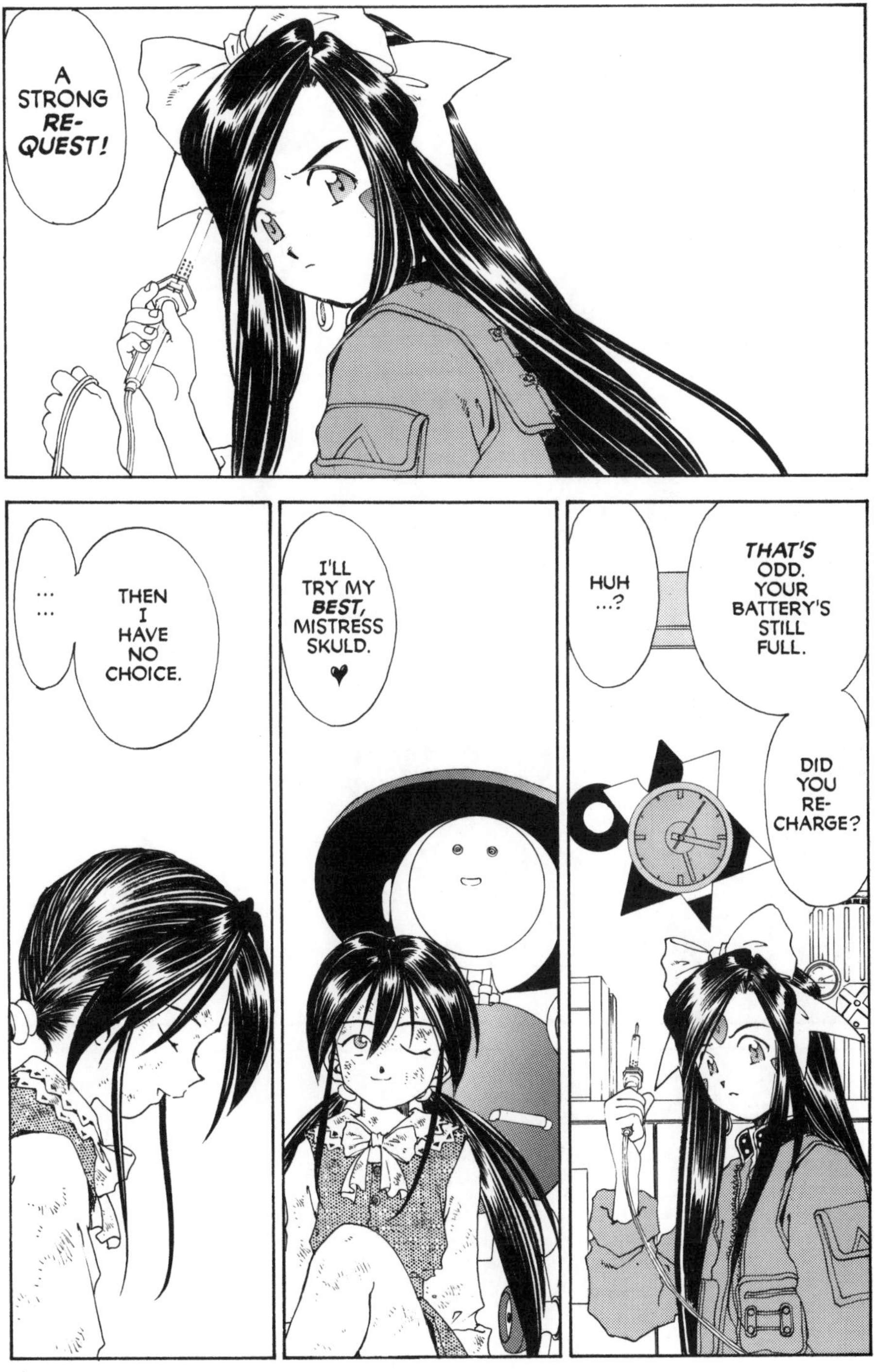
A STRONG ***RE-QUEST!***
......
THEN I HAVE NO CHOICE.
I'LL TRY MY ***BEST,*** MISTRESS SKULD. ♥
HUH ...?
THAT'S ODD. YOUR BATTERY'S STILL FULL.
DID YOU RE-CHARGE?

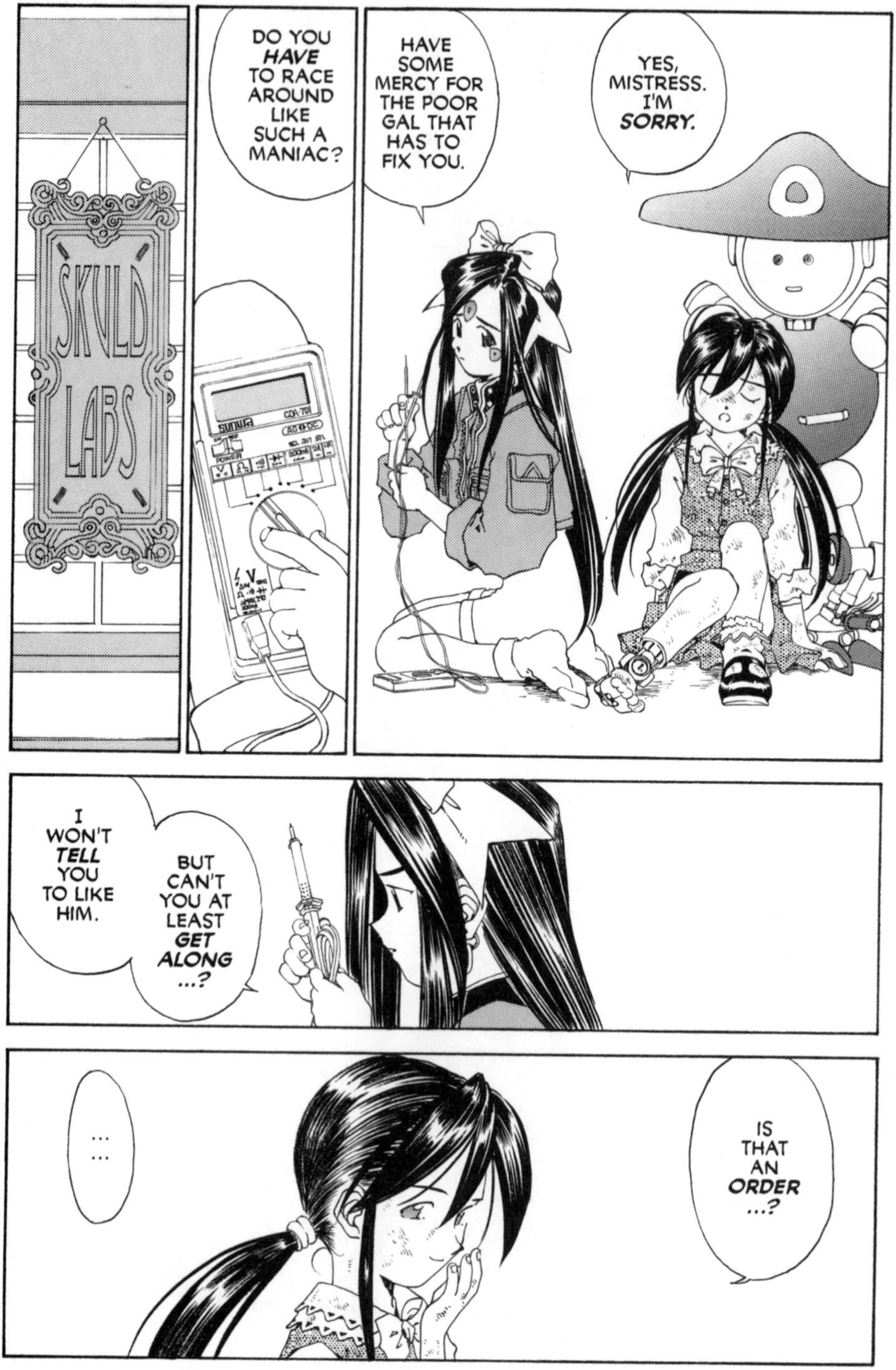
SKULD LABS
SUNWA CDA-701
DO YOU HAVE TO RACE AROUND LIKE SUCH A MANIAC?
HAVE SOME MERCY FOR THE POOR GAL THAT HAS TO FIX YOU.
YES, MISTRESS. I'M SORRY.
I WON'T TELL YOU TO LIKE HIM.
BUT CAN'T YOU AT LEAST GET ALONG ...?
... ...
IS THAT AN ORDER ...?

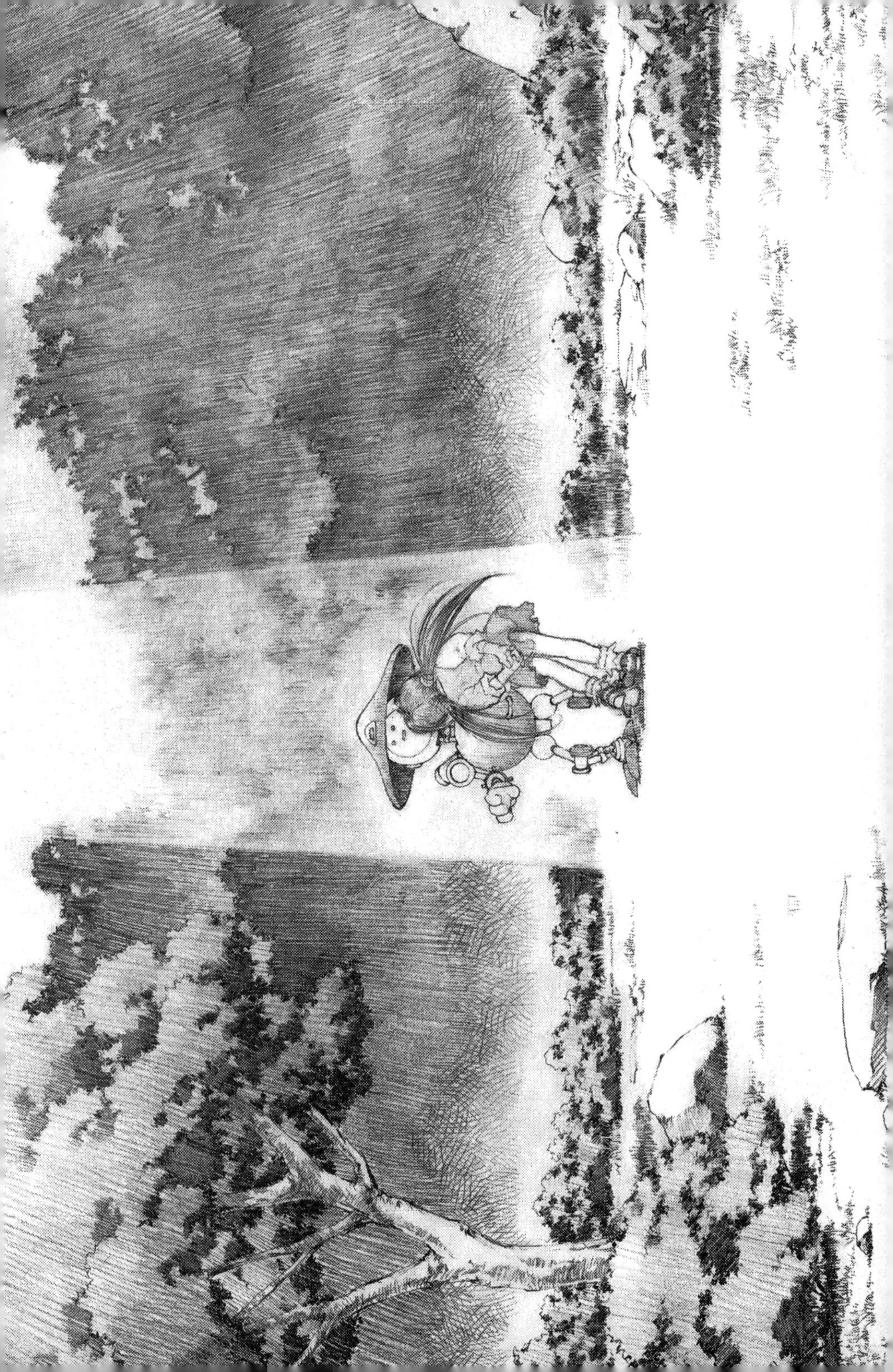

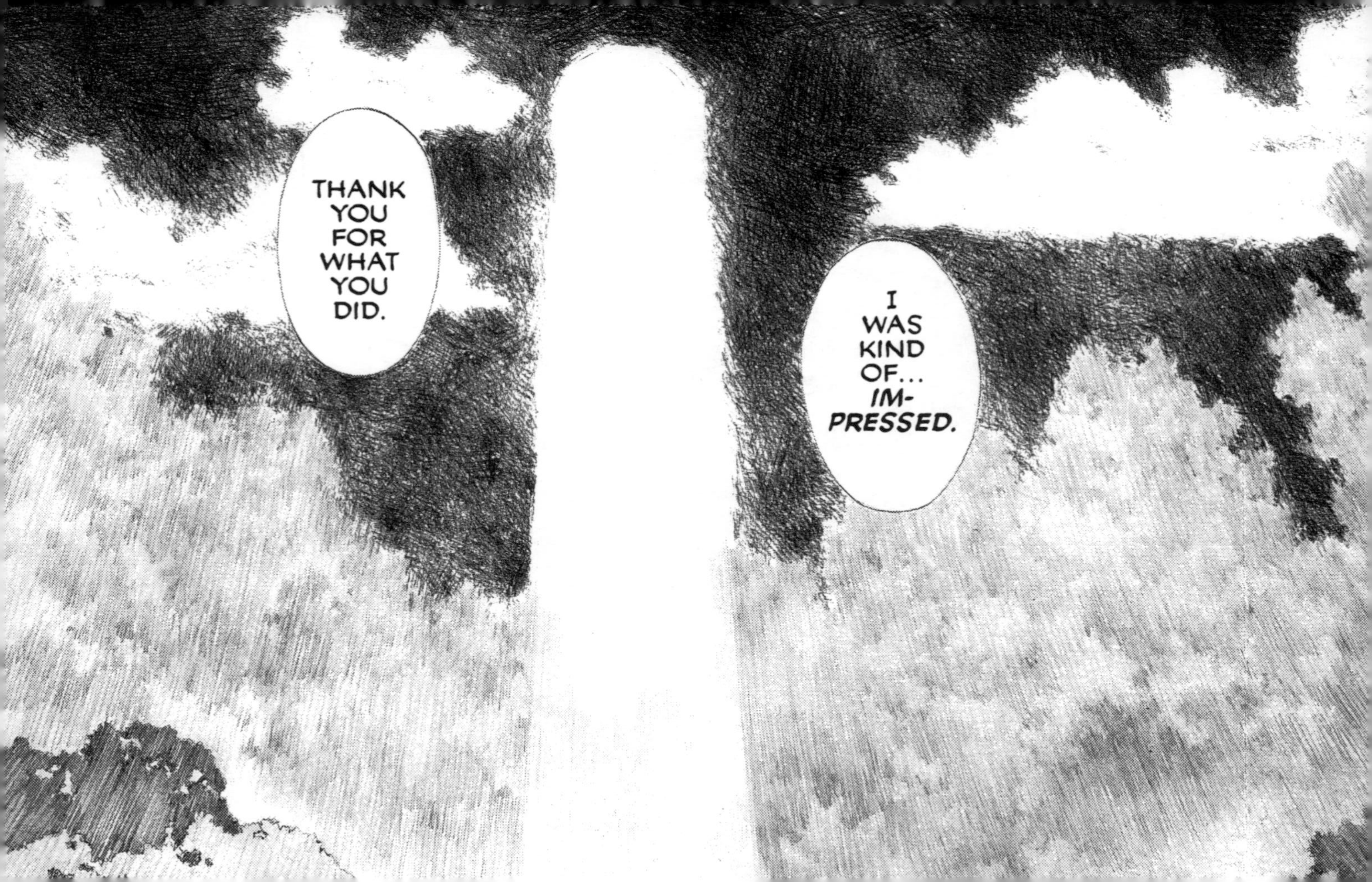
I WAS KIND OF... *IM-PRESSED.*
THANK YOU FOR WHAT YOU DID.

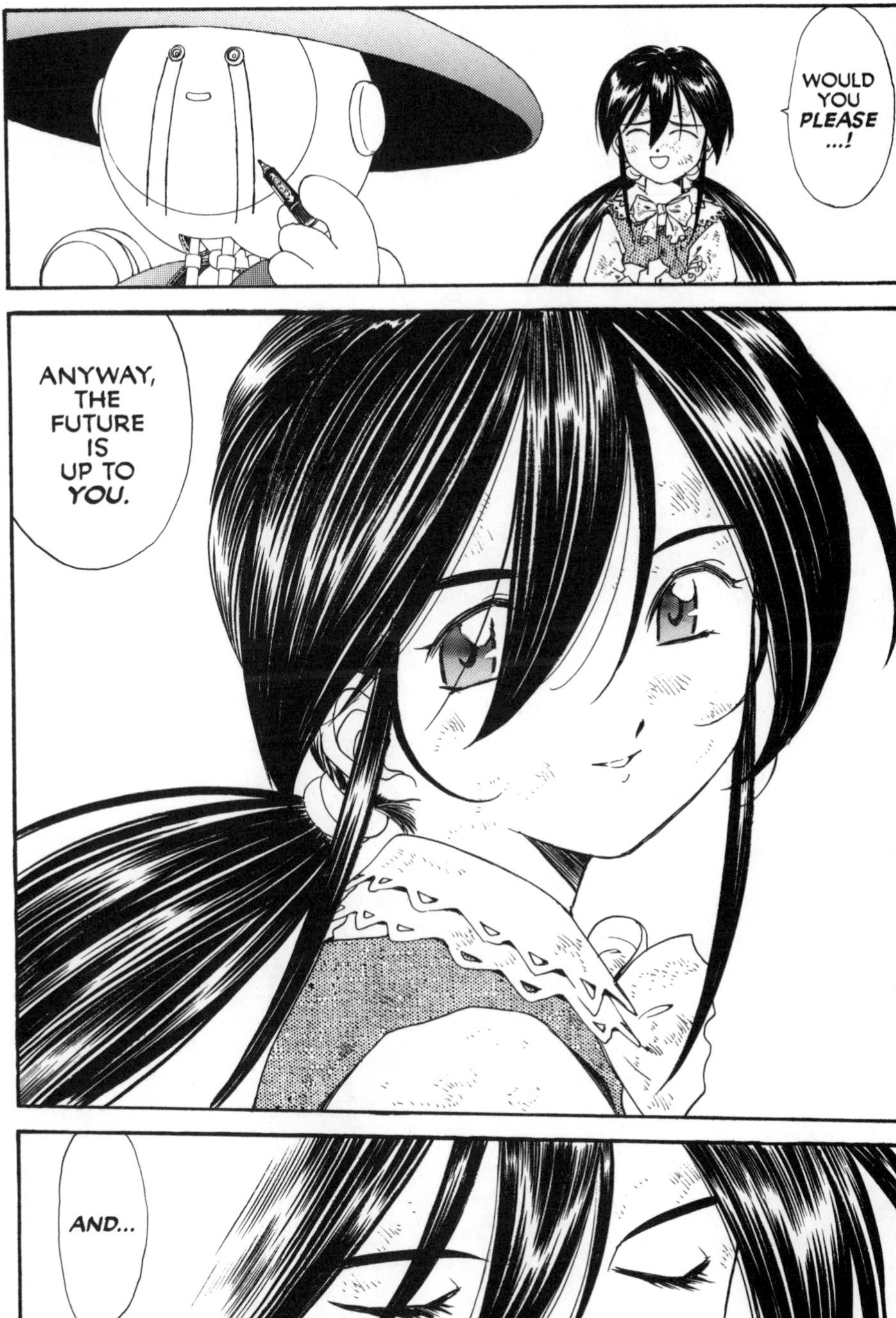
WOULD YOU PLEASE ...!
ANYWAY, THE FUTURE IS UP TO YOU.
AND...

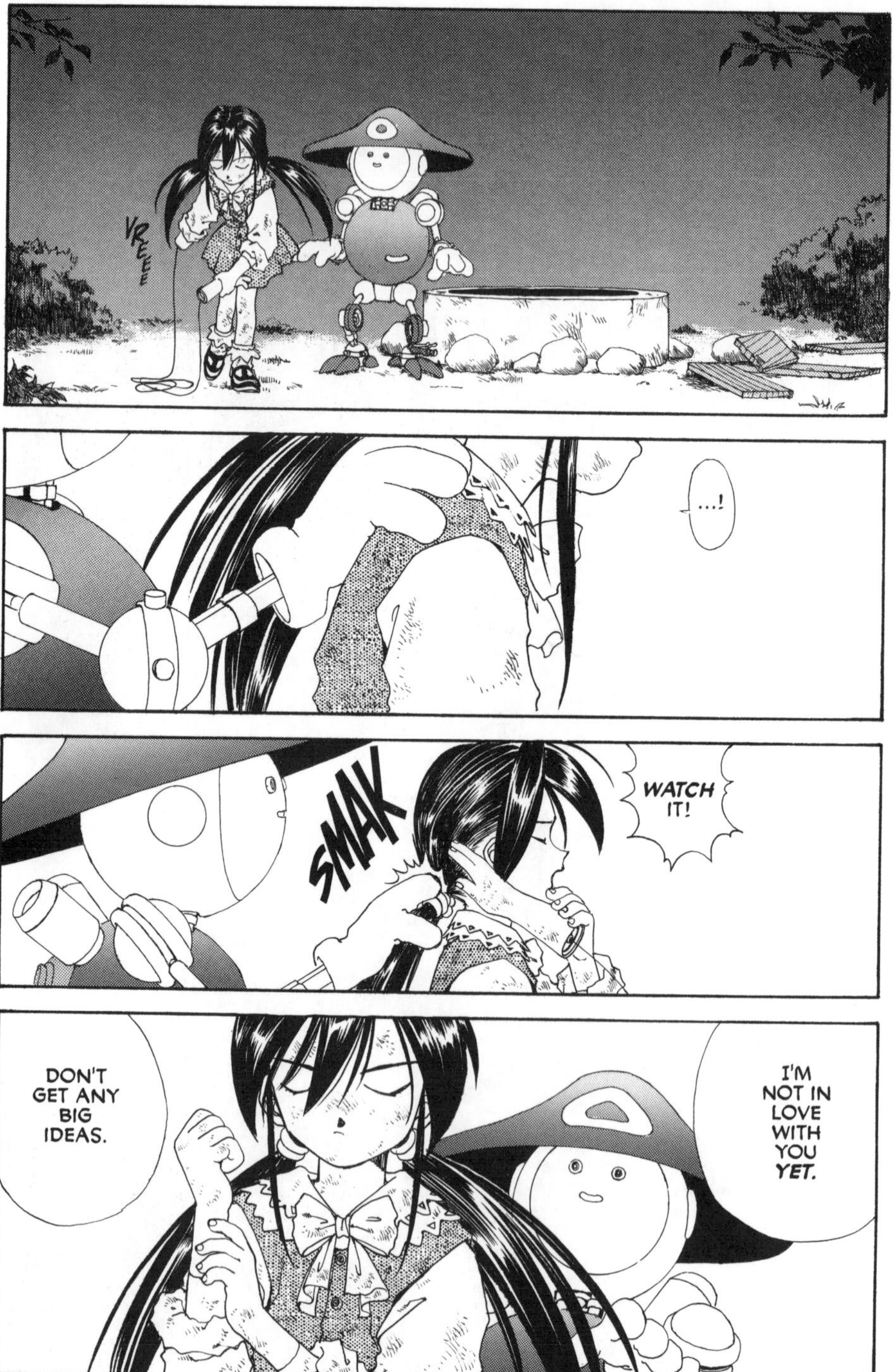
VREEEE
...!
SMAK
WATCH IT!
DON'T GET ANY BIG IDEAS.
I'M NOT IN LOVE WITH YOU *YET.*

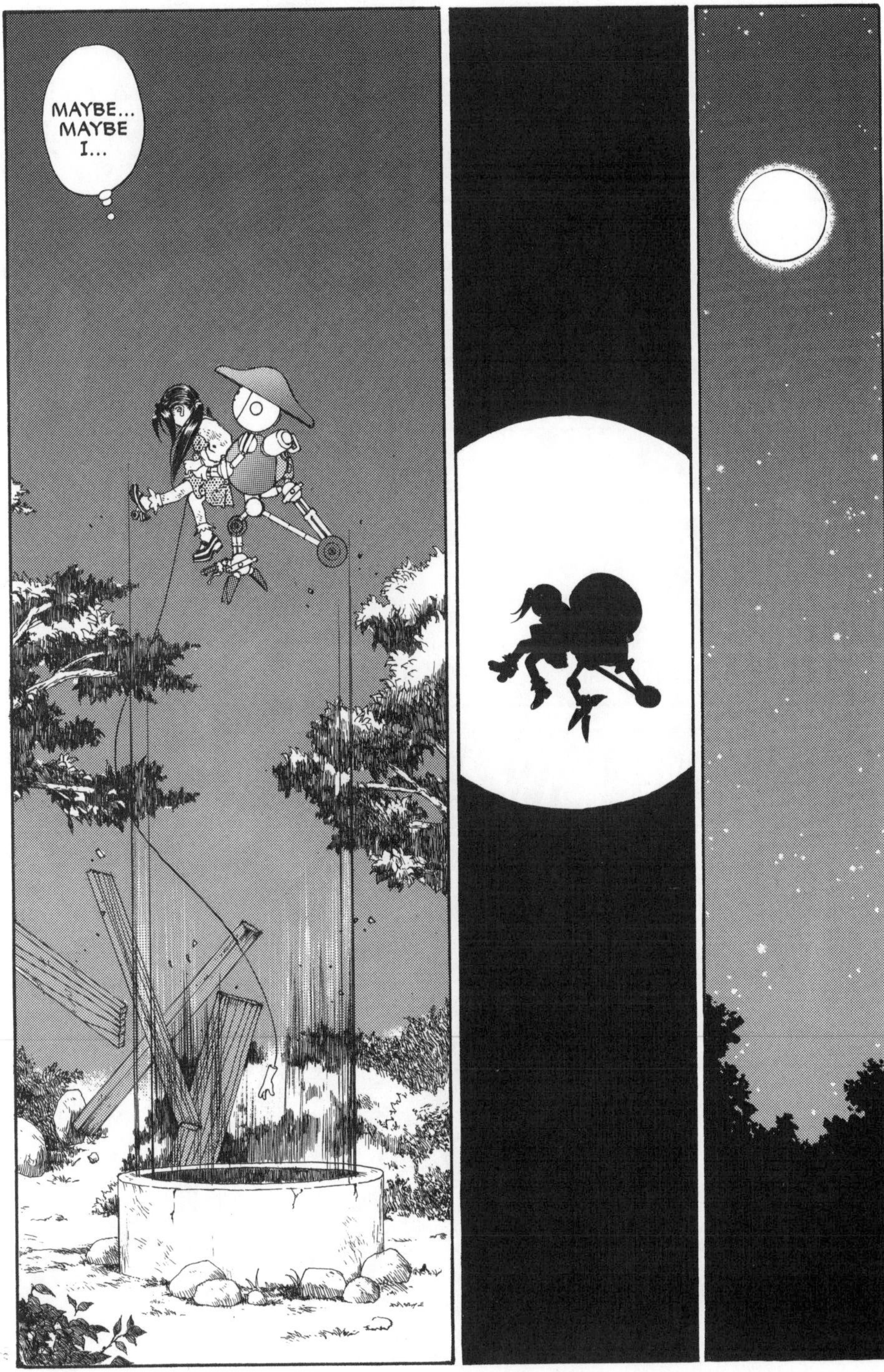
MAYBE... MAYBE I...

WHY DID I SAY THAT ...?
"DON'T LEAVE ME ALL ALONE!"

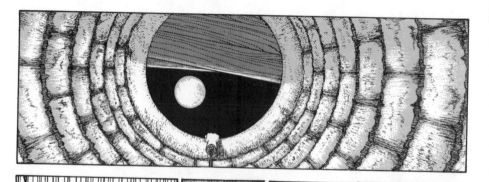

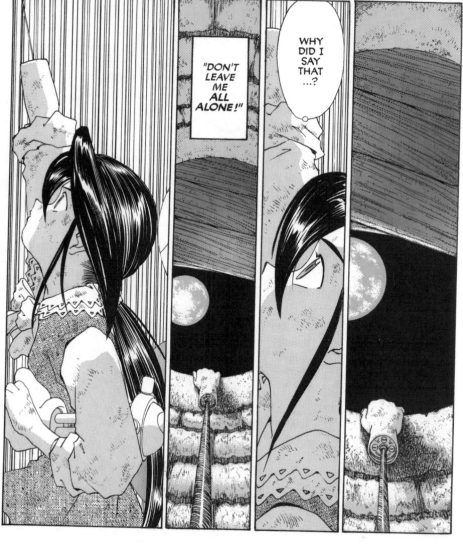

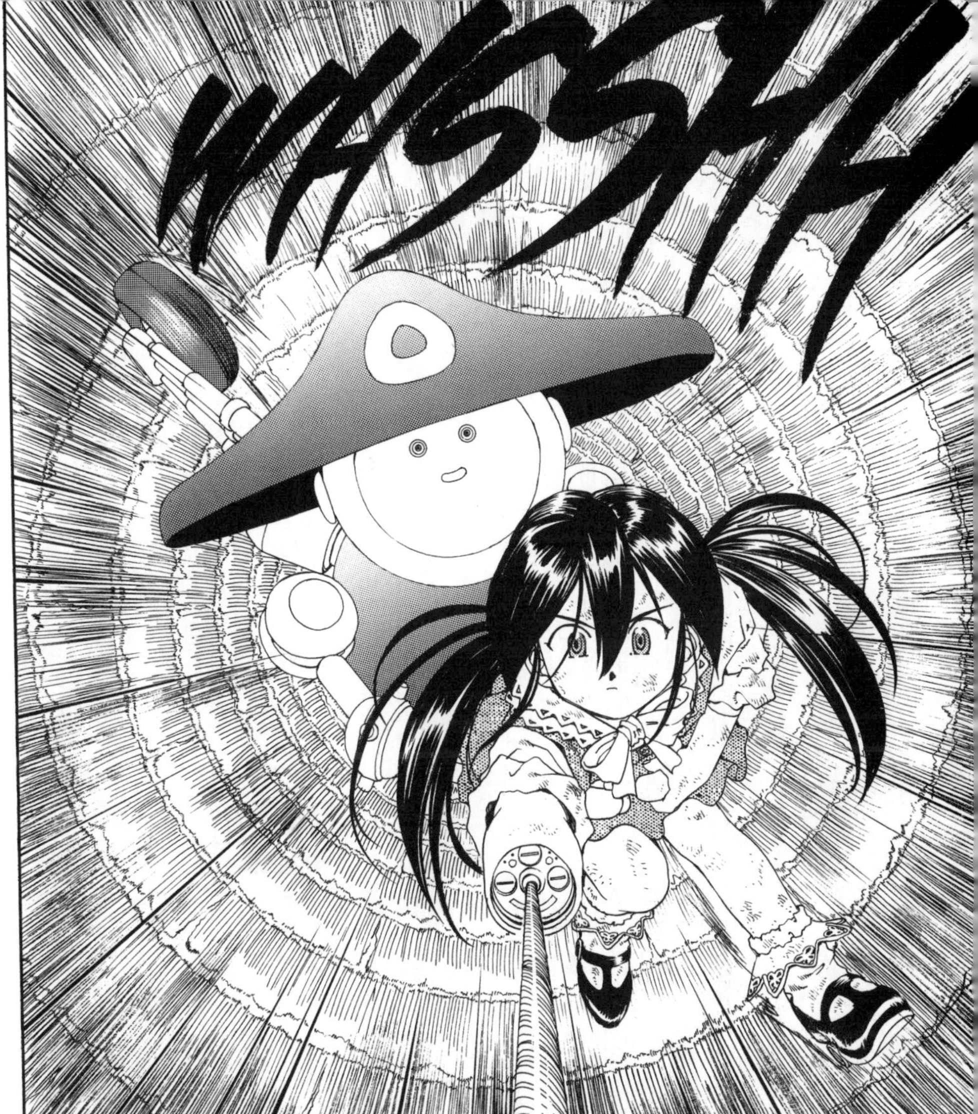
WHSSHH
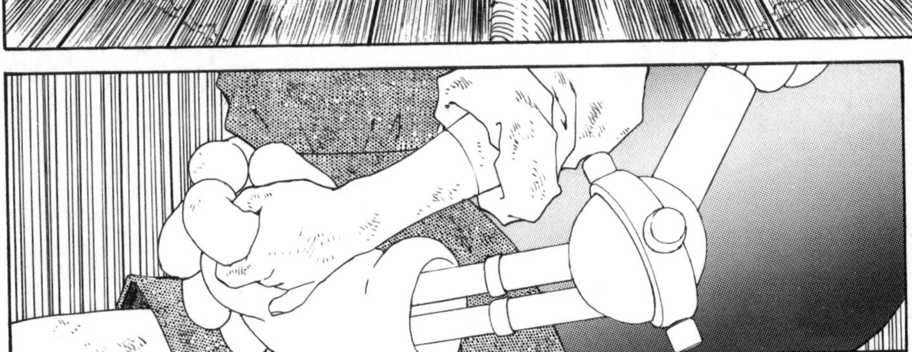

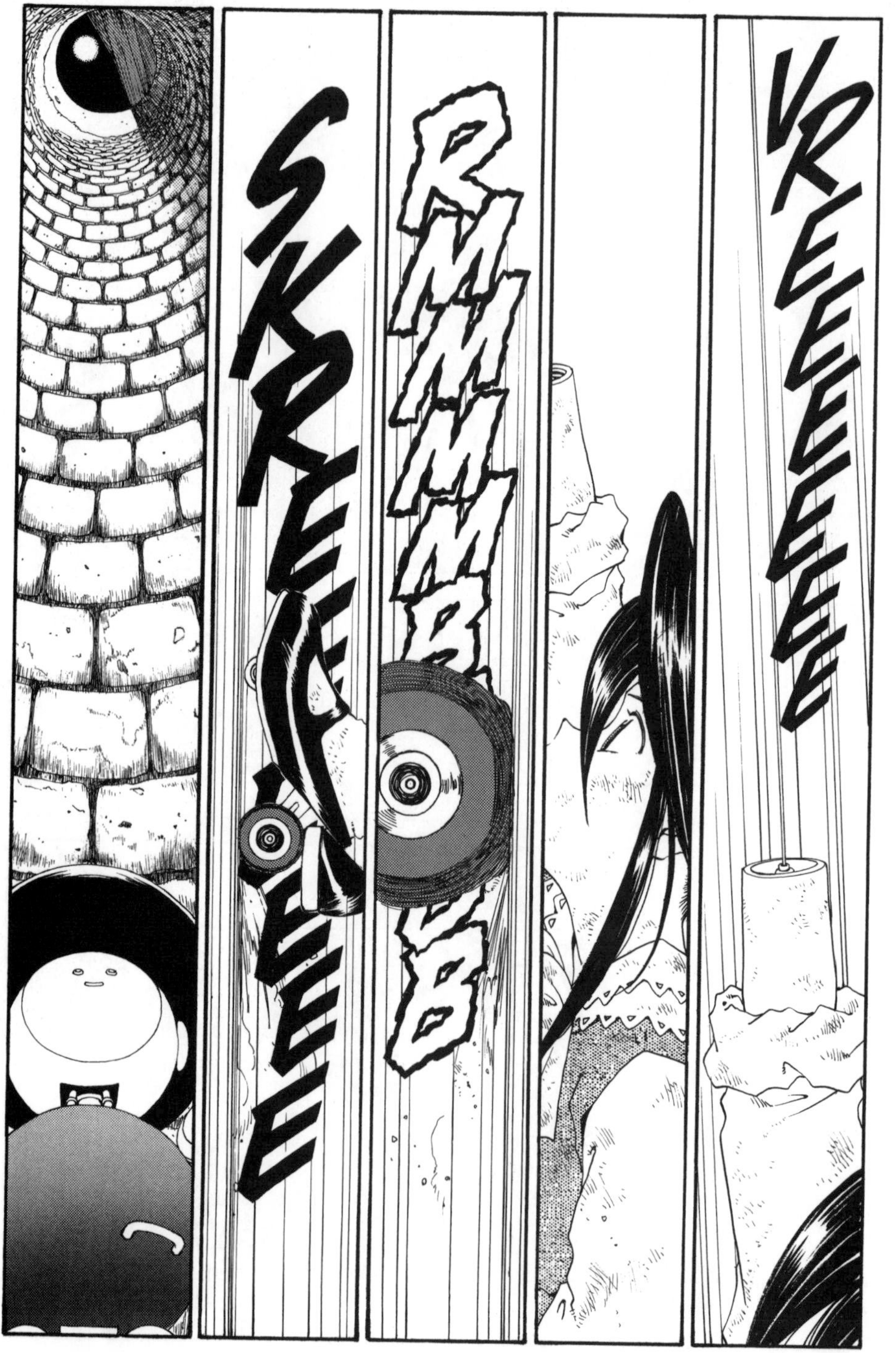
VREEEEEEEE
RMMMMBB
SKREEEEEEE

DIDN'T I TELL YOU TO *CUT THAT OUT?!*

IF YOU WASTE ANY MORE, YOU'LL RUN OUT FOR *SURE.*

AND NO, I'M *NOT* GOING TO GIVE THE FUSE BACK.

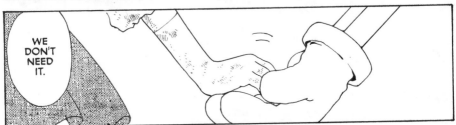

WE DON'T NEED IT.

IF WE HAVE *EACH OTHER.*

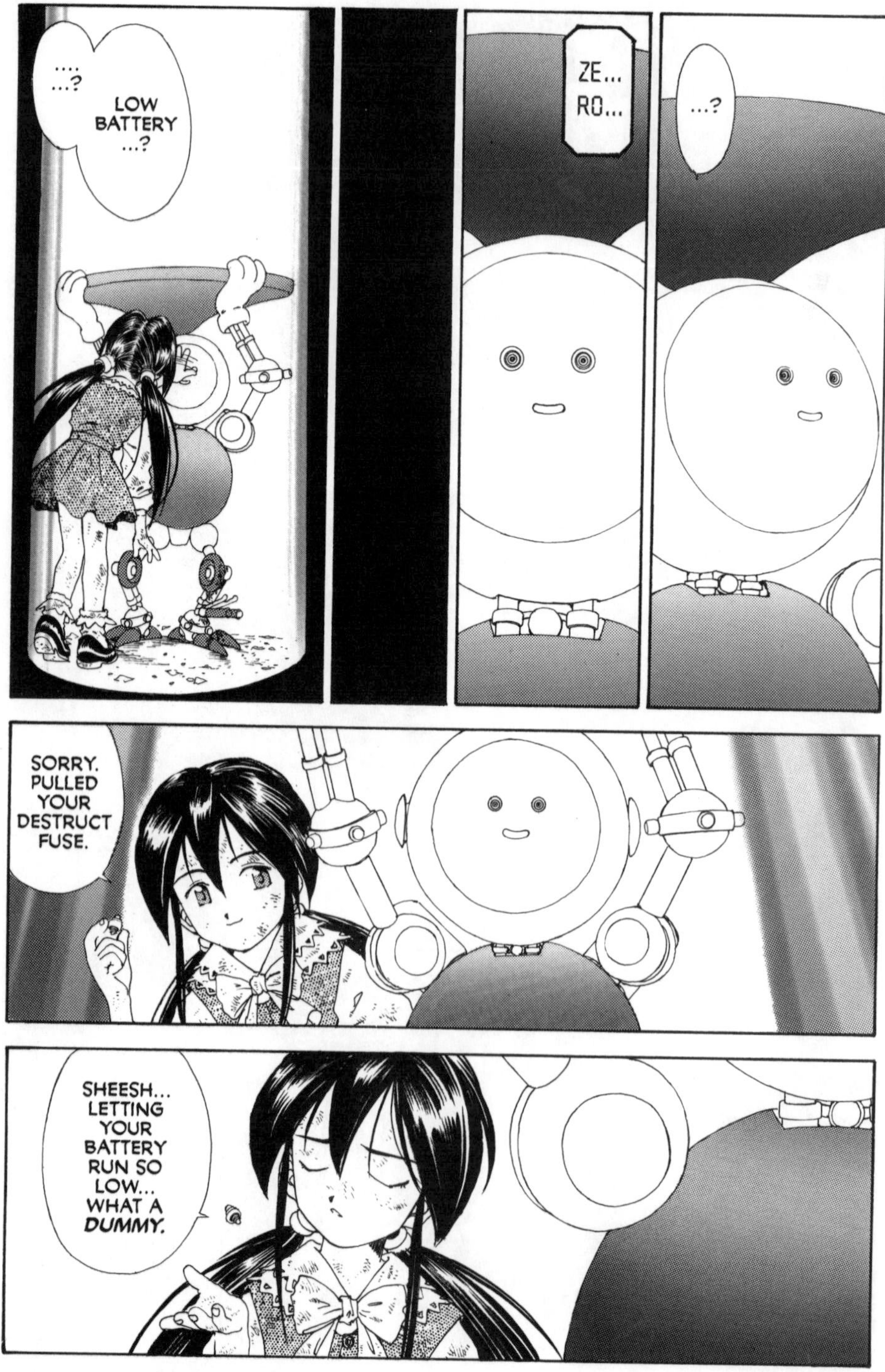
...?
ZE... RO...
....? LOW BATTERY ...?
SORRY. PULLED YOUR DESTRUCT FUSE.
SHEESH... LETTING YOUR BATTERY RUN SO LOW... WHAT A *DUMMY.*

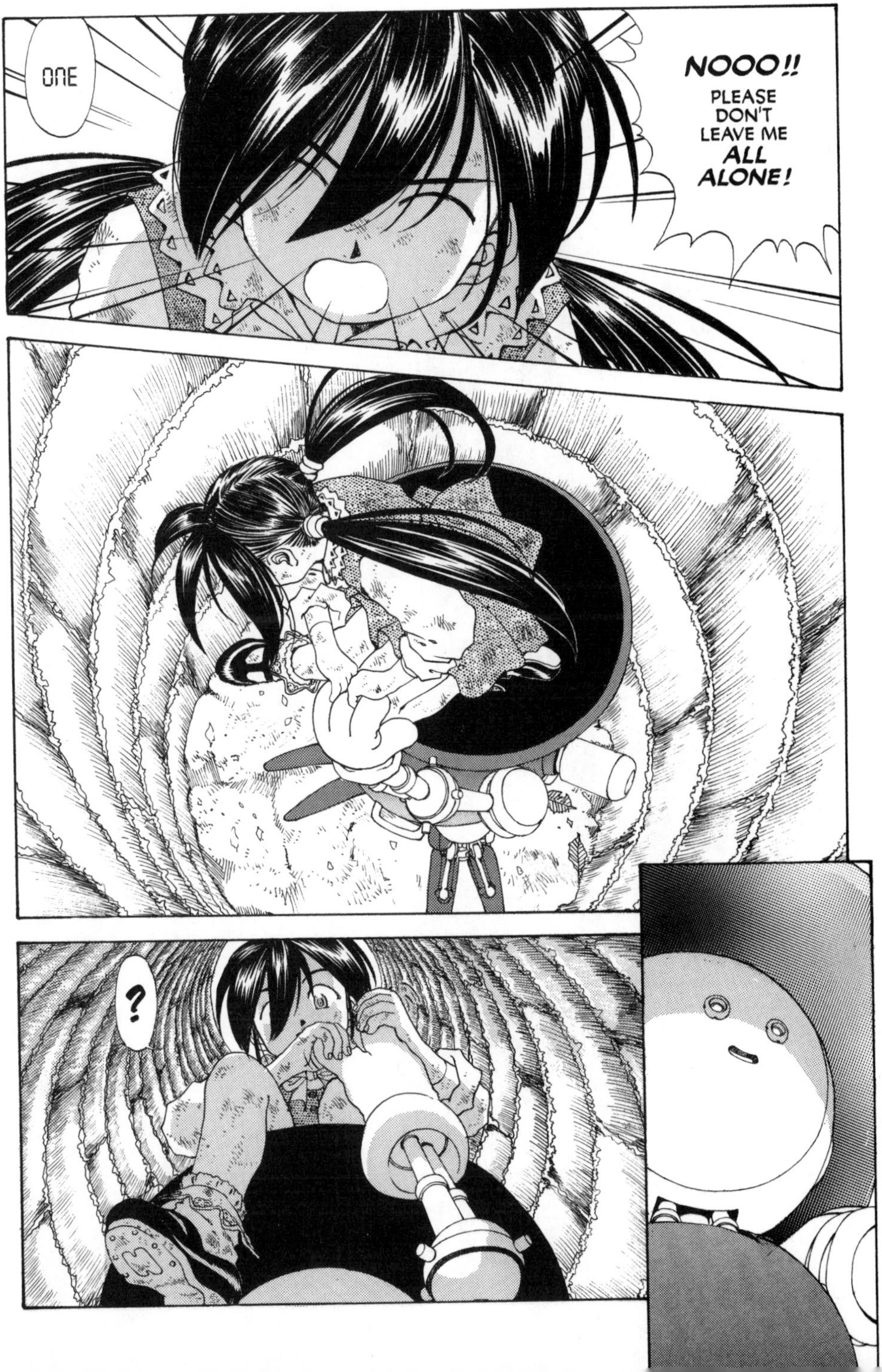
NOOO!! PLEASE DON'T LEAVE ME ALL ALONE!
ONE
?

MOVE IT-- I'M GETTING DOWN!

FIVE

FOUR FWAP

THREE

EEK!! GET YOUR HAND OFF ME, YOU... YOU PERVERT!

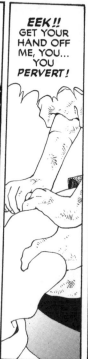

I...I'LL NEVER SPEAK TO YOU AGAIN!!

TWO

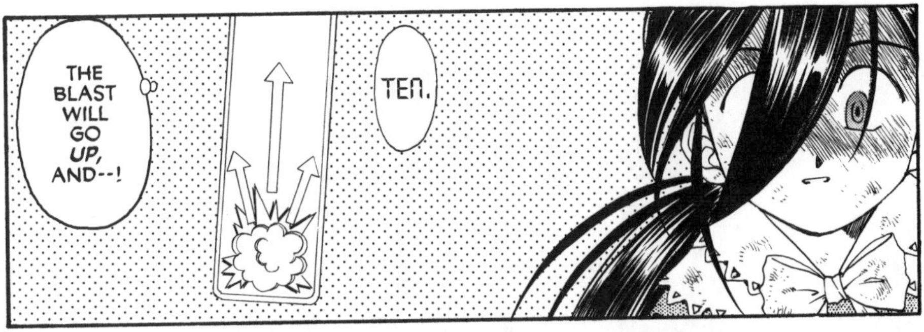
TEN.
THE BLAST WILL GO UP, AND--!

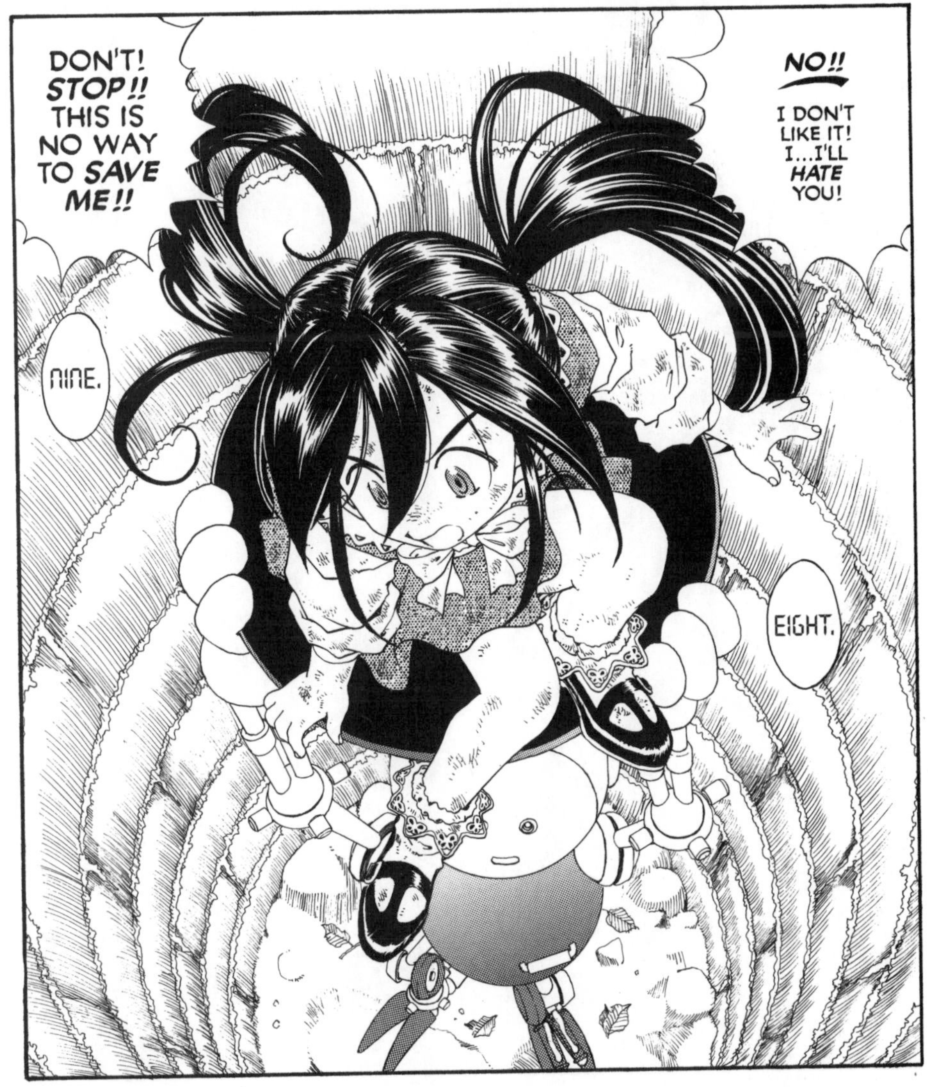
NO!! I DON'T LIKE IT! I...I'LL HATE YOU!
DON'T! STOP!! THIS IS NO WAY TO SAVE ME!!
NINE.
EIGHT.

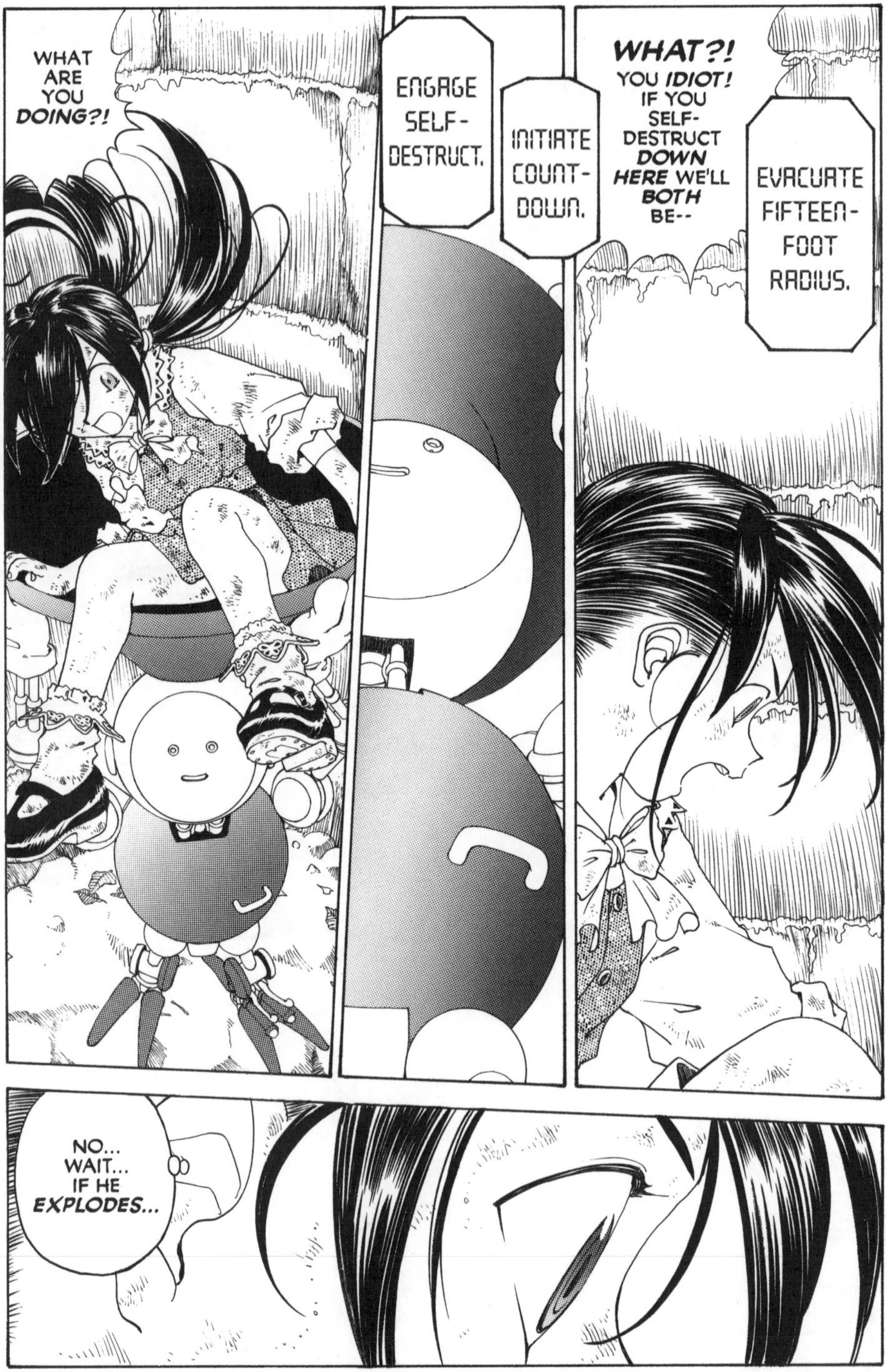
WHAT ARE YOU DOING?!
ENGAGE SELF-DESTRUCT.
INITIATE COUNT-DOWN.
WHAT?! YOU IDIOT! IF YOU SELF-DESTRUCT DOWN HERE WE'LL BOTH BE--
EVACUATE FIFTEEN-FOOT RADIUS.
NO... WAIT... IF HE EXPLODES...

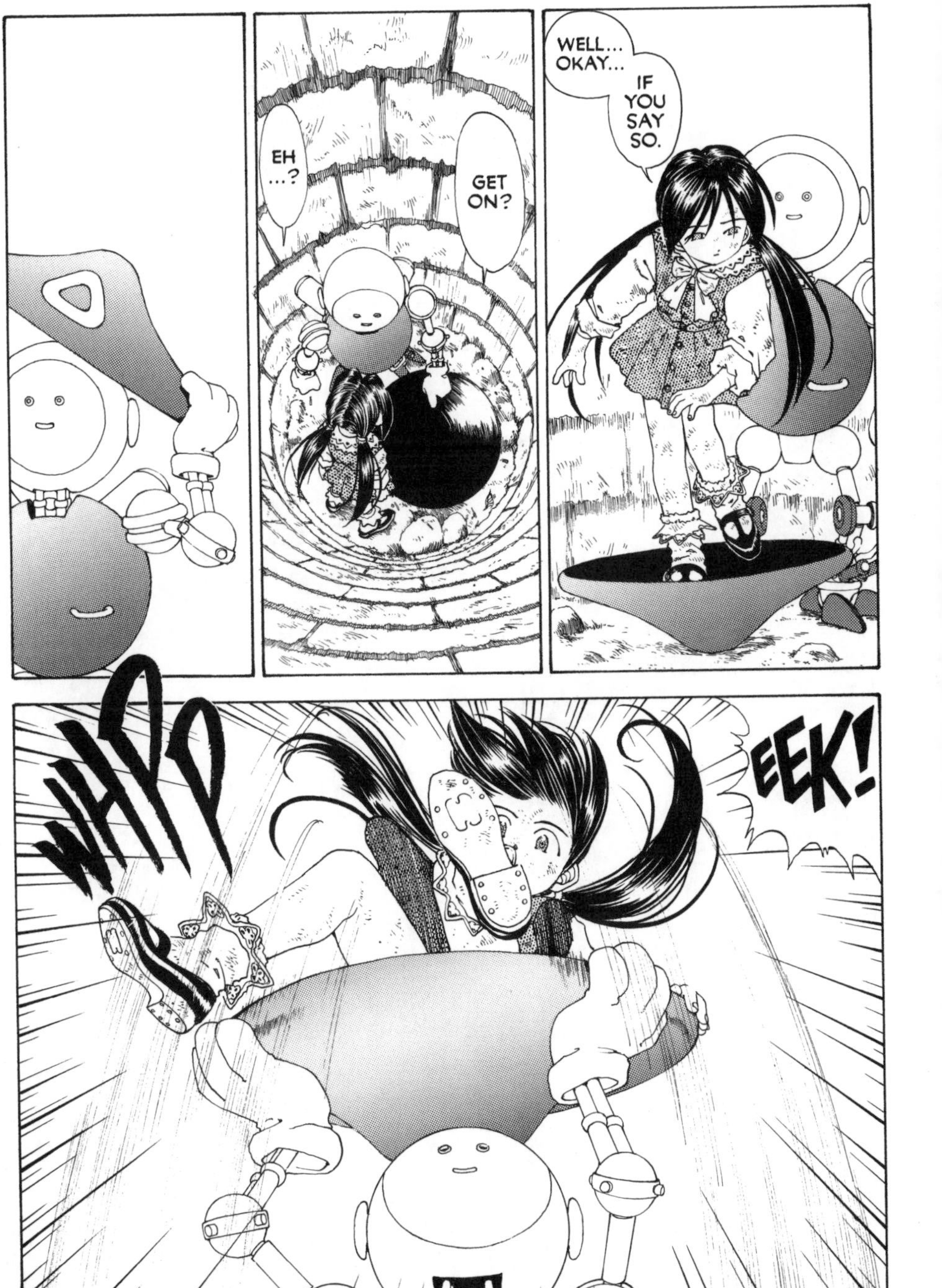
WELL... OKAY... IF YOU SAY SO.
GET ON?
EH ...?
EEK!
WHPP

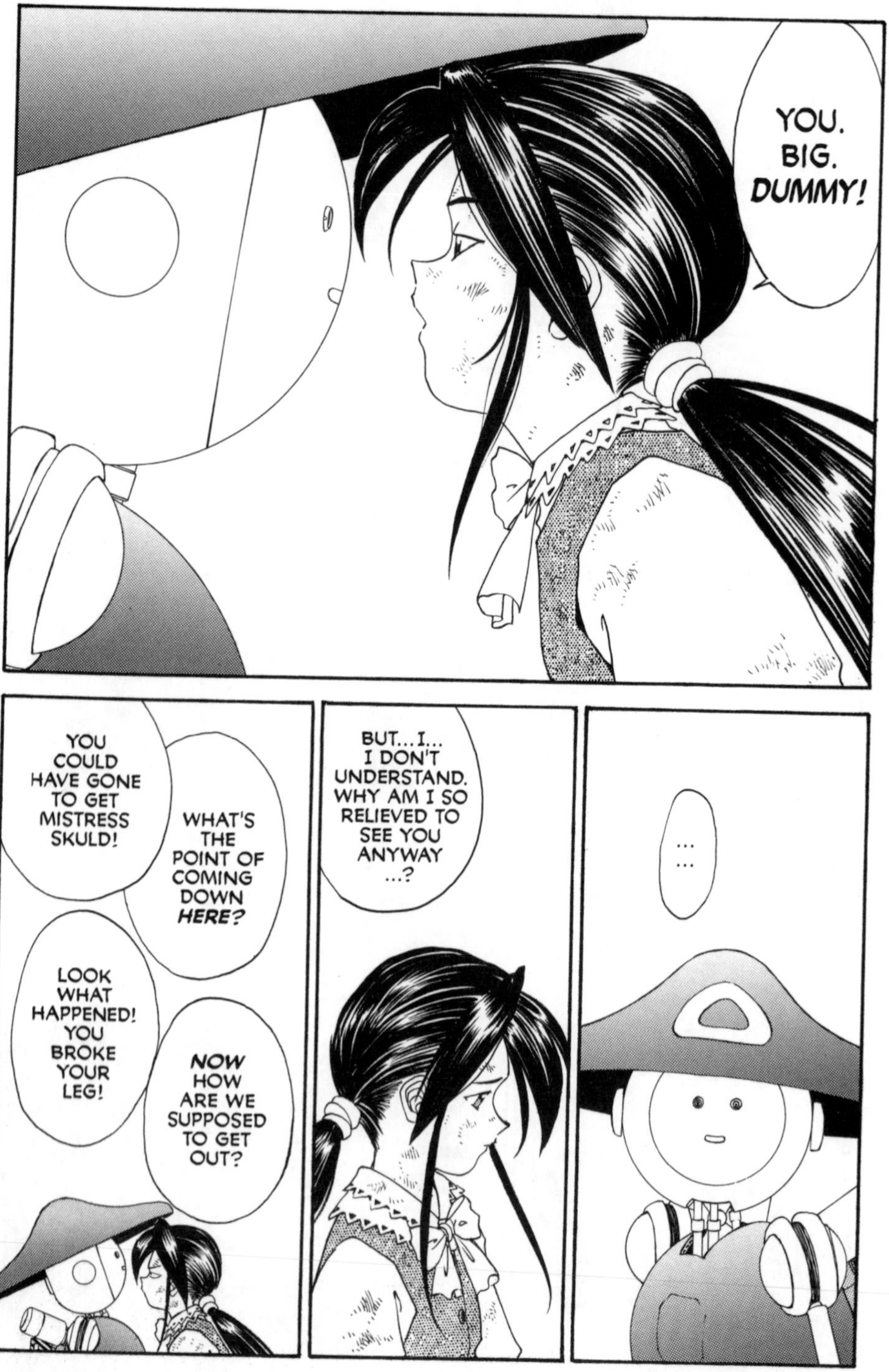
YOU. BIG. DUMMY!
YOU COULD HAVE GONE TO GET MISTRESS SKULD!
WHAT'S THE POINT OF COMING DOWN *HERE?*
LOOK WHAT HAPPENED! YOU BROKE YOUR LEG!
NOW HOW ARE WE SUPPOSED TO GET OUT?
BUT... I... I DON'T UNDERSTAND. WHY AM I SO RELIEVED TO SEE YOU ANYWAY ...?
... ...

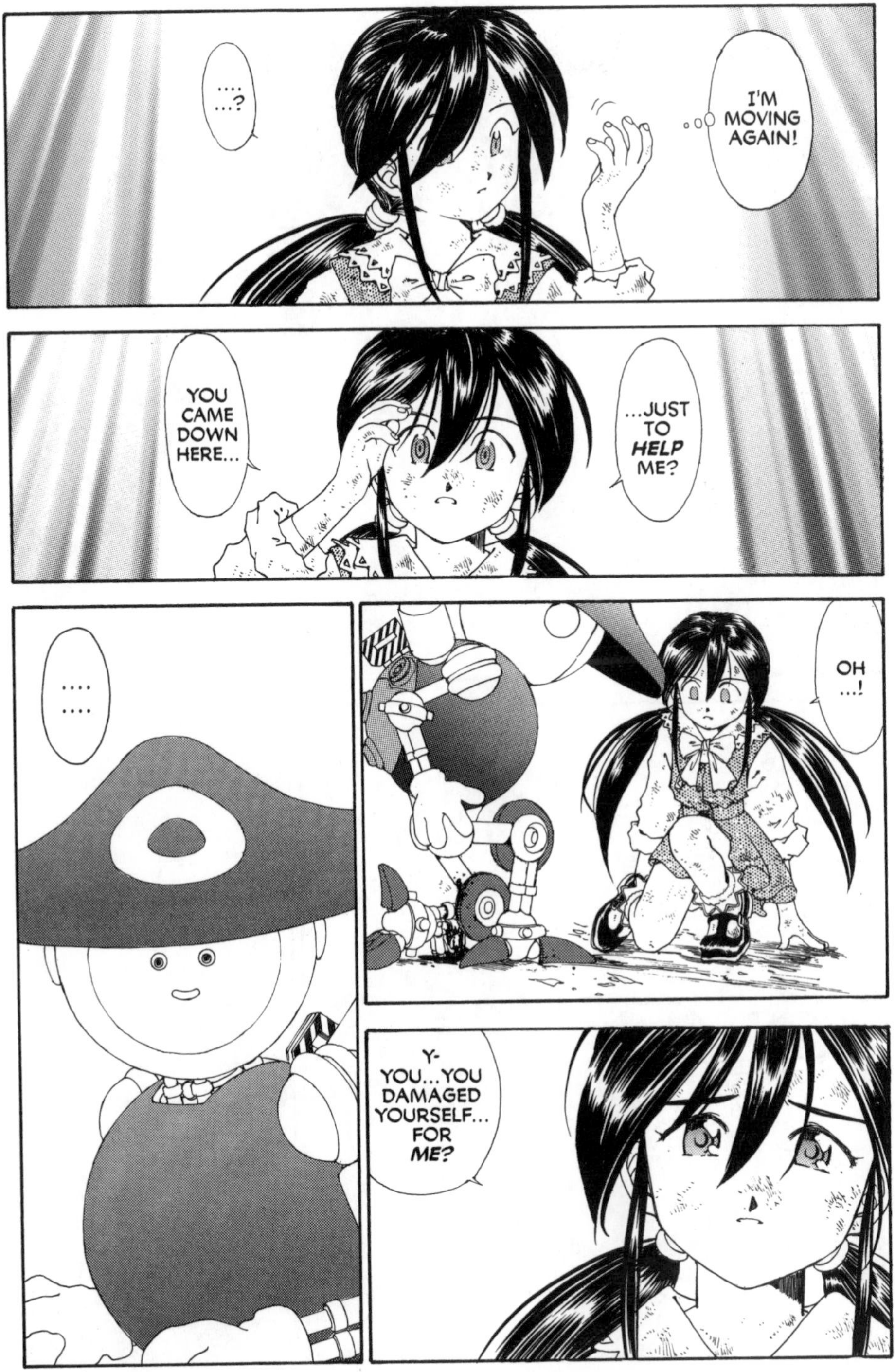
....
...?
I'M MOVING AGAIN!
YOU CAME DOWN HERE...
...JUST TO *HELP* ME?
....
....
OH ...!
Y-YOU...YOU DAMAGED YOURSELF... FOR *ME?*

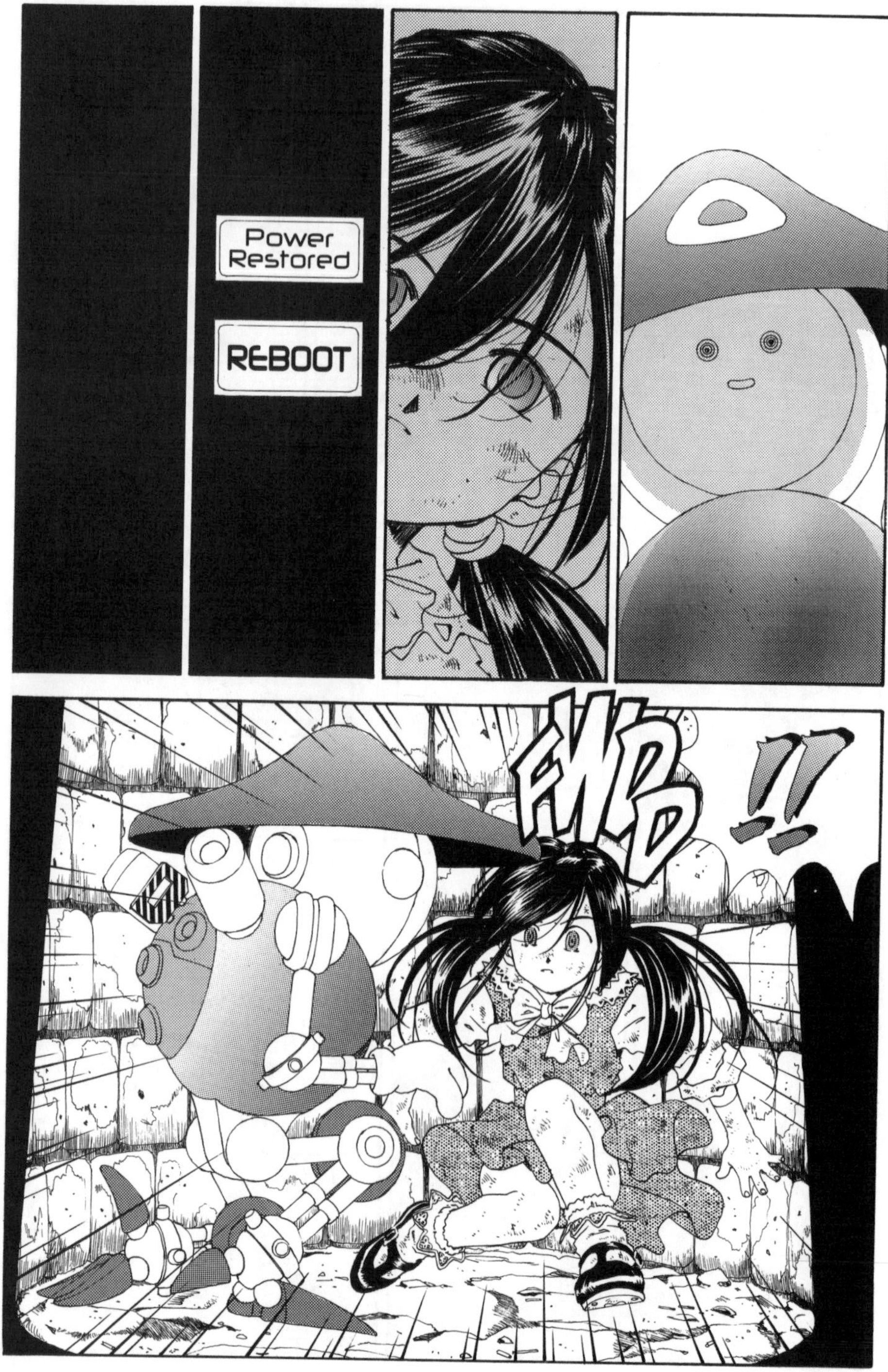
Power Restored
REBOOT
FWDD!!

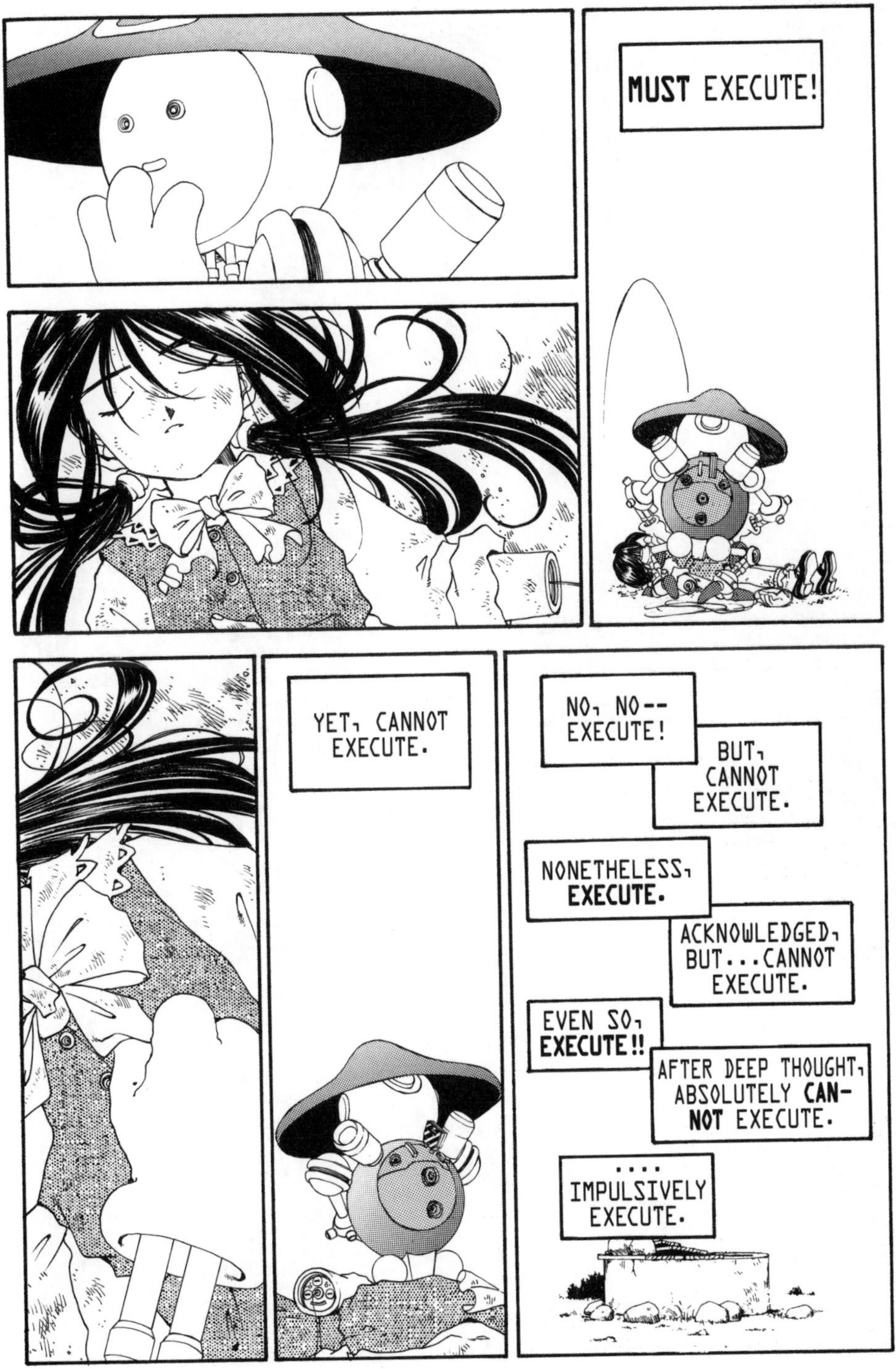
MUST EXECUTE!
YET, CANNOT EXECUTE.
NO, NO-- EXECUTE!
BUT, CANNOT EXECUTE.
NONETHELESS, EXECUTE.
ACKNOWLEDGED, BUT...CANNOT EXECUTE.
EVEN SO, EXECUTE!!
AFTER DEEP THOUGHT, ABSOLUTELY CAN-NOT EXECUTE.
.... IMPULSIVELY EXECUTE.

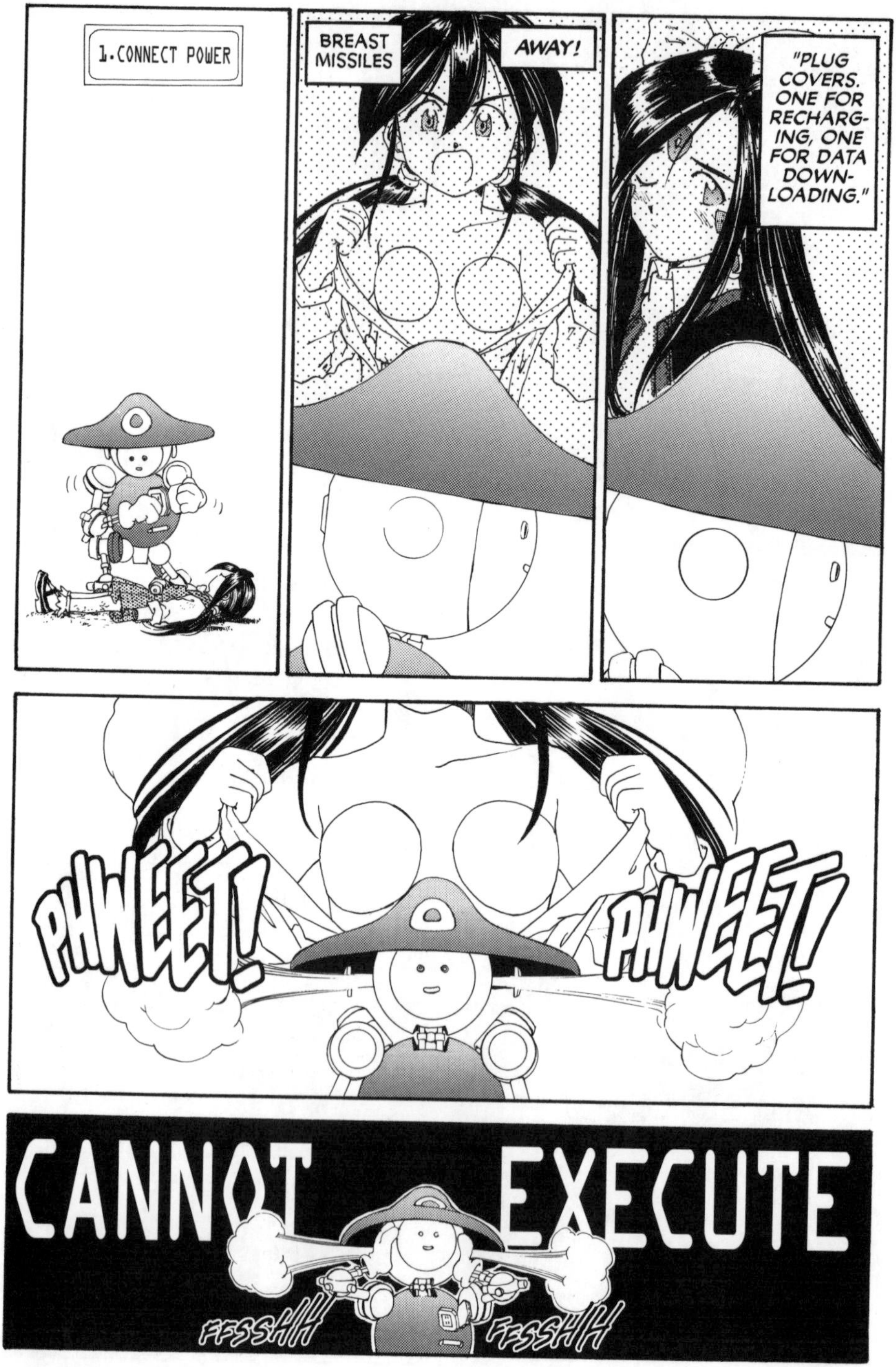
1. CONNECT POWER
BREAST MISSILES
AWAY!
"PLUG COVERS. ONE FOR RECHARG-ING, ONE FOR DATA DOWN-LOADING."
PHWEET!
PHWEET!
CANNOT EXECUTE
FFSSHH
FFSSHH

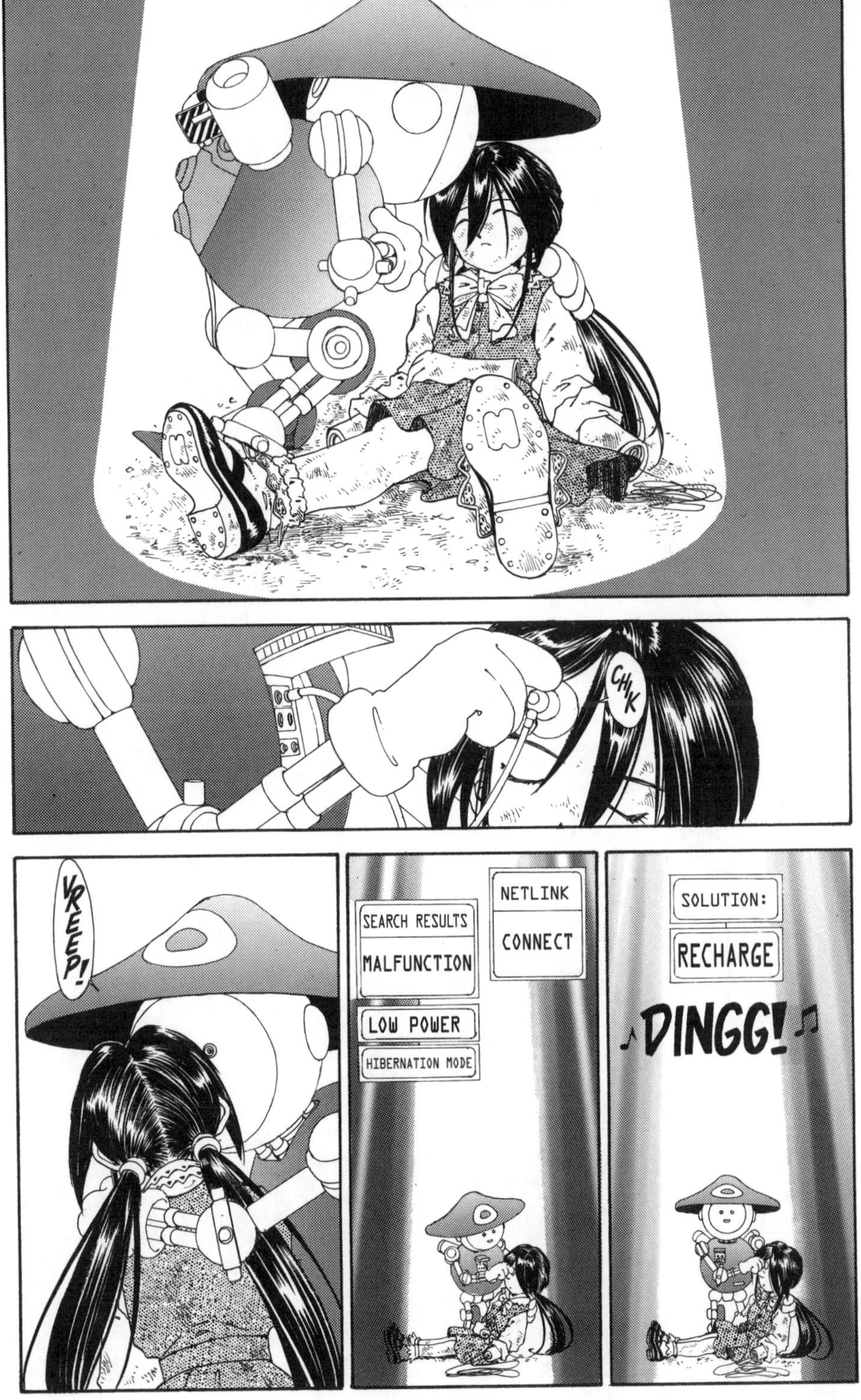
CHIK
VREEP!
NETLINK
CONNECT
SEARCH RESULTS
MALFUNCTION
LOW POWER
HIBERNATION MODE
SOLUTION:
RECHARGE
DINGG!

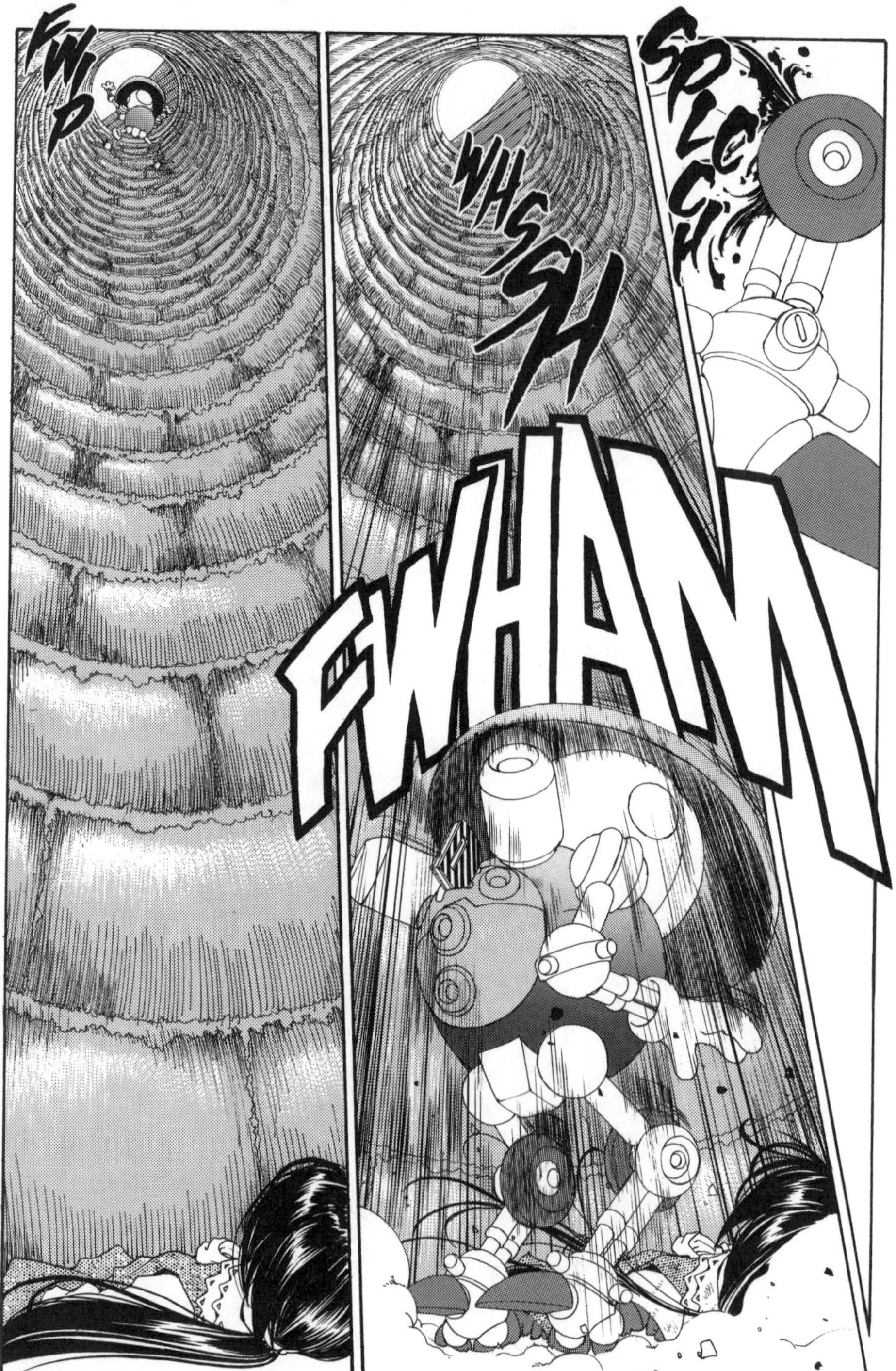
SPLECH
WHSSH
FWHAM
FWIP

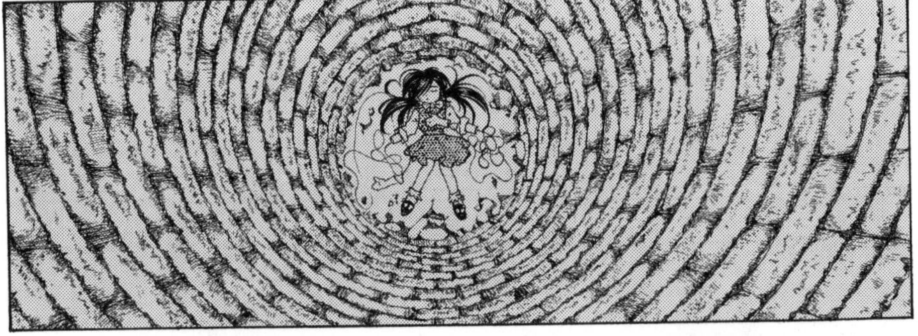
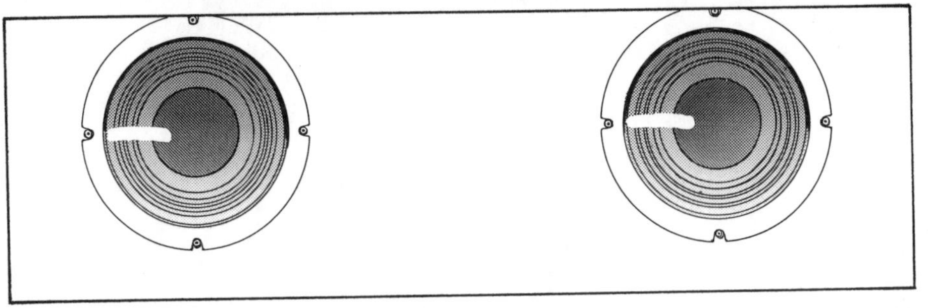
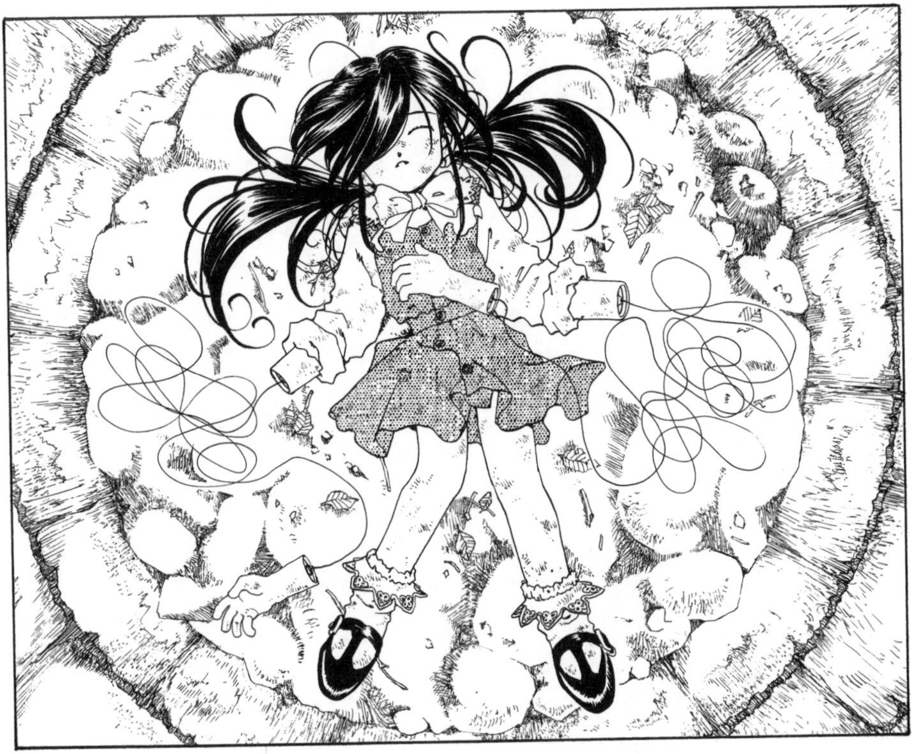

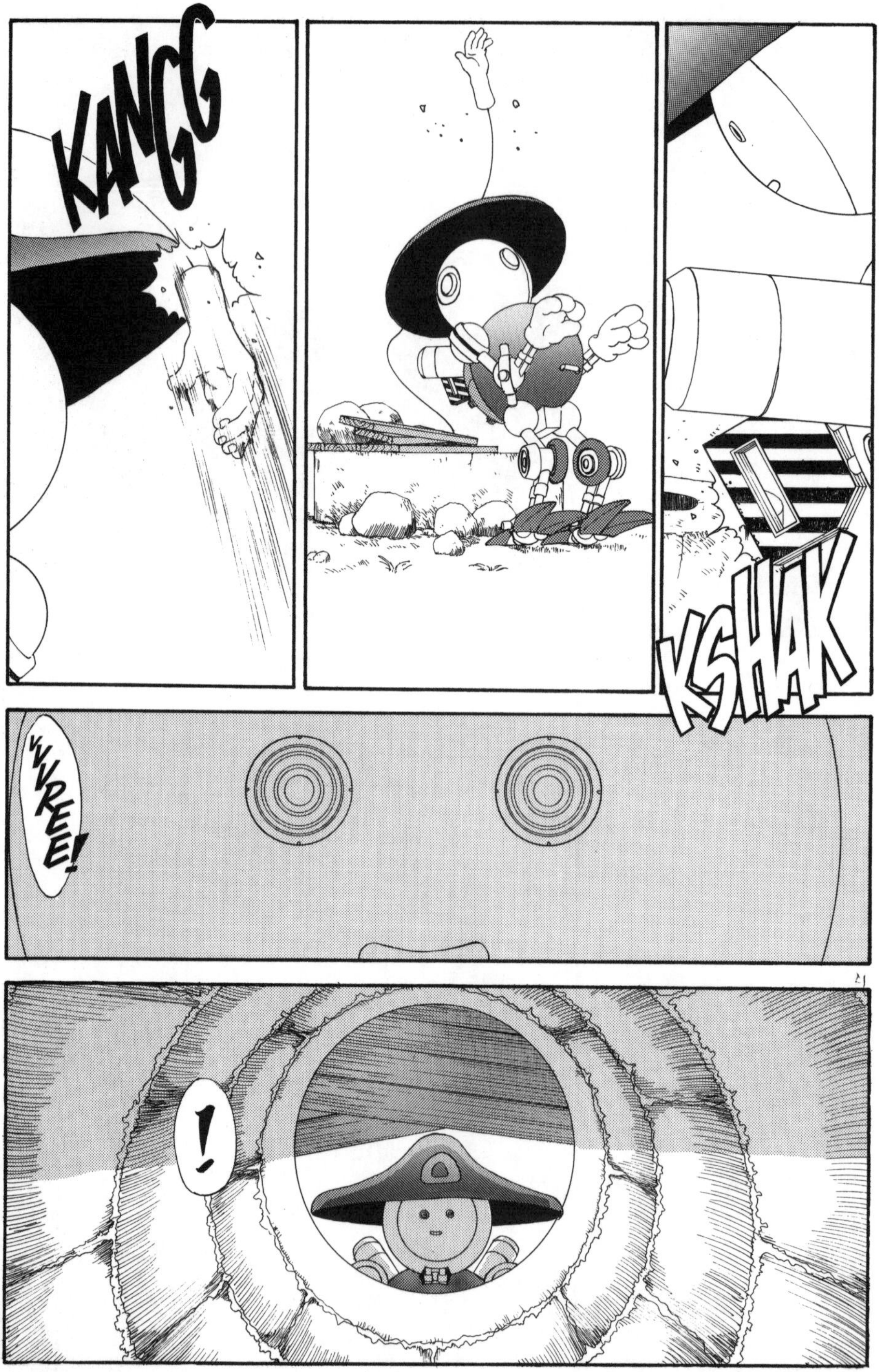
KSHAK
KANGG
VVVREE!
!

HIBERNATION
....
....
BEEEEEEEE
WH...
WHY?
WHY
DO I...
SEE *HIM*...
N-NOW...
.....
WHTT
SHINGG

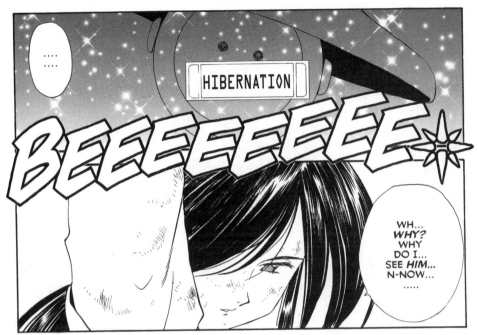

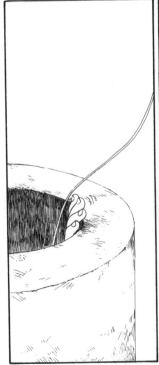

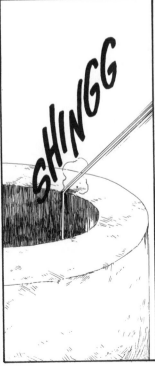

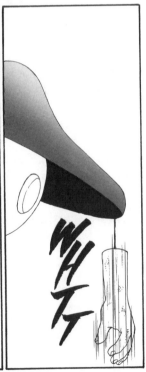

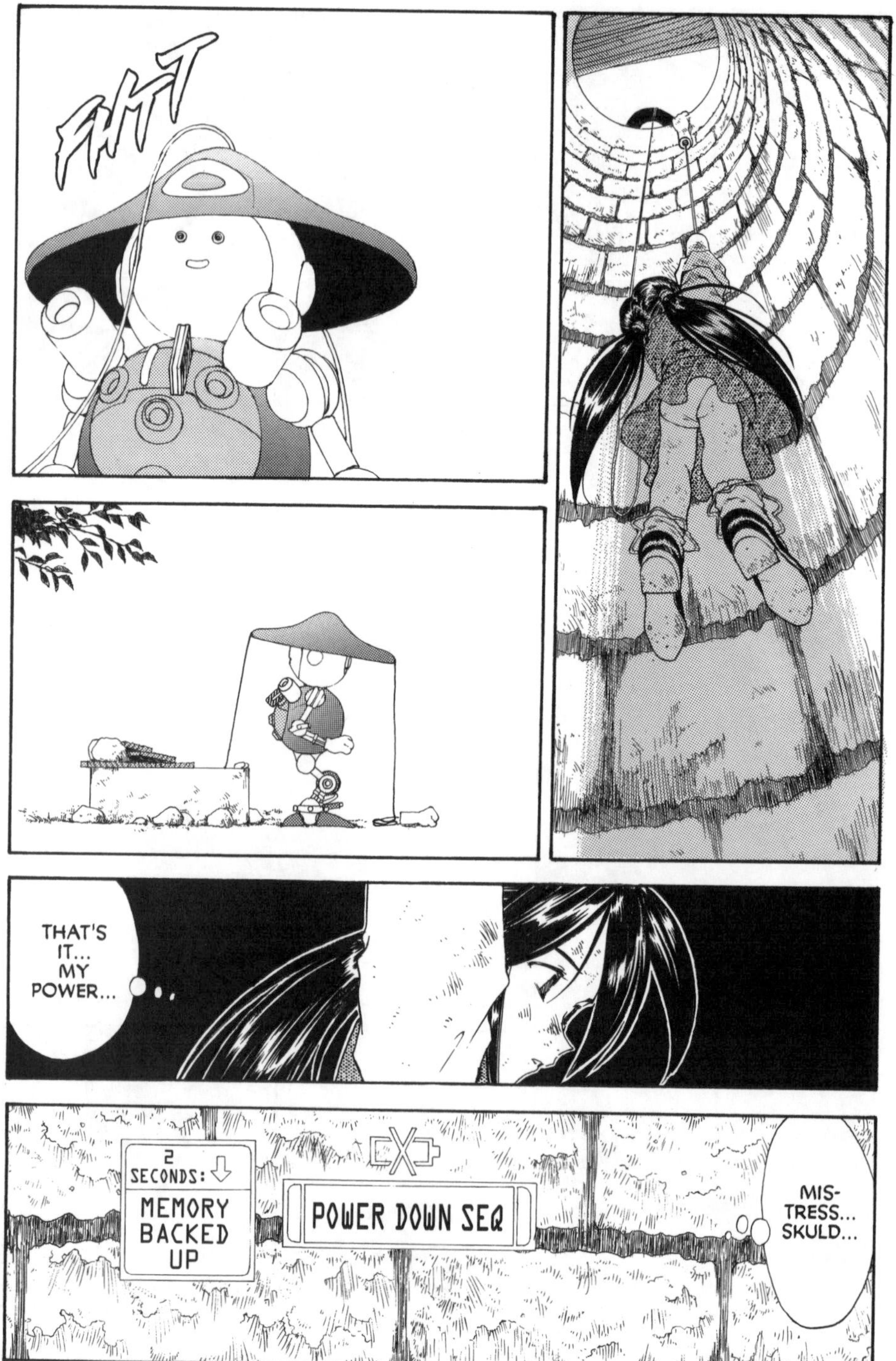
FLTTT
THAT'S IT... MY POWER...
MIS-TRESS... SKULD...
2 SECONDS: ⇩
MEMORY BACKED UP
POWER DOWN SEQ

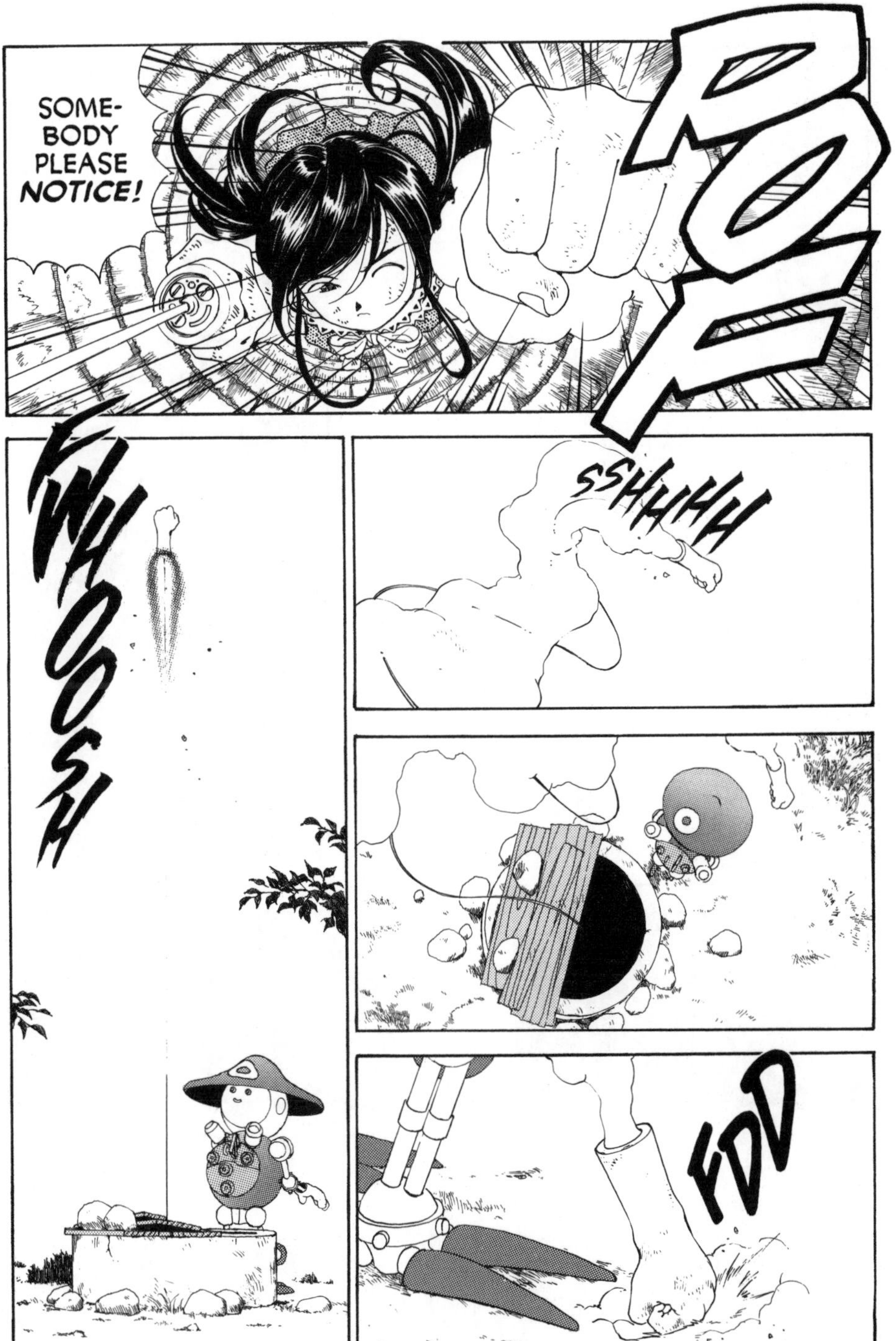
POW
SOME-BODY PLEASE NOTICE!
SSHHHH
FDD
WHOOOSH

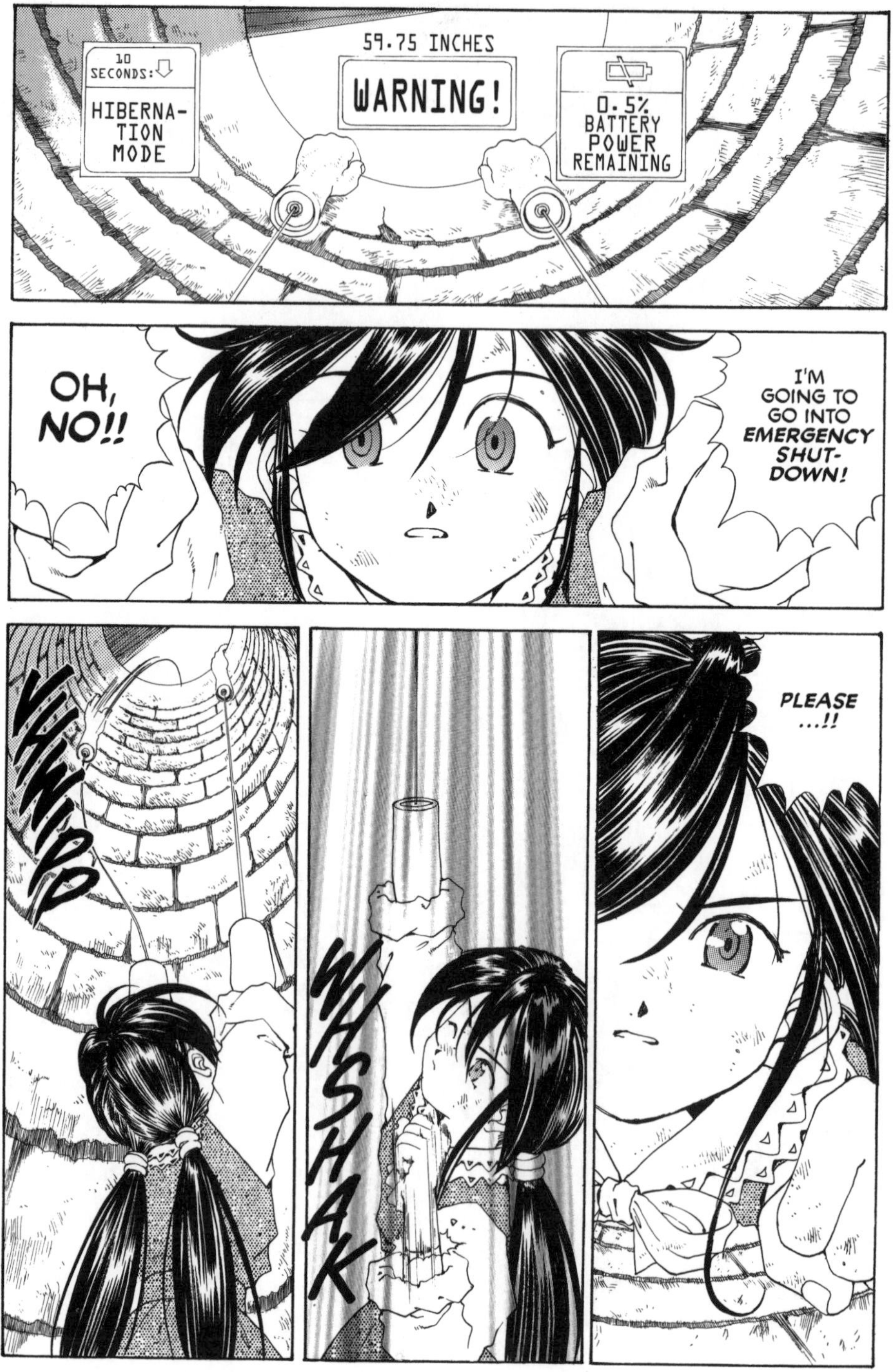
59.75 INCHES
WARNING!
0.5% BATTERY POWER REMAINING
10 SECONDS: ⇩
HIBERNATION MODE
I'M GOING TO GO INTO EMERGENCY SHUT-DOWN!
OH, NO!!
PLEASE ...!!
WHSHAK
VWHIPP

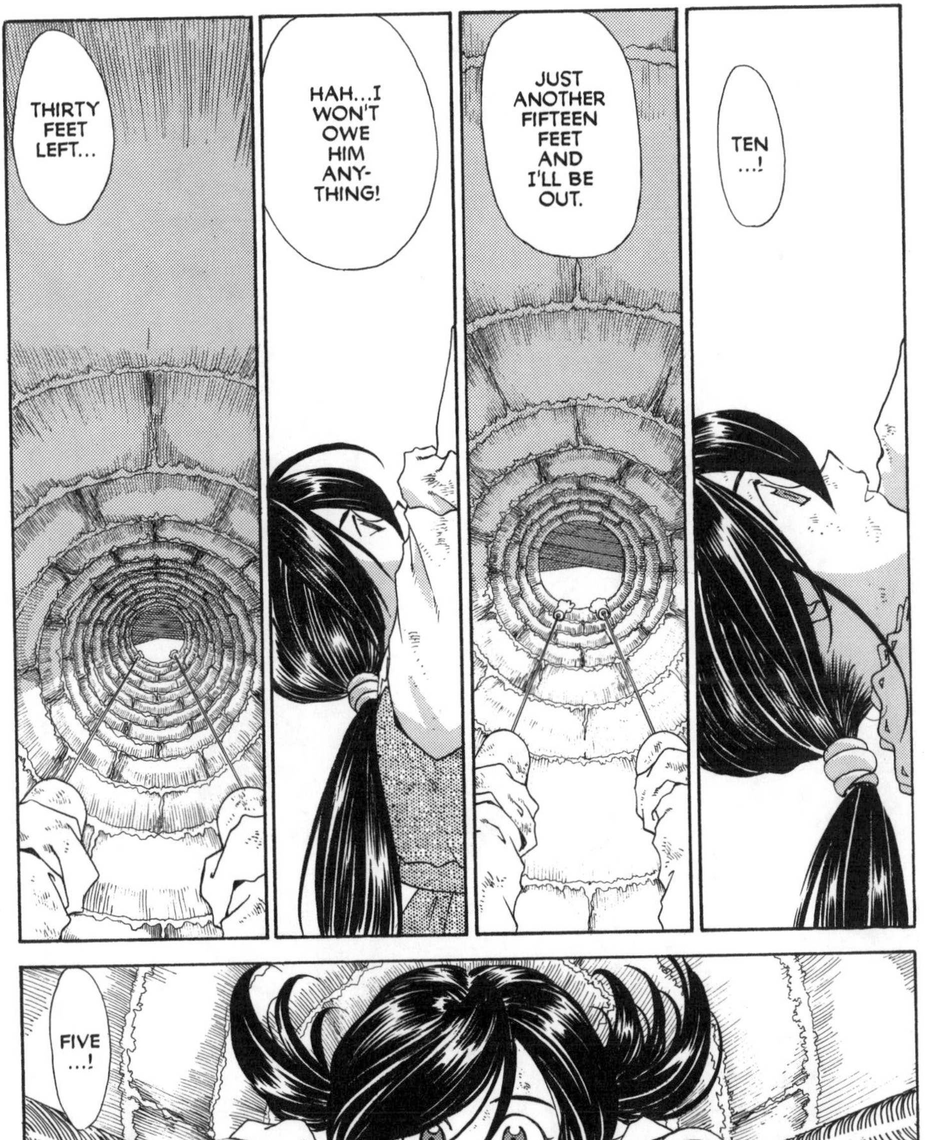
THIRTY FEET LEFT...
HAH...I WON'T OWE HIM ANY-THING!
JUST ANOTHER FIFTEEN FEET AND I'LL BE OUT.
TEN ...!
FIVE ...!

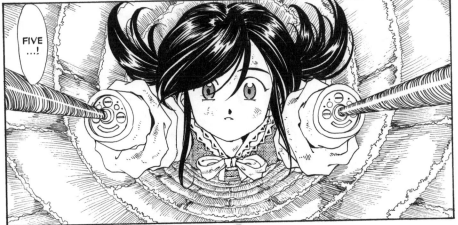

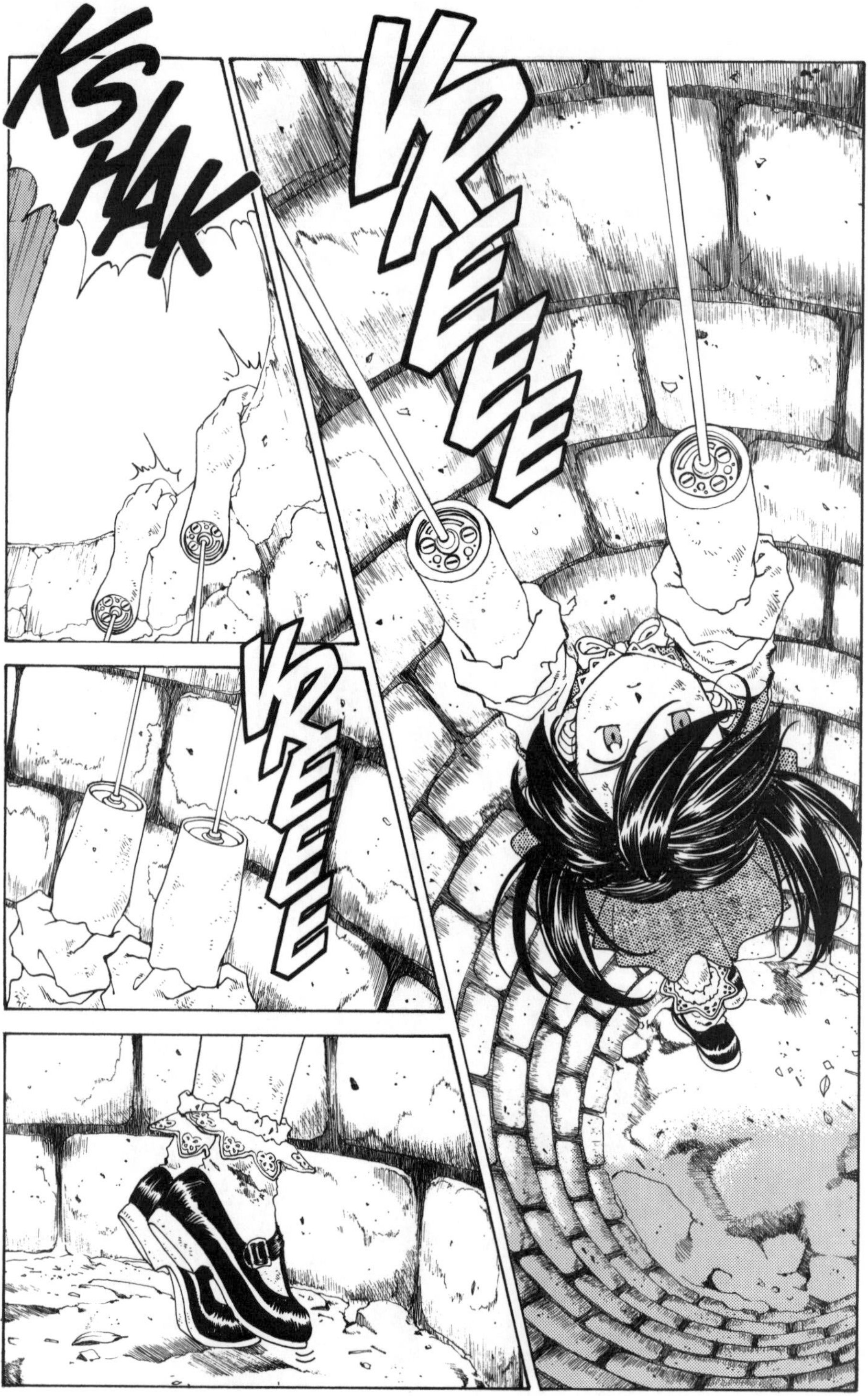
VREEEE
KSHAK
VREEEE

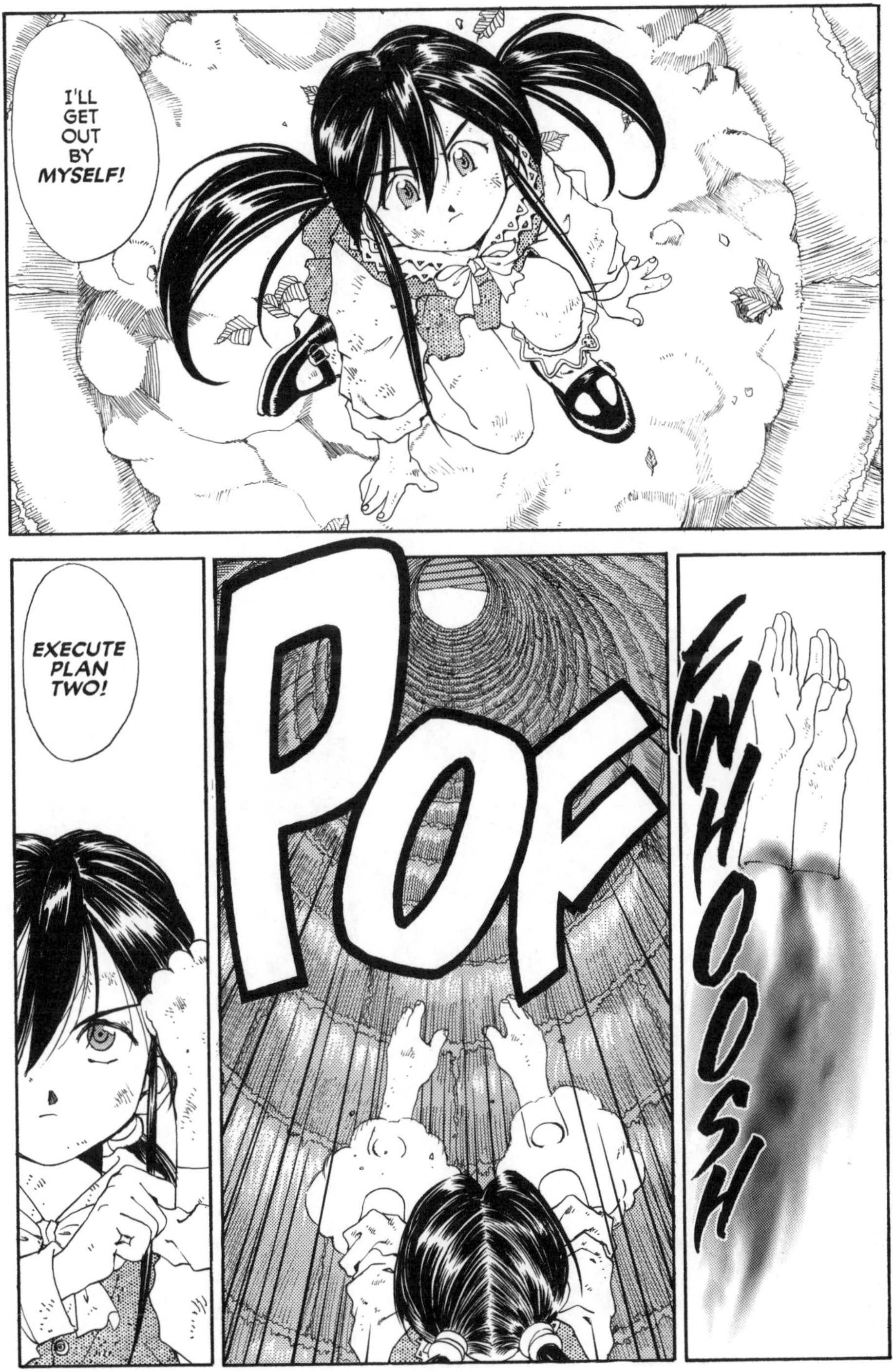
I'LL GET OUT BY *MYSELF!*
EXECUTE PLAN TWO!
POP
WHOOSH

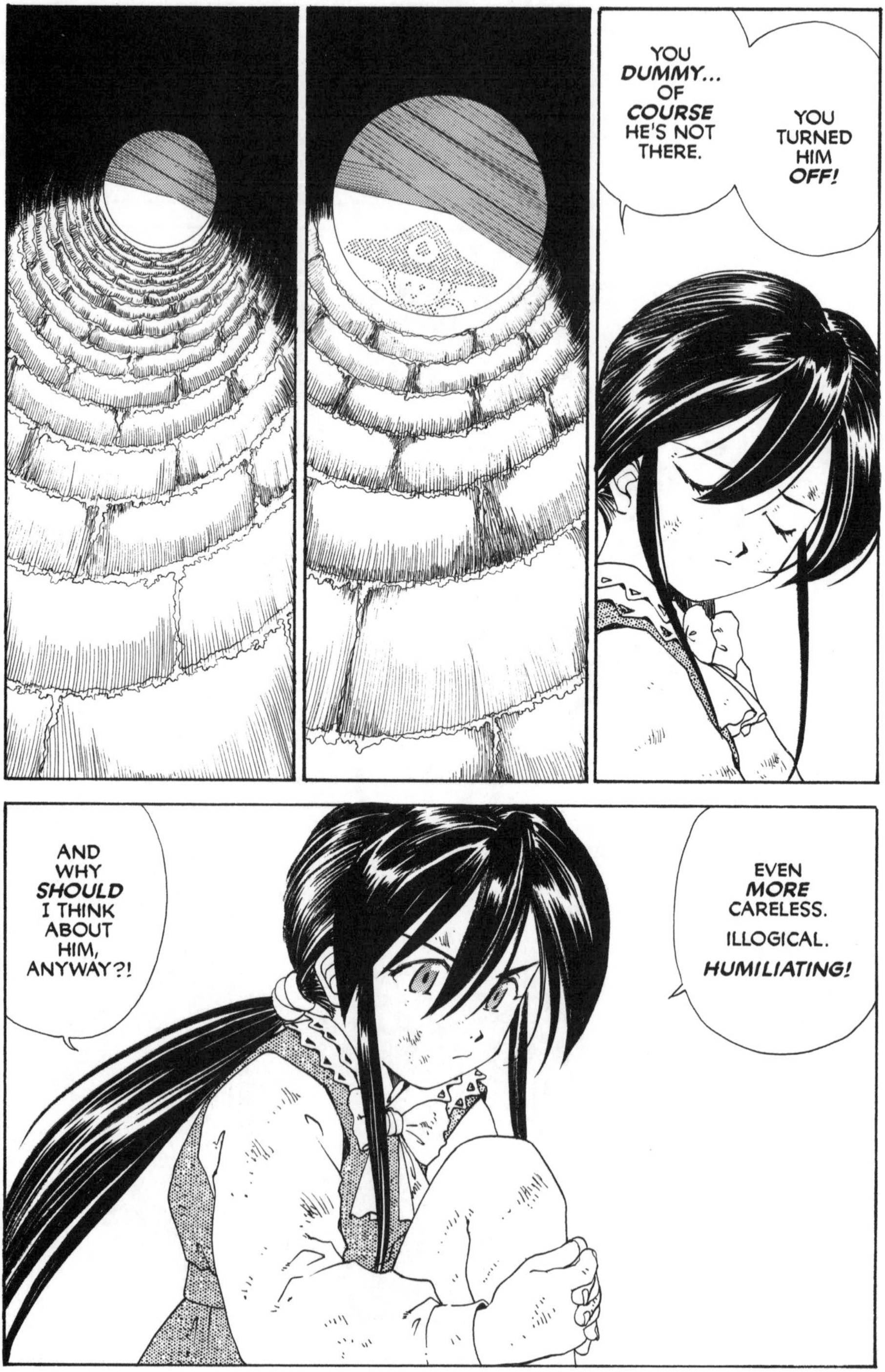
YOU TURNED HIM OFF!
YOU DUMMY... OF COURSE HE'S NOT THERE.
EVEN MORE CARELESS. ILLOGICAL. HUMILIATING!
AND WHY SHOULD I THINK ABOUT HIM, ANYWAY?!

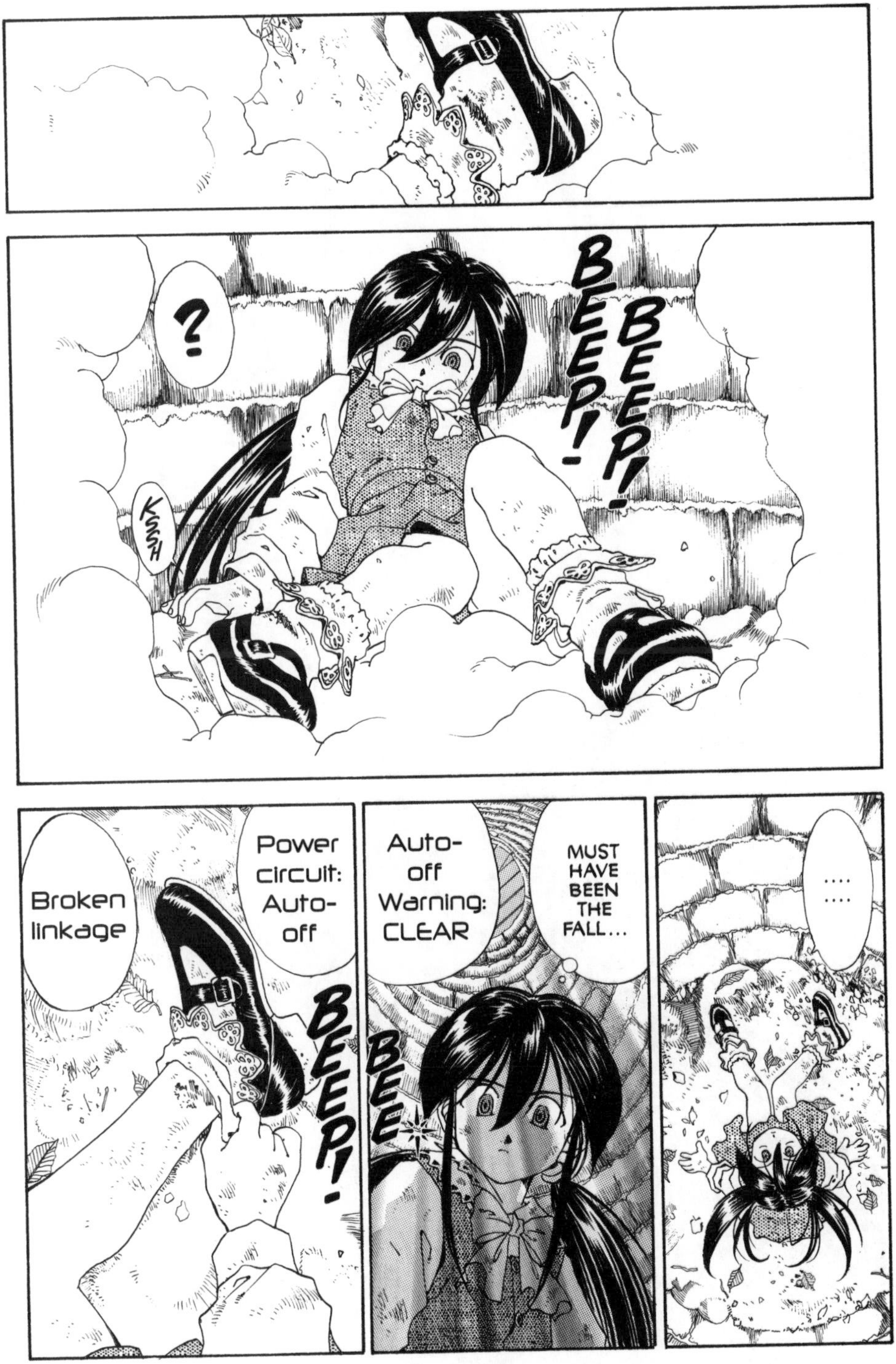
BEEP! BEEP!
?
KSSH
....
....
MUST HAVE BEEN THE FALL...
Auto-off Warning: CLEAR
BEE
Power circuit: Auto-off
Broken linkage
BEEP!

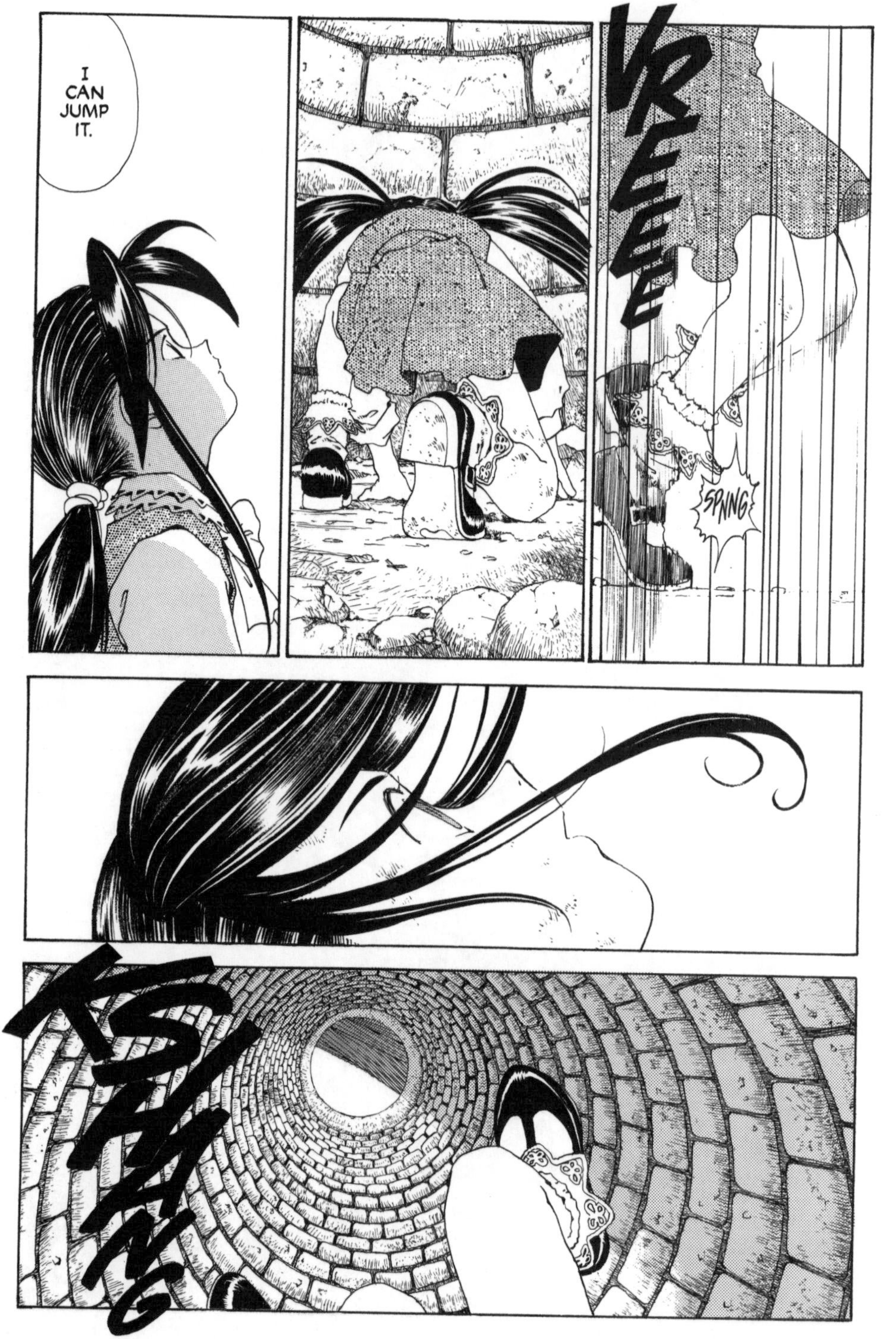
I CAN JUMP IT.
VREEEE
SPNNG
KSHANG

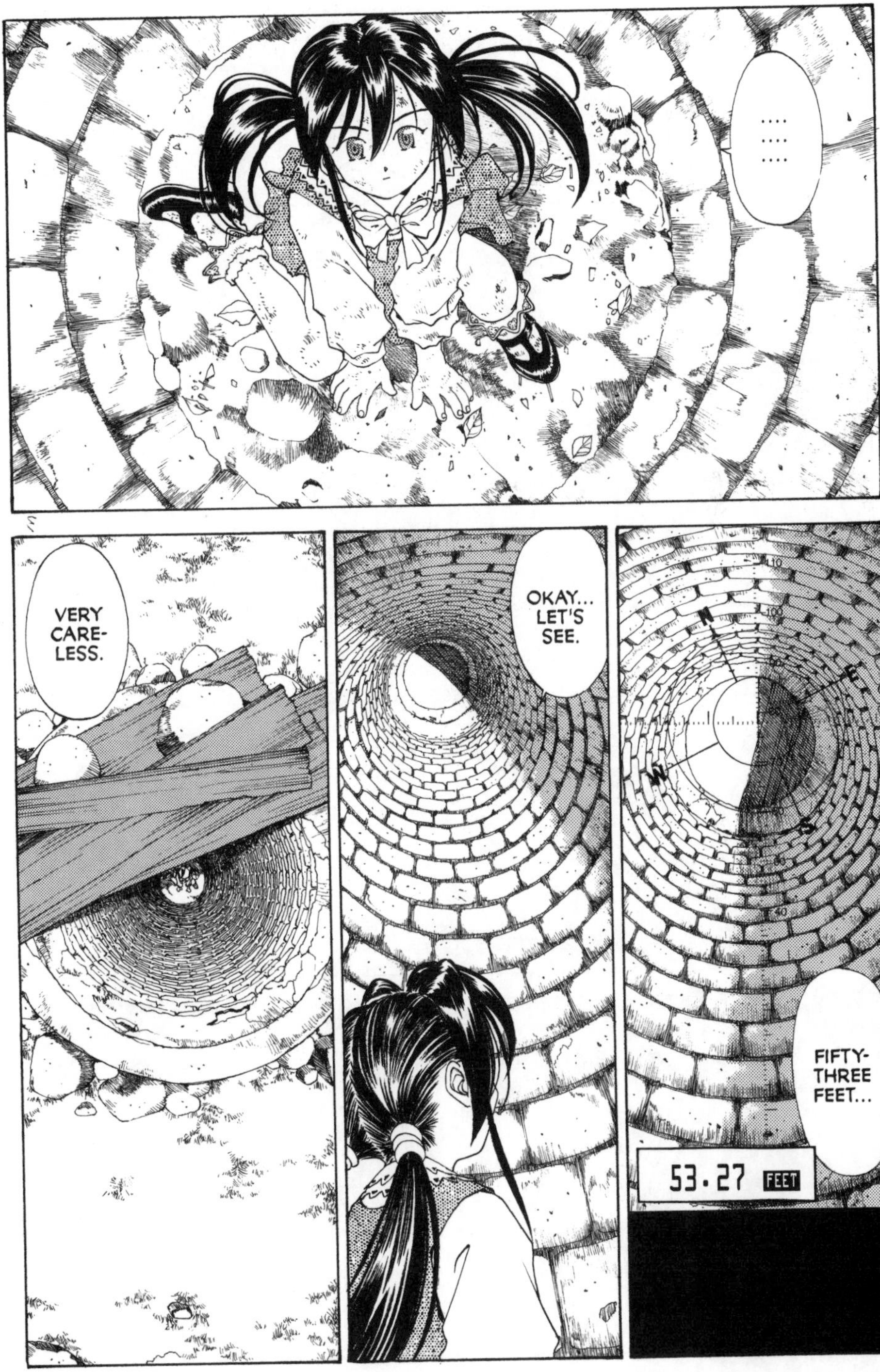

....
....
....
FIFTY-THREE FEET...
53.27 FEET
OKAY... LET'S SEE.
VERY CARE-LESS.

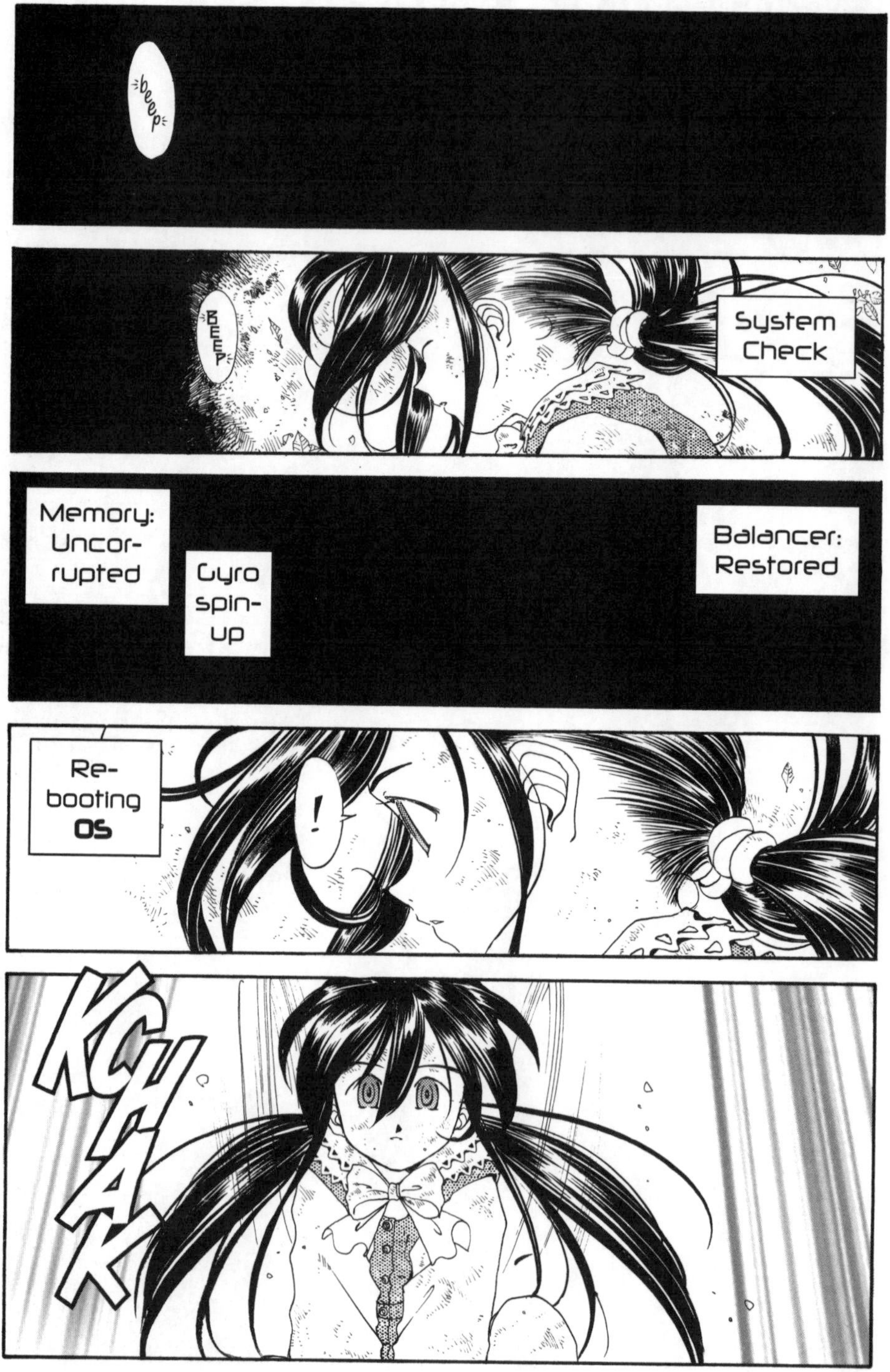
beep
System Check
BEEP
Balancer: Restored
Gyro spin-up
Memory: Uncor-rupted
!
Re-booting OS
KCHAK

ALMOST MY HERO

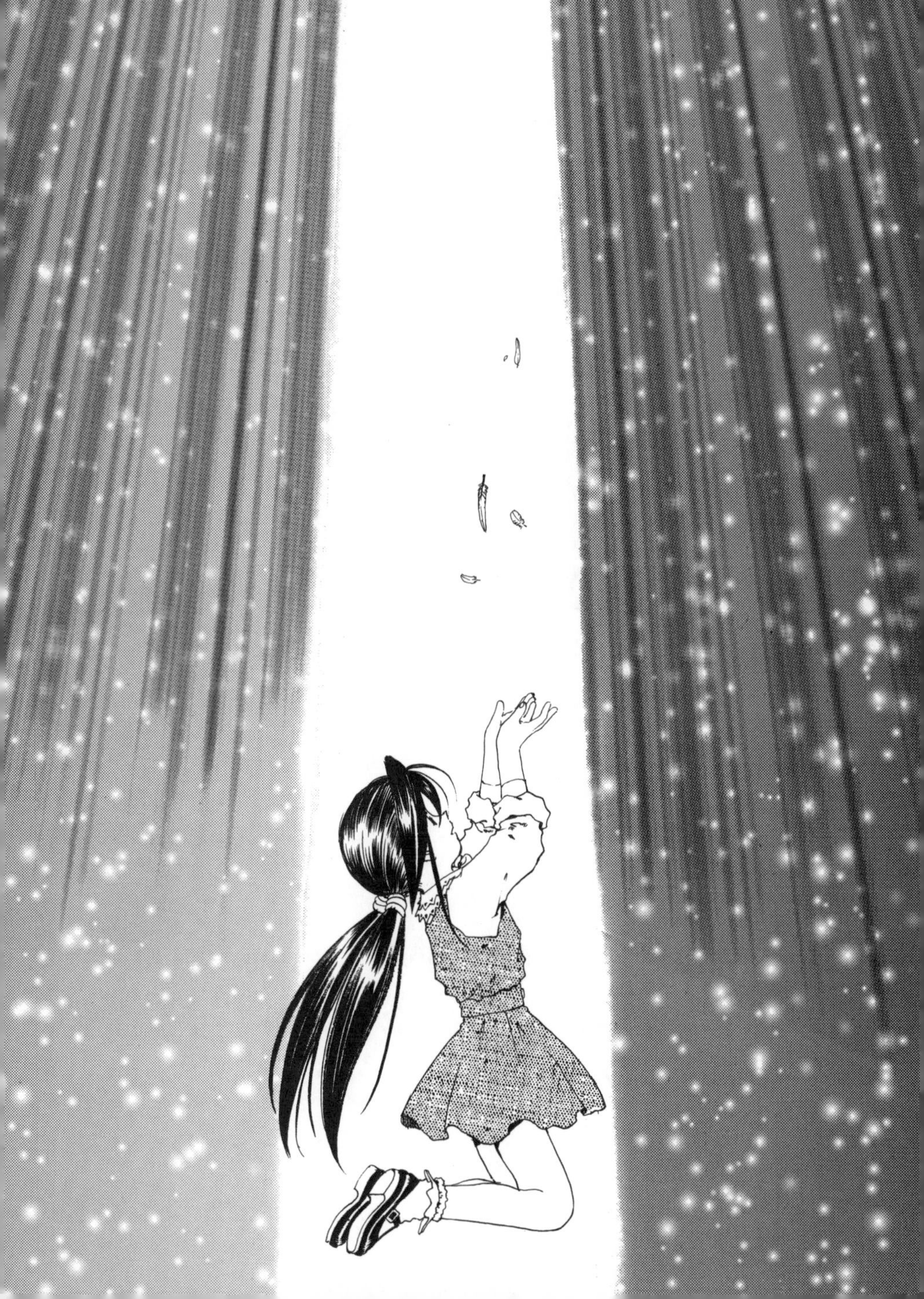

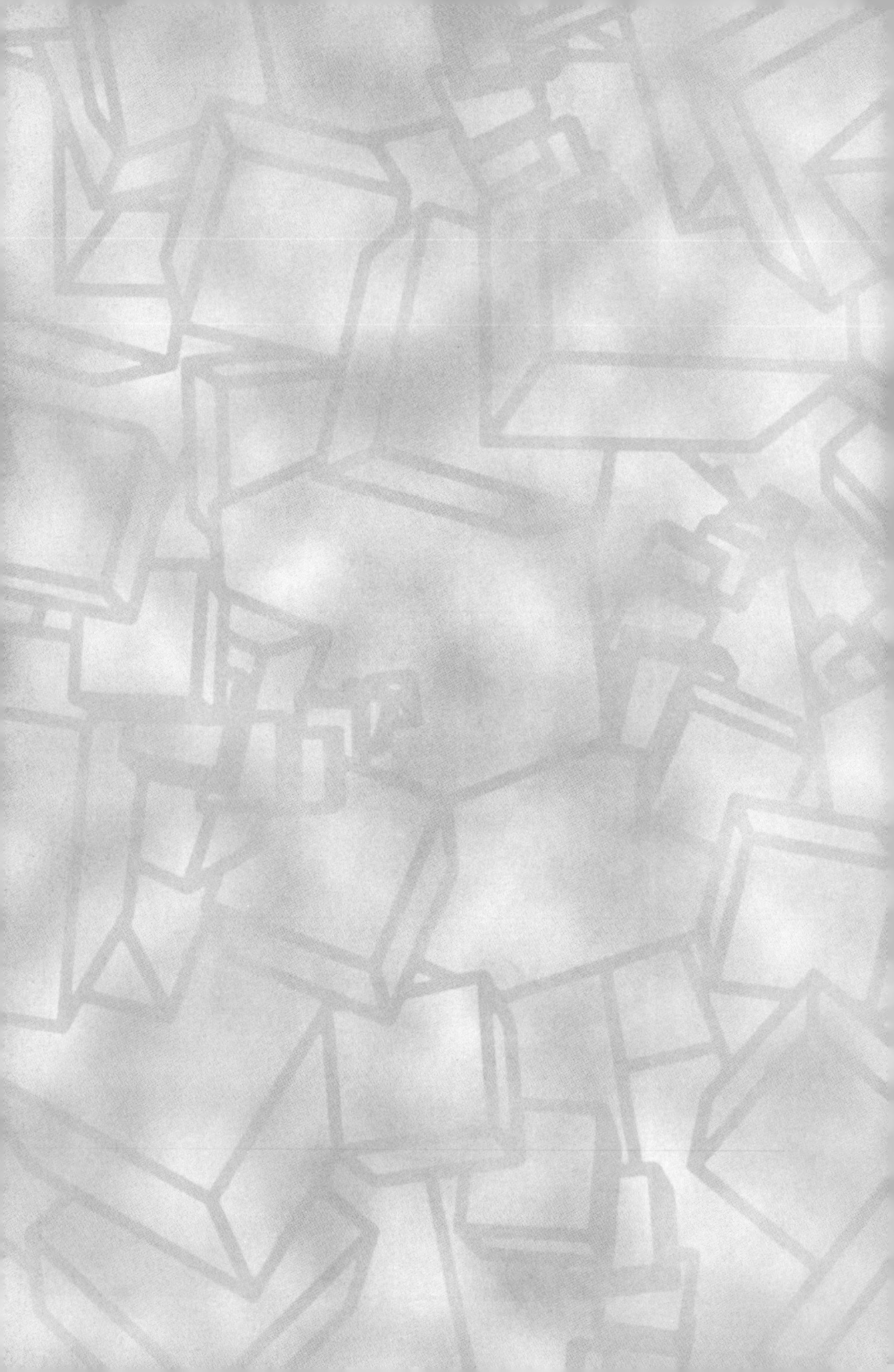

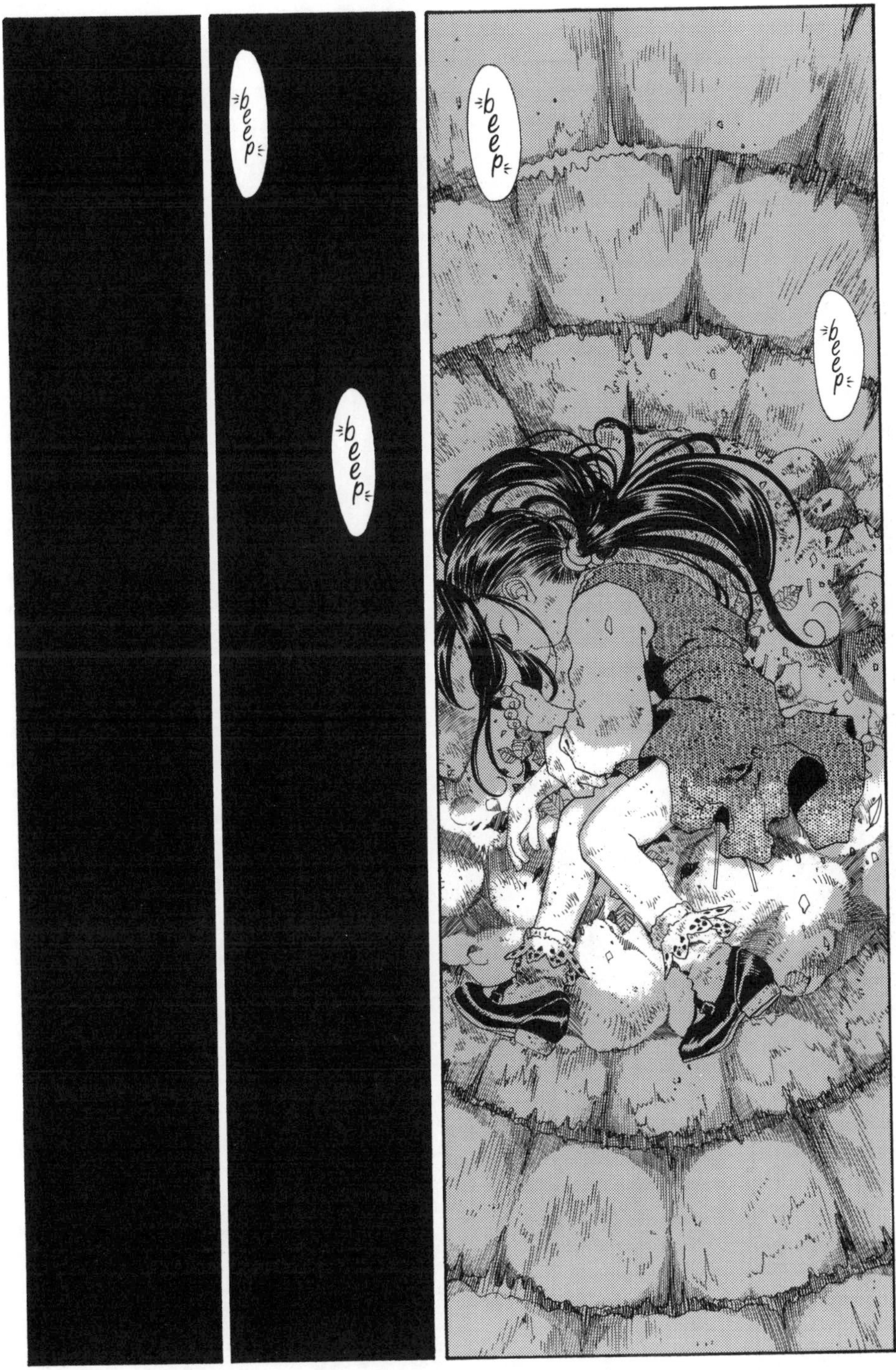
beep
beep
beep
beep

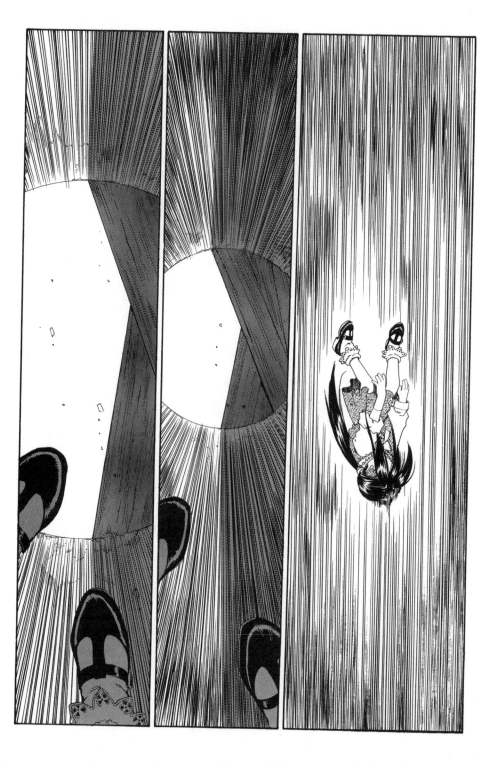

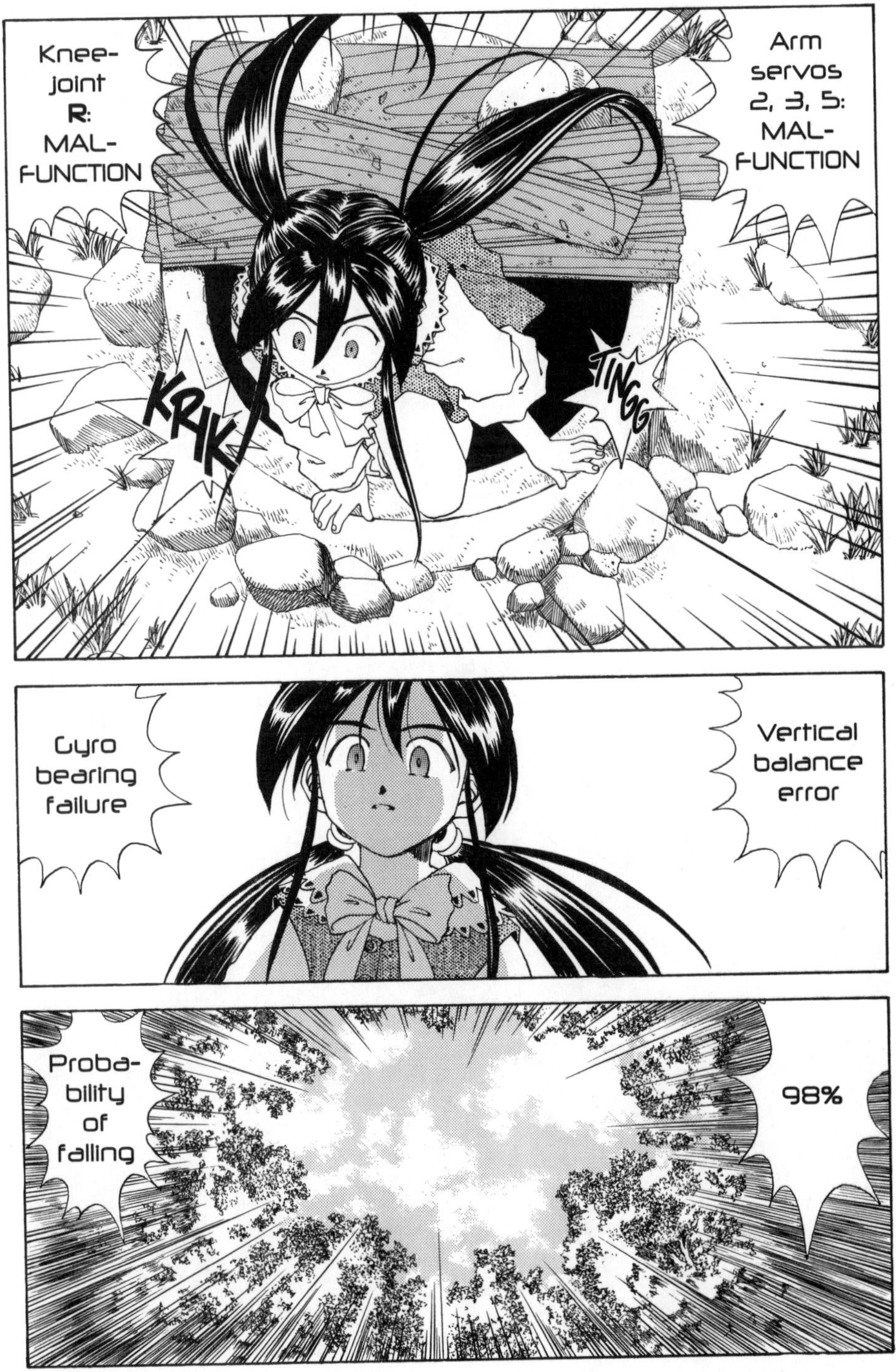
Knee-joint R: MAL-FUNCTION
KRIK
Arm servos 2, 3, 5: MAL-FUNCTION
TINGG
Gyro bearing failure
Vertical balance error
Probability of falling
98%

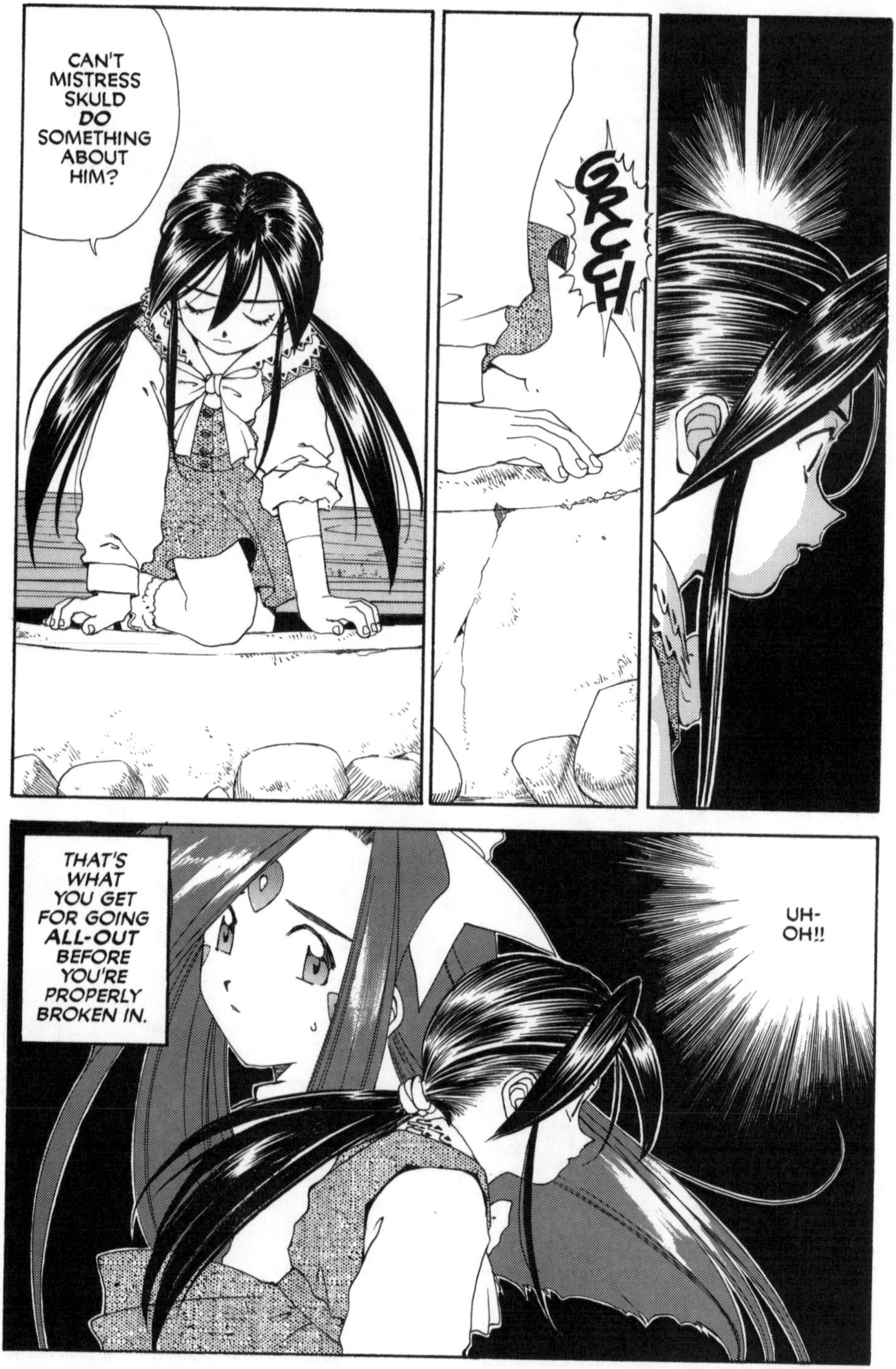
GRCCH
CAN'T MISTRESS SKULD *DO* SOMETHING ABOUT HIM?
UH-OH!!
*THAT'S WHAT YOU GET FOR GOING **ALL-OUT** BEFORE YOU'RE PROPERLY BROKEN IN.*

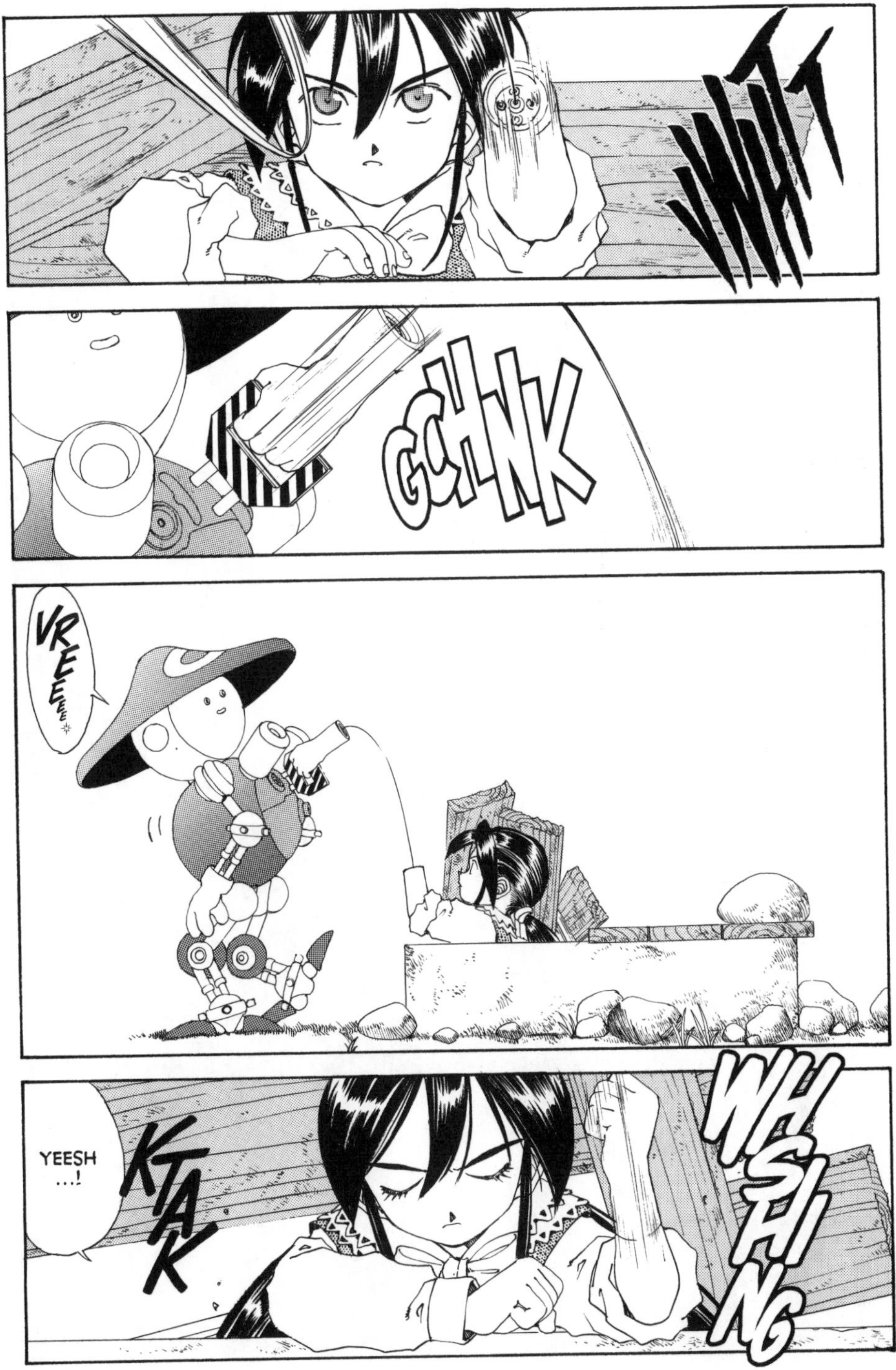
GCHNK
VREEEEE
WHSHING
KTAK
YEESH ...!

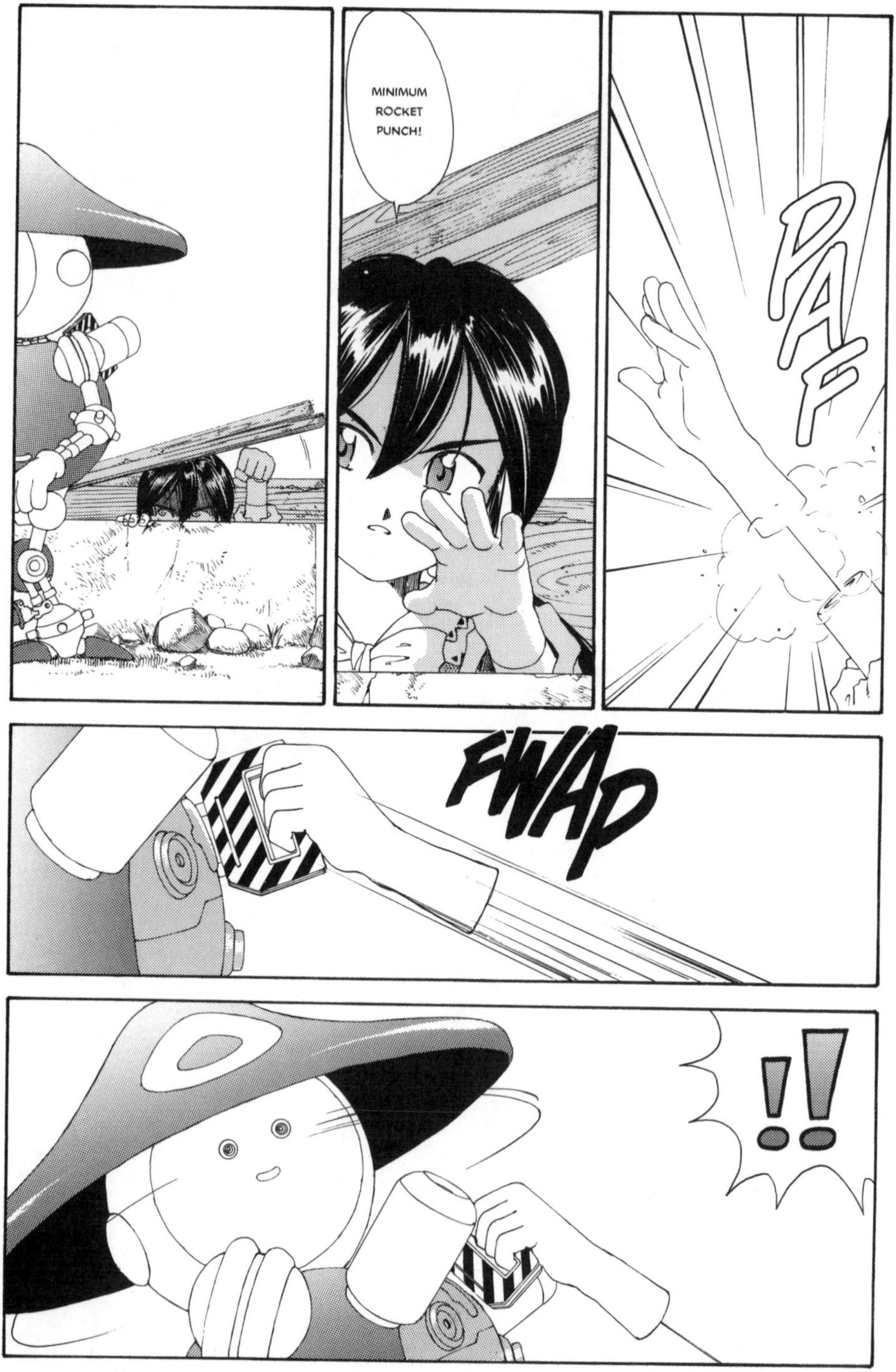
MINIMUM ROCKET PUNCH!
PAF
FWAP
!!

LEAVE
ME
ALONE!!

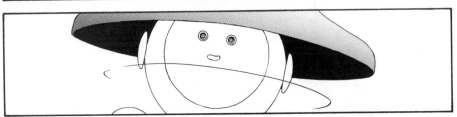

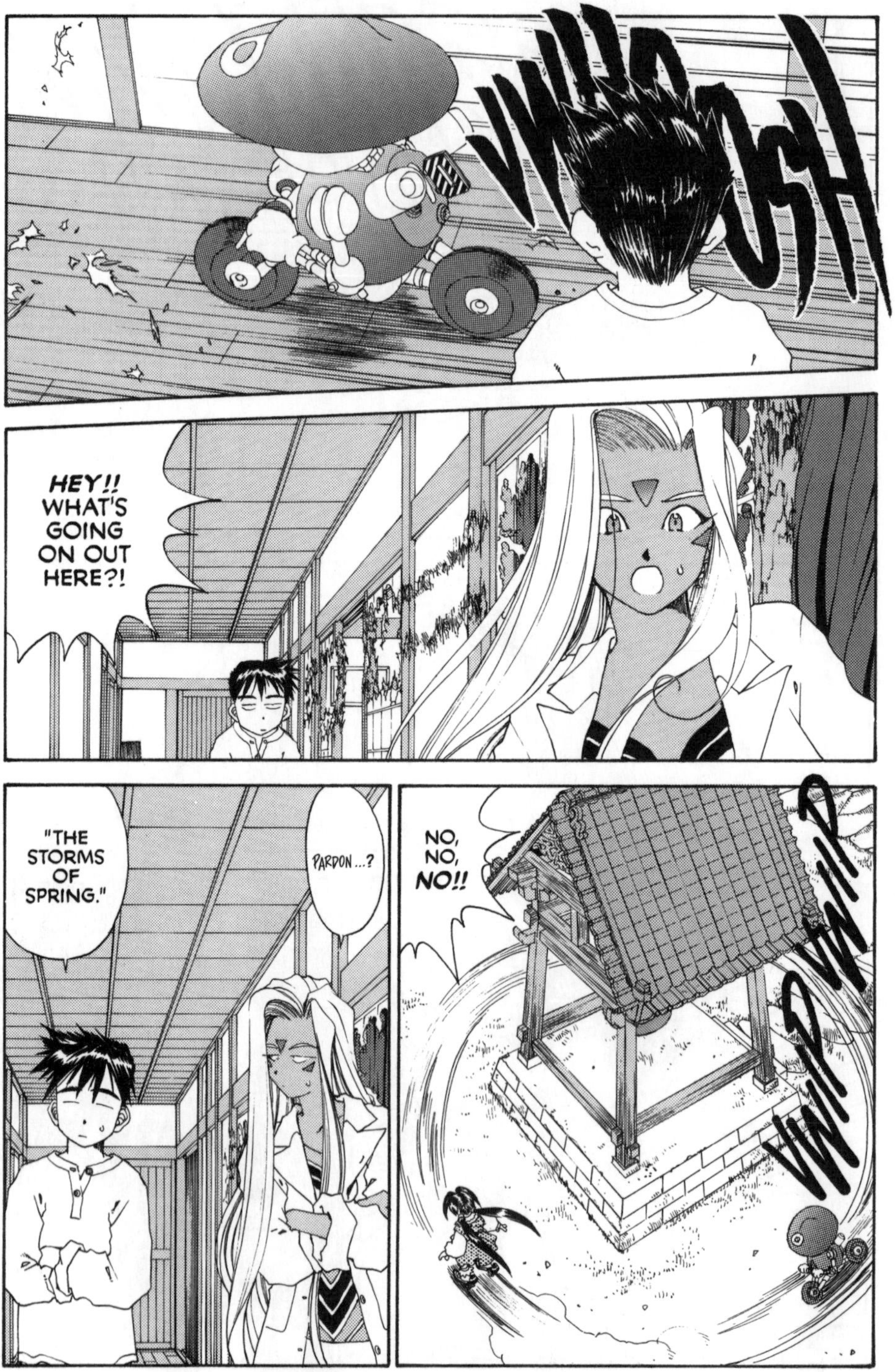
WHOOSH
HEY!! WHAT'S GOING ON OUT HERE?!
NO, NO, NO!!
WHIP WHIP
PARDON...?
"THE STORMS OF SPRING."

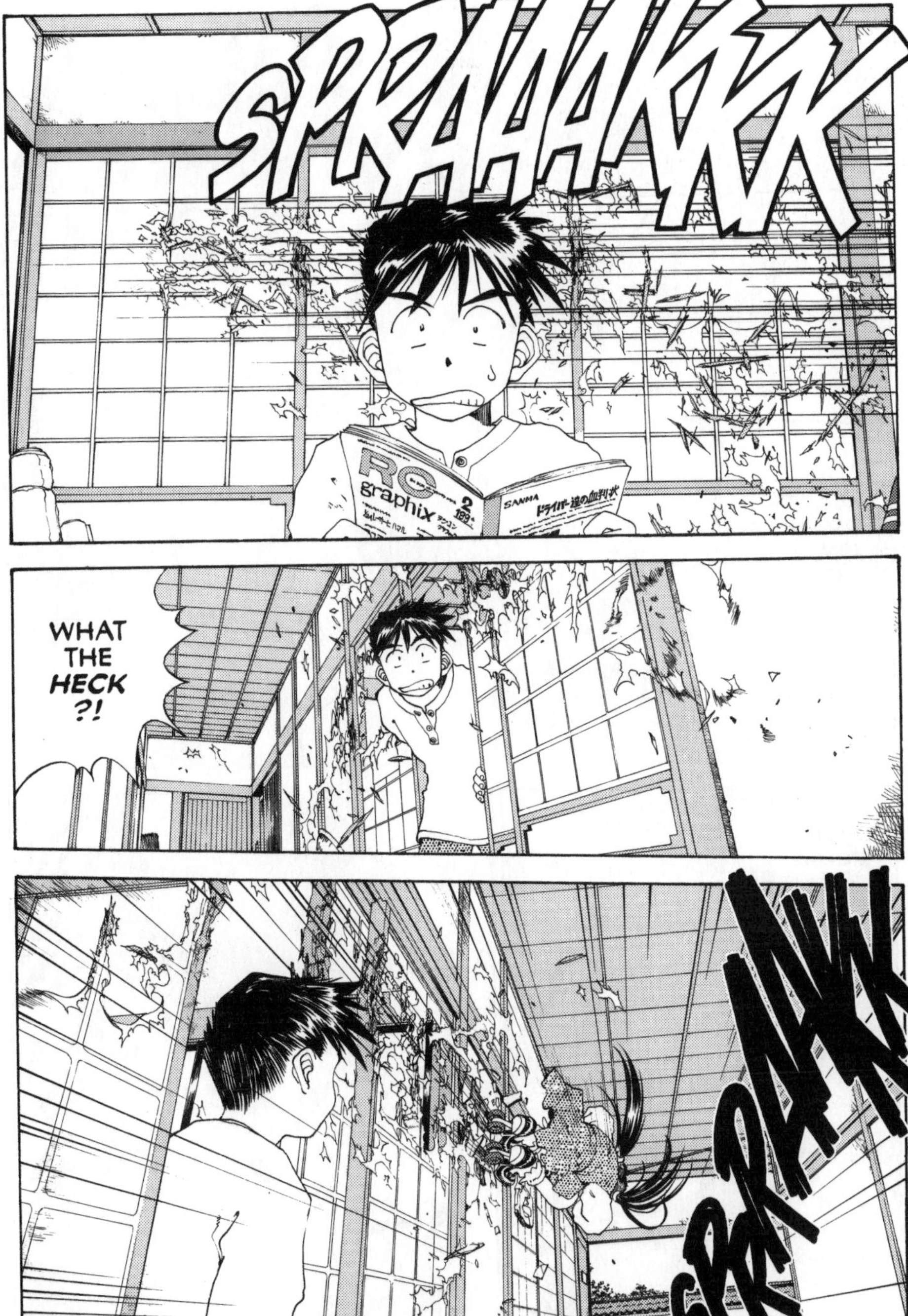

WHAT THE HECK ?!
SPRAKK

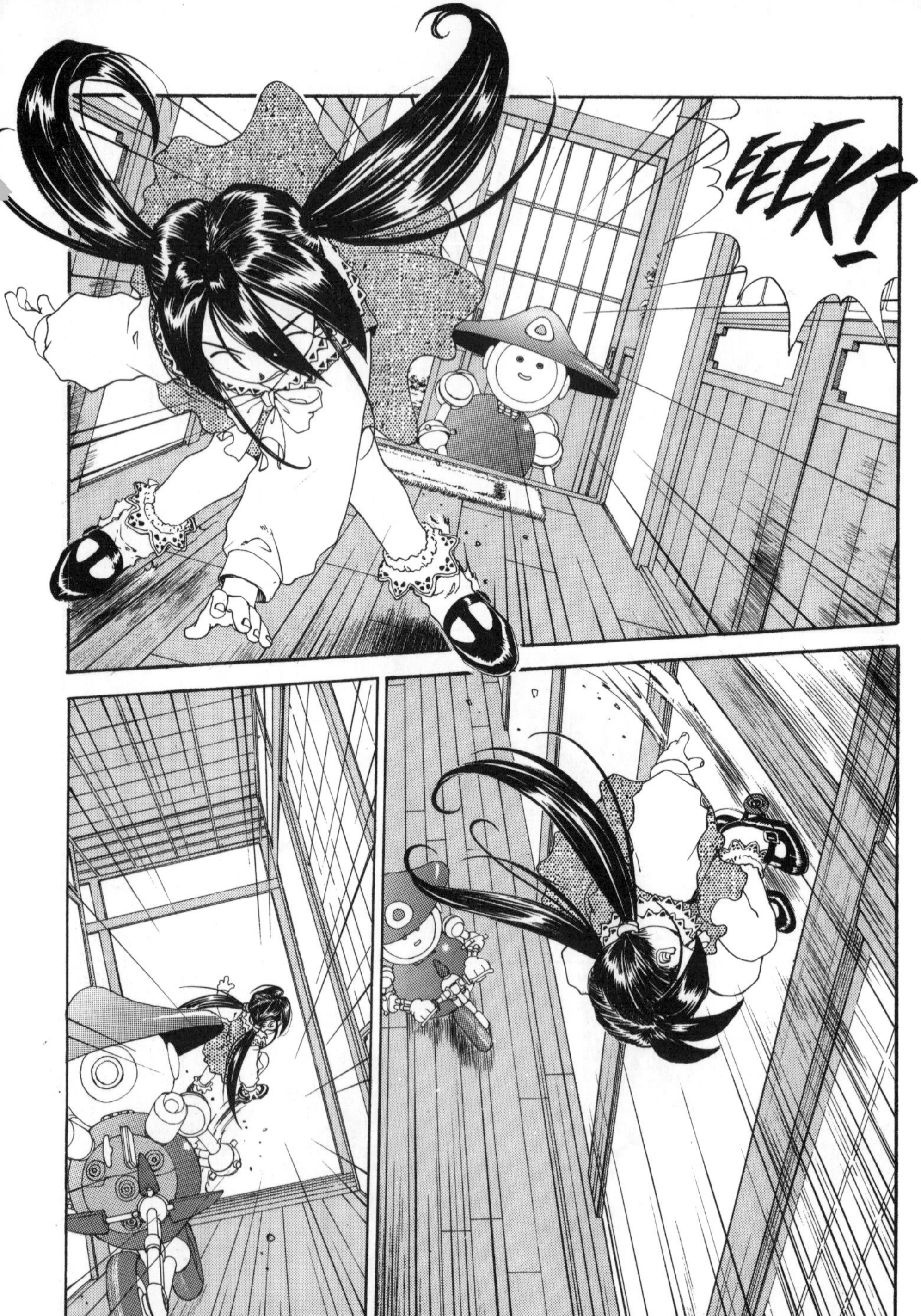
EEEK!

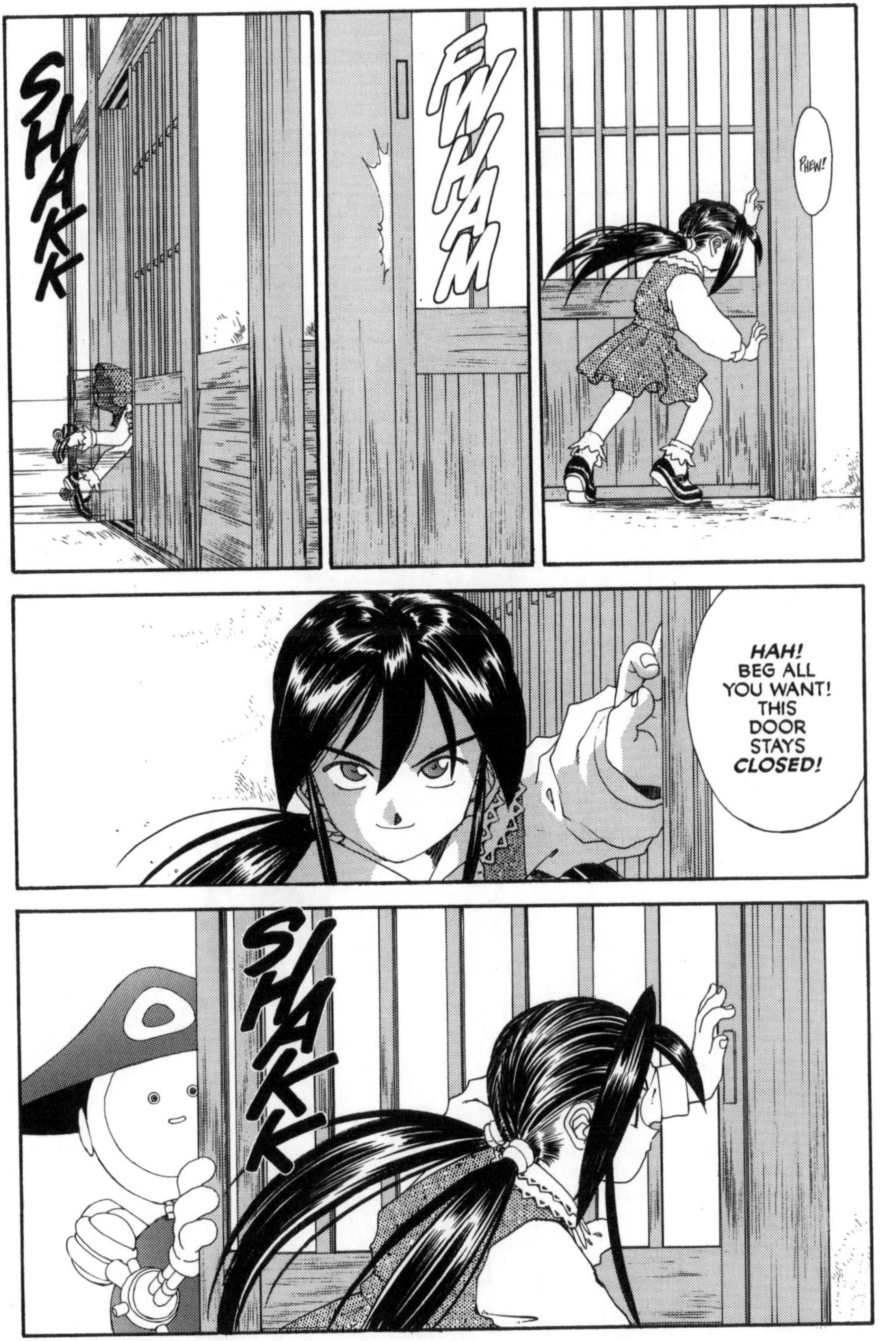
PHEW!
FWHAM
SHAKK
HAH! BEG ALL YOU WANT! THIS DOOR STAYS CLOSED!
SHAKK

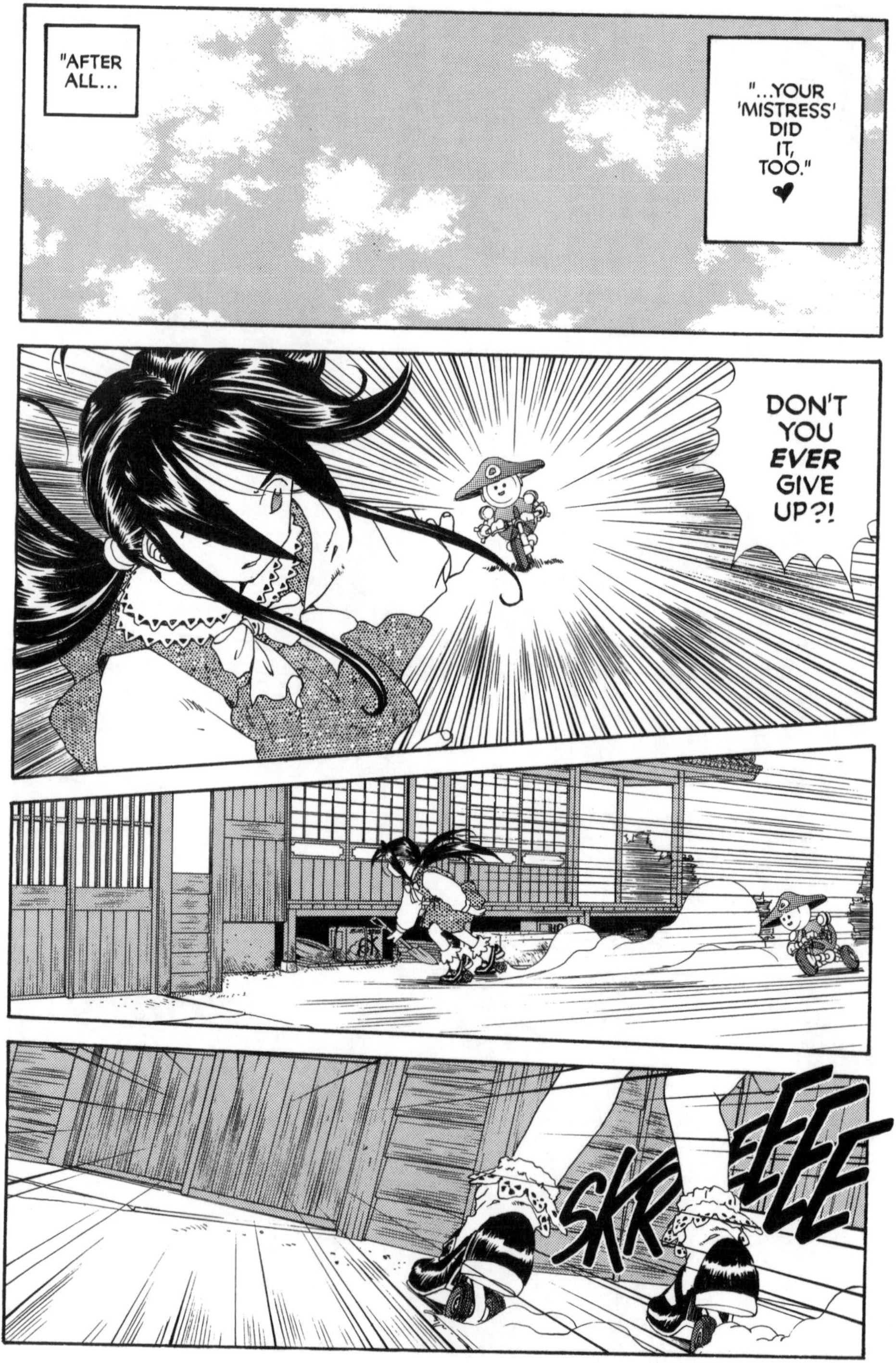
"...YOUR 'MISTRESS' DID IT, TOO." ♥
"AFTER ALL...
DON'T YOU EVER GIVE UP?!
SKREEEEE

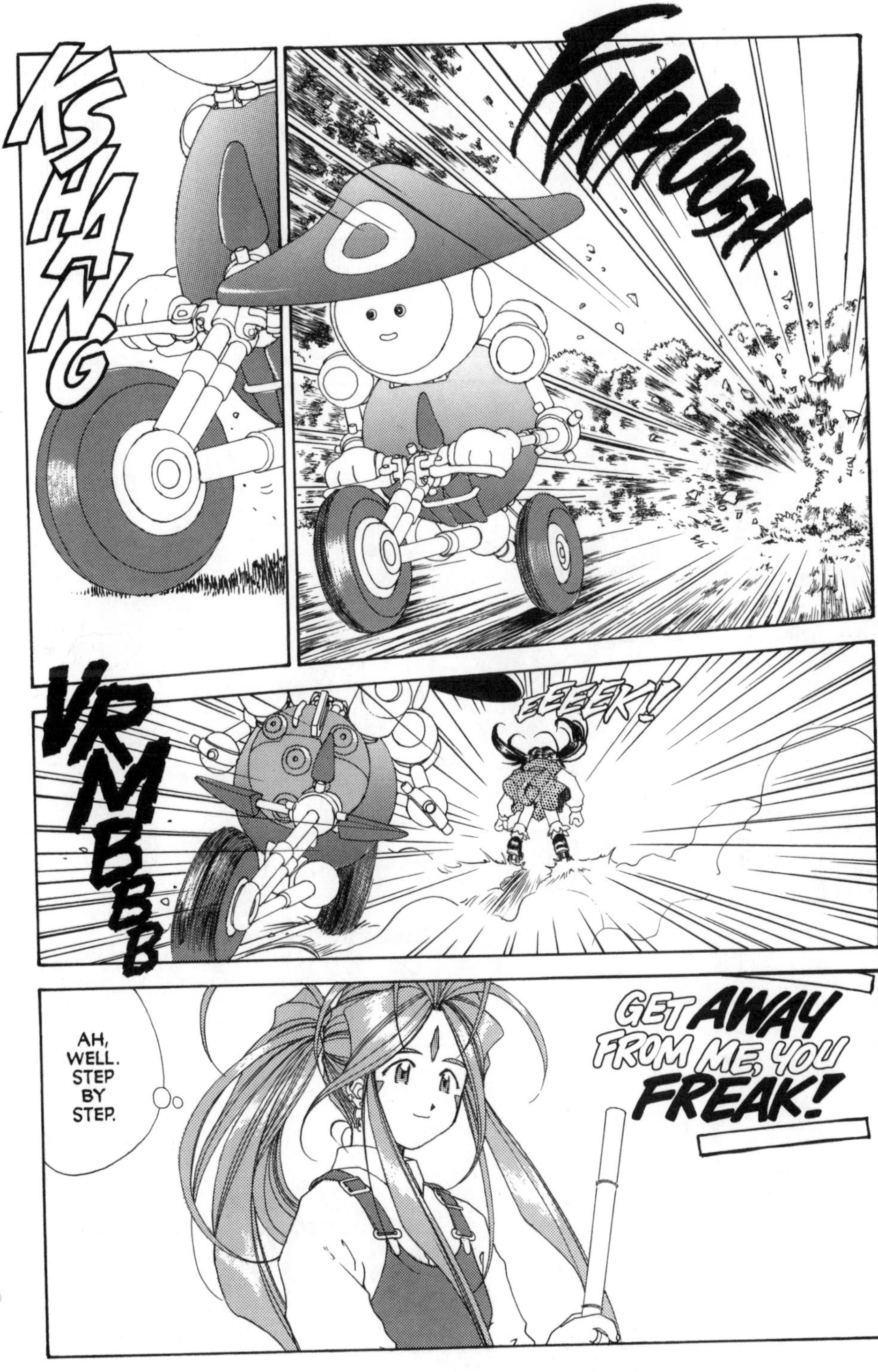
KSHANG
FWHOOSH
VRMBBB
EEEEK!
GET AWAY FROM ME, YOU FREAK!
AH, WELL. STEP BY STEP.

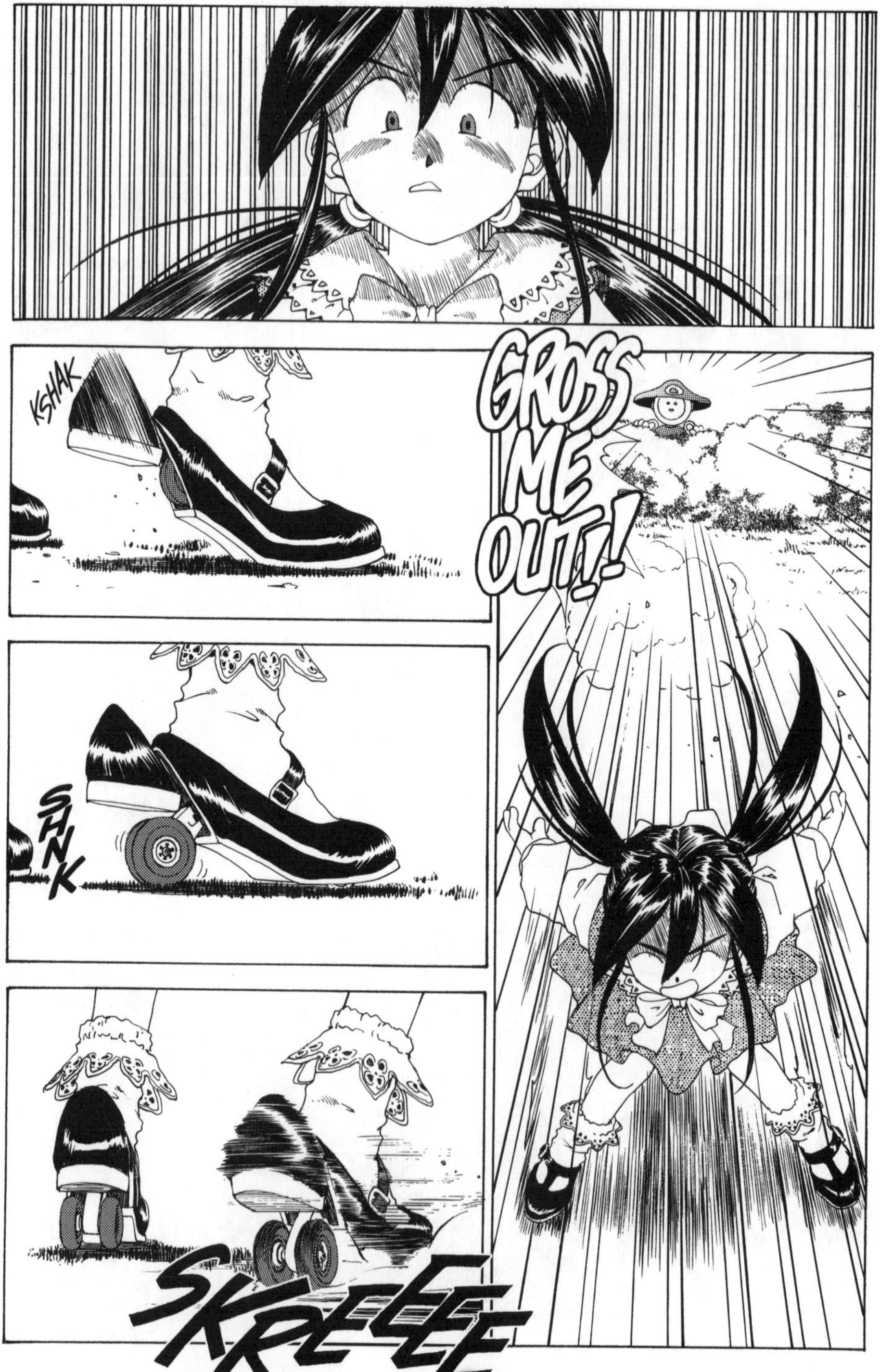
GROSS ME OUT!!
KSHAK
SHNK
SKREEEE

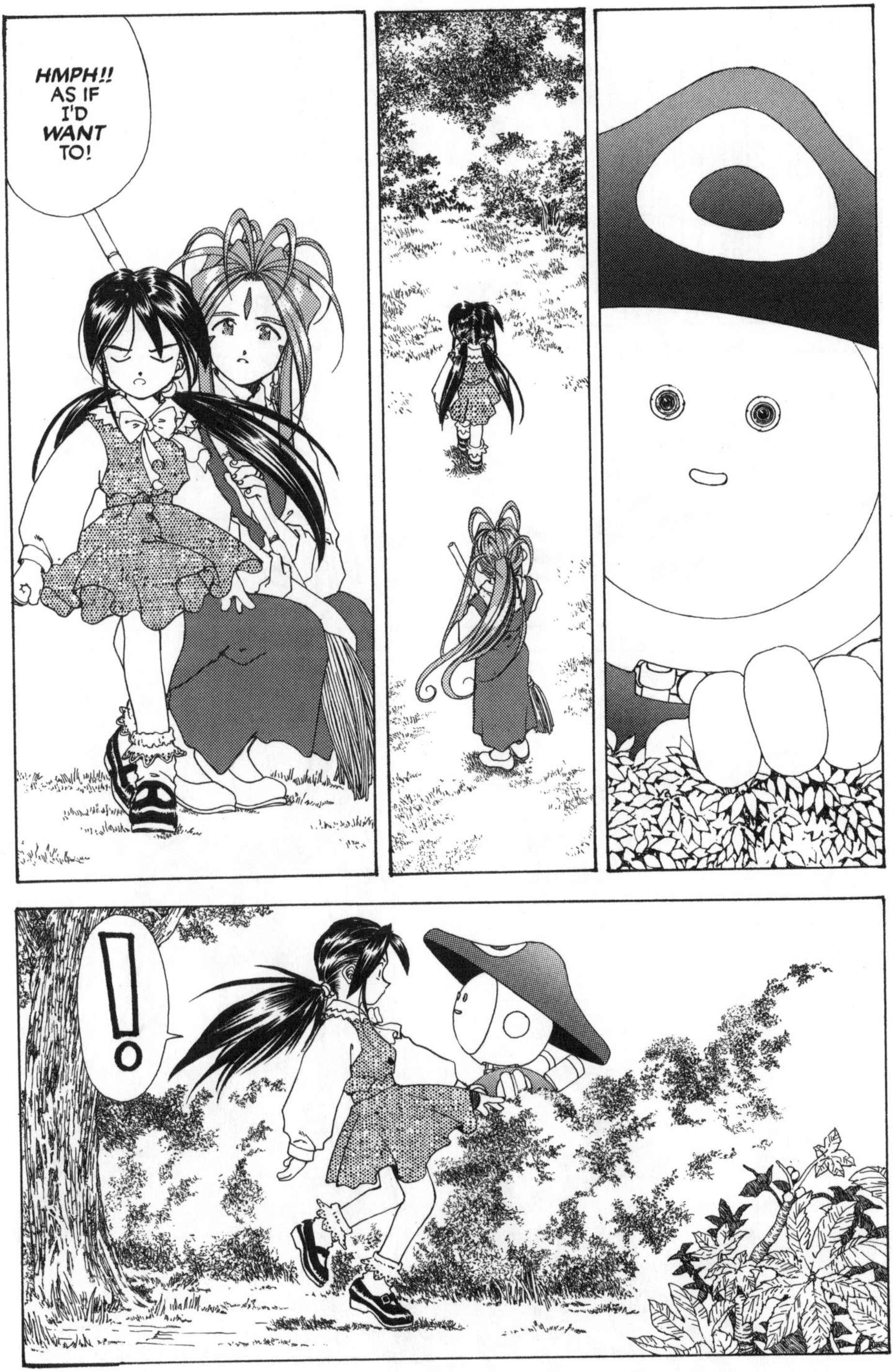
HMPH!! AS IF I'D WANT TO!
!

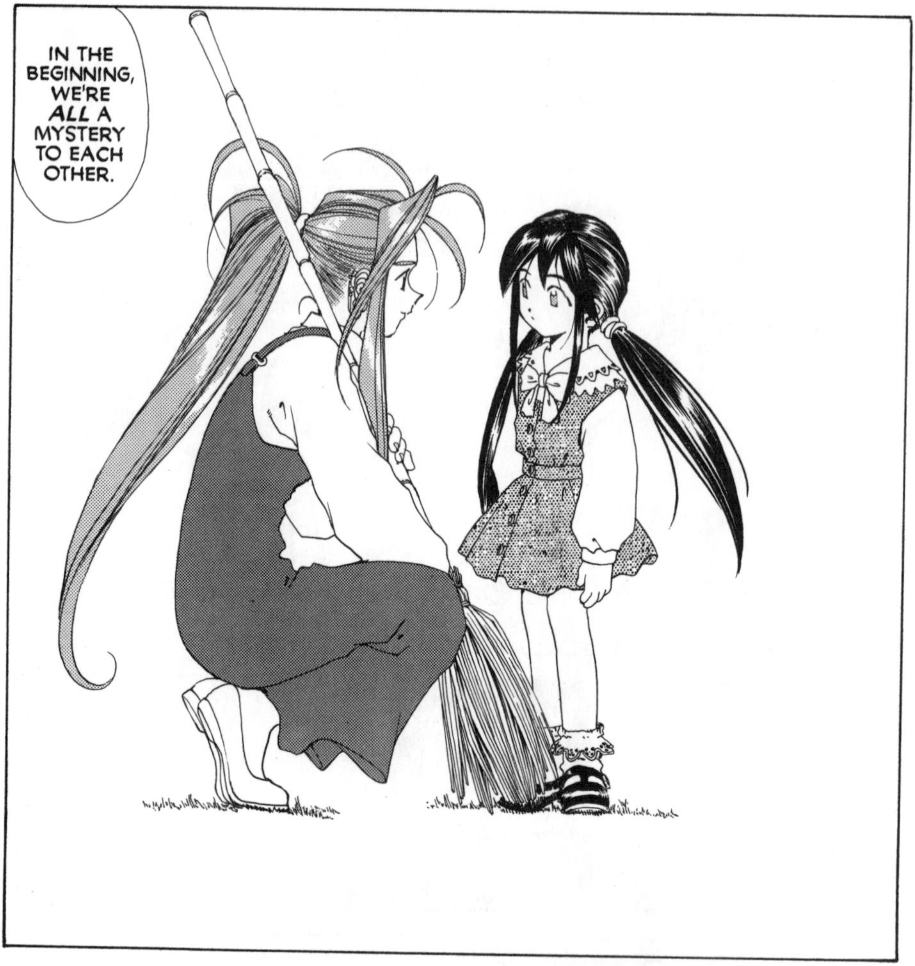
IN THE BEGINNING, WE'RE ALL A MYSTERY TO EACH OTHER.
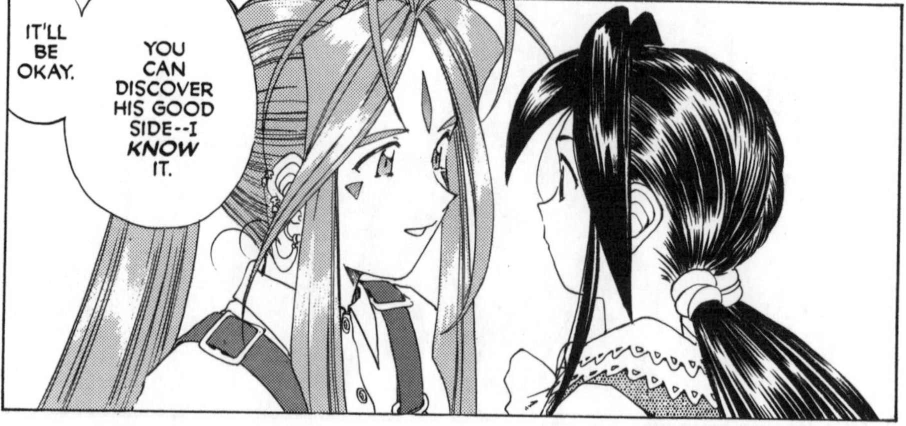
IT'LL BE OKAY. YOU CAN DISCOVER HIS GOOD SIDE--I KNOW IT.

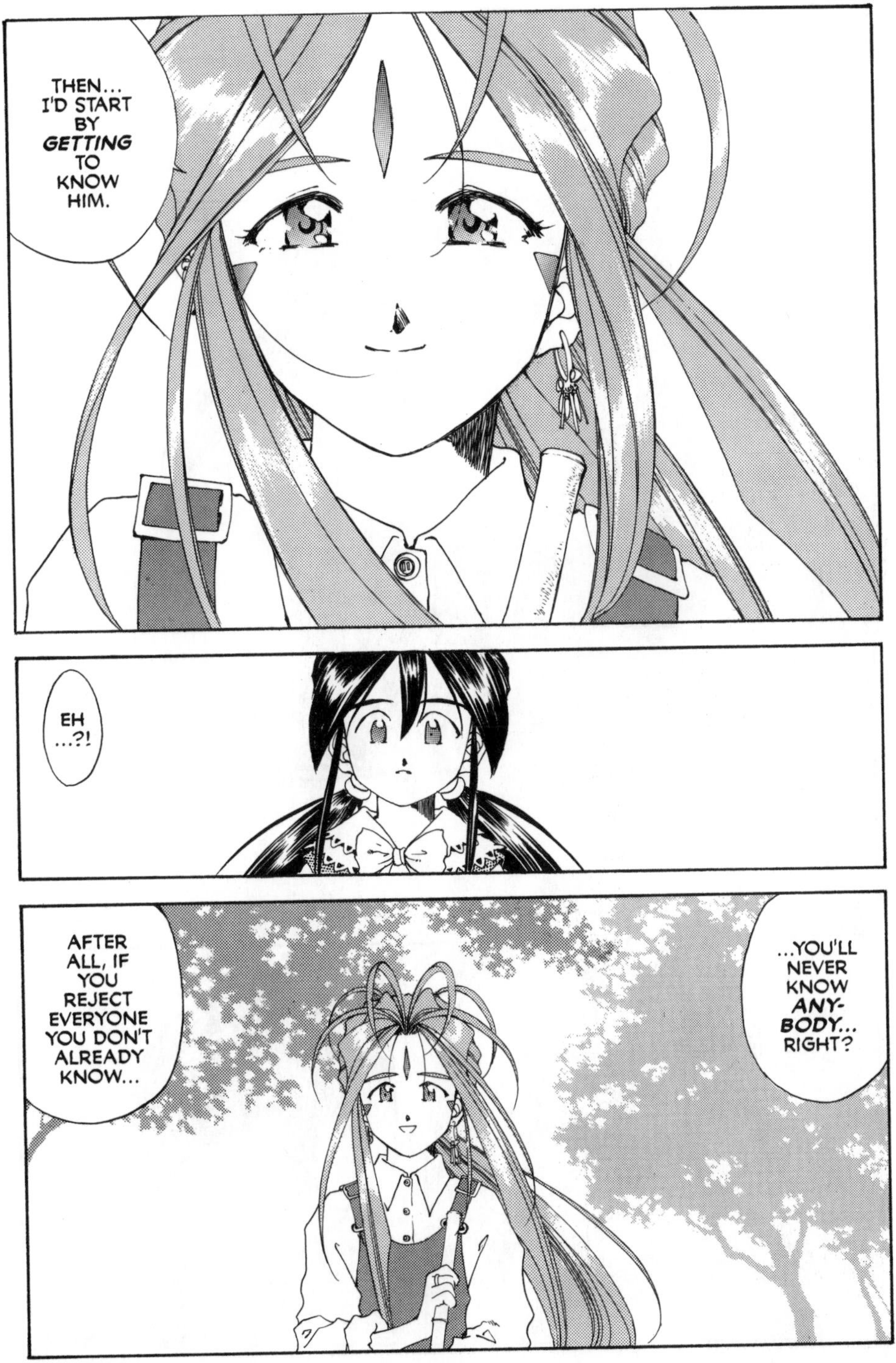
THEN... I'D START BY *GETTING* TO KNOW HIM.
EH ...?!
...YOU'LL NEVER KNOW *ANY-BODY*... RIGHT?
AFTER ALL, IF YOU REJECT EVERYONE YOU DON'T ALREADY KNOW...

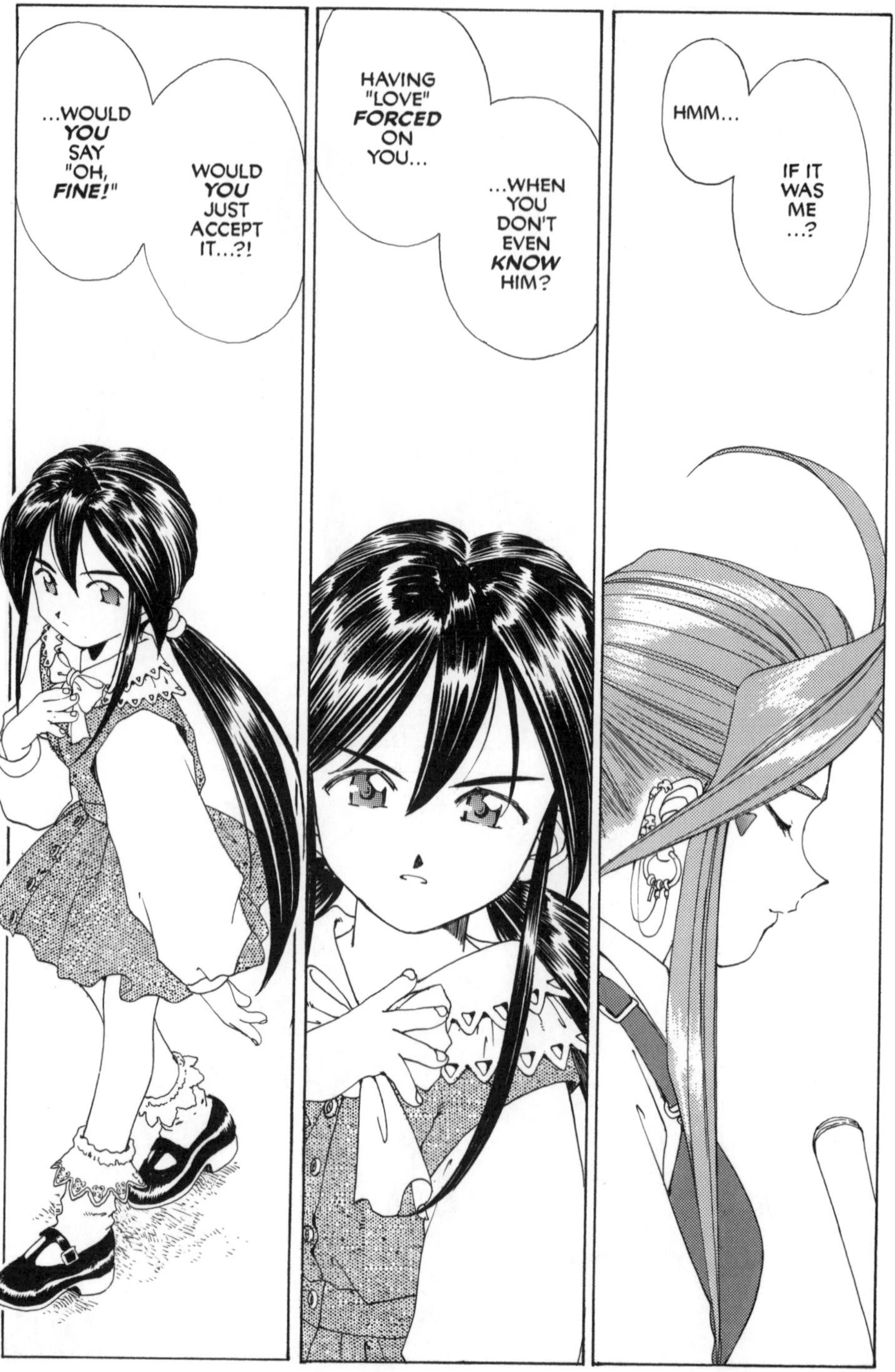
HMM...
IF IT WAS ME ...?
HAVING "LOVE" FORCED ON YOU...
...WHEN YOU DON'T EVEN KNOW HIM?
WOULD YOU JUST ACCEPT IT...?!
...WOULD YOU SAY "OH, FINE!"

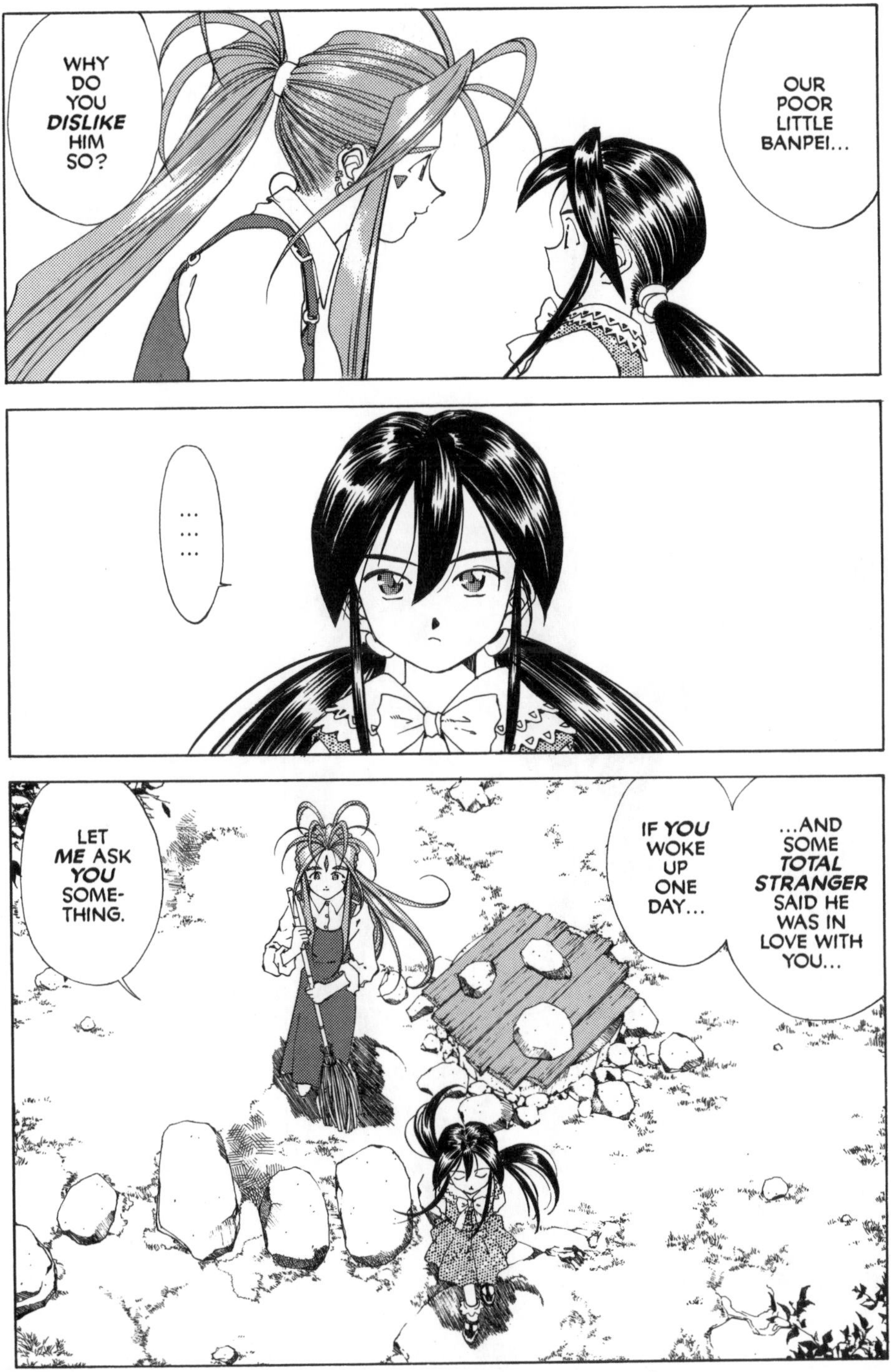
WHY DO YOU *DISLIKE* HIM SO?
OUR POOR LITTLE BANPEI...
......
......
......
LET *ME* ASK *YOU* SOME-THING.
IF *YOU* WOKE UP ONE DAY...
...AND SOME *TOTAL STRANGER* SAID HE WAS IN LOVE WITH YOU...

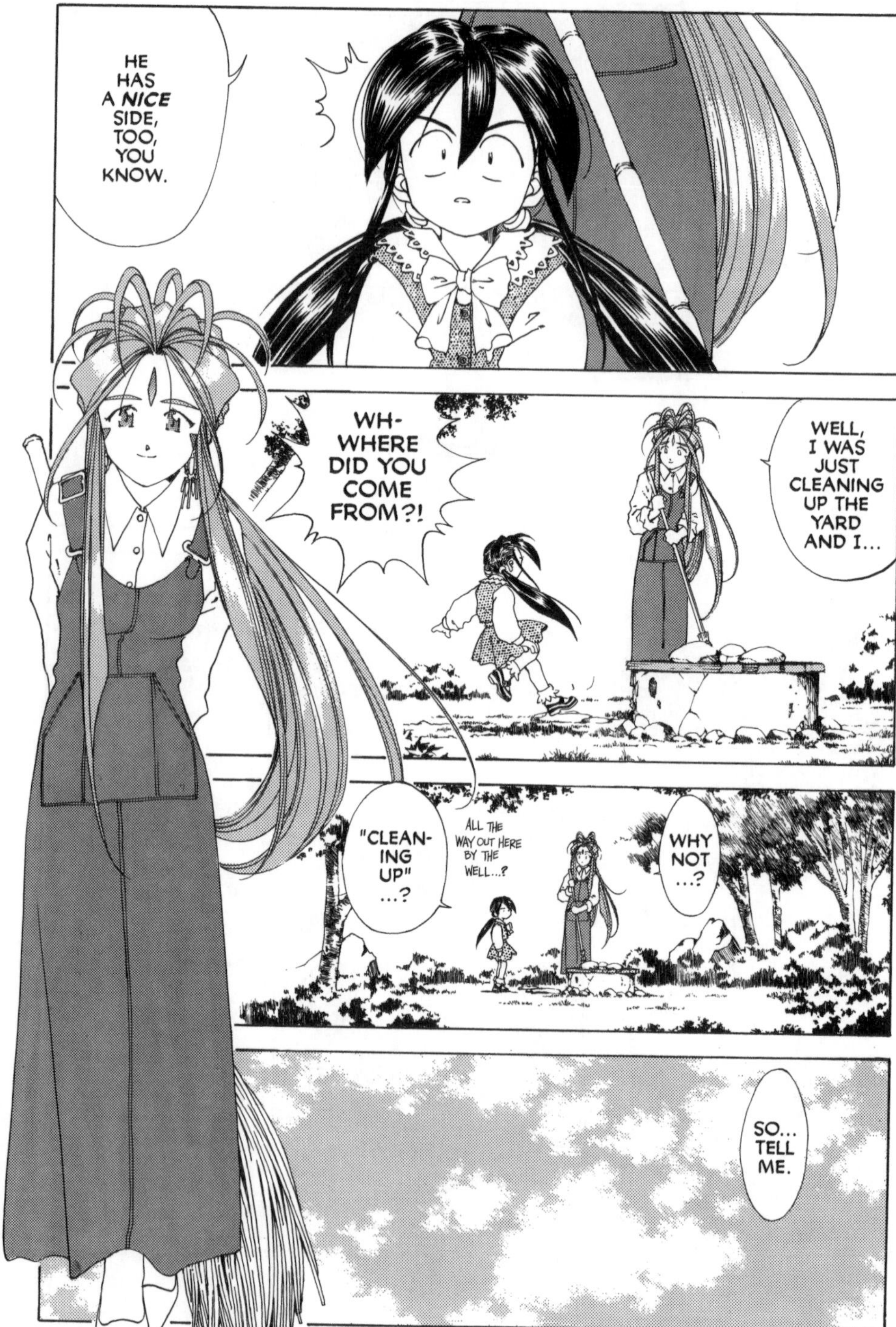
HE HAS A ***NICE*** SIDE, TOO, YOU KNOW.
WH- WHERE DID YOU COME FROM?!
WELL, I WAS JUST CLEANING UP THE YARD AND I...
"CLEAN- ING UP" ...?
ALL THE WAY OUT HERE BY THE WELL...?
WHY NOT ...?
SO... TELL ME.

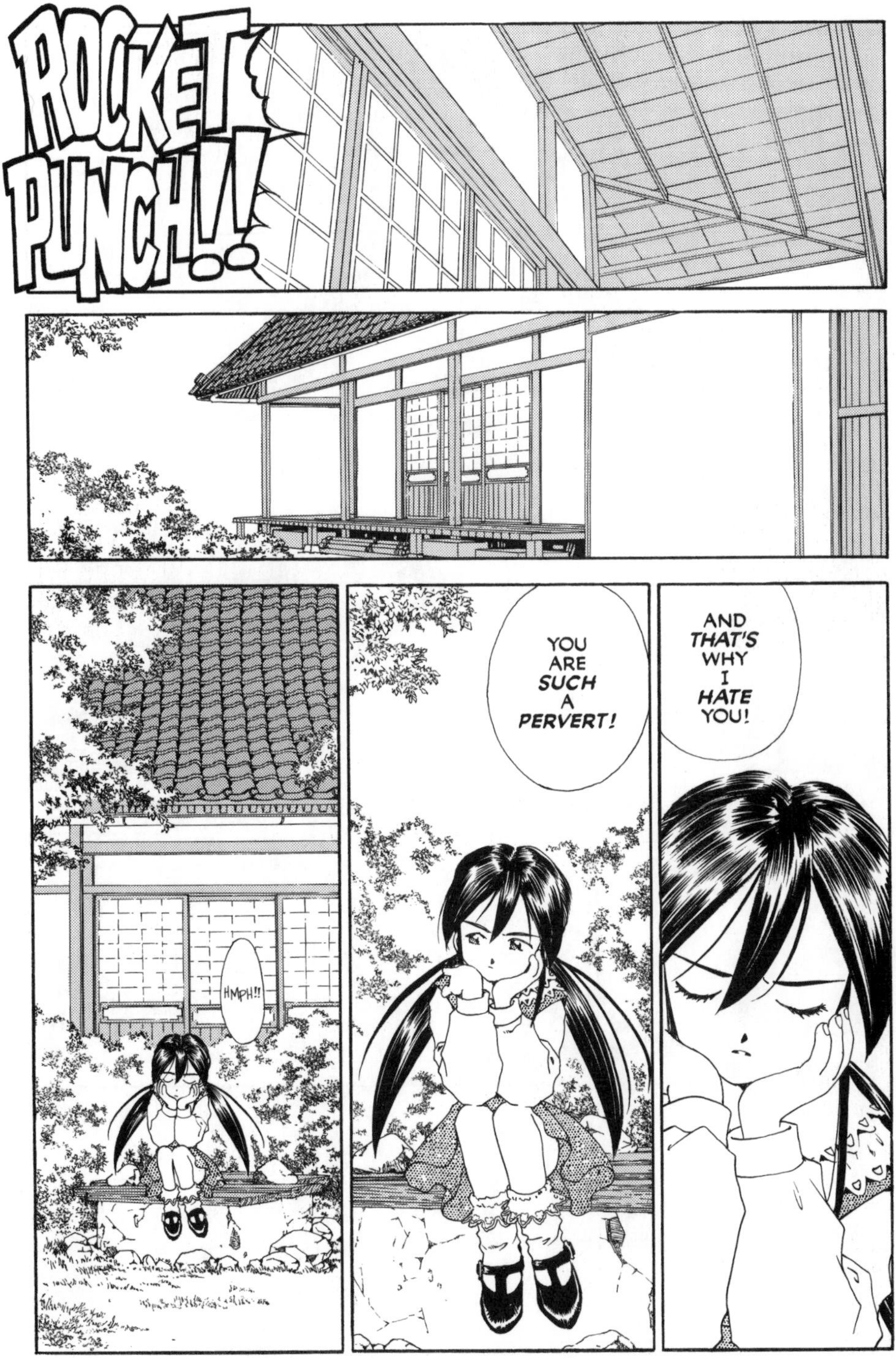
ROCKET PUNCH!!
AND THAT'S WHY I HATE YOU!
YOU ARE SUCH A PERVERT!
HMPH!!

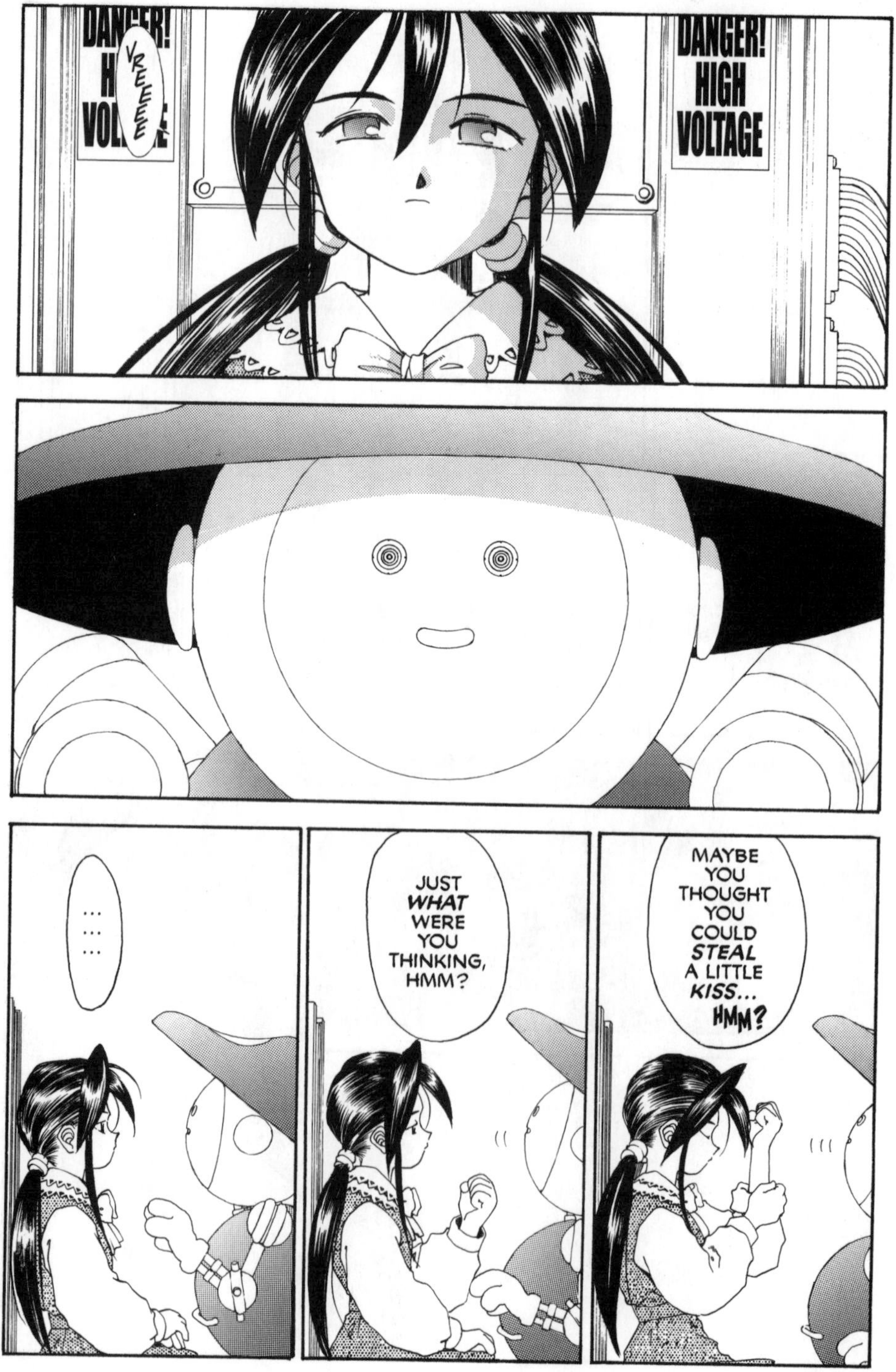
DANGER!
VREEEE
DANGER! HIGH VOLTAGE
...
...
...
JUST *WHAT* WERE YOU THINKING, HMM?
MAYBE YOU THOUGHT YOU COULD *STEAL* A LITTLE *KISS*... HMM?

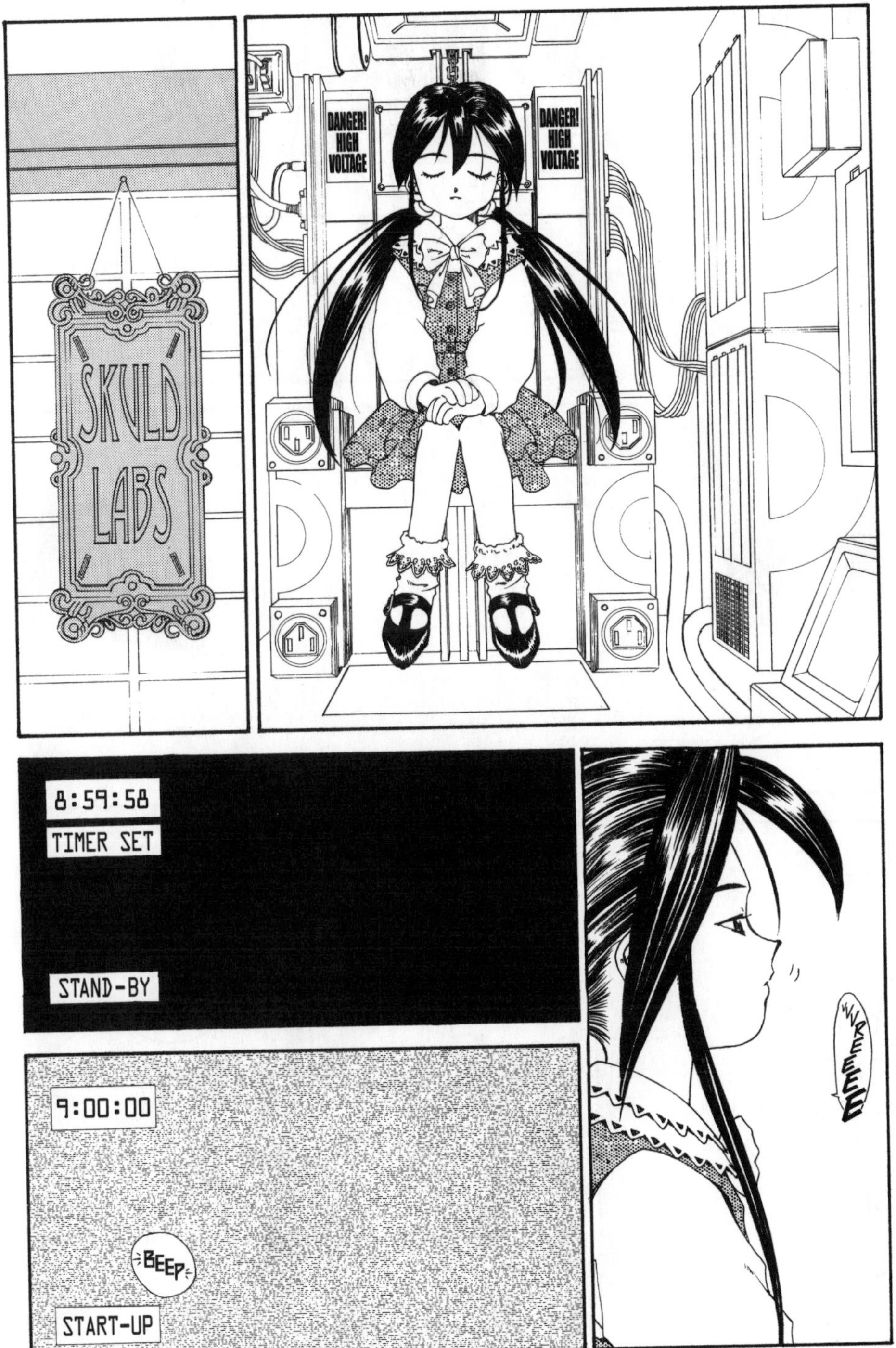
DANGER! HIGH VOLTAGE
DANGER! HIGH VOLTAGE
SKULD LABS
WWREEEE
8:59:58
TIMER SET
STAND-BY
9:00:00
BEEP
START-UP

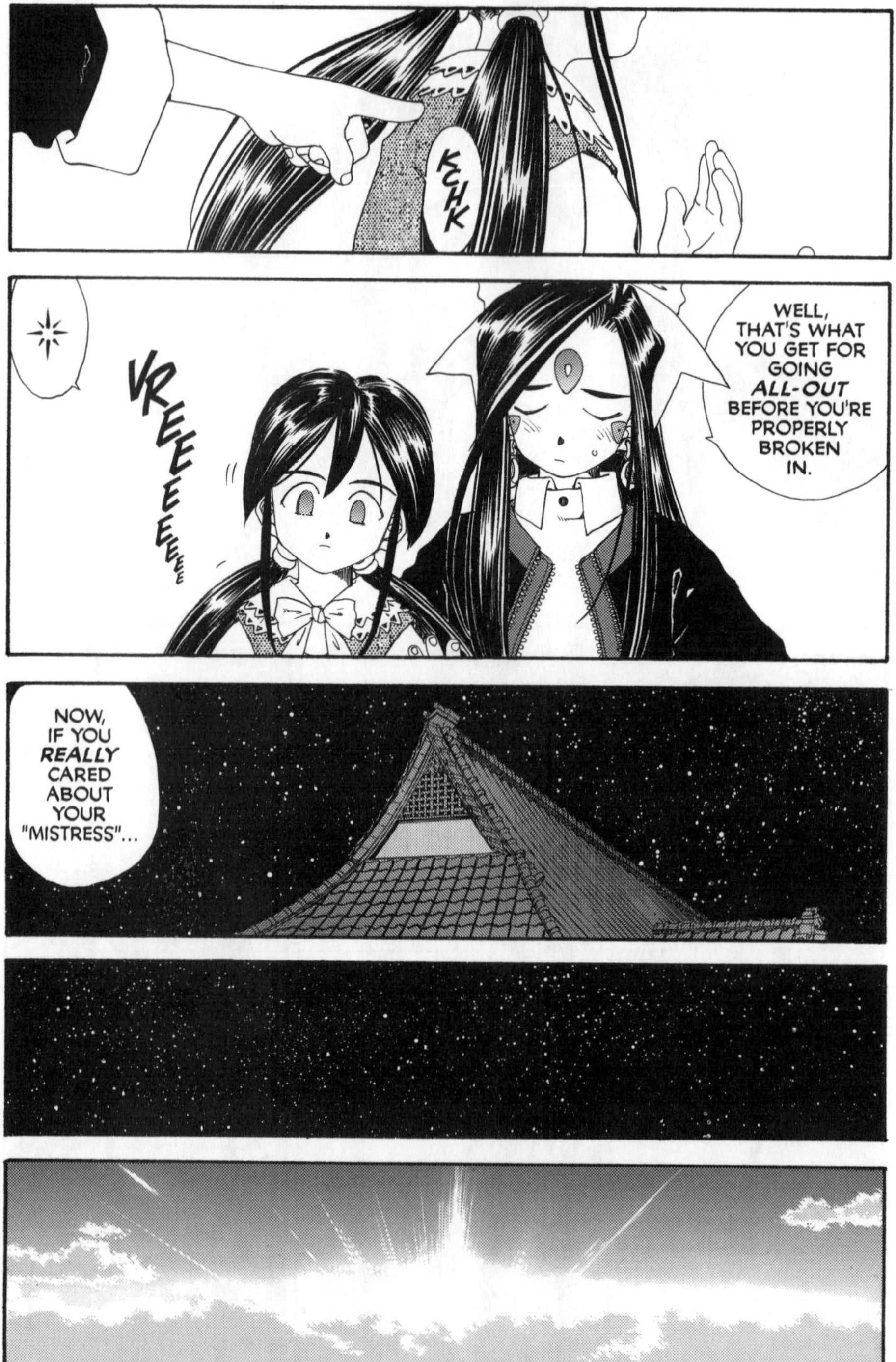
KCHK
WELL, THAT'S WHAT YOU GET FOR GOING ALL-OUT BEFORE YOU'RE PROPERLY BROKEN IN.
VREEEEEEEE
NOW, IF YOU REALLY CARED ABOUT YOUR "MISTRESS"...

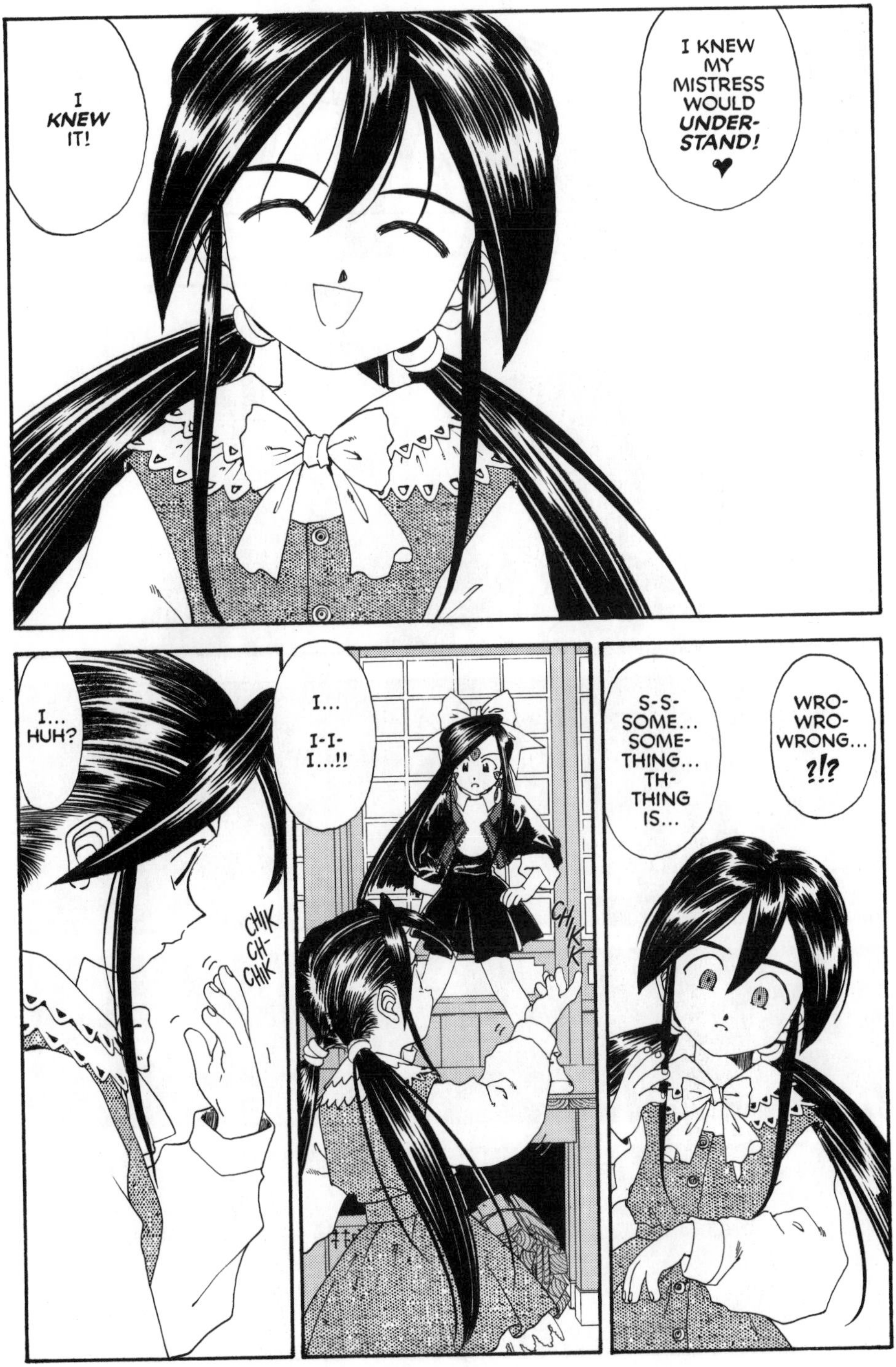
I KNEW MY MISTRESS WOULD UNDERSTAND! ♥
I KNEW IT!
WRO-WRO-WRONG... ?!?
S-S-SOME... SOMETHING... TH-THING IS...
I... I-I-I...!!
CHIKK
I... HUH?
CHIK CH-CHIK

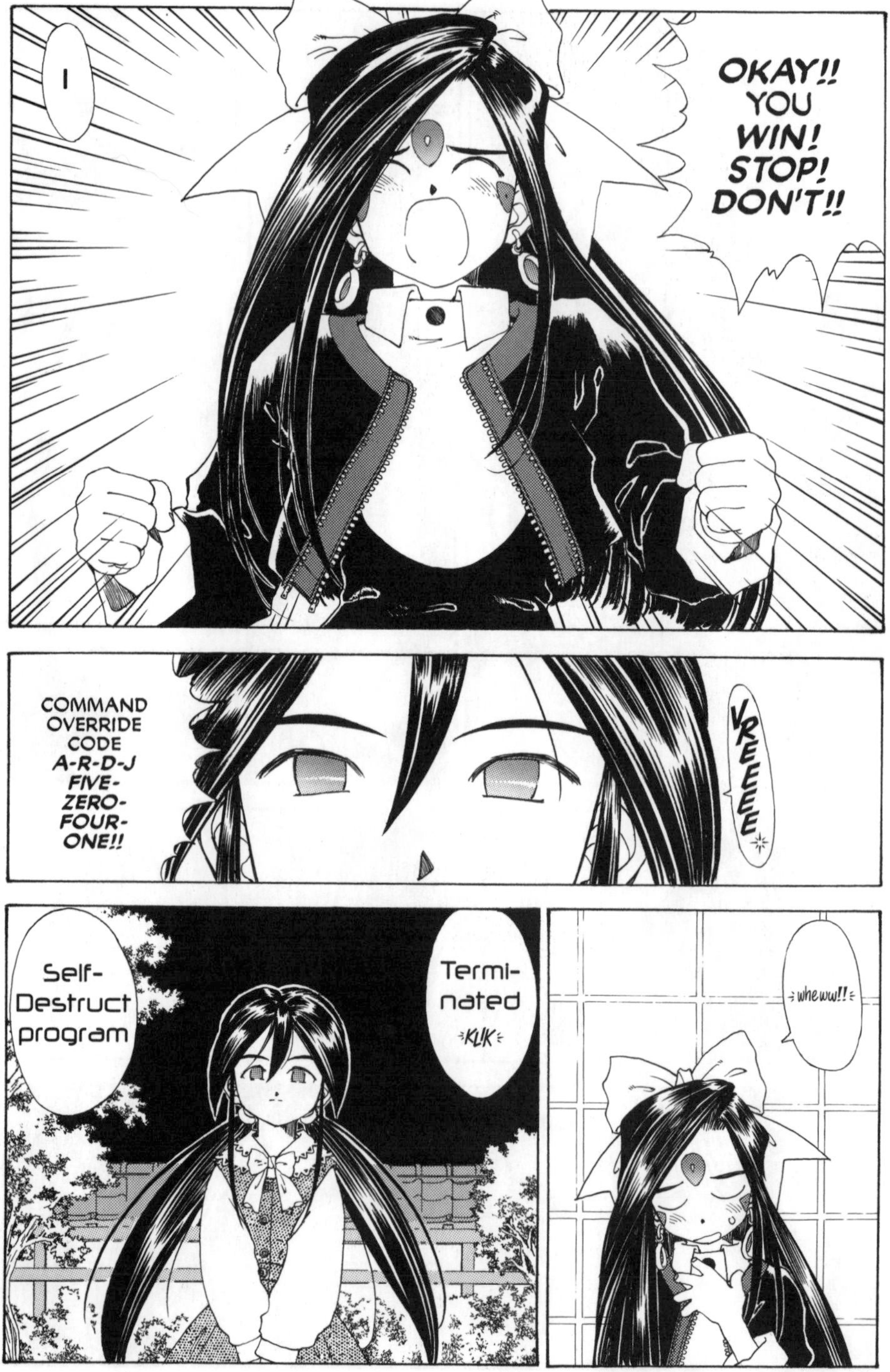
I
OKAY!! YOU WIN! STOP! DON'T!!
COMMAND OVERRIDE CODE A-R-D-J FIVE-ZERO-FOUR-ONE!!
VREEEE
Self-Destruct program
Terminated
KLIK
whewww!!

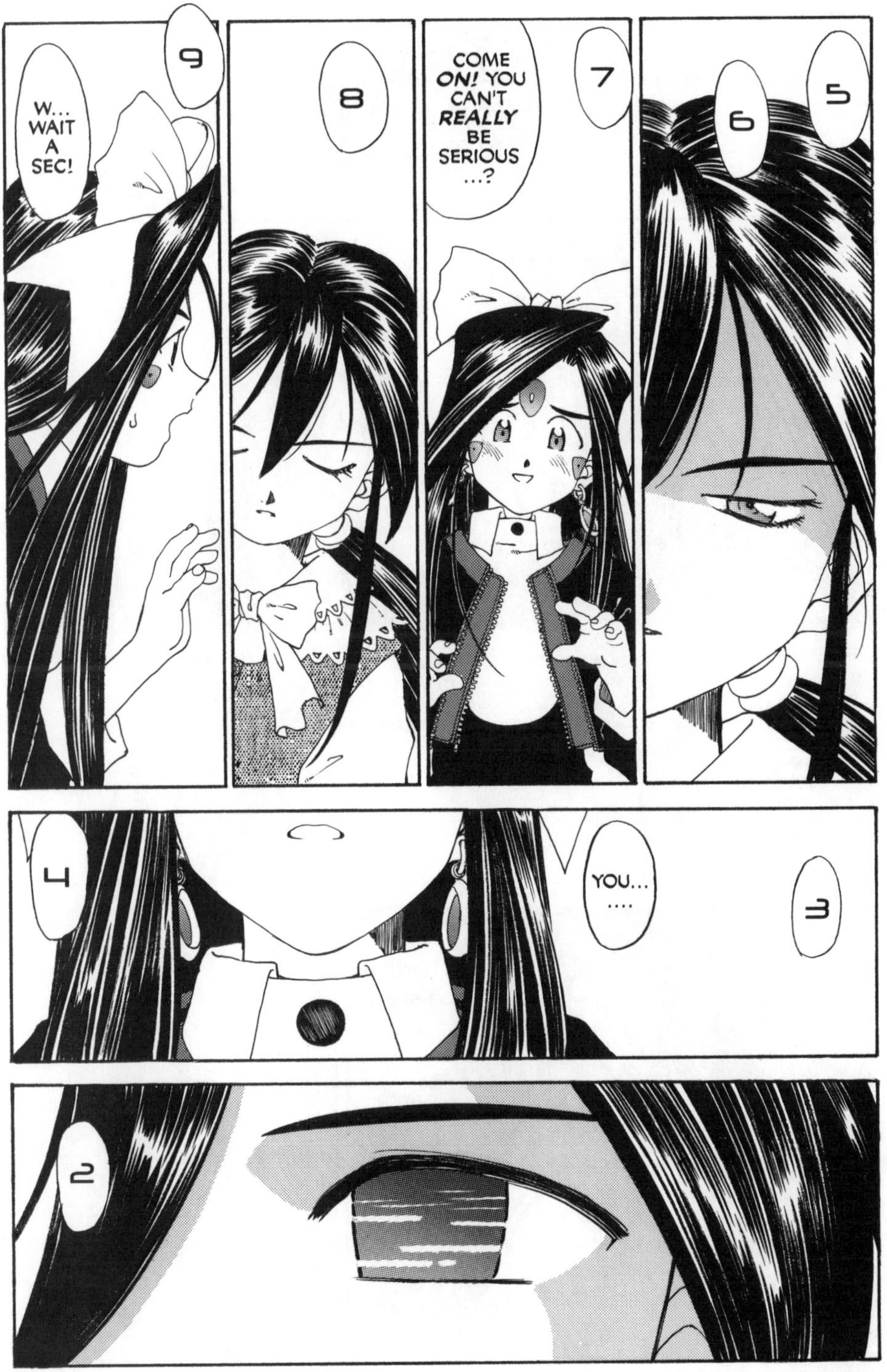
5
6
7
COME ON! YOU CAN'T REALLY BE SERIOUS ...?
8
9
W... WAIT A SEC!
3
YOU... ....
4
2

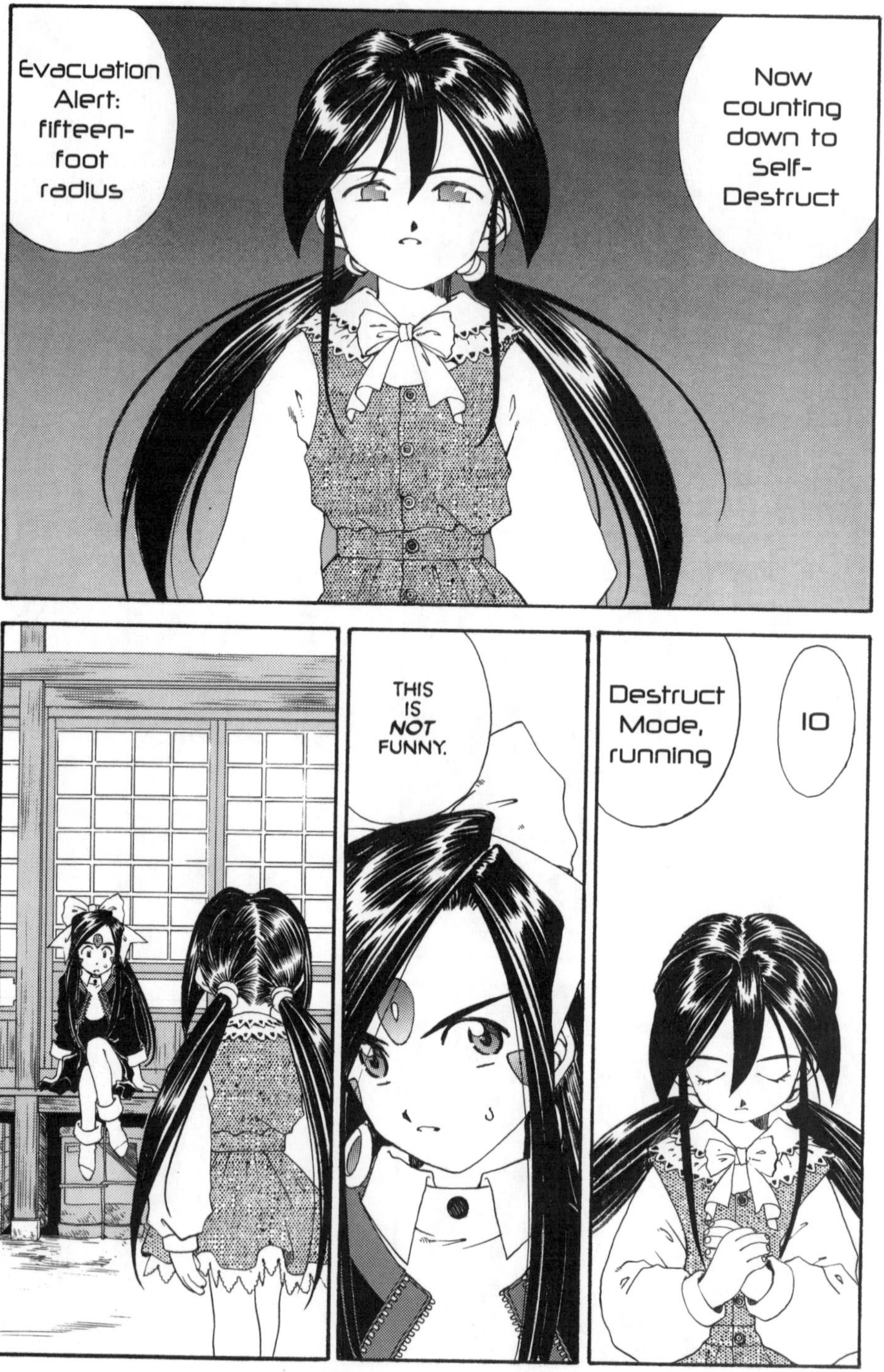
Now counting down to Self-Destruct
Evacuation Alert: fifteen-foot radius
Destruct Mode, running
10
THIS IS *NOT* FUNNY.

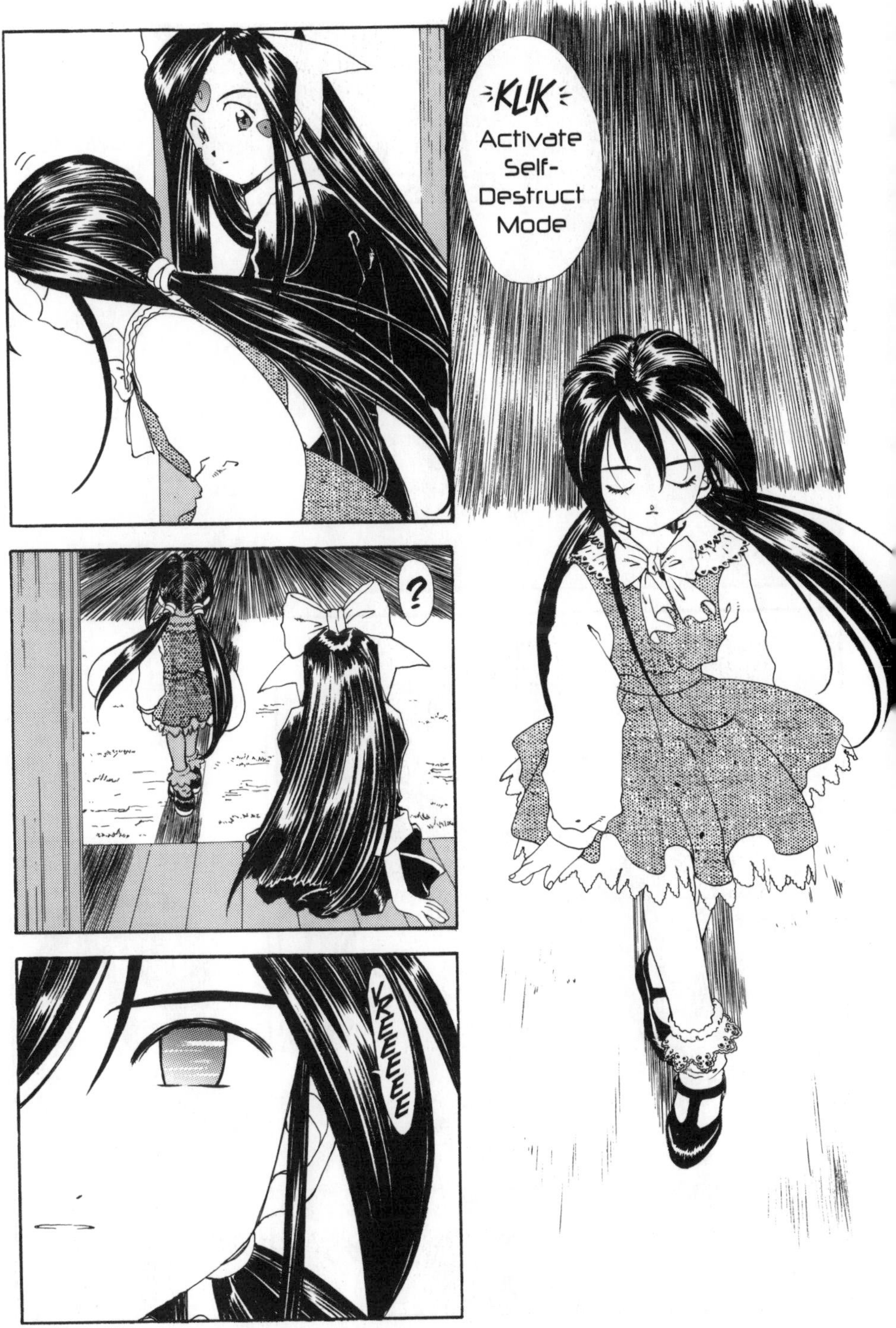

KLIK
Activate Self-Destruct Mode
?
VREEEEE

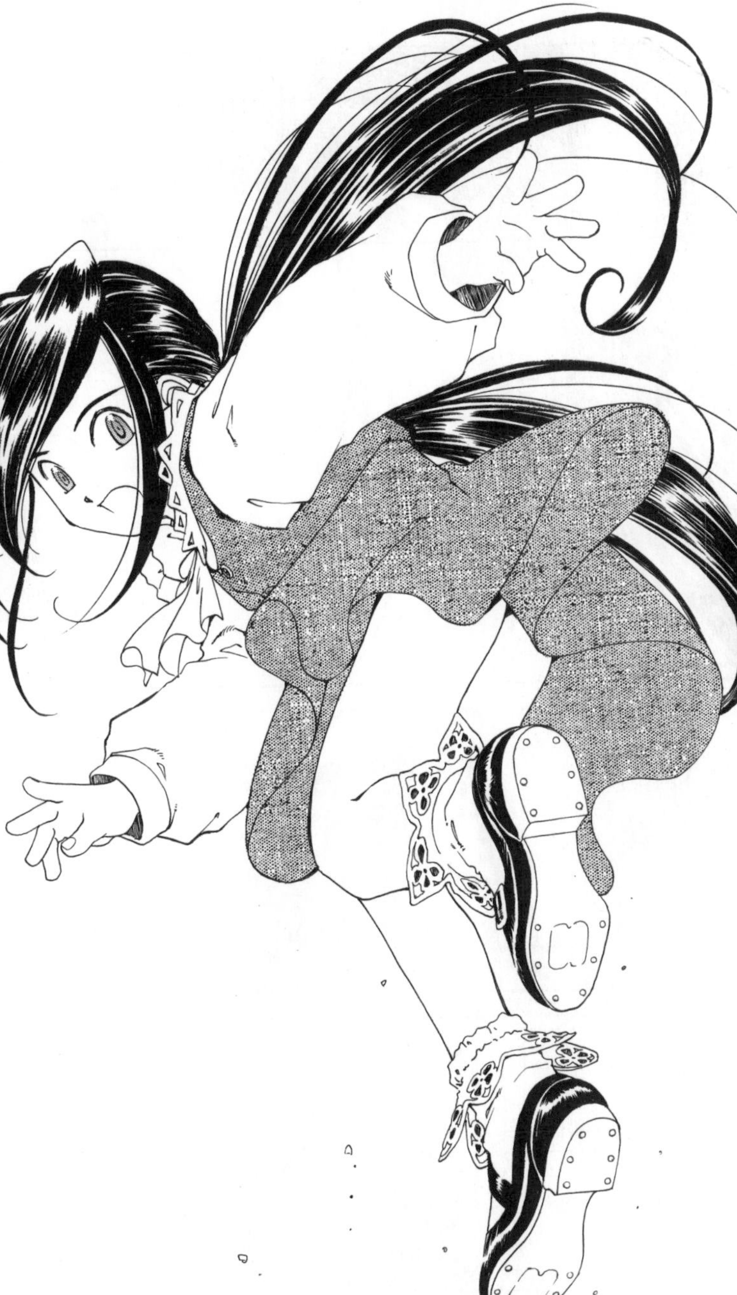

GETTING TO KNOW YOU

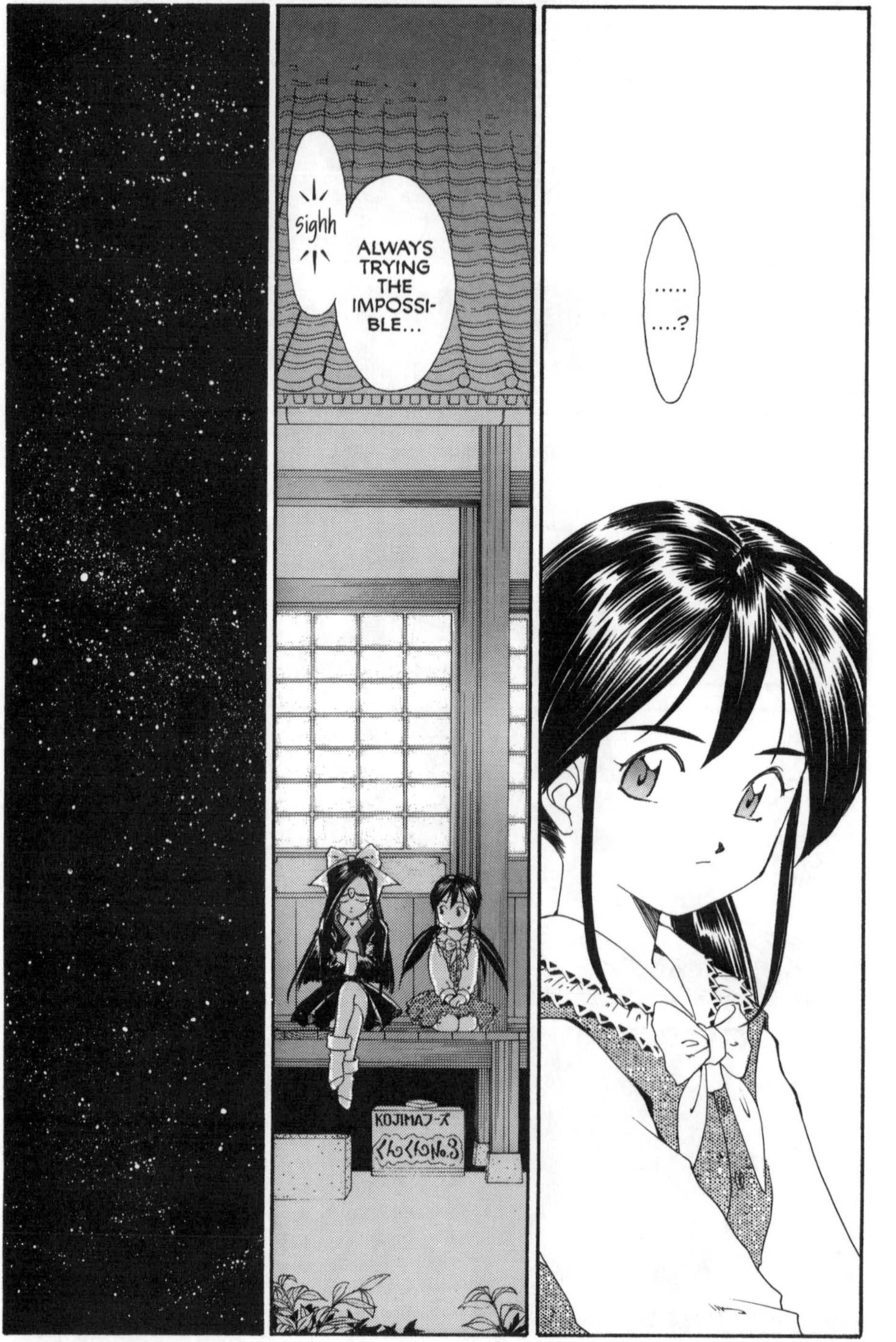
.....
....?
sighh
ALWAYS TRYING THE IMPOSSI-BLE...
KOJIMAフーズ
くんくんNo.3

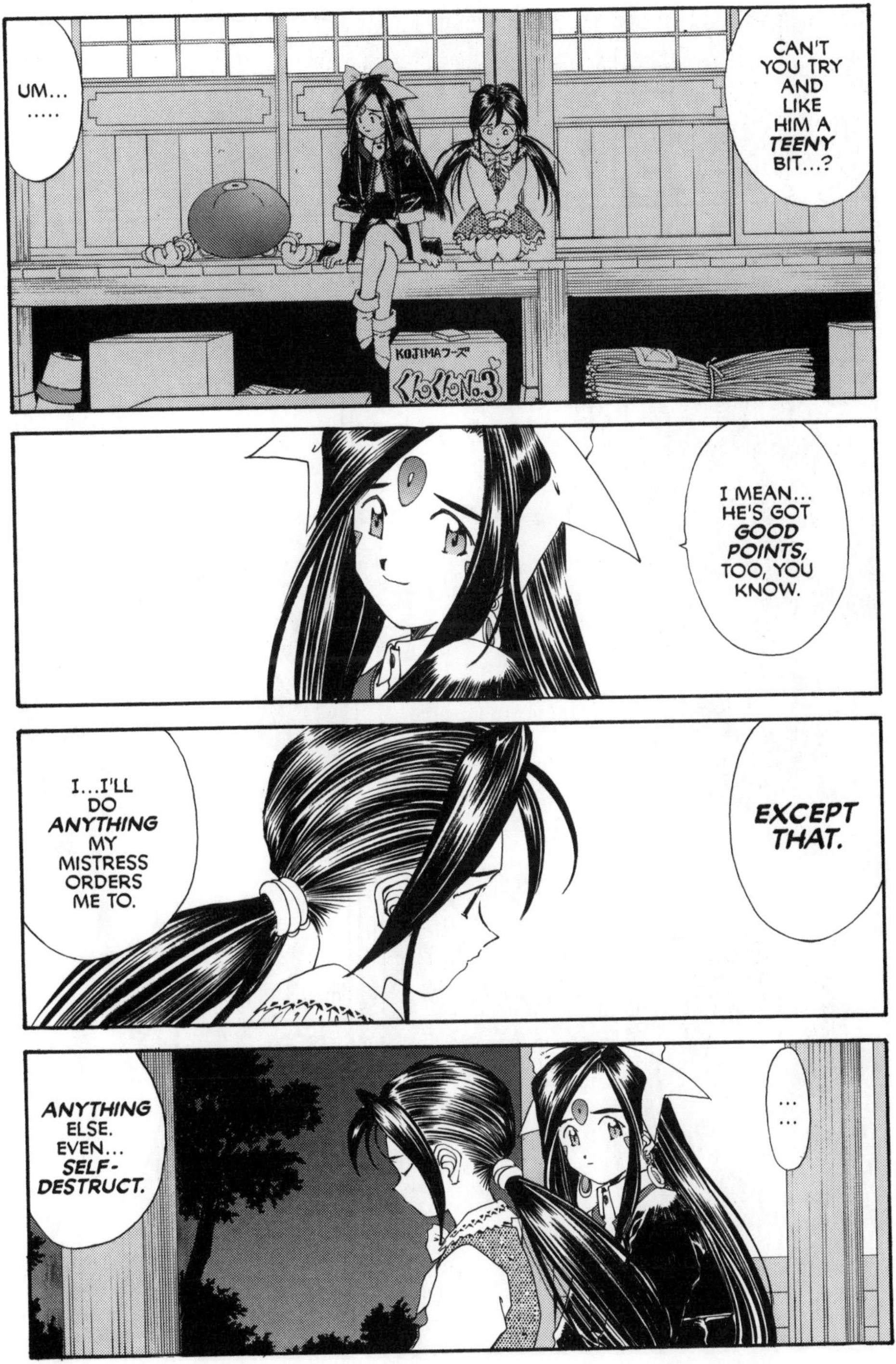
UM... .....
CAN'T YOU TRY AND LIKE HIM A *TEENY* BIT...?
I MEAN... HE'S GOT *GOOD POINTS,* TOO, YOU KNOW.
I...I'LL DO *ANYTHING* MY MISTRESS ORDERS ME TO.
EXCEPT THAT.
ANYTHING ELSE. EVEN... *SELF-DESTRUCT.*
... ...
KOJIMAフーズ
くんくんNo.3

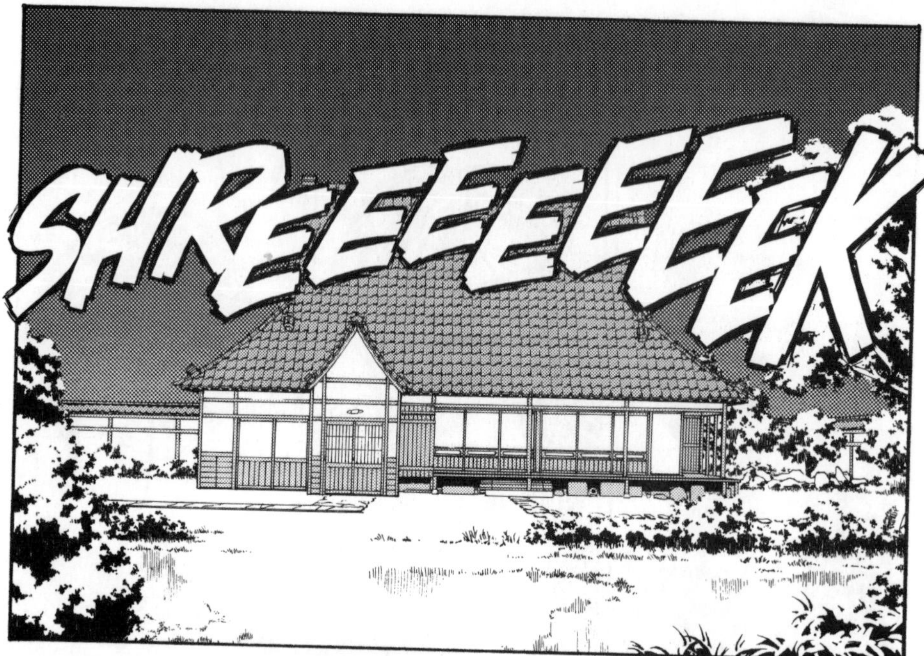
SHREEEEEEEK

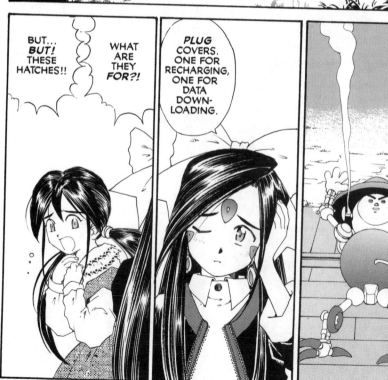

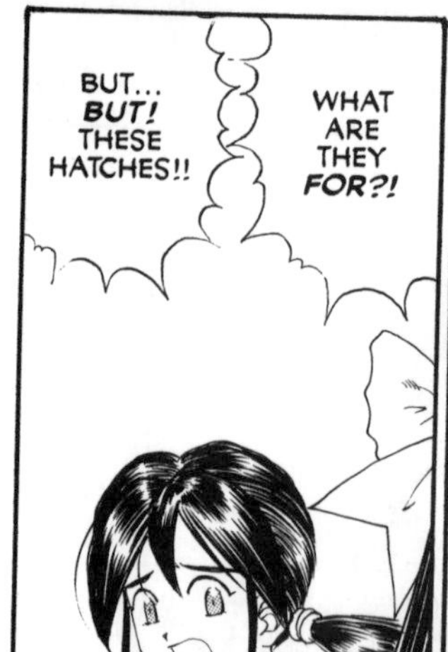
BUT... BUT! THESE HATCHES!!
WHAT ARE THEY FOR?!

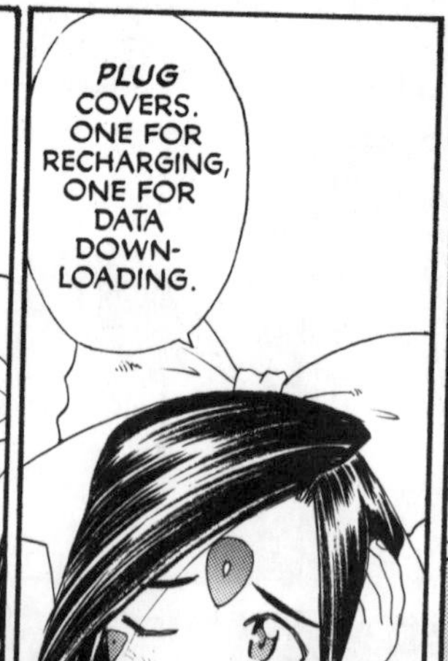
PLUG COVERS. ONE FOR RECHARGING, ONE FOR DATA DOWN-LOADING.

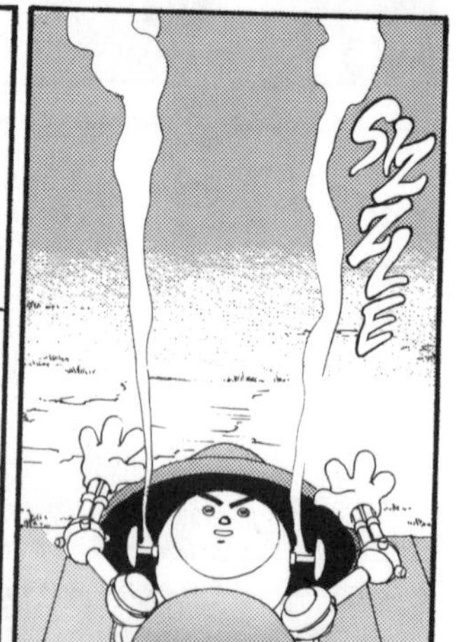
SIZZLE

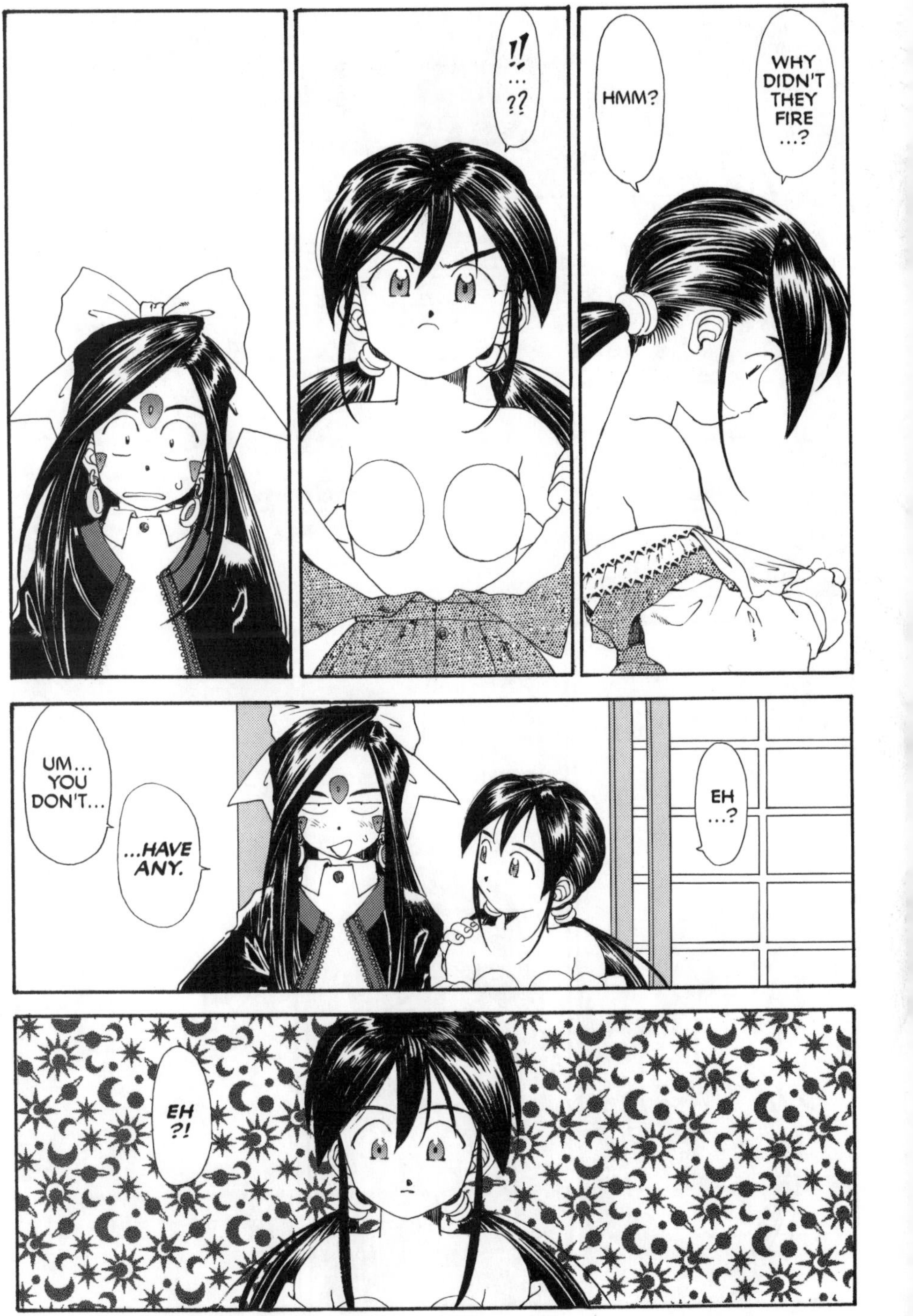
WHY DIDN'T THEY FIRE ...?
HMM?
!! ... ??
UM... YOU DON'T...
...HAVE ANY.
EH ...?
EH ?!

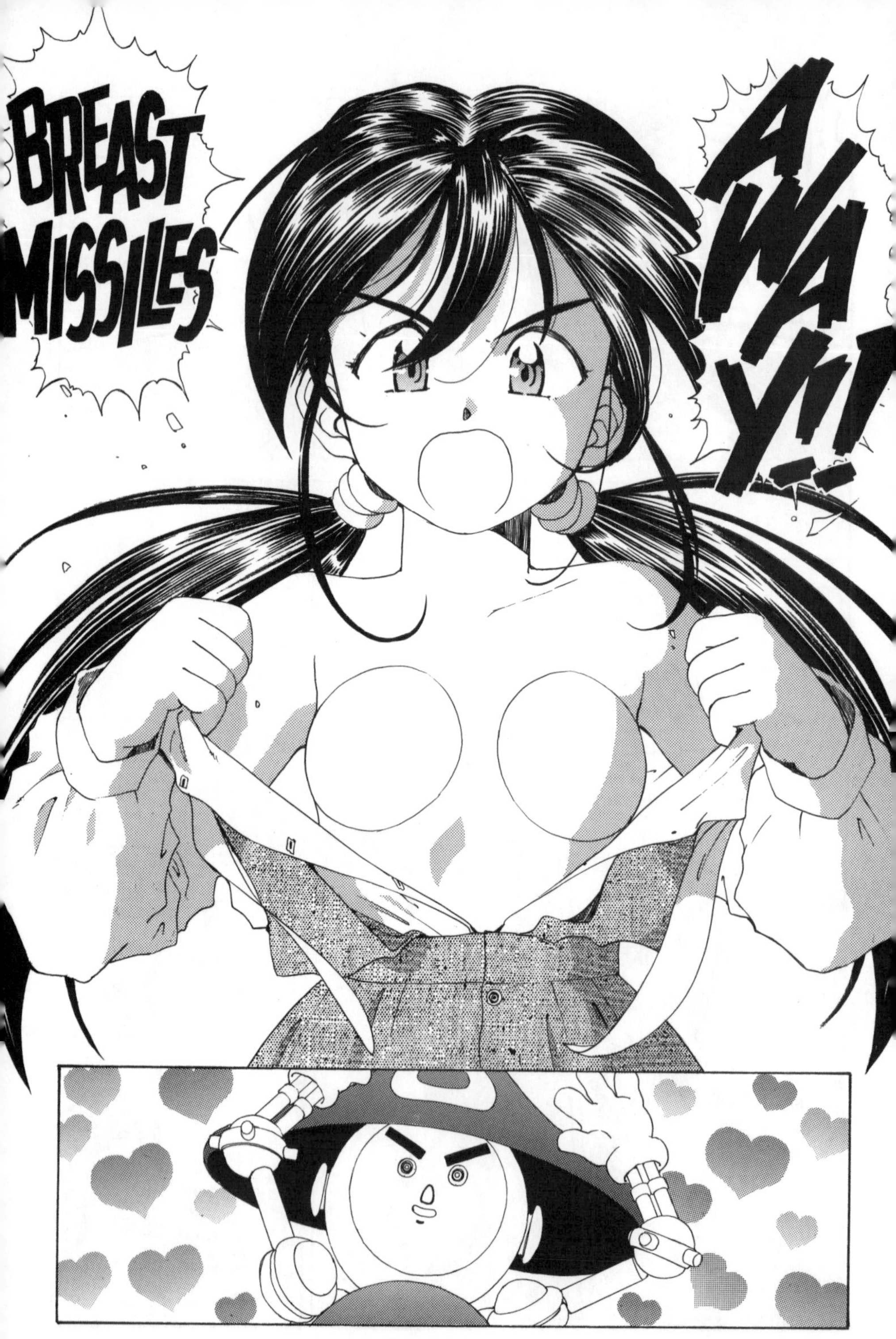

AWAYY!!
BREAST MISSILES

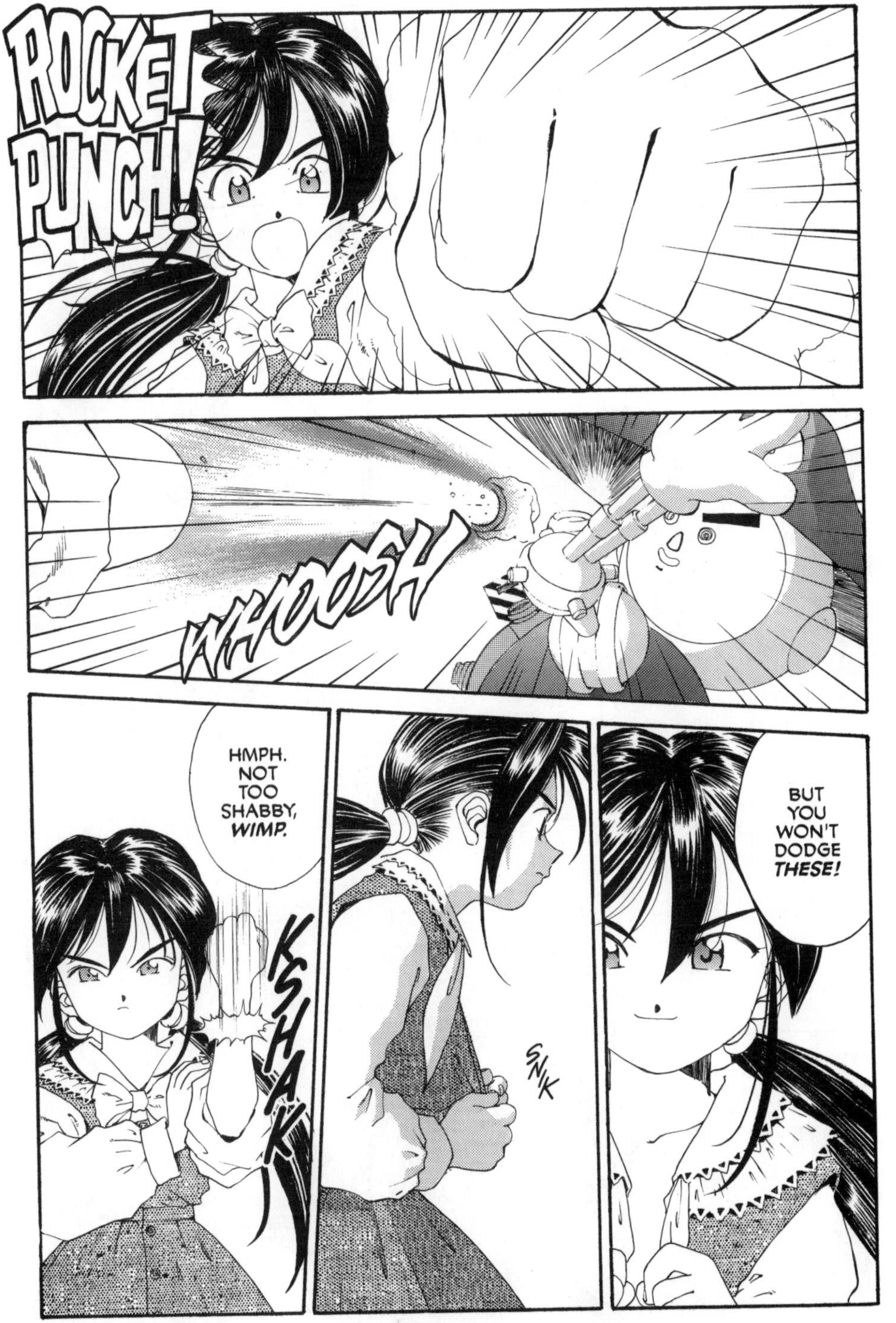
ROCKET PUNCH!
WHOOSH
BUT YOU WON'T DODGE *THESE!*
SNIK
HMPH. NOT TOO SHABBY, *WIMP.*
K'SHAK

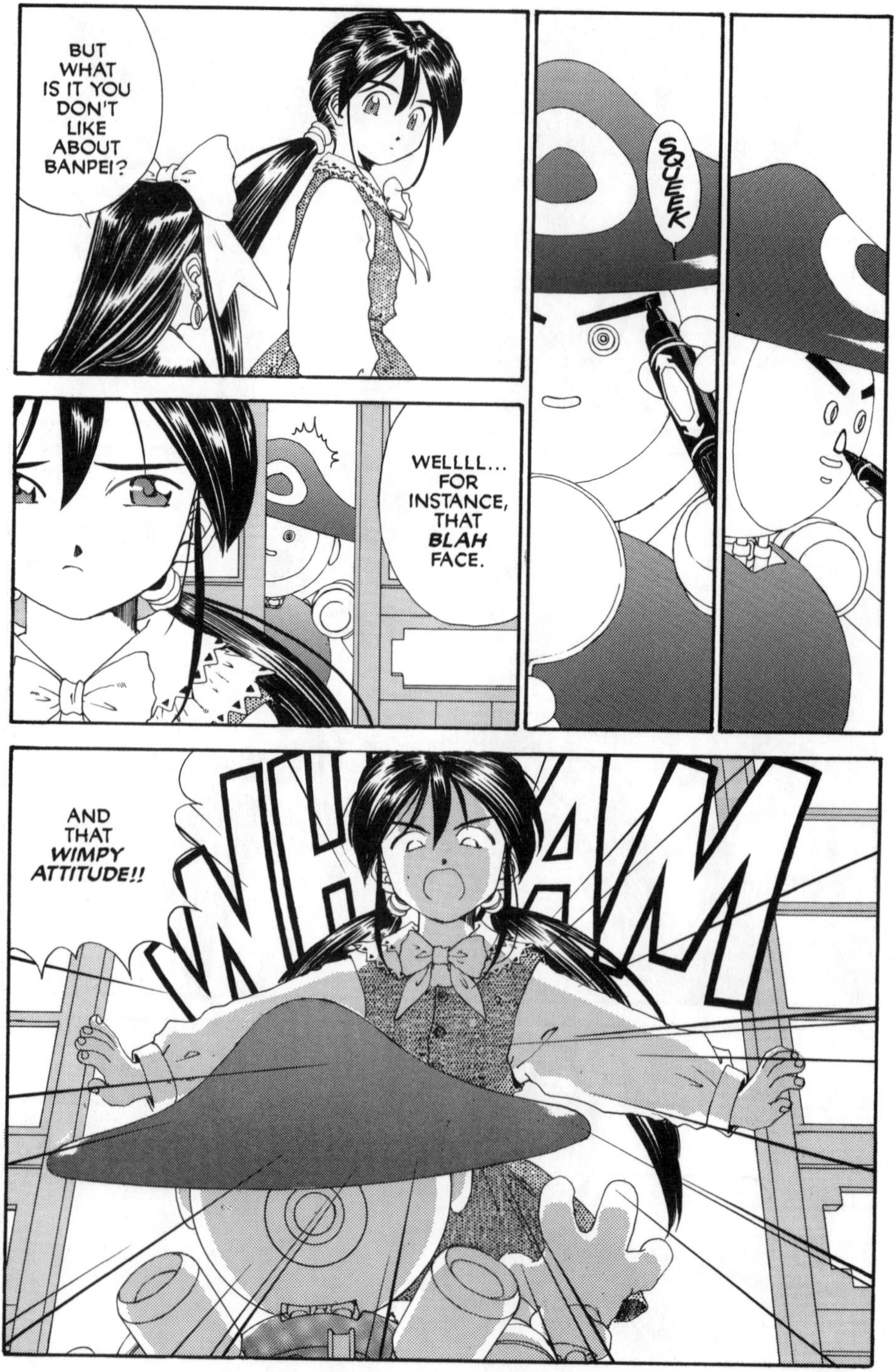
BUT WHAT IS IT YOU DON'T LIKE ABOUT BANPEI?
WELLLL... FOR INSTANCE, THAT *BLAH* FACE.
SQUEEK
AND THAT *WIMPY ATTITUDE!!*
WHAM

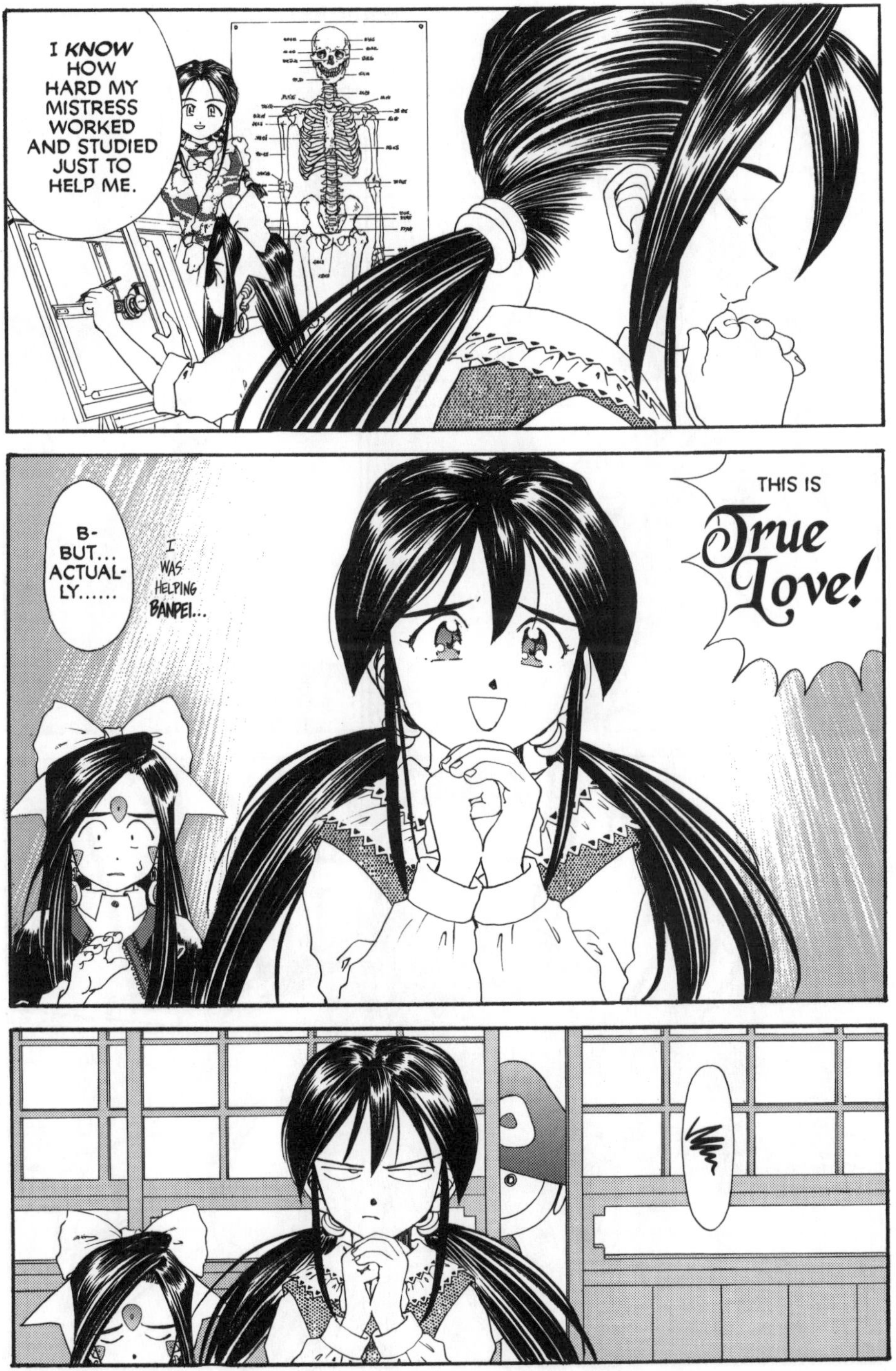
I KNOW HOW HARD MY MISTRESS WORKED AND STUDIED JUST TO HELP ME.
THIS IS True Love!
I WAS HELPING BANPEI...
B-BUT... ACTUAL-LY......

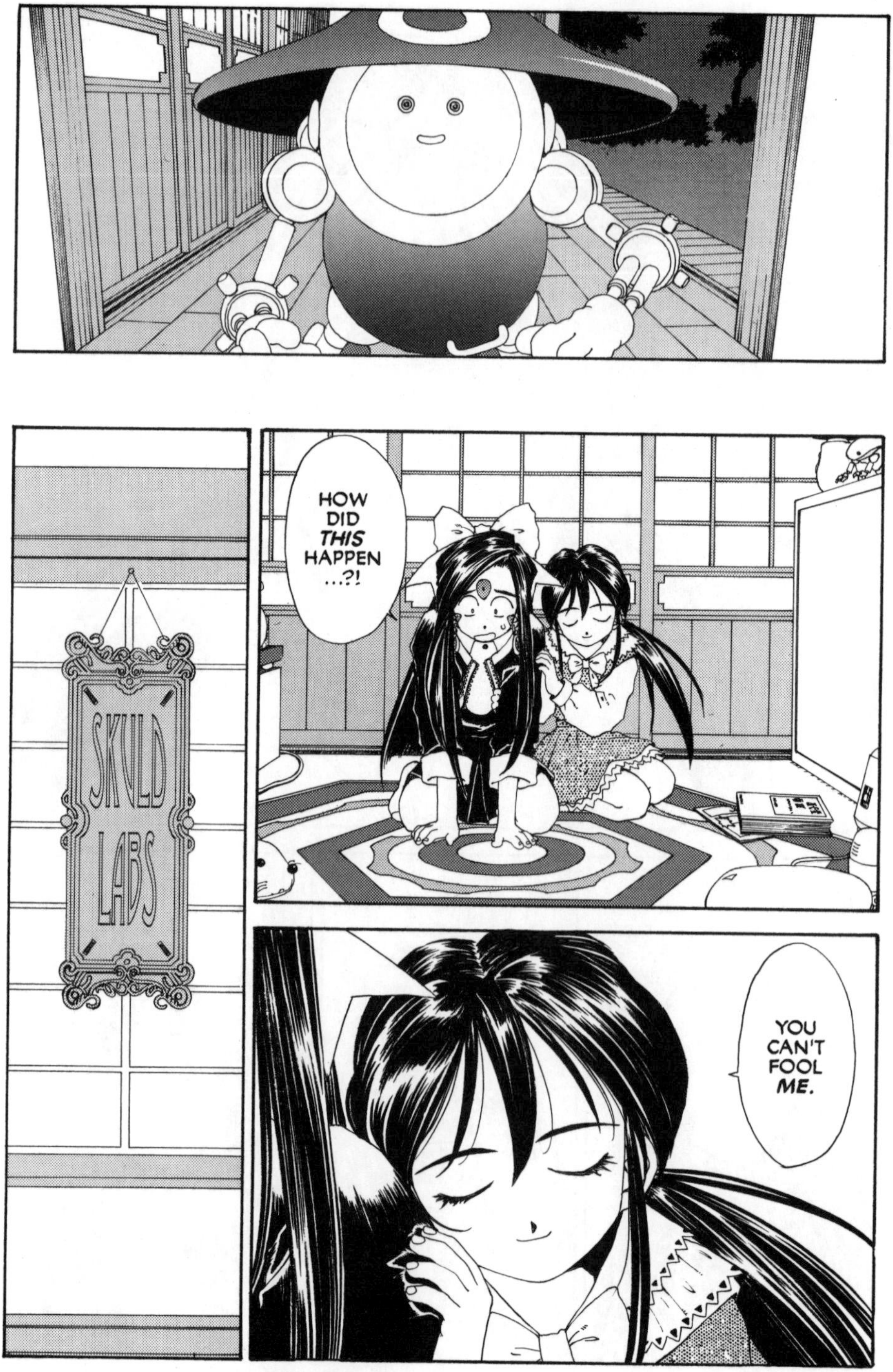
HOW DID *THIS* HAPPEN ...?!
YOU CAN'T FOOL *ME.*
SKULD LABS

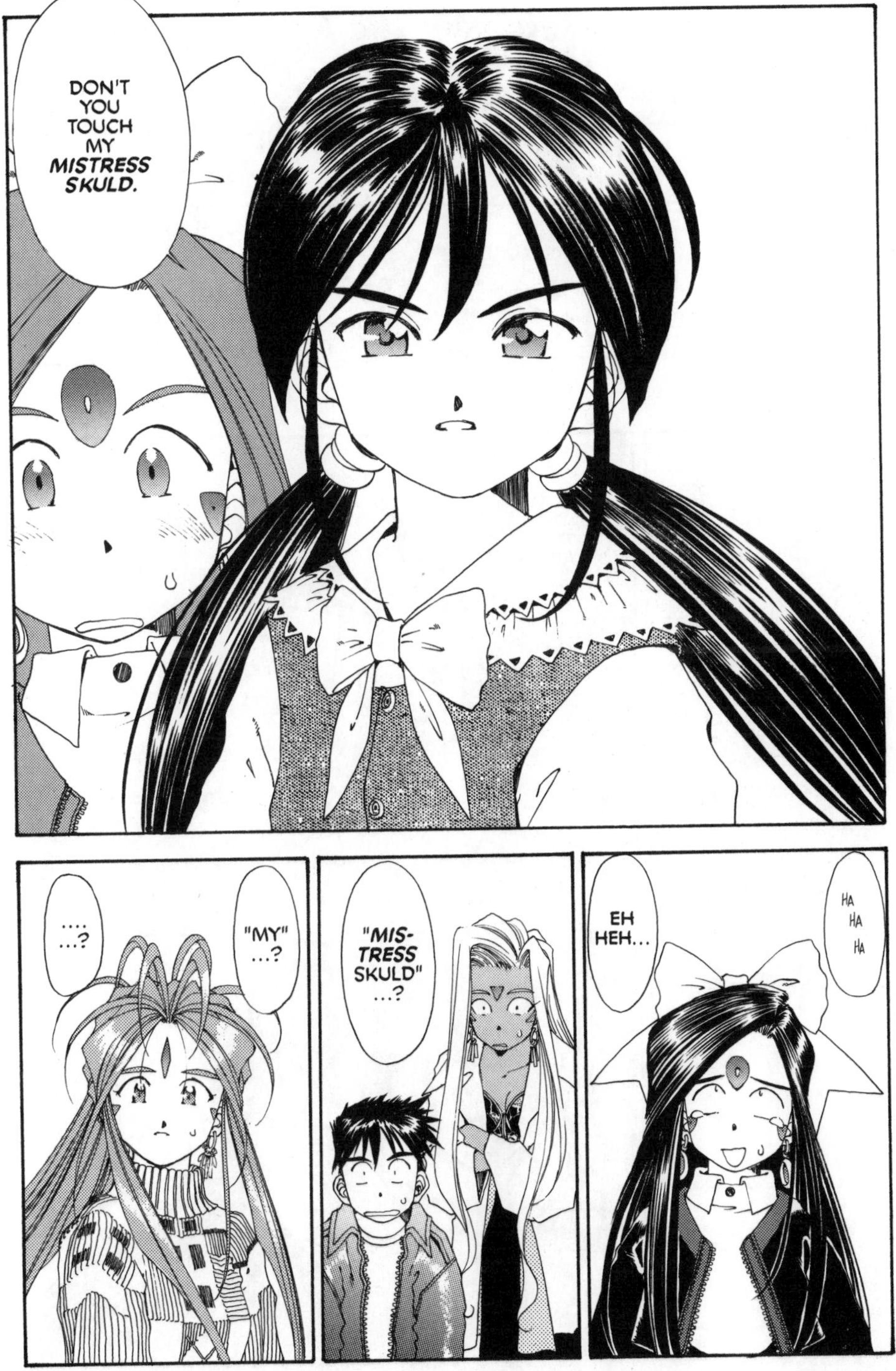
DON'T YOU TOUCH MY *MISTRESS SKULD.*
HA HA HA
EH HEH...
"*MIS-TRESS* SKULD" ...?
"MY" ...?
....?

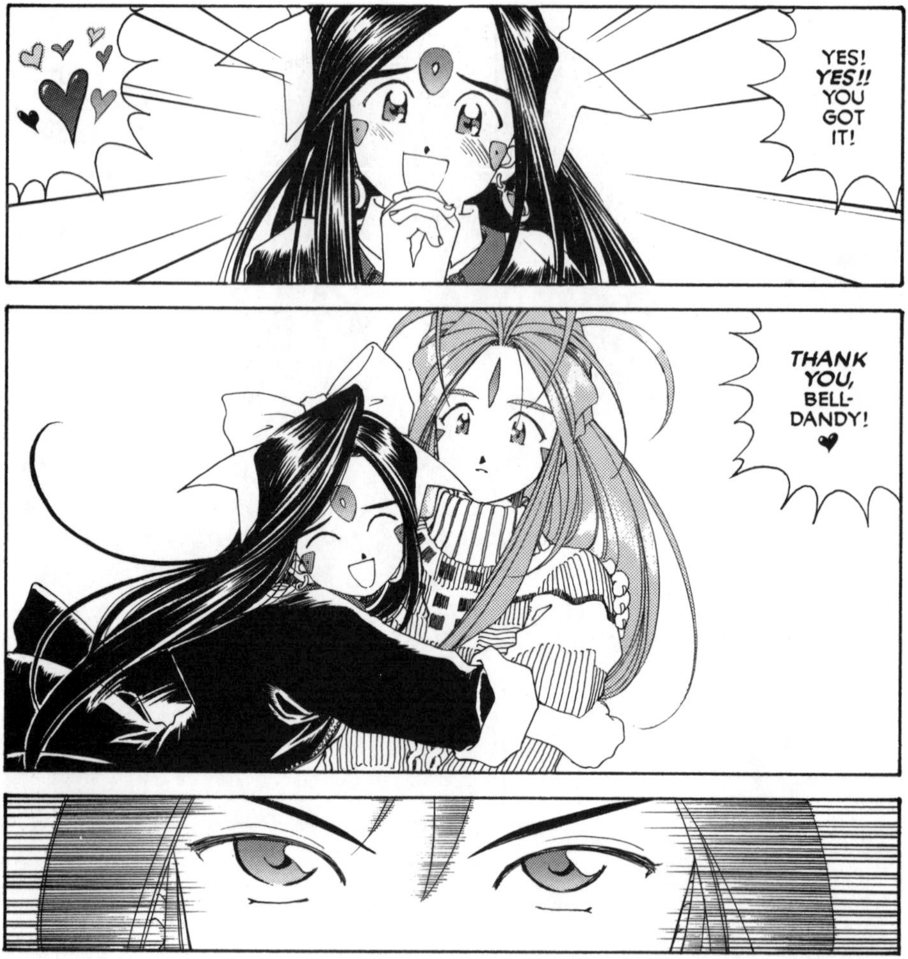
YES! YES!! YOU GOT IT!
THANK YOU, BELL-DANDY! ❤
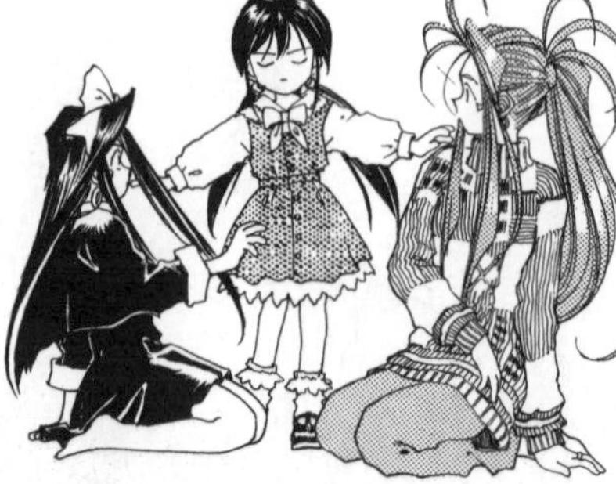

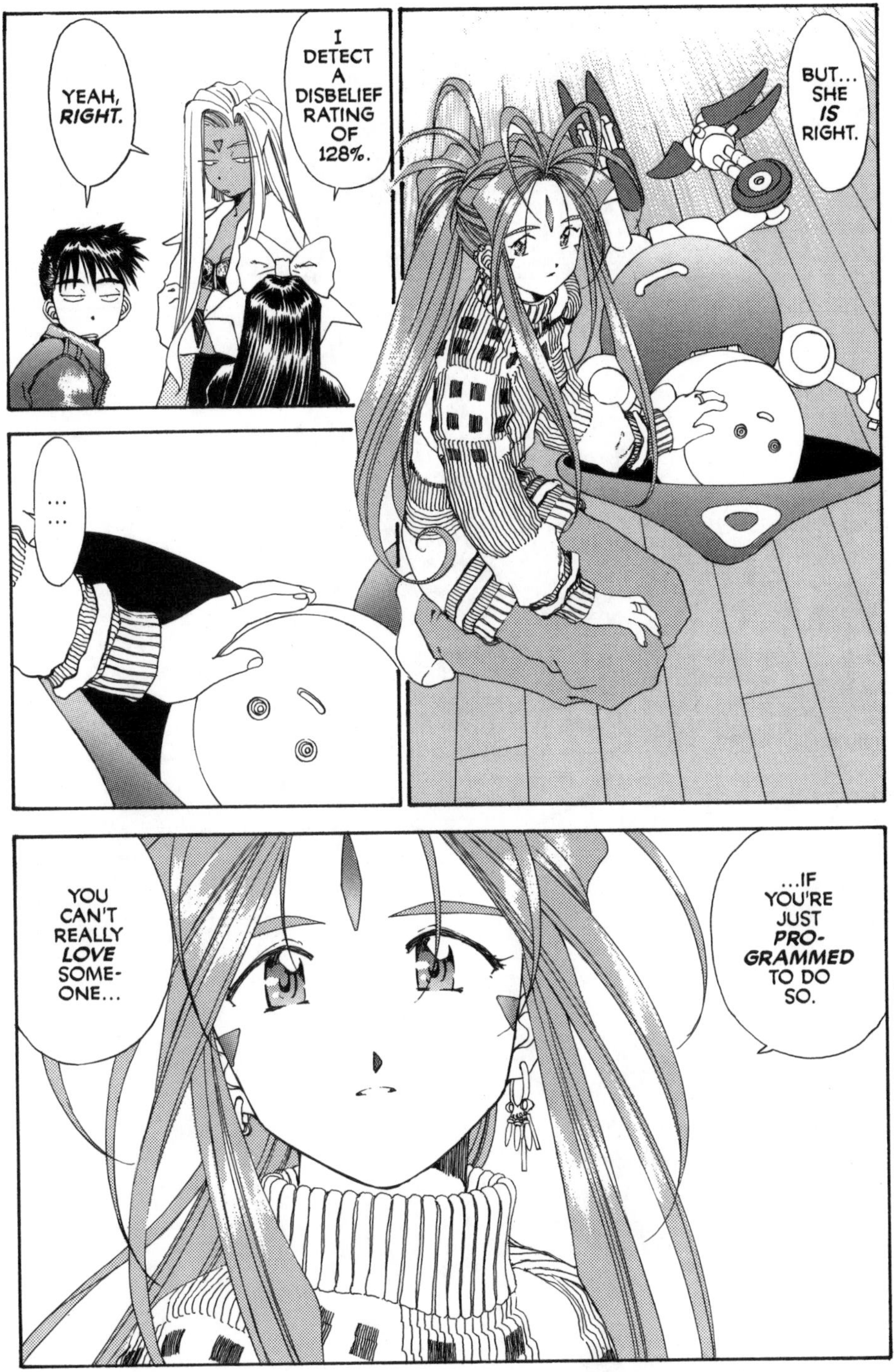
YEAH, *RIGHT*.
I DETECT A DISBELIEF RATING OF 128%.
......
BUT... SHE *IS* RIGHT.
YOU CAN'T REALLY *LOVE* SOME-ONE...
...IF YOU'RE JUST *PRO-GRAMMED* TO DO SO.

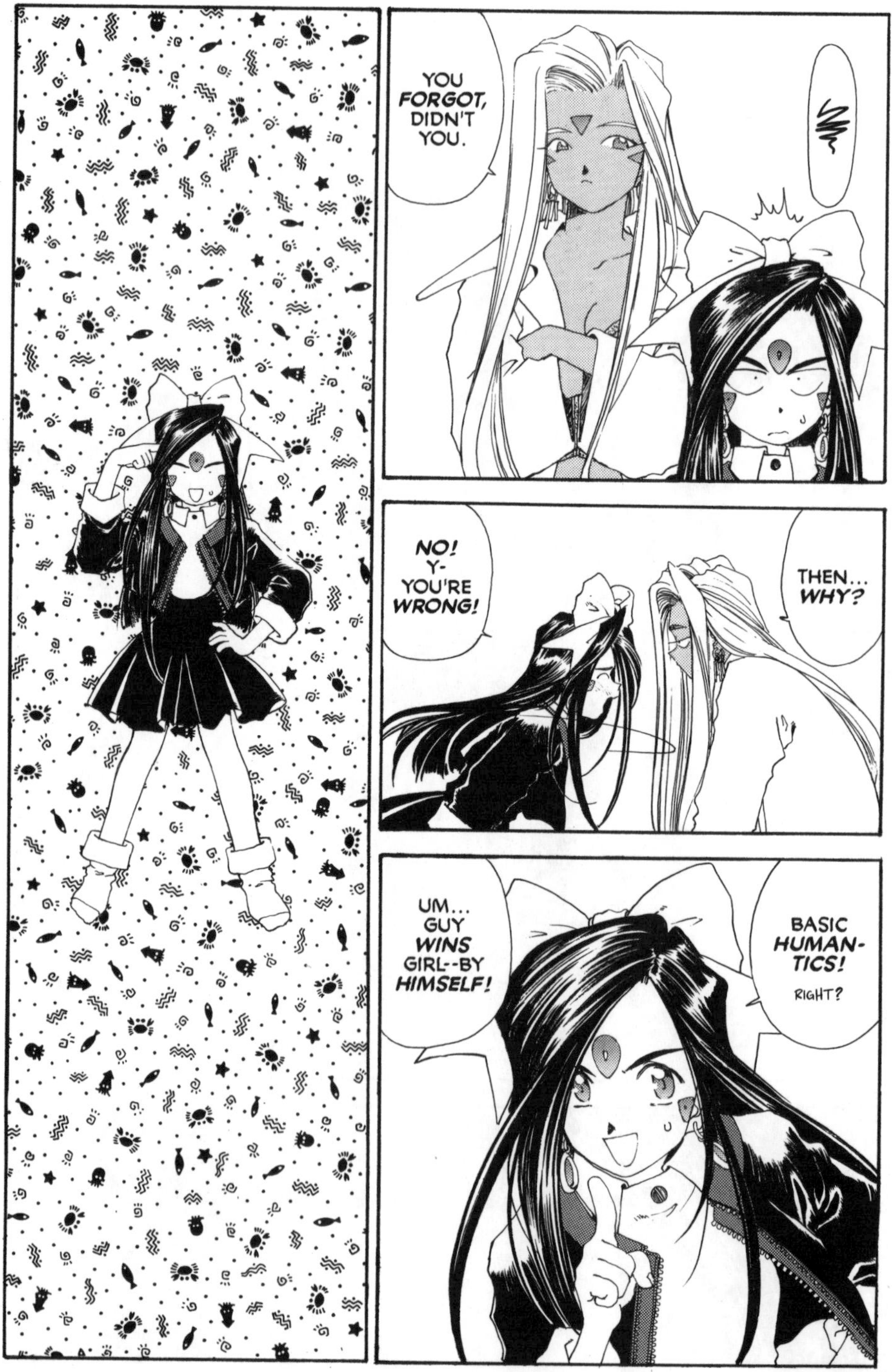

YOU *FORGOT*, DIDN'T YOU.
NO! Y- YOU'RE *WRONG!*
THEN... *WHY?*
UM... GUY *WINS* GIRL--BY *HIMSELF!*
BASIC *HUMAN-TICS!*
RIGHT?

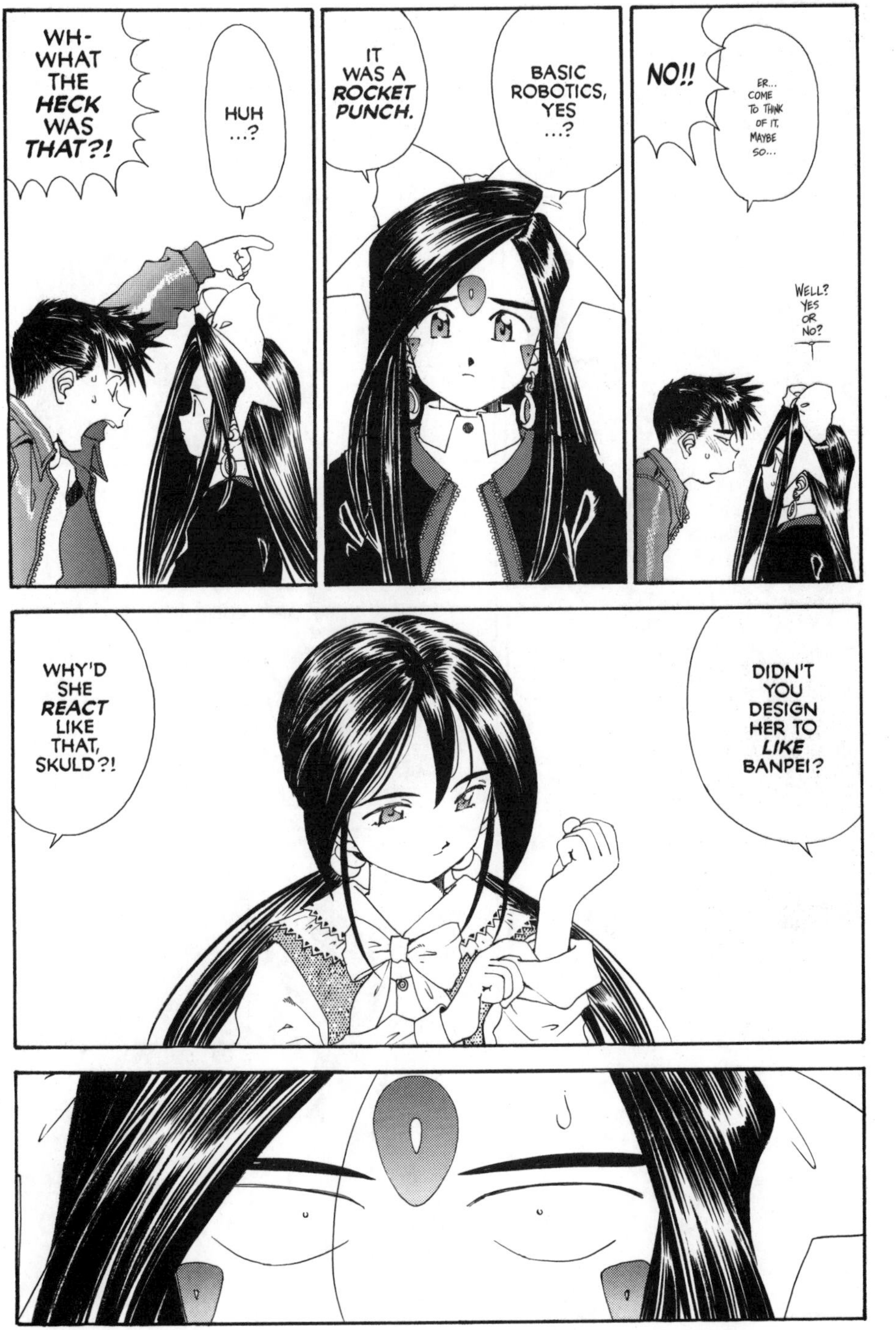
WH-WHAT THE HECK WAS THAT?!
HUH ...?
IT WAS A ROCKET PUNCH.
BASIC ROBOTICS, YES ...?
NO!!
ER... COME TO THINK OF IT, MAYBE SO...
WELL? YES OR NO?
WHY'D SHE REACT LIKE THAT, SKULD?!
DIDN'T YOU DESIGN HER TO LIKE BANPEI?

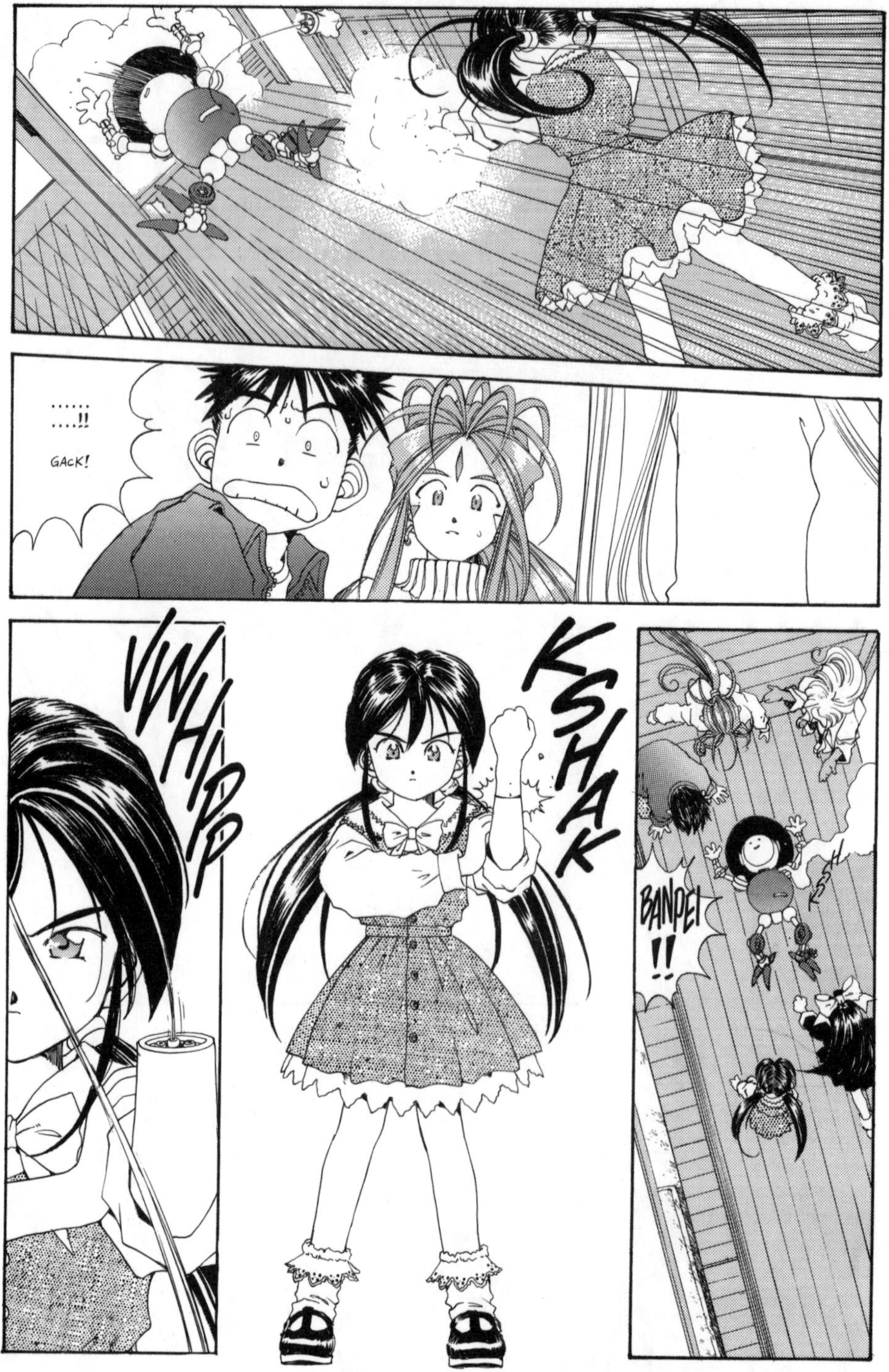
......
....!!
GACK!
BANPEI !!
KSSH
KSHAK
VWHIPP

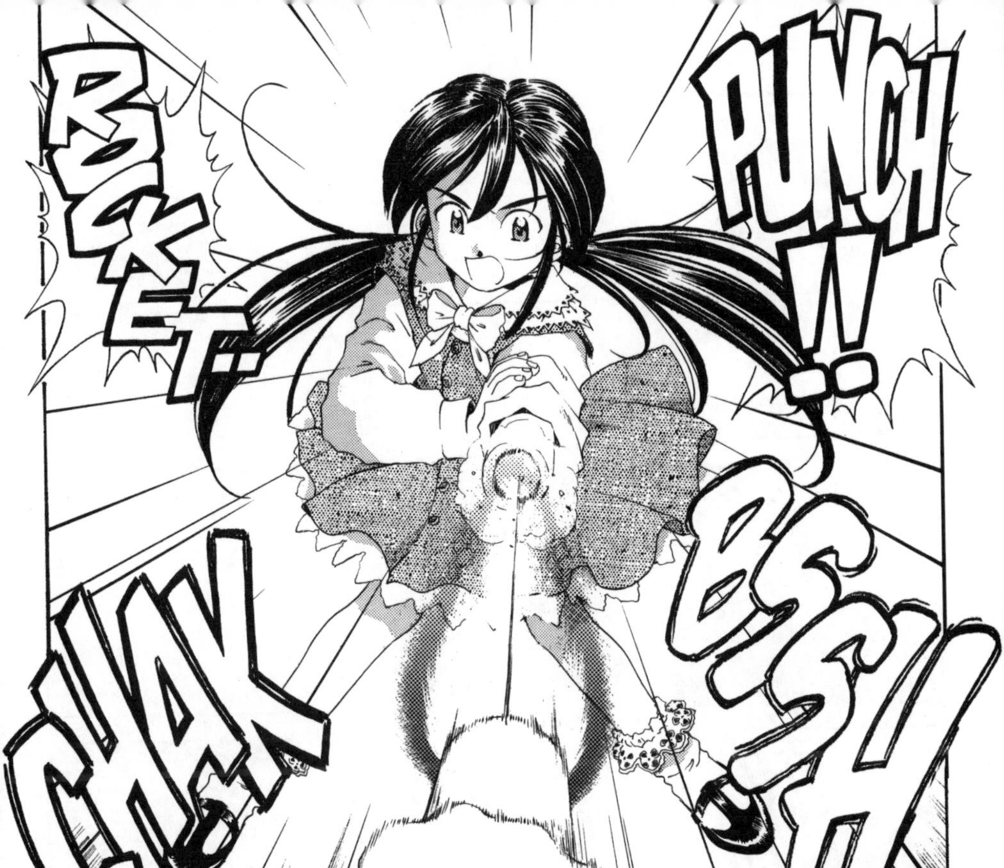
ROCKET...
PUNCH!!
BOSCH
CHAK
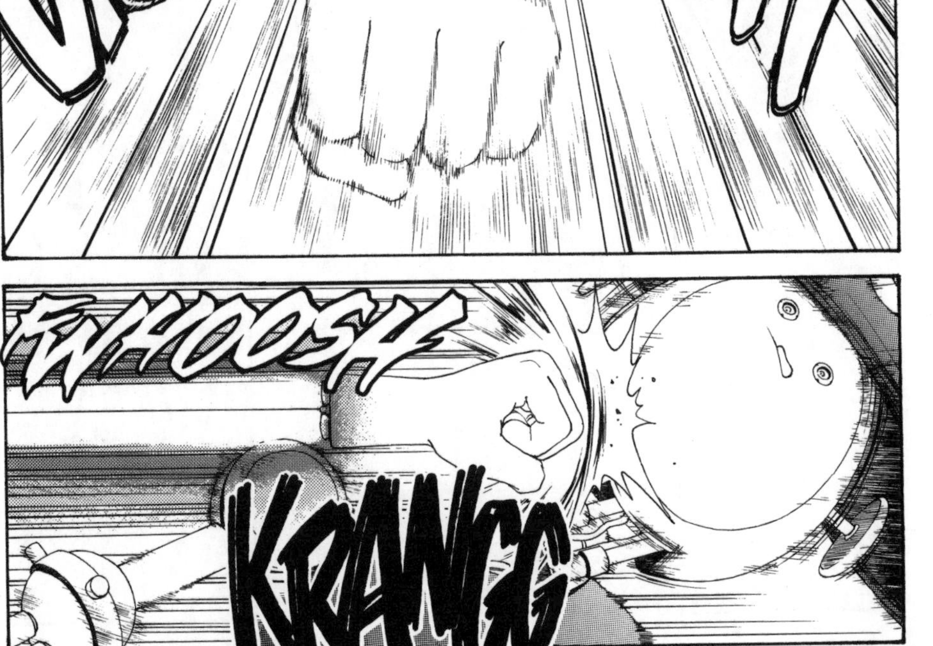
FWHOOSH
KRANGG

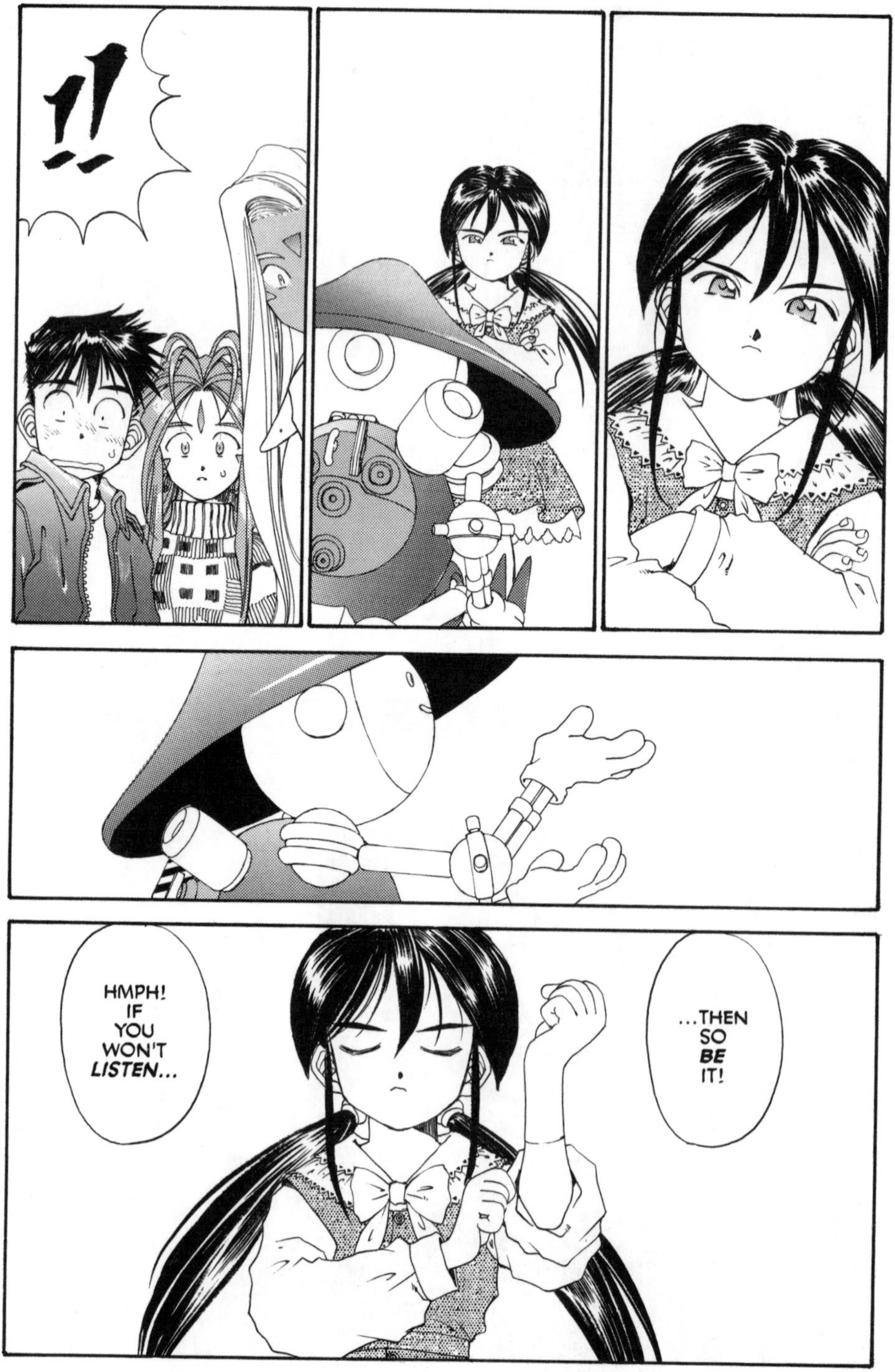
!!
HMPH! IF YOU WON'T *LISTEN*...
...THEN SO *BE* IT!

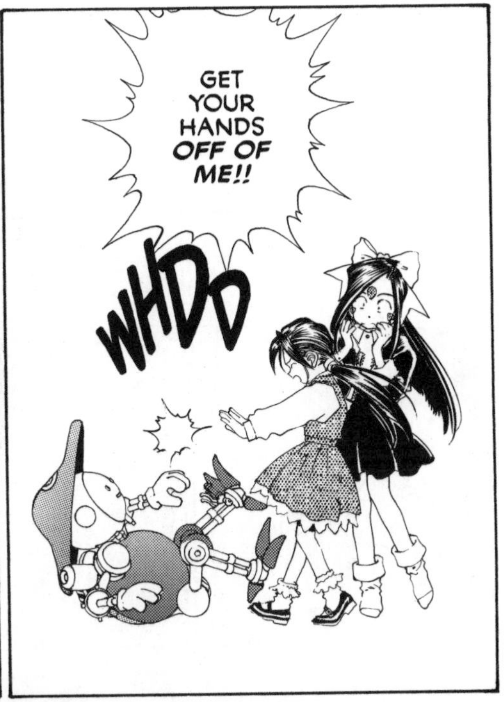
GET YOUR HANDS OFF OF ME!!
WHDD
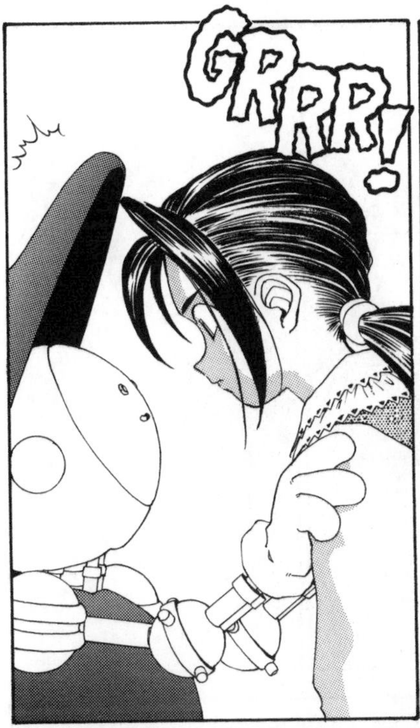
GRRR!
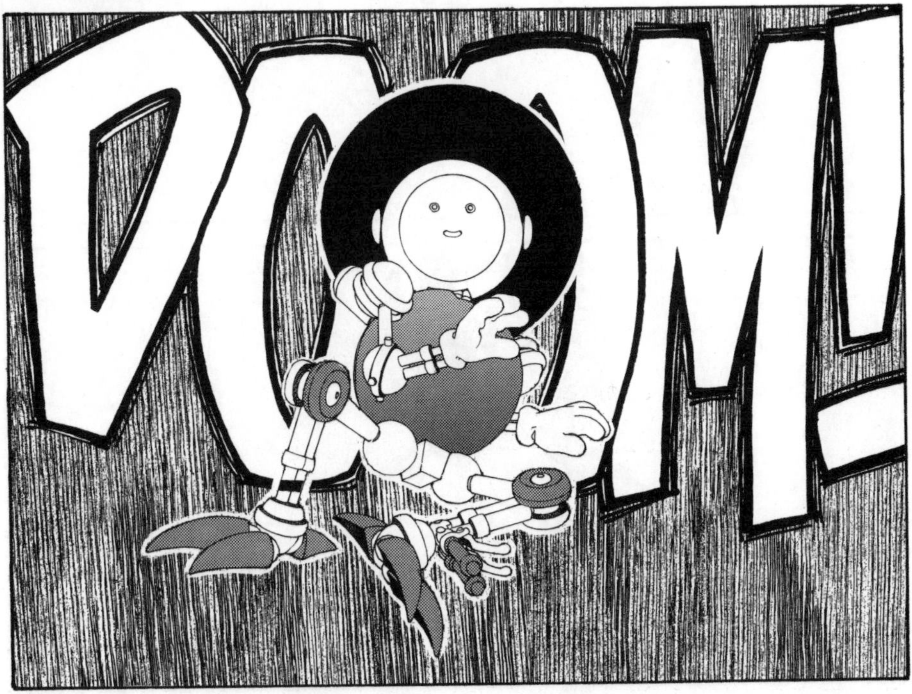
DOOM!

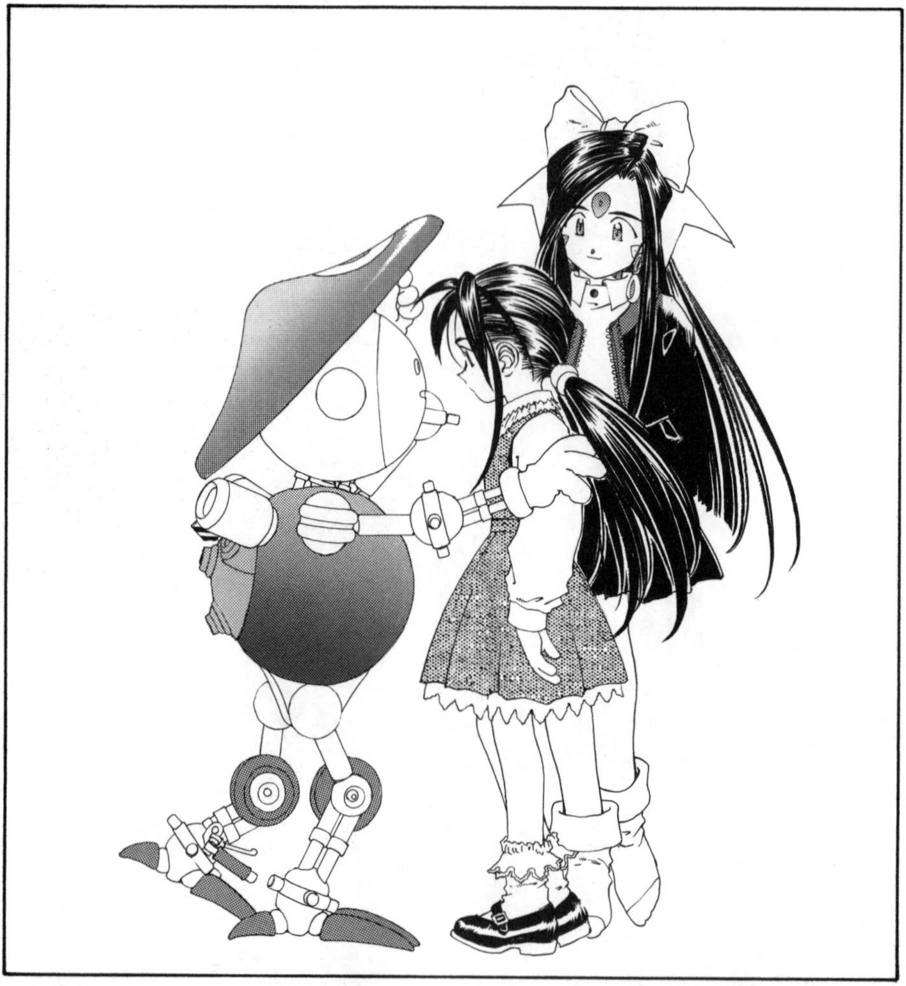

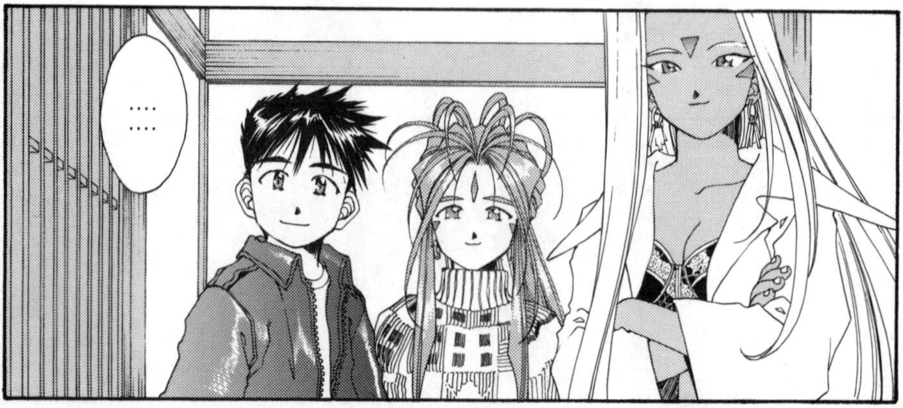
....
....

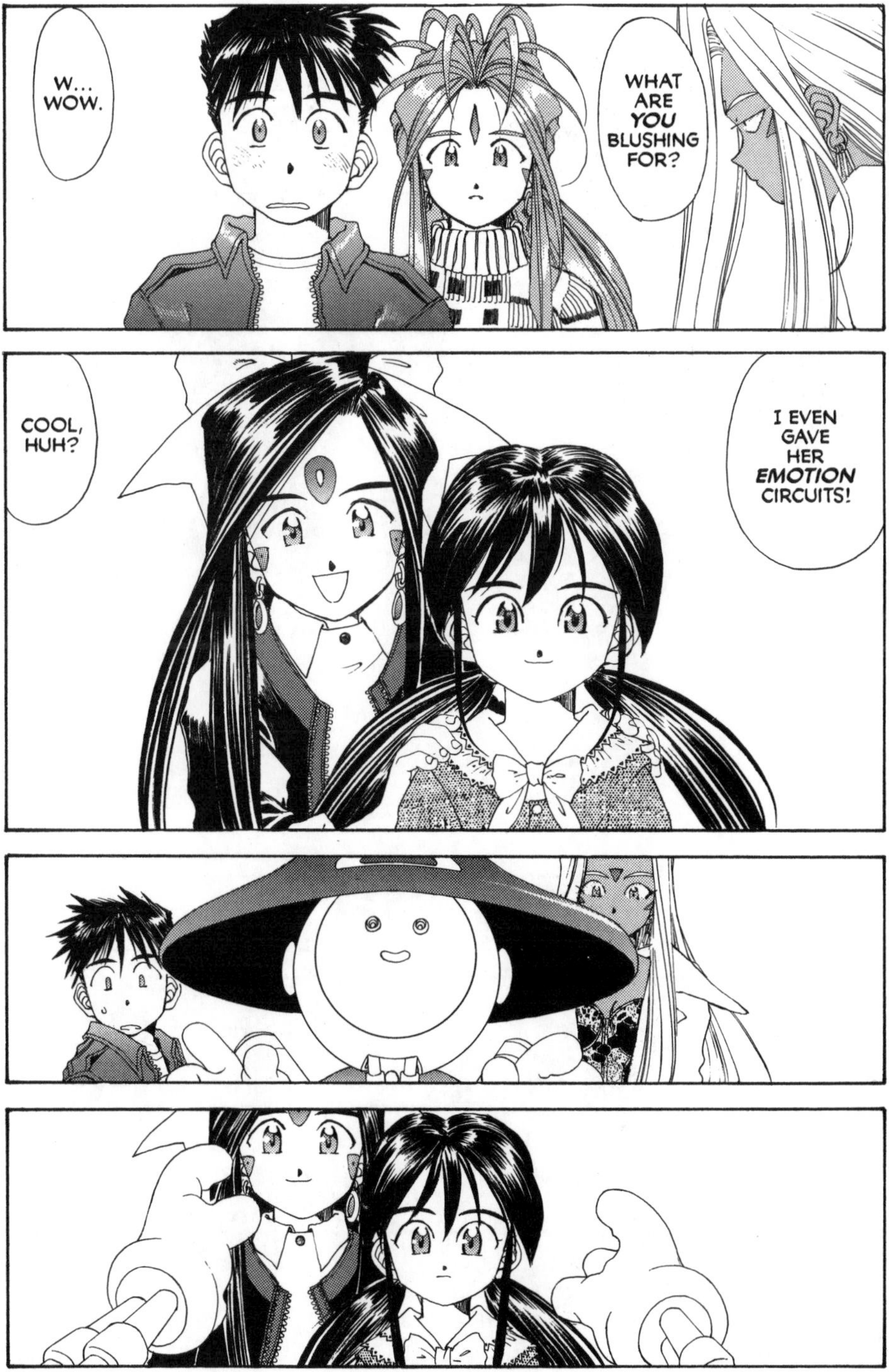
W... WOW.
WHAT ARE ***YOU*** BLUSHING FOR?
COOL, HUH?
I EVEN GAVE HER ***EMOTION*** CIRCUITS!

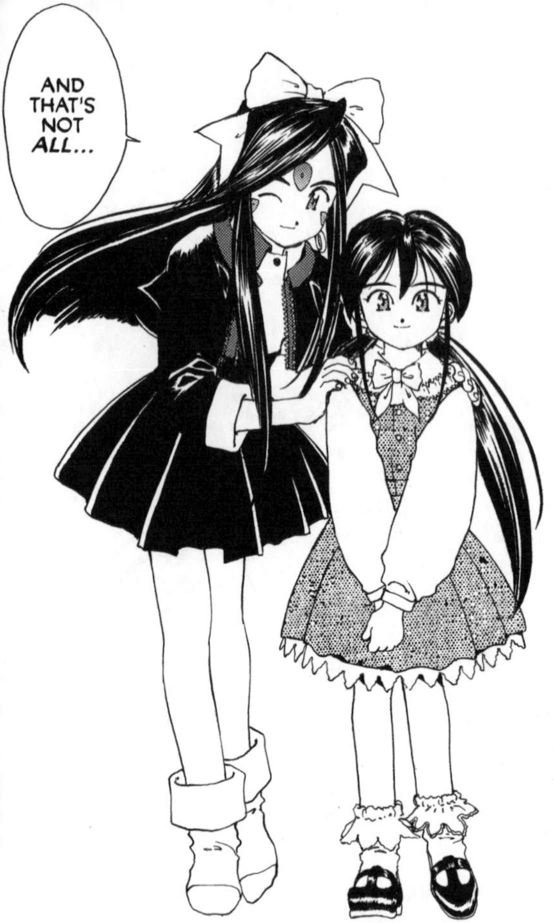
AND THAT'S NOT *ALL...*

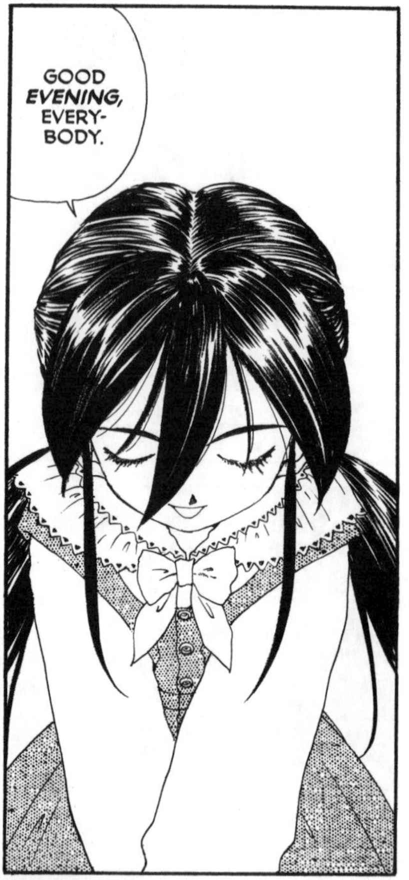
GOOD *EVENING,* EVERY-BODY.

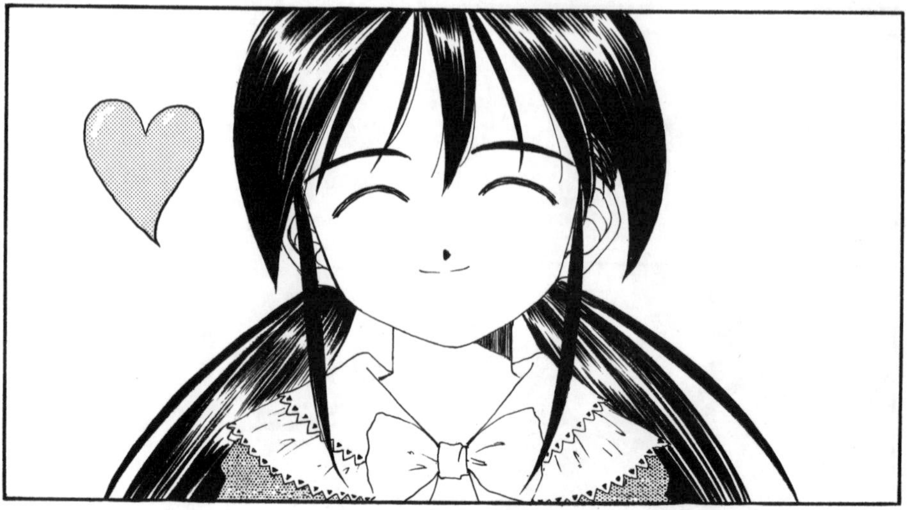

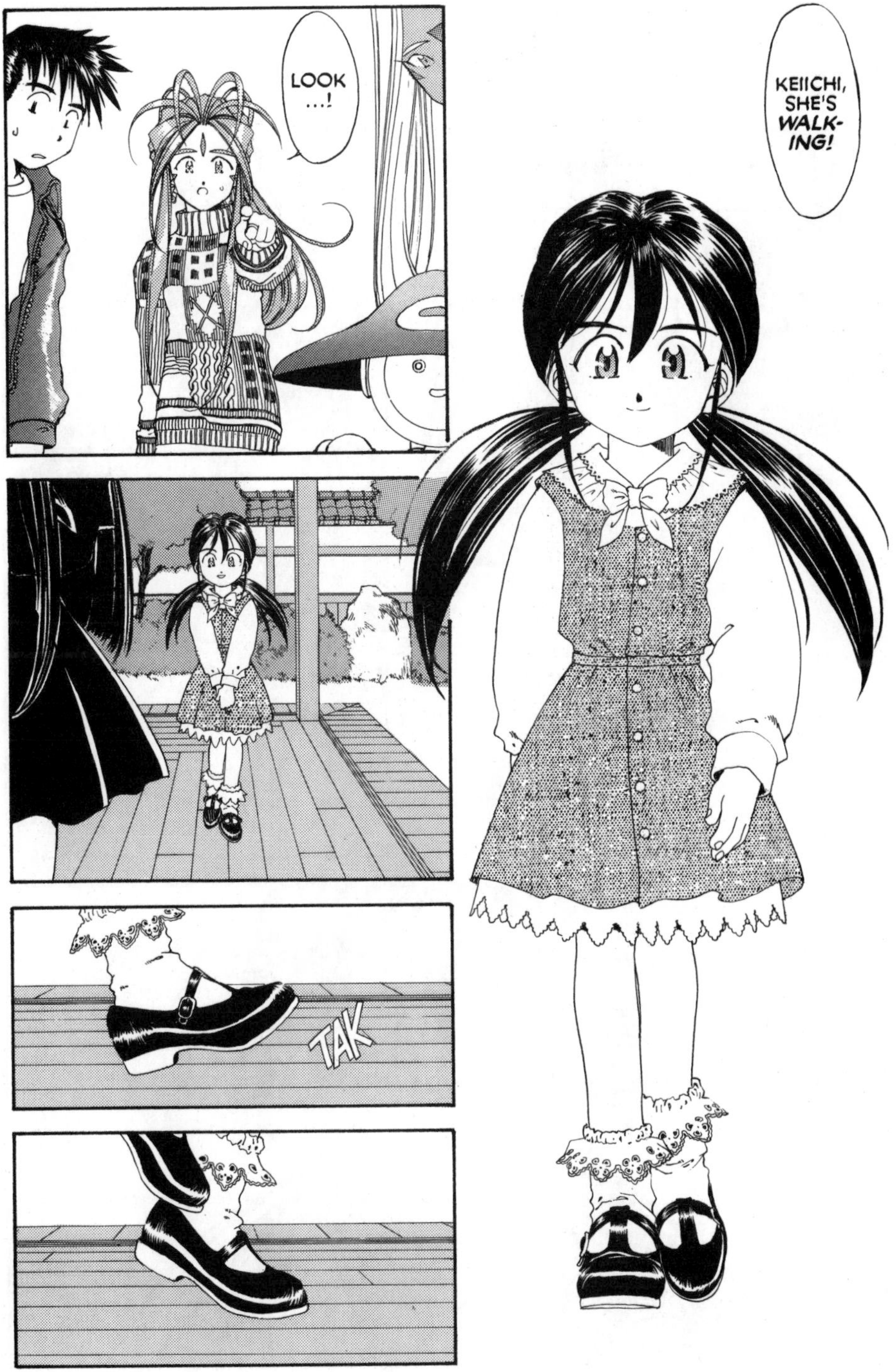
LOOK ...!
TAK
KEIICHI, SHE'S *WALKING!*

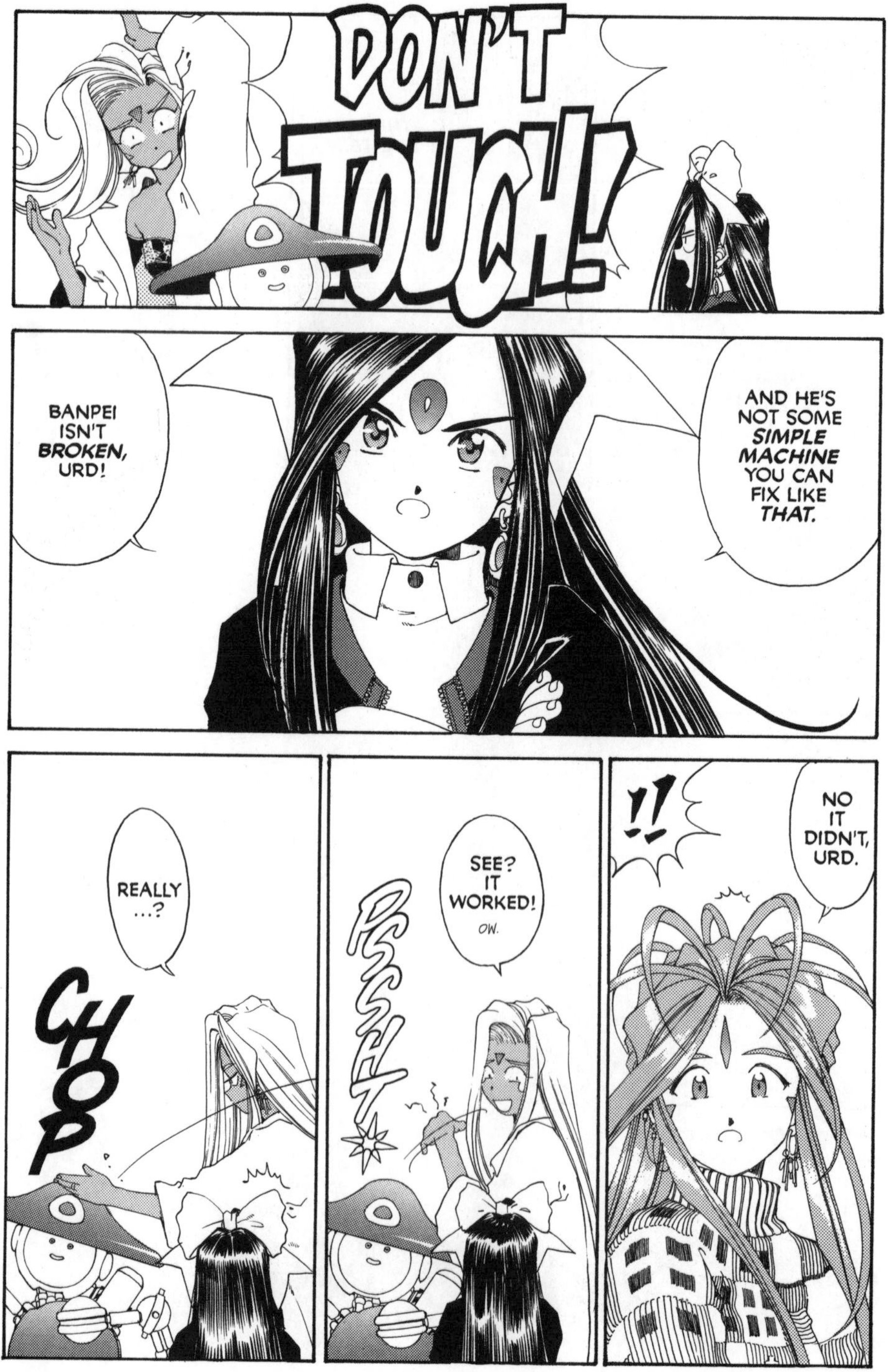
DON'T TOUCH!
BANPEI ISN'T BROKEN, URD!
AND HE'S NOT SOME SIMPLE MACHINE YOU CAN FIX LIKE THAT.
CHOP
REALLY ...?
PSSHH
SEE? IT WORKED!
OW.
!!
NO IT DIDN'T, URD.

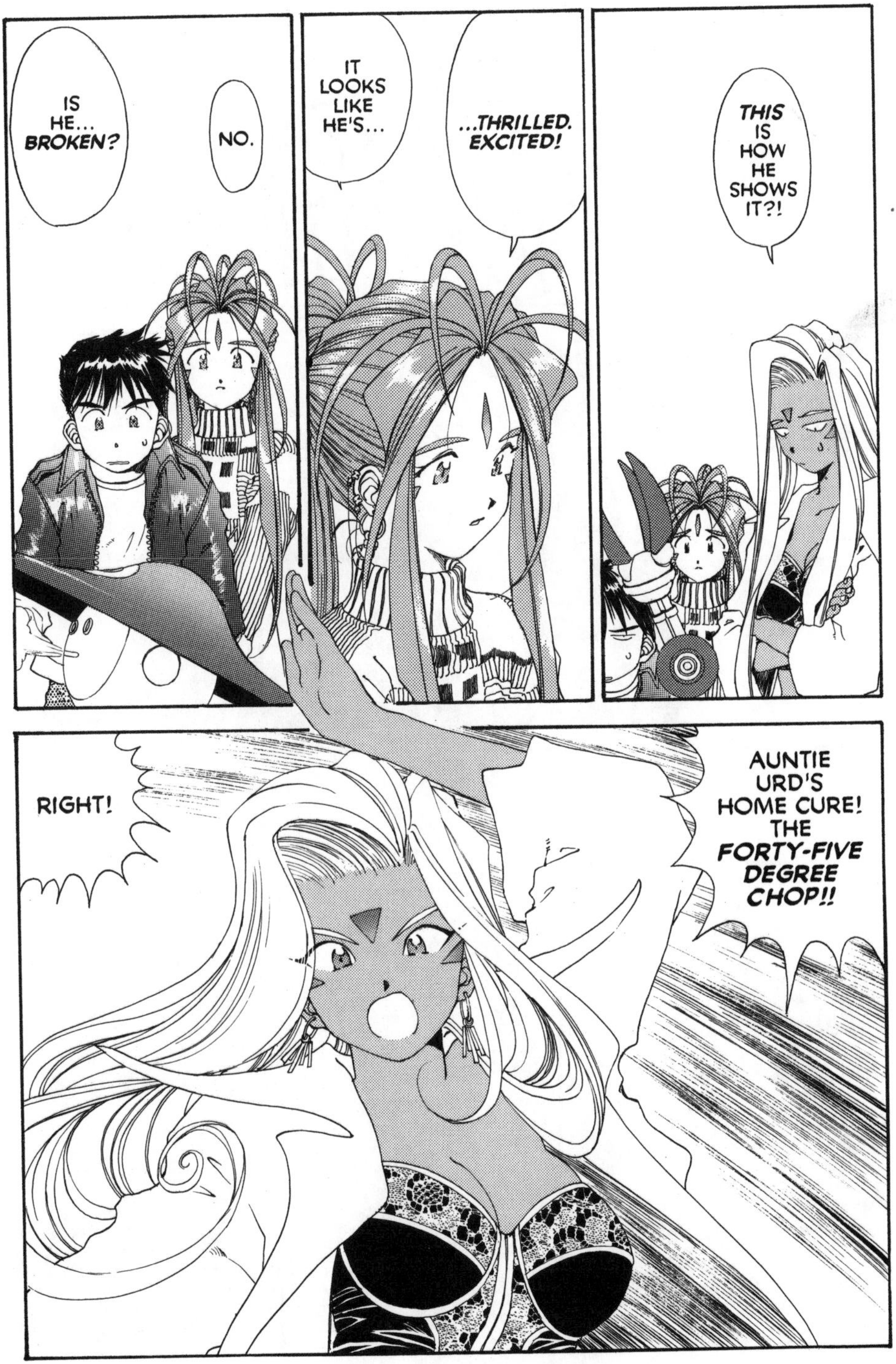
IS HE... BROKEN?
NO.
IT LOOKS LIKE HE'S...
...THRILLED. EXCITED!
THIS IS HOW HE SHOWS IT?!
RIGHT!
AUNTIE URD'S HOME CURE! THE FORTY-FIVE DEGREE CHOP!!

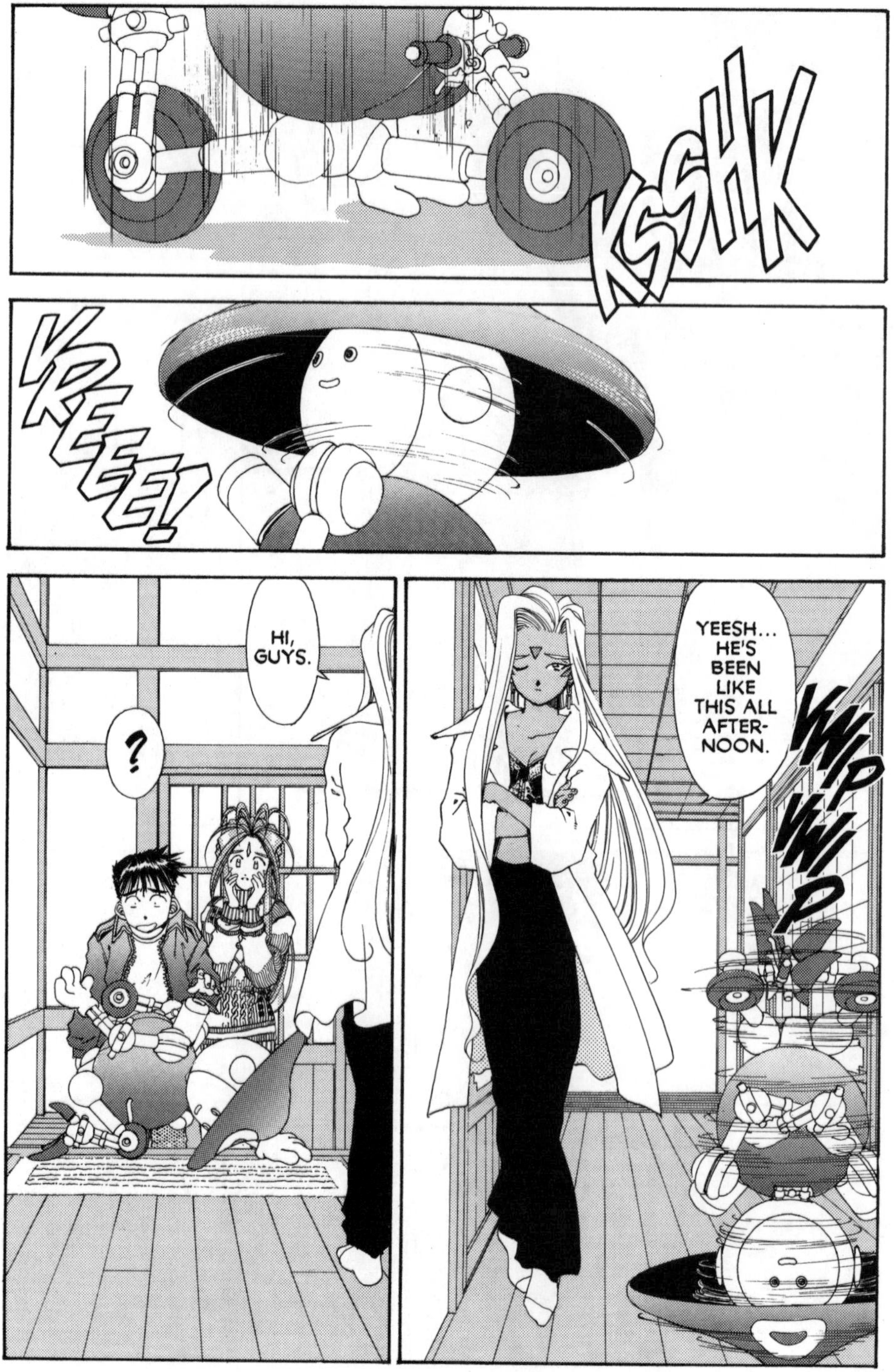
KSSHK
VREEEE!
HI, GUYS.
?
YEESH... HE'S BEEN LIKE THIS ALL AFTER-NOON.
VWIP VWIP

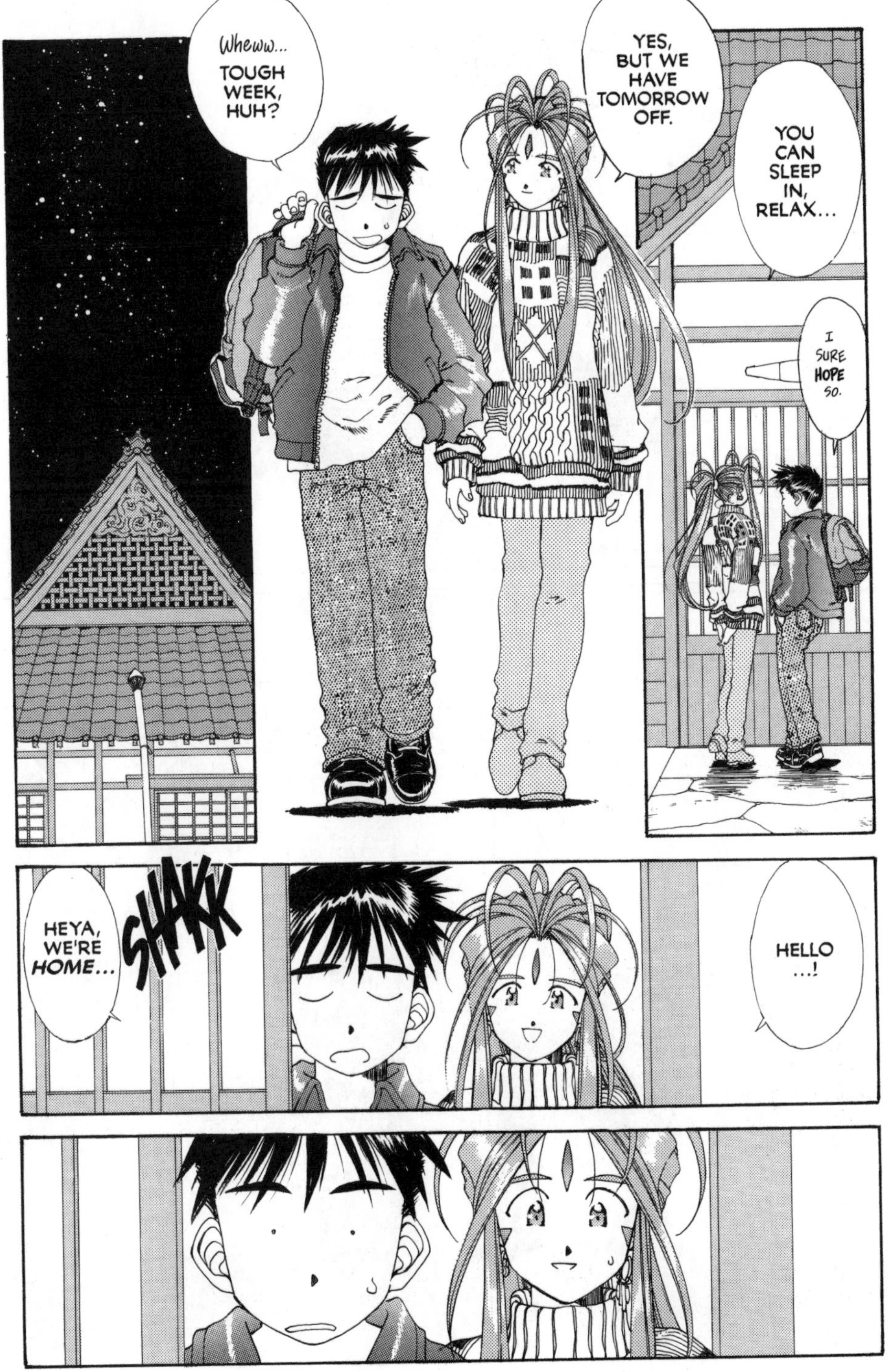
Wheww... TOUGH WEEK, HUH?
YES, BUT WE HAVE TOMORROW OFF.
YOU CAN SLEEP IN, RELAX...
I SURE HOPE SO.
HEYA, WE'RE HOME...
SHAKK
HELLO ...!

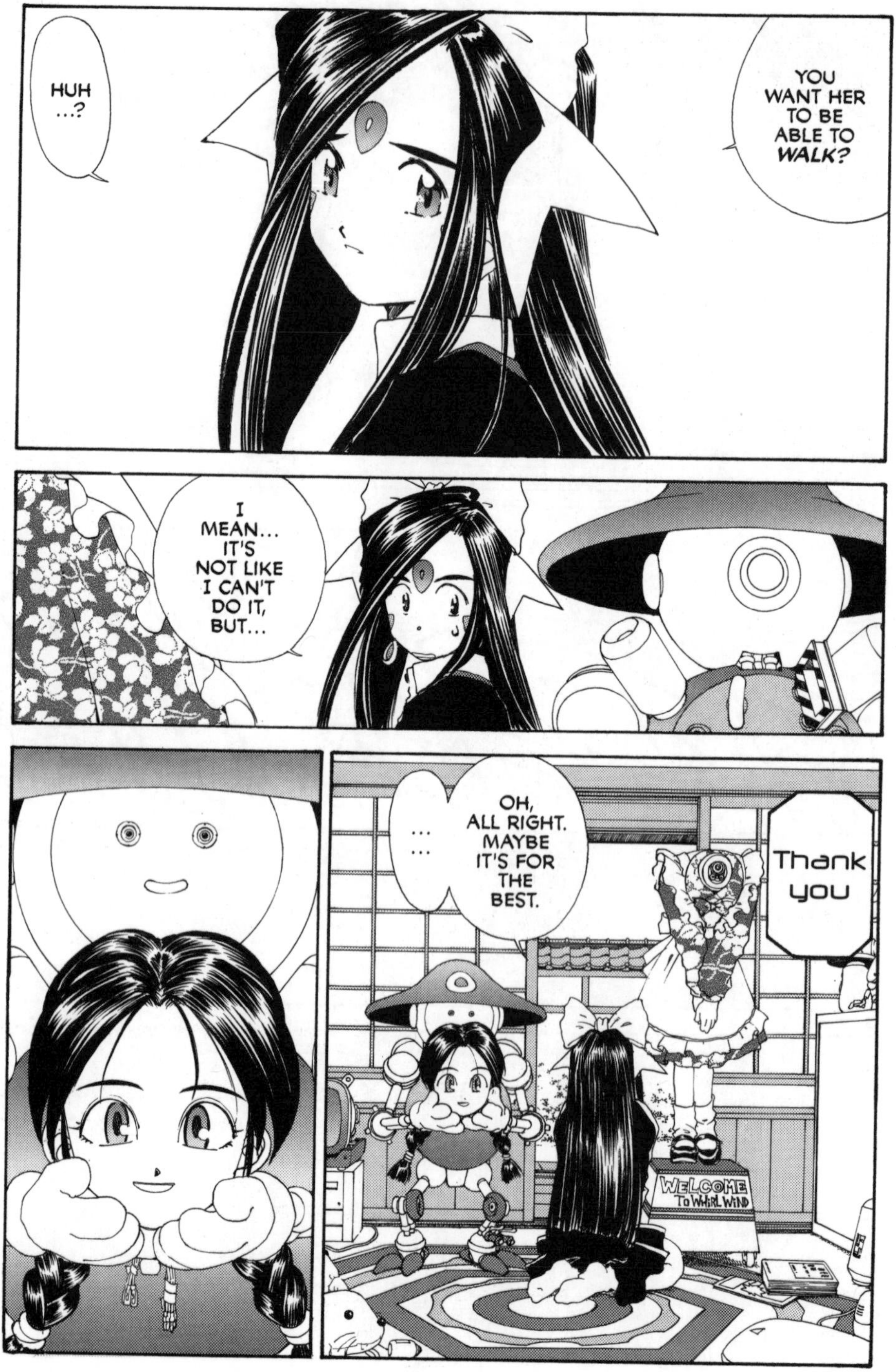
YOU WANT HER TO BE ABLE TO *WALK?*
HUH ...?
I MEAN... IT'S NOT LIKE I CAN'T DO IT, BUT...
Thank you
OH, ALL RIGHT. MAYBE IT'S FOR THE BEST.
... ...

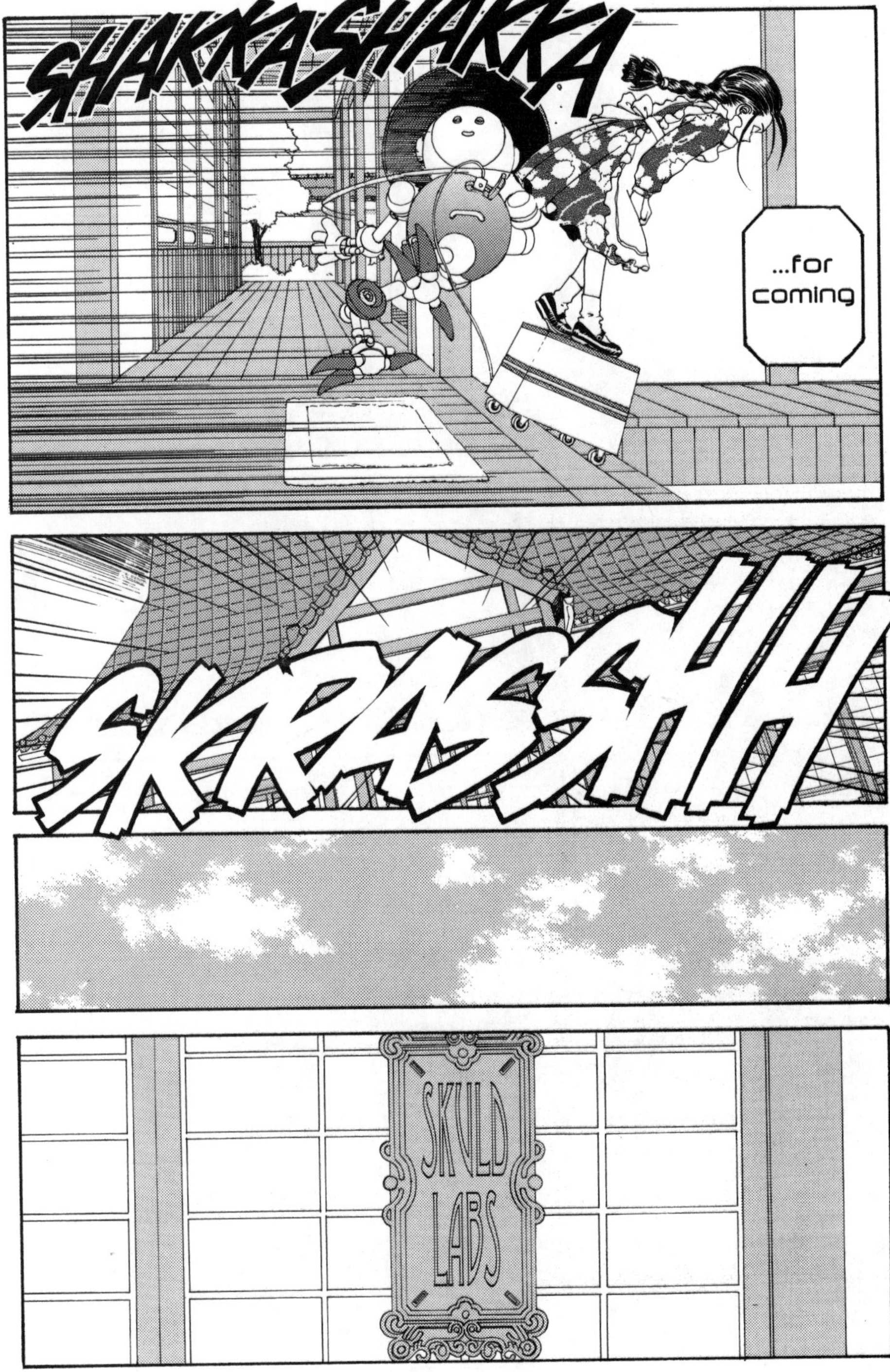

SHAKKASHAKKA
...for coming
SKRASSHH
SKULD LABS

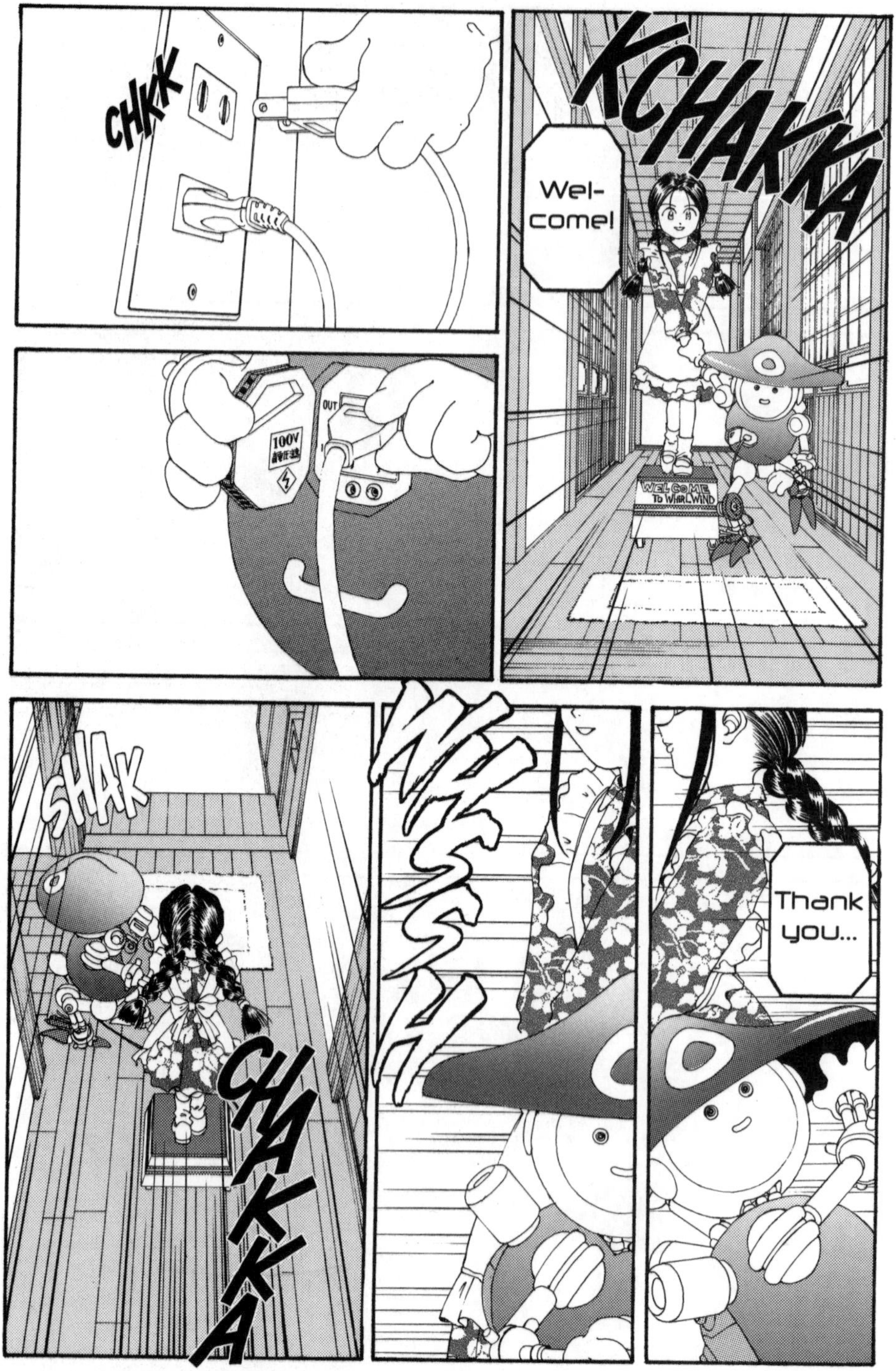
CHKK
100V
OUT
KCHAKKA
Wel-come!
WELCOME TO WHIRLWIND
SHAK
CHAKKA
WHSSH
Thank you...

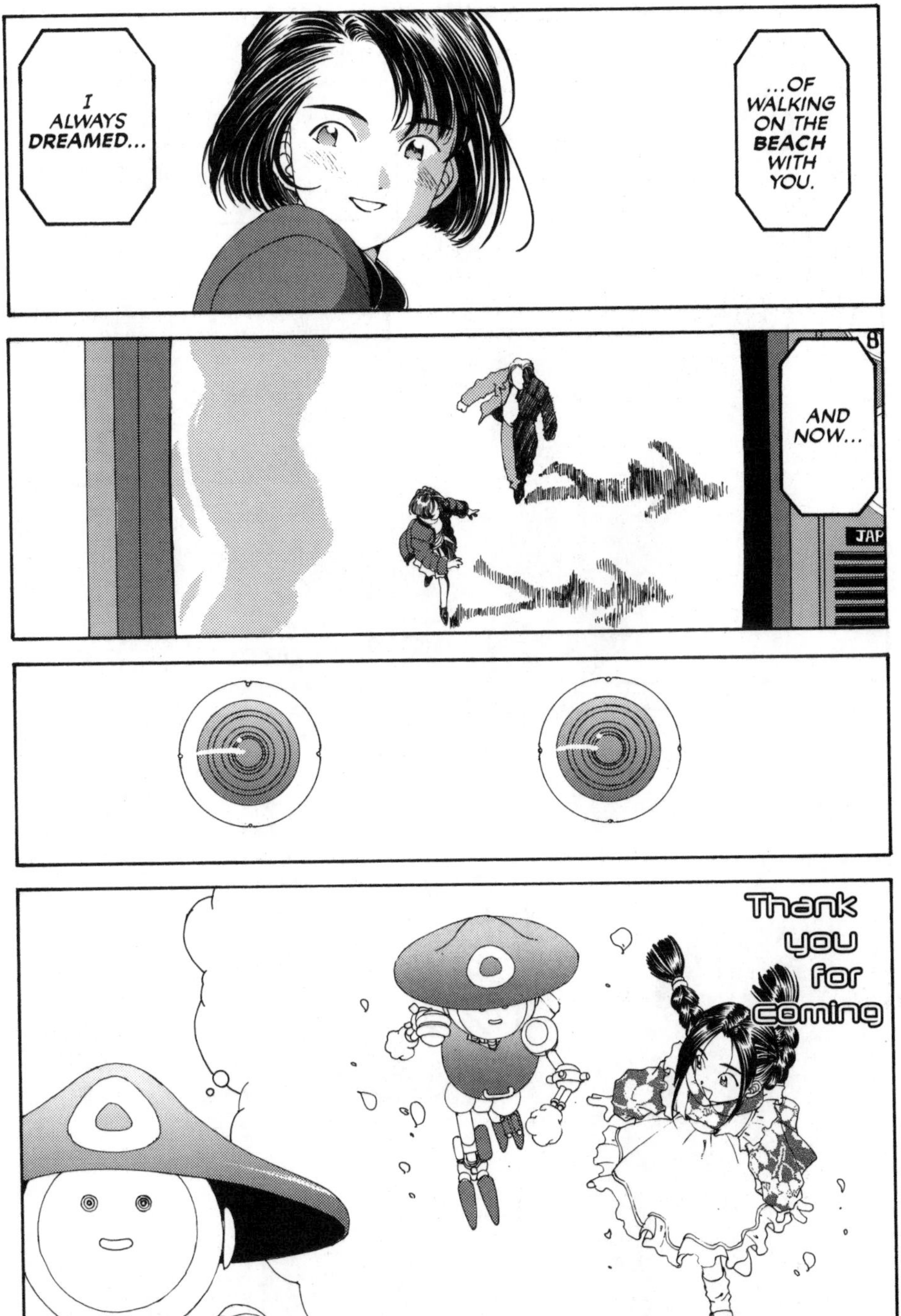
I ALWAYS DREAMED...
...OF WALKING ON THE BEACH WITH YOU.
AND NOW...
JAP
Thank you for coming

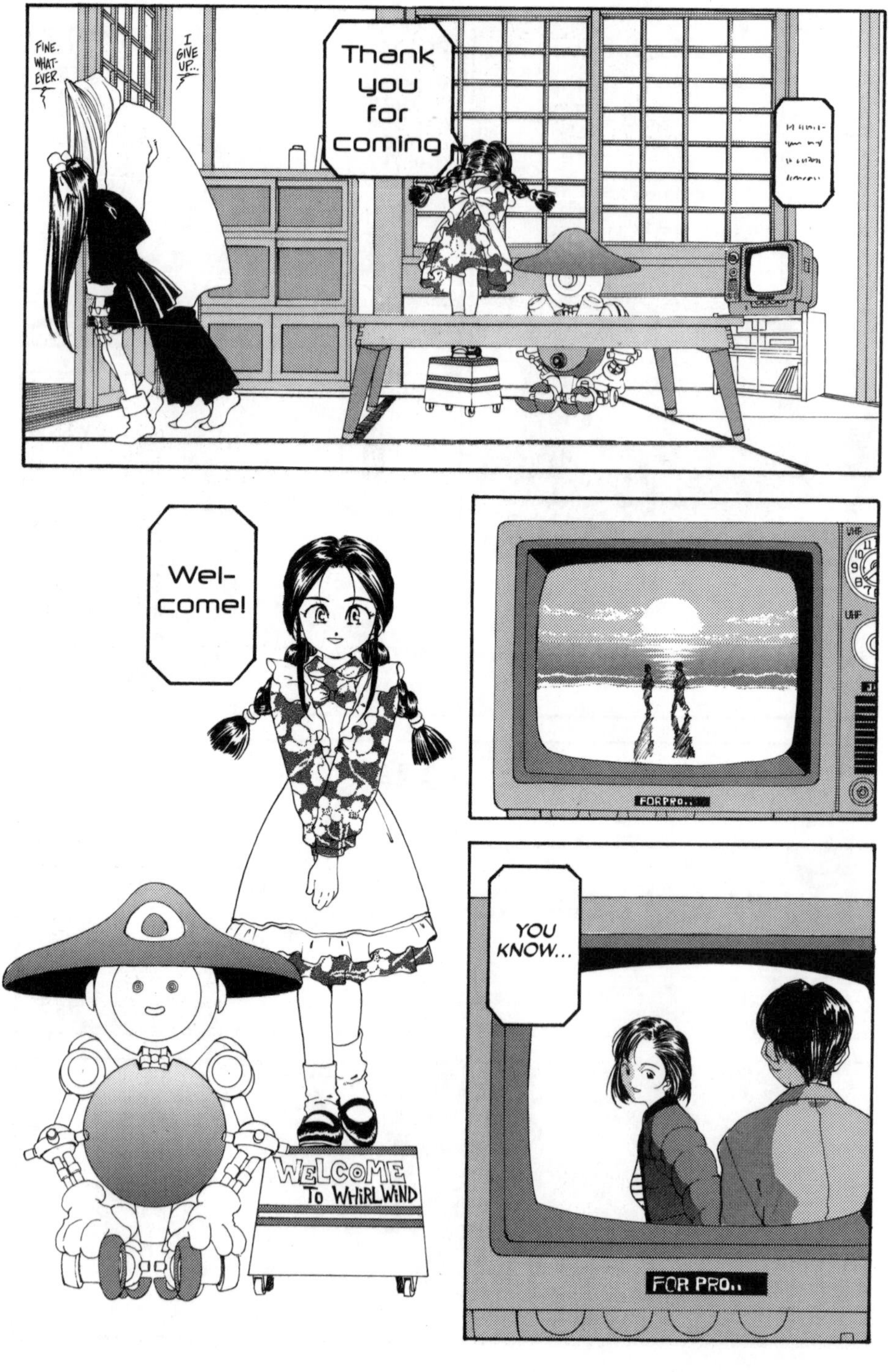
FINE. WHAT-EVER.
I GIVE UP...
Thank you for coming
Wel-come!
WELCOME To WHIRLWIND
FORPRO..
YOU KNOW...
FOR PRO..

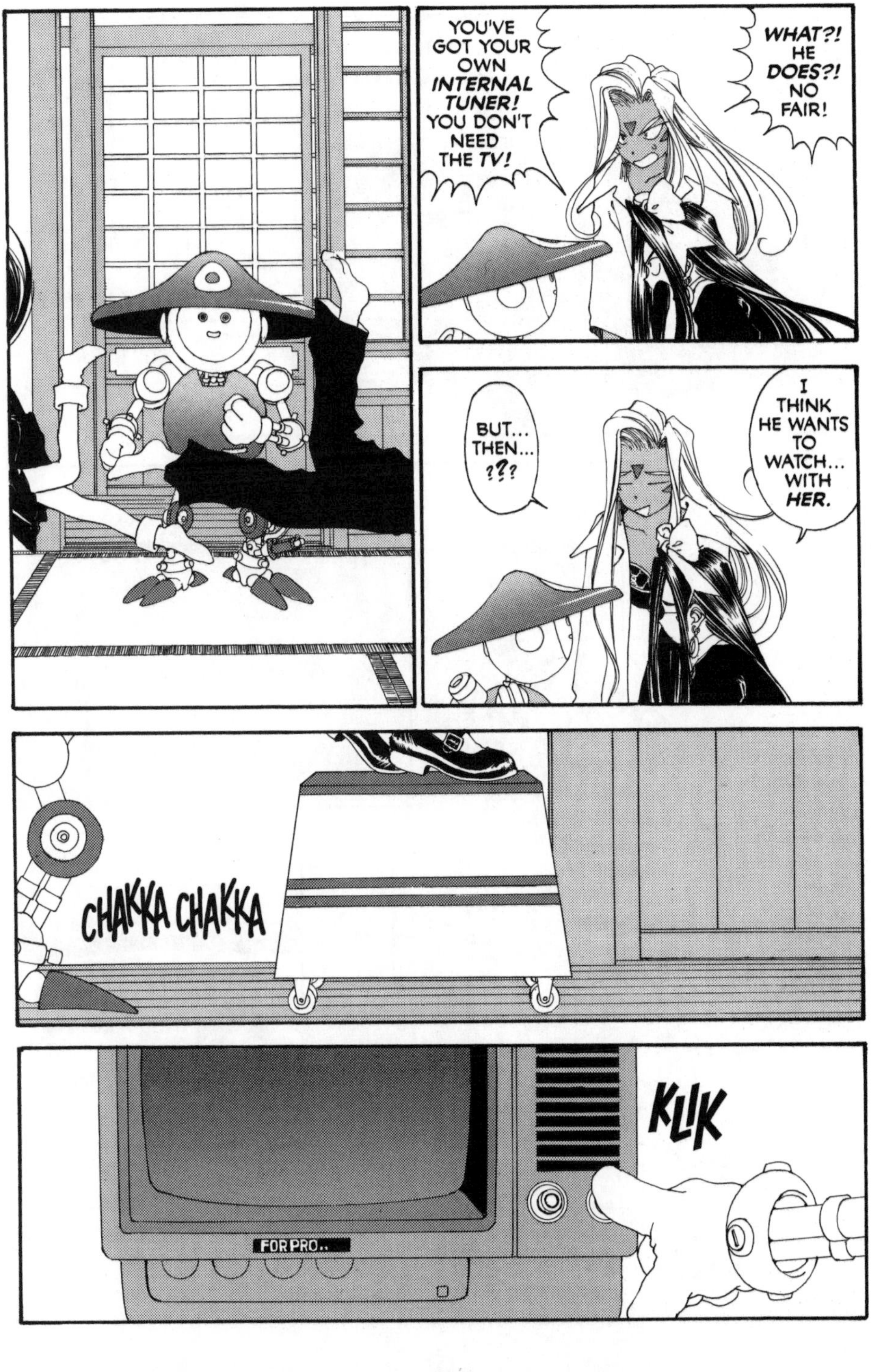
YOU'VE GOT YOUR OWN *INTERNAL TUNER!* YOU DON'T NEED THE *TV!*
WHAT?! HE *DOES?!* NO FAIR!
BUT... THEN... ???
I THINK HE WANTS TO WATCH... WITH *HER.*
CHAKKA CHAKKA
FOR PRO..
KLIK

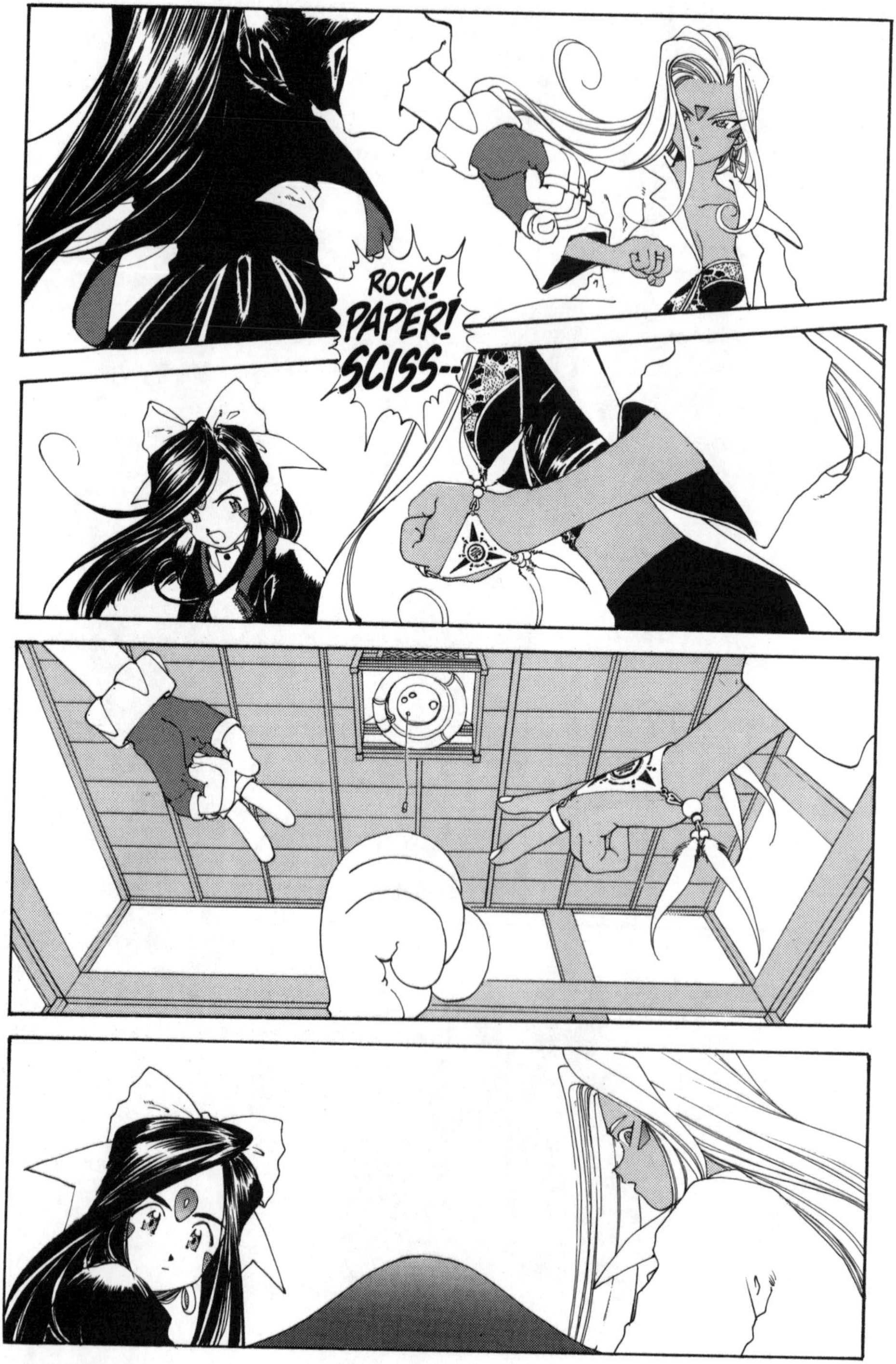
ROCK! PAPER! SCISS--

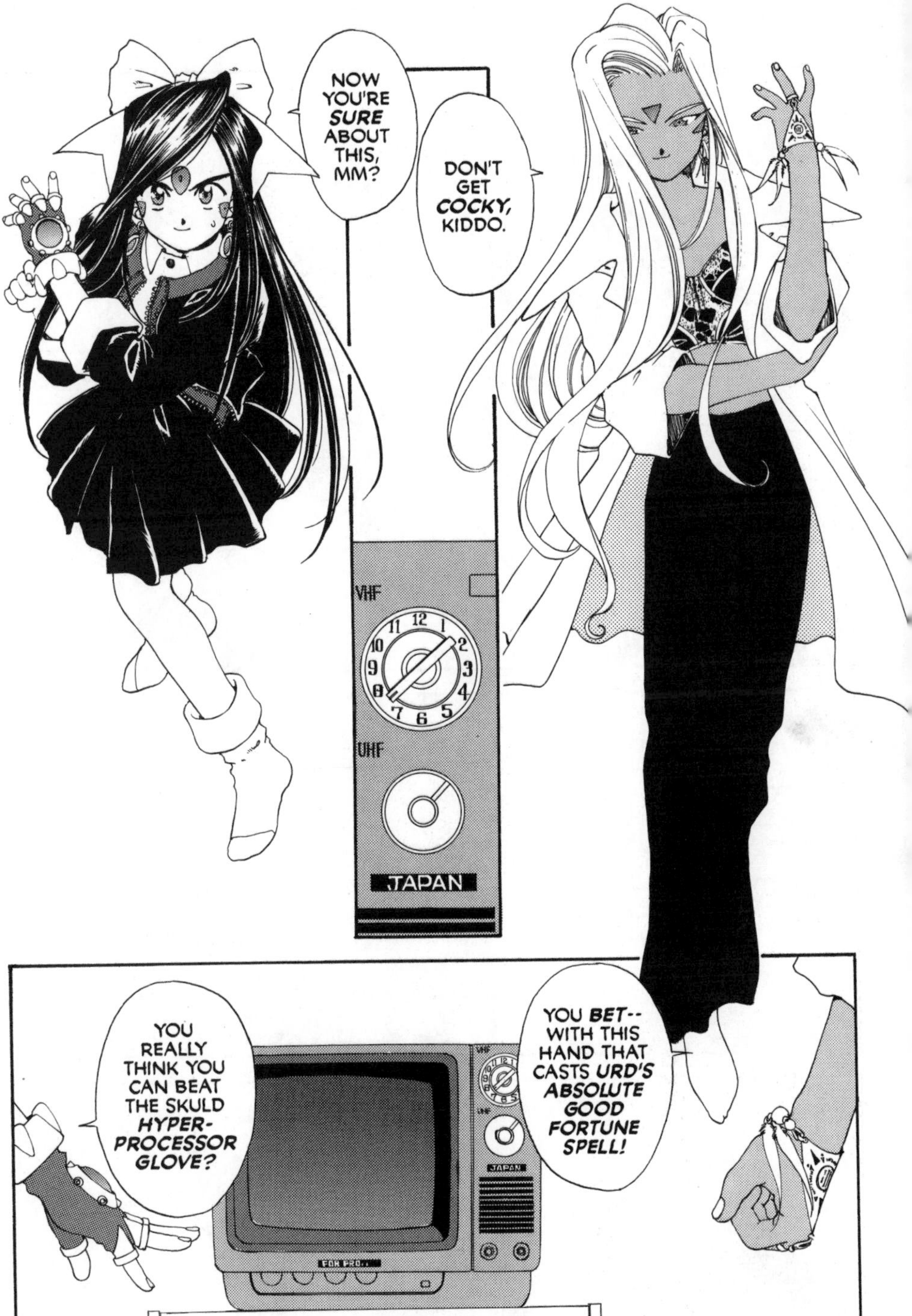
NOW YOU'RE *SURE* ABOUT THIS, MM?
DON'T GET *COCKY,* KIDDO.
VHF
UHF
JAPAN
YOU REALLY THINK YOU CAN BEAT THE SKULD *HYPER-PROCESSOR GLOVE?*
YOU *BET*-- WITH THIS HAND THAT CASTS *URD'S ABSOLUTE GOOD FORTUNE SPELL!*

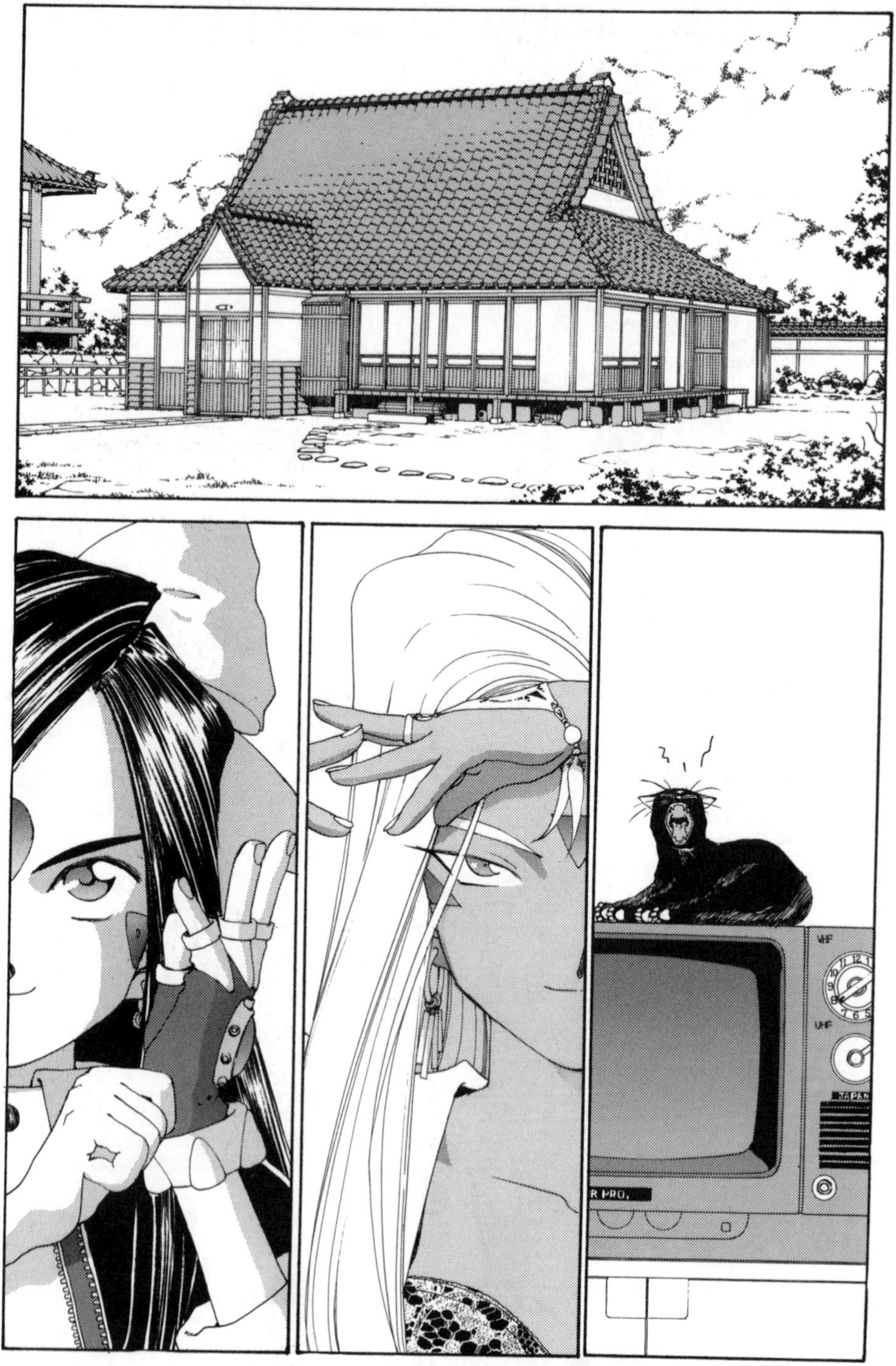
VHF
UHF
JAPAN
R PRO.

COME WALK WITH ME

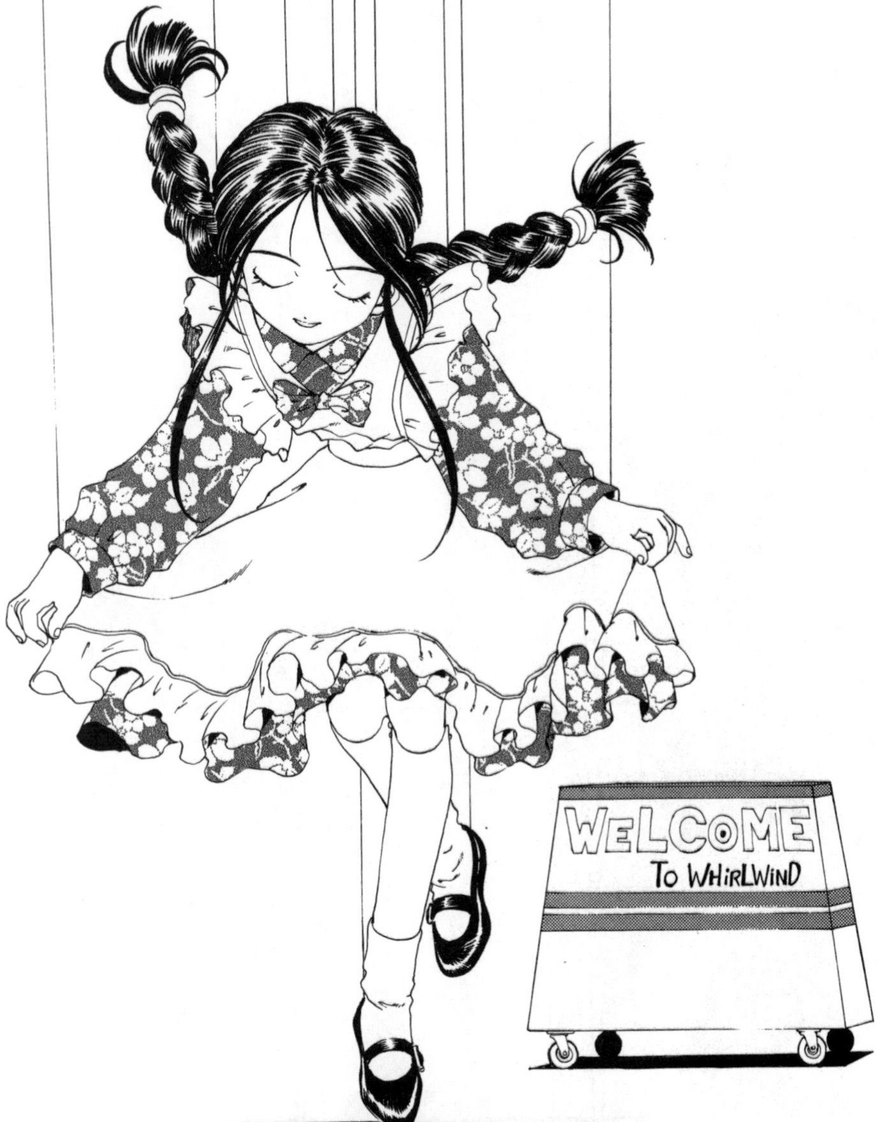

PUBLISHER
Mike Richardson

SERIES EDITOR
Tim Ervin-Gore

COLLECTION EDITOR
Chris Warner

COLLECTION DESIGNER
Amy Arendts

ART DIRECTOR
Mark Cox

English-language version produced by Studio Proteus
for Dark Horse Comics, Inc.

OH MY GODDESS Vol. XVII: Traveler

This volume collects issues eighty-eight through ninety-five of the Dark Horse comic book series *Oh My Goddess!*

Published by
Dark Horse Manga
A division of Dark Horse Comics, Inc.
10956 SE Main Street
Milwaukie, OR 97222

www.darkhorse.com

To find a comics shop in your area, call the Comic Shop
Locator Service toll-free at 1-888-266-4226

First edition: November 2003
ISBN: 1-56971-986-1

1 3 5 7 9 10 8 6 4 2
Printed in Canada

Oh My Goddess!

ああっ女神さまっ

TRAVELER

STORY AND ART BY

Kosuke Fujishima

TRANSLATION BY

Dana Lewis & Toren Smith

LETTERING AND TOUCH-UP BY

Susie Lee with Betty Dong & Tom2K

SONG LYRICS IN "MISSING TIME" BY

Matthew Sweet

DARK HORSE MANGA™

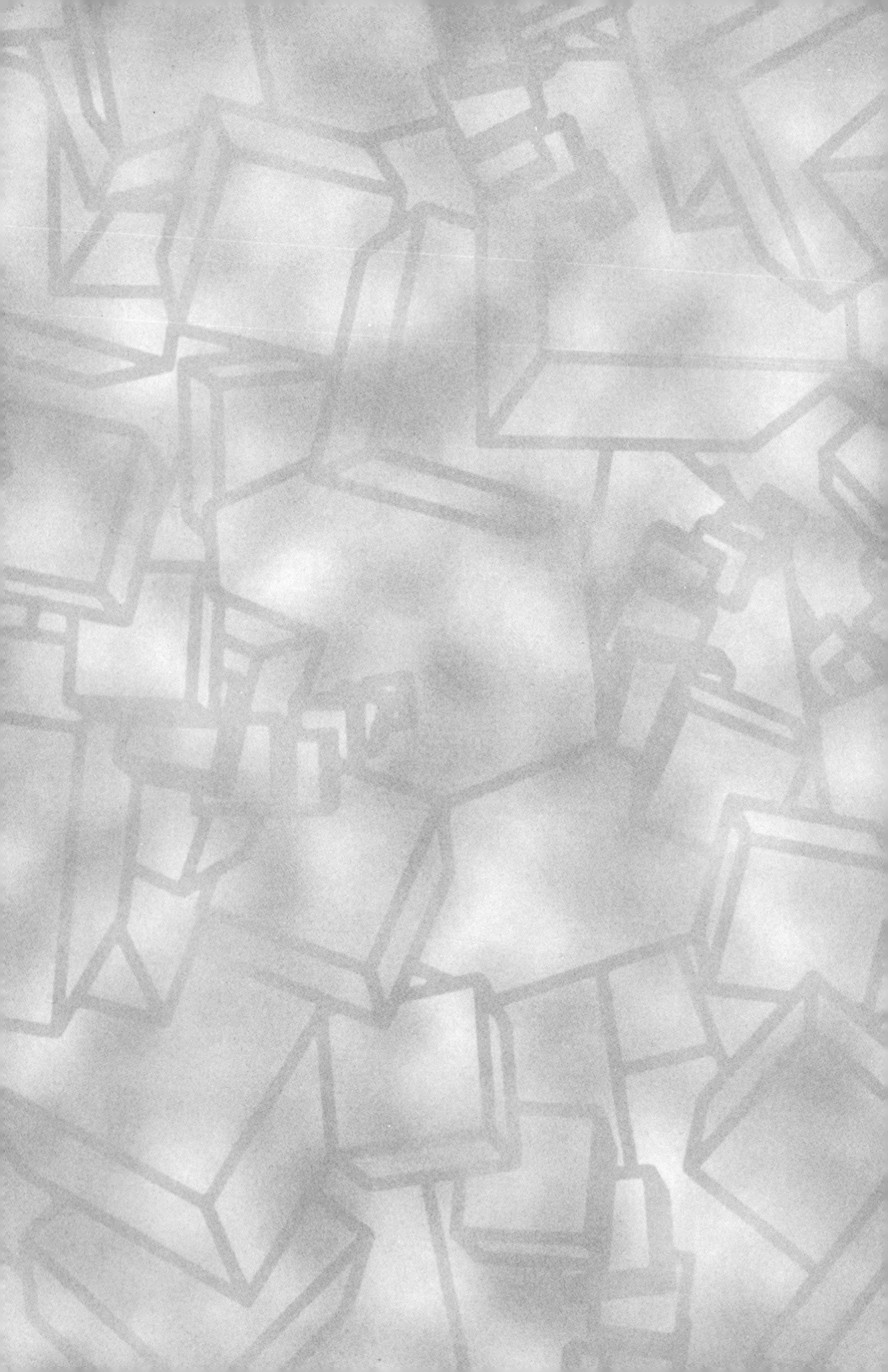

Oh My Goddess!

ああっ女神さまっ

TRAVELER